The O'Leary Series

Microsoft® Office Access 2007

Introductory Edition

The O'Leary Series

Computing Concepts

- *Computing Essentials 2007* Introductory & Complete Editions
- *Computing Essentials 2008* Introductory & Complete Editions

Microsoft® Office Applications

- *Microsoft® Office Word 2007* Brief & Introductory Editions
- *Microsoft® Office Excel 2007* Brief & Introductory Editions
- *Microsoft® Office Access 2007* Brief & Introductory Editions
- *Microsoft® Office PowerPoint 2007* Brief Edition

The O'Leary Series

Microsoft® Office Access 2007

Introductory Edition

Timothy J. O'Leary
Arizona State University

Linda I. O'Leary

Boston Burr Ridge, IL Dubuque, IA New York San Francisco St. Louis
Bangkok Bogotá Caracas Kuala Lumpur Lisbon London Madrid Mexico City
Milan Montreal New Delhi Santiago Seoul Singapore Sydney Taipei Toronto

The McGraw-Hill Companies

McGraw-Hill Higher Education

THE O'LEARY SERIES MICROSOFT® OFFICE ACCESS 2007 INTRODUCTORY EDITION
Published by McGraw-Hill, a business unit of The McGraw-Hill Companies, Inc., 1221 Avenue of the Americas, New York, NY, 10020.

Some ancillaries, including electronic and print components, may not be available to customers outside the United States.

This book is printed on acid-free paper.

4 5 6 7 8 9 0 QWD/QWD 0 9

ISBN 978-0-07-329455-1
MHID 0-07-329455-1

Vice President/Editor in Chief: *Elizabeth Haefele*
Vice President/Director of Marketing: *John E. Biernat*
Developmental editor: *Kelly L. Delso*
Marketing manager: *Sarah Wood*
Lead media producer: *Damian Moshak*
Media producer: *Benjamin Curless*
Director, Editing/Design/Production: *Jess Ann Kosic*
Project manager: *Marlena Pechan*
Production supervisor: *Jason Huls*
Designer: *Srdjan Savanovic*
Cover design: *© Asylum Studios*
Senior photo research coordinator: *Jeremy Cheshareck*
Typeface: *10.5/13 New Aster*
Compositor: *Laserwords Private Limited*
Printer: *Quebecor World Dubuque Inc.*

Library of Congress Cataloging-in-Publication Data

O'Leary, Timothy J., 1947-
Microsoft Office Access 2007 / Timothy J. O'Leary, Linda I. O'Leary.—Introductory ed.
p. cm.—(The O'Leary series)
Includes index.
ISBN-13: 978-0-07-329455-1 (alk. paper)
ISBN-10: 0-07-329455-1 (alk. paper)
1. Microsoft Access. 2. Database management. I. O'Leary, Linda I. II. Title.
QA76.9.D3O386 2008
005.75'65—dc22

2007028778

www.mhhe.com

Brief Contents

Labs

Detailed Contents

Lab 4 Importing and Querying Tables AC4.1

Lab 5 Creating Custom Forms AC5.1

Acknowledgments

We would like to extend our thanks to the professors who took time out of their busy schedules to provide us with the feedback necessary to develop the 2007 Edition of this text. The following professors offered valuable suggestions on revising the text:

Adida Awan, Savannah State University

Jacqueline Bakal, Felician College

Chet Barney, Southern Utah University

Bruce W. Bryant, University of Arkansas Community College Morrilton

Kelly D. Carter, Mercer University

Cesar Augusto Casas, St. Thomas Aquinas College

Sally Clements, St. Thomas Aquinas College

Donna N. Dunn, Beaufort County Community College

Donna Ehrhart, Genesee Community College

Saiid Ganjalizadeh, The Catholic University of America

Dr. Jayanta Ghosh, Florida Community College

Carol Grazette, Medgar Evers College/CUNY

Susan Gundy, University of Illinois at Springfield

Greg R. Hodge, Northwestern Michigan College

Christopher M. J. Hopper, Bellevue Community College

Ginny Kansas, Southwestern College

Robert Kemmerer, Los Angeles Mission College

Diana I. Kline, University of Louisville

Linda Klisto, Broward Community College North Campus

Nanette Lareau, University of Arkansas Community College Morrilton

Deborah Layton, Eastern Oklahoma State College

Keming Liu, Medgar Evers College/CUNY

J. Gay Mills, Amarillo College

Kim Moorning, Medgar Evers College/CUNY

Dr. Belinda J. Moses, University of Phoenix/Baker College/Wayne County Community College

Lois Ann O'Neal, Rogers State University

Andrew Perry, Springfield College

Michael Philipp, Greenville Technical College

Julie Piper, Bucks County Community College

Brenda Price, Bucks County Community College

Thali N. Rajashekhara, Camden County College

Dr. Marcel Marie Robles, Eastern Kentucky University

Jose (Joe) Sainz, Naugatuck Valley Community College

Pamela J. Silvers, Asheville-Buncombe Technical Community College

Glenna Stites, Johnson County Community College

Joyce Thompson, Lehigh Carbon Community College

Michelle G. Vlaich-Lee, Greenville Technical College

Mary A. Walthall, St. Petersburg College

We would like to thank those who took the time to help us develop the manuscript and ensure accuracy through pain-staking edits: Brenda Nielsen of Mesa Community College–Red Mountain, Rajiv Narayana of SunTech Info-Labs, and Craig Leonard.

Our thanks also go to Linda Mehlinger of Morgan State University for all her work on creating the PowerPoint presentations to accompany the text. We are grateful to Harry Knight of Franklin University, the author of the Instructor's Manual and Testbank, for his careful revision of these valuable resources and creation of online quizzing materials.

Finally, we would like to thank team members from McGraw-Hill, whose renewed commitment, direction, and support have infused the team with the excitement of a new project. Leading the team from McGraw-Hill are Sarah Wood, Marketing Manager, and Developmental Editor Kelly Delso.

The production staff is headed by Marlena Pechan, Project Manager, whose planning and attention to detail have made it possible for us to successfully meet a very challenging schedule; Srdjan Savanovic, Designer; Jason Huls, Production Supervisor; Ben Curless, Media Producer; Jeremy Cheshareck, Photo Researcher; and Betsy Blumenthal, copyeditor—team members whom we can depend on to do a great job.

Preface

The 20th century brought us the dawn of the digital information age and unprecedented changes in information technology. There is no indication that this rapid rate of change will be slowing—it may even be increasing. As we begin the 21st century, computer literacy is undoubtedly becoming a prerequisite in whatever career you choose.

The goal of the O'Leary Series is to provide you with the necessary skills to efficiently use these applications. Equally important is the goal to provide a foundation for students to readily and easily learn to use future versions of this software. This series does this by providing detailed step-by-step instructions combined with careful selection and presentation of essential concepts.

Times are changing, technology is changing, and this text is changing too. As students of today, you are different from those of yesterday. You put much effort toward the things that interest you and the things that are relevant to you. Your efforts directed at learning application programs and exploring the Web seem, at times, limitless.

On the other hand, students often can be shortsighted, thinking that learning the skills to use the application is the only objective. The mission of the series is to build upon and extend this interest by not only teaching the specific application skills but by introducing the concepts that are common to all applications, providing students with the confidence, knowledge, and ability to easily learn the next generation of applications.

Instructor's Resource CD-ROM

The **Instructor's Resource CD-ROM** contains a computerized Test Bank, an Instructor's Manual, and PowerPoint Presentation Slides. Features of the Instructor's Resource are described below.

- **Instructor's Manual CD-ROM** The Instructor's Manual, authored by Harry Knight of Franklin University, contains lab objectives, concepts, outlines, lecture notes, and command summaries. Also included are answers to all end-of-chapter material, tips for covering difficult materials, additional exercises, and a schedule showing how much time is required to cover text material.
- **Computerized Test Bank** The test bank, authored by Harry Knight, contains over 1,300 multiple choice, true/false, and discussion questions. Each question will be accompanied by the correct answer, the level of learning difficulty, and corresponding page references. Our flexible EZ Test software allows you to easily generate custom exams.

- **PowerPoint Presentation Slides** The presentation slides, authored by Linda Mehlinger of Morgan State University, include lab objectives, concepts, outlines, text figures, and speaker's notes. Also included are bullets to illustrate key terms and FAQs.

Online Learning Center/Web Site

Found at **www.mhhe.com/oleary,** this site provides additional learning and instructional tools to enhance the comprehension of the text. The OLC/Web site is divided into these three areas:

- **Information Center** Contains core information about the text, supplements, and the authors.
- **Instructor Center** Offers instructional materials, downloads, and other relevant links for professors.
- **Student Center** Contains data files, chapter competencies, chapter concepts, self-quizzes, flashcards, additional Web links, and more.

Simnet Assessment for Office Applications

Simnet Assessment for Office Applications provides a way for you to test students' software skills in a simulated environment. Simnet is available for Microsoft Office 2007 and provides flexibility for you in your applications course by offering:

Pre-testing options

Post-testing options

Course placement testing

Diagnostic capabilities to reinforce skills

Web delivery of test

MCAS preparation exams

Learning verification reports

For more information on skills assessment software, please contact your local sales representative, or visit us at **www.mhhe.com**.

O'Leary Series

The O'Leary Application Series for Microsoft Office is available separately or packaged with *Computing Essentials*. The O'Leary Application Series offers a step-by-step approach to learning computer applications and is available in both brief and introductory versions. The introductory books are MCAS Certified and prepare students for the Microsoft Certified Applications Specialist exam.

Computing Concepts

Computing Essentials 2008 offers a unique, visual orientation that gives students a basic understanding of computing concepts. *Computing Essentials* encourages "active" learning with exercises, explorations, visual illustrations, and inclusion of screen shots and numbered steps. While combining the "active" learning style with current topics and technology, this text provides an accurate snapshot of computing trends. When bundled with software application lab manuals, students are given a complete representation of the fundamental issues surrounding the personal computing environment.

GUIDE TO THE O'LEARY SERIES

The O'Leary Series is full of features designed to make learning productive and hassle free. On the following pages you will see the kind of engaging, helpful pedagogical features that have helped countless students master Microsoft Office Applications.

EASY-TO-FOLLOW INTRODUCTORY MATERIALS

INTRODUCTION TO MICROSOFT OFFICE 2007

Each text in the O'Leary Series opens with an Introduction to Office 2007, providing a complete overview of this version of the Microsoft Office Suite.

What Is the 2007 Microsoft Office System?

Microsoft's 2007 Microsoft Office System is a comprehensive, integrated system of programs, servers, and services designed to solve a wide array of business needs. Although the programs can be used individually, they are designed to work together seamlessly, making it easy to connect people and organizations to information, business processes, and each other. The applications include tools used to create, discuss, communicate, and manage projects. If you share a lot of documents with other people, these features facilitate access to common documents. This version has an entirely new user interface that is designed to make it easier to perform tasks and help users more quickly take advantage of all the features in the applications. In addition, the communication and collaboration features and integration with the World Wide Web have been expanded and refined.

The 2007 Microsoft Office System is packaged in several different combinations of programs or suites. The major programs and a brief description are provided in the following table.

Program	Description
Word 2007	Word Processor program used to create text-based documents
Excel 2007	Spreadsheet program used to analyze numerical data
Access 2007	Database manager used to organize, manage, and display a database
PowerPoint 2007	Graphics presentation program used to create presentation materials
Outlook 2007	Desktop information manager and messaging client
InfoPath 2007	Used to create XML forms and documents
OneNote 2007	Note-taking and information organization tools
Publisher 2007	Tools to create and distribute publications for print, Web, and e-mail
Visio 2007	Diagramming and data visualization tools
SharePoint Designer 2007	Web site development and management for SharePoint servers
Project 2007	Project management tools
Groove 2007	Collaboration program that enables teams to work together

The four main components of Microsoft Office 2007—Word, Excel, Access, and PowerPoint—are the applications you will learn about in this series of labs. They are described in more detail in the following sections.

I.2 Introduction to Microsoft Office 2007 www.mhhe.com/oleary

Word 2007

Overview of Microsoft Office Word 20

What Is Word Processing?

Office Word 2007 is a word processing software application whose p
is to help you create any type of written communication. A word pro
can be used to manipulate text data to produce a letter, a report, a
an e-mail message, or any other type of correspondence. Text data
letter, number, or symbol that you can type on a keyboard. The grou
the text data to form words, sentences, paragraphs, and pages
results in the creation of a document. Through a word processor, y
create, modify, store, retrieve, and print part or all of a document.

Word processors are one of the most widely used application software programs. Putting your thoughts in writing, from the simplest note to the most complex book, is a time-consuming process. Even more time-consuming is the task of editing and retyping the document to make it better. Word processors make errors nearly nonexistent—not because they are not made, but because they are easy to correct. Word processors let you throw away the correction fluid, scissors, paste, and erasers. Now, with a few keystrokes, you can easily correct errors, move paragraphs, and reprint your document.

Word 2007 Features

Word 2007 excels in its ability to change or edit a document. Editing involves correcting spelling, grammar, and sentence-structure errors. In addition, you can easily revise or update existing text by inserting or deleting text. For example, a document that lists prices can easily be updated to reflect new prices. A document that details procedures can be revised by deleting old procedures and inserting new ones. This is especially helpful when a document is used repeatedly. Rather than recreating the whole document, you change only the parts that need to be revised.

Revision also includes the rearrangement of selected areas of text. For example, while writing a report, you may decide to change the location of a single word or several paragraphs or pages of text. You can do it easily by cutting or removing selected text from one location, then pasting or placing the selected text in another location. The selection also can be copied from one document to another.

To help you produce a perfect document, Word 2007 includes many additional support features. The AutoCorrect feature checks the spelling and grammar in a document as text is entered. Many common errors are corrected automatically for you. Others are identified and a correction suggested. A thesaurus can be used to display alternative words that have a meaning similar or opposite to a word you entered. A Find and Replace feature can be used to quickly locate specified text and replace it with other text throughout a document. In addition, Word 2007 includes a

WDO.1

INTRODUCTION TO WORD 2007

Each text in the O'Leary Series also provides an overview of the specific application features.

ENGAGING LAB INTRODUCTIONS

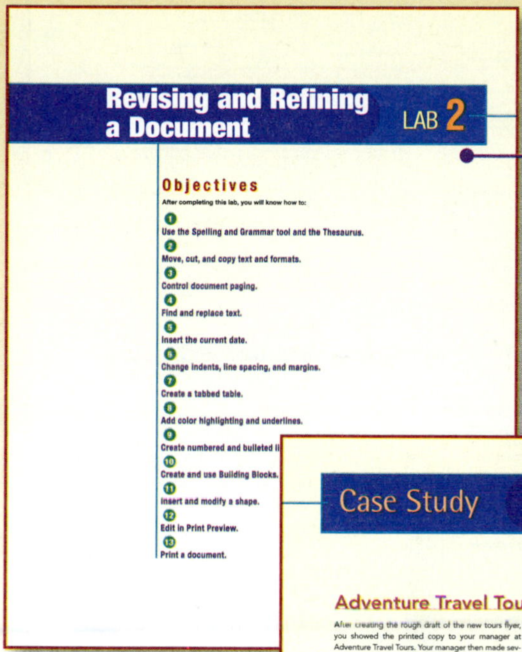

Revising and Refining a Document LAB 2

Objectives

After completing this lab, you will know how to:

1. Use the Spelling and Grammar tool and the Thesaurus.
2. Move, cut, and copy text and formats.
3. Control document paging.
4. Find and replace text.
5. Insert the current date.
6. Change indents, line spacing, and margins.
7. Create a tabbed table.
8. Add color highlighting and underlines.
9. Create numbered and bulleted li
10. Create and use Building Blocks.
11. Insert and modify a shape.
12. Edit in Print Preview.
13. Print a document.

OBJECTIVES

Each lab opens with a list of objectives clearly outlining skills covered in each lab.

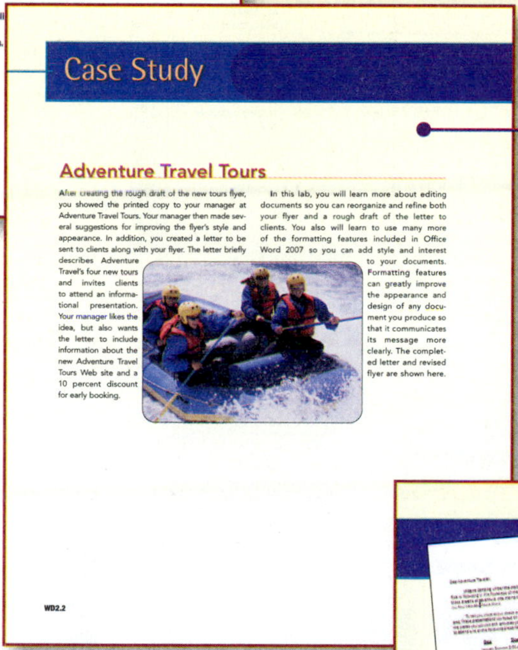

Case Study

Adventure Travel Tours

After creating the rough draft of the new tours flyer, you showed the printed copy to your manager at Adventure Travel Tours. Your manager then made several suggestions for improving the flyer's style and appearance. In addition, you created a letter to be sent to clients along with your flyer. The letter briefly describes Adventure Travel's four new tours and invites clients to attend an informational presentation. Your manager likes the idea, but also wants the letter to include information about the new Adventure Travel Tours Web site and a 10 percent discount for early booking.

In this lab, you will learn more about editing documents so you can reorganize and refine both your flyer and a rough draft of the letter to clients. You also will learn to use many more of the formatting features included in Office Word 2007 so you can add style and interest to your documents. Formatting features can greatly improve the appearance and design of any document you produce so that it communicates its message more clearly. The completed letter and revised flyer are shown here.

WD2.2

CASE STUDIES

Case studies introduce a real-life setting that is interwoven throughout the lab. Four separate running cases provide the basis for understanding the use of applications.

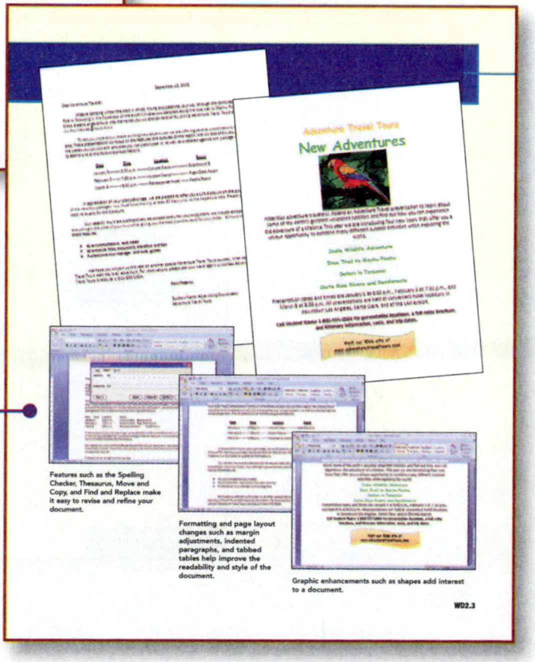

Adventure Travel Tours

New Adventures

Features such as the Spelling Checker, Thesaurus, Move and Copy, and Find and Replace make it easy to revise and refine your document.

Formatting and page layout changes such as margin adjustments, indented paragraphs, and tabbed tables help improve the readability and style of the document.

Graphic enhancements such as shapes add interest to a document.

WD2.3

FINAL SOLUTION

Screen shots of the major features and the final document allow you to preview what will be accomplished.

STEP-BY-STEP INSTRUCTION

NUMBERED AND BULLETED STEPS

Numbered and bulleted steps provide clear step-by-step instructions on how to complete a task, or series of tasks.

All steps and bullets appear in the left-hand margin, making it easy not to miss a step.

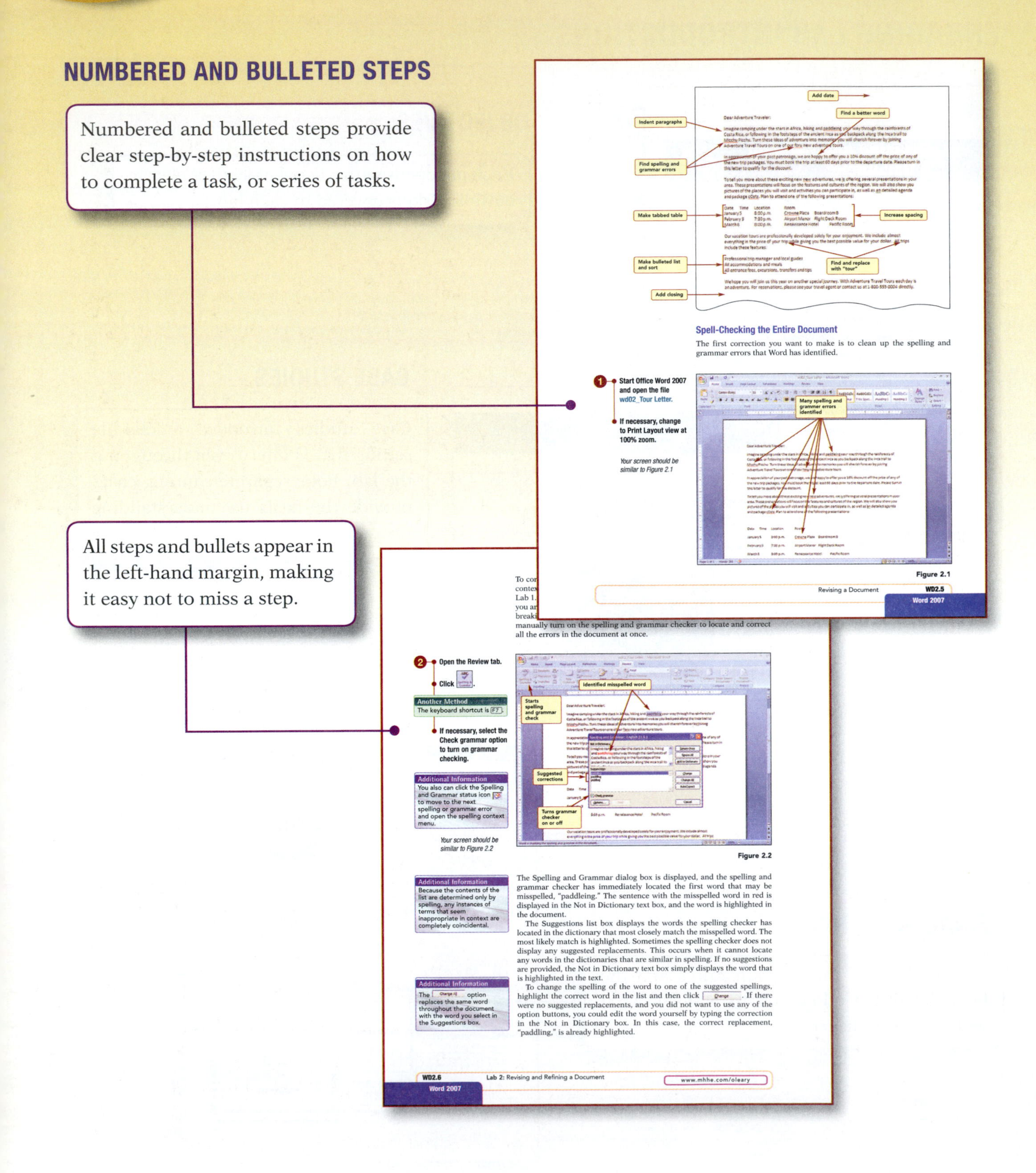

Spell-Checking the Entire Document

The first correction you want to make is to clean up the spelling and grammar errors that Word has identified.

1. **Start Office Word 2007 and open the file wd02_Tour Letter.**
   - **If necessary, change to Print Layout view at 100% zoom.**

Your screen should be similar to Figure 2.1

Figure 2.1

To co... conte... Lab 1... you a... break... manually turn on the spelling and grammar checker to locate and correct all the errors in the document at once.

2. **Open the Review tab.**
   - **Click [Spelling & Grammar].**

Another Method
The keyboard shortcut is F7.

   - **If necessary, select the Check grammar option to turn on grammar checking.**

Additional Information
You also can click the Spelling and Grammar status icon to move to the next spelling or grammar error and open the spelling context menu.

Your screen should be similar to Figure 2.2

Figure 2.2

Additional Information
Because the contents of the list are determined only by spelling, any instances of terms that seem inappropriate in context are completely coincidental.

Additional Information
The [Change All] option replaces the same word throughout the document with the word you select in the Suggestions box.

The Spelling and Grammar dialog box is displayed, and the spelling and grammar checker has immediately located the first word that may be misspelled, "paddleing." The sentence with the misspelled word in red is displayed in the Not in Dictionary text box, and the word is highlighted in the document.

The Suggestions list box displays the words the spelling checker has located in the dictionary that most closely match the misspelled word. The most likely match is highlighted. Sometimes the spelling checker does not display any suggested replacements. This occurs when it cannot locate any words in the dictionaries that are similar in spelling. If no suggestions are provided, the Not in Dictionary text box simply displays the word that is highlighted in the text.

To change the spelling of the word to one of the suggested spellings, highlight the correct word in the list and then click [Change]. If there were no suggested replacements, and you did not want to use any of the option buttons, you could edit the word yourself by typing the correction in the Not in Dictionary box. In this case, the correct replacement, "paddling," is already highlighted.

AND EASY-TO-FOLLOW DESIGN

TABLES

Tables provide quick summaries of concepts and procedures for specific tasks.

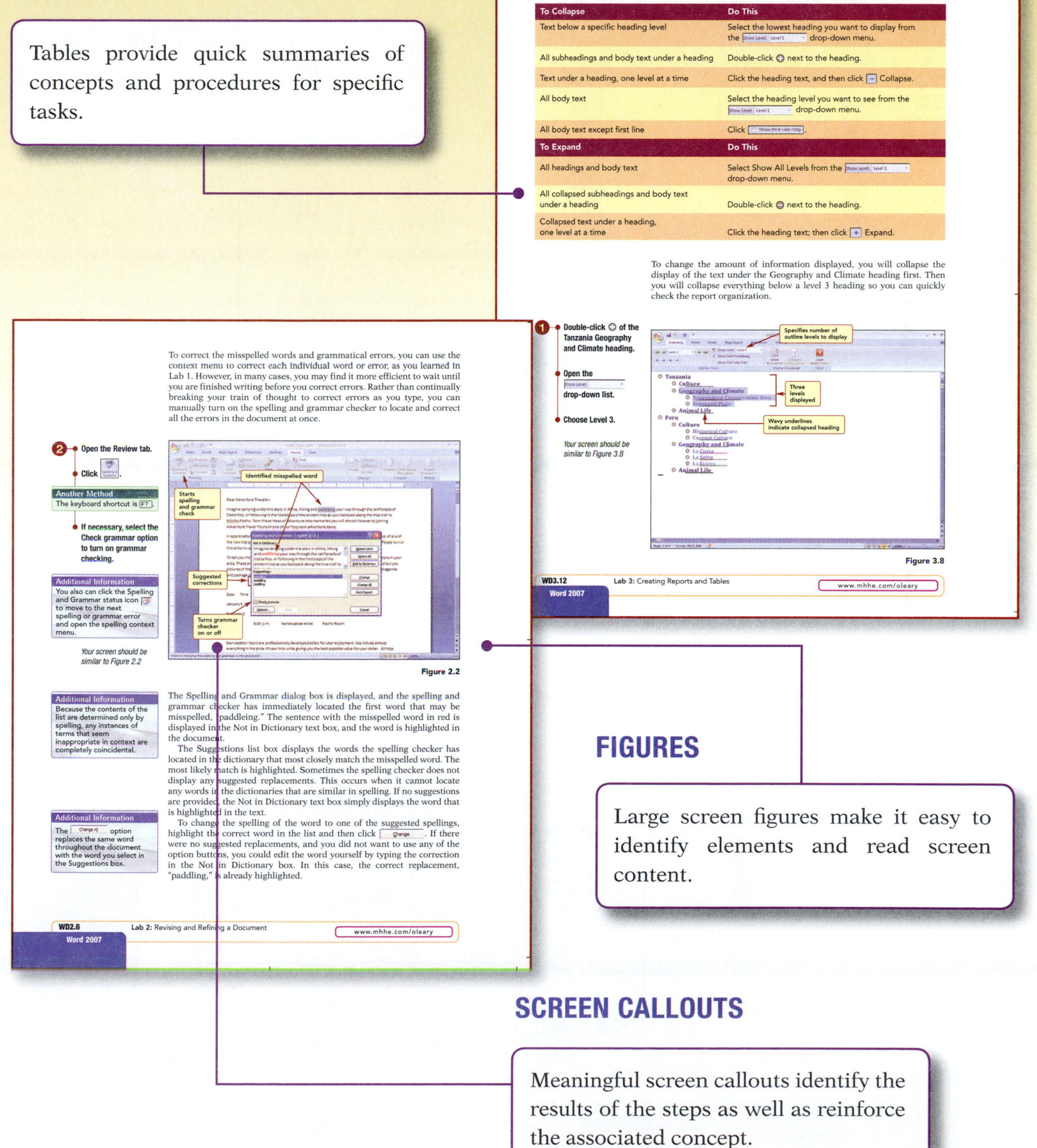

To Collapse	Do This
Text below a specific heading level	Select the lowest heading you want to display from the [Show Level: Level 1] drop-down menu.
All subheadings and body text under a heading	Double-click ⊕ next to the heading.
Text under a heading, one level at a time	Click the heading text, and then click [–] Collapse.
All body text	Select the heading level you want to see from the [Show Level: Level 1] drop-down menu.
All body text except first line	Click [Show First Line Only].
To Expand	**Do This**
All headings and body text	Select Show All Levels from the [Show Level: Level 1] drop-down menu.
All collapsed subheadings and body text under a heading	Double-click ⊖ next to the heading.
Collapsed text under a heading, one level at a time	Click the heading text; then click [+] Expand.

To change the amount of information displayed, you will collapse the display of the text under the Geography and Climate heading first. Then you will collapse everything below a level 3 heading so you can quickly check the report organization.

1. Double-click ⊕ of the Tanzania Geography and Climate heading.
   - Open the [Show Level] drop-down list.
   - Choose Level 3.

Your screen should be similar to Figure 3.8

Figure 3.8

To correct the misspelled words and grammatical errors, you can use the context menu to correct each individual word or error, as you learned in Lab 1. However, in many cases, you may find it more efficient to wait until you are finished writing before you correct errors. Rather than continually breaking your train of thought to correct errors as you type, you can manually turn on the spelling and grammar checker to locate and correct all the errors in the document at once.

2. Open the Review tab.
   - Click [Spelling & Grammar].

Another Method
The keyboard shortcut is F7.

- If necessary, select the Check grammar option to turn on grammar checking.

Additional Information
You also can click the Spelling and Grammar status icon to move to the next spelling or grammar error and open the spelling context menu.

Your screen should be similar to Figure 2.2

Figure 2.2

The Spelling and Grammar dialog box is displayed, and the spelling and grammar checker has immediately located the first word that may be misspelled, "paddleing." The sentence with the misspelled word in red is displayed in the Not in Dictionary text box, and the word is highlighted in the document.

The Suggestions list box displays the words the spelling checker has located in the dictionary that most closely match the misspelled word. The most likely match is highlighted. Sometimes the spelling checker does not display any suggested replacements. This occurs when it cannot locate any words in the dictionaries that are similar in spelling. If no suggestions are provided, the Not in Dictionary text box simply displays the word that is highlighted in the text.

Additional Information
Because the contents of the list are determined only by spelling, any instances of terms that seem inappropriate in context are completely coincidental.

To change the spelling of the word to one of the suggested spellings, highlight the correct word in the list and then click [Change]. If there were no suggested replacements, and you did not want to use any of the option buttons, you could edit the word yourself by typing the correction in the Not in Dictionary box. In this case, the correct replacement, "paddling," is already highlighted.

Additional Information
The [Change All] option replaces the same word throughout the document with the word you select in the Suggestions box.

FIGURES

Large screen figures make it easy to identify elements and read screen content.

SCREEN CALLOUTS

Meaningful screen callouts identify the results of the steps as well as reinforce the associated concept.

SUPPORTIVE MARGIN NOTES

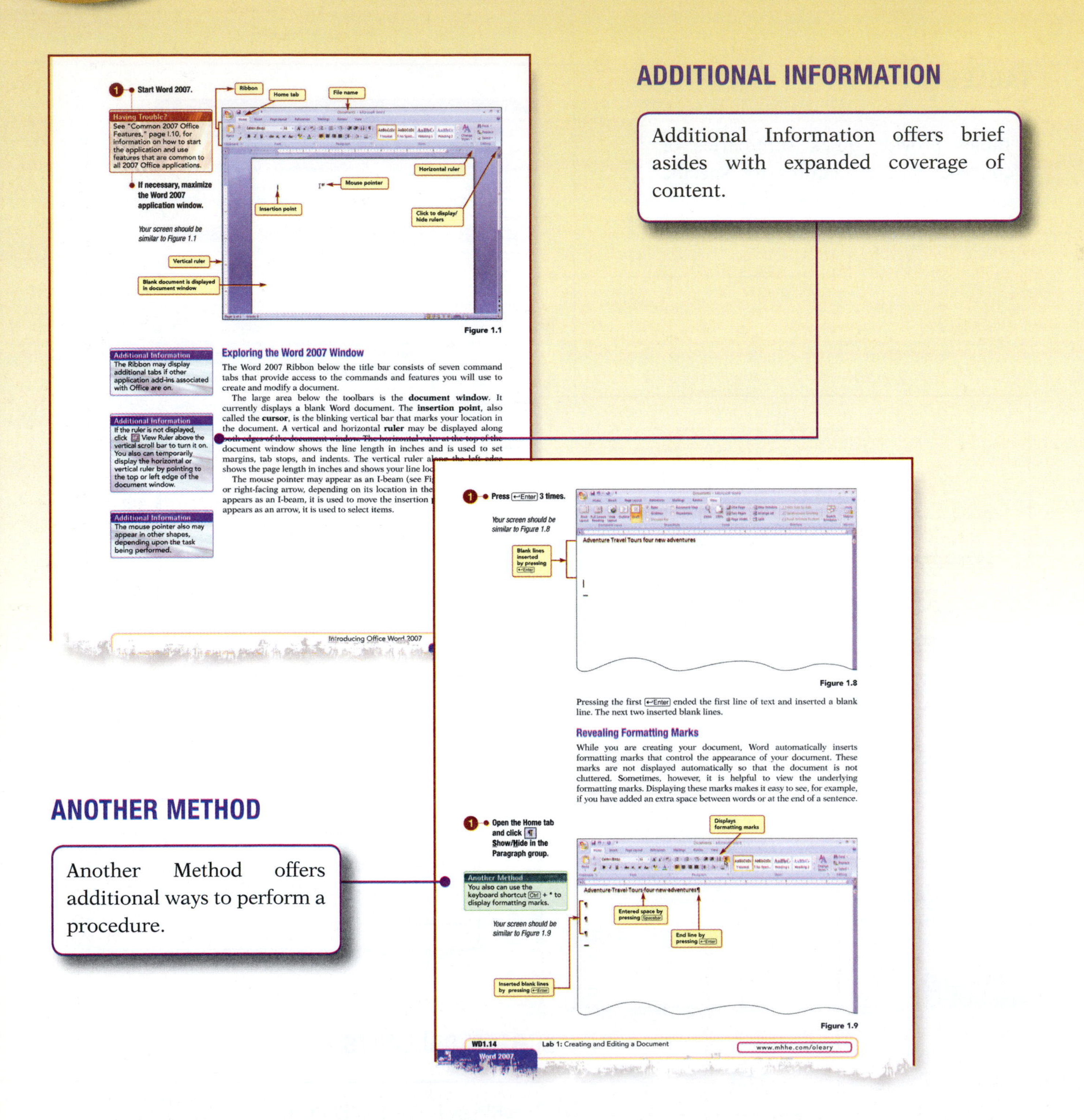

Start Word 2007.

Having Trouble? See "Common 2007 Office Features," page I.10, for information on how to start the application and use features that are common to all 2007 Office applications.

If necessary, maximize the Word 2007 application window.

Your screen should be similar to Figure 1.1

Figure 1.1

Additional Information The Ribbon may display additional tabs if other application add-ins associated with Office are on.

Additional Information If the ruler is not displayed, click View Ruler above the vertical scroll bar to turn it on. You also can temporarily display the horizontal or vertical ruler by pointing to the top or left edge of the document window.

Additional Information The mouse pointer also may appear in other shapes, depending upon the task being performed.

Exploring the Word 2007 Window

The Word 2007 Ribbon below the title bar consists of seven command tabs that provide access to the commands and features you will use to create and modify a document.

The large area below the toolbars is the **document window**. It currently displays a blank Word document. The **insertion point**, also called the **cursor**, is the blinking vertical bar that marks your location in the document. A vertical and horizontal **ruler** may be displayed along both edges of the document window. The horizontal ruler at the top of the document window shows the line length in inches and is used to set margins, tab stops, and indents. The vertical ruler along the left edge shows the page length in inches and shows your line loc...

The mouse pointer may appear as an I-beam (see Fi... or right-facing arrow, depending on its location in the... appears as an I-beam, it is used to move the insertion p... appears as an arrow, it is used to select items.

Introducing Office Word 2007

ADDITIONAL INFORMATION

Additional Information offers brief asides with expanded coverage of content.

Press ←Enter 3 times.

Your screen should be similar to Figure 1.8

Figure 1.8

Pressing the first ←Enter ended the first line of text and inserted a blank line. The next two inserted blank lines.

Revealing Formatting Marks

While you are creating your document, Word automatically inserts formatting marks that control the appearance of your document. These marks are not displayed automatically so that the document is not cluttered. Sometimes, however, it is helpful to view the underlying formatting marks. Displaying these marks makes it easy to see, for example, if you have added an extra space between words or at the end of a sentence.

Open the Home tab and click ¶ Show/Hide in the Paragraph group.

Another Method You also can use the keyboard shortcut Ctrl + * to display formatting marks.

Your screen should be similar to Figure 1.9

Figure 1.9

WD1.14 Word 2007 Lab 1: Creating and Editing a Document www.mhhe.com/oleary

ANOTHER METHOD

Another Method offers additional ways to perform a procedure.

SUPPORTIVE MARGIN NOTES (CONTINUED)

The document now displays the formatting marks. The ¶ character on the line above the insertion point represents the pressing of ←Enter that created the blank line. The ¶ character at the end of the text represents the pressing of ←Enter that ended the line and moved the insertion point to the beginning of the next line. Between each word, a dot shows where the Spacebar was pressed. Formatting marks do not appear when the document is printed. You can continue to work on the document while the formatting marks are displayed, just as you did when they were hidden.

You have decided you want the flyer heading to be on two lines, with the words "four new adventures" on the second line. To do this, you will insert a blank line after the word Tours. You will move the insertion point to the location in the text where you want to insert the blank line.

2
- **Click on the right side of the "s" in "Tours" before the dot for a space.**
- **Press ←Enter 2 times.**
- **Press Delete to remove the space at the beginning of the line.**
- **Press ↓.**

Your screen should be similar to Figure 1.10

Figure 1.10

As you continue to create a document, the formatting marks are automatically adjusted.

Identifying and Correcting Errors Automatically

Notice that a green wavy underline appears under the word "four." This indicates an error has been detected.

As you enter text, Word is constantly checking the document for spelling and grammar errors. The Spelling and Grammar Status icon in the status bar displays an animated pencil icon while you are typing, indicating Word is checking for errors as you type. When you stop typing, it displays either a blue checkmark, indicating the program does not detect any errors, or a red X, indicating the document contains an error.

Having Trouble?
If the green underline is not displayed, click Office Button, click Word Options, Proofing, and select the "Check spelling as you type", "Mark grammar errors as you type", and "Check grammar with spelling" options.

Identifying and Correcting Errors Automatically **WD1.15**

Word 2007

HAVING TROUBLE

Having Trouble helps resolve potential problems as students work through each lab.

MORE ABOUT

New to this edition, the More About icon directs students to the More About appendix found at the end of the book. Without interrupting the flow of the text, this appendix provides additional coverage required to meet MCAS certification.

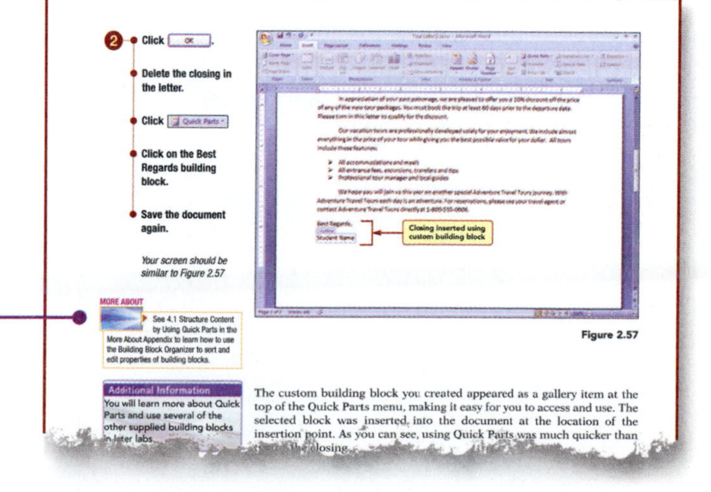

2
- **Click OK.**
- **Delete the closing in the letter.**
- **Click Quick Parts.**
- **Click on the Best Regards building block.**
- **Save the document again.**

Your screen should be similar to Figure 2.57

Figure 2.57

MORE ABOUT
See 4.1 Structure Content by Using Quick Parts in the More About Appendix to learn how to use the Building Block Organizer to sort and edit properties of building blocks.

Additional Information
You will learn more about Quick Parts and use several of the other supplied building blocks in later labs.

The custom building block you created appeared as a gallery item at the top of the Quick Parts menu, making it easy for you to access and use. The selected block was inserted into the document at the location of the insertion point. As you can see, using Quick Parts was much quicker than ... the closing.

REAL-WORLD APPLICATION

The default range setting, All, is the correct setting. In the Copies section, the default setting of one copy of the document is acceptable. You will print using the default print settings.

2 If you need to change the selected printer to another printer, open the Name drop-down list box and select the appropriate printer (your instructor will tell you which printer to select).

Click OK.

Your printer should be printing the document. The printed copy of the flyer should be similar to the document shown in the Case Study at the beginning of the lab.

Exiting Word

You are finished working on the flyer for now and want to save the last few changes you have made to the document and close the Word application. The Exit Word command in the File menu is used to quit the Word program. Alternatively, you can click the ✕ Close button in the application window title bar. If you attempt to close the application without first saving your document, Word displays a warning asking if you want to save your work. If you do not save your work and you exit the application, any changes you made since last saving it are lost.

Another Method
The keyboard shortcut for the Exit command is Alt + F4.

1 Click ✕ Close.

Click Yes to save the changes you made to the file.

The Windows desktop is visible again.

If multiple Word documents are open, clicking ✕ closes the application window containing the document you are viewing only.

Focus on Careers

EXPLORE YOUR CAREER OPTIONS

Food Service Manager

Have you noticed flyers around your campus advertising job positions? Many of these jobs are in the food service industry. Food service managers are traditionally responsible for overseeing the kitchen and dining room. However, these positions increasingly involve administrative tasks, including recruiting new employees. As a food service manager, your position would likely include creating newspaper notices and flyers to attract new staff. These flyers should be eye-catching and error-free. The typical salary range of a food service manager is $34,000 to $41,700. Demand for skilled food service managers is expected to increase through 2010.

Exiting Word **WD1.71**

Word 2007

FOCUS ON CAREERS

Focus on Careers provides an example of how the material covered may be applied in the "real world."

Each lab highlights a specific career, ranging from forensic science technician to food services manager, and presents job responsibilities and salary ranges for each.

Case Study

Adventure Travel Tours

Adventure Travel Tours provides information on their tours in a variety of forms. Travel brochures, for instance, contain basic tour information in a promotional format and are designed to entice potential clients to sign up for a tour. More detailed regional information packets are given to people who have already signed up for a tour, so they can prepare for their vacation. These packets include facts about each region's climate, geography, and culture. Additional informational formats include pages on Adventure Travel's Web site and scheduled group presentations.

Part of your responsibility as advertising coordinator is to gather the information that Adventure Travel will publicize about each regional tour. Specifically, you have been asked to provide background information for two of the new tours: the Tanzania Safari and the Machu Picchu trail. Because this information is used in a variety of formats, your research needs to be easily adapted. You will therefore present your facts in the form of a general report on Tanzania and Peru.

In this lab, you will learn to use many of the features of Office Word 2007 that make it easy to create an attractive and well-organized report. A portion of the completed report is shown here.

WD3.2

CONTINUING CASE STUDIES

Within each series application, the same Case Study is used to illustrate concepts and procedures.

AND INTEGRATION

WORKING TOGETHER LABS

At the completion of the brief and introductory texts, a final lab demonstrates the integration of Microsoft Office applications. Each Working Together lab also includes end-of-chapter materials.

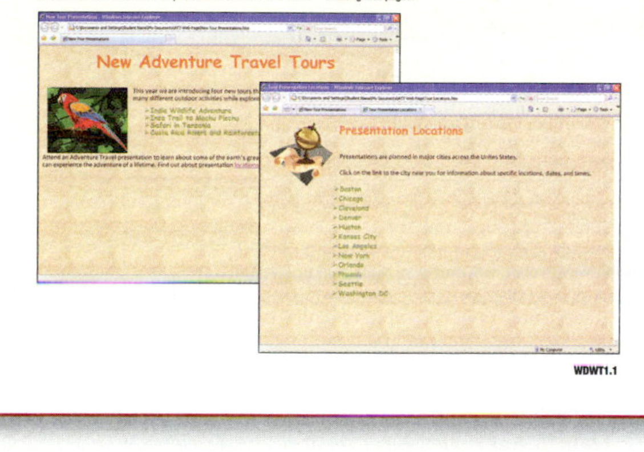

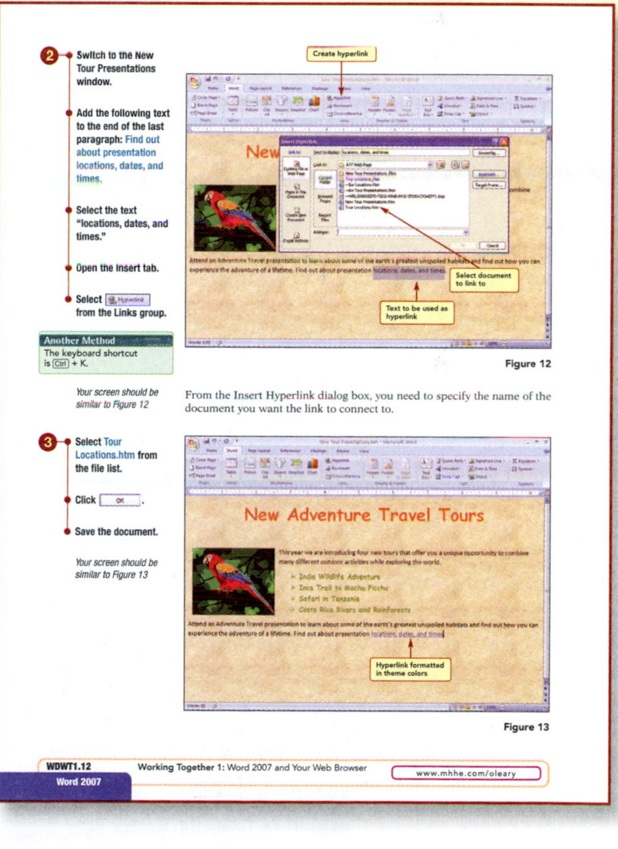

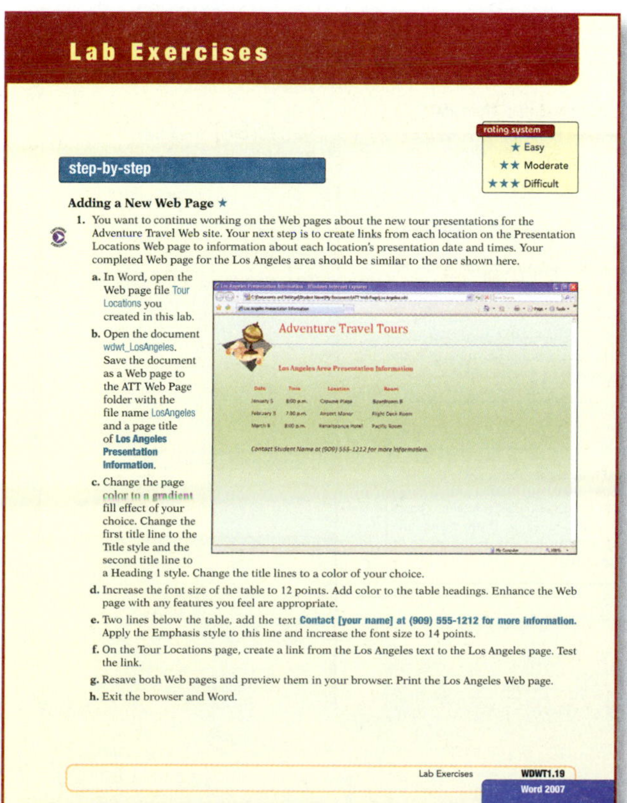

REINFORCED CONCEPTS

CONCEPT PREVIEW

Concept Previews provide an overview to the concepts that will be presented throughout the lab.

Concept Preview

The following concepts will be introduced in this lab:

1. **Grammar Checker** The grammar checker advises you of incorrect grammar as you create and edit a document, and proposes possible corrections.
2. **Spelling Checker** The spelling checker advises you of misspelled words as you create and edit a document, and proposes possible corrections.
3. **AutoCorrect** The AutoCorrect feature makes some basic assumptions about the text you are typing and, based on these assumptions, automatically corrects the entry.
4. **Word Wrap** The word wrap feature automatically decides where to end a line and wrap text to the next line based on the margin settings.
5. **Font and Font Size** Font, also commonly referred to as a typeface, is a set of characters with a specific design that has one or more font sizes.
6. **Alignment** Alignment is the positioning of text on a line between the margins or indents. There are four types of paragraph alignment: left, centered, right, and justified.
7. **Graphics** A graphic is a nontext element or object such as a drawing or picture that can be added to a document.

Introducing Office Word 2007

Adventure Travel Tours has recently upgraded their computer systems at all locations across the country. As part of the upgrade, they have installed the latest version of the Microsoft Office 2007 suite of applications. You are very excited to see how this new and powerful application can help you create professional letters and reports as well as eye-catching flyers and newsletters.

Starting Office Word 2007

...on Microsoft Office Word 2007 ...nd presentations.

www.mhhe.com/oleary

CONCEPT BOXES

Concept boxes appear throughout the lab providing clear, concise explanations and serving as a valuable study aid.

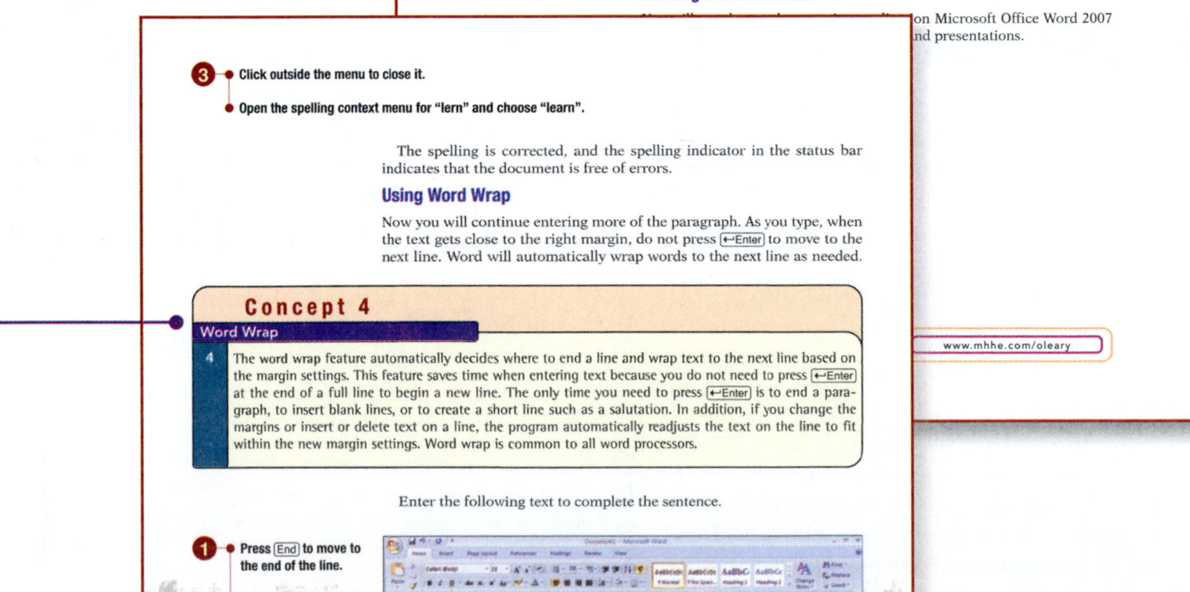

3. **Click outside the menu to close it.**
   Open the spelling context menu for "lern" and choose "learn".

The spelling is corrected, and the spelling indicator in the status bar indicates that the document is free of errors.

Using Word Wrap

Now you will continue entering more of the paragraph. As you type, when the text gets close to the right margin, do not press ←Enter to move to the next line. Word will automatically wrap words to the next line as needed.

Concept 4

Word Wrap

The word wrap feature automatically decides where to end a line and wrap text to the next line based on the margin settings. This feature saves time when entering text because you do not need to press ←Enter at the end of a full line to begin a new line. The only time you need to press ←Enter is to end a paragraph, to insert blank lines, or to create a short line such as a salutation. In addition, if you change the margins or insert or delete text on a line, the program automatically readjusts the text on the line to fit within the new margin settings. Word wrap is common to all word processors.

Enter the following text to complete the sentence.

1. **Press End to move to the end of the line.**

REINFORCED CONCEPTS (CONTINUED)

CONCEPT SUMMARIES

The Concept Summary offers a visual summary of the concepts presented throughout the lab.

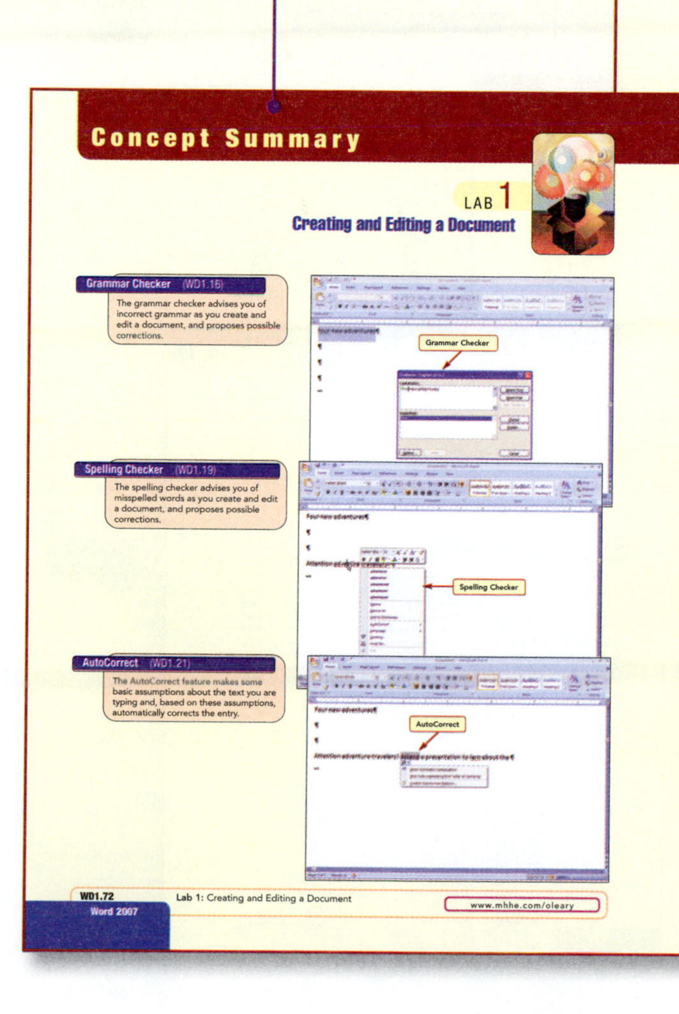

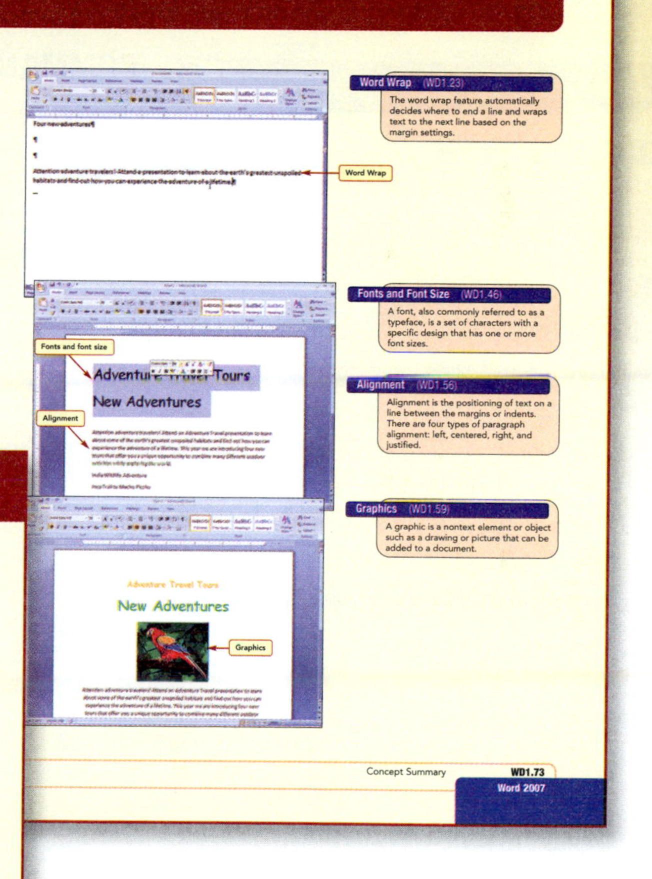

LAB REVIEW

KEY TERMS

Includes a list of all bolded terms with page references.

Lab Review

LAB 3
Creating Reports and Tables

key terms

bibliography WD3.41
caption WD3.55
cell WD3.62
citations WD3.41
Click and Type WD3.27
cross-reference WD3.55
Document Map WD3.37
document theme WD3.21
drawing layer WD3.52
endnote WD3.47
floating object WD3.52
footer WD3.79
footnote WD3.47
header WD3.79
heading style WD3.7
inline object WD3.52
navigation window WD3.37
note pane WD3.48
note reference mark WD3.47
note separator WD3.47
note text WD3.47
placeholder WD3.18
quick style WD3.7
section WD3.80
section break WD3.80
sort WD3.66
split window WD3.57
table WD3.62
table of contents WD3.33
table of figures WD3.72
table reference WD3.62
text box WD3.57
text wrapping WD3.52
thumbnails WD3.39

COMMAND SUMMARY

Command Summaries provide a table of commands, shortcuts, and their associated action for all commands used in the lab.

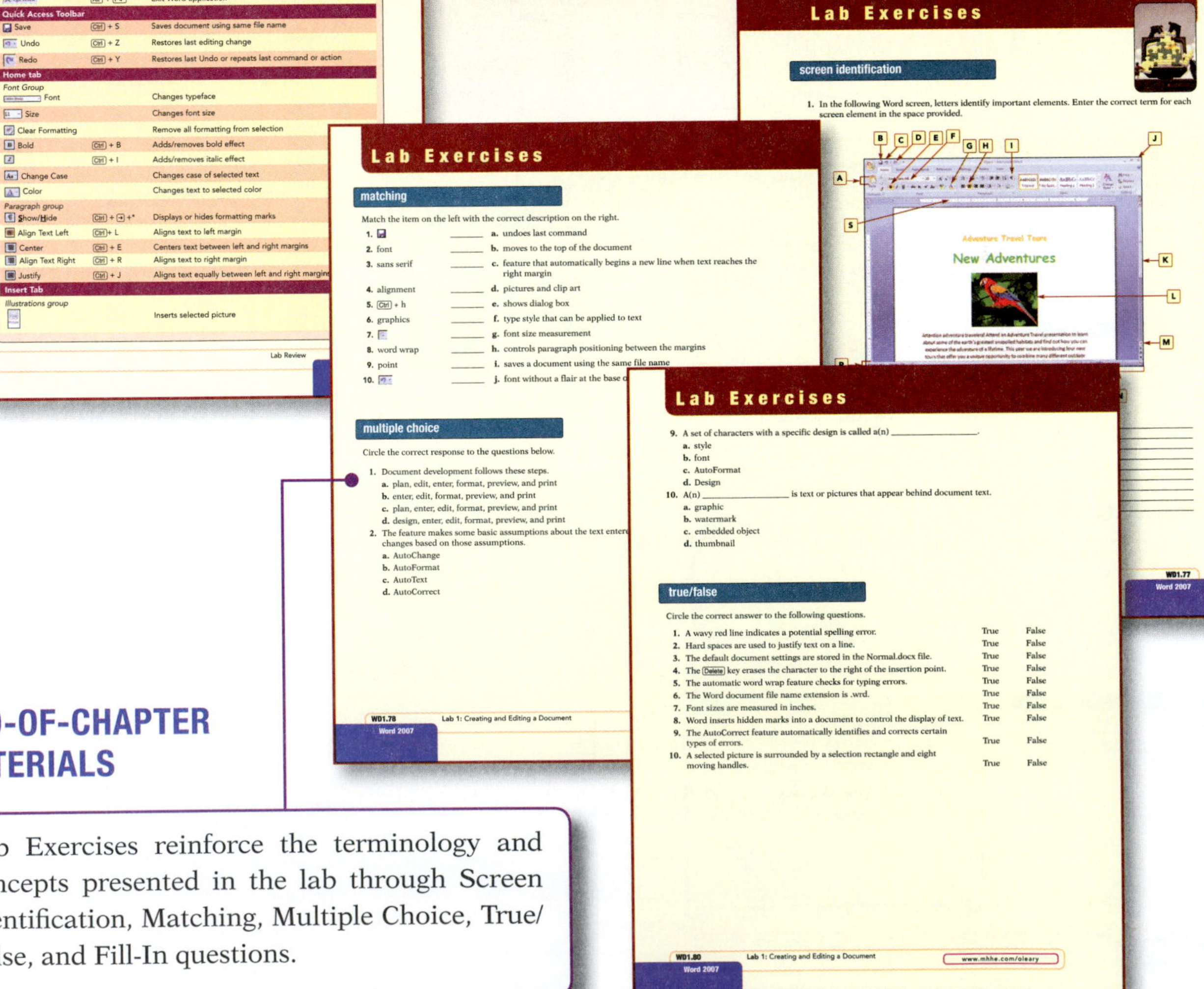

command summary

Command	Shortcut	Action
Office Button		Opens file menu
New	Ctrl + N	Opens new blank document
Open	Ctrl + O	Opens existing document file
Save	Ctrl + S	Saves document using same file name
Save As		Saves document using a new file name, type, and/or location
Print	Ctrl + P	Prints document
Prepare/Properties		Opens Document Information Panel
Close	Ctrl + F4	Closes document
Exit Word	Alt + F4	Exit Word application
Quick Access Toolbar		
Save	Ctrl + S	Saves document using same file name
Undo	Ctrl + Z	Restores last editing change
Redo	Ctrl + Y	Restores last Undo or repeats last command or action
Home tab		
Font Group		
Font		Changes typeface
Size		Changes font size
Clear Formatting		Remove all formatting from selection
Bold	Ctrl + B	Adds/removes bold effect
	Ctrl + I	Adds/removes italic effect
Change Case		Changes case of selected text
Color		Changes text to selected color
Paragraph group		
Show/Hide	Ctrl + ⇧ + *	Displays or hides formatting marks
Align Text Left	Ctrl + L	Aligns text to left margin
Center	Ctrl + E	Centers text between left and right margins
Align Text Right	Ctrl + R	Aligns text to right margin
Justify	Ctrl + J	Aligns text equally between left and right margins
Insert Tab		
Illustrations group		
		Inserts selected picture

Lab Exercises

screen identification

1. In the following Word screen, letters identify important elements. Enter the correct term for each screen element in the space provided.

Lab Exercises

matching

Match the item on the left with the correct description on the right.

1. ____ a. undoes last command
2. font ____ b. moves to the top of the document
3. sans serif ____ c. feature that automatically begins a new line when text reaches the right margin
4. alignment ____ d. pictures and clip art
5. Ctrl + h ____ e. shows dialog box
6. graphics ____ f. type style that can be applied to text
7. ____ g. font size measurement
8. word wrap ____ h. controls paragraph positioning between the margins
9. point ____ i. saves a document using the same file name
10. ____ j. font without a flair at the base

multiple choice

Circle the correct response to the questions below.

1. Document development follows these steps.
   a. plan, edit, enter, format, preview, and print
   b. enter, edit, format, preview, and print
   c. plan, enter, edit, format, preview, and print
   d. design, enter, edit, format, preview, and print
2. The feature makes some basic assumptions about the text entered and automatically makes changes based on those assumptions.
   a. AutoChange
   b. AutoFormat
   c. AutoText
   d. AutoCorrect

WD1.78 Word 2007 Lab 1: Creating and Editing a Document

Lab Exercises

9. A set of characters with a specific design is called a(n) ______________.
   a. style
   b. font
   c. AutoFormat
   d. Design
10. A(n) ______________ is text or pictures that appear behind document text.
   a. graphic
   b. watermark
   c. embedded object
   d. thumbnail

true/false

Circle the correct answer to the following questions.

1. A wavy red line indicates a potential spelling error. True False
2. Hard spaces are used to justify text on a line. True False
3. The default document settings are stored in the Normal.docx file. True False
4. The Delete key erases the character to the right of the insertion point. True False
5. The automatic word wrap feature checks for typing errors. True False
6. The Word document file name extension is .wrd. True False
7. Font sizes are measured in inches. True False
8. Word inserts hidden marks into a document to control the display of text. True False
9. The AutoCorrect feature automatically identifies and corrects certain types of errors. True False
10. A selected picture is surrounded by a selection rectangle and eight moving handles. True False

WD1.80 Word 2007 Lab 1: Creating and Editing a Document www.mhhe.com/oleary

WD1.77 Word 2007

END-OF-CHAPTER MATERIALS

Lab Exercises reinforce the terminology and concepts presented in the lab through Screen Identification, Matching, Multiple Choice, True/False, and Fill-In questions.

AND SKILL DEVELOPMENT

LAB EXERCISES

Lab Exercises provide hands-on practice and develop critical-thinking skills through step-by-step and on-your-own practice exercises. Many cases in the practice exercises tie to a running case used in another application lab. This helps demonstrate the use of the four applications across a common case setting. For example, the Adventure Tours case used in Word is continued in practice exercises in Excel, Access, and PowerPoint.

ON YOUR OWN

STEP-BY-STEP

Lab Exercises

on your own

Creating a Flyer ★

1. Adventure Travel Tours is offering a great deal on a Day of the Dead Bicycle Tour in Mexico. Research the Day of the Dead celebration using the Web as a resource. Then, using the features of Word you have learned so far, create a flyer that will advertise this tour. Be sure to use at least two colors of text, two sizes of text, and two kinds of paragraph alignment. Include a graphic from the Clip Organizer. Include your name at the bottom of the flyer. Include your name in the file properties as author and the file name as the title. Save the document as Mexico Adventure.

Creating a Swimming Pool Rules Flyer ★★

2. You work in the community pool and have been asked to create a flyer to post that identifies the rules swimmers should follow when using the pool. Create a flyer that explains the five most important rules to follow while swimming at the pool. Use a piece of clip art to liven up your flyer. Include different font sizes, paragraph alignments, and other formatting features to make the flyer attractive. Apply different font colors for each rule. Include a page border. Include your name at the bottom of the flyer. Include your name in the file properties as author and the file name as the title. Save the document as Pool Rules.

Astronomy Class Memo ★★

3. The city of Gilbert, Arizona, has recently built a $100,000 observatory that includes a $20,000 telescope in a local park. The observatory is open evenings for small groups of five to six people to take turns looking through the 16-inch telescope's eyepiece. The use of the observatory is free.
   The city has decided to offer classes for the community to learn how to use the telescope and to teach about astronomy. As a trial run, the class will first be offered to city employees and their families. You want to notify all employees about the observatory and the class by including a memo with their paycheck. Using Hands-On Exercise 1 as a model, provide information about when and where the class will be held. Include information about how people sign up for the class. Include your name in the file properties as author and the file name as the title. Save the memo as Astronomy Basics.

Volunteer Opportunities ★★★

4. Many community groups, hospitals, libraries, and churches are looking for volunteers to assist in their programs. Volunteering has rewards for both the volunteer and the community. Using the Web as a resource, research volunteer opportunities in your community. Then write a one-page report that includes information about two volunteer groups for which you would like to volunteer. Include information about what the organization does for the community. Also include the skills you have to offer and the amount of time you can commit as volunteer. Include a title at the top of the document and your name and the current date below the title. Center the title lines. Use at least two colors of text, two sizes of text, and two kinds of paragraph alignment. Include a graphic from the Clip Organizer. Include your name in the file properties as author and the file name as the title. Save the document as Volunteer Opportunities.

Writing a Career Report ★★★

5. Using the library or the Web, research information about your chosen career. Write a one-page report about your findings that includes information on three areas: Career Description; Educational Requirements; Salary and Employment projections. Include a title at the top of the document and your name and the current date below the title. Center the title lines. Justify the paragraphs. Include your name in the file properties as author and the file name as the title. Save the document as Career Report.

WD1.88 Word 2007 | Lab 1: Creating and Editing a Document | www.mhhe.com/oleary

Lab Exercises

Hands-On Exercises

rating system
★ Easy
★★ Moderate
★★★ Difficult

Step-by-Step

Asking for Input Memo ★

1. Adventure Travel Tours is planning to update its Web site in the near future. You have been asked to solicit suggestions from the travel agents about changes they would like to see made to the current Web site. You decide to send all the travel agents a memo asking them for their input. Your completed memo will be similar to the one shown here.
   a. Open a blank Word 2007 document and create the following memo in Draft view. Press Tab twice after you type the colons (:) following To in the memo header. Press Tab once after the From and Date lines. This will make the information following the colons line up evenly. Enter a blank line between paragraphs.

   To: Travel Agents
   From: Student Name
   Date: September, 15, 2008

   The Adventure Travel Tours Web site was designed with travel agents in mind. But as you know, the role of the travel agent is changing. In order to keep up with these changes we plan to begin work on updating the Adventure Travel Tours Web site.

   In preparation for this project, I would like your input about the content that will only be available to travel agents. In the next few days as you work with clients please note what can be changed to make it easier for you to book travel, and then send your comments back to me. All suggestions for changes are welcome and will be considered for our improved Web site.

   Thank you in advance for your input.

   To: Travel Agents
   From: Student Name
   Date: [Current date]

   The Adventure Travel Tours current Web site was designed with travel agents in mind but as you know, the role of the travel agent is changing. In order to keep up with these changes we plan to begin work on updating the current Adventure Travel Tours Web site. In preparation for this project, I would like your input about the content that will only be available to travel agents. As you work with clients please note what can be changed to make it easier for you to book travel, then send your comments back to me. All suggestions for changes are welcome and will be considered for our improved Web site.

   Thank you in advance for your input.
   b. Correct any spelling and grammar errors that are identified.
   c. Turn on the display of formatting marks. Check the document and remove any extra blank spaces between words or at the end of lines.
   d. Save the document as Web Site Memo in your data file location.
   e. Switch to Print Layout view.
   f. End the first sentence after the word "mind". Capitalize the following word, but. Insert the text

WD1.82 Word 2004 | Lab 1: Creating and Editing a Document | www.mhhe.com/oleary

RATING SYSTEM

These exercises have a rating system from easy to difficult and test your ability to apply the knowledge you have gained in each lab. Exercises that build off of previous exercises are noted with a Continuing Exercises icon.

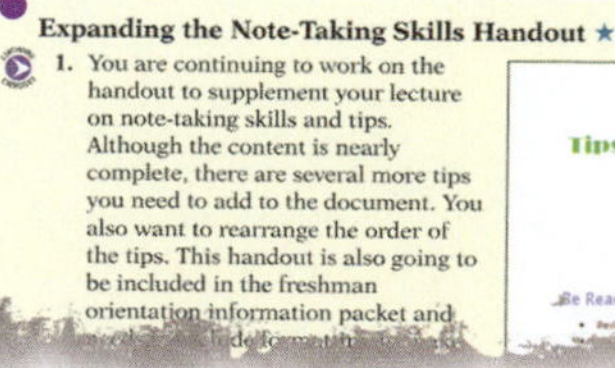

Expanding the Note-Taking Skills Handout ★

1. You are continuing to work on the handout to supplement your lecture on note-taking skills and tips. Although the content is nearly complete, there are several more tips you need to add to the document. You also want to rearrange the order of the tips. This handout is also going to be included in the freshman orientation information packet and

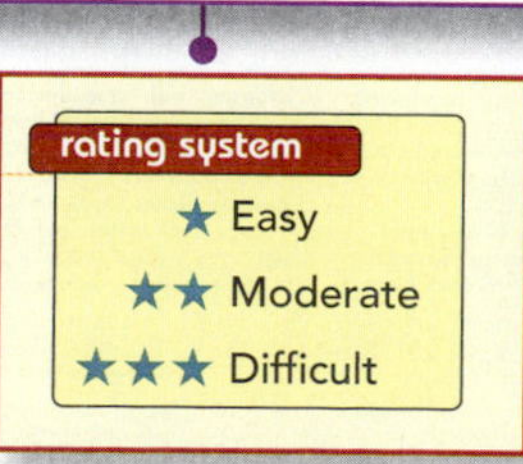

END-OF-BOOK RESOURCES

2007 Word Brief Command Summary

Command	Shortcut	Action
Office Button		**Opens File menu**
New	Ctrl + N	Opens new document
Open	Ctrl + O	Opens existing document file
Save	Ctrl + S	Saves document using same file name
Save As	F12	Saves document using a new file name, type, and/or location
Save as/Save As type/ Web Page		Saves file as a Web page document
Print	Ctrl + P	Specify print settings before printing document
Print/Print Preview		Displays document as it will appear when printed
Print/Quick Print		Prints document using default printer settings
Prepare/Properties		Opens Document Information Panel
Close	Ctrl + F4	Closes document
Word Options/Proofing		Changes settings associated with Spelling and Grammar checking
Word Options/Advanced/ Mark formatting inconsistencies		Checks for formatting inconsistencies
Exit Word	Alt + F4, X	Closes the Word application
Quick Access Toolbar		
Save		Saves document using same file name
Undo	Ctrl + Z	Restores last editing change
Redo	Ctrl + Y	Restores last Undo or repeats last command or action
Home tab		
Clipboard Group Cut	Ctrl + X	Cuts selection to Clipboard
Copy	Ctrl + C	Copies selection to Clipboard
Paste	Ctrl + V	Pastes item from Clipboard
Format Painter		Copies format to selection

2007 Word Brief Command Summary WDCS.1 Word 2007

COMPREHENSIVE COMMAND SUMMARY

Provides a table of commands, shortcuts, and their associated action for all commands used throughout each text in the O'Leary Series.

Glossary of Key Terms

active window The window containing the insertion point and that will be affected by any changes you make.

alignment How text is positioned on a line between the margins or indents. There are four types of paragraph alignment: left, centered, right, and justified.

antonym A word with the opposite meaning.

author The process of creating a Web page.

AutoCorrect A feature that makes basic assumptions about the text you are typing and automatically corrects the entry.

bibliography A listing of source references that appears at the end of the document.

browser A program that connects you to remote computers and displays the Web pages you request.

building blocks Document fragments that include text and formatting and that can be easily inserted into a document.

bulleted list Displays items that logically fall out from a paragraph into a list, with items preceded by bullets.

caption A title or explanation for a table, picture, or graph.

case sensitive The capability to distinguish between uppercase and lowercase characters.

cell The intersection of a column and row where data are entered in a table.

character formatting Formatting features such as bold and color that affect the selected characters only.

citations Parenthetical source references that give credit for specific information included in a document.

Click and Type A feature available in Print Layout and Web Layout views that is used to quickly insert text, graphics, and other items in a blank area of a document, avoiding the need to enter blank lines.

clip art Professionally drawn graphics.

control A graphic element that is a container for information or objects.

cross-reference A reference in one part of a document related to information in another part.

cursor The blinking vertical bar that shows you where the next character you type will appear. Also called the insertion point.

custom dictionary A dictionary of terms you have entered that are not in the main dictionary of the spelling checker.

default The initial Word document settings that can be changed to customize documents.

destination The location to which text is moved or copied.

Document Map A feature that displays the headings in the document in the navigation window.

document properties Details about a document that describe or identify it and are saved with the document content.

document theme A predefined set of formatting choices that can be applied to an entire document in one simple step.

document window The area of the application window that displays the contents of the open document.

drag and drop A mouse procedure that moves or copies a selection to a new location.

drawing layer The layer above or below the text layer where floating objects are inserted.

drawing object A simple object consisting of shapes such as lines and boxes.

edit The process of changing and correcting existing text in a document.

Glossary of Key Terms WDG.1 Word 2007

GLOSSARY

Bolded terms found throughout each text in the O'Leary Series are defined in the glossary.

END-OF-BOOK RESOURCES (CONTINUED)

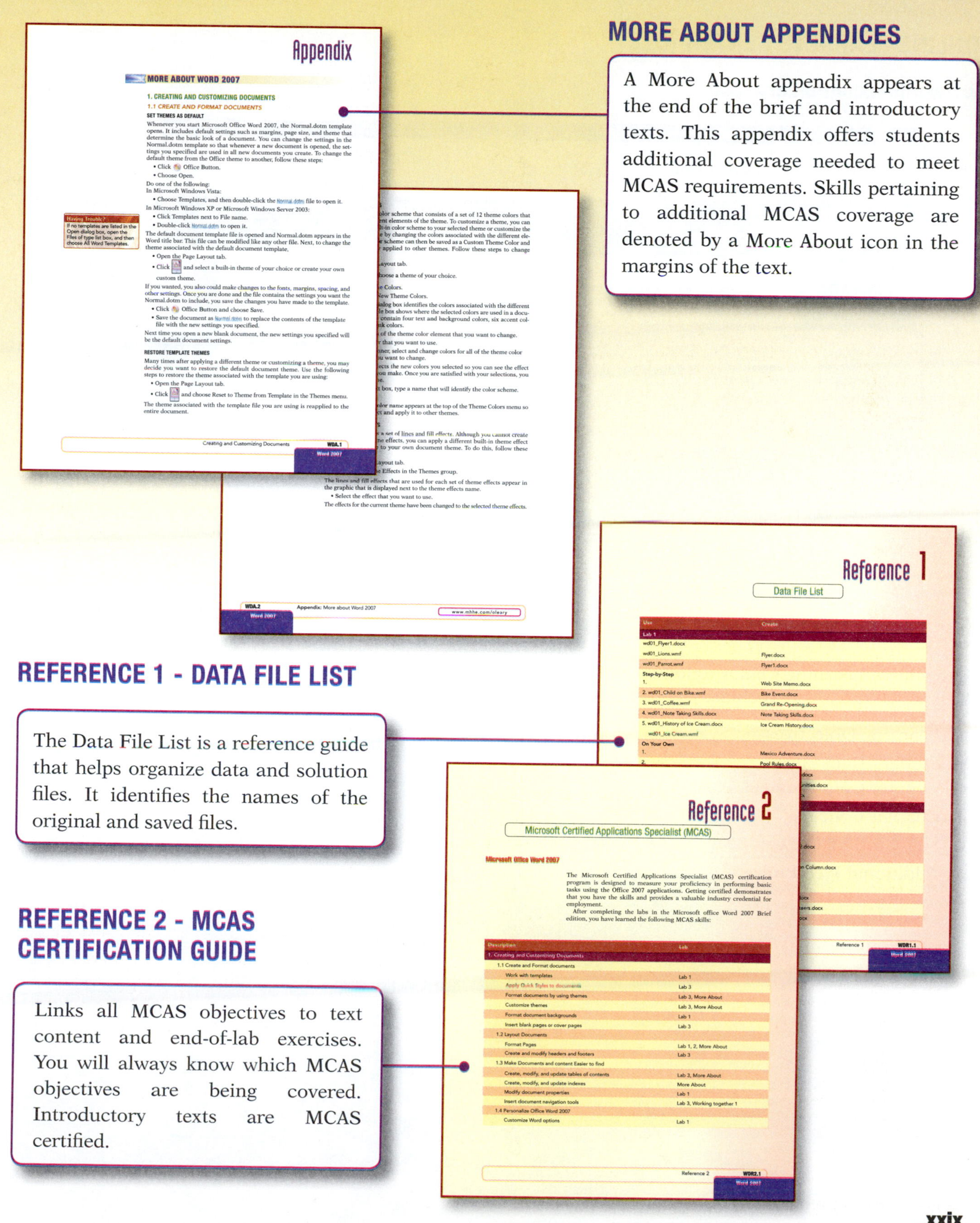

Appendix

MORE ABOUT WORD 2007

1. CREATING AND CUSTOMIZING DOCUMENTS

1.1 CREATE AND FORMAT DOCUMENTS

SET THEMES AS DEFAULT

Whenever you start Microsoft Office Word 2007, the Normal.dotm template opens. It includes default settings such as margins, page size, and theme that determine the basic look of a document. You can change the settings in the Normal.dotm template so that whenever a new document is opened, the settings you specified are used in all new documents you create. To change the default theme from the Office theme to another, follow these steps:

- Click Office Button.
- Choose Open.

Do one of the following:
In Microsoft Windows Vista:

- Choose Templates, and then double-click the Normal.dotm file to open it.

In Microsoft Windows XP or Microsoft Windows Server 2003:

- Click Templates next to File name.
- Double-click Normal.dotm to open it.

Having Trouble?
If no templates are listed in the Open dialog box, open the Files of type list box, and then choose All Word Templates.

The default document template file is opened and Normal.dotm appears in the Word title bar. This file can be modified like any other file. Next, to change the theme associated with the default document template.

- Open the Page Layout tab.
- Click and select a built-in theme of your choice or create your own custom theme.

If you wanted, you also could make changes to the fonts, margins, spacing, and other settings. Once you are done and the file contains the settings you want the Normal.dotm to include, you save the changes you have made to the template.

- Click Office Button and choose Save.
- Save the document as Normal.dotm to replace the contents of the template file with the new settings you specified.

Next time you open a new blank document, the new settings you specified will be the default document settings.

RESTORE TEMPLATE THEMES

Many times after applying a different theme or customizing a theme, you may decide you want to restore the default document theme. Use the following steps to restore the theme associated with the template you are using:

- Open the Page Layout tab.
- Click and choose Reset to Theme from Template in the Themes menu.

The theme associated with the template file you are using is reapplied to the entire document.

Creating and Customizing Documents WDA.1
Word 2007

Reference 1

Data File List

Use	Create
Lab 1	
wd01_Flyer1.docx	
wd01_Lions.wmf	Flyer.docx
wd01_Parrot.wmf	Flyer1.docx
Step-by-Step	
1.	Web Site Memo.docx
2. wd01_Child on Bike.wmf	Bike Event.docx
3. wd01_Coffee.wmf	Grand Re-Opening.docx
4. wd01_Note Taking Skills.docx	Note Taking Skills.docx
5. wd01_History of Ice Cream.docx	Ice Cream History.docx
wd01_Ice Cream.wmf	
On Your Own	
1.	Mexico Adventure.docx
2.	Pool Rules.docx

Reference 2

Microsoft Certified Applications Specialist (MCAS)

Microsoft Office Word 2007

The Microsoft Certified Applications Specialist (MCAS) certification program is designed to measure your proficiency in performing basic tasks using the Office 2007 applications. Getting certified demonstrates that you have the skills and provides a valuable industry credential for employment.

After completing the labs in the Microsoft office Word 2007 Brief edition, you have learned the following MCAS skills:

Description	Lab
1. Creating and Customizing Documents	
1.1 Create and Format documents	
Work with templates	Lab 1
Apply Quick Styles to documents	Lab 3
Format documents by using themes	Lab 3, More About
Customize themes	Lab 3, More About
Format document backgrounds	Lab 1
Insert blank pages or cover pages	Lab 3
1.2 Layout Documents	
Format Pages	Lab 1, 2, More About
Create and modify headers and footers	Lab 3
1.3 Make Documents and content Easier to find	
Create, modify, and update tables of contents	Lab 3, More About
Create, modify, and update indexes	More About
Modify document properties	Lab 1
Insert document navigation tools	Lab 3, Working together 1
1.4 Personalize Office Word 2007	
Customize Word options	Lab 1

Reference 2 WDR2.1
Word 2007

MORE ABOUT APPENDICES

A More About appendix appears at the end of the brief and introductory texts. This appendix offers students additional coverage needed to meet MCAS requirements. Skills pertaining to additional MCAS coverage are denoted by a More About icon in the margins of the text.

REFERENCE 1 - DATA FILE LIST

The Data File List is a reference guide that helps organize data and solution files. It identifies the names of the original and saved files.

REFERENCE 2 - MCAS CERTIFICATION GUIDE

Links all MCAS objectives to text content and end-of-lab exercises. You will always know which MCAS objectives are being covered. Introductory texts are MCAS certified.

ONLINE LEARNING CENTER (OLC)

www.mhhe.com/oleary

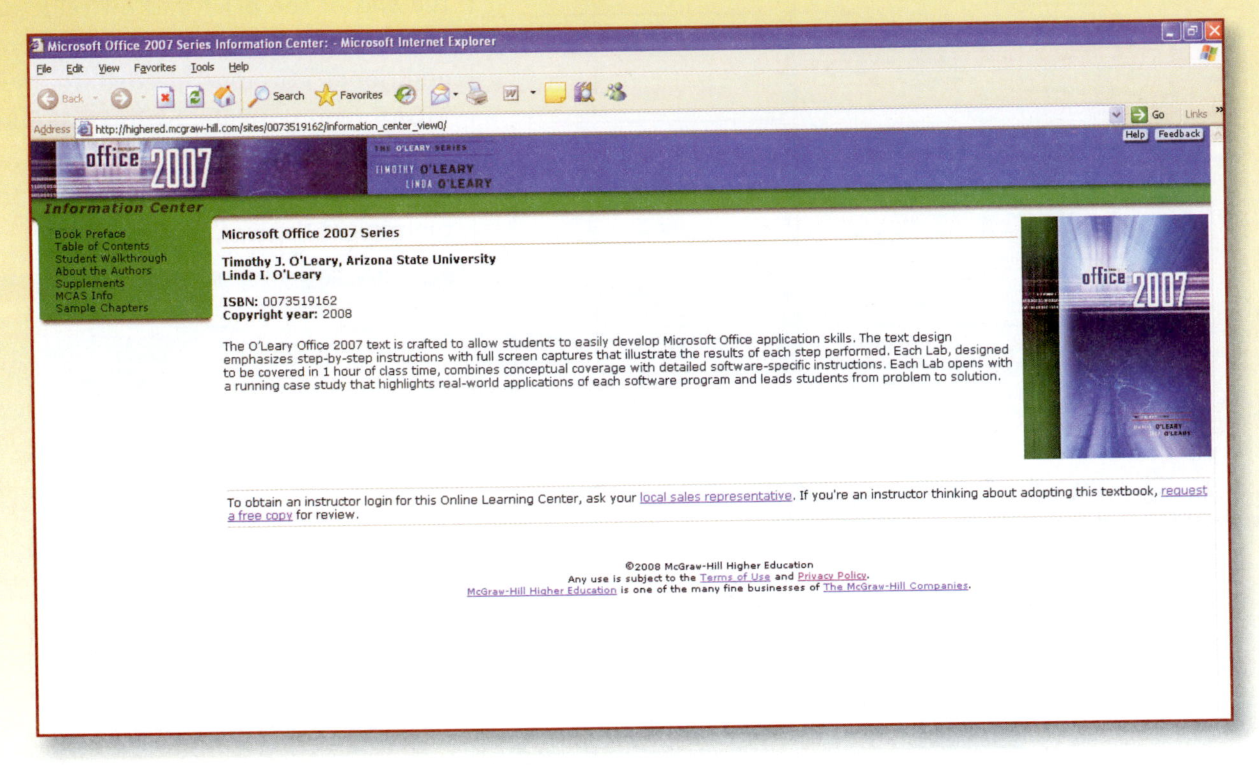

The Online Learning Center follows The O'Leary Series lab by lab, offering all kinds of supplementary help for you. OLC features include:

- Learning Objectives
- Student Data Files
- Chapter Competencies
- Chapter Concepts
- Self-Grading Quizzes
- Additional Web Links

ABOUT THE AUTHORS

Tim and Linda O'Leary live in the American Southwest and spend much of their time engaging instructors and students in conversation about learning. In fact, they have been talking about learning for over 25 years. Something in those early conversations convinced them to write a book, to bring their interest in the learning process to the printed page. Today, they are as concerned as ever about learning, about technology, and about the challenges of presenting material in new ways, in terms of both content and method of delivery.

A powerful and creative team, Tim combines his 25 years of classroom teaching experience with Linda's background as a consultant and corporate trainer. Tim has taught courses at Stark Technical College in Canton, Ohio, and at Rochester Institute of Technology in upstate New York, and is currently a professor at Arizona State University in Tempe, Arizona. Linda offered her expertise at ASU for several years as an academic advisor. She also presented and developed materials for major corporations such as Motorola, Intel, Honeywell, and AT&T, as well as various community colleges in the Phoenix area.

Tim and Linda have talked to and taught numerous students, all of them with a desire to learn something about computers and applications that make their lives easier, more interesting, and more productive.

Each new edition of an O'Leary text, supplement, or learning aid has benefited from these students and their instructors who daily stand in front of them (or over their shoulders). The O'Leary Series is no exception.

DEDICATION

We dedicate this edition to Nicole and Katie who have brought love and joy to our lives.

Introduction to Microsoft Office 2007

Objectives

After completing the Introduction to Microsoft Office 2007, you should be able to:

1. Describe the 2007 Microsoft Office System.
2. Describe the Office 2007 applications.
3. Start an Office 2007 application.
4. Recognize the basic application features.
5. Use menus, context menus, and shortcut keys.
6. Use the Ribbon, dialog boxes, and task panes.
7. Use Office Help.
8. Exit an Office 2007 application.

What Is the 2007 Microsoft Office System?

Microsoft's 2007 Microsoft Office System is a comprehensive, integrated system of programs, servers, and services designed to solve a wide array of business needs. Although the programs can be used individually, they are designed to work together seamlessly, making it easy to connect people and organizations to information, business processes, and each other. The applications include tools used to create, discuss, communicate, and manage projects. If you share a lot of documents with other people, these features facilitate access to common documents. This version has an entirely new user interface that is designed to make it easier to perform tasks and help users more quickly take advantage of all the features in the applications. In addition, the communication and collaboration features and integration with the World Wide Web have been expanded and refined.

The 2007 Microsoft Office System is packaged in several different combinations of programs or suites. The major programs and a brief description are provided in the following table.

Program	Description
Word 2007	Word Processor program used to create text-based documents
Excel 2007	Spreadsheet program used to analyze numerical data
Access 2007	Database manager used to organize, manage, and display a database
PowerPoint 2007	Graphics presentation program used to create presentation materials
Outlook 2007	Desktop information manager and messaging client
InfoPath 2007	Used to create XML forms and documents
OneNote 2007	Note-taking and information organization tools
Publisher 2007	Tools to create and distribute publications for print, Web, and e-mail
Visio 2007	Diagramming and data visualization tools
SharePoint Designer 2007	Web site development and management for SharePoint servers
Project 2007	Project management tools
Groove 2007	Collaboration program that enables teams to work together

The four main components of Microsoft Office 2007—Word, Excel, Access, and PowerPoint—are the applications you will learn about in this series of labs. They are described in more detail in the following sections.

Word 2007

Word 2007 is a word processing software application whose purpose is to help you create text-based documents. Word processors are one of the most flexible and widely used application software programs. A word processor can be used to manipulate text data to produce a letter, a report, a memo, an e-mail message, or any other type of correspondence.

Two documents you will produce in the first two Word 2007 labs, a letter and flyer, are shown here.

September 15, 2008

Dear Adventure Traveler:

Imagine camping under the stars in Africa, hiking and paddling your way through the rainforests of Costa Rica, or following in the footsteps of the ancient Inca as you backpack along the Inca trail to Machu Picchu. Turn these dreams of adventure into memories you will cherish forever by joining Adventure Travel Tours on one of our four new adventure tours.

To tell you more about these exciting new adventures, we are offering several presentations in your area. These presentations will focus on the features and cultures of the region. We will also show you pictures of the places you will visit and activities you can partici
to attend one of the following presentations:

Date	Time	
January 5	8:00 p.m.	Cro
February 3	7:30 p.m.	Air
March 8	8:00 p.m.	Re

In appreciation of your past patronage, we
of the new tour packages. You must book the trip at
letter to qualify for the discount.

Our vacation tours are professionally devel
everything in the price of your tour while giving you
these features:

- **All accommodations and meals**
- **All entrance fees, excursions, transfers and**
- **Professional tour manager and local guides**

We hope you will join us this year on anothe
Travel Tours each day is an adventure. For reservati
Travel Tours directly at 1-800-555-0004.

A letter containing a tabbed table, indented paragraphs, and text enhancements is quickly created using basic Word features.

Adventure Travel Tours

New Adventures

Attention adventure travelers! Attend an Adventure Travel presentation to learn about some of the earth's greatest unspoiled habitats and find out how you can experience the adventure of a lifetime. This year we are introducing four new tours that offer you a unique opportunity to combine many different outdoor activities while exploring the world.

India Wildlife Adventure

Inca Trail to Machu Picchu

Safari in Tanzania

Costa Rica Rivers and Rainforests

Presentation dates and times are January 5 at 8:00 p.m., February 3 at 7:30 p.m., and March 8 at 8:00 p.m. All presentations are held at convenient hotel locations in downtown Los Angeles, Santa Clara, and at the LAX airport.

Call Student Name 1-800-555-0004 for presentation locations, a full color brochure, and itinerary information, costs, and trip dates.

Visit our Web site at
www.adventuretraveltours.com

A flyer incorporating many visual enhancements such as colored text, varied text styles, and graphic elements is both eye-catching and informative.

The beauty of a word processor is that you can make changes or corrections as you are typing. Want to change a report from single spacing to double spacing? Alter the width of the margins? Delete some paragraphs and add others from yet another document? A word processor allows you to do all these things with ease.

Word 2007 includes many group collaboration features to help streamline how documents are developed and changed by group members. You also can create and send e-mail messages directly from within Word using all its features to create and edit the message. In addition, you can send an entire document as your e-mail message, allowing the recipient to edit the document directly without having to open or save an attachment.

Word 2007 is closely integrated with the World Wide Web, detecting when you type a Web address and automatically converting it to a hyperlink. You also can create your own hyperlinks to locations within documents, or to other documents, including those at external locations such as a Web site or file server. It also includes features that help you quickly create Web pages and blog entries.

Excel 2007

Excel 2007 is an electronic worksheet that is used to organize, manipulate, and graph numeric data. Once used almost exclusively by accountants, worksheets are now widely used by nearly every profession. Marketing professionals record and evaluate sales trends. Teachers record grades and calculate final grades. Personal trainers record the progress of their clients.

Excel 2007 includes many features that not only help you create a well-designed worksheet, but one that produces accurate results. Formatting features include visual enhancements such as varied text styles, colors, and graphics. Other features help you enter complex formulas and identify and correct formula errors. You also can produce a visual display of data in the form of graphs or charts. As the values in the worksheet change, charts referencing those values automatically adjust to reflect the changes.

Excel 2007 also includes many advanced features and tools that help you perform what-if analysis and create different scenarios. And like all Office 2007 applications, it is easy to incorporate data created in one application into another. Two worksheets you will produce in Labs 2 and 3 of Excel 2007 are shown on the next page.

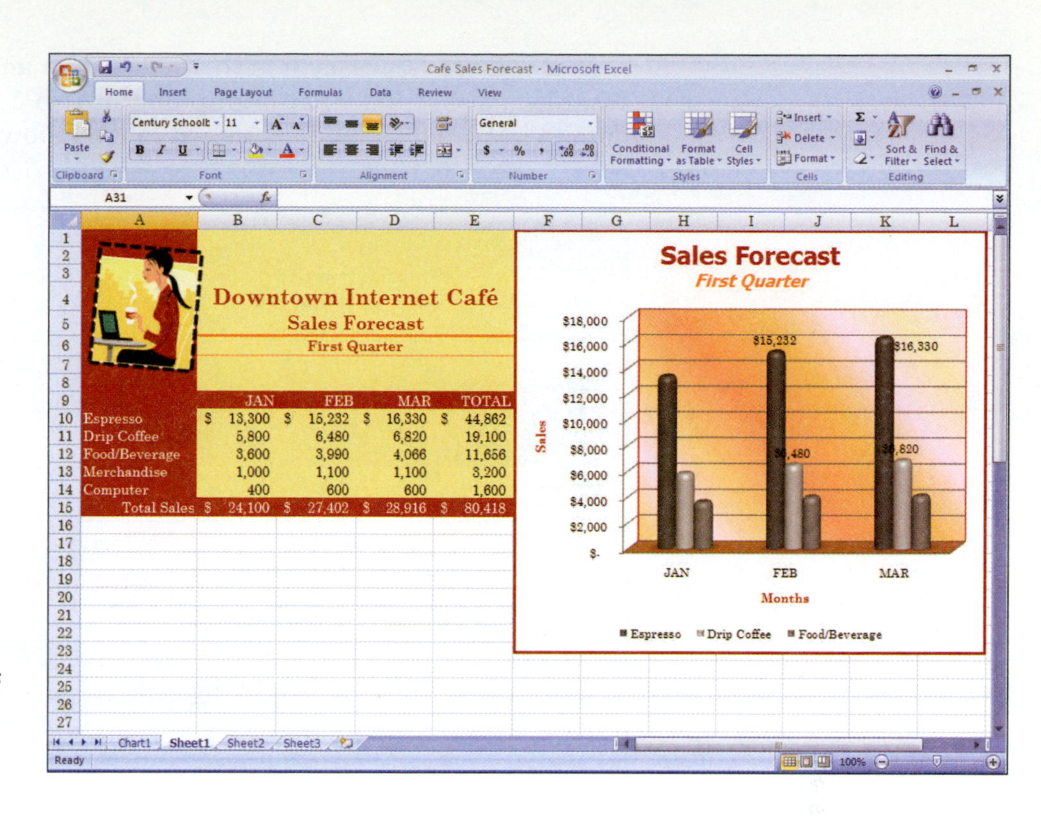

A worksheet showing the quarterly sales forecast containing a graphic, text enhancements, and a chart of the data is quickly created using basic Excel 2007 features.

Annual Forecast - Microsoft Excel

Downtown Internet Café
Annual Forecast

	JAN	FEB	MAR	APR	MAY	JUN	JUL	AUG	SEP	OCT	NOV
Sales											
Espresso	$13,300	$13,600	$14,200	$14,400	$15,200	$15,500	$15,200	$15,300	$15,800	$17,900	$18,5
Drip Coffee	$5,800	$6,000	$6,200	$6,200	$6,200	$6,200	$6,000	$6,000	$6,500	$6,900	$6,9
Food/Beverages	$3,600	$3,800	$3,800	$3,600	$3,800	$3,800	$4,000	$4,000	$4,000	$4,200	$4,4
Merchandise	$1,000	$1,100	$1,100	$1,500	$1,500	$1,500	$2,000	$2,000	$2,000	$2,000	$2,5
Computer	$400	$400	$400	$600	$600	$800	$800	$800	$600	$600	$6
Total Sales	**$24,100**	**$24,900**	**$25,700**	**$26,300**	**$27,300**	**$27,800**	**$28,000**	**$28,100**	**$28,900**	**$31,600**	**$32,9**
Expenses											
Cost of Goods	$7,225	$7,480	$7,690	$7,620	$7,940	$8,015	$8,000	$8,025	$8,300	$9,065	$9,3
Cost of Merchandise	$700	$770	$770	$1,050	$1,050	$1,050	$1,400	$1,400	$1,400	$1,400	$1,7
Payroll	$9,000	$9,000	$9,000	$7,860	$8,390	$8,740	$9,000	$9,000	$9,000	$9,000	$9,0
Internet	$325	$325	$325	$325	$325	$325	$325	$325	$325	$325	$3
Building	$2,100	$2,100	$2,100	$2,100	$2,100	$2,100	$2,100	$2,100	$2,100	$2,100	$2,1
Advertising	$600	$600	$600	$600	$600	$600	$600	$600	$600	$600	$6
Capital Assets	$1,500	$1,500	$1,500	$1,500	$1,500	$1,500	$1,500	$1,500	$1,500	$1,500	$1,5
Miscellaneous	$1,300	$1,300	$1,300	$1,300	$1,300	$1,300	$1,300	$1,300	$1,300	$1,300	$1,3
Total Expenses	**$22,750**	**$23,075**	**$23,285**	**$22,355**	**$23,205**	**$23,630**	**$24,225**	**$24,250**	**$24,525**	**$25,290**	**$25,9**
Income											
Net Income	$1,350	$1,825	$2,415	$3,945	$4,095	$4,170	$3,775	$3,850	$4,375	$6,310	$6,9
Profit Margin	5.60%	7.33%	9.40%	15.00%	15.00%	15.00%	13.48%	13.70%	15.14%	19.97%	21.2
		Quarter Profit Margin	12.38%			20.16%			20.26%		
		Income Year-To-Date	$ 9,250			$ 25,660			$ 42,885		

Year | First Quarter | Second Quarter | Third Quarter | Fourth Quarter

A large worksheet incorporating more complex formulas, visual enhancements such as colored text, varied text styles, and graphic elements is both informative and attractive.

You will see how easy it is to analyze data and make projections using what-if analysis and what-if graphing in Lab 3 and to incorporate Excel data in a Word document as shown in the following figures.

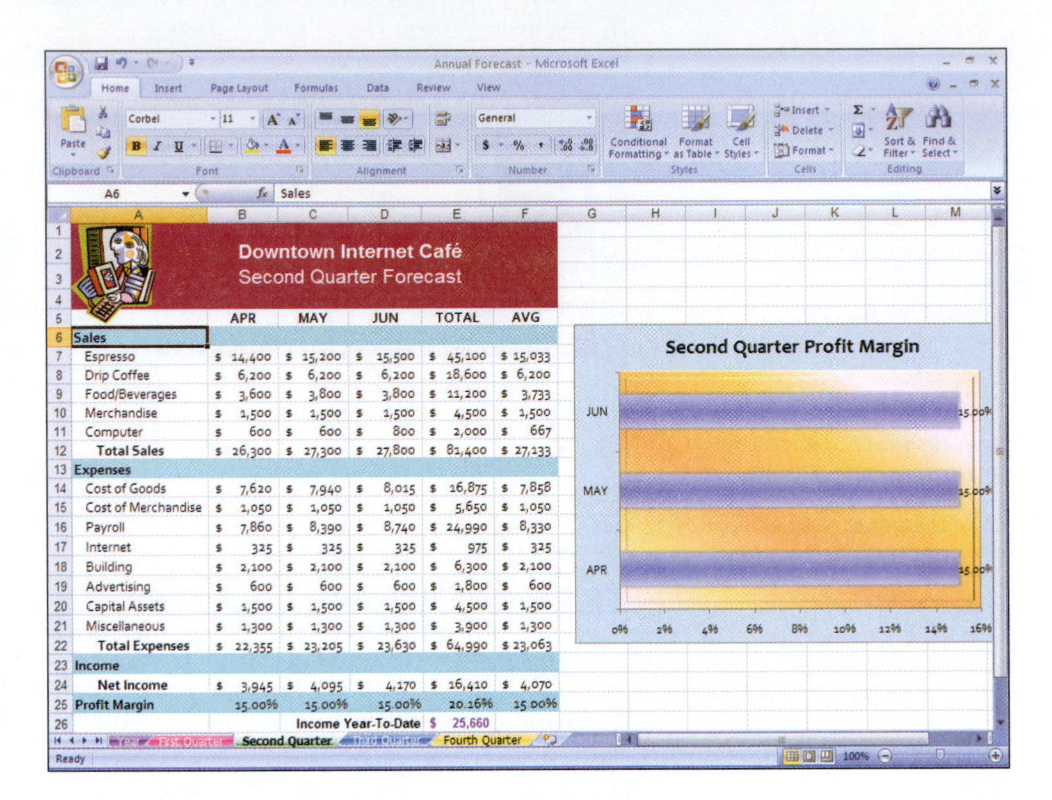

Changes you make in worksheet data while performing what-if analysis are automatically reflected in charts that reference that data.

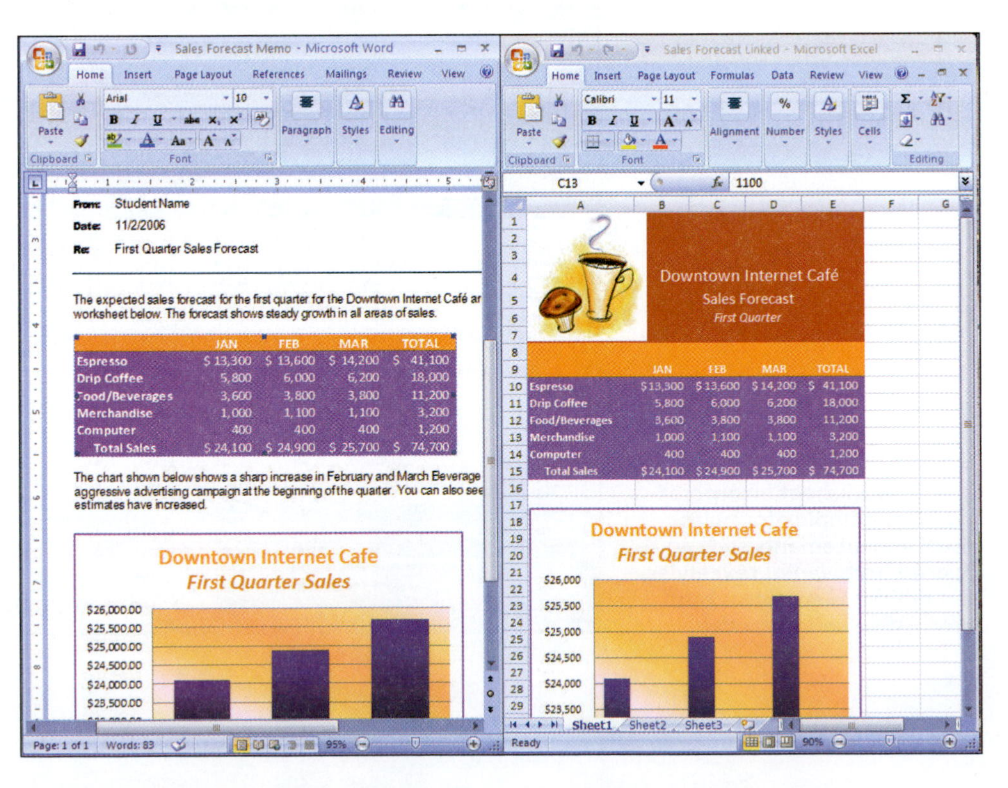

Worksheet data and charts can be copied and linked to other Office documents such as a Word document.

Access 2007

Access 2007 is a relational database management application that is used to create and analyze a database. A database is a collection of related data. In a relational database, the most widely used database structure, data is organized in linked tables. Tables consist of columns (called *fields*) and rows (called *records*). The tables are related or linked to one another by a common field. Relational databases allow you to create smaller and more manageable database tables, since you can combine and extract data between tables.

The program provides tools to enter, edit, and retrieve data from the database as well as to analyze the database and produce reports of the output. One of the main advantages of a computerized database is the ability to quickly add, delete, and locate specific records. Records also can be easily rearranged or sorted according to different fields of data, resulting in multiple table arrangements that provide more meaningful information for different purposes. Creation of forms makes it easier to enter and edit data as well. In the Access labs, you will create and organize the database table shown below.

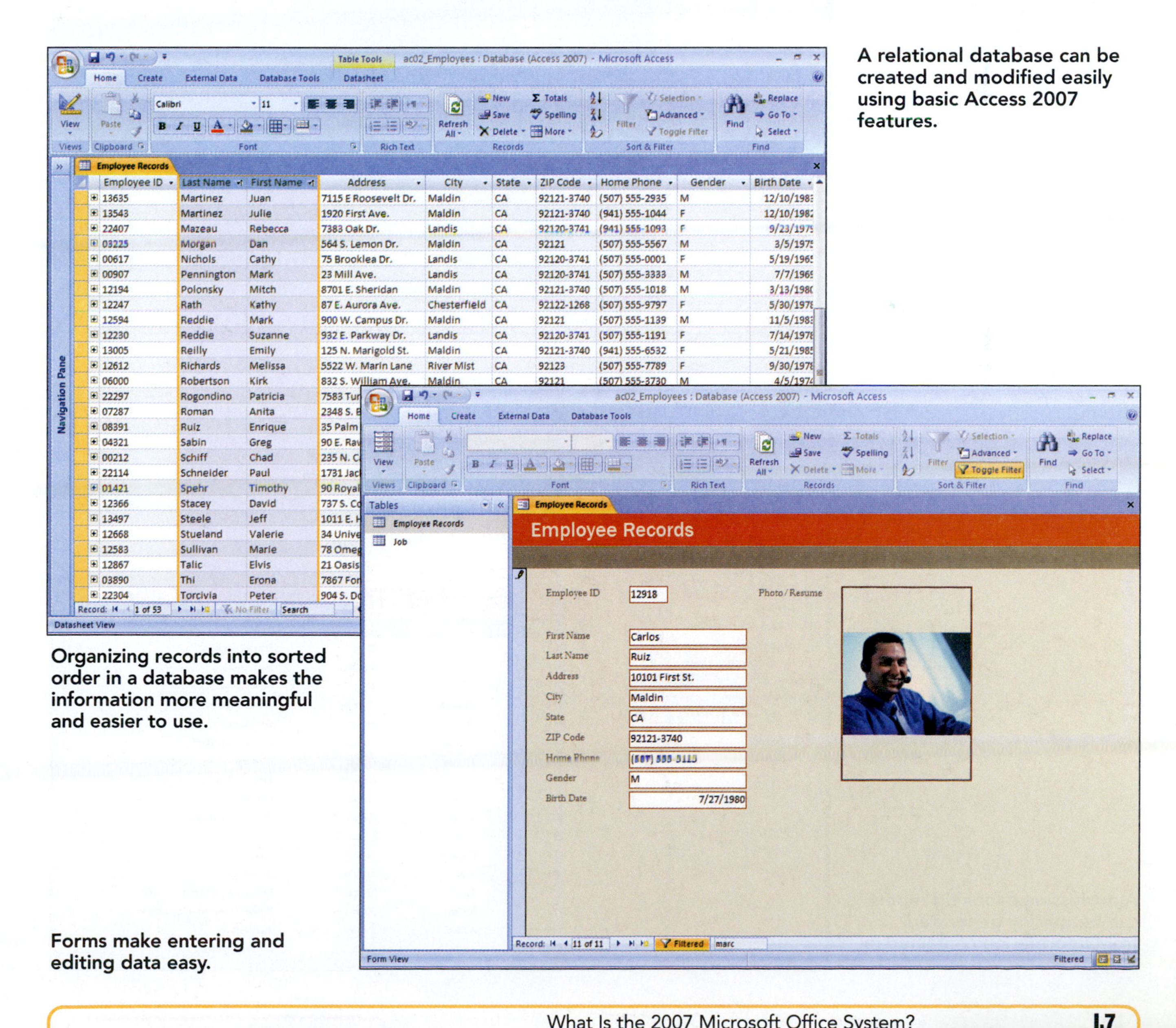

A relational database can be created and modified easily using basic Access 2007 features.

Organizing records into sorted order in a database makes the information more meaningful and easier to use.

Forms make entering and editing data easy.

Another feature is the ability to analyze the data in a table and perform calculations on different fields of data. Additionally, you can ask questions or query the table to find only certain records that meet specific conditions to be used in the analysis. Information that was once costly and time-consuming to get is now quickly and readily available. This information can then be quickly printed out in the form of reports ranging from simple listings to complex, professional-looking reports in different layout styles, or with titles, headings, subtotals, or totals.

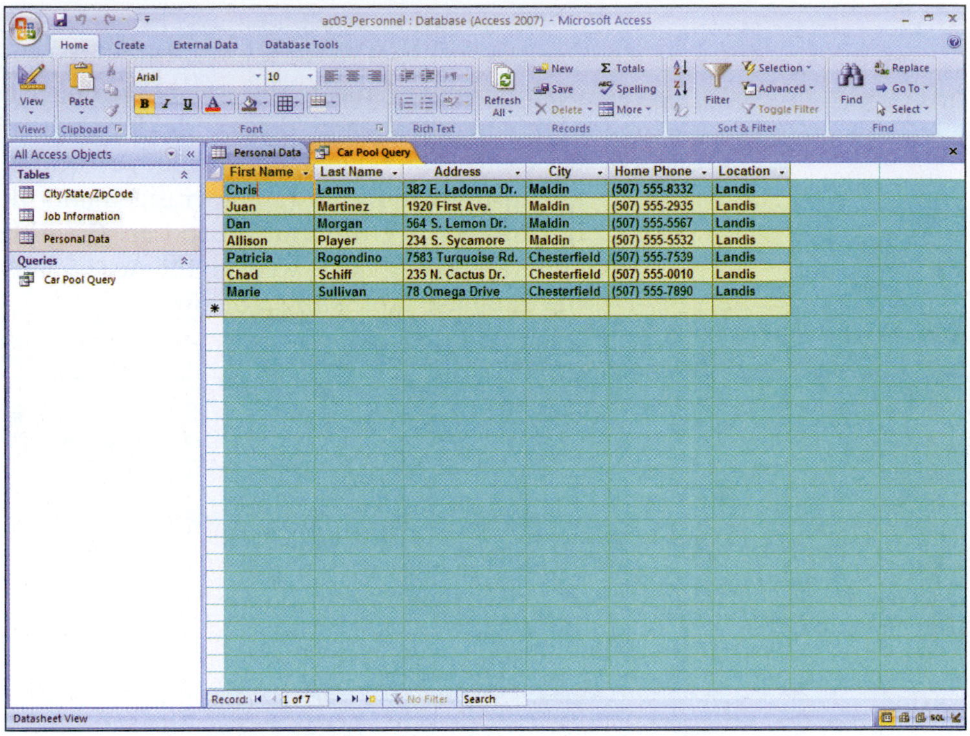

First Name	Last Name	Address	City	Home Phone	Location
Chris	Lamm	382 E. Ladonna Dr.	Maldin	(507) 555-8332	Landis
Juan	Martinez	1920 First Ave.	Maldin	(507) 555-2935	Landis
Dan	Morgan	564 S. Lemon Dr.	Maldin	(507) 555-5567	Landis
Allison	Player	234 S. Sycamore	Maldin	(507) 555-5532	Landis
Patricia	Rogondino	7583 Turquoise Rd.	Chesterfield	(507) 555-7539	Landis
Chad	Schiff	235 N. Cactus Dr.	Chesterfield	(507) 555-0010	Landis
Marie	Sullivan	78 Omega Drive	Chesterfield	(507) 555-7890	Landis

A database can be queried to locate and display only specified information.

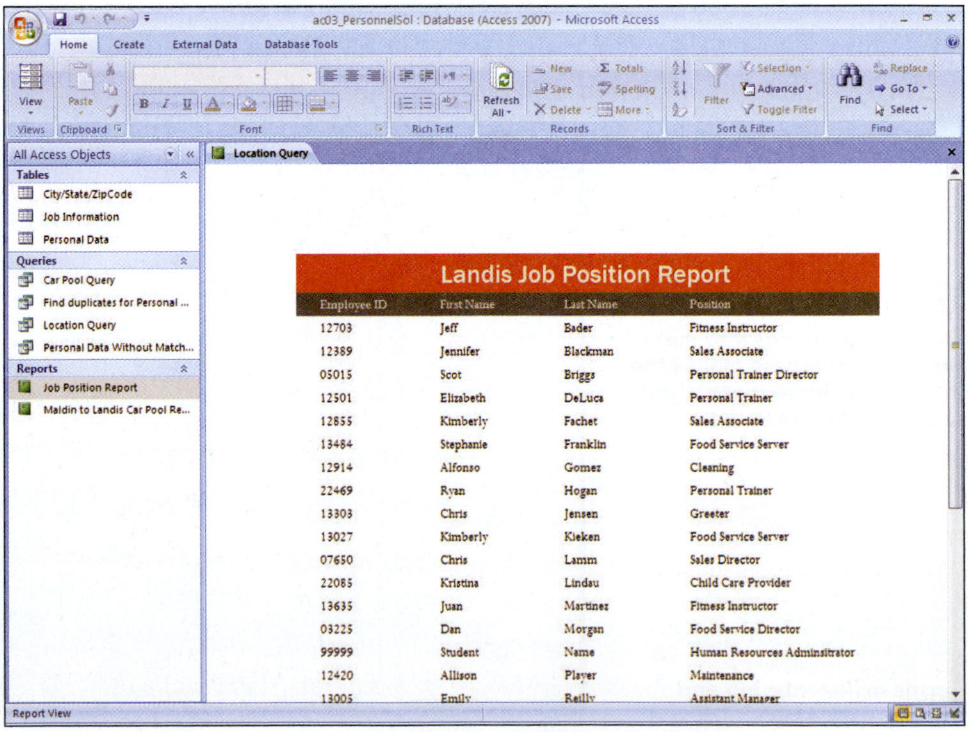

Landis Job Position Report

Employee ID	First Name	Last Name	Position
12703	Jeff	Bader	Fitness Instructor
12389	Jennifer	Blackman	Sales Associate
05015	Scot	Briggs	Personal Trainer Director
12501	Elizabeth	DeLuca	Personal Trainer
12855	Kimberly	Fachet	Sales Associate
13484	Stephanie	Franklin	Food Service Server
12914	Alfonso	Gomez	Cleaning
22469	Ryan	Hogan	Personal Trainer
13303	Chris	Jensen	Greeter
13027	Kimberly	Kieken	Food Service Server
07650	Chris	Lamm	Sales Director
22085	Kristina	Lindau	Child Care Provider
13635	Juan	Martinez	Fitness Instructor
03225	Dan	Morgan	Food Service Director
99999	Student	Name	Human Resources Administrator
12420	Allison	Player	Maintenance
13005	Emily	Reilly	Assistant Manager

A professional-looking report can be quickly generated from information contained in a database.

PowerPoint 2007

PowerPoint 2007 is a graphics presentation program designed to help you produce a high-quality presentation that is both interesting to the audience and effective in its ability to convey your message. A presentation can be as simple as overhead transparencies or as sophisticated as an on-screen electronic display. In the first two PowerPoint labs, you will create and organize the presentation shown below.

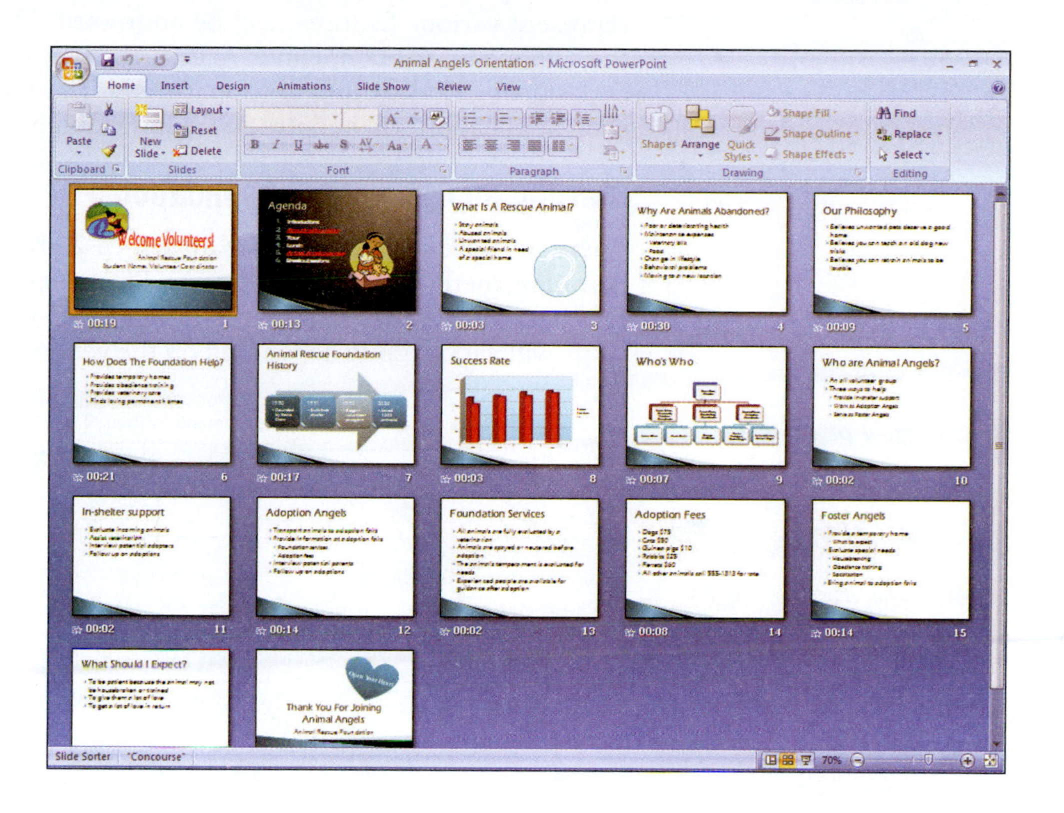

A presentation consists of a series of pages or "slides" presenting the information you want to convey in an organized and attractive manner.

When running an on-screen presentation, each slide of the presentation is displayed full-screen on your computer monitor or projected onto a screen.

Common Office 2007 Interface Features

Additional Information

Please read the Before You Begin and Instructional Conventions sections in the Overview of Microsoft Office Access 2007 (ACO.4) before starting this section.

Now that you know a little about each of the applications in Microsoft Office 2007, we will take a look at some of the interface features that are common to all Office 2007 applications. This is a hands-on section that will introduce you to the features and allow you to get a feel for how Office 2007 works. Although Word 2007 will be used to demonstrate how the features work, only common **user interface** features, a set of graphical images that represent various features, will be addressed. These features include using the File menu, Ribbon, Quick Access Toolbar, task panes, and Office Help, and starting and exiting an application. The features that are specific to each application will be introduced individually in each application text.

Starting an Office 2007 Application

There are several ways to start an Office 2007 application. The two most common methods are by using the Start menu or by clicking a desktop shortcut for the program if it is available. If you use the Start menu, the steps will vary slightly depending on the version of Windows you are using.

1. **Click start to display the Start menu.**

Having Trouble?

In Windows Vista, click

- **Choose Microsoft Office Word 2007.**

Having Trouble?

If you do not see the program name on the Start menu, select All Programs, select Microsoft Office, and then choose Microsoft Office Word 2007.

OR

1. **Double-click the shortcut on the desktop.**
2. **If necessary, click Maximize in the title bar to maximize the window.**

Your screen should be similar to Figure 1

Having Trouble?

Your screen may look slightly different based on your Windows operating system settings.

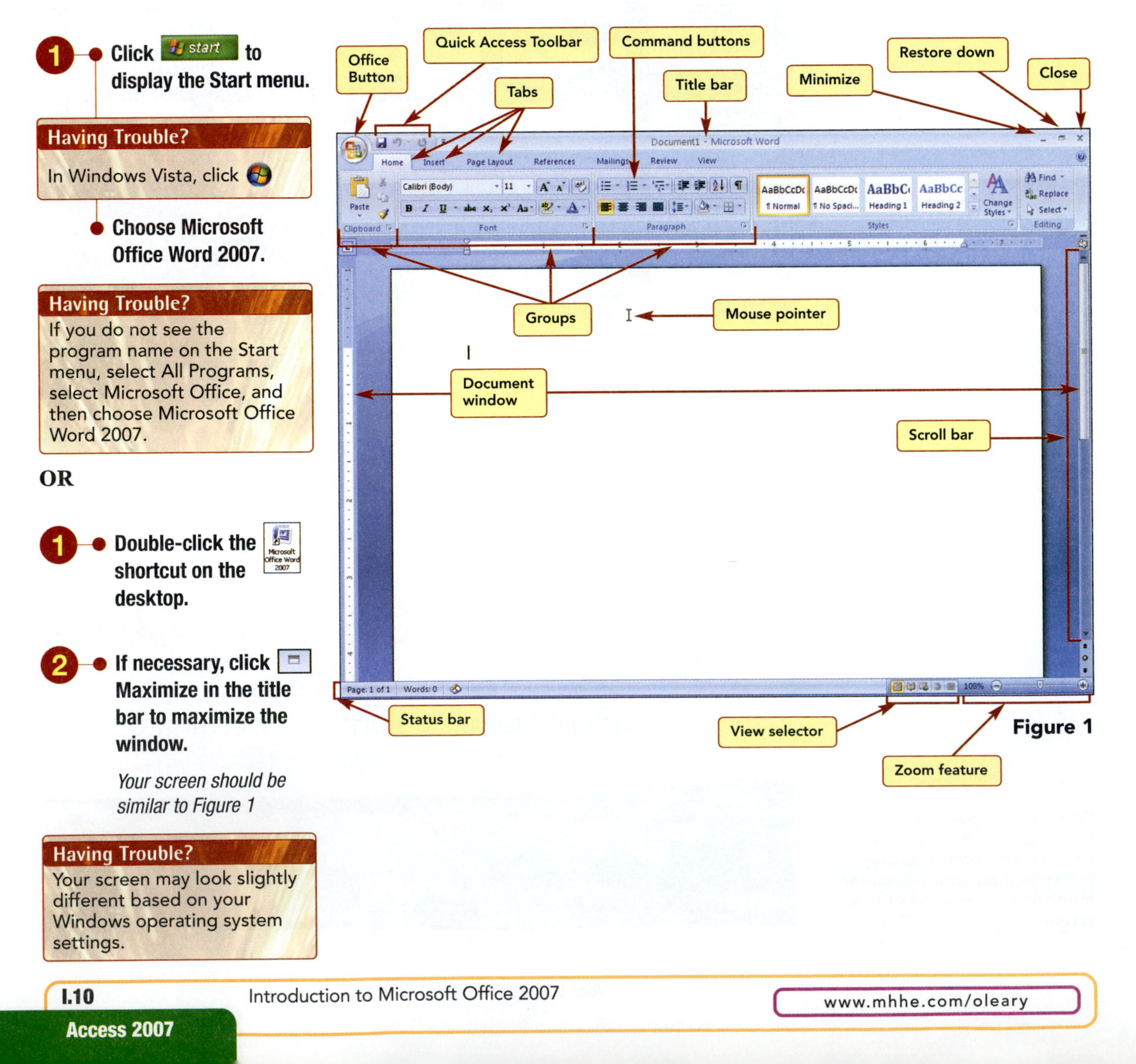

Figure 1

Additional Information
Application windows can be sized, moved, and otherwise manipulated like any other windows on the desktop.

The Word 2007 program is started and displayed in a window on the desktop. The application window title bar displays the file name followed by the program name, Microsoft Word. The right end of the title bar displays the Minimize, Restore Down, and Close buttons. They perform the same functions and operate in the same way as all Windows versions.

Below the title bar is the **Ribbon**, which provides a centralized area that makes it easy to find ways to work in your document. The Ribbon has three basic parts: tabs, groups, and commands. **Tabs** are used to divide the Ribbon into major activity areas. Each tab is then organized into **groups** that contain related items. The related items are commands that consist of command buttons, a box to enter information, or a menu. As you use the Office applications, you will see that the Ribbon contains many of the same groups and commands across the applications. You also will see that many of the groups and commands are specific to an application.

Additional Information
Because the Ribbon can adapt to the screen resolution and orientation, your Ribbon may look slightly different.

The upper left area of the window's title bar displays the Office Button and the Quick Access Toolbar. Clicking Office Button opens the File menu of commands that allows you to work *with* your document, unlike the Ribbon that allows you to work *in* your document. For example, it includes commands to open, save, and print files. The **Quick Access Toolbar** (QAT) provides quick access to frequently used commands. By default, it includes the Save, Undo, and Redo buttons, commands that Microsoft considers to be crucial. It is always available and is a customizable toolbar to which you can add your own favorite buttons.

The large center area of the program window is the **document window** where open application files are displayed. Currently, there is a blank Word document open. In Word, the mouse pointer appears as I when positioned in the document window and as a when it can be used to select items.

On the right of the document window is a vertical scroll bar. A **scroll bar** is used with a mouse to bring additional lines of information into view in a window. The vertical scroll bar is used to move up or down. A horizontal scroll bar is also displayed when needed and moves side to side in the window. At the bottom of the window is the **status bar**, a view selector, and a document zoom feature. Similar information and features are displayed in this area for different Office applications. You will learn how these features work in each individual application.

Using the File Menu

Clicking the Office Button opens the File menu of commands that are used to work with files.

1 Click Office Button to open the File menu.

Your screen should be similar to Figure 2

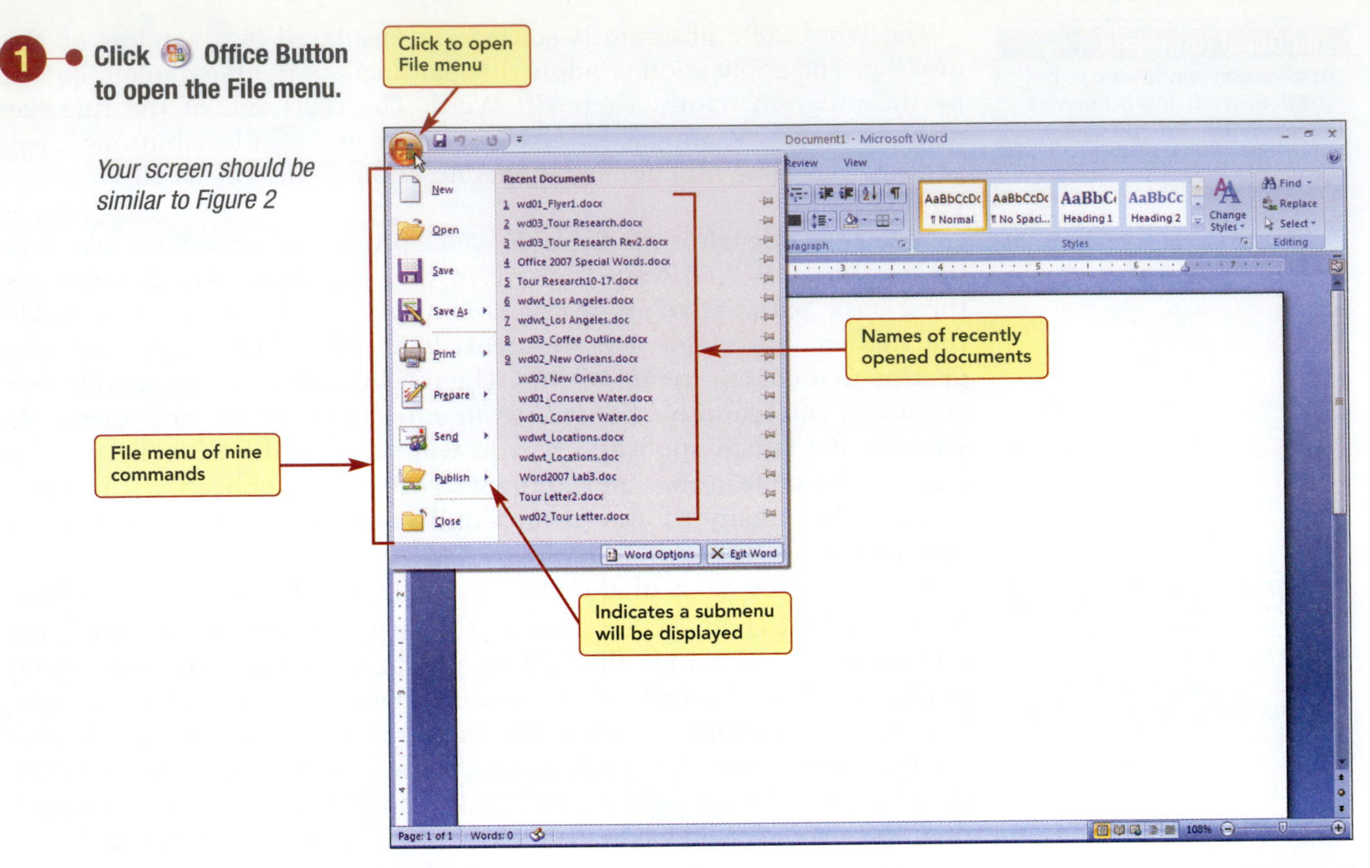

Figure 2

> **Additional Information**
>
> Clicking the [pin] next to a file name pins the file and permanently keeps the file name in the recently used list until it is unpinned.

The menu lists nine commands that are used to perform tasks associated with files. Notice that each command displays an underlined letter. This identifies the letter you can type to choose the command. Five commands display a ▸, which indicates the command includes a submenu of options. The right side of the command list currently displays the names of recently opened files (your list will display different file names). The default program setting displays a maximum of 17 file names. Once the maximum number of files is listed, when a new file is opened, the oldest is dropped from the list.

Once the File menu is open, you can select a command from the menu by pointing to it. A colored highlight bar, called the **selection cursor**, appears over the selected command.

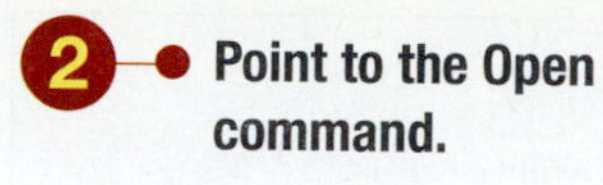
2
Point to the Open command.

Your screen should be similar to Figure 3

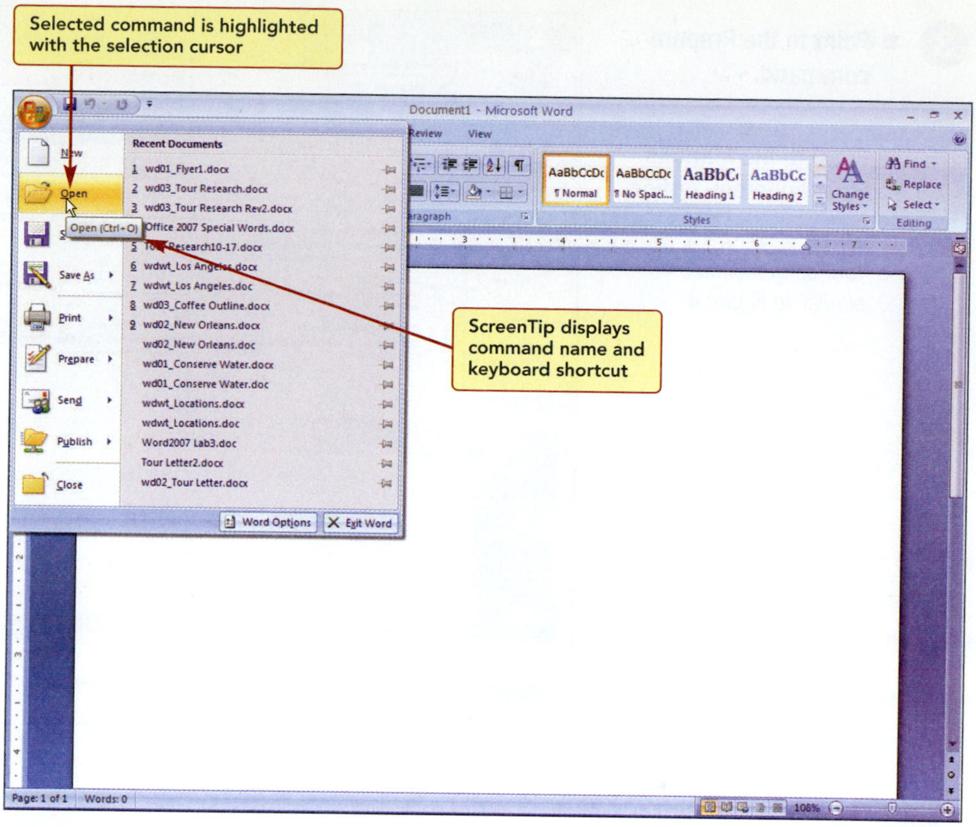

Selected command is highlighted with the selection cursor

ScreenTip displays command name and keyboard shortcut

Figure 3

A **ScreenTip**, also called a **tooltip**, briefly appears displaying the command name and the keyboard shortcut, Ctrl + O. The keyboard shortcut can be used to execute this command without opening the menu. In this case, if you hold down the Ctrl key while typing the letter O, you will access the Open command without having to open the File menu first. ScreenTips also often include a brief description of the action a command performs.

Next you will select a command that will display a submenu of options.

Point to the Prepare command.

Point to the Mark as Final submenu option.

Your screen should be similar to Figure 4

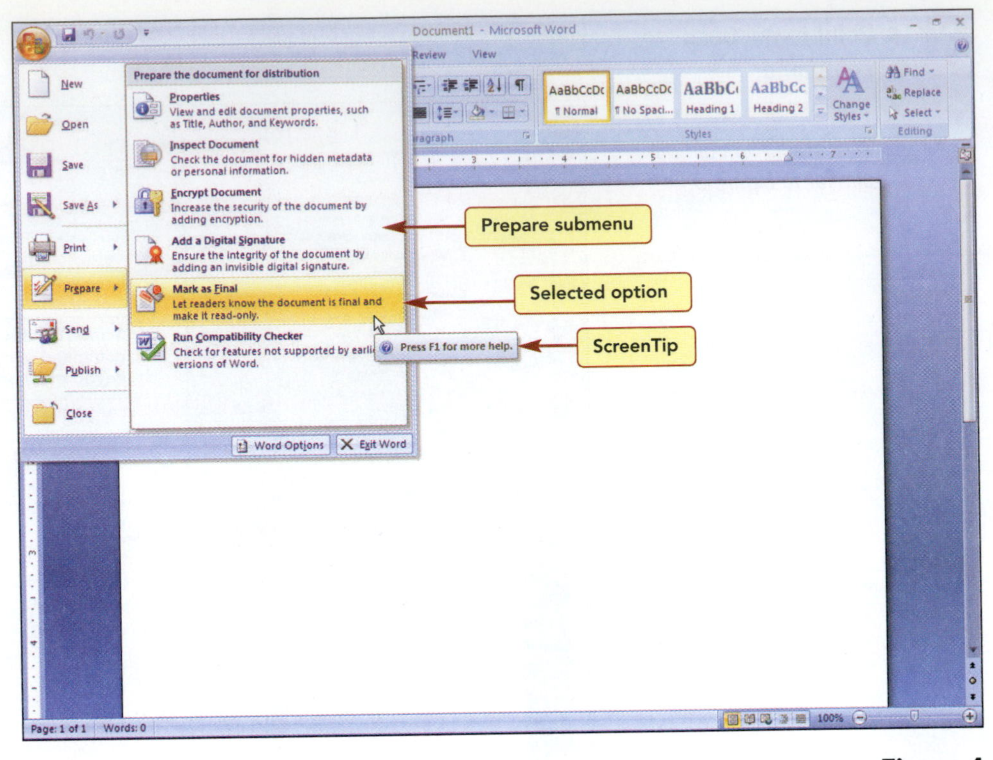

Figure 4

The submenu lists the six Prepare command submenu options and the Mark as Final option is selected. A ScreenTip provides information about how to get help on this feature. You will learn about using Help shortly.

4 Point to the Print command.

Point to the ▸ of the Print command.

Your screen should be similar to Figure 5

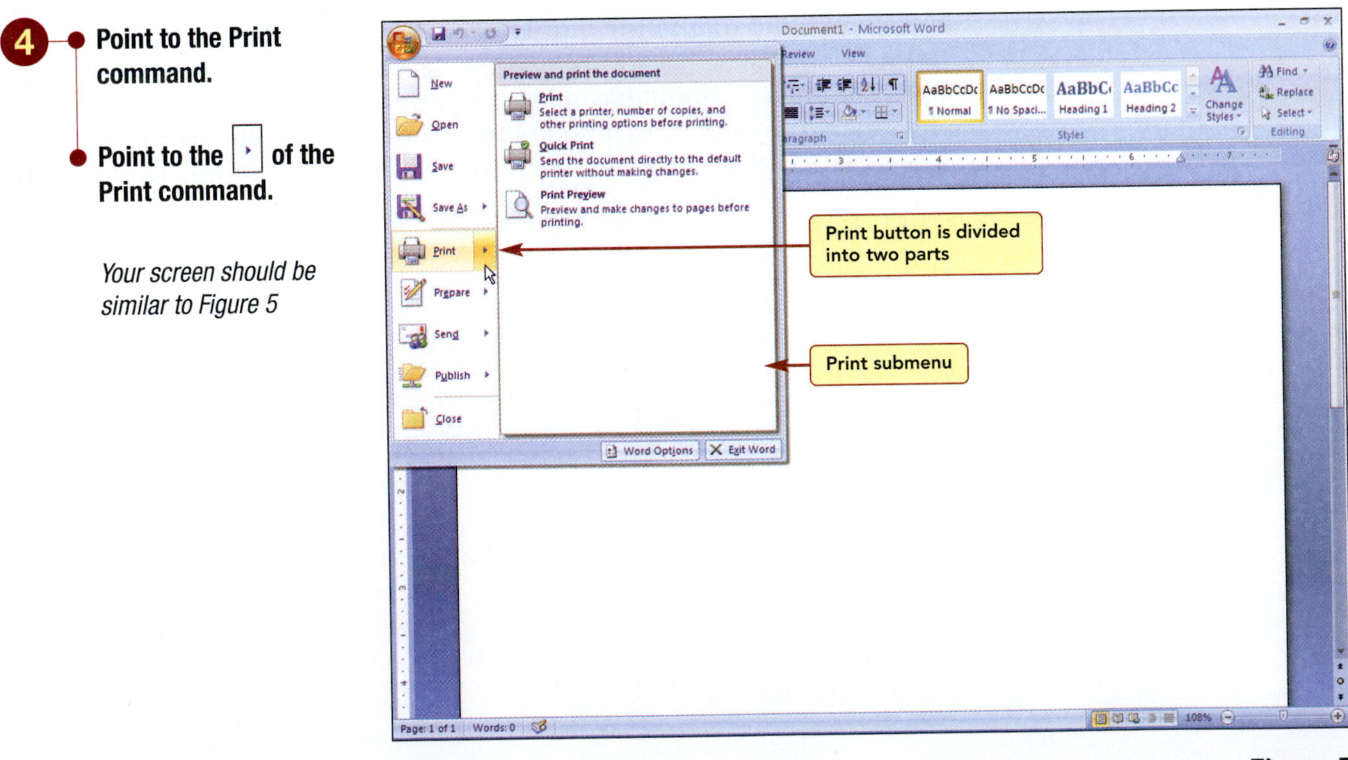

Figure 5

Another Method
You also can use the directional keys to move up, down, left, or right within the menu.

Another Method
You also can press ←Enter to choose a selected command.

So far you have only selected commands; you have not chosen them. To choose a command, you click on it. When the command is chosen, the associated action is performed. Notice the Print command is divided into two parts. Clicking the Print section on the left will choose the command and open the Print dialog box. Clicking ▸ in the right section has no effect and only the submenu is displayed.

5 Click the Print command.

Your screen should be similar to Figure 6

Print dialog box is used to specify print settings

Click to print document

Click to close dialog box without printing

Figure 6

In the Print dialog box, you would specify the print settings and click OK to actually print a document. In this case, you will cancel the action and continue to explore other features of the Office 2007 application.

6 Click Cancel.

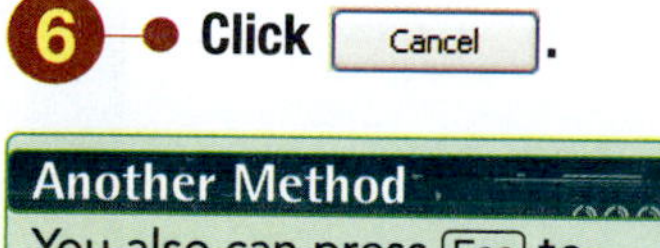

Another Method
You also can press Esc to cancel an action.

Using Context Menus

Another way to access some commands is to use a context menu. A **context menu** is opened by right-clicking on an item on the screen. This menu is context sensitive, meaning it displays only those commands relevant to the item. For example, right-clicking on the Quick Access Toolbar will display the commands associated with using the Quick Access Toolbar only. You will use this method to move the Quick Access Toolbar.

Point to the Quick Access Toolbar and right-click.

> **Another Method**
> You also can click ▾ at the end of the Quick Access toolbar to open the menu.

- **Click the Show Quick Access Toolbar below the Ribbon option.**

Your screen should be similar to Figure 7

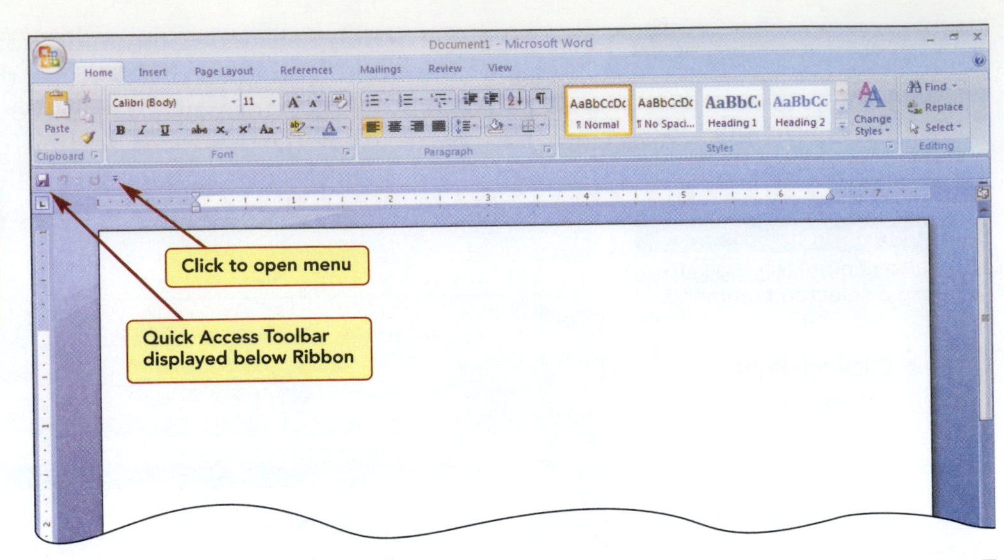

Figure 7

The Quick Access Toolbar is now displayed full size below the Ribbon. This is useful if you have many buttons on the toolbar; however, it takes up document viewing space. You will return it to its compact size using the toolbar's drop-down menu.

2 **Click ▾ on the right end of the Quick Access Toolbar.**

- **Choose Show Above the Ribbon.**

Your screen should be similar to Figure 8

Quick Access Toolbar displayed above Ribbon again

Figure 8

> **MORE ABOUT**
> See the More About appendix to learn how to customize the Quick Access Toolbar.

The Quick Access Toolbar is displayed above the Ribbon again. The toolbar's drop-down menu contains a list of commands that are often added to the toolbar. Clicking on the command selects it and adds it to the toolbar.

Using the Ribbon

The Ribbon displays tabs that organize similar features into groups. In Word, there are seven tabs displayed. To save space, some tabs, called **contextual** or **on-demand tabs**, are displayed only as needed. For example, when you are working with a picture, the Picture Tools tab appears. The contextual nature of this feature keeps the work area uncluttered when the feature is not needed and provides ready access to it when it is needed.

Opening Tabs

The Home tab is open when you first start the application or open a file. It consists of five groups: Clipboard, Font, Paragraph, Styles, and Editing. Each group contains command buttons that when clicked on perform their associated action or display a list of additional commands. The commands in the Home tab help you perform actions related to creating the content of your document.

1 Click on the Insert tab.

Additional Information
The open tab appears highlighted.

Your screen should be similar to Figure 9

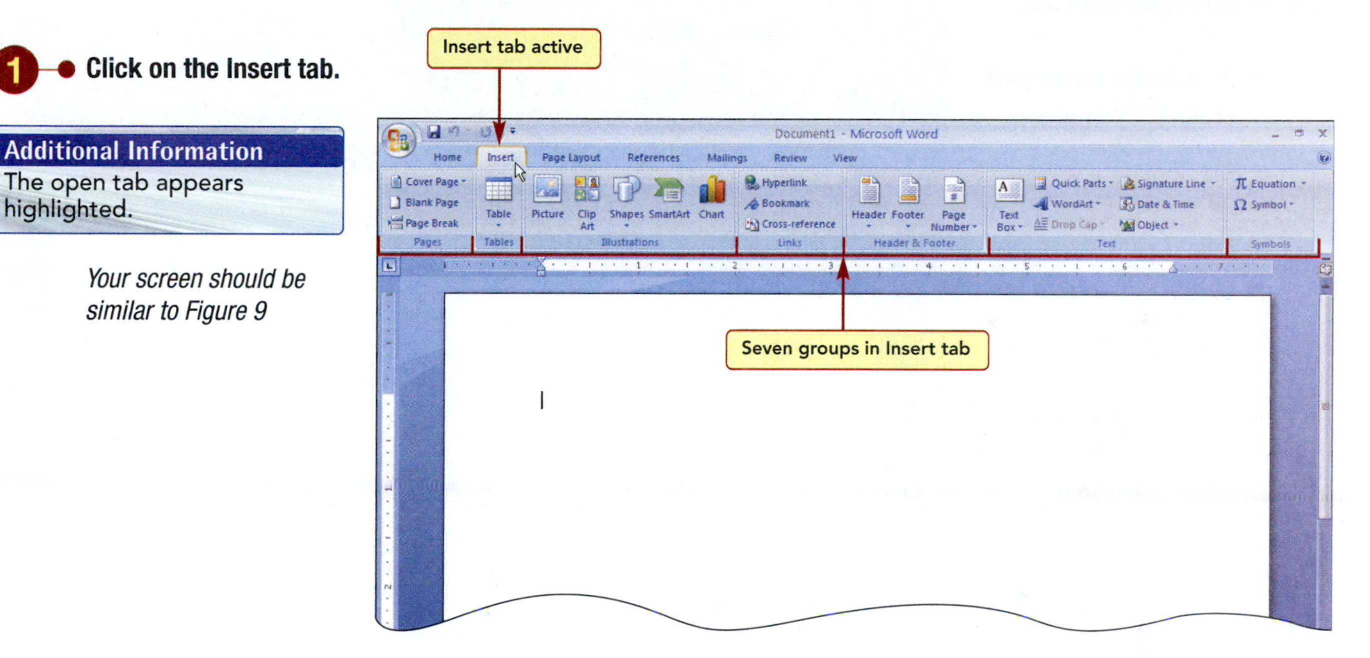

Figure 9

This Insert tab is now the active tab. It contains seven groups whose commands have to do with inserting items into a document.

2 Click on each of the other tabs, ending with the View tab, to see their groups and commands.

Your screen should be similar to Figure 10

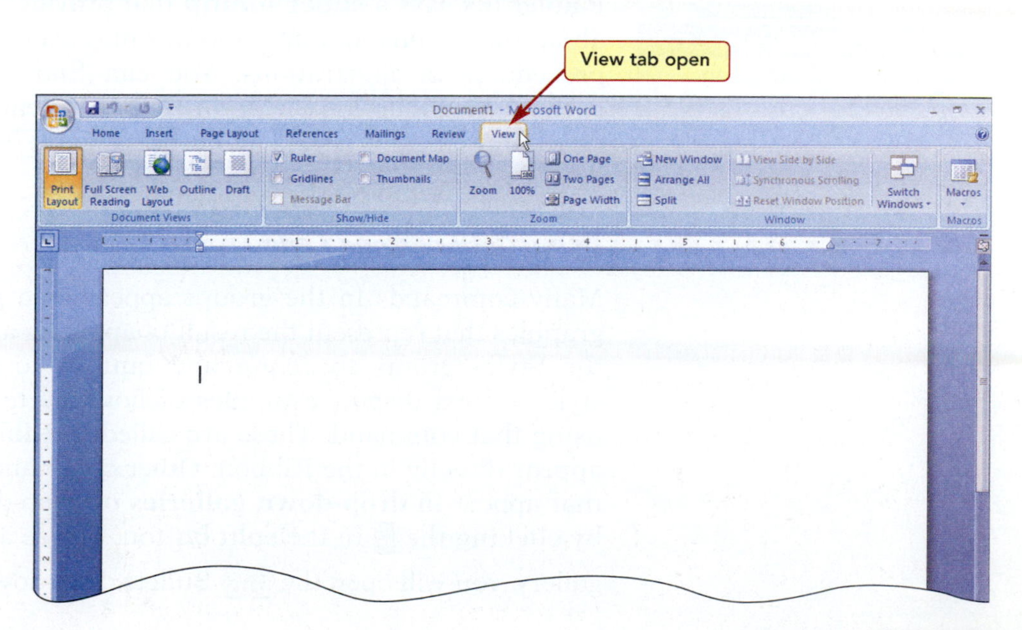

Figure 10

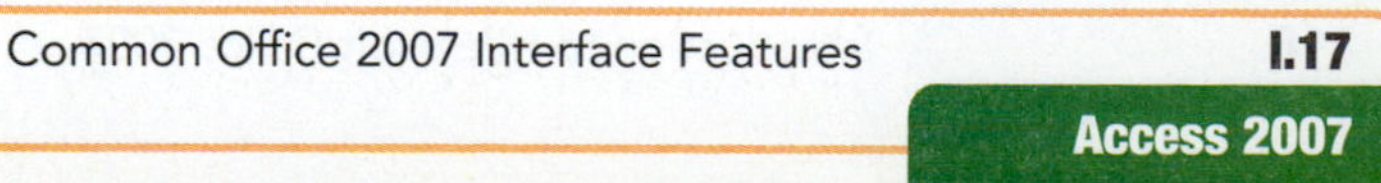

Each tab relates to a type of activity; for example, the View tab commands perform activities related to viewing the document. Within each tab, similar commands are grouped together to make finding the commands you want to use much easier.

Displaying Super Tooltips

Many command buttons immediately perform the associated action when you click on them. The buttons are graphic representations of the action they perform. To help you find out what a button does, you can display the button's ScreenTip.

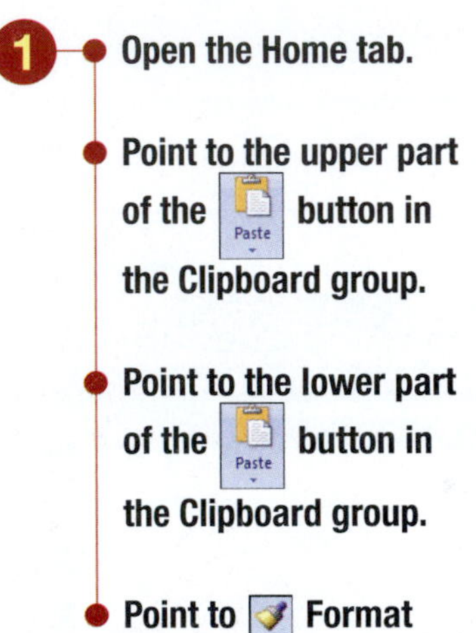

1. Open the Home tab.
   - Point to the upper part of the Paste button in the Clipboard group.
   - Point to the lower part of the Paste button in the Clipboard group.
   - Point to Format Painter in the Clipboard group.

Your screen should be similar to Figure 11

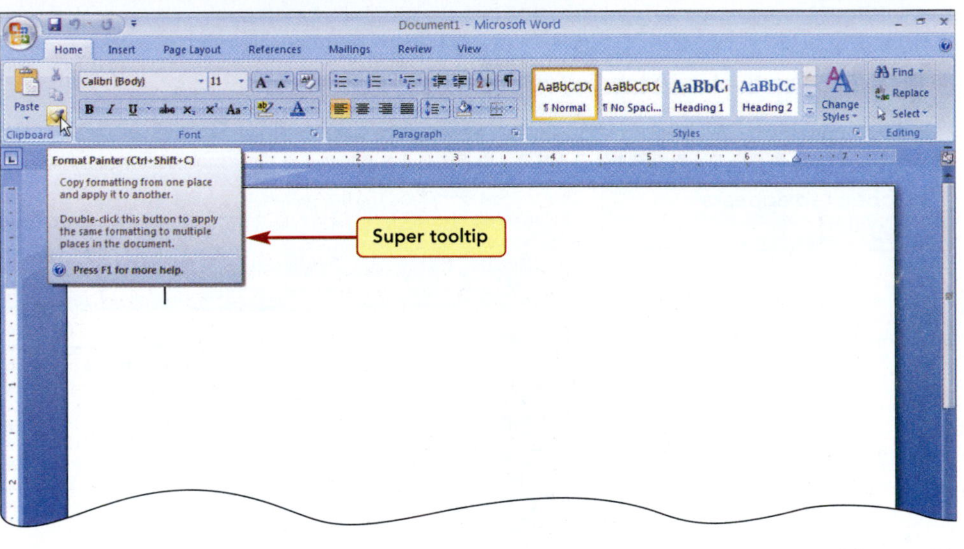

Figure 11

Additional Information
Not all commands have shortcut keys.

Additional Information
You will learn about using Help shortly.

The Paste button is a **split button.** Both parts of the button display tooltips containing the button name, the shortcut key combination, Ctrl + V, and a brief description of what clicking the button does. Pointing to Format Painter displays a **super tooltip** that provides more detailed information about the command. Super tooltips may even display information such as procedures or illustrations. You can find out what the feature does without having to look it up in Help. If a feature has a Help article, you can automatically access it by pressing F1 while the super tooltip is displayed.

Using Galleries and Lists

Many commands in the groups appear as a **gallery** that displays small graphics that represent the result of applying a command. For example, in the Styles group, the command buttons to apply different formatting styles to text display examples of how the text would look if formatted using that command. These are called **in-Ribbon galleries** because they appear directly in the Ribbon. Other commands include multiple options that appear in **drop-down galleries** or drop-down lists that are accessed by clicking the ▾ in the split button. To see an example of a drop-down gallery, you will open the Bullets drop-down gallery.

1 **Click ▾ in the ☰ ▾ Bullets button.**

Your screen should be similar to Figure 12

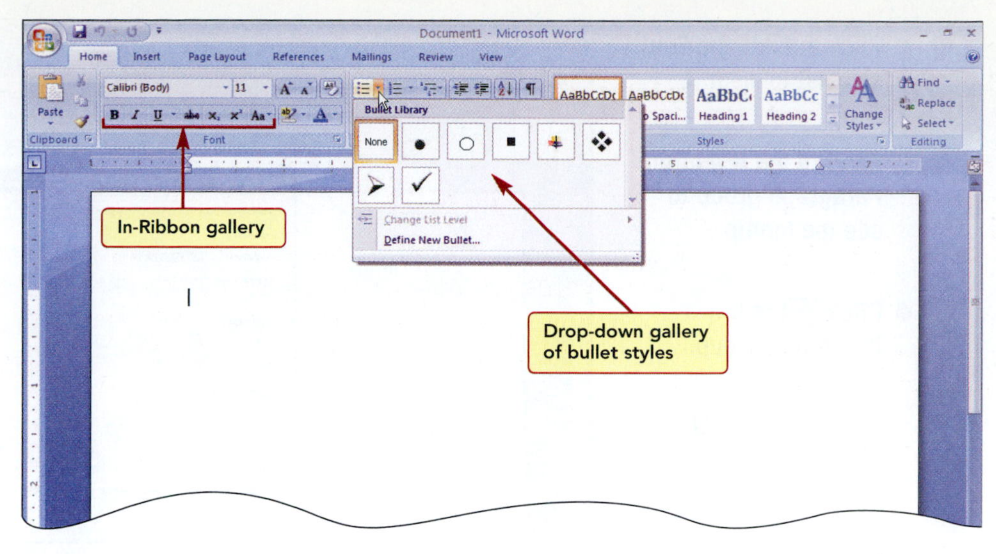

Figure 12

A drop-down gallery of different bullets is displayed. The drop-down gallery will disappear when you make a selection or click on any other area of the window. To see an example of a drop-down list, you will open the 11 ▾ Font Size drop-down list.

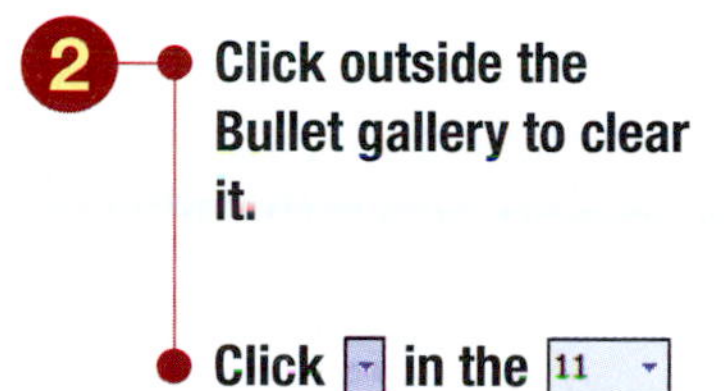
2 **Click outside the Bullet gallery to clear it.**

Click ▾ in the 11 ▾ Font Size button.

Your screen should be similar to Figure 13

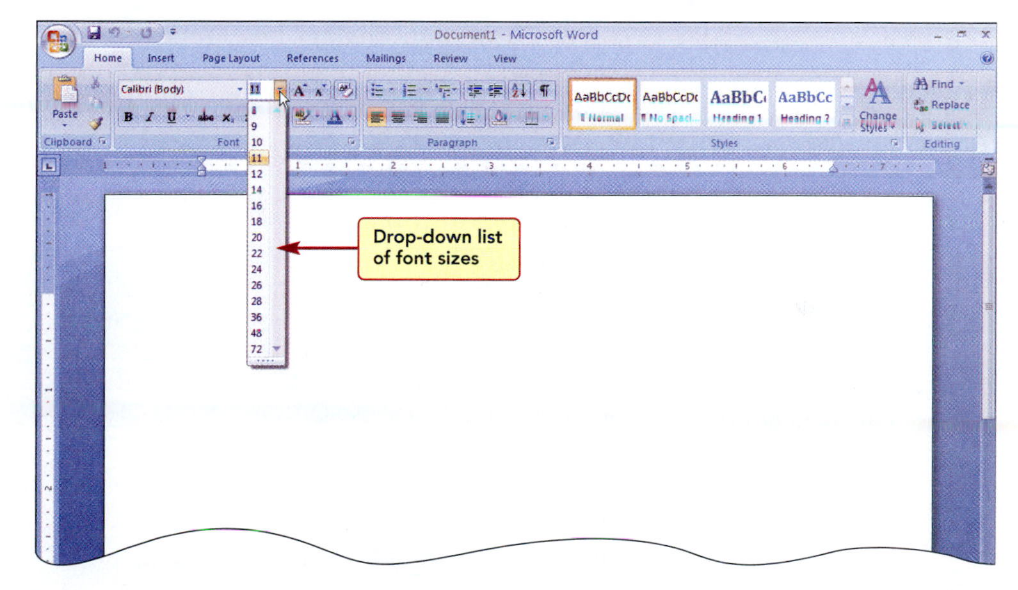

Figure 13

If you click on the button itself, not the ▾ section of the button, the associated command is performed.

Using the Dialog Box Launcher

Because there is not enough space, only the most used commands are displayed in the Ribbon. If there are more commands available, a ⧉ button, called the **dialog box launcher**, is displayed in the lower-right corner of the group. Clicking ⧉ opens a dialog box or **task pane** of additional options.

1 Click outside the Font size list to clear it.

- Point to the [dialog box launcher] of the Paragraph group to see the tooltip.
- Click [dialog box launcher] of the Paragraph group.

Your screen should be similar to Figure 14

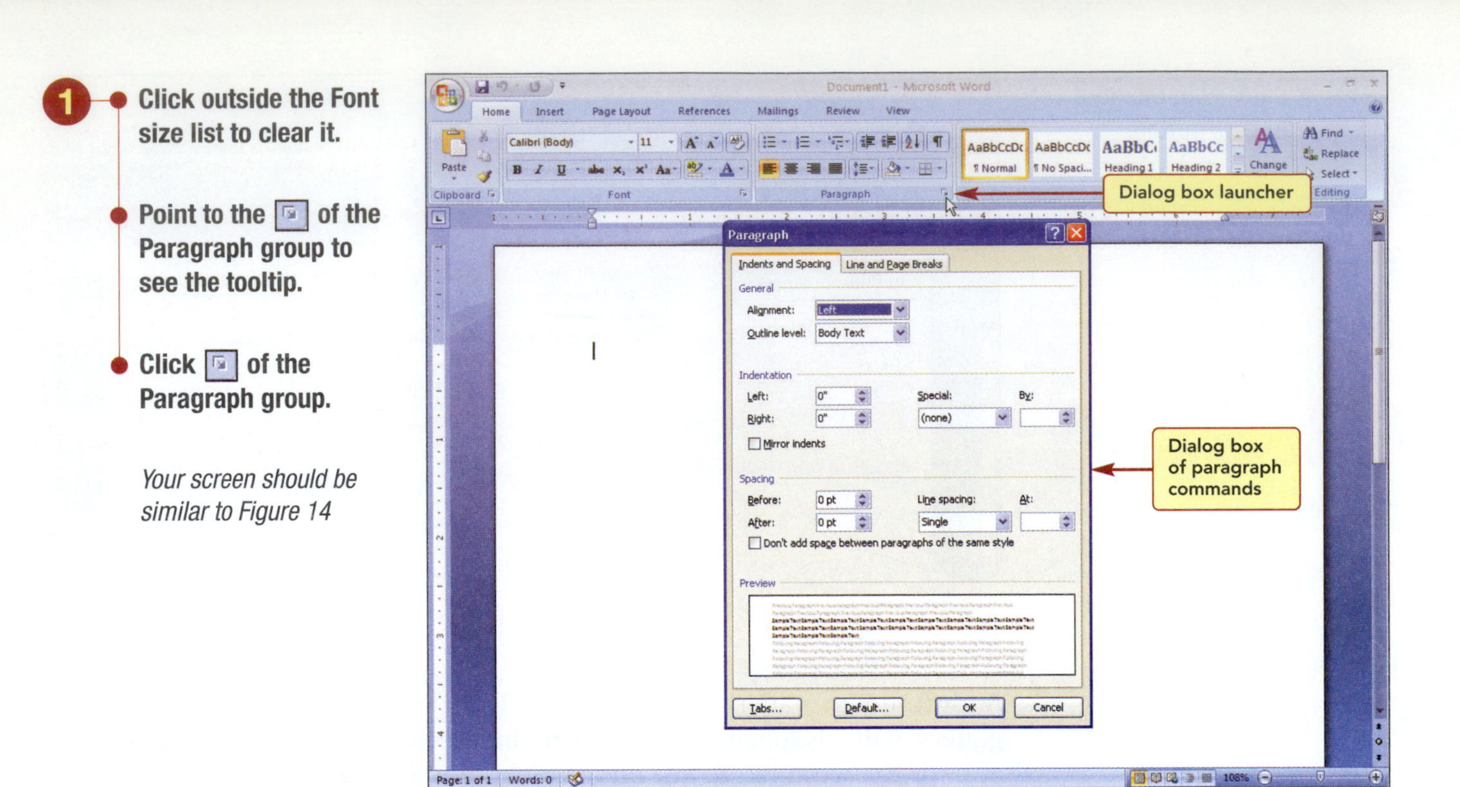

Figure 14

The Paragraph dialog box appears. It provides access to the more advanced paragraph settings features. Selecting options from the dialog box and clicking OK will close the dialog box and apply the settings as specified. To cancel the dialog box, you can click Cancel or ✕ in the dialog box title bar.

2 Click Cancel to close the dialog box.

- Click [dialog box launcher] in the Clipboard group.

Your screen should be similar to Figure 15

Clipboard task pane

Closes task pane

Dialog box launcher

Figure 15

Additional Information

You will learn about using dialog boxes, task panes, and the Clipboard as they are used in the labs.

A task pane is open that contains features associated with the Clipboard. Unlike dialog boxes, task panes remain open until you close them. This allows you to make multiple selections from the task pane while continuing to work on other areas of your document.

3 Click ✕ in the upper-right corner of the task pane to close it.

Using Access Key Shortcuts

Another way to use commands on the Ribbon is to display the access key shortcuts by pressing the Alt key and then typing the letter for the feature you want to use. Every Ribbon tab, group, and command has an access key.

1 Press Alt.

Another Method

You also can press F10 to display the access keys.

Your screen should be similar to Figure 16

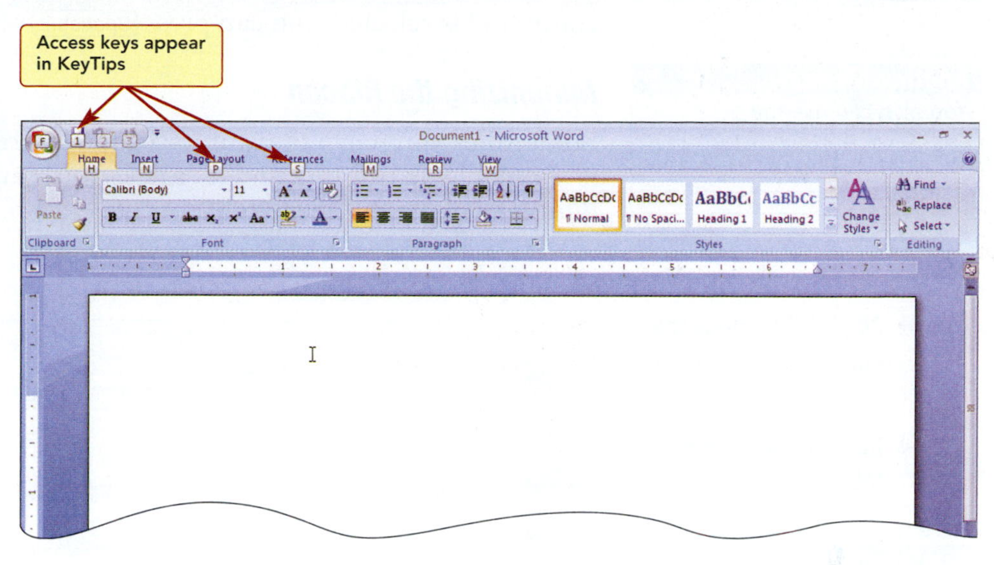

Figure 16

The letters are displayed in **KeyTips** over each available feature. Now typing a letter will access that feature. Then, depending on which letter you pressed, additional KeyTips may appear. To use a Ribbon command, press the key of the tab first, then the group, and then continue pressing letters until you press the letter of the specific command you want to use. You will use KeyTips to display the Paragraph dialog box again.

2 Type the letter H to access the Home tab.

Type the letters PG to access the Paragraph group and open the dialog box.

Your screen should be similar to Figure 17

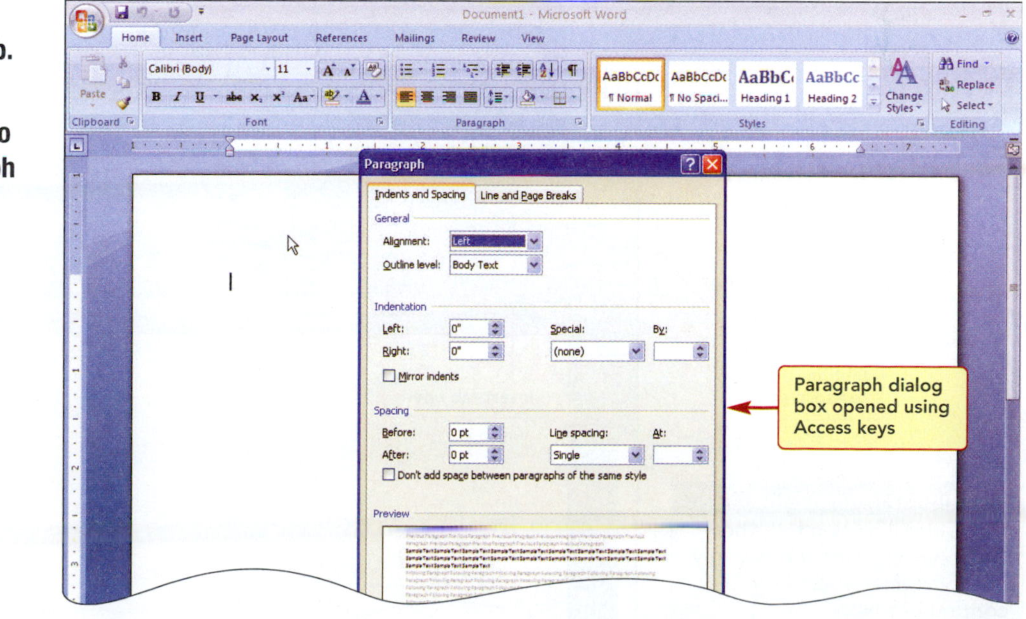

Figure 17

Three keystrokes opened the Paragraph dialog box.

Another Method

You also can press F6 to change the focus from the Ribbon to the document area to the View Toolbar.

Once the Access key feature is on, you can also use the ← or → directional key to move from one tab to another, and the ↓ key to move from a tab to a group and the ↑ key to move from a group to a tab. You can use all four directional keys to move among the commands in a Ribbon. Tab and ⇧Shift + Tab also can be used to move right or left. Once a command is selected, you can press Spacebar or ←Enter to activate it.

Another Method

You also can use the keyboard shortcut Ctrl + F1 to minimize and redisplay the Ribbon.

Minimizing the Ribbon

Sometimes you may not want to see the entire Ribbon so that more space is available in the document area. You can minimize the Ribbon by double-clicking the active tab.

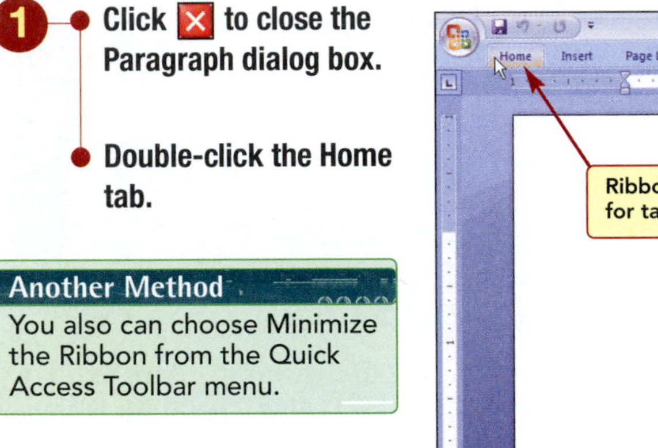

1 • **Click ☒ to close the Paragraph dialog box.**

• **Double-click the Home tab.**

Another Method

You also can choose Minimize the Ribbon from the Quick Access Toolbar menu.

Your screen should be similar to Figure 18

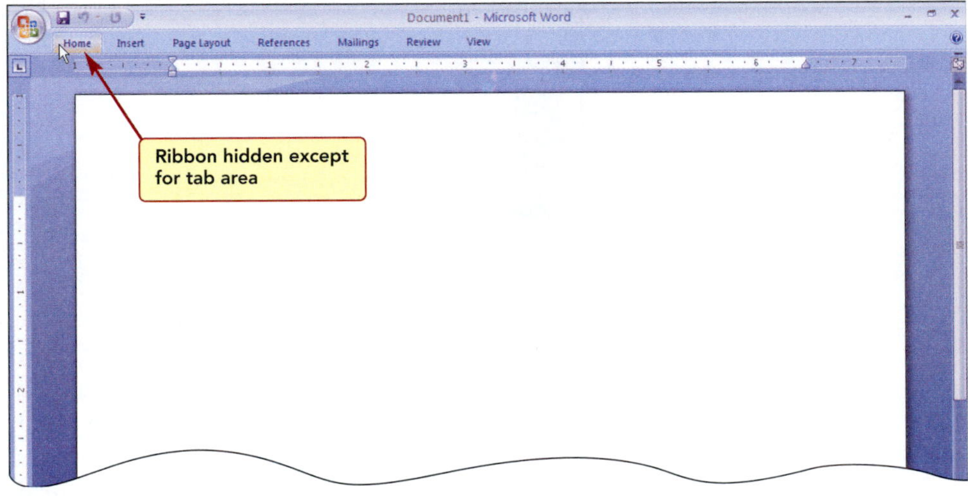

Figure 18

Now, the only part of the Ribbon that is visible is the tab area. This allows you to quickly reopen the Ribbon and, at the same time, open the selected tab.

2 • **Double-click the Insert tab.**

Your screen should be similar to Figure 19

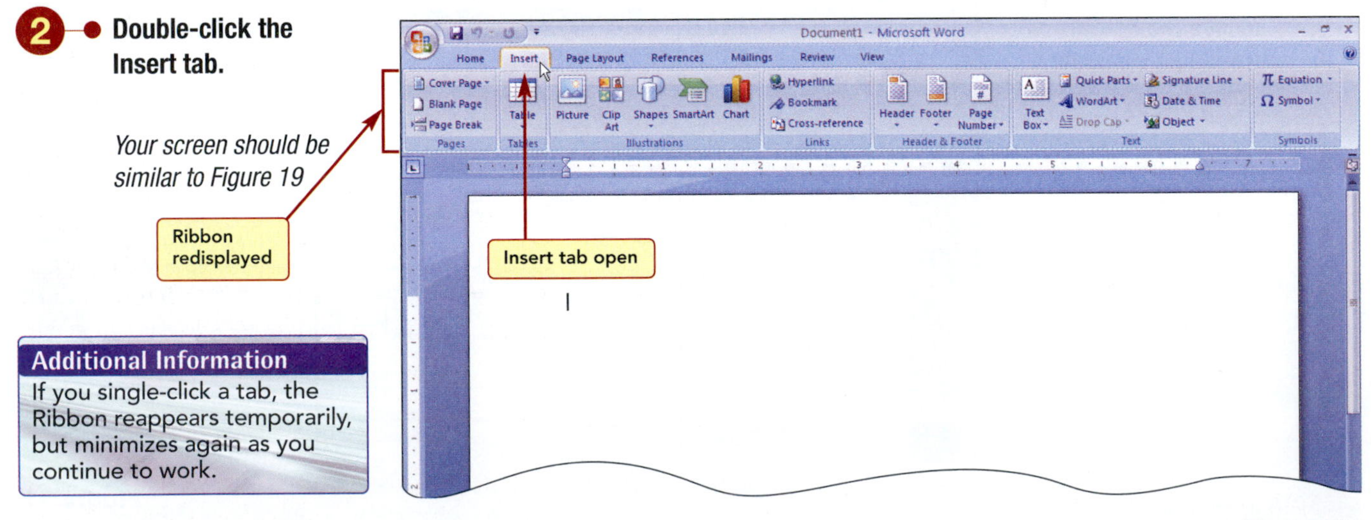

Figure 19

Additional Information

If you single-click a tab, the Ribbon reappears temporarily, but minimizes again as you continue to work.

The full Ribbon reappears and the Insert tab is open and ready for use.

Using the Mini Toolbar

Another method of accessing commands is through the Mini toolbar. The **Mini toolbar** appears automatically when you select text in a document and provides commands that are used to format (enhance) text. It also appears along with the context menu when you right-click an item in a document. Both the Mini toolbar and context menus are designed to make it more efficient to execute commands.

You can see what these features look like by right-clicking in a blank area of the document window.

1 Right-click the blank document window space.

Your screen should be similar to Figure 20

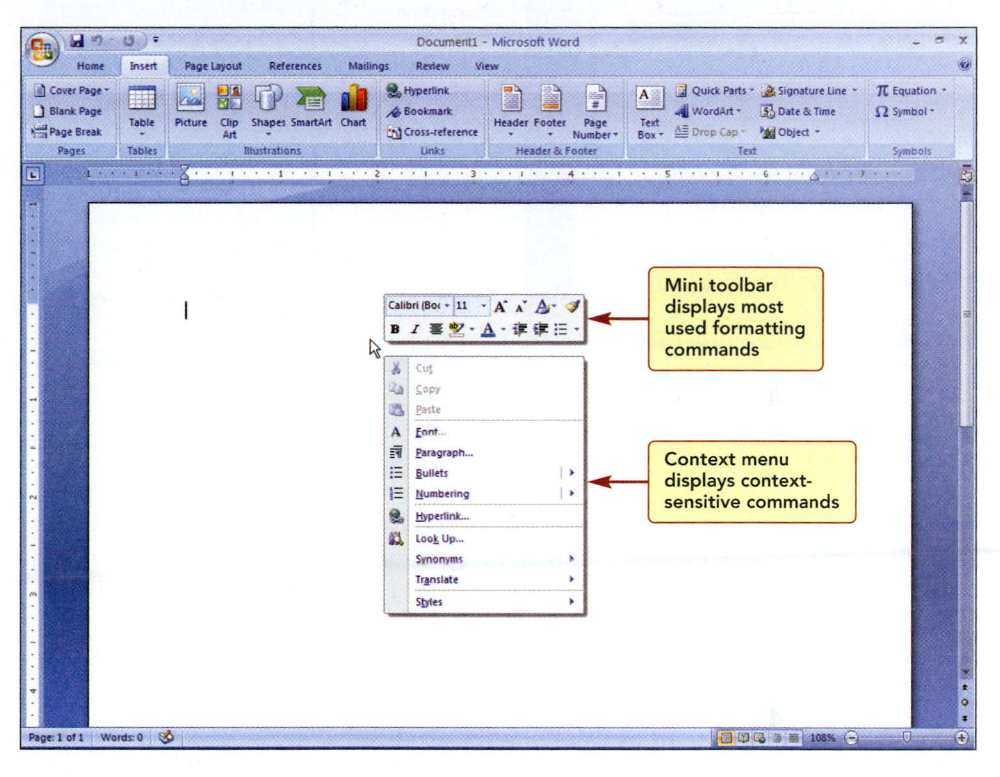

Figure 20

The Mini toolbar displays the most frequently used formatting commands. For example, when the Home tab is closed, you can use the commands in the Mini toolbar to quickly change selected text without having to reopen the Home tab to access the command. When the Mini toolbar appears automatically, it is faded so that it does not interfere with what you are doing, but changes to solid (as it is here) when you point at it.

The context menu below the Mini toolbar displays a variety of commands that are quicker to access than locating the command on the Ribbon. The commands that appear on this menu change depending on what you are doing at the time.

Using Office Help

Notice the [Help button] in the upper-right corner of the Ribbon. This button is used to access the Microsoft Help system. The Help button is always visible even when the Ribbon is hidden. Because you are using the Office Word 2007 application, Office Word Help will be accessed.

Another Method

You also can press F1 to access Help.

- Click Microsoft Office Word Help.
- If a Table of Contents list is displayed along the left side of the Help window, click in the Help window toolbar to close it.

Additional Information
You will learn about using the Table of Contents shortly.

Your screen should be similar to Figure 21

Additional Information
Clicking the scroll arrows scrolls the text in the window line by line, and dragging the scroll bar up or down moves to a general location within the window area.

Additional Information
Because Help is an online feature, the information is frequently updated. Your screens may display slightly different information than those shown in the figures in this lab.

Having Trouble?
In addition to being connected to the Internet, the feature to show content from the Internet must be selected. If necessary, click the Offline button at the bottom of the Help window and choose Show content from Office Online.

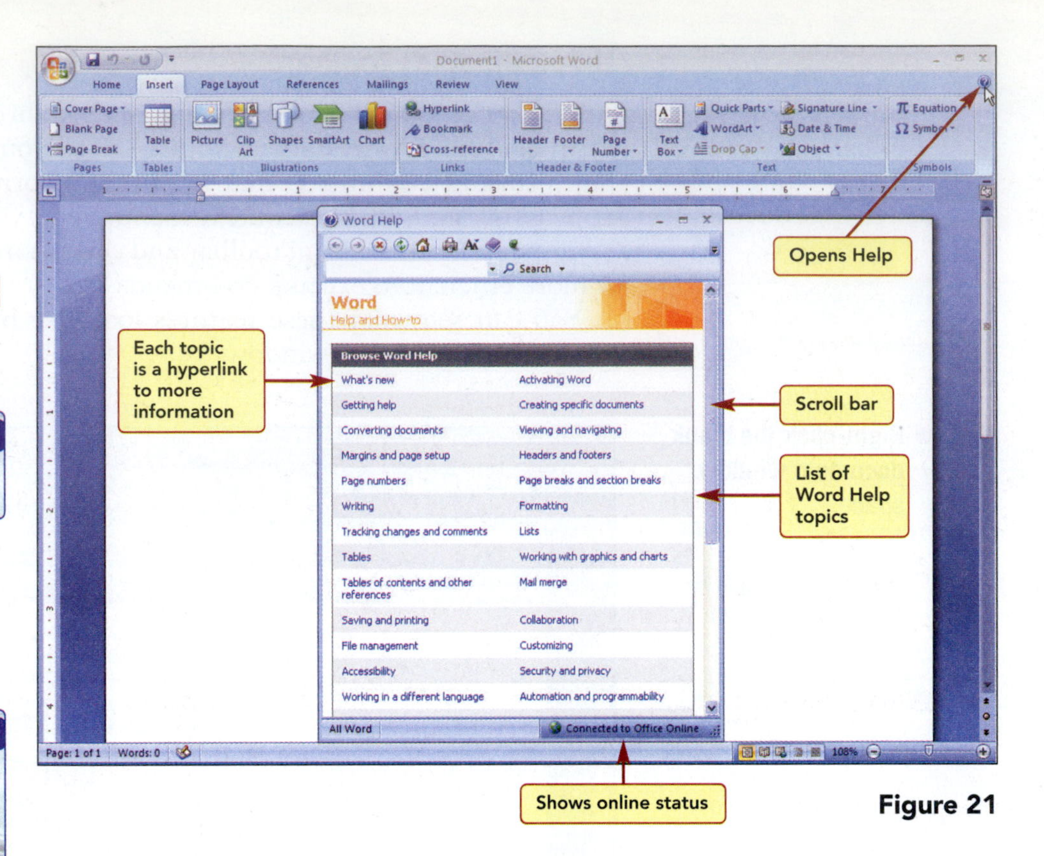

Figure 21

The Microsoft Word Help feature is opened and displayed in a separate window. The Help window on your screen will probably be a different size and arrangement than in Figure 21. Depending on the size of your Help window, you may need to scroll the window to see all the Help information provided.

It displays a listing of Help topics. If you are connected to the Internet, the Microsoft Office Online Web site is accessed and help information from this site is displayed in the window. If you are not connected, the offline help information that is provided with the application and stored on your computer is located and displayed. Generally, the listing of topics is similar but fewer in number.

Selecting Help Topics

There are several ways you can get help. The first is to select a topic from the listing displayed in the Help window. Each topic is a **hyperlink** or connection to the information located on the Online site or in Help on your computer. When you point to the hyperlink, it appears underlined and the mouse pointer appears as . Clicking the hyperlink accesses and displays the information associated with the hyperlink.

Click "Getting help."

Your screen should be similar to Figure 22

Document1 - Microsoft Word

Word Help

Word Home

Getting help

Subcategories of "Getting help"

Using Microsoft Office Online | Using Microsoft Office

Installing | Using Microsoft Windows

Topics in "Getting help" 15 items

Interactive: Word 2003 to Word 2007 command reference guide

2007 Microsoft Office System Beta 2 Technical Refresh Known Issues/ReadMe

2007 Microsoft Office System Known Issues/ReadMe

Reference: Locations of Word 2003 commands in Word 2007

Find the content you need in the Help window

Work with the Help window

Download training presentations about the 2007 Office system

Get targeted help on a program or feature

Change the appearance of a Help topic

All Word | Connected to Office Online

Listing of topics in "Getting help"

Hyperlink mouse pointer

Figure 22

A listing of topics about getting help is displayed. You will get help on using Microsoft Office and the Ribbon.

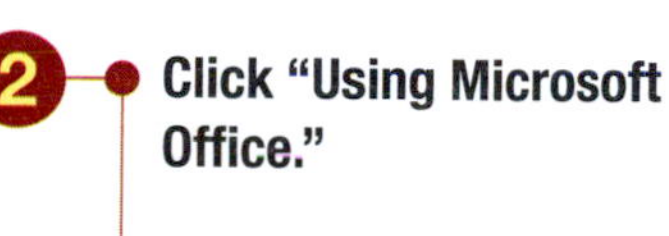

Click "Using Microsoft Office."

Click "Use the Ribbon."

Your screen should be similar to Figure 23

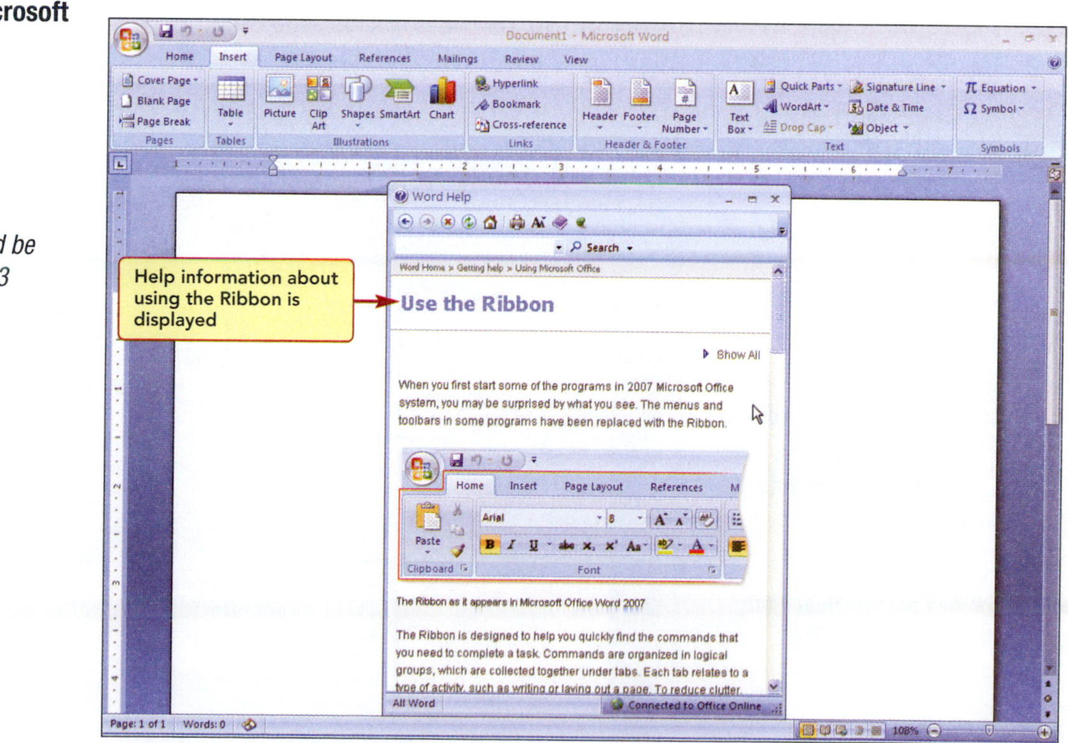

Figure 23

The information on the selected topic is displayed in the window.

3 Use the scroll bar to scroll the Help window to read the information about the Ribbon.

Display the "In this article" section of the window.

Your screen should be similar to Figure 24

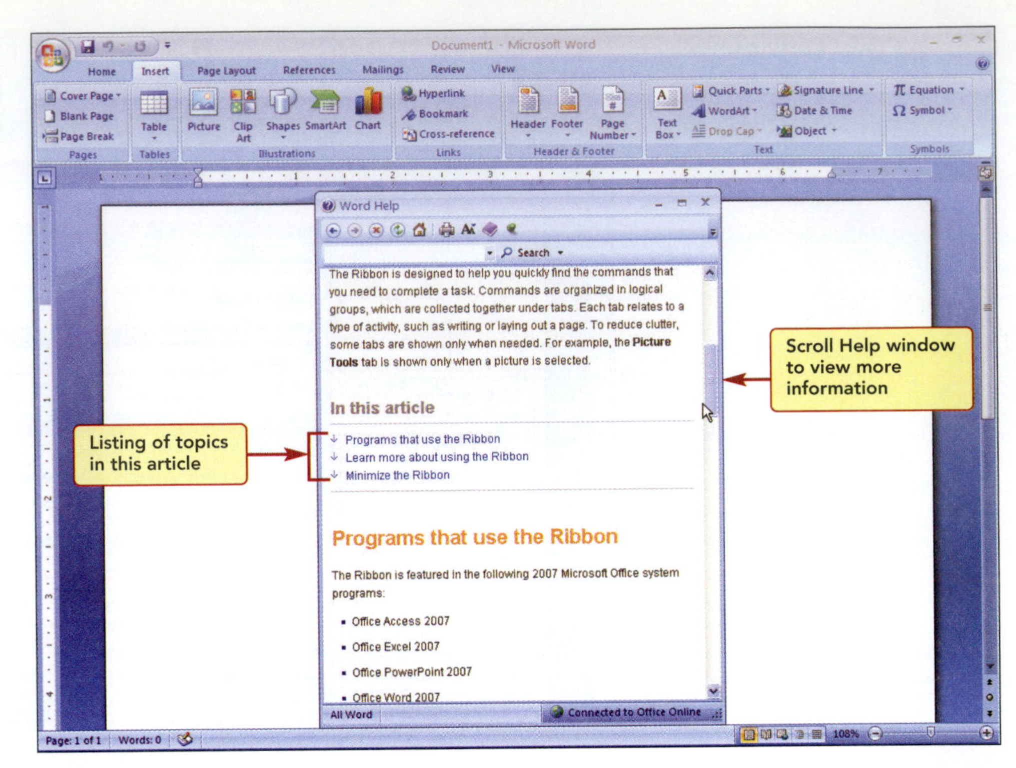

Figure 24

Additional Information
In Windows Vista, an unopened topic heading is preceded with +.

This area of the Help window provides a table of contents listing of the information in this window. Clicking on a link will take you directly to that location in the Help window. As you are reading the information in the window, you will see many topics preceded with ▶. This indicates the information in the topic is not displayed. Clicking on the topic heading displays the information about the topic.

4 Click "Learn more about using the Ribbon."

Click "Microsoft Office Word 2007."

If necessary, scroll the window to see all the information on this topic.

Your screen should be similar to Figure 25

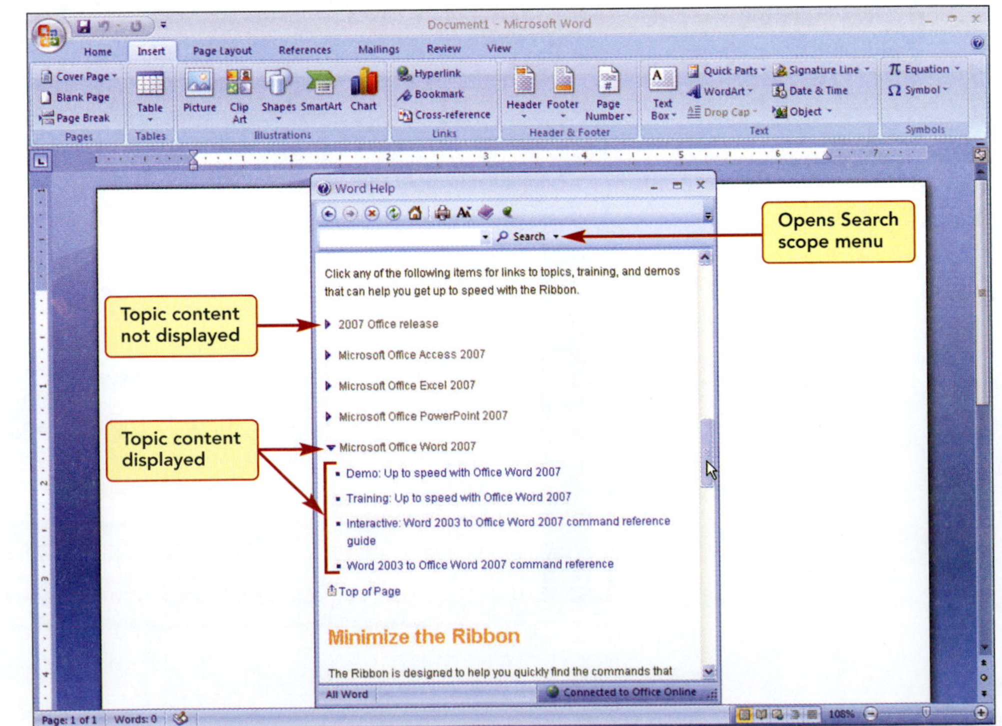

Figure 25

The information on the selected subtopic is displayed. Clicking the table of contents link jumped directly to this section of the window, saving you time by not having to scroll. The ▶ preceding the subtopic has changed to ▼, indicating the subtopic content is displayed.

You can continue to click on the subtopic headings to display the information about each topic individually. Likewise, clicking on an expanded topic hides the information. Additionally you can click Show All located at the top of the window to display all the available topic information and Hide All to hide all expanded information.

Additional Information

In Windows Vista, these buttons are Show All and Hide All.

Searching Help Topics

Another method to find Help information is to conduct a search by entering a sentence or question you want help on in the Search text box of the Help window. Although you also can simply enter a word in the Search box, the best results occur when you type a phrase, complete sentence, or question. A very specific search with 2–7 words will return the most accurate results.

When searching, you can specify the scope of the search by selecting from the Search scope drop-down menu. The broadest scope for a search, All Word, is preselected. You will narrow the scope to search Word Help only.

1

- Open the Search drop-down list.
- Click "Word Help."
- Click in the Search text box to display the insertion point.
- Type **What is the Ribbon**.
- Click Search.

Additional Information

You also could press ←Enter to start the search.

Your screen should be similar to Figure 26

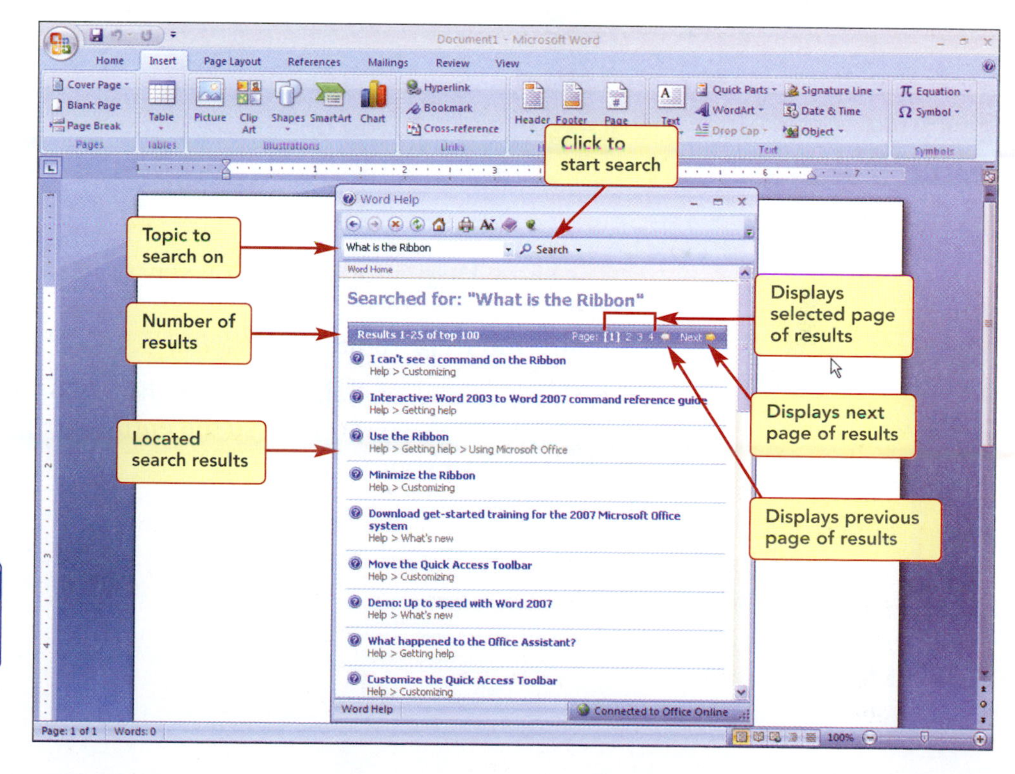

Figure 26

The first 25 located results of the top 100 are displayed in a window. There are four pages of results. The results are shown in order of relevance, with the most likely matches at the top of the list. Now you can continue to locate the information you need by selecting from the topic links provided. To see the next page of results, you can click Next or ➡ or click the specific page number you want to see from the Page count area. To see the previous page of results, click ⬅.

Topics preceded with [icon] indicate the window will display the related Help topic. Those preceded with a [icon] indicate a tutorial about the topic is available from the Microsoft Training Web site.

2 Click "Use the Ribbon."

Your screen should be similar to Figure 27

Figure 27

The same Help information you saw previously is displayed.

Using the Help Table of Contents

A third source of help is to use the Help table of contents. Using this method allows you to browse the entire list of Help topics to locate topics of interest to you.

1 **Click Home in the Help window toolbar to return to the opening Help window.**

Click Show Table of Contents from the Help window toolbar.

Additional Information

You also could click Back in the Help window toolbar to return to the previous page, page by page.

Your screen should be similar to Figure 28

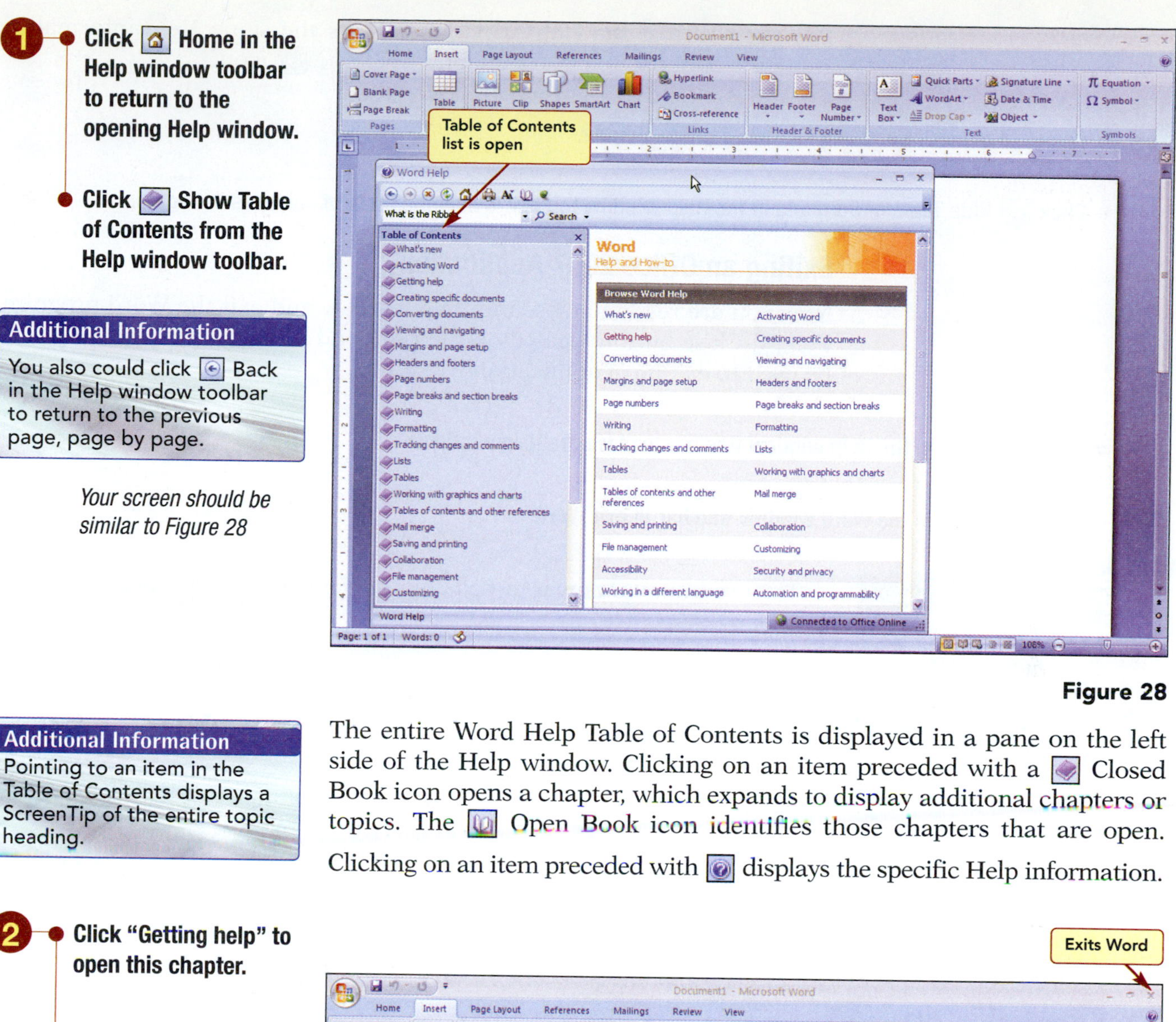

Figure 28

Additional Information

Pointing to an item in the Table of Contents displays a ScreenTip of the entire topic heading.

The entire Word Help Table of Contents is displayed in a pane on the left side of the Help window. Clicking on an item preceded with a Closed Book icon opens a chapter, which expands to display additional chapters or topics. The Open Book icon identifies those chapters that are open. Clicking on an item preceded with displays the specific Help information.

2 **Click "Getting help" to open this chapter.**

Click "Using Microsoft Office."

Scroll the table of contents list and click "Use the Ribbon."

Your screen should be similar to Figure 29

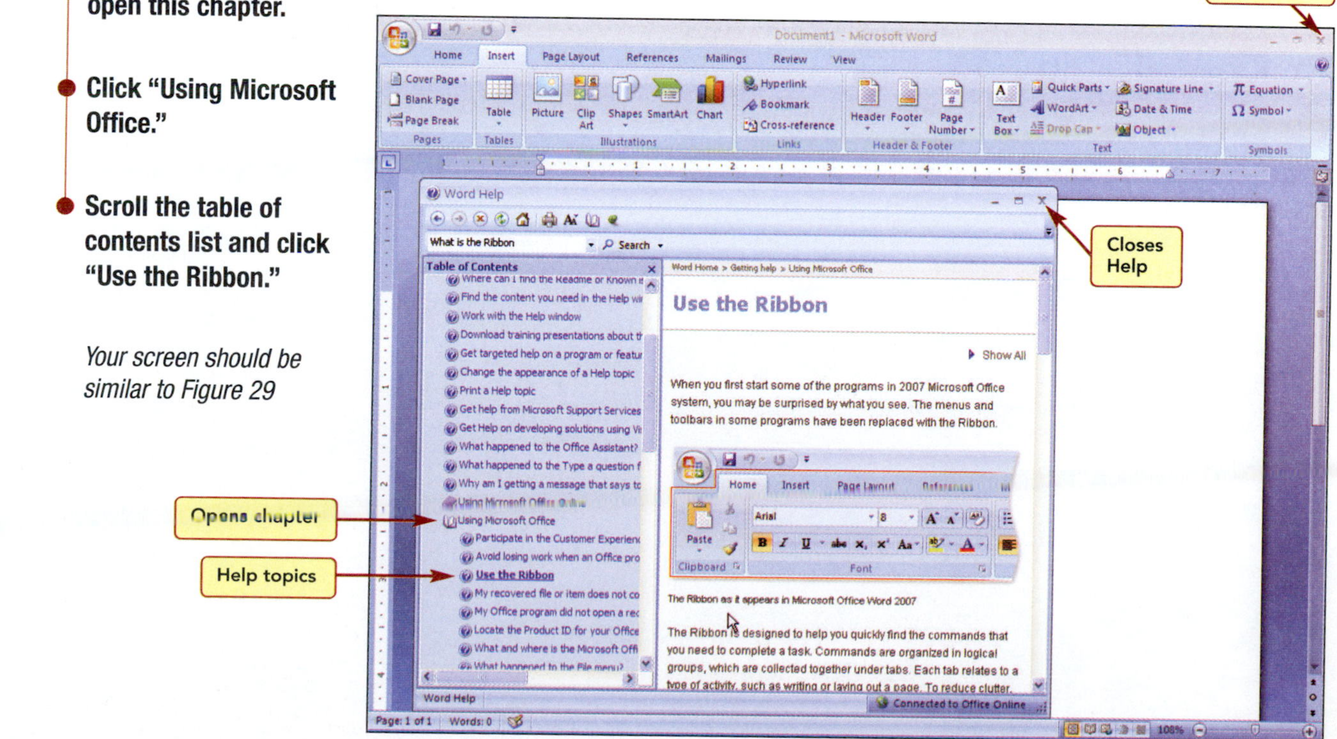

Figure 29

The right side of the Help window displays the same Help information about the Ribbon. To close a chapter, click the icon.

3 • Click to close the Using Microsoft Office chapter.

• Click Hide Table of Contents in the Help window toolbar to hide the table of contents list again.

Exiting an Office 2007 Application

Now you are ready to close the Help window and exit the Word program. The Close button located on the right end of the window title bar can be used to exit most application windows.

1 • Click Close in the Help window title bar to close the Help window.

• Click Close in the Word window title bar to exit Word.

Another Method

You also could choose / Exit Word or press Alt + F4 to exit an Office application.

The program window is closed and the desktop is visible again.

Lab Review

Introduction to Microsoft Office 2007

key terms

context menu I.15
contextual tabs I.16
dialog box launcher I.19
document window I.11
drop-down gallery I.18
gallery I.18
group I.11
hyperlink I.24
in-Ribbon gallery I.18
KeyTips I.21
Mini toolbar I.23
on-demand tab I.16
Quick Access Toolbar I.11
Ribbon I.11
ScreenTip I.13
scroll bar I.11
selection cursor I.12
split button I.18
status bar I.11
super tooltip I.18
tab I.11
task pane I.19
tooltip I.13
user interface I.10

command summary

Command/Button	Shortcut	Action
start		Opens the Start menu
Microsoft Office Word 2007		Starts the Word 2007 program
Office Button/ Exit Word	Alt + F4	Exits Office program
(Help button)	F1	Opens Help window

Lab Exercises

rating system
★ Easy
★★ Moderate
★★★ Difficult

step-by-step

Using an Office Application ★

1. All Office 2007 applications have a common user interface. You will explore the Excel 2007 application and use many of the same features you learned about while using Word 2007 in this lab.

   a. Use the Start menu or a shortcut icon on your desktop to start Office Excel 2007.

   b. What shape is the mouse pointer when positioned in the document window area? ________

   c. Excel has ________ tabs. Which tabs are not the same as in Word?
   ____

   d. Open the Formulas tab. How many groups are in the Formulas tab? ________

   e. Which tab contains the group to work with charts? ________

   f. From the Home tab, click the Number group dialog box launcher. What is the name of the dialog box that opens? How many number categories are there? ________ Close the dialog box.

   g. Display tooltips for the following buttons located in the Alignment group of the Home tab and identify what action they perform.

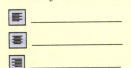

   h. Open the Excel Help window. Open the table of contents and locate the topic "What's new in Microsoft Office Excel 2007?" Open this topic and find information on the number of rows and columns in a worksheet. Answer the following questions:

   How many rows are in a worksheet? ________

   How many columns are in a worksheet? ________

   What are the letters of the last column? ________

   i. Close the table of contents. Close the Help window. Exit Excel.

on your own

Exploring Microsoft Help ★

1. In addition to the Help information you used in this lab, Office 2007 Online Help also includes many interactive tutorials. Selecting a Help topic that starts a tutorial will open the browser program on your computer. Both audio and written instructions are provided. You will use one of these tutorials to learn more about using Word 2007.

   Start Word 2007. Open Help and open the topic "What's New?" Click on the topic "Up to speed with Word 2007." Follow the directions in your browser to run the tutorial. When you are done, close the browser window, close Help, and exit Word 2007.

Overview of Microsoft Office Access 2007

What Is a Database?

Somewhere at home, or maybe in your office, you probably have a file cabinet or desk drawer filled with information. Perhaps you have organized the information into drawers of related information, and further categorized that information into file folders. This is a database.

As organized as you might be, it takes time to locate a specific piece of information by manually opening drawers and searching through the folders. You can just imagine how much time would be required for a large company to manually search through its massive amounts of data. These companies use electronic database management systems (DBMS). Now you too can use electronic database management systems to store, organize, access, manipulate, and present information in a variety of ways.

In this series of labs, you will learn how to design and create a computerized database using Access 2007 and you will quickly appreciate the many advantages of a computerized database.

Landis Job Position Report

Employee ID	First Name	Last Name	Position
12703	Jeff	Bader	Fitness Instructor
12389	Jennifer	Blackman	Sales Associate
05015	Scot	Briggs	Personal Trainer Director
12501	Elizabeth	DeLuca	Personal Trainer
12855	Kimberly	Fachet	Sales Associate
13484	Stephanie	Franklin	Food Service Server
12914	Alfonso	Gomez	Cleaning
22469	Ryan	Hog	
13303	Chris	Jens	
13027	Kimberly	Kiel	
07650	Chris	Lam	
22085	Kristina	Lind	
13635	Juan	Mar	
03225	Dan	Mor	
99999	Student	Nam	
12420	Allison	Play	
13005	Emily	Reil	
22297	Patricia	Rog	
07287	Anita	Rom	
12918	Carlos	Ruiz	
00212	Chad	Schi	
12583	Marie	Sulli	
03890	Erona	Thi	
12380	Jessica	Tho	

Tuesday, February 06, 2008

Table Tools ac03_PersonnelSol : Database (Access 2007) - Microsoft Access

Home Create External Data Database Tools Datasheet

View Paste Arial 10 Refresh All New Save Delete Totals Spelling More Filter Selection Advanced Toggle Filter Find Replace Go To Select

Views Clipboard Font Rich Text Records Sort & Filter Find

All Access Objects

Tables
City/State/ZipCode
Job Information
Personal Data

Queries
Car Pool Query
Find duplicates for Personal ...
Location Query
Personal Data Without Match...

Reports
Job Position Report
Maldin to Landis Car Pool Re...

Personal Data

Employee ID	Last Name	First Name	Address	Lookup Zip Code	Home Phone	Gender
00212	Schiff	Chad	235 N. Cactus Dr.	92122	(507) 555-0010	M
00617	Nichols	Cathy	75 Brooklea Dr.	92120-3741	(507) 555-0001	F
00907	Pennington	Mark	23 Mill Ave.	92120-3741	(507) 555-3333	M
01421	Spehr	Timothy	90 Royal Dr.	92121-3740	(507) 555-1038	M
03225	Morgan	Dan	564 S. Lemon Dr.	92121	(507) 555-5567	M
03406	Lopez	Mina	4290 E. Alameda Dr.	92121-3740	(507) 555-5050	F
03673	Walker	Aaron	76 Thomas Rd.	92123-2232	(507) 555-2222	M
03890	Thi	Erona	7867 Forest Ave.	92123-2232	(507) 555-1089	F
04321	Sabin	Greg	90 E. Rawhide Ave.	92122	(507) 555-4455	M
04731	Marchant	Roberta	564 Palm Avenue	92120-3741	(507) 555-6707	F
05015	Briggs	Scott	45 E. Camelback Rd.	92123-2232	(507) 555-9585	M
06000	Robertson	Kirk	832 S. William Ave.	92121	(507) 555-3730	M
07287	Roman	Anita	2348 S. Bala Dr.	92121-3740	(507) 555-9870	F
07450	Matsumoto	Tyrus	34 S. Onza Ave.	92122-1268	(507) 555-8372	M
07540	Pario	Ian	983 E. Carrage Ln.	92120-3741	(507) 555-2321	M
07550	Ernster	Barbara	1153 S. Wilson	92123-2232	(507) 555-3211	F
07650	Lamm	Chris	382 E. Ladonna Dr.	92121	(507) 555-8332	M
08000	Nelson	Samantha	2322 Trafalgar Ct.	92123-2232	(507) 555-0003	F
08391	Ruiz	Enrique	35 Palm St.	92122-1268	(507) 555-0091	M
08430	Smith	Brent	4321 Toledo St.	92123-2232	(507) 555-6464	M
09430	Robson	David	8584 Bryan Dr.	92123-2232	(507) 555-6666	M
11510	Sutton	Lisa	4389 S. Hayden Rd.	92121-0093	(507) 555-1950	F
11747	Lettow	Ryan	358 Maple Dr.	92121-3740	(507) 555-2805	M
12194	Polonsky	Mitch	8701 E. Sheridan	92120-3741	(507) 555-1018	M
12213	Young	Kim	89 College Ave.	92123-2232	(507) 555-1059	F
12230	Reddie	Suzanne	932 E. Parkway Dr.	92120-3741	(507) 555-1191	F
12247	Rath	Kathy	87 E. Aurora Ave.	92122-1268	(507) 555-9797	F
12258	Delano	Gordon	13101 N. Spindrift Dr.	92122-1268	(507) 555-8201	M
12366	Stacey	David	737 S. College Rd.	92122-1268	(507) 555-7784	M
12380	Thomas	Jessica	128 Marina Dr.	92123-2232	(507) 555-8513	F

Record: 1 of 70 Unfiltered Search

Unique 5-digit number assigned to each employee.

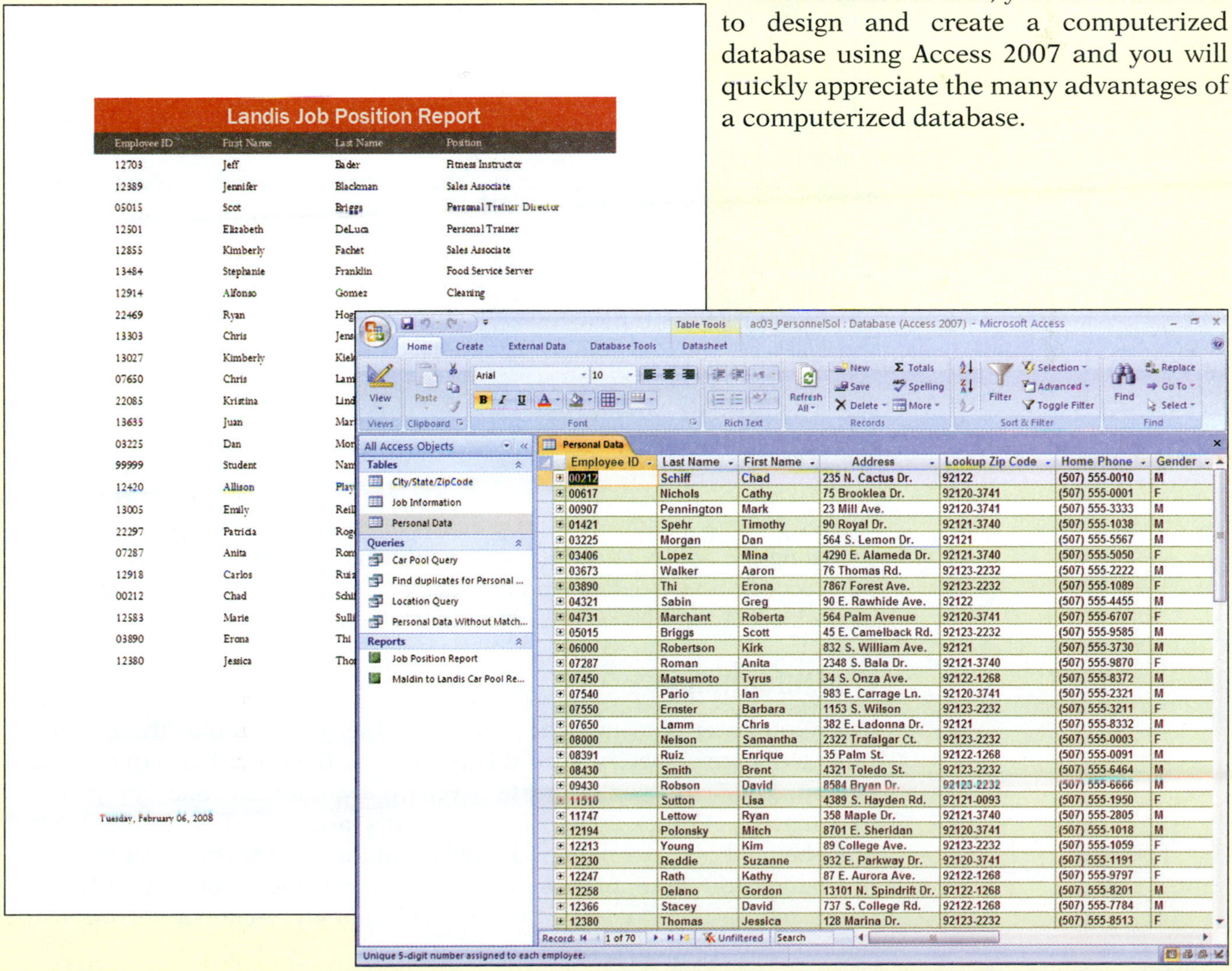

Access 2007 Features

Access 2007 is a relational database management system. In relational database systems, data is organized in tables that are related or linked to one another. Each table consists of rows, called records, and columns, called fields.

For example, a state's motor vehicle department database might have an address table. Each row (record) in the table would contain address information about one individual. Each column (field) would contain just one piece of information, for example, zip codes. The address table would be linked to other tables in the database by common fields. For example, the address table might be linked to a vehicle owner's table by name and linked to an outstanding citation table by license number (see example below).

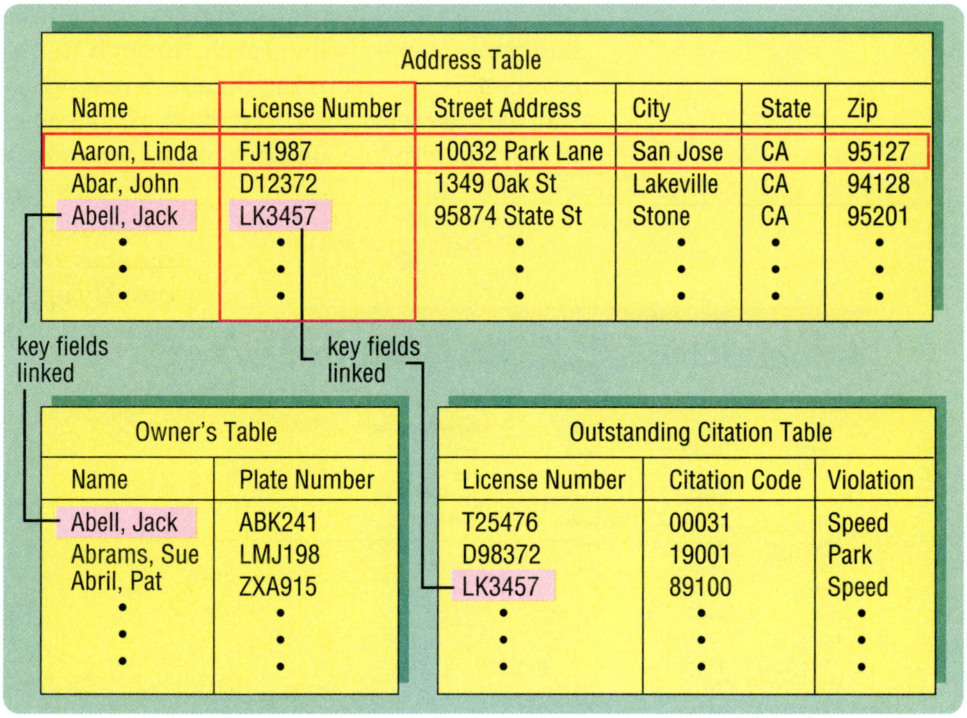

Address Table

Name	License Number	Street Address	City	State	Zip
Aaron, Linda	FJ1987	10032 Park Lane	San Jose	CA	95127
Abar, John	D12372	1349 Oak St	Lakeville	CA	94128
Abell, Jack	LK3457	95874 State St	Stone	CA	95201
⋮	⋮	⋮	⋮	⋮	⋮

key fields linked

key fields linked

Owner's Table

Name	Plate Number
Abell, Jack	ABK241
Abrams, Sue	LMJ198
Abril, Pat	ZXA915
⋮	⋮

Outstanding Citation Table

License Number	Citation Code	Violation
T25476	00031	Speed
D98372	19001	Park
LK3457	89100	Speed
⋮	⋮	⋮

Access 2007 is a powerful program with numerous easy-to-use features including the ability to quickly locate information; add, delete, modify, and sort records; analyze data; and produce professional-looking reports. Some of the basic Access 2007 features are described next.

Find Information

Once you enter data into the database table, you can quickly search the table to locate a specific record based on the data in a field. In a manual system, you can usually locate a record by knowing one key piece of information. For example, if the records are stored in a file cabinet alphabetically by last name, to quickly find a record, you must know the last name. In a computerized database, even if the records are sorted or organized by last name, you can still quickly locate a record using information in another field.

Add, Delete, and Modify Records

Using Access, it is also easy to add and delete records from the table. Once you locate a record, you can edit the contents of the fields to update the record or delete the record entirely from the table. You also can add new records to a table. When you enter a new record, it is automatically placed in the correct organizational location within the table.

Sort and Filter Records

The capability to arrange or sort records in the table according to different fields can provide more meaningful information. You can organize records by name, department, pay, class, or any other category you need at a particular time. Sorting the records in different ways can provide information to different departments for different purposes.

Additionally, you can isolate and display a subset of records by specifying filter criteria. The criteria specify which records to display based on data in selected fields.

Analyze Data

Using Access, you can analyze the data in a table and perform calculations on different fields of data. Instead of pulling each record from a filing cabinet, recording the piece of data you want to use, and then performing the calculation on the recorded data, you can simply have the database program perform the calculation on all the values in the specified field. Additionally, you can ask questions or query the table to find only certain records that meet specific conditions to be used in the analysis. Information that was once costly and time-consuming to get is now quickly and readily available.

Generate Reports

Access includes many features that help you quickly produce reports ranging from simple listings to complex, professional-looking reports. You can create a simple report by asking for a listing of specified fields of data and restricting the listing to records meeting designated conditions. You can create a more complex professional report using the same restrictions or conditions as the simple report, but you can display the data in different layout styles, or with titles, headings, subtotals, or totals.

Case Study for Office Access 2007 Labs

You have recently accepted a job as employment administrator for Lifestyle Fitness Club. The club has recently purchased Microsoft Access 2007, and you are using it to update their manual system for recording employee information.

Lab 1: You will learn how to design and create the structure for a computerized database and how to enter and edit records in the database. You also will print a simple report of the records you enter in the database file.

Lab 2: You will continue to build, modify, and use the employee database of records. You will learn how to sort the records in a database file to make it easier to locate records. You also will learn about filtering a table to display only the information you need. Additionally, you will create a form to make it easier to enter and edit data in the database file.

Lab 3: You will learn how to query the database to locate specific information. You also will learn how to create a report and link multiple tables.

Working Together: You will learn how to share information between applications by incorporating database information from Access into a Word memo.

Before You Begin

To the Student

The following assumptions have been made:

- Microsoft Access 2007 has been properly installed on your computer system.
- The data files needed to complete the series of labs and practice exercises are supplied by your instructor. These may be supplied by your instructor and are also available at the online learning center Web site found at www.mhhe.com/oleary.
- You are already familiar with how to use Microsoft Windows XP or Vista and a mouse.

To the Instructor

A complete installation of Microsoft Office 2007 is required in which all components are available to students while completing the labs. In several labs, an online connection to the Web is needed to fully access a feature.

Please be aware that the following settings are assumed to be in effect for the Office Access 2007 program. These assumptions are necessary so that the screens and directions in the labs are accurate. These settings are made using Office Button/ Access Options in the categories shown below.

Popular

- Always use ClearType is on.
- Show feature descriptions in ScreenTips is on.
- Show shortcut keys in ScreenTips is on.
- The Default file format is Access 2007.
- Default database folder is My Documents.
- New database sort order is General.

Current Database/Application Options

- Display Status Bar is on.
- Tabbed Documents is on.

- Display Document Tabs is on.
- Use Access Special Keys is on.
- Use Windows-themed Controls on Forms is on.
- Enable Layout View for this database is on.
- Enable design changes for tables in Datasheet view is on.
- Check for truncated number fields is on.
- Preserve source image format is on.

Current Database/Navigation

- Display Navigation Pane is on.
- Open objects with double-click is on.

Current Database/Ribbon and Toolbar Options

- Allow Full Menus is on.
- Allow Default Shortcut Menus is on.

Current Database/Name AutoCorrect Options

- Track name AutoCorrect info is on.
- Perform name AutoCorrect is on.

Datasheet/Default Colors

- All default colors are set to Automatic.

Datasheet/Gridlines and cell effects

- Default gridlines showing Horizontal and Vertical are on.
- Default cell effect is flat.
- Default column width is 1 inch.

Datasheet/Default font

- Font is Calibri.
- Font size is 11.
- Weight is Normal.

Object Designers/Table design

- Default field type is Text.
- Default text field size is 255.
- Default number field size is Long Integer.
- Show Property Update Options is on.

Object Designers/Query design

- Show table names is on.
- Enable AutoJoin is on.
- Query design font is Segoe UI with a point size of 8.

Object Designers/Forms/Reports

- Selection behavior is partially enclosed.
- Form and Report templates are Normal.

Object Designers/Error Checking

- All error checking options are on.
- Error indicator color is green.

Proofing

- All AutoCorrect options are on.
- Ignore words in Uppercase is on.
- Ignore words that contain numbers is on.
- Ignore Internet and file addresses is on.
- Flag repeated words is on.

Advanced/Editing

- Move after enter: Next field.
- Behavior entering field: Select entire field.
- Arrow key behavior: Next field.
- Default find/replace behavior: Fast search.
- All Confrim options are on.
- Default direction: Left-to-right.
- General Alignment: Interface mode.
- Cursor Movement: Logical.

Advanced/Display

- Show 9 recent documents.
- Display Status bar.
- Show animations is on.
- Show SmartTags on datasheets is on.
- Show SmartTags on forms and reports is on.

Advanced/Printing

- All margins are set to 0.25 inch.

Advanced/General

- No options are on.

Advanced/Advanced

- Default open mode is Shared.
- Default record locking is No locks.
- Open databases by using record-level locking is on.

Customize

- The Quick Access Toolbar displays the Save, Undo, and Redo buttons.
- Finally, the feature to access Online Help is on. (From the Help window, open the Connection Status menu and choose Show Content from Office Online.)

All figures in the text reflect the use of a display screen set at 1024 by 768 and the Windows XP operating system. If other monitor display settings are used, there may be more or fewer lines of information displayed in the windows than in the figures. If the Windows Vista operating system is used, some features may look slightly different.

Instructional Conventions

Hands-on instructions you are to perform appear as a sequence of numbered steps. Within each step, a series of bullets identifies the specific actions that must be performed. Step numbering begins over within each topic heading throughout the lab. Four types of marginal notes appear throughout the labs. Another Method notes provide alternate ways of performing the same command. Having Trouble? notes provide advice or cautions for steps that may cause problems. Additional Information notes provide more information about a topic. More About notes refer you to the More About appendix for additional information about related features.

Commands

Commands that are initiated using a command button and the mouse appear following the word "Click." The icon (and the icon name if the icon does not include text) is displayed following "Click." If there is another way to perform the same action, it appears in an Another Method margin note when the action is first introduced as shown in Example A.

When a feature has already been covered and you are more familiar with using the application, commands will appear as shown in Example B.

Example A

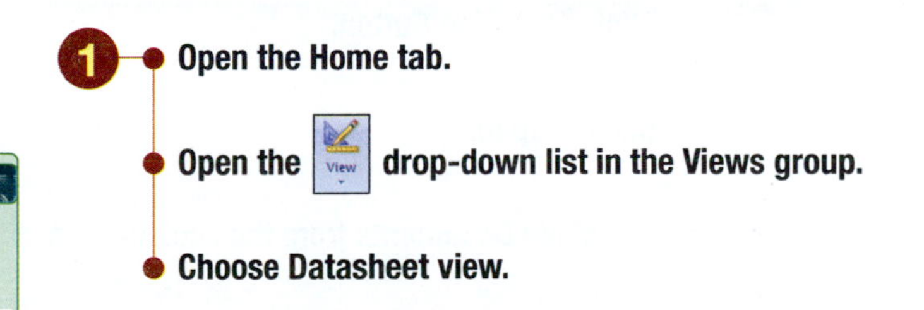

1
Open the Home tab.
Open the View drop-down list in the Views group.
Choose Datasheet view.

Another Method

You also can click Datasheet View in the status bar.

Example B

1. Click Datasheet View.

OR

1. Change the view to Datasheet View.

File Names and Information to Type

Plain blue text identifies file names you need to select or enter. Information you are asked to type appears in blue and bold. (See Example C.)

Example C

1. Open the database file ac02_Employees.
   - Type **9/23/01** in the Hire Date field.

Office Button Menu

Clicking Office Button opens the File menu of commands. File menu commands that you are to perform appear following the word "Choose." Items that need to be selected will follow the word "Select" and will appear in black text. You can select items with the mouse or directional keys. Initially these commands will appears as in Example A. As you become more familiar with the application, commands will appear as shown in Example B.

Example A

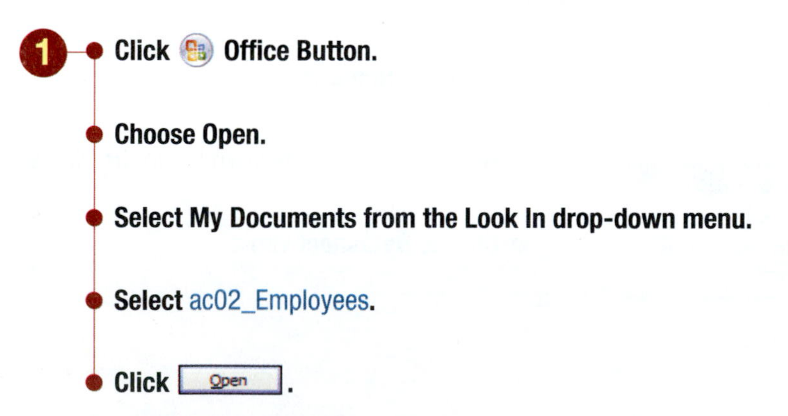

1. Click Office Button.
   - Choose Open.
   - Select My Documents from the Look In drop-down menu.
   - Select ac02_Employees.
   - Click Open.

Example B

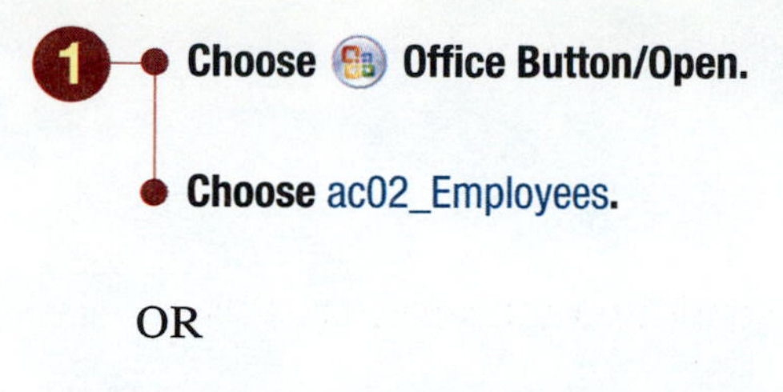
1
Choose Office Button/Open.
Choose ac02_Employees.

OR

1 — **Open the file** ac02_Employees**.**

Creating a Database LAB 1

Objectives

After completing this lab, you will know how to:

1. Plan, create, and modify a database.
2. Create and save a table structure.
3. Define field names, data types, field properties, and primary key fields.
4. Enter and edit data.
5. Add attachments.
6. Change views.
7. Adjust column widths.
8. Use the Best Fit feature.
9. Create a second table.
10. Create a Lookup field.
11. Delete records.
12. Preview and print a table.
13. Change page orientation.
14. Close and open a table and database.

Case Study

Lifestyle Fitness Club

You have recently accepted a job as a human resources administrator with Lifestyle Fitness Club. Like many fitness centers, Lifestyle Fitness Club includes exercise equipment, free weights, aerobics classes, tanning and massage facilities, swimming pool, steam room and sauna, and child-care facilities. In addition, it promotes a healthy lifestyle by including educational seminars on good nutrition and proper exercise. It also has a small snack bar that serves healthy drinks, sandwiches, and snacks.

The Lifestyle Fitness Clubs are a franchised chain of clubs that are individually owned. You work at a club owned by Felicity and Ryan Albright, who also own two others in California. Accounting and employment functions for all three clubs are handled centrally at the Landis location.

You are responsible for maintaining the employment records for all employees, as well as records for traditional employment activities such as hiring and benefits. Currently the club employment records are maintained on paper forms and are stored in file cabinets organized alphabetically by last name. Although the information is well organized, it still takes time to manually look through the folders to locate the information you need and to compile reports from this data.

The Club has recently purchased new computers, and the owners want to update the employee record-keeping system to an electronic database management system. The software tool you will use to create the database is the database application Office Access 2007. In this lab, you will learn about entering, editing, previewing, and printing information in the database you create for the Club.

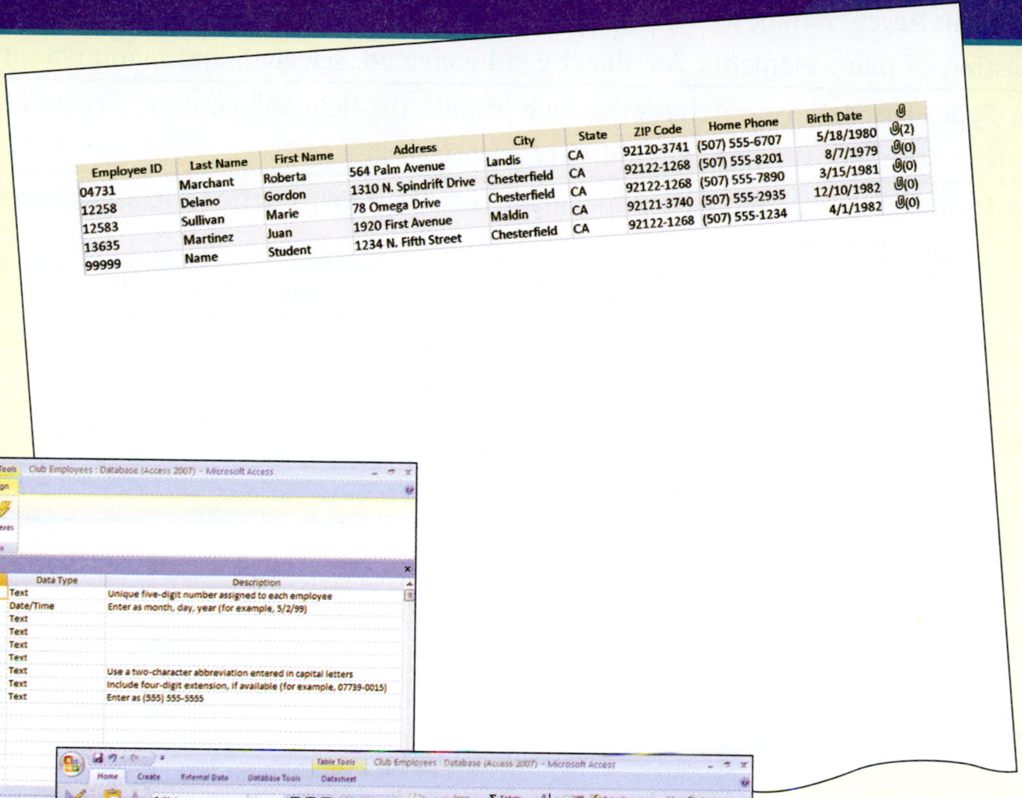

Employee ID	Last Name	First Name	Address	City	State	ZIP Code	Home Phone	Birth Date	📎
04731	Marchant	Roberta	564 Palm Avenue	Landis	CA	92120-3741	(507) 555-6707	5/18/1980	(2)
12258	Delano	Gordon	1310 N. Spindrift Drive	Chesterfield	CA	92122-1268	(507) 555-8201	8/7/1979	(0)
12583	Sullivan	Marie	78 Omega Drive	Chesterfield	CA	92122-1268	(507) 555-7890	3/15/1981	(0)
13635	Martinez	Juan	1920 First Avenue	Maldin	CA	92121-3740	(507) 555-2935	12/10/1982	(0)
99999	Name	Student	1234 N. Fifth Street	Chesterfield	CA	92122-1268	(507) 555-1234	4/1/1982	(0)

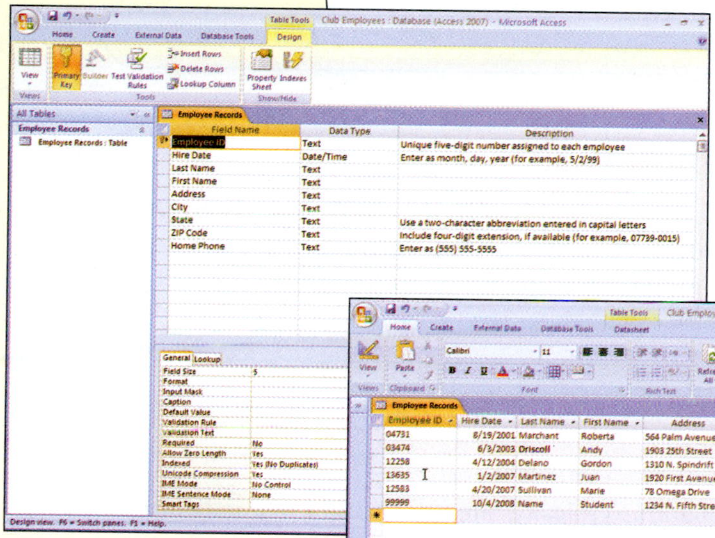

Designing the table structure consists of defining field names, data types, and field properties.

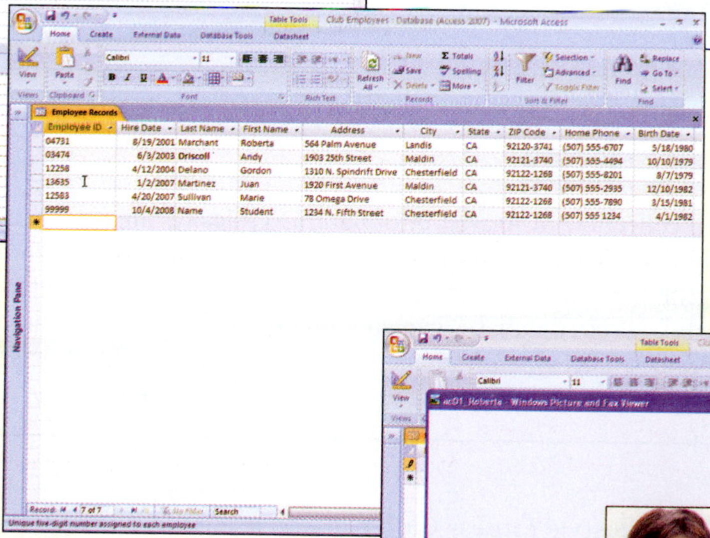

Entering data in a table creates records of information.

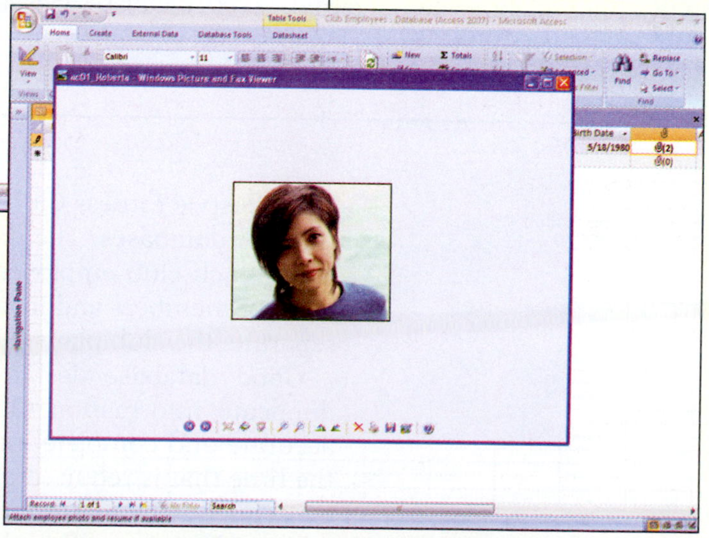

Fields can contain attachments, such as pictures or files.

Concept Preview

The following concepts will be introduced in this lab:

1. **Database** A database is an organized collection of related information.
2. **Object** An Access database is made up of several types of objects, such as a table or report, consisting of many elements. An object can be created, selected, and manipulated as a unit.
3. **Data Type** The data type defines the type of data the field will contain. Access uses the data type to ensure that the right kind of data is entered in a field.
4. **Field Property** A field property is a characteristic that helps define the appearance and behavior of a field.
5. **Primary Key** A primary key is a field that uniquely identifies each record.
6. **LookUp Field** A lookup field provides a list of values from which the user can choose to make entering data into that field simpler and more accurate.
7. **Subdatasheet** A subdatasheet is a data table nested in another data table that contains data related or joined to the table where it resides.

Designing a New Database

The Lifestyle Fitness Club recently purchased the 2007 Microsoft Office System software suite. You are very excited about learning to use the Access 2007 database management system to store and maintain the club's records.

Concept 1

Database

1 A **database** is an organized collection of related information. Typically, the information in a database is stored in a **table** consisting of vertical columns and horizontal rows. Each row contains a **record**, which is all the information about one person, thing, or place. Each column is a **field**, which is the smallest unit of information about a record. Access databases can contain multiple tables that can be linked to produce combined output from all tables. This type of database is called a **relational database**. See the "Overview of Microsoft Office Access 2007" for more information about relational databases.

The Lifestyle Fitness Club plans to use Access to maintain several different types of databases. The database you will create will contain information about each club employee. Other plans for using Access include keeping track of members and inventory. To keep the different types of information separate, the club plans to create a database for each group.

Good database design follows two basic principles: do not include duplicate information (also called redundant data) in tables and enter accurate and complete information. Redundant data wastes space, wastes the time that is required to enter the same information multiple times, and consequently increases the possibility of errors and inconsistencies between tables. The information that is stored in a database may be used to make business decisions and if the information is inaccurate, any decisions that are based on the information would be misinformed.

To attain these principles, the database design process is very important and consists of the following steps: plan, design, develop, implement, and refine and review. You will find that you will generally follow these steps in order as you create your database. However, you will probably retrace steps as the final database is developed.

Step	Description
Plan	The first step in the development of a database is to define the purpose of the database in writing. This includes establishing the scope of the database, determining its feasibility, and deciding how you expect to use it and who will use it.
Design	Using the information gathered during the planning step, you can create an implementation plan and document the functional requirements. This includes finding and organizing the information required for the database and deciding how this information should be divided into subject groups. You also need to think about the types of questions you might want the database to answer and determine the types of output you need such as reports and mailings.
Develop	Using the design you created, you are ready to create tables to hold the necessary data. Create separate tables for each of the major subjects to make it easier to locate and modify information. Define fields for each item that you want to store in each table. Determine how each table is related to another and include fields to clarify the relationships as needed. Try not to duplicate information in the different tables.
Implement	After setting up the tables, populate the tables by entering sample data to complete each record. Then work with the data to make sure it is providing the information you need.
Refine and Review	Refine the design by adding or removing fields and tables and continue to test the data and design. Apply the data normalization rules to see if the tables are structured correctly. Periodically review the database to ensure that the initial objectives have been met and to identify required enhancements.

As you develop the employee database for the Lifestyle Fitness Club, you will learn more about the details of the design steps and how to use Access 2007 to create a well-designed and accurate database.

Planning the Club Database

Your first step is to plan the design of your database tables: the number of tables, the data they will contain, and the relationship of the tables. You need to decide what information each table in the employee database should contain and how it should be structured or laid out.

You can obtain this information by analyzing the current record-keeping procedures used in the company. You need to understand the existing procedures so that your database tables will reflect the information that is maintained by different departments. You should be aware of the forms that are the basis for the data entered into the department records and of the information that is taken from the records to produce periodic reports. You also need to determine the information that the department heads would like to be able to obtain from the database that may be too difficult to generate with current procedures.

After looking over the existing record-keeping procedures and the reports that are created from the information, you decide to create several separate tables of data in the database file. Each table should only contain information about the subject of the table. Additionally, try not to duplicate information in different tables. If this occurs, create a separate table for this information. Creating several smaller tables of related data rather than one large table makes it easier to use the tables and faster to process data. This is because you can join several tables together as needed.

The main table will include the employee's basic information, such as employee number, name, birth date, and address. Another will contain the employee's job title and work location only. A third will contain data on pay rate and hours worked each week. To clarify the organization of the database, you sketched the structure for the employee database as shown below.

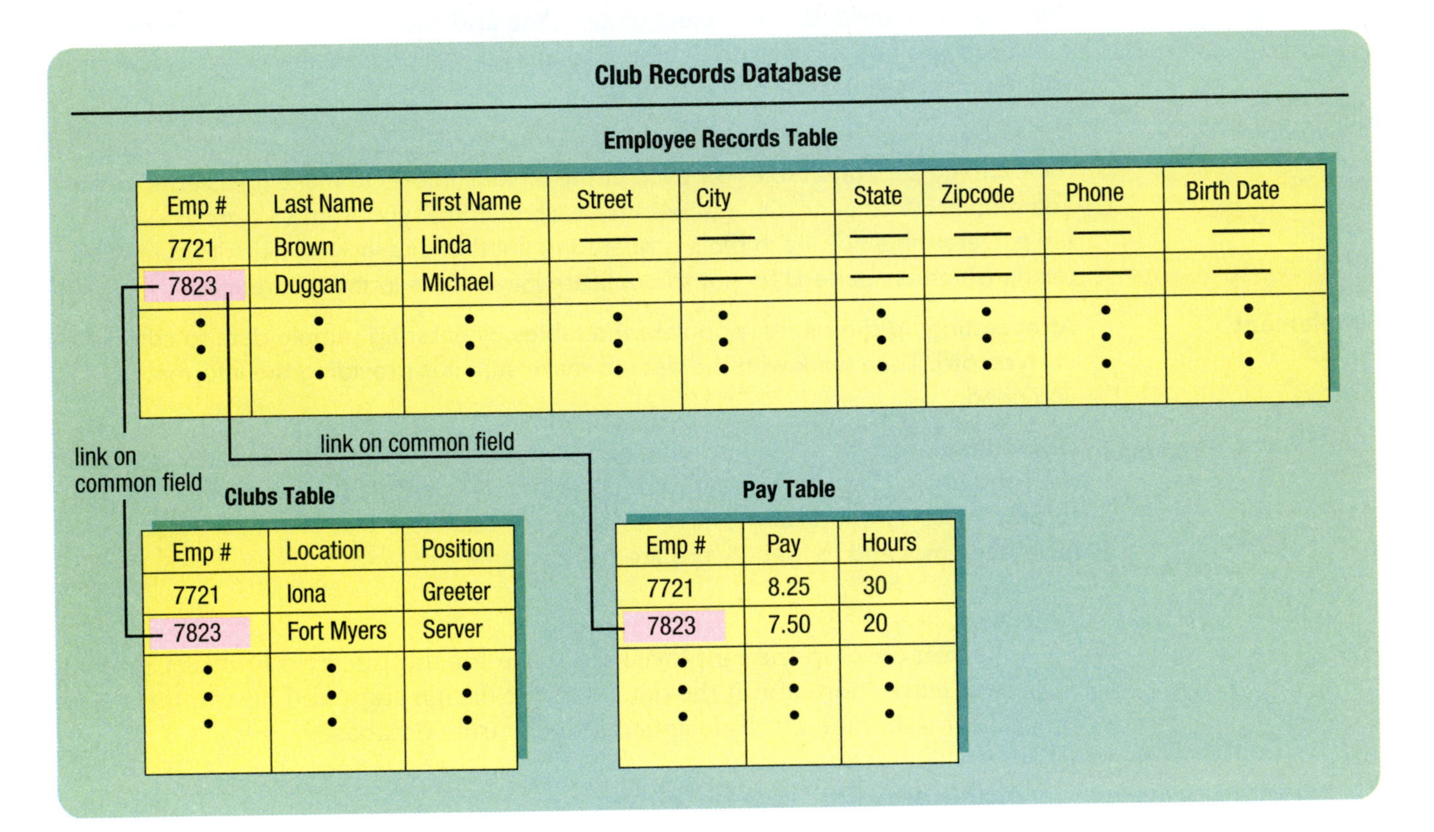

Creating and Naming the Database File

Now that you have decided on the information you want to include in the tables, you are ready to create a new database for the employee information using the Microsoft Office Access 2007 database management program.

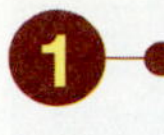

Start the Office Access 2007 application.

Having Trouble?

See "Introduction to 2007 Microsoft Office System" for information about starting the application and for a discussion of features that are common to all Office 2007 applications.

Your screen should be similar to Figure 1.1

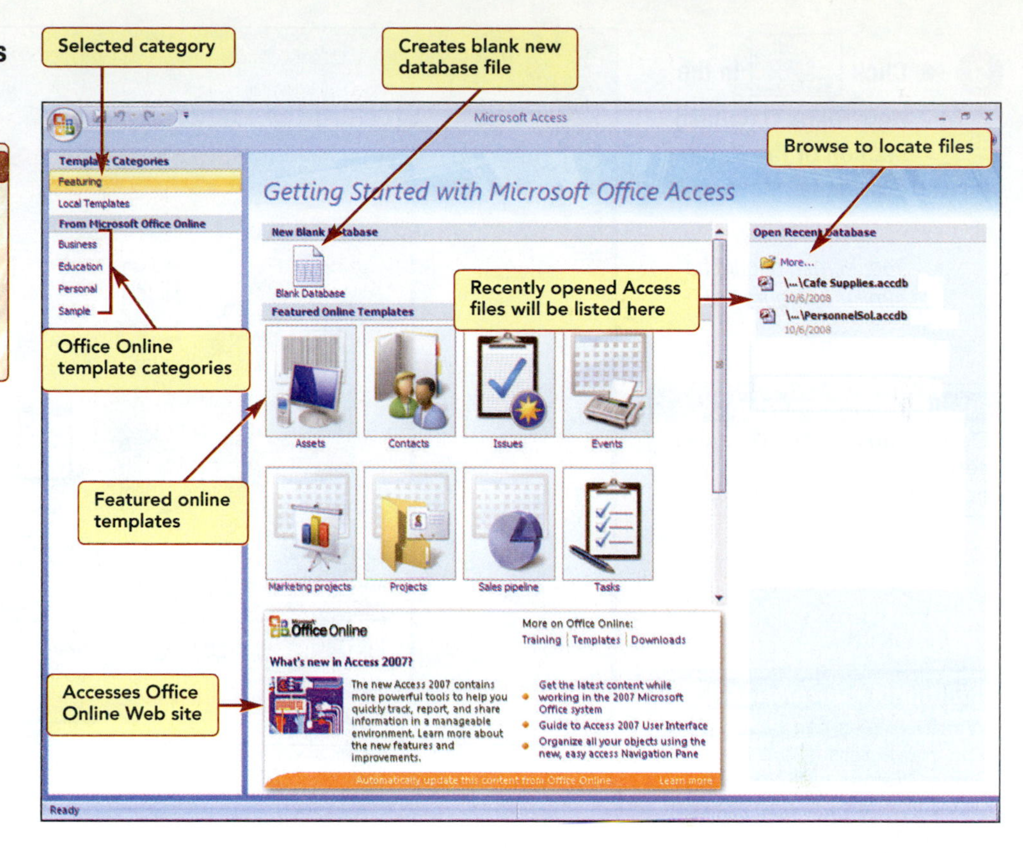

Figure 1.1

The Getting Started with Microsoft Office Access page is displayed. It is divided into several areas that provide a starting point for working with Access. It can be used to create a new database, open an existing database file, or access the Microsoft Office Online Web site. You want to create a new database.

Several methods can be used to create a new database. One method is to use one of the many templates that are provided by Microsoft as the basis for your new database. A **template** is a ready-to-use database that includes the data structure for the selected type of database. Another method is to start with a blank database that contains the basic database objects and then add your own content. A third is to copy or import data from another source into an Access database file. Finally, you can use a custom template that you created and saved as the basis for your new database.

Using the Getting Started with Microsoft Office Access page, you can create a new database by selecting a template design. The left side of the page displays the template categories. Currently, the Featuring category is selected and displays graphics of the featured templates in the middle of the page. Clicking on a different category in the list displays templates associated with that category. Although using a template is sometimes the fastest way to create a database, it often requires a lot of work to adapt the template to suit the needs of the existing data.

The Featuring category also provides access to the Blank Database template that includes the basic structure for a database file, but does not include a data structure that is specific to a type of database. You decide to create the club database from a blank database file.

2 Click **Blank Database** in the **New Blank Database section of the Getting Started window.**

Your screen should be similar to Figure 1.2

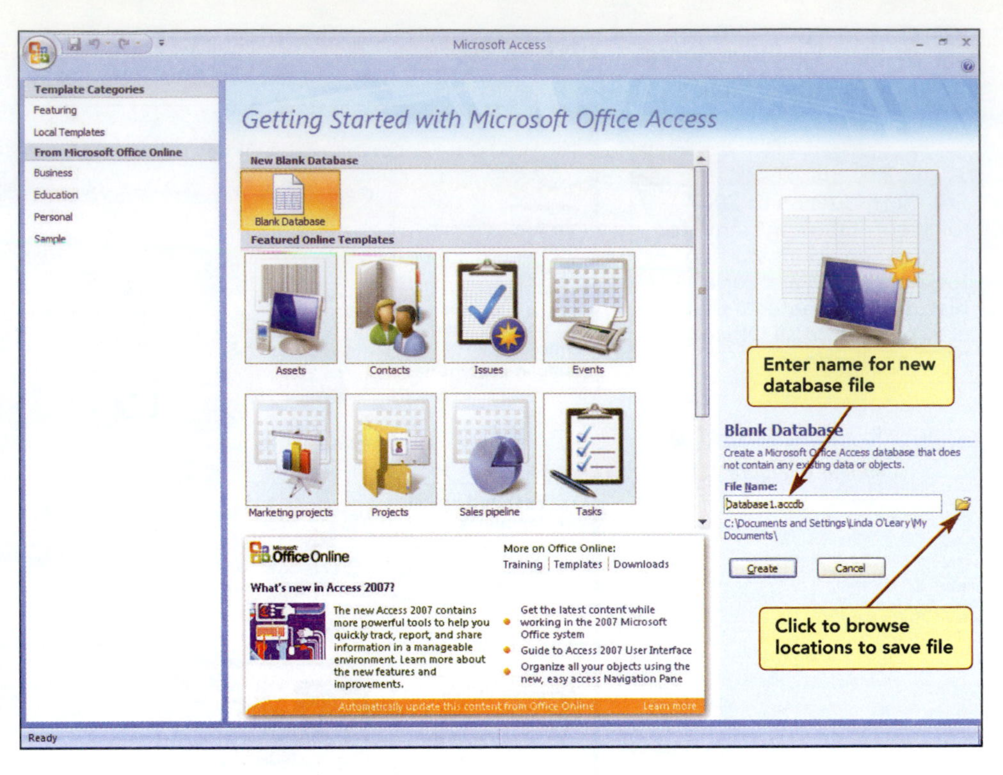

Figure 1.2

Additional Information

Depending on your Windows settings, your screens may not display file extensions.

Additional Information

Windows files can have up to 255 characters in the file name. Names can contain letters, numbers, and spaces; the symbols \, /, ?, :, *, ", <, and > cannot be used. The file name can be entered in either uppercase or lowercase letters and will appear exactly as you type it.

In the Blank Database section of the page, you need to enter a file name and specify the location on your computer where you want it saved. The File Name box displays Database1.accdb, the default database file name. The file extension .accdb identifies the file as an Access 2007 database.

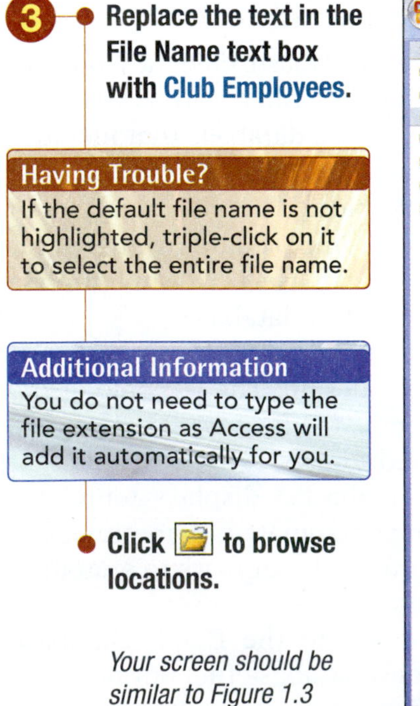

3 **Replace the text in the File Name text box with Club Employees.**

Having Trouble?

If the default file name is not highlighted, triple-click on it to select the entire file name.

Additional Information

You do not need to type the file extension as Access will add it automatically for you.

- **Click** [browse icon] **to browse locations.**

Your screen should be similar to Figure 1.3

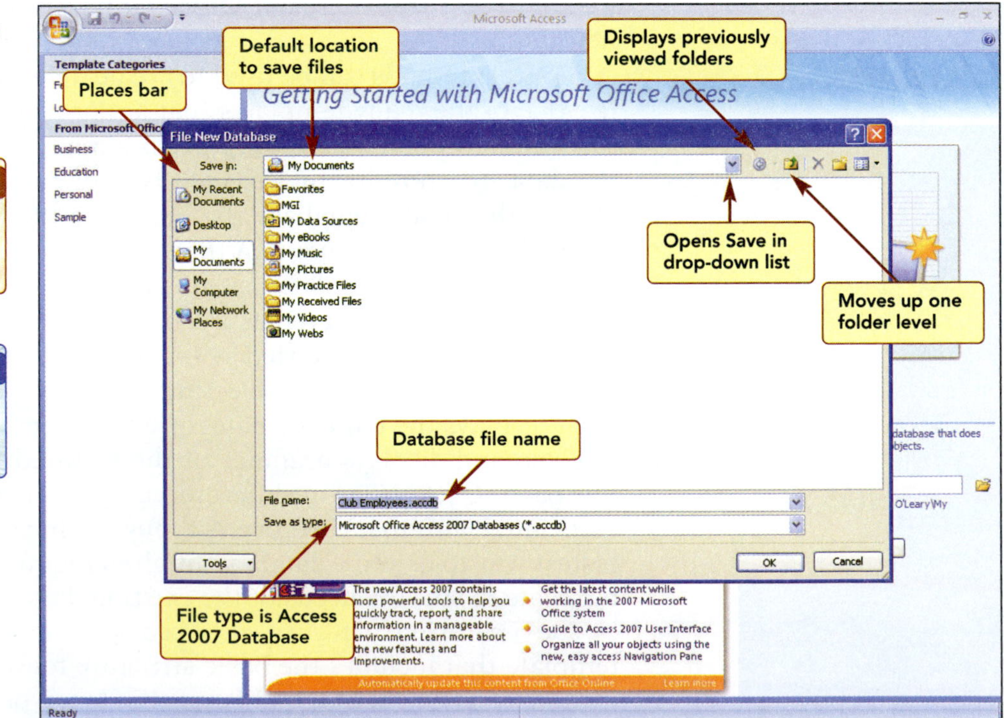

Figure 1.3

Having Trouble?

The default location, folders, and files displayed on your screen may be different from those shown here.

Having Trouble?

If you are using Windows Vista, the buttons in your dialog box will be different than those shown here.

More About

To learn how to save an Access database in another format, see "6 Managing and Maintaining Databases" in the More About appendix.

In the File New Database dialog box, you need to select the location where you want the database file saved. The Save in drop-down list box displays the default folder, My Documents, as the location where the file will be saved. You can use this drop-down list to specify another location. You also can select the location to save from the Places bar along the left side of the dialog box. The icons bring up a list of recently accessed files and folders (History), the contents of the My Documents and Favorites folders, items on the Windows desktop, and the locations on a network. You also can click the Back button in the toolbar to return to folders that were previously opened and Up One Level to move up a level in the folder hierarchy.

The file list section of the dialog box displays the names of folders and database files in the default location. Only Access 2007 database (.accdb) file names are displayed because this is the selected file type in the Save As Type text box. In addition to the .accdb file type, Access database files also can be saved in several different file formats that have different file extensions. The file type you select determines the file extension that will be automatically added to the file name when the file is saved. The new file name you specified appears in the File Name text box.

4

- **Open the Save in drop-down list.**
- **Select the appropriate drive and folder where you will save your database files (check with your instructor if you are not sure).**
- **Click OK.**
- **Click Create.**

Your screen should be similar to Figure 1.4

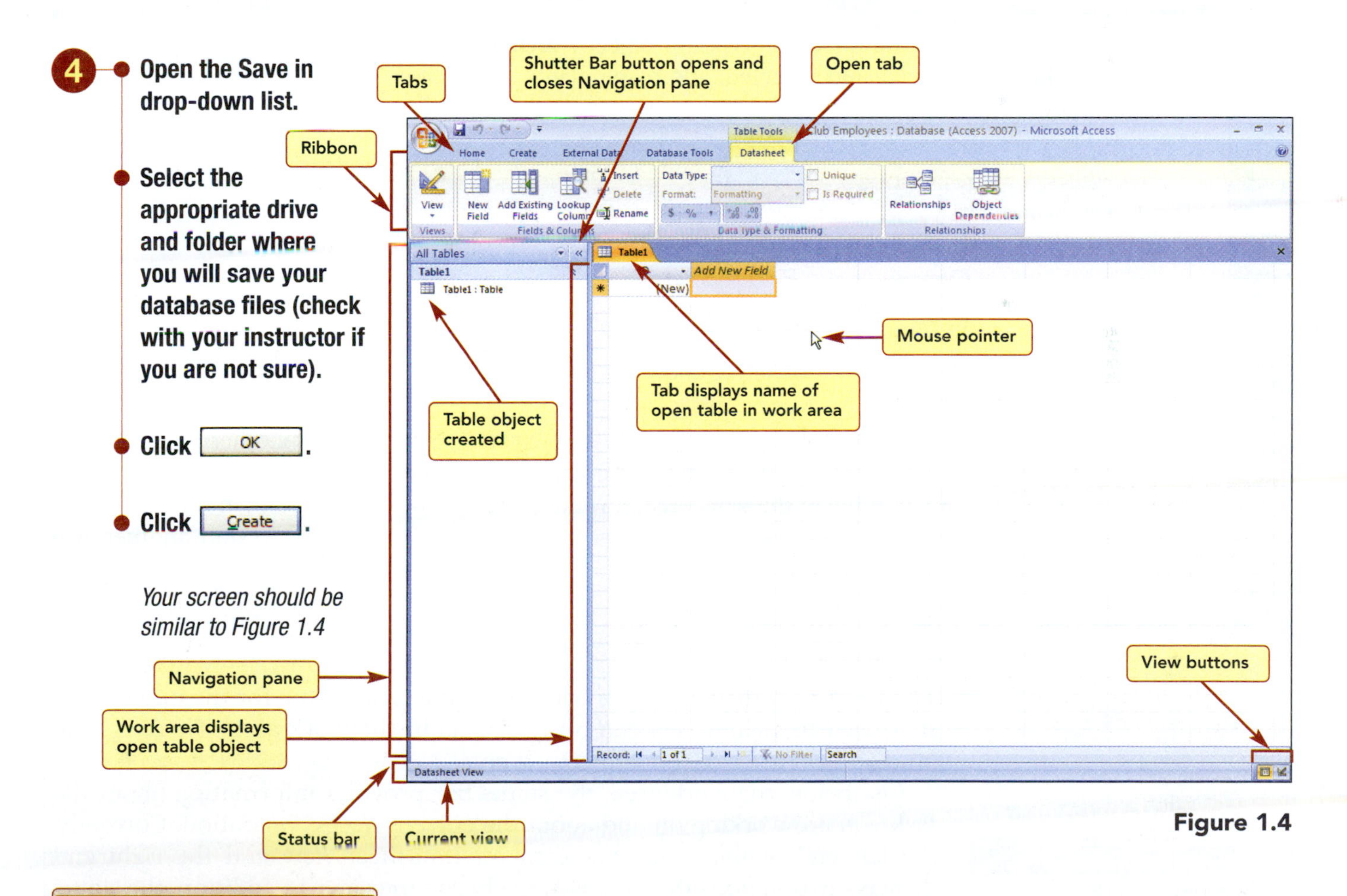

Figure 1.4

Having Trouble?

If your screen looks slightly different, this is because Access remembers settings that were on when the program was last used.

The blank database file is opened in the Access application window. The name of the database, Club Employees, followed by the application name appears in the window title bar.

Additional Information

Read "Common Office 2007 Interface Features" in the Introduction for more information about the File menu, Ribbon, galleries, and other features that are common to all Office applications.

Exploring the Access Window

The Access 2007 Ribbon, located below the title bar, currently consists of five tabs. These tabs contain the commands and features you will use to create and modify a database. Most tabs appear automatically as you perform different tasks and open different windows. The Table Tools Datasheet tab is open and contains buttons that are used to access basic database features.

The mouse pointer appears as on your screen. The mouse pointer changes shape depending upon the task you are performing or where the pointer is located in the window.

The large area below the Ribbon is the work area where different Access components are displayed as you are using the program. When the new database file is created, it includes one empty table named Table1. A table is one of several different database components or objects that can be included in the database file.

Concept 2

Object

2 An Access database is made up of several types of objects, such as a table or report, consisting of many elements. An **object** can be created, selected, and manipulated as a unit. The basic database objects are described below.

Object	Use
Table	Store data
Query	Find and display selected data
Form	View, add, and update data in tables
Report	Analyze and print data in a specific layout

The table object is the basic unit of a database and must be created first, before any other types of objects are created. Access displays each different type of object in its own window. You can open multiple objects from the same database file in the work area; however, you cannot open more than one database file at a time in a single instance of Access. To open a second database file, you need to start another instance of Access and open the database file in it.

The work area displays a tab containing the table name for the open table. It is used to switch between open objects in the work area. There is only one tab because only one object is open.

Just below the work area, the status bar provides information about the task you are working on and about the current Access operation. Currently, the left end of the status bar displays Datasheet view and the right end displays two buttons that are used to change the view. In addition, the status bar displays messages such as instructions to help you use the program more efficiently.

Additional Information

You will learn more about tables and the different database views shortly.

Using the Navigation Pane

The **Navigation pane** along the left edge of the work area displays all the objects in the database and is used to open and manage the objects. Because your database only contains one object, Table1, it is the only object listed in the pane. When there are many different objects, the pane organizes the objects into categories and groups within each category. It is used to quickly access the different objects.

The Navigation pane is always displayed, but can be collapsed to a bar to provide more space in the work area. The Shutter Bar close button «, located in the upper-right corner of the pane, is used to show or hide the pane.

Additional Information

The items in the Navigation pane can be organized differently by using the menu at the top of the pane.

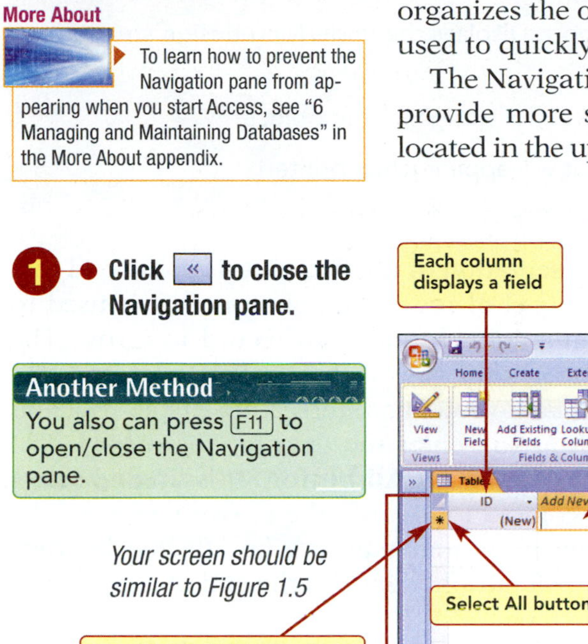

More About

To learn how to prevent the Navigation pane from appearing when you start Access, see "6 Managing and Maintaining Databases" in the More About appendix.

1 **Click « to close the Navigation pane.**

Another Method

You also can press F11 to open/close the Navigation pane.

Your screen should be similar to Figure 1.5

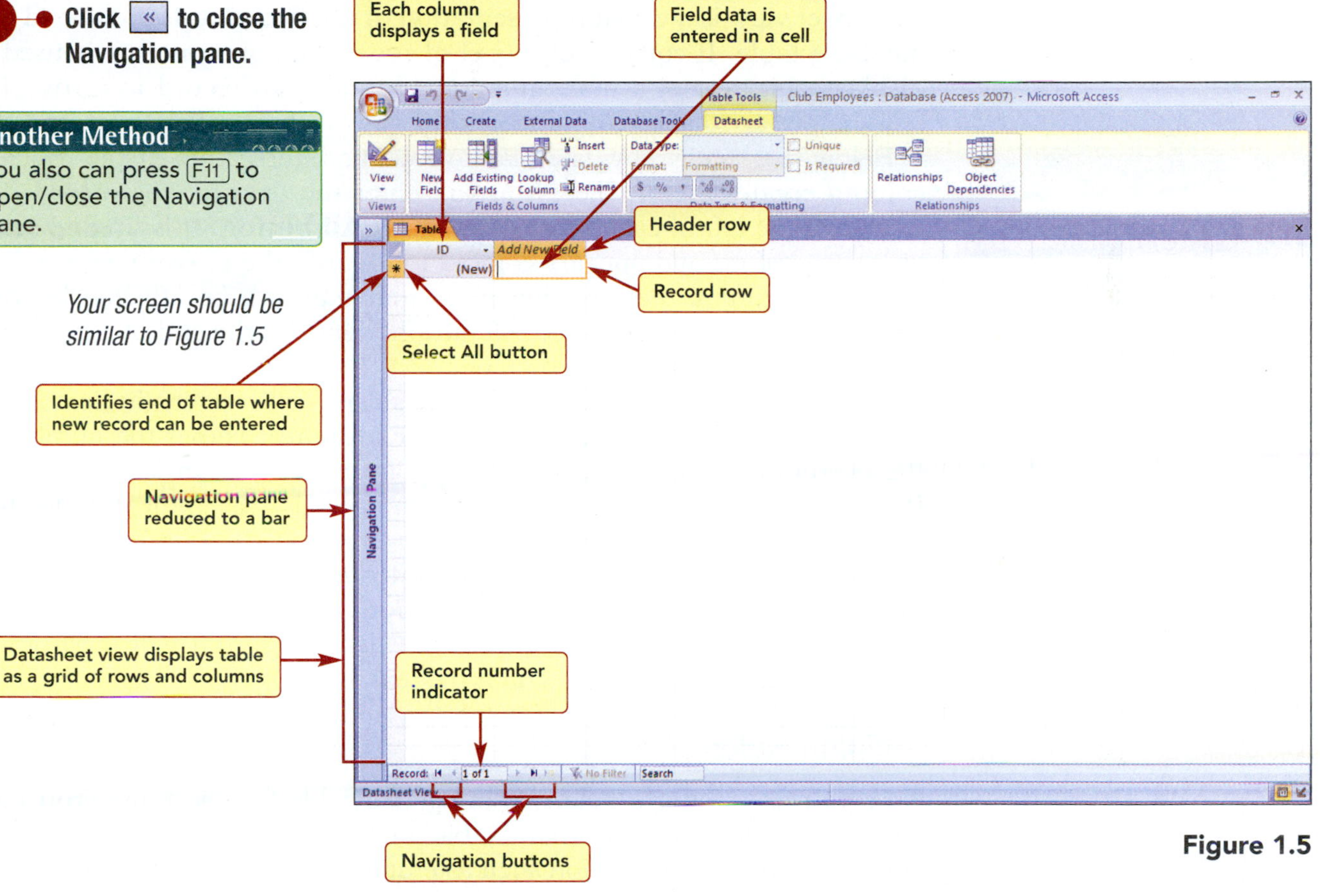

Figure 1.5

The Navigation pane is reduced to a bar along the left side of the window and the work area expands to fill the space. The pane can be easily displayed again by clicking ». You will learn more about using the Navigation pane throughout the labs.

Using Datasheet View

In anticipation of your entering information in the table, Access displays the blank table in Datasheet view, one of several different window formats, called **views,** that are used to display and work with the objects in a database. Each view includes its own Ribbon tab that includes commands that are designed to work with the object in that view. The available views change according to the type of object you are using. The basic views are described in the following table.

View	Purpose
Datasheet view	Provides a row-and-column view of the data in tables or query results.
Form view	Displays the records in a form.
Report view	Displays the table data in a report layout.
Design view	Used to create a table, form, query, or report. Displays the underlying design structure, not the data.
Layout view	Displays the object's data while in the process of designing the object.
Print Preview	Displays a form, report, table, or query as it will appear when printed.

Datasheet view is a visual representation of the data that is contained in a database table. It consists of a grid of rows and columns that is used to display each field of a table in a column and each record in a row. The field names are displayed in the **header row** at the top of the datasheet.

Below the header row is a blank row. The intersection of the row and column creates a **cell** where you will enter the data for the record. The square to the left of each row is the **Select All button.** It is used to select an entire record and appears colored to identify the **current record,** the record containing the insertion point and that will be affected by your next action. The * in the Select All button identifies the end of the table or where a new record can be entered.

Additional Information

Entering information in Datasheet view is very similar to working in a Microsoft Excel worksheet.

The bottom of the work area displays a record number indicator and navigation buttons. The **record number indicator** shows the number of the current record as well as the total number of records in the table. Because the table does not yet contain records, the indicator displays "Record: 1 of 1" in anticipation of your first entry. On both sides of the record number are the **navigation buttons,** which are used to move through records with a mouse. In addition, two buttons that are used to filter and search for data in a table are displayed. You will learn about using all these features throughout the text.

Defining Fields

Now you are ready to begin defining the fields for the table. You have already decided that the main table in this database will include the employee's basic information such as employee number, name, birth date, and address. Next, you need to determine what information you want to appear in each column (field) about the subject recorded in the table. For example, you know you want to include the employee's name. However, should the entire name be in a single column or should it appear as two separate columns: first name and last name? Because you may want to sort or search for information based on the employee's name, it is better to store the information in separate columns. Similarly, the address actually consists of four separate parts—address, city, state, and zip code—and it also makes sense to store them in separate columns.

Generally when deciding how to store the information about a subject in a table, break down the information into its smallest logical parts. If you combine more than one kind of information in a field, it is difficult to retrieve individual facts later.

A second factor that should be considered when adding fields to a table is to store only raw data, not the result of calculations, in the table. This is because you can have Access quickly perform the calculations when you want to see the result. This saves both time and space.

After looking at the information currently maintained in the personnel folder on each employee, you have decided to include the following fields in the table: Employee #, Hire Date, Last Name, First Name, Address, City, State, Zip, Home Phone, Birth Date, and Photo. The data for the first employee record you will enter is shown below.

Field Name	Data
Employee #	04731
Hire Date	August 19, 2001
Last Name	Marchant
First Name	Roberta
Address	564 Palm Avenue
City	Landis
State	CA
Zip	92120–3741
Home Phone	(507) 555–6707
Birth Date	May 18, 1980
Photo	Roberta.jpg

Entering Data

Notice that the first field in the table, ID, is already defined. This field is automatically included in each table when it is created. It automatically assigns a number to each record as it is added to a table and is useful for maintaining record order. The second column header displays Add New Field and is used to define a new field in the table.

In Datasheet view, you can enter data for a record and create a new field at the same time. The first field of data you will enter is the employee number, which is assigned to each employee when hired. Each new employee is given the next consecutive number, so that no two employees can have the same number. It is a maximum of five digits.

When you enter data in a record, it should be entered accurately and consistently. The data you enter in a field should be typed exactly as you want it to appear. This is important because any printouts of the data will display the information exactly as entered. It is also important to enter data in a consistent form. For example, if you decide to abbreviate the word "Avenue" as "Ave." in the Address field, then it should be abbreviated the same way in every record where it appears. Also be careful not to enter a blank space before or after a field entry. This can cause problems when using the table to locate information.

As you type, the insertion point shows your location in the entry. If you make a typing error, use the Backspace key to delete the characters back to the error and retype the entry.

1

- **Click in the blank cell below the Add New Field column header.**
- **Type 04731.**
- **Press ←Enter.**

Your screen should be similar to Figure 1.6

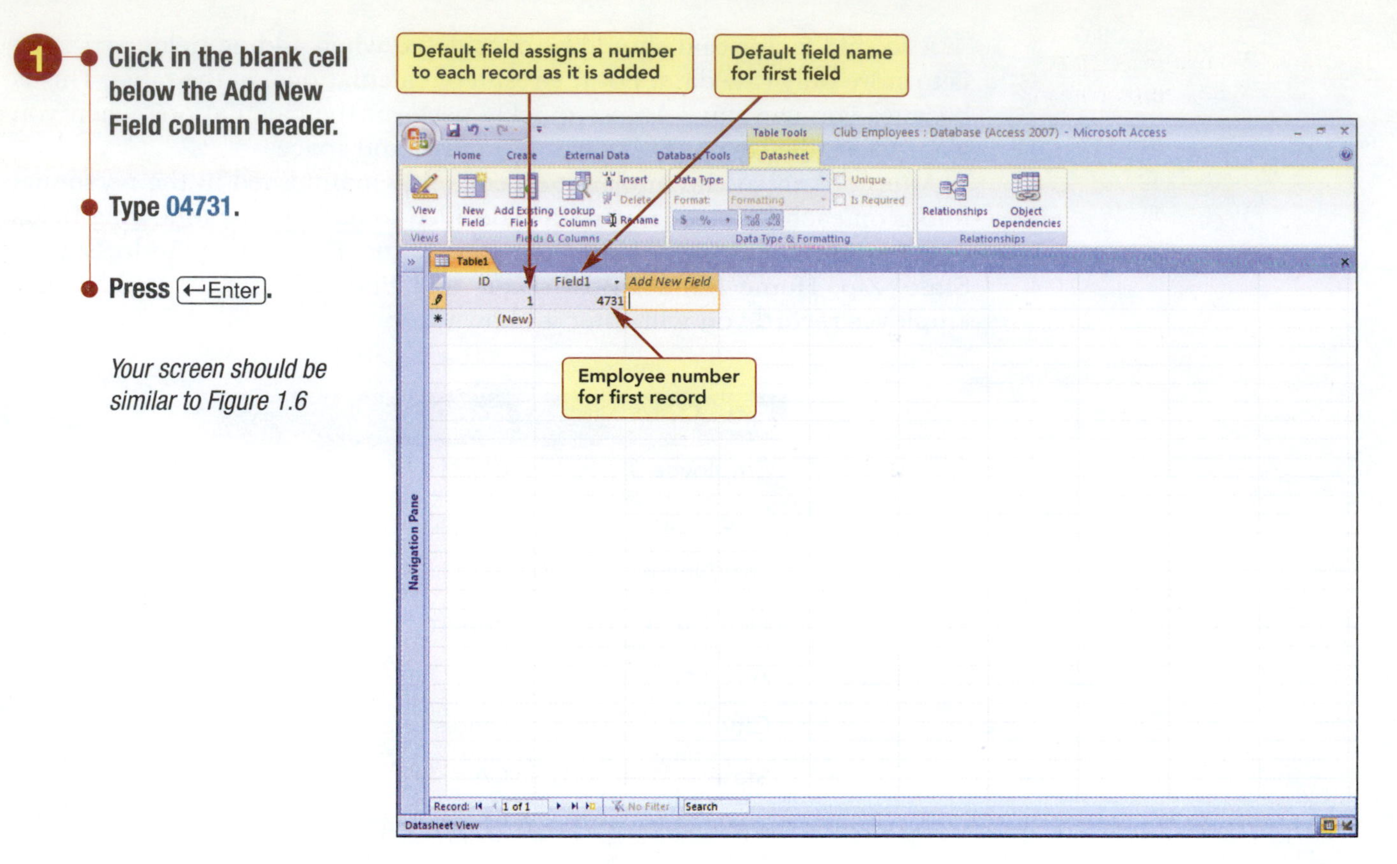

Figure 1.6

The employee number for the first record is entered in the table and Access is ready for you to enter the data for the next field. However, the number does not display the leading zero. You will learn the reason for this and how to correct it shortly.

The new field has been assigned the default field name of Field1. Also notice that the ID field displays the number 1 for the first record entered in the table.

Changing Field Names

Before entering more data, you want to replace the default field name with a more descriptive field name. A **field name** is used to identify the data stored in the field. A field name should describe the contents of the data to be entered in the field. It can be up to 64 characters long and can consist of letters, numbers, spaces, and special characters, except a period, an exclamation point, an accent grave (`), and brackets ([]). You also cannot start a field name with a space. It is best to use short field names to make the tables easier to manage.

1 **Double-click on the Field1 column header.**

Type Employee # (be sure to include a space before the #).

Another Method
You also can choose Rename Column from the column header's shortcut menu.

Additional Information
The field name can be typed in uppercase or lowercase letters. It will be displayed in your database table exactly as you enter it.

Your screen should be similar to Figure 1.7

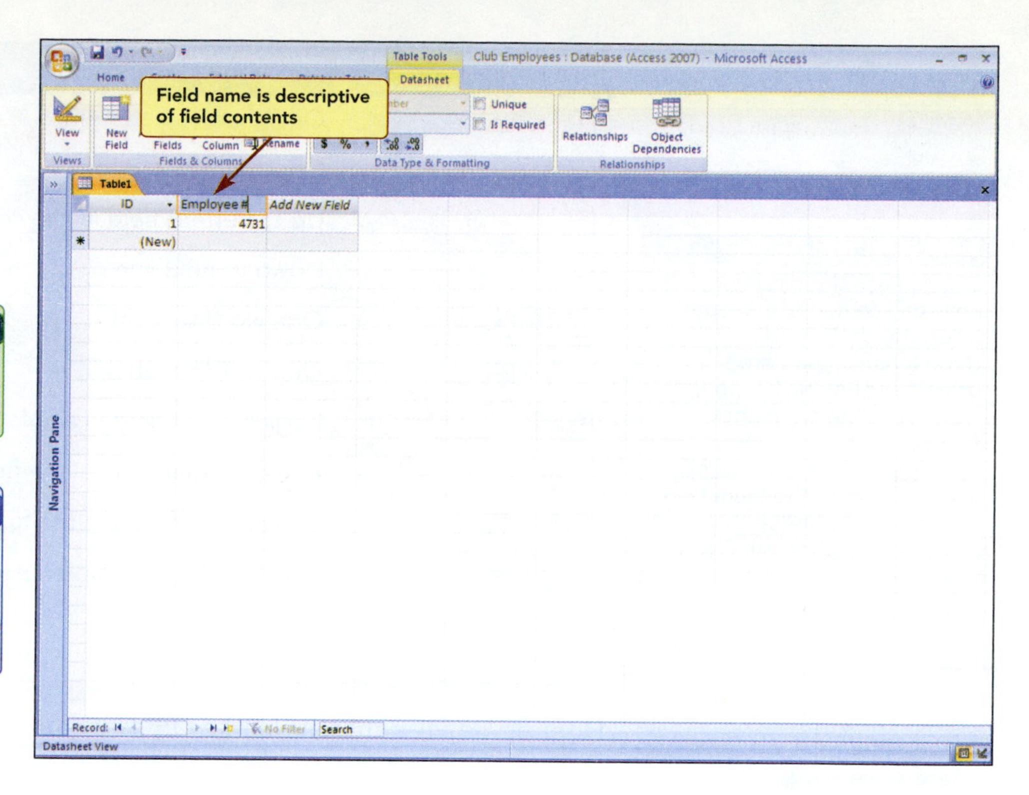

Field name is descriptive of field contents

Figure 1.7

The highlighted text is deleted and replaced by the new field name you typed. You realize that "Employee ID" is the more common term used on company forms, so you decide to use this as the field name instead.

Editing Entries

As you enter text, you are bound to make typing errors that need to be corrected. Other types of changes you may want to make are to edit or update information. In this case, you want to edit the field name entry you are currently working on. When editing, you need to position the insertion point in the entry at the location where you want to make the change. To position the insertion point using the mouse, simply click at the location where you want it to appear.

Additionally, the keyboard keys shown in the table below also can be used to move the insertion point in an entry.

Key	Movement
→	One character to right
←	One character to left
↑	Up to current field in previous record
↓	Down to next line
Ctrl + →	One word to right
Ctrl + ←	One word to left
Home	Beginning of field in single-line field
End	End of field in single-line field
Ctrl + Home	Beginning of field in multiple-line field
Ctrl + End	End of field in multiple-line field

Additional Information

You can use the directional keys on the numeric keypad or on the dedicated directional keypad area. If using the numeric keypad, make sure the Num Lock feature is off; otherwise, numbers will be entered in the document. The Num Lock indicator light above the keypad is lit when on. Press Num Lock to turn it off.

Additional Information

These same key and mouse movement procedures can be used in all Access views.

Holding down a directional key or key combination moves the insertion point quickly in the direction indicated, saving multiple presses of the key. Many of the insertion point movement keys can be held down to execute multiple moves.

Depending on what you are doing, one method may be more efficient than another. For example, if your hands are already on the keyboard as you are typing, it may be quicker to use the keyboard rather than take your hands off to use the mouse.

Once the insertion point is in the correct position, you can use the Backspace or Delete key to remove text. The Backspace key removes a character or space to the left of the insertion point. The Delete key removes the character or space to the right of the insertion point.

In this case, the insertion point is already in the correct position and you just need to delete the character to the left of it.

1

- **Press Backspace to delete the # symbol.**
- **Type ID.**
- **Press ←Enter.**
- **Click in the cell containing the Employee ID number.**

Your screen should be similar to Figure 1.8

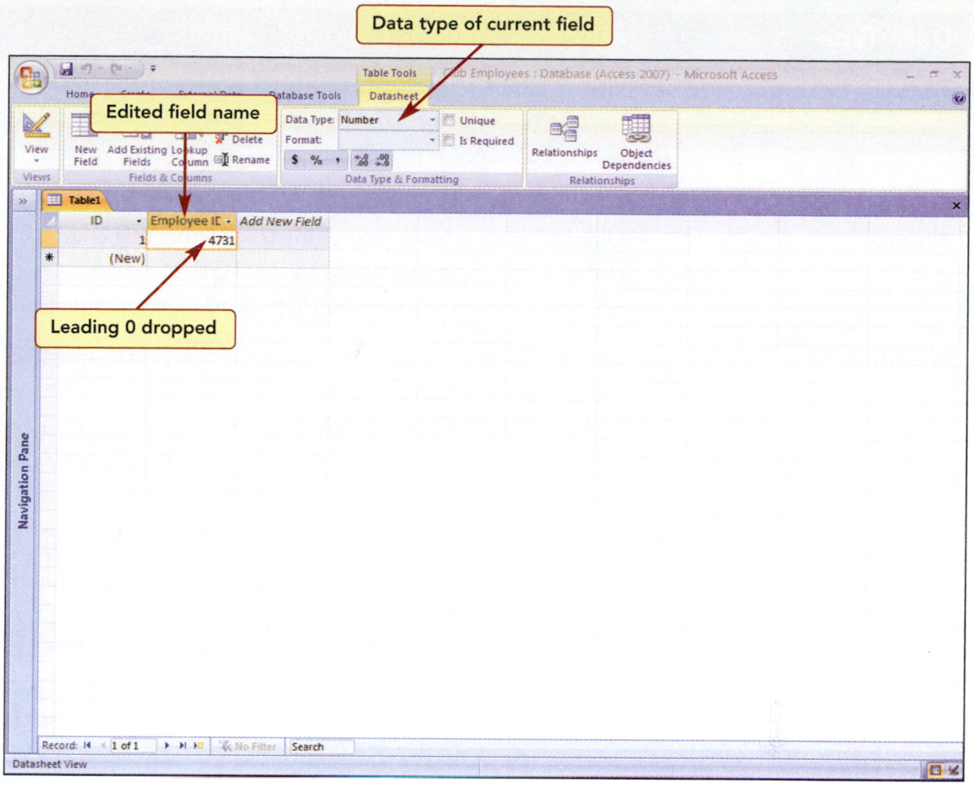

Data type of current field

Edited field name

Leading 0 dropped

Figure 1.8

The field name has been completed and it is now easy to know what the data in that column represents.

Defining Data Type

Notice the leading 0 of the Employee ID number has been dropped. This is because Access automatically detects and assigns a data type to each field based upon the data that is entered. In this case, the field entry consisted of numbers only, and Access assigned the field a Number data type. This data type drops any leading zeros.

Concept 3

Data Type

3 The **data type** defines the type of data the field will contain. Access uses the data type to ensure that the right kind of data is entered in a field. It is important to choose the right data type for a field before you start entering data in the table. You can change a data type after the field contains data, but if the data types are not compatible, such as a text entry in a field whose data type accepts numbers only, you may lose data. The data types are described in the following table.

Data Type	Purpose
Text	Use in fields that contain alphanumeric data (words, combinations of words and numbers, and numbers that are not used in calculations). Text field entries can be up to 255 characters in length. Names and phone numbers are examples of Text field entries. Text is the default data type.
Memo	Use in fields where you want to store more than 255 characters of alphanumeric data. A memo field holds up to 1GB of characters or 2GB of storage, of which 65,535 characters can be displayed. Text in this field can be formatted.
Number	Use in fields that contain numeric data only and that will be used to perform calculations on the values in the field. Number of units ordered is an example of a Number field entry. Leading zeros are dropped. Do not use in fields involving money or that require a high degree of accuracy because number fields round to the next highest value. Fields that contain numbers only but will not be used in calculations are usually assigned a Text data type.
Date/Time	Use in fields that will contain dates and times. Access allows dates from AD January 1, 100, to December 31, 9999. Access correctly handles leap years and checks all dates for validity. Even though dates and times are formatted to appear as a date or time, they are stored as **serial values** so that they can be used in calculations. The date serial values are consecutively assigned beginning with 1, which corresponds to the date January 1, 1900, and ending with 2958465, which is December 31, 9999.
Currency	Use in number fields that are monetary values or that you do not want rounded. Numbers are formatted to display decimal places and a currency symbol.
AutoNumber	Use when you need a unique, sequential number that is automatically incremented by one whenever a new record is added to a table. After a number is assigned to a record, it can never be used again, even if the record is deleted.
Yes/No	Use when the field contents can only be a Yes/No, True/False, or On/Off value. Yes values are stored as a 1 and No values as 0 so that they can be used in expressions.
OLE Object	Use in fields to store an object such as a graphic (picture), sound, document, or graph. The object is converted to a bitmap image and displayed in the table field, form, or report. An OLE server program must be on the computer that runs the database in order to render the object. Generally, use the Attachment field type rather than OLE Object because the objects are stored more efficiently and it does not require the supporting program.
Hyperlink	Use when you want the field to store a link to an object, document, Web page, or other destinations.
Attachment	Use to add multiple files of different types to a field. For example, you could add a photograph and set of resumes for each employee. Unlike OLE object fields, the files are not converted to bitmap images and additional software is not needed to view the object, thereby saving space. Attachments also can be opened and edited from within Access in their parent programs.

More About

To learn more about the Memo, Currency, Number, and Yes/No field types, see "2 Creating and Formatting Database Elements" in the More About appendix.

Additional Information

If Access does not have enough information to determine the data type, it sets the data type to Text.

Notice the Data Type box in the Data Type & Formatting group shows the current data type for the field is Number. Access accurately specified this data type because the Employee ID field contains numbers. However, unless the numbers are used in calculations, the field should be assigned the Text data type. This designation allows other characters, such as the parentheses or hyphens in a telephone number, to be included in the entry. Also, by specifying the type as Text, leading zeros will be preserved.

You need to override the data type decision and change the data type for this field to Text.

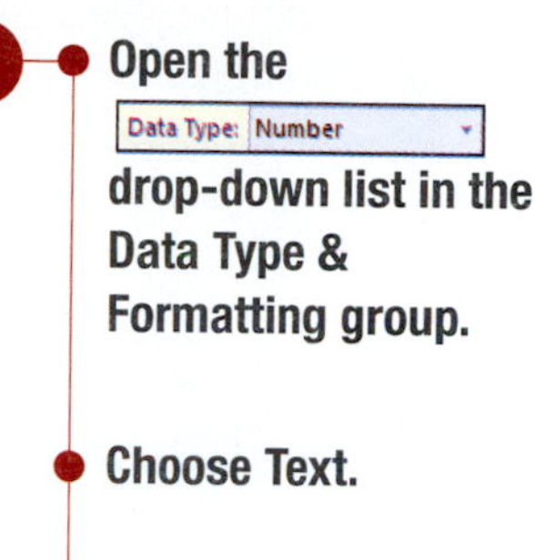

1. **Open the** Data Type: Number **drop-down list in the Data Type & Formatting group.**
   - **Choose Text.**
   - **Click at the beginning of the Employee ID entry to place the insertion point and type 0.**
   - **Press End to move to the end of the entry.**
   - **Press → to move to the next column.**

Your screen should be similar to Figure 1.9

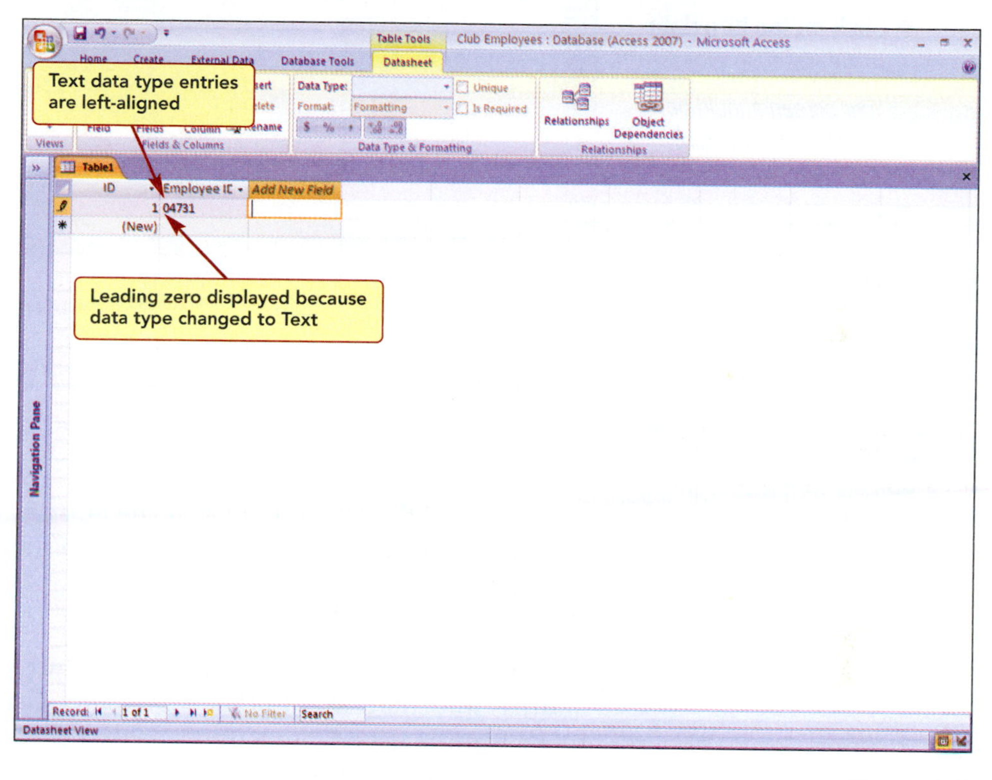

Figure 1.9

Additional Information

The Data Type list also contains a Lookup Wizard option, which is not actually a data type but instead is used to create lookup fields that let you choose from a list of values you enter or that are from another table or query.

The leading zero is now correctly displayed. Also notice that the entry is now left-aligned in the cell space whereas it was right-aligned when the data type was set to Number. Many data types also include formatting settings that control the appearance of the data in the field. In this case, the Text field format is to align the text with the left edge of the cell space. You will learn more about formatting later in the lab.

Now you are ready to enter the data for the next field, Hire Date.

2

- Type **Aug 19, 2001**.
- Click **Rename** in the **Fields & Columns** group.
- Type **Hire Date**.
- Press **←Enter**.
- Click on the hire date.

Your screen should be similar to Figure 1.10

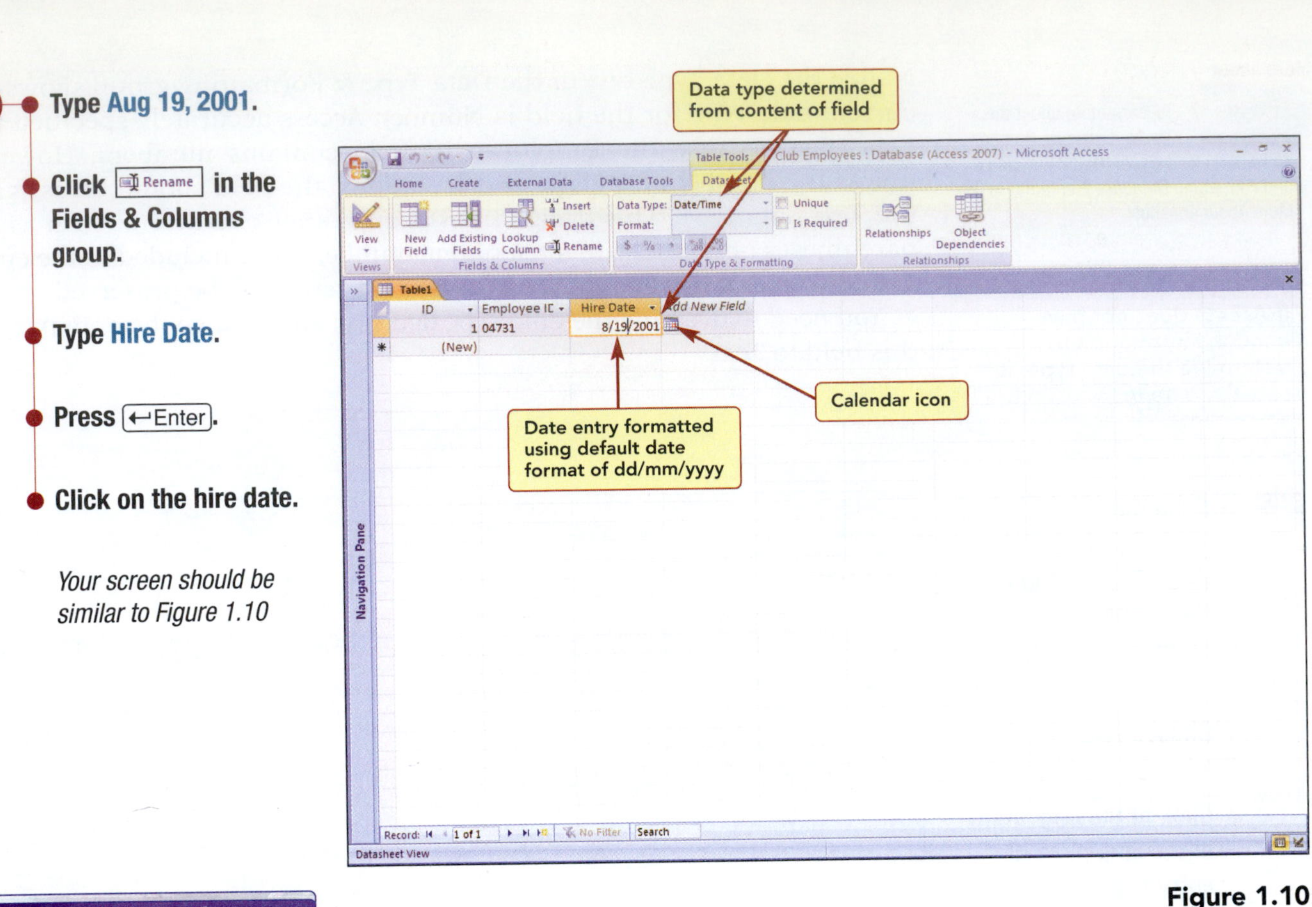

Figure 1.10

Additional Information

The calendar icon displays the month calendar for that date when you click on it.

Access correctly determined that the entry is a Date type and displays the date using the default date format of mm/dd/yyyy.

Using Field Templates

The next few fields you need to enter are for the employee name and address information. Another way you can specify field names is to select them from a list of predefined fields called **field templates.** Each field template definition includes a field name, a data type, and other settings that control the appearance and behavior of the field.

First you will add a field for the employee's last name.

Click New Field in the Fields & Columns group.

Your screen should be similar to Figure 1.11

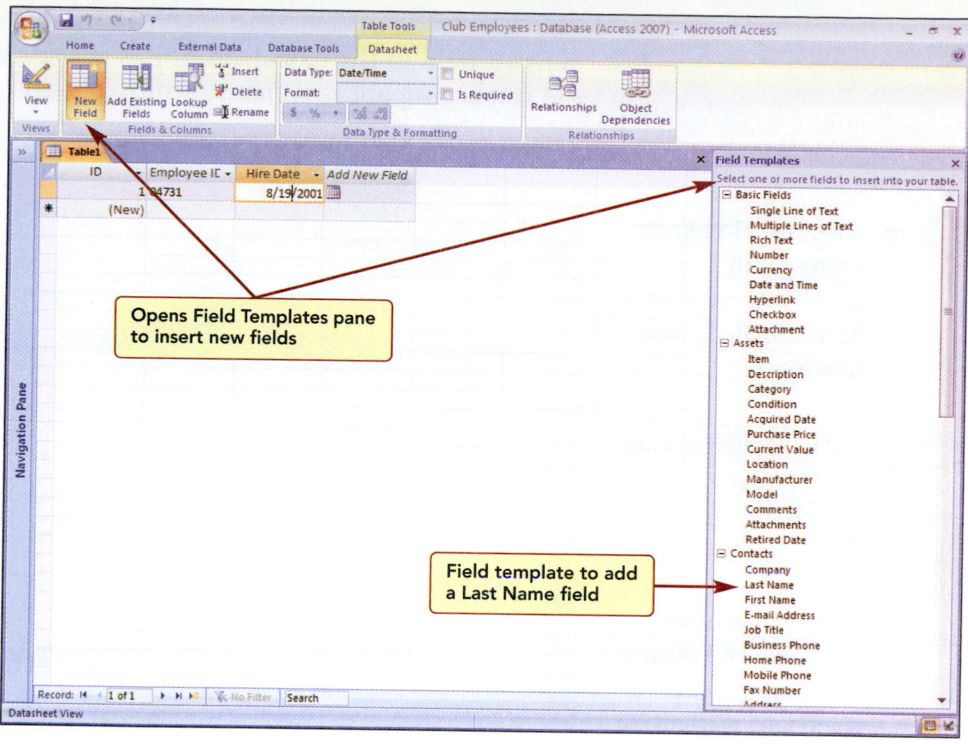

Figure 1.11

From the Field Templates pane, you can select and drag the field name to the table. When the insertion bar appears where you want the new field inserted, drop the field in position. You can also double-click on the field name and it will be inserted in the next empty field column in the datasheet.

2 Double-click Last Name in the Contacts section of the Field Templates list.

Your screen should be similar to Figure 1.12

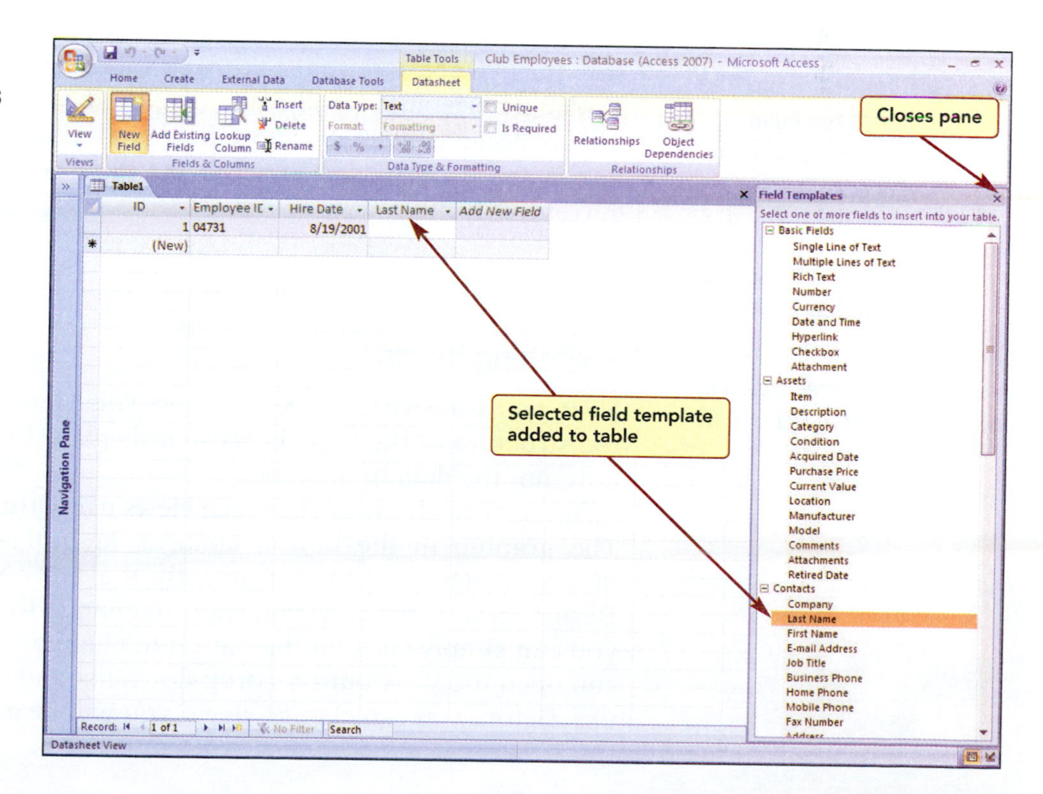

Figure 1.12

The Last Name field was inserted in the datasheet following the last defined field in the datasheet. It has a data type of Text. Next you will add the remaining address fields. Multiple field templates can be selected and inserted into the datasheet at the same time.

Select the First Name, Address, City, State/Province, and Zip/Postal Code field names.

Having Trouble?

Hold down Ctrl while selecting multiple field templates.

- **Drag them into the datasheet and release the mouse pointer when the insertion bar appears after the Last Name column.**
- **Move to the Add New Field column and double-click the Home Phone field to add it at that location.**
- **Click ☒ in the title bar of the Field Templates pane to close it.**
- **Move the horizontal scroll bar to the left.**

Your screen should be similar to Figure 1.13

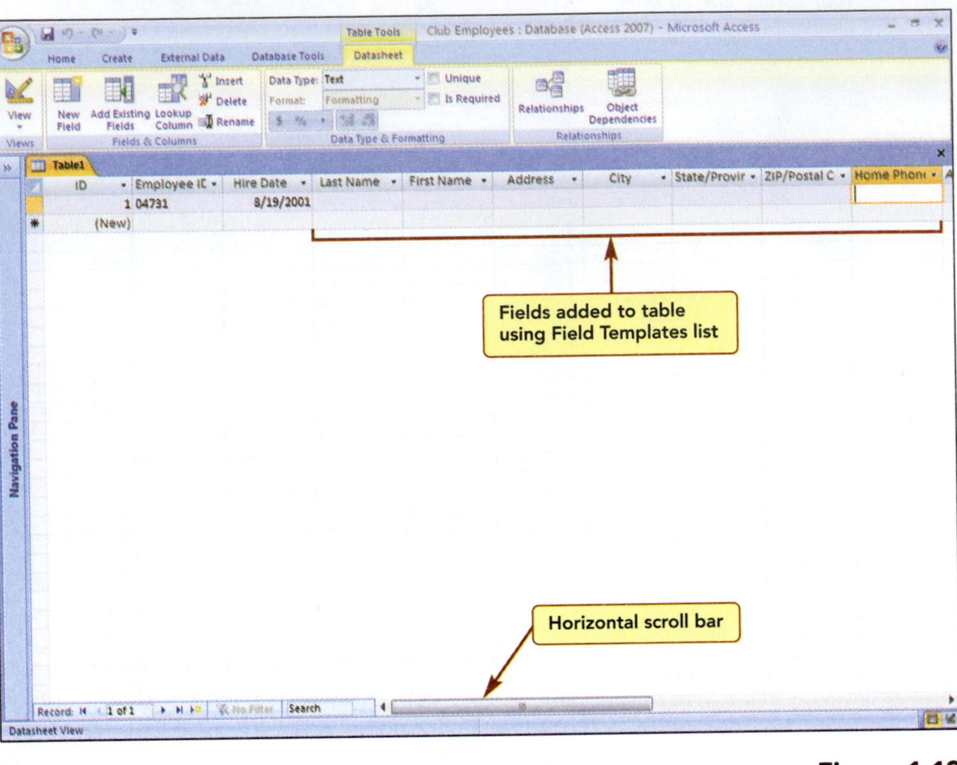

Figure 1.13

Using a field template saves time and provides the basis from which you can start. Once inserted, it can be modified like any other field name. Notice a horizontal scroll bar is displayed at the bottom of the work area. This is because there are more fields in the datasheet than can be viewed in the space. It is used to scroll the datasheet to see fields that are not currently visible.

Switching Views

Next, you will switch to Design view. This view makes it easier to focus on the structure of the table because it displays information about the fields only, not the data in the table.

You can easily switch between views using the button in the Ribbon. The graphic in the button changes to indicate the view that will be displayed when selected. Currently the button displays the graphic for Design view. If the view you want to change to is displayed in the button, you can simply click on the button to change to that view. Otherwise, you can open the View button's drop-down list and select the view you want to use. Before you can change views, you will be asked to save the table.

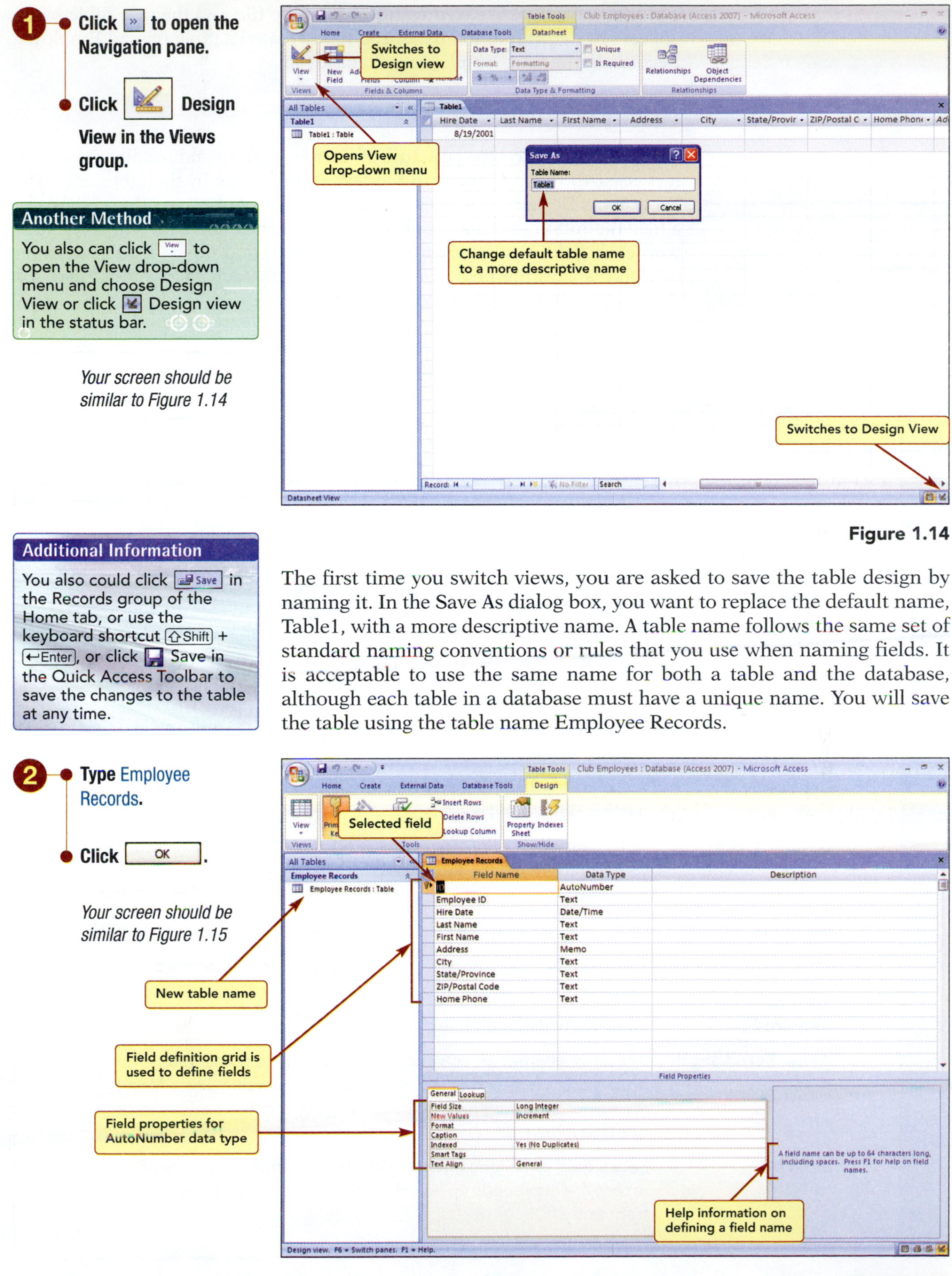

1 Click » to open the Navigation pane.

Click Design View in the Views group.

Another Method

You also can click View to open the View drop-down menu and choose Design View or click Design view in the status bar.

Your screen should be similar to Figure 1.14

Figure 1.14

Additional Information

You also could click Save in the Records group of the Home tab, or use the keyboard shortcut ⇧Shift + ←Enter, or click Save in the Quick Access Toolbar to save the changes to the table at any time.

The first time you switch views, you are asked to save the table design by naming it. In the Save As dialog box, you want to replace the default name, Table1, with a more descriptive name. A table name follows the same set of standard naming conventions or rules that you use when naming fields. It is acceptable to use the same name for both a table and the database, although each table in a database must have a unique name. You will save the table using the table name Employee Records.

2 Type Employee Records.

Click OK.

Your screen should be similar to Figure 1.15

Figure 1.15

The table structure is saved with the database file and the new table name appears in the Navigation pane. You have created a table named Employee Records in the Club Employees database file.

Using Design View

Design view displays the structure of the table, not the table data. Therefore, it is used to make changes to the layout and fields in the table only. The Table Tools Design tab is displayed and open. The upper section consists of a field definition grid that displays the field names, the data type associated with each field, and an area to enter a description of the field. The lower section displays the properties associated with each field and a Help box that provides information about the current task.

Additional Information

You can get more Help information about the current selection by pressing F1 to open Access Help.

Concept 4

Field Property

4 A **field property** is a characteristic that helps define the appearance and behavior of a field. Each field has a set of field properties associated with it, and each data type has a different set of field properties. Setting field properties enhances the way your table works. Some of the more commonly used properties and their functions are described in the following table.

Field Property	Description
Field Size	Sets the maximum number of characters that can be entered in the field.
Format	Specifies the way data displays in a table and prints.
Input Mask	Simplifies data entry by controlling the data that is required in a field and the way the data is to be displayed.
Caption	Specifies a field label other than the field name that is used in queries, forms, and reports.
Default Value	Automatically fills in a certain value for this field in new records as you add to the table. You can override a default value by typing a new value into the field.
Validation Rule	Limits data entered in a field to values that meet certain requirements.
Validation Text	Specifies the message to be displayed when the associated Validation Rule is not satisfied.
Required	Specifies whether a value must be entered in a field.
Allow Zero Length	Specifies whether an entry containing no characters is valid. This property is used to indicate that you know no value exists for a field. A zero-length string is entered as "" with no space between the quotation marks.
Indexed	Sets a field as an index field (a field that controls the order of records). This speeds up searches on fields that are searched frequently.

More About

For information on other field properties, see "2 Creating and Formatting Database Elements" in the More About appendix.

The first field in the field definition grid, ID, is the selected field or **current field** and will be affected by any changes you make. It has a data type of AutoNumber. The properties associated with the current field are displayed in the Field Properties section.

You will look at the properties associated with the first field you added to the table. Positioning the insertion point in any column of the field definition grid will select that field and display the associated field properties.

1 Select Employee ID.

Your screen should be similar to Figure 1.16

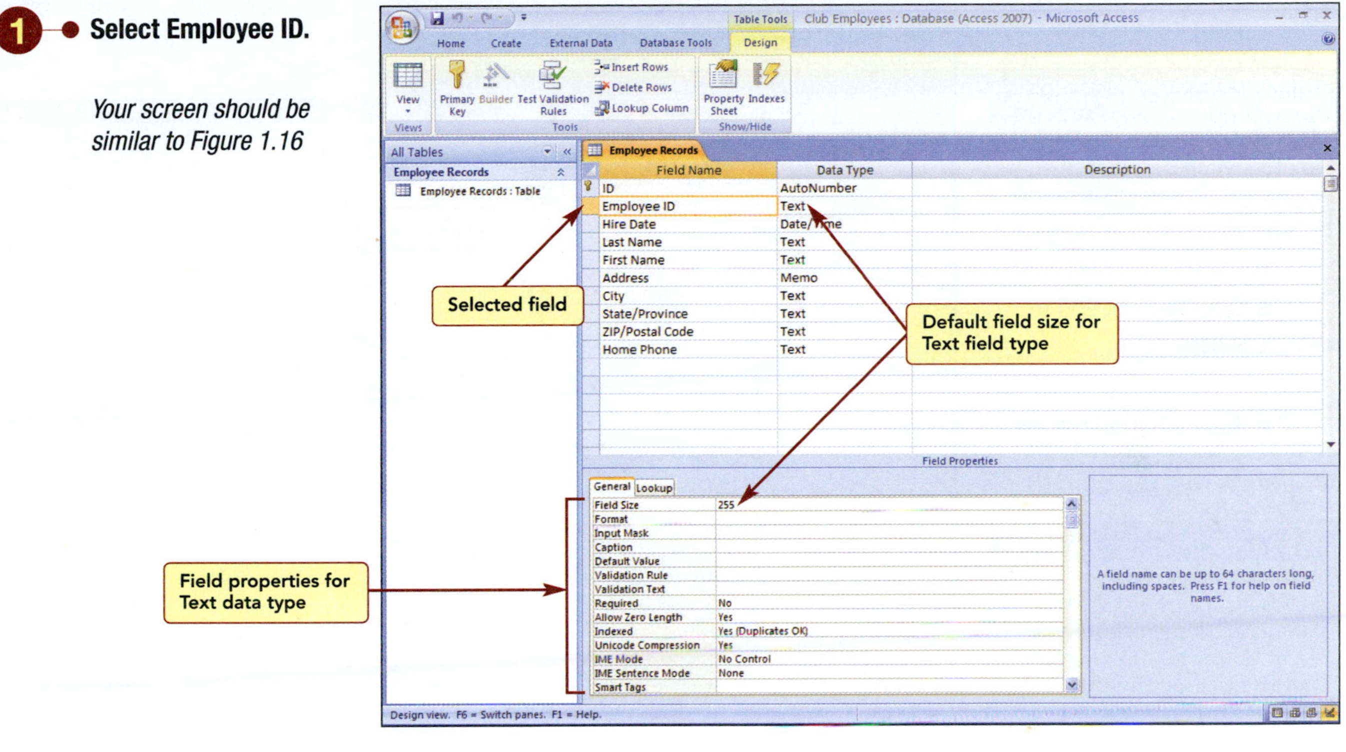

Figure 1.16

The data type of this field is Text and the default properties associated with a Text data type are displayed in the Field Properties area. Although some of the properties are the same as those for the AutoNumber data type, most are different. Access sets the field size for a Text field to 255 characters. It also sets the Required property to no, which allows the field to be blank. The Allow Zero Length property is set to yes, which allows entries with no characters. The Indexed property is also set to yes, meaning indexing is on, and duplicate entries are allowed in the field, as, for example, the same name could be entered in the Name field of multiple records. All these settings seem appropriate, except for the field size, which is much too large.

Modifying Field Properties

Although Access uses only the amount of storage space necessary for the text you actually store in a Text field, setting the field size to the smallest possible size can decrease the processing time required by the program. Additionally, if the field data to be entered is a specific size, setting the field size to that number restricts the entry to the maximum number.

Because the employee number will never be more than five digits long, you will change the field size from the default of 255 to 5. Another way to edit text is to select (highlight by dragging or double-clicking) a character or characters (including complete words and sentences) and press the Delete key to erase the selection.

1 **Click the Field Size property text box.**

Another Method

You also can press the F6 key to switch between the upper and lower areas of the Design window.

Double-click 255 to select it.

Type 5 to replace the default entry.

Additional Information

You can cancel changes you are making in the current field at any time before you move on to the next field. Just press Esc, and the original entry is restored.

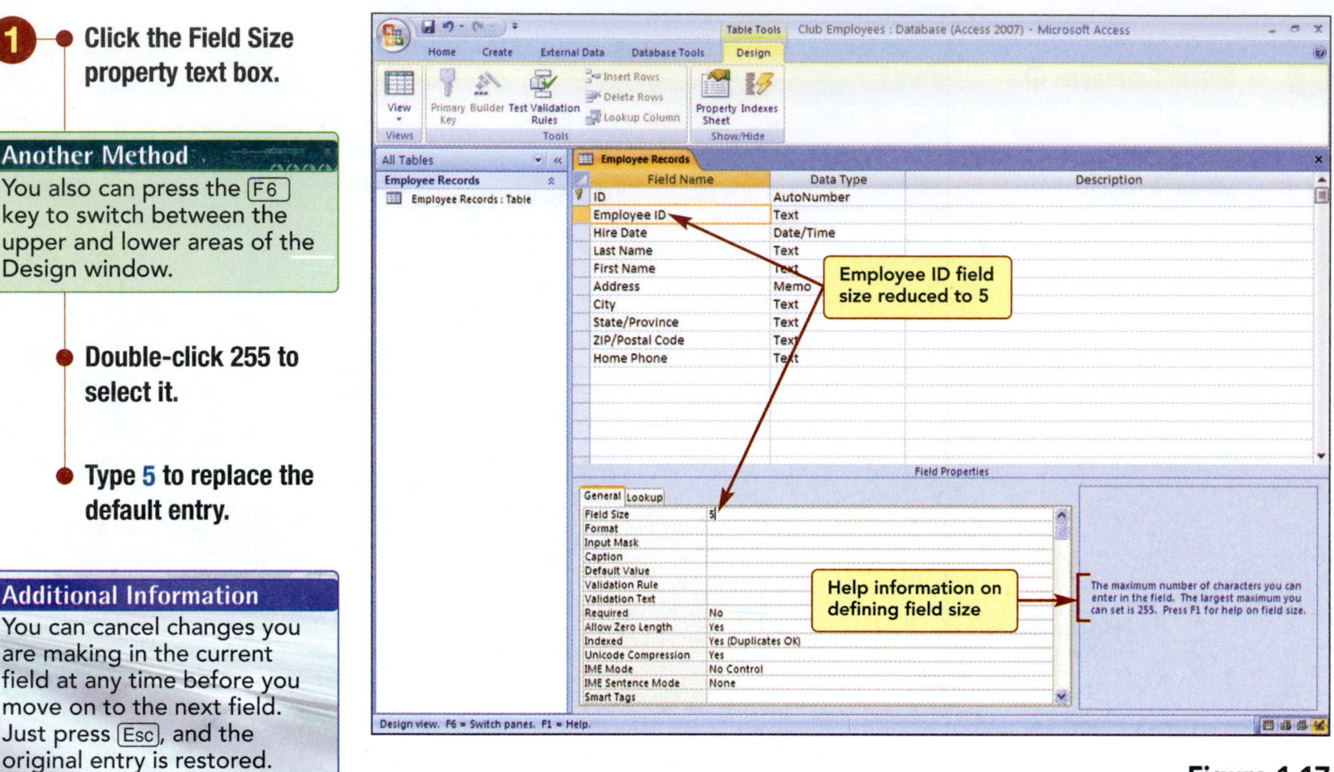

Employee ID field size reduced to 5
Help information on defining field size
The maximum number of characters you can enter in the field. The largest maximum you can set is 255. Press F1 for help on field size.

Figure 1.17

Your screen should be similar to Figure 1.17

The maximum number of characters that can be entered in this field is now restricted to 5. Notice the Help box displays a brief description of the selected property.

Likewise, you will adjust the field sizes of several other fields.

2 Change the field sizes to those shown for the fields in the following table.

Field	Size
Last Name	25
First Name	25
City	25
ZIP/Postal Code	10
Home Phone	15

Your screen should be similar to Figure 1.18

Table Tools Club Employees : Database (Access 2007) - Microsoft Access
Home Create External Data Database Tools Design
View Primary Key Builder Test Validation Rules Insert Rows Delete Rows Lookup Column Property Sheet Indexes
Views Tools Show/Hide
All Tables
Employee Records
Employee Records : Table
Employee Records

Field Name	Data Type	Description
ID	AutoNumber	
Employee ID	Text	
Hire Date	Date/Time	
Last Name	Text	
First Name	Text	
Address	Memo	
City	Text	
State/Province	Text	
ZIP/Postal Code	Text	
Home Phone	Text	

Memo data type not appropriate

Field Properties
General Lookup

Field Size	15
Format	
Input Mask	
Caption	
Default Value	
Validation Rule	
Validation Text	
Required	No
Allow Zero Length	No
Indexed	No
Unicode Compression	Yes
IME Mode	Off
IME Sentence Mode	Phrase Predict
Smart Tags	

Field size changed
The maximum number of characters you can enter in the field. The largest maximum you can set is 255. Press F1 for help on field size.
Design view. F6 = Switch panes. F1 = Help.

Figure 1.18

Changing Data Type

As you look at the field definitions, you see that the Address field type was set to Memo by the field template. This setting allows text entries longer than 255 characters and lets you add formatting to the text, such as bold or italics. You do not feel this data type is appropriate for the field and will change it to Text with a field size of 50.

1 Click in the Data Type column for the Address field.

- Click [▾] to open the drop-down list and choose Text.
- Change the field size to 50.

Your screen should be similar to Figure 1.19

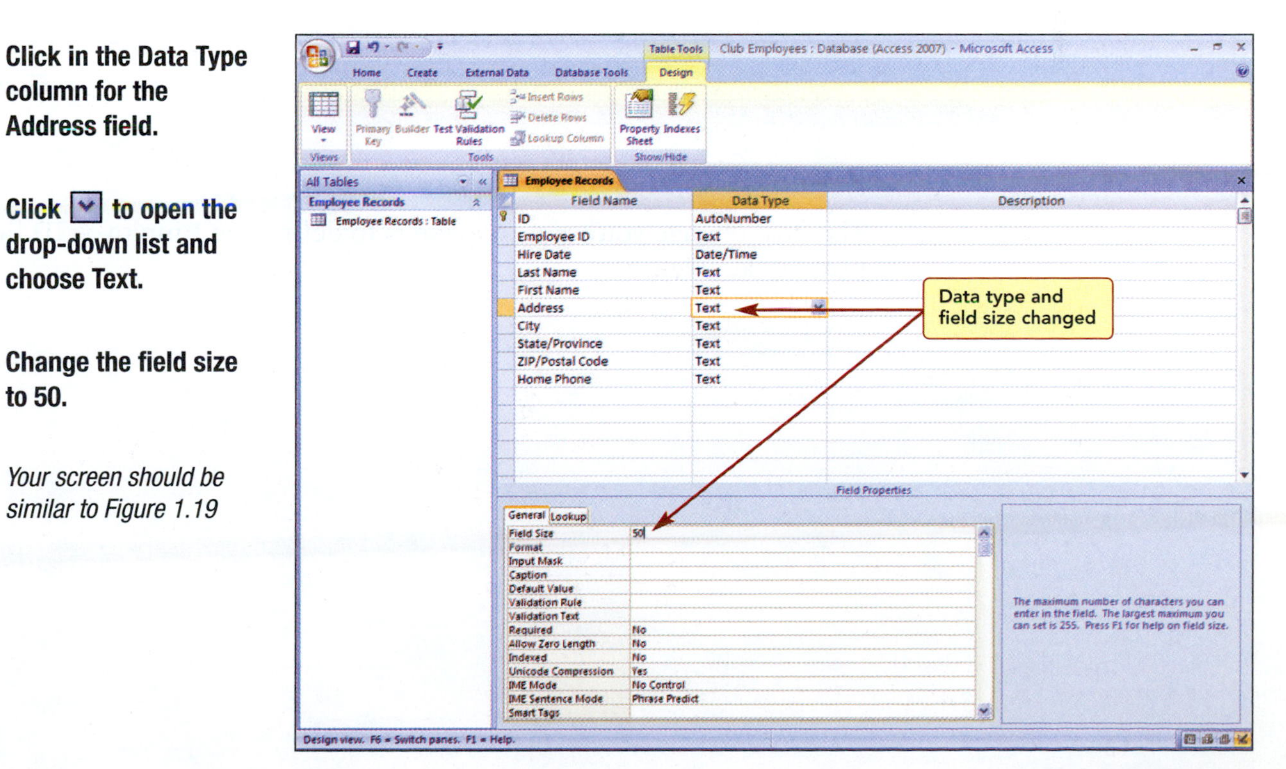

Figure 1.19

Notice that even though this field has a text data type, the property settings are different. For example, the Allow Zero Length and Indexed properties are both set to No. This is because the fields were defined using field templates that included these settings.

Editing Field Names

As you continue to look over the fields, you decide to change several of the field names that were assigned when you selected the field templates.

1

- **Change the State/Province field name to State.**
- **Change the ZIP/Postal Code field name to ZIP Code.**

Having Trouble?
Double-click on the field name to select it.

Your screen should be similar to Figure 1.20

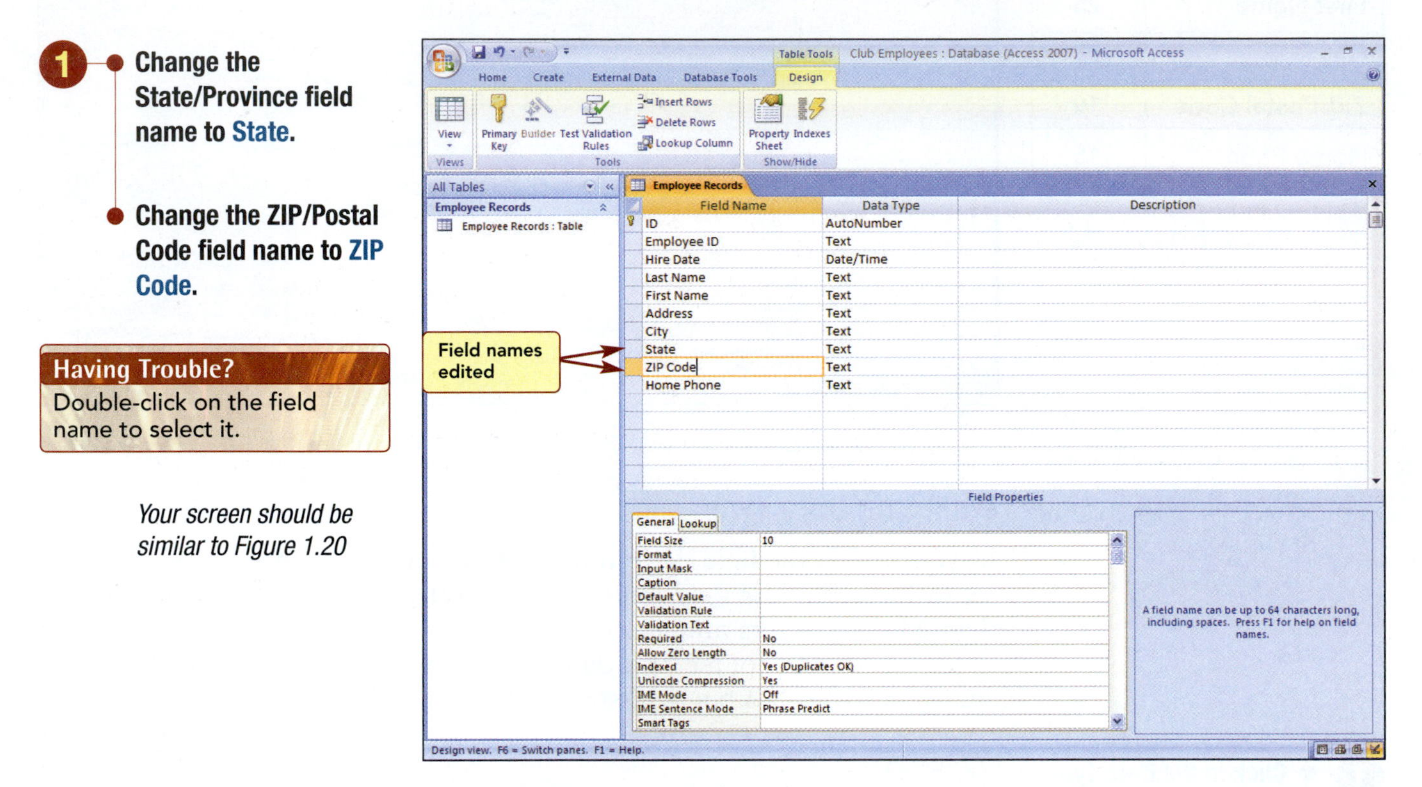

Figure 1.20

Defining a Primary Key Field

The next change you want to make is to define the Employee ID field as a primary key field.

Concept 5

Primary Key

5

A **primary key** is a field that uniquely identifies each record and is used to associate data from multiple tables. To qualify as a primary key field, the data in the field must be unique for each record. For example, a Social Security Number field could be selected as the primary key because the data in that field is unique for each employee. Other examples of a primary key field are parts numbers or catalog numbers. (One example of a field that should not be used as the primary key is a name field, because more than one person can have the same last or first name.) A second requirement is that the field can never be empty or null. A third is that the data in the field never, or rarely, changes.

A primary key prevents duplicate records from being entered in the table and is used to control the order in which records display in the table. This makes it faster for databases to locate records in the table and to process other operations.

Most tables have at least one field that is selected as the primary key. Some tables may use two or more fields that, together, provide the primary key of a table. When a primary key uses more than one field, it is called a **composite key**.

More About

For information about defining multifield primary keys, see "1.3 Add, Set, Change, or Remove Primary Keys" in the More About appendix.

Notice the icon that is displayed to the left of the ID field. This indicates that this field is a primary key field. You want to define the Employee ID field as the primary key field so that duplicate employee ID numbers will not be allowed.

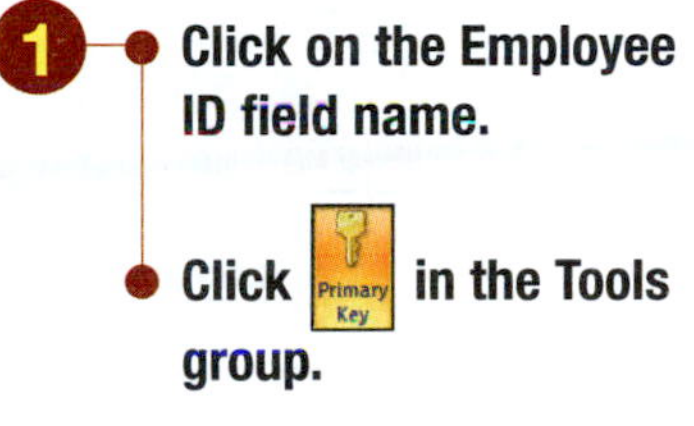

1 **Click on the Employee ID field name.**

Click Primary Key in the Tools group.

Your screen should be similar to Figure 1.21

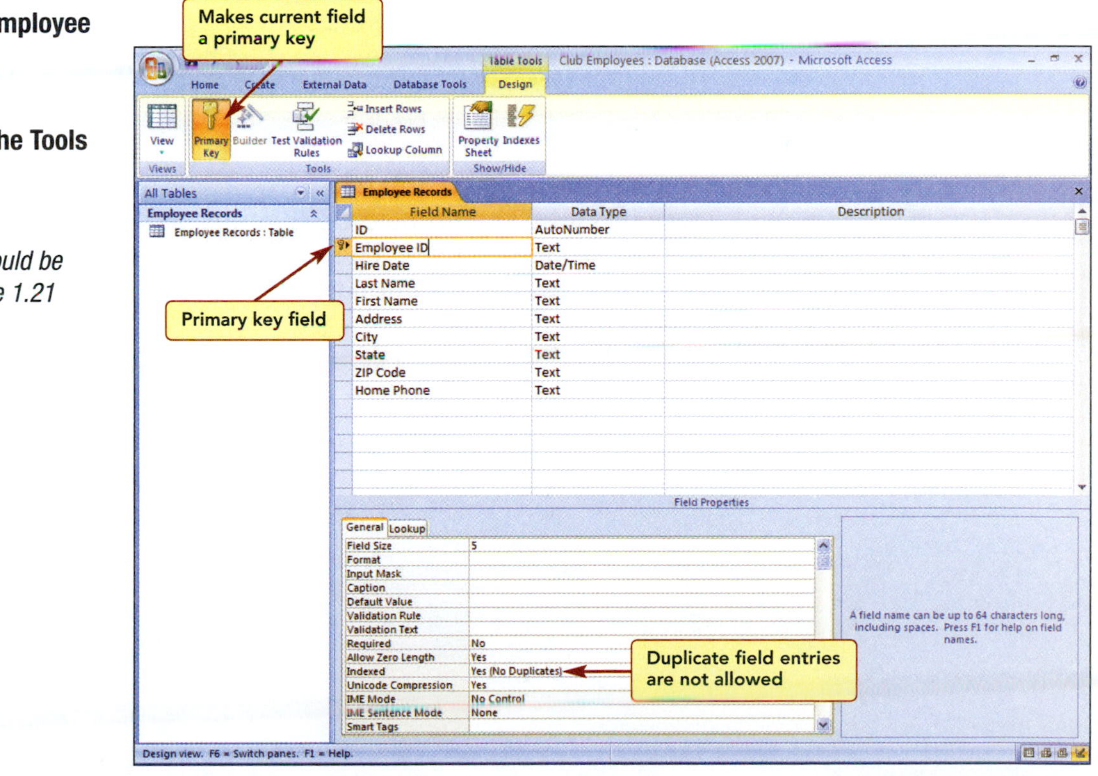

Figure 1.21

Notice the Indexed property setting for this field has changed to Yes (No Duplicates) because the field is defined as the primary key field. This setting prohibits duplicate values in a field. Also, the primary key status has been removed from the default ID field.

Entering a Field Description

To continue defining the Employee ID field, you will enter a brief description of the field. Although it is optional, a field description makes the table easier to understand and update because the description is displayed in the status bar when you enter data into the table.

1

- **Click the Description text box for the Employee ID field.**
- **Type Unique five-digit number assigned to each employee.**

Additional Information

The Description box scrolls horizontally as necessary to accommodate the length of the text entry. The maximum length is 255 characters.

Your screen should be similar to Figure 1.22

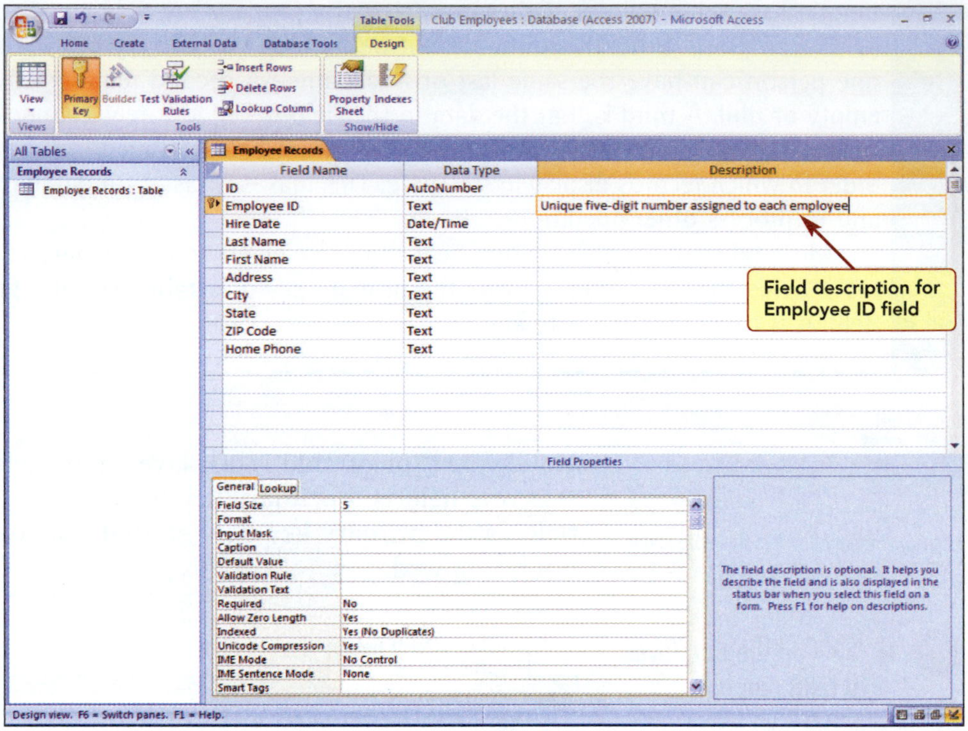

Figure 1.22

You also want to add field descriptions to several other fields. As you do, the Property Update Options button appears. Clicking on this button opens a menu whose option will update the description in the status bar everywhere it is used.

2 **Add descriptions to the fields shown in the table below.**

Your screen should be similar to Figure 1.23

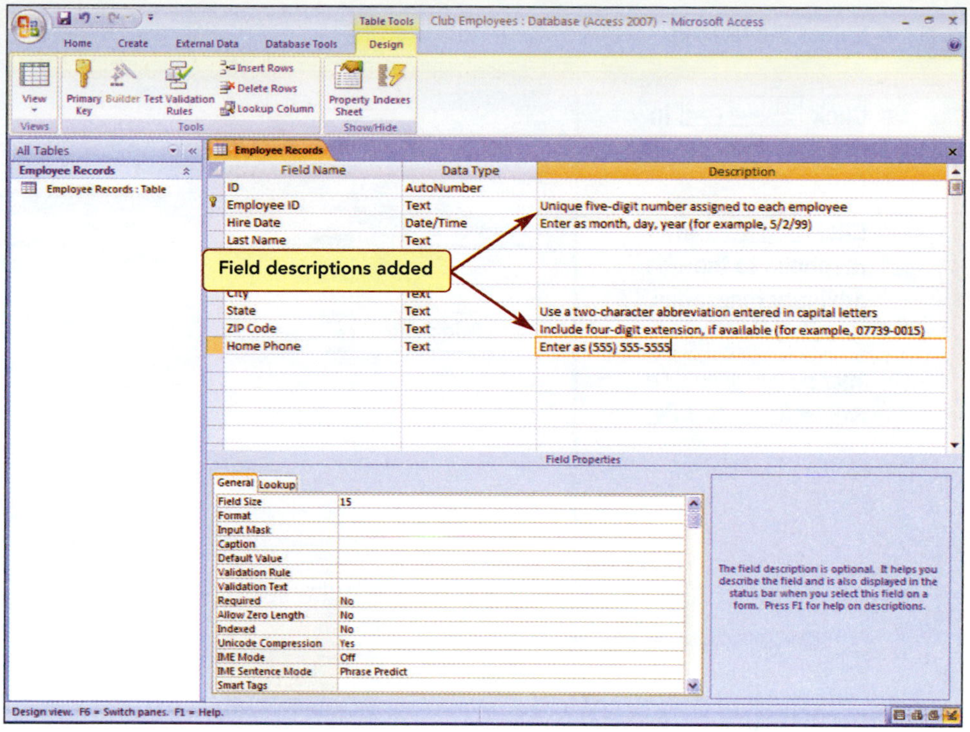

Figure 1.23

Field	Description
Hire Date	Enter as month, day, year (for example, 5/2/99)
State	Use a two-character abbreviation entered in capital letters
ZIP Code	Include four-digit extension, if available (for example, 07739-0015)
Home Phone	Enter as (555) 555-5555

Additional Information

In a table that contains a lot of data, it is a good idea to create a backup copy of the table before you delete a field in case you need to recover the deleted data.

Deleting a Field

Because the ID field essentially duplicates the purpose of the Employee ID field, you will delete the ID field. Deleting a field permanently removes the field column and all the data in the field from the table.

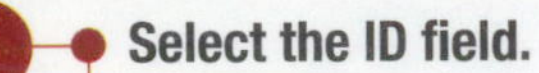

1. Select the ID field.
   - Click Delete Rows in the Tools group.
   - Click Yes in response to the advisory messages.

Your screen should be similar to Figure 1.24

Figure 1.24

Another Method

You also can delete a field in Datasheet view by choosing Delete Column from the shortcut menu or Delete in the Fields & Columns group of the Table Tools Datasheet tab for the column you want to delete.

The field is permanently removed from the table.

Defining Additional Fields

You still need to add two fields to the table: one for the employee's date of birth and the other to display the employee photo. You will add the new fields and define their properties in Design view.

1. Click in the blank Field Name row below the Home Phone field name.
   - Type **Birth Date**.
   - Press ←Enter, Tab, or → to move to the Data Type column.
   - Open the Data Type drop-down list and choose Date/Time.

Another Method

You also can enter the data type by typing the first character of the type you want to use. For example, if you type D, the Date/Time data type will be automatically selected and displayed in the field.

   - Enter the field description **Enter as month, day, year (for example, 5/2/74)**.

Your screen should be similar to Figure 1.25

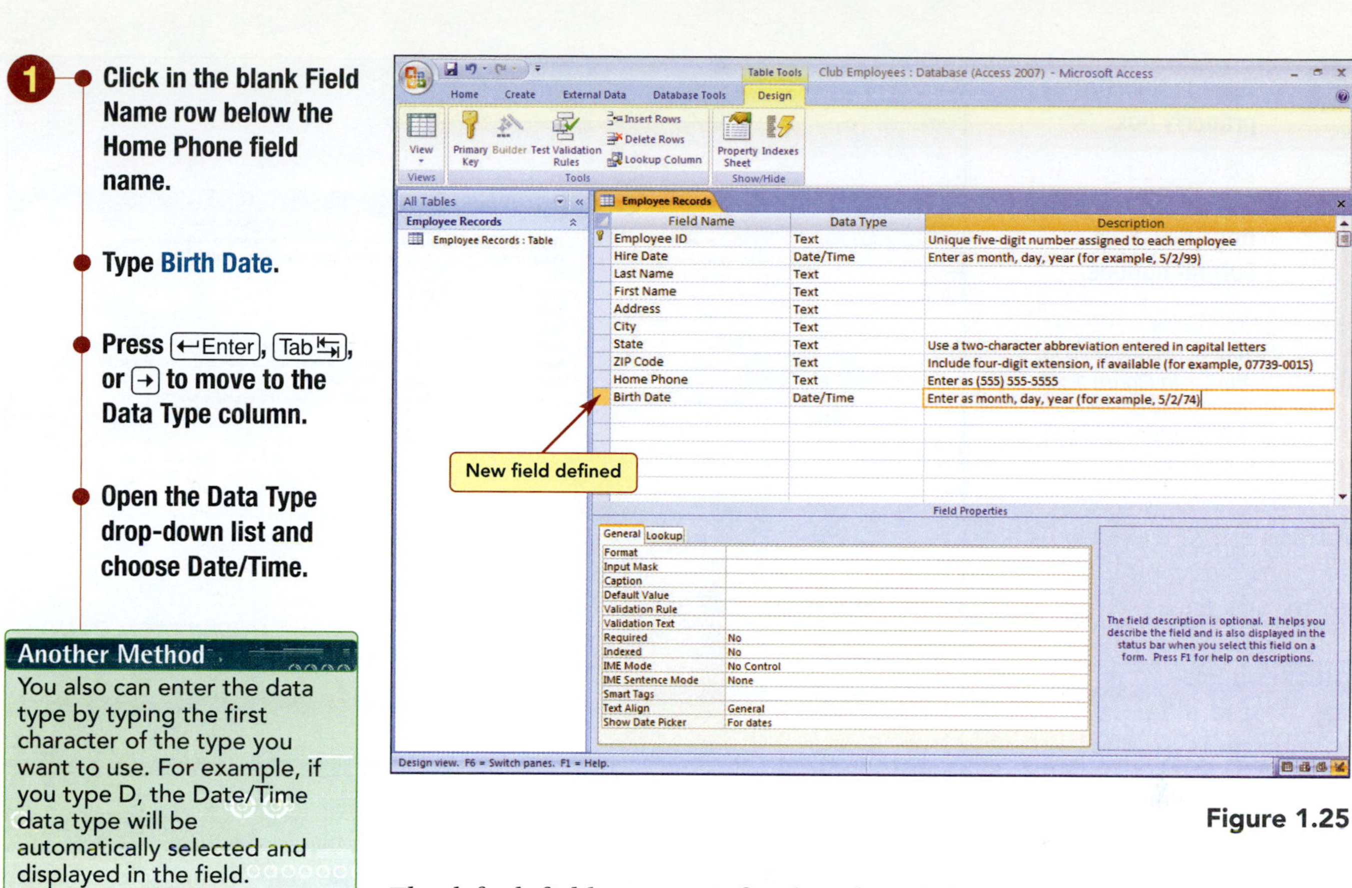

Figure 1.25

The default field properties for the selected data type are displayed. Because the format line is blank, you decide to check the format to make sure that the date will display as you want.

- **Click in the Format property box.**
- **Click [▾] to open the drop-down list of Format options.**

Your screen should be similar to Figure 1.26

Date/time formats

Figure 1.26

The names of the seven predefined layouts for the Date/Time field type are displayed in the list. An example of each layout appears to the right of the name. The General Date format is the default format. It displays dates using the Short Date format. If a time value is entered, it also will display the time in the Long Time format.

Choose General Date.

Your screen should be similar to Figure 1.27

Additional Information

Access automatically assumes the first two digits of a year entry. If you enter a year that is between /30 and /99, Access reads this as a 20th century date (1930 to 1999). A year entry between /00 and /29 is assumed to be a 21st century date (2000 to 2029).

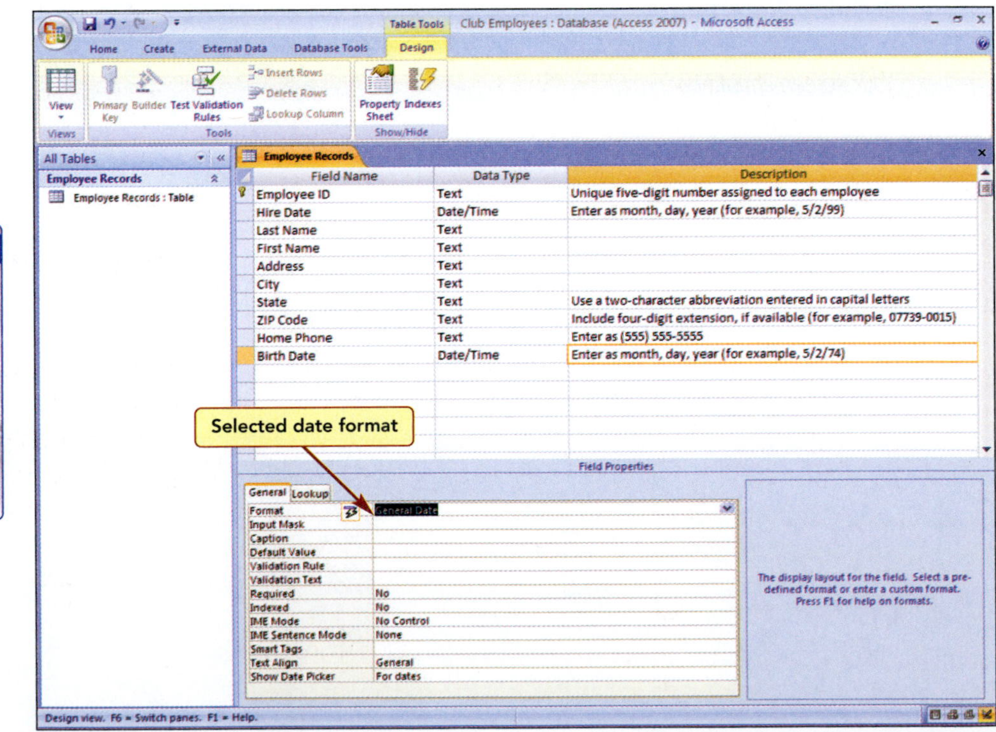

Figure 1.27

The Date property setting is now displayed in the Format text box.

The last field you will enter will display a photo and resume if available of each employee. The data type for this type of input is Attachment. Once a field has been assigned, this data type cannot be changed. You can, however, delete the field and then redefine it if you think you made an error.

4

- **In the next blank field name row, enter the field name Photo/ Resume with a data type of Attachment.**
- **Include the description Attach employee photo and resume if available.**

Your screen should be similar to Figure 1.28

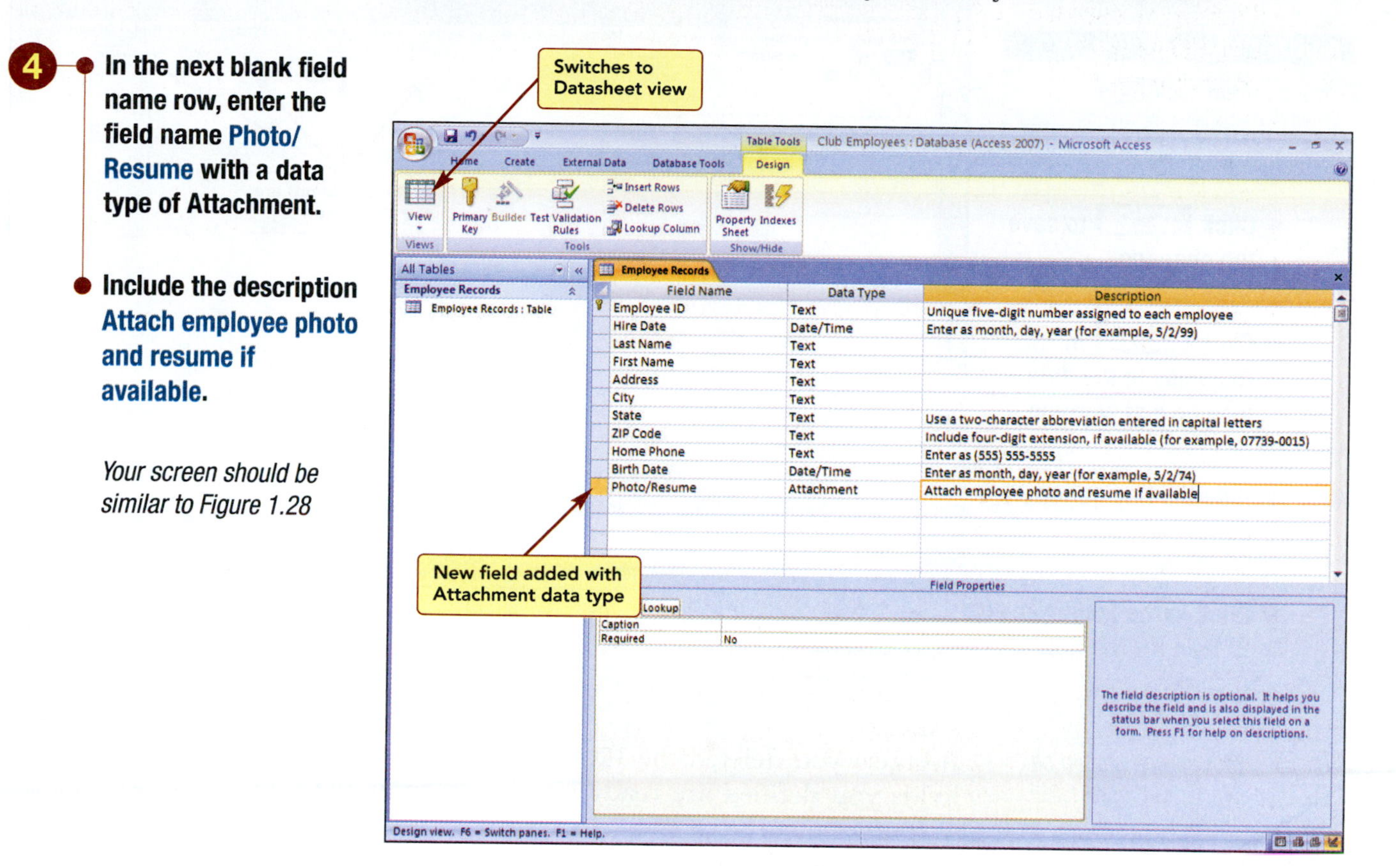

Figure 1.28

Specifying the Attachment data type allows you to store multiple files of different file types in a single field.

Entering and Editing Data

Now that the table structure is complete, you want to continue entering the employee data into the table. To do this, you need to switch back to Datasheet view.

Because you have made many changes to the table design, you will be asked to save the changes before you switch views. You also will be advised that data may be lost because you decreased field sizes in several fields. Since there is very little data in the table, this is not a concern.

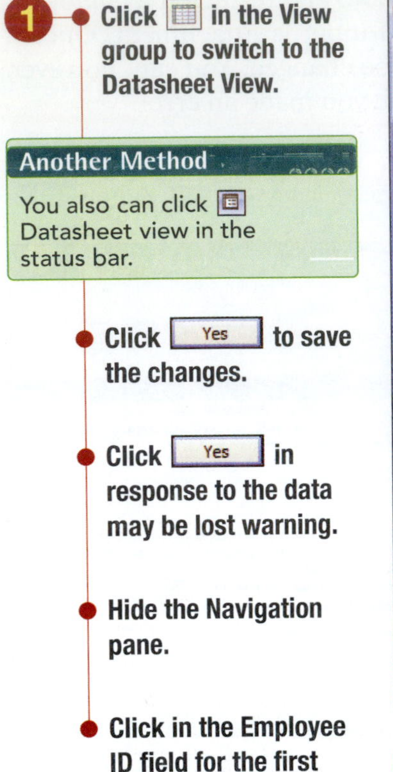

1 Click in the View group to switch to the Datasheet View.

Another Method

You also can click Datasheet view in the status bar.

- Click **Yes** to save the changes.
- Click **Yes** in response to the data may be lost warning.
- Hide the Navigation pane.
- Click in the Employee ID field for the first record.

Your screen should be similar to Figure 1.29

Orange identifies current field and record

All field columns are the same width

Field description appears in status bar

Figure 1.29

Because you deleted the ID field, it is no longer displayed and the new fields you defined are ready for you to enter the remaining data for the first record.

The first field, Employee ID, of the first record is outlined in orange, indicating that the program is ready to accept data in this field. The field name and Select All button also are highlighted in orange to identify the current field and current record. The status bar displays the description you entered for the field.

Additional Information

You will learn how to change the column width shortly.

Notice also in this view that the column widths are all the same, even though you set different field sizes in the Table Design window. This is because the Table Datasheet view has its own default column width setting.

Verifying Data Accuracy and Validity

To see how field properties help ensure data accuracy, you will reenter the employee number for the first record and try to enter a number that is larger than the field size of five that you defined in Table Design view.

1 If necessary, double-click on the number to select it.

- Type **047310**.

Your screen should be similar to Figure 1.30

Figure 1.30

The program accepted only the first five digits and would not let you type a sixth. The field size restriction helps control the accuracy of data by not allowing an entry larger than specified. Notice also that the current record symbol has changed to [pencil icon]. The pencil symbol means the record is in the process of being entered or edited and has not yet been saved.

Next, you will intentionally enter an invalid date to see what happens.

2 Press ←Enter, Tab, or → to move to the Hire Date field.

- Type **8/32/01**.
- Press ←Enter, Tab, or →.

Your screen should be similar to Figure 1.31

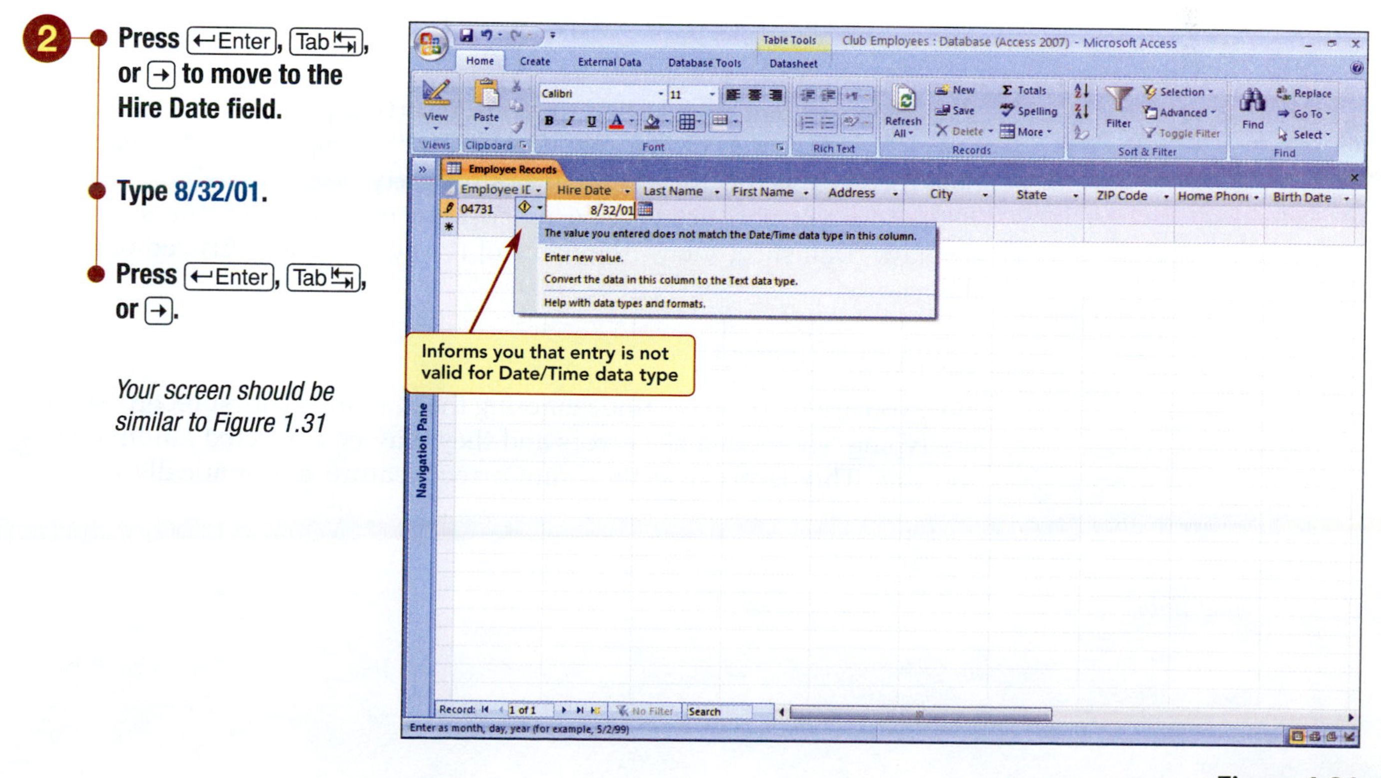

Figure 1.31

An informational message box is displayed advising you that the entry is not valid. In this case, the date entered (8/32/01) could not be correct because a month cannot have 32 days. Access automatically performs some basic checks on the data as it is entered based upon the field type specified in the table design. This is another way that Access helps you control data entry to ensure the accuracy of the data.

You will need to edit the date entry to correct it.

3

- **Select Enter new value from the message box.**
- **Double-click on 32 to select it.**
- **Type 19.**
- **Press Tab.**

Your screen should be similar to Figure 1.32

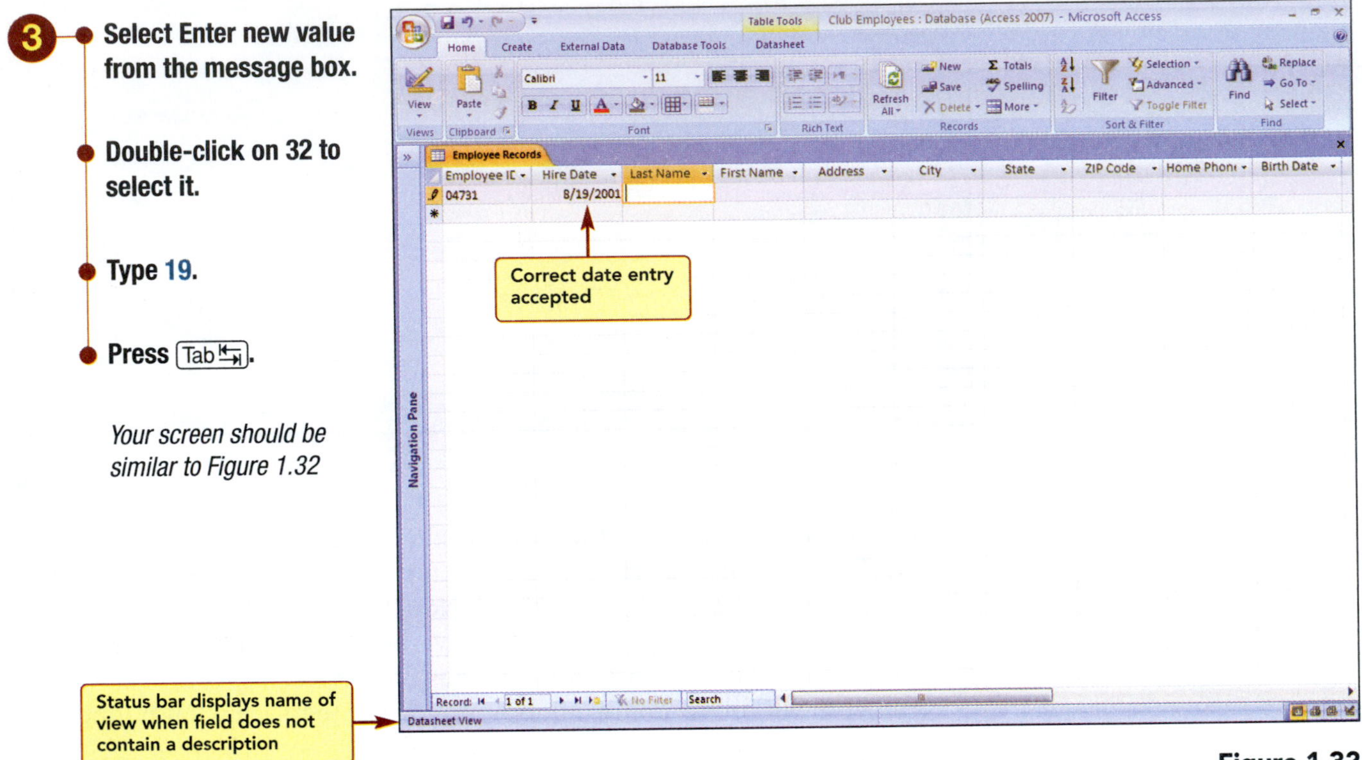

Figure 1.32

The corrected date is accepted, and the insertion point moves to the Last Name field. The year in the date changed to four digits, which reflects the date format you specified in the field's property.

Because you did not enter a description for this field, the status bar displays "Datasheet View," the name of the current view, instead of a field description.

Using AutoCorrect

Now you are ready to continue entering the data for the first record. As you are typing, you may make errors and they may be corrected automatically for you. This is because the AutoCorrect feature automatically corrects obvious errors such as capitalizing names of days, the first letter of sentences, and other common typing errors and misspellings such as words starting with two initial capital letters. The AutoCorrect Options button will appear next to any text that was corrected. You have the option of undoing the correction or leaving it as is. Most times the typing error is not corrected, and you will need to fix it manually.

To see how this works, you will enter the last name incorrectly by typing the first two letters using capital letters.

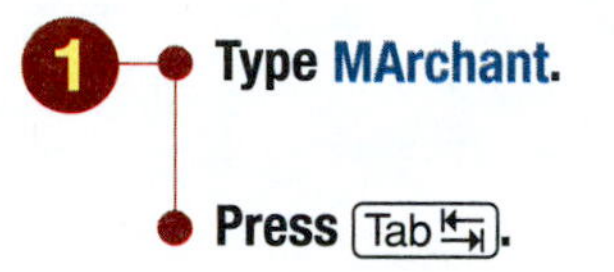

1

- **Type MArchant.**
- **Press Tab.**

Your screen should be similar to Figure 1.33

Figure 1.33

The name was automatically corrected and the AutoCorrect Options button appears. You will leave the correction as is and continue to enter data for this record.

Enter the data shown in the table below for the remaining fields, typing the information exactly as it appears.

> **Additional Information**
> The fields will scroll on the screen as you move to the right in the record.

Your screen should be similar to Figure 1.34

Identifies field as an Attachment data type field

Figure 1.34

Field Name	Data
First Name	**Roberta**
Address	**564 Palm Avenue**
City	**Landis**
State	**CA**
ZIP Code	**92120–3741**
Home Phone	**(507) 555–6707**
Birth Date	**May 18, 1980** (press Tab ↹ to complete the entry)

All the information for the first record is now complete, except for the last field for the employee photo and resume.

Attaching a File

Notice the field name in the header for this field is not Photo/Resume, as you defined in Design view. This is because Access does not allow field names for Attachment data types. Instead it displays a paperclip icon in the field header to show that the field has an Attachment data type. The field description that appears in the status bar is particularly important because there is no descriptive field name.

To complete the information for this field, you plan to attach the employee photo and a copy of the employee's resume if it is available. A photo is one of several different types of graphic objects that can be added to a database table. A **graphic** is a nontext element or object. A graphic can be a simple **drawing object** consisting of shapes such as lines and boxes that can be created using a drawing program such as Paint or it can be a picture. A **picture** is an illustration such as a scanned photograph. A resume is a text document that is typically created using a word processor application.

Because you have not organized all the employees' badge photographs yet, you will only insert the photo for Roberta Marchant to demonstrate this feature to the club owners. You also will attach a sample resume that was created using Word 2007.

1 Double-click on the Attachment field cell for this record.

Another Method

You also can choose Manage Attachments from the field's shortcut menu.

Your screen should be similar to Figure 1.35

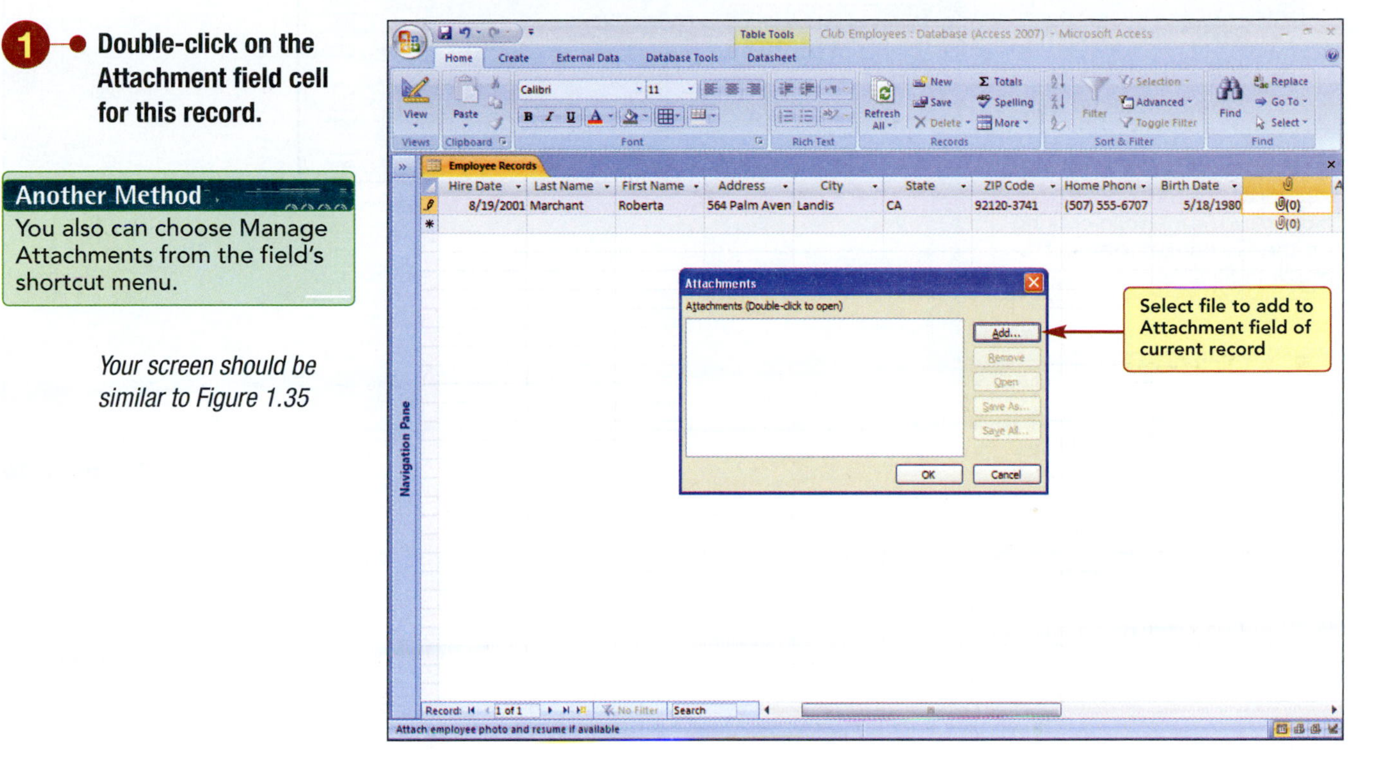

Figure 1.35

The Attachments box is used to manage the items that are in an attachment field. Because there are currently no attachments associated with this field, it is empty. You will select the photo and resume files you want to add to the field.

2 Click Add... .

- If necessary, open the Look in drop-down list box and specify the location of your data files.

- Select ac01_Roberta and ac01_Resume from the file list box.

Having Trouble?

Hold down Ctrl while clicking on the file names to select multiple files.

- Click Open .

Your screen should be similar to Figure 1.36

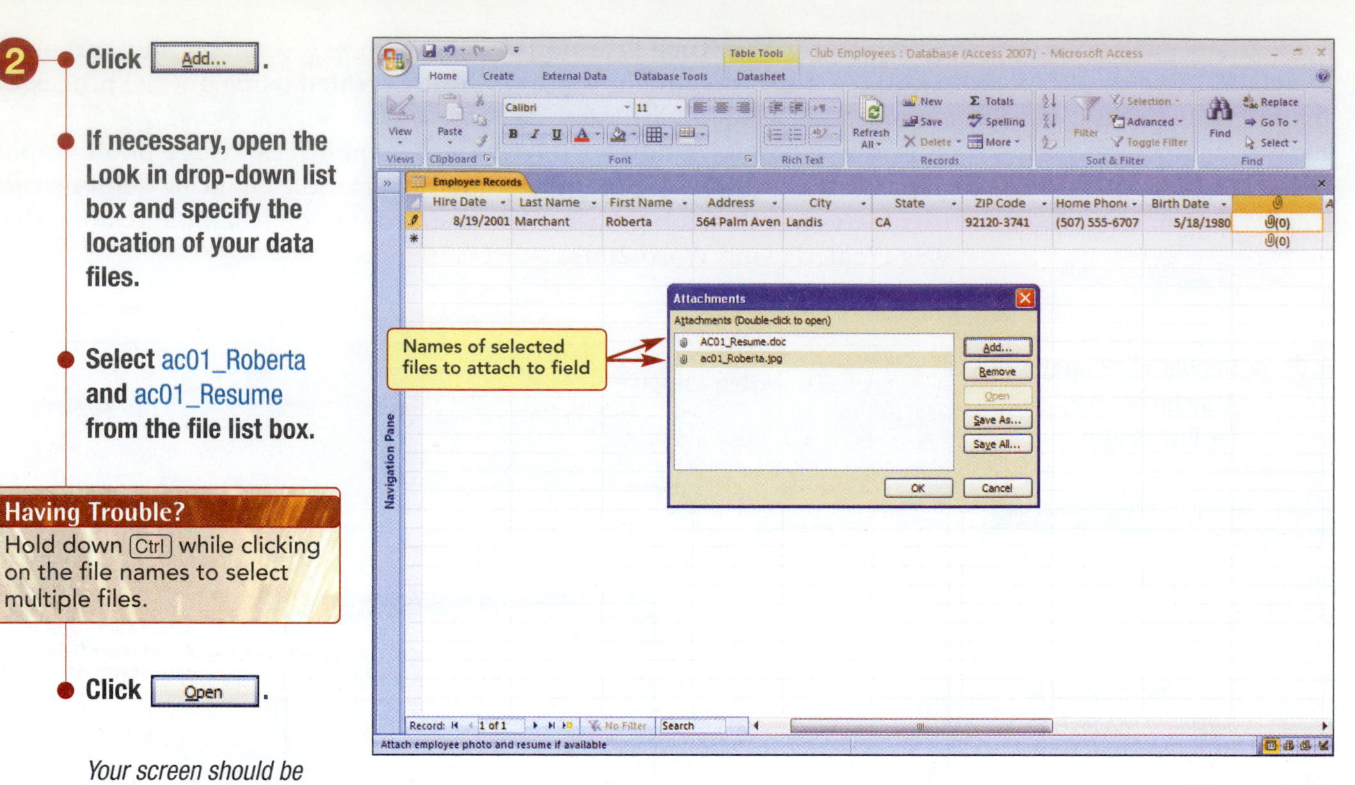

Figure 1.36

Additional Information

To remove a file from the attachment field, select the file name from the list and click Remove .

More About

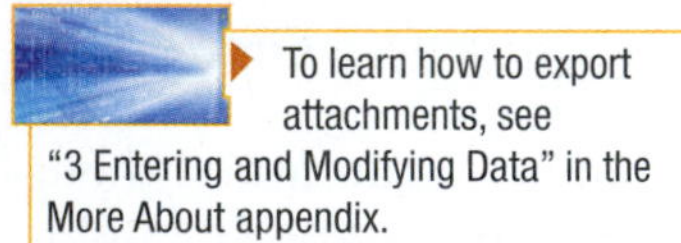

To learn how to export attachments, see "3 Entering and Modifying Data" in the More About appendix.

The Attachments dialog box is displayed again and now displays the names of the selected files.

3 **Click OK.**

Your screen should be similar to Figure 1.37

Table Tools
Club Employees : Database (Access 2007) - Microsoft Access
Home Create External Data Database Tools Datasheet
View Paste Calibri 11 Refresh All New Save Delete Totals Spelling More Filter Toggle Filter Select
Views Clipboard Font Rich Text Records Sort & Filter Find

Two attachments in field

Employee Records

Hire Date	Last Name	First Name	Address	City	State	ZIP Code	Home Phone	Birth Date	
8/19/2001	Marchant	Roberta	564 Palm Aven	Landis	CA	92120-3741	(507) 555-6707	5/18/1980	(2)
									(0)

Navigation Pane

Record: 1 of 1 No Filter Search

Attach employee photo and resume if available

Figure 1.37

The selected files are inserted as attachments and identified with the number 2 in the cell. The number indicates how many attachments have been added to the field. You will now display the photograph from the Attachment field to check that it has been inserted properly.

4 **Double-click the cell.**

Select the ac01_Roberta file from the Attachments dialog box.

Click Open.

Another Method

You also can double-click the file to both select and open it.

Your screen should be similar to Figure 1.38

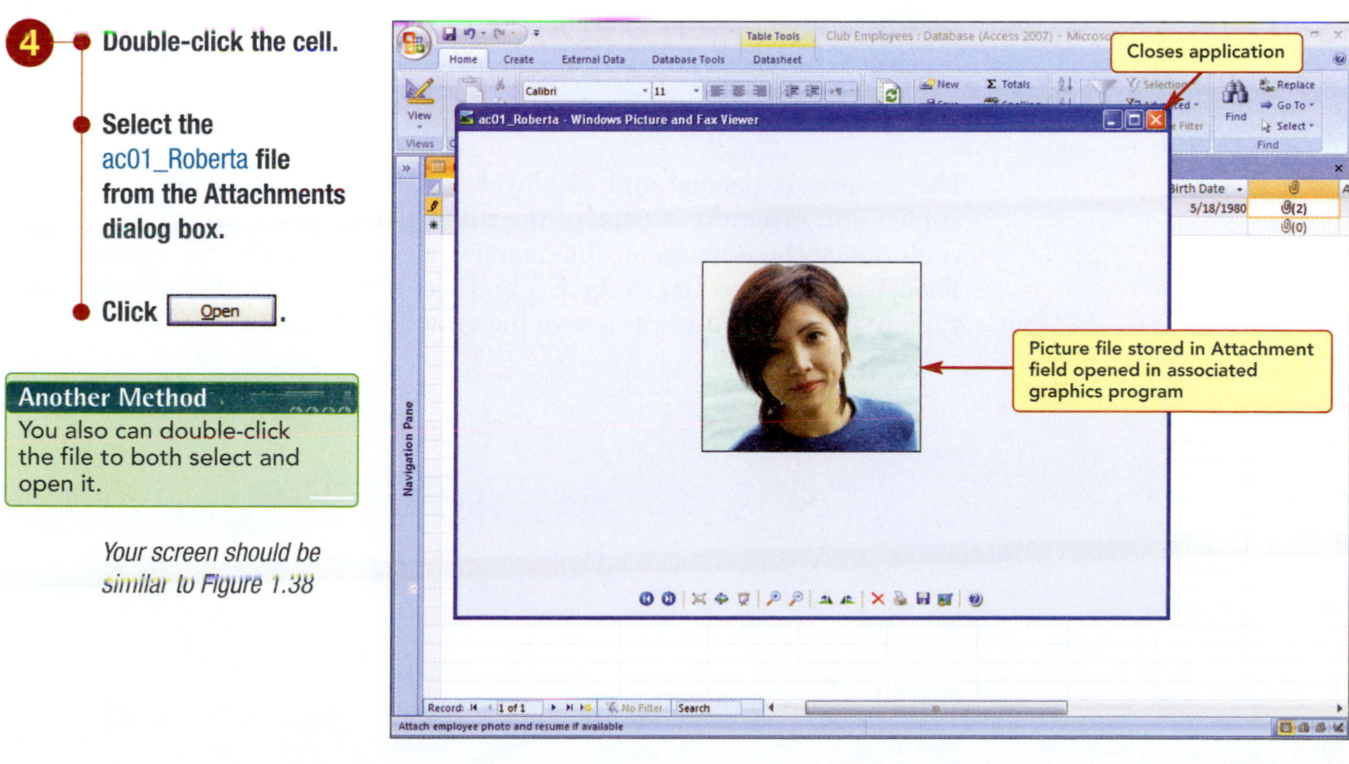

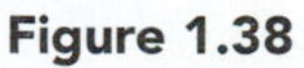

Figure 1.38

Additional Information

Image files that open in Microsoft Picture and Fax Viewer can only be viewed, not edited. If you wanted to edit the image, right-click on the image and choose Edit. The program used to create the file, if available on your computer, is opened.

The picture object is opened and displayed in the graphics program that is associated with this type of file—in this case, Windows Picture and Fax Viewer. Yours may open and display in a different graphics program such as Paint. The application that opens is not necessarily the application in which the file was created. If the application in which it opens includes features that can be used to edit the file, you will be prompted to save any changes before closing the Attachments dialog box. If you do not save them, the changes will be lost.

5

- **Click Close in the graphics application window title bar to close the application.**
- **Select and open the** ac01_Resume **attachment.**

Your screen should be similar to Figure 1.39

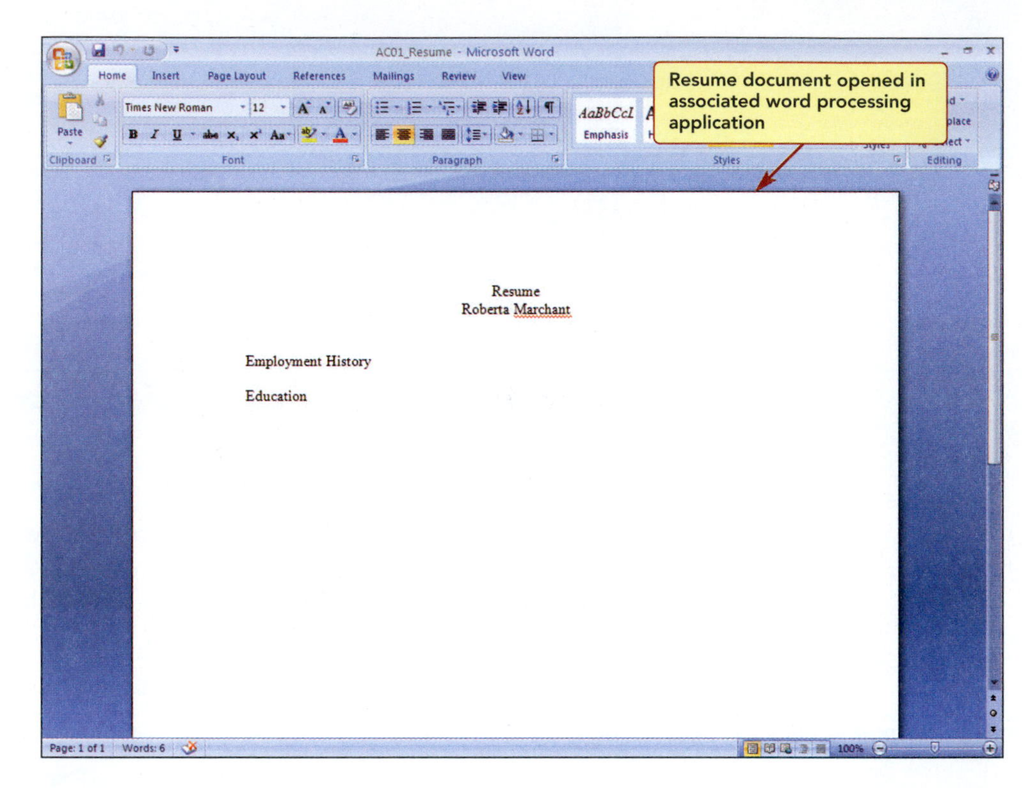

Figure 1.39

The resume is opened and displayed in the associated word processing application program. A copy of the file is placed in a temporary folder. If you change the document, the changes are saved to the temporary copy. Then when you return to Access and close the Attachments dialog box, you are asked if you want to save the attached file again.

6 **Click ☒ Close in the application window title bar to close the application.**

- **Click ☒ Close to close the Attachments dialog box.**
- **Press ←Enter to move to the beginning of the next record.**

Your screen should be similar to Figure 1.40

Data for record 1 is complete
Second record is ready for input
Current record of a total of 2 records in table

Figure 1.40

The data for the first record is now complete. The insertion point moves to the first field in the next row and waits for input of the employee number for the next record. As soon as the insertion point moves to another record, the data is saved to the table file and the number of the new record appears in the status bar. The second record was automatically assigned the record number 2.

Moving between Fields

Next, you will check the first record for accuracy. To quickly move from one field to another in a record, you can first select (highlight) the entire field contents and then you can use the keyboard keys shown in the following table to move quickly between field columns.

Key	Movement
→ or Tab	Next field
← or ⇧Shift + Tab	Previous field
↓	Current field in next record
↑	Current field in previous record
Home	First field in record
End	Last field in record

You will select the Employee ID field for the first record and then move to the Address field to check its contents.

1 Point to the left end of the Employee ID field for the first record. When the mouse pointer appears as ✚, click the mouse button.

Press → four times.

Your screen should be similar to Figure 1.41

Contents of entire field is selected

Figure 1.41

> **Additional Information**
> If you press Delete or Backspace while the entire field is selected, the entire field contents will be deleted.

Because the entire field contents are selected, you need to be careful that you do not type a character as that will delete the selection and replace it with the new text. To switch back to editing, you need to display the insertion point in the field and then edit the entry.

2 Click the Address field with the mouse pointer shape as an I-beam.

Your screen should be similar to Figure 1.42

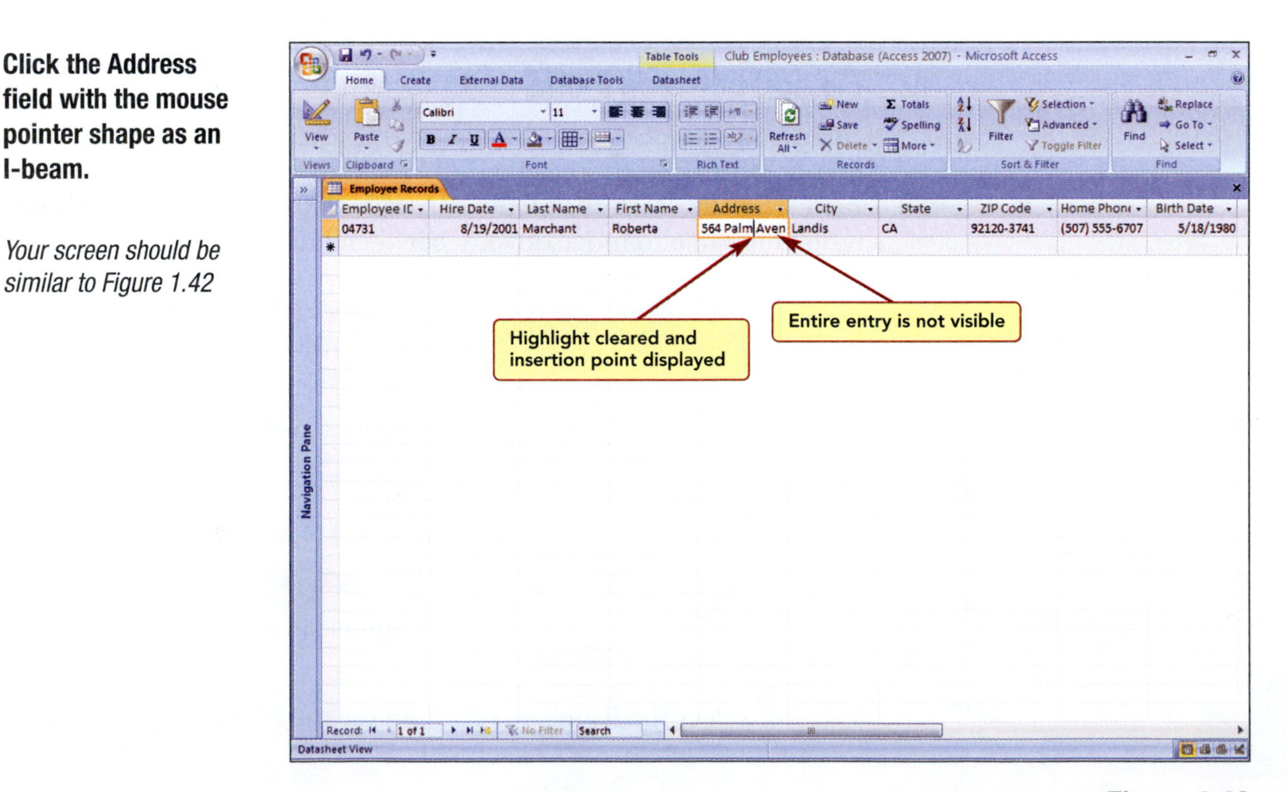

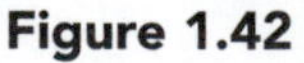

Figure 1.42

Additional Information

You can press F2 to switch between editing an entry (the insertion point is displayed) and navigating (the field is selected) through the datasheet.

The highlight is cleared and the insertion point is visible in the field. Now, using the directional keys moves the insertion point within the field and you can edit the field contents if necessary.

Zooming a Field

The beginning of the field looks fine, but because the column width is too narrow, you cannot see the entire entry. You will move the insertion point to the end of the address so you can check the rest of the entry.

1 Press End.

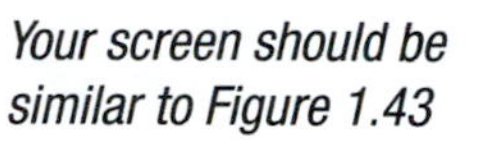

Your screen should be similar to Figure 1.43

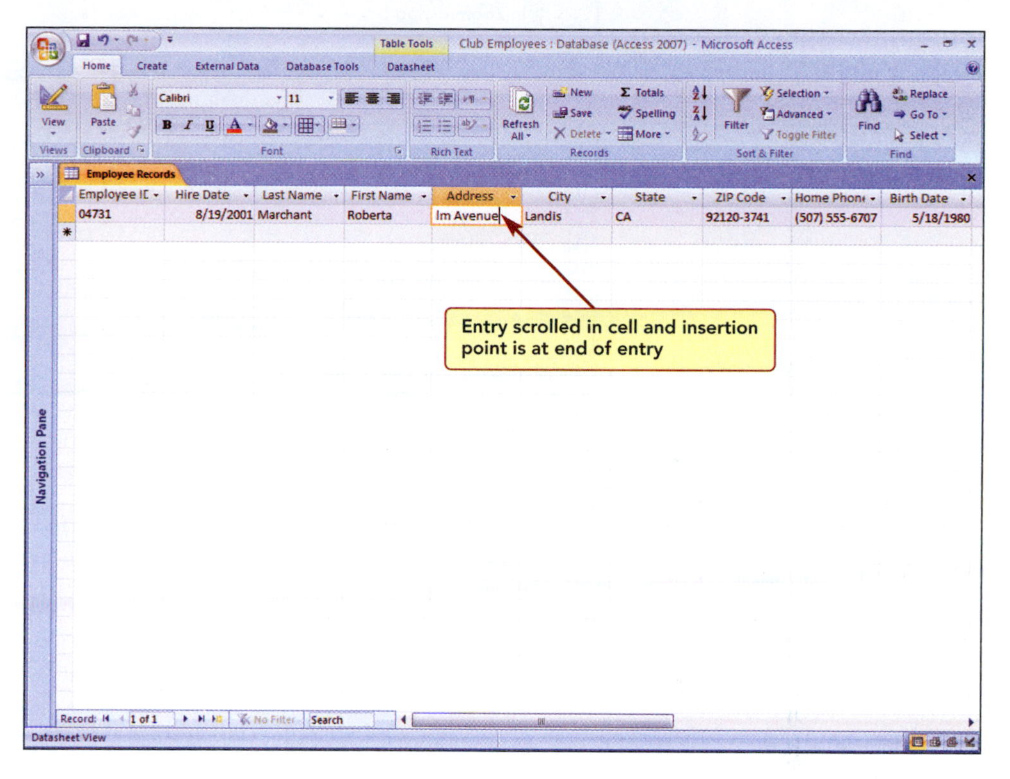

Figure 1.43

The text scrolled in the field, and the insertion point is positioned at the end of the entry. However, now you cannot see the beginning of the entry, which makes it difficult to edit. Another way to view the field's contents is to expand the field.

 **Press** Shift + F2.

Your screen should be similar to Figure 1.44

Figure 1.44

The entry is fully displayed in the Zoom dialog box. You can edit in the dialog box just as you can in the field.

3 • **If the entry contains an error, correct it.**

• **Click** OK.

• **Press** Tab.

Additional Information

You also can use the horizontal scroll bar to scroll the window and check fields that are not currently visible.

• **Continue to check the first record for accuracy and edit as needed.**

• **Enter the data shown in the table for the second record (you will leave the attachment field empty).**

• **Check the second record for accuracy and edit it if necessary.**

• **Move to the first field of the blank record row.**

Your screen should be similar to Figure 1.45

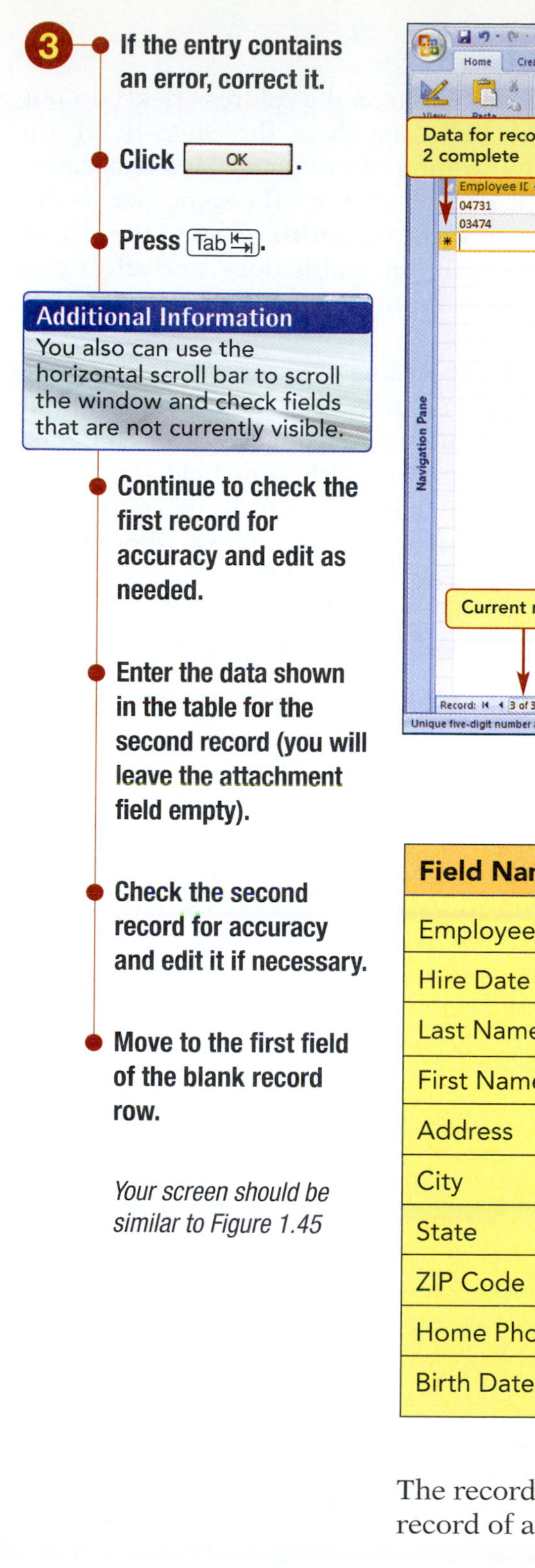

Figure 1.45

Field Name	Data
Employee ID	**03474**
Hire Date	**June 3, 2003**
Last Name	**Driscoll**
First Name	**Andy**
Address	**1903 25th Street**
City	**Maldin**
State	**CA**
ZIP Code	**92121-3740**
Home Phone	**(507) 555-4494**
Birth Date	**October 10, 1979**

The record indicator in the status bar tells you that record 3 is the current record of a total of three records.

Changing Column Width

As you have noticed, some of the fields (such as the Address field) do not display the entire entry, while other fields (such as the State field) are much larger than the field's column heading or contents. This is because the default width of a column in the datasheet is not the same size as the field sizes you specified in Design view. **Column width** refers to the size of a field column in a datasheet. The column width does not affect the amount of data you can enter into a field, but it does affect the data that you can see.

> **Additional Information**
> The default datasheet column width is set to display 15.6667 characters.

You can adjust the column width to change the appearance of the datasheet. Usually you should adjust the column width so that the column is slightly larger than the column heading or longest field contents, whichever is longer. Do not confuse column width with field size. Field size is a property associated with each field; it controls the maximum number of characters that you can enter in the field. If you shorten the field size, you can lose data already entered in the field.

Resizing a Column

The first thing you want to do is make the Address column wider so that you can see each complete field entry without having to move to the field and scroll or expand the field box. There are several ways that you can manipulate the rows and columns of a datasheet so that it is easier to view and work with the table data.

To quickly resize a column, simply drag the right column border line in the field selector in either direction to increase or decrease the column width. The mouse pointer shape is ↔ when you can drag to size the column. As you drag, a column line appears to show you the new column border. When you release the mouse button, the column width will be set. First you will increase the width of the Address field so that the entire address will be visible.

1

- **Point to the right column border line in the field selector for the Address field.**
- **When the mouse pointer is ↔, click and drag to the right until you think the column width will be wide enough to display the field contents.**
- **Adjust the column width again if it is too wide or not wide enough.**

Another Method

You also can adjust the column width to a specific number of characters using More in the Records group of the Home tab and choosing Column Width. This command is also on the shortcut menu when an entire column is selected.

Your screen should be similar to Figure 1.46

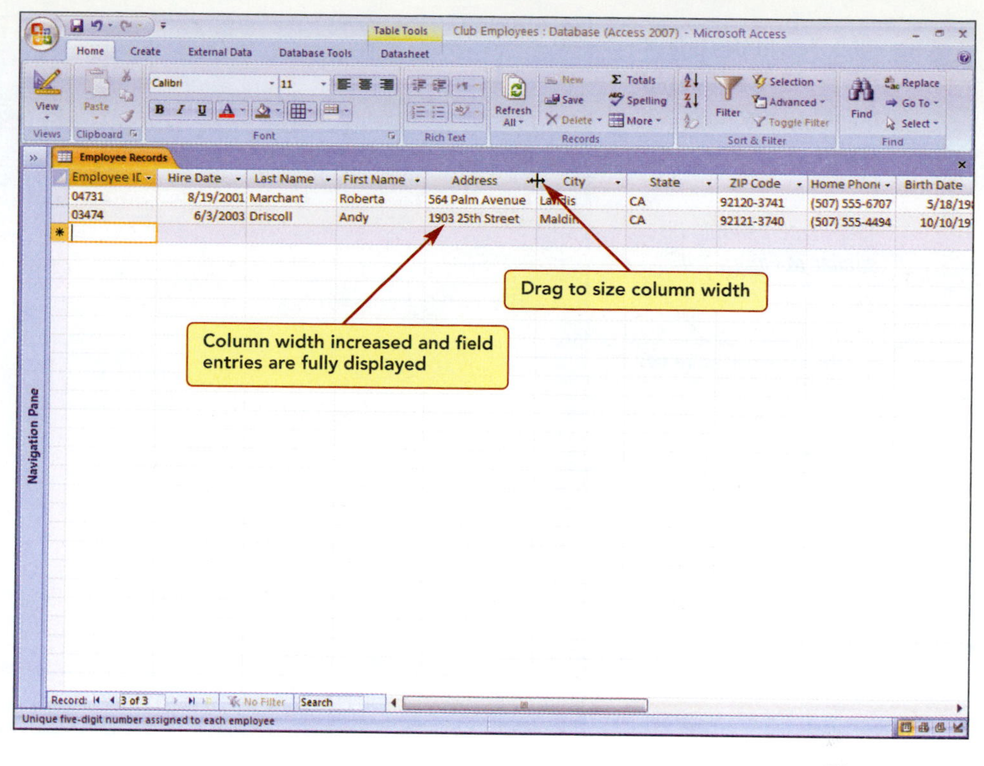

Figure 1.46

Using Best Fit

Rather than change the widths of all the other columns individually, you can select all columns and change their widths at the same time using the **Best Fit** feature. To select multiple columns, point to the column heading in the header row of the first or last column you want to select. Then, when the mouse pointer changes to ⬇, click, and without releasing the mouse button, drag in either direction across the column headings.

1 Click ▢ to the left of the first field name to quickly select the entire table.

Your screen should be similar to Figure 1.47

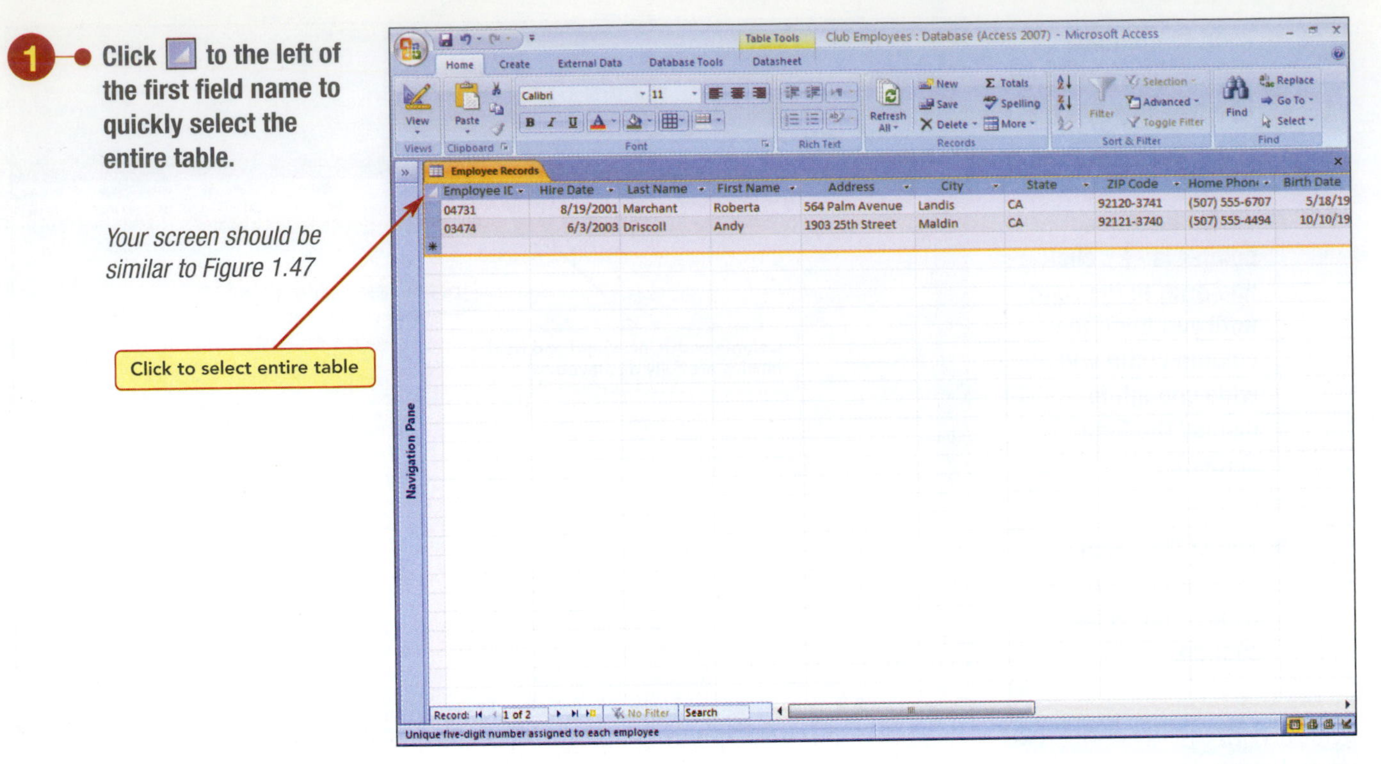

Figure 1.47

All the table columns are highlighted. Now, if you were to drag the column border of any selected column, all the selected columns would change to the same size. However, you want the column widths to be adjusted appropriately to fit the data in each column. To do this, you can double-click the column border to activate the Best Fit feature. The Best Fit feature automatically adjusts the column widths of all selected columns to accommodate the longest entry or column heading in each of the selected columns.

2 **Double-click any column border line (in the field selector row) when the mouse pointer is ↔.**

Click anywhere on the table to deselect the datasheet.

Another Method

You also can use More in the Records group of the Home tab and choose Column Width/Best Fit.

Your screen should be similar to Figure 1.48

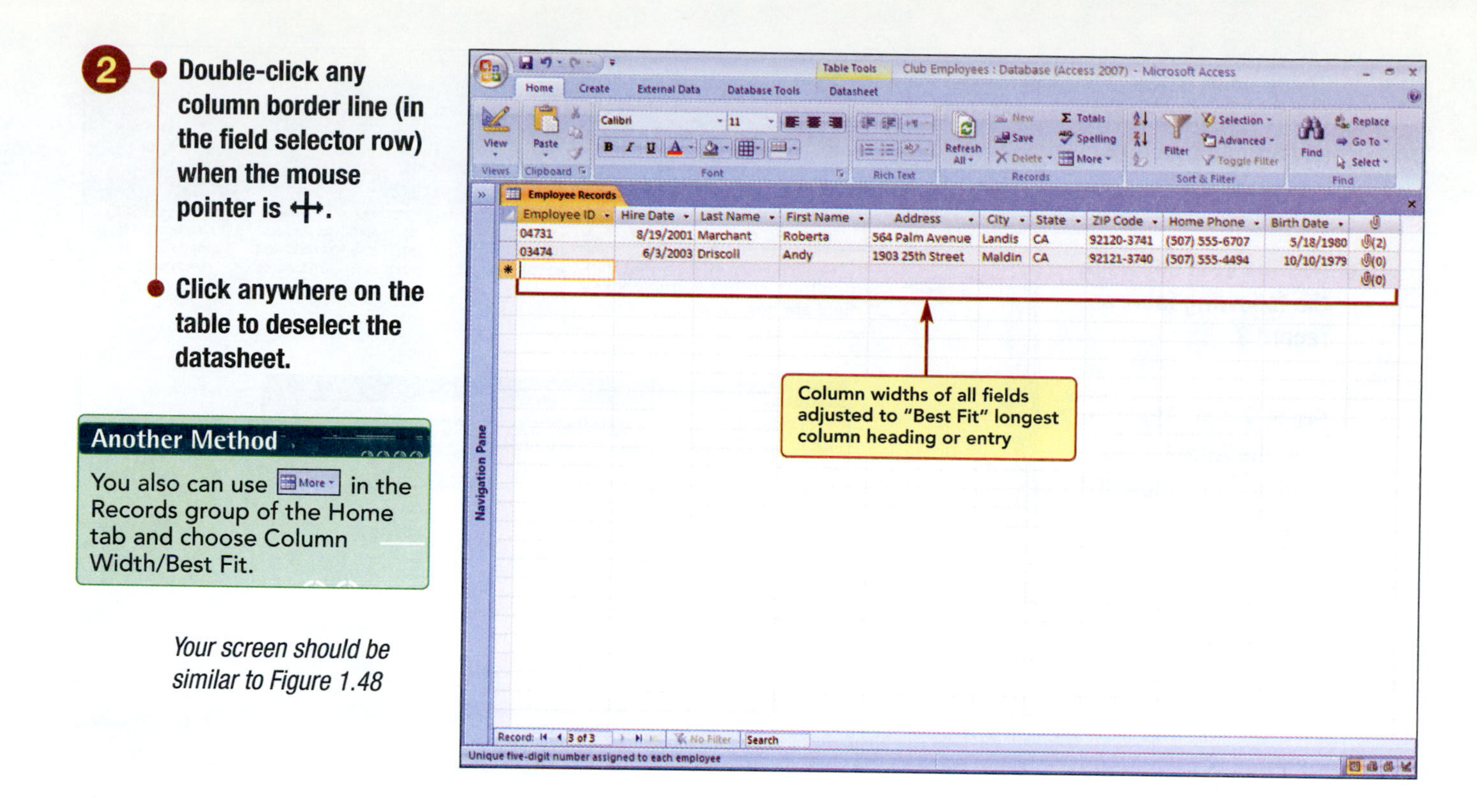

Figure 1.48

The column widths for each field have been sized to accommodate the longest entry or column heading. As you add more records to the table that contain longer field entries, you will need to use Best Fit again to readjust the column widths.

- **Check each of the records again and edit any entries that are incorrect.**
- **Add the data shown in the following table as record 3.**
- **Press ←Enter twice to skip the Attachment field and complete the record.**

Your screen should be similar to Figure 1.49

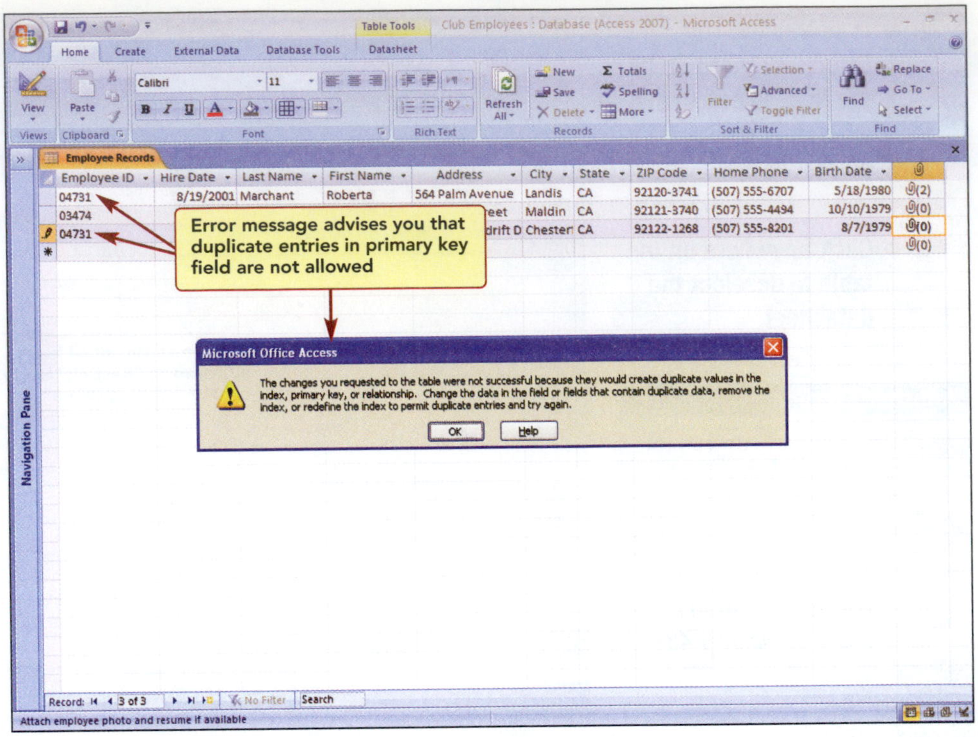

Figure 1.49

Field Name	Data
Employee ID	**04731**
Hire Date	**April 12, 2004**
Last Name	**Delano**
First Name	**Gordon**
Address	**1310 N. Spindrift Drive**
City	**Chesterfield**
State	**CA**
ZIP Code	**92122-1268**
Phone	**(507) 555-8201**
Birth Date	**August 7, 1979**

As soon as you complete the record, an error message dialog box appears indicating that Access has located a duplicate value in a key field. The key field is Employee ID. You realize you were looking at the employee number from Roberta Marchant's record when you entered the employee number for this record. You need to clear the message and enter the correct number.

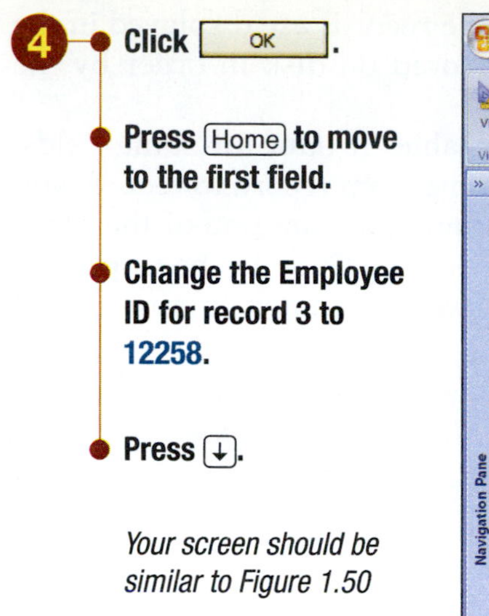

4 Click OK.

- Press Home to move to the first field.
- Change the Employee ID for record 3 to **12258**.
- Press ↓.

Your screen should be similar to Figure 1.50

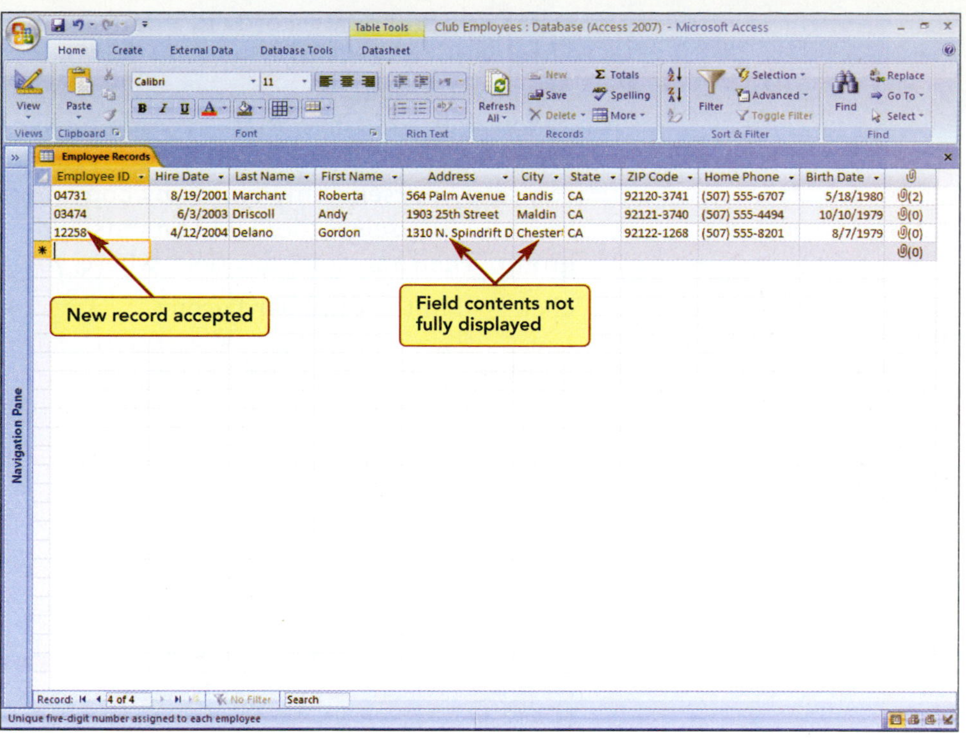

Figure 1.50

The record is accepted with the new employee number. However, you notice that the address and city for this record are not fully displayed in the fields.

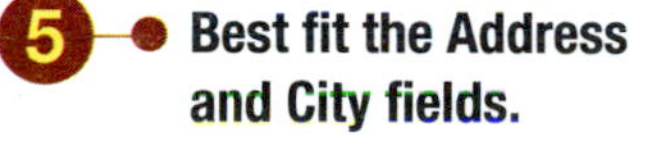

5 Best fit the Address and City fields.

Your screen should be similar to Figure 1.51

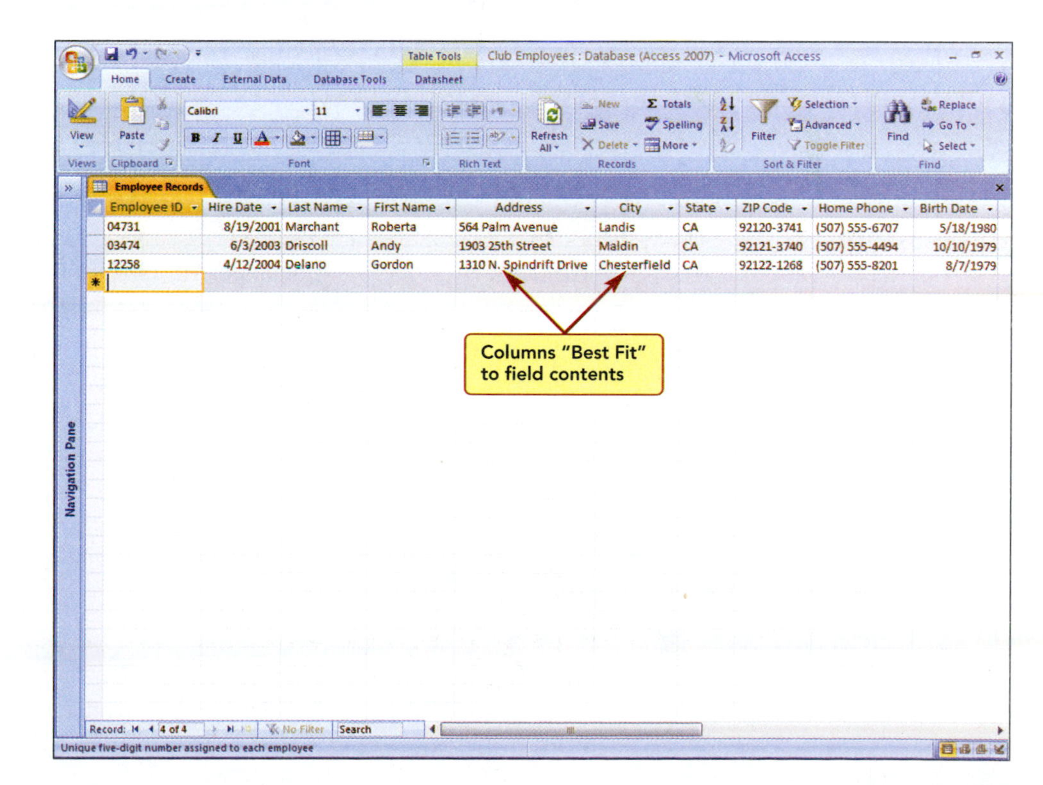

Figure 1.51

When you add new records in a datasheet, the records are displayed in the order you enter them. However, they are stored on disk in order by the primary key field.

You will add three more records to the table. If data for some fields, such as the City, State, or ZIP Code, is the same from record to record, you can save yourself some typing by copying the data from one of the other records. Just select the field contents and click Copy in the Clipboard group. Then move to the field where you want the copy to appear and click Paste in the Clipboard group.

6 Enter the data for the two records shown in the following table.

Field	Record 4	Record 5
Employee ID	13635	12583
Hire Date	January 2, 2007	April 20, 2007
Last Name	Martinez	Sullivan
First Name	Juan	Marie
Address	1920 First Avenue	78 Omega Drive
City	Maldin	Chesterfield
State	CA	CA
ZIP Code	92121-3740	92122-1268
Phone	(507) 555-2935	(507) 555-7890
Birth Date	December 10, 1982	March 15, 1981

7. **Enter a final record using your first and last names. Enter 99999 as your employee number and the current date as your date hired. The information you enter in all other fields can be fictitious.**

- **Check each of the records and correct any entry errors.**

Your screen should be similar to Figure 1.52

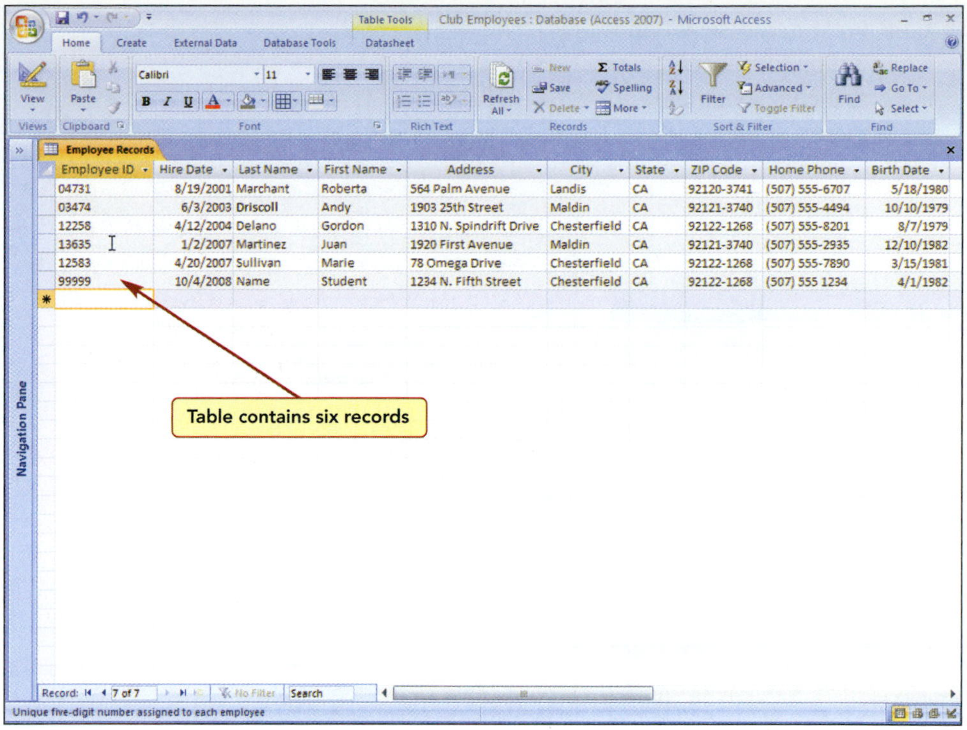

Club Employees : Database (Access 2007) - Microsoft Access
Table Tools
Home Create External Data Database Tools Datasheet
Employee Records
Employee ID Hire Date Last Name First Name Address City State ZIP Code Home Phone Birth Date
04731 8/19/2001 Marchant Roberta 564 Palm Avenue Landis CA 92120-3741 (507) 555-6707 5/18/1980
03474 6/3/2003 Driscoll Andy 1903 25th Street Maldin CA 92121-3740 (507) 555-4494 10/10/1979
12258 4/12/2004 Delano Gordon 1310 N. Spindrift Drive Chesterfield CA 92122-1268 (507) 555-8201 8/7/1979
13635 1/2/2007 Martinez Juan 1920 First Avenue Maldin CA 92121-3740 (507) 555-2935 12/10/1982
12583 4/20/2007 Sullivan Marie 78 Omega Drive Chesterfield CA 92122-1268 (507) 555-7890 3/15/1981
99999 10/4/2008 Name Student 1234 N. Fifth Street Chesterfield CA 92122-1268 (507) 555 1234 4/1/1982
Table contains six records
Navigation Pane
Record: 7 of 7
Unique five-digit number assigned to each employee

Figure 1.52

There are now a total of six records in the table

Deleting Records

While you are entering the employee records, you find a memo from one of your managers stating that Andy Driscoll is no longer working at the club and asking you to remove his record from the employee files.

You can remove records from a table by selecting the entire record and pressing the Delete key. After pressing Delete, you will be asked to confirm that you really want to delete the selected record. This is because this action cannot be reversed.

Another Method

You also can move to the record and choose Select from the Select drop-down list in the Find group of the Home tab.

Additional Information

You can select multiple noncontiguous records by holding down Ctrl while clicking the Select All button of each record. To select contiguous records, click and drag along the Select All buttons.

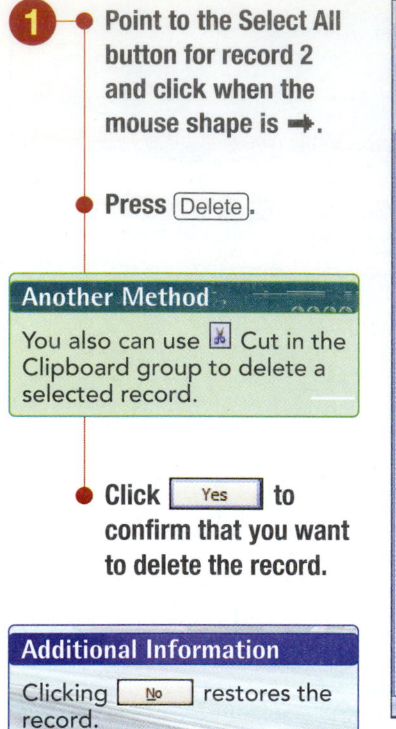

1. Point to the Select All button for record 2 and click when the mouse shape is ➡.
   - Press Delete.

Another Method

You also can use Cut in the Clipboard group to delete a selected record.

   - Click Yes to confirm that you want to delete the record.

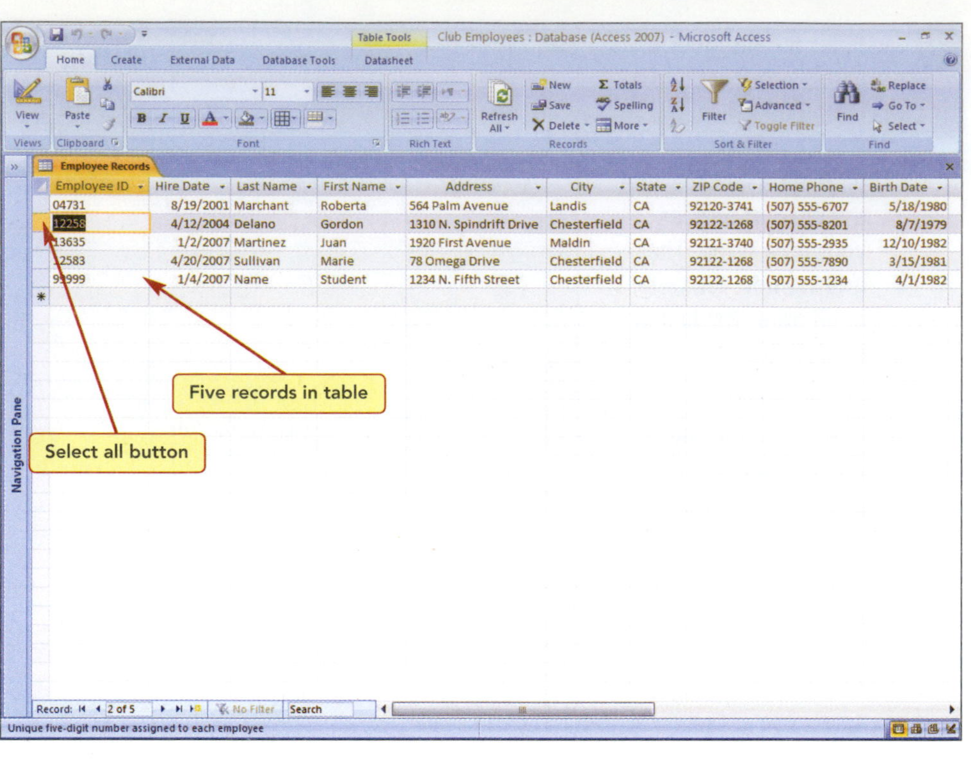

Additional Information

Clicking No restores the record.

Figure 1.53

Your screen should be similar to Figure 1.53

The table now consists of five employee records.

Another Method

You also can choose Delete Record from the Delete drop-down list in the Records group of the Home tab. The current record is both selected and deleted at the same time.

Creating a Second Table

Following your plan for the employee database, you will add another table to the existing database file. This table will hold information about the employee's work location and job title.

There are several ways to create a new table in an existing database. You can insert a blank table and define the fields in datasheet view as you already did or you can create a table based on a table template. You also can import from or link to data from another source, such as another database, an Excel worksheet, or a SharePoint list. Finally, you can create a new table starting in Design view. You will use this last method to define the two fields in the table, club location and job title.

Additional Information

A SharePoint list is a list of data that is stored on a SharePoint server and is available to others in an organization.

1. Open the Create tab and click Table Design in the Tables group.

   - Define the fields using the settings shown in the following table.

Your screen should be similar to Figure 1.54

Figure 1.54

Field Name	Data Type	Field Size
Location	Text	20
Job Title	Text	50

The new table has a default table name of Table1 displayed in the table tab.

Adding an Existing Field

As you look at the design, you realize you need to include a field that will be used to refer back to the primary key field of the Employee Records table in order to create an association between the two tables. A field that refers to the primary key field in another table is called a **foreign key** field. The new table will use the same field as the Employee Records table, employee number, as the foreign key field. The field names of these two fields do not have to match, although their data types must be the same. Instead of recreating the field, you will copy it from the Employee Records table into the new table.

1. Switch to Datasheet view.
   - Click Yes to save the table.
   - Enter **Job** as the table name and click OK.
   - Click No in response to the prompt to create a primary key.
   - Display the Navigation pane.
   - Open the Table Tools Datasheet tab and click Add Existing Fields from the Fields & Columns group.

Your screen should be similar to Figure 1.55

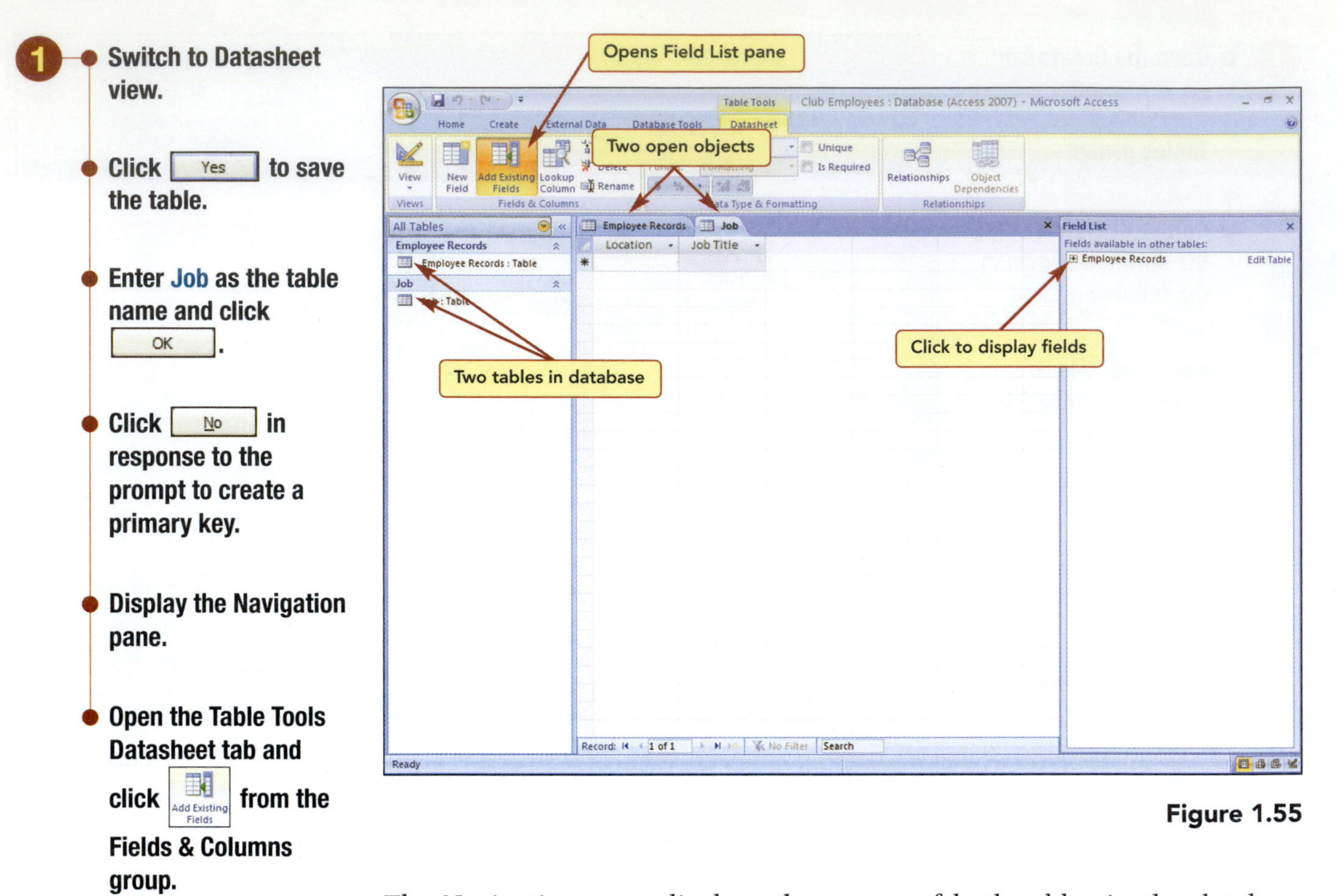

Figure 1.55

The Navigation pane displays the names of both tables in the database and a tab for both open objects appears above the work area. A Field List pane appears on the right side of the work area. It displays the name of the only other table in the database, Employee Records. Clicking the ⊞ next to the table name will display a list of the fields in the table. Then you can select and drag the field name to the new table, much as you did when using the Field Templates pane. When the insertion bar appears where you want the new field inserted, drop the field in position. You also can double-click on the field name and it will be inserted in the next empty field column in the datasheet.

2

- **Click ⊞ to display the field names.**
- **Select the Employee ID field.**
- **Drag the field from the pane and drop it to the left of the Location field.**

Your screen should be similar to Figure 1.56

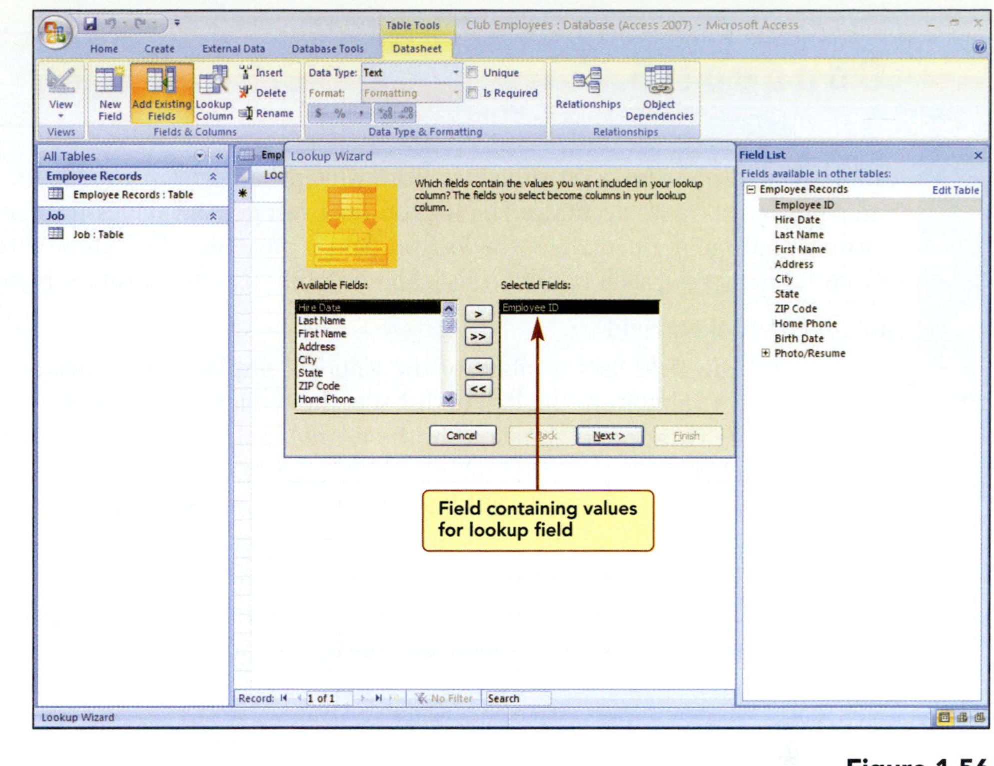

Figure 1.56

Using the Lookup Wizard

The **Lookup Wizard** automatically starts and is used to create a lookup field that will allow you to select from a list of values when entering the employee number into the new table. A **wizard** is a feature that guides you step by step through the process to perform a task.

Concept 6

Lookup Field

6 A **lookup field** provides a list of values from which the user can choose to make entering data into that field simpler and more accurate. The lookup field can get the values from an existing table or a fixed set of values that are defined when the lookup field is created. A lookup field that uses another table as the **source** for values is called a **lookup list**, and one that uses fixed values is called a **value list**.

Lookup List Lookup Field

When the lookup field uses a table for the values it displays, an association is created between the two tables. Picking a value from the lookup list sets the foreign key value in the current record to the primary key value of the corresponding record in the related table. A foreign key is a field in one table that refers to the primary key field in another table and indicates how the tables are related. The field names of these two fields do not have to match, although their data types must be the same.

The related table displays but does not store the data in the record. The foreign key is stored but does not display. For this reason, any updates made to the data in the related table will be reflected in both the list and records in the table containing the lookup field. You must define a lookup list field from the table that will contain the foreign key and display the lookup list.

Value List Lookup Field

A lookup field that uses a fixed list of values looks the same as a lookup field that uses a table, except the fixed set of values is entered when the lookup field is created. A value list should be used only for values that will not change very often and do not need to be stored in a table. For example, a list for a Salutation field containing the abbreviations Mr., Mrs., or Ms. would be a good candidate for a value list. Choosing a value from a value list will store that value in the record—it does not create an association to a related table. For this reason, if you change any of the original values in the value list later, they will not be reflected in records added before this change was made.

Additional Information

You will create a value list lookup field in Lab 2.

In the first Lookup Wizard dialog box, you specify the source for the values for the lookup field. The Employee ID field is already correctly selected.

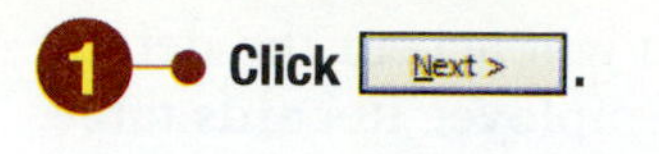

Your screen should be similar to Figure 1.57

Figure 1.57

The next step is to specify a sort order. Since the items will automatically appear in the same order as in the Employee Records table, you can skip this step and move to the next step to specify the column width. Again, you want to use the same width setting you established in the Employee Records table so you will skip this step as well.

Your screen should be similar to Figure 1.58

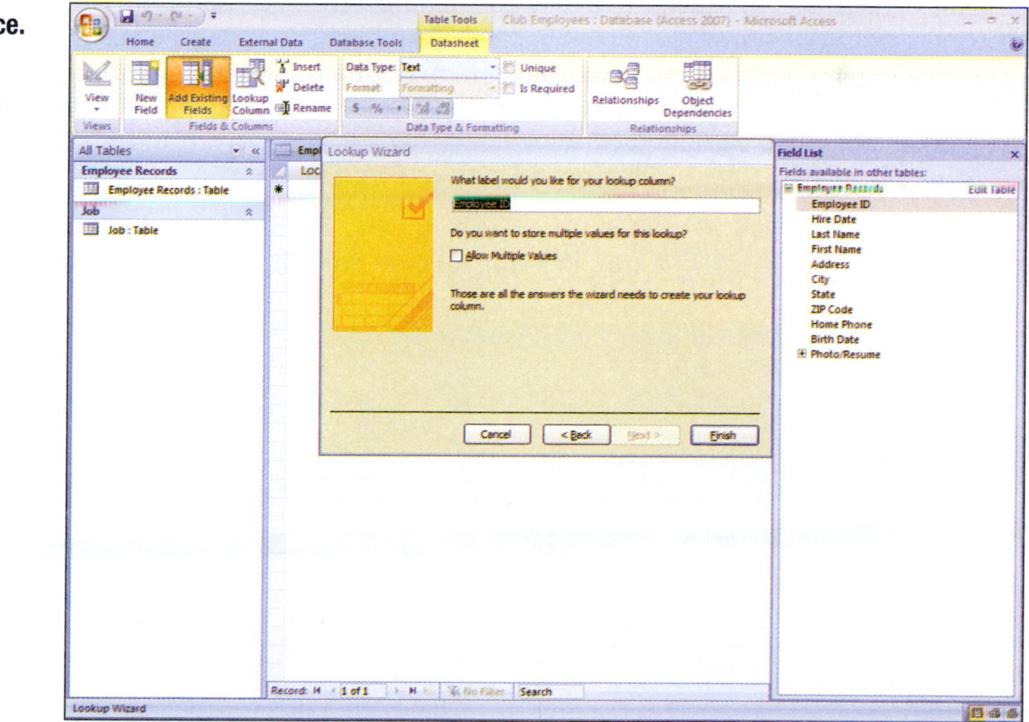

Figure 1.58

Finally, you are asked to specify a field name. You will accept the default name, which is the same as the name used in the Employee Records table.

3 **Click** Finish.

- **Close the Field List pane.**
- **Switch to Design view.**
- **Select the Employee ID field.**
- **Open the Lookup tab in the Field Properties area.**

Your screen should be similar to Figure 1.59

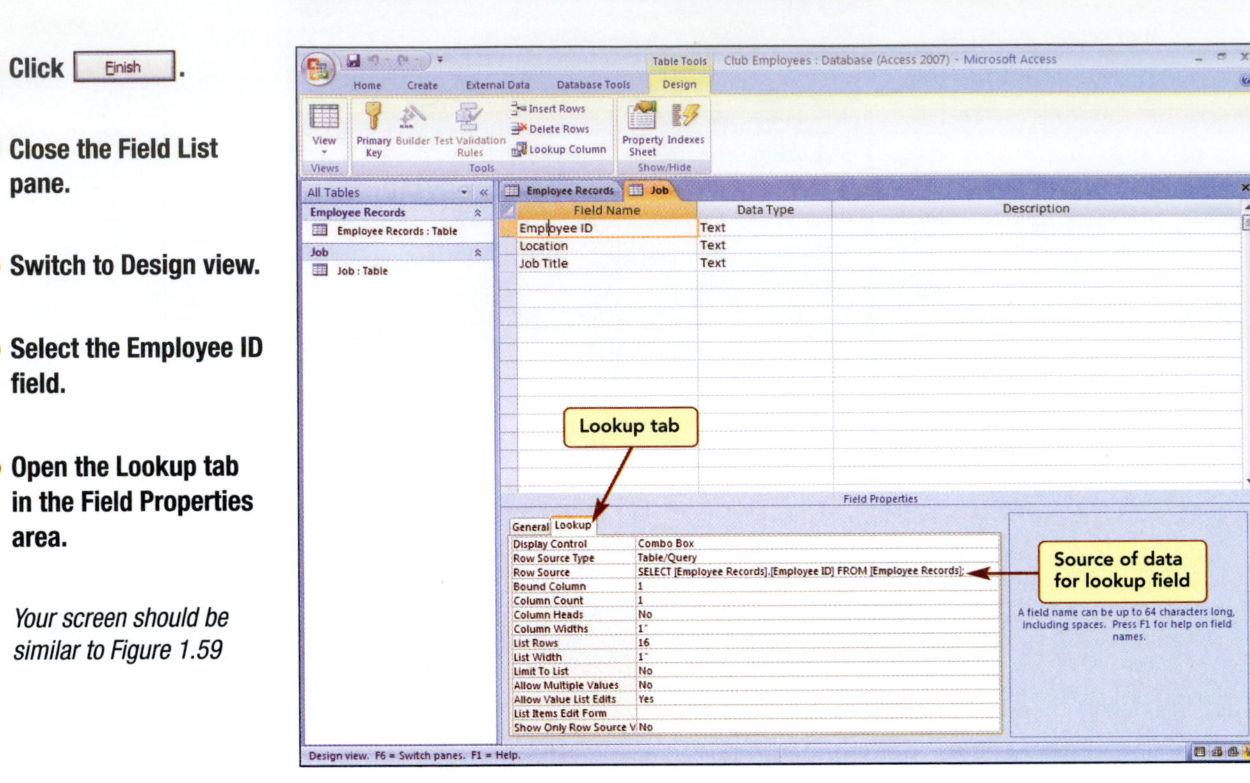

Figure 1.59

The new field has been added to the table and includes the same properties as the Employee ID field in the Employee Records table. It is a primary key field with a field size of 5. In addition, an association between the two tables has been established, as can be seen in the Row Source row of the Lookup properties, which identifies the source of the data for this row as the Employee Records table.

Additional Information
You will learn about table relationships in later labs.

Using a Lookup Field

Next, you will use the Employee ID lookup field to enter the employee numbers for each record. Then you will complete the information for each record.

1

- **Switch to Datasheet view.**
- **If necessary, click in the Employee ID field to make it active.**
- **Click ▼ at the end of the box to open the drop-down list of options.**

Your screen should be similar to Figure 1.60

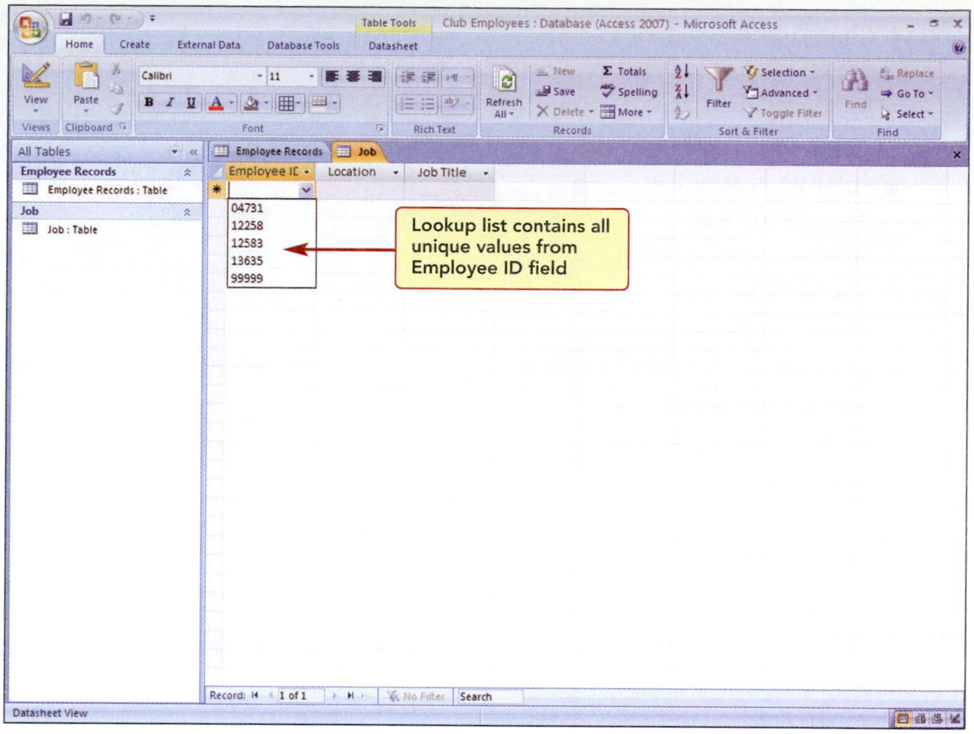

Figure 1.60

The lookup list displays a drop-down list of all the values in the Employee ID field of the Employee Records table. Clicking on an entry in the list inserts it into the field.

- Choose 04731 and press ←Enter to move to the Location field.
- Enter **River Mist** for the location and **Fitness Coordinator** for the job title.
- In a similar manner, add the remaining records (shown below) to the table.
- Best fit the columns.

Your screen should be similar to Figure 1.61

Field data added to table

Figure 1.61

ID	Location	Position
12258	Chesterfield	Food Service Manager
12583	Landis	Greeter
13635	Landis	Fitness Instructor
99999	Landis	Records Administrator

The table now includes information on the location and job titles for the same five records as in the Employee Records table.

Inserting a Field

As you consider the contents of the two tables, you realize that the Hire Date information also should be in the Job table because the subject matter is related to the employee's job, not to his or her personal information.

1

- Move to any row in the Location field.
- Click Insert in the Fields & Columns group of the Table Tools Datasheet tab to insert a blank field column to the left of the current column.
- Name the field **Hire Date**.
- Change the data type to Date/Time.
- Click Format: in the Data Type & Formatting group and choose Short Date.

Your screen should be similar to Figure 1.62

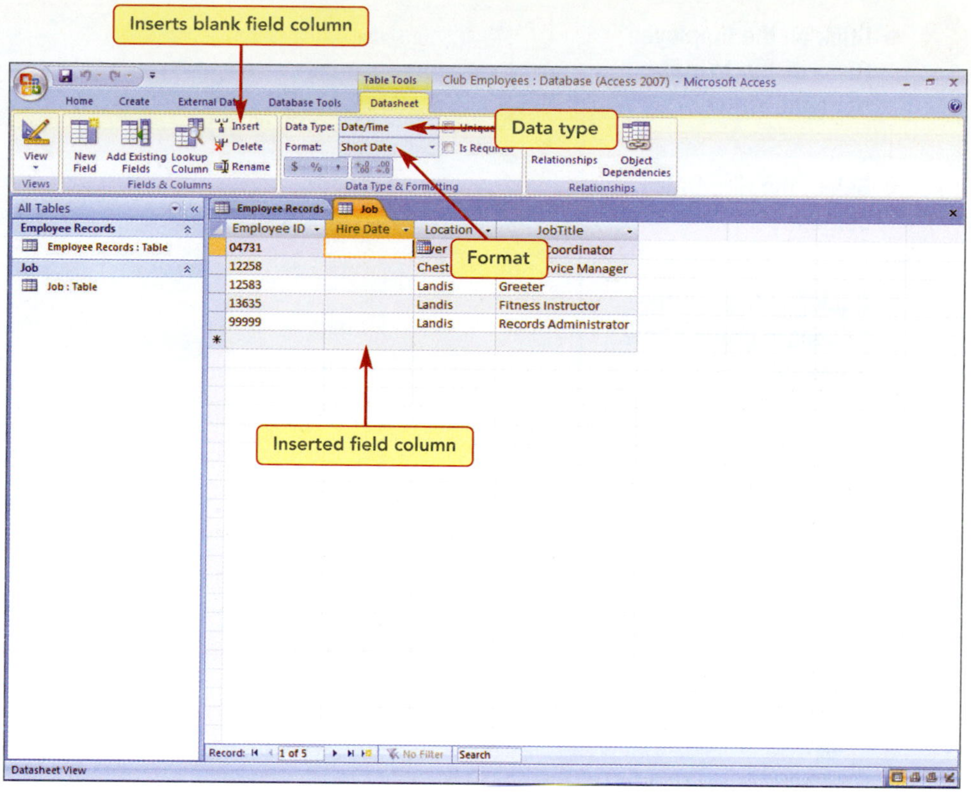

Inserts blank field column

Data type

Format

Inserted field column

Figure 1.62

The new field has been inserted and defined.

Copying Field Content

Next, you will copy the data from the Hire Date field in the Employee Records table to the new field in the Job table. A selection that is copied creates a duplicate of the original, called the *source*, and stores it in the **Clipboard,** a temporary storage area in memory. Then, to insert the copied data from the Clipboard, you paste it in a new location, called the **destination.**

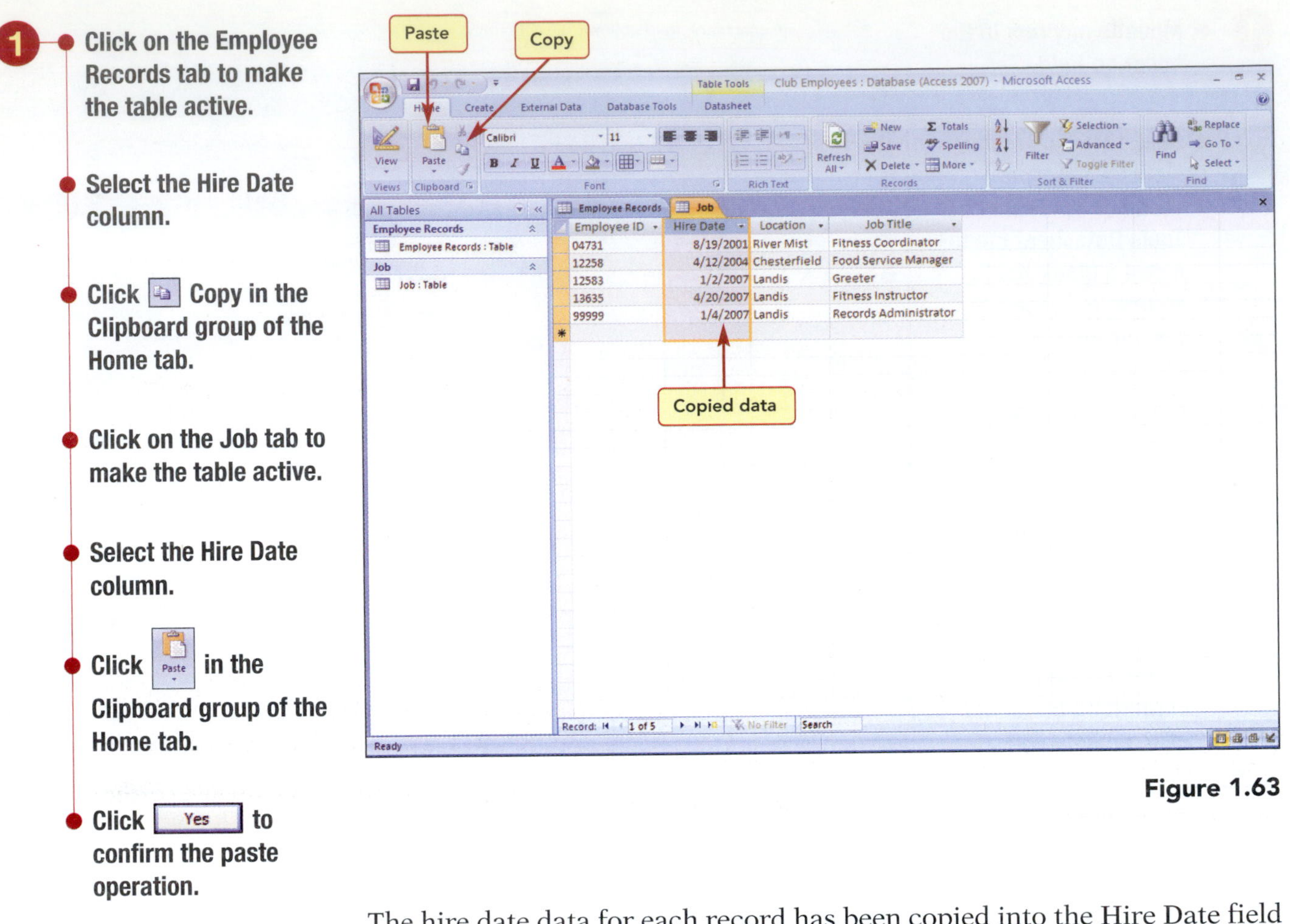

1

- **Click on the Employee Records tab to make the table active.**
- **Select the Hire Date column.**
- **Click Copy in the Clipboard group of the Home tab.**
- **Click on the Job tab to make the table active.**
- **Select the Hire Date column.**
- **Click Paste in the Clipboard group of the Home tab.**
- **Click Yes to confirm the paste operation.**

Your screen should be similar to Figure 1.63

Figure 1.63

The hire date data for each record has been copied into the Hire Date field of the Job table. All you need to do now is delete the Hire Date field in the Employee Records table.

2

- **Make the Employee Records table active.**
- **Delete the Hire Date field from the table.**

Now, the Employee Records table only contains the employee's personal information and the Job table contains information about the employee's job.

Previewing and Printing a Table

Now that you have completed designing and entering some sample data in the two tables, you want to print a copy of the tables to get your managers' approval before you begin entering more employee records. Before printing the tables, you will preview them onscreen to see how they will look when printed.

Previewing the Table

Previewing a table displays each page in a reduced size so you can see the layout. Then, if necessary, you can make changes to the layout before printing, to both save time and avoid wasting paper.

1

- **Make the Job table active.**
- **Click Office Button.**
- **Select Print and choose Print Preview.**
- **Hide the Navigation pane.**

Your screen should be similar to Figure 1.64

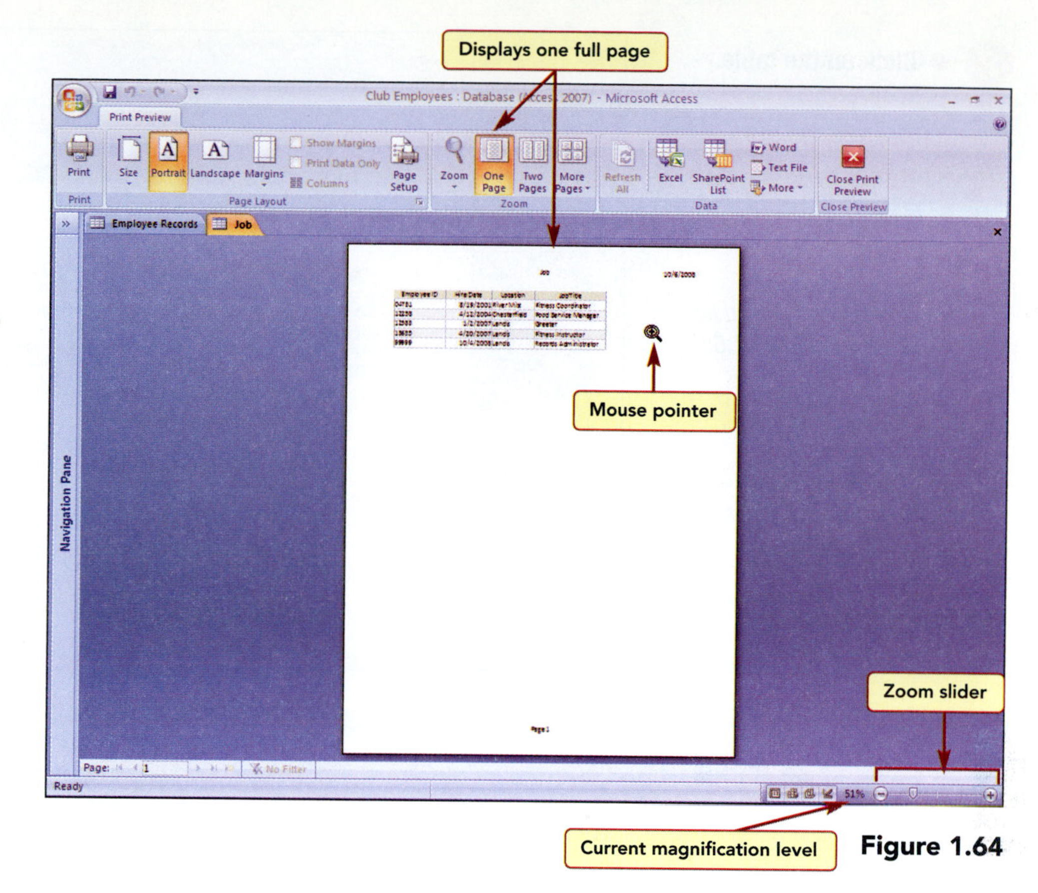

Figure 1.64

The Print Preview window displays how the table will appear when printed. The Print Preview tab is open and includes commands that are used to modify the print settings.

To see the information in the table more clearly, you can change the magnification level of the preview window. The current setting, One Page, adjusts the magnification to display an entire page in the preview window. You can drag the zoom slider in the status bar to increase the onscreen character size up to 10 times the normal display (1000 percent) or reduce the character size to 10 percent. Clicking ⊖ or ⊕ on the zoom slider increases or decreases the magnification by 10 percent increments.

> **Additional Information**
> The current magnification level is displayed in the status bar.

Notice that the mouse pointer is a magnifying glass when it is positioned on the page. This indicates that you can click on the page to switch between the One Page setting and the last-used magnification level (initially 100%).

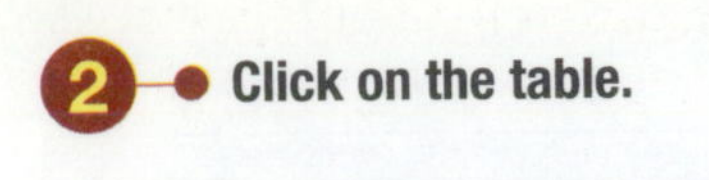

2 Click on the table.

Additional Information

The location where you click will determine the area that is displayed initially.

Your screen should be similar to Figure 1.65

Page displayed at 100% magnification

Figure 1.65

The table appears in 100 percent magnification. This is the size it will appear when printed.

Printing a Table

The Print button in the Print group is used to define the printer settings and print the document.

1 If necessary, make sure your printer is on and ready to print.

Click Print.

Another Method

The keyboard shortcut is Ctrl + P.

Your screen should be similar to Figure 1.66

Having Trouble?

Please consult your instructor for printing procedures that may differ from the directions given here.

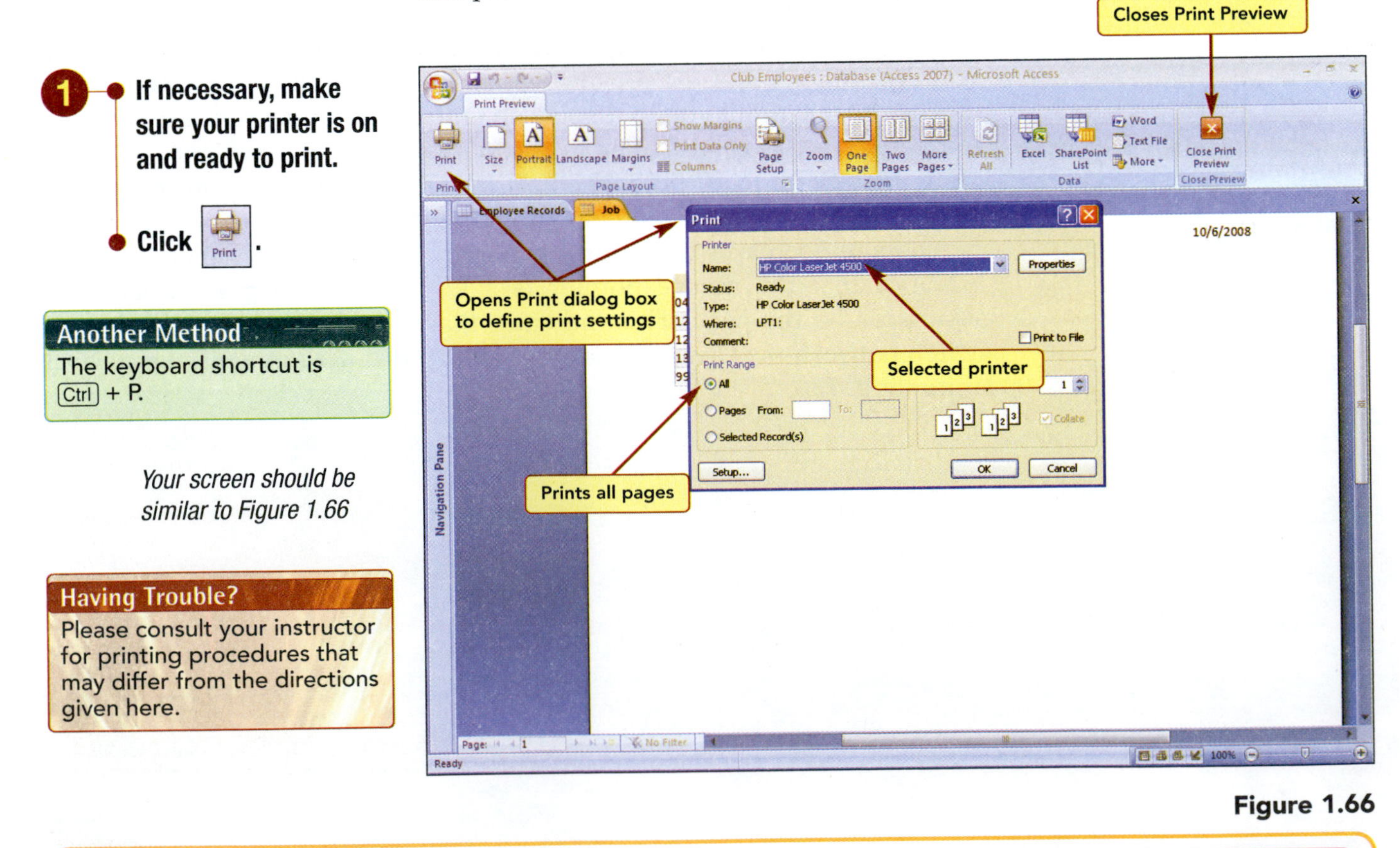

Figure 1.66

From the Print dialog box, you specify the printer you will be using and the document settings. The printer that is currently selected is displayed in the Name drop-down list box in the Printer section of the dialog box.

The Print Range area of the Print dialog box lets you specify the amount of the document you want printed. The range options are described in the following table.

Option	Action
All	Prints the entire document.
Pages	Prints pages you specify by typing page numbers in the text box.
Selected Records	Prints selected records only.

You will print the entire document.

2

- **If you need to change the selected printer to another printer, open the Name drop-down list box and select the appropriate printer (your instructor will tell you which printer to select).**
- **Click OK.**

A status message box is displayed briefly, informing you that the table is being printed. Your printed copy should be similar to the printout shown in the Case Study at the beginning of the lab.

Changing the Page Orientation and Margins

Next, you will preview and print the Employee Records table.

1

- **Click Close Print Preview in the Close Preview group.**
- **Make the Employee Records table active.**
- **Click Office Button.**
- **Select Print and choose Print Preview.**
- **Click on the table to zoom the preview.**

Your screen should look similar to Figure 1.67

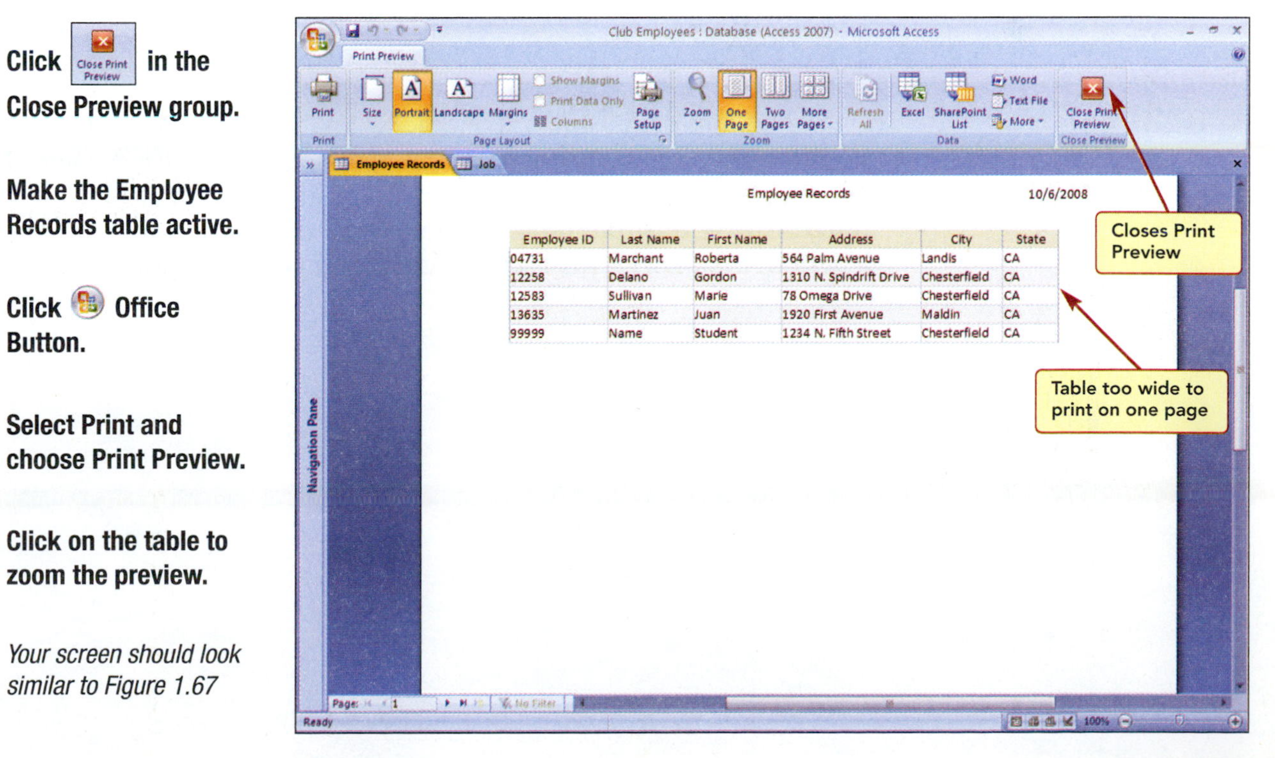

Figure 1.67

Notice that because the table is too wide to fit across the width of a page, only the first six fields are displayed on the page. Tables with multiple columns are typically too wide to fit on an 8$^1/_2$ by 11 piece of paper. You would like to see both pages displayed onscreen.

2 **Click** Two Pages **in the Zoom group.**

Your screen should be similar to Figure 1.68

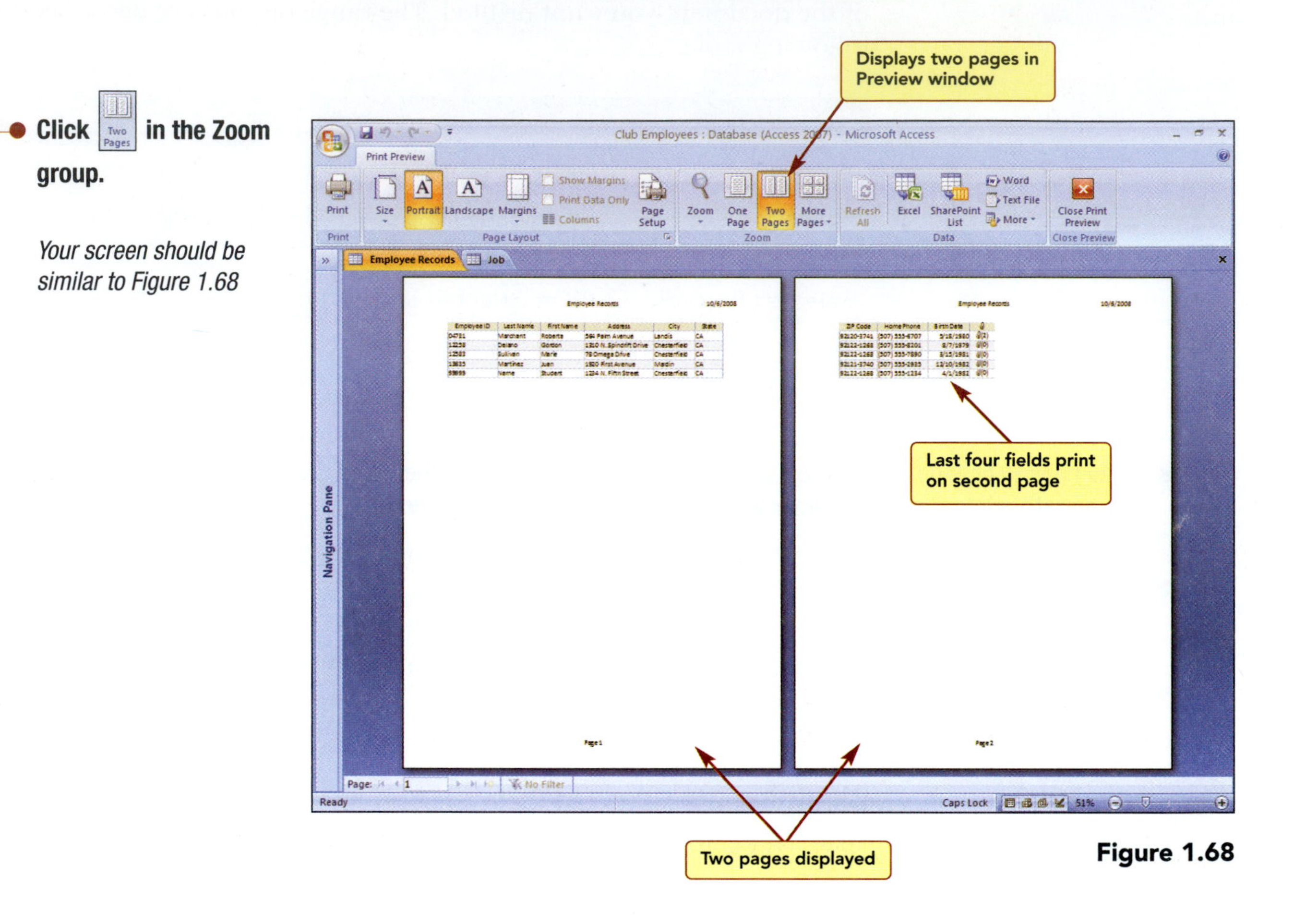

Figure 1.68

Rather than print the table on two pages, you decide to see whether changing the orientation of the table will allow you to print it on one page. **Orientation** refers to the direction that text prints on a page. Normal orientation is to print across the width of an 8$^1/_2$-inch page. This is called **portrait orientation.** You can change the orientation to print across the length of the paper. This is called **landscape orientation.**

3 Click [Landscape] in the Page Layout group.

Additional Information

Clicking [Portrait] changes the orientation to portrait.

Your screen should be similar to Figure 1.69

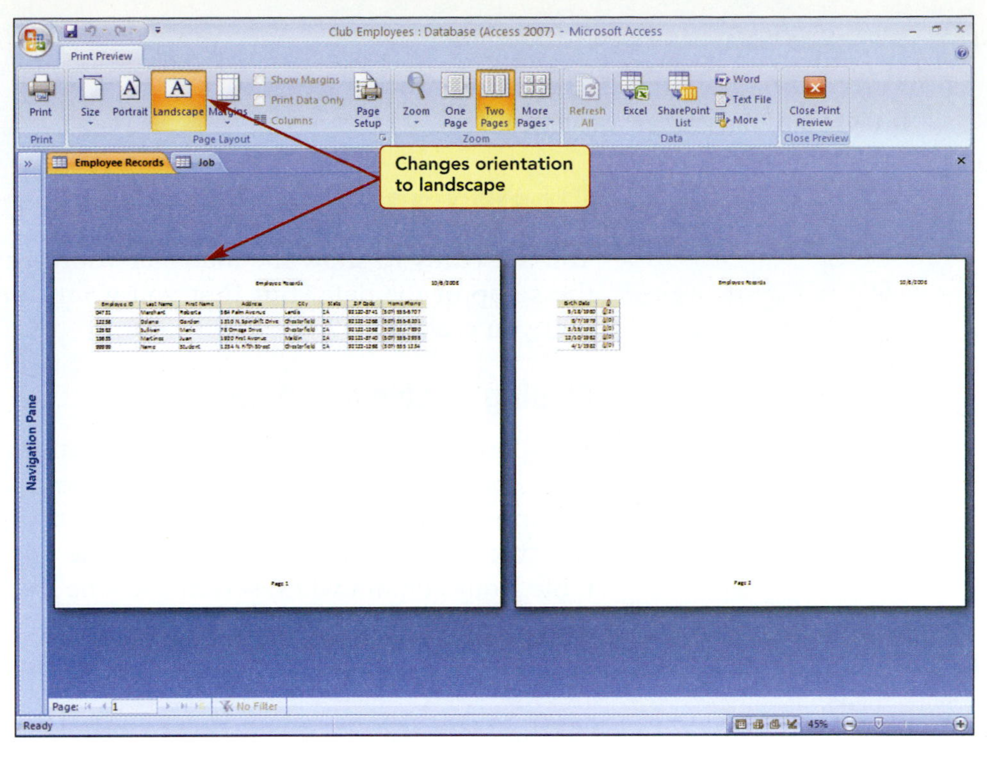

Figure 1.69

Although this helps, there are still two fields that do not fit on the page. To fix this, you will try reducing the size of the page margins. The **margin** is the blank space around the edge of a page. You will decrease the right and left margin settings to 0.25 inch to see if this helps all fields fit on the page.

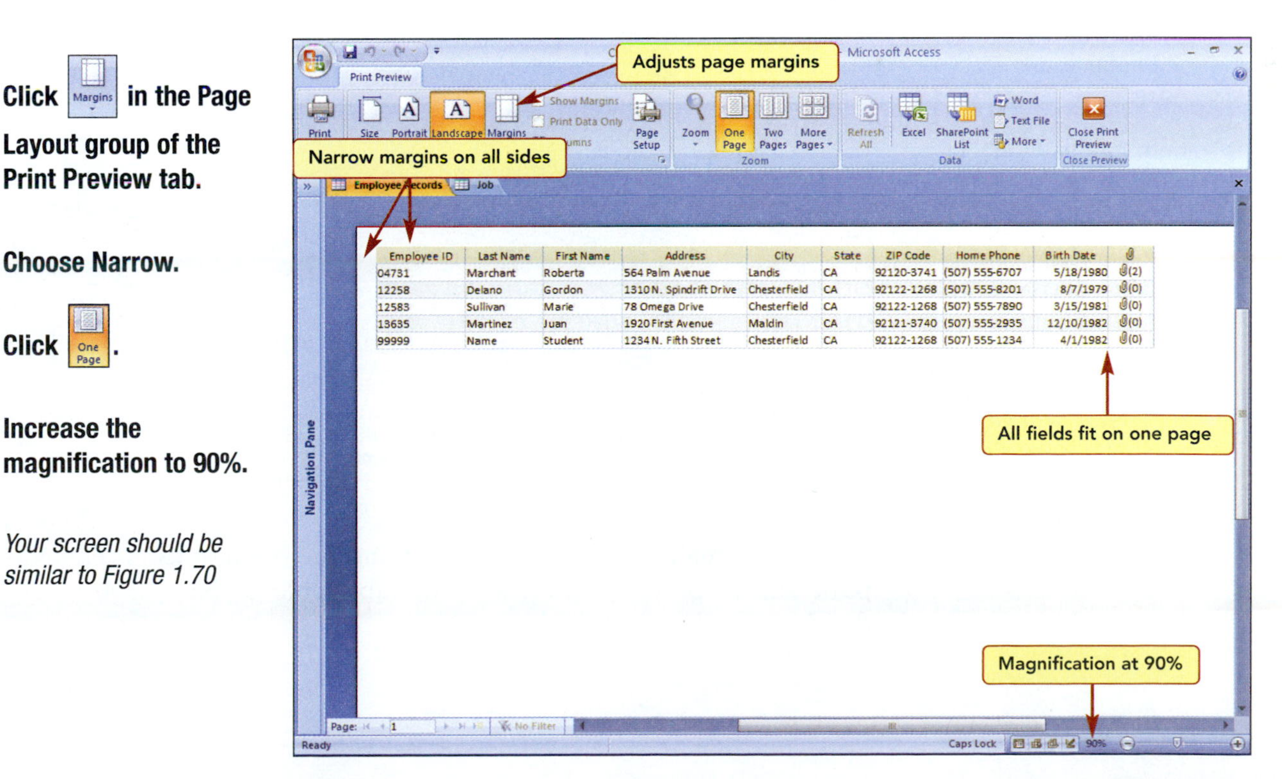

4 Click [Margins] in the Page Layout group of the Print Preview tab.

- Choose Narrow.
- Click [One Page].
- Increase the magnification to 90%.

Your screen should be similar to Figure 1.70

Figure 1.70

You can now see that all the fields will print on one page.

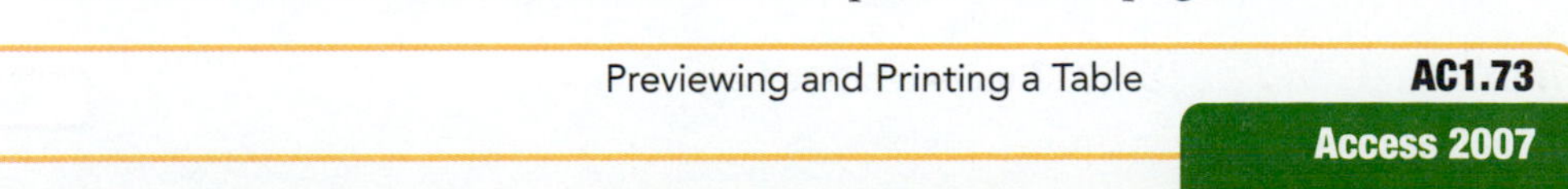

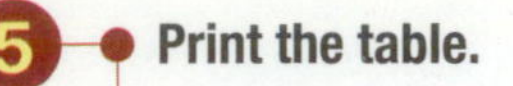

5 Print the table.

- Close the Print Preview window.

Closing and Opening a Table and Database

You are ready to show the manager your printed table to get approval on the setup of the data. But first you want to close the table and database that you created.

Closing a Table and Database

You close a table by closing its window and saving any layout changes you have made since your last Access session. Because you changed the column widths of the table in Datasheet view, you will be prompted to save the layout changes before the table is closed. If you do not save the table, your column width settings will be lost.

1 Display the Navigation pane.

- Click ☒ Close 'Employee Records' in the datasheet window.
- If necessary, click Yes in response to the prompt to save the table.
- In a similar manner, close the Job table.

Your screen should be similar to Figure 1.71

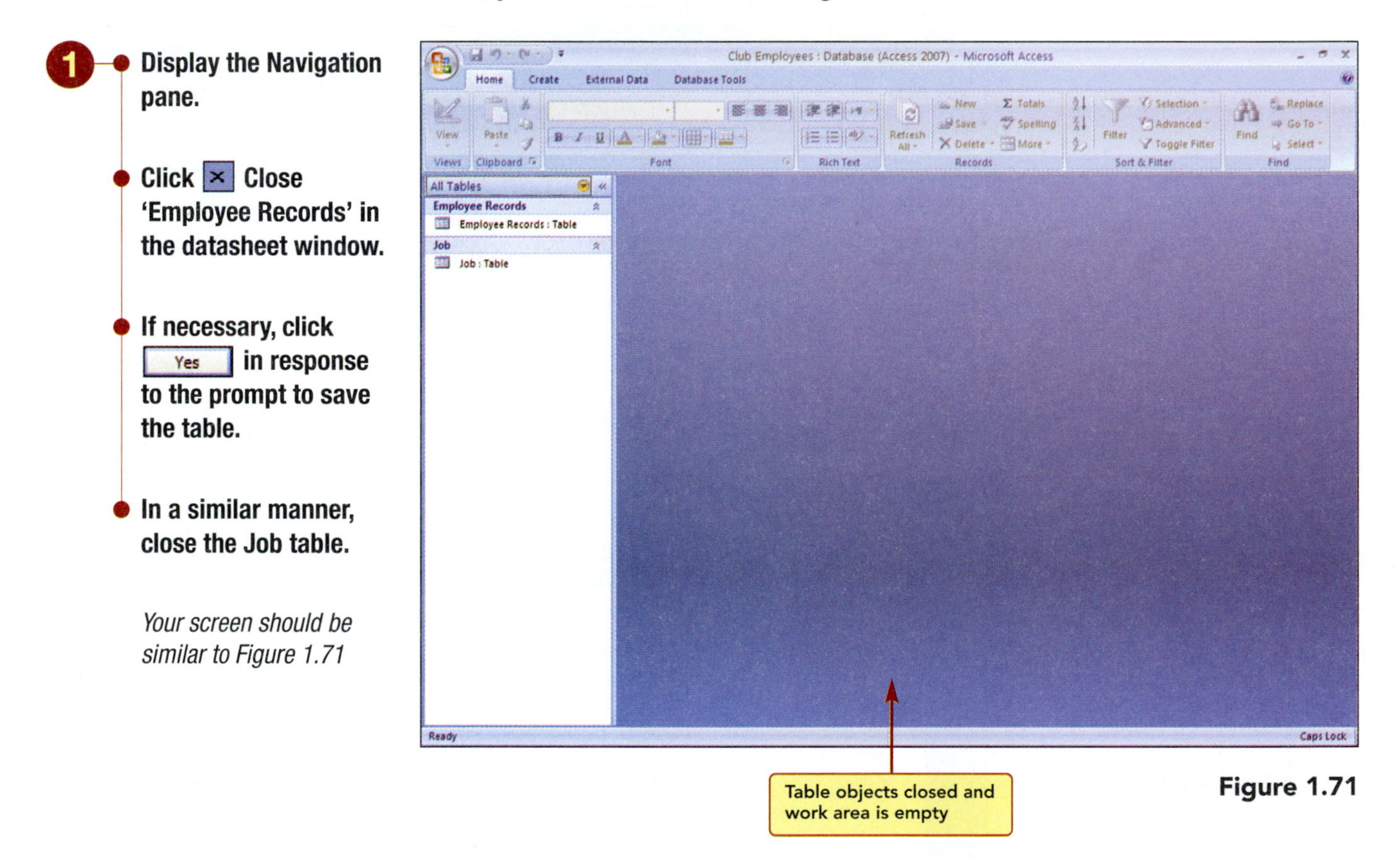

Figure 1.71

The work area is empty because there are no open objects. The Navigation pane still displays the names of the table objects. Next, you will close the database.

Click Office Button and choose Close Database.

Another Method

Do not click Close in the Access window title bar as this will exit the application.

Your screen should be similar to Figure 1.72

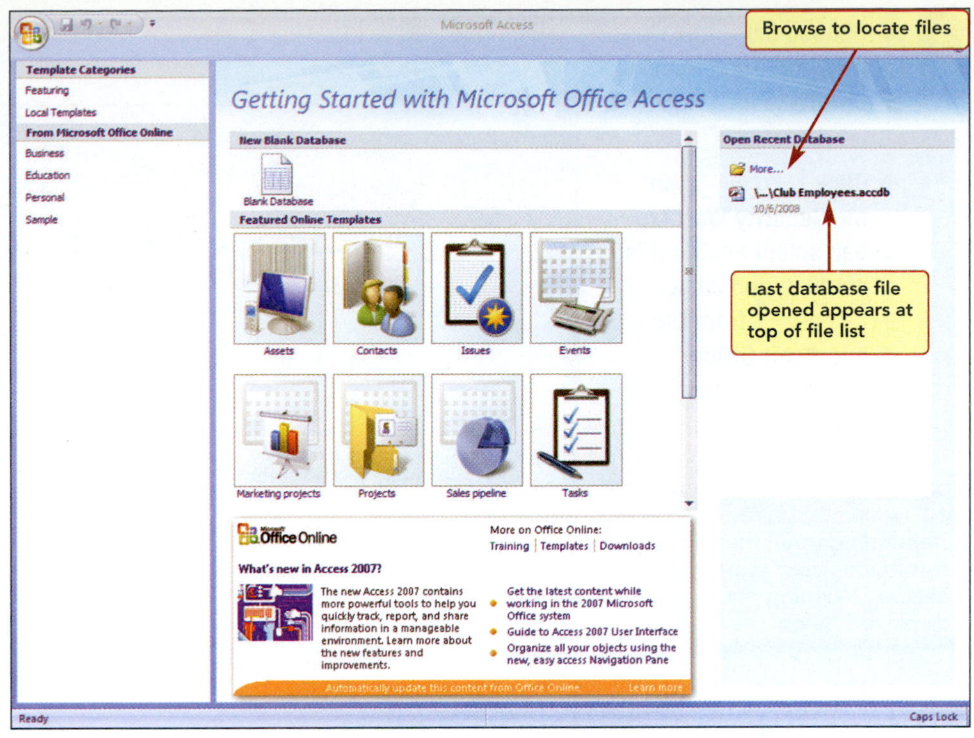

Figure 1.72

The Getting Started window is displayed again so you can open another existing database file or create a new one.

More About

See "6 Managing and Maintaining Databases" in the More About appendix to learn how to save databases as a previous version.

Opening a Table and Database

You want to make sure that you know how to access your table of employee records, so you will reopen it and then close it again. Because opening a file is a very common task, there are many ways to do it. You can select the file name from the Open Recent Database list, which displays the names of the last nine recently used files. If the file name is not listed, you can click More... to browse your computer to locate the file.

You also can open database files that were created in previous versions of Access that used the .mdb file extension. It must be converted to Access 2007 file format, however, if you want to take advantage of the new features in Access 2007. If you plan to share a file with someone using Access 2003 or earlier, you can save the file using the .mdb file type; however, some features may be lost. Otherwise, if you save it as an .accdb file type, the recipient will not be able to open the file.

Another Method

You also can click Office Button and select the file name from the Recent Document list or choose Open to browse your computer to locate the file. You also can use the keyboard shortcut Ctrl + O to browse for files.

Additional Information

The default setting is to display the last nine recently used files. This setting can be changed using Office Button/Access Options/Advanced/Display.

1 Choose Club Employees from the Open Recent Database list.

- Click Options... in the Security Warning bar, select Enable this content, and click OK from the Microsoft Office Security Options dialog box.

Having Trouble?
Depending upon the security settings on your system, a Security Warning may not be displayed below the Ribbon.

- Double-click on the Employee Records table.

Another Method
You also can drag the object from the Navigation pane to the work area to open it.

Your screen should be similar to Figure 1.73

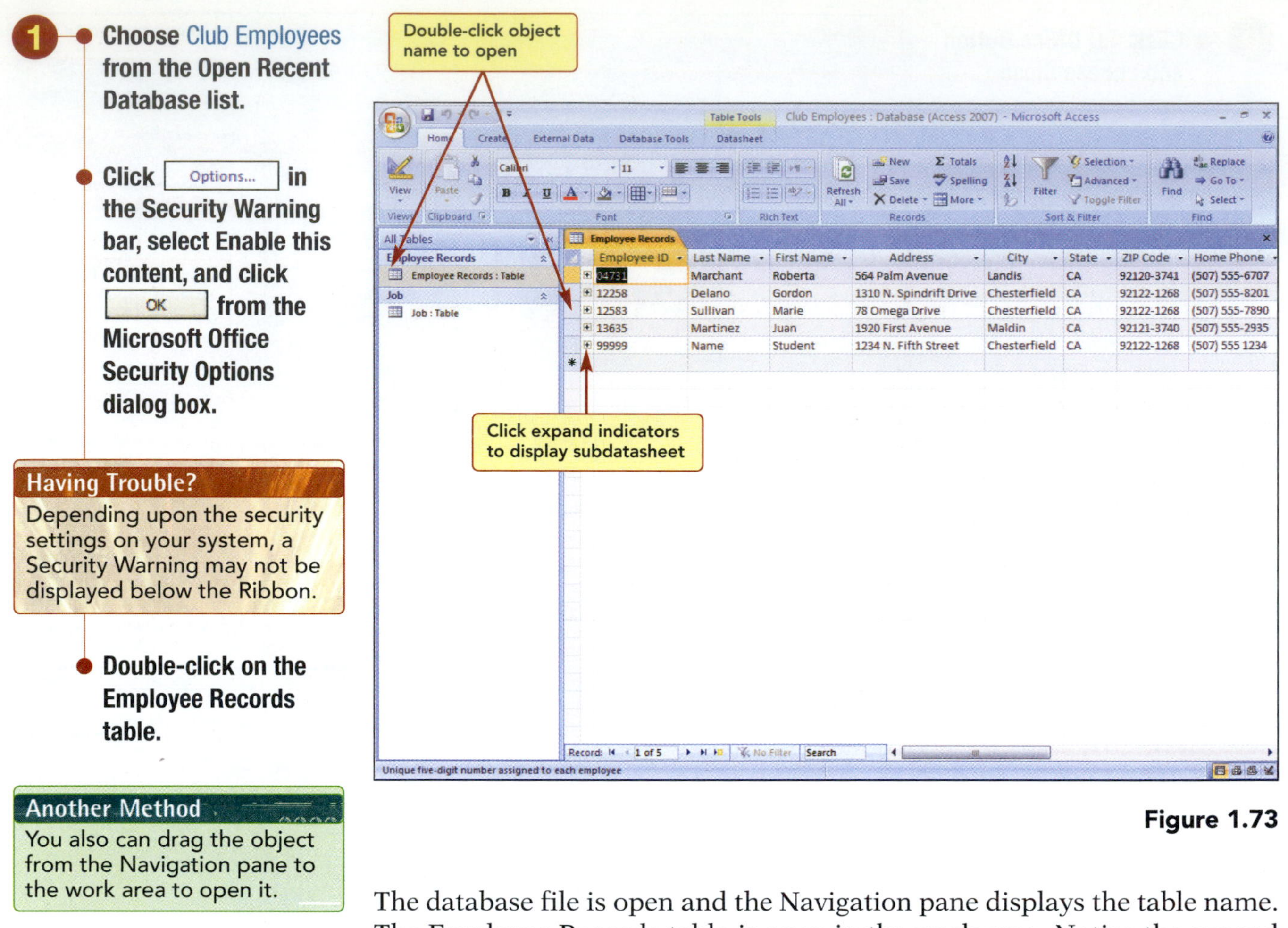

Figure 1.73

The database file is open and the Navigation pane displays the table name. The Employee Records table is open in the work area. Notice the expand indicators ⊞ at the beginning of each row. This indicates there is a subdatasheet linked to the records in this table.

Concept 7

Subdatasheet

7 A **subdatasheet** is a data table nested in another data table that contains data related or joined to the table where it resides. A subdatasheet allows you to easily view and edit related data. Subdatasheets are created automatically whenever relationships are established between tables.

In this case, the subdatasheet is to the Job table. Clicking ⊞ will expand the table to show the information in the subdatasheet table, Job.

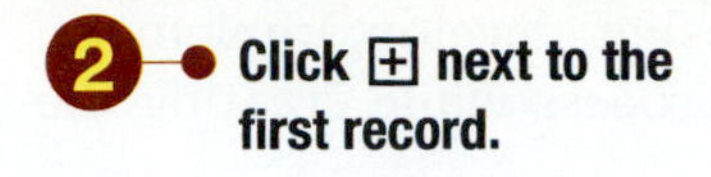

Click ⊞ next to the first record.

Your screen should be similar to Figure 1.74

Figure 1.74

> **Additional Information**
> You will learn more about relationships and subdatasheets in later labs.

A subdatasheet appears and displays the location and job title information contained in the Job table for Roberta Marchant. Then, to hide or collapse the subdatasheet again, you click the collapse indicator ⊟.

Click ⊟ next to the first record.

You have created a database file that contains two tables and that follows the two basic principles of database design: do not include redundant information in tables and enter accurate and complete information. Although you may think the employee number is redundant data, it is the only way the information in the two tables can be associated. The database attains the goals of **normalization,** a design technique that identifies and eliminates redundancy by applying a set of rules to your tables to confirm that they are structured properly. These rules ensure that your design meets the **normal form** standards, a set of constraints that must be satisfied. There are five sequential normal form levels; however, meeting the third level, commonly called 3NF, is the level that is required for most database designs. This level requires that every nonkey column be dependent on the primary key and that nonkey columns are independent of each other.

You also have followed the five steps (plan, design, develop, implement, and refine and review) of the database design process while creating the database.

Exiting Access

You will continue to build and use the database of employee records in the next lab. Until then, you can exit Access.

1. **Click ☒ Close in the Access window title bar.**

Another Method

You also can click Office Button and choose Exit Access.

Notice that this time you were not prompted to save the table because you did not make any changes to it since last opening it. If you had made changes, you would be prompted to save the file before exiting Access.

Focus on Careers

EXPLORE YOUR CAREER OPTIONS

Admitting Nurse

Can you imagine trying to organize the information of hundreds of patients in a busy emergency room? This is the job of an admitting nurse. They have to be able to enter, edit, and format data; add and delete records; and so on. This information is used by all departments of the hospital, from the doctors, to the pharmacy, and to the billing department. Without a proper understanding of database software, a hospital cannot run efficiently. The average salary of an admitting nurse is in the $40,000 to $50,000 range. The demand for nurses is expected to remain high.

Concept Summary

LAB 1

Creating a Database

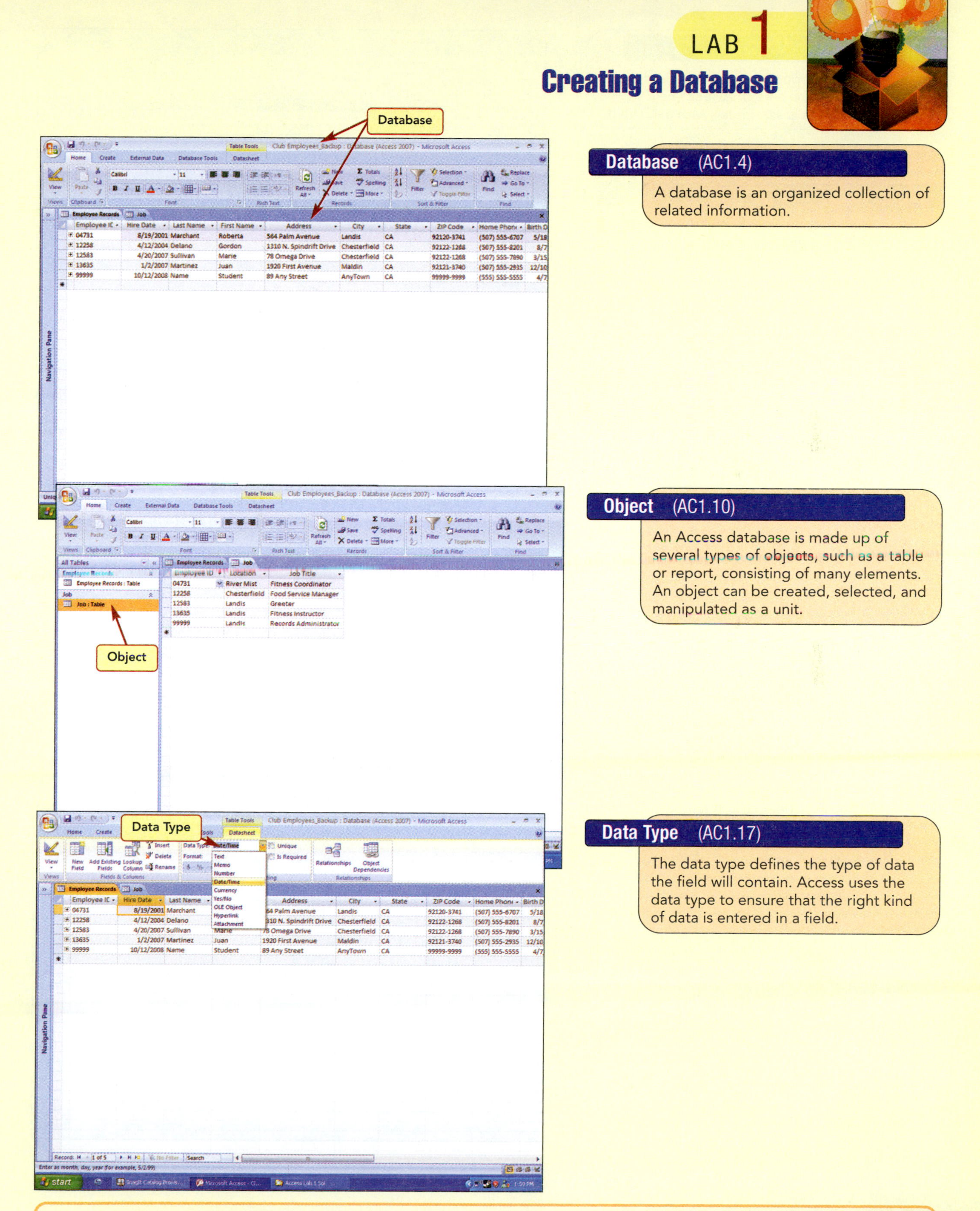

Database (AC1.4)

A database is an organized collection of related information.

Object (AC1.10)

An Access database is made up of several types of objects, such as a table or report, consisting of many elements. An object can be created, selected, and manipulated as a unit.

Data Type (AC1.17)

The data type defines the type of data the field will contain. Access uses the data type to ensure that the right kind of data is entered in a field.

Concept Summary

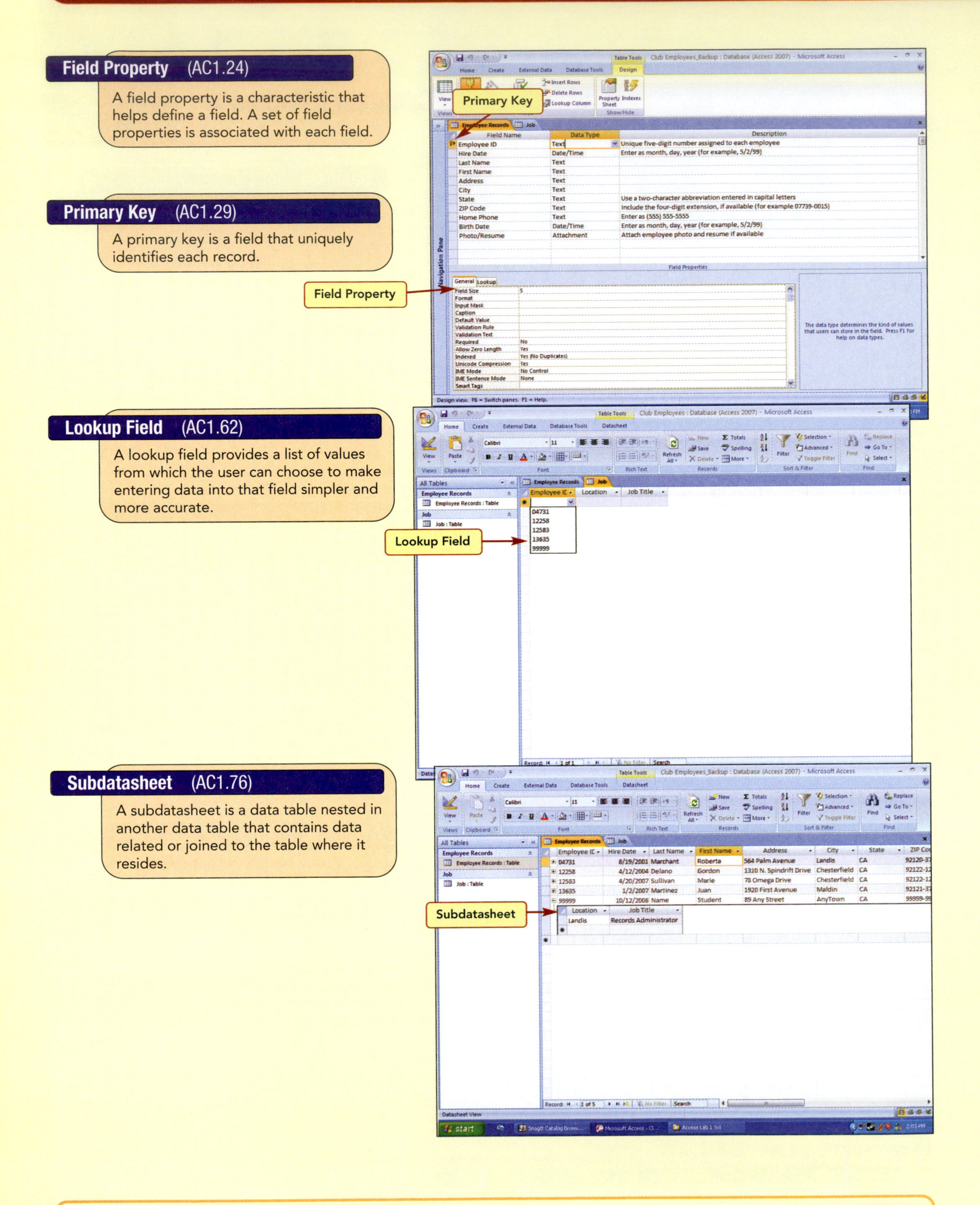

Field Property (AC1.24)

A field property is a characteristic that helps define a field. A set of field properties is associated with each field.

Primary Key (AC1.29)

A primary key is a field that uniquely identifies each record.

Lookup Field (AC1.62)

A lookup field provides a list of values from which the user can choose to make entering data into that field simpler and more accurate.

Subdatasheet (AC1.76)

A subdatasheet is a data table nested in another data table that contains data related or joined to the table where it resides.

Lab Review

LAB 1

Creating a Database

key terms

- **Allow Zero Length property** AC1.24
- **Attachment data type** AC1.18
- **AutoNumber data type** AC1.18
- **Best Fit feature** AC1.51
- **Caption property** AC1.24
- **cell** AC1.12
- **Clipboard** AC1.67
- **column width** AC1.50
- **composite key** AC1.29
- **Currency data type** AC1.18
- **current field** AC1.25
- **current record** AC1.12
- **data type** AC1.17
- **database** AC1.4
- **Datasheet view** AC1.12
- **Date/Time data type** AC1.18
- **Default Value property** AC1.24
- **Design view** AC1.12
- **destination** AC1.67
- **drawing object** AC1.40
- **field** AC1.4
- **field name** AC1.14
- **field property** AC1.24
- **Field Size property** AC1.24
- **field template** AC1.20
- **foreign key** AC1.59
- **form** AC1.10
- **Form view** AC1.12
- **Format property** AC1.24
- **graphic** AC1.40
- **header row** AC1.12
- **Hyperlink data type** AC1.18
- **Indexed property** AC1.24
- **Input Mask property** AC1.24
- **landscape orientation** AC1.72
- **Layout view** AC1.12
- **lookup field** AC1.62
- **lookup list** AC1.62
- **Lookup Wizard** AC1.61
- **margin** AC1.73
- **Memo data type** AC1.18
- **navigation buttons** AC1.12
- **Navigation pane** AC1.11
- **normal form** AC1.77
- **normalization** AC1.77
- **Number data type** AC1.18
- **object** AC1.10
- **OLE Object data type** AC1.18
- **orientation** AC1.72
- **picture** AC1.41
- **portrait orientation** AC1.72
- **primary key** AC1.29
- **Print Preview** AC1.12
- **query** AC1.10
- **record** AC1.4
- **record number indicator** AC1.12
- **relational database** AC1.4
- **report** AC1.10
- **Report view** AC1.12
- **Required property** AC1.24
- **Select All button** AC1.12
- **serial value** AC1.18
- **source** AC1.62
- **subdatasheet** AC1.76
- **table** AC1.4
- **template** AC1.7
- **Text data type** AC1.18
- **Validation Rule property** AC1.24
- **Validation Text property** AC1.24
- **value list** AC1.62
- **view** AC1.11
- **wizard** AC1.61
- **Yes/No data type** AC1.18

MCAS Skills

The Microsoft Certified Applications Specialist (MCAS) certification program is designed to measure your proficiency in performing basic tasks using the Office 2007 applications. Getting certified demonstrates that you have the skills and provides a valuable industry credential for employment. See Reference 2: Microsoft Certified Applications Specialist (MCAS) for a complete list of the skills that were covered in Lab 1.

command summary

Command	Shortcut	Action
Office Button		
New		Opens a new blank database
Open	Ctrl + O	Opens an existing database
Save	Ctrl + S	Saves database object
Print/Print	Ctrl + P	Specifies print settings and prints current database object
Print/Print Preview		Displays file as it will appear when printed
Close Database		Closes open window
Exit Access		Closes Access
Home tab		
Views group Design View		Displays object in Design view
Datasheet View		Displays object in Datasheet view
Clipboard group Cut	Ctrl + X	Removes selected item and copies it to the Clipboard
Copy	Ctrl + C	Duplicates selected item and copies to the Clipboard
Paste	Ctrl + V	Inserts copy of item from Clipboard
Records group Delete	Delete	Deletes current record
More/Column Width		Adjusts width of selected column
Find group Select/Select		Selects current record
Table Tools Datasheet tab		
Views group Design View		Displays table in Design view
Datasheet View		Displays table in Datasheet view
Fields & Columns group New Field		Inserts a new field
Delete		Removes selected field column

command summary

Command	Shortcut	Action
Rename		Renames selected field
Data Type & Formatting group		
Data Type: Text		Changes the data type for current field
Format: Formatting		Sets the display format of the selected field
Table Tools Design Tab		
Views group		
Design View		Displays table in Design view
Datasheet View		Displays table in Datasheet view
Tools group		
Primary Key		Makes current field a primary key field
Delete Rows		Deletes selected field row
Print Preview Tab		
Print group		
Print		Prints displayed object
Page Layout group		
Portrait		Changes print orientation to portrait
Landscape		Changes print orientation to landscape
Zoom group		
One Page		Displays one entire page in Print Preview
Two Pages		Displays two entire pages in Print Preview
Close Preview group		
Close Print Preview		Closes Print Preview window

Lab Exercises

screen identification

1. In the following Access screen, several items are identified by letters. Enter the correct term for each item in the spaces provided.

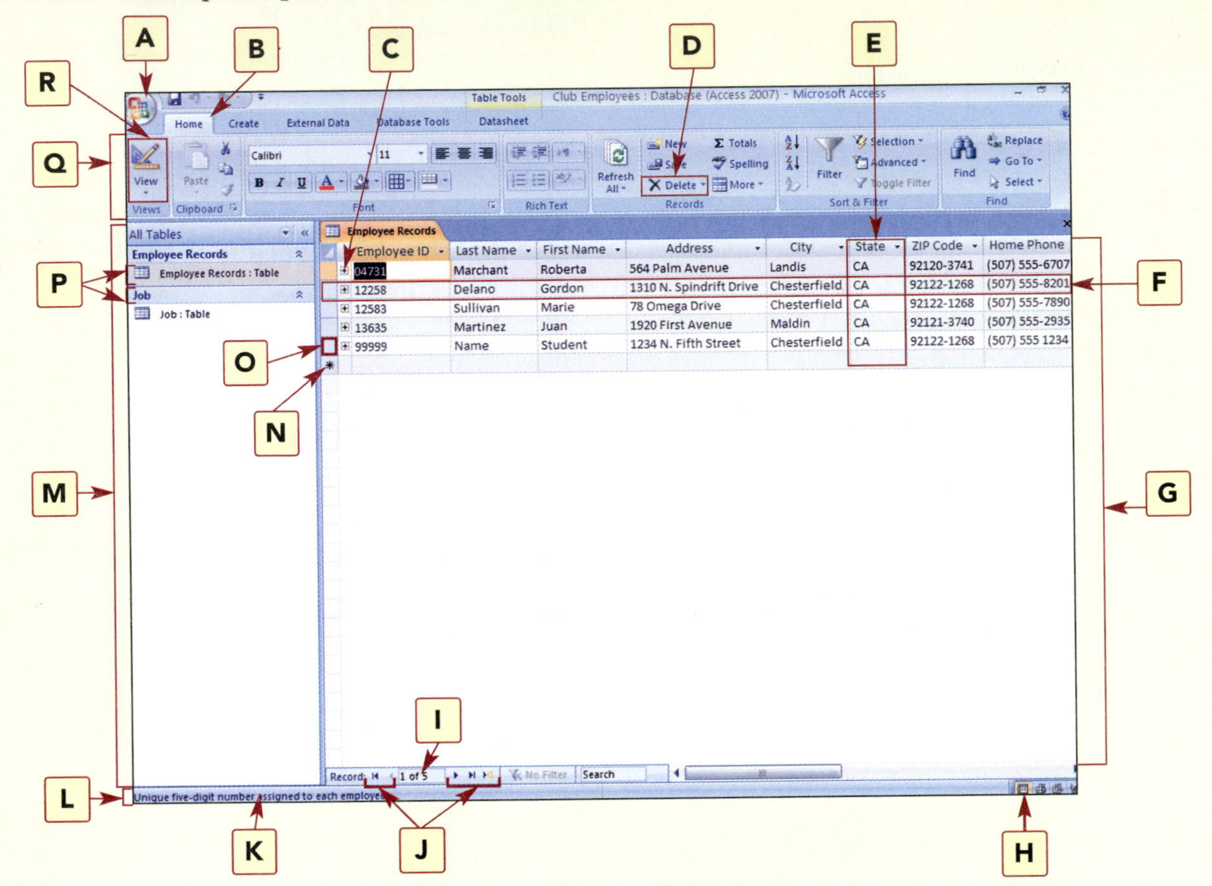

Possible answers for the screen identification are:

Design view	Select All button
Cell	Primary key indicator
Record number indicator	Navigation buttons
Field name	Datasheet View button
Work area	Status bar
Ribbon	Tabs
Object	Delete record
Field description	Field
End of table indicator	Navigation pane
Open tab	Record
	File menu

A. ______________________ J. ______________________
B. ______________________ K. ______________________
C. ______________________ L. ______________________
D. ______________________ M. ______________________
E. ______________________ N. ______________________
F. ______________________ O. ______________________
G. ______________________ P. ______________________
H. ______________________ Q. ______________________
I. ______________________ R. ______________________

matching

Match the numbered item with the correct lettered description.

1. primary key	________	**a.** collection of related fields
2. Navigation pane	________	**b.** a unit of a database
3. Datasheet view	________	**c.** contains multiple tables linked by a common field
4. Attachment	________	**d.** used to define the table structure
5. Design view	________	**e.** used to open and manage database objects
6. field size	________	**f.** a data type that stores multiple files of different file types in a single field
7. data type	________	**g.** field that uniquely identifies each record
8. object	________	**h.** displays table in row and column format
9. record	________	**i.** defines the type of data the field will contain
10. relational database	________	**j.** controls the maximum number of characters that can be entered in a field

fill-in

Complete the following statements by filling in the blanks with the correct terms.

1. You use the ________ located at the left of the work area to select the type of object you want to work with.
2. The ________ field property specifies how data displays in a table.
3. A field name is used to identify the ________ stored in a field.
4. The ________ data type restricts data to digits only.
5. Using ________ orientation prints across the length of the paper.
6. The field property that limits a text data type to a certain size is called a(n) ________.
7. A ________ is a data table nested in another data table that contains data related or joined to the table where it resides.
8. An Access database is made up of several types of ________.
9. The ________ is a field that uniquely identifies each record.
10. The ________ data type can be used to store a graphic file in a field.

Lab Exercises

true/false

Circle the correct answer to the following statements.

1.	A field description is a required part of the field definition.	True	False
2.	Interactive databases define relationships between tables by having common data in the tables.	True	False
3.	A field contains information about one person, thing, or place.	True	False
4.	The data type defines the information that can be entered in a field.	True	False
5.	You can format the text in a Memo field.	True	False
6.	A foreign key is a field in one table that refers to the primary key field in another table and indicates how the tables are related.	True	False
7.	Tables and queries are two types of database objects.	True	False
8.	A lookup field that uses another table as the source for values is called a value list.	True	False
9.	A table is a required object in a database.	True	False
10.	Changing the column width in the datasheet changes the field size.	True	False

multiple choice

Circle the letter of the correct response.

1. The last step of database development is ___________.
   - **a.** design
   - **b.** develop
   - **c.** review
   - **d.** plan
2. ___________ is a design technique that identifies and eliminates redundancy by applying a set of rules to your tables.
   - **a.** Database development
   - **b.** Normalization
   - **c.** Validation
   - **d.** Orientation
3. A ___________ is often used as the primary key.
   - **a.** phone number
   - **b.** catalog number
   - **c.** last name
   - **d.** first name

4. You may lose data if your data and __________ are incompatible.
   a. field name
   b. data type
   c. default value
   d. field size
5. __________ affects the amount of data that you can enter into a field.
   a. Column width
   b. Field size
   c. Format
   d. Description size
6. A __________ is a field in one table that refers to the primary key field in another table and indicates how the tables are related.
   a. foreign key
   b. common key
   c. related key
   d. data key
7. A(n) __________ provides a list of values from which the user can choose.
   a. value field
   b. lookup field
   c. related field
   d. attachment field
8. Graphics can be inserted into a field that has a(n) __________ data type.
   a. graphic
   b. text
   c. attachment
   d. memo
9. The basic database objects are __________.
   a. panes, tables, queries, and reports
   b. tables, queries, forms, and reports
   c. forms, reports, data, and files
   d. portraits, keys, tables, and views
10. __________ view is only used to modify the table structure.
   a. Design
   b. Report
   c. Datasheet
   d. Query

Hands-On Exercises

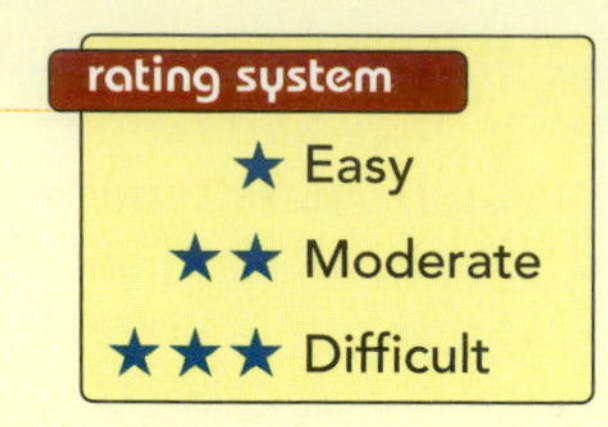

step-by-step

Oak Ridge School Parent Contact Database ★

CONTINUING EXERCISES

1. Oak Ridge Elementary School has decided to set up a database with the contact information for all students. As a parent, you have volunteered to do the initial database creation and teach the secretary at the school to maintain it. The database table you create will have the following information: student's last name, student's first name, guardian's name, home address, and home phone number. When you have finished, a printout of your completed database table should look similar to the one shown here.

ID	Student Last Name	Student First Name	Guardian	Street Address	City	State	ZIP Code	Home Phone	Alternate Phone
1	Roderick	Smithy	Shannon Roderick	1293 Hillview Rd.	Oak Ridge	UT	22301	(802) 555-0914	
3	Salazar	Gloria	Betha Salazar	103 Oak Ave.	Oak Ridge	UT	22301	(802) 555-8411	
4	Name	Student	Ricardo Ramirez	107 Oak Ave.	Oak Ridge	UT	22301	(802) 555-8632	(802) 555-9711

a. Create a blank database named **Oak Ridge School.** Design a table in Design view named Students using the following field information. Make the ID field the primary key field.

Field Name	Data Type	Description	Field Size
ID	AutoNumber		**Long Integer**
Student Last Name	Text	**Student's legal last name**	**25**
Student First Name	Text	**Include student's nickname in parentheses**	**25**
Guardian	Text	**First and last name of primary guardian**	**55**
Street Address	Text		**75**
City	Text		**20**
State	Text	**Two-letter abbreviation**	**2**
ZIP Code	Text		**5**
Home Phone	Text		**15**

b. Enter the following records into the table, using Copy and Paste for fields that have the same data (such as the city):

Record 1	Record 2	Record 3
Roderick	**Avery**	**Salazar**
Smithy	**Wilson**	**Gloria**
Shannon Roderick	**Rita Avery-Montoya**	**Betha Salazar**
1293 Hillview Rd.	**102 4th Street**	**103 Oak Ave.**
Oak Ridge	**Oak Ridge**	**Oak Ridge**
UT	**UT**	**UT**
22301	**22301**	**22301**
(802) 555-0914	**(802) 555-3375**	**(802) 555-8411**

c. Adjust the column widths appropriately.

d. Delete record 2. Add another record with the following data:

[Your last name]

[Your first name]

Ricardo Ramirez

107 Oak Ave.

Oak Ridge

UT

22301

(802) 555-8632

e. Add a new field after the Home Phone field with the following definitions:

Field Name: **Alternate Phone**

Data Type: Text

Field Size: **15**

f. Change the ZIP Code field size to **10**.

g. Enter the Alternate Phone number of **(802) 555-9711** and the ZIP Code of **22301-4459** for the record with ID number 4.

h. Best fit all columns.

i. View the table in Print Preview; change the page orientation to landscape and margins to Narrow.

j. Print, save, and close the table.

EchoPlex Records Database ★★

2. Your record collection has expanded beyond a hobby into an online business. In order to meet the needs of your expanding client base, you need to get your inventory cataloged. When you are finished, your printed database table should be similar to the one shown here.

Records 10/6/2008

Catalog Number	Item	Title	Acquired Date	📎
1	LP	Up	8/13/2002	📎(1)
3	12'	Forever Blue	7/8/2005	📎(0)
4	LP	Definitive Collection	3/3/2003	📎(0)
5		Student Name	10/6/2008	📎(0)

a. Create a blank database named EchoPlex.
b. From the Assets Field Templates list, add the following fields to the table:

Item

Description

Acquired Date

Attachments

c. Switch to Design view. Save the table as **Records**.
d. Change the ID Field Name to **Catalog Number**. Change the Description Field Name to **Title**.
e. Change the Field Size of the Item field to **4**.
f. Return to Datasheet view. Add the following records to the table:

Item	LP	12"	12"	LP
Title	Up	Rank	Forever Blue	Definitive Collection
Acquired Date	8/13/2002	4/1/2006	7/8/2005	3/3/2003

g. Insert the image file ac01_Guitar in the Attachment field of the first record.
h. Adjust the column widths using the Best Fit feature.
i. Delete the record for the title Rank. Add a new record and enter your name in the Title field and the current date in the Acquired Date field.
j. Preview and print the table in portrait orientation with wide margins.
k. Save and close the table. Exit Access.

Library Catalog Database ★★

3. You are a volunteer at a small county library. The library recently received a large collection of young adult books and would like to keep better track of the titles. The library is still using an antiquated method for cataloging most its books. Because of your computer skills, you have been asked to create a database containing the catalog number, title, author, and copyright date of each

of the new books. The young adult titles database will serve as a model for the library's entire collection; after it is done, the database will make search, tracking, and inventory functions much easier. Your printed database table should be similar to the one shown here.

Catalog 10/6/2008

Catalog #	Title	Description	Acquired Date	ISBN	Location	Condition
1	Speak	Paperback	8/12/2006	340817623	Building	Binding loose
3	Hoot	Paperback	8/17/2006	375821813	Building	
4	Artemis Fowl	Hardcover	8/17/2006	141312122	Bookmobile	Missing dust jacket
5	Wolfie	Hardcover	9/29/2008	299389231	Bookmobile	

a. Create a blank database named County Library.
b. Add fields using the following field templates from the Assets list:

Item
Description
Acquired Date
Manufacturer

c. Switch to Design view. Save the table as **Catalog**.
d. Edit the field properties using the following information:

Field Name	Data Type	Description	Field Size
Change ID to Catalog #	AutoNumber		
Change Item to Title	Text	**Include complete title**	**150**
Description	Text	**Hardcover or paperback**	**15**
Change Manufacturer to ISBN	Text	**Unique 10-digit number**	**10**

e. Add the following new fields:

Field Name	Data Type	Description	Field Size
Location	Text	**Building or Bookmobile**	**30**
Condition	Memo	**Describe condition of book if needed**	

f. Switch to Datasheet view and enter the following records into the table:

	Record 1	Record 2	Record 3	Record 4
Title	**Speak**	**Freak the Mighty**	**Hoot**	**Artemis Fowl**
Description	**Paperback**	**Paperback**	**Paperback**	**Hardcover**
Acquired Date	**8/12/2006**	**8/12/2006**	**8/17/2006**	**8/17/2006**
ISBN	**0340817623**	**0439286069**	**0375821813**	**0141312122**
Location	**Building**	**Bookmobile**	**Building**	**Bookmobile**
Condition	**Binding loose**			**Missing dust jacket**

g. Best Fit all column widths.

h. Delete record 2. Add another record with the following data:

Title:	**Wolfie**
Description:	**Hardcover**
Acquired Date:	**9/29/08**
ISBN:	**0299389231**
Location:	**Bookmobile**

i. Check the table in Print Preview. Change the page layout to landscape with wide margins. Print, save, and close the table. Exit Access.

DownTown Internet Café Inventory Database ★★★

4. The Downtown Internet Café, which you helped get off the ground, is an overwhelming success. The clientele is growing every day, as is the demand for the beverages the café serves. Up until now, the information about the vendors has been kept in an alphabetical card file. This has become quite unwieldy, however, and Evan, the owner, would like a more sophisticated tracking system. He would like you to create a database containing each supply item and the contact information for the vendor that sells that item. When you are finished, your database tables should be similar to those shown here.

Suppliers 10/6/2008

ID	Vendor	Contact First Name	Contact Last Name	Business Phone	E-mail Address
1	Cuppa Jo	Leila	Brooks	(502) 555-9090	Leila.Brooks@cuppajoe.c
2	Natural Nectars	Estrella	Ramirez	(206) 555-5986	estrella@nnectar.com
3	Tea Time	Audry	Chischillie	(206) 555-6100	ac@teatime.com
4	Paper Products e	Student	Name	(206) 555-9999	studentname@paperpro

Stock 2/6/2008

Item	Description	Vendor	📎
197	Café Mocha	Cuppa Jo	📎(0)
198	Mango Strawberry Flavoring	Natural Nectars	📎(1)
199	Chamomile Tea Leaves	Cuppa Jo	📎(0)
200	Napkins	Paper Products etc.	📎(0)

a. Create a blank database named Cafe Inventory.
b. Design a table using the **Item** and **Description** field templates from the Assets list:
c. Switch to Design view. Save the table as **Stock**.
d. Delete the ID field. Make Item the primary key field.
e. Add the following information to the field properties:

Field Name	Data Type	Description	Field Size
Item	Text	**Unique three-digit product number**	**3**
Description	Text	**Name of product**	**50**

f. Create a second table using the following field templates from the Contacts list:

Company
First Name
Last Name
Business Phone
E-mail Address

g. Switch to Design view. Save the table as **Suppliers**.
h. Edit the field properties as shown here:

Field Name	Data Type	Description	Field Size
Change Company to Vendor	Text	**Company name of supplier**	**50**
Change First Name to Contact First Name	Text		**50**
Change Last Name to Contact Last Name	Text		**50**
Business Phone	Text	**Include the area code in parentheses: (800) 555-5555**	**15**
Change E-mail Address to E-mail	Text	**E-mail address of contact person**	**50**

i. Enter the following records into the Stock and Suppliers tables:

Stock table			
Record 1	Record 2	Record 3	
197	198	199	
Café Mocha	Mango Strawberry Flavoring	Chamomile Tea Leaves	
Suppliers table			
Record 1	Record 2	Record 3	Record 4
Cuppa Jo	Natural Nectars	Tea Time	Paper Products etc.
Leila	Estrella	Audry	Enter your first name
Brooks	Ramirez	Chischillie	Enter your last name
(502) 555-9090	(206) 555-5986	(206) 555-6001	(206) 555-9999
lbrooks@cuppajo.com	estrella@nnectar.com	ac@teatime.com	Yourname@paperproducts.com

j. Add the existing field, Vendor, from the Suppliers table as the last field in the Stock table.
k. In the Stock table, select Cuppa Jo as the vendor for the first record, Natural Nectars for the second record, and Tea Time for the third record.
l. In the Suppliers table, edit the record for ID 1 by changing the E-mail address to **Leila.Brooks@cuppajo.com**.
m. Add a new field to the Stock table named **Picture.** Make the data type Attachment. For item number 198 insert the file ac01_Flavoring.
n. Add the following new item to the Stock file.

Item:	**200**
Description:	**Napkins**
Vendor:	**Paper Products etc.**

o. Adjust the column widths in both tables using Best Fit.
p. Preview the Suppliers table. Change to landscape orientation. Change the margins to wide and print the table.
q. Close the database. Exit Access.

Kodiak Construction Database ★★★

5. You have just been hired by Kodiak Paint and Construction to create and maintain a database containing information about their clients and jobs. The company has grown rapidly and they need ready access to information about jobs spread across the city. When you are finished, your tables should be similar to those shown here.

ID	Job	Client Last Name	Begin Date	Forema	Job Description	Job Location	Job Estimate
010	Ridgeline Condos	Foss	2/18/2008	Pisano	New construction of 75 condo units	Aurora	$2,500,000.00
053	R Bar C Ranch	Sanchez	7/18/2008	Englan	Private home guest addition	Glendale	$125,000.00
062	Sandalwood Villa	McGhee	9/15/2008	Name	Remodel restaurant	Aurora	$750,000.00
112	Williams Retreat	Bortle	12/13/2008	Valdez	New construction	Golden	$925,000.00

Foremen 10/6/2008

ID	Foreman First Name	Foreman Last Name	Mobile Phone	📎
1	Jonathan	Hedly	(303) 555-1480	📎(0)
2	Hector	Valdez	(303) 555-7677	📎(1)
3	Bob	England	(303) 555-6123	📎(0)
4	Ricky	Pisano	(303) 555-9438	📎(0)
5	Student	Name	(303) 555-7712	📎(0)

Clients 10/6/2008

ID	First Name	Last Name	Address	City	State	ZIP Code	Business Phone
1	Joe	Bortle	20032 W. 13th Place	Lakewood	CO	80215	(303) 555-1232
2	Timothy	McGhee	135 Mountain Peak Rd.	Aurora	CO	80011	(303) 555-7922
3	Charlotte	Foss	39 Avery Rd.	Denver	CO	80246	(303) 555-2525
4	Miguel	Sanchez	7218 N Crestview St.	Glendale	CO	80246	(303) 555-0932
5	Alan	Chang	82 Pine Land	Denver	CO	80002	(303) 555-0048

a. Create a blank database named Kodiak Construction. Design a table using the following field templates from the Projects list:

Project Name

Begin Date

End Date

b. Add the following additional fields to the table.

Field Name	Type
Job Description	Memo
Job Location	Text
Job Estimate	Currency

c. Save the table as **Jobs**. Switch to Design view.

d. Change the Project Name field name to **Job**. Delete the End Date field. Add field descriptions and make the changes to the field properties shown in the following table:

Field Name	Data Type	Description	Field Size	Format
ID	Text	Unique three-digit job ID	3	
Job		Project Name	75	
Begin Date				General date
Job Description		Brief description of project		
Job Location	Text	Enter city only	25	

e. Enter the following records into the table:

Record 1	Record 2	Record 3	Record 4	Record 5
034	062	010	053	112
Summit Lakes	Sandalwood Villa	Ridgeline Condos	R Bar C Ranch	Williams Retreat
4/13/2008	9/15/2008	2/18/2008	7/18/2008	12/13/2008
Remodel golf club	Remodel restaurant	New construction of 75 condo units	Private home guest addition	New construction
Denver	Aurora	Aurora	Glendale	Golden
1,200,000	750,000	2,500,000	125,000	925,000

f. Adjust the column widths using Best Fit.
g. Delete the record for the Summit Lakes job.
h. Create a second table for the client information using the following field templates from the Contacts list:

    First Name
    Last Name
    Address
    City
    State/Province
    ZIP/Postal Code
    Business Phone

i. Save the table as **Clients**.
j. Add field descriptions and make the changes to the field properties shown in the following table:

Field Name	Data Type	Description	Field Size
First Name		**First name of client**	**25**
Last Name		**Last name of client**	**25**
Address	Text		**50**
Change State/Province to State		**Use two character abbreviation**	**2**
Change ZIP/Postal Code to ZIP Code		**Enter 10 digit code, if available**	**10**
Business Phone		**Enter phone as (###) ###-####**	**14**

k. Add the following client information:

	Record 1	Record 2	Record 3	Record 4	Record 5
First Name	**Joe**	**Timothy**	**Charlotte**	**Miguel**	**Alan**
Last Name	**Bortle**	**McGhee**	**Foss**	**Sanchez**	**Chang**
Address	**20032 W. 13th Place**	**135 Mountain Peak Rd.**	**39 Avery Rd.**	**7218 N. Crestview St.**	**82 Pine Lane**
City	**Lakewood**	**Aurora**	**Denver**	**Glendale**	**Denver**
State	**CO**	**CO**	**CO**	**CO**	**CO**
ZIP Code	**80215**	**80011**	**80012**	**80246**	**80002**
Business Phone	**(303) 555-1232**	**(303) 555-7922**	**(303) 555-2525**	**(303) 555-0932**	**(303) 555-0048**

l. Create a third table for the foreman information with the following fields:

Field Name	Data Type	Description	Field Size
Foreman First Name	Text		**25**
Foreman Last Name	Text		**25**
Mobile Phone	Text	**Enter phone as (###) ###-####**	**14**
Picture	Attachment	**Photo of foreman**	

m. Save the table as **Foremen.**

n. Enter the following information for the five foremen.

Jonathan Hedly	**Hector Valdez**	**Bob England**	**Ricky Pisano**	**Your Name**
(303) 555-1480	**(303) 555-7677**	**(303) 555-6123**	**(303) 555-9438**	**(303) 555-7712**

o. Add the file ac01_Valdez to the attachment field for Hector Valdez.

p. Add the existing field Foreman Last Name from the Foremen table to the Jobs table after the Begin Date field.

q. Enter the following foremen for each job:

Job	Foreman
010	Pisano
053	England
062	Your Name
112	Valdez

r. Add the existing field Last Name from the Clients table to after the Job field in the Jobs table. Rename the field **Client Last Name.**

s. Enter the following clients for each job:

Job	Client
010	Foss
053	Sanchez
062	McGhee
112	Bortle

t. Best fit all fields in all tables.

u. Preview and print the Jobs table in landscape orientation with narrow margins. Print the Foremen table in portrait orientation with wide margins.

v. Save and close all tables and exit Access.

on your own

Valley View Newsletter Advertising Database ★

CONTINUING EXERCISES

1. Your homeowner's association distributes a monthly newsletter, *Valley View News,* to keep residents up to date with neighborhood news. In the past year, there has been rapid growth in building, including more houses and small office complexes. There are also plans to build an elementary school, fire station, and shopping center in the community. Consequently, the newsletter is now the size of a small newspaper, and the homeowners' dues are not covering the expense of publishing it.

The editorial staff has already begun selling ad space in the newsletter to local businesses, and, based on your background in database management, they have asked you to set up a database to keep track of the advertiser contact information. You agree to design such a database, called Valley View News, and tell them you will have something to show them at the next meeting. Your finished database should include each advertiser's billing number, business name and address, and contact name and phone number in a table named **Advertisers**. Enter 10 records and include a record that has your name as the contact name. Preview and print the table when you are finished.

Music Collection Database ★

2. You have just purchased a 200-disk CD carousel and now you would like to organize and catalog your CDs. You realize that without an updatable list, it will be difficult to maintain an accurate list of what is in the changer. To get the most out of your new purchase, you decide a database is in order. Create a new database called Music Collection and a table called **CD Catalogue**. The table you create should include the Artist's Name, Album Title, Genre, and Position Number. Make the Position Number field the primary key (because you may have multiple CDs by a given artist). Enter at least 15 records. Include an entry that has your name as the artist. Preview and print the table when you are finished.

Patient Database ★

3. You are the manager of a newly opened dental office. As one of your first projects, you need to create a patient database. Create a database called Dental Patients and a table named **Personal Information**. The database table you set up should contain patient identification numbers, last and first names, addresses, and phone numbers. Also include a field named "Referred by" and another field named "Patient since". Use appropriate field sizes and make the ID number field the primary key. Enter at least ten records, adjusting the column widths as necessary. Include a record that contains your name as the patient. Preview and print the table.

Old Watch Database Using the Web ★★

4. You have a small online business, Timeless Treasures, that locates and sells vintage wrist and pocket watches. Your business and inventory has grown large enough now that you have decided to use a database to track your inventory. Create a simple database named Timeless Treasures with a table named **Watches** that contains identification numbers, manufacturer (Waltham, Hamilton, Melrose), category (pocket watch, wrist watch), description, price, and quantity on hand. Size the fields appropriately and assign a primary key to one of them. Enter at least 10 records in the table. To obtain data about watches to include in your table, search the Web on "old watches". Use the information you locate to complete the data for the records in your table. Adjust column widths as necessary. Include your name as the manufacturer in one of the records. Preview and print the table.

Expense Tracking Database ★★★

5. You work in the accounting department at a start-up company called EMP Enterprises. One of your duties is to process, which up until now was a simple task of having the employees fill out a form and submit it to you for payment. You would then cut a check for them and charge it to the general expense fund of the company. However, the company has grown tremendously in the last year, adding employees and departments at a rapid rate, and the executive team has decided that it is time to start managing the income and expenses on a much more detailed level. To this end, you

need to create a database that includes the employee ID, employee name, submission date, expense type, and expense amount for each expense report that is turned in. Name the database EMP Enterprises. Create two tables, one for the employee information named **Employee Info** and the other for employee expenses named **Employee Expenses**. Include the Employee ID, First Name and Last Name fields in the Employee Info table. Include the Employee ID, Submission Date, Expense Type and Expense Amount fields in the Employee Expenses table. Use the Currency data type for the Expense Amount field, and appropriate data types for all other fields. Size the fields appropriately. Delete the ID field from the Employee Info table and make the Employee ID field the primary key. Enter at least 15 records. Adjust the column widths as necessary. Delete one of the records you just entered, and then edit one of the remaining records so it contains your name as the employee. Enter 10 records in the Employee Expenses table (one should be an expense record for the record containing your name.) Preview and print both tables.

Modifying and Filtering a Table and Creating a Form

LAB 2

Objectives

After completing this lab, you will know how to:

1. Navigate a large table.
2. Change field format properties.
3. Set default field values.
4. Insert a field.
5. Define validation rules.
6. Hide and redisplay fields.
7. Create a lookup field.
8. Find and replace data.
9. Sort records.
10. Format a datasheet.
11. Filter a table.
12. Create, modify, and use a form.
13. Preview, print, close, and save a form.
14. Identify object dependencies.
15. Add file and object documentation.

Case Study

Lifestyle Fitness Club

The Lifestyle Fitness Club owners, Ryan and Felicity, are very pleased with your plans for the organization of the database and with your progress in creating the first table of basic employee data. As you have seen, creating a database takes planning and a great deal of time to set up the structure and enter the data. As you have continued to add more employee records to the table, you have noticed several errors. You also realize that you forgot to include a field for the employee's gender. Even with the best of planning and care, errors occur and the information may change. You will see how easy it is to modify the database structure and to customize field properties to provide more control over the data that is entered in a field.

Even more impressive, as you will see in this lab, is the program's ability to locate information in the database. This is where all the hard work of entering data pays off. With a click of a button, you can find data that might otherwise take hours to locate. The result saves time and improves the accuracy of the output.

You also will see how you can make the data you are looking at onscreen more pleasing and easier to read by creating and using a form.

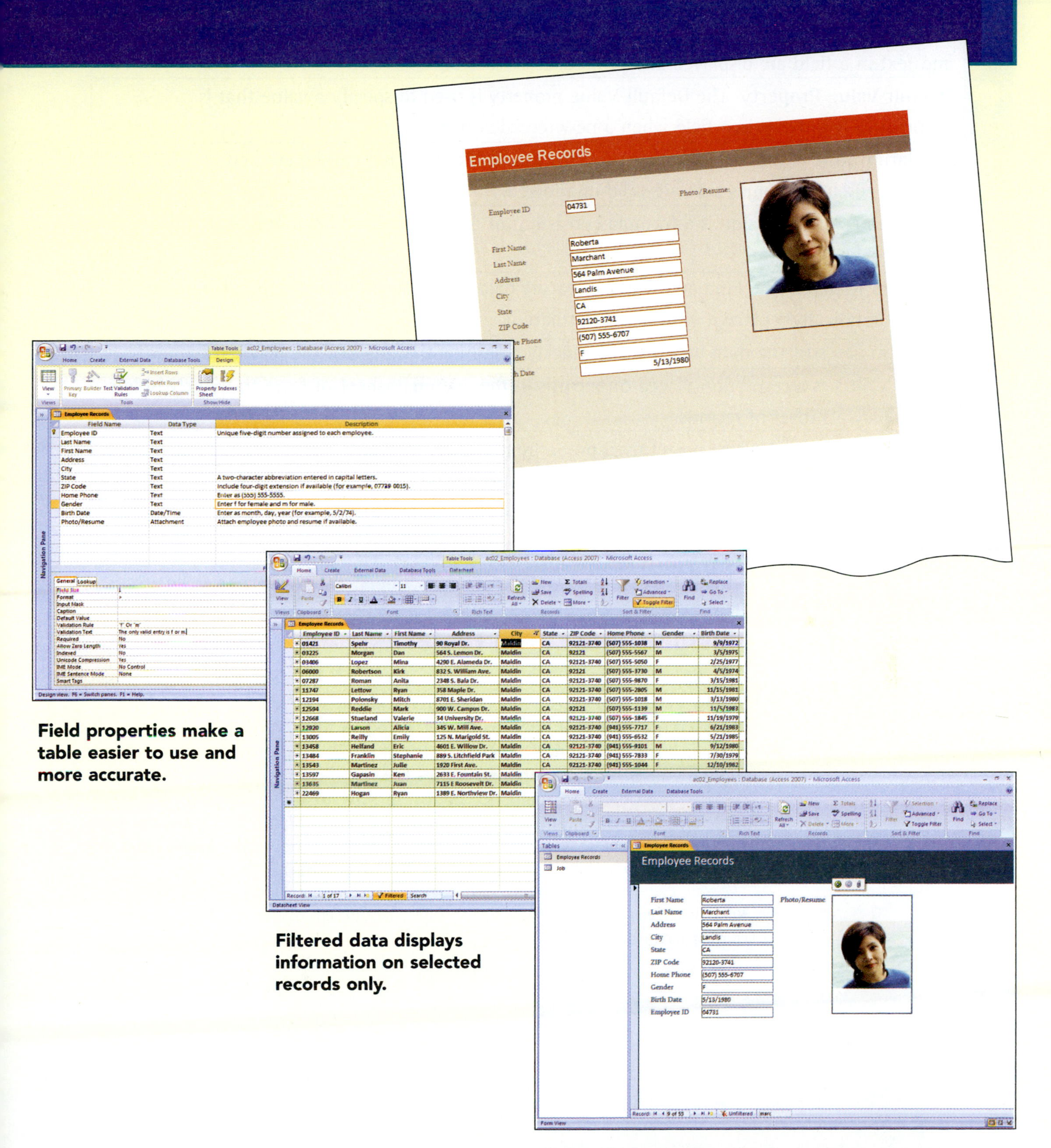

Field properties make a table easier to use and more accurate.

Filtered data displays information on selected records only.

Forms can be used to display information in an easy-to-read manner and make data entry easier.

Concept Preview

The following concepts will be introduced in this lab:

1. **Format Property** The Format property is used to specify the way that numbers, dates, times, and text in a field are displayed and printed.
2. **Default Value Property** The Default Value property is used to specify a value that is automatically entered in a field when a new record is created.
3. **Validation Rule** Validation rules are used to control the data that can be entered in a field by defining the input values that are valid or allowed.
4. **Expression** An expression is a formula consisting of a combination of symbols that will produce a single value.
5. **Find and Replace** The Find and Replace feature helps you quickly find specific information and automatically replace it with new information.
6. **Sort** You can sort the data in a table to quickly rearrange the order of the records.
7. **Filter** A filter is a restriction placed on records in the open datasheet or form to quickly isolate and display a subset of records.
8. **Form** A form is a database object used primarily to display records onscreen to make it easier to enter new records and to make changes to existing records.
9. **Controls** Controls are objects that display information, perform actions, or enhance the design of a form or report.

Navigating a Large Table

You have continued to add more records to the Lifestyle Fitness Club employee database. As you entered the data, you know you made data entry errors that still need to be corrected. Additionally, you have found that with the addition of records, it takes much longer to move around in the datasheet. Typical database tables are very large and consequently can be very inefficient to navigate. Learning how to move around in a large table will save time and help you get the job done faster. You want to open the expanded database that you saved using a new file name, and to continue working on and refining the Records table.

Note: Before you begin, you may want to create a backup copy of the ac02_Employees file by copying and renaming it.

1. **Start Office Access 2007.**
   - **In the Open Recent Database list, click** More... **.**
   - **Change the location to the location containing your data files.**
   - **Double-click** ac02_Employees**.**
   - **Click** Options... **in the Security Warning bar just below the ribbon.**
   - **Choose Enable this content and click** OK **.**
   - **Open the Employee Records table.**

Your screen should be similar to Figure 2.1

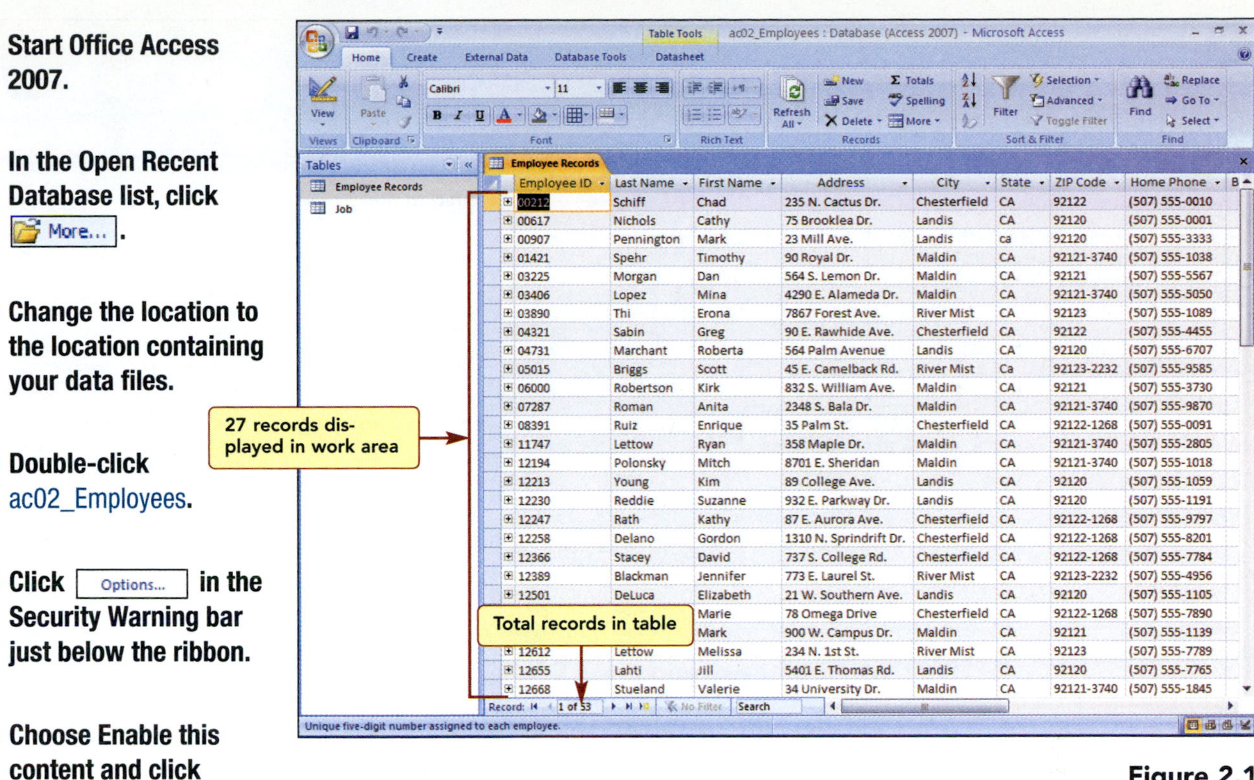

Figure 2.1

> **Having Trouble?**
> Your screen may display a different number of records depending on your monitor settings.

By default, the table is displayed in Datasheet view. As you can see from the record number indicator, the updated table now contains 53 records.

Moving Using the Keyboard

In a large table, there are many methods you can use to quickly navigate through records in Datasheet view. You can always use the mouse to move from one field or record to another. However, if the information is not visible in the window, you must scroll the window using the scroll bar first. The following table presents several keyboard methods that will help you move around in the datasheet.

Keys	Effect
Page Down	Down one window
Page Up	Up one window
Ctrl + Page Up	Left one window
Ctrl + Page Down	Right one window
Ctrl + End	Last field of last record
Ctrl + Home	First field of first record
Ctrl + ↑	Current field of first record
Ctrl + ↓	Current field of last record

Currently, records 1 through 27 are displayed in the work area. You can easily move from one window of records to the next.

Press Page Down.

Having Trouble?

If your screen displays a different number of records, this is because your monitor and system setup may be different than those used to create the figures in the text.

Your screen should be similar to Figure 2.2

Table Tools — ac02_Employees : Database (Access 2007) - Microsoft Access

Employee Records

Current record

Records 27–53 displayed in work area

Employee ID	Last Name	First Name	Address	City	State	ZIP Code	Home Phone
12668			34 University Dr.	Maldin	CA	92121-3740	(507) 555-1845
12703			947 S. Forest St.	Landis	CA	92120	(941) 555-7789
12855	Fachet	Kimberly	923 E. Baseline Rd.	River Mist	CA	92123	(941) 555-0018
12867	Talic	Elvis	21 Oasis St.	River Mist	CA	92123-2232	(941) 555-5985
12914	Gomez	Alfonso	3429 S. Grandview St.	Landis	CA	92120-3741	(941) 555-2395
12920	Larson	Alicia	345 W. Mill Ave.	Maldin	CA	92121-3740	(941) 555-7717
13005	Reilly	Emily	125 N. Marigold St.	Maldin	CA	92121-3740	(941) 555-6532
13027	Kieken	Kimberly	942 S. Golf Dr.	Landis	CA	92120	(941) 555-7564
13297	Delucchi	Bill	950 S. Terrace Dr.	Chesterfield	CA	92122-1268	(941) 555-8195
13303	Jensen	Chris	601 Alpha Dr.	River Mist	CA	92123-2232	(941) 555-0018
13416	Lembi	Damon	4389 S. Rita Ln.	Landis	CA	92120	(941) 555-4747
13458	Helfand	Eric	4601 E. Willow Dr.	Maldin	CA	92121-3740	(941) 555-9101
13484	Franklin	Stephanie	889 S. Litchfield Park	Maldin	CA	92121-3740	(941) 555-7833
13497	Steele	Jeff	1011 E. Holly Ln.	River Mist	CA	92123-2232	(941) 555-1912
13543	Martinez	Julie	1920 First Ave.	Maldin	CA	92121-3740	(941) 555-1044
13597	Gapasin	Ken	2633 E. Fountain St.	Maldin	CA	92121-3740	(941) 555-0589
13635	Martinez	Juan	7115 E Roosevelt Dr.	Maldin	CA	92121-3740	(507) 555-2935
22085	Lindau	Kristina	1947 E. Watson	Landis	CA	92120	(941) 555-6363
22091	Fromthart	Lisa	32 Redcoat Rd.	Chesterfield	CA	92122-1268	(941) 555-0110
22100	Vaccaro	Louis	289 E. Heather Ave.	River Mist	CA	92123-2232	(941) 555-3758
22114	Schneider	Paul	1731 Jackson Ave.	Landis	CA	92120	(941) 555-7440
22297	Rogondino	Patricia	7583 Turquoise	Chesterfield	CA	92122-1268	(941) 555-7539
22304	Torcivia	Peter	904 S. Dorsey Dr.	Chesterfield	CA	92122-1268	(941) 555-9870
22407	Mazeau	Rebecca	7383 Oak Dr.	Landis	CA	92120	(941) 555-1093
22425	Ferguson	Robby	4232 Tuller Ave.	River Mist	CA	92123-2232	(941) 555-7039
22469	Hogan	Ryan	1389 E. Northview Dr.	Maldin	CA	92121-3740	(941) 555-1010
22473	Harvey	Sarah	73 Lakeview Dr.	Chesterfield	CA	92122-1268	(941) 555-7144

Record: 27 of 53

Unique five-digit number assigned to each employee.

Figure 2.2

Now records 27 through 53 are displayed in the window. The first record in the window is now the current record.

Because of the number and width of the fields, all of the fields cannot be displayed in the window at the same time. Rather than scrolling the window horizontally to see the additional fields, you can quickly move to the right a window at a time.

Press Ctrl + Page Down.

Your screen should be similar to Figure 2.3

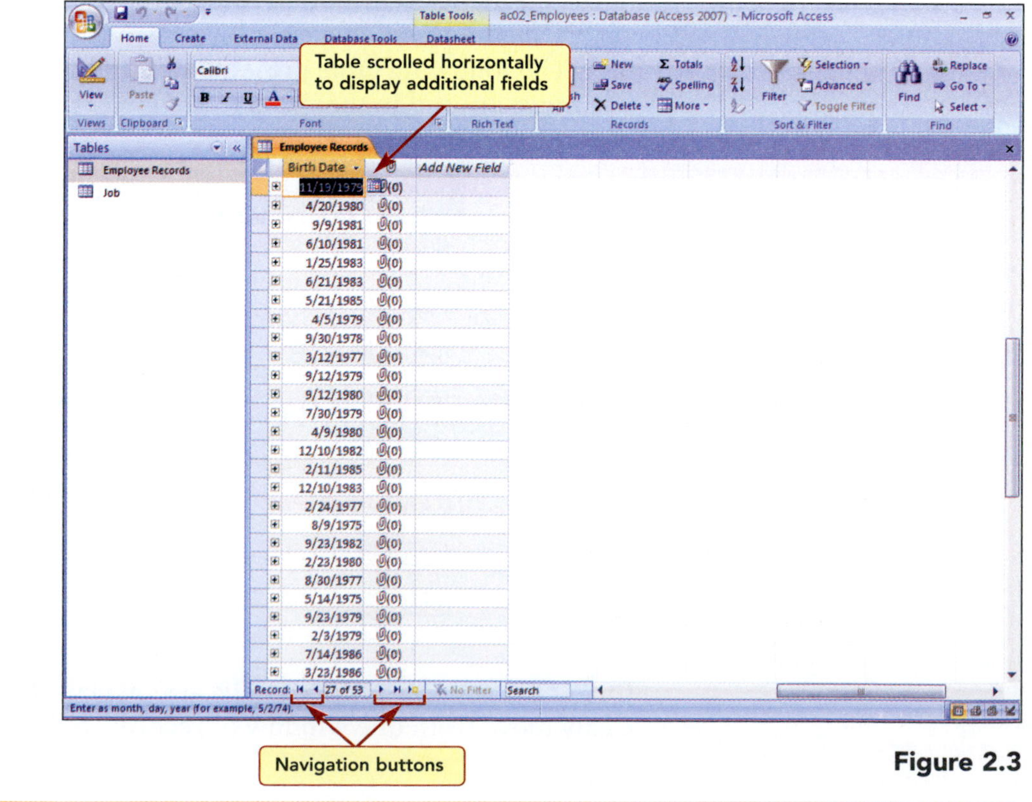

Figure 2.3

The table scrolled horizontally one window to the right and the last two fields in the table are now visible.

Moving Using the Navigation Buttons

The navigation buttons in the status bar also provide navigation shortcuts. These buttons are described in the following table.

Another Method

You also can use Go To in the Find group of the Home tab to access the navigation buttons.

Button	Effect
⏮	First record, same field
◀	Previous record, same field
▶	Next record, same field
⏭	Last record, same field
▶*	New (blank) record

Additional Information

You can move to a specific record by typing the record number in the Record Number Indicator box.

You will use the navigation buttons to move to the same field that is currently selected in the last record, and then back to the same field of the first record. Then you will move to the first field of the first record.

1. **Click ⏭ Last Record.**
   Click ⏮ First Record.
   Press Home.

Your screen should be similar to Figure 2.4

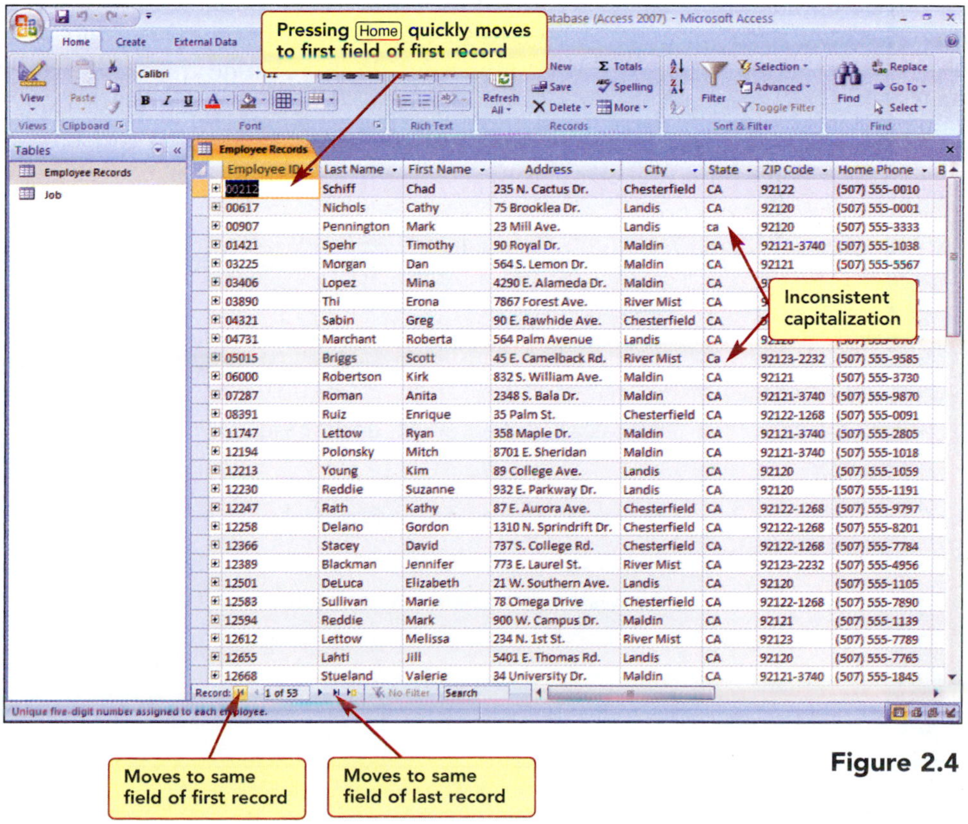

Pressing Home quickly moves to first field of first record

Inconsistent capitalization

Moves to same field of first record

Moves to same field of last record

Figure 2.4

The first field of the first record is selected.

Customizing and Inserting Fields

As you looked through the records, you noticed that record 3 has a lowercase entry in the State field and that record 10 has a mixed-case entry. You want all the State field entries to be consistently entered in all uppercase letters. Also, because all the club locations are in California, it is unlikely that any club employees live in another state. Rather than repeatedly entering the same state for each record, you want the State field to automatically display CA. You will make these changes to the State field by modifying its properties.

Additionally, you realize that you forgot to include a field for each employee's gender. While developing a table, you can modify and refine how the table operates. You can easily add and delete fields and add restrictions on the data that can be entered in a field as well as define the way that the data entered in a field will be displayed.

Setting Display Formats

You will begin by fixing the display of the entries in the State field. Instead of manually editing each field, you will fix the entries by defining a display format for the field to customize the way the entry is displayed.

Concept 1

Format Property

1

The **Format property** is used to specify the way that numbers, dates, times, and text in a field are displayed and printed. Format properties do not change the way Access stores data, only the way the data is displayed. To change the format of a field, you can select from predefined formats or create a custom format by entering different symbols in the Format text box. Text and Memo data types can use any of the four symbols shown in the following table.

Symbol	Meaning	Example
@	Requires a text character or space	@@@-@@-@@@ would display 123456789 as 123-45-6789. Nine characters or spaces are required.
>	Forces all characters to uppercase	> would display SMITH whether you entered SMITH, smith, or Smith.
<	Forces all characters to lowercase	< would display smith whether you entered SMITH, smith, or Smith.
&	Allows an optional text character	@@-@@& would display 12345 as 12-345 and 12.34 as 12-34. Four out of five characters are required, and a fifth is optional.

You want to change the format of the State field to display the entries in all uppercase characters.

1

- **Click Design View.**
- **Click the State field to make it the current field.**
- **Move to the Format field property text box.**
- **Type >.**

Your screen should be similar to Figure 2.5

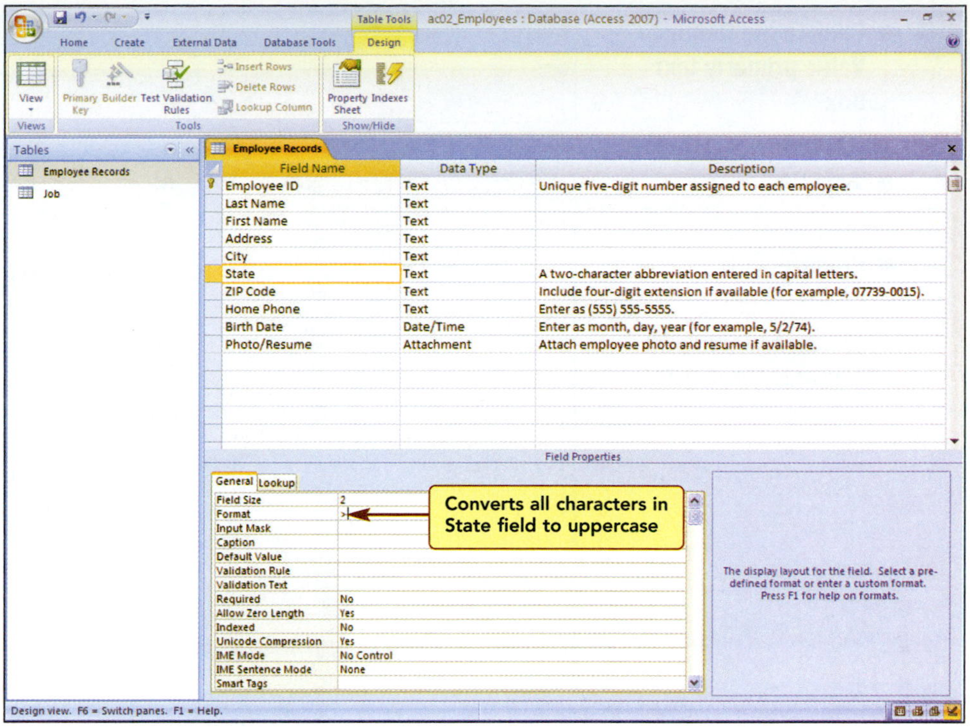

Converts all characters in State field to uppercase

Figure 2.5

Setting Default Values

Next, you want to change the State field for new records to automatically display CA. To do this, you specify a default value property.

Concept 2

Default Value Property

2 The **Default Value property** is used to specify a **value** that is automatically entered in a field when a new record is created. This property is commonly used when most of the entries in a field will be the same for the entire table. That default value is then displayed automatically in the field. When users add a record to the table, they can either accept this value or enter another value. This saves time while entering data.

You will set the State field's default value to display CA.

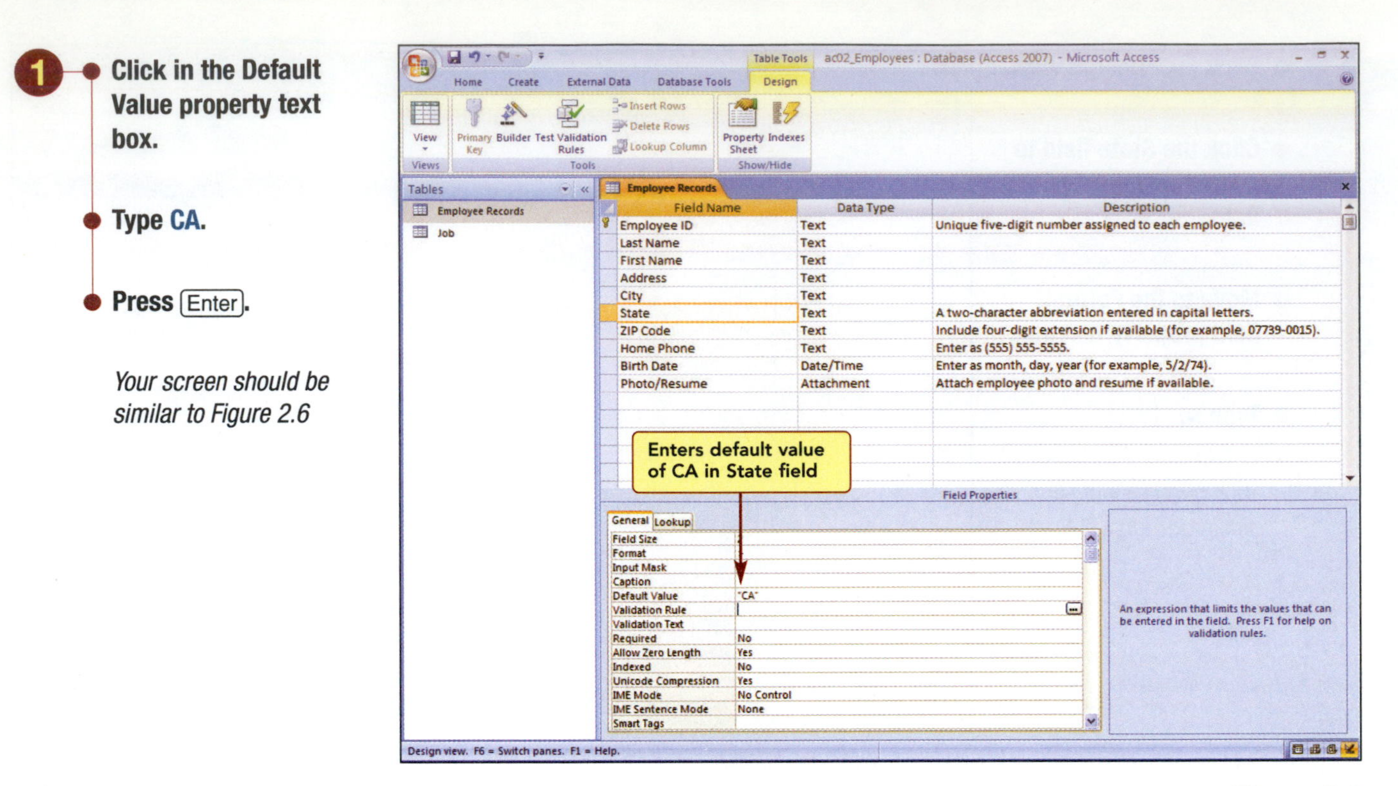

1 Click in the Default Value property text box.

Type **CA**.

Press Enter.

Your screen should be similar to Figure 2.6

Figure 2.6

The default value is automatically enclosed in quotation marks to identify the entry as a group of characters called a **character string.** To see the effect on the table of setting a default value, you will return to Datasheet view and look at a new blank record.

Next, you want to see the effect of the modifications to the State field's properties on the table.

2 Click Datasheet View.

Click Yes to save the table.

Hide the Navigation pane.

Your screen should be similar to Figure 2.7

Figure 2.7

You can see that records 3 (Mark Pennington) and 10 (Scot Briggs) now correctly display the state in capital letters. Setting the format for the field will prevent this type of error from occurring again.

3 **Click New (blank) Record on the status bar to move to a new record.**

Your screen should be similar to Figure 2.8

Employee ID	Last Name	First Name	Address	City	State	ZIP Code	Home Phone	Birth Date	
12855	Fachet	Kimberly	923 E. Baseline Rd.	River Mist	CA	92123	(941) 555-0018	9/9/1981	(0)
12867	Talic	Elvis	21 Oasis St.	River Mist	CA	92123-2232	(941) 555-5985	6/10/1981	(0)
12914	Gomez	Alfonso	3429 S. Grandview St.	Landis	CA	92120-3741	(941) 555-2395	1/25/1983	(0)
12920	Larson	Alicia	345 W. Mill Ave.	Maldin	CA	92121-3740	(941) 555-7717	6/21/1983	(0)
13005	Reilly	Emily	125 N. Marigold St.	Maldin	CA	92121-3740	(941) 555-6532	5/21/1985	(0)
13027	Kieken	Kimberly	942 S. Golf Dr.	Landis	CA	92120	(941) 555-7564	4/5/1979	(0)
13297	Delucchi	Bill	950 S. Terrace Dr.	Chesterfield	CA	92122-1268	(941) 555-8195	9/30/1978	(0)
13303	Jensen	Chris	601 Alpha Dr.	River Mist	CA	92123-2232	(941) 555-0018	3/12/1977	(0)
13416	Lembi	Damon	4389 S. Rita Ln.	Landis	CA	92120	(941) 555-4747	9/12/1979	(0)
13458	Helfand	Eric	4601 E. Willow Dr.	Maldin	CA	92121-3740	(941) 555-9101	9/12/1980	(0)
13484	Franklin	Stephanie	889 S. Litchfield Park	Maldin	CA	92121-3740	(941) 555-7833	7/30/1979	(0)
13497	Steele	Jeff	1011 E. Holly Ln.	River Mist	CA	92123-2232	(941) 555-1912	4/9/1980	(0)
13543	Martinez	Julie	1920 First Ave.	Maldin	CA	92121-3740	(941) 555-1044	12/10/1982	(0)
13597	Gapasin	Ken	2633 E. Fountain St.	Maldin	CA	92121-3740	(941) 555-0589	2/11/1985	(0)
13635	Martinez	Juan	7115 E Roosevelt Dr.	Maldin	CA	92121-3740	(507) 555-2935	12/10/1983	(0)
22085	Lindau	Kristina	1947 E. Watson	Landis	CA	92120	(941) 555-6363	2/24/1977	(0)
22091	Fromthart	Lisa	32 Redcoat Rd.	Chesterfield	CA	92122-1268	(941) 555-0110	8/9/1975	(0)
22100	Vaccaro	Louis	289 E. Heather Ave.	River Mist	CA	92123-2232	(941) 555-3758	9/23/1982	(0)
22114	Schneider	Paul	1731 Jackson Ave.	Landis	CA	92120	(941) 555-7440	2/23/1980	(0)
22297	Rogondino	Patricia	7583 Turquoise	Chesterfield	CA	92122-1268	(941) 555-7539	8/30/1977	(0)
22304	Torcivia	Peter	904 S. Dorsey Dr.	Chesterfield	CA	92122-1268	(941) 555-9870	5/14/1975	(0)
22407	Mazeau	Rebecca	7383 Oak Dr.	Landis	CA	92120	(941) 555-1093	9/23/1979	(0)
22425	Ferguson	Robby	4232 Tuller Ave.	River Mist	CA	92123-2232	(941) 555-7039	2/3/1979	(0)
22469	Hogan	Ryan	1389 E. Northview Dr.	Maldin	CA	92121-3740	(941) 555-1010	7/14/1986	(0)
22473	Harvey	Sarah	73 Lakeview Dr.	Chesterfield	CA	92122-1			
					CA				

Default value displayed in State field of new record

New (blank) record button

Figure 2.8

The new blank record at the end of the table displays CA as the default value for the State field. If you did need to enter a different state, it would display in all capital letters because of the format property setting associated with the field.

Another Method

You also can insert a field in Datasheet view by moving to the location where you want to insert the new field and using Insert on the Datasheet tab. However, you still need to switch to Design view to set the new field's properties.

Inserting a Field

Now you want to add the new field to hold each employee's gender. Although it is better to include all the necessary fields when creating the table structure, it is possible to add fields to a table at a later time. After looking at the order of the fields, you decide to add the Gender field between the Home Phone and Birth Date fields. To do so, you will switch to Design view to insert the new field in the table.

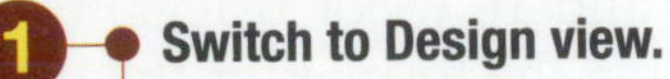

1 Switch to Design view.

- Make the Birth Date field current.
- Click Insert Rows in the Tools group of the Design tab.

Another Method

You also can use Insert Rows on the shortcut menu.

Your screen should be similar to Figure 2.9

Inserts blank field row above current row

Blank field row inserted

Figure 2.9

A new blank row is inserted into the table. Next, you will name the field and set its properties.

2 Enter the new field definitions from the table shown here:

Field Name	Gender
Data Type	Text
Description	Enter f for female and m for male.
Field Size	1
Format	>

Your screen should be similar to Figure 2.10

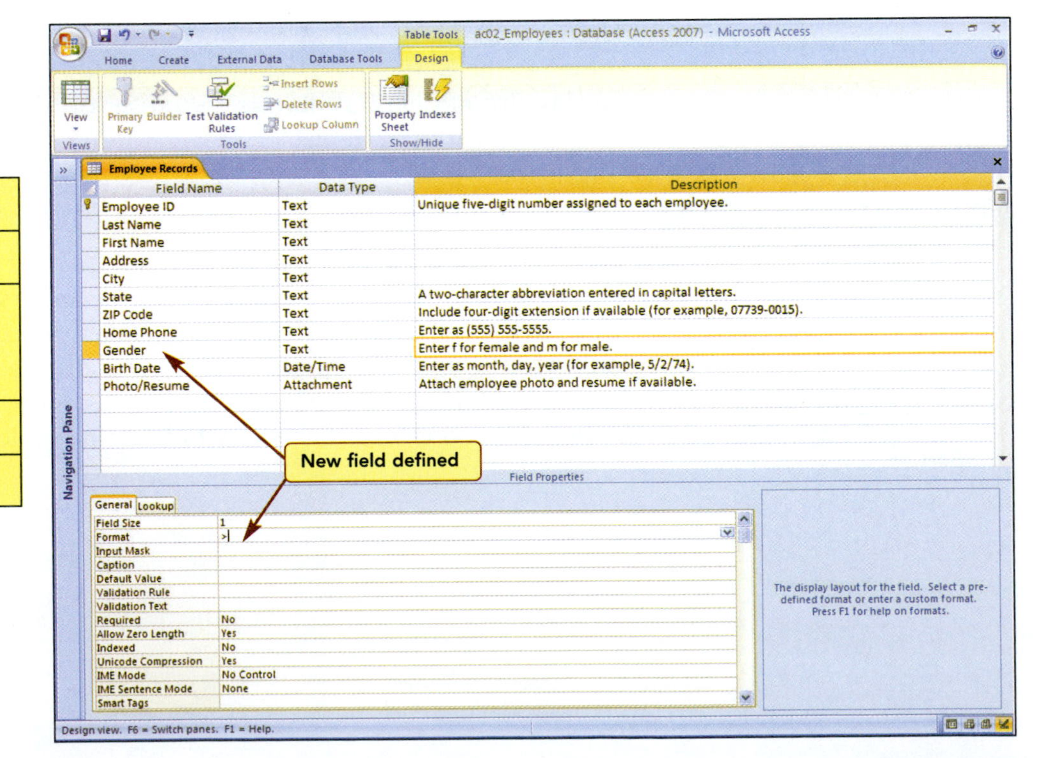

Figure 2.10

Defining Validation Rules

The only two characters you want the Gender field to accept are F for female and M for male. To specify that these two characters are the only entries acceptable in the Gender field, you will add a validation rule to the field's properties.

Concept 3

Validation Rule

3

Validation rules are used to control the data that can be entered in a field by defining the input values that are valid or allowed. Certain checks on the validity of the data that is entered in a field are performed automatically based on the field's data type and size. For example, in a field whose data type is Number and size is five, the type of data that can be entered in the field is restricted to a maximum of five numeric entries. You can further refine these basic restrictions by adding a validation rule to the field's properties that defines specific restrictions for the type of data that can be entered in the field.

You also can include a validation text message. **Validation text** is an explanatory message that appears if a user attempts to enter invalid information in a text field for which there is a validity check. If you do not specify a message, Access will display a default error message, which may not clearly describe the reason for the error.

You will create a validation rule for the Gender field to restrict the data entry to the two valid characters. A validation rule is specified by entering an expression in the validation rule property that limits the values that can be entered in the field.

Concept 4

Expression

4 An **expression** is a formula consisting of a combination of symbols that will produce a single value. You create an expression by combining identifiers, operators, and values to produce the desired results. An **identifier** is an element that refers to the value of a field, a graphical object, or a property. In the expression [Sales Amount] + [Sales Tax], [Sales Amount] and [Sales Tax] are identifiers that refer to the values in the Sales Amount and Sales Tax fields. Identifiers are separated by dots or exclamation points. Each part of an identifier is surrounded by square brackets.

An **operator** is a symbol or word that indicates that an operation is to be performed. Common mathematical operators are + for addition, - for subtraction, * for multiplication, and / for division. A **comparison operator** is a symbol that allows you to make comparisons between two items. The following table describes the comparison operators:

Operator	Meaning
=	Equal to
<>	Not equal to
<	Less than
>	Greater than
<=	Less than or equal to
>=	Greater than or equal to

In addition, the OR and AND operators allow you to enter additional criteria in the same field or different fields.

Values are numbers, dates, or character strings. Character strings such as "F", "M", or "Workout Gear" are enclosed in quotation marks. Dates are enclosed in pound signs (#), as in #1/1/99#.

The following table shows some examples of possible expressions.

Expression	Result
[Sales Amount] + [Sales Tax]	Sums values in two fields.
"F" OR "M"	Restricts entry to the letters F or M only.
>= #1/1/99# AND <= #12/31/99#	Restricts entries to dates greater than or equal to 1/1/99 and less than or equal to 12/31/99.
"Workout Gear"	Allows the entry Workout Gear only.

You will enter the expression to restrict the data entry in the Gender field to the letters "f" or "m."

1. **Move to the Validation Rule field property text box.**
   - **Type f or m.**

Additional Information

The AND and OR operators can be entered using uppercase or lowercase characters.

   - **Press Enter.**
   - **For the validation text, type The only valid entry is f or m.**

Your screen should be similar to Figure 2.11

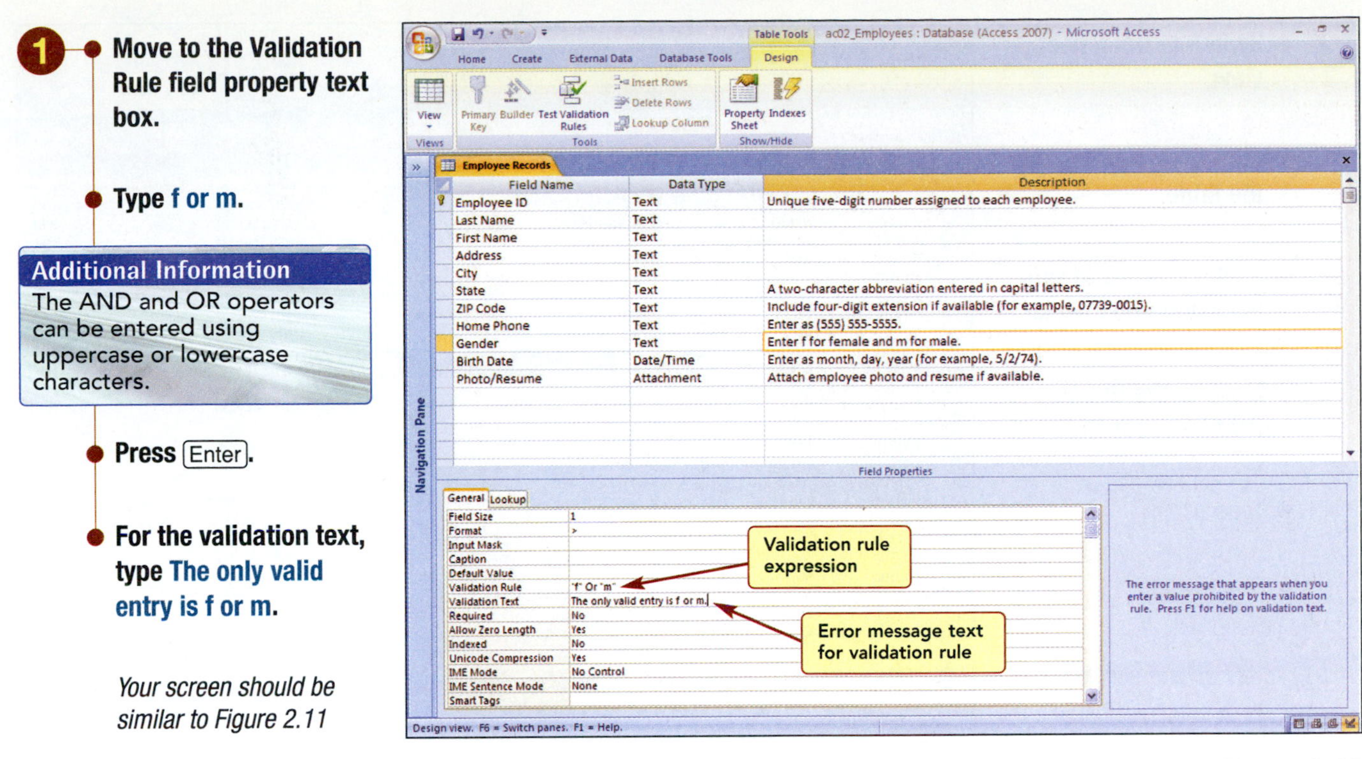

Figure 2.11

The expression states that the acceptable values can only be equal to an F or an M. Notice that Access automatically added quotation marks around the two character strings and changed the "o" in "or" to uppercase. Because the Format property has been set to convert all entries to uppercase, this means that an entry of f or m is as acceptable as F or M.

Next, you will switch back to Datasheet view to test the validation rule by entering data for the Gender field. In addition to a message box asking whether you want to save the design changes, another message box will appear to advise you that the data integrity rules have been changed. When you restructure a table, you often make changes that could result in a loss of data. Changes such as shortening field sizes, creating validity rules, or changing field types can cause existing data to become invalid. Because the field is new, it has no data values to verify, and a validation check is unnecessary at this time.

2 **Switch to Datasheet view.**

- **Click** Yes **to save the table.**
- **Click** No **to skip the validation check.**
- **Move to the Gender field for record 1.**
- **Type p.**
- **Press** Enter.

Your screen should be similar to Figure 2.12

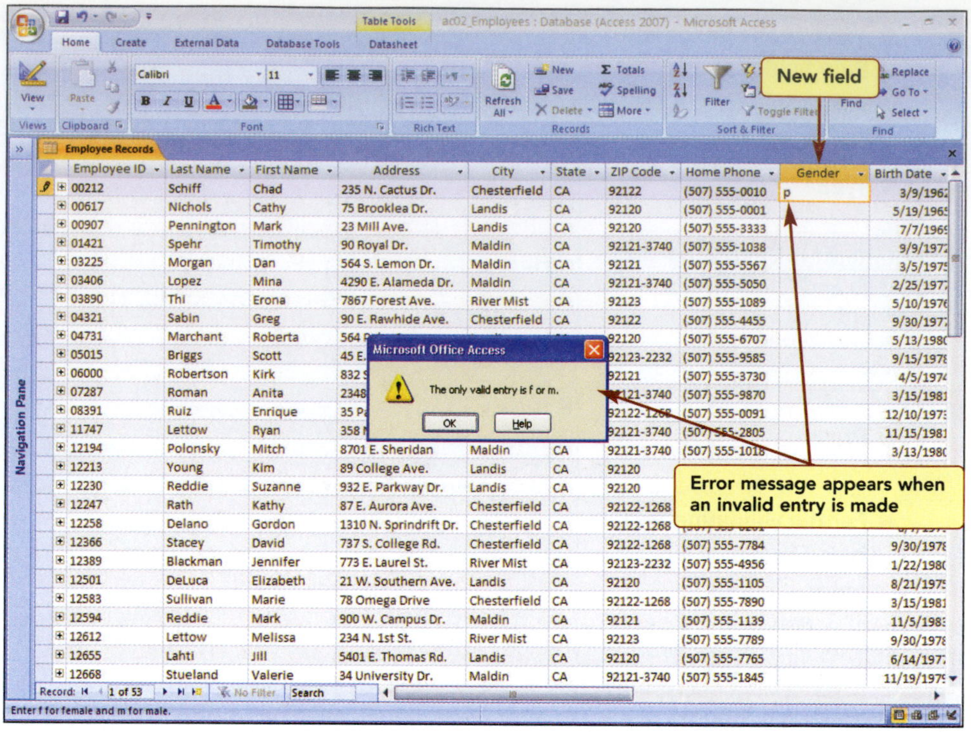

Table Tools ac02_Employees : Database (Access 2007) - Microsoft Access

New field

Employee Records

Employee ID	Last Name	First Name	Address	City	State	ZIP Code	Home Phone	Gender	Birth Date
00212	Schiff	Chad	235 N. Cactus Dr.	Chesterfield	CA	92122	(507) 555-0010	p	3/9/1962
00617	Nichols	Cathy	75 Brooklea Dr.	Landis	CA	92120	(507) 555-0001		5/19/1965
00907	Pennington	Mark	23 Mill Ave.	Landis	CA	92120	(507) 555-3333		7/7/1969
01421	Spehr	Timothy	90 Royal Dr.	Maldin	CA	92121-3740	(507) 555-1038		9/9/1972
03225	Morgan	Dan	564 S. Lemon Dr.	Maldin	CA	92121	(507) 555-5567		3/5/1975
03406	Lopez	Mina	4290 E. Alameda Dr.	Maldin	CA	92121-3740	(507) 555-5050		2/25/1977
03890	Thi	Erona	7867 Forest Ave.	River Mist	CA	92123	(507) 555-1089		5/10/1976
04321	Sabin	Greg	90 E. Rawhide Ave.	Chesterfield	CA	92122	(507) 555-4455		9/30/1972
04731	Marchant	Roberta	564 P			92120	(507) 555-6707		5/13/1980
05015	Briggs	Scott	45 E.			92123-2232	(507) 555-9585		9/15/1978
06000	Robertson	Kirk	832 S			92121	(507) 555-3730		4/5/1974
07287	Roman	Anita	2348			21-3740	(507) 555-9870		3/15/1981
08391	Ruiz	Enrique	35 P			92122-1268	(507) 555-0091		12/10/1973
11747	Lettow	Ryan	358 M			92121-3740	(507) 555-2805		11/15/1981
12194	Polonsky	Mitch	8701 E. Sheridan	Maldin	CA	92121-3740	(507) 555-1018		3/13/1980
12213	Young	Kim	89 College Ave.	Landis	CA	92120			
12230	Reddie	Suzanne	932 E. Parkway Dr.	Landis	CA	92120			
12247	Rath	Kathy	87 E. Aurora Ave.	Chesterfield	CA	92122-1268			
12258	Delano	Gordon	1310 N. Sprindrift Dr.	Chesterfield	CA	92122-1268			
12366	Stacey	David	737 S. College Rd.	Chesterfield	CA	92122-1268	(507) 555-7784		9/30/1978
12389	Blackman	Jennifer	773 E. Laurel St.	River Mist	CA	92123-2232	(507) 555-4956		1/22/1980
12501	DeLuca	Elizabeth	21 W. Southern Ave.	Landis	CA	92120	(507) 555-1105		8/21/1975
12583	Sullivan	Marie	78 Omega Drive	Chesterfield	CA	92122-1268	(507) 555-7890		3/15/1981
12594	Reddie	Mark	900 W. Campus Dr.	Maldin	CA	92121	(507) 555-1139		11/5/1983
12612	Lettow	Melissa	234 N. 1st St.	River Mist	CA	92123	(507) 555-7789		9/30/1978
12655	Lahti	Jill	5401 E. Thomas Rd.	Landis	CA	92120	(507) 555-7765		6/14/1972
12668	Stueland	Valerie	34 University Dr.	Maldin	CA	92121-3740	(507) 555-1845		11/19/1979

Microsoft Office Access

The only valid entry is f or m.

OK Help

Error message appears when an invalid entry is made

Record: 1 of 53 No Filter Search

Enter f for female and m for male.

Figure 2.12

The new field was added to the table between the Home Phone and Birth Date fields. Because the letter p is not a valid entry, Access displays the error message you entered as the Validation Text for the field. You will clear the error message and correct the entry.

3 **Click** OK.

- **Press** ←Backspace.
- **Type m.**
- **Press** ↓.

Your screen should be similar to Figure 2.13

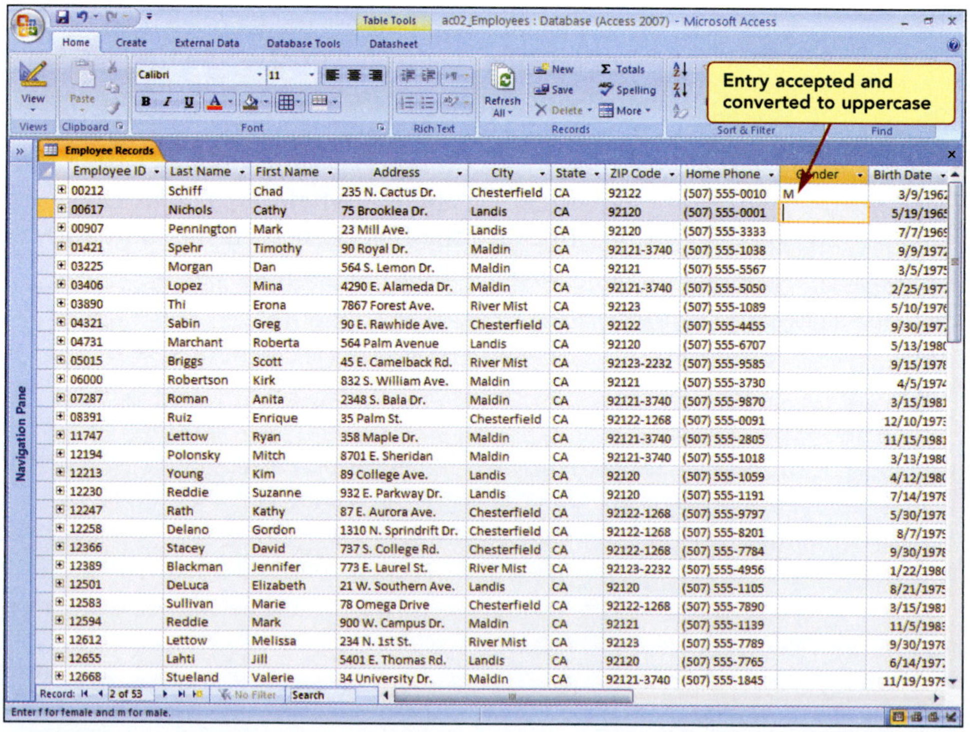

Table Tools ac02_Employees : Database (Access 2007) - Microsoft Access

Entry accepted and converted to uppercase

Employee Records

Employee ID	Last Name	First Name	Address	City	State	ZIP Code	Home Phone	Gender	Birth Date
00212	Schiff	Chad	235 N. Cactus Dr.	Chesterfield	CA	92122	(507) 555-0010	M	3/9/1962
00617	Nichols	Cathy	75 Brooklea Dr.	Landis	CA	92120	(507) 555-0001		5/19/1965
00907	Pennington	Mark	23 Mill Ave.	Landis	CA	92120	(507) 555-3333		7/7/1969
01421	Spehr	Timothy	90 Royal Dr.	Maldin	CA	92121-3740	(507) 555-1038		9/9/1972
03225	Morgan	Dan	564 S. Lemon Dr.	Maldin	CA	92121	(507) 555-5567		3/5/1975
03406	Lopez	Mina	4290 E. Alameda Dr.	Maldin	CA	92121-3740	(507) 555-5050		2/25/1977
03890	Thi	Erona	7867 Forest Ave.	River Mist	CA	92123	(507) 555-1089		5/10/1976
04321	Sabin	Greg	90 E. Rawhide Ave.	Chesterfield	CA	92122	(507) 555-4455		9/30/1972
04731	Marchant	Roberta	564 Palm Avenue	Landis	CA	92120	(507) 555-6707		5/13/1980
05015	Briggs	Scott	45 E. Camelback Rd.	River Mist	CA	92123-2232	(507) 555-9585		9/15/1978
06000	Robertson	Kirk	832 S. William Ave.	Maldin	CA	92121	(507) 555-3730		4/5/1974
07287	Roman	Anita	2348 S. Bala Dr.	Maldin	CA	92121-3740	(507) 555-9870		3/15/1981
08391	Ruiz	Enrique	35 Palm St.	Chesterfield	CA	92122-1268	(507) 555-0091		12/10/1973
11747	Lettow	Ryan	358 Maple Dr.	Maldin	CA	92121-3740	(507) 555-2805		11/15/1981
12194	Polonsky	Mitch	8701 E. Sheridan	Maldin	CA	92121-3740	(507) 555-1018		3/13/1980
12213	Young	Kim	89 College Ave.	Landis	CA	92120	(507) 555-1059		4/12/1980
12230	Reddie	Suzanne	932 E. Parkway Dr.	Landis	CA	92120	(507) 555-1191		7/14/1978
12247	Rath	Kathy	87 E. Aurora Ave.	Chesterfield	CA	92122-1268	(507) 555-9797		5/30/1978
12258	Delano	Gordon	1310 N. Sprindrift Dr.	Chesterfield	CA	92122-1268	(507) 555-8201		8/7/1979
12366	Stacey	David	737 S. College Rd.	Chesterfield	CA	92122-1268	(507) 555-7784		9/30/1978
12389	Blackman	Jennifer	773 E. Laurel St.	River Mist	CA	92123-2232	(507) 555-4956		1/22/1980
12501	DeLuca	Elizabeth	21 W. Southern Ave.	Landis	CA	92120	(507) 555-1105		8/21/1975
12583	Sullivan	Marie	78 Omega Drive	Chesterfield	CA	92122-1268	(507) 555-7890		3/15/1981
12594	Reddie	Mark	900 W. Campus Dr.	Maldin	CA	92121	(507) 555-1139		11/5/1983
12612	Lettow	Melissa	234 N. 1st St.	River Mist	CA	92123	(507) 555-7789		9/30/1978
12655	Lahti	Jill	5401 E. Thomas Rd.	Landis	CA	92120	(507) 555-7765		6/14/1972
12668	Stueland	Valerie	34 University Dr.	Maldin	CA	92121-3740	(507) 555-1845		11/19/1979

Record: 2 of 53 No Filter Search

Enter f for female and m for male.

Figure 2.13

The entry for the first record is accepted and displayed as an uppercase M.

Hiding and Redisplaying Fields

To enter the gender data for the rest of the fields, you will use the First Name field as a guide. Unfortunately, the First Name and Gender fields are currently on opposite sides of the screen and will require you to look back and forth across each record. You can eliminate this problem by hiding the fields you do not need to see, and then redisplaying them when you have finished entering the gender data.

Hiding Fields

A quick way to view two fields side by side (in this case, the First Name and Gender fields) is to hide the fields that are in between (the Address through Home Phone fields).

1

- **Select the Address field through the Home Phone field.**

Additional Information

Drag along the column heads when the mouse pointer is ⬇ to select the fields.

- **Right-click on the selection.**
- **Choose Hide Columns from the shortcut menu.**

Another Method

You also can click More in the Records group of the Home tab and choose Hide Columns.

Your screen should be similar to Figure 2.14

Address through Home Phone fields hidden

Figure 2.14

Now that the First Name and Gender columns are next to each other, you can refer to the first name in each record to enter the correct gender data.

2 **Enter the Gender field values for the remaining records by looking at the First Name field to determine whether the employee is male or female.**

Reduce the size of the Gender column using the Best Fit command.

Having Trouble?

Remember, to best fit data in a column, you double-click its right border.

Your screen should be similar to Figure 2.15

Field column width reduced

Gender data entered for all records

Figure 2.15

Redisplaying Hidden Fields

After you have entered the gender data for all of the records, you can redisplay the hidden fields.

1 **Right-click on any column header.**

Choose Unhide columns from the shortcut menu.

Another Method

You also can click More in the Records group of the Home tab and choose Unhide Columns.

Your screen should be similar to Figure 2.16

Hidden fields are not selected

Figure 2.16

You use the Unhide Columns dialog box to select the currently hidden columns you want to redisplay. A checkmark in the box next to a column name indicates that the column is currently displayed; column names with no checkmarks indicate that they are currently hidden. You want to unhide all hidden columns in your table.

2 • **Select the five column names that do not display checkmarks.**

Additional Information
Notice that as you make each selection, the corresponding column reappears in the table datasheet behind the dialog box.

• **Click** Close.

Your screen should be similar to Figure 2.17

Fields that were hidden are redisplayed

Employee Records

Employee ID	Last Name	First Name	Address	City	State	ZIP Code	Home Phone	Gender	Birth Date
12855	Fachet	Kimberly	923 E. Baseline Rd.	River Mist	CA	92123	(941) 555-0018	F	9/9/1981
12867	Talic	Elvis	21 Oasis St.	River Mist	CA	92123-2232	(941) 555-5985	M	6/10/1981
12914	Gomez	Alfonso	3429 S. Grandview St.	Landis	CA	92120-3741	(941) 555-2395	M	1/25/1983
12920	Larson	Alicia	345 W. Mill Ave.	Maldin	CA	92121-3740	(941) 555-7717	F	6/21/1983
13005	Reilly	Emily	125 N. Marigold St.	Maldin	CA	92121-3740	(941) 555-6532	F	5/21/1985
13027	Kieken	Kimberly	942 S. Golf Dr.	Landis	CA	92120	(941) 555-7564	F	4/5/1979
13297	Delucchi	Bill	950 S. Terrace Dr.	Chesterfield	CA	92122-1268	(941) 555-8195	M	9/30/1978
13303	Jensen	Chris	601 Alpha Dr.	River Mist	CA	92123-2232	(941) 555-0018	M	3/12/1977
13416	Lembi	Damon	4389 S. Rita Ln.	Landis	CA	92120	(941) 555-4747	M	9/12/1979
13458	Helfand	Eric	4601 E. Willow Dr.	Maldin	CA	92121-3740	(941) 555-9101	M	9/12/1980
13484	Franklin	Stephanie	889 S. Litchfield Park	Maldin	CA	92121-3740	(941) 555-7833	F	7/30/1979
13497	Steele	Jeff	1011 E. Holly Ln.	River Mist	CA	92123-2232	(941) 555-1912	M	4/9/1980
13543	Martinez	Julie	1920 First Ave.	Maldin	CA	92121-3740	(941) 555-1044	F	12/10/1982
13597	Gapasin	Ken	2633 E. Fountain St.	Maldin	CA	92121-3740	(941) 555-0589	M	2/11/1985
13635	Martinez	Juan	7115 E Roosevelt Dr.	Maldin	CA	92121-3740	(507) 555-2935	M	12/10/1983
22085	Lindau	Kristina	1947 E. Watson	Landis	CA	92120	(941) 555-6363	F	2/24/1977
22091	Fromthart	Lisa	32 Redcoat Rd.	Chesterfield	CA	92122-1268	(941) 555-0110	F	8/9/1975
22100	Vaccaro	Louis	289 E. Heather Ave.	River Mist	CA	92123-2232	(941) 555-3758	M	9/23/1982
22114	Schneider	Paul	1731 Jackson Ave.	Landis	CA	92120	(941) 555-7440	M	2/23/1980
22297	Rogondino	Patricia	7583 Turquoise	Chesterfield	CA	92122-1268	(941) 555-7539	F	8/30/1977
22304	Torcivia	Peter	904 S. Dorsey Dr.	Chesterfield	CA	92122-1268	(941) 555-9870	M	5/14/1975
22407	Mazeau	Rebecca	7383 Oak Dr.	Landis	CA	92120	(941) 555-1093	F	9/23/1979
22425	Ferguson	Robby	4232 Tuller Ave.	River Mist	CA	92123-2232	(941) 555-7039	M	2/3/1979
22469	Hogan	Ryan	1389 E. Northview Dr.	Maldin	CA	92121-3740	(941) 555-1010	M	7/14/1986
22473	Harvey	Sarah	73 Lakeview Dr.	Chesterfield	CA	92122-1268	(941) 555-7144	F	3/23/1986
					CA				

Record: 1 of 53 No Filter Search

Enter f for female and m for male.

Figure 2.17

All of the fields are displayed again.

Creating a Lookup Field

Next you decide to change the Location field in the Job table to a lookup field that will make entering the location information easier, faster, and less prone to errors. There are three club locations: Landis, Chesterfield, and River Mist. You want the club locations to be listed so that anyone entering a new employee record will merely have to choose from this list to enter the club location for that employee.

Having Trouble?
Refer to Concept 6 in Lab 1 to review Lookup fields.

You will use the Lookup Wizard to change the existing Location field to a lookup field that uses fixed values.

1

- **Display the Navigation pane and open the Job table.**
- **Hide the Navigation pane and switch to Design view.**
- **Make the Location field active.**
- **Open the Data Type drop-down list and choose Lookup Wizard.**

Your screen should be similar to Figure 2.18

Figure 2.18

Additional Information

Using [Lookup Column] in the Fields & Columns group of the Datasheet tab inserts a new field column and starts the Lookup Wizard.

In the first Lookup Wizard dialog box, you specify the source for the values for the lookup field. You will enter your own values, the club locations, for this field.

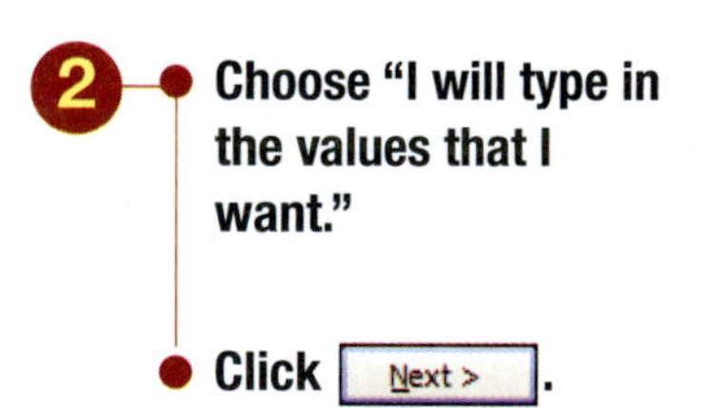

2

- **Choose "I will type in the values that I want."**
- **Click [Next >].**

Your screen should be similar to Figure 2.19

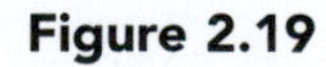

Figure 2.19

The next step is to enter the values you want listed in the lookup field. You also can add columns and adjust their widths to fit the values you enter, if necessary. You only need one column, and the current width is sufficient for the values you will enter.

3

- **Click the entry box under Col1.**
- **Type Landis.**
- **Press Tab.**
- **Enter Chesterfield and River Mist locations next, pressing Tab to go from one cell to the next.**

Having Trouble?
You can correct these entries the same way you do when entering data into any other field.

Your screen should be similar to Figure 2.20

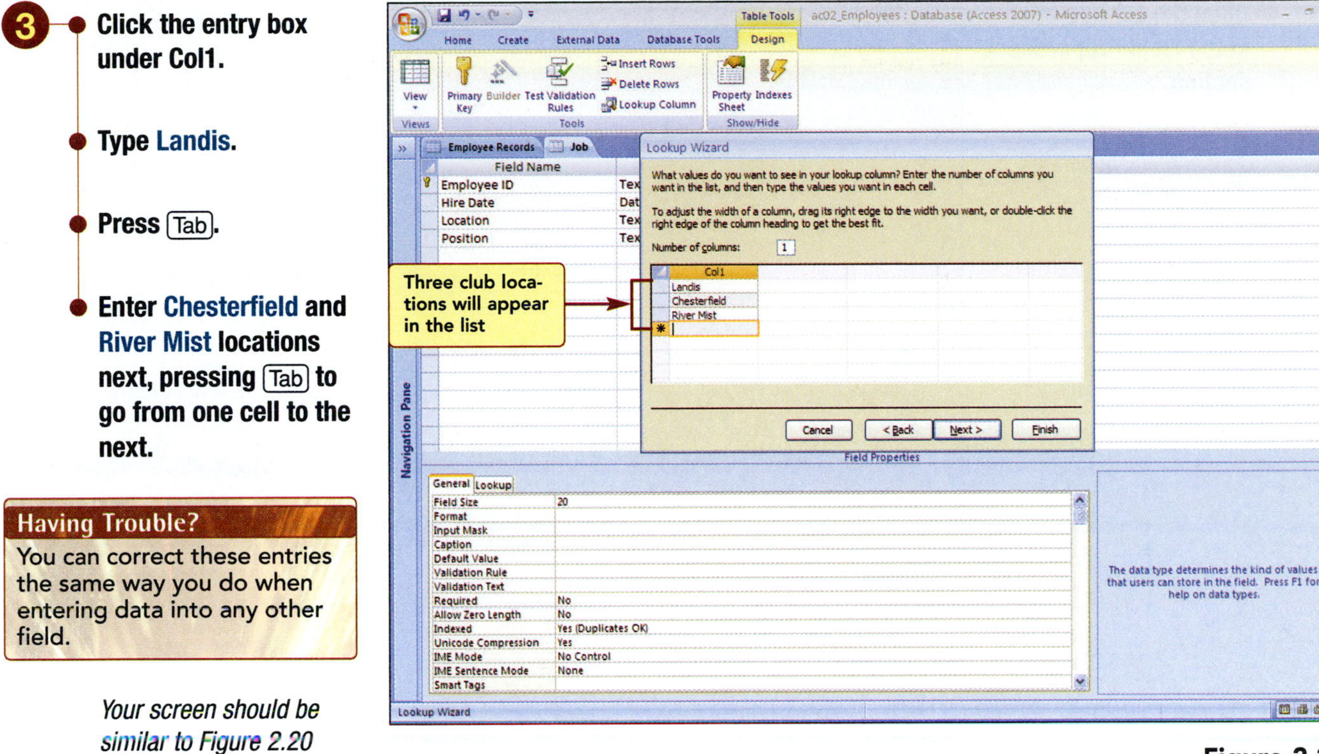

Figure 2.20

After entering the field values, you will move to the next step to enter a field name and finish the wizard. You will leave the field name as Location. Then you will check the field property settings established for this field to see whether any changes are necessary.

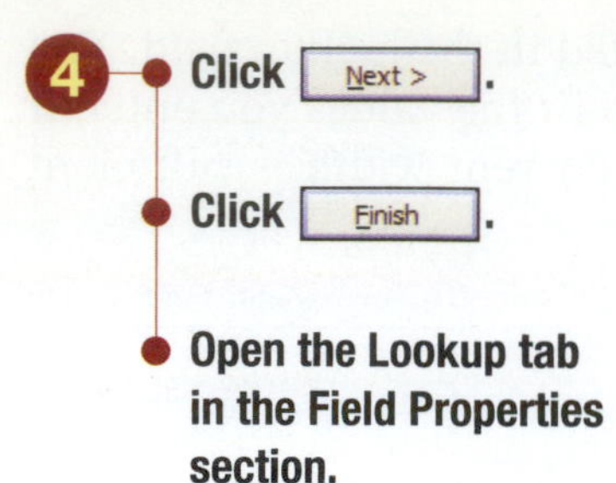

4 Click Next >.

Click Finish.

Open the Lookup tab in the Field Properties section.

Your screen should be similar to Figure 2.21

Table Tools | ac02_Employees : Database (Access 2007) - Microsoft Access

Home | Create | External Data | Database Tools | Design

View | Primary Key | Builder | Test Validation Rules | Insert Rows | Delete Rows | Lookup Column | Property Sheet | Indexes

Views | Tools | Show/Hide

Employee Records | Job

Field Name	Data Type	Description
Employee ID	Text	
Hire Date	Date/Time	Enter as month, day, year (for example, 5/2/99)
Location	Text	
Position	Text	

Navigation Pane

Field Properties

General | Lookup

Display Control	Combo Box
Row Source Type	Value List
Row Source	"Landis";"Chesterfield";"River Mist"
Bound Column	1
Column Count	1
Column Heads	No
Column Widths	1"
List Rows	16
List Width	1"
Limit To List	No
Allow Multiple Values	No
Allow Value List Edits	No
List Items Edit Form	
Show Only Row Source V	No

The data type determines the kind of values that users can store in the field. Press F1 for help on data types.

Type of control

List values

Allows other entries

Design view. F6 = Switch panes. F1 = Help.

Figure 2.21

The lookup list will display in a combo box (drop-down list) control on forms. It gets its list values from the value list containing the values you specified as the source. The other properties are set to the defaults for lookup fields. The only change you want to make is to restrict the data entry in that field to values in the lookup list. Then you will test that the Location field is performing correctly.

- **Change the Limit to List property to Yes.**

Having Trouble?

Select the property and click ▾ at the end of the box to open the drop-down list of options.

- **Save the table design and switch to Datasheet view.**

Additional Information:

If you do not save the table design before switching views, Access will prompt you to save it. Click Yes to continue.

- **Click in the Location field of the first record.**
- **Replace the current location with Maldin and press Enter.**

Your screen should be similar to Figure 2.22

Table Tools ac02_Employees : Database (Access 2007) - Microsoft Access

Home Create External Data Database Tools Datasheet

View Paste Calibri 11 Refresh All New Save Delete Totals Spelling More Filter Selection Advanced Toggle Filter Find Replace Go To Select

Views Clipboard Font Rich Text Records Sort & Filter Find

Employee Records Job

Employee ID	Hire Date	Location	Position	Add New Field
00212	2/1/1999	Maldin	Club Director	
00617	7/8/1999	Chesterfield	Club Manager	
00907	12/12/1999	River Mist	Club Manager	
01421	1/10/2000	River Mist	Assistant Manager	
03225	5/1/2000	Landis	Food Service Director	
03406	5/5/2000	Chesterfield	Assistant Manager	
03890	7/5/2001	Landis	Fitness Director	
04321	8/5/2001	Chesterfield	Assistant Manager	
04731	8/19/2001	Ri		
05015	1/4/2002	La		
06000	2/10/2002	Ch		
07287	3/15/2002	La		
08391	6/4/2002	Ri		
11747	7/9/2002	Ch		
12194	1/12/2003	Chesterfield	Personal Trainer	
12213	1/17/2003	River Mist	Sales Associate	
12230	3/2/2003	River Mist	Personal Trainer	
12247	3/10/2003	River Mist	Fitness Instructor	
12258	4/12/2003	Chesterfield	Food Service Manager	
12366	6/1/2003	River Mist	Fitness Instructor	
12389	8/4/2003	Landis	Sales Associate	
12501	10/5/2003	Landis	Personal Trainer	
12583	4/20/2003	Landis	Greeter	
12594	12/21/2003	River Mist	Food Service Server	
12612	1/14/2004	Chesterfield	Cleaning	
12655	1/16/2004	Chesterfield	Fitness Instructor	
12668	2/4/2004	Chesterfield	Sales Associate	

Microsoft Office Access

The text you entered isn't an item in the list.

Select an item from the list, or enter text that matches one of the listed items.

OK

Entry does not match one of the items in list

Navigation Pane

Record: 1 of 53 No Filter Search

Ready

Figure 2.22

A warning box advises you that the entry is not one of the listed items because you restricted the field entries in the Location field to the lookup values you specified.

6

- **Click OK.**

- **Select Landis from the list of values.**
- **Press Enter.**

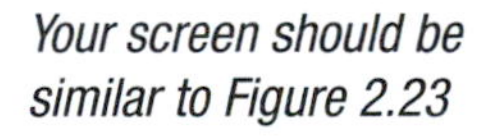

Your screen should be similar to Figure 2.23

Table Tools ac02_Employees : Database (Access 2007) - Microsoft Access

Home Create External Data Database Tools Datasheet

View Paste Calibri 11 Refresh All New Save Delete Totals Spelling More Filter Selection Advanced Toggle Filter Find Replace Go To Select

Views Clipboard Font Rich Text Records Sort & Filter Find

Entry accepted

Employee Records Job

Employee ID	Hire Date	Location	Position	Add New Field
00212	2/1/1999	Landis	Club Director	
00617	7/8/1999	Chesterfield	Club Manager	
00907	12/12/1999	River Mist	Club Manager	
01421	1/10/2000	River Mist	Assistant Manager	
03225	5/1/2000	Landis	Food Service Director	
03406	5/5/2000	Chesterfield	Assistant Manager	
03890	7/5/2001	Landis	Fitness Director	
04321	8/5/2001	Chesterfield	Assistant Manager	
04731	8/19/2001	River Mist	Fitness Coordinator	
05015	1/4/2002	Landis	Personal Trainer Director	
06000	2/10/2002	Chesterfield	Child Care Coordinator	
07287	3/15/2002	Landis	Child Care Director	
08391	6/4/2002	River Mist	Personal Trainer Coordinator	
11747	7/9/2002	Chesterfield	Personal Trainer	
12194	1/12/2003	Chesterfield	Personal Trainer	
12213	1/17/2003	River Mist	Sales Associate	
12230	3/2/2003	River Mist	Personal Trainer	
12247	3/10/2003	River Mist	Fitness Instructor	
12258	4/12/2003	Chesterfield	Food Service Manager	
12366	6/1/2003	River Mist	Fitness Instructor	
12389	8/4/2003	Landis	Sales Associate	
12501	10/5/2003	Landis	Personal Trainer	
12583	4/20/2003	Landis	Greeter	
12594	12/21/2003	River Mist	Food Service Server	
12612	1/14/2004	Chesterfield	Cleaning	
12655	1/16/2004	Chesterfield	Fitness Instructor	
12668	2/4/2004	Chesterfield	Sales Associate	

Navigation Pane

Record: 1 of 53 No Filter Search

Ready

Figure 2.23

The Location lookup field is working correctly. Using a lookup field makes entering repetitive information faster and more accurate.

Finding and Replacing Data

Over the past few days, you have received several change-request forms to update the employee records. Rather than have to scroll through all the records to locate the ones that need to be modified, you can use the Find and Replace feature.

Concept 5

Find and Replace

5 The **Find and Replace** feature helps you quickly find specific information and automatically replace it with new information. The Find command will locate all specified values in a field, and the Replace command will both find a value and automatically replace it with another. For example, in a table containing supplier and item prices, you may need to increase the price of all items supplied by one manufacturer. To quickly locate these items, you would use the Find command to locate all records with the name of the manufacturer and then update the price appropriately. Alternatively, you could use the Replace command if you knew that all items priced at $11.95 were increasing to $15.99. This command would locate all values matching the original price and replace them with the new price.

Finding and replacing data is fast and accurate, but you need to be careful when replacing not to replace unintended matches.

Finding Data

The first change request is for Melissa Lettow, who recently married and has both a name and address change. To quickly locate this record, you will use the Find command.

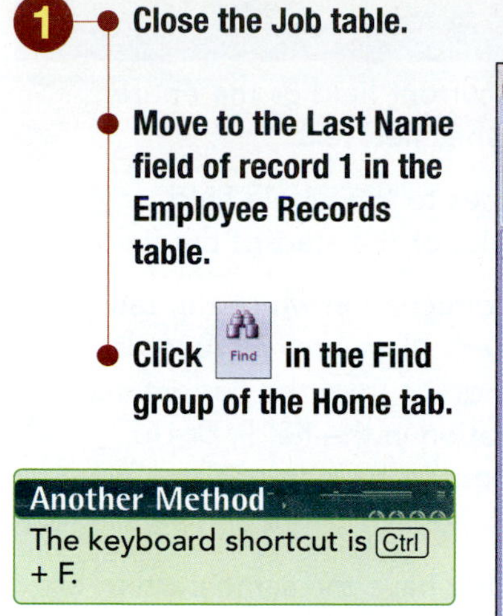

1. - Close the Job table.
   - Move to the Last Name field of record 1 in the Employee Records table.
   - Click Find in the Find group of the Home tab.

Another Method

The keyboard shortcut is Ctrl + F.

Your screen should be similar to Figure 2.24

Figure 2.24

You use the Find and Replace dialog box to specify the information you are looking for and the way that you want Access to search the table. In the Find What text box, you specify the **criteria** or a set of limiting conditions records must meet by entering the text you want to locate. You can enter a specific character string or use wildcards to specify the criteria. **Wildcards** are symbols that are used to represent characters. The * symbol represents any collection of characters and the ? symbol represents any individual character. For example, ?ar will locate any three-letter text such as bar, far, and car. In contrast, *ar will locate the same text, but in addition will expand the criteria to locate any text ending with ar, such as star, popular, and modular.

You can further refine your search by using the options described in the following table.

Option	Effect
Look In	Searches the current field or the entire table for the specified text.
Match	Locates matches to the whole field, any part of the field, or the start of the field.
Search	Specifies the direction in which the table will be searched: All (search all records), Down (search down from the current insertion point location in the field), or Up (search up from the current insertion point location in the field).
Match Case	Finds words that have the same pattern of uppercase letters as entered in the Find What text box. Using this option makes the search case sensitive.
Search Fields as Formatted	Finds data based on its display format.

Because the insertion point is already in the field you want to search, the Look In location is correctly specified. If you wanted to search on a different field, you could click on the field you want in the datasheet without closing the dialog box. You also can select the table name from the Look In list if you want to search the entire table.

The other default options, to match the whole field and to search all records, are also appropriately set.

First, you will use the * wildcard to find all records whose last name begins with "l".

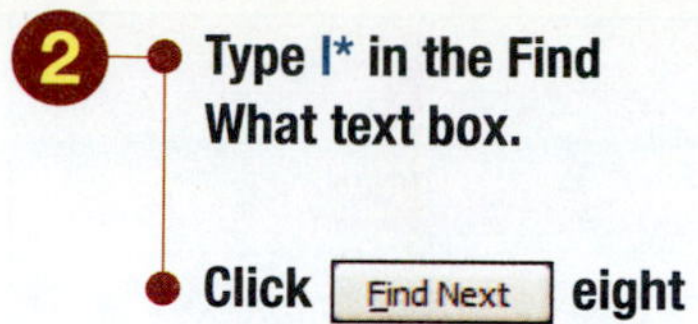

2 Type l* in the Find What text box.

Click Find Next eight times to move from one located record to the next.

Your screen should be similar to Figure 2.25

Table Tools ac02_Employees : Database (Access 2007) - Microsoft Access

Home Create External Data Database Tools Datasheet

View Paste Calibri 11 Refresh All New Save Delete Totals Spelling More Filter Selection Advanced Toggle Filter Find Replace Go To Select

Views Clipboard Font Rich Text Records Sort & Filter Find

Employee Records

Employee ID	Last Name	First Name	Address	City	State	ZIP Code	Home Phone	Gender	Birth Date
13416	Lembi	Damon	4389 S. Rita Ln.	Landis	CA	92120	(941) 555-4747	M	9/12/197
13458	Helfand	Eric	4601 E. Willow Dr.	Maldin	CA	92121-3740	(941) 555-9101	M	9/12/198
13484	Franklin	Stephanie	889 S. Litchfield Park	Maldin	CA	92121-3740	(941) 555-7833	F	7/30/197
13497	Steele	Jeff	1011 E. Holly Ln.	River Mist	CA	92123-2232	(941) 555-1912	M	4/9/198
13543	Martinez	Julie	1920 First Ave.	Maldin	CA	92121-3740	(941) 555-1044	F	12/10/198
13597	Gapasin	Ken	2633 E. Fountain St.	Maldin	CA	92121-3740	(941) 555-0589	M	2/11/198
13635	Martinez	Juan						M	12/10/198
22085	Lindau	Kristin						F	2/24/197
22091	Fromthart	Lisa						F	8/9/197
22100	Vaccaro							M	9/23/198
								M	2/23/198
								F	8/30/197
							5-9870	M	5/14/197
							5-1093	F	9/23/197
22425	Ferguson						5-7039	M	2/3/197
22469	Hogan						5-1010	M	7/14/198
22473							5-7144	F	3/23/198

Microsoft Office Access

Microsoft Office Access finished searching the records. The search item was not found.

OK

Find What: l*

Find Next

Cancel

Look In: Last Name

Match: Whole Field

Search Fields As Formatted

Last entry beginning with "L"

Wildcard character

Record: 44 of 53 No Filter Search

Searching. Press CTRL+BREAK to stop.

Figure 2.25

Using the wildcard located seven records whose last name starts with the letter l. The more specific you can make your criteria, the quicker you can locate the information you want to find. In this case, you want to find a specific last name, so you will enter the complete name in the Find What text box.

- **Click OK to close the finished searching informational box.**

- **Click on the entry in the Find What text box to select it and type lettow.**

Additional Information

Because the Match Case option is not selected in the Find and Replace dialog box, you can enter the text to be located in uppercase, lowercase, or mixed-case letters—Access will ignore the case and look for the specified text.

- **Click** **.**

Your screen should be similar to Figure 2.26

Having Trouble?

If the Find command did not locate this record, try it again. Make sure that you entered the name "lettow" (uppercase or lowercase) correctly and that Last Name is the selected field in the Look In box.

Figure 2.26

Access searches the table and moves to the first located occurrence of the entry you specified. The Last Name field is highlighted in record 14. You need to change the last name from Lettow to Richards.

- Click in the Last Name field of record 14.

Additional Information

You do not need to close the Find and Replace dialog box before you make a change to the table. You will be using this dialog box again to perform more searches, so leave it open for now.

- Double-click Lettow to select the entry.
- Type Richards.
- Press Enter.

Your screen should be similar to Figure 2.27

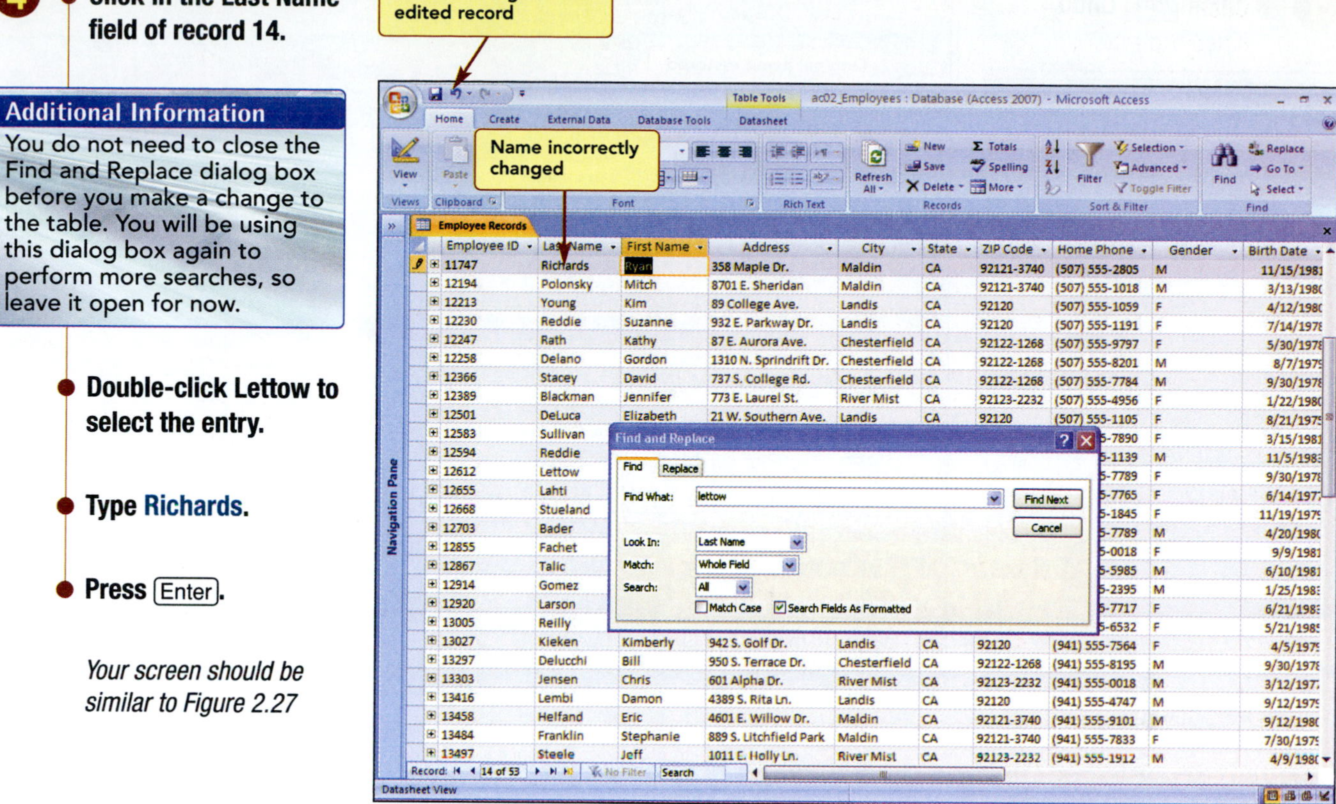

Figure 2.27

Now that the highlight is on the First Name field, you notice that this is the record for Ryan Lettow, not Melissa. You changed the wrong record. You will use the Undo command next to quickly fix this error.

Using Undo

Undo will cancel your last action as long as you have not made any further changes to the table. Even if you save the record or the table, you can undo changes to the last edited record by clicking Undo. After you have changed another record or moved to another window, however, the earlier change cannot be undone. You will use Undo to return Ryan's record to the way it was before you made the change.

1 Click Undo.

Another Method

The keyboard shortcut is Ctrl + Z.

Your screen should be similar to Figure 2.28

Table Tools ac02_Employees : Database (Access 2007) - Microsoft Access

Home Create External Data Database Tools Datasheet

View | Clipboard | Font | Rich Text | Refresh All | New Save Delete | Totals Spelling More | Records | Filter | Selection Advanced Toggle Filter | Sort & Filter | Find | Replace Go To Select | Find

Original name restored

Employee Records

Employee ID	Last Name	First Name	Address	City	State	ZIP Code	Home Phone	Gender	Birth Date
11747	Lettow	Ryan	358 Maple Dr.	Maldin	CA	92121-3740	(507) 555-2805	M	11/15/1981
12194	Polonsky	Mitch	8701 E. Sheridan	Maldin	CA	92121-3740	(507) 555-1018	M	3/13/198
12213	Young	Kim	89 College Ave.	Landis	CA	92120	(507) 555-1059	F	4/12/198
12230	Reddie	Suzanne	932 E. Parkway Dr.	Landis	CA	92120	(507) 555-1191	F	7/14/197
12247	Rath	Kathy	87 E. Aurora Ave.	Chesterfield	CA	92122-1268	(507) 555-9797	F	5/30/197
12258	Delano	Gordon	1310 N. Sprindrift Dr.	Chesterfield	CA	92122-1268	(507) 555-8201	M	8/7/197
12366	Stacey	David	737 S. College Rd.	Chesterfield	CA	92122-1268	(507) 555-7784	M	9/30/197
12389	Blackman	Jennifer	773 E. Laurel St.	River Mist	CA	92123-2232	(507) 555-4956	F	1/22/198
12501	DeLuca	Elizabeth	21 W. Southern Ave.	Landis	CA	92120	(507) 555-1105	F	8/21/197
12583	Sullivan						5-7890	F	3/15/1981
12594	Reddie						5-1139	M	11/5/198
12612	Lettow						5-7789	F	9/30/197
12655	Lahti						5-7765	F	6/14/197
12668	Stueland						5-1845	F	11/19/197
12703	Bader						5-7789	M	4/20/198
12855	Fachet						5-0018	F	9/9/1981
12867	Talic						5-5985	M	6/10/1981
12914	Gomez						5-2395	M	1/25/198
12920	Larson						5-7717	F	6/21/198
13005	Reilly						5-6532	F	5/21/198
13027	Kieken	Kimberly	942 S. Golf Dr.	Landis	CA	92120	(941) 555-7564	F	4/5/197
13297	Delucchi	Bill	950 S. Terrace Dr.	Chesterfield	CA	92122-1268	(941) 555-8195	M	9/30/197
13303	Jensen	Chris	601 Alpha Dr.	River Mist	CA	92123-2232	(941) 555-0018	M	3/12/197
13416	Lembi	Damon	4389 S. Rita Ln.	Landis	CA	92120	(941) 555-4747	M	9/12/197
13458	Helfand	Eric	4601 E. Willow Dr.	Maldin	CA	92121-3740	(941) 555-9101	M	9/12/198
13484	Franklin	Stephanie	889 S. Litchfield Park	Maldin	CA	92121-3740	(941) 555-7833	F	7/30/197
13497	Steele	Jeff	1011 E. Holly Ln.	River Mist	CA	92123-2232	(941) 555-1912	M	4/9/198

Find and Replace

Find | Replace

Find What: lettow

Find Next

Cancel

Look In: First Name

Match: Whole Field

Search: All

Match Case   Search Fields As Formatted

Record: 14 of 53   No Filter   Search

Datasheet View

Figure 2.28

The original field value of Lettow is restored. Now, you want to continue the search to locate the next record with the last name of Lettow.

2

- Move back to the Last Name field of record 14.
- Click Find Next in the Find and Replace dialog box.
- When Access locates the record for Melissa Lettow (record 25), change her last name to **Richards** and the Address to **5522 W. Marin Lane**.

Having Trouble?

If necessary, move the Find and Replace dialog box.

Your screen should be similar to Figure 2.29

Table Tools ac02_Employees : Database (Access 2007) - Microsoft Access

Home Create External Data Database Tools Datasheet

View | Paste | Clipboard | Calibri | Font | Rich Text | Refresh All | New Save Delete | Totals Spelling More | Records | Filter | Selection Advanced Toggle Filter | Sort & Filter | Find | Replace Go To Select | Find

Name and address updated

Employee Records

Employee ID	Last Name	First Name	Address	City	State	ZIP Code	Home Phone	Gender	Birth Date
12612	Richards	Melissa	5522 W. Marin Lane	River Mist	CA	92123	(507) 555-7789	F	9/30/197
12655	Lahti	Jill	5401 E. Thomas Rd.	Landis	CA	92120	(507) 555-7765	F	6/14/197
12668	Stueland	Valerie	34 University Dr.	Maldin	CA	92121-3740	(507) 555-1845	F	11/19/197
12703	Bader	Jeff	947 S. Forest St.	Landis	CA	92120	(941) 555-7789	M	4/20/198
12855	Fachet	Kimberly	923 E. Baseline Rd.	River Mist	CA	92123	(941) 555-0018	F	9/9/1981
12867	Talic	Elvis	21 Oasis St.	River Mist	CA	92123-2232	(941) 555-5985	M	6/10/1981
12914	Gomez	Alfonso	3429 S. Grandview St.	Landis	CA	92120-3741	(941) 555-2395	M	1/25/198
12920	Larson	Alicia	345 W. Mill Ave.	Maldin	CA	92121-3740	(941) 555-7717	F	6/21/198
13005	Reilly	Emily	125 N. Marigold St.	Maldin	CA	92121-3740	(941) 555-6532	F	5/21/198
13027	Kieken						5-7564	F	4/5/197
13297	Delucchi						5-8195	M	9/30/197
13303	Jensen						5-0018	M	3/12/197
13416	Lembi						5-4747	M	9/12/197
13458	Helfand						5-9101	M	9/12/198
13484	Franklin						5-7833	F	7/30/197
13497	Steele						5-1912	M	4/9/198
13543	Martinez						5-1044	F	12/10/198
13597	Gapasin						5-0589	M	2/11/198
13635	Martinez						5-2935	M	12/10/198
22085	Lindau						5-6363	F	2/24/197
22091	Fromthart	Lisa	32 Redcoat Rd.	Chesterfield	CA	92122-1268	(941) 555-0110	F	8/9/197
22100	Vaccaro	Louis	289 E. Heather Ave.	River Mist	CA	92123-2232	(941) 555-3758	M	9/23/198
22114	Schneider	Paul	1731 Jackson Ave.	Landis	CA	92120	(941) 555-7440	M	2/23/198
22297	Rogondino	Patricia	7583 Turquoise	Chesterfield	CA	92122-1268	(941) 555-7539	F	8/30/197
22304	Torcivia	Peter	904 S. Dorsey Dr.	Chesterfield	CA	92122-1268	(941) 555-9870	M	5/14/197
22407	Mazeau	Rebecca	7383 Oak Dr.	Landis	CA	92120	(941) 555-1093	F	9/23/197
22425	Ferguson	Robby	4232 Tuller Ave.	River Mist	CA	92123-2232	(941) 555-7039	M	2/3/197

Find and Replace

Find | Replace

Find What: lettow

Find Next

Cancel

Look In: Last Name

Match: Start of Field

Search: All

Match Case   Search Fields As Formatted

Record: 25 of 53   No Filter   Search

Datasheet View

Figure 2.29

The Find method works well when you need to locate an individual field in order to view the data and/or modify it. However, when you need to make the same change to more than one record, the Replace command is the quicker method because it both finds and replaces the data.

Replacing Data

You have checked with the U.S. Postal Service and learned that all zip codes of 92120 have a four-digit extension of 3741. To locate all the records with this zip code, you could look at the ZIP Code field for each record to find the match and then edit the field to add the extension. If the table is small, this method would be acceptable. For large tables, however, this method could be quite time consuming and more prone to errors. A more efficient way is to search the table to find specific values in records and then replace the entry with another.

1
- **Move to the ZIP Code field of record 1.**
- **Open the Replace tab.**

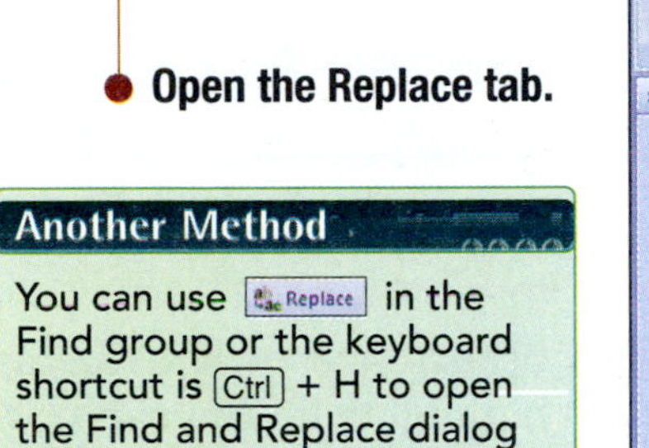

Another Method
You can use Replace in the Find group or the keyboard shortcut is Ctrl + H to open the Find and Replace dialog box and display the Replace tab.

Your screen should be similar to Figure 2.30

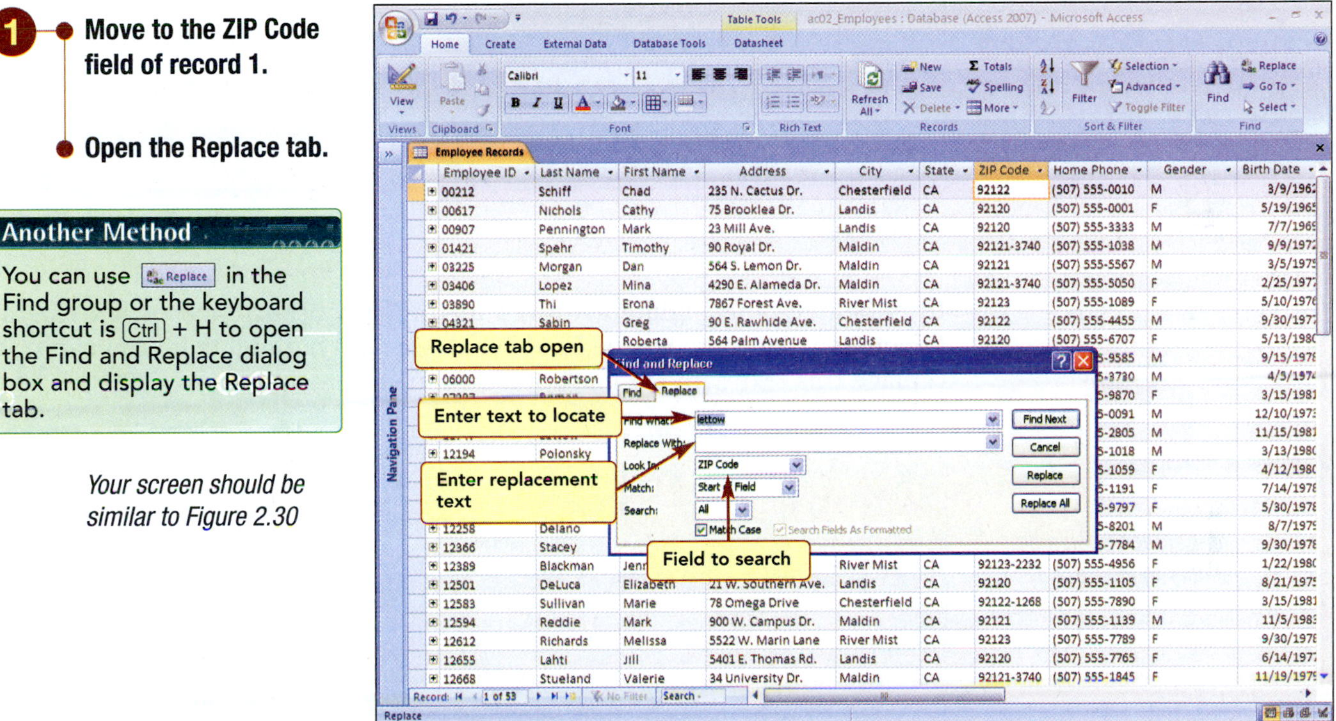

Figure 2.30

The options in the Replace tab are the same as those in the Find tab, with the addition of a Replace With text box, where you enter the replacement text exactly as you want it to appear in your table.

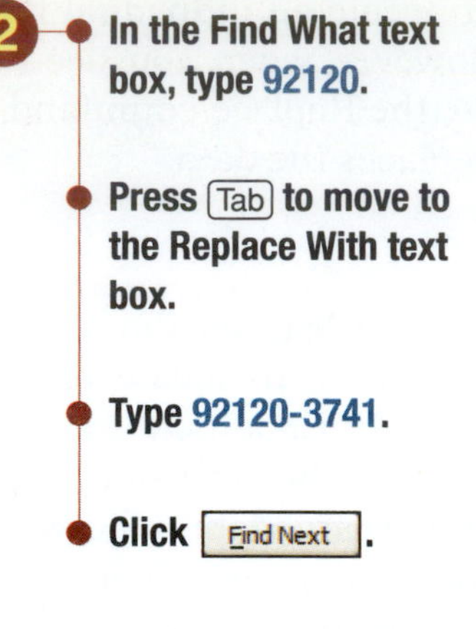

2 • **In the Find What text box, type 92120.**

• **Press Tab to move to the Replace With text box.**

• **Type 92120-3741.**

• **Click Find Next.**

Your screen should be similar to Figure 2.31

Having Trouble?

If necessary, move the dialog box so you can see the highlighted entry.

Figure 2.31

Immediately, the highlight moves to the first occurrence of text in the document that matches the Find What text and highlights it. You can now replace this text with the click of a button.

3 • **Click Replace.**

Your screen should be similar to Figure 2.32

Figure 2.32

The original zip code entry is replaced with the new zip code. The program immediately continues searching and locates a second occurrence of the entry. You decide that the program is locating the values accurately and that it will be safe to replace all finds with the replacement value.

4

- **Click Replace All.**
- **Click Yes in response to the advisory message.**
- **Close the Find and Replace dialog box.**

Your screen should be similar to Figure 2.33

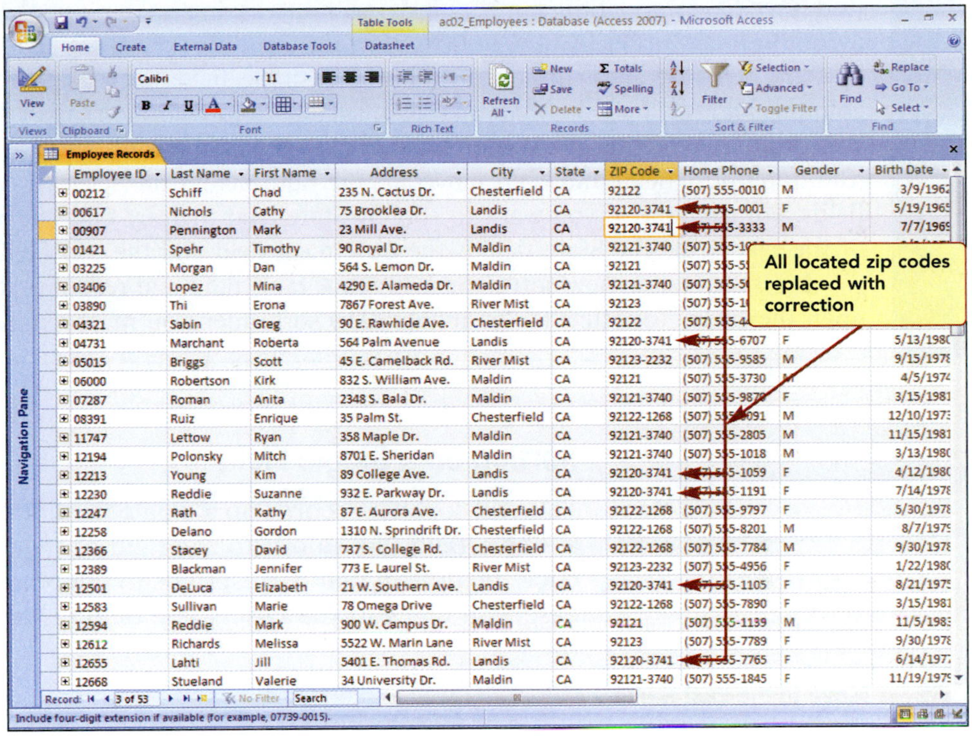

All located zip codes replaced with correction

Figure 2.33

All matches are replaced with the replacement text. It is much faster to use Replace All than to confirm each match separately. However, exercise care when using Replace All, because the search text you specify might be part of another field and you may accidentally replace text you want to keep.

Sorting Records

As you may recall from Lab 1, the records are ordered according to the primary key field, Employee ID. The accounting manager, however, has asked you for an alphabetical list of all employees. To do this, you will sort the records in the table.

Concept 6

Sort

6 You can **sort** the data in a table to quickly rearrange the order of the records. Sorting data helps you find specific information more quickly without having to browse the data. You can sort data in **ascending sort order** (A to Z or 0 to 9) or **descending sort order** (Z to A or 9 to 0).

You can sort all records in a table by a single field, such as State, or you can select adjacent columns and sort by more than one field, such as State and then City. When sorting on multiple fields, you begin by selecting the columns to sort. Access sorts records starting with the column farthest left (the outermost field) and then moves to the right across the selected columns to sort the innermost fields. For example, if you want to sort by State, and then by City, the State field must be to the left of the City field. The State field is the outermost field and the city field is the innermost field.

Access saves the new sort order with your table data and reapplies it automatically each time you open the table. To return to the primary key sort order, you must remove the temporary sort.

Sorting on a Single Field

You will sort the records on a single field, Last Name. To perform a sort on a single field, you move to the field on which you will base the sort and click the button that corresponds to the type of sort you want to do. In this case, you will sort the Last Name field in ascending alphabetical order.

1 **Move to the Last Name field of any record.**

Click Ascending in the Sort & Filter group.

Additional Information

Clicking Descending arranges the data in descending sort order.

Your screen should be similar to Figure 2.34

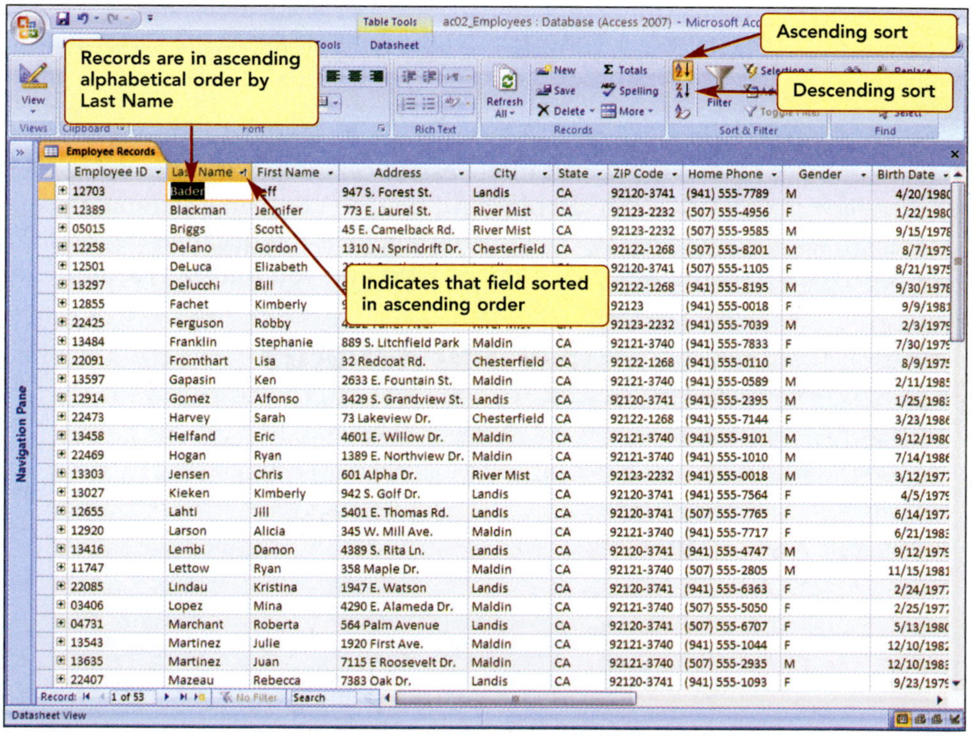

Figure 2.34

The employee records are displayed in alphabetical order by last name. The Last Name field header displays a to show that the field is in ascending sorted order. Next, you want to check the rest of the table to see if there is anything else you need to do.

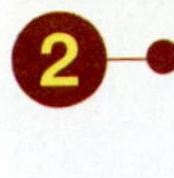

Use the scroll box to scroll down to record 25.

Additional Information

As you drag the scroll box, the record location is displayed in a Screen Tip (for example, "Record 25 of 53").

Your screen should be similar to Figure 2.35

Records with same last name not sorted by first name

Employee ID	Last Name	First Name	Address	City	State	ZIP Code	Home Phone	Gender	Birth Date
13543	Martinez	Julie	1920 First Ave.	Maldin	CA	92121-3740	(941) 555-1044	F	12/10/198
13635	Martinez	Juan	7115 E Roosevelt Dr.	Maldin	CA	92121-3740	(507) 555-2935	M	12/10/198
22407	Mazeau	Rebecca	7383 Oak Dr.	Landis	CA	92120-3741	(941) 555-1093	F	9/23/197
03225	Morgan	Dan	564 S. Lemon Dr.	Maldin	CA	92121	(507) 555-5567	M	3/5/197
00617	Nichols	Cathy	75 Brooklea Dr.	Landis	CA	92120-3741	(507) 555-0001	F	5/19/196
00907	Pennington	Mark	23 Mill Ave.	Landis	CA	92120-3741	(507) 555-3333	M	7/7/196
12194	Polonsky	Mitch	8701 E. Sheridan	Maldin	CA	92121-3740	(507) 555-1018	M	3/13/198
12247	Rath	Kathy	87 E. Aurora Ave.	Chesterfield	CA	92122-1268	(507) 555-9797	F	5/30/197
12230	Reddie	Suzanne	932 E. Parkway Dr.	Landis	CA	92120-3741	(507) 555-1191	F	7/14/197
12594	Reddie	Mark	900 W. Campus Dr.	Maldin	CA	92121	(507) 555-1139	M	11/5/198
13005	Reilly	Emily	125 N. Marigold St.	Maldin	CA	92121-3740	(941) 555-6532	F	5/21/198
12612	Richards	Melissa	5522 W. Marin Lane	River Mist	CA	92123	(507) 555-7789	F	9/30/197
06000	Robertson	Kirk	832 S. William Ave.	Maldin	CA	92121	(507) 555-3730	M	4/5/197
22297	Rogondino	Patricia	7583 Turquoise	Chesterfield	CA	92122-1268	(941) 555-7539	F	8/30/197
07287	Roman	Anita	2348 S. Bala Dr.	Maldin	CA	92121-3740	(507) 555-9870	F	3/15/198
08391	Ruiz	Enrique	35 Palm St.	Chesterfield	CA	92122-1268	(507) 555-0091	M	12/10/197
04321	Sabin	Greg	90 E. Rawhide Ave.	Chesterfield	CA	92122	(507) 555-4455	M	9/30/197
00212	Schiff	Chad	235 N. Cactus Dr.	Chesterfield	CA	92122	(507) 555-0010	M	3/9/196
22114	Schneider	Paul	1731 Jackson Ave.	Landis	CA	92120-3741	(941) 555-7440	M	2/23/198
01421	Spehr	Timothy	90 Royal Dr.	Maldin	CA	92121-3740	(507) 555-1038	M	9/9/197
12366	Stacey	David	737 S. College Rd.	Chesterfield	CA	92122-1268	(507) 555-7784	M	9/30/197
13497	Steele	Jeff	1011 E. Holly Ln.	River Mist	CA	92123-2232	(941) 555-1912	M	4/9/198
12668	Stueland	Valerie	34 University Dr.	Maldin	CA	92121-3740	(507) 555-1845	F	11/19/197
12583	Sullivan	Marie	78 Omega Drive	Chesterfield	CA	92122-1268	(507) 555-7890	F	3/15/198
12867	Talic	Elvis	21 Oasis St.	River Mist	CA	92123-2232	(941) 555-5985	M	6/10/198
03890	Thi	Erona	7867 Forest Ave.	River Mist	CA	92123	(507) 555-1089	F	5/10/197
22304	Torcivia	Peter	904 S. Dorsey Dr.	Chesterfield	CA	92122-1268	(941) 555-9870	M	5/14/197

Figure 2.35

Now, you can see that the records for Julie and Juan Martinez are sorted by last name but not by first name. You want all records that have the same last name to be further sorted by first name. To do this, you need to sort using multiple sort fields.

Sorting on Multiple Fields

Additional Information

If the columns to sort were not already adjacent, you would hide the columns that are in between. If the columns were not in the correct order, you would move the columns. You will learn how to do this in Lab 3.

When sorting on multiple fields, the fields must be adjacent to each other in order to designate the inner and outer sort fields. The outer sort field (primary field in the sort) must be to the left of the inner sort field. The Last Name and First Name fields are already in the correct locations for the sort you want to perform. To specify the fields to sort on, both columns must be selected.

1. Select the Last Name and First Name field columns.
   - Click Ascending.
   - Scroll down to record 25 again.

Your screen should be similar to Figure 2.36

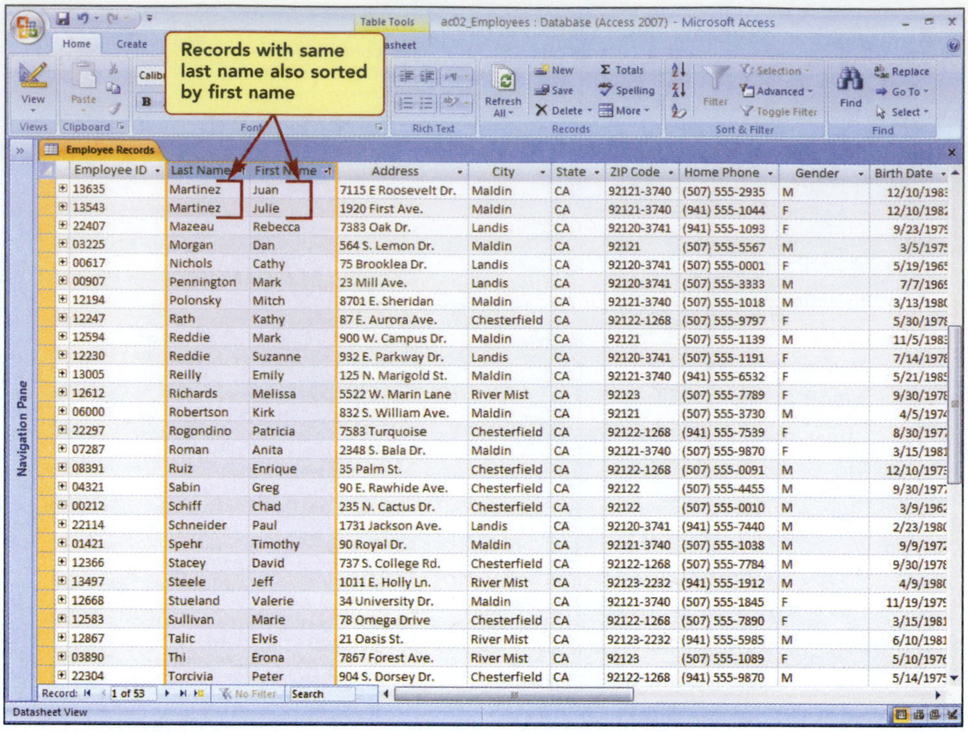

Records with same last name also sorted by first name

Figure 2.36

The record for Juan Martinez now appears before the record for Julie. As you can see, sorting is a fast, useful tool. The sort order remains in effect until you remove the sort or replace it with a new sort order. Although Access remembers your sort order even when you exit the program, it does not actually change the table records.

You can remove the sort at any time to restore the records to the primary key sort order. You decide to return to primary key sort order and resort the table alphabetically for the Accounting department later, after you have finished making changes to it.

2 • **Click Clear All Sorts.**

• **Click anywhere in the datasheet to clear the selection.**

Your screen should be similar to Figure 2.37

Employee ID	Last Name	First Name	Address	City	State	ZIP Code	Home Phone	Gender	Birth Date
00212	Schiff	Chad	235 N. Cactus Dr.	Chesterfield	CA	92122	(507) 555-0010	M	3/9/196
00617	Nichols	Cathy	75 Brooklea Dr.	Landis	CA	92120-3741	(507) 555-0001	F	5/19/196
00907	Pennington	Mark	23 Mill Ave.	Landis	CA	92120-3741	(507) 555-3333	M	7/7/196
01421	Spehr	Timothy	90 Royal Dr.	Maldin	CA	92121-3740	(507) 555-1038	M	9/9/197
03225	Morgan	Dan	564 S. Lemon Dr.	Maldin	CA	92121	(507) 555-5567	M	3/5/197
03406	Lopez	Mina	4290 E. Alameda Dr.	Maldin	CA	92121-3740	(507) 555-5050	F	2/25/197
03890	Thi	Erona	7867 Forest Ave.	River Mist	CA	92123	(507) 555-1089	F	5/10/197
04321	Sabin	Greg	90 E. Rawhide Ave.	Chesterfield	CA	92122	(507) 555-4455	M	9/30/197
04731	Marchant	Roberta	564 Palm Avenue	Landis	CA	92120-3741	(507) 555-6707	F	5/13/198
05015	Briggs	Scott	45 E. Camelback Rd.	River Mist	CA	92123-2232	(507) 555-9585	M	9/15/197
06000	Robertson	Kirk	832 S. William Ave.	Maldin	CA	92121	(507) 555-3730	M	4/5/197
07287	Roman	Anita	2348 S. Bala Dr.	Maldin	CA	92121-3740	(507) 555-9870	F	3/15/1981
08391	Ruiz	Enrique	35 Palm St.	Chesterfield	CA	92122-1268	(507) 555-0091	M	12/10/197
11747	Lettow	Ryan	358 Maple Dr.	Maldin	CA	92121-3740	(507) 555-2805	M	11/15/1981
12194	Polonsky	Mitch	8701 E. Sheridan	Maldin	CA	92121-3740	(507) 555-1018	M	3/13/198
12213	Young	Kim	89 College Ave.	Landis	CA	92120-3741	(507) 555-1059	F	4/12/198
12230	Reddie	Suzanne	932 E. Parkway Dr.	Landis	CA	92120-3741	(507) 555-1191	F	7/14/197
12247	Rath	Kathy	87 E. Aurora Ave.	Chesterfield	CA	92122-1268	(507) 555-9797	F	5/30/197
12258	Delano	Gordon	1310 N. Sprindrift Dr.	Chesterfield	CA	92122-1268	(507) 555-8201	M	8/7/197
12366	Stacey	David	737 S. College Rd.	Chesterfield	CA	92122-1268	(507) 555-7784	M	9/30/197
12389	Blackman	Jennifer	773 E. Laurel St.	River Mist	CA	92123-2232	(507) 555-4956	F	1/22/198
12501	DeLuca	Elizabeth	21 W. Southern Ave.	Landis	CA	92120-3741	(507) 555-1105	F	8/21/197
12583	Sullivan	Marie	78 Omega Drive	Chesterfield	CA	92122-1268	(507) 555-7890	F	3/15/1981
12594	Reddie	Mark	900 W. Campus Dr.	Maldin	CA	92121	(507) 555-1139	M	11/5/198
12612	Richards	Melissa	5522 W. Marin Lane	River Mist	CA	92123	(507) 555-7789	F	9/30/197
12655	Lahti	Jill	5401 E. Thomas Rd.	Landis	CA	92120-3741	(507) 555-7765	F	6/14/197
12668	Stueland	Valerie	34 University Dr.	Maldin	CA	92121-3740	(507) 555-1845	F	11/19/197

Figure 2.37

All the sorts are cleared and the data in the table is now in order by the primary key field, Employee ID.

Formatting the Datasheet

Finally, you want to **format** or enhance the appearance of the datasheet on the screen to make it more readable or attractive by applying different effects. Datasheet formats include settings that change the appearance of the cell, gridlines, background and gridline colors, and border and line styles. In addition, you can change the text color and add text effects such as bold and italics to the datasheet. Datasheet formats affect the entire datasheet appearance and cannot be applied to separate areas of the datasheet.

Changing Background and Gridline Color

The default datasheet format displays alternate rows in white and light gray backgrounds with a gridline color of blue. The text color is set to black. You want to see the effect of changing the color of the alternate rows and gridlines in the datasheet.

Click Datasheet Formatting in the Font group of the Home tab.

Your screen should be similar to Figure 2.38

Opens Datasheet Formatting dialog box

Default datasheet formatting settings

Sample of current selections

Home Create External Data Database Tools

View Paste Calibri 11 Refresh All Save Delete Totals Spelling More Filter Selection Advanced Toggle Filter Find Replace Go To Select

Views Clipboard Font Rich Text Records Sort & Filter Find

Employee Records

Datasheet Formatting

Cell Effect: Flat / Raised / Sunken

Gridlines Shown: Horizontal / Vertical

OK Cancel

Background Color: Alternate Background Color: Gridline Color:

Sample:

Border and Line Styles: Datasheet Border Solid

Direction: Left-to-right Right-to-left

Employee ID	Last Name	First Name	Address	City	State	Zip Code	Home Phone	Gender	Birth Date
00212	Schiff	Chad					(507) 555-0010	M	3/9/1962
		Cathy					(507) 555-0001	F	5/19/1965
		Mark					(507) 555-3333	M	7/7/1969
		Timothy					(507) 555-1038	M	9/9/1972
		Dan					(507) 555-5567	M	3/5/1975
03406	Lopez	Mina					(507) 555-5050	F	2/25/1977
03890	Thi	Erona					(507) 555-1089	F	5/10/1976
		Greg					(507) 555-4455	M	9/30/1974
		Roberta					(507) 555-6707	F	5/13/1980
		Scott					(507) 555-9585	M	9/15/1978
06000	Robertson	Kirk					(507) 555-3730	M	4/5/1974
07287	Roman	Anita					(507) 555-9870	F	3/15/1981
08391	Ruiz	Enrique					(507) 555-0091	M	12/10/1973
11747	Lettow	Ryan					(507) 555-2805	M	11/15/1981
12194	Polonsky	Mitch					(507) 555-1018	M	3/13/1980
12213	Young	Kim					(507) 555-1059	F	4/12/1980
12230	Reddie	Suzanne	932 E. Parkway Dr.	Landis	CA	92120-3741	(507) 555-1191	F	7/14/1978
12247	Rath	Kathy	87 E. Aurora Ave.	Chesterfield	CA	92122-1268	(507) 555-9797	F	5/30/1978
12258	Delano	Gordon	1310 N. Sprindrift Dr.	Chesterfield	CA	92122-1268	(507) 555-8201	M	8/7/1975
12366	Stacey	David	737 S. College Rd.	Chesterfield	CA	92122-1268	(507) 555-7784	M	9/30/1978
12389	Blackman	Jennifer	773 E. Laurel St.	River Mist	CA	92123-2232	(507) 555-4956	F	1/22/1980
12501	DeLuca	Elizabeth	21 W. Southern Ave.	Landis	CA	92120-3741	(507) 555-1105	F	8/21/1975
12583	Sullivan	Marie	78 Omega Drive	Chesterfield	CA	92122-1268	(507) 555-7890	F	3/15/1981
12594	Reddie	Mark	900 W. Campus Dr.	Maldin	CA	92121	(507) 555-1139	M	11/5/1983
12612	Richards	Melissa	5522 W. Marin Lane	River Mist	CA	92123	(507) 555-7789	F	9/30/1978
12655	Lahti	Jill	5401 E. Thomas Rd.	Landis	CA	92120-3741	(507) 555-7765	F	6/14/1977
12668	Stueland	Valerie	34 University Dr.	Maldin	CA	92121-3740	(507) 555-1845	F	11/19/1975

Record: 1 of 53 No Filter Search

Unique five-digit number assigned to each employee.

Figure 2.38

The default datasheet formatting settings are displayed in the dialog box and the Sample area shows how the settings will appear in the datasheet. You will leave the background color white and change the color of the alternate rows.

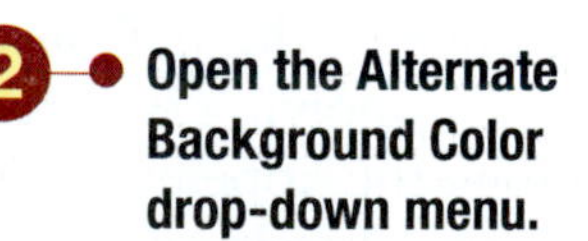

Open the Alternate Background Color drop-down menu.

Your screen should be similar to Figure 2.39

Opens the Alternate Background Color drop-down menu

Theme colors

Green 2

Standard colors

Table Tools ac02_Employees : Database (Access 2007) - Microsoft Access

Home Create External Data Database Tools Datasheet

Datasheet Formatting

Automatic

Access Theme Colors

Standard Colors

No Color

More Colors...

Employee ID	Last Name	First Name
00212	Schiff	Chad
00617	Nichols	Cathy
00907	Pennington	Mark
01421	Spehr	Timothy
03225	Morgan	Dan
03406	Lopez	Mina
03890	Thi	Erona
04321	Sabin	Greg
04731	Marchant	Roberta
05015	Briggs	Scott
06000	Robertson	Kirk
07287	Roman	Anita
08391	Ruiz	Enrique

Figure 2.39

The color gallery displays the Access Theme Colors in the upper section and standard colors in the lower section. **Theme colors** are a combination of coordinating colors that are used in the default datasheet. Each color is assigned to a different area of the datasheet, such as label text or table background. Pointing to a color identifies where it is used in a ScreenTip. The colors in the Standard Colors gallery are not assigned to specific areas on the datasheet. Pointing to a Standard Color displays the name assigned to the color.

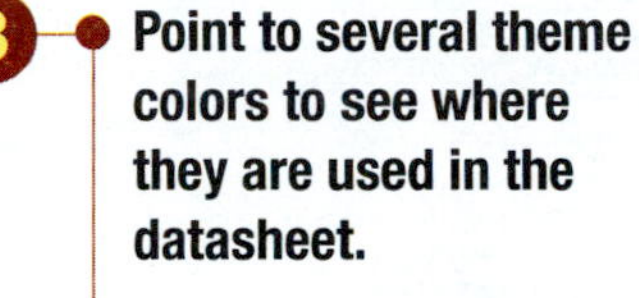

3

- **Point to several theme colors to see where they are used in the datasheet.**
- **Click on the Green 2 color in the Standard Colors area.**

Another Method

You also can use Alternate Fill/Back Color in the Font group to change the color.

Your screen should be similar to Figure 2.40

Changes gridline color

Changes alternate fill background color

Table Tools | Microsoft Access

Home | Create | External Data | Database Tools | Datasheet

View | Paste | Calibri | 11 | B I U | Refresh All | New | Save | Delete | Totals | Spelling | More | Filter | Selection | Advanced | Toggle Filter | Find | Replace | Go To | Select

Views | Clipboard | Font | Rich Text | Records | Sort & Filter | Find

Employee Records

Datasheet Formatting

Cell Effect: Flat, Raised, Sunken

Gridlines Shown: Horizontal, Vertical

OK | Cancel

Background Color: | Alternate Background Color: | Gridline Color:

Green 2 color selected

Sample:

Sample shows use of color in alternate rows

Border and Line Styles: Datasheet Border | Solid

Direction: Left-to-right | Right-to-left

Employee ID	Last Name	First Name					Home Phone	Gender	Birth Date
00212	Schiff	Chad					(507) 555-0010	M	3/9/1962
00617	Nichols	Cathy				41	(507) 555-0001	F	5/19/1965
00907	Pennington	Mark				41	(507) 555-3333	M	7/7/1969
01421	Spehr	Timothy				40	(507) 555-1038	M	9/9/1972
03225	Morgan	Dan							3/5/1975
03406	Lopez	Mina							2/25/1977
03890	Thi	Erona					(507) 555-1089	F	5/10/1976
04321	Sabin	Greg					(5		197
04731	Marchant	Roberta				41			198
05015	Briggs	Scott				32	(5		197
06000	Robertson	Kirk					(507) 555-3730	M	4/5/1974
07287	Roman	Anita				40	(507) 555-9870	F	3/15/1981
08391	Ruiz	Enrique				68	(507) 555-0091	M	12/10/1973
11747	Lettow	Ryan				40	(507) 555-2805	M	11/15/1981
12194	Polonsky	Mitch				40	(507) 555-1018	M	3/13/1980
12213	Young	Kim				41	(507) 555-1059	F	4/12/1980
12230	Reddie	Suzanne	932 E. Parkway Dr.	Landis	CA	92120-3741	(507) 555-1191	F	7/14/1978
12247	Rath	Kathy	87 E. Aurora Ave.	Chesterfield	CA	92122-1268	(507) 555-9797	F	5/30/1978
12258	Delano	Gordon	1310 N. Sprindrift Dr.	Chesterfield	CA	92122-1268	(507) 555-8201	M	8/7/1979
12366	Stacey	David	737 S. College Rd.	Chesterfield	CA	92122-1268	(507) 555-7784	M	9/30/1978
12389	Blackman	Jennifer	773 E. Laurel St.	River Mist	CA	92123-2232	(507) 555-4956	F	1/22/1980
12501	DeLuca	Elizabeth	21 W. Southern Ave.	Landis	CA	92120-3741	(507) 555-1105	F	8/21/1975
12583	Sullivan	Marie	78 Omega Drive	Chesterfield	CA	92122-1268	(507) 555-7890	F	3/15/1981
12594	Reddie	Mark	900 W. Campus Dr.	Maldin	CA	92121	(507) 555-1139	M	11/5/1982
12612	Richards	Melissa	5522 W. Marin Lane	River Mist	CA	92123	(507) 555-7789	F	9/30/1978
12655	Lahti	Jill	5401 E. Thomas Rd.	Landis	CA	92120-3741	(507) 555-7765	F	6/14/1977
12668	Stueland	Valerie	34 University Dr.	Maldin	CA	92121-3740	(507) 555-1845	F	11/19/1975

Record: 1 of 53 | No Filter | Search

Unique five-digit number assigned to each employee.

Figure 2.40

The sample area displays how the selection will appear in the datasheet. You like the green shading and want to change the gridline color to a darker shade of the same green.

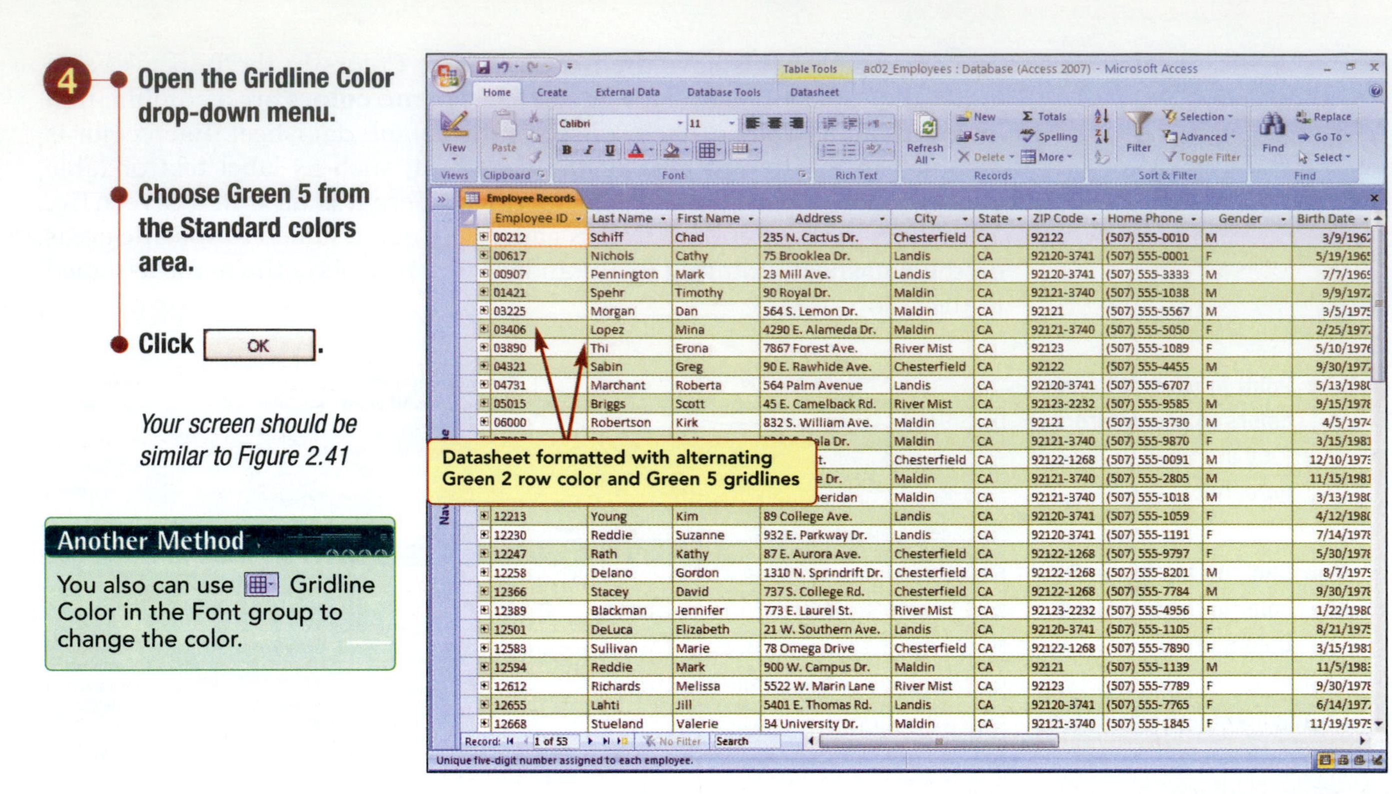

4 **Open the Gridline Color drop-down menu.**

- **Choose Green 5 from the Standard colors area.**
- **Click OK.**

Your screen should be similar to Figure 2.41

Another Method

You also can use Gridline Color in the Font group to change the color.

Figure 2.41

The selected alternating row and gridline color formatting has been applied to the datasheet.

Changing the Text Color

The datasheet background colors brighten the screen appearance, but you think the text is a little light, making it difficult to read. You will change the text color to a dark blue and bold.

1 Open the **A** Font Color drop-down menu in the Font group.

Select Dark Blue from the Standard Colors section of the color gallery.

Click **B** Bold in the Font group.

Your screen should be similar to Figure 2.42

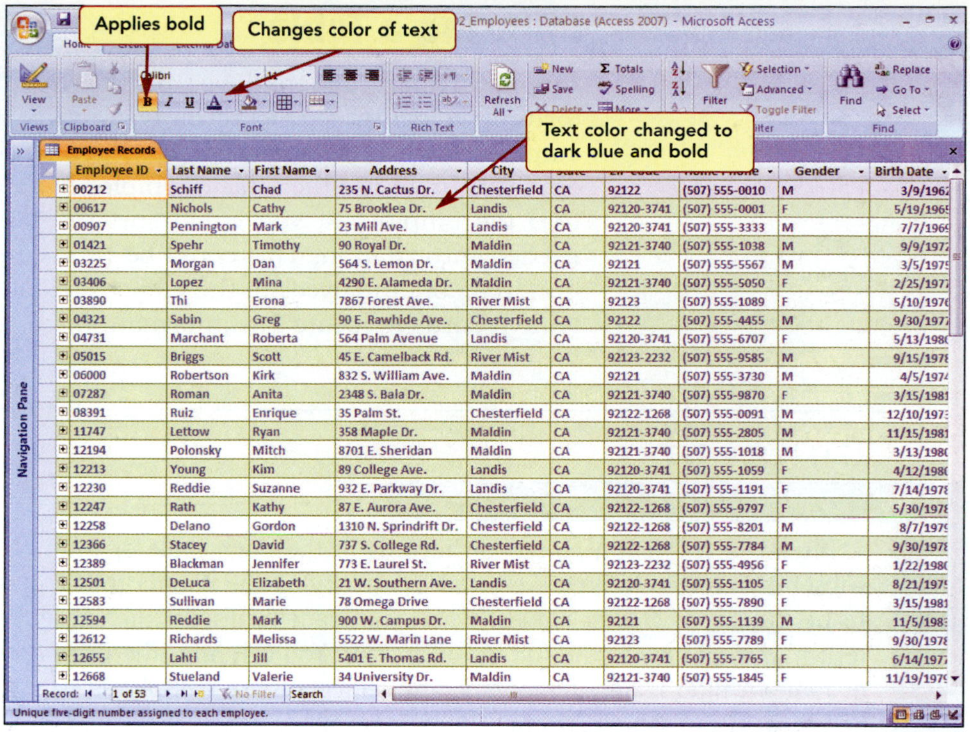

Applies bold

Changes color of text

Text color changed to dark blue and bold

Employee ID	Last Name	First Name	Address	City	State	ZIP Code	Home Phone	Gender	Birth Date
00212	Schiff	Chad	235 N. Cactus Dr.	Chesterfield	CA	92122	(507) 555-0010	M	3/9/196
00617	Nichols	Cathy	75 Brooklea Dr.	Landis	CA	92120-3741	(507) 555-0001	F	5/19/196
00907	Pennington	Mark	23 Mill Ave.	Landis	CA	92120-3741	(507) 555-3333	M	7/7/196
01421	Spehr	Timothy	90 Royal Dr.	Maldin	CA	92121-3740	(507) 555-1038	M	9/9/197
03225	Morgan	Dan	564 S. Lemon Dr.	Maldin	CA	92121	(507) 555-5567	M	3/5/197
03406	Lopez	Mina	4290 E. Alameda Dr.	Maldin	CA	92121-3740	(507) 555-5050	F	2/25/197
03890	Thi	Erona	7867 Forest Ave.	River Mist	CA	92123	(507) 555-1089	F	5/10/197
04321	Sabin	Greg	90 E. Rawhide Ave.	Chesterfield	CA	92122	(507) 555-4455	M	9/30/197
04731	Marchant	Roberta	564 Palm Avenue	Landis	CA	92120-3741	(507) 555-6707	F	5/13/198
05015	Briggs	Scott	45 E. Camelback Rd.	River Mist	CA	92123-2232	(507) 555-9585	M	9/15/197
06000	Robertson	Kirk	832 S. William Ave.	Maldin	CA	92121	(507) 555-3730	M	4/5/197
07287	Roman	Anita	2348 S. Bala Dr.	Maldin	CA	92121-3740	(507) 555-9870	F	3/15/198
08391	Ruiz	Enrique	35 Palm St.	Chesterfield	CA	92122-1268	(507) 555-0091	M	12/10/197
11747	Lettow	Ryan	358 Maple Dr.	Maldin	CA	92121-3740	(507) 555-2805	M	11/15/198
12194	Polonsky	Mitch	8701 E. Sheridan	Maldin	CA	92121-3740	(507) 555-1018	M	3/13/198
12213	Young	Kim	89 College Ave.	Landis	CA	92120-3741	(507) 555-1059	F	4/12/198
12230	Reddie	Suzanne	932 E. Parkway Dr.	Landis	CA	92120-3741	(507) 555-1191	F	7/14/197
12247	Rath	Kathy	87 E. Aurora Ave.	Chesterfield	CA	92122-1268	(507) 555-9797	F	5/30/197
12258	Delano	Gordon	1310 N. Sprindrift Dr.	Chesterfield	CA	92122-1268	(507) 555-8201	M	8/7/197
12366	Stacey	David	737 S. College Rd.	Chesterfield	CA	92122-1268	(507) 555-7784	M	9/30/197
12389	Blackman	Jennifer	773 E. Laurel St.	River Mist	CA	92123-2232	(507) 555-4956	F	1/22/198
12501	DeLuca	Elizabeth	21 W. Southern Ave.	Landis	CA	92120-3741	(507) 555-1105	F	8/21/197
12583	Sullivan	Marie	78 Omega Drive	Chesterfield	CA	92122-1268	(507) 555-7890	F	3/15/198
12594	Reddie	Mark	900 W. Campus Dr.	Maldin	CA	92121	(507) 555-1139	M	11/5/198
12612	Richards	Melissa	5522 W. Marin Lane	River Mist	CA	92123	(507) 555-7789	F	9/30/197
12655	Lahti	Jill	5401 E. Thomas Rd.	Landis	CA	92120-3741	(507) 555-7765	F	6/14/197
12668	Stueland	Valerie	34 University Dr.	Maldin	CA	92121-3740	(507) 555-1845	F	11/19/197

Record: 1 of 53

Unique five-digit number assigned to each employee.

Figure 2.42

You do not like how the blue text color looks and want to change it back to the default color. You cannot use Undo to remove formatting, so you will need to select the text color again.

2 Open the **A** Font Color drop-down menu.

Choose Automatic to restore the default font color.

Your screen should be similar to Figure 2.43

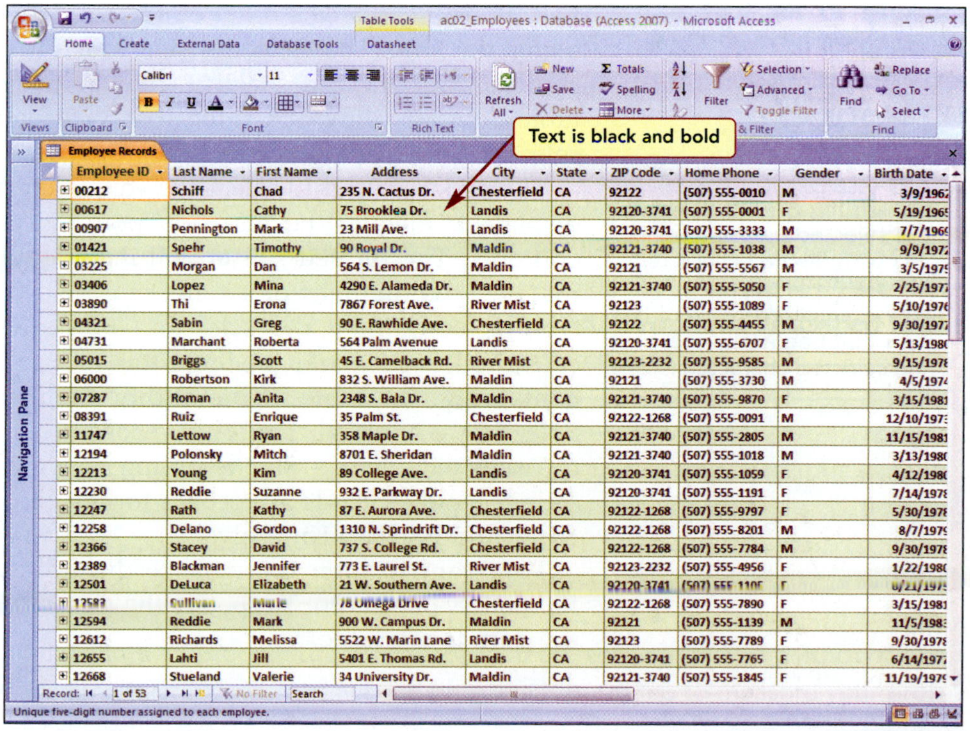

Text is black and bold

(Datasheet identical to Figure 2.42, shown in black bold text.)

Figure 2.43

The black text color is restored. The text is still bolded and is easier to read.

Filtering a Table

Juan Martinez, an employee at the Landis location, is interested in forming a car pool. He recently approached you about finding other employees who also may want to carpool. You decide this would be a great opportunity to use the table of employee data to find this information. To find the employees, you could sort the table and then write down the needed information. This could be time-consuming, however, if you had hundreds of employees in the table. A faster way is to apply a filter to the table records to locate this information.

Concept 7

Filter

7 A **filter** is a restriction placed on records in the open table or form to quickly isolate and display a subset of records. A filter is created by specifying the criteria that you want records to meet in order to be displayed. A filter is ideal when you want to display the subset for only a brief time and then return immediately to the full set of records. You can print the filtered records as you would any form or table. A filter is only temporary, and all records are redisplayed when you remove the filter or close and reopen the table or form. The filter results cannot be saved. However, the last filter criteria you specify can be saved with the table, and the results quickly redisplayed.

Using Filter by Selection

Juan lives in Maldin and works at the Lifestyle Fitness Club located in Landis. You can locate other employees who live in Maldin quite easily by using the Filter by Selection feature. Filter by Selection displays only records containing a specific value. This method is effective when the table contains only one value that you want to use as the criterion for selecting and displaying records.

Additional Information

If the selected part of a value starts with the first character in the field, the subset displays all records with values that begin with the same selected characters.

The process used to select the value determines the results that will be displayed. Placing the insertion point in a field selects the entire field contents. The filtered subset will include all records containing an exact match. Selecting part of a value in a field (by highlighting it) displays all records containing the selection. For example, in a table for a book collection, you could position the mouse pointer anywhere in a field containing the name of the author Stephen King, choose the Filter by Selection command, and only records for books whose author matches the selected name, "Stephen King," would be displayed. Selecting just "King" would include all records for authors Stephen King, Martin Luther King, and Barbara Kingsolver.

You want to filter the table to display only those records with a City field entry of Maldin. To specify the city to locate, you select an example of the data in the table.

1 • **Move to the City field of record 4.**

• **Click Selection in the Sort & Filter group of the Home tab.**

Your screen should be similar to Figure 2.44

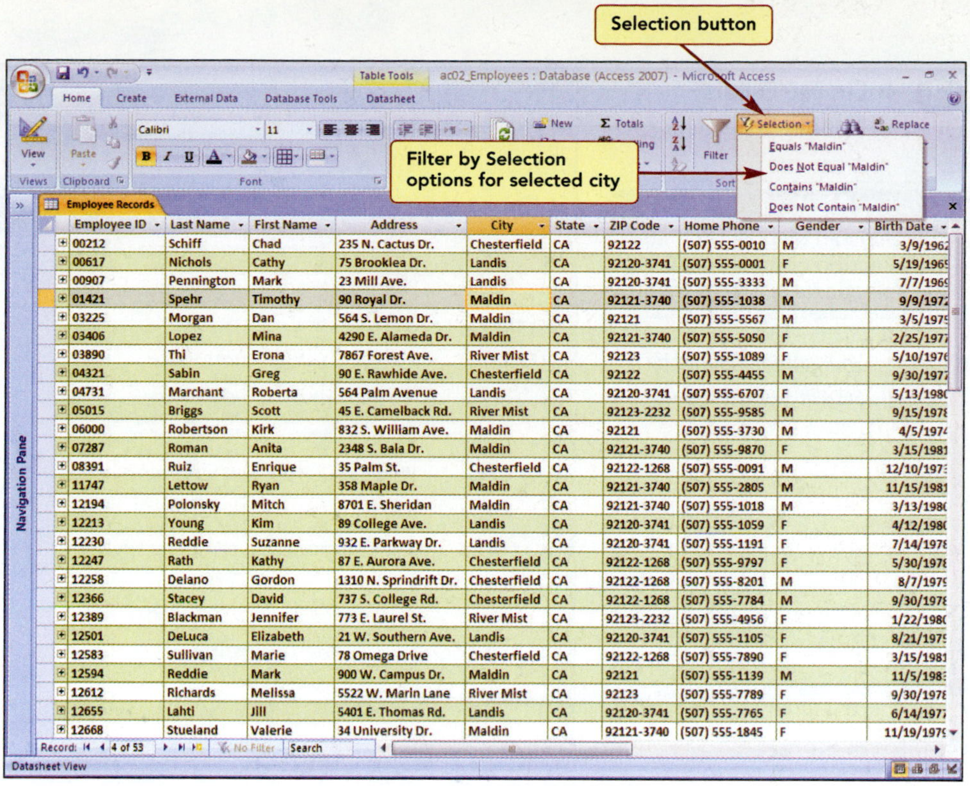

Selection button

Table Tools ac02_Employees : Database (Access 2007) - Microsoft Access

Home Create External Data Database Tools Datasheet

Selection · New · Totals · Filter · Replace

Equals "Maldin"
Does Not Equal "Maldin"
Contains "Maldin"
Does Not Contain "Maldin"

Filter by Selection options for selected city

Employee Records

Employee ID	Last Name	First Name	Address	City	State	ZIP Code	Home Phone	Gender	Birth Date
00212	Schiff	Chad	235 N. Cactus Dr.	Chesterfield	CA	92122	(507) 555-0010	M	3/9/196
00617	Nichols	Cathy	75 Brooklea Dr.	Landis	CA	92120-3741	(507) 555-0001	F	5/19/196
00907	Pennington	Mark	23 Mill Ave.	Landis	CA	92120-3741	(507) 555-3333	M	7/7/196
01421	Spehr	Timothy	90 Royal Dr.	Maldin	CA	92121-3740	(507) 555-1038	M	9/9/197
03225	Morgan	Dan	564 S. Lemon Dr.	Maldin	CA	92121	(507) 555-5567	M	3/5/197
03406	Lopez	Mina	4290 E. Alameda Dr.	Maldin	CA	92121-3740	(507) 555-5050	F	2/25/197
03890	Thi	Erona	7867 Forest Ave.	River Mist	CA	92123	(507) 555-1089	F	5/10/197
04321	Sabin	Greg	90 E. Rawhide Ave.	Chesterfield	CA	92122	(507) 555-4455	M	9/30/197
04731	Marchant	Roberta	564 Palm Avenue	Landis	CA	92120-3741	(507) 555-6707	F	5/13/198
05015	Briggs	Scott	45 E. Camelback Rd.	River Mist	CA	92123-2232	(507) 555-9585	M	9/15/197
06000	Robertson	Kirk	832 S. William Ave.	Maldin	CA	92121	(507) 555-3730	M	4/5/197
07287	Roman	Anita	2348 S. Bala Dr.	Maldin	CA	92121-3740	(507) 555-9870	F	3/15/1981
08391	Ruiz	Enrique	35 Palm St.	Chesterfield	CA	92122-1268	(507) 555-0091	M	12/10/197
11747	Lettow	Ryan	358 Maple Dr.	Maldin	CA	92121-3740	(507) 555-2805	M	11/15/1981
12194	Polonsky	Mitch	8701 E. Sheridan	Maldin	CA	92121-3740	(507) 555-1018	M	3/13/198
12213	Young	Kim	89 College Ave.	Landis	CA	92120-3741	(507) 555-1059	F	4/12/198
12230	Reddie	Suzanne	932 E. Parkway Dr.	Landis	CA	92120-3741	(507) 555-1191	F	7/14/197
12247	Rath	Kathy	87 E. Aurora Ave.	Chesterfield	CA	92122-1268	(507) 555-9797	F	5/30/197
12258	Delano	Gordon	1310 N. Sprindrift Dr.	Chesterfield	CA	92122-1268	(507) 555-8201	M	8/7/197
12366	Stacey	David	737 S. College Rd.	Chesterfield	CA	92122-1268	(507) 555-7784	M	9/30/197
12389	Blackman	Jennifer	773 E. Laurel St.	River Mist	CA	92123-2232	(507) 555-4956	F	1/22/198
12501	DeLuca	Elizabeth	21 W. Southern Ave.	Landis	CA	92120-3741	(507) 555-1105	F	8/21/197
12583	Sullivan	Marie	78 Omega Drive	Chesterfield	CA	92122-1268	(507) 555-7890	F	3/15/1981
12594	Reddie	Mark	900 W. Campus Dr.	Maldin	CA	92121	(507) 555-1139	M	11/5/198
12612	Richards	Melissa	5522 W. Marin Lane	River Mist	CA	92123	(507) 555-7789	F	9/30/197
12655	Lahti	Jill	5401 E. Thomas Rd.	Landis	CA	92120-3741	(507) 555-7765	F	6/14/197
12668	Stueland	Valerie	34 University Dr.	Maldin	CA	92121-3740	(507) 555-1845	F	11/19/197

Record: 4 of 53 No Filter Search

Datasheet View

Figure 2.44

The drop-down list of commands contains the current selected value in the field. The commands that appear will vary depending on the data type of the selected value. Also, the commands will vary depending on how much of the value is selected. If the selection is a partial selection, the commands allow you to specify a filter using the beginning, middle, or end of a field value. In this case, the entire value is selected and the four commands allow you to specify whether you want the selection to equal, not equal, contain, or not contain the value.

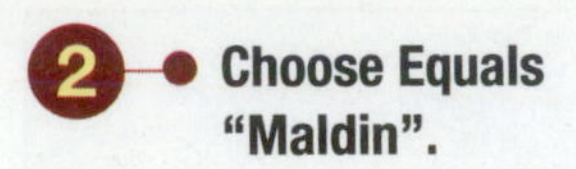

Choose Equals "Maldin".

Another Method

You also can display the Filter by Selection commands using the selection's shortcut menu.

Your screen should be similar to Figure 2.45

Filter displays only those records meeting the criterion of City equal to Maldin

Identifies filtered field

Employee ID	Last Name	First Name	Address	City	State	ZIP Code	Home Phone	Gender	Birth Date
01421	Spehr	Timothy	90 Royal Dr.	Maldin	CA	92121-3740	(507) 555-1038	M	9/9/1972
03225	Morgan	Dan	564 S. Lemon Dr.	Maldin	CA	92121	(507) 555-5567	M	3/5/1975
03406	Lopez	Mina	4290 E. Alameda Dr.	Maldin	CA	92121-3740	(507) 555-5050	F	2/25/1977
06000	Robertson	Kirk	832 S. William Ave.	Maldin	CA	92121	(507) 555-3730	M	4/5/1974
07287	Roman	Anita	2348 S. Bala Dr.	Maldin	CA	92121-3740	(507) 555-9870	F	3/15/1981
11747	Lettow	Ryan	358 Maple Dr.	Maldin	CA	92121-3740	(507) 555-2805	M	11/15/1981
12194	Polonsky	Mitch	8701 E. Sheridan	Maldin	CA	92121-3740	(507) 555-1018	M	3/13/1980
12594	Reddie	Mark	900 W. Campus Dr.	Maldin	CA	92121	(507) 555-1139	M	11/5/1983
12668	Stueland	Valerie	34 University Dr.	Maldin	CA	92121-3740	(507) 555-1845	F	11/19/1979
12920	Larson	Alicia	345 W. Mill Ave.	Maldin	CA	92121-3740	(941) 555-7717	F	6/21/1983
13005	Reilly	Emily	125 N. Marigold St.	Maldin	CA	92121-3740	(941) 555-6532	F	5/21/1985
13458	Helfand	Eric	4601 E. Willow Dr.	Maldin	CA	92121-3740	(941) 555-9101	M	9/12/1980
13484	Franklin	Stephanie	889 S. Litchfield Park	Maldin	CA	92121-3740	(941) 555-7833	F	7/30/1979
13543	Martinez	Julie	1920 First Ave.	Maldin	CA	92121-3740	(941) 555-1044	F	12/10/1982
13597	Gapasin	Ken	2633 E. Fountain St.	Maldin	CA	92121-3740	(941) 555-0589	M	2/11/1985
13635	Martinez	Juan	7115 E Roosevelt Dr.	Maldin	CA	92121-3740	(507) 555-2935	M	12/10/1983
22469	Hogan	Ryan	1389 E. Northview Dr.	Maldin	CA	92121-3740	(941) 555-1010	M	7/14/1986
*					CA				

Record: 1 of 17 Filtered Search

Number of records that meet filter criterion

Status of datasheet is filtered

Figure 2.45

Additional Information

You can print a filtered datasheet just like any other table.

The table displays only those records that contain the selected city. All other records are temporarily hidden. The status bar displays the Filtered button to show that the datasheet is filtered and the record number indicator shows that the total number of filtered records is 17. The City field name also displays a filter icon to identify the field on which the table was filtered.

After seeing how easy it was to locate this information, you want to locate employees who live in Chesterfield. This information may help in setting up the car pool, because the people traveling from the city of Maldin pass through Chesterfield on the way to the Landis location.

Removing and Deleting Filters

Before creating the new filter, you will remove the current filter and return the table to its full display.

1. Click Toggle Filter in the Sort & Filter group.

Another Method

You also can use Filtered in the record navigator bar to apply and remove a filter.

Your screen should be similar to Figure 2.46

Figure 2.46

The filter is temporarily removed from the field and all the records are displayed again. The navigator bar displays Unfiltered. The filter is still available and can be reapplied quickly by clicking Toggle Filter or Unfiltered.

You will reapply the filter and then you will permanently remove these filter settings.

2.
- **Click Toggle Filter to redisplay the filtered datasheet.**
- **Click Advanced in the Sort & filter group.**
- **Choose Clear All Filters.**

The filter is removed and all the records are redisplayed. The Toggle Filter button is dimmed because the table does not include any filter settings.

Filtering Using Common Filters

To filter the employee data by two cities, Chesterfield and Maldin, you can select from a list of several popular filters. Using this list allows you to perform filters on multiple criteria within a single field.

Click on the ▾ in the City column header to open the field's drop-down menu.

Another Method

You also can move to the field to filter on and click Filter in the Sort & Filter group to display the Filter list.

Your screen should be similar to Figure 2.47

Dimmed button shows no filter settings stored with table

Employee Records

Employee ID	Last Name	First Name	Address	City	State	ZIP Code	Home Phone	Gender	Birth Date
00212	Schiff	Chad	235 N. Cactus Dr.	Chesterfiel				M	3/9/1962
00617	Nichols	Cathy	75 Brooklea Dr.	Landis				F	5/19/1965
00907	Pennington	Mark	23 Mill Ave.	Landis				M	7/7/1969
01421	Spehr	Timothy	90 Royal Dr.	Maldin				M	9/9/1972
03225	Morgan	Dan	564 S. Lemon Dr.	Maldin				M	3/5/1975
03406	Lopez	Mina	4290 E. Alameda Dr.	Maldin				F	2/25/1977
03890	Thi	Erona	7867 Forest Ave.	River Mist					5/10/1976
04321	Sabin	Greg	90 E. Rawhide Ave.	Chesterfiel					9/30/1977
04731	Marchant	Roberta	564 Palm Avenue	Landis					5/13/1980
05015	Briggs	Scott	45 E. Camelback Rd.	River Mist					9/15/1978
06000	Robertson	Kirk	832 S. William Ave.	Maldin				M	4/5/1974
07287	Roman	Anita	2348 S. Bala Dr.	Maldin				F	3/15/1981
08391	Ruiz	Enrique	35 Palm St.	Chesterfiel				M	12/10/1973
11747	Lettow	Ryan	358 Maple Dr.	Maldin				M	11/15/1981
12194	Polonsky	Mitch	8701 E. Sheridan	Maldin				M	3/13/1980
12213	Young	Kim	89 College Ave.	Landis				F	4/12/1980
12230	Reddie	Suzanne	932 E. Parkway Dr.	Landis	CA	92120-3741	(507) 555-1191	F	7/14/1978
12247	Rath	Kathy	87 E. Aurora Ave.	Chesterfield	CA	92122-1268	(507) 555-9797	F	5/30/1978
12258	Delano	Gordon	1310 N. Sprindrift Dr.	Chesterfield	CA	92122-1268	(507) 555-8201	M	8/7/1979
12366	Stacey	David	737 S. College Rd.	Chesterfield	CA	92122-1268	(507) 555-7784	M	9/30/1978
12389	Blackman	Jennifer	773 E. Laurel St.	River Mist	CA	92123-2232	(507) 555-4956	F	1/22/1980
12501	DeLuca	Elizabeth	21 W. Southern Ave.	Landis	CA	92120-3741	(507) 555-1105	F	8/21/1979
12583	Sullivan	Marie	78 Omega Drive	Chesterfield	CA	92122-1268	(507) 555-7890	F	3/15/1981
12594	Reddie	Mark	900 W. Campus Dr.	Maldin	CA	92121	(507) 555-1139	M	11/5/1983
12612	Richards	Melissa	5522 W. Marin Lane	River Mist	CA	92123	(507) 555-7789	F	9/30/1978
12655	Lahti	Jill	5401 E. Thomas Rd.	Landis	CA	92120-3741	(507) 555-7765	F	6/14/1977
12668	Stueland	Valerie	34 University Dr.	Maldin	CA	92121-3740	(507) 555-1845	F	11/19/1979

Sort A to Z
Sort Z to A
Clear filter from City
Text Filters
(Select All)
(Blanks)
Chesterfield
Landis
Maldin
River Mist
OK Cancel

List of unique field values

Record: 1 of 53 No Filter Search
Datasheet View

Figure 2.47

A list of all the unique values that are stored in the current field is displayed. Selecting a value from the list filters the table based on the selected value. Depending on the data type of the selected value, you may be able to filter for a range of values by clicking on a value and specifying the appropriate range. In this case, because the field is not filtered, all the values are selected. You will first clear the selection from all values, and then select the names of the two cities you want displayed in the filtered list.

2

- **Click the Select All check box to clear the selection from all values.**
- **Click the Chesterfield and Maldin check boxes to select them.**
- **Click OK.**

Your screen should be similar to Figure 2.48

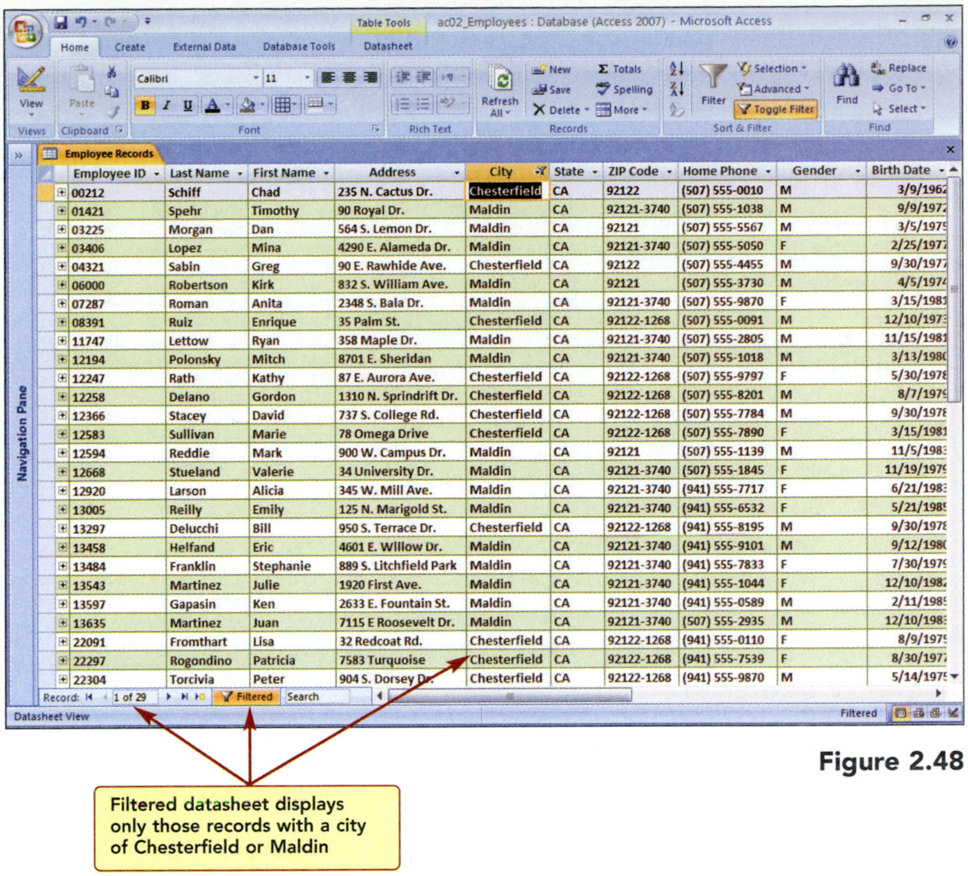

Table Tools ac02_Employees : Database (Access 2007) - Microsoft Access

Home Create External Data Database Tools Datasheet

Views Clipboard Font Rich Text Records Sort & Filter Find

Employee Records

Employee ID	Last Name	First Name	Address	City	State	ZIP Code	Home Phone	Gender	Birth Date
00212	Schiff	Chad	235 N. Cactus Dr.	Chesterfield	CA	92122	(507) 555-0010	M	3/9/1962
01421	Spehr	Timothy	90 Royal Dr.	Maldin	CA	92121-3740	(507) 555-1038	M	9/9/1972
03225	Morgan	Dan	564 S. Lemon Dr.	Maldin	CA	92121	(507) 555-5567	M	3/5/1975
03406	Lopez	Mina	4290 E. Alameda Dr.	Maldin	CA	92121-3740	(507) 555-5050	F	2/25/1977
04321	Sabin	Greg	90 E. Rawhide Ave.	Chesterfield	CA	92122	(507) 555-4455	M	9/30/1977
06000	Robertson	Kirk	832 S. William Ave.	Maldin	CA	92121	(507) 555-3730	M	4/5/1974
07287	Roman	Anita	2348 S. Bala Dr.	Maldin	CA	92121-3740	(507) 555-9870	F	3/15/1981
08391	Ruiz	Enrique	35 Palm St.	Chesterfield	CA	92122-1268	(507) 555-0091	M	12/10/1973
11747	Lettow	Ryan	358 Maple Dr.	Maldin	CA	92121-3740	(507) 555-2805	M	11/15/1981
12194	Polonsky	Mitch	8701 E. Sheridan	Maldin	CA	92121-3740	(507) 555-1018	M	3/13/1980
12247	Rath	Kathy	87 E. Aurora Ave.	Chesterfield	CA	92122-1268	(507) 555-9797	F	5/30/1978
12258	Delano	Gordon	1310 N. Sprindrift Dr.	Chesterfield	CA	92122-1268	(507) 555-8201	M	8/7/1979
12366	Stacey	David	737 S. College Rd.	Chesterfield	CA	92122-1268	(507) 555-7784	M	9/30/1978
12583	Sullivan	Marie	78 Omega Drive	Chesterfield	CA	92122-1268	(507) 555-7890	F	3/15/1981
12594	Reddie	Mark	900 W. Campus Dr.	Maldin	CA	92121	(507) 555-1139	M	11/5/1983
12668	Stueland	Valerie	34 University Dr.	Maldin	CA	92121-3740	(507) 555-1845	F	11/19/1979
12920	Larson	Alicia	345 W. Mill Ave.	Maldin	CA	92121-3740	(941) 555-7717	F	6/21/1983
13005	Reilly	Emily	125 N. Marigold St.	Maldin	CA	92121-3740	(941) 555-6532	F	5/21/1985
13297	Delucchi	Bill	950 S. Terrace Dr.	Chesterfield	CA	92122-1268	(941) 555-8195	M	9/30/1978
13458	Helfand	Eric	4601 E. Willow Dr.	Maldin	CA	92121-3740	(941) 555-9101	M	9/12/1980
13484	Franklin	Stephanie	889 S. Litchfield Park	Maldin	CA	92121-3740	(941) 555-7833	F	7/30/1979
13543	Martinez	Julie	1920 First Ave.	Maldin	CA	92121-3740	(941) 555-1044	F	12/10/1982
13597	Gapasin	Ken	2633 E. Fountain St.	Maldin	CA	92121-3740	(941) 555-0589	M	2/11/1985
13635	Martinez	Juan	7115 E Roosevelt Dr.	Maldin	CA	92121-3740	(507) 555-2935	M	12/10/1983
22091	Fromthart	Lisa	32 Redcoat Rd.	Chesterfield	CA	92122-1268	(941) 555-0110	F	8/9/1975
22297	Rogondino	Patricia	7583 Turquoise	Chesterfield	CA	92122-1268	(941) 555-7539	F	8/30/1977
22304	Torcivia	Peter	904 S. Dorsey Dr.	Chesterfield	CA	92122-1268	(941) 555-9870	M	5/14/1975

Record: 1 of 29 Filtered Search

Datasheet View Filtered

Filtered datasheet displays only those records with a city of Chesterfield or Maldin

Figure 2.48

The filtered datasheet displays the records for all 29 employees who live in the city of Chesterfield or Maldin.

Filtering on Multiple Fields

As you look at the filtered results, you decide to further refine the list by restricting the results to those records that have the same zip code as Juan's zip code of 92121. Although you can only specify one filter per field, you can specify a different filter for each field that is present in the view.

1

- **Open the ZIP Code field's drop-down menu to display the field list.**
- **Clear the checkmark from the 92121-3740 value.**
- **Click** **.**

Your screen should be similar to Figure 2.49

Second filter on ZIP Code further restricts displayed records to ZIP Code not equal to 92121-3740

Figure 2.49

Now there are only 15 records displayed in the filtered table. Applying the second filter refined the results by removing all records from the filtered list that had a zip code of 92121-3740.

Although you would like to provide a copy of this information to Juan, you realize that it contains more information about each employee than someone would need (or should even have access to) in order to form a car pool. Also, because you are not finished adding records to the employee database, these findings may not be complete.

You will redisplay all the records in the table, but you will not clear the filter settings. If you do not clear the filters, the filter criteria you last specified are stored with the table, and the results can be redisplayed simply by applying the filter again.

2

- **Click Toggle Filter to display the unfiltered datasheet.**
- **Close the table, saving your design changes.**
- **Redisplay the Navigation pane.**

The table is closed and the work area is empty. Next you will learn how to create and use a form in Access.

Note: If you are ending your session now, close the database file and exit Access. When you begin again, start Access and open the ac02_Employees database file.

Creating and Using Forms

One of your objectives is to make the database easy to use. You know from experience that long hours of viewing large tables can be tiring. Therefore, you want to create an onscreen form to make this table easier to view and use.

Concept 8

Form

8

A **form** is a database object used primarily to display records onscreen and to make it easier to enter new records and to make changes to existing records. Forms can control access to data, such as which fields or rows of data are displayed. That way, any unnecessary fields of data are not displayed, which makes it easier for people using the database. They enable people to use the data in the tables without having to sift through many lines of data to find the exact record.

Forms are based on an underlying table and can include design elements such as descriptive text, titles, labels, lines, boxes, and pictures. Forms also can use calculations to summarize data that is not listed on the actual table, such as a sales total. The layout and arrangement of information can be customized in a form. Using these features creates a visually attractive form that makes working with the database more enjoyable, more efficient, and less prone to data-entry errors.

You want the onscreen form to be similar to the paper form that is completed by each new employee when hired (shown below). The information from that form is used as the source of input for the new record that will be added to the table for the new employee.

EMPLOYEE DATA

Employee ID ____________________

First Name ____________________ Last Name ____________________
Street ____
City ____________________ State ______ Zip __________
Phone Number ____________________
Gender ________
Birth Date __________________

MORE ABOUT

To learn how to create a datasheet form, see "2 Creating and Formatting Database Elements" in the More About appendix.

There are several different methods you can use to create forms as described in the following table. The method you use depends on the type of form you want to create.

Method	Use to
Form Tool	Create a form containing all the fields in the table.
Split Form tool	Create a form that displays the form and datasheet in a single window
Blank Form tool	Build a form from scratch by adding the fields you select from the table
Datasheet tool	Create a form using all the fields in the table and display it in Datasheet view
Multiple Items tool	Create a form that displays multiple records but is more customizable than a datasheet
Form Wizard	Create a form using a wizard that guides you through the steps to create a complex form that displays selected fields, data groups, sorted records, and data from multiple tables

Using the Form Tool

Using the Form tool is the quickest method to create a simple form. You decide to see if the Form tool will create the form you need.

1

- **If necessary, select the Employee Records table in the Navigation pane.**
- **Open the Create tab.**
- **Click Form in the Forms group.**

Your screen should be similar to Figure 2.50

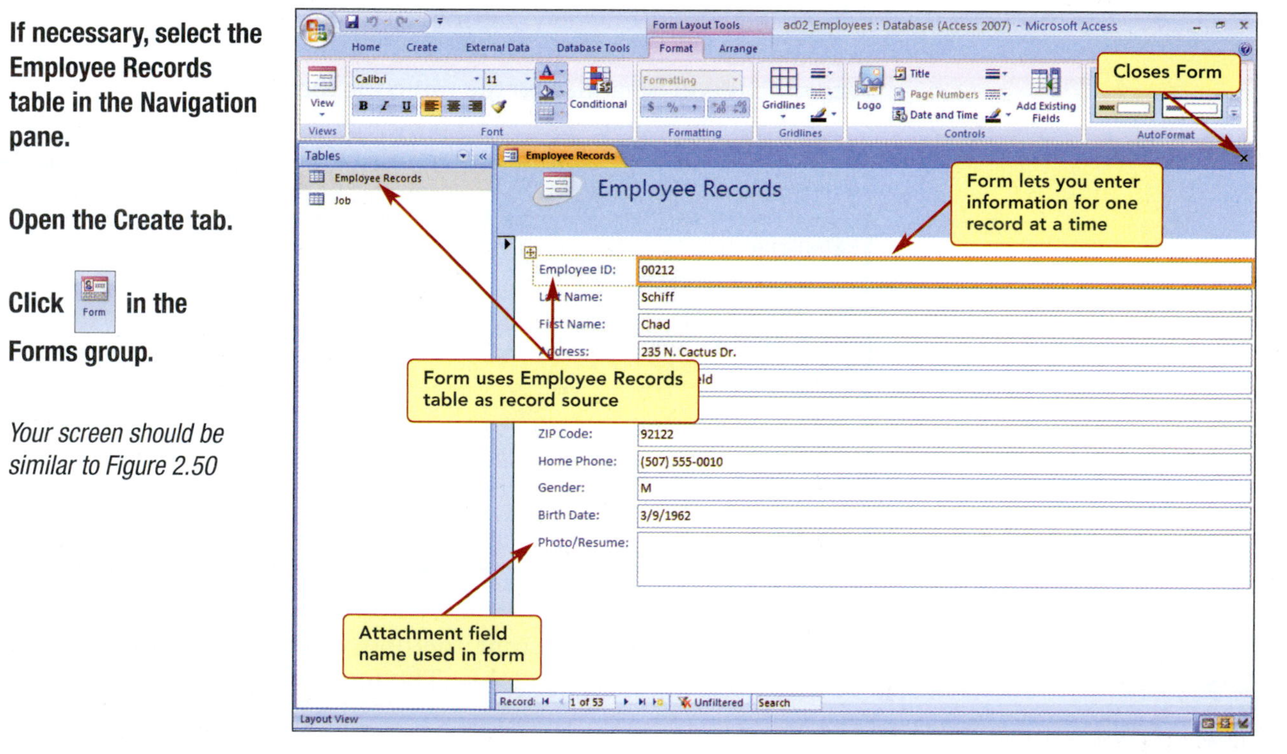

Figure 2.50

A form that allows you to enter data for one record at a time was quickly created. The fields from the Employee Records table were used to create the form because it was the selected object in the Navigation pane. The underlying table that is used to create a form is called the **record source.**

The fields are in the same order as in the datasheet. Notice the field name you specified for the Attachment field is used in the form, although it is not used in the table.

This form does not quite meet your needs and you decide to try another method to create the form.

2 • **Close the form.**

• **Click No to the prompt to save the form.**

Using the Multiple Items Tool

Next, you will use the Multiple Items tool to create a form.

1 • **If necessary, open the Create tab.**

• **Click Multiple Items in the Forms group.**

Your screen should be similar to Figure 2.51

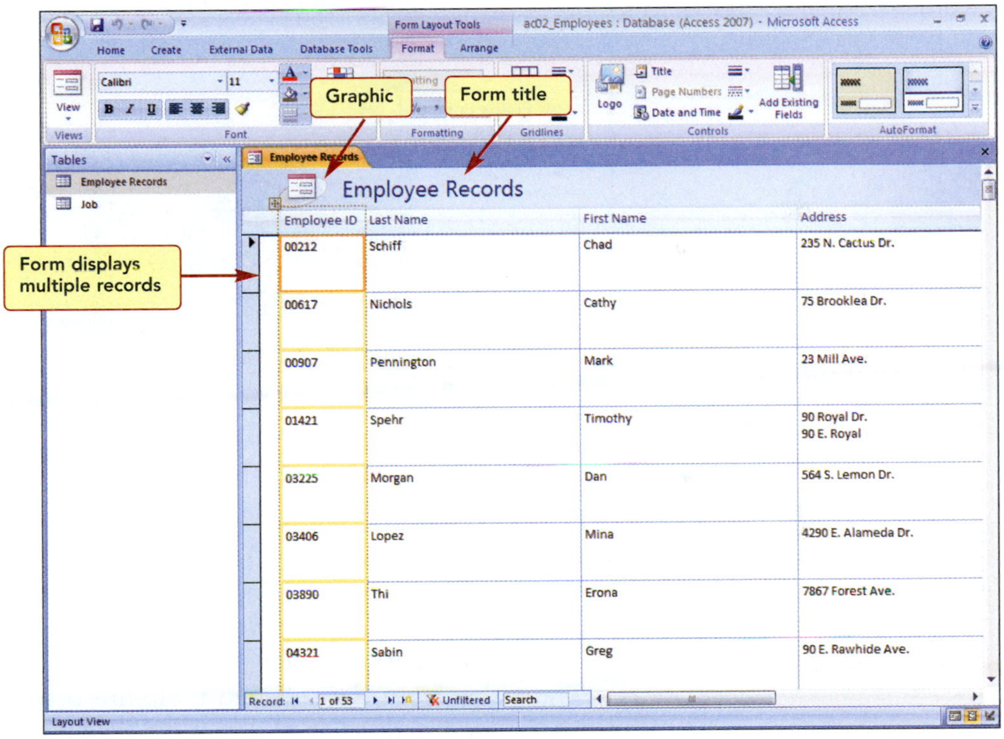

Figure 2.51

A form that displays multiple records at a time was quickly created. Although it looks similar to datasheet view, it is easier to read and includes a title and graphic. However, this form still does not work and you decide to use the Form Wizard to create a form that is closer to your needs.

2 • **Close the form.**

• **Click No to the prompt to save the form.**

Using the Form Wizard

The Form Wizard will help you create a form that is closer to your needs by guiding you through a series of steps that allow you to specify different form features.

1 **Click More Forms in the Forms group of the Create tab.**

Choose Form Wizard.

Your screen should be similar to Figure 2.52

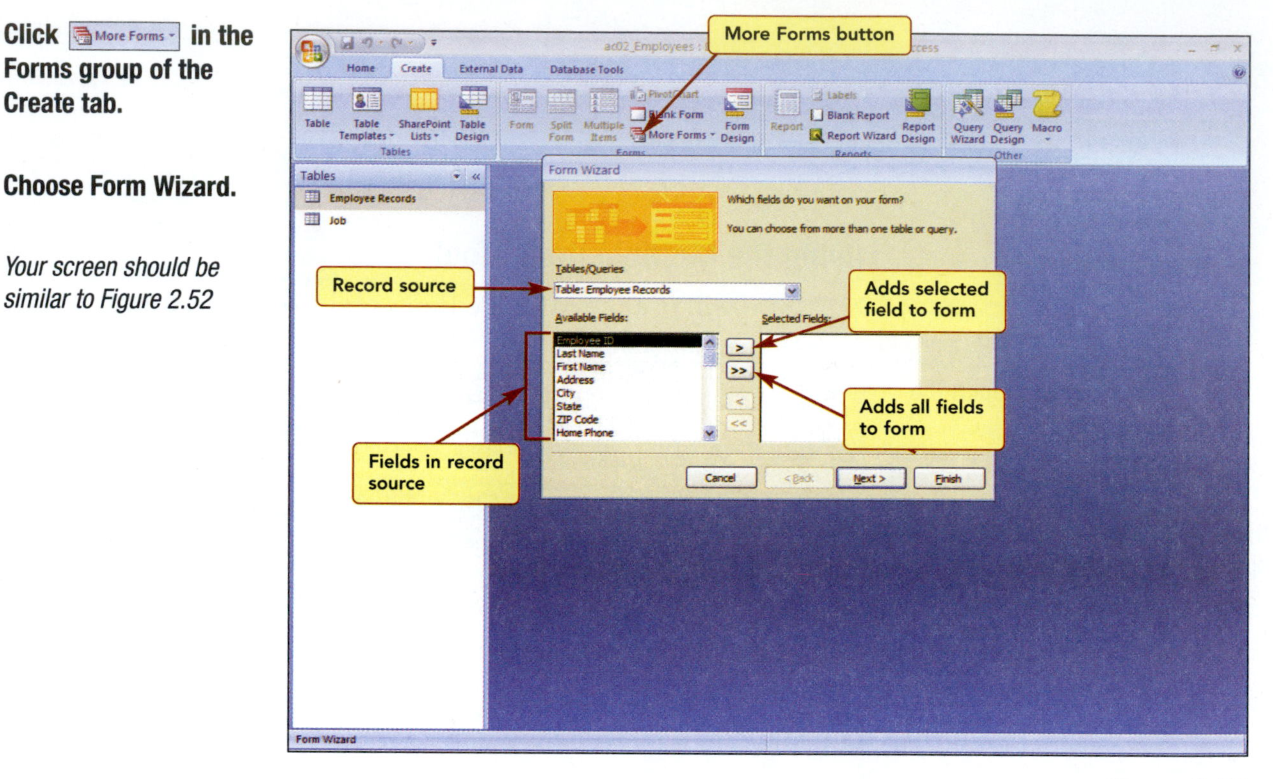

Figure 2.52

The Form Wizard dialog box displays the name of the current table, Employee Records, in the Tables/Queries list box. This is the table that will be used as the record source. If you wanted to use a different table as the record source, you could open the Tables/Queries drop-down list to select the appropriate table.

The fields from the selected table are displayed in the Available Fields list box. You use this box to select the fields you want included on the form, in the order that you want them to appear. This order is called the **tab order** because it is the order that the highlight will move through the fields on the form when you press the Tab key during data entry. You decide that you want the fields to be in the same order as they are on the paper form shown in the illustration on the previous page.

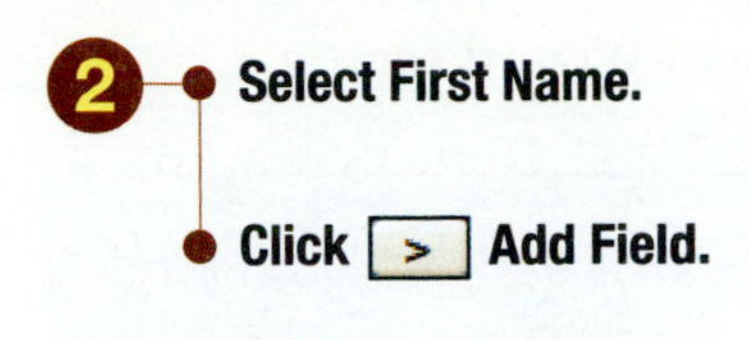

Select First Name.

Click [>] Add Field.

Another Method

You also can double-click on each field name in the Available Fields list box to move the field name to the Selected Fields list box.

Additional Information

The [>>] Add All Fields button adds all available fields to the Selected Fields list, in the same order that they appear in the Available Fields list.

Your screen should be similar to Figure 2.53

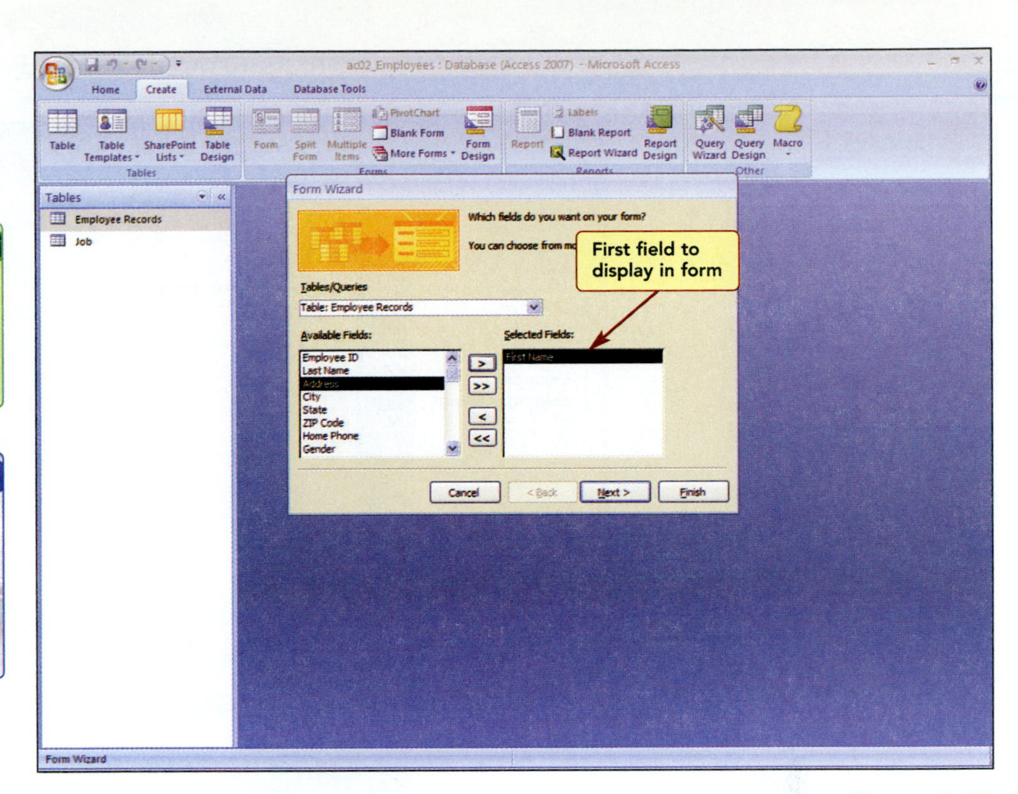

Figure 2.53

The First Name field is removed from the Available Fields list and added to the top of the Selected Fields list box. It will be the first field in the form.

3 **In the same manner, add the following fields to the Selected Fields list in the order shown here:**

Last Name

Address

City

State

ZIP Code

Home Phone

Gender

Birth Date

Employee ID

Photo/Resume

Your screen should be similar to Figure 2.54

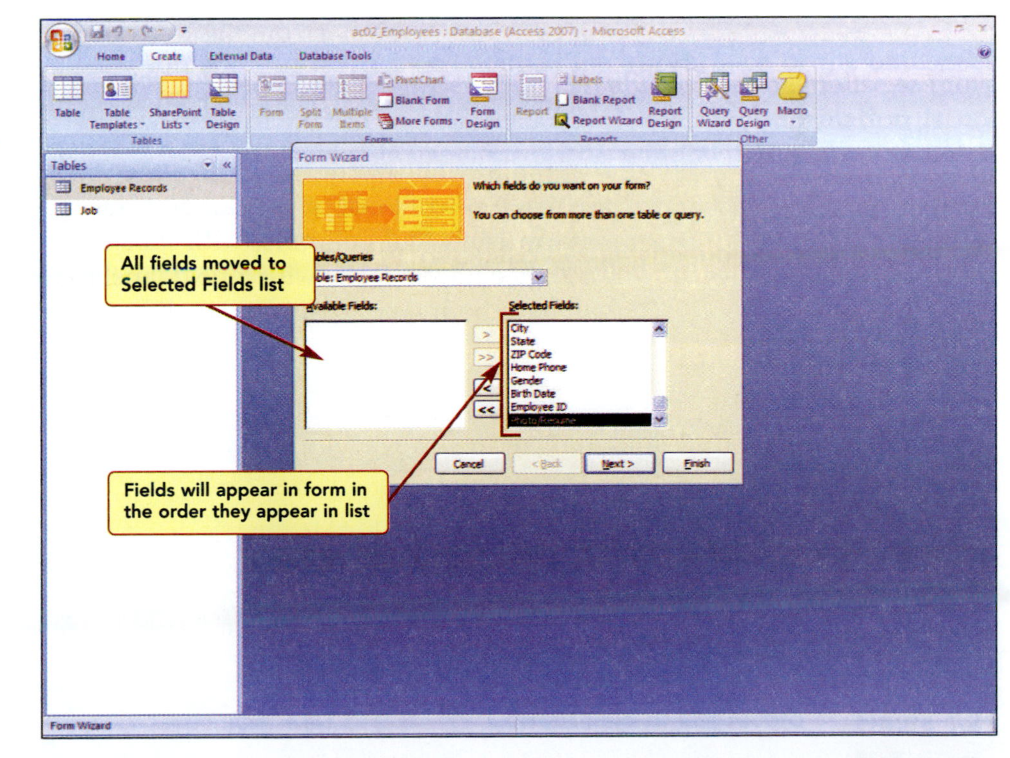

Figure 2.54

When finished, the Available Fields list box is empty and the Selected Fields list box lists the fields in the selected order.

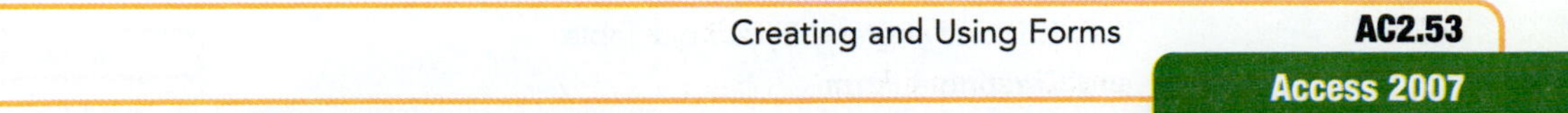

You are now ready to move on to the next Form Wizard screen.

4 Click .

Your screen should be similar to Figure 2.55

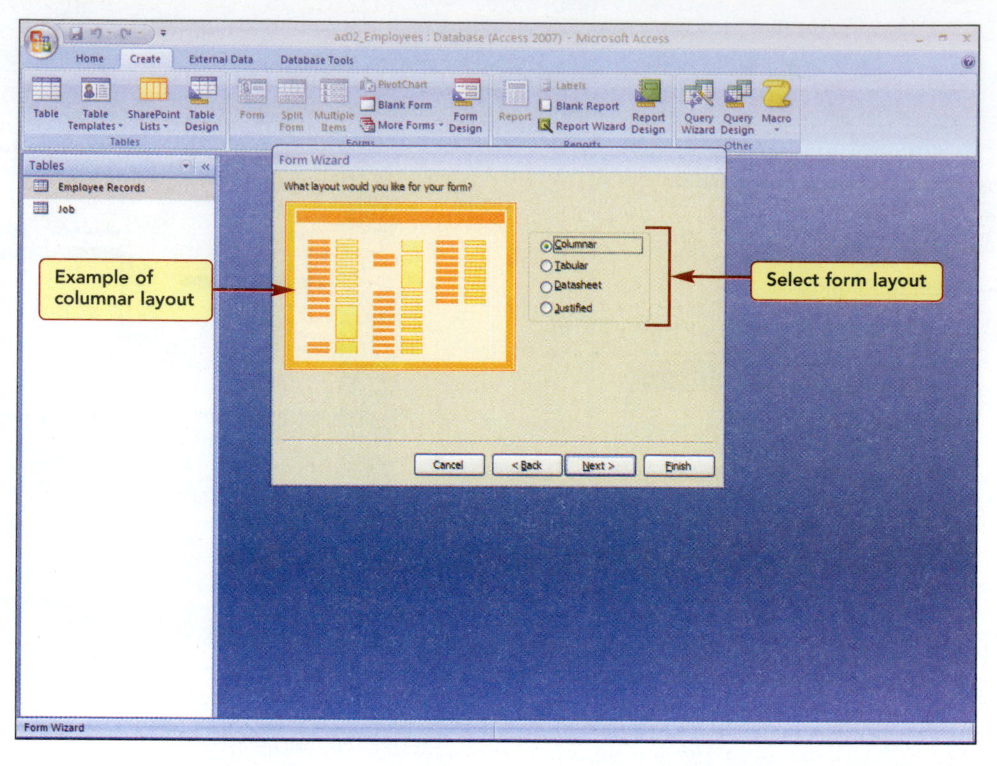

Figure 2.55

In this Form Wizard screen, you are asked to select the control layout for the form. **Layouts** control how the data is displayed in the form by aligning the items horizontally or vertically to give the form a uniform appearance.

The controls are contained in a control layout that was created automatically when the form was created. A control layout aligns controls horizontally and vertically to give the form a uniform appearance. There are two types of layouts: tabular and stacked. **Tabular layouts** arrange the data in rows and columns, with labels across the top. **Stacked layouts** arrange data vertically with a field label to the left of the field data. A form can have both types of layouts in different sections.

The four form layouts offered by the Form Wizard are variations of the two basic layouts as described in the following table.

Form	Layout Style	Description
Columnar		This is a stacked layout that presents data for the selected fields in columns. The field name labels are displayed down the left side of the column with the data for each field just to the right of the corresponding label. A single record is displayed in each Form window.
Tabular		This is the basic tabular layout that presents data with field name labels across the top of the page and the corresponding data in columns under each heading. Multiple records are displayed in the Form window, each on a single row. All fields are displayed across the top of the Form window.
Datasheet		This is a tabular layout that displays data in rows and columns similar to the Table Datasheet view. It displays multiple records, one per row, in the Form window. You may need to scroll the form horizontally to see all the fields.
Justified		This is a tabular layout that displays data in rows, with field name labels across the top of the row and the corresponding field data below it. A single record may appear in multiple rows in the Form window in order to fully display the field name label and data. A single record is displayed in each Form window.

Additional Information

Using [Form] in the Forms group creates a form using the stacked layout.

The columnar layout appears most similar to the paper form currently in use by the club, so you decide to use that layout for your form.

5 • If necessary, choose Columnar.

• Click Next >.

Your screen should be similar to Figure 2.56

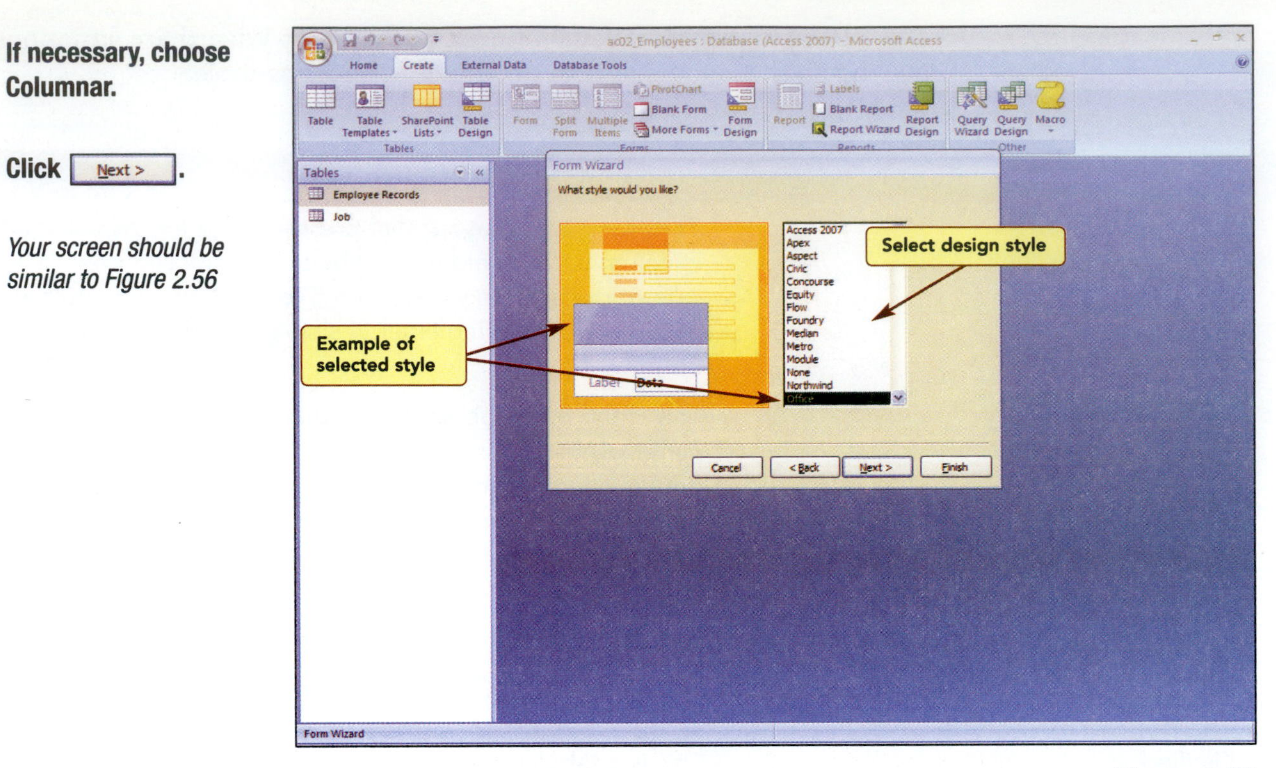

Figure 2.56

Next you select a design style for your form. Design styles consist of different combinations of colors, fonts, and graphic elements. A sample of each style as it is selected is displayed on the left side of the dialog box. None is the default selection. You will create the form using the Flow style.

6 • Choose several design styles to view the example.

• Choose the Flow design style.

• Click Next >.

Your screen should be similar to Figure 2.57

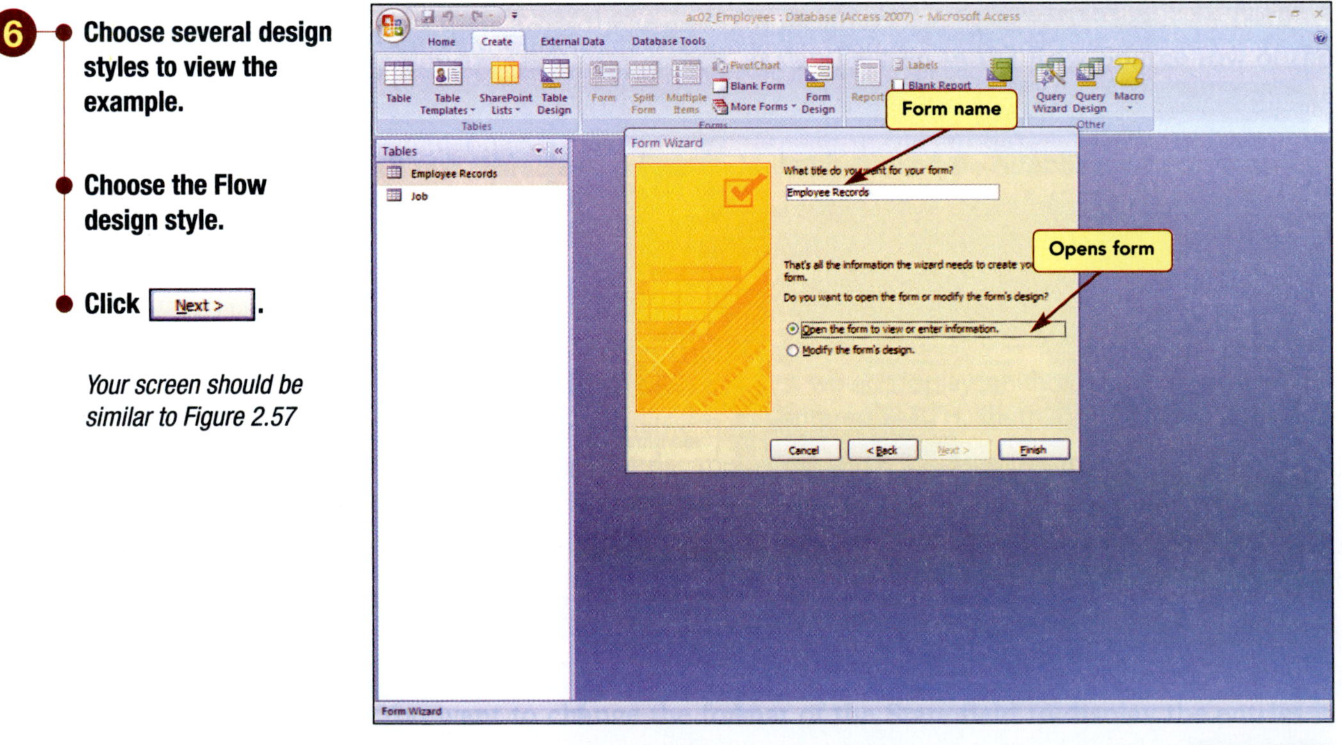

Figure 2.57

In the final Form Wizard dialog box, you can enter a form title to be used as the name of the form, and you can specify whether to open the form or to modify it. The Form Wizard uses the name of the table as the default form title. You will keep the proposed form title and the default of opening the form.

7 Click .

Your screen should be similar to Figure 2.58

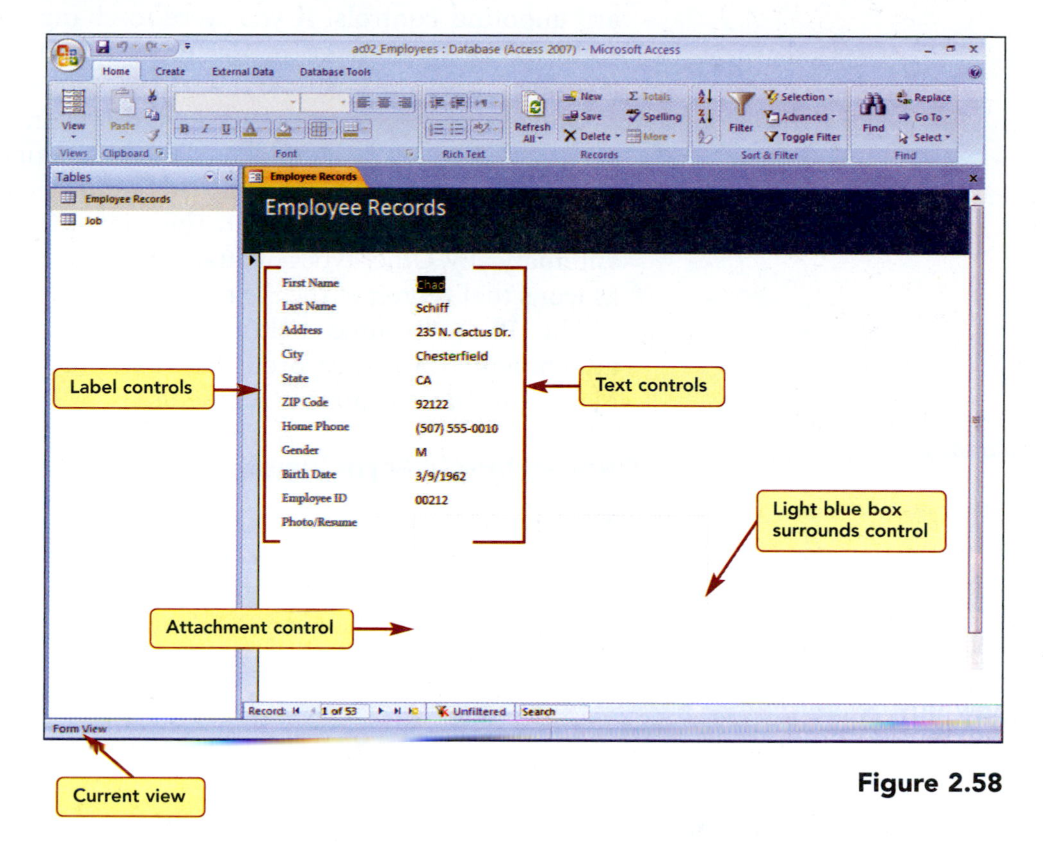

Figure 2.58

Having Trouble?

Do not be concerned if your Photo/Resume field appears in a second column to the right.

The completed form is displayed in the work area in Form view. The form title appears at the top of the form. The employee information for Chad Schiff, the first record in the table, is displayed in the form.

The form displays the selected fields in columnar layout using the Flow design style. A single column displays the field name labels down the left side of the column with the data for each field displayed just to the right of the corresponding label.

Each item in the form is a separate object contained in boxes, called controls.

Concept 9

Controls

Controls are objects that display information, perform actions, or enhance the design of a form or report. Access provides controls for many types of objects, including labels, text boxes, check boxes, list boxes, command buttons, lines, rectangles, option buttons, and more. The most common controls are **text controls** and **label controls.** Text controls display the information in the field from the record source. Label controls display descriptive labels.

There are two basic types of controls: bound and unbound. A **bound control** is linked to a field in an underlying table. An example of a bound control is a text control that is linked to the record source (usually a field from a table) and displays the field entry in the form or report. An **unbound control** is not connected to an underlying record source. Examples of unbound controls are labels such as the title of a form or elements that enhance the appearance of the form such as lines, boxes, and pictures.

> **Additional Information**
> You will learn about reports in Lab 3.

This form contains two types of controls: label controls that display the field names and text controls that display the field data. The text controls are bound controls. Changing information in the text controls will change the data for the record in the underlying table. Even though the label controls display the field names that are used in the underlying table, they are unbound controls. If you were to change the text in the form's label control, the field name in the table would not change. The columnar layout controls the layout and position of these controls.

Notice the Photo/Resume field control is an **attachment control** that is surrounded by a very light blue box. It is a bound control that allows you to add, edit, remove, and save attached files to the field directly from the form, just as you can in the datasheet. The attachment control displays image files automatically. Other types of attachments, such as Word documents, appear as icons that represent the file type and must be opened to view them.

The Photo/Resume field's control is empty because there are no attachments for this record. You would like to see the record for Roberta Marchant that contains attachments.

Navigating in Form View

You use the same navigation keys in Form view that you used in Datasheet view. You can move between fields in the form by using the Tab, Enter, and Shift + Tab keys. The → and ← keys are used to move character by character through the entry. You can use Page Up and Page Down, as well as the navigation buttons at the bottom of the form, to move between records.

You will try out several of these navigation keys as you try to locate the record for Roberta Marchant.

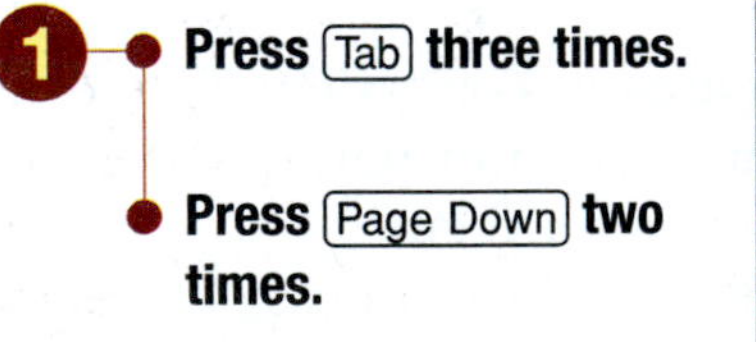

1 **Press Tab three times.**

Press Page Down two times.

Your screen should be similar to Figure 2.59

Pressing Tab moves to the next field

Pressing Page Down moves to the next record

Figure 2.59

First you moved down three fields to the City field in the current record. Then you moved down two records to record three. The field that was selected in the previous record remains the selected field when you move between records. As you navigate the form, it automatically scrolls to display additional controls. To view controls that are no larger visible, simply use the vertical scroll bar.

Searching in Form View

A quicker way to locate a record is to use the Find command or the Search feature. The Find command works just as it does in Datasheet view. The Search feature simply locates information in a table by searching every field for a match to the text you enter in the Search box. It begins a search with the first field of the first record in the table. To try this out, you will search for the record for Roberta Marchant by entering the characters of her last name in the Search box.

1 • **Click in the Search text box at the bottom of the work area.**

• **Type m.**

Additional Information
The Search feature is not case sensitive.

Your screen should be similar to Figure 2.60

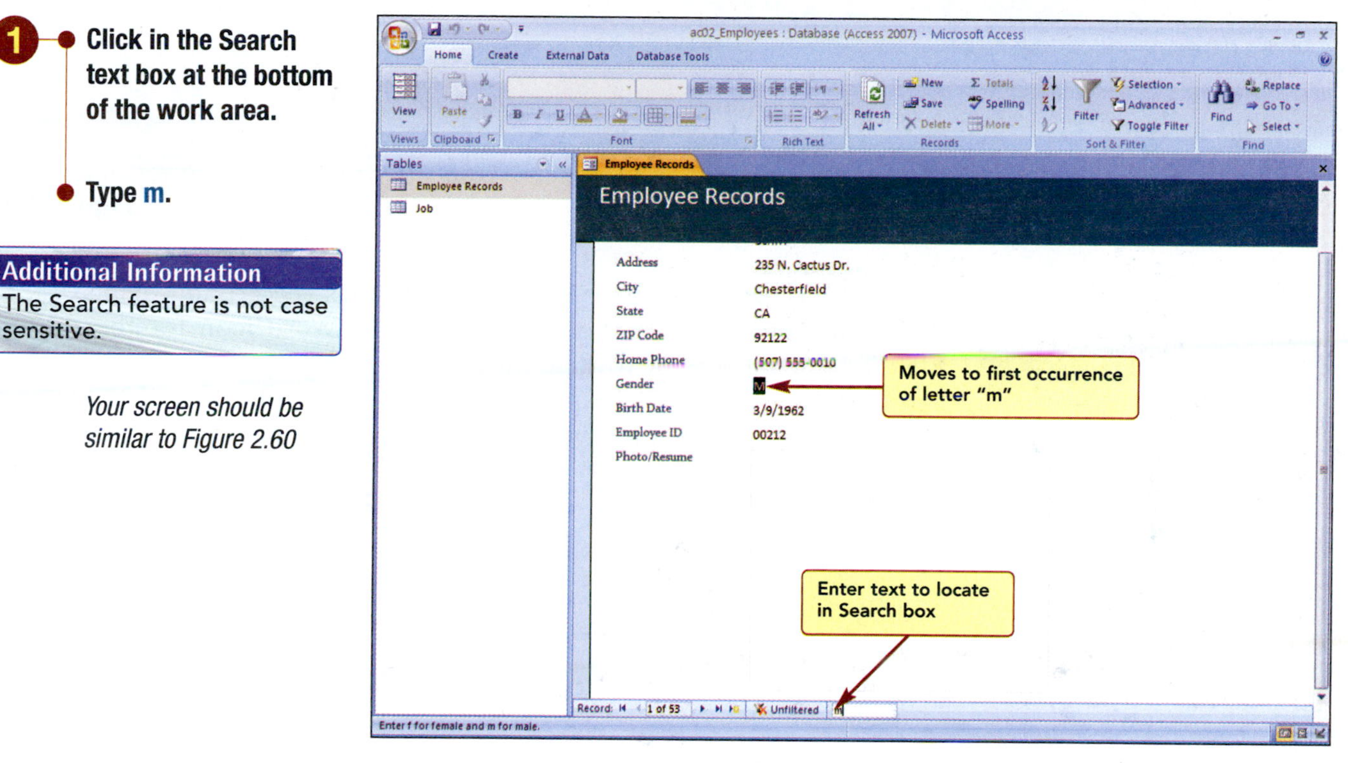

Figure 2.60

The first occurrence of the letter "m" in the table is located and highlighted. The more characters you type in the search text box, the more refined the search becomes. You will type more characters to continue looking for Roberta Marchant's record. As you type the characters, watch how the search advances through the table and highlights matching text.

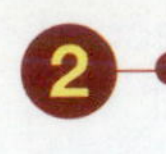

Type arc in the Search box.

Your screen should be similar to Figure 2.61

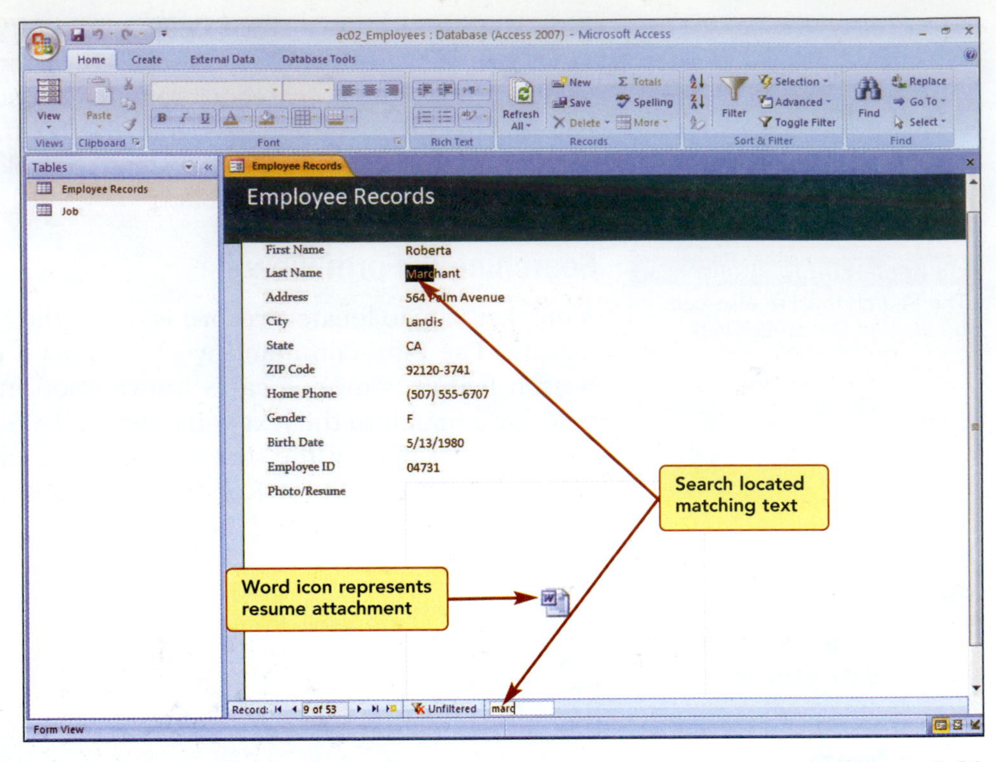

Figure 2.61

> **Additional Information**
> The Mini Toolbar appears dimmed until you point to it.

The Search feature located Roberta Marchant's record and displays it in the form. The Photo/Resume field displays a Word icon for the resume file. To move to the next attachment, you make the attachment control active to display the Mini Toolbar. It contains three buttons that are used to work with attachment controls. You can scroll through attached files using the [back] and [forward] buttons or add or view attachments using [paperclip] to open the Attachments dialog box.

- **Click on the Photo/Resume field to make it active.**
- **Point to the Mini Toolbar and click [button] to move to the next attachment.**

Your screen should be similar to Figure 2.62

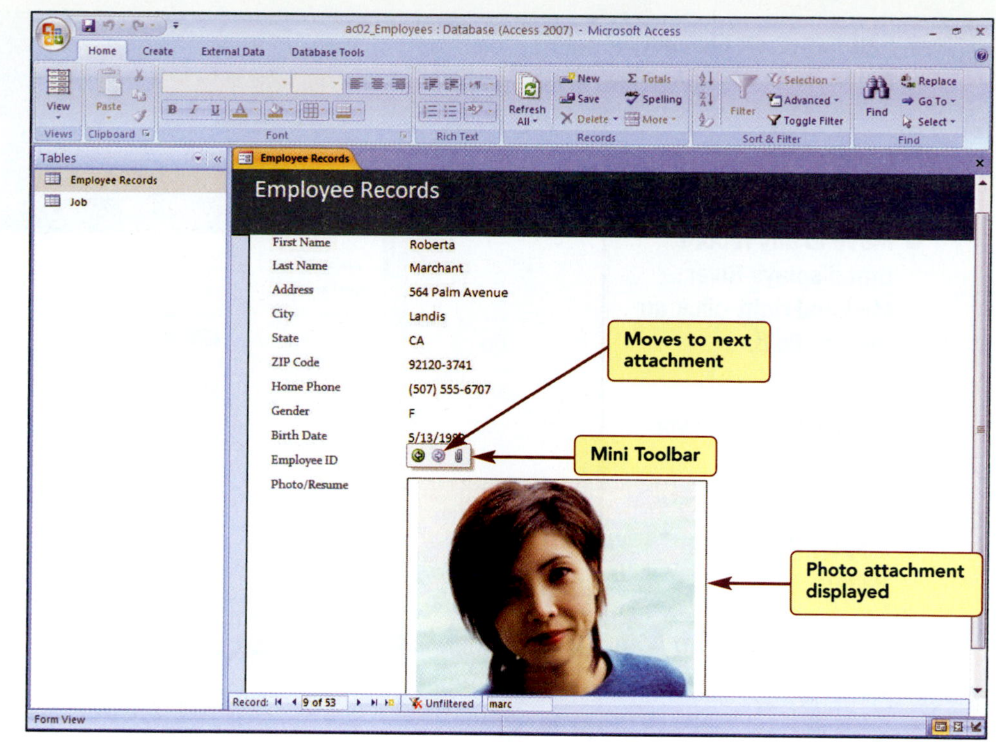

Figure 2.62

Now the photo is displayed in the Photo/Resume field control.

Sorting and Filtering Data in a Form

Just as in the table datasheet, you can sort and filter the data that is displayed in a form. You will use these features to sort the records in alphabetical order by last name and display only those records who live in River Mist.

1. Right-click on the Last Name field.
   - Choose Sort A to Z.
   - Move to any record that displays River Mist and right-click on the city field.
   - Choose Equals "River Mist".
   - Display the last record.

Your screen should be similar to Figure 2.63

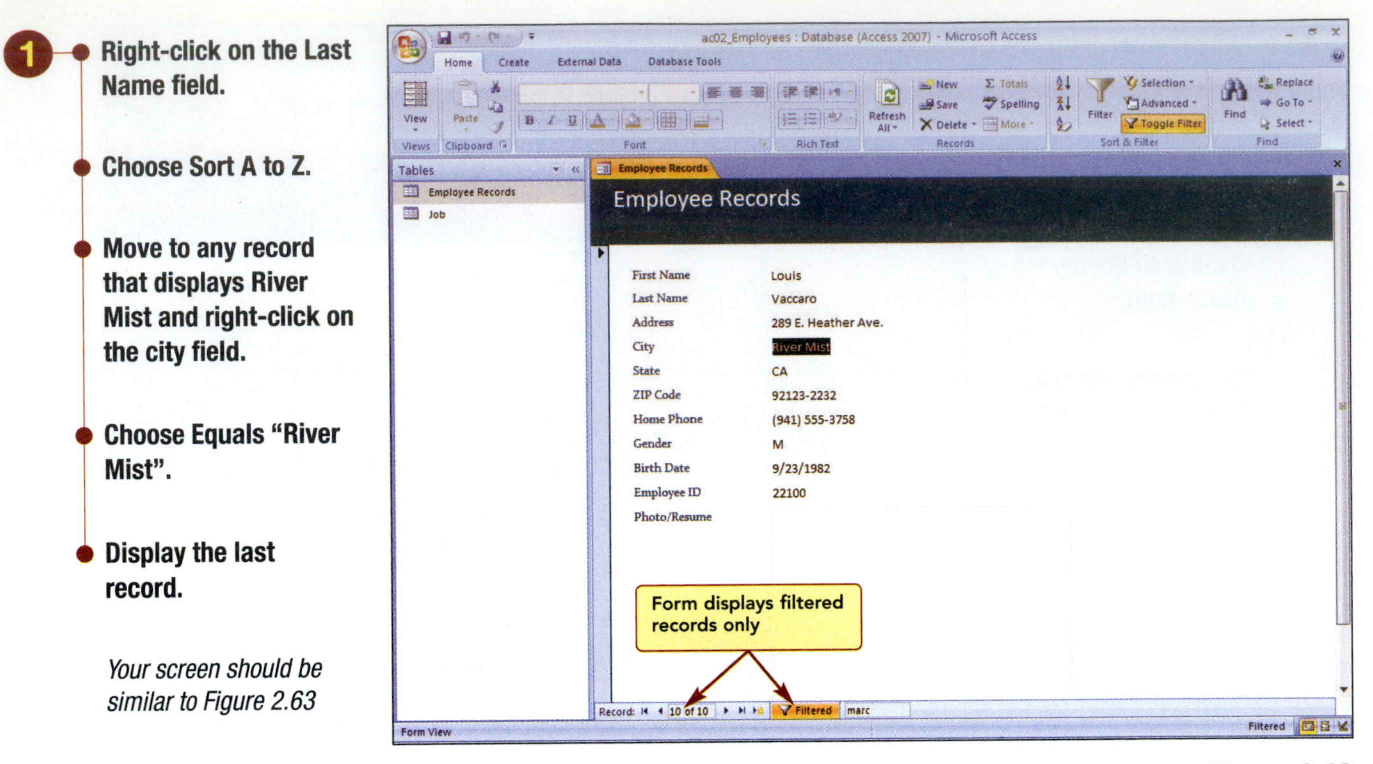

Figure 2.63

The record indicator tells you that there are only 10 records and the table is filtered. The records are also in sorted order by last name. The sort and filter settings apply only to the object in which they were specified, in this case the form.

Working with Controls

Although you are generally satisfied with the look of the form, there are a few changes that you want to make. The first change is to move the Employee ID field to the top of the form and size it to fit the data. Then, if necessary, you will move the Photo/Resume control to the right of the other controls so that it is easier to see.

You can use Form Layout view or Form Design view to modify the design and layout of a form. As in Datasheet Design view, Form Design view displays the structure of the form, not the data in the form. It is used to make extensive changes to the form. Form Layout view displays the underlying data and allows you to make many basic modifications. You will use this view because you want to be able to see the data in the Employee ID field as you adjust the size of the field box.

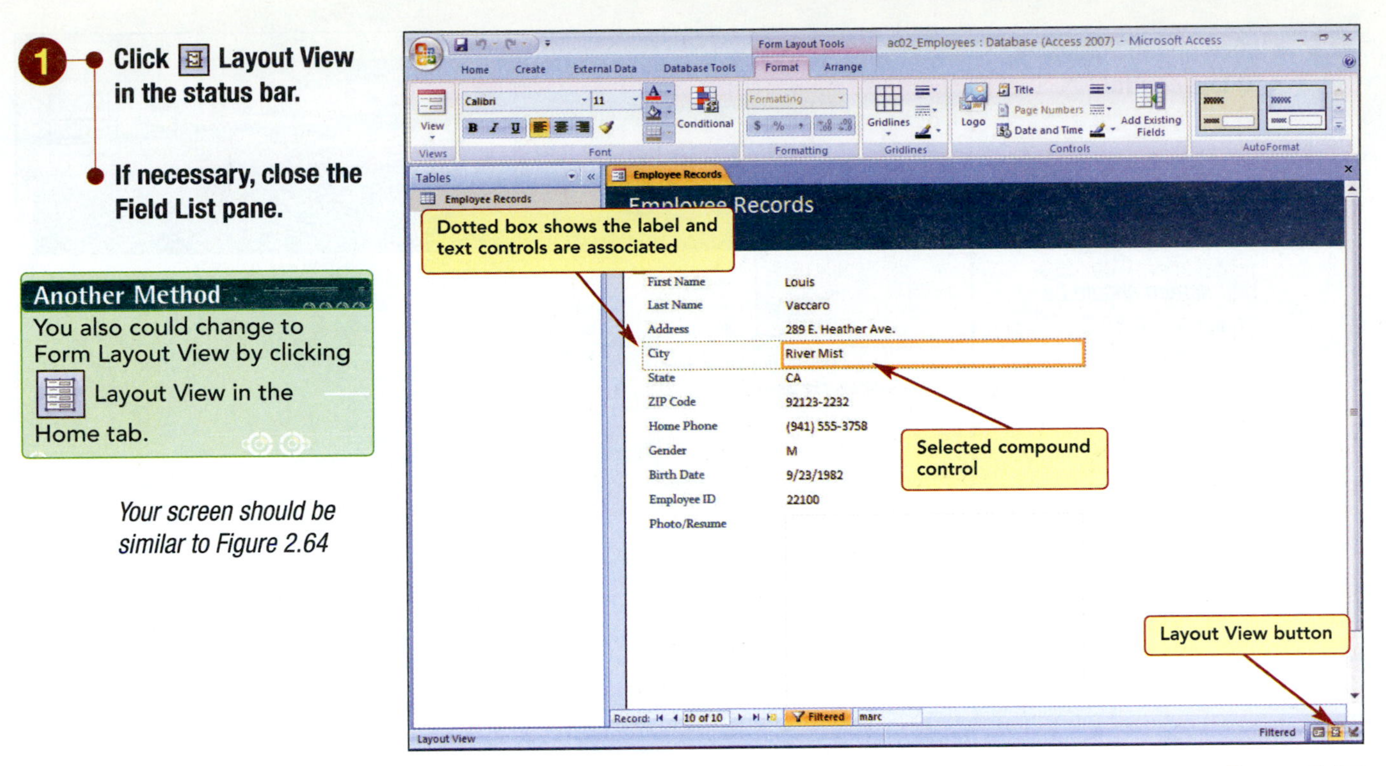

1 **Click Layout View in the status bar.**

If necessary, close the Field List pane.

Another Method

You also could change to Form Layout View by clicking Layout View in the Home tab.

Your screen should be similar to Figure 2.64

Figure 2.64

Additional Information

You will learn much more about selecting and modifying controls in Lab 3.

The Form Layout Tools Format and Arrange tabs are now available to help you modify the form design. Currently, the City text box control is surrounded with a solid orange box indicating the control is selected and is the control that will be affected by your actions. The dotted box around the label and text box controls shows they are associated. When the two parts of a control are associated, it is called a **compound control.**

First, you will select the Employee ID control to modify its size.

Click on the Employee ID text control.

Having Trouble?

The mouse pointer must be ✥ when selecting controls.

Your screen should be similar to Figure 2.65

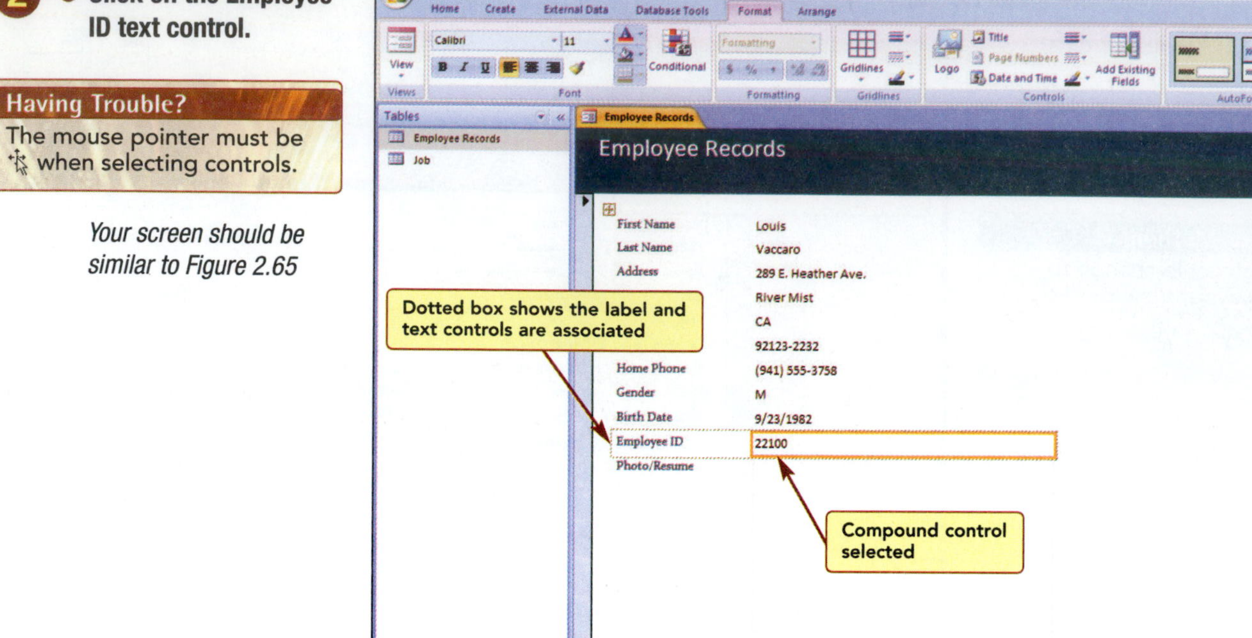

Figure 2.65

The text control of the Employee ID compound control is selected and surrounded in an orange box. Once controls are selected, they can be moved, sized, deleted, or modified. You will move the control to above the First Name control. When you point to the selected control and the mouse pointer appears as ✥, you can move the control by dragging it. A solid orange line appears and shows you where the object will be placed when you stop dragging.

3

- **Point to the selected control and drag upward to move the control.**
- **When the solid orange line appears above the First Name control, release the mouse button to drop the control in the new location.**

Your screen should be similar to Figure 2.66

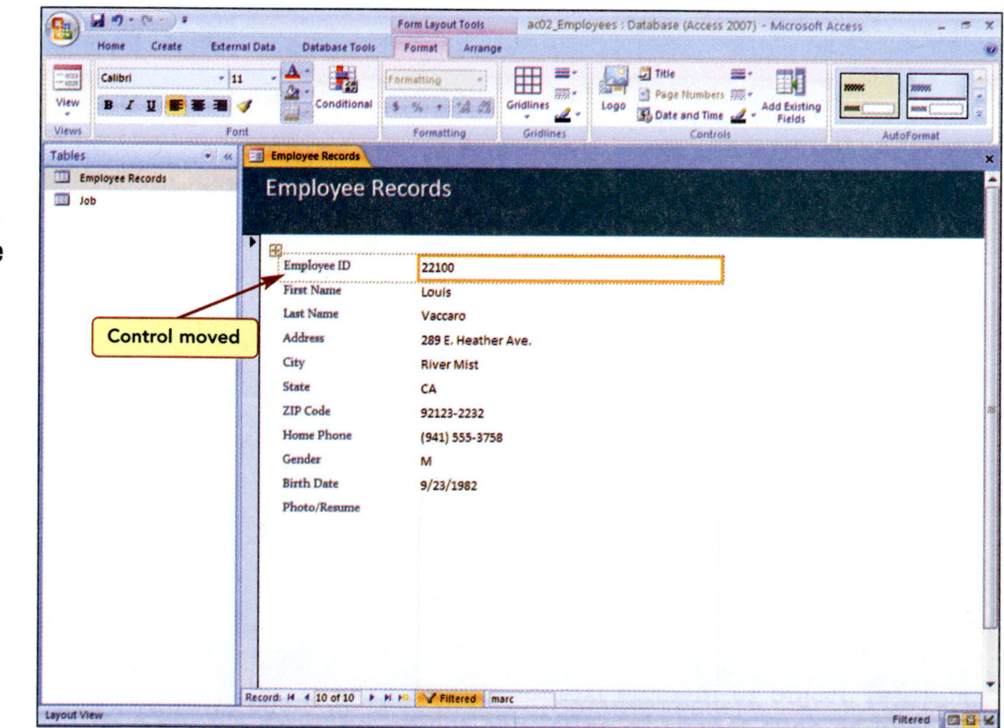

Figure 2.66

Next, you want to reduce the size of the Employee ID text control to match the size of the entry. When you position the mouse pointer on the orange box surrounding the selected control, the pointer changes to ↔ and can be used to size the control. The direction of the arrow indicates in which direction dragging the mouse will alter the shape of the object. This action is similar to sizing a window.

4 • **If necessary, click on the text box part of the Employee ID control to select it.**

Having Trouble?

The selected part of the control is contained in the orange box.

• **Point to the right edge of the selection box and, when the mouse pointer is ↔, drag to the left to decrease the size of the control as in Figure 2.67.**

Your screen should be similar to Figure 2.67

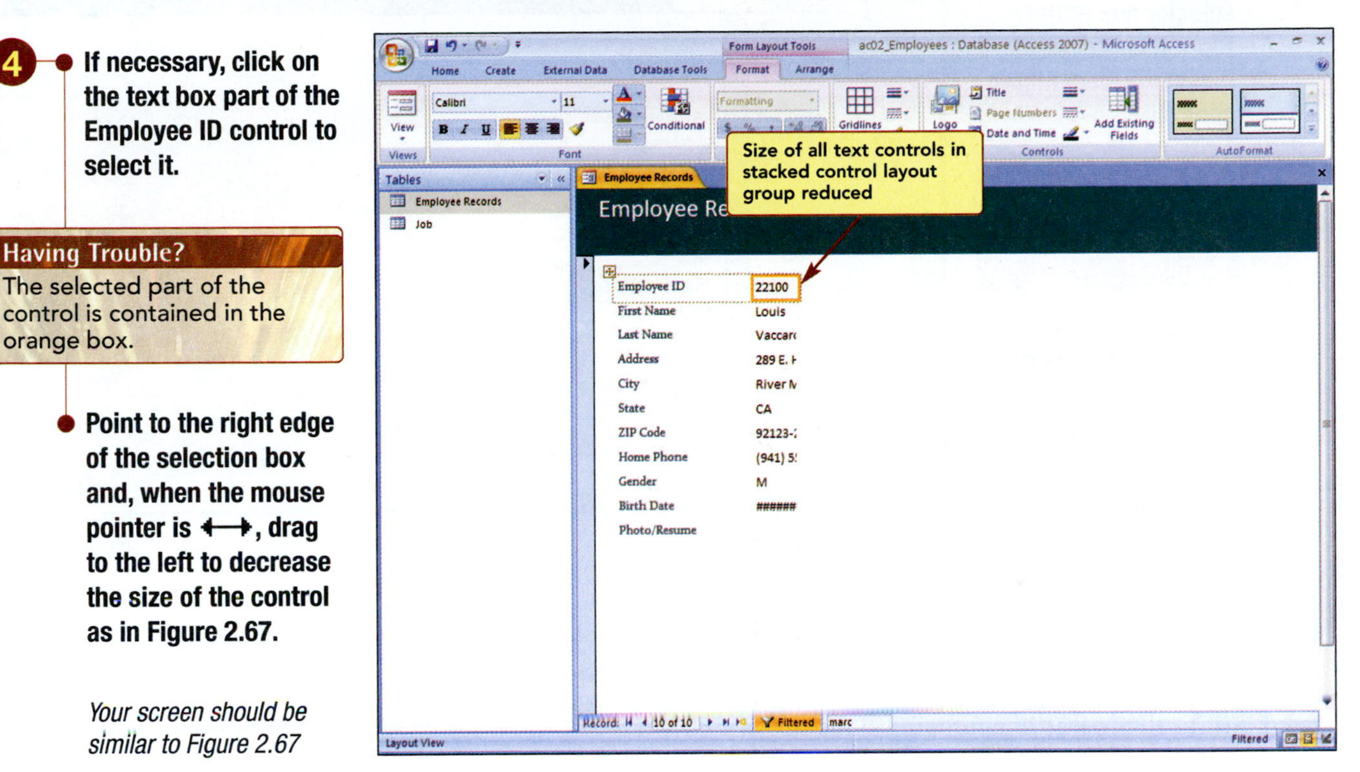

Figure 2.67

Unfortunately, the size of all the text box controls has been reduced. This is because in order for the stacked control layout to maintain the uniform appearance, it groups the controls so that they size as a unit. To size a control individually or move it outside the layout group, it must be removed from the group.

You want to move the Employee ID control outside the group so that it stands alone at the top of the form. Then you will size it to fit the contents. To make space at the top of the form, you will move all the controls in the group down first.

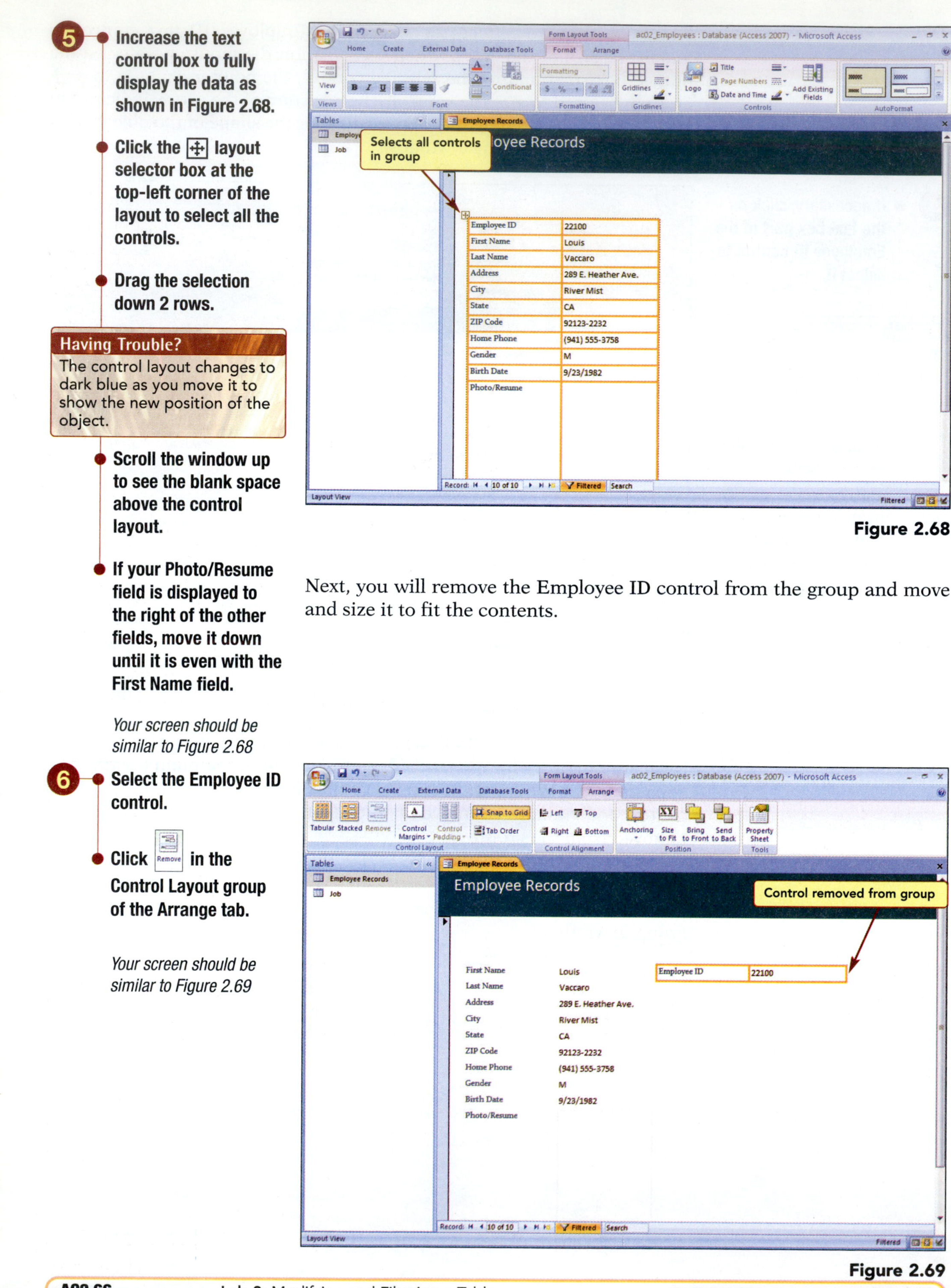

5 ● **Increase the text control box to fully display the data as shown in Figure 2.68.**

● **Click the layout selector box at the top-left corner of the layout to select all the controls.**

● **Drag the selection down 2 rows.**

Having Trouble?

The control layout changes to dark blue as you move it to show the new position of the object.

● **Scroll the window up to see the blank space above the control layout.**

● **If your Photo/Resume field is displayed to the right of the other fields, move it down until it is even with the First Name field.**

Your screen should be similar to Figure 2.68

Figure 2.68

Next, you will remove the Employee ID control from the group and move and size it to fit the contents.

6 ● **Select the Employee ID control.**

● **Click Remove in the Control Layout group of the Arrange tab.**

Your screen should be similar to Figure 2.69

Figure 2.69

The Employee ID is now two separate objects that can be modified individually. Next, you will move the Employee ID control above the other controls.

7 **Drag the Employee ID object to the position shown in Figure 2.70.**

Select the Employee ID text control and reduce its size as in Figure 2.70.

Your screen should be similar to Figure 2.70

Figure 2.70

Now the Employee ID is clearly separate from the personal data on the form. Next, you will move the Photo/Resume control to the right of the other controls.

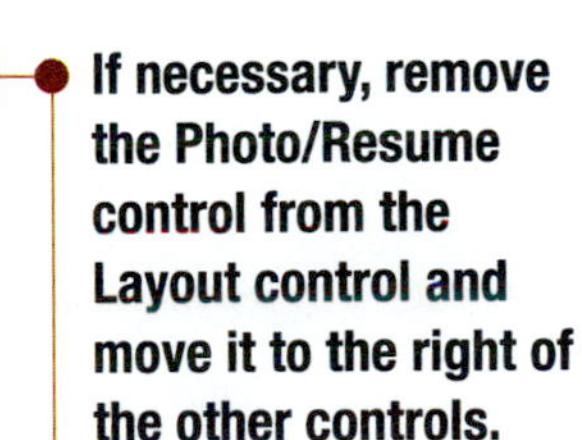

8 **If necessary, remove the Photo/Resume control from the Layout control and move it to the right of the other controls.**

Reposition the controls as in Figure 2.71.

Your screen should be similar to Figure 2.71

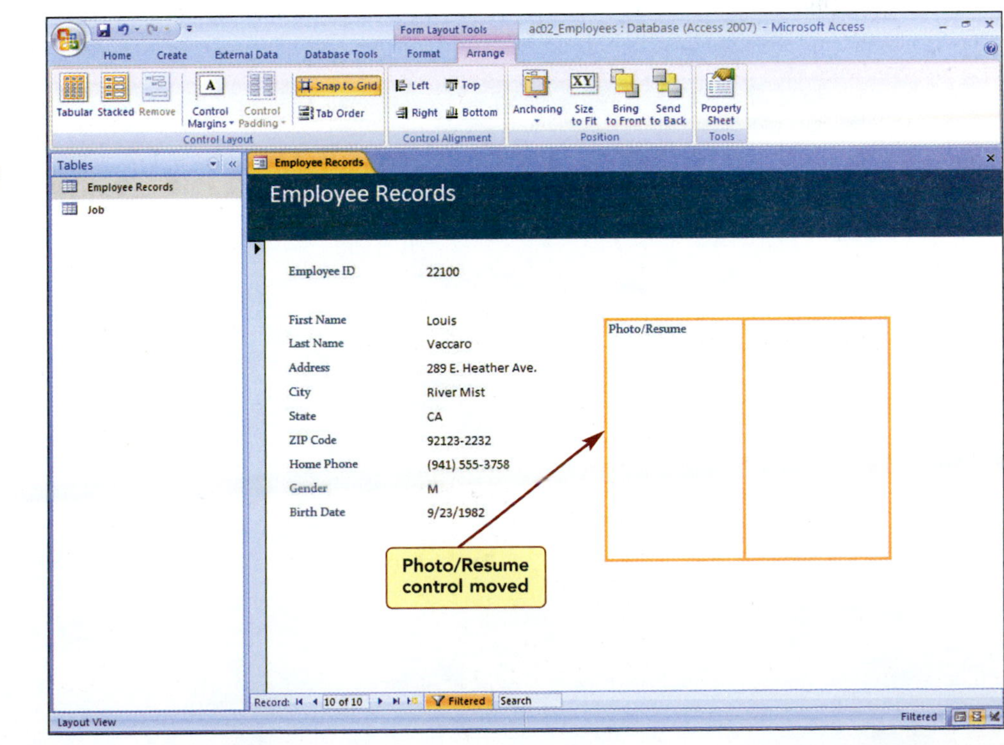

Figure 2.71

Changing the Form Design Style

Finally, you decide to change the form design style to another more colorful style.

1 Open the Form Layout Tools Format tab.

Click More in the AutoFormat group.

Your screen should be similar to Figure 2.72

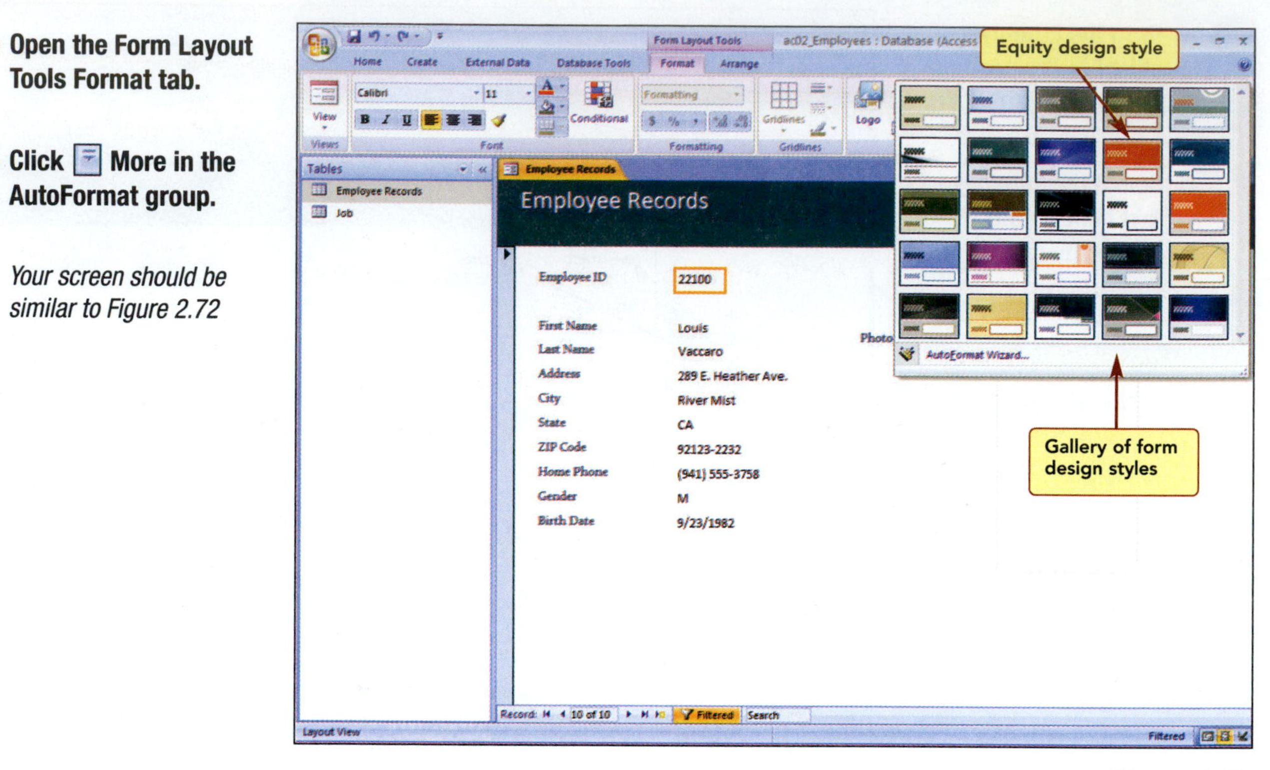

Figure 2.72

The gallery of the form design styles is displayed. You think the Equity design will be more interesting.

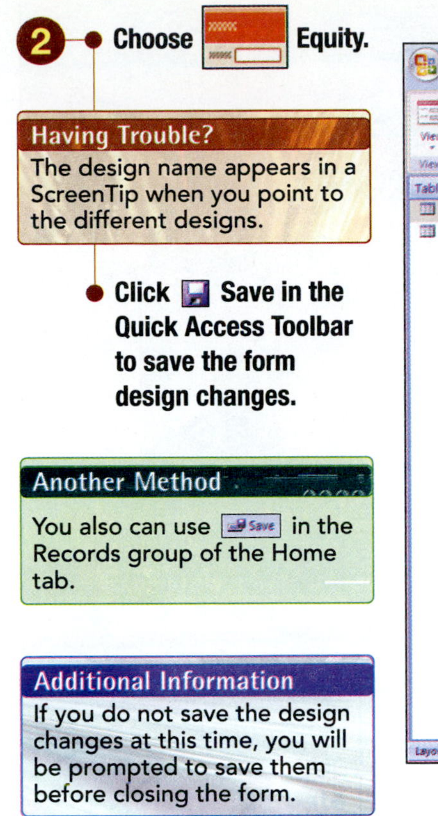

2 • Choose Equity.

Having Trouble?
The design name appears in a ScreenTip when you point to the different designs.

• **Click Save in the Quick Access Toolbar to save the form design changes.**

Another Method
You also can use Save in the Records group of the Home tab.

Additional Information
If you do not save the design changes at this time, you will be prompted to save them before closing the form.

Figure 2.73

Your screen should be similar to Figure 2.73

The selected design was applied to the form.

Adding Records Using a Form

Now, you need to add a new employee record to the database whose paper employee record form is shown here. You will add the record in Form view using the information on the paper form for the field entry data. You also will attach a picture to the Photo/Resume field.

Additional Information
You will learn more about working with form design and layout in later labs.

EMPLOYEE DATA

Employee ID 12918

First Name Carlos Last Name Ruiz
Street 10101 First St.
City Maldin State CA Zip Code 92121-3740
Phone Number (507) 555-5125
Gender M
Birth Date July 27, 1980

1 **Click** [View icon] **in the View group.**

> **Another Method**
> You also could click [Form icon] Form View in the status bar.

- **Click** [New (blank) icon] **New (blank) record to display a new blank entry form.**

> **Another Method**
> You also can use [New] in the Records group of the Home tab or Ctrl + + to add a new record.

- **Enter the data shown in Figure 2.74 into the new record.**
- **Double-click on the Attachment field control.**

> **Another Method**
> You also could choose Manage Attachments from the shortcut menu or click [Attachments icon] Attachments on the Mini Toolbar.

- **Add the file** ac02_Carlos **from your data file location.**

Your screen should be similar to Figure 2.74

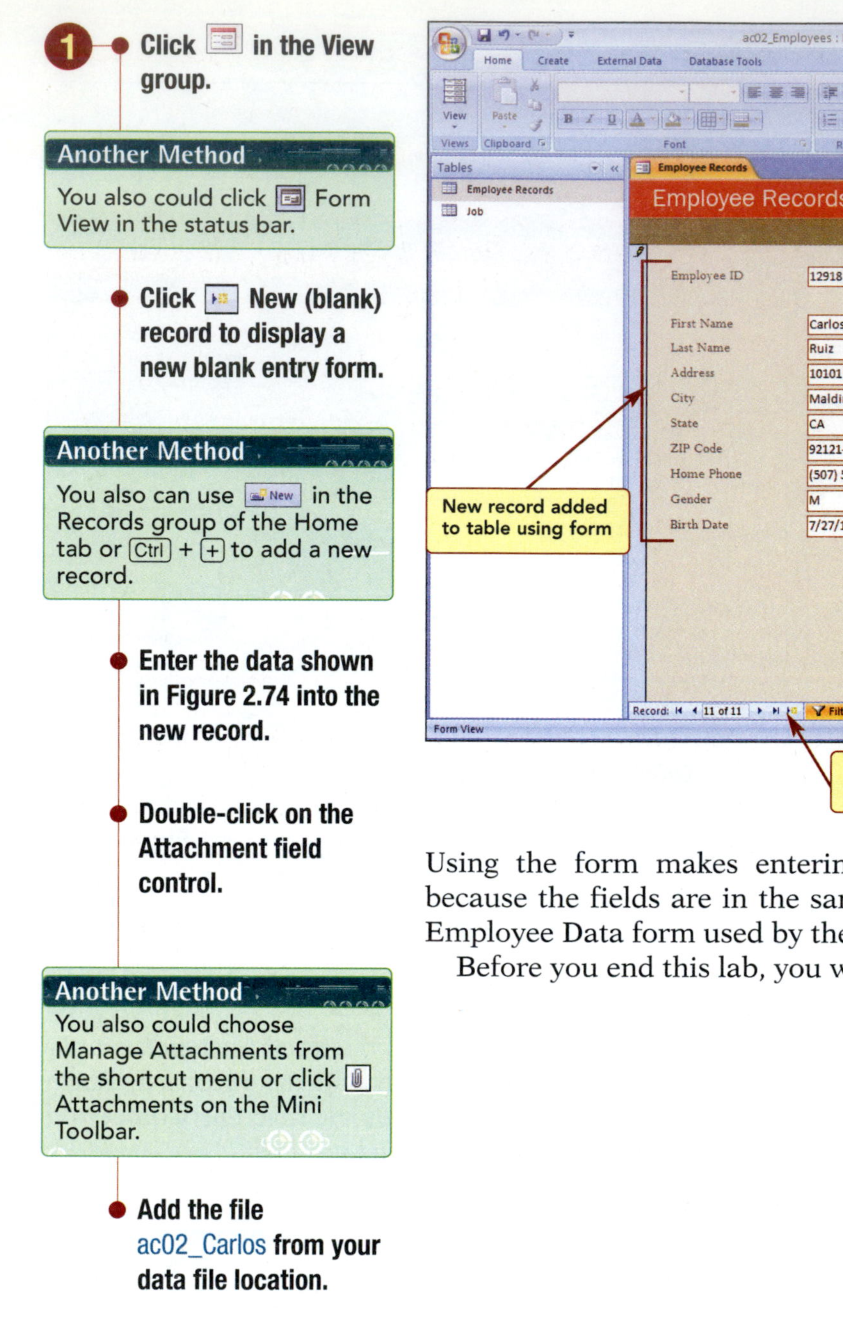

Figure 2.74

Using the form makes entering the new employee data much faster because the fields are in the same order as the information in the paper Employee Data form used by the personnel department.

Before you end this lab, you will add a record for yourself.

2 • **Enter another record using your special Employee ID 99999 and your first and last names. The data in all other fields can be fictitious.**

• **Remove the filter.**

The table now contains 55 records. Next, you need to add these two records to the Job table.

Organizing the Navigation Pane

Notice the name of the form does not appear in the Navigation pane. This is because initially the pane is set to display table objects only. To display other objects in the pane, you can change what objects are displayed in the pane and how they are grouped.

1 • **Click**

at the top of the Navigation pane to open the Tables drop-down menu.

Your screen should be similar to Figure 2.75

Figure 2.75

The upper section of the menu contains categories and the lower section contains groups. The groups change as you select different categories. Currently, Object Type is the selected category and Tables is the selected group. You want to keep the category selection as Object Type but want to change the group selection to display all object types in the pane at the same time.

2 **From the Filter by Group section, choose All Access Objects.**

Double-click the Job table in the Navigation pane.

Another Method
You also can drag an object from the Navigation pane to the work area to open it.

Add the two records in the following table.

Your screen should be similar to Figure 2.76

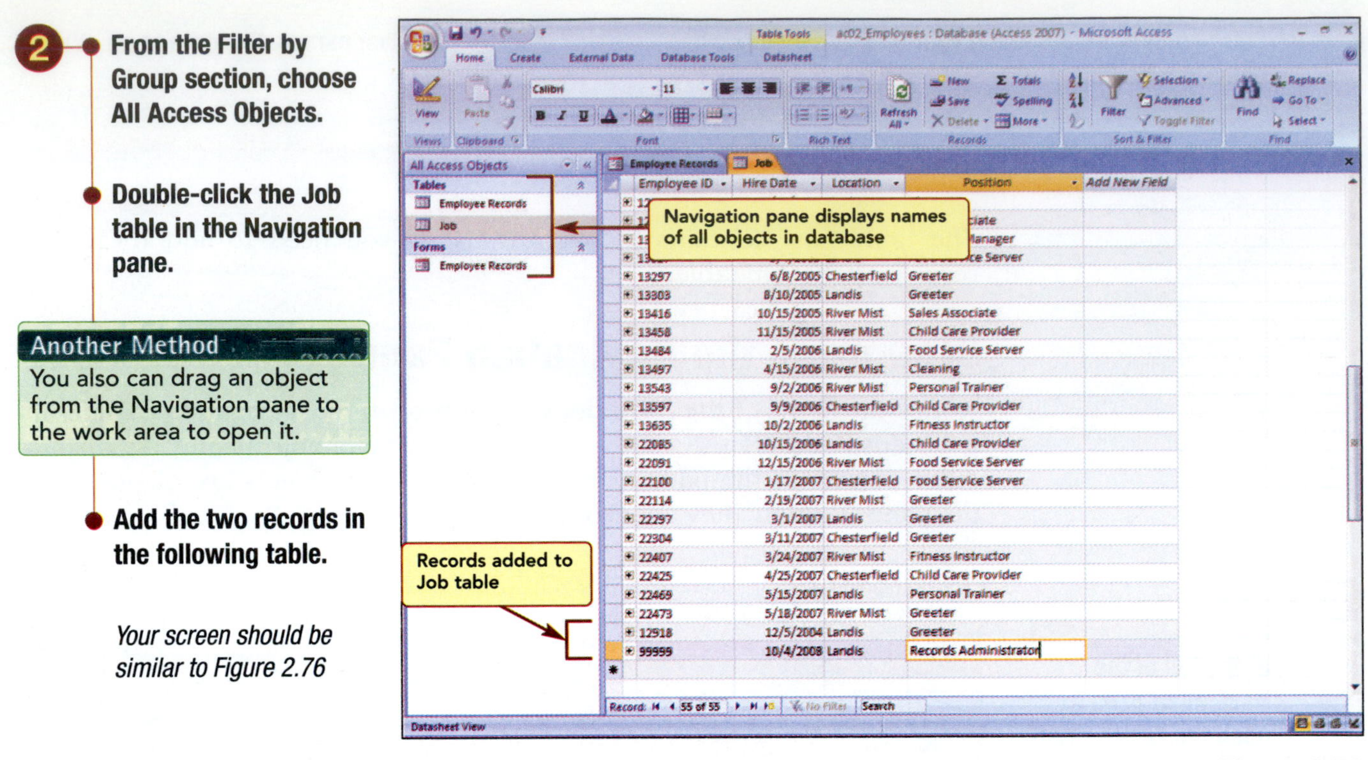

Figure 2.76

Employee ID	**12918**	**99999**
Hire Date	**12/5/2004**	**Today's date**
Location	**Landis**	**Landis**
Position	**Greeter**	**Records Administrator**

Additional Information
You will learn in later labs how to create a single form to update both tables.

Now both tables contain 55 records.

Previewing and Printing a Form

You want to preview and print only the form that displays your record.

1. **Click the Employee Records tab to display the form.**

   Click Office Button and choose Print/Print Preview.

   Your screen should be similar to Figure 2.77

Having Trouble?
Your form may display fewer records than in Figure 2.77.

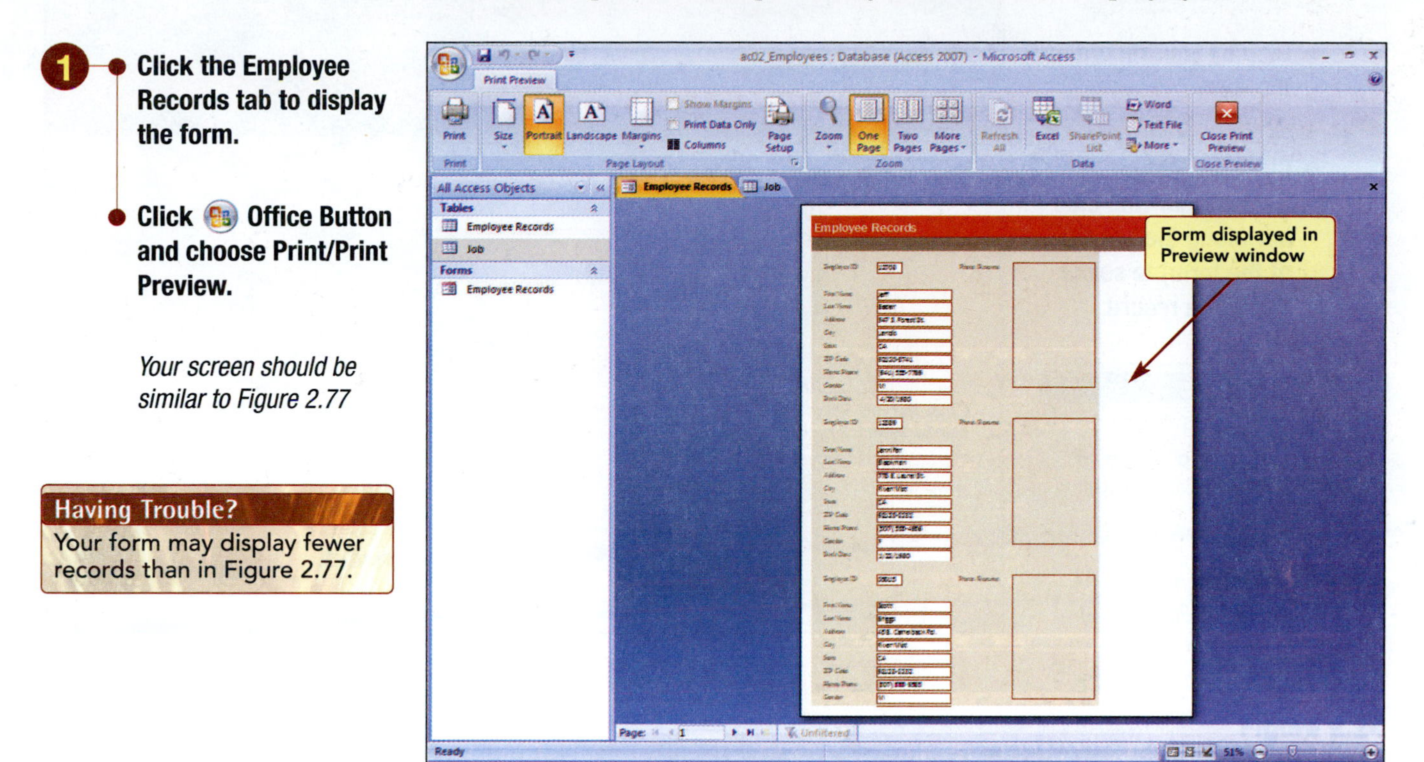

Figure 2.77

Print Preview displays the current object. In this case, because you were last in Form view, the form is displayed in the Preview window.

Printing a Selected Record

Access prints as many records as can be printed on a page using the Form layout. You want to print only the form displaying your record. To do this, you need to select your record first in Form view.

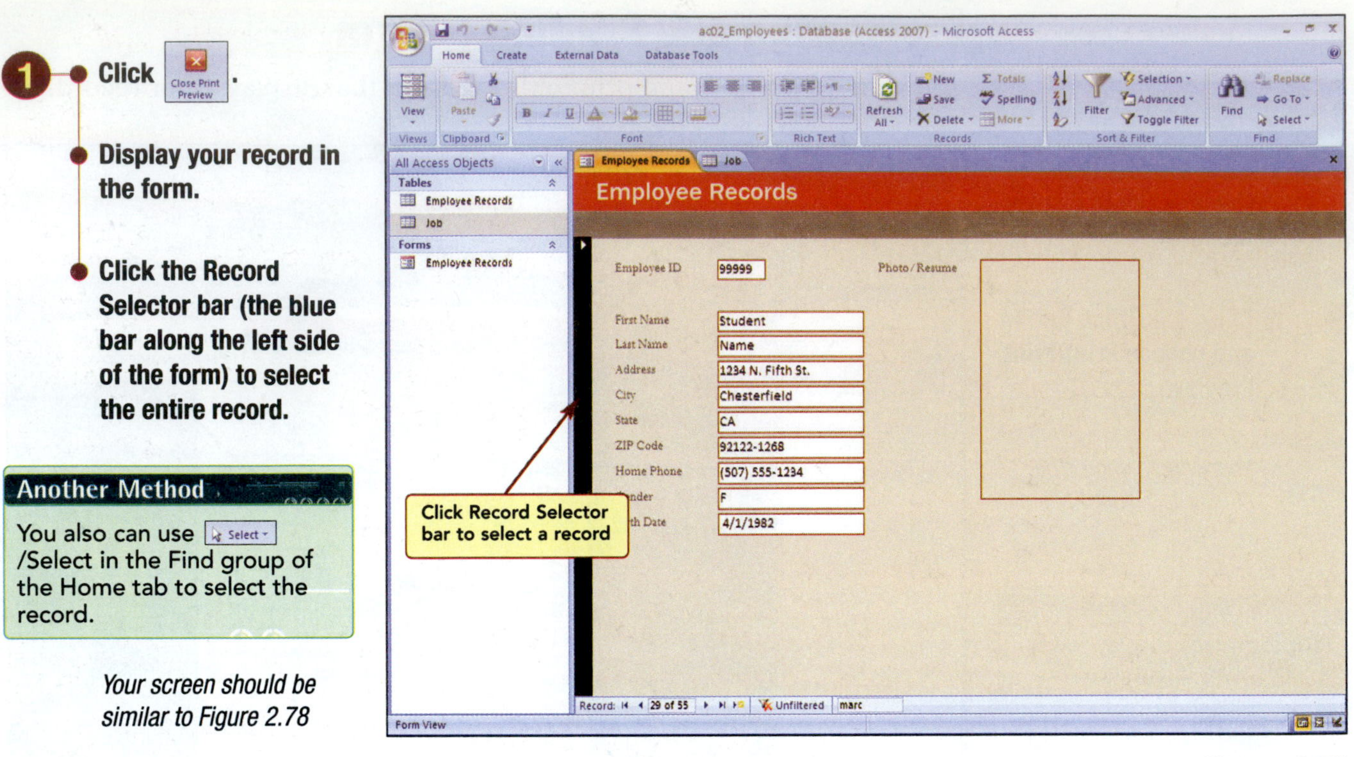

1. Click Close Print Preview.
   - Display your record in the form.
   - Click the Record Selector bar (the blue bar along the left side of the form) to select the entire record.

Another Method

You also can use Select /Select in the Find group of the Home tab to select the record.

Your screen should be similar to Figure 2.78

Figure 2.78

Now that the record is selected, you can print the record. The record will print using the current view, in this case, Form view.

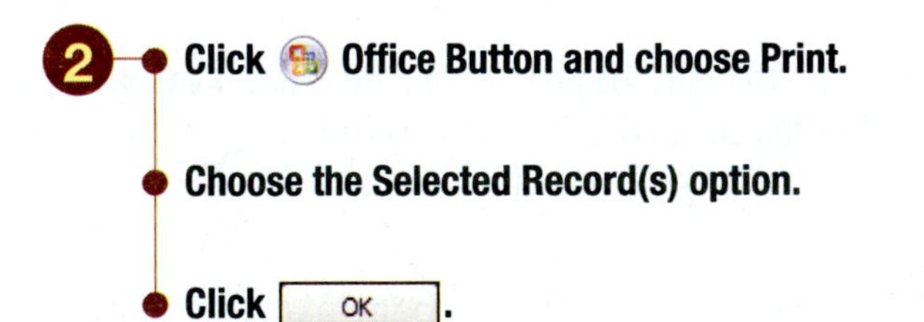

2. Click Office Button and choose Print.
   - Choose the Selected Record(s) option.
   - Click OK.

Identifying Object Dependencies

The form is the third database object that has been added to the file. Many objects that you create in a database are dependent upon other objects for their content. In this case, the form is dependent upon the Employee Records database table for its content. Sometimes it is helpful to be able to find out what objects an object is dependent on or that depend on it. To help in these situations, you can display the object dependencies.

1 Select the Employee Records table object in the Navigation pane.

- Open the Database Tools tab.
- Click [Object Dependencies] in the Show/Hide group.
- If necessary, select "Objects that depend on me" from the Object Dependencies task pane.

Your screen should be similar to Figure 2.79

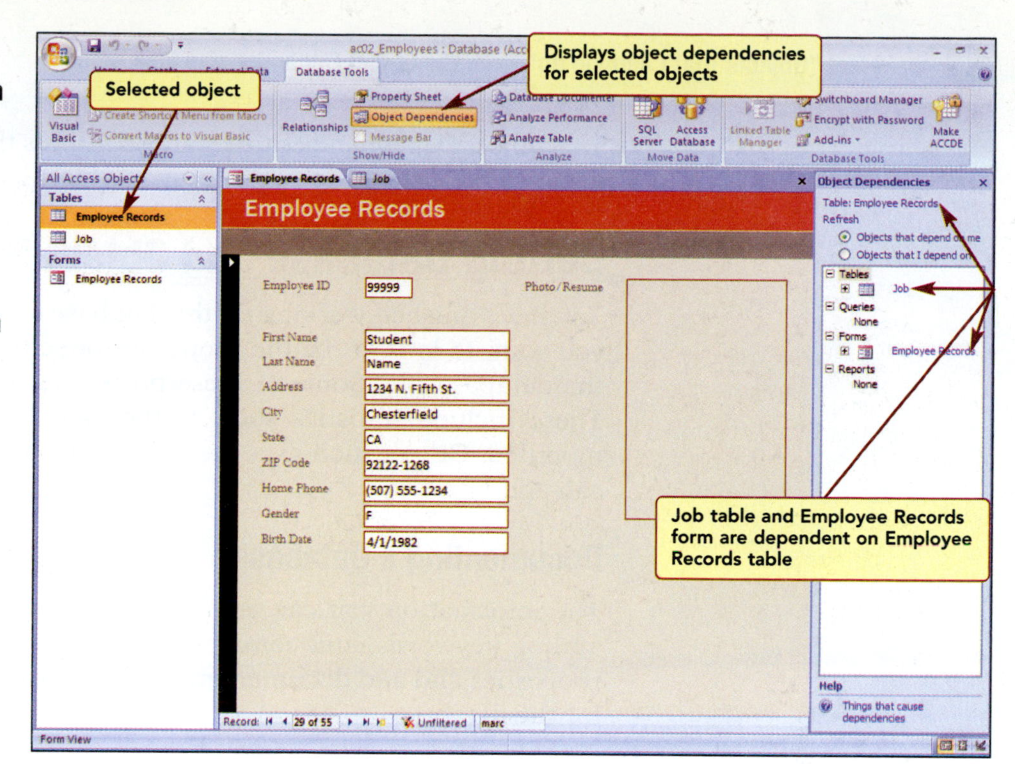

Figure 2.79

The Object Dependencies task pane identifies the two objects that are dependent on the table: the Job table and the Employee Records form. Next, you will see which objects depend on the Employee Records form.

2 Select Employee Records in the Forms category of the Navigation pane.

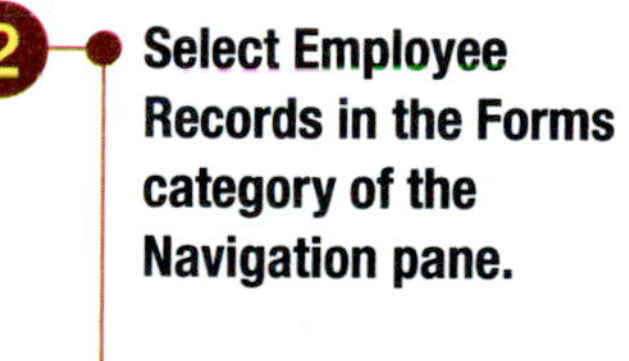

- Click Refresh in the Object Dependencies task pane.

Your screen should be similar to Figure 2.80

Updates information in task pane

No objects dependent on Employee Records form

Figure 2.80

You can now see that the Employee Records object does not have any objects dependent on it.

3 Select "Objects that I depend on" from the Object Dependencies task pane.

The Object Dependencies task pane identifies the only object that the form depends on is the Employee Records table.

Setting Database and Object Properties

You have finished working on the database for now. Before exiting Access, you want to look at the file properties or settings that are associated with the database file. Some of these properties are automatically generated. These include statistics such as the date the file was created and last modified. Others such as a description of the file are properties that you can add.

Documenting a Database

The information you can associate with the file includes a title, subject, author, keywords, and comments about the file. You will look at the file properties and add documentation to identify you as the author and a title for the database.

1

- **Close the Object Dependencies task pane.**
- **Click Office Button and choose Manage/Database Properties.**
- **Select each tab in the Properties dialog box and look at the recorded information.**
- **Display the Summary tab.**
- **Enter the following information in the Summary tab.**

Title **Lifestyle Fitness Employee Database**

Author **Your Name**

Having Trouble?

The Title and Author text boxes may be blank or may already show information. Clear the existing contents first if necessary.

Your screen should be similar to Figure 2.81

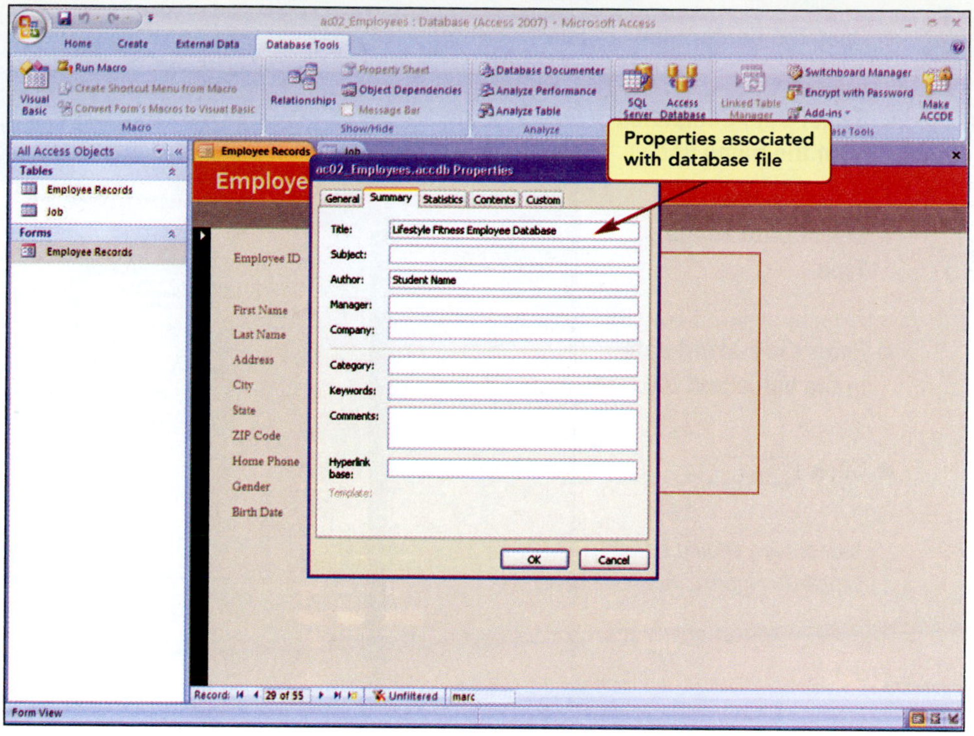

Properties associated with database file

Figure 2.81

You also want to create a custom property to identify the completion date.

2 Open the Custom tab.

- Select Date Completed from the Name list.
- Select Date as the Type.
- Enter the current date in the Value text box.
- Click Add.

Your screen should be similar to Figure 2.82

Figure 2.82

You have completed adding the properties to the file. You also can add limited documentation to each object in a database. You will add documentation to the Employee Records table object.

3 Click OK.

- Select the Employee Records table object.
- Select Property Sheet from the Show/Hide group.
- In the Description text box, type **This table is under construction and currently contains 55 records.**

Your screen should be similar to Figure 2.83

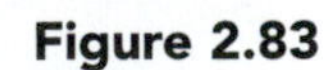

Figure 2.83

MORE ABOUT

For information about creating a report using the Database Documenter that details the properties of an entire database or any of its objects, see "6.2 Manage Databases" in the More About appendix.

You have added property information to both the database file and the Employee Records table.

4
- **Click OK to close the Properties dialog box.**
- **Close the form and table objects.**
- **Exit Access.**

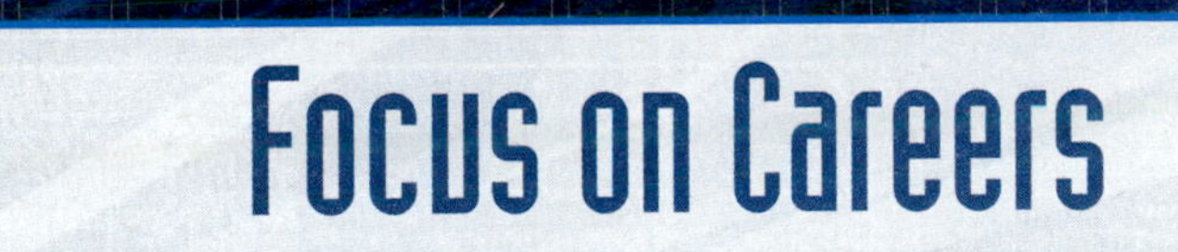

Focus on Careers

EXPLORE YOUR CAREER OPTIONS

Administrative Assistant

Administrative assistants are typically responsible for the efficient management of office operations. This position may involve conducting research, training new staff, scheduling meetings, and maintaining databases. As an administrative assistant, you could be responsible for updating an inventory or staffing database. The typical salary range of an administrative assistant is $24,000 to $35,000. Demand for experienced administrative assistants, especially in technology and health fields, is expected to increase through 2010.

Concept Summary

LAB 2

Modifying and Filtering a Table and Creating a Form

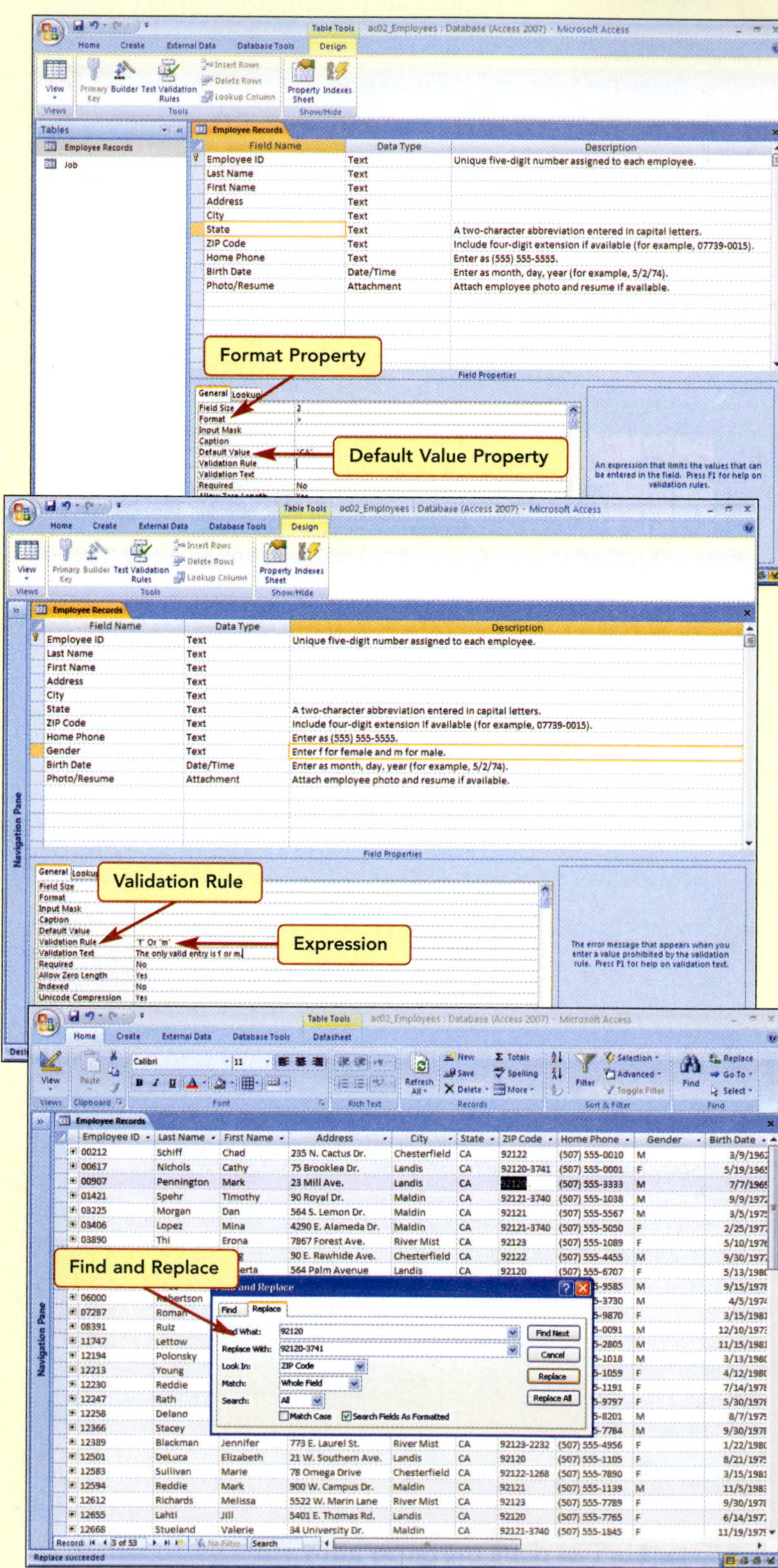

Format Property (AC2.8)

The Format property is used to specify the way that numbers, dates, times, and text in a field are displayed and printed.

Default Value Property (AC2.9)

The Default Value property is used to specify a value that is automatically entered in a field when a new record is created.

Validation Rule (AC2.13)

Validation rules are used to control the data that can be entered in a field by defining the input values that are valid or allowed.

Expression (AC2.14)

An expression is a formula consisting of a combination of symbols that will produce a single value.

Find and Replace (AC2.24)

The Find and Replace feature helps you quickly find specific information and automatically replace it with new information.

Sort

Table Tools · ac02_Employees : Database (Access 2007) - Microsoft Access

Home · Create · External Data · Database Tools · Datasheet

Employee Records

Employee ID	Last Name	First Name	Address	City	State	ZIP Code	Home Phone	Gender	Birth Date
13635	Martinez	Juan	7115 E Roosevelt Dr.	Maldin	CA	92121-3740	(507) 555-2935	M	12/10/198
13543	Martinez	Julie	1920 First Ave.	Maldin	CA	92121-3740	(941) 555-1044	F	12/10/198
22407	Mazeau	Rebecca	7383 Oak Dr.	Landis	CA	92120-3741	(941) 555-1093	F	9/23/197
03225	Morgan	Dan	564 S. Lemon Dr.	Maldin	CA	92121	(507) 555-5567	M	3/5/197
00617	Nichols	Cathy	75 Brooklea Dr.	Landis	CA	92120-3741	(507) 555-0001	F	5/19/196
00907	Pennington	Mark	23 Mill Ave.	Landis	CA	92120-3741	(507) 555-3333	M	7/7/196
12194	Polonsky	Mitch	8701 E. Sheridan	Maldin	CA	92121-3740	(507) 555-1018	M	3/13/198
12247	Rath	Kathy	87 E. Aurora Ave.	Chesterfield	CA	92122-1268	(507) 555-9797	F	5/30/197
12594	Reddie	Mark	900 W. Campus Dr.	Maldin	CA	92121	(507) 555-1139	M	11/5/198
12230	Reddie	Suzanne	932 E. Parkway Dr.	Landis	CA	92120-3741	(507) 555-1191	F	7/14/197
13005	Reilly	Emily	125 N. Marigold St.	Maldin	CA	92121-3740	(941) 555-6532	F	5/21/198
12612	Richards	Melissa	5522 W. Marin Lane	River Mist	CA	92123	(507) 555-7789	F	9/30/197
06000	Robertson	Kirk	832 S. William Ave.	Maldin	CA	92121	(507) 555-3730	M	4/5/197
22297	Rogondino	Patricia	7583 Turquoise	Chesterfield	CA	92122-1268	(941) 555-7539	F	8/30/197
07287	Roman	Anita	2348 S. Bala Dr.	Maldin	CA	92121-3740	(507) 555-9870	F	3/15/198
08391	Ruiz	Enrique	35 Palm St.	Chesterfield	CA	92122-1268	(507) 555-0091	M	12/10/197
04321	Sabin	Greg	90 E. Rawhide Ave.	Chesterfield	CA	92122	(507) 555-4455	M	9/30/197
00212	Schiff	Chad	235 N. Cactus Dr.	Chesterfield	CA	92122	(507) 555-0010	M	3/9/196
22114	Schneider	Paul	1731 Jackson Ave.	Landis	CA	92120-3741	(941) 555-7440	M	2/23/198
01421	Spehr	Timothy	90 Royal Dr.	Maldin	CA	92121-3740	(507) 555-1038	M	9/9/197
12366	Stacey	David	737 S. College Rd.	Chesterfield	CA	92122-1268	(507) 555-7784	M	9/30/197
13497	Steele	Jeff	1011 E. Holly Ln.	River Mist	CA	92123-2232	(941) 555-1912	M	4/9/198
12668	Stueland	Valerie	34 University Dr.	Maldin	CA	92121-3740	(507) 555-1845	F	11/19/197
12583	Sullivan	Marie	78 Omega Drive	Chesterfield	CA	92122-1268	(507) 555-7890	F	3/15/198
12867	Talic	Elvis	21 Oasis St.	River Mist	CA	92123-2232	(941) 555-5985	M	6/10/198
03890	Thi	Erona	7867 Forest Ave.	River Mist	CA	92123	(507) 555-1089	F	5/10/197
22304	Torcivia	Peter	904 S. Dorsey Dr.	Chesterfield	CA	92122-1268	(941) 555-9870	M	5/14/197

Record: 1 of 53 · No Filter · Search

Datasheet View

Sort (AC2.34)

You can sort the data in a table to quickly rearrange the order of the records.

Filter

Table Tools · ac02_Employees : Database (Access 2007) - Microsoft Access

Employee Records

Employee ID	Last Name	First Name	Address	City	State	ZIP Code	Home Phone	Gender	Birth Date
01421	Spehr	Timothy	90 Royal Dr.	Maldin	CA	92121-3740	(507) 555-1038	M	9/9/1972
03225	Morgan	Dan	564 S. Lemon Dr.	Maldin	CA	92121	(507) 555-5567	M	3/5/1975
03406	Lopez	Mina	4290 E. Alameda Dr.	Maldin	CA	92121-3740	(507) 555-5050	F	2/25/1977
06000	Robertson	Kirk	832 S. William Ave.	Maldin	CA	92121	(507) 555-3730	M	4/5/1974
07287	Roman	Anita	2348 S. Bala Dr.	Maldin	CA	92121-3740	(507) 555-9870	F	3/15/1981
11747	Lettow	Ryan	358 Maple Dr.	Maldin	CA	92121-3740	(507) 555-2805	M	11/15/1981
12194	Polonsky	Mitch	8701 E. Sheridan	Maldin	CA	92121-3740	(507) 555-1018	M	3/13/1980
12594	Reddie	Mark	900 W. Campus Dr.	Maldin	CA	92121	(507) 555-1139	M	11/5/1983
12668	Stueland	Valerie	34 University Dr.	Maldin	CA	92121-3740	(507) 555-1845	F	11/19/1979
12920	Larson	Alicia	345 W. Mill Ave.	Maldin	CA	92121-3740	(941) 555-7717	F	6/21/1983
13005	Reilly	Emily	125 N. Marigold St.	Maldin	CA	92121-3740	(941) 555-6532	F	5/21/1985
13458	Helfand	Eric	4601 E. Willow Dr.	Maldin	CA	92121-3740	(941) 555-9101	M	9/12/1980
13484	Franklin	Stephanie	889 S. Litchfield Park	Maldin	CA	92121-3740	(941) 555-7833	F	7/30/1979
13543	Martinez	Julie	1920 First Ave.	Maldin	CA	92121-3740	(941) 555-1044	F	12/10/1982
13597	Gapasin	Ken	2633 E. Fountain St.	Maldin	CA	92121-3740	(941) 555-0589	M	2/11/1985
13635	Martinez	Juan	7115 E Roosevelt Dr.	Maldin	CA	92121-3740	(507) 555-2935	M	12/10/1983
22469	Hogan	Ryan	1389 E. Northview Dr.	Maldin	CA	92121-3740	(941) 555-1010	M	7/14/1986
					CA				

Record: 1 of 17 · Filtered · Search

Datasheet View

Filter (AC2.42)

A filter is a restriction placed on records in the open table or form to quickly isolate and display a subset of records.

Form Layout Tools · ac02_Employees : Database (Access 2007) - Microsoft Access

Tables: Employee Records · Job

Form

Employee Records

First Name	Louis
Last Name	Vaccaro
Address	289 E. Heather Ave.
City	River Mist
State	CA
ZIP Code	92123-2232
Home Phone	(941) 555-3758
Gender	M
Birth Date	9/23/1982
Employee ID	22100

Photo/Resume

Controls

Record: 10 of 10 · Filtered

Layout View

Form (AC2.49)

A form is a database object used primarily to display records onscreen to make it easier to enter new records and to make changes to existing records.

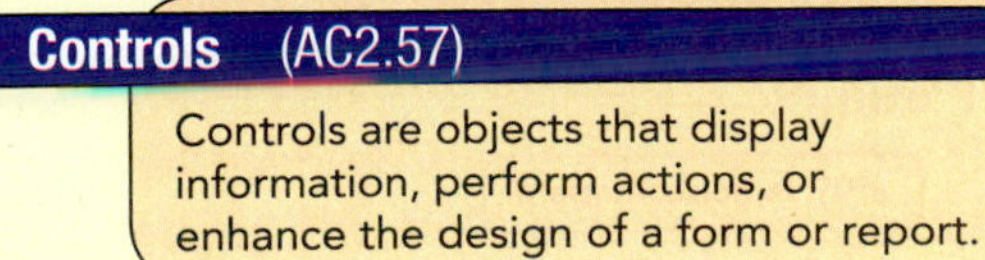

Controls (AC2.57)

Controls are objects that display information, perform actions, or enhance the design of a form or report.

Lab Review

LAB 2

Modifying and Filtering a Table and Creating a Form

key terms

ascending sort order AC2.34
attachment control AC2.58
bound control AC2.57
character string AC2.10
comparison operator AC2.14
compound control AC2.63
control AC2.57
criteria AC2.25
Default Value property AC2.9
descending sort order AC2.34
expression AC2.14
filter AC2.42
Find and Replace AC2.24
form AC2.49
format AC2.37
Format property AC2.8
identifier AC2.14
label control AC2.57
layout AC2.54
operator AC2.14
record source AC2.50
sort AC2.34
stacked layout AC2.54
tab order AC2.52
tabular layout AC2.54
text control AC2.57
theme colors AC2.39
unbound control AC2.57
Validation Rule property AC2.13
Validation Text property AC2.13
value AC2.9
wildcards AC2.25

MCAS Skills

The Microsoft Certified Applications Specialist (MCAS) certification program is designed to measure your proficiency in performing basic tasks using the Office 2007 applications. Getting certified demonstrates that you have the skills and provides a valuable industry credential for employment. See Reference 2: Microsoft Certified Applications Specialist (MCAS) for a complete list of the skills that were covered in Lab 2.

command summary

Command	Shortcut	Action
Office Button		
Manage/Database Properties		Allows changes to database properties
Quick Access Toolbar		
Undo	Ctrl + Z	Cancels last action
Save	Ctrl + S	Saves the current object
Home tab		
Views group		
Form View		Changes to Form view
Form Layout View		Changes to Form Layout view
Font group		
Bold	Ctrl + B	Applies bold effect to all text in datasheet
Font Color		Applies selected color to all text in datasheet
Gridlines		Changes gridline color of datasheet
Alternate Fill/Back Color		Changes background color of datasheet
Records group		
Save	Shift + Enter	Saves changes to object design
New	Ctrl + +	Adds new record
More/Hide Columns		Hides columns in Datasheet view
More/Unhide Columns		Redisplays hidden columns
Sort & Filter group		
Ascending		Changes sort order to ascending
Descending		Changes sort order to descending
Clear All Sorts		Clears all sorts and returns sort order to primary key order
Filter		Allows multiple filter criteria in a single field
Selection/Equals		Displays only those records containing selected value

Lab Review

command summary

Command	Shortcut	Action
Advanced /Clear all Filters		Removes all filters from table
Toggle Filter		Applies and removes filter from table
Find group		
Find	Ctrl + F	Locates specified data
Replace	Ctrl + H	Locates specified data and replaces it with specified replacement text
Go To		Moves to First, Previous, Next, Last, or New record location
Select /Select		Selects current record
Select /Select All		Selects all records in database
Create tab		
Tables group		
Table		Creates a new table in Datasheet view
Table Design		Creates a new table in Design view
Forms group		
Form		Creates a new form using all the fields from the underlying table
Blank Form		Displays a blank form to which you add the fields from the table that you want to appear on the form
More Forms /Form Wizard		Creates a new form by following the steps in the Form Wizard
Database Tools tab		
Show/Hide group		
Property Sheet		Specifies general properties associated with the database file
Object Dependencies		Shows the objects in the database that use the selected object

command summary

Command	Shortcut	Action
Table Tools Design tab		
Tools group		
Insert Rows		Inserts a new field in Table Design view
Table Tools Datasheet tab		
Fields & Columns group		
Lookup Column		Creates a lookup column
Form Layout Tools Format tab		
AutoFormat group		
More		Opens gallery of design styles
Form Layout Tools Arrange tab		
Control Layout group		
Remove		Removes selected control
Position group		
Bring to Front		Brings selected control to top of stack

Lab Exercises

matching

Match the numbered item with the correct lettered description.

1. *	______	**a.**	locates specified values in a field
2. filter	______	**b.**	an expression
3. tab order	______	**c.**	database object used primarily for onscreen display
4. character string	______	**d.**	order that the selection point moves in a form when Tab is used
5. find	______	**e.**	temporarily displays subset of records
6. >=	______	**f.**	operator
7. ascending sort	______	**g.**	a group of characters
8. ="Y" Or "N"	______	**h.**	rearranges records in A to Z or 0 to 9 order
9. record source	______	**i.**	wildcard character
10. form	______	**j.**	underlying table for a form

fill-in

Complete the following statements by filling in the blanks with the correct terms.

1. The upper section of the Navigation pane contains ______ and the lower section contains______.
2. A(n) ______ is a symbol or word that indicates that an operation is to be performed.
3. ______ restrict the type of data that can be entered in a field.
4. ______ is displayed when an invalid entry is entered.
5. Format ______ is used to create custom formats that change the way numbers, dates, times, and text display and print.
6. The ______ property changes the way data appears in a field.
7. The most common controls are ______ controls and ______ controls.
8. A(n) ______ control is linked to the data in the resource table.
9. The ______ property is used to specify a value that is automatically entered in a field when a new record is created.
10. The two basic form layouts are ______ and ______.

true/false

Circle the correct answer to the following statements.

1.	The Default Value property determines the value automatically entered into a field of a new record.	True	False
2.	Forms are database objects used primarily for viewing data.	True	False
3.	Text controls display descriptive labels.	True	False
4.	Values are numbers, dates, or pictures.	True	False
5.	An expression is a sequence of characters (letters, numbers, or symbols) that must be handled as text, not as numeric data.	True	False
6.	Label controls are bound controls.	True	False
7.	A contrast operator is a symbol that allows you to make comparisons between two items.	True	False
8.	A validation rule is an expression that defines acceptable data entry values.	True	False
9.	Filter results can be saved with the database and quickly redisplayed.	True	False
10.	When the two parts of a control are associated, it is called a compound control.	True	False

multiple choice

Circle the letter of the correct response.

1. ___________ control(s) how data is displayed in a form.
- **a.** Design styles
- **b.** Controls
- **c.** Layouts
- **d.** Tab order

2. A form is ___________ an underlying table for its content.
- **a.** independent of
- **b.** reliant on
- **c.** contingent on
- **d.** dependent on

3. ___________ layouts arrange data vertically with a field label to the left of the field data.
- **a.** Datasheet
- **b.** Justified
- **c.** Tabular
- **d.** Stacked

4. A ___________ is a temporary restriction placed on a table to display a subset of records.
- **a.** wildcard
- **b.** control
- **c.** filter
- **d.** sort

5. The ___________ is used to specify a value that is automatically entered in a field when a new record is created.
   a. Default Value property
   b. Sort property
   c. field value
   d. Format property

6. ___________ is/are an explanatory message that appears if a user attempts to enter invalid information in a text field.
   a. Validation text
   b. Validation rule
   c. Expressions
   d. Validity checks

7. A(n) ___________ control is linked to its underlying data source.
   a. bound
   b. label
   c. field
   d. unbound

8. A ___________ is a feature that guides you step by step through a process.
   a. dialog box
   b. wizard
   c. task pane
   d. gallery

9. ___________ properties change the way that data is displayed.
   a. Format
   b. Field
   c. Data
   d. Record

10. The ___________ property is commonly used when most of the entries in a field will be the same for the entire table.
    a. AutoNumber
    b. Default Value
    c. Field Data
    d. Best Fit

Hands-On Exercises

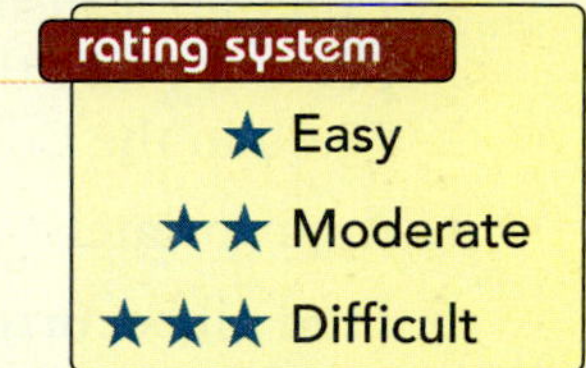

step-by-step

Note: Before you begin, you may want to create a backup copy of each data file by copying and renaming it.

Second Time Around Inventory Database ★

1. You have already set up an inventory database for the Second Time Around consignment shop. It currently contains the item number, description, price, and consignor last name fields, and it has records for the inventory currently in stock. The owner of the shop is quite pleased with the database as it stands but has asked you to change the name of the existing price field to show that it is the original price and add a new field for the current selling price of the item. Also, she would like you to modify some existing records, create a form to ease data entry, and print a copy of the form. Your completed table and form will be similar to those shown here.

Antiques Inventory 12/6/2008

Item Number	Description	Consignment Price	Sale Price	Consignor Last Name
34	Arts & Crafts Style Inlaid Dining Table	$4,500.00	$6,750.00	Ward
23	5 shelf Etagere	$4,500.00	$6,750.00	Bennett
72	Machine Age Refracting Telescope	$4,800.00	$6,700.00	Student Name
37	Robot Bar	$4,800.00	$7,200.00	Cooper
14	1980's Italian Rubber and Anodized Aluminum coffee table	$5,800.00	$8,700.00	Long
58	Monumental 20th c Polished Aluminum Bridge Lights	$6,500.00	$9,750.00	Perez
21	French Iron Floor Safe Circa 1860	$6,500.00	$[illegible],750.00	Ross
8	Polished Aluminum Portable Lighthouse Circa 1930	$7,200.00	$10,800.00	Griffin
53	Jules Wabbes lounge suite	$7,500.00	$11,250.00	Parker
19	Francois Monet Coffee Table	$8,600.00	$12,900.00	Henderson

a. Open the database named ac02_Second Time Around and the table named Antiques Inventory.

b. Change the Price field name to **Consignment Price**. Change the Data Type for this field to Currency.

c. Insert the following field before the Consignor Last Name field:

Field name:	**Sale Price**
Data type:	Currency

Antiques Inventory

Item Number: 72
Description: Machine Age Refracting Telescope
Consignment Price: $4,800.00
Sale Price: $6,700.00
Consignor Last Name: Student Name

d. Make all fields except Sale Price required. (Hint: Set the Required property to Yes.) Reduce the field size of the Consignor Last Name field to **25.**

e. Switch to Datasheet view and respond "yes" to all prompts and warnings when saving the design changes.

f. Update the table by entering **0.00** in the Consignment Price field for all records that have a blank entry in this field. (Hint: Use copy and paste).

g. Enter appropriate values in the Sale Price field for each record. (Generally the sale price is 33 percent more than the consignment price.) Leave the Sale Price field blank for those items with $0.00 in the Consignment Price field.

h. Appropriately size all columns to fully display the data.

i. Find all occurrences of dates that include an apostrophe (1930's) and are preceded with the word circa. Manually delete the 's from each located item.

j. Filter the table to display all records with a consignment price greater than or equal to $4,500. Sort the filtered records in ascending sort order by consignment price.

k. Format the datasheet using alternate row fill colors. Close the table object.

l. Use the Form tool to create a simple form for the Antiques Inventory table.

m. Display the form in Layout view. Change the form design style to another style of your choice. Reduce the size of all the text controls (they will size together as a group).

n. Use the new form to enter the following records:

Record 1	Record 2
Machine Age Refracting Telescope	Mid Century School House Globe
$4,800	$1,100
$6,700	$3,150
[Your Last Name]	Lewis

o. Print the form for the record containing your name. Close the form, saving it as Inventory.

p. Open the table and rerun the filter to display your record in the results. Print the filtered datasheet in landscape orientation using the normal margin setting. Close the table.

q. Display all object types in the Navigation pane.

r. Add object documentation for the form. Add your name to the database properties and exit Access.

Enterprise Employment Client Database ★★

2. You work for a private employment agency as an administrative assistant. As part of your responsibilities, you maintain a client database that contains the job candidates' basic contact information: name, address, and phone number. The office manager has asked you to add to the database the date each candidate applied at your office, the date they were placed with an employer, and the employer's name. Also, because the database is getting rather large, you decide to create a form to make it easier to enter and update records. Your completed table and form will be similar to those shown here.

   a. Open the database named **ac02_Enterprise Employment Agency** and the table named Candidates.

   b. Reduce the State field size to **2**. Change the State field Format property to display all entries in uppercase. Make the Default Value for the state field **FL**.

   c. Change the Zip Code data type to Text with a field size of **10**.

   d. Insert the following field after the Application # field.

      Field name: **Application Date**
      Data type: Date/Time
      Format: Short Date

   e. Add the following two fields to the end of the table:

      Field name: **Hire Date**
      Data type: Date/Time
      Format: Short Date
      Field name: **Employed By**
      Data type: Text
      Description: **Enter the name of the employer**
      Field size: **45**

   f. Switch to Datasheet view and save the table design changes.

   g. All zip codes of 72725 need to be changed to **72725-1016**. Use Find and Replace to make this change in the database. Best fit the columns.

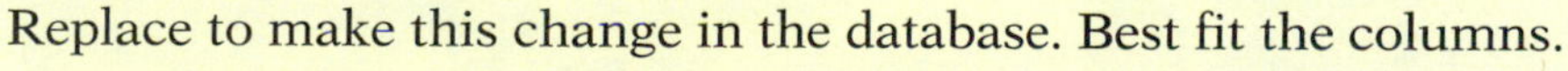

   h. Use the Form Wizard to create a form for the Candidates table. Include all the table fields in their current order. Use the Columnar layout and a style of your choice. Title the form **Candidate Information**.

Candidates 12/28/2008

Application #	Application Date	First Name	Last Name	Hire Date	Employed By
000263	2/15/2008	Bob	Alvarez	2/28/2008	Mantego Bay Electronics
000209	2/7/2008	Lily	Hammond	2/21/2008	Paper Products etc.
001098	1/5/2007	Frank	Montanaro	1/13/2007	Tamara Manufacturing
037623	1/7/2008	Student	Name	1/11/2008	Vistion Graphics
000199	2/12/2008	Terence	Pratt	3/2/2008	Quality Vision

Candidate Information

Application #	037623
Application Date	1/7/2008
First Name	Student
Last Name	Name
Address	802 Valimara Way
City	Palmdale
State	FL
ZIP Code	72725-1016
Phone	(726) 555-0909
Hire Date	1/11/2008
Employed By	Vistion Graphics

i. Use the new form to enter the following records:

Application #	001098	037623
Application Date	1/5/08	1/7/08
First Name	Frank	Your first name
Last Name	Montanaro	Your last name
Address	124 Beach Front Way	802 Valimara Way
City	Lexington	Palmdale
State	FL	FL
ZIP Code	72724	72725-1016
Phone	(726) 555-7623	(726) 555-0909
Hire Date	1/13/08	1/11/08
Employed By	Tamara Manufacturing	Vistion Graphics

j. Use the Search feature to locate the following records and update their data.

Locate	Application Date	Hire Date	Employed By
Lilly Hammond	2/7/08	2/21/08	Paper Products etc.
Terrence Pratt	2/12/08	3/2/08	Quality Vision
Bob Alvarez	2/15/08	2/28/08	Mantego Bay Electronics

k. Display all object types in the Navigation pane.

l. Print the form for the record containing your name.

m. Filter the Candidates table to display only those records displaying a hire date. Sort the records in ascending order by last name. Hide the Address through Phone columns.

n. Print the filtered datasheet using the Normal margin setting in landscape orientation.

o. Remove the filter and unhide the columns.

p. Add your name to the database properties. Close all objects and exit Access.

ARF Tracking Database ★★

3. You have created a database for tracking the animals that come into and go out of the Animal Rescue Foundation. Now you need to modify the database structure and customize field properties to control the data entered by the foundation's volunteers who are assigned this task. You also want to create a form to make it easier for the volunteers to enter the necessary information. Your completed datasheet and form will be similar to those shown here.

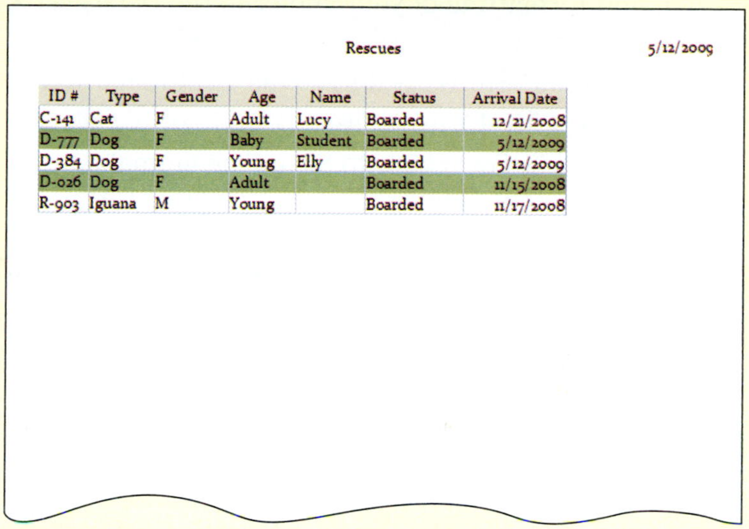

Rescues 5/12/2009

ID #	Type	Gender	Age	Name	Status	Arrival Date
C-141	Cat	F	Adult	Lucy	Boarded	12/21/2008
D-777	Dog	F	Baby	Student	Boarded	5/12/2009
D-384	Dog	F	Young	Elly	Boarded	5/12/2009
D-026	Dog	F	Adult		Boarded	11/15/2008
R-903	Iguana	M	Young		Boarded	11/17/2008

Animals

ID #	D-777
Type	Dog
Gender	F
Age	Baby
Name	Student Name
Status	Boarded
Arrival Date	5/12/2009
Foster Date	
Adoption Date	

Photo

a. Open the file ac02_ARF Database and the table Rescues in Datasheet view.

b. Use Find to locate ID # R-904. Add the adoption date **6/13/2007**.

c. Use Search to locate the animal named Spreckels and change the age to B and enter **12/01/2007** as the Foster Date.

d. Add the following field before the Arrival Date field:

Field name:	**Status**
Data type:	Lookup
Description:	**Select Boarded, Foster Care or Adopted**
Field size:	**15**

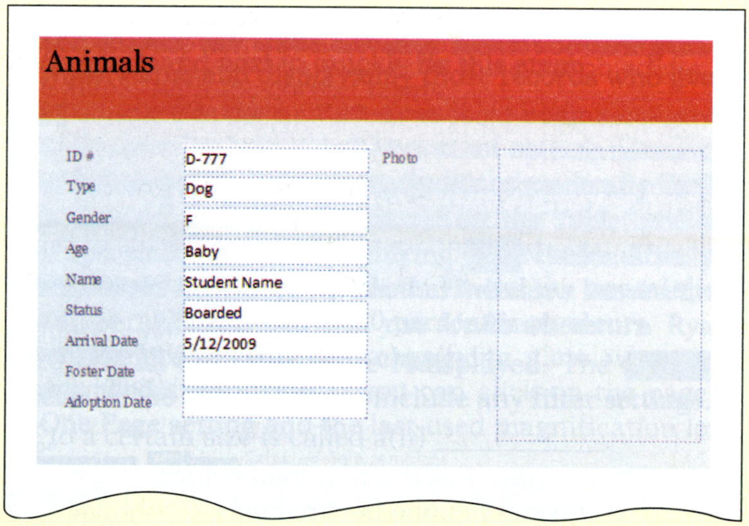

e. Make the following additional changes to the database structure:

- Restrict the entries in the Status field to list items only. Make Boarded the default value for Status.
- Add a validation rule and validation text to the Gender field to accept only M or F (male or female). Format the field to display the information in uppercase.
- Change the Age field to Lookup data type to accept only Baby, Young, or Adult. Increase the field size to **5**. Restrict the entries to items on the list only.

f. In Datasheet view, complete the data for the Status by entering F (if there is a Foster Date only), A (if there is an adoption date), or B (if there is neither a foster or an adoption date). Best fit the columns.

g. Change the data in the Age column by selecting from the list for each record.

h. Best fit all columns.

i. Add formatting of your choice to the Datasheet. Change the font of the datasheet to Constantia, 12 point.

j. Use the Form Wizard to create a columnar form. Include all the fields in their current order and use a style of your choice. Title the form **Animals**.

k. Search in Form view to locate the animal named Titus and add the picture ac02_WhiteDog to the Attachment field.

l. Adjust the size of the attachment control in Form Layout view. Change the form design style to another and make any adjustments to controls that are needed.

m. Add two records using the new form. Use the current date as the arrival date and make the status Boarded. In the Name field of the second record you add, enter your name, so your name appears on the printed output.

n. Save the form and print the record with your name as the animal name.

o. Filter the Rescues datasheet to display only those animals with a status of Boarded. Sort the filtered datasheet by Type. Hide the Foster Date, Adoption Date, and Attachment columns. Print the Rescues datasheet in portrait orientation using the Wide margin setting.

p. Unhide all columns. Clear all sorts and remove the filter.

q. Display all object types in the Navigation pane.

r. Identify object dependencies.

s. Add your name to the database properties. Close all objects and exit Access.

Kodiak Construction Database ★★★

CONTINUING EXERCISES

4. Although the database you designed for the expanding Kodiak Construction Company was well received, you have been asked to make several additions and improvements to the original design. In addition, they have asked you to create a form to make the process of entering new records in the database easier. Your completed database table and form will be similar to those shown here.

Jobs   11/6/2008

ID	Job	Priority	Client Last Name	Begin Date
296	Amberly Oaks	1 (High)		4/28/2007
884	Bella Greens	1 (High)		4/7/2006
163	Frisco Lake View	1 (High)	King	11/4/2006
489	Historia	1 (High)		12/10/2005
587	Pinewood Glen	1 (High)		3/5/2006
254	Shadow Hills	1 (High)		5/7/2006
999	Student Name private res	1 (High)	Name	11/6/2008
985	Willow Shoreline	1 (High)		3/21/2007

a. Open the file ac02_Kodiak Construction.

b. Open the Clients table and switch to Design view. Insert a new field before the Business Phone field named **Home Phone**. Include a description. Set the field size to **14**.

c. Enter the following Home Phone numbers into the table. Hide the fields between the Last Name and Home Phone fields. Use Find to locate the records. Unhide the columns when you are done.

Last Name	Home Phone
Lopez	**(303) 555-3772**
Miller	**(303) 555-8831**
Walker	**(303) 555-6613**
Young	**(303) 555-0912**

Jobs

ID	999
Job	Student Name private residence
Priority	1 (High)
Client Last Name	Name
Begin Date	11/6/2008
Foreman Last Name	Valdez
Job Location	
Job Estimate	
Job Description	

d. Change the City column to a Lookup Field data type. Include the following cities as the lookup list values: Aurora, Denver, Glendale, Lakewood, Littleton, Parker.

e. Open the City field drop-down list for each record and select a city.

f. Make the default value for the State field **CO**. Change the format to uppercase.

Next, you want to add a field for the job priority to the Jobs table. This field can only contain three possible values: High, Normal, or Low. Instead of typing this information in the field, you will make the field a Lookup field.

g. Open the Jobs table and insert the new field named **Priority** after the Job field. Select the Lookup Wizard from the Data Type list. Select the "I will type in the values that I want" option. In column 1, enter **High** in the first cell, **Normal** in the second cell, and **Low** in the third cell. Accept the field name. Set the field's size to **15** and the default value to Normal. Limit entries to values from the list.

h. Switch to Datasheet view, saving your design changes.

i. Open the Priority field drop-down list for each record and select a priority level.

j. Best fit the columns.

k. Add formatting of your choice to the Jobs datasheet. Change the font to Arial. Close the table.

l. Use the Form Wizard to create a form for the Jobs table. Include all of the fields from the Jobs table in order. Use the columnar form layout. Select a style of your choice and accept the default form name (**Jobs**).

m. In Form Layout view, search for the record for R Bar C Ranch. Change the foreman to **Valdez**.

n. Appropriately size the label and text controls (they will size together as a group).

o. Create similar forms for the Clients and Foremen tables. Size the controls appropriately.

p. Using the form, add a new record to the Client table using your first and last names as the client name. Save the changes and close the form.

q. Using the form, add a new record to the Jobs table with **999** as the ID and **[your last name] private residence** as the job; select your name as the Client Last Name, priority of High, the current date as the Begin Date, and a foreman of your choice.

r. Print your record in the form.

s. Open the Jobs table. Filter the records to display only those with a High priority. Sort the filtered records by Job in ascending sort order. Hide the Job Location, Job Estimate, and Job Description columns.

t. Print the filtered Jobs datasheet in landscape orientation.

u. Unhide all columns. Clear all sorts and remove the filter.

v. Display all object types in the Navigation pane.

w. Add your name to the database properties. Save and close the database.

EchoPlex Database ★★★

5. EchoPlex is an online record store that specializes in rare and collectible vinyl. You recently expanded the business and created a database to manage your inventory. The database initially began as a list of available titles, but with use you saw a need for more information. You changed the original database file design and have been using it for several weeks now, but it still needs some additional changes that you feel will make inventory control and data entry even easier. The completed database and form are shown here.

Records 10/6/2008

ID	Title	Artist	Condition	Purchase Price	Sold Price	Shipped
42	The Doors	The Doors	Excellent	$10.00	$0.00	N
41	Never Mind the Bollocks	The Sex Pistols	Excellent	$10.00	$0.00	N
56	Songs in the Key of Life	Stevie Wonder	Excellent	$12.00	$0.00	N
102	My Record	Student Name	Excellent	$38.00	$50.00	Y
6	What's Going On	Marvin Gaye	Excellent	$50.00	$86.00	Y
51	Bridge Over Troubled Water	Simon and Garfunkel	Excellent	$50.00	$0.00	N
10	The Beatles ("The White Album")	The Beatles	Excellent	$50.00	$0.00	N
15	Are You Experienced?	The Jimi Hendrix Experience	Excellent	$50.00	$0.00	N
81	Graceland	Paul Simon	Excellent	$87.00	$0.00	N

ID 102

Title: My Record
Artist: Student Name
Condition: Excellent
Purchase Price: $38.00
Sold Price: $50.00
Shipped: Y
Comments: Sold to Bernard.
Attachments:

a. Open the database file ac02_EchoPlex and the table Records.

b. Change the Format property of the Sold Price field to Currency.

c. Use Search to find the record for Neil Young's *Harvest*. Enter the sold price of **155**.

d. Unhide the Comments field.

e. You want to add a new field to show the condition of each item. This field can only contain four possible values: Excellent, Good, Fair, or Poor. Insert a new field after Artist named **Condition**. Use a data type of Lookup and enter the following as the list values: **Excellent**, **Good**, **Fair**, and **Poor**. Accept the field name. Set the field's Default Value to **Good** and limit entries to list items.

f. Switch to Datasheet view and select a condition for each record.

g. Enter the following information as a new record:

Title:	**School House Rocker**
Artist:	**Kate Lansbergen**
Condition:	**Fair**
Purchase Price:	**$45.00**
Sold Price:	**$47.00**
Comments:	**Traded to SearchLight Records for $47.00 in store credit.**

h. Insert a new field after the Sold Price field named **Shipped** with a data type of Text. Add **"Y or N"** as a validation rule. Add **Must be Y or N** as the Validation text. Format the field to display in uppercase.

i. Sort the list by Sold Price. For all of the entries with $0.00, enter **N** in the Shipped field. For entries with a Sold Price, enter **Y** in the Shipped field. Remove the sort.

j. Find all instances of Beatles in the Artist field and replace with **The Beatles**.

k. Hide the Comments and Attachments fields.

l. Add formatting of your choice to the datasheet. Change the font of the datasheet to one of your choice.

m. Use the Form Wizard to create a form for the Records table. Include all of the fields from the Records table in order. Use the columnar form. Apply a style of your choice to the form and accept the default form name (**Records**).

n. Switch to Layout view. Select another design style. Move the grouped controls down on the form. Remove the ID field from the group. Move the ID field above the grouped controls. Size the ID field to fit the data. Adjust the size of the other form controls as needed (they will size together as a group). Move and size the Attachment label and text controls as needed.

o. Use the form to enter a new record with a title of your choice and your name as the artist. Include a condition of Excellent, a purchase price of $38, and a sold price of $50.

p. Preview and print the form for your record. Save and close the form.

q. Filter the records to display only those records with a condition of Excellent and a purchase price of $10 or more. Sort the records in ascending order by Purchase Price. Best fit the fields. Print the filtered datasheet in landscape orientation with Normal margins.

r. Display all object types in the Navigation pane.

s. Add your name to the database properties. Save the database and exit Access.

on your own

Adventure Travel Packages Form ★

1. You have heard from the employees of Adventure Travel Tours that the database table you created is a bit unwieldy for them to enter the necessary data, because it now contains so many fields that it requires scrolling across the screen to locate them. You decide to create a form that will make entering data not only easier, but more attractive as well. Open the ac02_ATT Database. Best fit the columns. Change the order of the Length and Description field columns in Design view. Apply formatting of your choice to the datasheet. Sort the table on Destination in ascending order. Use the Form Wizard to create a form called **Travel Packages** for the Packages table. Use the form to enter five new records with tour package information of your choice (use the newspaper travel section or the Web for ideas). Enter your name as the Contact in one of the new records. Print the form containing your name. Print the datasheet in landscape orientation.

EMP Account Tracking ★★

2. While creating the database table for EMP Enterprises, you learned that some employees have been receiving advances for anticipated expenses (such as for travel). You have also been informed that the CEO wants to start tracking the expenses by department. Open the database file **EMP Enterprise** (Lab 1, On Your Own 5). Add a new field named Advanced Amount with a currency data type to the Employee Expenses table. Also add a Yes/No field named Payment Made to record whether or not the expense has been paid, with a corresponding validation rule and message. In The Employee Info table, add a new field named Department to enter the department's charge code number. Update both tables to include appropriate values in the new fields in the existing records. Apply formatting of your choice to the Employee Expenses datasheet. Sort the Employee Expenses table on the Expense Amount field in Descending sort order. Close the table, saving the changes. Use the Form Wizard to create a form named **Expenses** for the Employee Expenses table. Include the form title Your Name Expenses. To test the form, enter a new expense record using the employee ID number for the record containing your name in the Employee Info table. Select your record in the form and print it.

Dental Patient Database Update ★★

3. The dentist office for which you created a patient database has expanded to include a second dentist and receptionist. The two dentists are Dr. Jones and Dr. Smith. You now need to modify the database to identify required fields and to add a new field that identifies which patient is assigned to which dentist. You also decide that creating a form for the database would make it easier for both you and the other receptionist to enter and locate patient information. Open the Dental Patients database (Lab 1, On Your Own 3) and the Personal Information table. Make the patient identification number, name, and phone number required fields. Add a Dentist Name Lookup list field, with the two dentists' names and an appropriate validation rule and message. Update the table to "assign" some of the patients to one of the dentists and some patients to the other dentist. Assign the record containing your name to Dr. Jones. Sort the table by dentist name to see the results of your new assignments. "Reassign" one of the displayed patients and then remove the sort. Filter the table to display only those patients for Dr. Jones. Apply formatting of your choice to the datasheet. Print the filtered datasheet and then remove the filter. Create a form called **Patient Data** for the table using the Form Wizard. Enter two new records, one for each of the dentists. Use the Search feature to locate the record that has your name as the patient, and then select and print the displayed record in the form.

Lewis & Lewis Employee Database ★★

4. You work in the Human Resource Management department at Lewis & Lewis, Inc. You recently created a simple database containing information on the employees Department and work telephone extension. Several of your co-employees also want to use the database. You decide to add a field for the employees job title and enhance the table. You also want to create a form that will make it easier for others to update the information in the database as well. Open the ac02_Lewis Personnel database and **Phone List** table and add the Job Title field after the Department field. Update the table to include information in the new field for the existing records. Add a new record that includes your name. Apply formatting of your choice to the datasheet. Sort the table by Department and Last Name. Use the Search feature to locate and delete the record for Anna Tai who has left the company. Print the datasheet in landscape orientation, Remove the sort and

close the table, saving the changes. Create a form called **Phone List** for the Phone List table using the Form Wizard. Enter five new records. Use the Replace command to locate and change the last name for Alexa Hirsch to Alexa Muirhead who has gotten married since you first created the database. Use the Search feature to locate the record form that has your name as the employee. Select and print the displayed record.

Timeless Treasures Inventory Database ★★★

5. You realize that you have left out some very important fields in the Inventory table you created in the Timeless Treasures database (On Your Own Exercise 4 of Lab 1)—fields that identify the sources where you can obtain the vintage watches your customers are looking for. Repeat your Web search for old watches and note the resources (for example, online shopping services, specialty stores, or individual collectors who are offering these items at online auctions) for the watches in your table. Add a Source Name field, a Source E-mail field and a Source Phone field to the table. Update the table to include this information in the existing records. Apply formatting of your choice to the datasheet. Sort the records according to the source name field and adjust the column widths to accommodate the new information. Print the datasheet. Remove the sort and close the table, saving the changes. Now, to make data entry easier, create a form named **Watches** using the Form Wizard. Use the form to locate the record with your name as the manufacturer, and then print it.

Querying Tables and Creating Reports

LAB 3

Objectives

After completing this lab, you will know how to:

1. Evaluate table design.
2. Establish relationships.
3. Enforce referential integrity.
4. Create and modify a simple query.
5. Query two tables.
6. Filter a query.
7. Find unmatched and duplicate records.
8. Create a Parameter query.
9. Create reports from tables and queries.
10. Display a Totals row.
11. Modify a report design.
12. Select, move, and size controls.
13. Change page margins.
14. Preview and print a report.
15. Compact and back up a database.

Case Study

Lifestyle Fitness Club

After modifying the structure of the table of Personal Data, you have continued to enter many more records. You also have created a second table in the database that contains employee information about location and job titles. Again, the owners are very impressed with the database. They are eager to see how the information in the database can be used.

As you have seen, compiling, storing, and updating information in a database is very useful. The real strength of a database program, however, is its ability to find the information you need quickly, and to manipulate and analyze it to answer specific questions. You will use the information in the tables to provide the answers to several inquiries about the club employees. As you learn about the analytical features, imagine trying to do the same task by hand. How long would it take? Would it be as accurate or as well presented? In addition, you will create several reports that present the information from the database attractively.

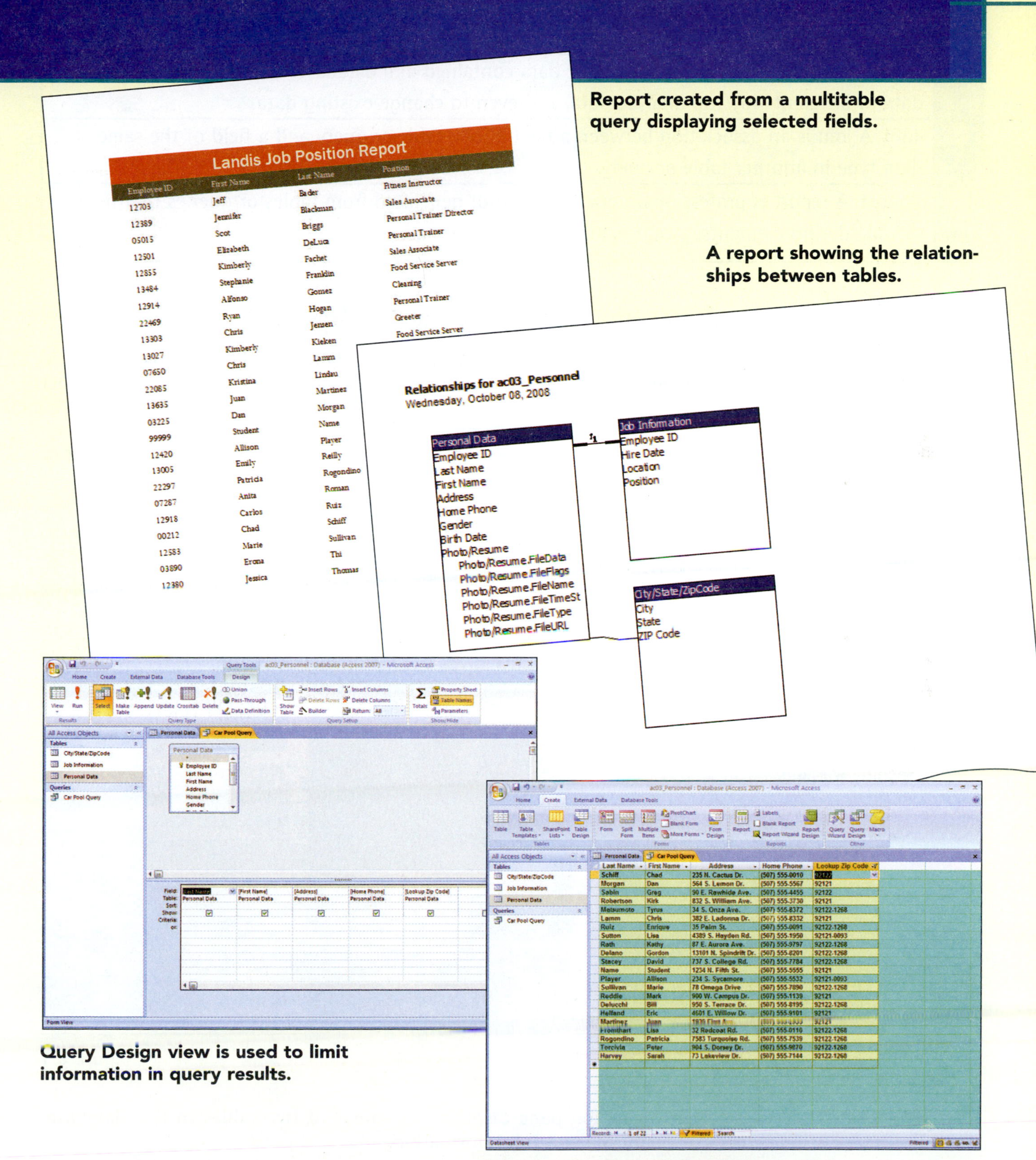

Landis Job Position Report

Employee ID	First Name	Last Name	Position
12703	Jeff	Bader	Fitness Instructor
12389	Jennifer	Blackman	Sales Associate
05015	Scot	Briggs	Personal Trainer Director
12501	Elizabeth	DeLuca	Personal Trainer
12855	Kimberly	Fachet	Sales Associate
13484	Stephanie	Franklin	Food Service Server
12914	Alfonso	Gomez	Cleaning
22469	Ryan	Hogan	Personal Trainer
13303	Chris	Jensen	Greeter
13027	Kimberly	Kieken	Food Service Server
07650	Chris	Lamm	
22085	Kristina	Lindau	
13635	Juan	Martinez	
03225	Dan	Morgan	
99999	Student	Name	
12420	Allison	Player	
13005	Emily	Reilly	
22297	Patricia	Rogondino	
07287	Anita	Roman	
12918	Carlos	Ruiz	
00212	Chad	Schiff	
12583	Marie	Sullivan	
03890	Erona	Thi	
12380	Jessica	Thomas	

Report created from a multitable query displaying selected fields.

A report showing the relationships between tables.

Query Design view is used to limit information in query results.

Last Name	First Name	Address	Home Phone	Lookup Zip Code
Schiff	Chad	235 N. Cactus Dr.	(507) 555-0010	92122
Morgan	Dan	564 S. Lemon Dr.	(507) 555-5567	92121
Sabin	Greg	90 E. Rawhide Ave.	(507) 555-4455	92122
Robertson	Kirk	832 S. William Ave.	(507) 555-3730	92121
Matsumoto	Tyrus	34 S. Onza Ave.	(507) 555-8372	92122-1268
Lamm	Chris	382 E. Ladonna Dr.	(507) 555-8332	92121
Ruiz	Enrique	35 Palm St.	(507) 555-0091	92122-1268
Sutton	Lisa	4389 S. Hayden Rd.	(507) 555-1950	92121-0093
Roth	Kathy	87 E. Aurora Ave.	(507) 555-9797	92122-1268
Delano	Gordon	13101 N. Spindrift Dr.	(507) 555-8201	92122-1268
Stacey	David	737 S. College Rd.	(507) 555-7784	92122-1268
Name	Student	1234 N. Fifth St.	(507) 555-5555	92121
Player	Allison	234 S. Sycamore	(507) 555-5532	92121-0093
Sullivan	Marie	78 Omega Drive	(507) 555-7890	92122-1268
Reddie	Mark	900 W. Campus Dr.	(507) 555-1139	92121
Delucchi	Bill	950 S. Terrace Dr.	(507) 555-8195	92122-1268
Helfand	Eric	4601 E. Willow Dr.	(507) 555-9101	92121
Martinez	Juan	[illegible]	[illegible]	92121
Fromthart	Lisa	32 Redcoat Rd.	(507) 555-0110	92122-1268
Rogondino	Patricia	7583 Turquoise Rd.	(507) 555-7539	92122-1268
Torcivia	Peter	904 S. Dorsey Dr.	(507) 555-9870	92122-1268
Harvey	Sarah	73 Lakeview Dr.	(507) 555-7144	92122-1268

Creating queries of data limits the information that is displayed in the results.

Concept Preview

The following concepts will be introduced in this lab:

1. **Relationship** A relationship establishes the association between common fields in two tables.
2. **Query** A query is a request for specific data contained in a database. Queries are used to view data in different ways, to analyze data, and even to change existing data.
3. **Join** A join is an association between a field in one table or query and a field of the same data type in another table or query.
4. **Report** A report is professional-appearing output generated from tables or queries that may include design elements, groups, and summary information.

Refining the Database Design

You have continued to enter Personal Data into the Records table. The updated table has been saved for you as Personal Data in the ac03_Personnel database file.

Note: Before you begin, you may want to create a backup copy of the ac03_Personnel file by copying and renaming it.

1. **Start Office Access 2007.**
   - **Open the ac03_Personnel database file.**
   - **If necessary, respond appropriately to the Security Warning.**

Your screen should be similar to Figure 3.1

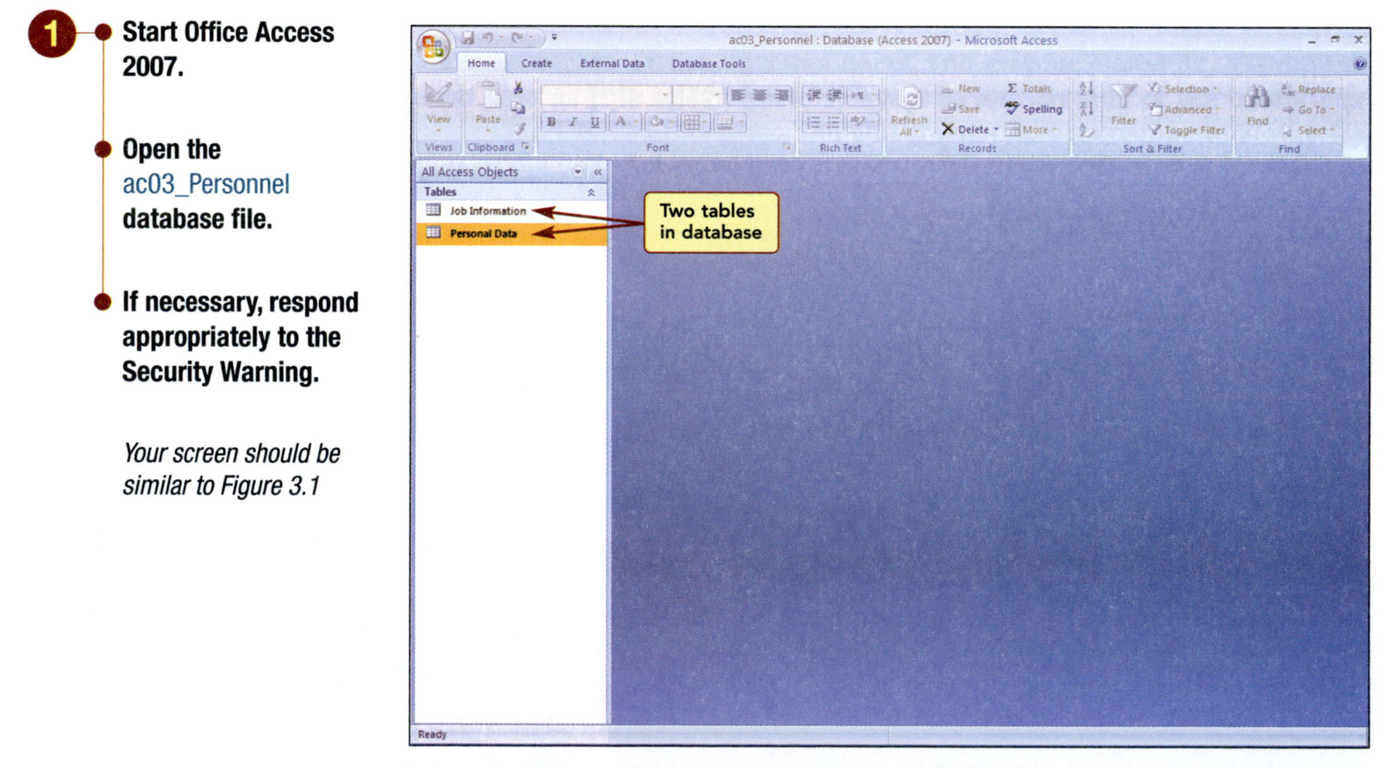

Figure 3.1

The Navigation pane displays the names of two tables in this database: Personal Data and Job Information.

Open the Personal Data table.

Add your information as record number 70 using your special ID number 99999 and your name. Enter Maldin as the city and 92121 as the zip code. Fill in the remaining fields as desired.

Return to the first field of the first record.

Hide the Navigation pane.

Your screen should be similar to Figure 3.2

Personal Data

Employee ID	Last Name	First Name	Address	City	State	ZIP Code	Home Phone	Gender	Birth Date
00212	Schiff	Chad	235 N. Cactus Dr.	Chesterfield	CA	92122	(507) 555-0010	M	3/9/196
00617	Nichols	Cathy	75 Brooklea Dr.	Landis	CA	92120-3741	(507) 555-0001	F	5/19/196
00907	Pennington	Mark	23 Mill Ave.	Landis	CA	92120-3741	(507) 555-3333	M	7/7/196
01421	Spehr	Timothy	90 Royal Dr.	Maldin	CA	92121-3740	(507) 555-1038	M	9/9/197
03225	Morgan	Dan	564 S. Lemon Dr.	Maldin	CA	92121	(507) 555-5567	M	3/5/197
03406	Lopez	Mina	4290 E. Alameda Dr.	Maldin	CA	92121-3740	(507) 555-5050	F	2/25/197
03673	Walker	Aaron	76 Thomas Rd.	River Mist	CA	92123-2232	(507) 555-2222	M	8/1/197
03890	Thi	Erona	7867 Forest Ave.	River Mist	CA	92123-2232	(507) 555-1089	F	5/10/197
04321	Sabin	Greg	90 E. Rawhide Ave.	Chesterfield	CA	92122	(507) 555-4455	M	9/30/197
04731	Marchant	Roberta	564 Palm Avenue	Landis	CA	92120-3741	(507) 555-6707	F	5/13/198
05015	Briggs	Scott	45 E. Camelback Rd.	River Mist	CA	92123-2232	(507) 555-9585	M	9/15/197
06000	Robertson	Kirk	832 S. William Ave.	Maldin	CA	92121	(507) 555-3730	M	4/5/197
07287	Roman	Anita	2348 S. Bala Dr.	Maldin	CA	92121-3740	(507) 555-9870	F	3/15/198
07450	Matsumoto	Tyrus	34 S. Onza Ave.	Chesterfield	CA	92122-1268	(507) 555-8372	M	6/23/198
07540	Pario	Ian	983 E. Carrage Ln.	Landis	CA	92120-3741	(507) 555-2321	M	4/23/197
07550	Ernster	Barbara	1153 S. Wilson	River Mist	CA	92123-2232	(507) 555-3211	F	5/30/197
07650	Lamm	Chris	382 E. Ladonna Dr.	Maldin	CA	92121	(507) 555-8332	M	8/3/197
08000	Nelson	Samantha	2322 Trafalgar Ct.	River Mist	CA	92123-2232	(507) 555-0003	F	10/30/197
08391	Ruiz	Enrique	35 Palm St.	Chesterfield	CA	92122-1268	(507) 555-0091	M	12/10/197
08430	Smith	Brent	4321 Toledo St.	River Mist	CA	92123-2232	(507) 555-6464	M	11/4/197
09430	Robson	David	8584 Bryan Dr.	River Mist	CA	92123-2232	(507) 555-6666	M	12/5/197
11510	Sutton	Lisa	4389 S. Hayden Rd.	Maldin	CA	92121-0093	(507) 555-1950	F	6/14/197
11747	Lettow	Ryan	358 Maple Dr.	Maldin	CA	92121-3740	(507) 555-2805	M	11/15/197
12194	Polonsky	Mitch	8701 E. Sheridan	Landis	CA	92120-3741	(507) 555-1018	M	3/13/197
12213	Young	Kim	89 College Ave.	River Mist	CA	92123-2232	(507) 555-1059	F	4/12/198
12230	Reddie	Suzanne	932 E. Parkway Dr.	Landis	CA	92120-3741	(507) 555-1191	F	7/14/197
12247	Rath	Kathy	87 E. Aurora Ave.	Chesterfield	CA	92122-1268	(507) 555-9797	F	5/30/197
12258	Delano	Gordon	13101 N. Spindrift Dr.	Chesterfield	CA	92122-1268	(507) 555-8201	M	8/7/197
12366	Stacey	David	737 S. College Rd.	Chesterfield	CA	92122-1268	(507) 555-7784	M	9/30/197
12380	Thomas	Jessica	128 Marina Dr.	River Mist	CA	92123-2232	(507) 555-8513	F	1/22/198

Record: 1 of 70 Unfiltered Search

Unique 5-digit number assigned to each employee.

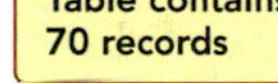

Figure 3.2

Evaluating Table Design

As you continue to use and refine the database, you have noticed that you repeatedly enter the same city, state, and zip code information in the Personal Data table. You decide there may be a better way to organize the table information and will use the Table Analyzer tool to help evaluate the design of the Personal Data table.

Open the Database Tools tab.

Click Analyze Table in the Analyze group.

Your screen should be similar to Figure 3.3

Table Analyzer Wizard

The Table Analyzer: Looking At the Problem

Your table or spreadsheet may store the same information many times. Duplicating information can cause problems.

First, duplicating information wastes space.

Show me an example.

Second, duplicating information can lead to mistakes.

Show me an example.

Supplier name is misspelled.

Supplier information is repeated.

Cancel < Back Next > Finish

Introductory information

Figure 3.3

The first two windows of Table Analyzer Wizard are introductory pages that review the process that will be used. First it will analyze the information stored in the table by looking for duplicate information. Then, if duplicates are located, it will split the original table and create new tables to store the information a single time to solve the problem.

2 **Click Next > to see the next introductory page.**

Click Next > to move to the first step.

Your screen should be similar to Figure 3.4

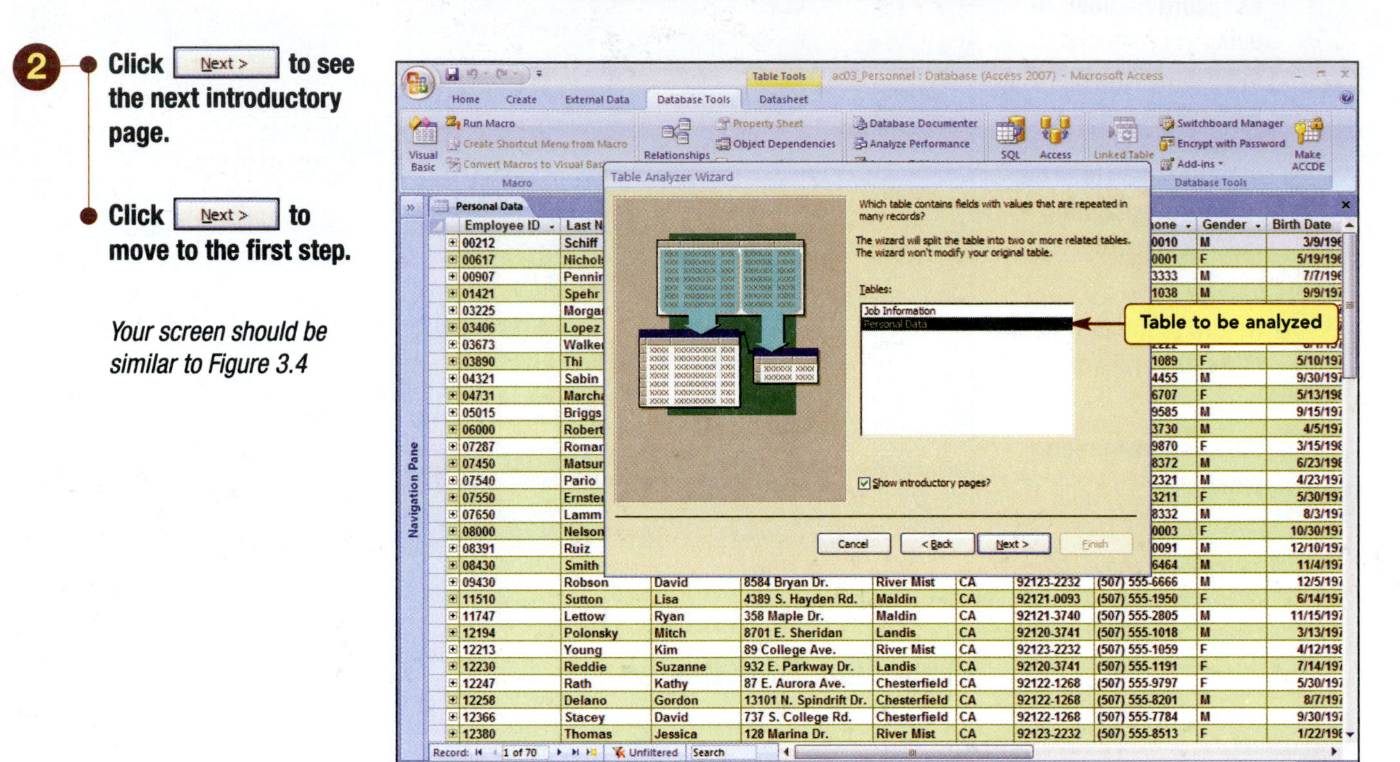

Figure 3.4

In the next two steps, you identify the table you want to evaluate and whether you want the wizard to decide what fields to place in the new table or to make that determination yourself.

3 • Click Next > to accept analyzing the Personal Data table.

• Click Next > to accept letting the wizard decide.

Your screen should be similar to Figure 3.5

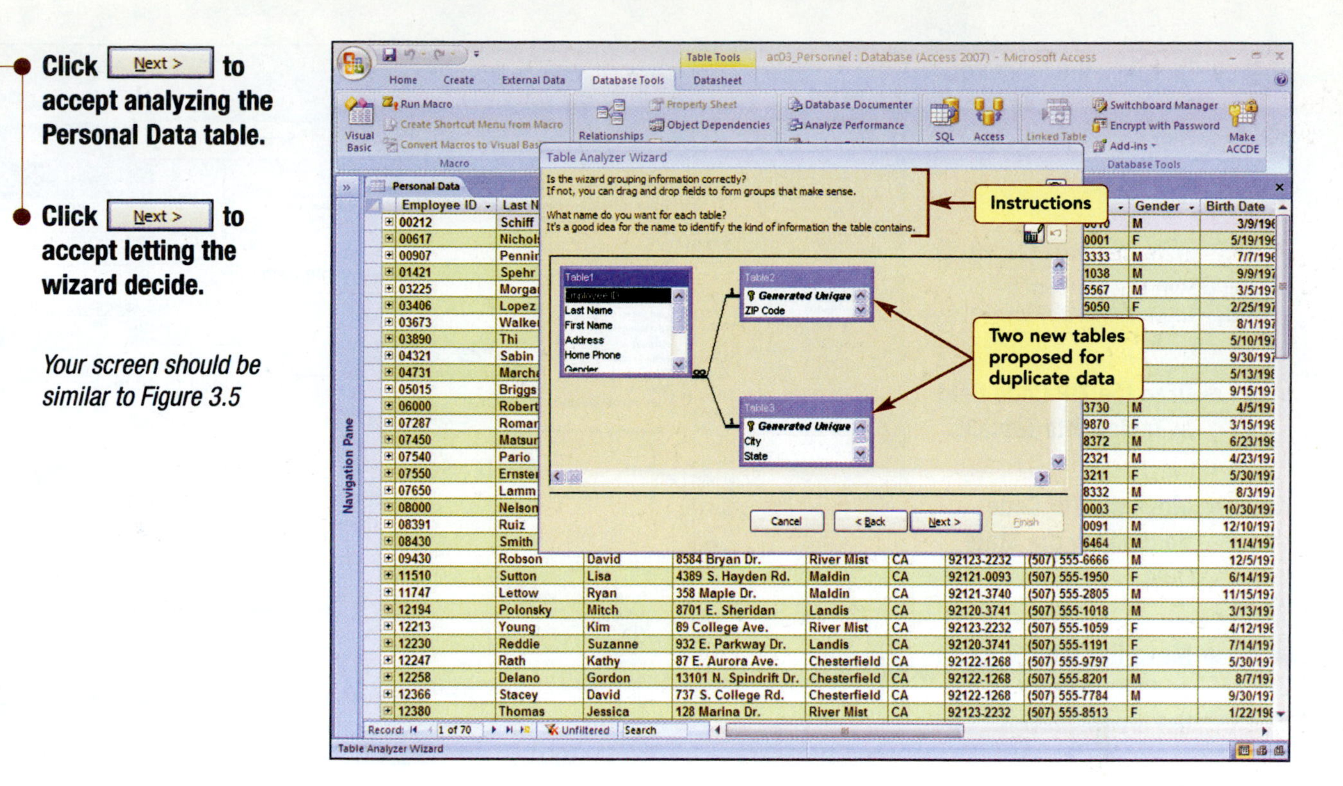

Figure 3.5

The wizard has identified duplicate data in the zip code, city, and state fields and proposes to move these fields into two additional tables: one for zip codes and the other for city and state where the information would be stored only once. The instructions at the top of the Table Analyzer Wizard box ask you to revise the grouping if needed and to create names for the tables. You decide that creating one new table containing the three fields will prevent the duplicate data and will revise the grouping by adding the ZIP Code field to Table3. You will then rename the new table and move to the next step.

Increase the length of the Table1 list to display all the field names.

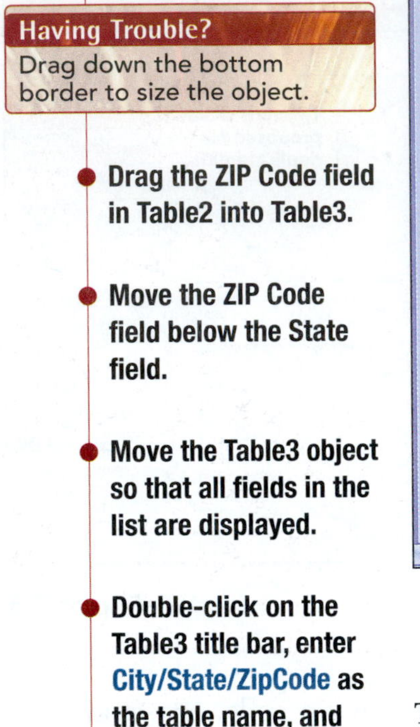

Having Trouble?

Drag down the bottom border to size the object.

- **Drag the ZIP Code field in Table2 into Table3.**
- **Move the ZIP Code field below the State field.**
- **Move the Table3 object so that all fields in the list are displayed.**
- **Double-click on the Table3 title bar, enter City/State/ZipCode as the table name, and click OK.**
- **Click Next > to move to the next step.**

Your screen should be similar to Figure 3.6

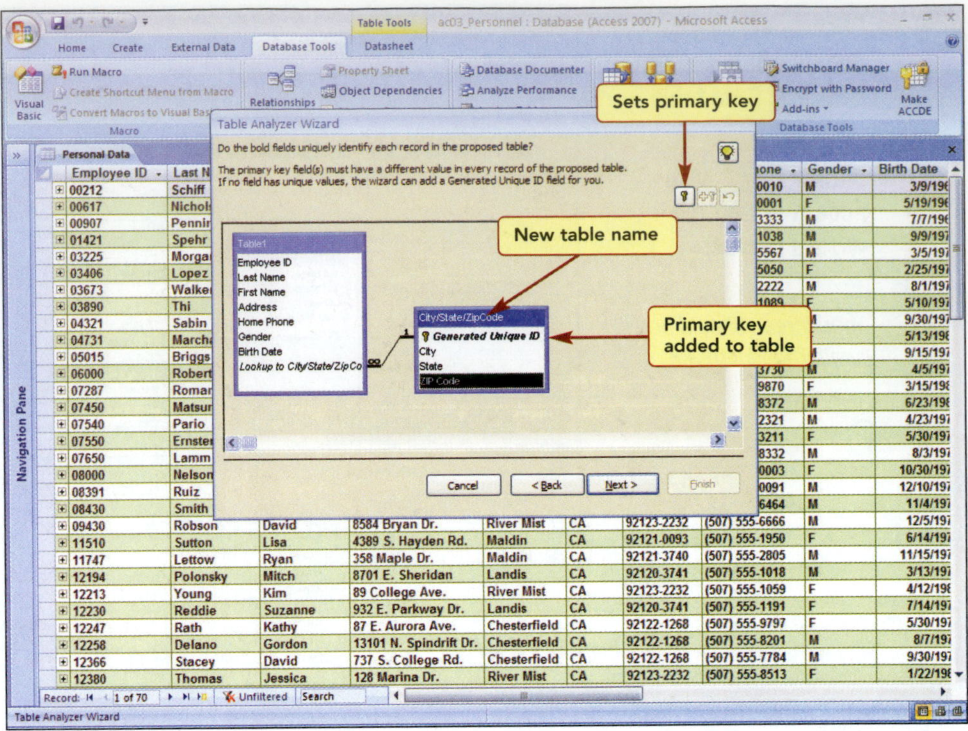

Figure 3.6

This step identifies the fields to use as a primary key in the new tables by bolding the field name. The wizard automatically added a Generated Unique ID field (AutoNumber) to the new table. You will define the ZIP Code field as the primary key field, which will also remove the Unique ID field.

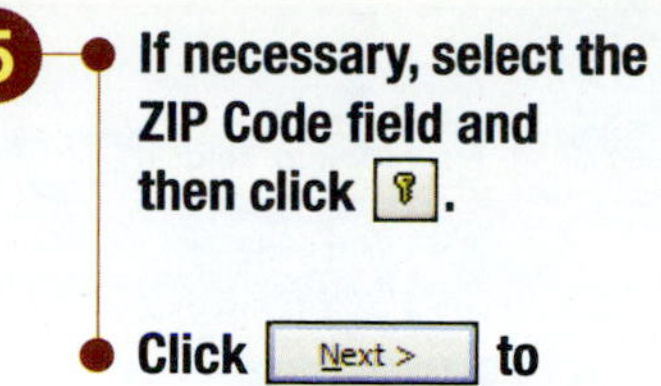

5

- **If necessary, select the ZIP Code field and then click [key button].**
- **Click Next > to move to the next step.**

Your screen should be similar to Figure 3.7

Table Tools ac03_Personnel : Database (Access 2007) - Microsoft Access
Home Create External Data Database Tools Datasheet
Visual Basic Run Macro Create Shortcut Menu from Macro Convert Macros to Visual Basic Macro
Relationships Property Sheet Object Dependencies
Database Documenter Analyze Performance
SQL Access Linked Table
Switchboard Manager Encrypt with Password Add-ins Make ACCDE Database Tools
Personal Data
Navigation Pane

Table Analyzer Wizard
That's all the information the wizard needs to create related tables.
After the wizard creates new tables, it can create a query that looks like your original table but does much more.
If you choose to create a query:
. Forms and reports based on your original table will continue to work.
- The wizard will give the query the name of your original table, and rename your original table.
Do you want a query?
(•) Yes, create the query.
( ) No, don't create the query.
Cancel < Back Next > Finish

Employee ID	Last N...						...one	Gender	Birth Date
00212	Schiff						0010	M	3/9/196
00617	Nichol						0001	F	5/19/196
00907	Pennir						3333	M	7/7/196
01421	Spehr						1038	M	9/9/197
03225	Morgai						5567	M	3/5/197
03406	Lopez						5050	F	2/25/197
03673	Walke						2222	M	8/1/197
03890	Thi						1089	F	5/10/197
04321	Sabin						4455	M	9/30/197
04731	Marcha						6707	F	5/13/198
05015	Briggs						9585	M	9/15/197
06000	Robert						3730	M	4/5/197
07287	Romar						9870	F	3/15/198
07450	Matsur						8372	M	6/23/198
07540	Pario						2321	M	4/23/197
07550	Ernste						3211	F	5/30/197
07650	Lamm						8332	M	8/3/197
08000	Nelson						0003	F	10/30/197
08391	Ruiz						0091	M	12/10/197
08430	Smith						6464	M	11/4/197
09430	Robson	David	8584 Bryan Dr.	River Mist	CA	92123-2232	(507) 555-6666	M	12/5/197
11510	Sutton	Lisa	4389 S. Hayden Rd.	Maldin	CA	92121-0093	(507) 555-1950	F	6/14/197
11747	Lettow	Ryan	358 Maple Dr.	Maldin	CA	92121-3740	(507) 555-2805	M	11/15/197
12194	Polonsky	Mitch	8701 E. Sheridan	Landis	CA	92120-3741	(507) 555-1018	M	3/13/197
12213	Young	Kim	89 College Ave.	River Mist	CA	92123-2232	(507) 555-1059	F	4/12/198
12230	Reddie	Suzanne	932 E. Parkway Dr.	Landis	CA	92120-3741	(507) 555-1191	F	7/14/197
12247	Rath	Kathy	87 E. Aurora Ave.	Chesterfield	CA	92122-1268	(507) 555-9797	F	5/30/197
12258	Delano	Gordon	13101 N. Spindrift Dr.	Chesterfield	CA	92122-1268	(507) 555-8201	M	8/7/197
12366	Stacey	David	737 S. College Rd.	Chesterfield	CA	92122-1268	(507) 555-7784	M	9/30/197
12380	Thomas	Jessica	128 Marina Dr.	River Mist	CA	92123-2232	(507) 555-8513	F	1/22/198

Record: 1 of 70 Unfiltered Search
Table Analyzer Wizard

Figure 3.7

The final wizard step asks if you want to create a query. You will be learning about queries shortly so you will not create a query at this time.

6

- **Choose No, don't create the query.**
- **Click Finish.**
- **If an informational message appears, click OK to continue.**

Your screen should be similar to Figure 3.8

Two new tables

Table Tools ac03_Personnel : Database (Access 2007) - Microsoft Access
Home Create External Data Database Tools Datasheet
Visual Basic Run Macro Create Shortcut Menu from Macro Convert Macros to Visual Basic Macro
Relationships Property Sheet Object Dependencies Message Bar Show/Hide
Database Documenter Analyze Performance Analyze Table Analyze
SQL Server Access Database Move Data
Linked Table Manager Switchboard Manager Encrypt with Password Add-ins Make ACCDE Database Tools
Personal Data Table1 City/State/ZipCode
Navigation Pane

City	State	ZIP Code	Add New Field
Landis	CA	92120-3741	
Maldin	CA	92121	
Maldin	CA	92121-0093	
Maldin	CA	92121-3740	
Chesterfield	CA	92122	
Chesterfield	CA	92122-1268	
River Mist	CA	92123-2232	

Record: 1 of 7 No Filter Search
Table Analyzer Wizard

Figure 3.8

The two new tables are opened and the City/State/ZipCode table is displayed. The ZIP Code field is the primary key field and has been associated with the data in the new Table1.

7 **Display Table1 and move to the Lookup to City/State/ZipCode field for the first record.**

Best fit the field column.

Your screen should be similar to Figure 3.9

Figure 3.9

The Lookup field displays the zip code, city, and state information from the associated table and the individual fields that stored this information for each record have been deleted. You can now see how using a separate table to store this data saves space by not duplicating the information and also makes data entry more accurate. The zip code field appears first because it is the primary key field.

Creating a Table List Lookup Field

Now your database contains two tables that hold duplicate data, Table1 and Personal Data, and you need to decide which table to keep. You notice that Table1 did not maintain the association to the Job table and the field and datasheet formatting. Rather than make these same changes again to Table1, you decide to modify the Personal Data table by creating a lookup field to the City/State/ZipCode table.

1. Display the Personal Data table.

- Right-click on the Add New Field column and choose Lookup Column.

- Run the Lookup Wizard and specify the following settings:
  - Look up the values in a table or query.
  - Use the City/State/ZipCode table.
  - Add all three columns to the selected fields list.
  - Do not specify a sort order.
  - Clear the checkmark from the Hide key column option to display all three columns.
  - Store the ZIP Code value in the lookup column.
  - Enter the field name **Lookup Zip Code**.

- Click .

- Click in the Lookup field for the first record and display the drop-down list.

Your screen should be similar to Figure 3.10

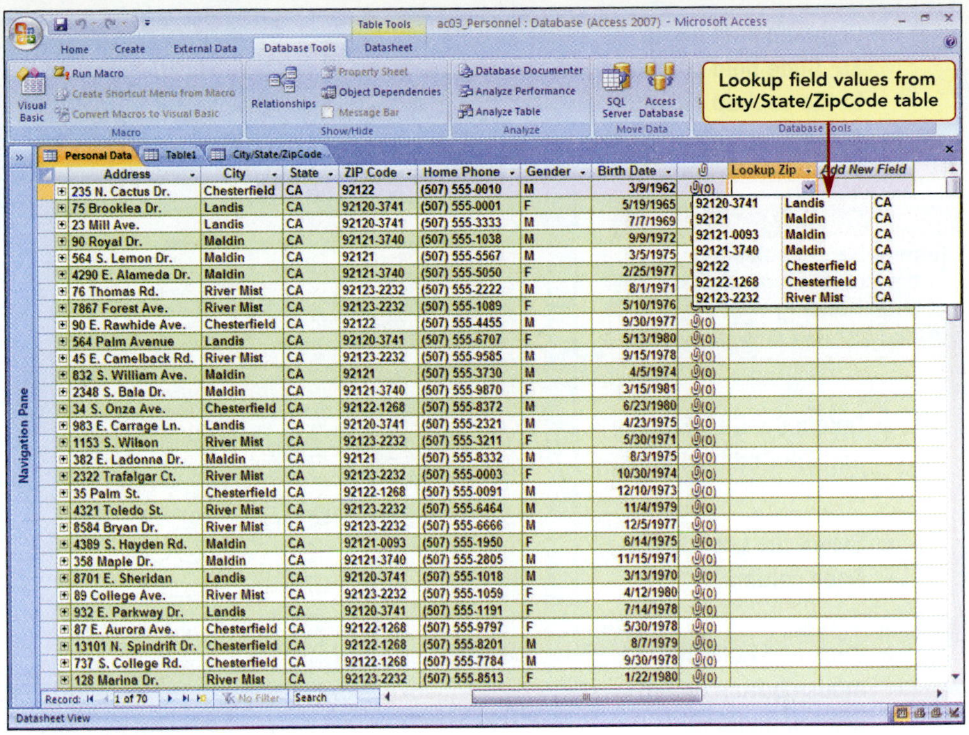

Lookup field values from City/State/ZipCode table

Figure 3.10

Now you need to add the data for this column. Instead of selecting each zip code, you will copy the data in the existing ZIP Code field column into the lookup column. Then, because you will no longer need them, you will delete the City, State, and ZIP Code fields. Finally, you will move the Lookup column after the Address column. You can move a column by selecting it and then dragging it to its new location.

Copy the data in the ZIP Code field column to the Lookup Zip Code column.

Having Trouble?

Remember, to select an entire column, you click on its column heading when the mouse pointer is ⬇.

- **Delete the City, State, and ZIP Code columns.**
- **Select the Lookup Zip Code column.**
- **Click and hold the mouse button on the column heading.**

Additional Information

When the mouse pointer is ⇱, it indicates that you can drag to move the selection.

- **Drag the Lookup column to the left until a thick line is displayed between the Address and Home Phone columns.**
- **Release the mouse button.**
- **Best fit the Lookup Zip Code column.**

Your screen should be similar to Figure 3.11

Three fields deleted and replaced by lookup field

Column moved

Personal Data | Table1 | City/State/ZipCode

Employee ID	Last Name	First Name	Address	Lookup Zip Code	Home Phone	Gender	Birth Date		Add
00212	Schiff	Chad	235 N. Cactus Dr.	92122	(507) 555-0010	M	3/9/1962	(0)	
00617	Nichols	Cathy	75 Brooklea Dr.	92120-3741	(507) 555-0001	F	5/19/1965	(0)	
00907	Pennington	Mark	23 Mill Ave.	92120-3741	(507) 555-3333	M	7/7/1969	(0)	
01421	Spehr	Timothy	90 Royal Dr.	92121-3740	(507) 555-1038	M	9/9/1972	(0)	
03225	Morgan	Dan	564 S. Lemon Dr.	92121	(507) 555-5567	M	3/5/1975	(0)	
03406	Lopez	Mina	4290 E. Alameda Dr.	92121-3740	(507) 555-5050	F	2/25/1977	(0)	
03673	Walker	Aaron	76 Thomas Rd.	92123-2232	(507) 555-2222	M	8/1/1971	(0)	
03890	Thi	Erona	7867 Forest Ave.	92123-2232	(507) 555-1089	F	5/10/1976	(0)	
04321	Sabin	Greg	90 E. Rawhide Ave.	92122	(507) 555-4455	M	9/30/1977	(0)	
04731	Marchant	Roberta	564 Palm Avenue	92120-3741	(507) 555-6707	F	5/13/1980	(0)	
05015	Briggs	Scott	45 E. Camelback Rd.	92123-2232	(507) 555-9585	M	9/15/1978	(0)	
06000	Robertson	Kirk	832 S. William Ave.	92121	(507) 555-3730	M	4/5/1974	(0)	
07287	Roman	Anita	2348 S. Bala Dr.	92121-3740	(507) 555-9870	F	3/15/1981	(0)	
07450	Matsumoto	Tyrus	34 S. Onza Ave.	92122-1268	(507) 555-8372	M	6/23/1980	(0)	
07540	Pario	Ian	983 E. Carrage Ln.	92120-3741	(507) 555-2321	M	4/23/1975	(0)	
07550	Ernster	Barbara	1153 S. Wilson	92123-2232	(507) 555-3211	F	5/30/1971	(0)	
07650	Lamm	Chris	382 E. Ladonna Dr.	92121	(507) 555-8332	M	8/3/1975	(0)	
08000	Nelson	Samantha	2322 Trafalgar Ct.	92123-2232	(507) 555-0003	F	10/30/1974	(0)	
08391	Ruiz	Enrique	35 Palm St.	92122-1268	(507) 555-0091	M	12/10/1973	(0)	
08430	Smith	Brent	4321 Toledo St.	92123-2232	(507) 555-6464	M	11/4/1979	(0)	
09430	Robson	David	8584 Bryan Dr.	92123-2232	(507) 555-6666	M	12/5/1977	(0)	
11510	Sutton	Lisa	4389 S. Hayden Rd.	92121-0093	(507) 555-1950	F	6/14/1975	(0)	
11747	Lettow	Ryan	358 Maple Dr.	92121-3740	(507) 555-2805	M	11/15/1971	(0)	
12194	Polonsky	Mitch	8701 E. Sheridan	92120-3741	(507) 555-1018	M	3/13/1970	(0)	
12213	Young	Kim	89 College Ave.	92123-2232	(507) 555-1059	F	4/12/1980	(0)	
12230	Reddie	Suzanne	932 E. Parkway Dr.	92120-3741	(507) 555-1191	F	7/14/1978	(0)	
12247	Rath	Kathy	87 E. Aurora Ave.	92122-1268	(507) 555-9797	F	5/30/1978	(0)	
12258	Delano	Gordon	13101 N. Spindrift Dr.	92122-1268	(507) 555-8201	M	8/7/1979	(0)	
12366	Stacey	David	737 S. College Rd.	92122-1268	(507) 555-7784	M	9/30/1978	(0)	
12380	Thomas	Jessica	128 Marina Dr.	92123-2232	(507) 555-8513	F	1/22/1980	(0)	

Record: 1 of 70 No Filter Search

Datasheet View

Figure 3.11

Deleting a Table

Now that the Personal Data table is modified, you will delete the duplicate Table1.

1. Close all tables, saving changes when prompted.
   - Redisplay the Navigation pane.
   - Select Table1 and click Delete in the Records group of the Home tab.
   - Click Yes to confirm the deletion from all groups.

Another Method

You also could press Delete or choose Delete from the object's shortcut menu.

Your screen should be similar to Figure 3.12

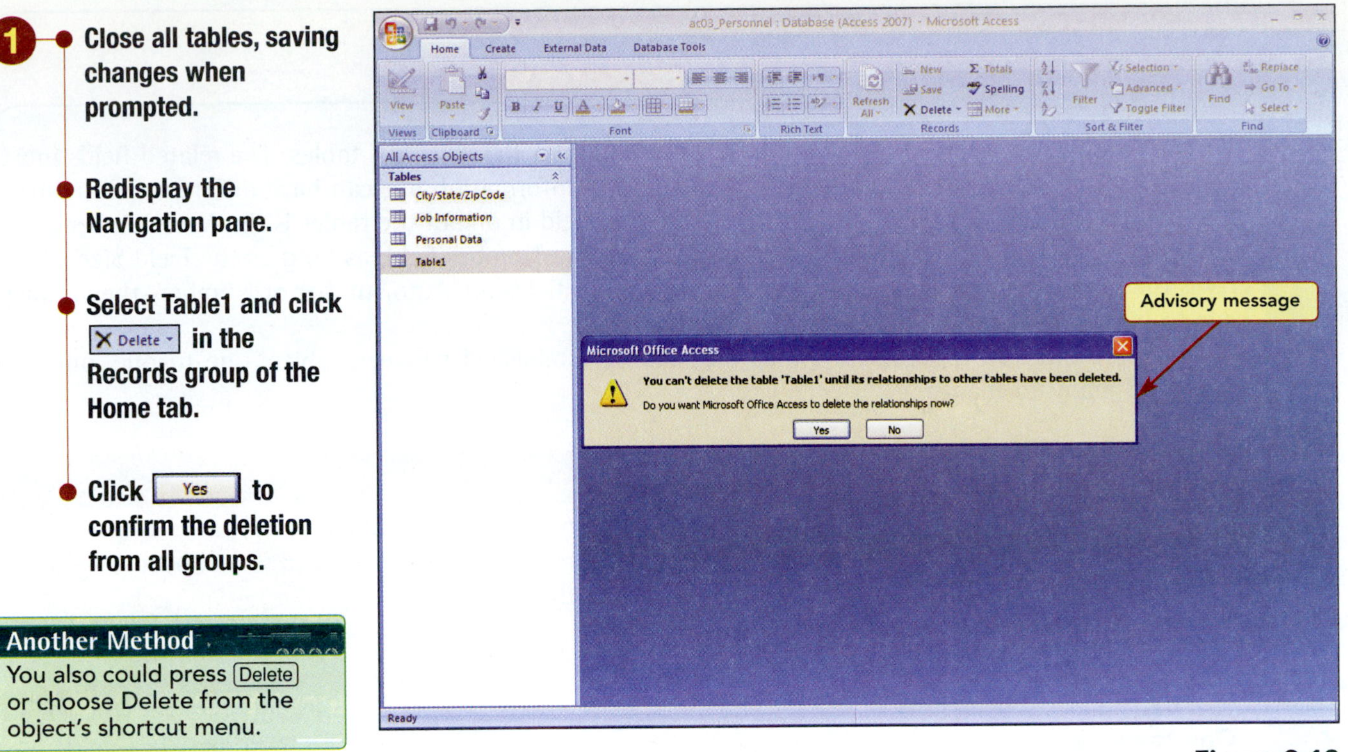

Figure 3.12

The advisory message warns that the table cannot be deleted until its relationships to other tables have been deleted. Rather than have the program remove the relationships for you, you will look at the relationships that have been created between all tables first.

2. Click No.
   - Click OK.

Defining and Modifying Relationships

The Relationships window is used to create and edit relationships.

1. Click Relationships in the Show/Hide group of the Database Tools tab.
   - Click All Relationships in the Relationships group of the Relationship Tools Design tab.

Your screen should be similar to Figure 3.13

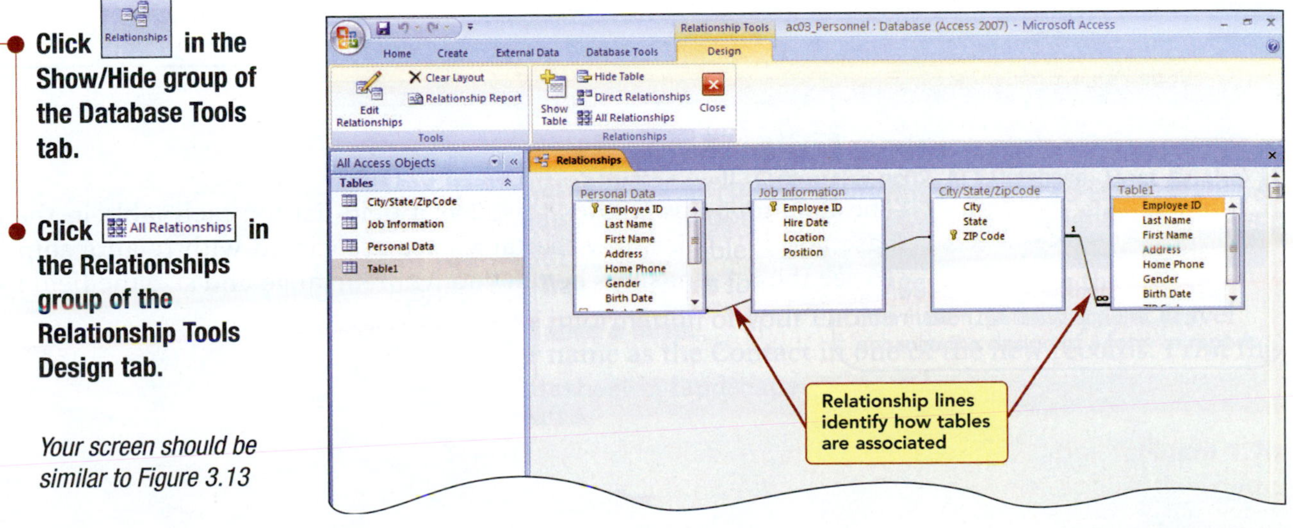

Figure 3.13

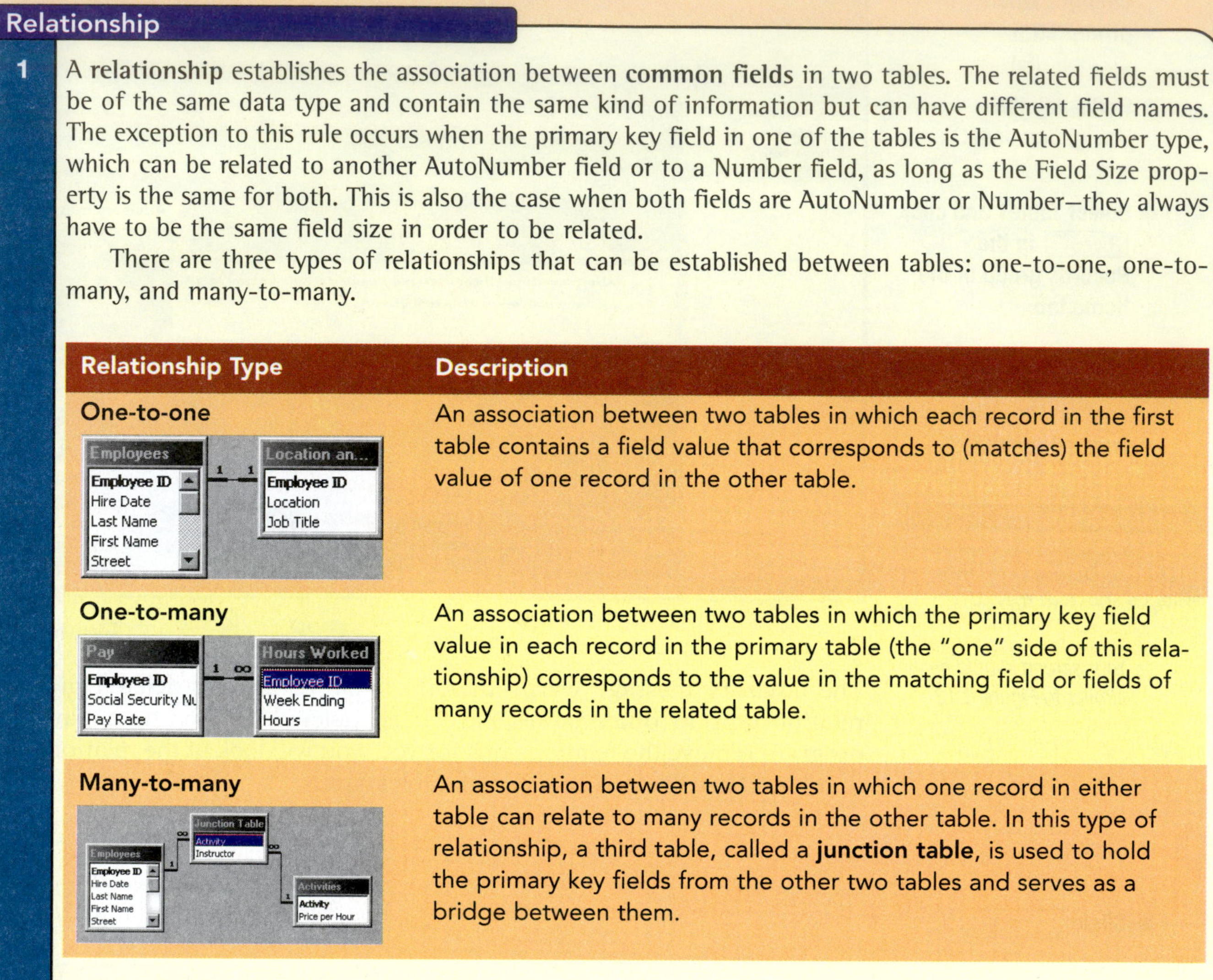

Concept 1

Relationship

1 A **relationship** establishes the association between **common fields** in two tables. The related fields must be of the same data type and contain the same kind of information but can have different field names. The exception to this rule occurs when the primary key field in one of the tables is the AutoNumber type, which can be related to another AutoNumber field or to a Number field, as long as the Field Size property is the same for both. This is also the case when both fields are AutoNumber or Number—they always have to be the same field size in order to be related.

There are three types of relationships that can be established between tables: one-to-one, one-to-many, and many-to-many.

Relationship Type	Description
One-to-one	An association between two tables in which each record in the first table contains a field value that corresponds to (matches) the field value of one record in the other table.
One-to-many	An association between two tables in which the primary key field value in each record in the primary table (the "one" side of this relationship) corresponds to the value in the matching field or fields of many records in the related table.
Many-to-many	An association between two tables in which one record in either table can relate to many records in the other table. In this type of relationship, a third table, called a **junction table**, is used to hold the primary key fields from the other two tables and serves as a bridge between them.

Once relationships are established, rules can be enforced, called the rules of **referential integrity**, to ensure that relationships between tables are valid and that related data is not accidentally changed or deleted. The rules ensure that a record in a primary table cannot be deleted if matching records exist in a related table, and a primary key value cannot be changed in the primary table if that record has related records.

Viewing Relationships

The Relationships window displays a field list for each table in the database and identifies how the tables are associated with relationship lines. To see the relationships better, you will rearrange and size the field lists in the window.

1 Click on the City/State/Zip Code field list title bar and drag the field list below the Job Information field list.

- Move the Table1 field list to the right of the City/State/ZipCode field list.

- Increase the length of the Personal Data field list so that all fields are displayed.

- Increase the length of the Table1 field list so that all fields are displayed.

Your screen should be similar to Figure 3.14

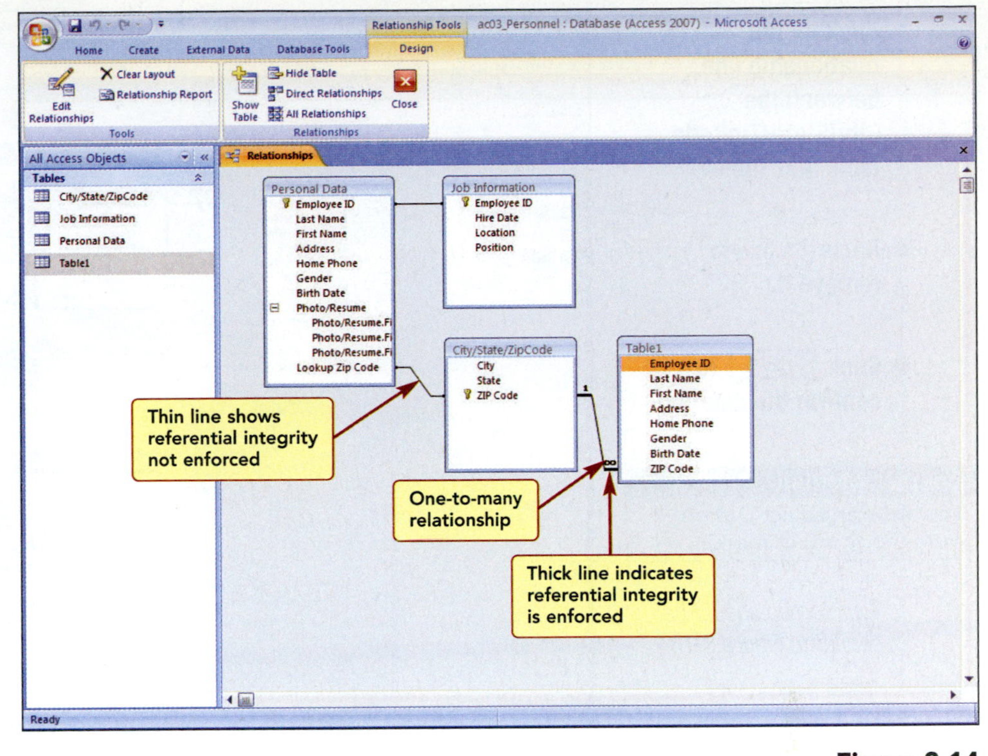

Figure 3.14

Now it is easier to follow the relationship lines. The Personal Data and the Job Information tables are related by the Employee ID fields and are connected by a thin relationship line. This relationship was established when you created the Job Information table by copying an existing field to a new table.

There is also a relationship between the Lookup Zip Code field and the ZIP Code field in the City/State/ZipCode table. A thin line between common fields shows the relationship does not support referential integrity.

The third relationship that exists is between the ZIP Code field in the City/State/ZipCode table and the ZIP Code field in Table1. This line is thicker at both ends, which indicates that referential integrity has been enforced. It also displays a 1 at one end of the line and an infinity symbol (∞) over the other end. This tells you the relationship is a one-to-many type relationship.

Deleting Relationships

The first relationship change you want to make is to remove the relationship between the City/State/ZipCode table and Table1 so that you can delete the table. To edit or delete a relationship, click on the relationship line to select it. It will appear thicker to show it is selected. Then it can be modified.

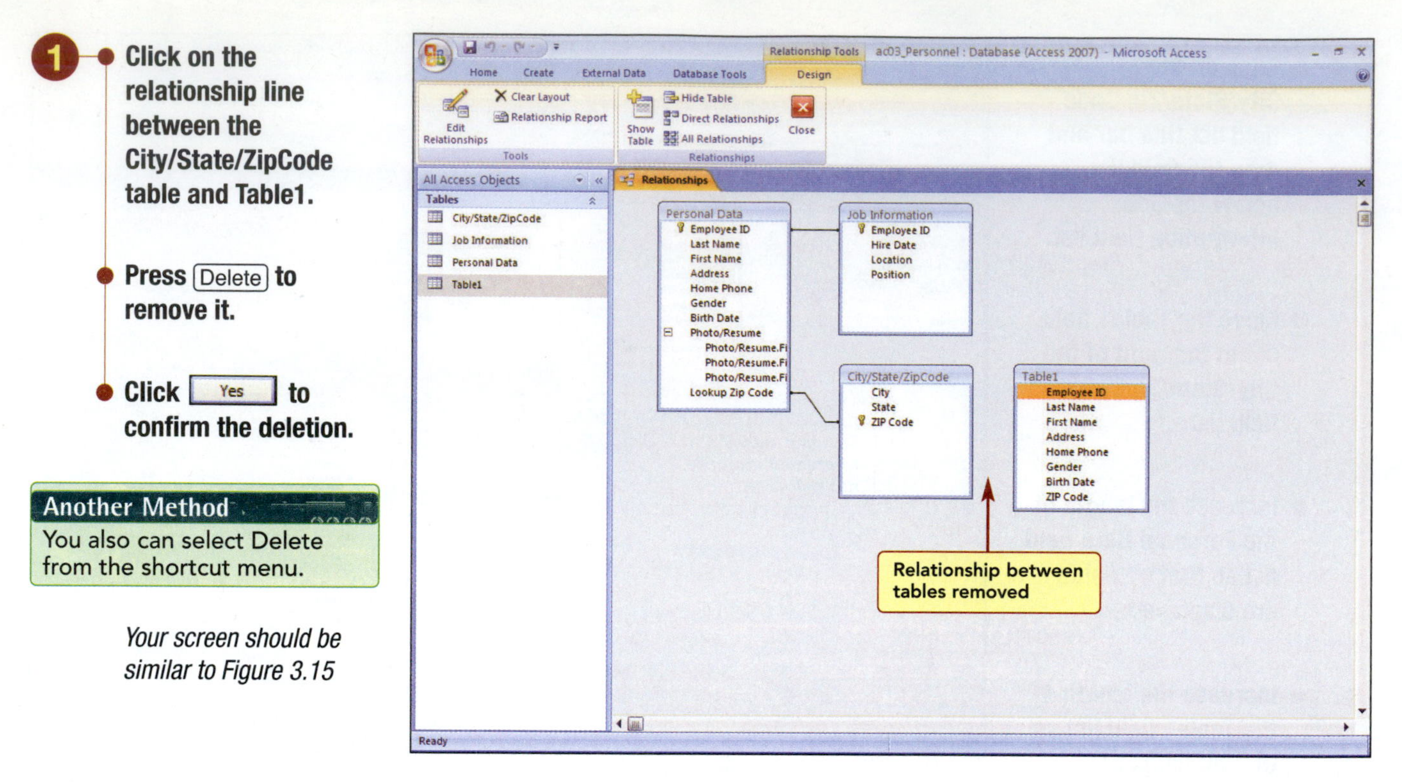

1 Click on the relationship line between the City/State/ZipCode table and Table1.

Press Delete to remove it.

Click Yes to confirm the deletion.

Another Method

You also can select Delete from the shortcut menu.

Your screen should be similar to Figure 3.15

Figure 3.15

The relationship line has been removed between the tables. Now you can delete the table.

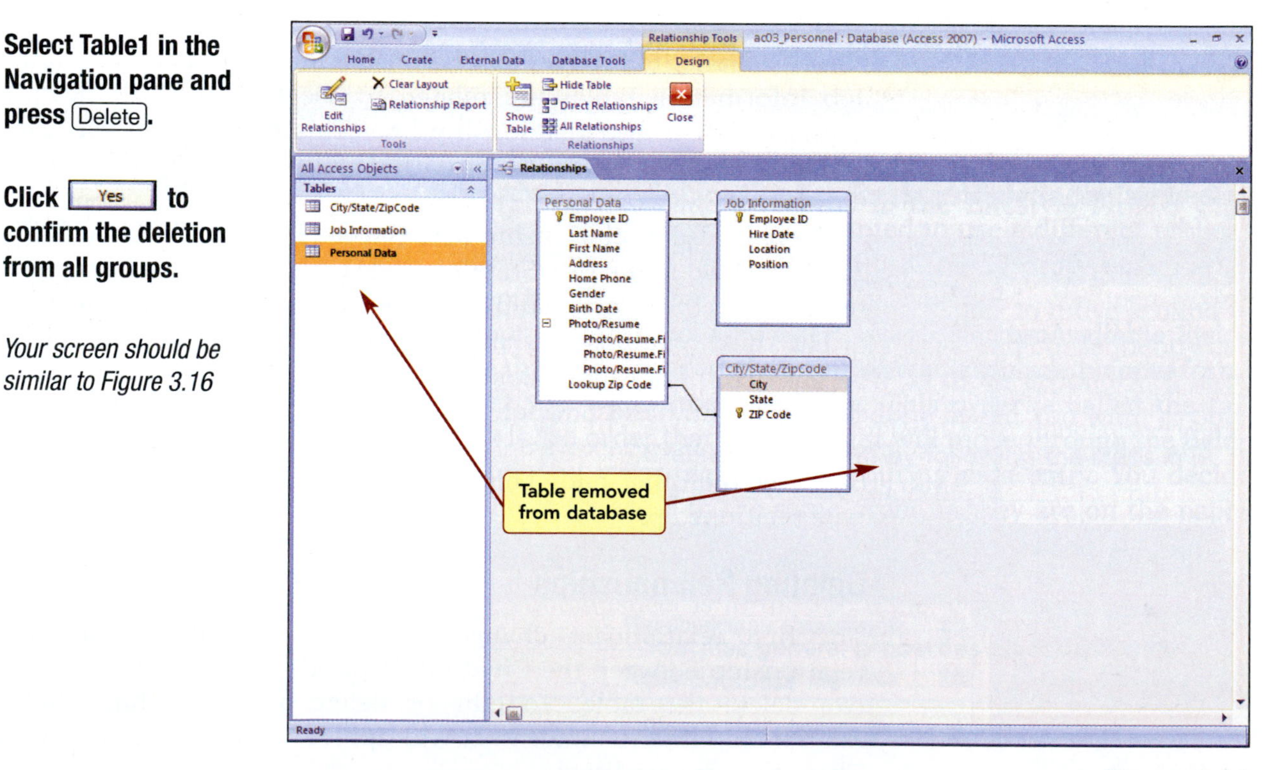

2 Select Table1 in the Navigation pane and press Delete.

Click Yes to confirm the deletion from all groups.

Your screen should be similar to Figure 3.16

Figure 3.16

The Table1 field list is removed from the Relationships window and the table object is removed from the Navigation pane, showing the table has been deleted from the database.

Enforcing Referential Integrity

Next, you want to change the relationship between the Employee ID fields to support referential integrity.

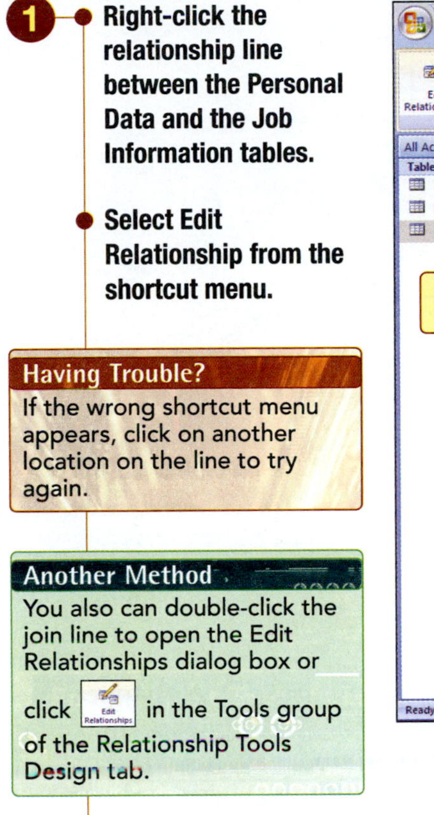

1

- **Right-click the relationship line between the Personal Data and the Job Information tables.**
- **Select Edit Relationship from the shortcut menu.**

Having Trouble?

If the wrong shortcut menu appears, click on another location on the line to try again.

Another Method

You also can double-click the join line to open the Edit Relationships dialog box or click [Edit Relationships] in the Tools group of the Relationship Tools Design tab.

- **Select Enforce Referential Integrity.**

Your screen should be similar to Figure 3.17

Figure 3.17

The Edit Relationships dialog box shows the tables and their current relationship. Selecting the Enforce Referential Integrity option also makes the Cascade Update and Cascade Delete options available. Selecting these options ensures that if you change a primary key or delete a record, all fields that reference the primary key of that record are likewise updated or deleted in both tables. This prevents inconsistent and orphaned records (records that do not have a matching primary key record in the associated table). You will select both these options. In addition, you can see the relationship type is one-to-one.

2

- **Choose Cascade Update Related Fields.**
- **Choose Cascade Delete Related Records.**
- **Click OK.**
- **Click on the Job Information field list to remove the selection from the relationship line.**

Your screen should be similar to Figure 3.18

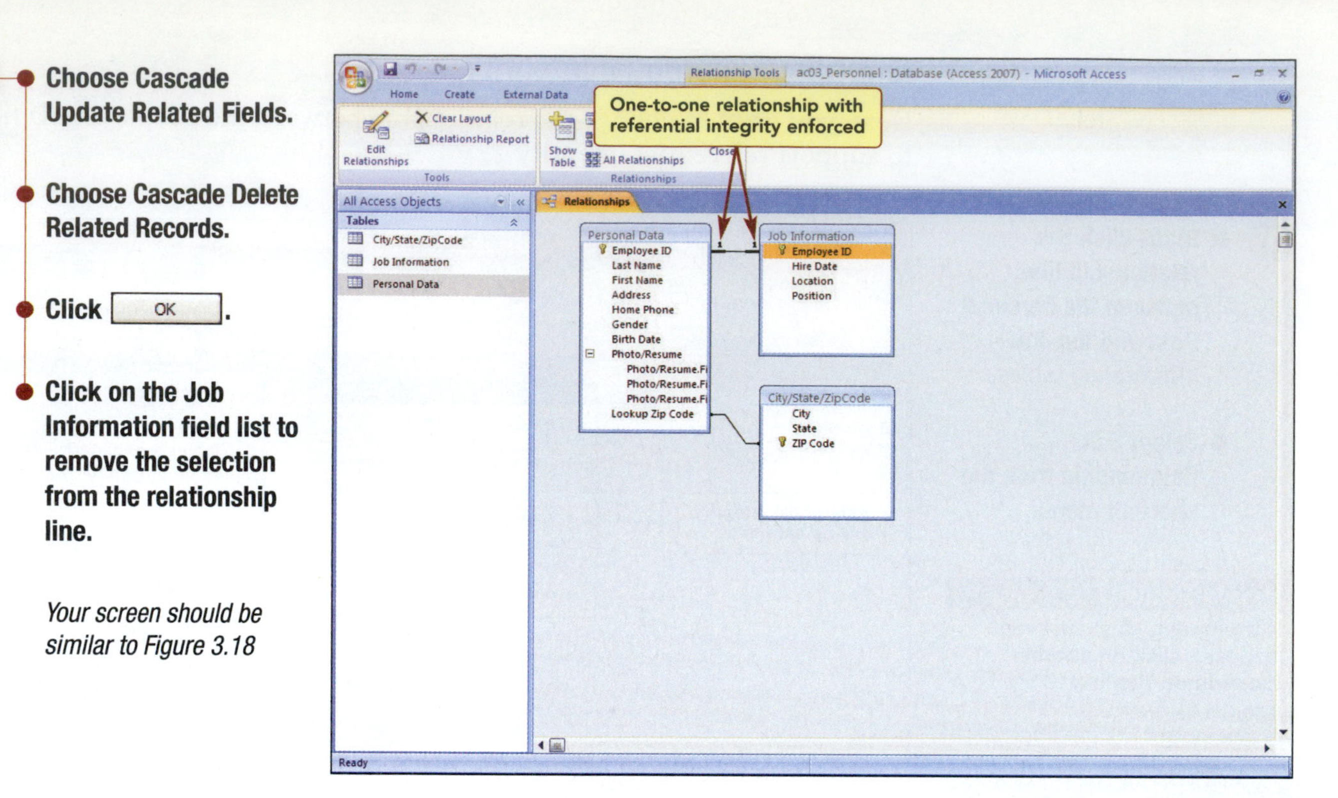

Figure 3.18

Once referential integrity is enforced, the relationship line changes and identifies the type of relationship. The relationship line appears thicker at each end indicating that referential integrity is enforced. Also, the type of relationship is identified. The number 1 next to each table above the relationship line shows a one-to-one relationship exists between these tables.

Creating a Relationship

Although the Lookup Zip Code relationship is already created, you will delete it and then create it again to learn how to create relationships. To do this, you drag the field that you want to relate from one table to the other related field in the other table.

1
- **Select and delete the ZIP Code relationship.**
- **Drag the Lookup Zip Code field from the Personal Data table to the ZIP Code field in the City/State/ZipCode table.**
- **Click Create.**

Your screen should be similar to Figure 3.19

Figure 3.19

The related tables again have a relationship line connecting them. The relationship type is one-to-many because there are many records in the Personal Data table that use the same zip code value and only one record in the City/State/ZipCode table for each zip code. Referential integrity was not enforced because you will want to remove records in the Personal Data table that have matching data in the City/State/ZIPCode table.

The tables in your database are now all related. Once referential integrity has been enforced, a warning message is automatically displayed if one of the rules is broken, and you are not allowed to complete the action you are trying to do.

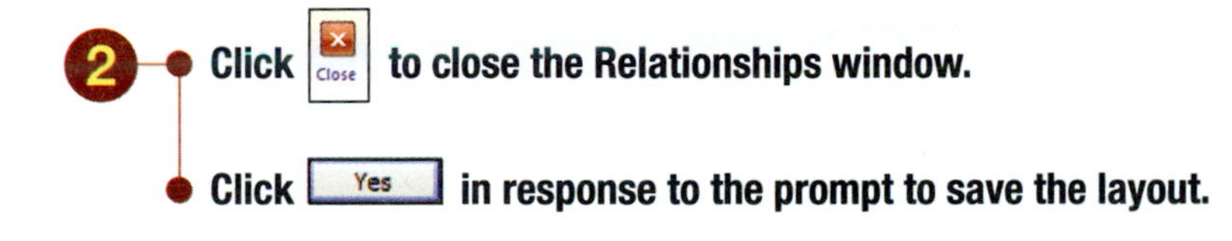

2
- **Click Close to close the Relationships window.**
- **Click Yes in response to the prompt to save the layout.**

The relationships and layout are saved.

Creating a Filter

Now you are ready to start gathering some information from the database again. You have added many more records to the database tables and you decide to continue working on the list of employees to help Juan create a car pool. Because the table no longer contains a separate City field, you will need to create a new filter using the ZIP Code field.

1. **Open the Personal Data table.**
   - **Open the Lookup Zip Code field's drop-down menu**
   - **Choose Select all to clear all the selections and then select only the 92121, 92121-0093, 92122, and 92122-1268 values.**
   - **Click OK.**

Your screen should be similar to Figure 3.20

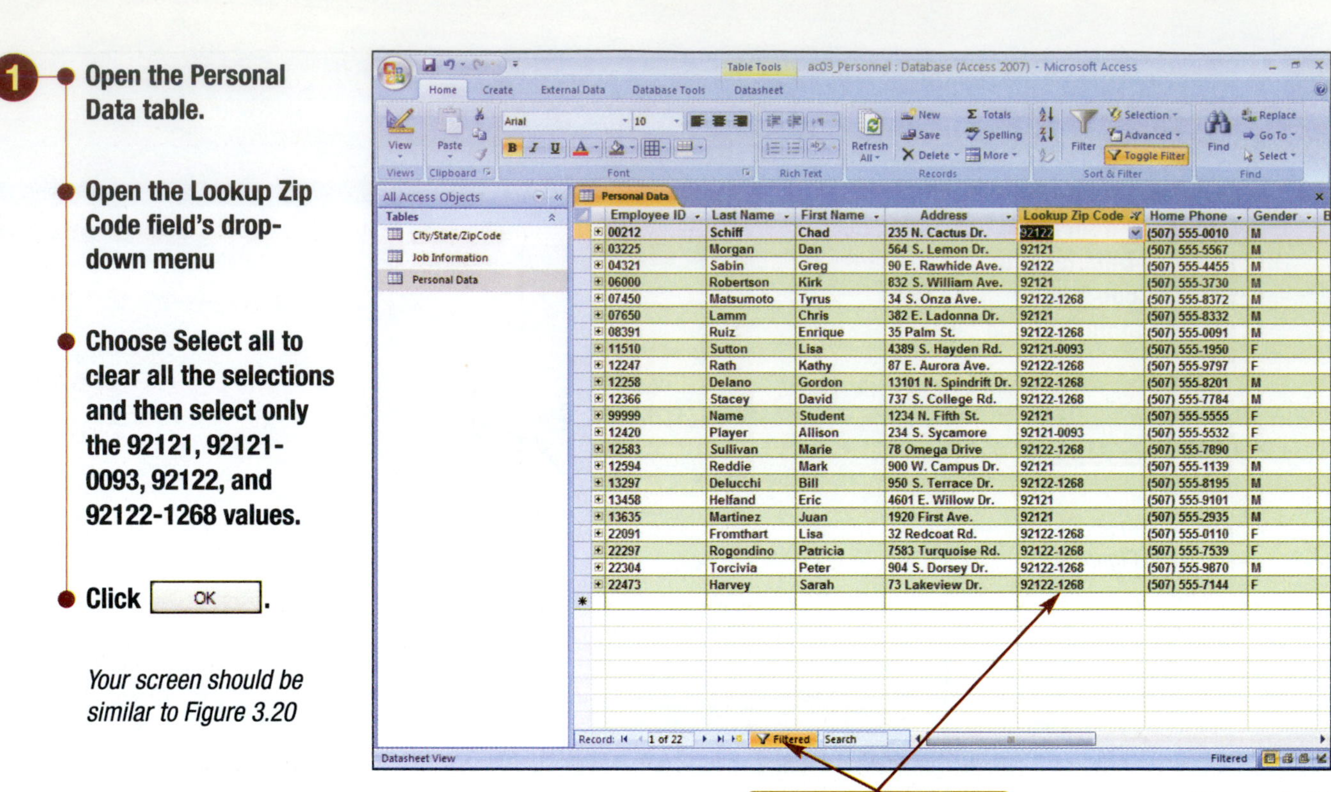

Employee ID	Last Name	First Name	Address	Lookup Zip Code	Home Phone	Gender
00212	Schiff	Chad	235 N. Cactus Dr.	92122	(507) 555-0010	M
03225	Morgan	Dan	564 S. Lemon Dr.	92121	(507) 555-5567	M
04321	Sabin	Greg	90 E. Rawhide Ave.	92122	(507) 555-4455	M
06000	Robertson	Kirk	832 S. William Ave.	92121	(507) 555-3730	M
07450	Matsumoto	Tyrus	34 S. Onza Ave.	92122-1268	(507) 555-8372	M
07650	Lamm	Chris	382 E. Ladonna Dr.	92121	(507) 555-8332	M
08391	Ruiz	Enrique	35 Palm St.	92122-1268	(507) 555-0091	M
11510	Sutton	Lisa	4389 S. Hayden Rd.	92121-0093	(507) 555-1950	F
12247	Rath	Kathy	87 E. Aurora Ave.	92122-1268	(507) 555-9797	F
12258	Delano	Gordon	13101 N. Spindrift Dr.	92122-1268	(507) 555-8201	M
12366	Stacey	David	737 S. College Rd.	92122-1268	(507) 555-7784	M
99999	Name	Student	1234 N. Fifth St.	92121	(507) 555-5555	F
12420	Player	Allison	234 S. Sycamore	92121-0093	(507) 555-5532	F
12583	Sullivan	Marie	78 Omega Drive	92122-1268	(507) 555-7890	F
12594	Reddie	Mark	900 W. Campus Dr.	92121	(507) 555-1139	M
13297	Delucchi	Bill	950 S. Terrace Dr.	92122-1268	(507) 555-8195	M
13458	Helfand	Eric	4601 E. Willow Dr.	92121	(507) 555-9101	M
13635	Martinez	Juan	1920 First Ave.	92121	(507) 555-2935	M
22091	Fromthart	Lisa	32 Redcoat Rd.	92122-1268	(507) 555-0110	F
22297	Rogondino	Patricia	7583 Turquoise Rd.	92122-1268	(507) 555-7539	F
22304	Torcivia	Peter	904 S. Dorsey Dr.	92122-1268	(507) 555-9870	M
22473	Harvey	Sarah	73 Lakeview Dr.	92122-1268	(507) 555-7144	F

Figure 3.20

Twenty-two records meet these criteria. However, the filtered datasheet still includes more information about each employee than Juan needs to contact people about car pooling.

Querying a Database

To obtain the exact information you need to give Juan for his car pool, you will use a query.

Concept 2

Query

2 A **query** is a request for specific data contained in a database. Queries are used to view data in different ways, to analyze data, and even to change existing data. Because queries are based on tables, you also can use a query as the source for forms and reports. The five types of queries are described in the following table.

Query Type	Description	
Select query	Retrieves the specific data you request from one or more tables, then displays the data in a query datasheet in the order you specify. This is the most common type of query.	
Crosstab query	Summarizes large amounts of data in an easy-to-read, row-and-column format.	
Parameter query	Displays a dialog box prompting you for information, such as the **criteria** for locating data. For example, a parameter query might request the beginning and ending dates, then display all records matching dates between the two specified values.	
Action query	Used to make changes to many records in one operation. There are four types of action queries:	
	Type	**Description**
	Make-table query	Creates a new table from selected data in one or more tables
	Update query	Makes update changes to records, when, for example, you need to raise salaries of all sales staff by 7 percent
	Append query	Adds records from one or more tables to the end of other tables
	Delete query	Deletes records from a table or tables
SQL query	Created using SQL (Structured Query Language), an advanced programming language used in Access.	

You will create a simple select query to obtain the results for the car pool. Creating a query adds a query object to the database file. It is a named object, just like a form, that can be opened, viewed, and modified at any time.

Using the Query Wizard

Query Design view or the Query Wizard can be used to create a query. The process is much like creating a table or form. You will first use the Query Wizard to guide you through the steps.

1 Click [Query Wizard] in the Other group of the Create tab.

- Click [Yes] in response to the prompt to save the table.

Your screen should be similar to Figure 3.21

Figure 3.21

From the New Query dialog box, you select the type of query you want to create using the wizard.

Query Wizard	Type of Query
Simple	Select query
Crosstab	Crosstab query
Find Duplicates	Locates all records that contain duplicate values in one or more fields in the specified tables
Find Unmatched	Locates records in one table that do not have records in another. For example, you could locate all employees in one table who have no hours worked in another table.

You will use the Simple Query Wizard to create a select query to see if it gives you the results you want.

2 • If necessary, select Simple Query Wizard.

• Click OK.

Your screen should be similar to Figure 3.22

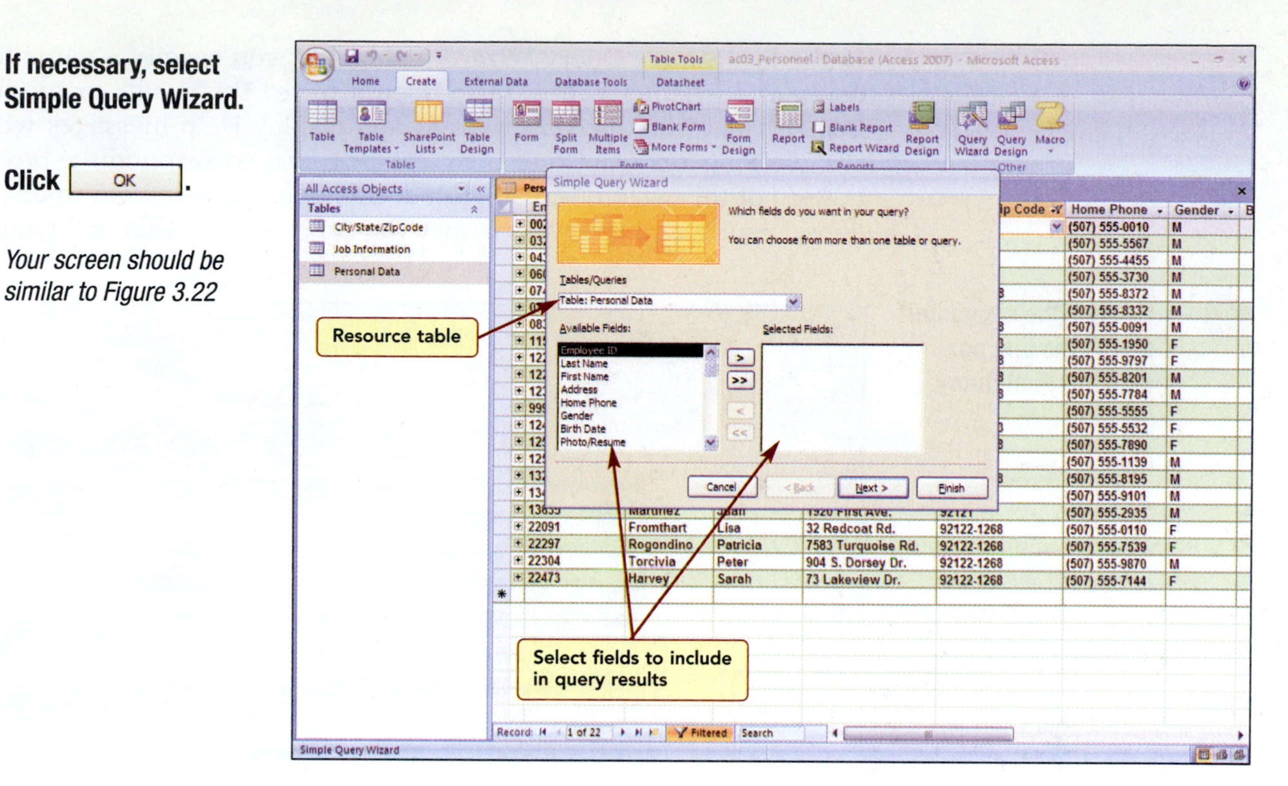

Figure 3.22

In the first Simple Query Wizard dialog box, you specify the resource table that will be used to supply the data and the fields that you want displayed in the query result, just as you did when creating a form. You will use the Personal Data table as the resource table and select the fields you want displayed in the query output.

3 • If necessary, select the Personal Data table from the Table/Queries drop-down list.

• Add the Last Name, First Name, Address, Home Phone, and Lookup Zip Code fields to the Selected Fields list.

Additional Information

The quickest way to add a field to the Selected Fields list is to double-click its field name in the Available Fields list.

• Click Next >.

Your screen should be similar to Figure 3.23

Enter descriptive name for query

Displays query results

Figure 3.23

In the last Simple Query Wizard dialog box, you specify a name for your query and whether you want to open it to see the results or modify it in Design view. You also can have Access display Help messages while you are working on your query by clicking the corresponding box at the bottom of this wizard screen. You decide that you just want to display the query results, and you want to give the query a name that will identify it.

4 **Replace the suggested title in the text box with Car Pool Query.**

Click Finish.

Your screen should be similar to Figure 3.24

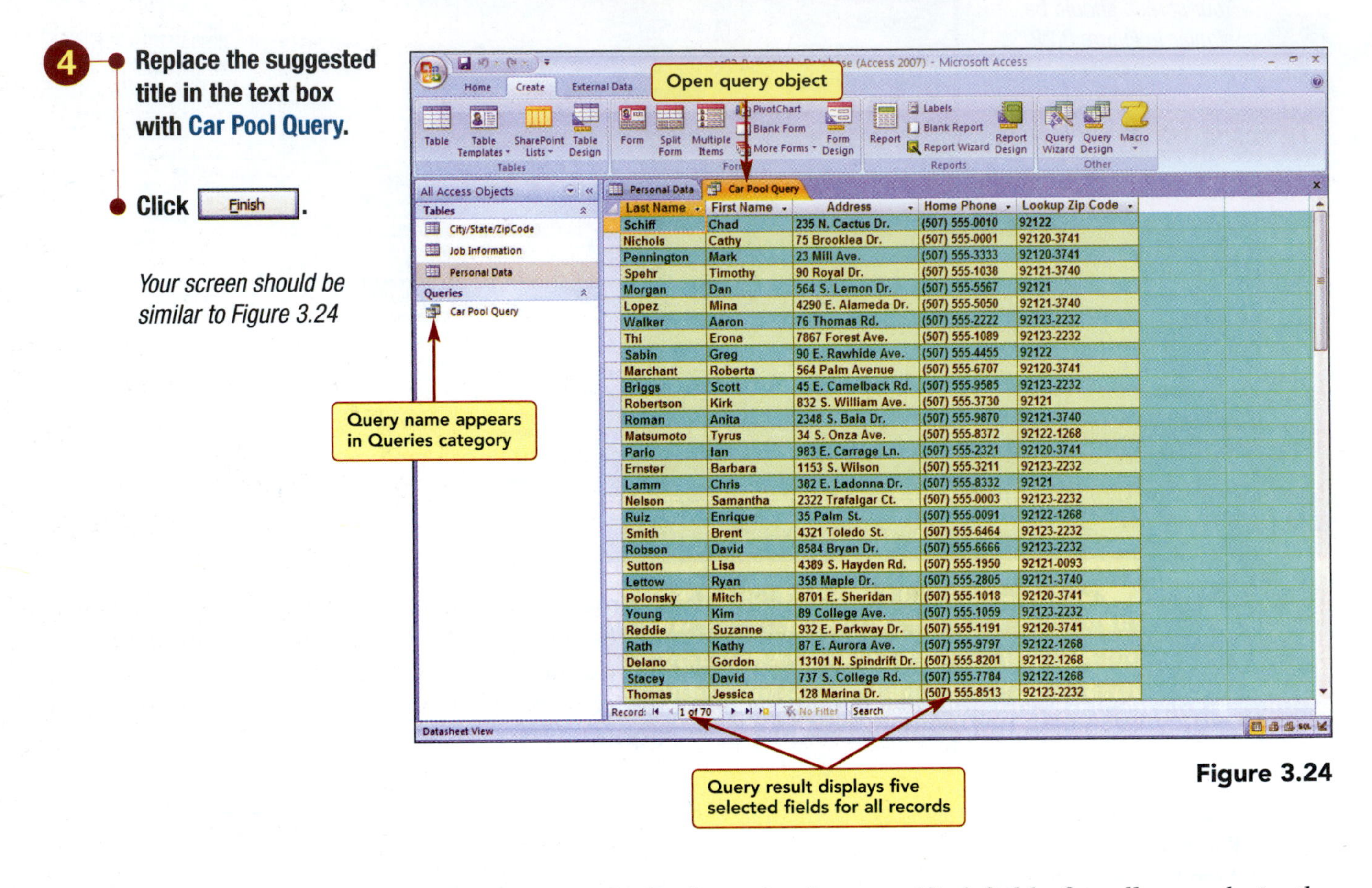

Figure 3.24

The query result displays the five specified fields for all records in the table in a new query datasheet object. The object's tab displays the query name. The Navigation pane also displays the name of the new query object in the Queries category.

Filtering a Query

Although the query result displays only the fields you want to see, it includes all the records in the table. To display only those records in the zip code areas needed for Juan, you can filter the query results. The filter criteria are available with the Personal Data table only and need to be recreated to apply to the query results.

Filter the query to display only records with zip codes of 92121, 92121-0093, 92122, and 92122-1268.

Your screen should be similar to Figure 3.25

Last Name	First Name	Address	Home Phone	Lookup Zip Code
Schiff	Chad	235 N. Cactus Dr.	(507) 555-0010	92122
Morgan	Dan	564 S. Lemon Dr.	(507) 555-5567	92121
Sabin	Greg	90 E. Rawhide Ave.	(507) 555-4455	92122
Robertson	Kirk	832 S. William Ave.	(507) 555-3730	92121
Matsumoto	Tyrus	34 S. Onza Ave.	(507) 555-8372	92122-1268
Lamm	Chris	382 E. Ladonna Dr.	(507) 555-8332	92121
Ruiz	Enrique	35 Palm St.	(507) 555-0091	92122-1268
Sutton	Lisa	4389 S. Hayden Rd.	(507) 555-1950	92121-0093
Rath	Kathy	87 E. Aurora Ave.	(507) 555-9797	92122-1268
Delano	Gordon	13101 N. Spindrift Dr.	(507) 555-8201	92122-1268
Stacey	David	737 S. College Rd.	(507) 555-7784	92122-1268
Name	Student	1234 N. Fifth St.	(507) 555-5555	92121
Player	Allison	234 S. Sycamore	(507) 555-5532	92121-0093
Sullivan	Marie	78 Omega Drive	(507) 555-7890	92122-1268
Reddie	Mark	900 W. Campus Dr.	(507) 555-1139	92121
Delucchi	Bill	950 S. Terrace Dr.	(507) 555-8195	92122-1268
Helfand	Eric	4601 E. Willow Dr.	(507) 555-9101	92121
Martinez	Juan	1920 First Ave.	(507) 555-2935	92121
Fromthart	Lisa	32 Redcoat Rd.	(507) 555-0110	92122-1268
Rogondino	Patricia	7583 Turquoise Rd.	(507) 555-7539	92122-1268
Torcivia	Peter	904 S. Dorsey Dr.	(507) 555-9870	92122-1268
Harvey	Sarah	73 Lakeview Dr.	(507) 555-7144	92122-1268

Filtered query results

Switches to Query Design view

Figure 3.25

Now the Car Pool Query results display the same 22 records as the filtered Personal Data table. Although these results are closer to what you need, you are still not satisfied. You want the results to display the city as well as the zip code. Additionally, it does not tell you which employees work at the Landis location. To make these refinements to the query, you need to use Query Design view.

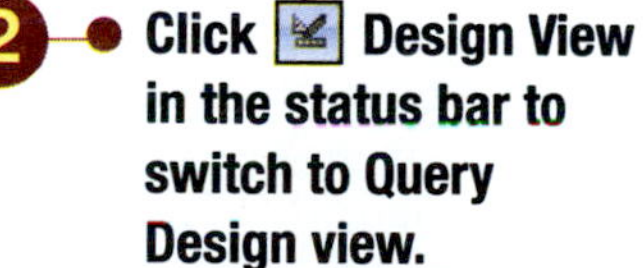

Click Design View in the status bar to switch to Query Design view.

Your screen should be similar to Figure 3.26

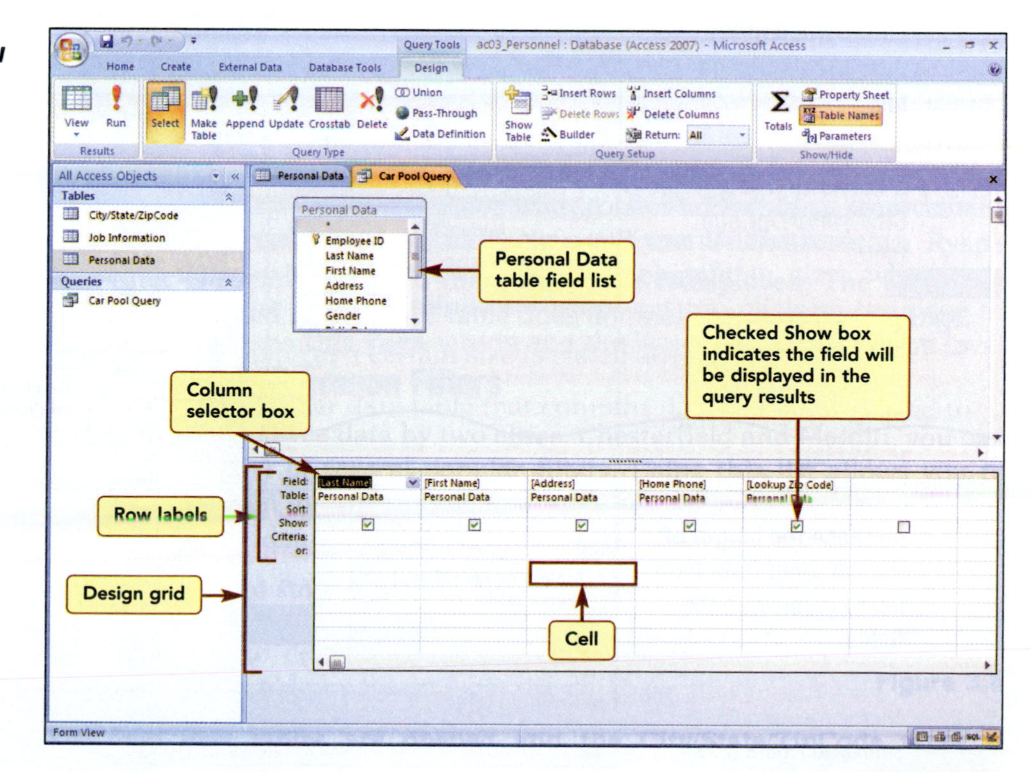

Figure 3.26

Using Query Design View

Query Design view can be used to create a new query as well as modify the structure of an existing query. This view automatically displays the Query Tools Design tab, which contains commands that are used to create, modify, and run queries.

Query Design view is divided into two areas. The upper area displays a list box of all the fields in the selected table. This is called the **field list.** The lower portion of the window displays the **design grid** where you enter the settings that define the query. Each column in the grid holds the information about each field to be included in the query datasheet. The design grid automatically displays the fields that are specified when a query is created using a Query Wizard.

Above the field names is a narrow bar called the **column selector bar,** which is used to select an entire column. Each **row label** identifies the type of information that can be entered. The intersection of a column and row creates a cell where you enter expressions to obtain the query results you need.

The boxes in the Show row are called Show boxes. The **Show box** for a field lets you specify whether you want that field displayed in the query result. A checked box indicates that the field will be displayed; an unchecked box means that it will not.

Adding a Second Table to the Query

To display the city information for each employee in the query results, you need to add the City/State/ZipCode table to the query design. A query that uses information from two or more tables to get the results is called a **multitable query.**

1

- **Click Show Table in the Query Setup group of the Query Tools Design tab.**
- **If necessary, select the City/State/ZipCode table.**
- **Click Add.**
- **Close the Show Table dialog box.**
- **Increase the length of the Personal Data field list to display all the fields.**

Your screen should be similar to Figure 3.27

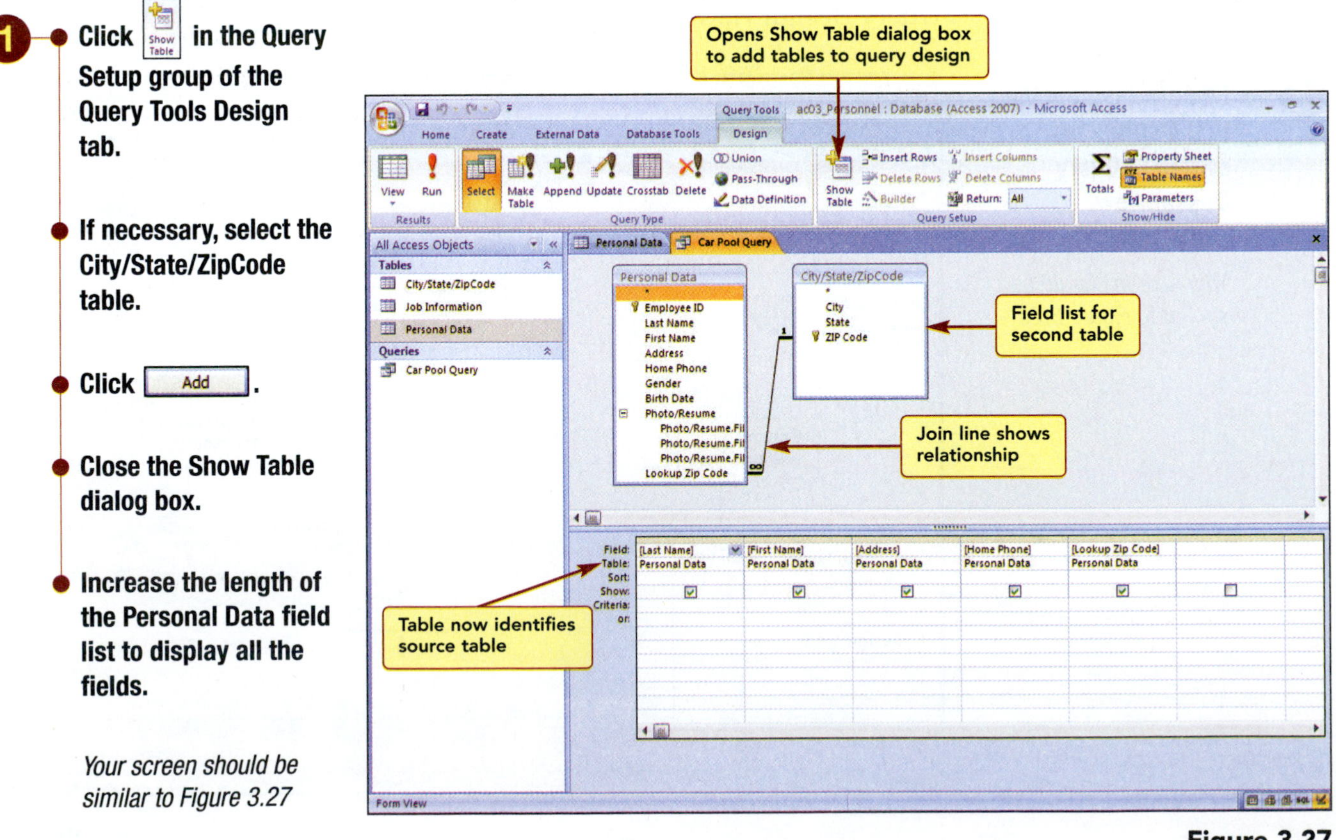

Figure 3.27

The field list for the second table has been added to the Query Design window. When multiple tables are added to a query, Access automatically creates joins between the tables.

Concept 3

Join

3

A **join** is an association that is created in a query between a field in one table or query and a field of the same data type in another table or query. The join is based on the relationships that have already been defined between tables. A **join line** between the field lists identifies the fields on which the relationship is based.

If a table did not already have a relationship defined, a join would be created between common fields in the tables if one of the common fields is a primary key. If the common fields have different names, however, Access does not automatically create the join. In those cases, you would create the join between the tables using the same procedure that is used to create table relationships.

The difference between a relationship line and a join line in a query is that the join line creates a temporary relationship that establishes rules that the data must match to be included in the query results. Joins also specify that each pair of rows that satisfy the join conditions will be combined in the results to form a single row.

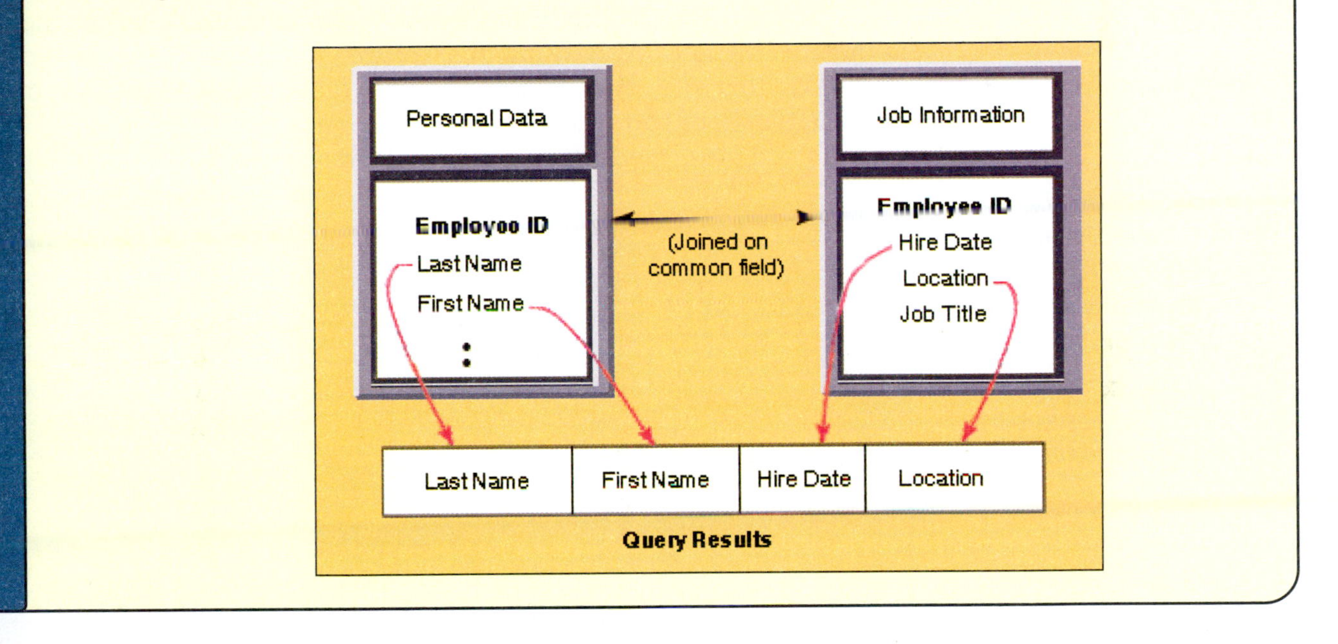

Having Trouble?

If the Table row is not displayed, click Table Names in the Show/Hide group.

MORE ABOUT

Sometimes you may want to add a second copy of the same table to a query. To learn how to do this, see "4 Creating and Modifying Queries" in the More About appendix.

In this case, the join line correctly indicates that the two tables are related and that the ZIP Code is the common field.

Additionally a Table row has been added to the grid. It displays the name of the table from which each field is selected.

Adding Fields

You want the query results to display the City information for each record. To do this, you need to add the City field from the City/State/ZipCode field list to the design grid. You can use the following methods to add fields to the design grid:

- Select the field name and drag it from the field list to the grid. To select several adjacent fields, press ⇧Shift while you click the field names. To select nonadjacent fields, press Ctrl while clicking the field names. To select all fields, double-click the field list title bar. You can then drag all the selected fields into the grid, and Access will place each field in a separate column.

- Double-click on the field name. The field is added to the next available column in the grid.

- Select the Field cell drop-down arrow in the grid, and then choose the field name.

In addition, if you select the asterisk in the field list and add it to the grid, Access displays the table or query name in the field row followed by a period and asterisk. This indicates that all fields in the table will be included in the query results. Also, using this feature will automatically include any new fields that may later be added to the table, and will exclude deleted fields. You cannot sort records or specify criteria for fields, however, unless you also add those fields individually to the design grid.

1 Double-click City in the City/State/ZipCode field list to add it to the grid.

Your screen should be similar to Figure 3.28

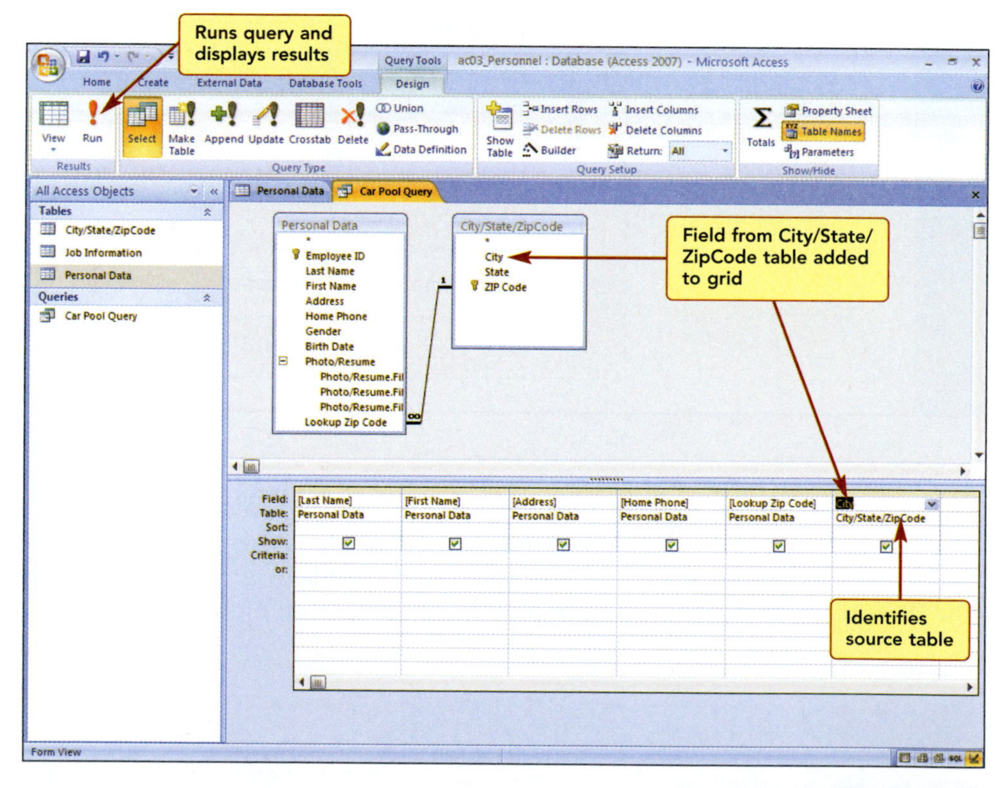

Figure 3.28

Notice the Table row displays the name of the table from which the City field was drawn. Sometimes when multiple tables are specified in a query, they have fields with the same names. For example, two tables may have fields named Address; however, the address in one table may be a personal address and the other table may be a business address. It is important to select the appropriate field from a table that contains the data you want to appear in the query. The Table row makes it clear from which table a field was drawn.

Now, you want to see the query results. To do this, you run the query.

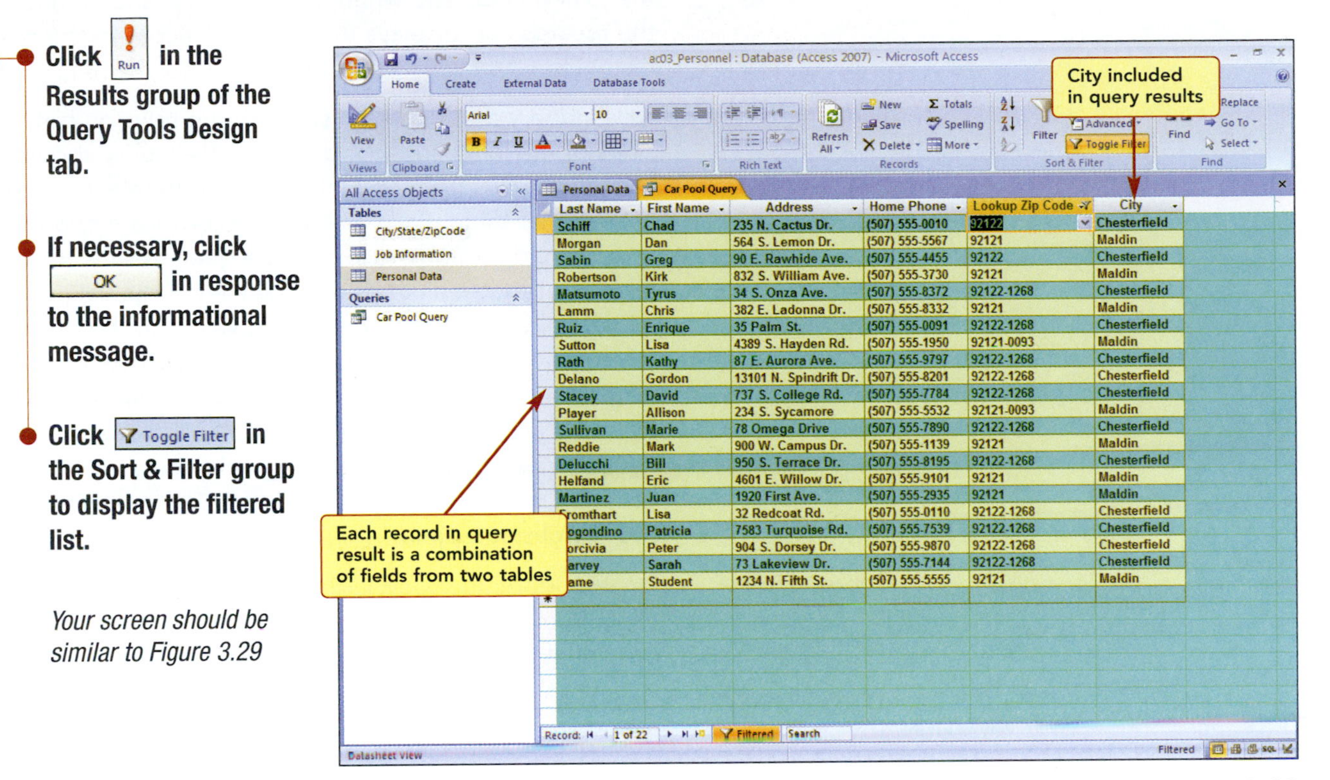

2

- **Click [Run] in the Results group of the Query Tools Design tab.**
- **If necessary, click [OK] in response to the informational message.**
- **Click [Toggle Filter] in the Sort & Filter group to display the filtered list.**

Your screen should be similar to Figure 3.29

Figure 3.29

The city for each record is displayed in the results. Now, each record in the query result datasheet includes information from both tables. This is because of the type of join used in the query. There are three basic types of joins, as described in the following table.

Join Type	Description
Inner join	Tells a query that rows from one of the joined tables corresponds to rows in the other table on the basis of the data in the joined fields. Checks for matching values in the joined fields and when it finds matches, combines the records and displays them as one record in the query results.
Outer join	Tells a query that although some of the rows on both sides of the join correspond exactly, the query should include all rows from one table even if there is no match in the other table. Each matching record from two tables is combined into one record in the query results. One table contributes all of its records even if the values in its joined field do not match the field values in the other table. Outer joins can be left outer joins or right outer joins. In a query with a left outer join, all rows in the left table are included in the results and only those rows from the other table where the joining field contains values common to both tables are included. The reverse is true with a right outer join.
Unequal joins	Records to be included in the query results are based on the value in one join field being greater than, less than, not equal to, greater than or equal to, or less than or equal to the value in the other join field.

MORE ABOUT

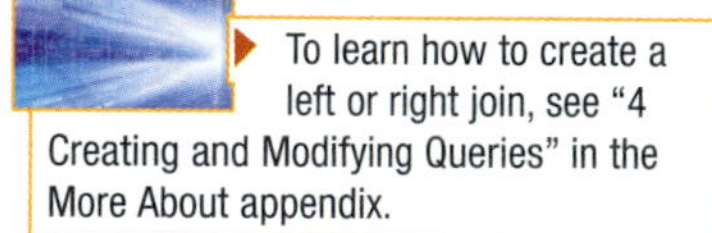

To learn how to create a left or right join, see "4 Creating and Modifying Queries" in the More About appendix.

In a query, the default join type is an inner join. In this case, it checked for matching values in the ZIP Code fields, combined matching records, and displayed them as one record in the query result.

Additionally, by applying the filter, only those records meeting the filter criteria are displayed.

Each time you run the query, you would need to reapply the filter. Rather than do this, you can specify the criteria in the query design and they would automatically be used each time the query is run.

Specifying Criteria

Additional Information
Refer to Lab 2 for a review of expressions and operators.

The Criteria row is used to enter the criteria expression (field value or values) and a comparison operator. A **criteria expression** is an expression that will select only records that meet certain limiting criteria. First, you will enter criteria in the City field to locate and display only those records where the city is Maldin. In the Criteria row of the City column, you will enter the criteria expression to select only those records. It is not necessary to enter = (equal to) in the criteria, because it is the assumed comparison operator.

1 **Click Design View.**

- **Move to the City Criteria cell.**
- **Type Maldin.**

Additional Information

The criteria expression is not case-sensitive.

- **Press ←Enter.**

Another Method

As with other Access tables and forms, you can use ←Enter, Tab, and the arrow keys to move from cell to cell in the Query Design grid.

Your screen should be similar to Figure 3.30

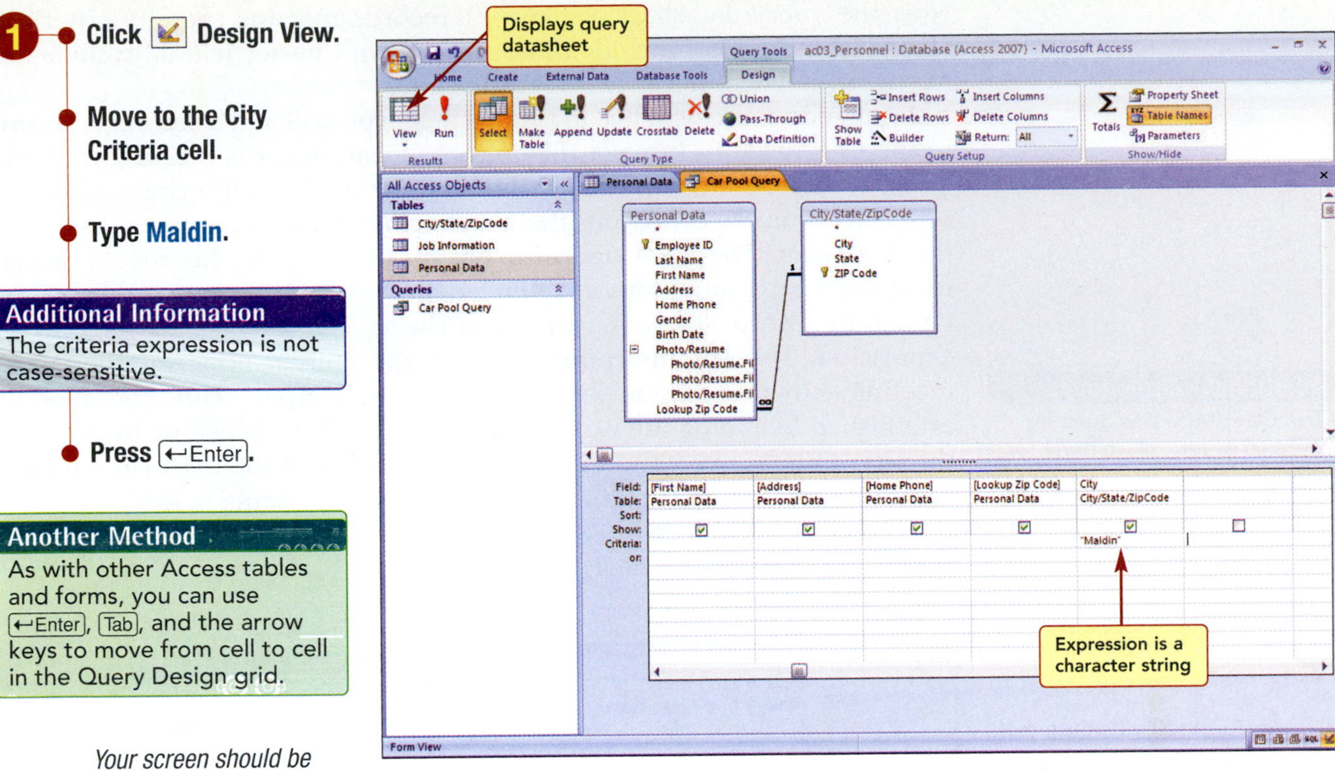

Figure 3.30

The expression is enclosed in quotation marks because it is a character string. To display the query results, you will run the query. Another way to run a query is to change to Datasheet view.

2 **Click Datasheet View.**

- **If necessary, click OK in response to the informational message.**

Your screen should be similar to Figure 3.31

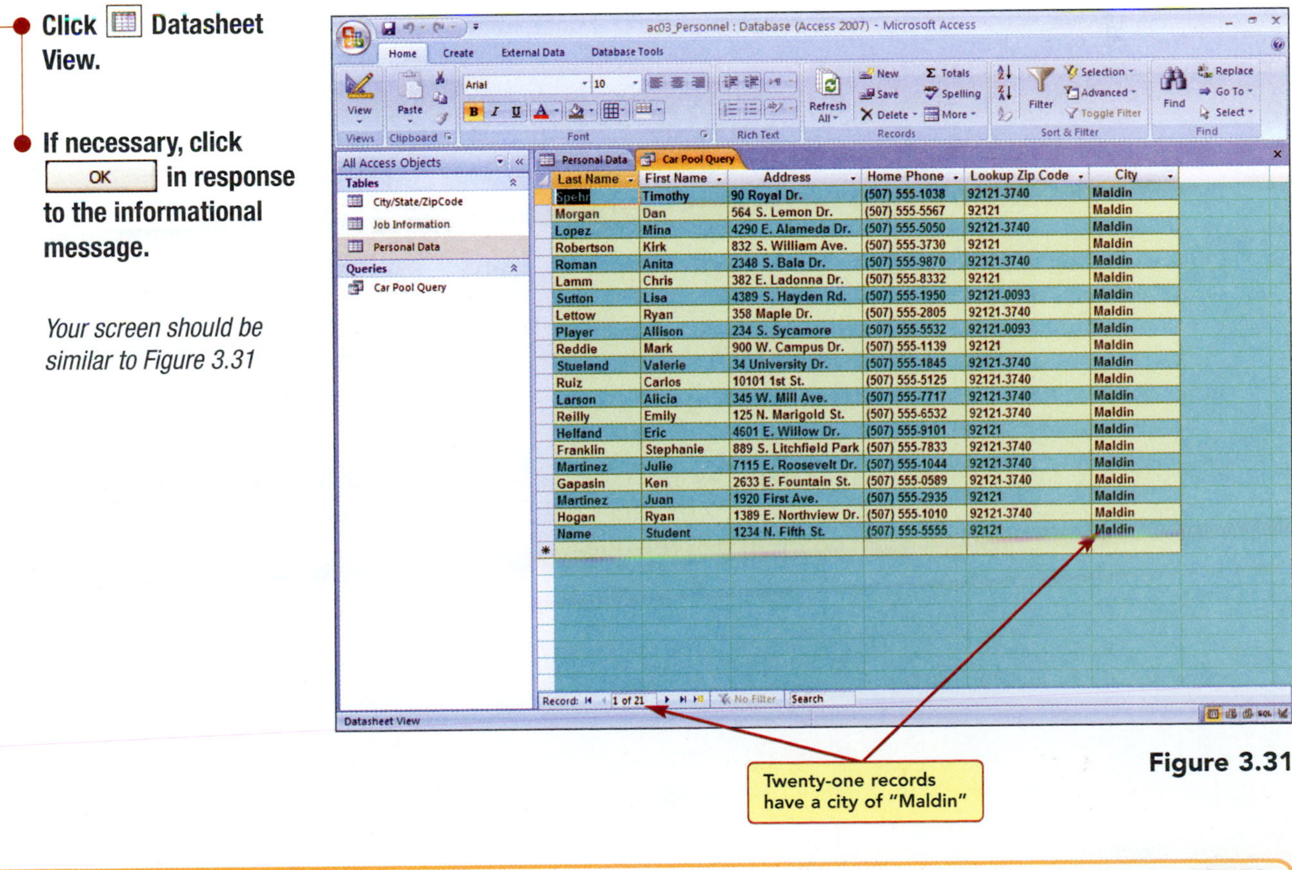

Figure 3.31

Now the query datasheet displays 21 records meeting the city criterion. However, it does not include those who live in Chesterfield or exclude the people who live in the 92121-3740 zip code.

To include those who live in Chesterfield, you will add a second criterion to the City field. To instruct the query to locate records meeting multiple criteria, you use a **compound criterion.** The AND or OR criterion is used to specify multiple conditions that must be met for the records to display in the datasheet. The **AND operator** narrows the search, because a record must meet both conditions to be included. This condition is established by typing the word "and" in a field's Criteria cell as part of its criteria expression. The **OR operator** broadens the search, because any record meeting either condition is included in the output. This condition is established by typing the word "or" in a field's Criteria cell or by entering the first criteria expression in the first Criteria cell for the field, and the second expression in the Or criteria row cell for the same field.

Additional Information

The Or criteria row must be used to enter "or" criteria for different fields.

Because you want to display the records for employees who live in either city, you will use the OR operator.

3 **Switch to Design view.**

- **In the City Criteria cell, continue the criteria by typing or Chesterfield.**
- **Press ←Enter.**

Another Method

You also could type Chesterfield in the Or cell of the City column.

Your screen should be similar to Figure 3.32

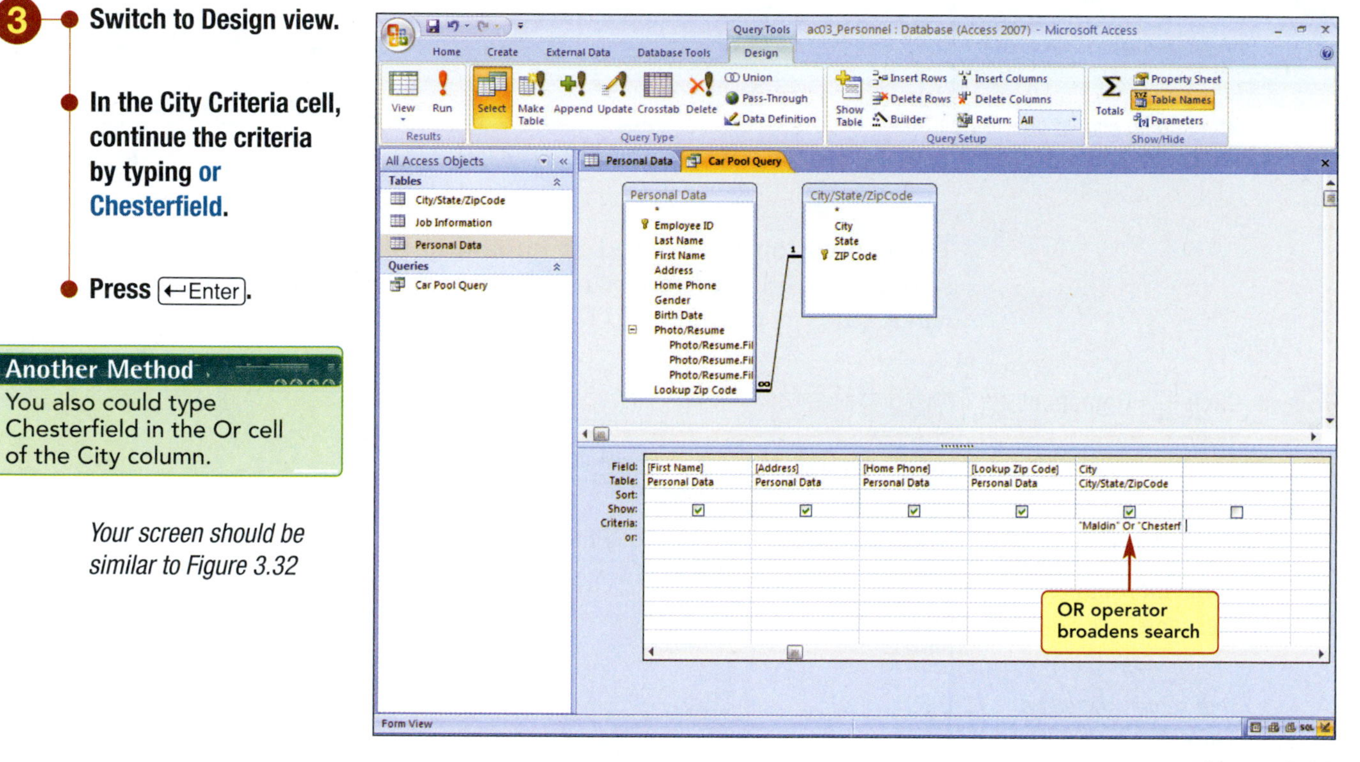

Figure 3.32

"Chesterfield" is now set as the Or condition. Next you will enter the criteria in the ZIP Code field to exclude the zip code of 92121-3740 and then you will run the query.

4 • Enter <>92121-3740 in the LookUp Zip Code criteria cell.

• Run the query.

• If necessary, click OK in response to the informational message.

> **Additional Information**
> If an expression is entered incorrectly, an informational box that indicates the source of the error will be displayed when the query is run.

Your screen should be similar to Figure 3.33

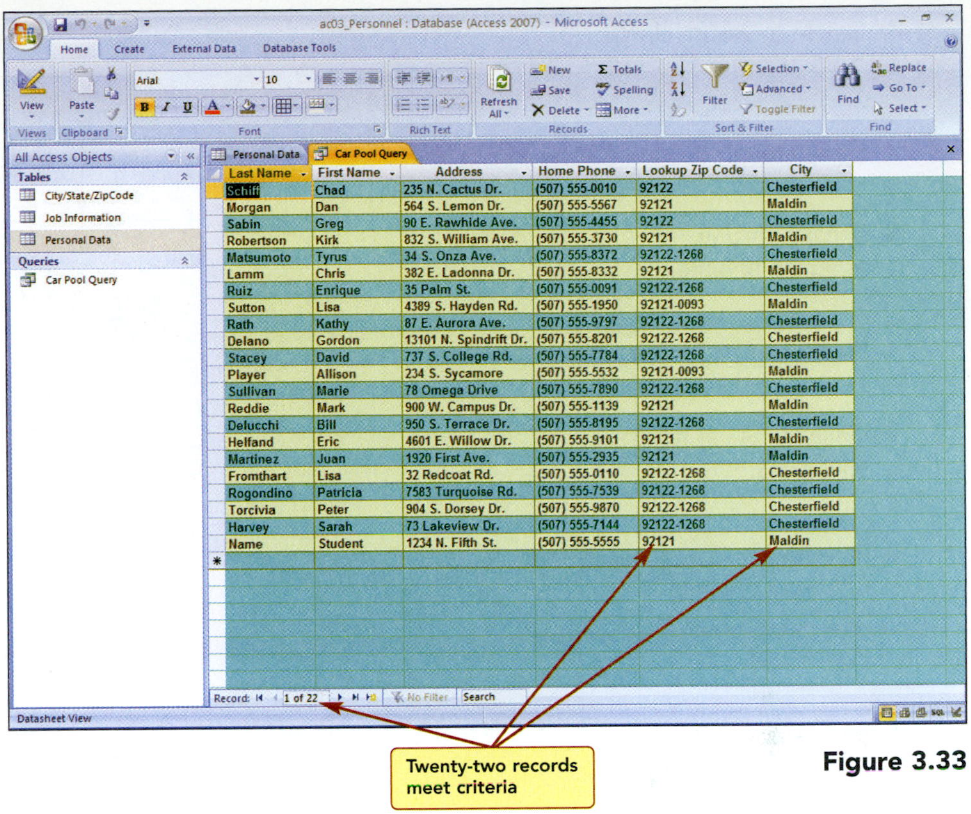

ac03_Personnel : Database (Access 2007) - Microsoft Access

Home | Create | External Data | Database Tools

All Access Objects

Tables: City/State/ZipCode; Job Information; Personal Data

Queries: Car Pool Query

Personal Data | Car Pool Query

Last Name	First Name	Address	Home Phone	Lookup Zip Code	City
Schiff	Chad	235 N. Cactus Dr.	(507) 555-0010	92122	Chesterfield
Morgan	Dan	564 S. Lemon Dr.	(507) 555-5567	92121	Maldin
Sabin	Greg	90 E. Rawhide Ave.	(507) 555-4455	92122	Chesterfield
Robertson	Kirk	832 S. William Ave.	(507) 555-3730	92121	Maldin
Matsumoto	Tyrus	34 S. Onza Ave.	(507) 555-8372	92122-1268	Chesterfield
Lamm	Chris	382 E. Ladonna Dr.	(507) 555-8332	92121	Maldin
Ruiz	Enrique	35 Palm St.	(507) 555-0091	92122-1268	Chesterfield
Sutton	Lisa	4389 S. Hayden Rd.	(507) 555-1950	92121-0093	Maldin
Rath	Kathy	87 E. Aurora Ave.	(507) 555-9797	92122-1268	Chesterfield
Delano	Gordon	13101 N. Spindrift Dr.	(507) 555-8201	92122-1268	Chesterfield
Stacey	David	737 S. College Rd.	(507) 555-7784	92122-1268	Chesterfield
Player	Allison	234 S. Sycamore	(507) 555-5532	92121-0093	Maldin
Sullivan	Marie	78 Omega Drive	(507) 555-7890	92122-1268	Chesterfield
Reddie	Mark	900 W. Campus Dr.	(507) 555-1139	92121	Maldin
Delucchi	Bill	950 S. Terrace Dr.	(507) 555-8195	92122-1268	Chesterfield
Helfand	Eric	4601 E. Willow Dr.	(507) 555-9101	92121	Maldin
Martinez	Juan	1920 First Ave.	(507) 555-2935	92121	Maldin
Fromthart	Lisa	32 Redcoat Rd.	(507) 555-0110	92122-1268	Chesterfield
Rogondino	Patricia	7583 Turquoise Rd.	(507) 555-7539	92122-1268	Chesterfield
Torcivia	Peter	904 S. Dorsey Dr.	(507) 555-9870	92122-1268	Chesterfield
Harvey	Sarah	73 Lakeview Dr.	(507) 555-7144	92122-1268	Chesterfield
Name	Student	1234 N. Fifth St.	(507) 555-5555	92121	Maldin

Record: 1 of 22 | No Filter | Search

Datasheet View

Twenty-two records meet criteria

Figure 3.33

The query located 22 records that met the specified criteria. These are the same results you obtained using a filter, except that only the fields you want displayed are included in the datasheet.

The final criterion you need to add to the query is to display only those employees who work at the Landis location. To do this, you need to add the Job Information table to the query design.

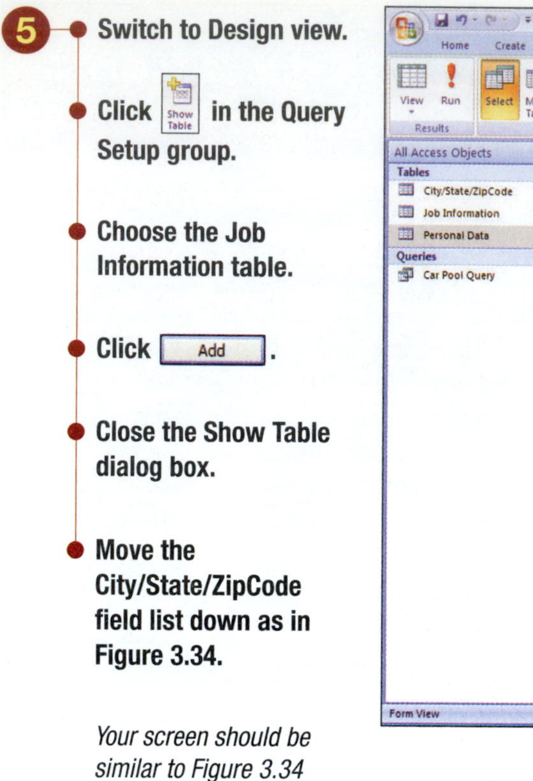

5 Switch to Design view.

- Click **Show Table** in the Query Setup group.
- Choose the Job Information table.
- Click **Add**.
- Close the Show Table dialog box.
- Move the City/State/ZipCode field list down as in Figure 3.34.

Your screen should be similar to Figure 3.34

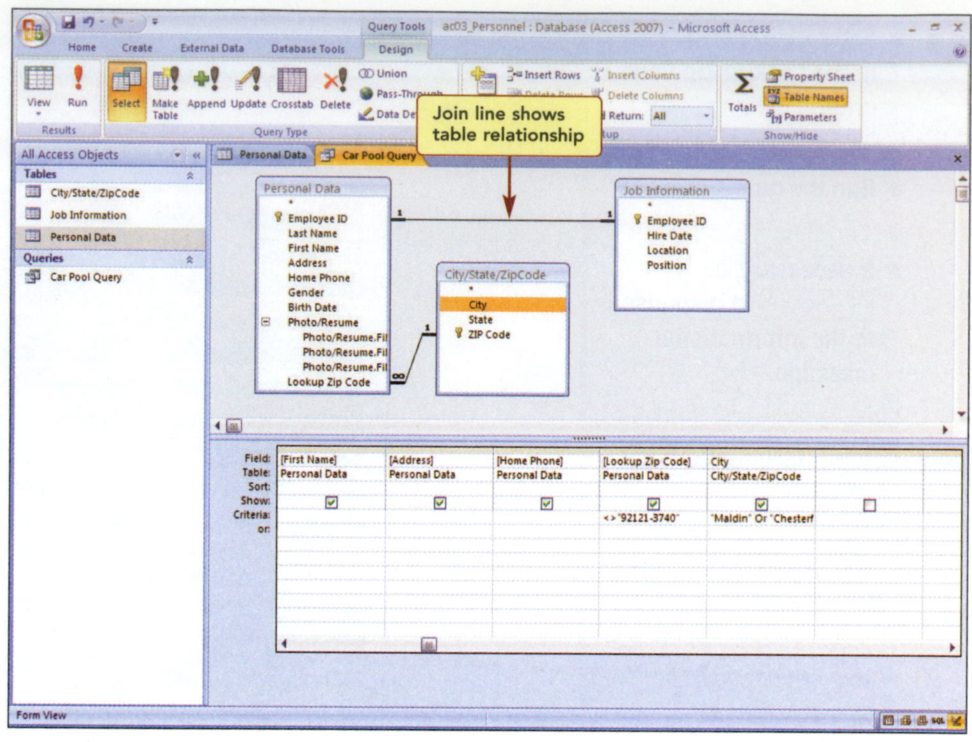

Figure 3.34

The field list for the third table was added to the Query Design window and the join line correctly links the Personal Data and Job Information field lists on the Employee ID fields.

6 Add the Location field to the design grid.

- Enter **Landis** in the Location Criteria cell.

Your screen should be similar to Figure 3.35

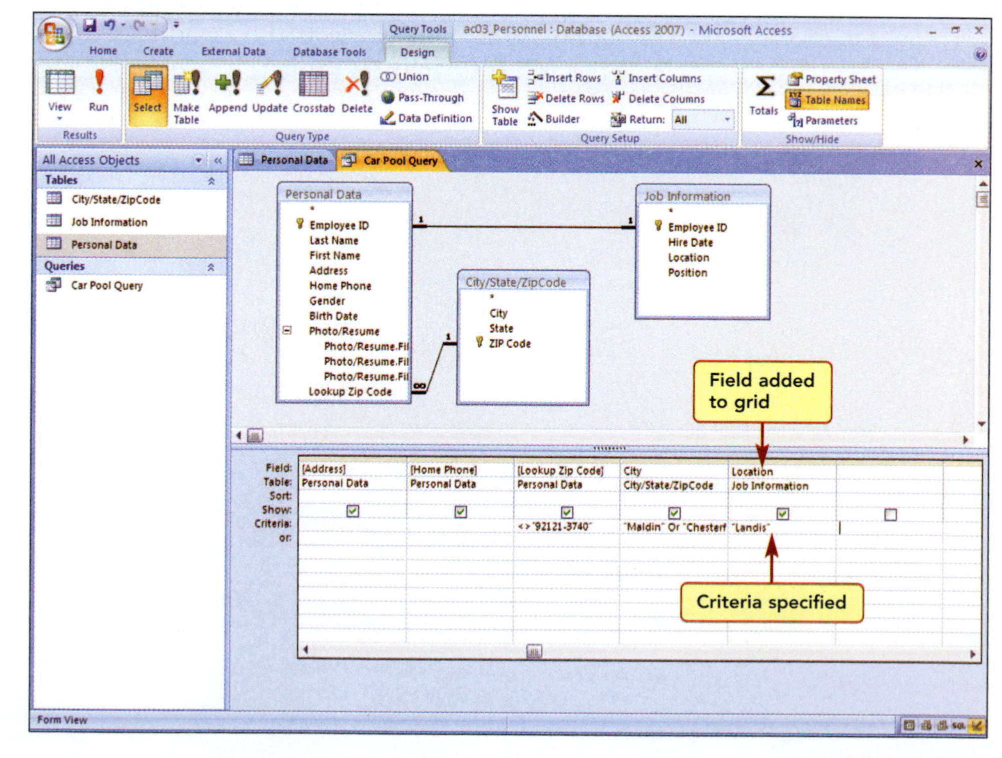

Figure 3.35

Hiding and Sorting Columns

Before running the query, you want to make a few additional changes to the query design. You do not want the ZIP Code field displayed in the results and would like the results to be sorted by last name and city.

1

- **Click the Show box of the Lookup Zip Code field to clear the checkmark.**

- **Click in the Sort row of the Last Name field.**

Having Trouble?

Scroll the grid to bring field columns into view.

- **Open the Sort drop-down menu and choose Ascending.**

Your screen should be similar to Figure 3.36

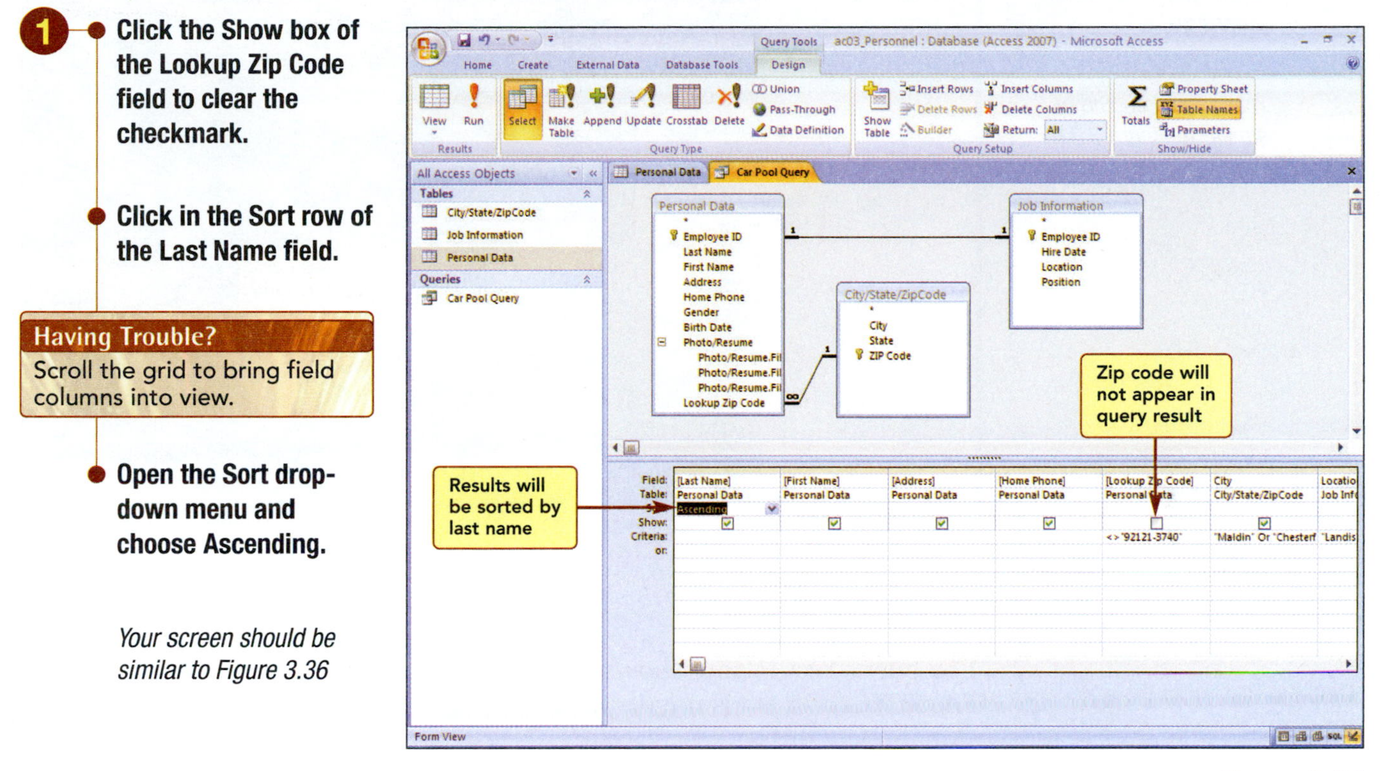

Figure 3.36

Now you can display the results.

Run the query.

If necessary, click OK in response to the informational message.

Your screen should be similar to Figure 3.37

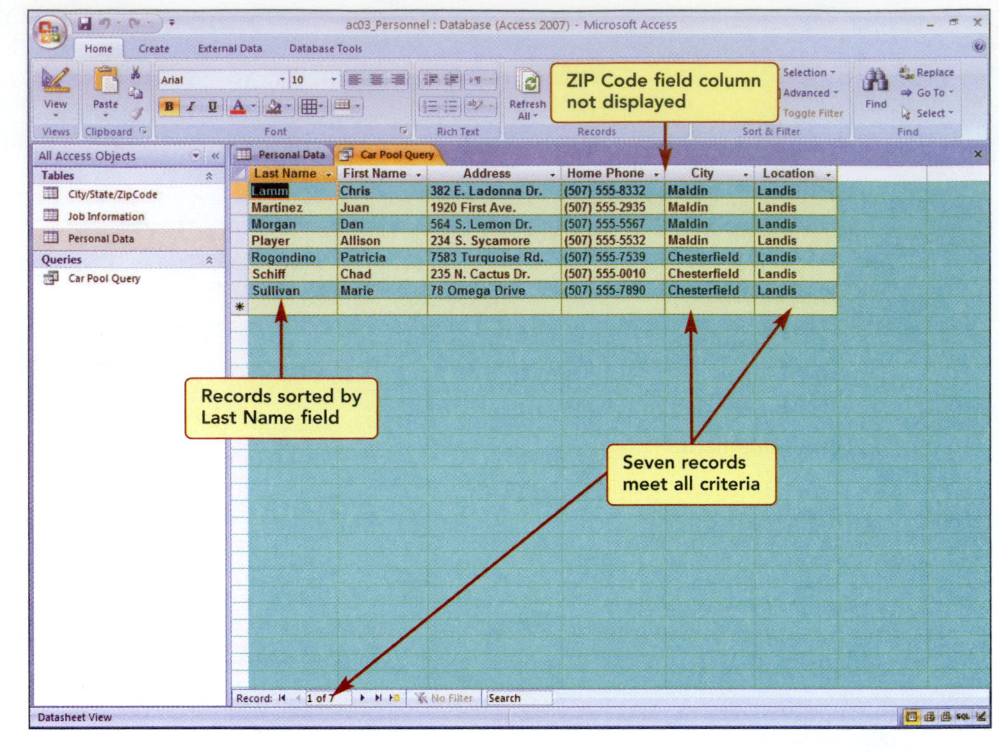

Figure 3.37

The query result now shows that seven employees meet all the criteria. The ZIP Code field is not displayed and last names are sorted in ascending alphabetical order.

Rearranging the Query Datasheet

The order of the fields in the query datasheet reflects the order in which they were placed in the Selected Fields list. You think the results will be easier to read if the Last Name field column followed the First Name column and the City column followed the Address column. You will then size the fields to fit the contents.

Moving a field column in the query datasheet is the same as in a table datasheet. Changing the column order in the query datasheet does not affect the field order in the resource table, which is controlled by the table design.

- **Select the Last Name column.**

Having Trouble?

Remember, to select an entire column, you click on its column heading when the mouse pointer is ↓.

- **Click and hold the mouse button on the Last Name column heading.**

Additional Information

When the mouse pointer is ⇱, it indicates that you can drag to move the selection.

- **Drag the Last Name column to the right until a thick line is displayed between the First Name and Address columns.**
- **Release the mouse button.**
- **Move the City column to the right of the Address column.**

Additional Information

You can move fields in Table Datasheet view in the same way.

- **Best fit the five columns.**
- **Clear the selection.**

Your screen should be similar to Figure 3.38

Columns moved and "Best Fit"

First Name	Last Name	Address	City	Home Phone	Location
Chris	Lamm	382 E. Ladonna Dr.	Maldin	(507) 555-8332	Landis
Juan	Martinez	1920 First Ave.	Maldin	(507) 555-2935	Landis
Dan	Morgan	564 S. Lemon Dr.	Maldin	(507) 555-5567	Landis
Allison	Player	234 S. Sycamore	Maldin	(507) 555-5532	Landis
Patricia	Rogondino	7583 Turquoise Rd.	Chesterfield	(507) 555-7539	Landis
Chad	Schiff	235 N. Cactus Dr.	Chesterfield	(507) 555-0010	Landis
Marie	Sullivan	78 Omega Drive	Chesterfield	(507) 555-7890	Landis

Figure 3.38

This is the information Juan needs to form his car pool. However, as you look at the results, you realize your record should have been included in the list because you live in Maldin and work at the Landis location. You need to determine why your record was not included.

2. Display the Personal Data table.
   - Remove the filter.
   - Scroll to the bottom of the table to see your record.

You can see that the Personal Data table has 70 records from the record indicator and that your record is the last record. Now, however, you realize that you did not add your information to the Job Location table.

Finding Unmatched Records

You will check the Job Information table to see how many records it contains.

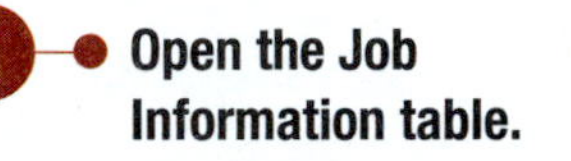

1. Open the Job Information table.

Your screen should be similar to Figure 3.39

Figure 3.39

This table has 68 records, whereas the Personal Data table has 70. You know your record is one of the missing records, but you need to locate the other missing record. You can do this quickly using the Find Unmatched Query Wizard.

2 Click [Query Wizard] in the Other group of the Create tab.

- Choose Find Unmatched Query Wizard.
- Click OK.

Your screen should be similar to Figure 3.40

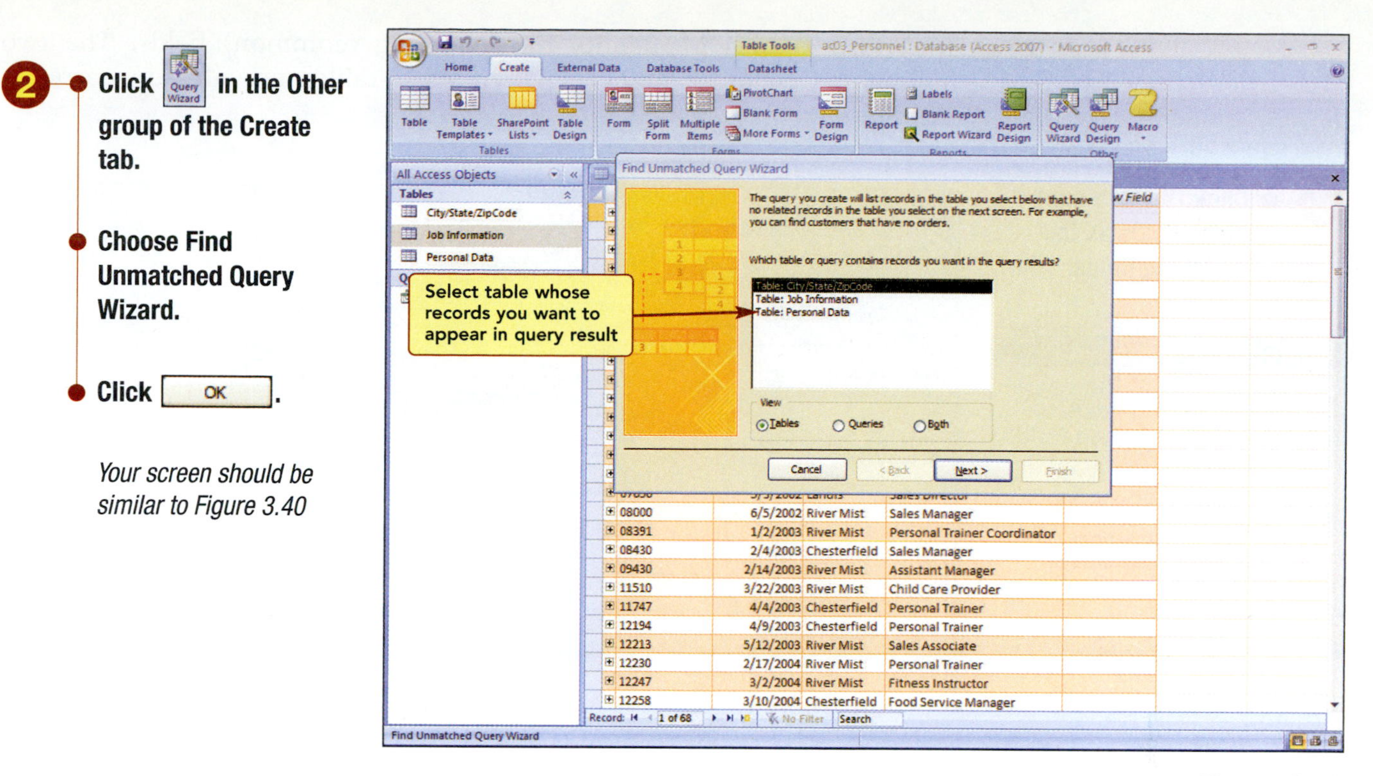

Figure 3.40

In the first wizard dialog box, you select the table that contains records you want to appear in the results. In this case, you will select the Personal Data table first because it is the primary table and has more records than the Job Information table, and these are the records you want to appear in the results. In the second dialog box, you will select the table to compare the first table to. This establishes the join between the tables.

3 Select Table: Personal Data.

- Click Next >.
- Select Table: Job Information.
- Click Next >.

Your screen should be similar to Figure 3.41

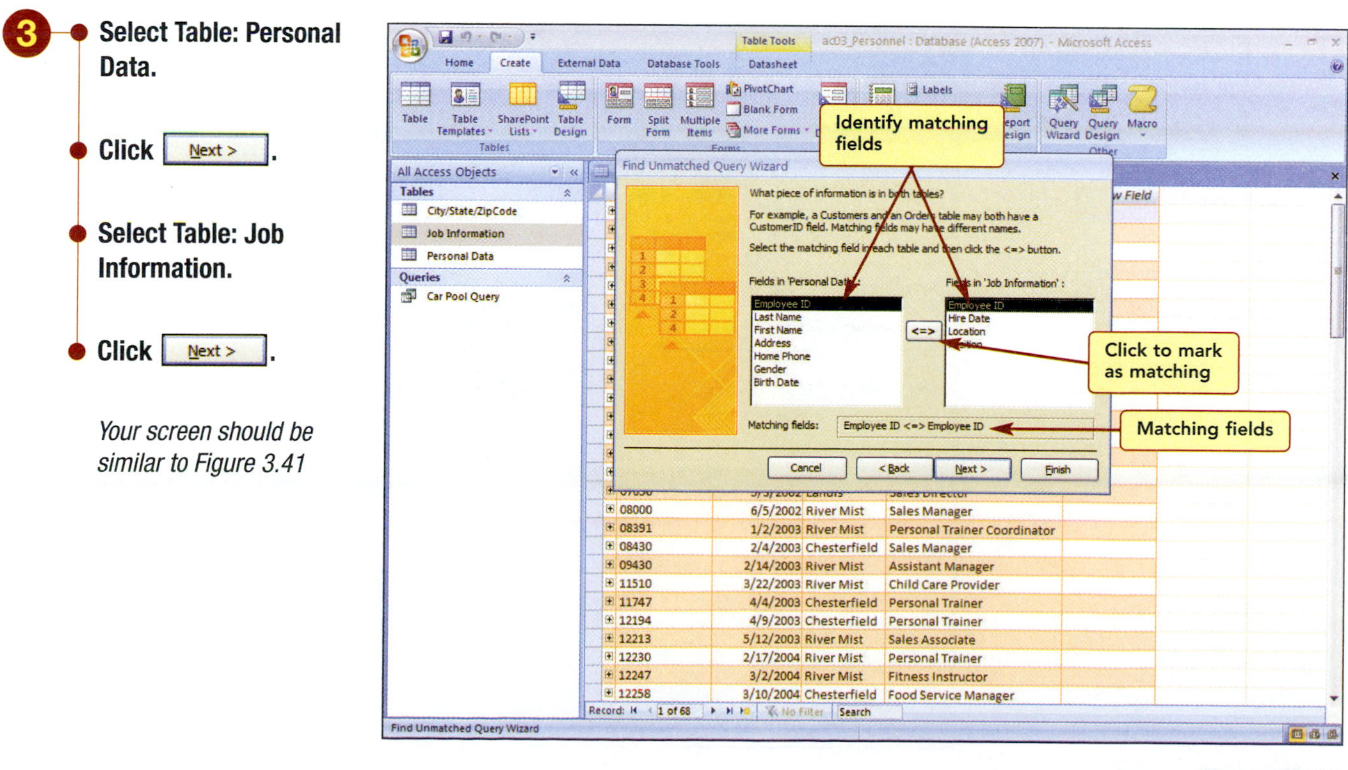

Figure 3.41

The third step is to identify the matching (common) fields. The two highlighted fields, Employee ID, in both tables are already correctly highlighted.

4 **Click [<=>] to mark these fields as the matching fields.**

Additional Information

The field names of the selected matching fields appear in the Matching Fields text box.

Click [Next >].

Your screen should be similar to Figure 3.42

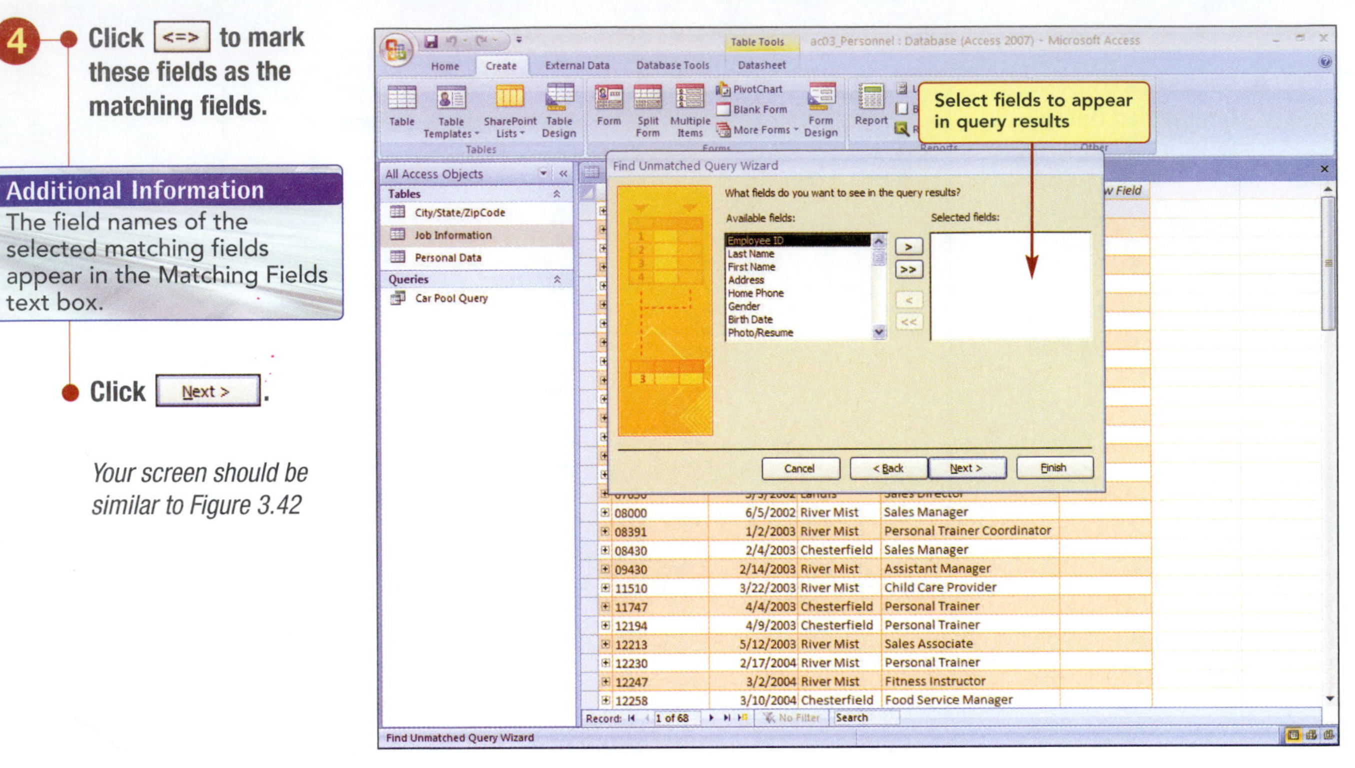

Figure 3.42

Next, you need to identify the fields you want to appear in the query results.

5 **Click [>>] to add all the fields to the Selected Fields list.**

Click [Next >].

Click [Finish].

Your screen should be similar to Figure 3.43

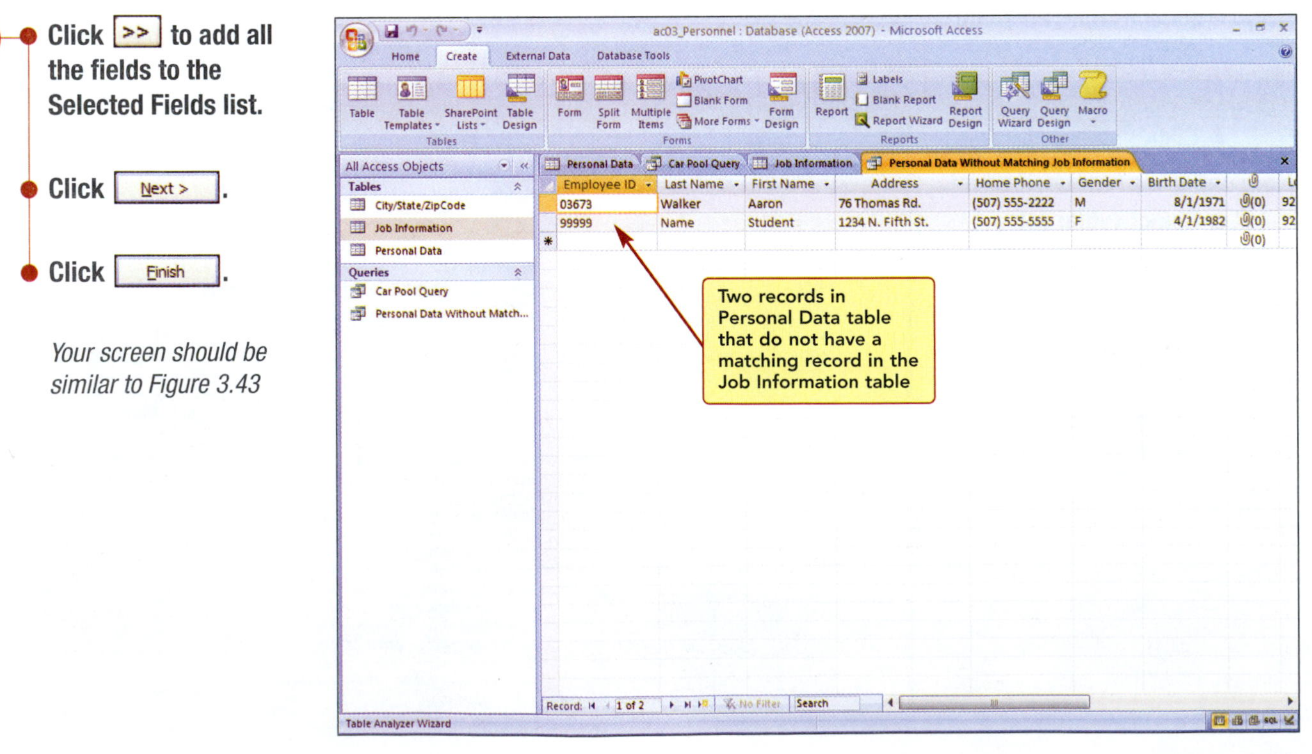

Figure 3.43

The two records in the Personal Data table that do not have matching records in the Job Information table are displayed in the query results. One record is the matching information for your own record that you added earlier to the Personal Data table. Now, you just need to add the information to the Job Information table for these two employees.

6

- **Close the Query window.**
- **Add the following records to the Job Information table:**

Employee ID	Hire Date	Location	Position
03673	2/10/2001	River Mist	Greeter
99999	2/25/08	Landis	Human Resources Administrator

- **Best fit the Position field.**

Your screen should be similar to Figure 3.44

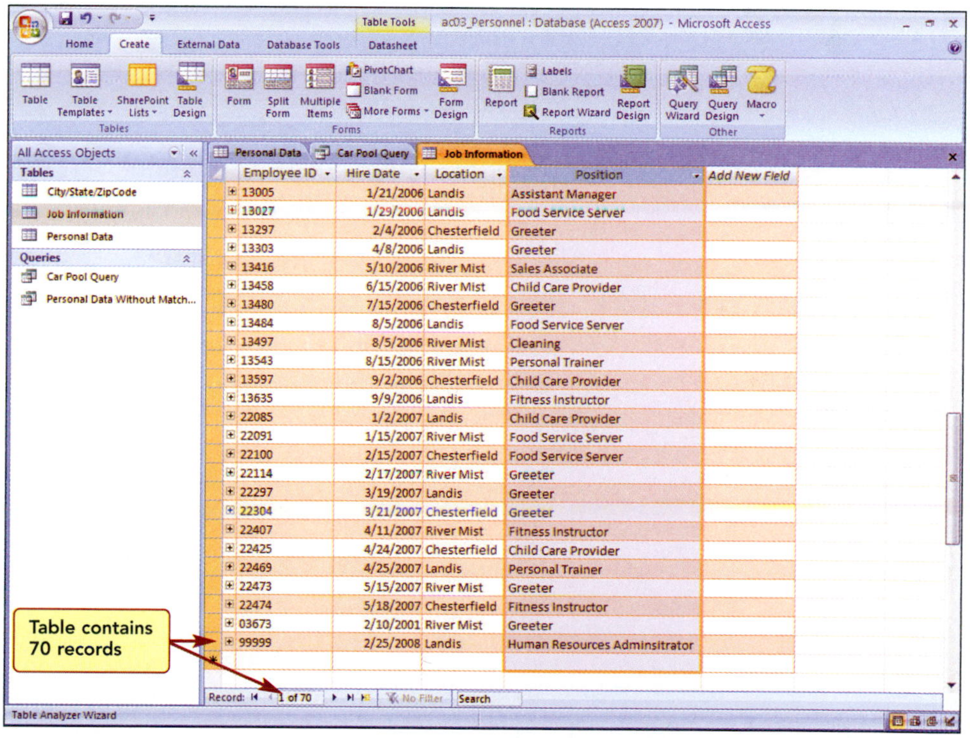

Table contains 70 records

Figure 3.44

Both tables now contain 70 records. Notice that the Unmatched Records query was automatically saved and the object is listed in the Queries group of the Navigation pane. If you were to rerun this query, no results would be located because there are no longer any missing records.

Finally, you want to update all objects that use the Location table as the underlying record source to reflect the addition of the new records.

7 **Display the Car Pool Query datasheet.**

- **Click** Refresh All **in the Records group of the Home tab.**

Your screen should be similar to Figure 3.45

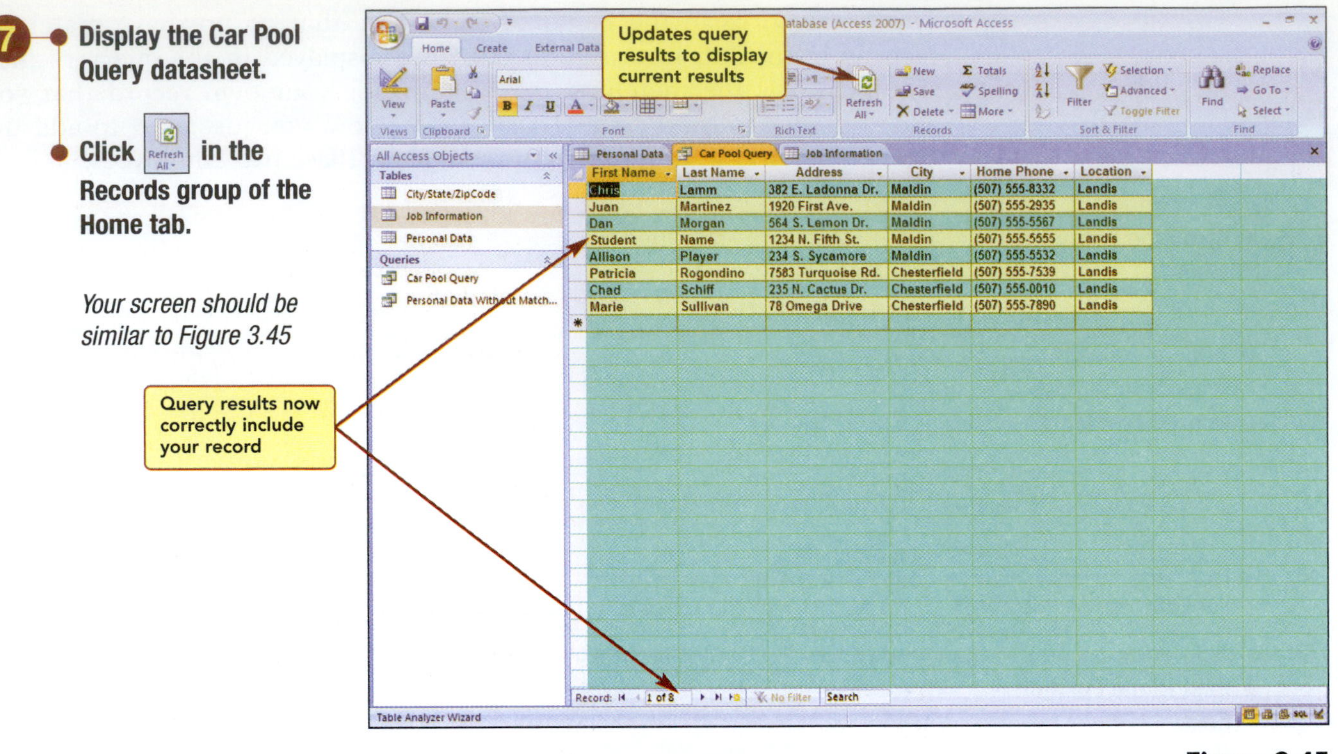

Figure 3.45

The query results list eight records that meet the criteria and now correctly include your record.

Finding Duplicate Records

Next, you want to check the Personal Data table for possible duplicate records. Even though this table uses the Employee ID as the primary key, it is possible to enter the same record with two different IDs. To check for duplication, you will use the Find Duplicates Query Wizard.

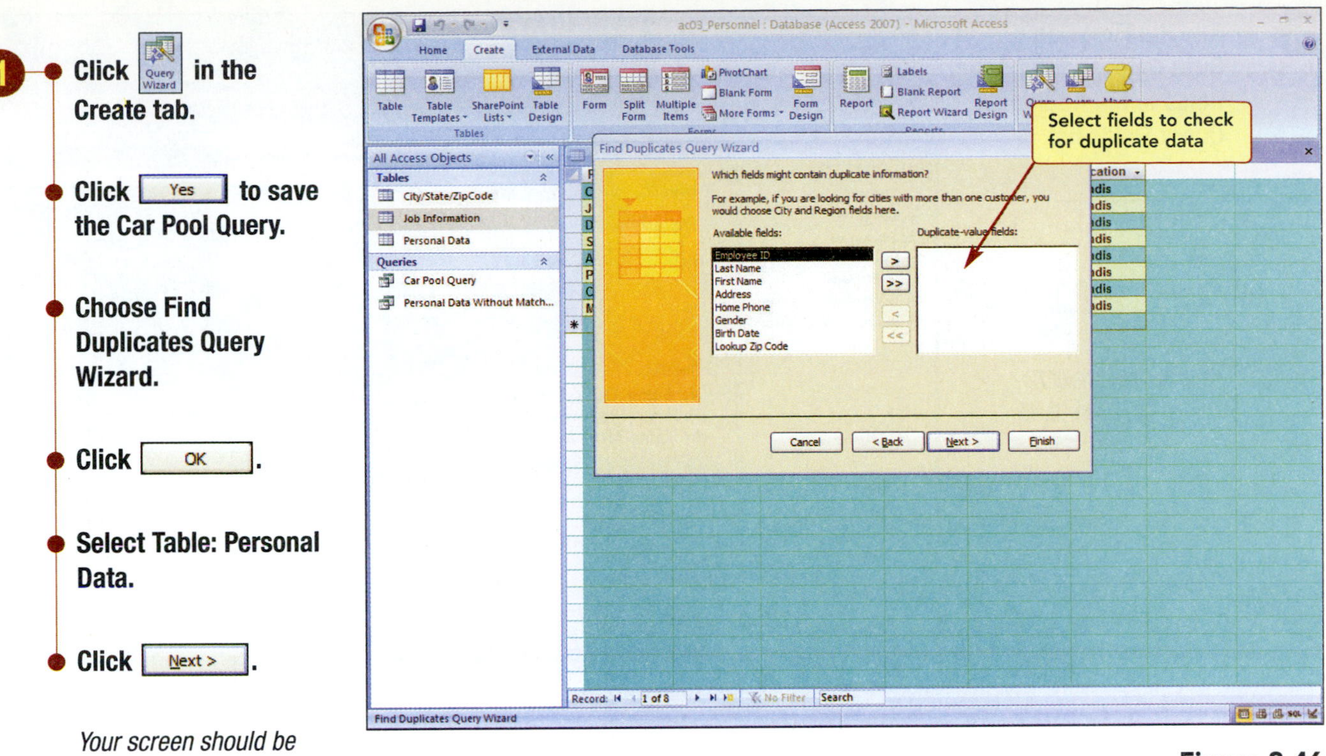

1 • Click [Query Wizard] in the Create tab.

• Click [Yes] to save the Car Pool Query.

• Choose Find Duplicates Query Wizard.

• Click [OK].

• Select Table: Personal Data.

• Click [Next >].

Your screen should be similar to Figure 3.46

Figure 3.46

In this wizard dialog box, you identify the fields that may contain duplicate data. In this case, you will check the Last Name fields for duplicate values.

2 • Add the Last Name field to the Duplicate-value fields list.

• Click [Next >].

Your screen should be similar to Figure 3.47

Select additional fields to appear in query results

Figure 3.47

Next, you need to identify the additional fields you want to appear in the query results.

3 **Add the First Name, Birth Date, and Gender fields to the Additional Query Fields list.**

Click Next >.

Click Finish.

Your screen should be similar to Figure 3.48

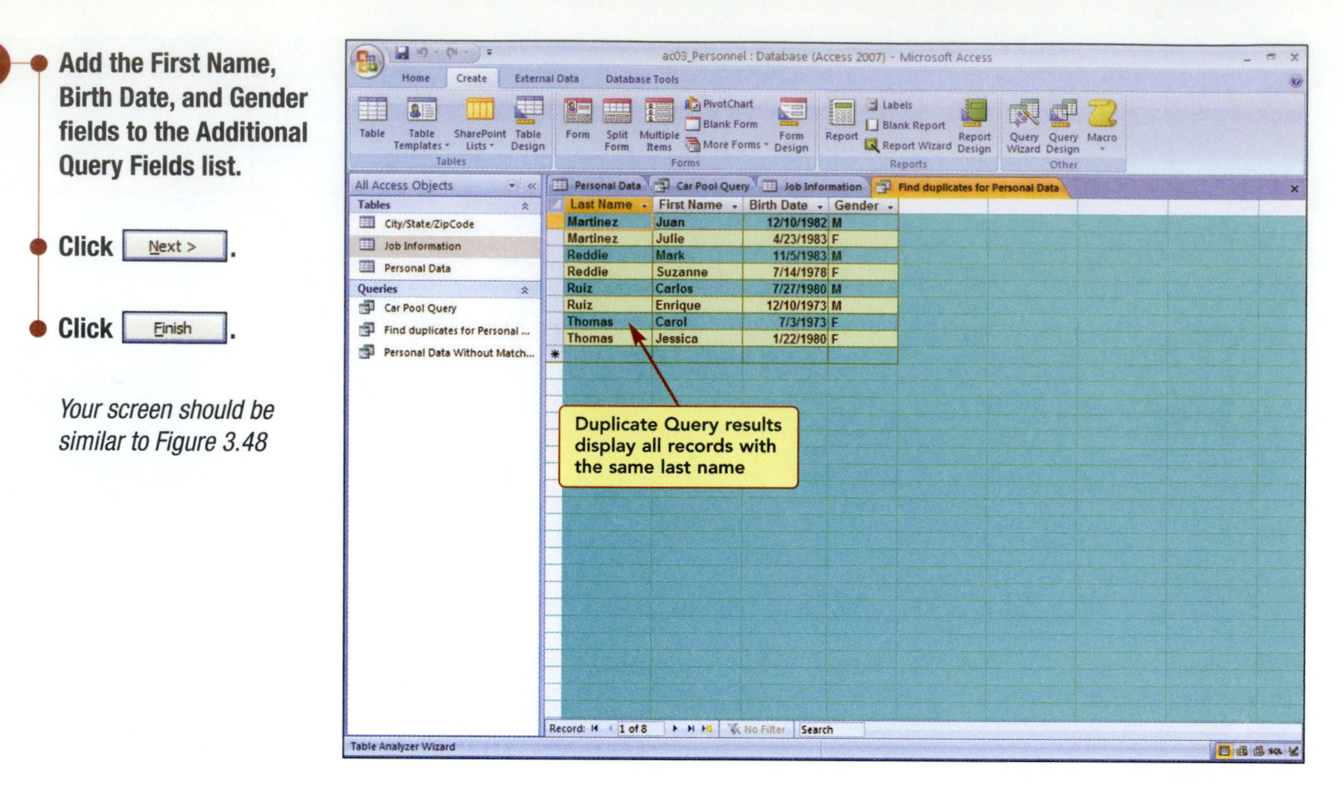

Figure 3.48

All records with the same last name are listed. These all look like valid records, so you will not make any changes.

Creating a Parameter Query

Periodically the club director wants to know the employee number and names of the employees at each club and their job position. To find this information, you will create a simple query and sort the location field to group the records.

To create this query, you will modify the existing Car Pool Query design since it already includes the two tables, Personal Data and Job Information, that you need to use. You will remove the City/State/ZipCode table field list because you do not need any information from that table. Then you will clear the design grid and save the modified query using a new name.

1 Display the Car Pool Query in Design view.

- Right-click on the title bar of the City/State/ZipCode table field list and choose Remove Table from the shortcut menu.
- Drag across the top of the six fields in the grid to select them and press Delete.
- Click Office Button and choose Save As/Save Object As.
- Enter **Location Query** as the new query name and click OK.

Your screen should be similar to Figure 3.49

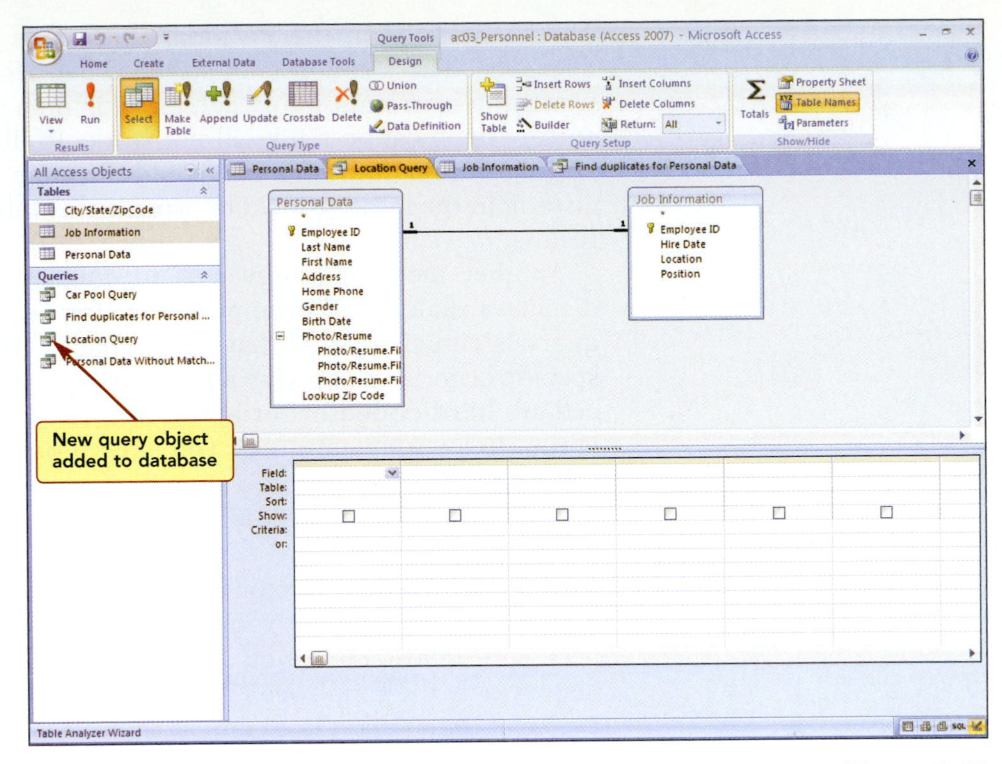

Figure 3.49

The query object is added to the Navigation pane and you are ready to define the query. You will add all the fields from the Personal Data table to the grid and the Location field from the Job Information table.

2 Double-click * in the Personal Data field list.

- Double-click Location in the Job Information table.
- Sort the Location field in ascending sort order.
- Run the query.
- Hide the Navigation pane.

Your screen should be similar to Figure 3.50

Query results display all fields from Personal Data table and Location field from Job Information table

Sorted in ascending order

Employee ID	Last Name	First Name	Address	Home Phone	Gender	Birth Date		Lookup Zip Code	Locati
08430	Smith	Brent	4321 Toledo St.	(507) 555-6464	M	11/4/1979	(0)	92123-2232	Cheste
12668	Stueland	Valerie	34 University Dr.	(507) 555-1845	F	11/19/1979	(0)	92121-3740	Cheste
12867	Talic	Elvis	21 Oasis St.	(507) 555-5985	M	6/10/1981	(0)	92123-2232	Cheste
12920	Larson	Alicia	345 W. Mill Ave.	(507) 555-7717	F	6/21/1983	(0)	92121-3740	Cheste
13297	Delucchi	Bill	950 S. Terrace Dr.	(507) 555-8195	M	9/30/1978	(0)	92122-1268	Cheste
12258	Delano	Gordon	13101 N. Spindrift Dr.	(507) 555-8201	M	8/7/1979	(0)	92122-1268	Cheste
12194	Polonsky	Mitch	8701 E. Sheridan	(507) 555-1018	M	3/13/1970	(0)	92120-3741	Cheste
11747	Lettow	Ryan	358 Maple Dr.	(507) 555-2805	M	11/15/1971	(0)	92121-3740	Cheste
12655	Lahti	Jill	5401 E. Thomas Rd.	(507) 555-7765	F	6/14/1977	(0)	92123-2232	Cheste
13480	Burke	Ellen	234 N. First St.	(507) 555-6122	F	7/30/1979	(0)	92123-2232	Cheste
12612	Richards	Melissa	5522 W Marin Ln.	(507) 555-7789	F	9/30/1978	(0)	92123-2232	Cheste
07550	Ernster	Barbara	1153 S. Wilson	(507) 555-3211	F	5/30/1971	(0)	92123-2232	Cheste
13597	Gapasin	Ken	2633 E. Fountain St.	(507) 555-0589	M	2/11/1985	(0)	92121-3740	Cheste
03406	Lopez	Mina	4290 E. Alameda Dr.	(507) 555-5050	F	2/25/1977	(0)	92121-3740	Cheste
00617	Nichols	Cathy	75 Brooklea Dr.	(507) 555-0001	F	5/19/1965	(0)	92120-3741	Cheste
06000	Robertson	Kirk	832 S. William Ave.	(507) 555-3730	M	4/5/1974	(0)	92121	Cheste
22100	Vaccaro	Louis	289 E. Heather Ave.	(507) 555-3758	M	9/23/1982	(0)	92123-2232	Cheste
04321	Sabin	Greg	90 E. Rawhide Ave.	(507) 555-4455	M	9/30/1977	(0)	92122	Cheste
22304	Torcivia	Peter	904 S. Dorsey Dr.	(507) 555-9870	M	5/14/1975	(0)	92122-1268	Cheste
22425	Ferguson	Robby	4232 Tuller Ave.	(507) 555-7039	M	2/3/1979	(0)	92123-2232	Cheste
07450	Matsumoto	Tyrus	34 S. Onza Ave.	(507) 555-8372	M	6/23/1980	(0)	92122-1268	Cheste
22474	Tillman	Kevin	89 E. Southern Dr.	(507) 555-3434	M	4/13/1978	(0)	92120-3741	Cheste
99999	Name	Student	1234 N. Fifth St.	(507) 555-5555	F	4/1/1982	(0)	92121	Landis
12583	Sullivan	Marie	78 Omega Drive	(507) 555-7890	F	3/15/1981	(0)	92122-1268	Landis
00212	Schiff	Chad	235 N. Cactus Dr.	(507) 555-0010	M	3/9/1962	(0)	92122	Landis
12501	DeLuca	Elizabeth	21 W. Southern Ave.	(507) 555-1105	F	8/21/1975	(0)	92123-2232	Landis
12420	Player	Allison	234 S. Sycamore	(507) 555-5532	F	5/5/1971	(0)	92121-0093	Landis
03225	Morgan	Dan	564 S. Lemon Dr.	(507) 555-5567	M	3/5/1975	(0)	92121	Landis
07650	Lamm	Chris	382 E. Ladonna Dr.	(507) 555-8332	M	8/3/1975	(0)	92121	Landis
12380	Thomas	Jessica	128 Marina Dr.	(507) 555-8513	F	1/22/1980	(0)	92123-2232	Landis

Record: 1 of 70

Figure 3.50

All the fields from the Personal Data table and the Location field are displayed. The location is in sorted order. However, because the director wants the information for each location on a separate page when printed, sorting the location field will not work. To display only the records for a single location at a time, you could filter the location field or change the criteria in the location field to provide this information and then print the results.

Another method, however, is to create a parameter query that will display a dialog box prompting you for location information when the query is run. This saves having to change to Design view and enter the specific criteria or applying a filter. Criteria that are entered in the criteria cell are **hard-coded criteria,** meaning they are used each time the query is run. In a parameter query, you enter a **parameter value** in the Criteria cell rather than a specific value. The parameter value tells the query to prompt you for the specific criteria you want to use when you run the query.

Additionally, the director does not need all the information from the Personal Data table, so you will change the design to include only the necessary fields. First, you will change the fields in the design grid to display only the Employee ID and the First and Last Name fields from the Personal Data table.

3 — **Display Design view.**

- **Select and delete the Personal Data column in the design grid.**
- **Select the Employee ID, Last Name, and First Name fields in the Personal Data table and drag them to before the Location field in the design grid.**

Having Trouble?
Hold down ⇧Shift while clicking on each field name to select all three.

- **Remove the Sort from the Location field.**
- **Type [Enter Location] in the Location Criteria cell.**

Your screen should be similar to Figure 3.51

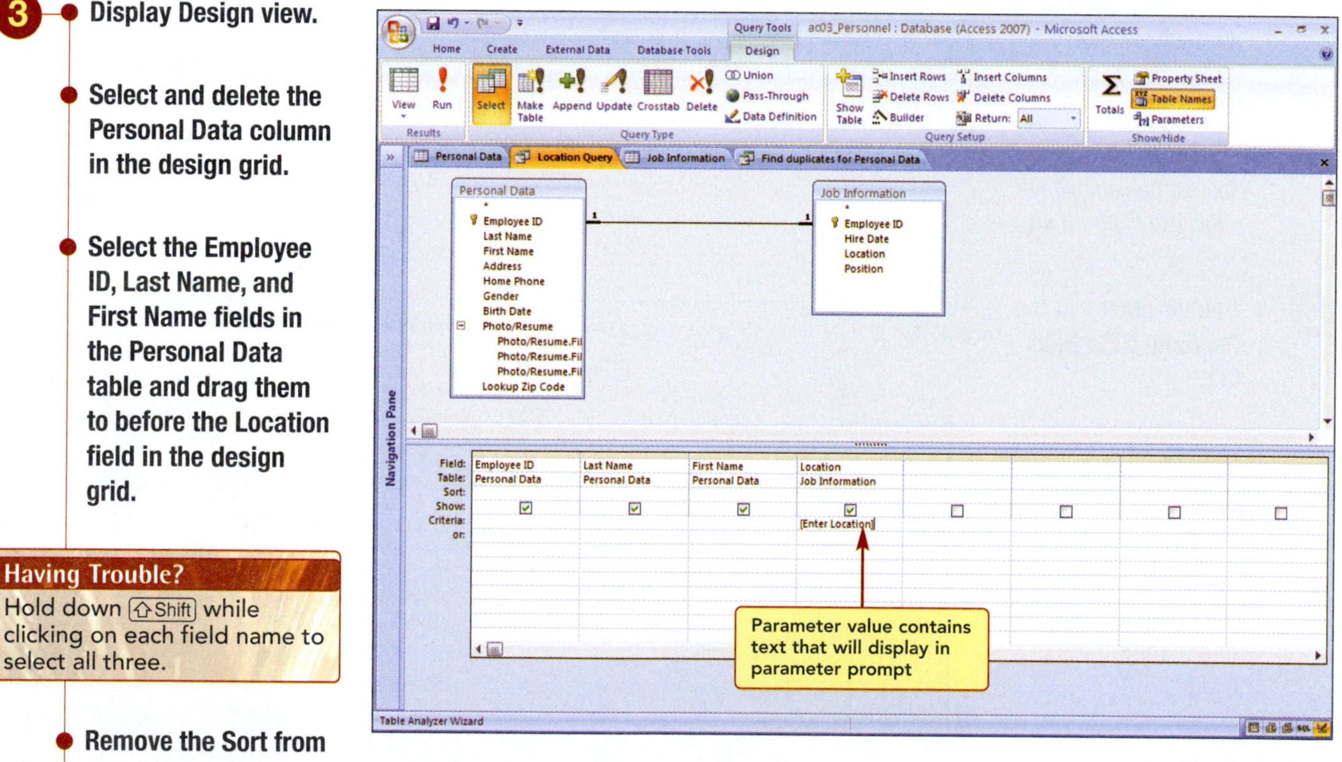

Figure 3.51

The Location criterion you entered is the parameter value. Parameter values are enclosed in square brackets and contain the text you want to appear when the parameter prompt is displayed. The parameter value cannot be a field name, because Access will assume you want to use that particular field and will not prompt for input.

4 **Run the query and type Landis in the Enter Parameter Value dialog box.**

Click OK.

Your screen should be similar to Figure 3.52

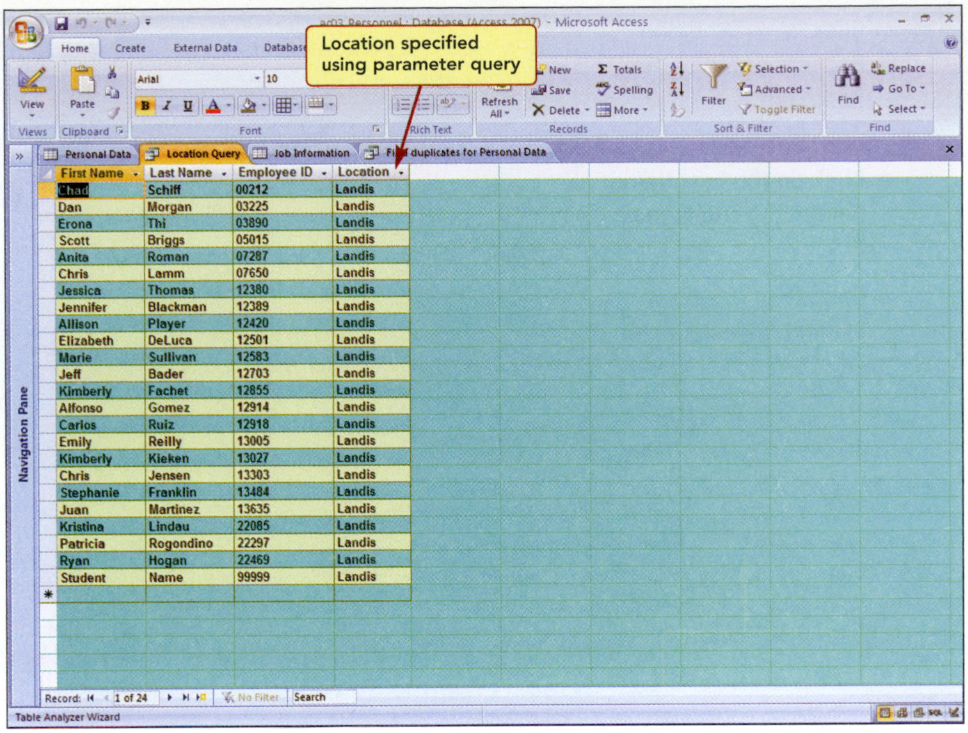

Location specified using parameter query
Personal Data
Location Query
Job Information
First Name
Last Name
Employee ID
Location
Chad Schiff 00212 Landis
Dan Morgan 03225 Landis
Erona Thi 03890 Landis
Scott Briggs 05015 Landis
Anita Roman 07287 Landis
Chris Lamm 07650 Landis
Jessica Thomas 12380 Landis
Jennifer Blackman 12389 Landis
Allison Player 12420 Landis
Elizabeth DeLuca 12501 Landis
Marie Sullivan 12583 Landis
Jeff Bader 12703 Landis
Kimberly Fachet 12855 Landis
Alfonso Gomez 12914 Landis
Carlos Ruiz 12918 Landis
Emily Reilly 13005 Landis
Kimberly Kieken 13027 Landis
Chris Jensen 13303 Landis
Stephanie Franklin 13484 Landis
Juan Martinez 13635 Landis
Kristina Lindau 22085 Landis
Patricia Rogondino 22297 Landis
Ryan Hogan 22469 Landis
Student Name 99999 Landis
Record: 1 of 24
Navigation Pane
Table Analyzer Wizard

Figure 3.52

Only those records whose location is Landis are displayed. Additionally, only the fields you specified are included in the result. Now, each time you run the query, you simply need to specify the location in the parameter dialog box to obtain results for the different locations.

Displaying a Totals Row

As you look at the query results, you can see the record indicator tells you there are 24 records. The record indicator is a simple count of the total number of records in the table and only appears when you view the datasheet. You decide to display a Totals row in the datasheet that will display this information when you print the datasheet.

In addition to count totals, the Totals row can perform other types of calculations such as averages and sums on a column of data. Calculations that are performed on a range of data are called **aggregate functions.** Because aggregate functions perform calculations, the data type in a column must be a number, decimal, or currency data type. The Personal Data table does not use any of these data types. However, the Count function can be used on all data types.

Additional Information

Some functions can use a Date/Time data type also.

You will add a Totals row and then use the Count aggregate function to display the record count. The Totals row appears below the star (new record) row in the table and remains fixed on the window as you scroll the table. Clicking in a column of the Totals row selects the field to be calculated. Then, you open the drop-down list to select the function you want to use. For text data types, only the Count function is listed.

Additional Information

You will learn more about using the other aggregate functions in later labs.

1 Click [Σ Totals] in the Records group of the Home tab.

- Click on the Last Name field in the Totals row.
- Open the drop-down list and choose Count.

Your screen should be similar to Figure 3.53

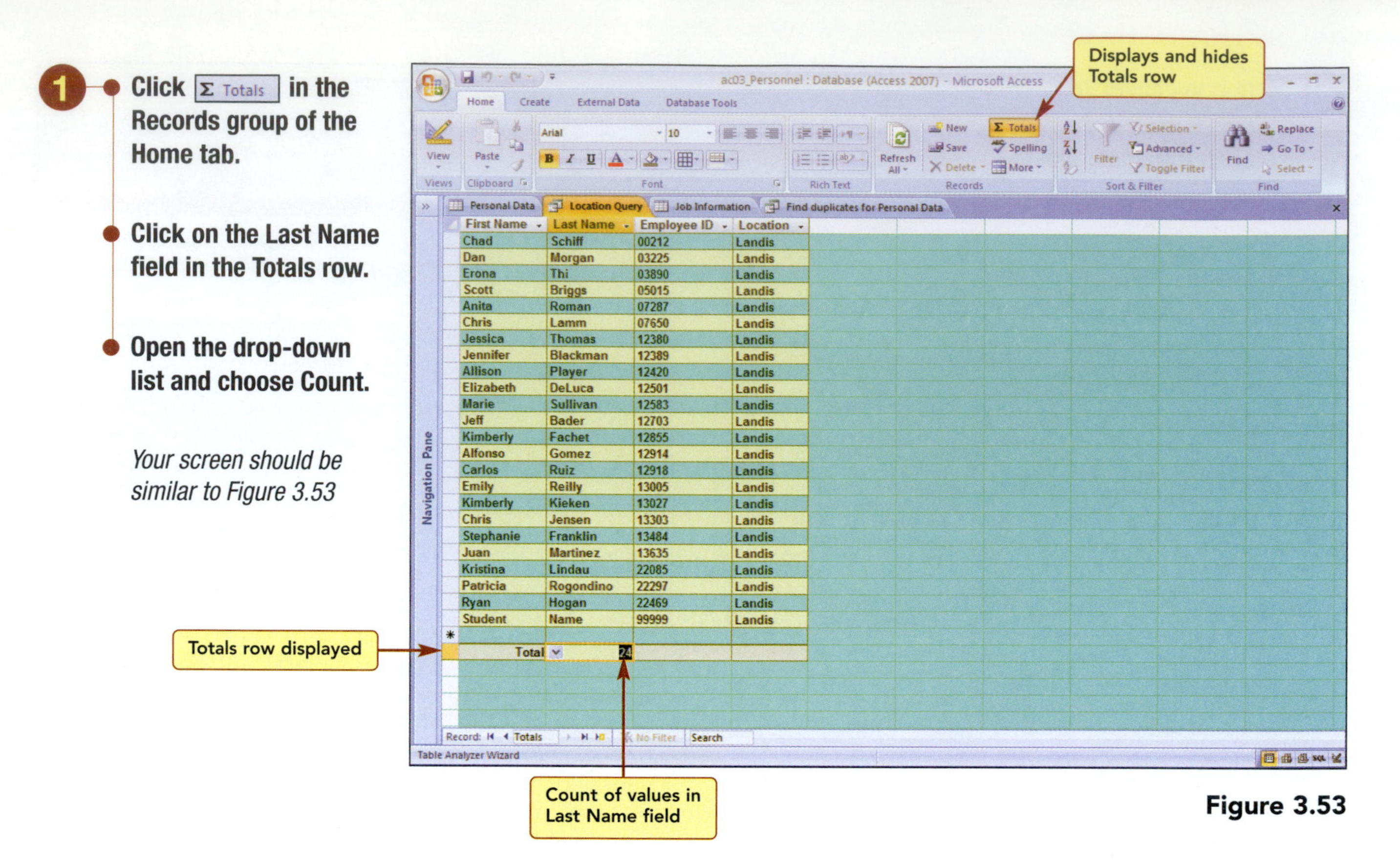

Figure 3.53

> **Additional Information**
> If you select a function in the first column of the Totals row, the label is removed and the value displayed.

The Totals row displays 24 as the number of values in the column. The Totals label in the first column identifies the meaning of this value.

You can turn the display of the Totals row on and off any time by clicking [Σ Totals]. When you redisplay the row, any functions that were selected are displayed again. A Totals row also can be displayed in a table datasheet.

You will print this query datasheet and then close all open objects.

2 Preview and then print the query datasheet.

- Close the query, saving changes when prompted.
- Close all remaining open objects, saving when prompted.
- Display the Navigation pane.

> **MORE ABOUT**
> You also can save a filter as a query. To learn about this feature, see "4 Creating and Modifying Queries" in the More About appendix.

Note: If you are running short on time, this is an appropriate point to end your Access session. When you begin again, open the ac03_Personnel database.

Creating Reports

As you know, you can print the table and query datasheets to obtain a simple printout of the data. However, there are many times when you would like the output to look more professional. To do this, you can create custom reports of this information.

Concept 4

Report

4 A **report** is professional-appearing output generated from tables or queries that may include design elements, groups, and summary information. A report can be a simple listing of all the fields in a table, or it might be a list of selected fields based on a query. Reports generally include design elements such as formatted labels, report titles, and headings, as well as different design styles, layouts, and graphics that enhance the display of information. In addition, when creating a report, you can group data to achieve specific results. You can then display summary information such as totals by group to allow the reader to further analyze the data. Creating a report displays the information from your database in a more attractive and meaningful format.

The first step to creating a report is to decide what information you want to appear in the report. Then you need to determine the tables or queries (the report's record source) that can be used to provide this information. If all the fields you want to appear in the report are in a single table, then simply use that table. However, if the information you want to appear in the report is contained in more than one table, you first need to create a query that specifically fits the needs of the report.

There are several different methods you can use to create reports as described in the following table. The method you use depends on the type of report you need to create.

Report Tool	Creates a simple report containing all the fields in the table
Blank Report Tool	Builds a report from scratch in Report Layout view by adding the fields you select from the table
Report Design	Builds a report from scratch in Report Design view by adding the fields you select from the table
Report Wizard	Guides you through the steps to create a report

Using the Report Tool

Although you could give Juan a simple printout of the carpool query results, you decide to create a report of this information. Since the fastest way to create a report is to use the Report tool, you decide to try this method first. This tool uses the selected or displayed table or query object as the report source.

1

- Select the Car Pool Query in the Navigation bar.
- Click Report in the Reports group of the Create tab.
- If necessary, click OK in response to the informational dialog box.
- Hide the Navigation pane

Your screen should be similar to Figure 3.54

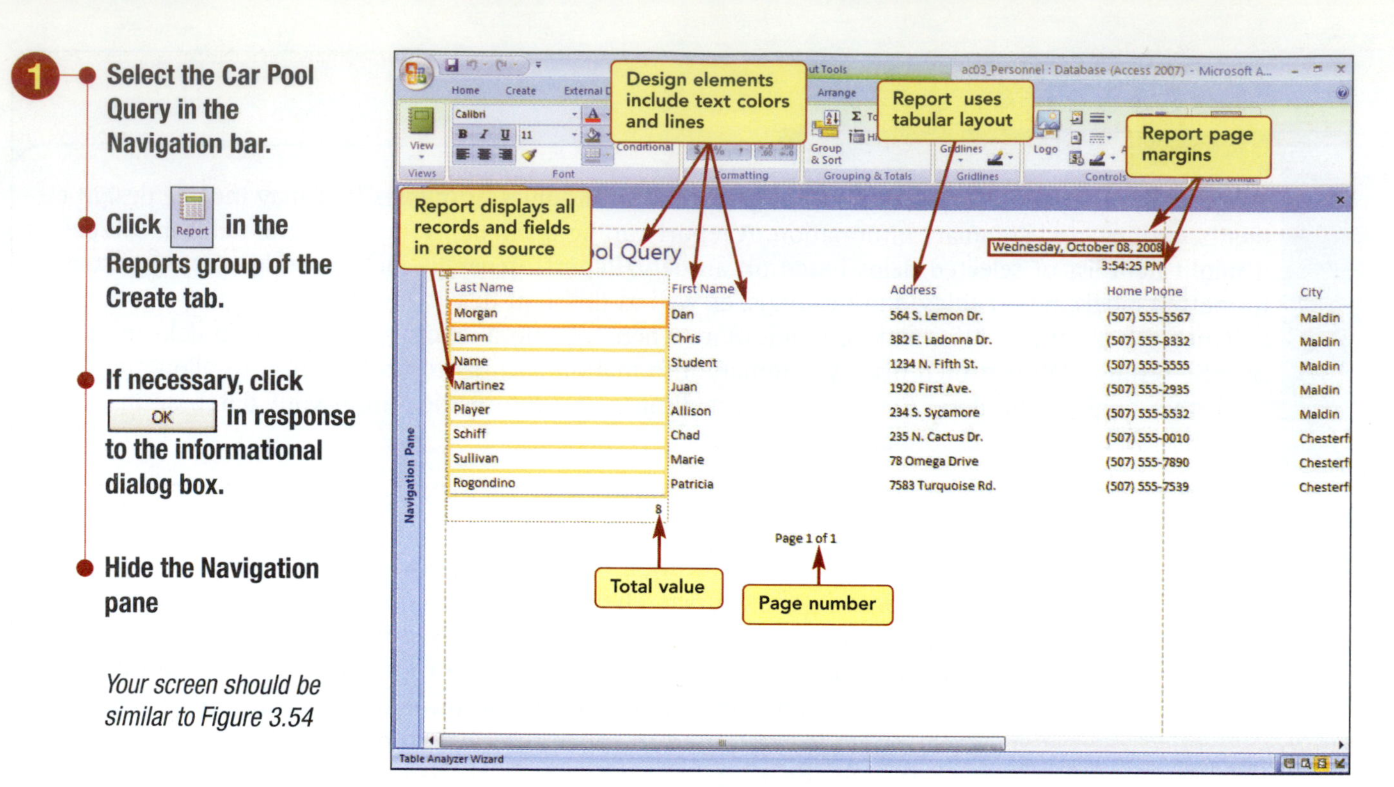

Figure 3.54

The Report tool creates a report that displays all fields and records from the record source in a predesigned report layout and style. It uses a tabular layout in which each field name appears at the top of the column and each record appears in a line, much like in Datasheet view. The fields are displayed in the order they appear in the table. It also displays the object name as the report title and the current date and time in the title area. The report design elements include blue font color for the report title and field names and a horizontal blue line below the field names. The title is also in a larger text size. The last row displays a total value of the number of records in the report. The dotted lines identify the report page margins and show that the Home Phone field data will be split between two pages.

Viewing the Report

The report is displayed in Layout view. As in Form Layout view, you could modify the report design if needed in this view. Instead, you will switch to Report view to see how the report will look when printed.

1 **Click Report View in the Views group of the Report Layout Tools Format tab.**

- **Scroll to the right to see the last field column.**

Your screen should be similar to Figure 3.55

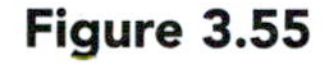
Report view displays data as it will appear when printed

Figure 3.55

Additional Information
The report date and time will reflect the current date and time on your computer.

Report view displays the data in the report as it will appear when printed. It does not show how the data will fit on a page. This view is useful if you want to copy data from the report and paste it into another document such as a Word file. It also can be used to temporarily change what data is displayed in the report, by applying a filter.

The last view you can use is Print Preview. This view will show you exactly how the report will look when printed and can be used to modify the page layout and print-related settings. Another way to display this view is from the object's shortcut menu.

2 **Right-click on the report tab or an empty area of the report and choose Print Preview.**

- **Click** Two Pages.

> **Another Method**
> You also can right-click an object in the Navigation pane to display this shortcut menu.

Your screen should be similar to Figure 3.56

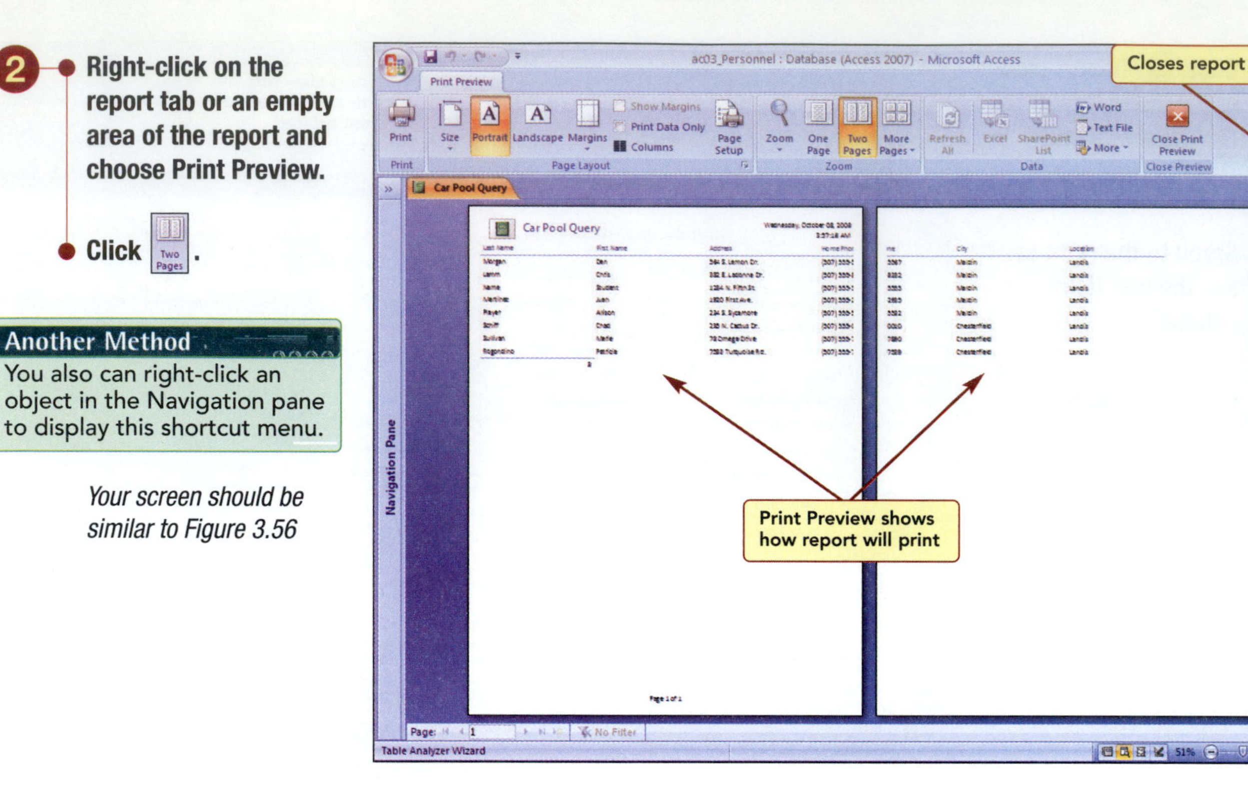

Figure 3.56

It is now easy to see exactly how the report will look when printed. After looking over the report, you decide that although the tabular layout is appropriate for your report, you do not want the report to include all the fields from the query. Rather than modify the report design by removing the unneeded fields, you will close this report without saving it and then use the Report Wizard to create a report that is more appropriate for your needs.

3 **Close Print Preview.**

- **Click** ✕ **to close the report.**
- **Click** No **in response to the dialog box to save the report.**

Using the Report Wizard

Using the Report Wizard, you can easily specify the fields you want to include in the report. The Report Wizard consists of a series of dialog boxes, much like those in the Form and Query Wizards. In the first dialog box, you specify the table or query to be used in the report and add the fields to be included. The Car Pool Query object is already correctly specified as the object that will be used to create the report.

1 • Click [Report Wizard] in the Reports group of the Create tab.

• Add the First Name field to the Selected Fields list.

• Add all the remaining fields to the list. Remove the Location field.

• Click [Next >].

Your screen should be similar to Figure 3.57

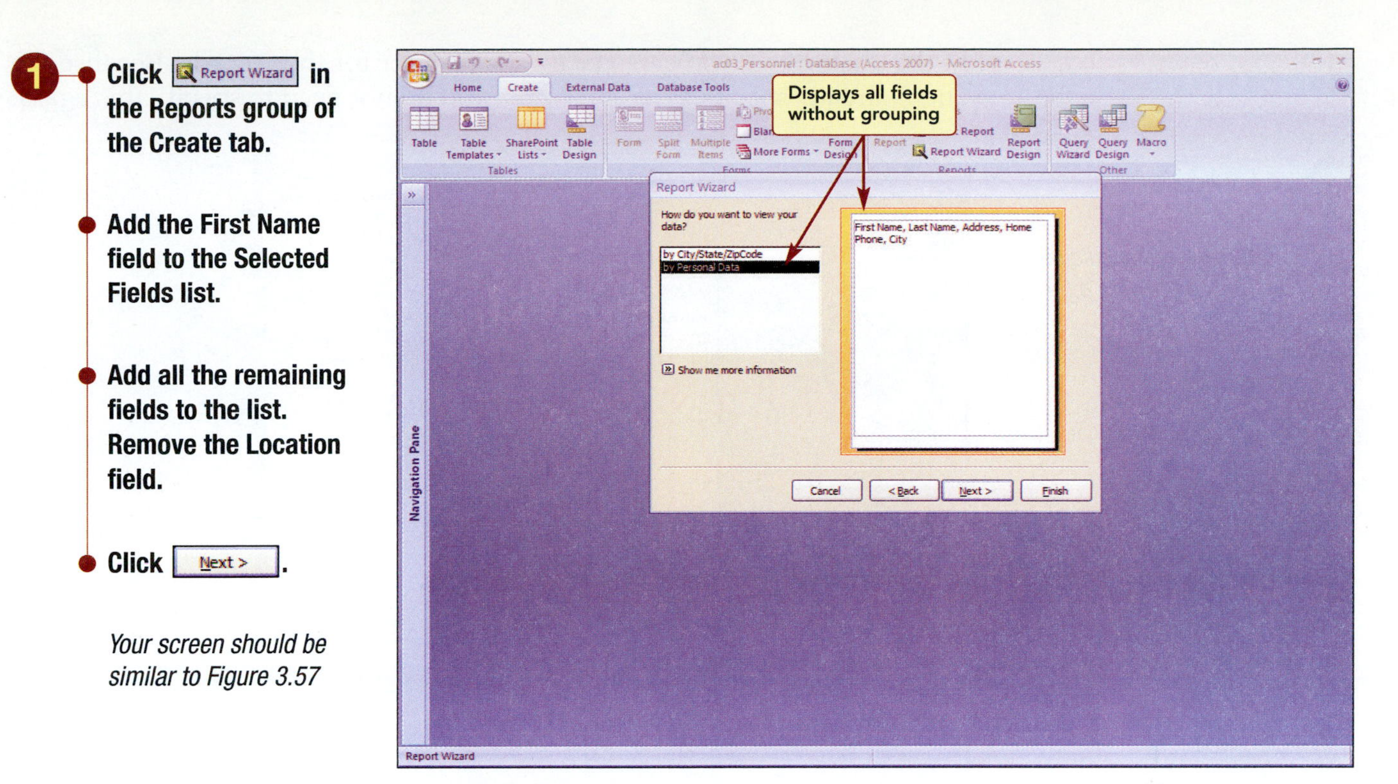

Figure 3.57

This dialog box asks you to decide how to display or group the data in the report based on the relationships between the tables. The selected option, by Personal Data, is appropriate for your needs and allows you to specify the fields you may want to group yourself. In the following dialog box, you will be asked if you want to add any grouping levels to the report. You do not want the report grouped by any category, so you do not need to do anything in this dialog box.

2 • Click [Next >] twice.

Your screen should be similar to Figure 3.58

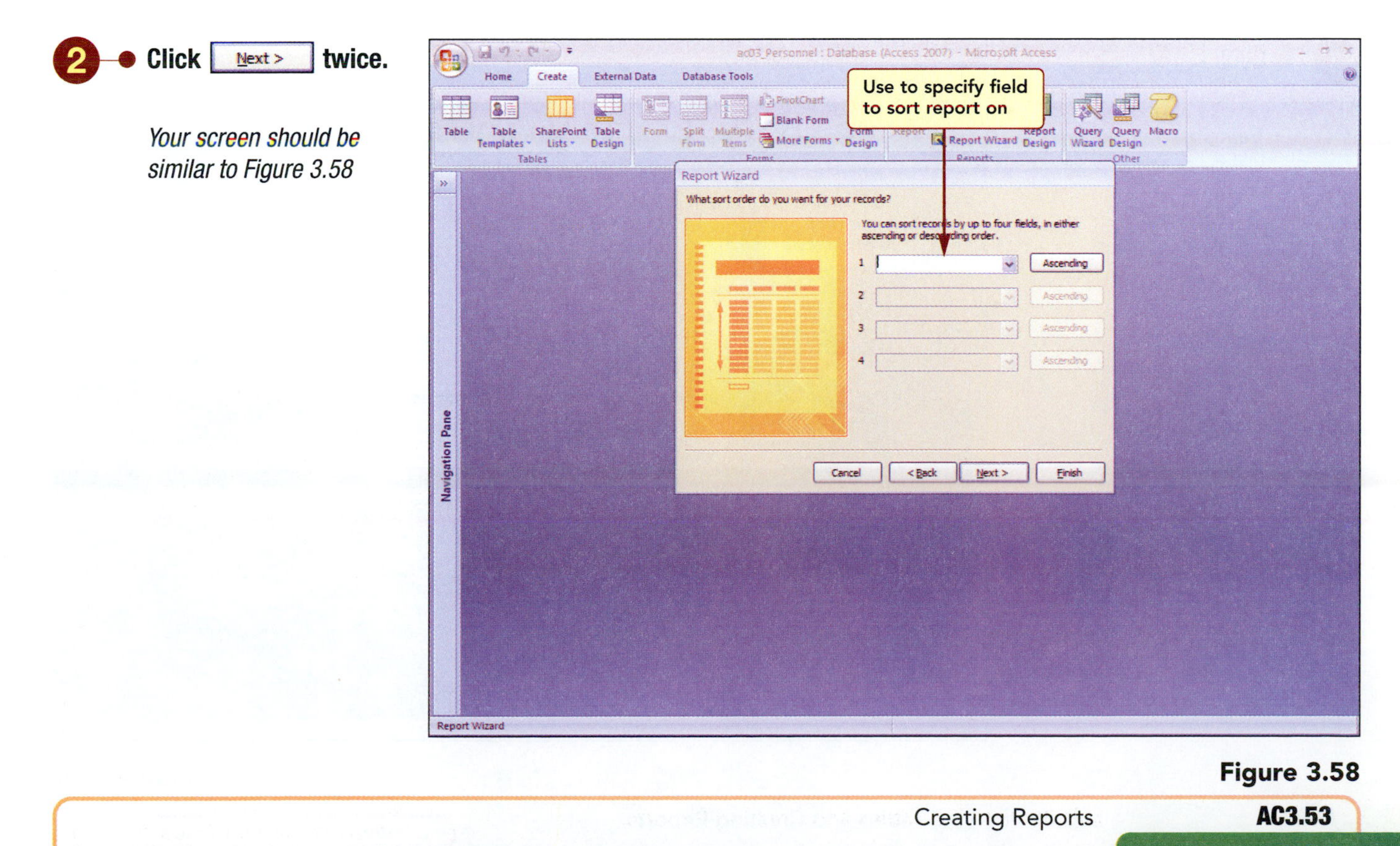

Figure 3.58

In this dialog box, you can specify a sort order for the records. Because the query already specifies the sort order, you do not need to specify this again.

3 Click .

Your screen should be similar to Figure 3.59

Creates a tabular report in portrait orientation

Fits report on one page

Figure 3.59

This dialog box is used to change the report layout and orientation. The default report settings create a tabular layout using portrait orientation. In addition, the option to adjust the field width so that all fields fit on one page is selected. The default settings are acceptable.

Additional Information

Reports use the same layouts as Forms.

4 Click 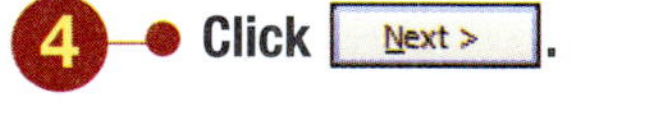.

Your screen should be similar to Figure 3.60

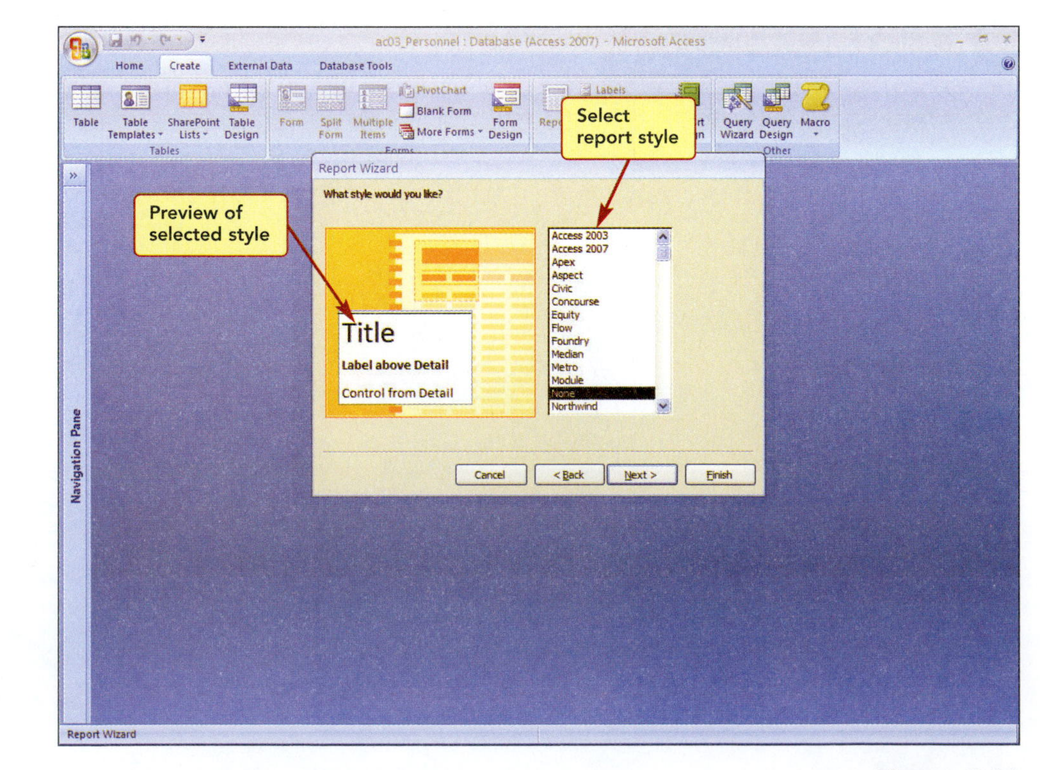

Figure 3.60

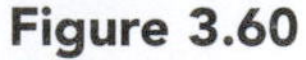

From this dialog box, you select a design style for the report. The preview area displays a sample of each style as it is selected.

5
- **Select each style to preview the style options.**
- **Select Northwind.**
- **Click Next >.**

Your screen should be similar to Figure 3.61

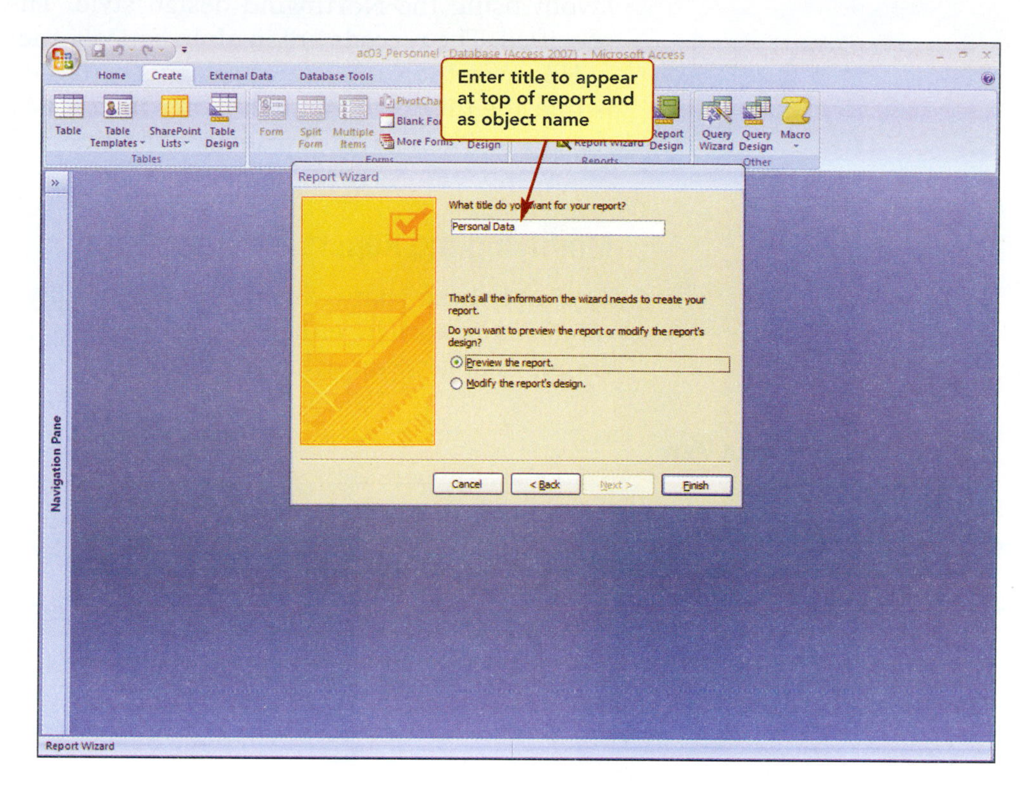

Figure 3.61

The last Report Wizard dialog box is used to add a title to the report and to specify how the report should be displayed after it is created. The only change you want to make is to replace the query name with a more descriptive report title.

6
- **Enter Maldin to Landis Car Pool Report as the title.**
- **Click Finish.**

Your screen should be similar to Figure 3.62

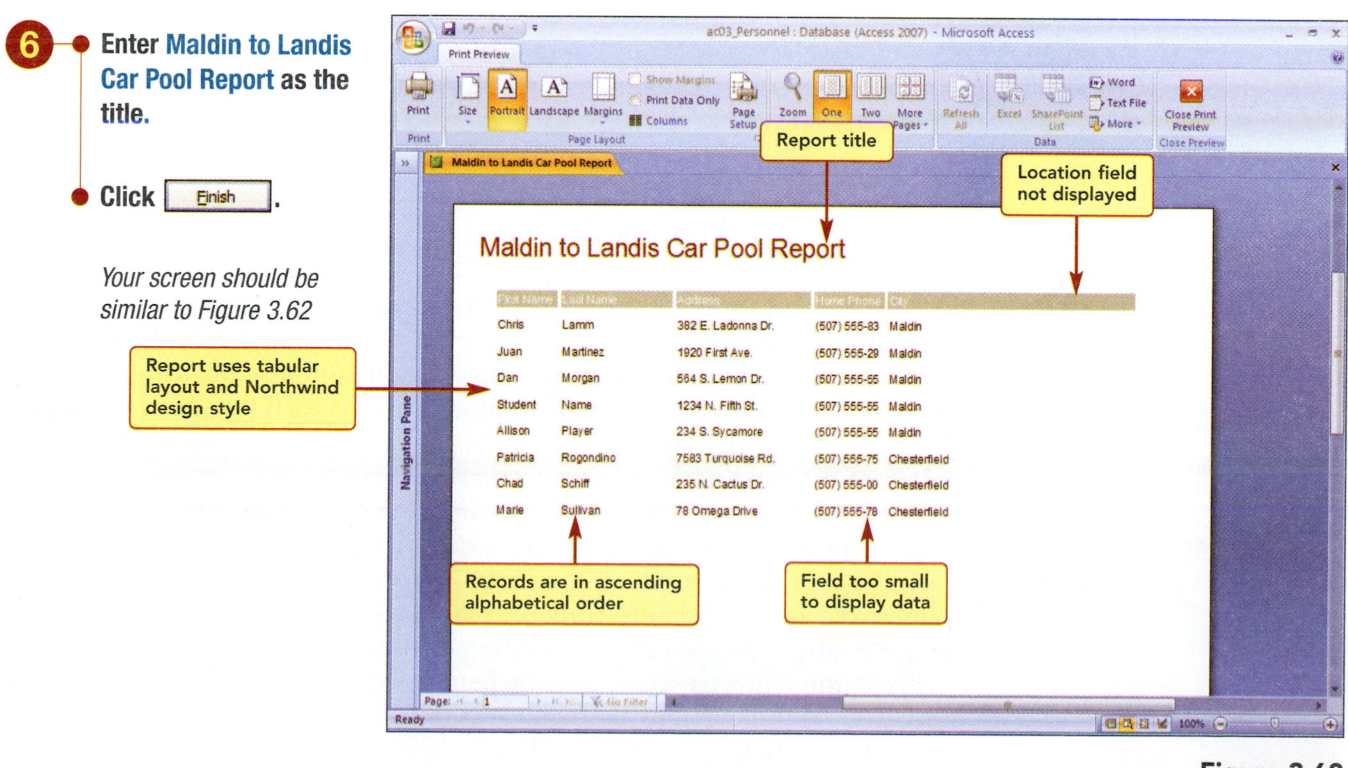

Figure 3.62

In a few moments, the completed report with the data from the resource query is displayed in Print Preview. The report appears in the tabular layout using the Northwind design style. The title reflects the title you specified. The records are in alphabetical order as specified by the query.

However, there are a few problems with the design. The most noticeable is that the City field is much larger than it needs to be and, consequently, the Home Phone field is truncated. Additionally, you want the City field to follow the Address field.

Modifying the Report in Layout View

To make these changes, you need to modify the report design. You can modify a report in either Design view or Layout view. To make these simple changes, you will use Layout view.

1 **Click Layout View in the status bar.**

If necessary, close the Field list pane.

Your screen should be similar to Figure 3.63

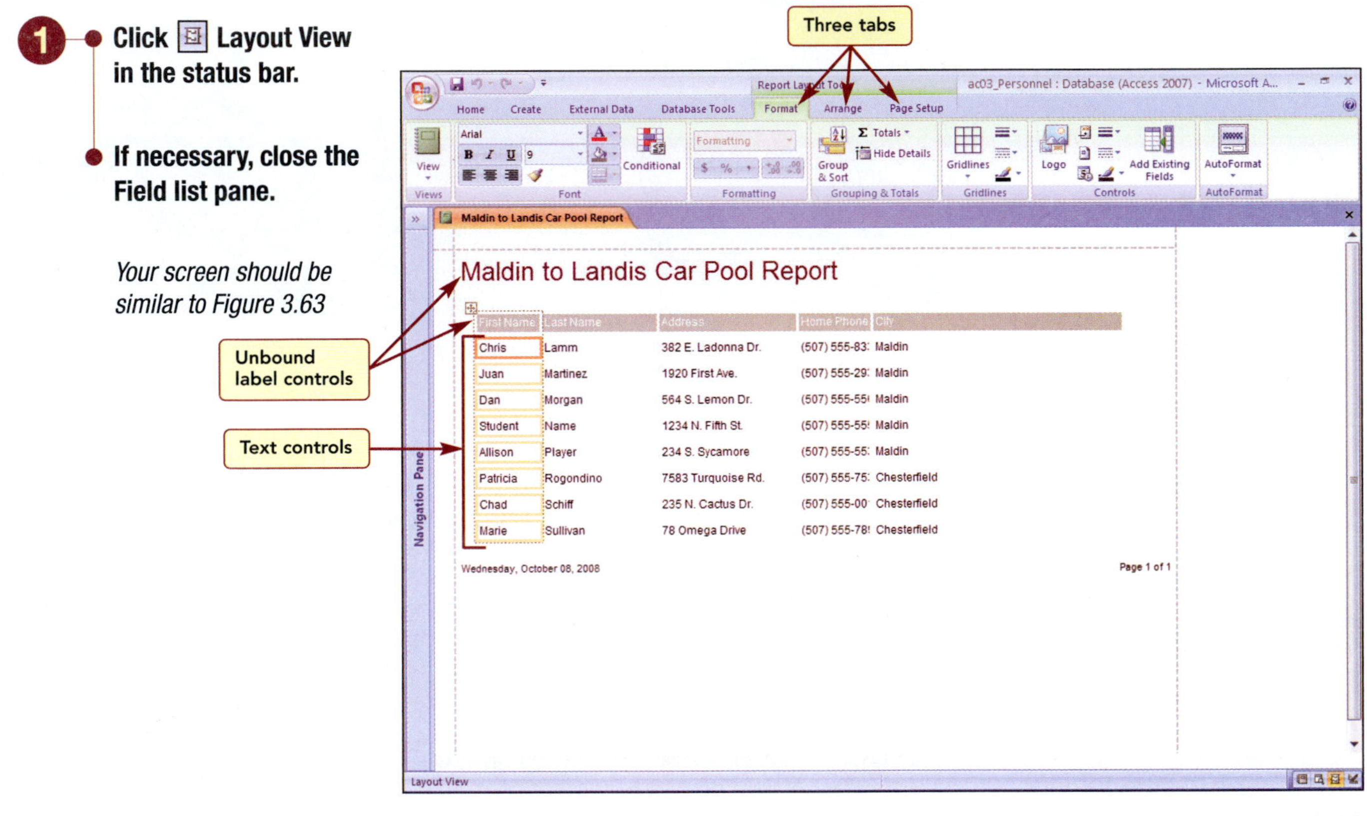

Figure 3.63

In Layout view, three tabs are available to help you modify the report. The Format tab contains commands that are used to make text enhancements such as fonts and colors, as well as to add and modify report design objects. The Arrange tab is used to modify the overall layout of the report or of individual elements. The Page Setup tab is used to control the page layout of the report for printing purposes.

Just as in forms, each item in the report is a separate control. The field names are label controls and the field information is a text control. The text controls are bound to the data in the underlying table. The field names and report title are unbound label controls. The columnar report layout controls the layout and position of these controls.

The same features you learned when working in Form Layout view are available in Report Layout view. You will begin by sizing the City and Home Phone fields. Then you will move the Home Phone field.

Having Trouble?

See Concept 8 in Lab 2 to review controls.

Click on the City field.

Additional Information

The dotted box around the label and text box controls shows they are a compound control.

- **Reduce the size of the field to fit the contents.**
- **Click on the Home Phone field and increase the size of the field to display the contents.**
- **Drag the Home Phone field object to the right of the City field.**
- **Adjust the size of the fields as in Figure 3.64.**

Your screen should be similar to Figure 3.64

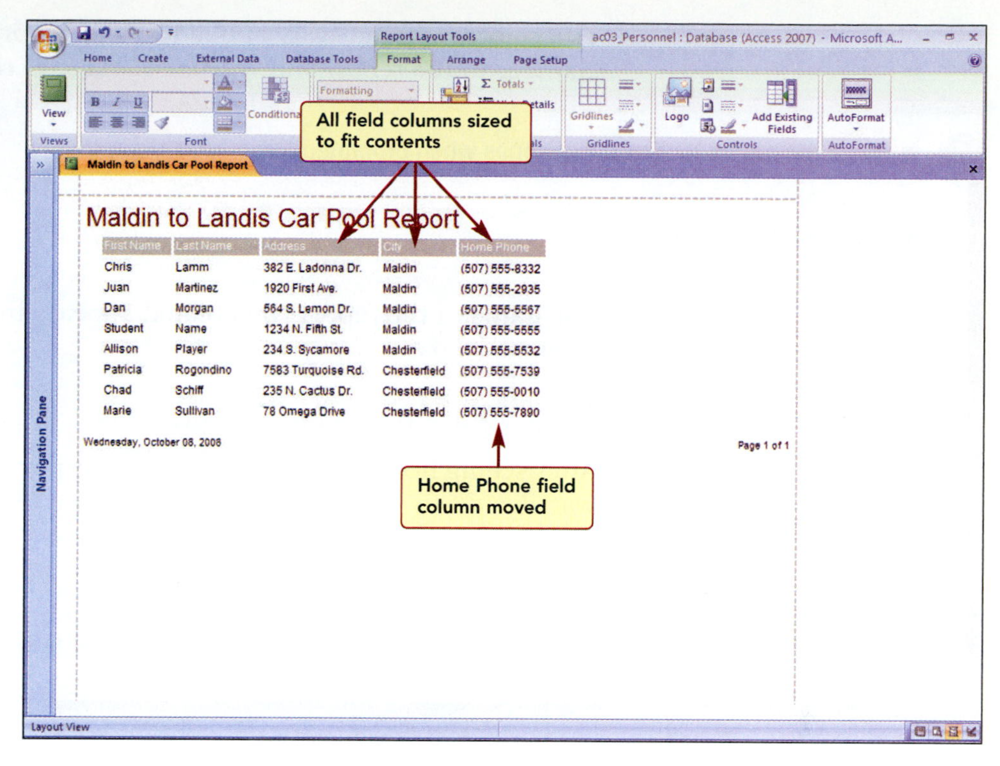

Figure 3.64

The last changes you want to make are to the appearance of the report. You decide to change the report design style to another more colorful style. This feature works similarly to the Form AutoFormat feature. The same selection of report design styles that were available in the wizard are displayed in the AutoFormat gallery.

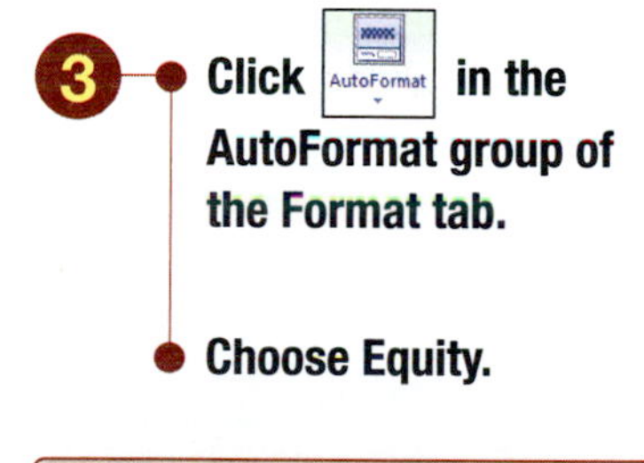

3 **Click AutoFormat in the AutoFormat group of the Format tab.**

- **Choose Equity.**

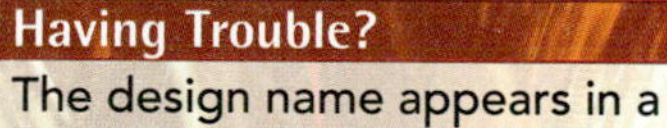

Having Trouble?

The design name appears in a ScreenTip when you point to the different designs.

Your screen should be similar to Figure 3.65

Displays predefined report formats

Equity design format applied to table

Figure 3.65

The selected design was applied to the report. You are finished making changes to the report and will close and save the report.

4

- **Close the report, saving the changes when prompted.**
- **Display the Navigation pane.**

The name of the report you created appears in the Reports category of the Navigation pane.

Modifying a Report in Design View

After seeing how easy it was to create a report for the carpool information, you decide to create a custom report for the job position and location information requested by the club director.

1

- **Select the Location Query from the Queries category and click Report Wizard in the Create tab.**
- **Add all the fields to the report.**
- **Click Finish.**
- **Enter River Mist as the location and click OK.**

Your screen should be similar to Figure 3.66

Figure 3.66

Rather than moving through each step of the wizard, if you know that you will be using the default or last-used settings, you can end the wizard at any point. The report displays the specified fields and uses the tabular layout and the Equity design style. This style was used because it was the last style used in the database.

As you look at the report, you realize you forgot to include the Position field. You will modify the query and then add this field in Design view to the report.

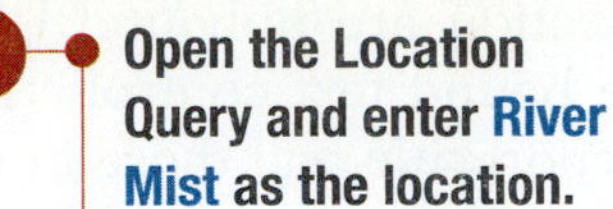

- Open the Location Query and enter **River Mist** as the location.
- Change to Design view and add the Position field to the design grid.
- Click [Save icon] Save in the Quick Access Toolbar to save the query design changes.
- Display the Location Query report and click [Close Print Preview].
- Hide the Navigation pane.
- If the Field List pane is not displayed, click [Add Existing Fields] in the Tools group of the Design tab.

Another Method

You also can use the shortcut key (Alt) + (F8) to hide and display the Field List pane.

Your screen should be similar to Figure 3.67

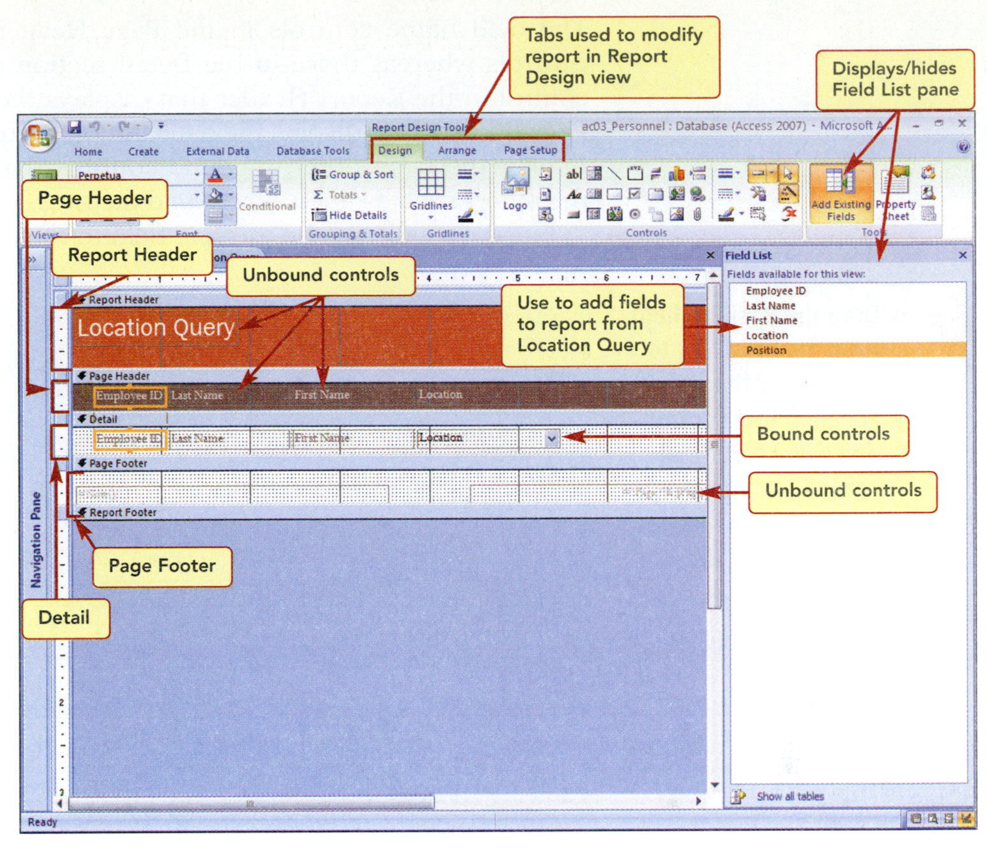

Figure 3.67

The report is displayed in Report Design view. It includes three tabs that help you modify the report. The Design tab contains commands that are used to make text enhancements such as fonts and colors, as well as to add and modify report design objects. The Arrange tab is used to modify the overall layout of the report or of individual elements. The Page Setup tab is used to control the page layout of the report for printing purposes.

Additionally, the Field List task pane displays the field names from the design grid of the Location Query and is used to add fields to the report.

The Report Design window is divided into five sections: Report Header, Page Header, Detail, Page Footer, and Report Footer. The contents of each section appear below the horizontal bar that contains the name of that section. The sections are described in the following table.

Section	Description
Report Header	Contains information to be printed once at the beginning of the report. The report title is displayed in this section.
Page Header	Contains information to be printed at the top of each page. The column headings are displayed in this section.
Detail	Contains the records of the table. The field column widths are the same as the column widths set in the table design.
Page Footer	Contains information to be printed at the bottom of each page such as the date and page number.
Report Footer	Contains information to be printed at the end of the report. The Report Footer section currently contains no data.

The field name controls in the Page Header section are unbound label controls whereas those in the Detail section are bound text controls. The control in the Report Header that displays the report title and those in the Page Footers that display the date and page numbers are unbound controls. Finally, there are other unbound controls that enhance the appearance of the report such as lines, boxes, and pictures.

First you will add the missing field to the report.

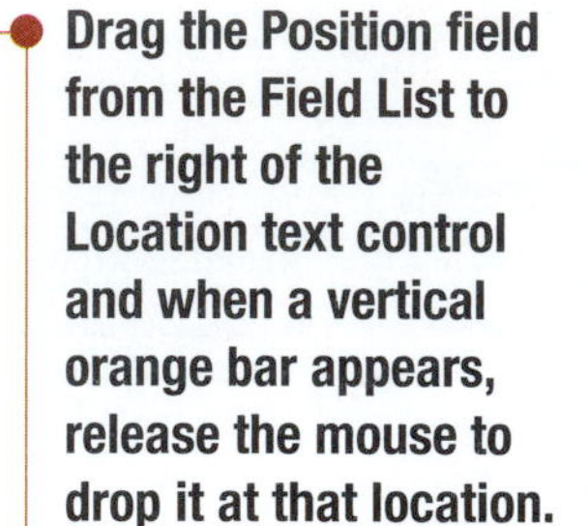

3. **Drag the Position field from the Field List to the right of the Location text control and when a vertical orange bar appears, release the mouse to drop it at that location.**

- **Close the Field List pane.**

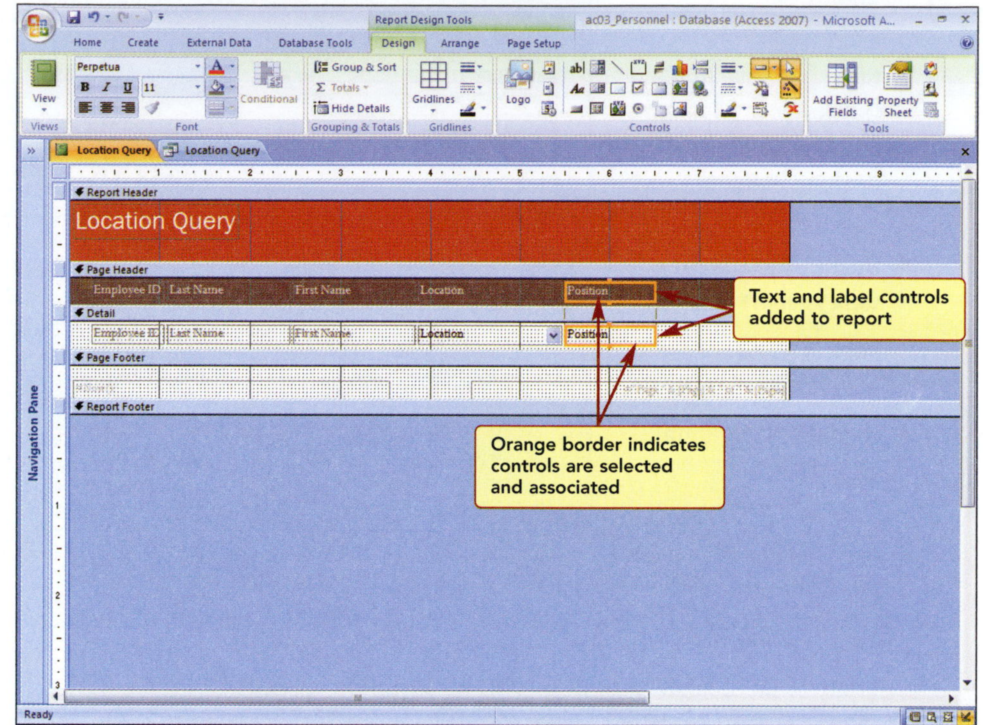

Figure 3.68

Additional Information

You also can double-click on the field from the field list to move it into the report design.

Your screen should be similar to Figure 3.68

Position text and label controls have been added to the report. The Position label control was inserted in the Page Header section and the Position text control in the Detail section. This is because the controls were inserted into the tabular control layout and comply with the horizontal and vertical alignment settings of the layout.

Both controls are surrounded by an orange border indicating that they are selected and that they are **compound controls.** This means the controls are associated, and that the two controls will act as one when moved. Additionally, the text control is a bound control that is tied to the Position field data.

Now you want to move the Last Name controls to the right of the First Name controls. Controls can be moved to any location within the control layout by clicking on the control to select it and then dragging it to the new location. The mouse pointer changes to ✥ to indicate that a selected control can be moved.

Additional Information

If you want to move a control out of the control layout, it needs to be removed from the group as you did when designing the form.

Another Method

You also can move controls using Ctrl + the directional arrow keys.

- **Select the Last Name text control.**
- **Point to the control and when the mouse pointer changes to ✥, drag it to the right of the First Name text control.**

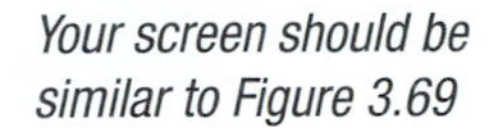

Your screen should be similar to Figure 3.69

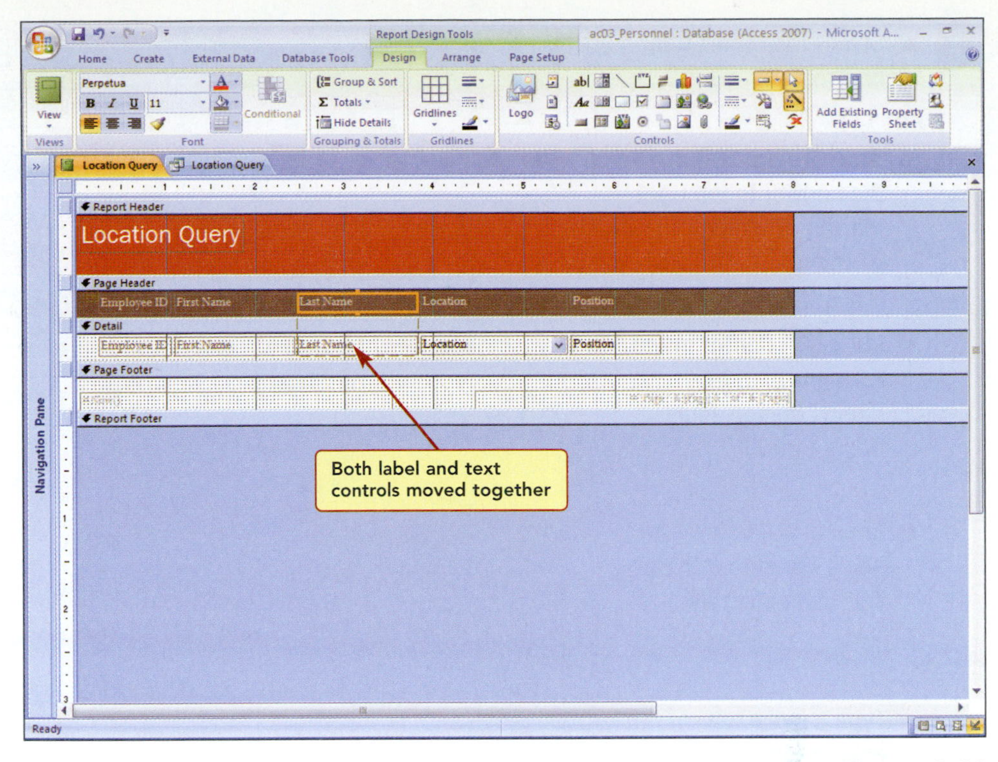

Figure 3.69

Notice that the Last Name label control in the Page Header area also moved and was automatically placed and aligned above the Last Name text control. The controls in both the Page Header and Detail sections are horizontally and vertically aligned and spaced an equal distance apart.

Format Controls

Next, you decide to change the text of the report title and center it over the report. First you will enlarge the title control to extend the width of the report and then center the text within the control.

- Select the report title control.
- Drag the right edge of the control to the right margin (8" ruler position).
- Click Center in the Font group of the Report Design Tools Design tab.
- Click in the control to place the cursor in the text and select the text.
- Type **Landis Job Position Report**.

Having Trouble?

The title text is difficult to see because it is white on a white background when the text is selected.

- Click outside the report design area to clear the selection.

Your screen should be similar to Figure 3.70

Figure 3.70

The revised title is centered over the report columns. Changing the title text does not change the name of the report object.

Now you want to see the effects of your changes. You will be prompted to enter the location. This time, you will enter Landis as the location because the report title now includes the location.

Switch to Layout view.

Enter the location of Landis.

Your screen should be similar to Figure 3.71

Figure 3.71

The report is really shaping up. However, there are still a few changes you need to make. You want to remove the Location field because the title now identifies the location. Then you will adjust the sizes of the fields to make the report fill more of the width of the page.

Deleting a Field

You will delete the field and resize the other fields in Layout view so you can see the field content and layout while sizing them.

1. Select the Location field and press Delete.

- Increase the size of the Position field to fully display the field contents.

Having Trouble?

Scroll to the end of the report to make sure that the largest Position name is fully displayed.

- Increase the size of the Employee ID field to approximately the same size as the name fields.

Your screen should be similar to Figure 3.72

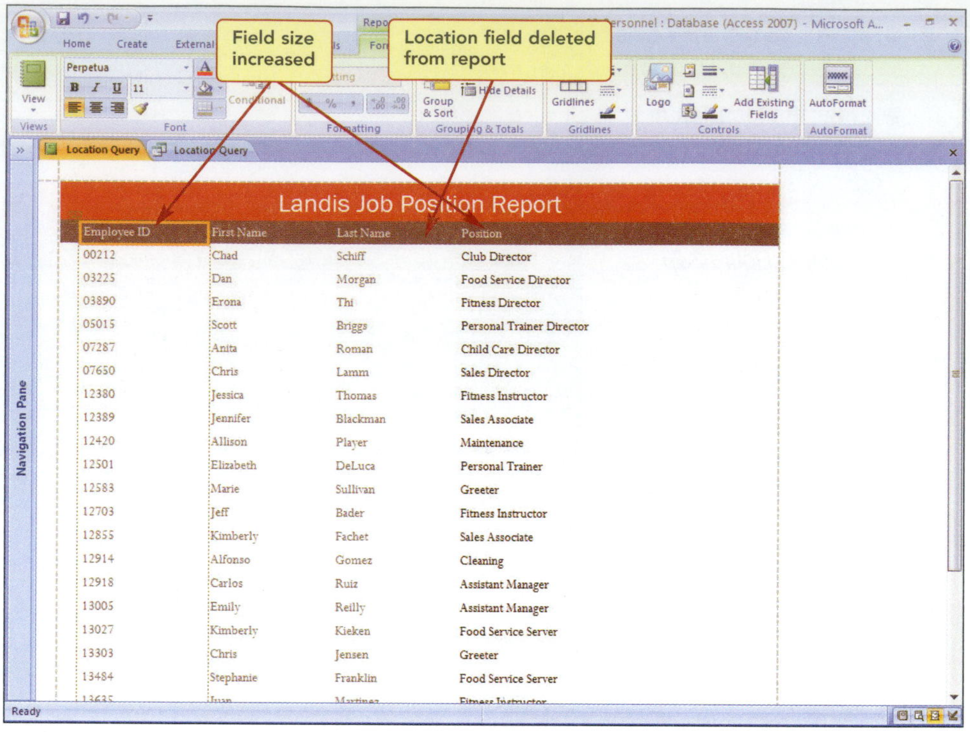

Field size increased

Location field deleted from report

Figure 3.72

Now, each time you run the report, you simply need to change the location in the title to reflect the location you specify as the query parameter.

Sorting and Filtering Data in a Report

You also notice that the records in the report are in Employee ID order. This is because a sort order was not specified in the query or the report when they were created. Just as in a table datasheet, query, or form, you can sort and filter the data that is displayed in a report. You will use these features to sort the records in alphabetical order by last name and display only those records whose job is a fitness instructor.

1. Right-click on the Last Name field of any record.
   - Choose Sort A to Z.
   - Right-click on the Position field of any record that displays Fitness Instructor.
   - Choose Equals "Fitness Instructor".

Your screen should be similar to Figure 3.73

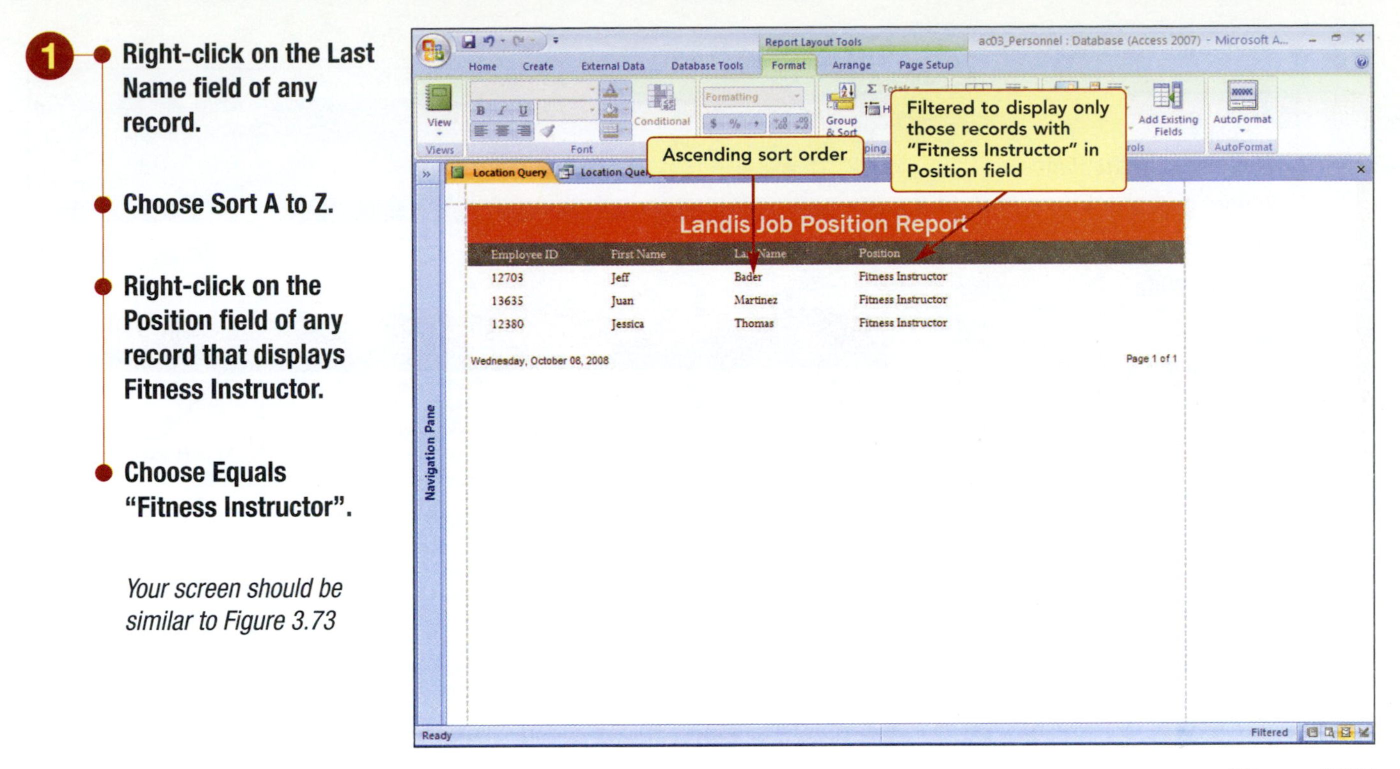

Figure 3.73

Only the three records meeting the filter requirements are displayed in the report. They are in alphabetical order by last name. You will remove the filter but maintain the sorted record order.

2. Right-click on the Position field of any record.
   - Choose Clear filter from Position.

> **Additional Information**
> You also can click Toggle Filter in the Home tab to remove the filter.

All the records are redisplayed again.

Preparing Reports for Printing

You can print the report from any view or even when the report is closed. However, unless you are sure the page settings are correct, it is a good idea to open the report and check its layout in Layout view or Print Preview first. In Layout view, you can easily make any adjustments to the report if you find the changes you make to the page layout affect how the report will print.

Modifying the Page Setup

As you look at the layout of the report on the page, you see the columns are not centered on the page. This is because the first column starts at the default left margin setting of 0.25 inch. You decide to increase the size of the margins, which will push the columns to the right and better center them on the page.

1 Open the Page Setup tab.

Click Margins in the Page Layout group.

Choose Wide.

Your screen should be similar to Figure 3.74

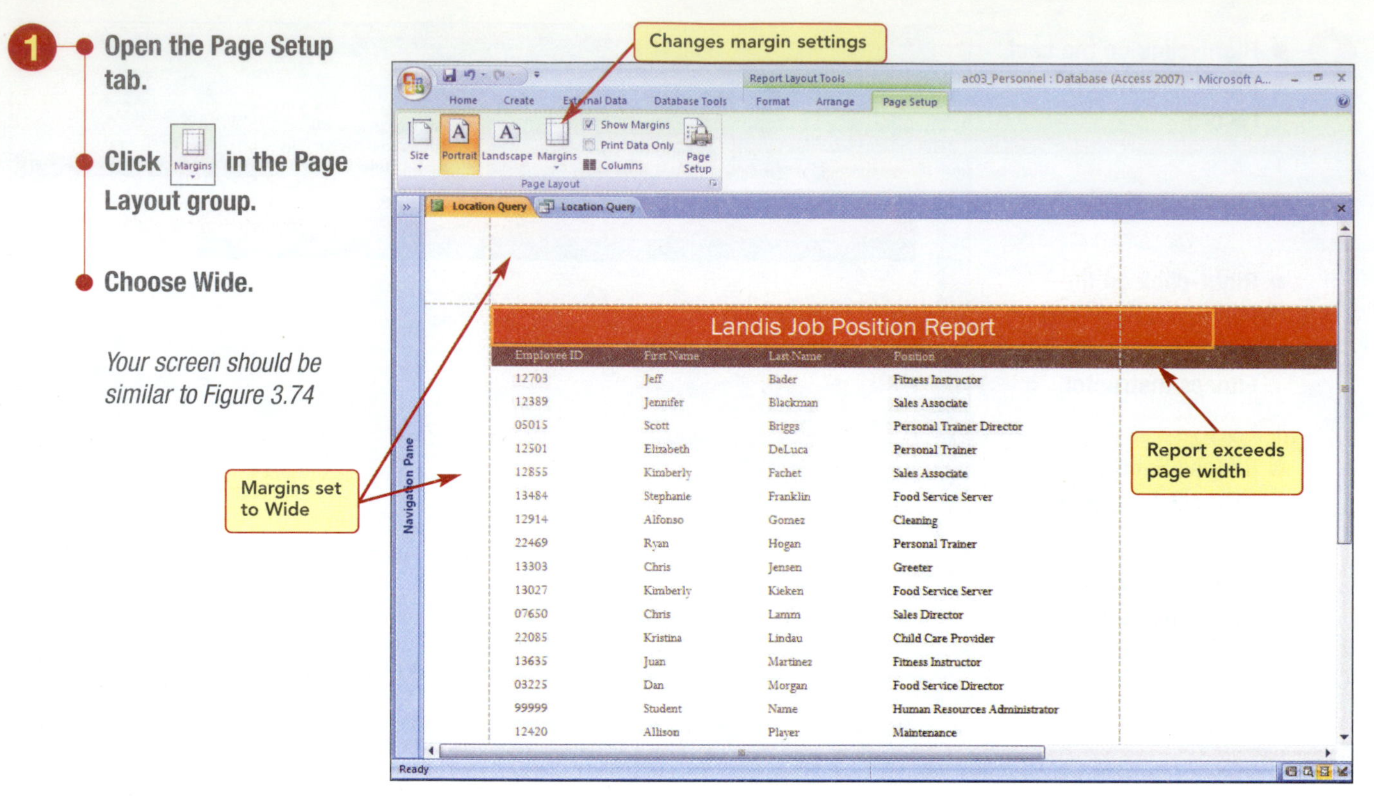

Figure 3.74

The Wide margin option increases the left and right margins to 0.75 inch. The columns now begin at the left margin and the report appears more balanced on the page; however, now the report width exceeds a single page. This is because some of the controls in the report exceed the new page margins. Additionally, the title is no longer centered because the control is wider than the new page width. These problems can be quickly fixed by reducing the size of the controls that are causing the problem. You decide to increase the margins to 1 inch and then make the adjustments to the controls to fit the new page width. To do this, you will set a custom left and right margin.

2

- **Click [Page Setup] in the Page Layout group.**
- **Enter 1 in the Left and Right Margin text boxes.**
- **Click**  **OK.**
- **Click on the title control and size the control to fit the new page width.**
- **Scroll to the bottom of the report and click on the page number control in the footer.**
- **Reduce the control size (from the right edge) until it is inside the right margin line.**
- **If the report still exceeds the margins, click on the Position column and reduce the size of the column.**
- **Scroll to the top of the report.**

Your screen should be similar to Figure 3.75

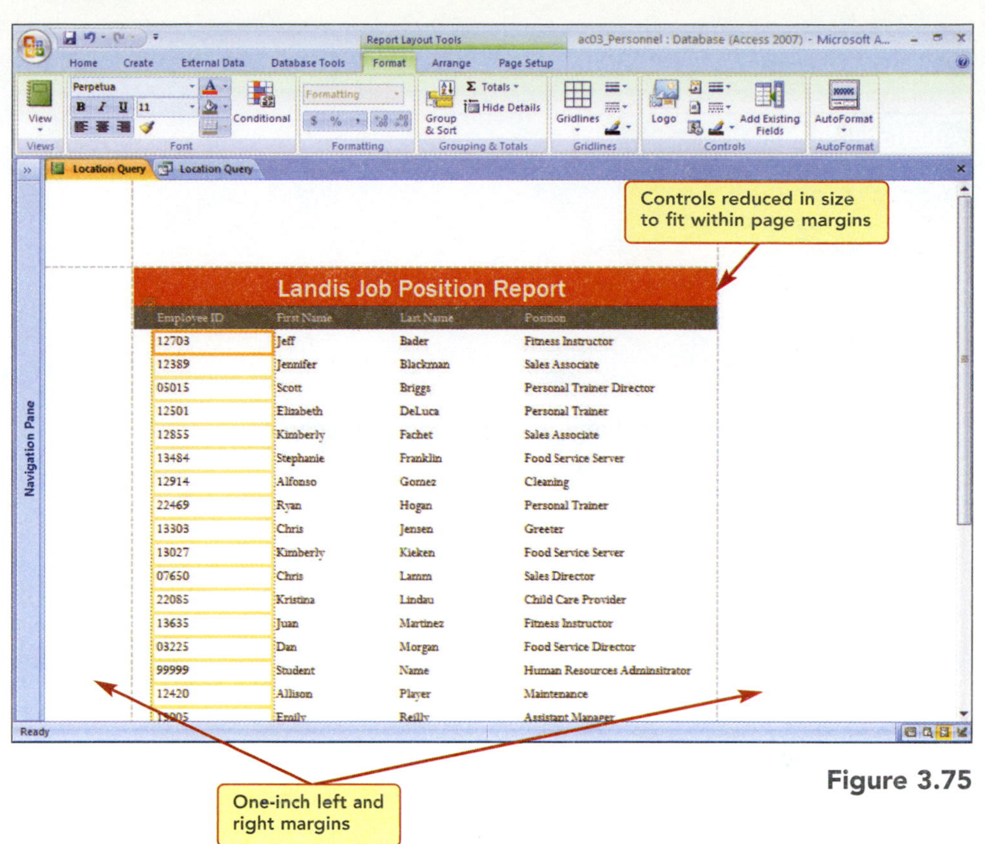

Figure 3.75

Now the columns are spaced attractively across the page. The page layout settings you specify are saved with the report, so unless you make changes to the report design, you only need to set them once.

Previewing and Printing Reports

Although you believe the report is ready to print, you will preview it first and then print it.

1. Click Print Preview in the status bar to change the view to Print Preview.

Additional Information
You also can specify margins and page setup using the same features in the Print Preview ribbon.

- Click Print.
- Specify your printer settings and then print the report.
- Close the report, saving the changes.
- Close the query.
- Open the Navigation pane and rename the Location Query report **Job Position Report**.

Your printed report should look like the one shown in the Case Study at the beginning of the lab.

Printing a Relationships Report

Before exiting Access, you want to print a report that shows the relationships between the tables in your database.

1. Open the Database Tools tab.
- Click Relationships.
- If necessary, click All Relationships to show all table relationships.
- Click Relationship Report in the Tools group of the Relationship Tools Design tab.
- Click Margins and select Last Custom Setting from the drop-down menu.
- Print the report.

Your screen should be similar to Figure 3.76

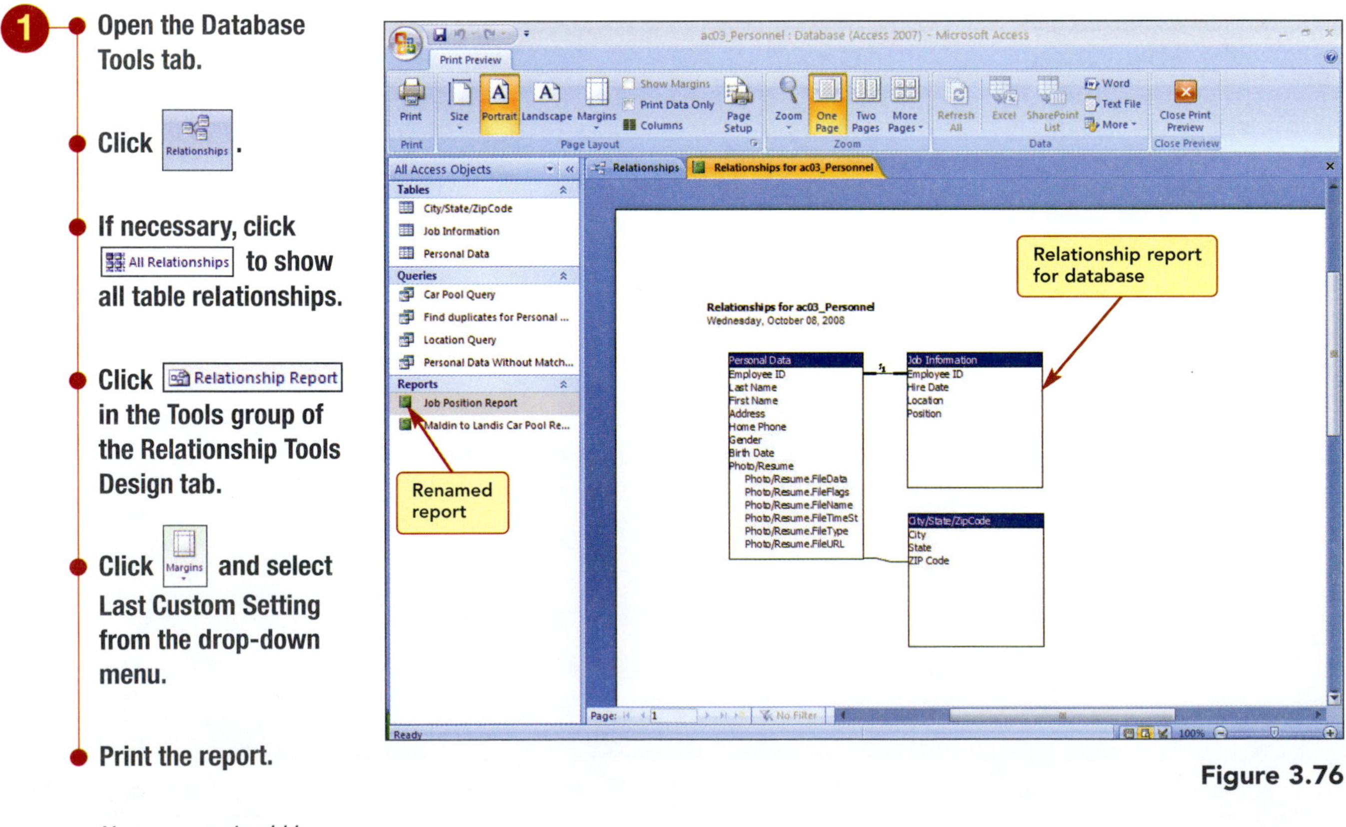

Figure 3.76

A preview of how the report will look when printed is displayed on the screen. The database name and creation date are automatically used as the report header. You can print this report as well as save it for future reference.

2 Close the relationship report without saving it.

Close the Relationships window.

> **Additional Information**
> A file is fragmented when it becomes too large for your computer to store in a single location on your hard disk. When this happens, the file is split up and stored in pieces in different locations on the disk, making access slower.

Compacting and Backing Up the Database

As you modify a database, the changes are saved to your disk. When you delete data or objects, the database file can become fragmented and use disk space inefficiently. To make the database perform optimally, you should **compact** the database on a regular basis. Compacting makes a copy of the file and rearranges the way that the file is stored on your disk.

1 Click Office Button and choose Manage/Compact and Repair Database.

Although it appears that nothing has happened, the database file has been compacted and repaired as needed. It is also a good idea to back up your databases periodically. This will ensure that you have a copy of each database in case of a power outage or other system failure while you are working on a file, or in case you need to access a previous version of a database that you have changed.

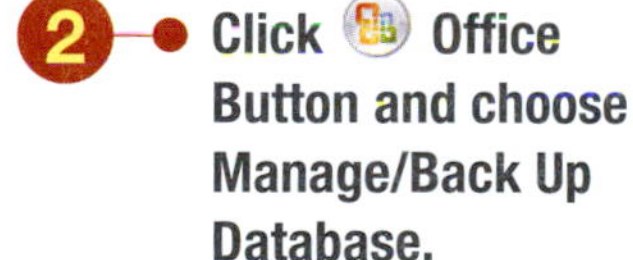

2 Click Office Button and choose Manage/Back Up Database.

Your screen should be similar to Figure 3.77

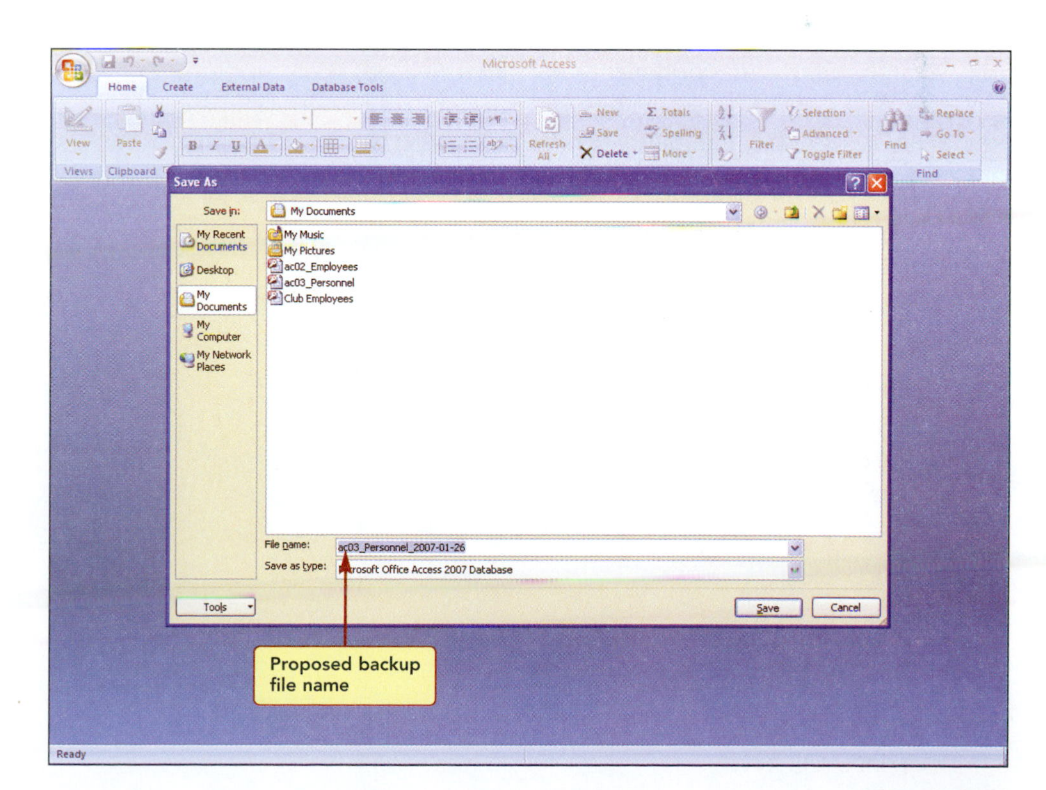

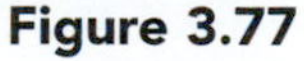
Figure 3.77

The Save As dialog box displays your database name (which in this case is ac03_Personnel) with the current date appended to it. This is a good way to keep track of when you performed the backup on the database, so you will not change this file name.

3
- **If necessary, change the Save In location to your data file location.**
- **Click Save.**
- **Close the database and exit Access.**

The backup database file has been saved to your data file location. If you need to restore a backed up database, you just change the name of the backup file (so it does not conflict with another file of the same name that you may have created since the backup) and then open it in Access.

Focus on Careers

EXPLORE YOUR CAREER OPTIONS

Database Administrator

Database administrators are responsible for organizing and maintaining an organization's information resources. This position generally involves training new users to use the database, testing new objects, and backing up the data. As a database administrator, your position also would include safeguarding the system from threats. The typical salary range of a database administrator is $40,000 to $65,000. A bachelor's degree in computer science is typically preferred in addition to practical experience. Demand for skilled database administrators is expected to make it one of the fastest-growing occupations.

Concept Summary

LAB 3

Querying Tables and Creating Reports

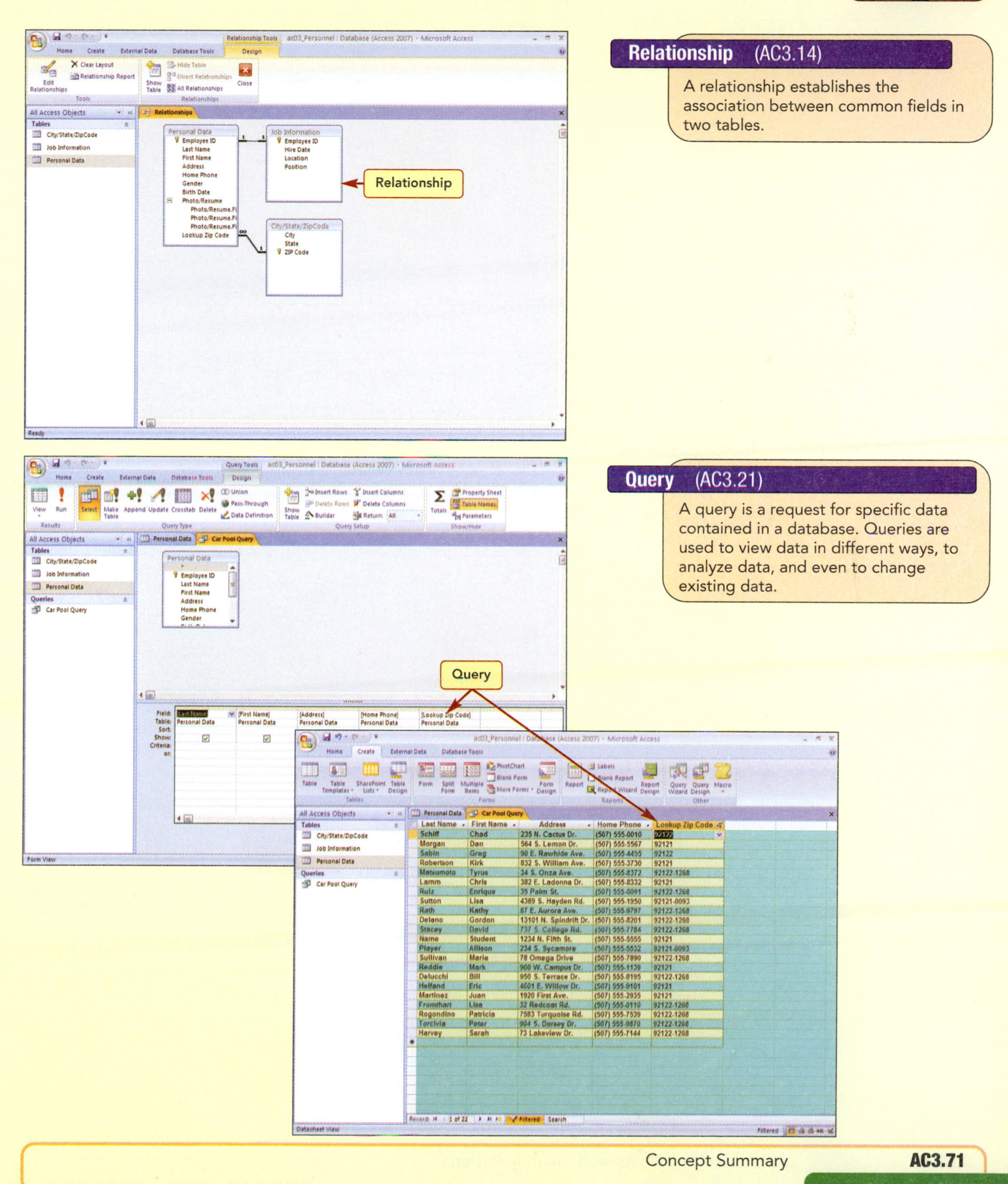

Relationship (AC3.14)

A relationship establishes the association between common fields in two tables.

Query (AC3.21)

A query is a request for specific data contained in a database. Queries are used to view data in different ways, to analyze data, and even to change existing data.

Concept Summary

Join (AC3.27)

A join is an association between a field in one table or query and a field of the same data type in another table or query.

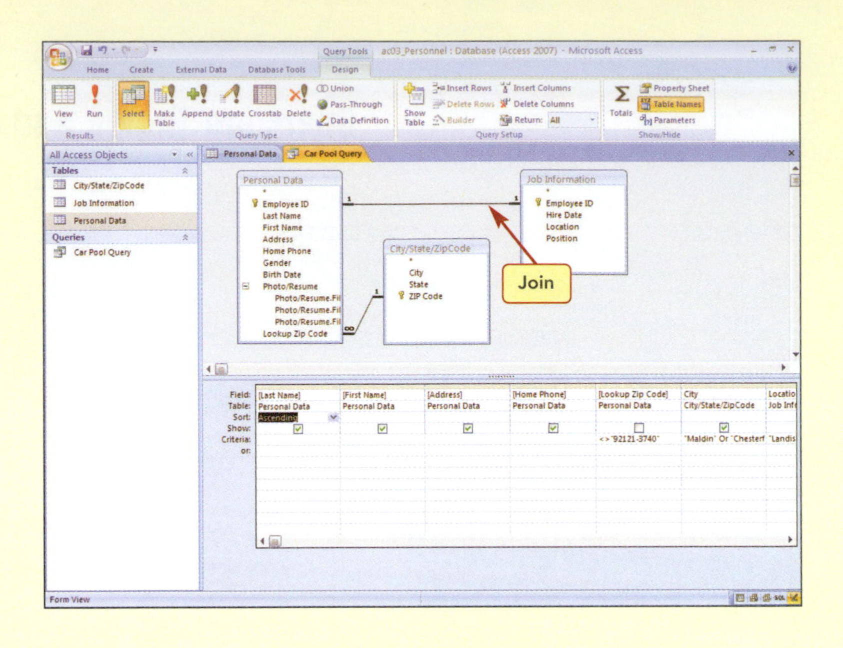

Report (AC3.49)

A report is professional-appearing output generated from tables or queries that may include design elements, groups, and summary information.

Report

Landis Job Position Report

Employee ID	First Name	Last Name	Location	Position
00212	Chad	Schiff	Landis	Club Director
03225	Dan	Morgan	Landis	Food Service Dire
03890	Erona	Thi	Landis	Fitness Director
05015	Scot	Briggs	Landis	Personal Trainer
07287	Anita	Roman	Landis	Child Care Direc
07650	Chris	Lamm	Landis	Sales Director
12380	Jessica	Thomas	Landis	Fitness Instructor
12389	Jennifer	Blackman	Landis	Sales Associate
12420	Allison	Player	Landis	Maintenance
12501	Elizabeth	DeLuca	Landis	Personal Trainer
12583	Marie	Sullivan	Landis	Greeter
12703	Jeff	Bader	Landis	Fitness Instructor
12855	Kimberly	Fachet	Landis	Sales Associate
12914	Alfonso	Gomez	Landis	Cleaning
12918	Carlos	Ruiz	Landis	Assistant Manager

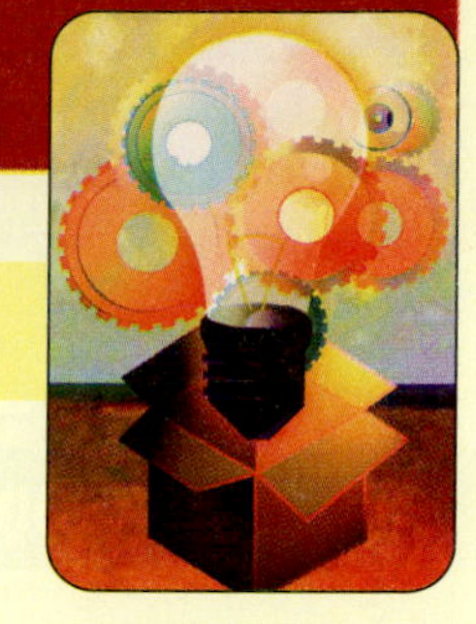

LAB 3

Querying Tables and Creating Reports

key terms

Action query AC3.21
aggregate functions AC3.47
AND operator AC3.32
column selector bar AC3.26
common field AC3.14
compact AC3.69
compound control AC3.60
compound criterion AC3.32
criteria AC3.21
criteria expression AC3.30
Crosstab query AC3.21
design grid AC3.26
field list AC3.26
hard-coded criteria AC3.46
inner join AC3.30
join AC3.27
join line AC3.18
junction table AC3.14
many-to-many AC3.14
multitable query AC3.26
one-to-many AC3.14
one-to-one AC3.14
OR operator AC3.32
outer join AC3.30
Parameter query AC3.21
parameter value AC3.46
query AC3.21
referential integrity AC3.14
relationship AC3.14
report AC3.49
row label AC3.26
Select query AC3.21
Show box AC3.26
SQL query AC3.21
unequal join AC3.30

MCAS skills

The Microsoft Certified Applications Specialist (MCAS) certification program is designed to measure your proficiency in performing basic tasks using the Office 2007 applications. Getting certified demonstrates that you have the skills and provides a valuable industry credential for employment. See Reference 2: Microsoft Certified Applications Specialist (MCAS) for a complete list of the skills that were covered in Lab 3.

Lab Review

command summary

Command	Shortcut	Action
Office Button		
Save As		Saves database object with a new file name
Manage/Back Up Database		Backs up database
Manage/Compact and Repair		Compacts and repairs database file
Home tab		
Views group		
Report View		Displays report in Report view
Report Layout View		Displays report in Layout view
Records group		
Refresh All		Updates selected object
Σ Totals		Displays/hides Totals row
Create tab		
Reports group		
Report		Creates a report using all fields in current table
Blank Report		Creates a report using Report Design view
Report Wizard		Creates a report using the Report Wizard
Other group		
Query Wizard		Creates a query using the Query Wizard
Query Design		Creates a query using Query Design view
Database Tools tab		
Show/Hide group		
Object Dependencies		Evaluates table design and suggests modifications
Relationships		Defines how the data in tables is related

command summary

Command	Shortcut	Action
Analyze group Analyze Table		Evaluates table design
Query Tools Design tab		
Results group Run		Displays query results in Query Datasheet view
Query Setup group Show Table		Displays/hides Show Table dialog box
Show/Hide group Table Names		Displays/hides the Tables row
Report Layout Tools Format tab		
Font group Center		Centers text in selected control
Controls group Add Existing Fields		Displays/hides Add Existing Fields task pane
AutoFormat group AutoFormat		Applies selected predesigned styles to report
Report Layout Tools Page Setup tab		
Page Layout group Margins		Sets margins of printed report
Page Setup		Sets features related to the page layout of printed report

command summary

Command	Shortcut	Action
Report Design Tools Design tab		
Font group		
Center		Centers text in selected control
		Sizes text in selected control
Tools group		
Add Existing Fields		Displays/hides the Fields List task pane
Relationship Tools Design tab		
Tools group		
Relationship Report		Creates a report of the displayed relationships
Print Preview tab		
Page Layout group		
Margins		Adjusts margins in printed output

Lab Exercises

matching

Match the numbered item with the correct lettered description.

1. one-to-many	______	**a.** intersection of a column and row
2. compact	______	**b.** calculations that are performed on a range of data
3. multitable query	______	**c.** runs a query and displays a query datasheet
4. aggregate functions	______	**d.** a type of table relationship
5. query	______	**e.** makes a copy of the file and rearranges the way that the file is stored on your disk
6. cell	______	**f.** an association between fields in related tables
7. ! Run	______	**g.** used to ask questions about database tables
8. referential integrity	______	**h.** query that uses data from more than one table
9. criteria	______	**i.** set of limiting conditions
10. parameter value	______	**j.** prompts you for the specific criteria you want to use when you run the query

fill-in

Complete the following statements by filling in the blanks with the correct terms.

1. Enforcing ______ ensures that relationships between tables are valid and that related data is not accidentally changed or deleted.
2. The ______ operator narrows the search for records that meet both conditions.
3. A(n) ______ control is used to enter multiple criteria.
4. A(n) ______ is a request for specific data contained in a database.
5. A(n) ______ is used to display the results of a query.
6. A(n) ______ is an association that tells Access how data between tables is related.
7. The ______ is where you enter the settings that define the query.
8. In a report, a(n) ______ is not connected to a field.
9. ______ are the set of limiting conditions used in filters and queries.
10. To be joined, the tables must have at least one ______ field.

Lab Exercises

true/false

Circle the correct answer to the following statements.

1.	Values that tell Access how to filter the criteria in a query are called filter expressions.	True	False
2.	Queries are used to view data in different ways, to analyze data, and to change existing data.	True	False
3.	Reports can be generated from tables only.	True	False
4.	Fields in different tables must have the same name to create a relationship.	True	False
5.	A compound control consists of two controls that are associated.	True	False
6.	A join line shows how different tables are related.	True	False
7.	Related fields are fields that have the same data type and the same kind of information, but different field names.	True	False
8.	A compound criterion is created using the AND operator.	True	False
9.	A Select query is the most common type of query.	True	False
10.	Hard-coded criteria are used each time the query is run.	True	False

multiple choice

Circle the letter of the correct response.

1. A join line creates a ___________ relationship that establishes rules that the data must match to be included in the query results.
   a. permanent
   b. partial
   c. temporary
   d. complete
2. The query ___________ is where you enter the settings that define the query.
   a. field list
   b. Show box
   c. design grid
   d. objects
3. The ___________ operator is assumed when you enter criteria in multiple fields.
   a. OR
   b. AND
   c. BETWEEN
   d. EQUAL TO

4. A report title is a(n) __________ control because it is not connected to a field.
   a. bound
   b. associated
   c. unbound
   d. text
5. A(n) __________ query prompts you for the specific criteria you want to use when you run the query.
   a. Parameter
   b. SQL
   c. Update
   d. Append
6. __________ view is used to create and modify the structure of a query.
   a. Design
   b. Update
   c. Layout
   d. Datasheet
7. When a file is __________, it uses disk space inefficiently.
   a. broken
   b. fragmented
   c. compacted
   d. repaired
8. __________ view can be used to view the data in a report and modify the report design and layout.
   a. Layout
   b. Design
   c. Print Preview
   d. Datasheet
9. The operator that broadens the filter, because any record meeting either condition is included in the output, is __________.
   a. AND
   b. OR
   c. MOST
   d. ALL
10. Bound and unbound are types of __________.
   a. buttons
   b. forms
   c. properties
   d. controls

Hands-On Exercises

rating system
★ Easy
★★ Moderate
★★★ Difficult

step-by-step

Scensations Spa Database ★

1. The Scensations Salon and Day Spa offers hair and spa treatments exclusively for women. The owner of the spa is offering a new spa package that would include various anti-aging skin treatments and massages. She wants to send an announcement about this package to her clients who are over the age of 40. You will get this information for her from the client information that is stored in an Access 2007 database file. Your printed report will be similar to that shown here.

   a. Open the database file named ac03_Scensations Spa and the table named Clients.

   b. Find and delete any duplicate records using the Last Name field as the field to check for duplicate data.

   c. Use the Table Analyzer Wizard to create a second table containing the City, State, and Zip Code information. Name the new table **City/State/Zip**. Make the Zip Code field the primary key in this table.

   d. Delete the Clients table. Rename Table1 **Clients**. Move the Lookup field after the Address field. Best fit all the fields in the table.

   e. Query the Clients table to display the First Name, Last Name, Address, and City/State/Zip fields for those records with a birth date before 1/1/69.

   f. Display a Totals row showing a count of the Last Name field. Save the query as **40+ Clients**. Print the query results.

40+ Clients

Wednesday, October 08, 2008
9:34:05 AM

First Name	Last Name	Address	Lookup to City/Sate/Zip
Mary	Smith	560 E. West	89430, Smith Valley , NV
Patricia	Johnson	24486 S. 11th	89430, Smith Valley , NV
Linda	Williams	495 W. Cherry	89430, Smith Valley , NV
Barbara	Jones	738 N. Eighth	89430, Smith Valley , NV
Elizabeth	Brown	1008 E. Adams	89430, Smith Valley , NV
Jennifer	Davis	984 N. 7th	89430, Smith Valley , NV
Maria	Miller	448 E. Williams	89430, Smith Valley , NV
Margaret	Moore	246 N. 1st	89430, Smith Valley , NV
Dorothy	Taylor	1238 E. Fifth	89430, Smith Valley , NV
Lisa	Anderson	7428 S. Hill	89447, Yerington , NV
Nancy	Thomas	6190 E. Main	89447, Yerington , NV
Karen	Jackson	4952 S. Ridge	89706, Mound House , NV
Betty	White	3714 E. Washington	89706, Mound House , NV
Helen	Harris	246 N. 6th	89706, Mound House , NV
Heather	Morris	385 E. 5th	89403, Dayton , NV
Teresa	Rogers	55 N. 2nd	89403, Dayton , NV
Doris	Reed	10494 N. Forest	89403, Dayton , NV
Gloria	Cook	224 E. Laurel	89403, Dayton , NV
Evelyn	Morgan	6190 N. Ninth	89403, Dayton , NV
Mildred	Bailey	31482 E. Smith	89403, Dayton , NV
Katherine	Rivera	123 N. Willow	89403, Dayton , NV
Christina	Ramirez	492 N. First	89403, Dayton , NV
Beverly	Brooks	13992 S. River	89403, Dayton , NV
Andrea	Henderson	8666 N. 9th	89403, Dayton , NV
Kathryn	Coleman	784 E. Fourteenth	89403, Dayton , NV
Anne	Powell	112 E. Forest	89408, Fernley , NV
Tina	Simmons	27984 W. 14th	89408, Fernley , NV
Phyllis	Foster	27984 W. Dogwood	89408, Fernley , NV
Norma	Gonzales	9904 E. Elm	89408, Fernley , NV
Diana	Alexander	246 E. 9th	89408, Fernley , NV

Page 1 of 2

g. Use the Report tool to create a report based on the 40+ Clients query.

h. Change the report margins to Normal. Adjust the controls to fit the report on a single page width-wise.

i. Add a new record to the Clients table that includes your name in the first and last name fields and a birth date of 2/11/68.

j. Refresh the query and report to update them.

k. Save the report as **40+ ClientsReport**. Print the report.

l. Compact and repair the database. Back up the database.

m. Close the database, saving as needed, and exit Access.

EchoPlex Reports ★

CONTINUING EXERCISES

2. Your vinyl record hobby has grown into a full-fledged online business catering to collectors across the globe. With the database you created (Step-by-Step Exercise 5 of Lab 2), you will enhance the inventory system you created with two new queries. The database you designed to help control inventory has made shipping orders easier than it was in the past, but you would like to make additional changes to help in this process. You would like to create a query that will help you determine which titles move quickly, so that future purchasing is more on target. Your completed query will be similar to that shown here.

Shipping List 10/8/2008

Title	Artist	Sold Price	Shipped
Four Walls Bending	Emily Bezar	$35.00	N
Now or Never	Student Name	$16.00	N
Imagine	John Lennon	$76.00	N
Total	3	$127.00	

a. Open the database file named ac02_EchoPlex that you modified in Step-by-Step Exercise 5 of Lab 2. Open the Records table.

b. Make **N** the default value for the Shipped field. Save the changes to the table.

c. You have sold Fleetwood Mac's *Rumours* for $16.00. Change the record accordingly. Enter **Y** in the Shipped field. You also have sold John Lennon's *Imagine* for $76.00. Adjust the record and leave N in the Shipped field.

d. Using the Records form, add the following new records to the table:

ID		
Title	**Four Walls Bending**	**Now or Never**
Artist	**Emily Bezar**	**[Your Name]**
Condition	**Good**	**Poor**
Purchase Price	**$15.00**	**$4.00**
Sold Price	**$35.00**	**$16.00**
Shipped	**N**	**N**
Comments		
Attachments		

e. Create a query that displays inventory that has a sold price but has not been shipped yet. Include the Title, Sold Price, and Shipped fields. Name the query **Shipping List**. Add the Artist field after the Title field to the query. Best fit the query datasheet columns. Display a Total row with a count in the Artist field column and a Sum in the Sold Price column. Print the query results.

f. Close all objects. Compact and repair the database. Exit Access.

Downtown Internet Café Inventory ★★

CONTINUING EXERCISES

3. The Inventory database you created for the Downtown Internet Café (Lab 1, Step-by-Step Exercise 4) has been in use several weeks now and is working well. During this time, you have modified the table design and added more information to the table. Evan, the owner, has asked you to submit a daily report on all low-quantity items so he can place the necessary orders. You will use the database to monitor inventory levels and respond to Evan's request. First you decide to run a query to find the low-stock items, and then you can generate the requested report from the query. Your completed report should look similar to the report below.

Stock Report

Supplier	Description	In Stock	Special Order?	Contact	Phone Number	E-mail
ABC Restaurant Supply	Sugar	26	N	Richard Price	(206) 555-0037	brs@email.net
ABC Restaurant Supply	Cups-large	27	N	Richard Price	(206) 555-0037	brs@email.net
ABC Restaurant Supply	Cups-medium	28	N	Richard Price	(206) 555-0037	brs@email.net
ABC Restaurant Supply	Cups-small	29	N	Richard Price	(206) 555-0037	brs@email.net
Aquatics	Bottled water	14	N	Lee Branson	(207) 555-1122	thirst@net.com
By Design	T-Shirts	12	Y	Anna Parker	(502) 555-6973	design@email.
Cuppa Jo	Italian Roast	12	N	Student Name	(206) 555-9090	jo@dial.com
Cuppa Jo	Espresso	11	Y	Student Name	(206) 555-9090	jo@dial.com
Cuppa Jo	Kona coffee	10	N	Student Name	(206) 555-9090	jo@dial.com
Tea and Toast, Inc.	Darjeeling Tea	13	Y	Mavis Dunhill	(206) 555-6001	tea@net.com

a. Open the database file named ac03_Café Inventory. Open the Stock table to view its content. Replace the contact name for Cuppa Jo with your name in the Suppliers table.

b. Use the Query Wizard to create a query based on the Stock table. Include all fields, except Item, in their current order. Name the query **Low Stock**.

c. In Query Design view, enter the criteria to display only those records with an In Stock value less than 30, and run the query.

d. Upon reviewing the datasheet, you realize that it needs to include the contact name, phone, and e-mail addresses for Evan to use when he places orders. Add these fields to the query design.

e. Use the Report Wizard to create a report based on the Low Stock query. Include all the fields in the order listed. Select Supplier as the only sort field. Select the Tabular layout and a design style of your choice. Name the report **Stock Report**.

f. In Report Layout view, change the report design to Opulent. Change the title font color to a color of your choice. Adjust the column widths as needed to appropriately display the data. Center the data in the Special Order column. Change the margin setting to Normal and resize or move any controls that cause the report to overlap to a second page.

g. Preview and print the report. Close the Report window, saving the changes.

h. Compact and repair the database.

i. Back up the database. Exit Access.

Kodiak Construction Reports ★★

CONTINUING EXERCISES

4. The database you created for Kodiak Construction (Step-by-Step Exercise 4 of Lab 2) has been very well received. Now that the database has been in use for a few months, several new requests have been made. You will create a query and a report to fulfill these requests. Your completed report should look similar to the report below.

Job Priority Report

Begin Date	ID	Job	Priority	Foreman Last Name
2/2/2007	21	Ancho Homestead	High	
5/10/2007	51	Madeira Highlands	High	
5/18/2007	54	Stone Creek Ranch	High	
9/23/2007	89	Glenbrooks	High	
2/1/2008	109	Solera Greens	High	
2/3/2008	999	Student Name private residence	High	Valdez
6/12/2008	116	Riverwood Hills	High	
9/3/2008	127	Mesquite Trails	High	

a. Open the database file named ac02_Kodiak Construction that you modified in Step-by-Step Exercise 4 of Lab 2.

b. Create a Parameter query named **Priority** that displays all fields from the Jobs table that have a high priority.

c. Create a report using the Priority query for those jobs with a high priority. Include the ID, Job, Priority, Begin Date, and Foreman Last Name fields. Sort the report by Begin Date. Use the tabular layout in portrait orientation and the Foundry style. Name the report **Job Priority Report**.

d. Change the page margins to Wide. Adjust the size of the report controls in Layout view to appropriately display the data on one page.

e. Preview and print the report.

f. Close all objects.

g. Display the database relationships. Edit relationships as needed. Enforce referential integrity for all relationships. Create and print a relationships report.

h. Compact and repair the database. Save the changes and exit Access.

ARF Reports ★★★

5. The Animal Rescue Foundation volunteers are successfully using the database you created to enter information for all the rescued animals. Meanwhile, you created another table containing information about the foster homes (including names, addresses, and phone numbers). The Animal Rescue Foundation management has now asked you for a report, shown below, of all animals placed in foster homes in the past year (2008) and the names and addresses of those providing foster care, so the appropriate thank you notes can be sent. Your completed report will be similar to the report shown here.

2008 Foster Parents Report

Foster First Name	Foster Last Name	Foster Street	Foster City	Foster State	Foster Zip	Type
Gloria	Atherton	808 McDonald Rd.	Mesa	AZ	85205-0346	Dog
Bonnie	Brookfield	7 N. Williams Ave.	Tempe	AZ	86301-1268	Dog
Bonnie	Brookfield	7 N. Williams Ave.	Tempe	AZ	86301-1268	Cat
Fran	Calco	799 Summer St.	Tempe	AZ	86301-1268	Cat
Betty	Cavender	453 Orange St.	Tempe	AZ	85201-1268	Cat
Theresa	Fox	959 Price Rd.	Tempe	AZ	85201-1268	Cat
Theresa	Fox	959 Price Rd.	Tempe	AZ	85201-1268	Dog
Judith	Gold	683 Alameda Dr.	Scottsdale	AZ	85201-6760	Dog
Judith	Gold	683 Alameda Dr.	Scottsdale	AZ	85201-6760	Cat
Lucy	Granger	61 Lincoln Blvd.	Mesa	AZ	85205-0346	Pig
Bradley	Hawkins	789 University Ave.	Tempe	AZ	85201-1268	Dog
Mark	Lemon	900 Thomas Rd.	Phoenix	AZ	82891-9999	Dog
Susan	Malik	22 Sunrise Dr.	Mesa	AZ	85205-0346	Cat
Calvin	Summerset	912 N. Central Ave.	Phoenix	AZ	82891-9999	Goat
Calvin	Summerset	912 N. Central Ave.	Phoenix	AZ	82891-9999	Monkey
Ned	Young	387 Rawhide Rd.	Chandler	AZ	83174-2311	Cat

a. Open the database file named ac03_ARF3. Open both tables to review their content.

b. Find and delete any duplicate records in the Fosters table using the Last Name field as the field to check for duplicate data. Delete the duplicate records that have the highest Foster ID number.

c. Add your name as a new foster parent with the ID number 999.

d. To generate the requested information, you need to add a new field to the Rescues table that identifies the foster person that was assigned to the animal. Instead of checking the Fosters table to find the number and then entering the number in the Rescues table, you will make the new field a Lookup field that will display values from the Fosters table.

   In Design view, add the **Foster ID#** field after the ID# field of the Rescues table. Select Lookup Wizard from the Data Type list. Select the following options from the LookUp Wizard:

   - Look up values in a table.
   - Use the Fosters table
   - Display the Foster ID, Foster Last Name, and Foster First Name fields.
   - Sort by the last and first names.
   - Clear the Hide Key column option.
   - Select Foster ID as the value to store.
   - Use the Foster ID# field name.

e. Switch to Datasheet view. Now you need to enter the Foster ID for all animals that were sent to a foster home. Query the datasheet to display only those records with a 2008 foster date or F in the Status column. Display the Foster ID, Status, and Foster Date columns only. From the Foster ID drop-down list, select a foster name for each record. Select your name as the foster parent for the last animal.

f. Next you will modify the query to display the information you need in the report. Add the Fosters tables to the query grid. Delete the Foster ID field from the grid. Add the following fields from the tables specified in the order listed below.

   Rescues table

   - Type

   Fosters table

   - Foster First Name
   - Foster Last Name
   - Foster Street
   - Foster City
   - Foster State
   - Foster Zip

g. Sort the Foster Last Name column in ascending order. Hide the Status field. Run the query and review the resulting datasheet. Save the query as **2008 Foster Parents**.

h. Use the Report Wizard to create a report based on the 2008 Foster Parents query you just saved. Include the following fields in the order listed below:

- Foster First Name
- Foster Last Name
- Foster Street
- Foster City
- Foster State
- Foster Zip
- Type

i. View the data by Rescues, use the tabular layout, landscape orientation, and the Apex style. Name the report **2008 Foster Parents Report**.

j. Center the Report Header control at the top of the page. Change the design style to another of your choice. Change the page margin setting to Wide. Size the controls as needed to enhance the report appearance and fit the entire report on a single page.

k. Preview and then print the report. Close the report window, saving the changes you made.

l. Compact and repair the database.

m. Back up the database and exit Access.

on your own

Timeless Treasures Report ★

1. The owners of Timeless Treasures have decided to expand their offerings to include vintage clocks as well as watches. Open the database file Timeless Treasures that you worked on in Lab 2, On your Own exercise 5. Revisit the Web to obtain information on vintage clocks. Create a second table in the database with the same fields as the Watches table to use for maintaining the clock inventory. Name this table **Clocks**. Enter 10 records in the new table. Create an inventory report called **Timeless Treasures Watches Inventory** that displays the identification number, description, price and quantity on hand fields of information. Use a design style and layout of your choice. Modify the report design as needed to improve its appearance. Create the same report for the Clocks table and name it **Timeless Treasures Clocks Inventory**. Preview and print both reports. Compact and back up the database.

P&P W2 Forms ★

2. As an administrative assistant at Parker & Pisaño, Inc., you are responsible for sending out W2 forms to all of the employees. Create a database named P&P Employees and a table named **Employees** that includes fields for the employee ID number, first and last names and home contact information (Street, City, State, Zip Code and Phone). Enter 15 records in the table. Include your name as the employee name in one of the records. Then use this table to create a query that includes only the employee first and last name and home address fields of information. Sort the query by last name. Save the query as **Employee Addresses**. Create a report named **Employee Addresses** using the query as the record source. Use a design style and layout of your choice. Modify the report design as needed to improve its appearance. Compact and back up the database.

Learnsoft Developers ★★

3. Learnsoft Inc. develops computer-based curriculum for grades K-8. The company uses a database to track which software titles that have been worked on by the project managers. The program manager for the Learnsoft company wants a report of this information so he can use it for the employee reviews the following week. Open the database file ac03_Learnsoft and the table named Software. Add a new field named Project Manager before the Release Date field to include the name of the project manager for each title. Make this field a Lookup list field that will lookup the names of the five project managers. (Use names of your choice, but include your name as one of the project managers.) Complete the data for this field by selecting a project manager for each record. Assign your name as project manager to one of

the records with a release date in 2010. Create a report named **Project Manager Report** that shows the titles, subject and project manager names for the years 2009 through 2010. Use a design style and layout of your choice. Modify the report design as needed to improve its appearance. Compact and back up the database.

ARF Adoptions Report ★★★

4. The Animal Rescue Foundation would like you to create a report showing foster information. Open the database file ac03_ARF3 and the Rescues table. Add a new field before the Foster Date field named Foster Parent. Make it a Lookup field to the Foster ID field in the Fosters table. Edit the relationship to enforce referential integrity. Open the Fosters table and change the name for Foster ID F-001 to your name. For each record in the Rescues table that has a Foster Date entry, specify a Foster Parent by selecting a Foster ID. Make sure to include your Foster ID in at least one record. Add the Foster Parent field to above the Foster Date field in the ARF Animals form. Create a query that displays all fields from the Rescues table except the Photo Attachment field and the Foster First Name and Foster Last Name fields from the Fosters table. Sort the query by Foster Parent. Display the Foster First Name and Foster Last Name fields after the Foster Parent field. Name the query **Animal-Foster Query**. Create a report based on the Animal-Foster query that shows the Foster Date, Foster First Name, Foster Last Name, Type, Gender, Age and Name. Use a design style and layout of your choice. Modify the report design as needed to improve its appearance. Name the report **Foster Report**. Preview and print the report.

EMP Expense Account Report ★★

5. One of the department managers at EMP Enterprises has requested a report showing who in her department has submitted an expense reimbursement request but has not yet been paid. You decide this would be a good report to generate for all departments. In the EMP Enterprises database, open the Employee Expenses table you updated in On Your Own Exercise 2 of Lab 2. Create a one-to-many relationship between the Employee Info table and the Employee Expenses table based on the Employee ID fields. Enforce referential integrity and select the Cascade Update option. Create a query that displays all fields from both tables, sorted by Department. View the query results. Modify the query to not show the Employee ID field and to display only those employees who have not been paid. Apply an ascending sort to the Submission Date field. Save the query as **Pending Payment**. Use the Report Wizard to create a report named **Open Expense Requests** based on the Pending Payment query. Use a design style and layout of your choice. Modify the report design as needed to improve its appearance. Preview and print the report. Compact and back up the database.

Working Together 1: Exporting Data

Case Study

Lifestyle Fitness Club

Periodically, the club director wants to know the names of the employees at each club and their job position. You created a parameter query to obtain this information and then a custom report to display it professionally. Now you want to provide this information to the director.

You will learn about exporting Access data to Excel and Word using the Export Wizard. Then you will learn how to copy and paste objects and selections between Access and Word to create a memo to the director.

Your memo containing a copy of the query results and the report generated by Access will look like the one shown here.

Note: This tutorial assumes that you already know how to use Office Word 2007 and that you have completed Lab 3 of Access 2007.

Lifestyle Fitness Club

Memo

To: Club Director
From: Student Name
Date: October 8, 2008
Re: Job Positions

You recently asked me for a list of employees at each Club location and their job positions. I was easily able to gather this information using Access 2007. This memo contains the information for the Landis location. Below this paragraph is the output from the query I used to gather this information.

Location Query

Employee ID	First Name	Last Name	Location	Position
00212	Chad	Schiff	Landis	Club Director
03225	Dan	Morgan	Landis	Food Service Director
03890	Erona	Thi	Landis	Fitness Director
05015	Scot	Briggs	Landis	Personal Trainer Director
07287	Anita	Roman	Landis	Child Care Director
07650	Chris	Lamm	Landis	Sales Director
12380	Jessica	Thomas	Landis	Fitness Instructor
12389	Jennifer	Blackman	Landis	Sales Associate
12420	Allison	Player	Landis	Maintenance
12501	Elizabeth	DeLuca	Landis	Personal Trainer
12583	Marie	Sullivan	Landis	Greeter
12703	Jeff	Bader	Landis	Fitness Instructor
12855	Kimberly	Fachet	Landis	Sales Associate
12914	Alfonso	Gomez	Landis	Cleaning
12918	Carlos	Ruiz	Landis	Assistant Manager
13005	Emily	Reilly	Landis	Assistant Manager
13027	Kimberly	Kieken	Landis	Food Service Server
13303	Chris	Jensen	Landis	Greeter
13484	Stephanie	Franklin	Landis	Food Service Server
13635	Juan	Martinez	Landis	Fitness Instructor
22085	Kristina	Lindau	Landis	Child Care Provider
22297	Patricia	Rogondino	Landis	Greeter
22469	Ryan	Hogan	Landis	Personal Trainer
99999	Student	Name	Landis	Human Resources Administrator

Below this paragraph is a report that was generated from the Landis Location query. It displays the same information in a professional style report.

Job Position Report

Employee ID	First Name	Position	Last Name
00212	Chad	Club Director	Schiff
03225	Dan	Food Service Director	Morgan
03890	Erona	Fitness Director	Thi
05015	Scot	Personal Trainer Director	Briggs
07287	Anita	Child Care Director	Roman
07650	Chris	Sales Director	Lamm
12380	Jessica	Fitness Instructor	Thomas
12389	Jennifer	Sales Associate	Blackman
12420	Allison	Maintenance	Player
12501	Elizabeth	Personal Trainer	DeLuca
12583	Marie	Greeter	Sullivan
12703	Jeff	Fitness Instructor	Bader
12855	Kimberly	Sales Associate	Fachet
12914	Alfonso	Cleaning	Gomez
12918	Carlos	Assistant Manager	Ruiz
13005	Emily	Assistant Manager	Reilly
13027	Kimberly	Food Service Server	Kieken
13303	Chris	Greeter	Jensen
13484	Stephanie	Food Service Server	Franklin
13635	Juan	Fitness Instructor	Martinez
22085	Kristina	Child Care Provider	Lindau
22297	Patricia	Greeter	Rogondino
22469	Ryan	Personal Trainer	Hogan
99999	Student	Human Resources Administrator	Name

I have also found that I can easily provide the same information to you in and Excel workbook. This is convenient if you want to analyze the information. Please let me know which of the above two formats you would like me to use to provide the information for the other locations in and if you would also like it as an Excel workbook.

MORE ABOUT

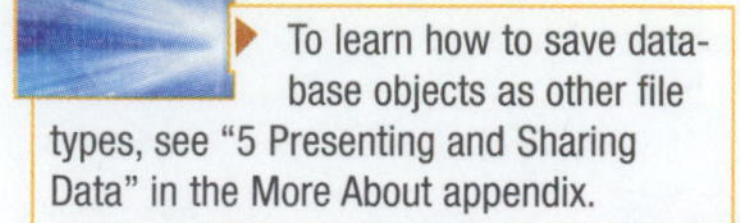

To learn how to save database objects as other file types, see "5 Presenting and Sharing Data" in the More About appendix.

Exporting Data

There are often circumstances when you will want to provide data from an Access database to someone else to use. The process of copying this information to a file outside the database is called **exporting.** There are a variety of methods you can use, depending upon the type of output needed. The most common export types are described below:

Export to	Description
Excel	Creates a copy of the selected data, table, query, or form object and stores the copy in an Excel worksheet.
Word	Creates a copy of the selected data, table, query, form, or report, including formatting, in a new Word (*.rtf) file.
Access database	Creates a copy of the table definition and data or just the table definition in another Access database.
Text file	Creates a copy of the selected data, table, query, form, or report, approximating formatting if possible, in a new text file (*.txt) document.
SharePoint site	Creates a copy of a table or query and stores it on a SharePoint site as a list.

MORE ABOUT

To learn about exporting to another Access database, see "2.2 Create Tables" in the More About appendix.

The director does not have Access 2007 installed on his computer, so you need to export the data in either Word 2007 or Excel 2007 format. You will try both methods to see what the output in each application looks like.

The Export Wizard is used for all types of exports. In addition, in some cases, you can copy and paste an object in another application. The file that you export from is the **source file** and the file that is created is the **destination file.**

Additional Information

Only one object can be exported at a time.

Additional Information

If you want to export a selection, you need to open the object and select the records you want to export.

Exporting to Excel 2007

When exporting to Excel, the database file you want to copy from must be open in Access. Then you select the object you want to export. The Export Wizard can copy selected data, a table, a query, or a form object, but it cannot export a report to Excel. Because you cannot export a report, you will export the Job Positions query instead.

1

- **Start Access 2007 and open the database file** acwt1_Personnel **from your data file location.**
- **If necessary, respond appropriately to the Security Warning.**
- **Select the Location Query in the Navigation pane.**
- **Click Excel in the Export group of the External Data tab.**

Your screen should be similar to Figure 1

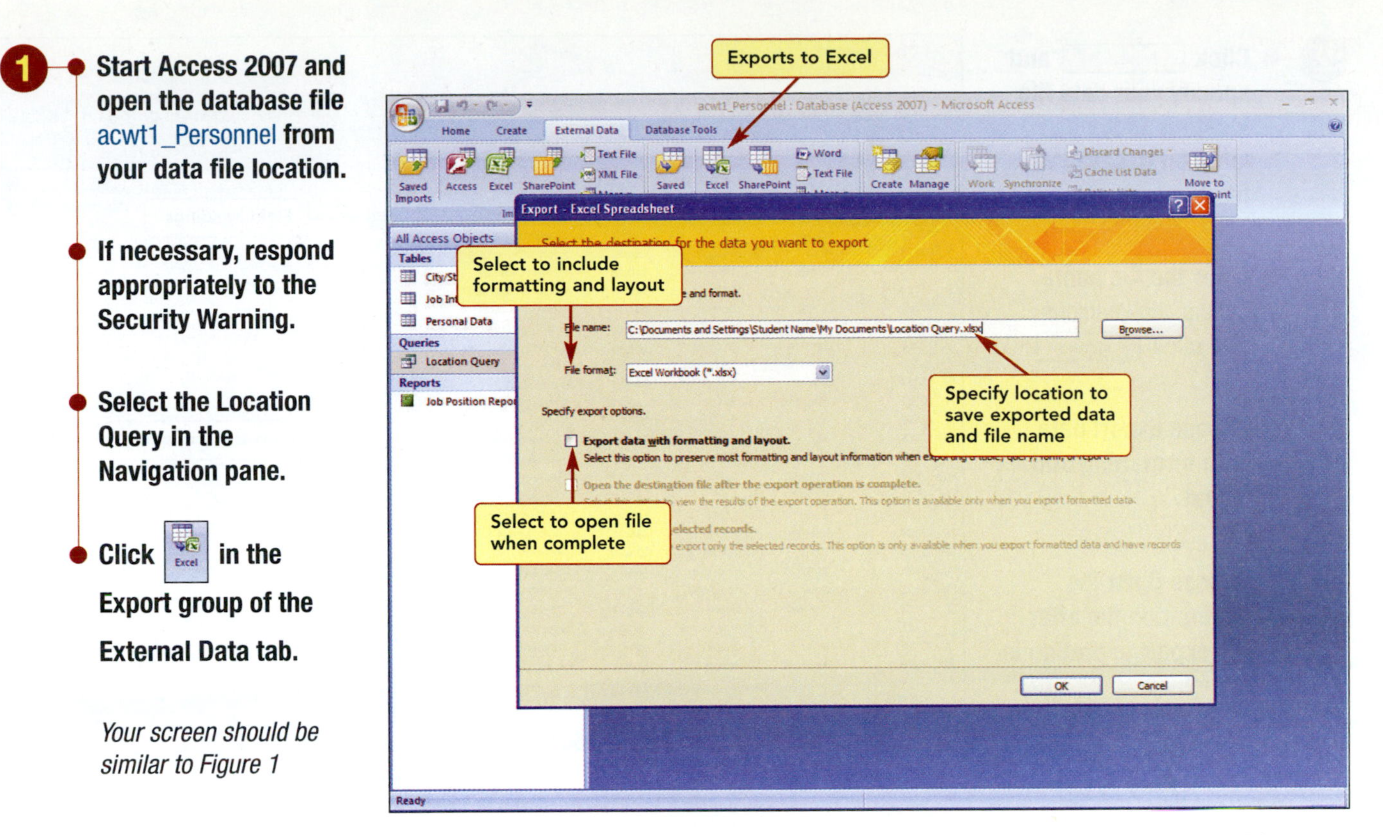

Figure 1

In the first Export - Excel Spreadsheet wizard dialog box, you specify the name of the destination file and the file format. The default file format of an Excel 2007 workbook file is acceptable; however, you need to change the file location and name. In addition, you want to include the formatting from the query object and want to see the new Excel workbook file after it is created. Because the query is a parameter query, you also will be asked to enter the location you want to copy to the destination.

2 Click [Browse...] and specify your data file location as the location to save the file.

- Enter the file name Landis Job Positions and click [Save].
- Choose Export data with formatting and layout.
- Choose Open the destination file after the export operation is complete.
- Click [OK].
- Enter Landis in the Parameter Value dialog box.
- Click [OK].
- If necessary, maximize the Excel application window.

Your screen should be similar to Figure 2

Landis Job Positions.xlsx - Microsoft Excel

	A	B	C	D	E
1	Employee ID	First Name	Last Name	Location	Position
2	00212	Chad	Schiff	Landis	Club Director
3	03225	Dan	Morgan	Landis	Food Service Director
4	03890	Erona	Thi	Landis	Fitness Director
5	05015	Scot	Briggs	Landis	Personal Trainer Director
6	07287	Anita	Roman	Landis	Child Care Director
7	07650	Chris	Lamm	Landis	Sales Director
8	12380	Jessica	Thomas	Landis	Fitness Instructor
9	12389	Jennifer	Blackman	Landis	Sales Associate
10	12420	Allison	Player	Landis	Maintenance
11	12501	Elizabeth	DeLuca	Landis	Personal Trainer
12	12583	Marie	Sullivan	Landis	Greeter
13	12703	Jeff	Bader	Landis	Fitness Instructor
14	12855	Kimberly	Fachet	Landis	Sales Associate
15	12914	Alfonso	Gomez	Landis	Cleaning
16	12918	Carlos	Ruiz	Landis	Assistant Manager
17	13005	Emily	Reilly	Landis	Assistant Manager
18	13027	Kimberly	Kieken	Landis	Food Service Server
19	13303	Chris	Jensen	Landis	Greeter
20	13484	Stephanie	Franklin	Landis	Food Service Server
21	13635	Juan	Martinez	Landis	Fitness Instructor
22	22085	Kristina	Lindau	Landis	Child Care Provider
23	22297	Patricia	Rogondino	Landis	Greeter
24	22469	Ryan	Hogan	Landis	Personal Trainer
25	99999	Student	Name	Landis	Human Resources Administrator

Location Query

Field headings

Records from query

Taskbar button for each open application

Figure 2

Now there are two applications open, Excel and Access, and application buttons for both open windows are displayed in the taskbar. The Excel 2007 application window is displayed and the exported data has been copied into a worksheet of the new workbook file. The field headings appear formatted in the first row of the worksheet and each following row is a record from the query datasheet. Notice that the Microsoft Access button in the taskbar is flashing. This is to tell you that the wizard is not yet done.

Click on the Microsoft Access button in the taskbar to switch to the Access application window.

Your screen should be similar to Figure 3

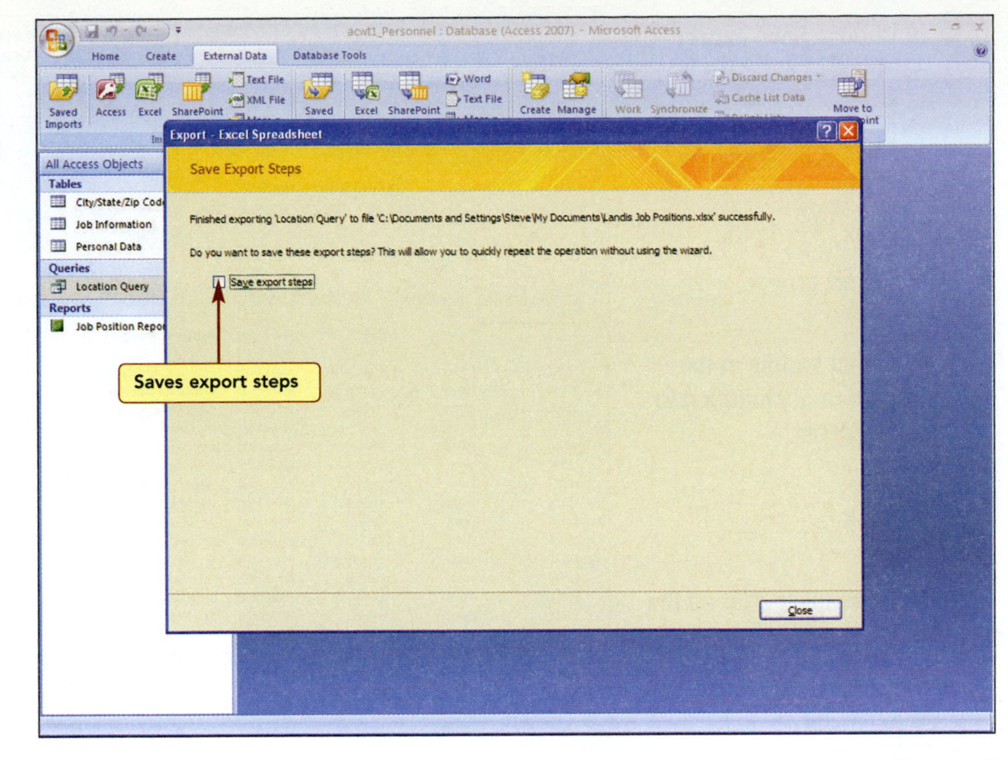

Figure 3

The final step tells you the export has been completed successfully and asks if you want to save the export steps. Saving the steps is useful if you think you will be running the same export operation on a routine basis. Since you need to repeat this operation for each location, you will save the steps using the suggested name. The wizard also can add a reminder for you in Outlook to run the export if you need to generate the results on a routine basis. You will not include this feature at this time.

Next, you will rerun the export operation to export the River Mist location data by selecting the name of the saved export steps from a list of saved exports. You also will need to edit the file name to reflect the location data and to save the exported data to a new file.

4 • **Choose Save export steps.**

• **Click** Save Export **.**

• **Click** Saved Exports **in the Export group.**

• **Select Landis in the path and change it to** River Mist**.**

• **Click** Run **.**

• **Enter River Mist as the location parameter.**

• **Click** OK **.**

Your screen should be similar to Figure 4

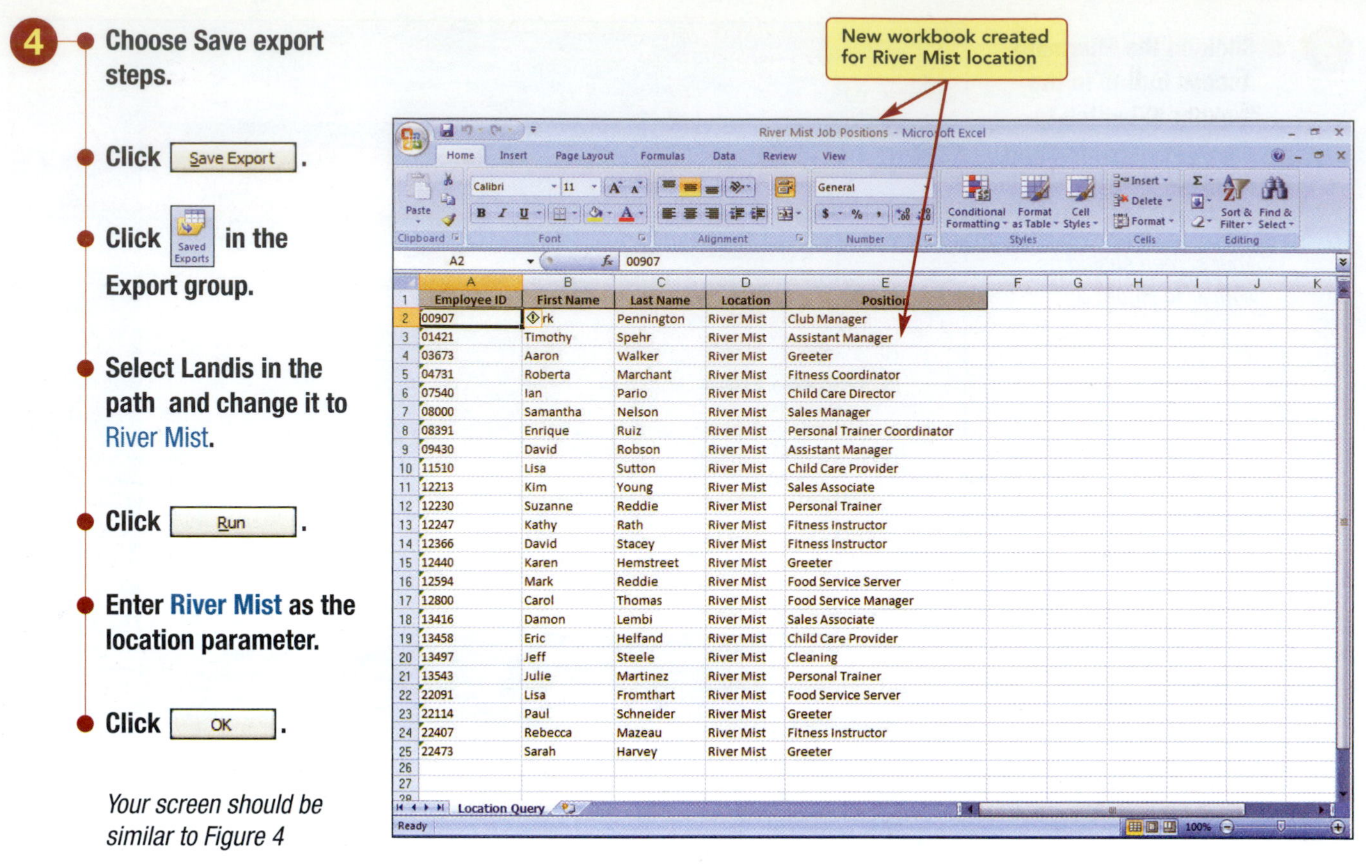

	A	B	C	D	E
1	Employee ID	First Name	Last Name	Location	Position
2	00907	rk	Pennington	River Mist	Club Manager
3	01421	Timothy	Spehr	River Mist	Assistant Manager
4	03673	Aaron	Walker	River Mist	Greeter
5	04731	Roberta	Marchant	River Mist	Fitness Coordinator
6	07540	Ian	Pario	River Mist	Child Care Director
7	08000	Samantha	Nelson	River Mist	Sales Manager
8	08391	Enrique	Ruiz	River Mist	Personal Trainer Coordinator
9	09430	David	Robson	River Mist	Assistant Manager
10	11510	Lisa	Sutton	River Mist	Child Care Provider
11	12213	Kim	Young	River Mist	Sales Associate
12	12230	Suzanne	Reddie	River Mist	Personal Trainer
13	12247	Kathy	Rath	River Mist	Fitness Instructor
14	12366	David	Stacey	River Mist	Fitness Instructor
15	12440	Karen	Hemstreet	River Mist	Greeter
16	12594	Mark	Reddie	River Mist	Food Service Server
17	12800	Carol	Thomas	River Mist	Food Service Manager
18	13416	Damon	Lembi	River Mist	Sales Associate
19	13458	Eric	Helfand	River Mist	Child Care Provider
20	13497	Jeff	Steele	River Mist	Cleaning
21	13543	Julie	Martinez	River Mist	Personal Trainer
22	22091	Lisa	Fromthart	River Mist	Food Service Server
23	22114	Paul	Schneider	River Mist	Greeter
24	22407	Rebecca	Mazeau	River Mist	Fitness Instructor
25	22473	Sarah	Harvey	River Mist	Greeter

Figure 4

A separate workbook file was created and contains the data for the River Mist location. Now, all the Excel features can be used to analyze the data in the worksheets. After exporting each location to a workbook, you could combine the workbooks by copying the worksheet data from each worksheet into one workbook file.

5 • **Close both workbook files and exit the Excel application.**

• **Click** OK **to acknowledge the export is finished.**

• **Close the Manage Data Tasks dialog box.**

Exporting to Word 2007

Next, you will try exporting the Job Position Report to a Word document. When you use the Export Wizard to do this, a copy of the object's data is inserted into a Microsoft Word Rich Text Format file (.rtf).

1

- **Select the Job Position Report in the Navigation pane.**
- **Click [Word] in the Export group.**
- **If necessary, change the file location to your data file location.**

> **Having Trouble?**
> The report will be saved using the default file name of Job Position Report.

- **Choose Open the destination files after the export operation is complete.**
- **Click [OK].**
- **Enter Landis in the Enter Parameter Value dialog box.**
- **Click [OK].**

Your screen should be similar to Figure 5

> **Having Trouble?**
> If WordPad is the open application, this is because your system has associated .rtf file types with this application. You could close WordPad and open the document in Word 2007.

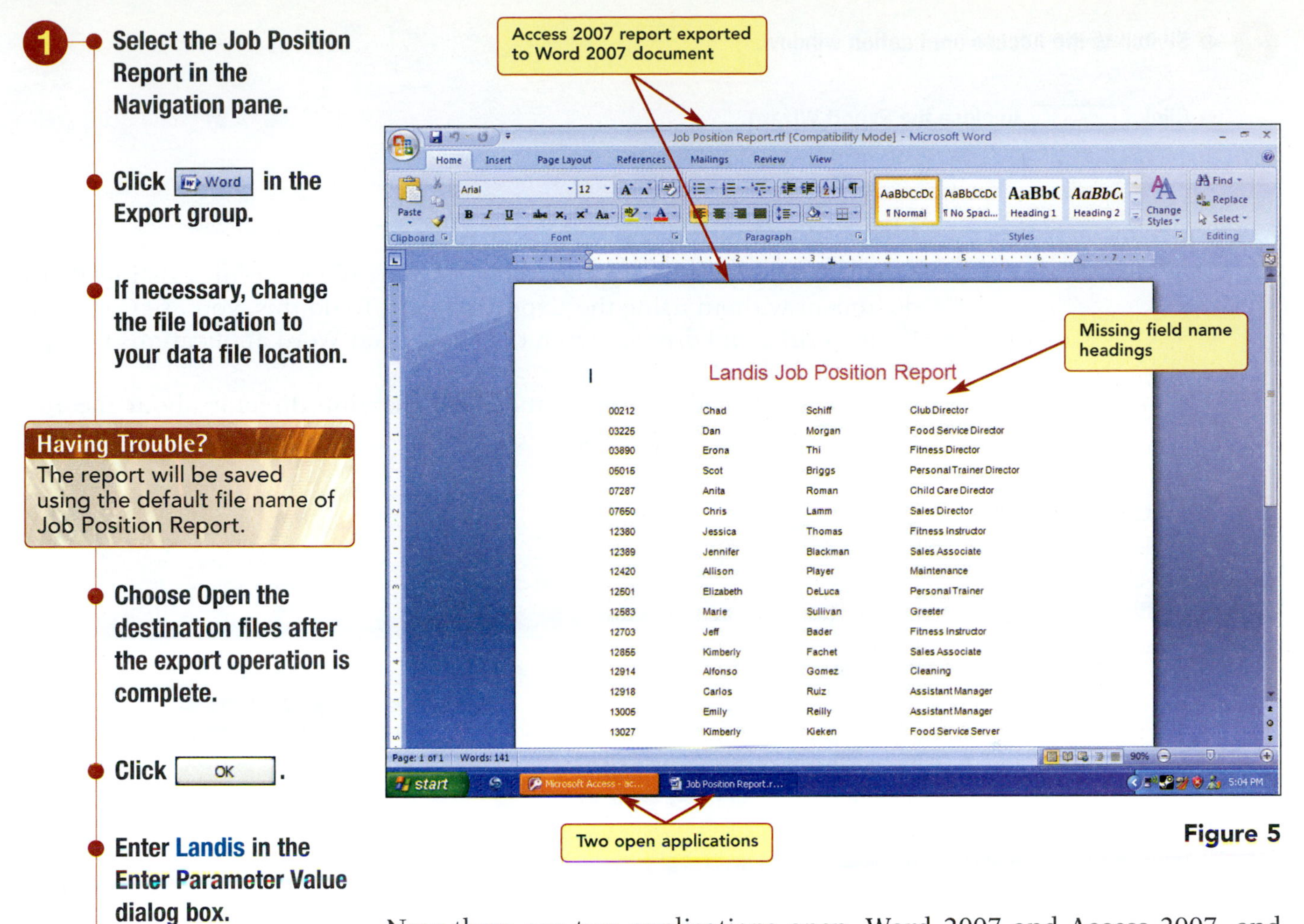

Figure 5

Now there are two applications open, Word 2007 and Access 2007, and application buttons for both open windows are displayed in the taskbar. The Word 2007 application window is displayed and the exported data has been copied into a document file and saved as Job Positions Report. The report resembles the Access report as closely as possible. The problem with the exported report is that the field name headings are missing.

Again, the Microsoft Access button in the taskbar is flashing. This time you will not save the steps.

2 Switch to the Access application window.

- Click Close to close the Export Wizard.

Copying a Query Object to Word 2007

Finally, you decide to try copying an Access object to an existing Word document without using the Export Wizard. To do this, you use Copy and Paste or drag and drop between the Access and Word applications to copy a database object.

You have already started a memo to the club director about the Job Position query and report you created.

1 Switch to the Word application window and close the Job Position Report document.

- Open the document acwt1_Job Positions.

- In the memo header, replace Student Name with your name.

Your screen should be similar to Figure 6

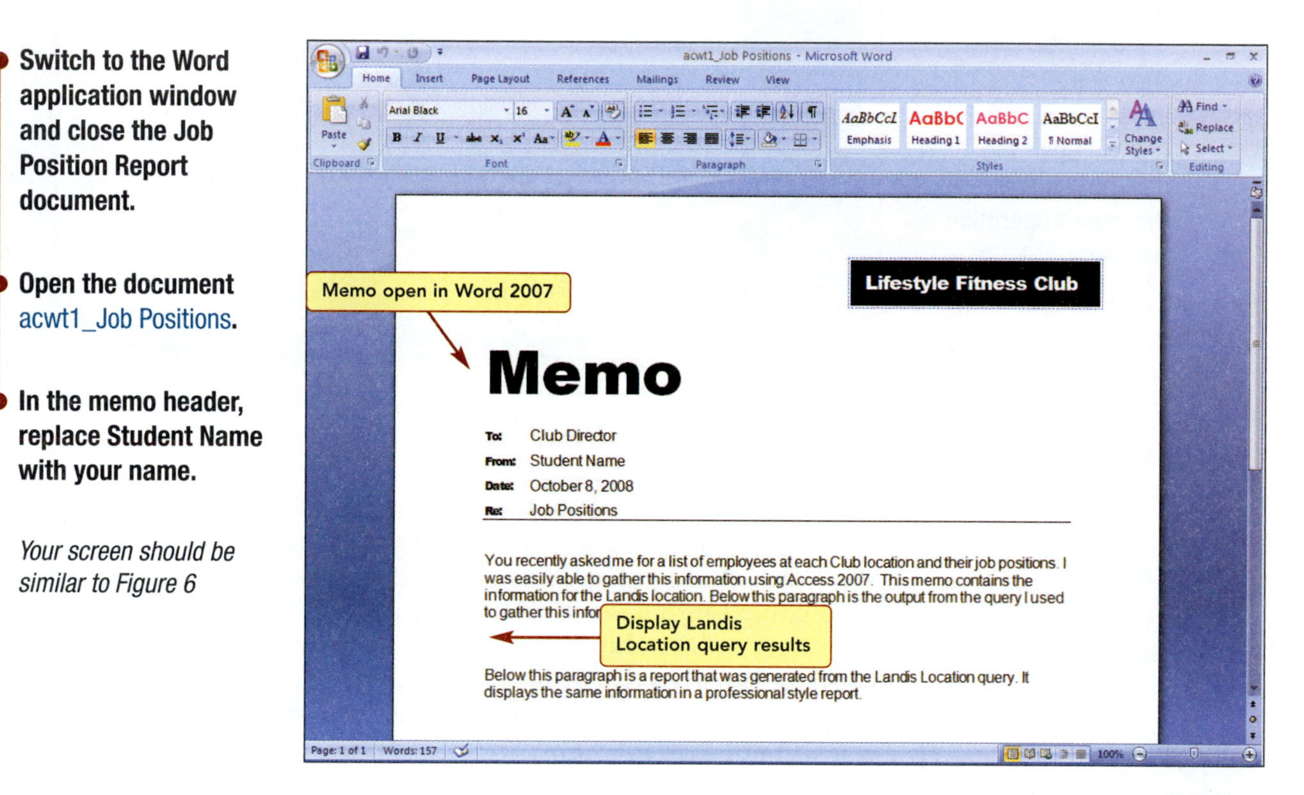

Figure 6

This document contains the text of the memo to the director. Below the first paragraph, you want to copy the output from the Landis Location query results using drag and drop. To do this, both applications must be open and visible, which you will do by tiling the application windows.

2

- **Right-click on a blank area of the taskbar to open the shortcut menu.**

Having Trouble?

If your taskbar is hidden, point to the thin line at the bottom of the screen to redisplay it.

- **Choose Tile Windows Vertically.**
- **Click in the Word application window.**

Your screen should be similar to Figure 7

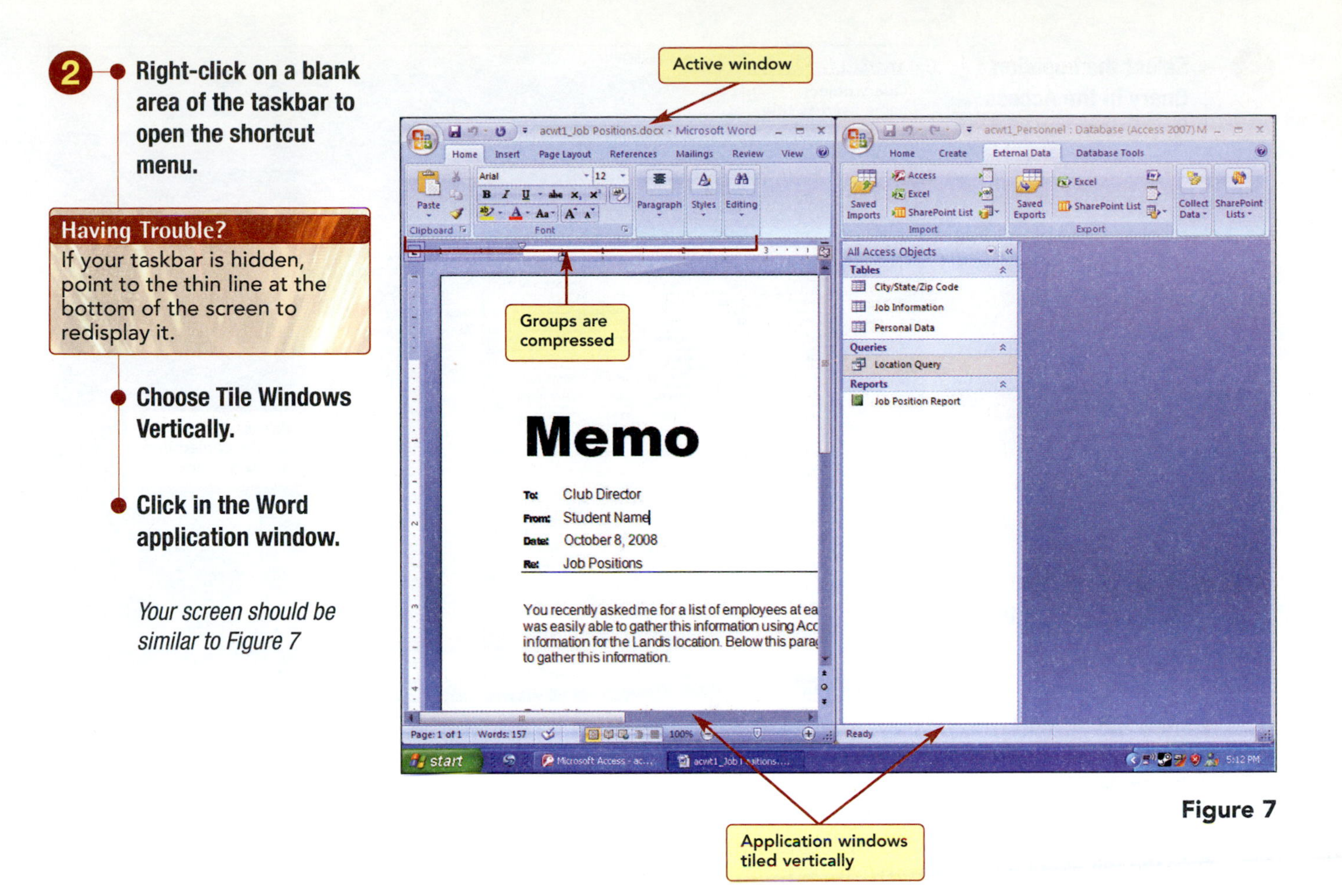

Figure 7

You can now see the contents of both the Access and Word applications. The Word document contains the insertion point and the window title bar text is not dimmed, which indicates that it is the **active window,** or the window in which you can work. Simply clicking on the other document makes it active. Because the windows are side by side and there is less horizontal space in each window, the Ribbon groups are compressed. To access commands in these groups, simply click on the group button and the commands appear in a drop-down list.

You will copy the query results to below the first paragraph of the memo.

3

- **Select the Location Query in the Access Navigation pane.**
- **Drag the selected object to the blank line below the first paragraph of the memo.**

Having Trouble?

An insertion point appears and the mouse pointer is ⧉ when you can release the mouse.

- **Enter Landis as the Location parameter and click OK.**
- **Click in the Word document to deselect the table.**
- **Scroll the document to see the table.**

Your screen should be similar to Figure 8

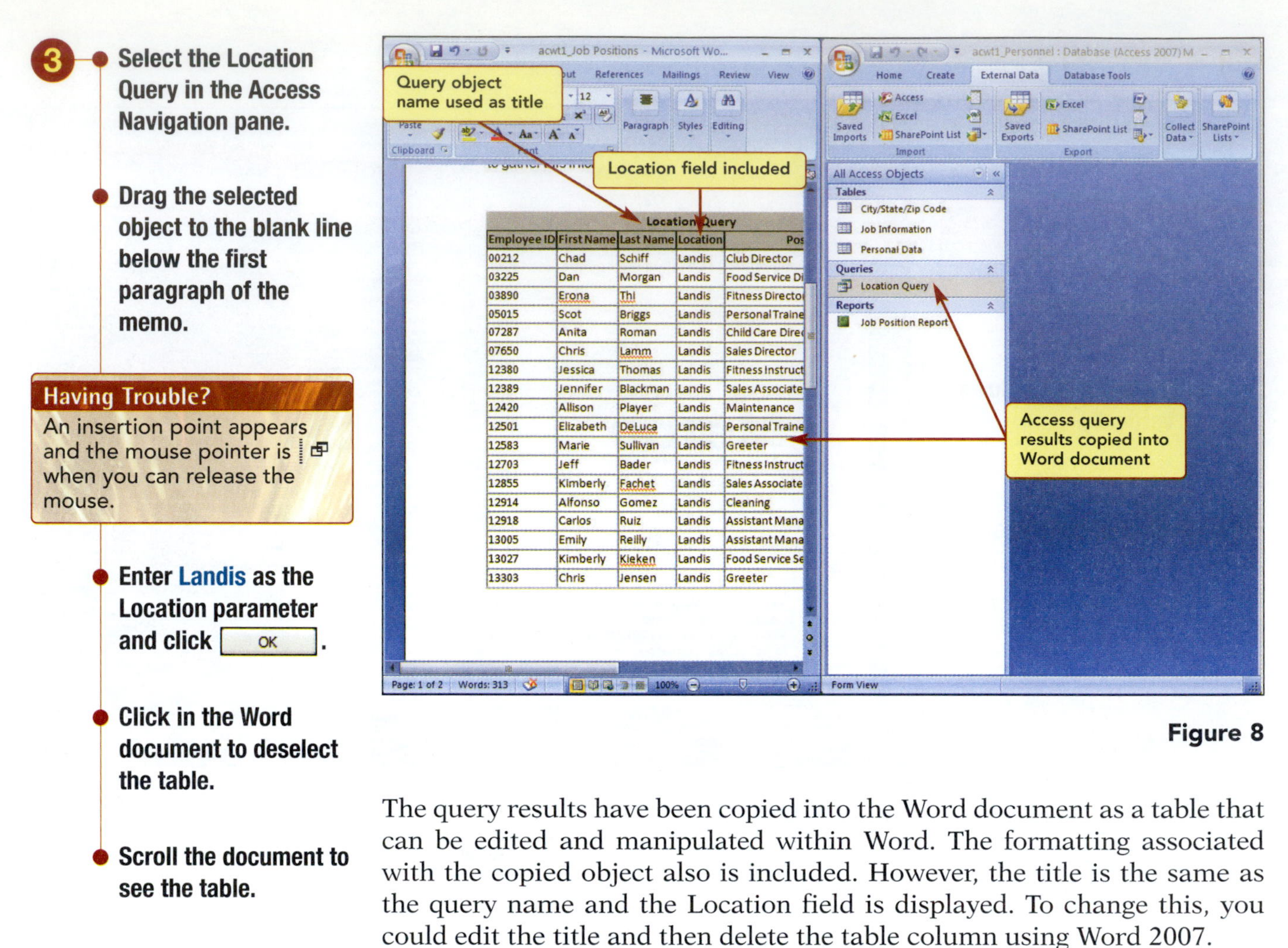

Figure 8

The query results have been copied into the Word document as a table that can be edited and manipulated within Word. The formatting associated with the copied object also is included. However, the title is the same as the query name and the Location field is displayed. To change this, you could edit the title and then delete the table column using Word 2007.

Copying a Report

Instead, you want to copy the report into the memo to see how it will look. To copy report data, you run the report in Access and then use copy and paste to copy the contents to a Word document.

1

- **Open the Job Position Report in Access using Landis as the location.**
- **Hide the Navigation pane.**
- **Select the report title and drag downward along the left edge of the rows to select the entire report, excluding the footer information.**
- **Open the Home tab and click Copy in the Clipboard group.**

Your screen should be similar to Figure 9

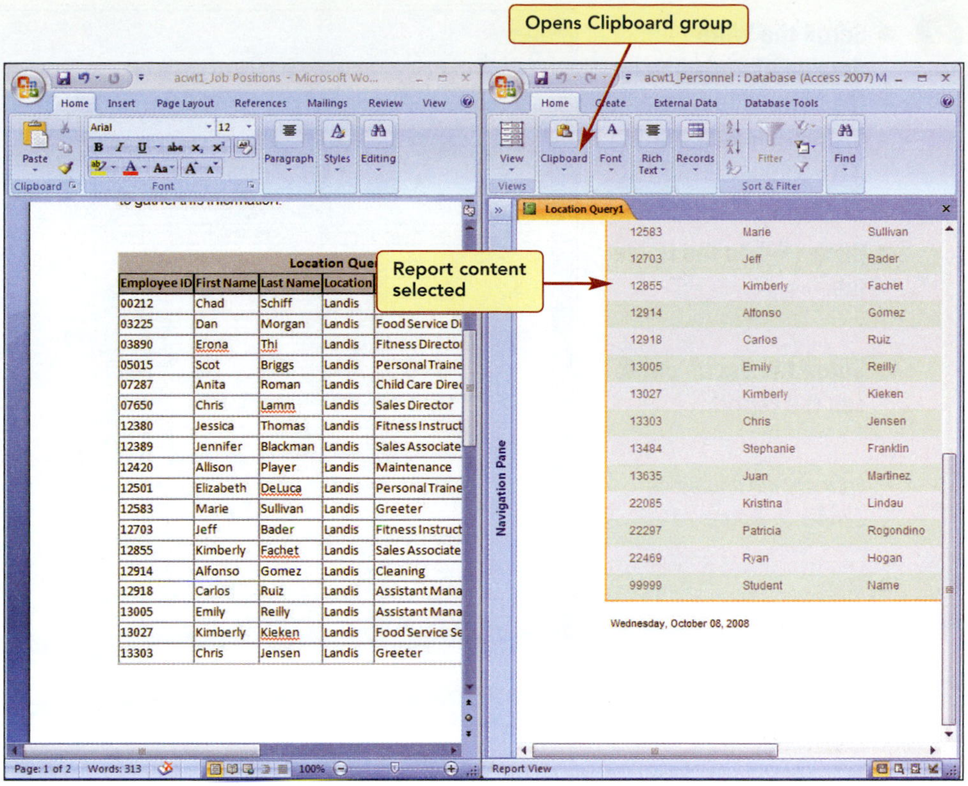

Opens Clipboard group

Report content selected

Figure 9

Next, you need to select the location in the memo where you want the copied data inserted.

2

- **Scroll the Word document and click on the blank line between the second and third paragraphs.**
- **Click Paste in the Home tab.**
- **Scroll the document to see the report.**

Your screen should be similar to Figure 10

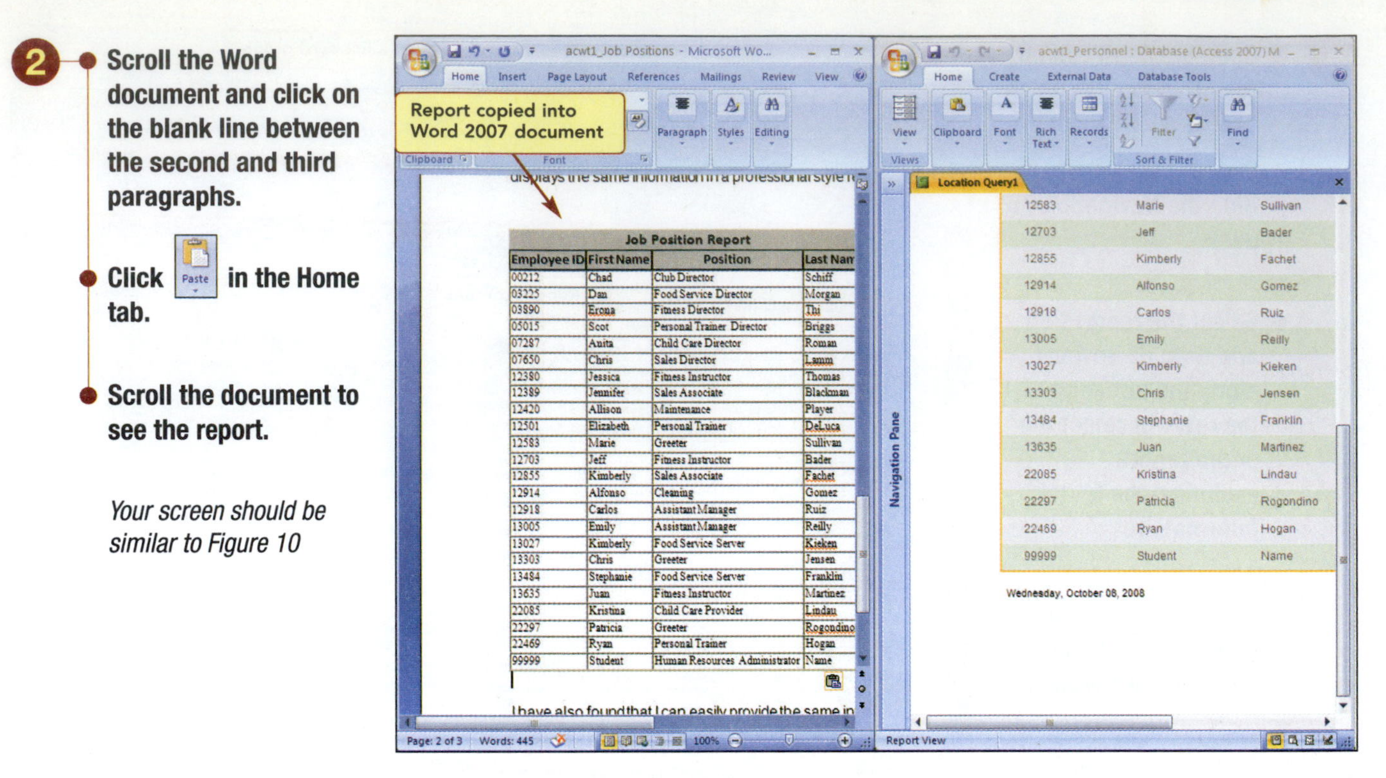

Figure 10

The copied report is similar to the copied query, except the correct title was included and the Location row is not included as specified by the report settings.

3

- **Close the report in Access.**
- **Click No to not save the copied data that was placed on the Clipboard.**
- **Display the Navigation pane.**
- **Undo the tiled windows.**

Having Trouble?
Choose Undo Tile from the taskbar shortcut menu.

- **Exit Access.**
- **Delete the blank line above both tables in the memo.**
- **Save the memo as Job Positions.**
- **Preview, and then print the memo.**
- **Exit Word.**

Your printed memo should look similar to the one shown in the Case Study at the beginning of this lab.

WORKING TOGETHER 1
Exporting Data

key terms

active window ACWT1.9
destination file ACWT1.2
export ACWT1.2
source file ACWT1.2

MCAS skills

The Microsoft Certified Applications Specialist (MCAS) certification program is designed to measure your proficiency in performing basic tasks using the Office 2007 applications. Getting certified demonstrates that you have the skills and provides a valuable industry credential for employment. See Reference 2: Microsoft Certified Applications Specialist (MCAS) for a complete list of the skills that were covered in this lab.

command summary

Command	Shortcut	Action
Home tab		
Clipboard group		
Copy	Ctrl + C	Copies selection to Clipboard
External Data tab		
Saved Exports		View and run saved exports
Excel		Exports selected object to an Excel workbook
Word		Exports selected object to a Rich Text Format file

Hands-On Exercises

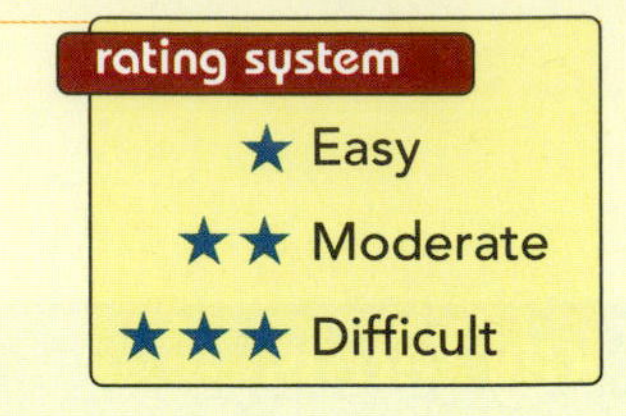

step-by-step

Spa Marketing Memo ★

CONTINUING EXERCISES

1. The Scensations Salon and Spa database has been used extensively. The owner asked you for a list of clients who are over the age of 40 to get an idea of how much interest there would be in an anti-aging spa package she is considering offering. You already filtered the Clients table to locate this information and now want to include the results in a memo to Latisha. The first page of the memo is shown here.

   a. Open the ac03_Scensations Spa database file and the Clients table that you modified in Step-by-Step Exercise 1 of Lab 3. Display the results of the 40+ Clients query.

   b. Start Word 2007 and enter the following text in a new document.

      To: Latisha Pine

      From: [Your Name]

      Date: [current date]

      Here is the information you requested on the clients who are over the age of 40:

   c. Select the query results and copy them into the Word document.

   d. Save the memo as 40+ Spa Clients. Print the memo.

   e. Close the document and exit Word.

   f. Close the table and database.

To: Latisha Pine
From: Student Name
Date: Current Date

Here is the information you requested on the clients who are over the age of 40:

40+ Clients			
First Name	Last Name	Address	Lookup to City/Sate/Zip
Mary	Smith	560 E. West	89430, Smith Valley, NV
Patricia	Johnson	24486 S. 11th	89430, Smith Valley, NV
Linda	Williams	495 W. Cherry	89430, Smith Valley, NV
Barbara	Jones	738 N. Eighth	89430, Smith Valley, NV
Elizabeth	Brown	1008 E. Adams	89430, Smith Valley, NV
Jennifer	Davis	984 N. 7th	89430, Smith Valley, NV
Maria	Miller	448 E. Williams	89430, Smith Valley, NV
Margaret	Moore	246 N. 1st	89430, Smith Valley, NV
Dorothy	Taylor	1238 E. Fifth	89430, Smith Valley, NV
Lisa	Anderson	7428 S. Hill	89447, Yerington, NV
Nancy	Thomas	6190 E. Main	89447, Yerington, NV
Karen	Jackson	4952 S. Ridge	89706, Mound House, NV
Betty	White	3714 E. Washington	89706, Mound House, NV
Helen	Harris	246 N. 6th	89706, Mound House, NV
Heather	Morris	385 E. 5th	89403, Dayton, NV
Teresa	Rogers	55 N. 2nd	89403, Dayton, NV
Doris	Reed	10494 N. Forest	89403, Dayton, NV
Gloria	Cook	224 E. Laurel	89403, Dayton, NV
Evelyn	Morgan	6190 N. Ninth	89403, Dayton, NV
Mildred	Bailey	31482 E. Smith	89403, Dayton, NV
Katherine	Rivera	123 N. Willow	89403, Dayton, NV
Christina	Ramirez	492 N. First	89403, Dayton, NV
Beverly	Brooks	13992 S. River	89403, Dayton, NV
Andrea	Henderson	8666 N. 9th	89403, Dayton, NV
Kathryn	Coleman	784 E. Fourteenth	89403, Dayton, NV
Anne	Powell	112 E. Forest	89408, Fernley, NV
Tina	Simmons	27984 W. 14th	89408, Fernley, NV
Phyllis	Foster	27984 W. Dogwood	89408, Fernley, NV
Norma	Gonzales	9904 E. Elm	89408, Fernley, NV
Diana	Alexander	246 E. 9th	89408, Fernley, NV
Annie	Russell	123 E. 3rd	89408, Fernley, NV
Emily	Diaz	330 N. 3rd	89408, Fernley, NV

Low Stock Analysis ★★

CONTINUING EXERCISES

2. Evan, the owner of the Downtown Internet Café, continues to be impressed with the cafe's inventory database (Step-by-Step Exercise 3 of Lab 3). He has asked you for a list of all special-order items and how many of these items are currently in stock. He wants this information as an Excel 2007 worksheet so that he can further analyze the data. You will provide this information by exporting the data from Access 2007 to Excel 2007. Your completed worksheet of this data should be similar to that shown here.

Description	In Stock	Special Order?	Supplier
Powdered cream	31	Y	ABC Restaurant Supply
T-Shirts	10	Y	By Design
Decaf Viennese	33	Y	Pure Processing
Decaf Sumatra	35	Y	Pure Processing
Business cards	43	Y	Pro Printing
Coffee mints	30	Y	Sweet Stuff
French Roast	47	Y	Café Ole
Guatamala coffee	45	Y	Cuppa Jo
Java coffee	46	Y	Cuppa Jo
Arabian coffee	47	Y	Cuppa Jo
Espresso	11	Y	Cuppa Jo
Darjeeling Tea	13	Y	Tea and Toast, Inc.

a. Open the ac03_Cafe Inventory database that you modified in Step-by-Step Exercise 3 of Lab 3.

b. Create a new query named Special Orders that will display items with Y in the Special Order? field, and include the Description, In Stock, Special Order?, and Supplier fields (in that order). Run the query. Save the query.

c. Export the data to Excel using the file name Special Orders. Close the workbook file.

d. Save the export steps.

e. Change the In-Stock in the query for T-Shirts to **10** and Coffee mints to **30**. Rerun the export using the saved steps, replacing the Special Orders file.

f. Print the worksheet. Exit Excel.

g. Save the query. Close the table and database.

Top Priority Jobs Memo ★★

3. The Job Priority report you created for Kodiak Construction needs to be sent to the company president. (See Step-by-Step Exercise 4 of Lab 3.) You want to include a brief note with the report and decide to export the report to a memo you create using Word. Your completed memo should be similar to that shown here.

   a. Open the ac02_Kodiak Construction database and the Priority query showing the high-priority jobs that you created in Step-by-Step Exercise 4 of Lab 3. Modify the query to show only the ID, Job, Begin Date, and Foreman Last Name fields and beginning dates of 2008 only.

   b. Export the Priority query results to a Word document named Kodiak Top Priority.

To: Kevin Lindquist, President

From: Student Name

Date: Current Date

Here is the information you requested on high priority jobs that were started in 2008.

ID	Job	Begin Date	Foreman Last Name
109	Solera Greens	2/1/2008	
116	Riverwood Hills	6/12/2008	
127	Mesquite Trails	9/3/2008	
999	Student Name private residence	2/3/2008	Valdez

   c. Enter the following text above the table in the document.

      To: Kevin Lindquist, President

      From: [Your Name]

      Date: [current date]

      Here is the information you requested on high priority jobs that were started in 2008.

   d. Apply formatting of your choice to the table. Size and center the table appropriately.

   e. Save the memo. Print the document.

   f. Save the query changes. Close the table and database.

Importing and Querying Tables

LAB 4

Objectives

After completing this lab, you will know how to:

1. Import a table.
2. Import data from Excel.
3. Save import steps.
4. Create an input mask.
5. Make fields required.
6. Create and use action queries.
7. Add a calculated field to a query.
8. Create a subquery.
9. Create a Top-Values query.
10. Create a crosstab query.

Case Study

Lifestyle Fitness Club

You have created an employee database and several simple queries and reports related to this database for the Lifestyle Fitness Club. This has made recordkeeping at the club much easier than it used to be when everything was done manually. Based on the success of this database, the club owners would like you to also include the employees' pay information and hours worked in the database. The hours worked data is submitted to and maintained by the payroll department, who use the information to generate bimonthly paychecks. Pay rates are set by the management and provided to the payroll department by you. Many times the same information in an organization is used by different departments. How you set up a database can make sharing this data between departments much easier.

Once you have added the necessary data to the database, the club owners want you to update the pay rates to reflect the annual pay increases. Specifically, you have been told to award a 3.2 percent increase to all employees. Additionally, recently the club has experienced turnover in personal trainer jobs because of market demand. To counteract this turnover, they want to give all personal trainer positions an additional 5 percent pay increase. Once these adjustments are made, the club owners want to see a gross pay report for the current pay period.

While creating the new table and queries, you will learn about features such as applying input masks and required properties to fields to ensure that the correct information is entered. You also will learn how to create a field to calculate numerical data in a query and to create a crosstab query that displays table data in tabular format. The crosstab and gross pay reports are shown here.

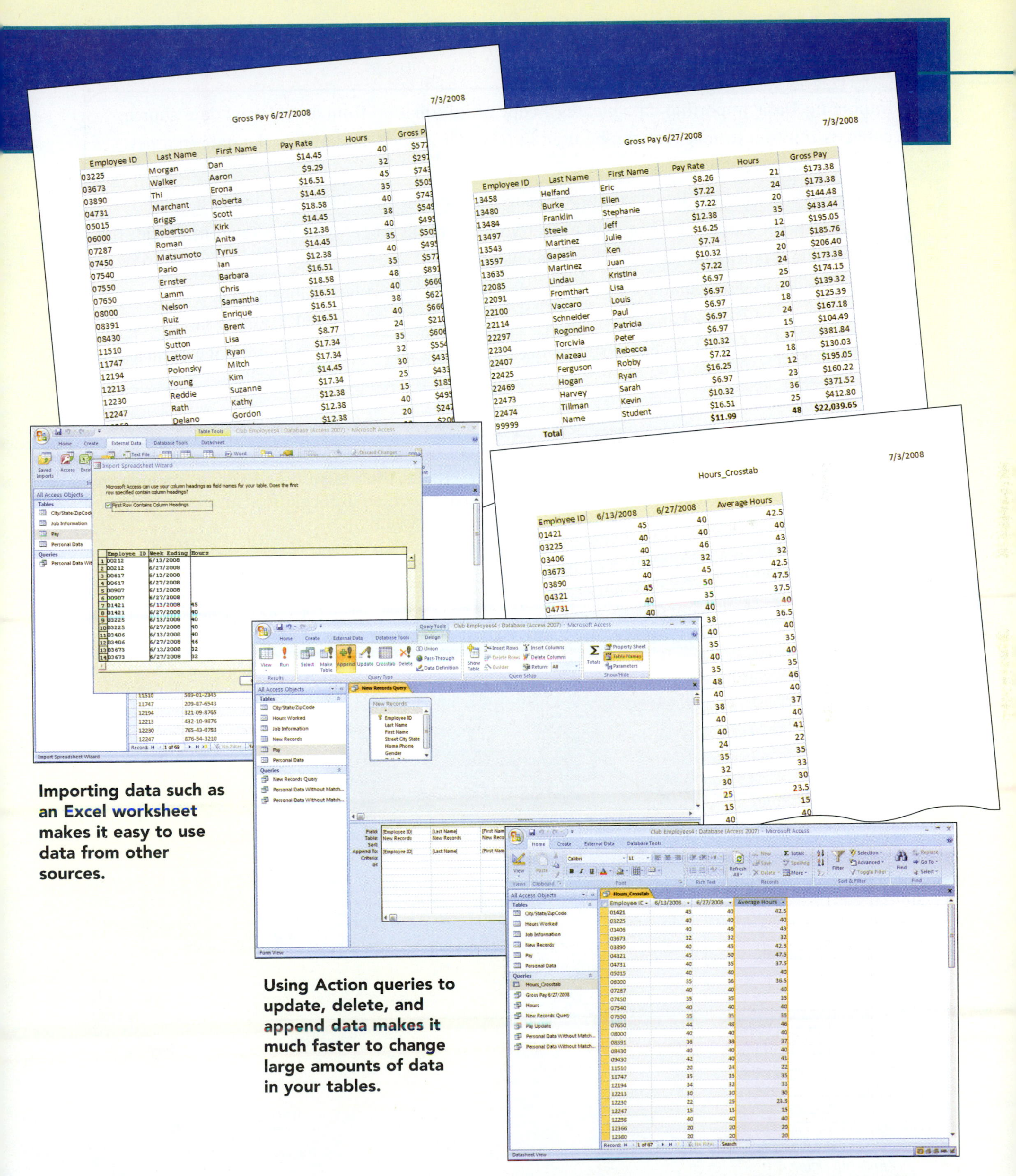

Importing data such as an **Excel worksheet** makes it easy to use data from other sources.

Using Action queries to update, delete, and append data makes it much faster to change large amounts of data in your tables.

Using a crosstab query, you can quickly summarize data and display it in a tabular format.

Concept Preview

The following concepts will be introduced in this lab:

1. **Importing Data** Importing data creates a copy of information from an external data source, converts it into a format that can be used in Access if needed, and inserts the data in a new table in your Access database.
2. **Required Property** The Required property specifies whether a value is required in a field.
3. **Input Mask** An input mask is a field property that controls where data is entered in a field, the kind of data, and the number of allowable characters.
4. **Calculated Field** A calculated field displays the result of a calculation in a query.
5. **SQL (Structured Query Language)** SQL is the most common relational database language.
6. **Crosstab Query** A crosstab query summarizes table data and displays it in a tabular format.

Importing Data

The owners of the Lifestyle Fitness Club have asked you to include the employees' pay rate and hours worked information in the Employees database. You will create the Pay table first.

1

- **In Windows, create a copy of the ac04_Club Employees file and rename it Club Employees4.**
- **Start Access and open the Club Employees4 database file.**
- **Enable the content.**

Having Trouble?

Click Options... and choose Enable this content.

- **Open the Personal Data table.**
- **Replace Student Name with your name in the last record (70) of the table.**

Your screen should be similar to Figure 4.1

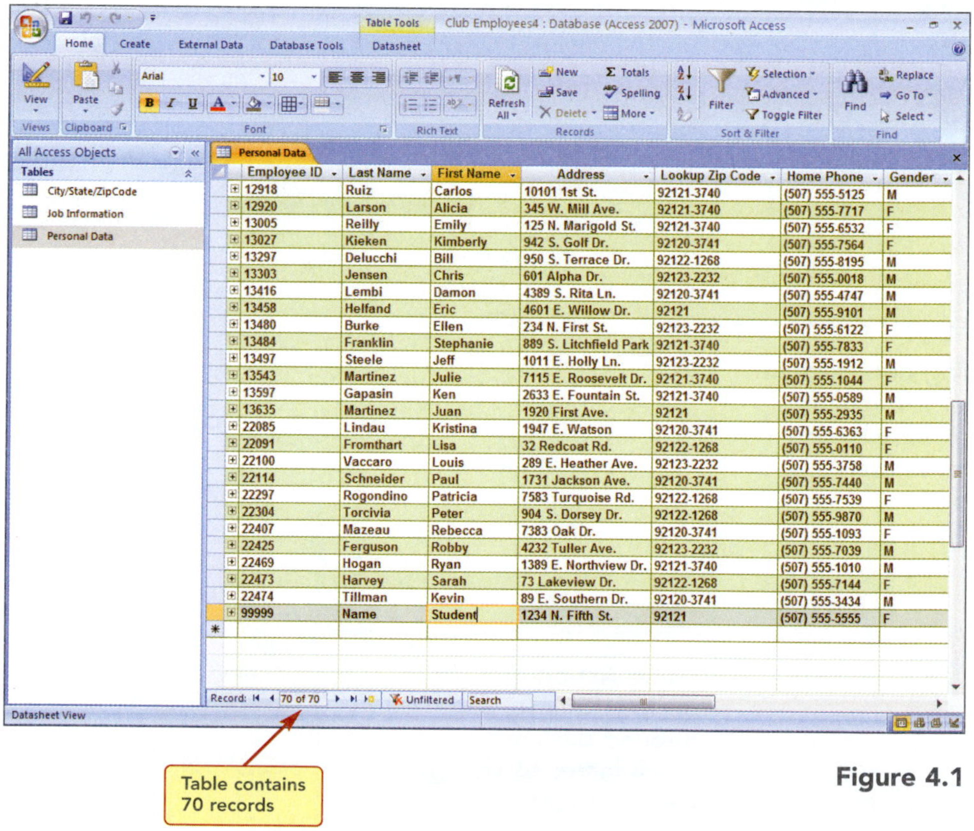

Employee ID	Last Name	First Name	Address	Lookup Zip Code	Home Phone	Gender
12918	Ruiz	Carlos	10101 1st St.	92121-3740	(507) 555-5125	M
12920	Larson	Alicia	345 W. Mill Ave.	92121-3740	(507) 555-7717	F
13005	Reilly	Emily	125 N. Marigold St.	92121-3740	(507) 555-6532	F
13027	Kieken	Kimberly	942 S. Golf Dr.	92120-3741	(507) 555-7564	F
13297	Delucchi	Bill	950 S. Terrace Dr.	92122-1268	(507) 555-8195	M
13303	Jensen	Chris	601 Alpha Dr.	92123-2232	(507) 555-0018	M
13416	Lembi	Damon	4389 S. Rita Ln.	92120-3741	(507) 555-4747	M
13458	Helfand	Eric	4601 E. Willow Dr.	92121	(507) 555-9101	M
13480	Burke	Ellen	234 N. First St.	92123-2232	(507) 555-6122	F
13484	Franklin	Stephanie	889 S. Litchfield Park	92121-3740	(507) 555-7833	F
13497	Steele	Jeff	1011 E. Holly Ln.	92123-2232	(507) 555-1912	M
13543	Martinez	Julie	7115 E. Roosevelt Dr.	92121-3740	(507) 555-1044	F
13597	Gapasin	Ken	2633 E. Fountain St.	92121-3740	(507) 555-0589	M
13635	Martinez	Juan	1920 First Ave.	92121	(507) 555-2935	M
22085	Lindau	Kristina	1947 E. Watson	92120-3741	(507) 555-6363	F
22091	Fromthart	Lisa	32 Redcoat Rd.	92122-1268	(507) 555-0110	F
22100	Vaccaro	Louis	289 E. Heather Ave.	92123-2232	(507) 555-3758	M
22114	Schneider	Paul	1731 Jackson Ave.	92120-3741	(507) 555-7440	M
22297	Rogondino	Patricia	7583 Turquoise Rd.	92122-1268	(507) 555-7539	F
22304	Torcivia	Peter	904 S. Dorsey Dr.	92122-1268	(507) 555-9870	M
22407	Mazeau	Rebecca	7383 Oak Dr.	92120-3741	(507) 555-1093	F
22425	Ferguson	Robby	4232 Tuller Ave.	92123-2232	(507) 555-7039	M
22469	Hogan	Ryan	1389 E. Northview Dr.	92121-3740	(507) 555-1010	M
22473	Harvey	Sarah	73 Lakeview Dr.	92122-1268	(507) 555-7144	F
22474	Tillman	Kevin	89 E. Southern Dr.	92120-3741	(507) 555-3434	M
99999	Name	Student	1234 N. Fifth St.	92121	(507) 555-5555	F

Table contains 70 records

Figure 4.1

There are 70 records in the Personal Data table. Your first project is to create a table to hold the pay data for each of these records.

Importing an Access Table

The Pay table will contain three fields of information: Employee ID, Social Security Number, and Pay Rate. This information is currently maintained in a table in another database that is used to generate payroll. Instead of recreating the table, you will import it from the other database.

Concept 1

Importing Data

1 **Importing** data creates a copy of information from an external data source, converts it into a format that can be used in Access if needed, and inserts the data in a new table in your Access database. The source table or file is not altered in this process. Data can be imported from an Excel workbook, another Access database, or text files such as Word documents. You also can import database objects other than tables, such as forms or reports, from another Access database.

When importing data, you cannot add the imported data to a table that already contains records (except when importing spreadsheet or text files). However, once you have imported a table into an Access database you can perform an Append query to add the table's data to another table.

Imported data also can be linked to the source data. This creates a table that displays the information in the source but does not actually store the data in Access. Changes made to the source are reflected in the linked table. However, you can only view, not change, the data from within Access. The linked data can be used in creating queries and reports. You may want to link rather than import when the source data changes frequently and you do not want to maintain the data in the destination Access database.

Having Trouble?
To review exporting data, refer to the Working Together 1 lab.

The process of importing files is similar to exporting files. When importing files, you need to first specify the source and destination files. The information you want to import is contained in another Access database file.

1 **Open the External Data tab and click Access in the Import group.**

Your screen should be similar to Figure 4.2

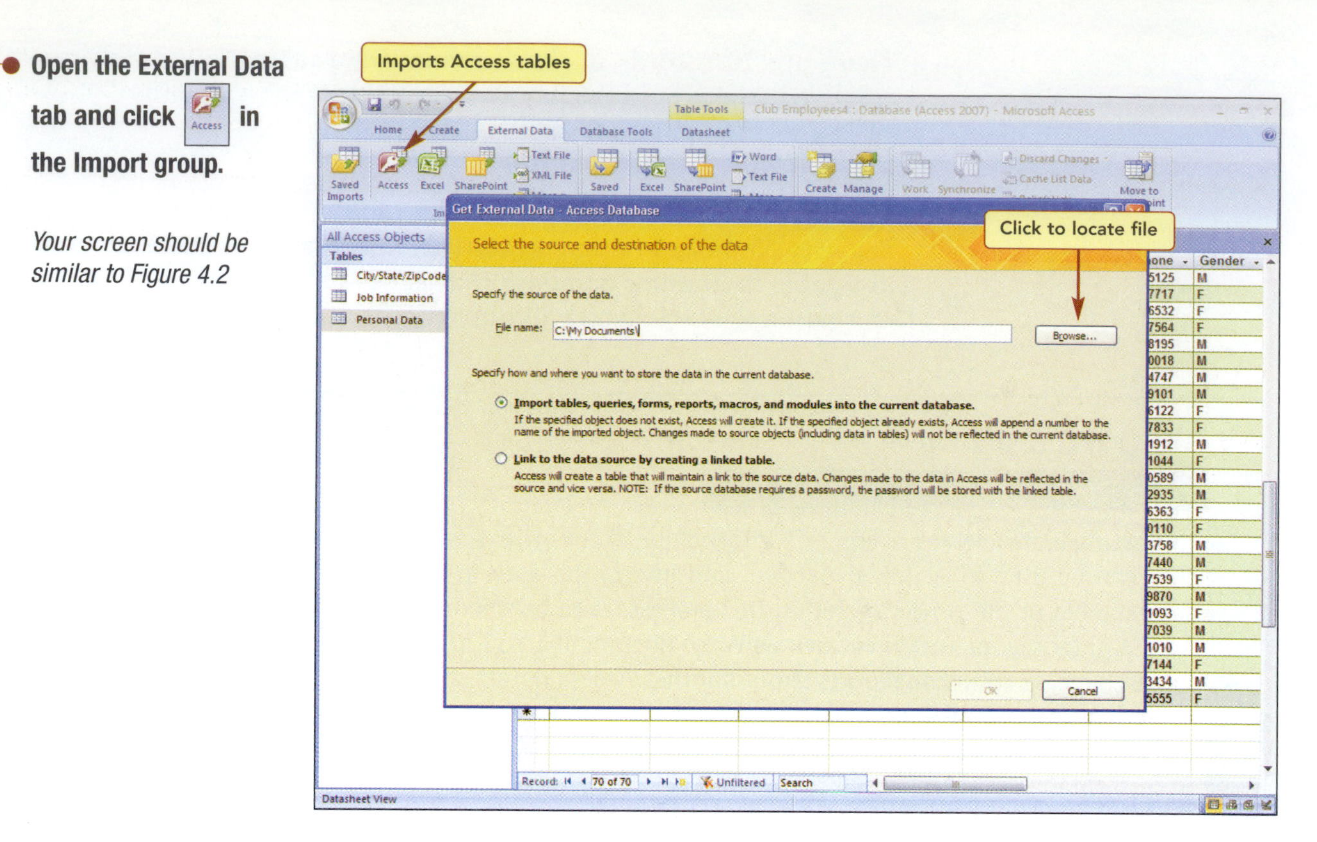

Figure 4.2

First, you need to specify the source of the data you want to import. Then you specify how and where you want to store the data.

2 **Click Browse... and select the** ac04_Employee Pay **database file from your data file location.**

Click Open.

If necessary, choose the Import tables, queries, forms, reports, macros, and modules into the current database option.

Click OK.

Your screen should be similar to Figure 4.3

Select object to import

Figure 4.3

From the Import Objects dialog box, you select the objects from the database that you want to import. In this case, the database only includes a single table, named Table1, which you will select.

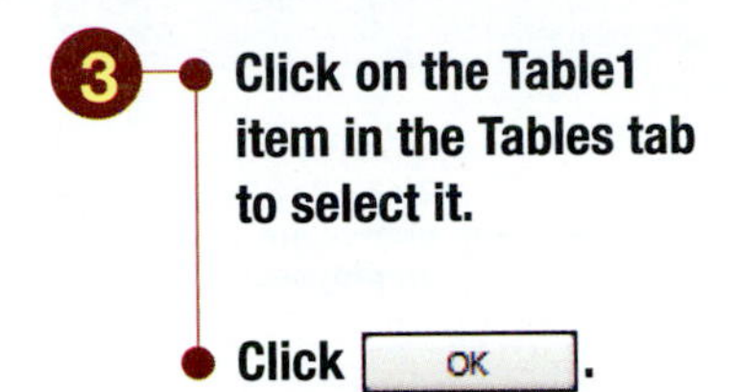

3 **Click on the Table1 item in the Tables tab to select it.**

Click OK.

Your screen should be similar to Figure 4.4

Figure 4.4

Finally, you are asked if you want to save the import steps so that you could quickly rerun the import. You will save the steps so that you can reuse the import operation shortly to import another table. Then you will open the new Pay table to review the contents of the table before starting to use it to make sure that everything looks correct.

4 ● **Choose Save Import Steps.**

Additional Information

You could specify a different name in the Save as text box as the name for the saved import steps.

● **Click Save Import to save the steps using the suggested name.**

● **Rename the new table Pay.**

● **Open the Pay table.**

Your screen should be similar to Figure 4.5

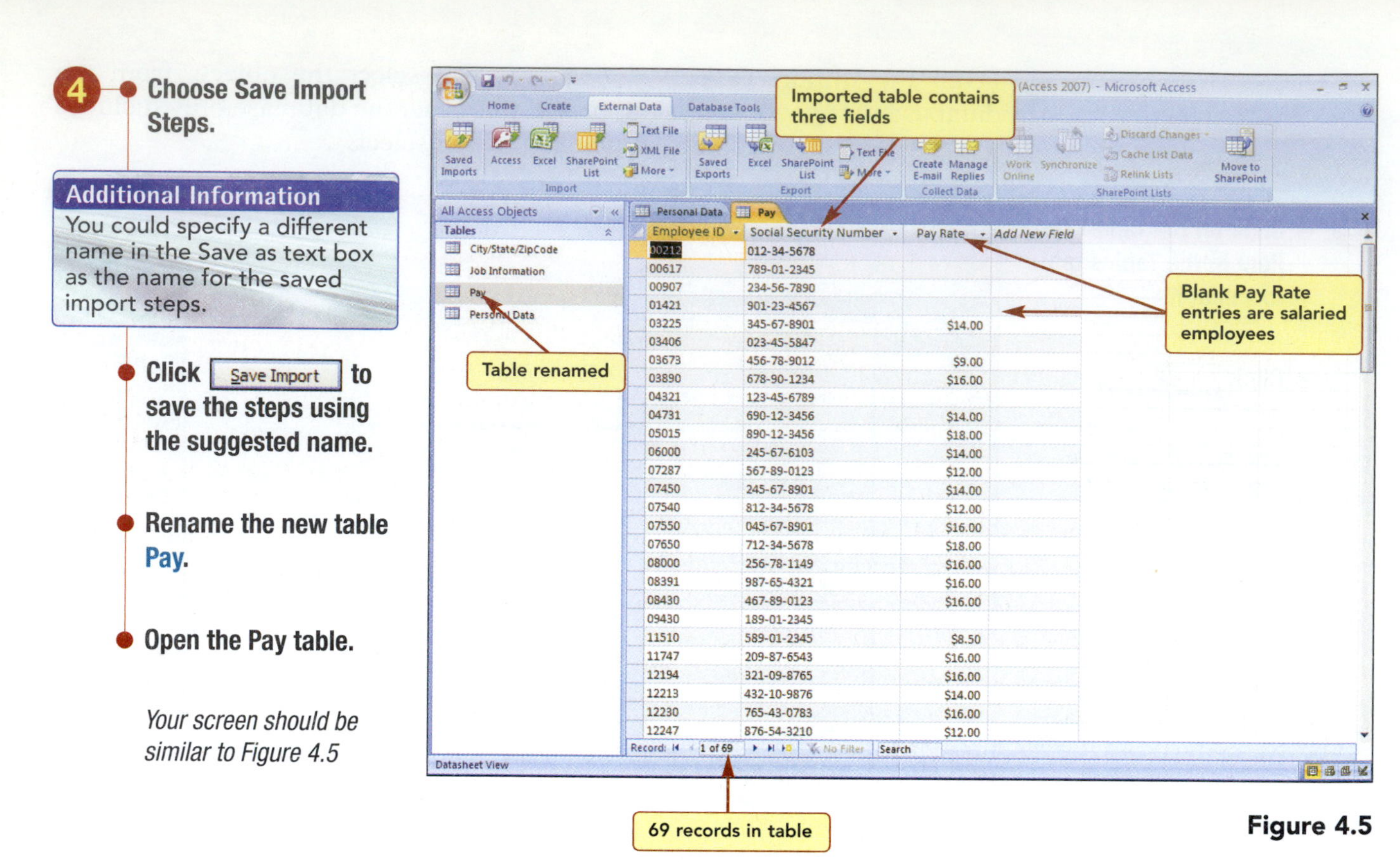

Figure 4.5

The Pay table consists of three fields: Employee ID, Social Security Number, and Pay Rate. Those records with a blank in the Pay Rate field are salaried employees. The Pay table contains 69 records and you know the Personal Data table contains 70 records. You will use the Find Unmatched Query Wizard to locate the missing record.

5 ● **Use the Find Unmatched Query Wizard to locate the missing record. Show all fields in the results.**

Having Trouble?

See Lab 3 to review using the Find Unmatched Query Wizard.

Your screen should be similar to Figure 4.6

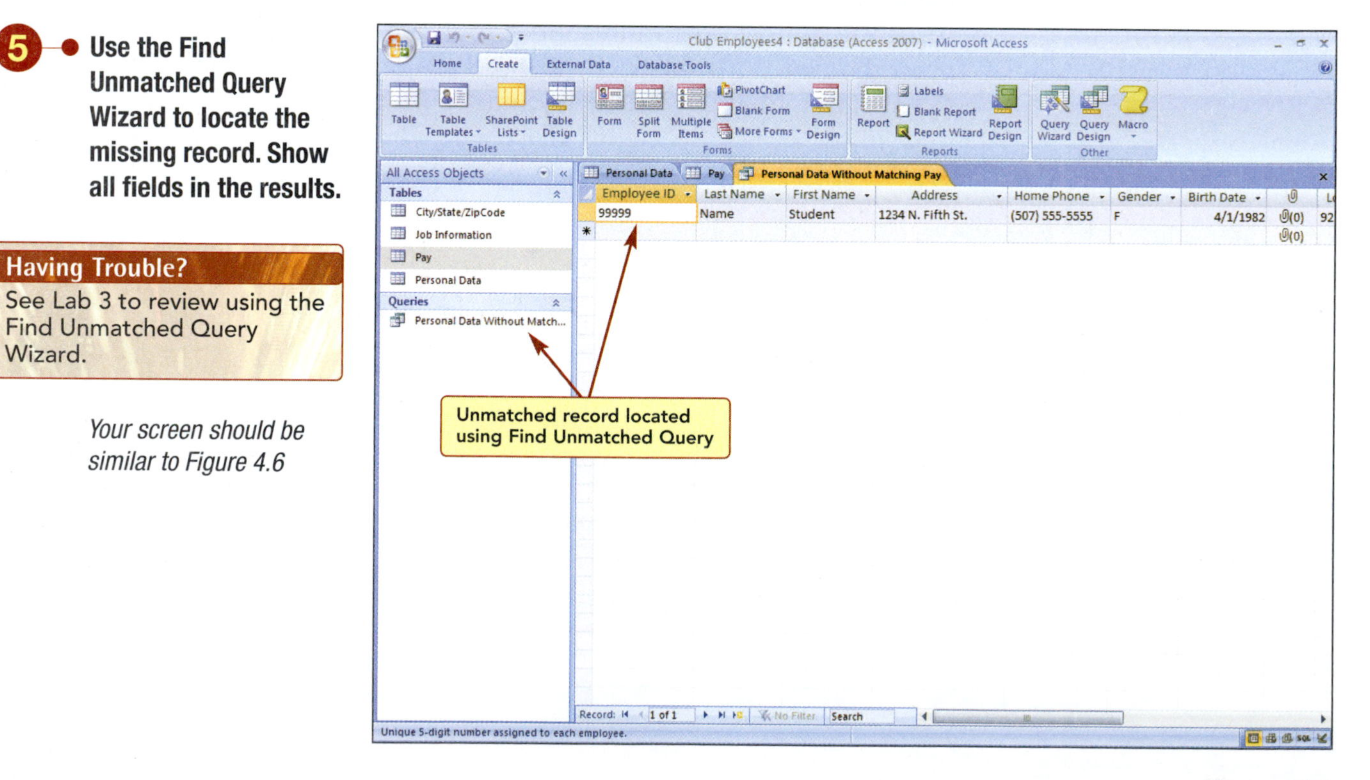

Figure 4.6

You see the missing data is for your record. You will add this data shortly.

6 **Close the Query window.**

Importing Data from Another Application

You are now ready to create a second table to hold the hours worked data. The club's payroll department has provided you with an Excel workbook file that includes the employee ID number, Week Ending dates, and hours worked information for all employees in sorted order by employee number. Again, you will import this information into the Club Employees database.

The process is similar to importing Access data. You select the file containing the data to import and specify whether to save this data in a new table or an existing table. You will create a new table.

> **Additional Information**
> When importing worksheet data to an existing table, the source data must be in the same field order as in the destination table and the destination table must be empty and closed.

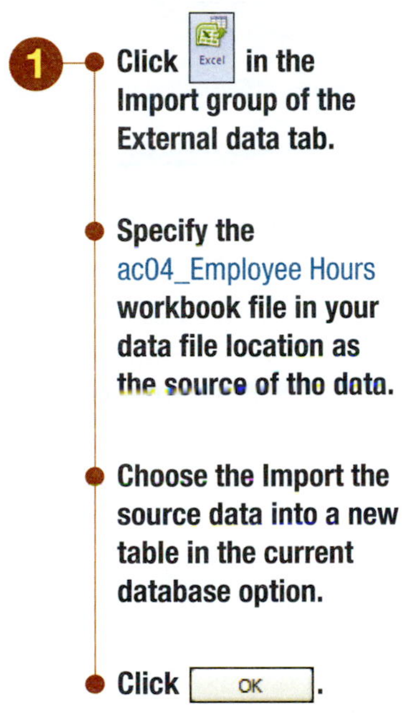

1 **Click** Excel **in the Import group of the External data tab.**

Specify the ac04_Employee Hours **workbook file in your data file location as the source of the data.**

Choose the Import the source data into a new table in the current database option.

Click OK**.**

Your screen should be similar to Figure 4.7

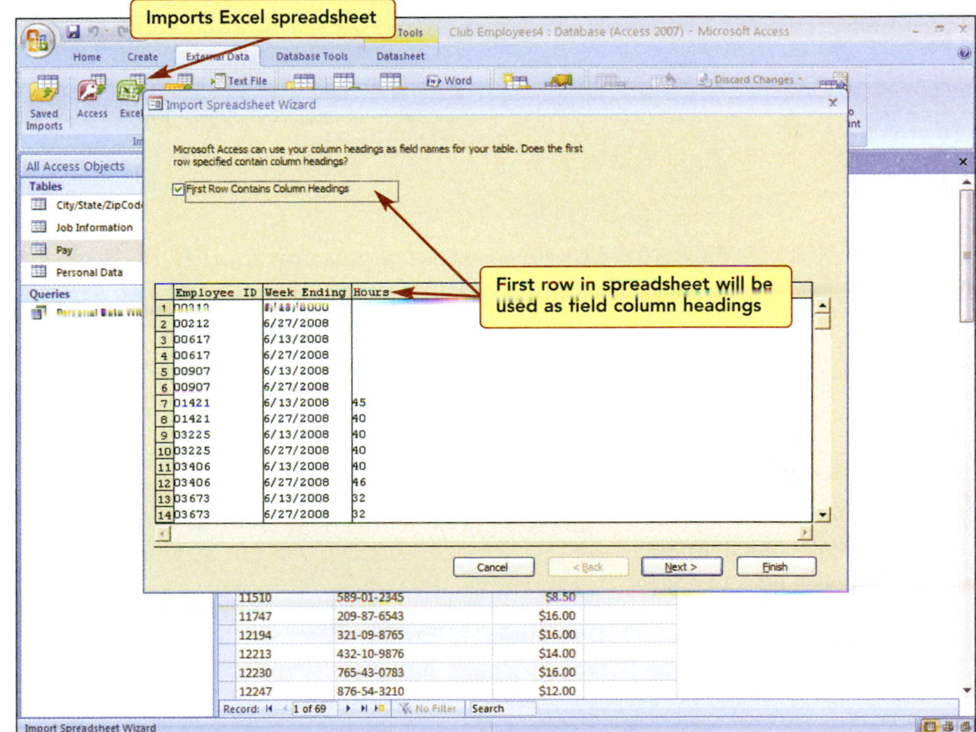

Figure 4.7

> **Additional Information**
> When importing to an existing table, the column headings in the imported file must match the column headings in the existing table.

The Import Spreadsheet Wizard starts and leads you through the steps to import the data. First you specify whether to use the column headings in the worksheet as the field names. The preview area shows how the data in the worksheet is set up so you can easily confirm that the first row contains information you want to use as column headings.

2 **If necessary, choose First Row Contains Column Headings.**

Click Next > **.**

Your screen should be similar to Figure 4.8

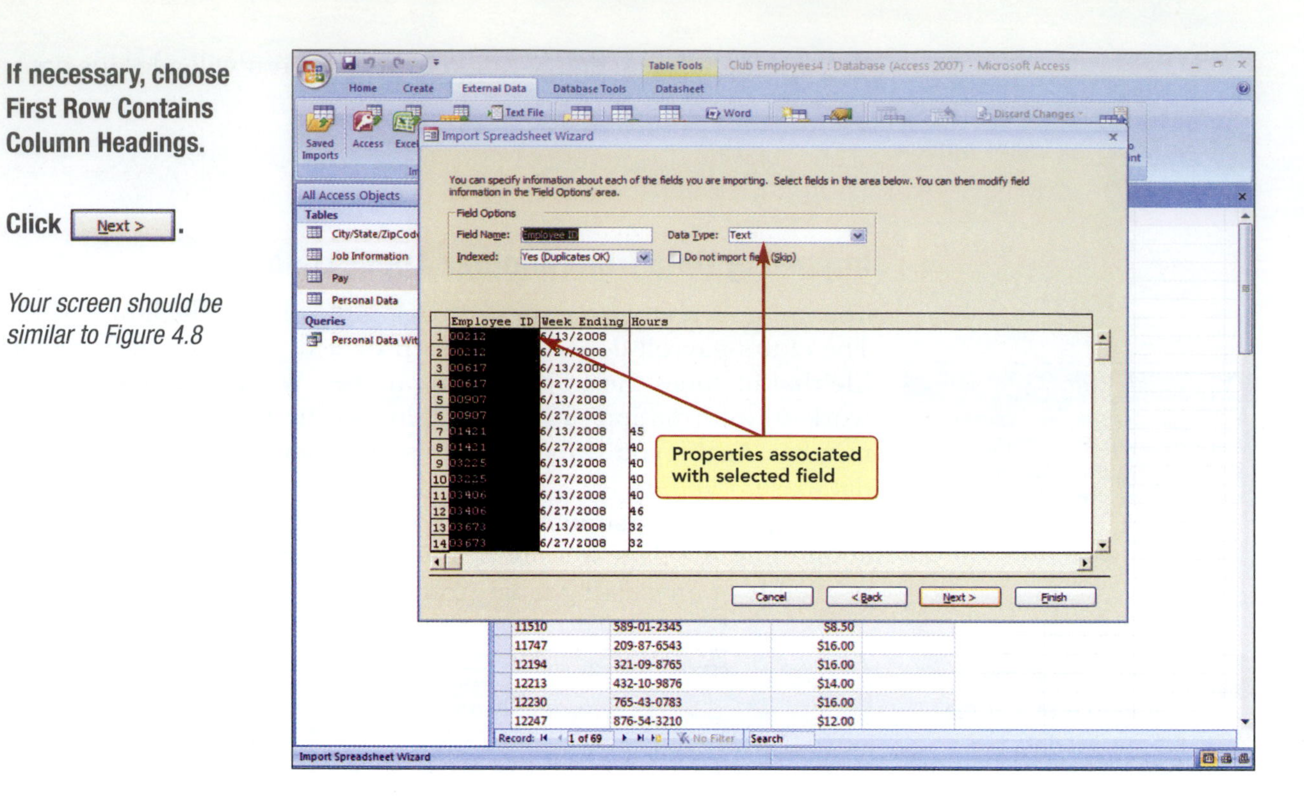

Figure 4.8

In the next step, you can modify the field information, including the field name and data type. The Employee ID field is the selected field and is highlighted in the preview area. The field options associated with the Employee ID field are displayed in the Field Options area of the dialog box. This field will have a Text data type, which is correct, and the field name is appropriate.

3 **Click on the Week Ending column in the preview area to review its properties.**

Click on the Hours column.

Your screen should be similar to Figure 4.9

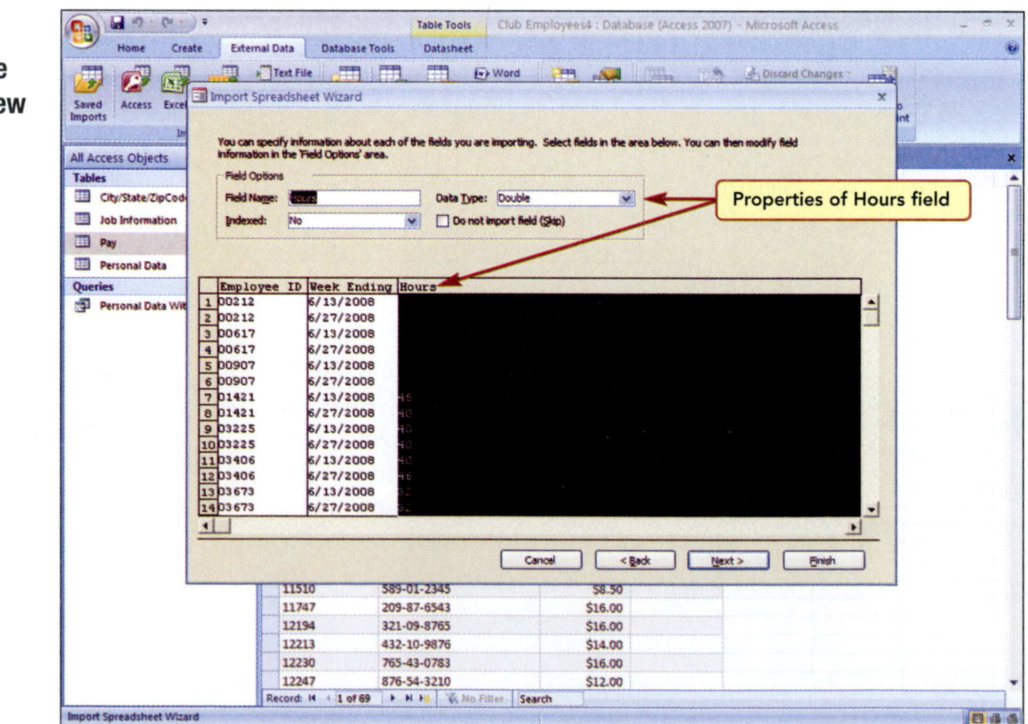

Figure 4.9

Access determines the data type by looking at the first eight rows in each column and suggests an appropriate data type. Most often, this is the Text data type. You can choose a different data type; however, if the values are not compatible with the data type you choose, they will be ignored or converted incorrectly. The Hours data type is set to Double, a numeric data type with a field size of two digits. You will accept the data types as suggested.

Your screen should be similar to Figure 4.10

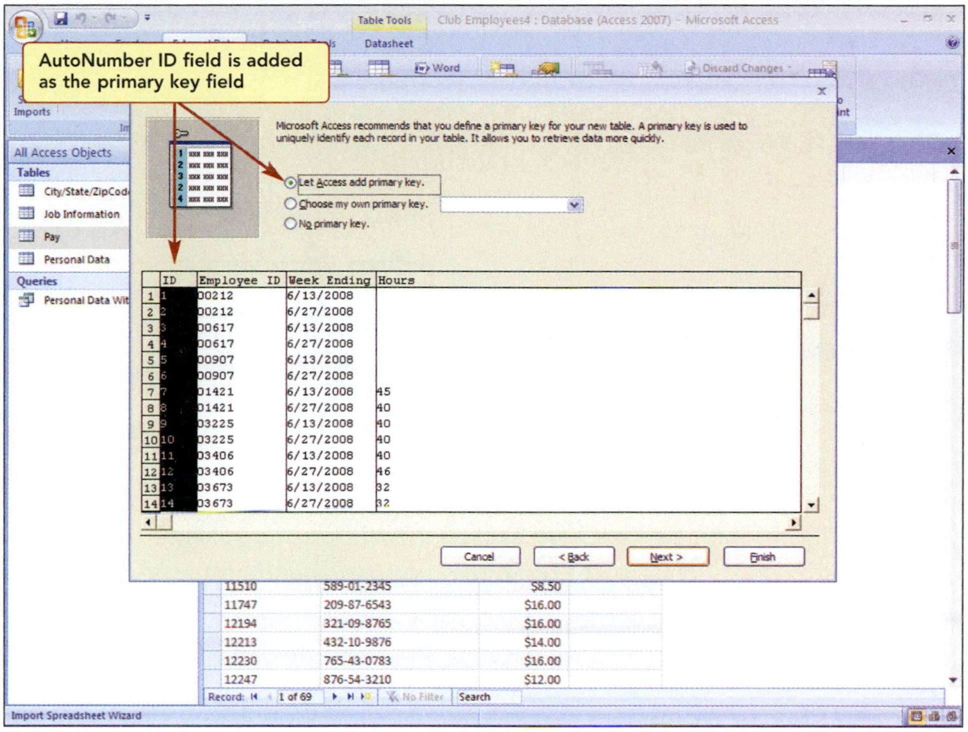

AutoNumber ID field is added as the primary key field

Figure 4.10

In this step, you are asked to specify a primary key field. Initially, Access adds an AutoNumber data type ID field to the table and uses it as the primary key field. Because there are duplicate ID numbers in the Employee ID field, this field cannot be used as a primary key field. Therefore, you will accept the default.

5 Click Next >.

Your screen should be similar to Figure 4.11

Figure 4.11

The final step is to specify a name for the new table.

6 Enter **Hours Worked** as the table name.

Click Finish.

Your screen should be similar to Figure 4.12

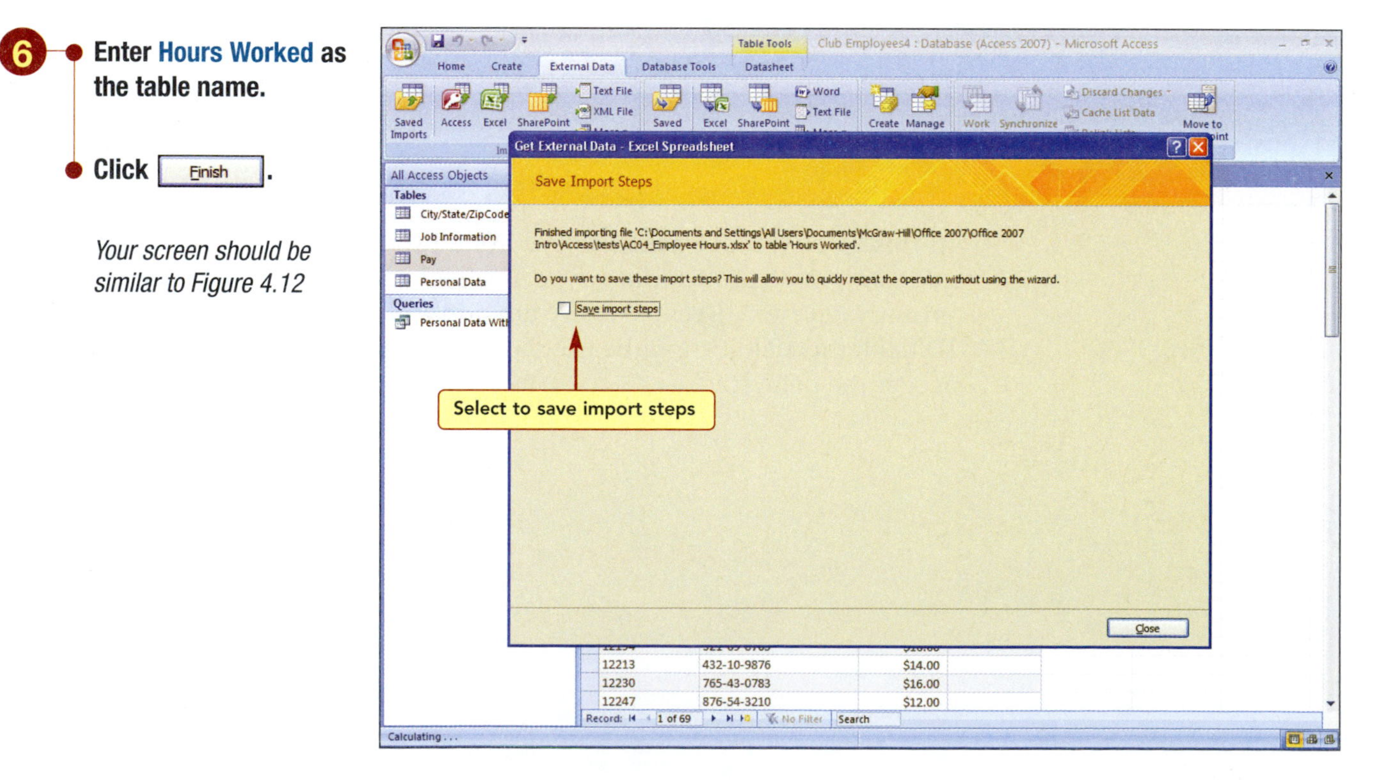

Figure 4.12

The dialog box informs you that the Excel data was successfully imported into the Hours Worked table. You decide you want to save these steps, since you may want to import this data periodically if the managers want a report generated using this information on a routine basis. Then you will open the new table.

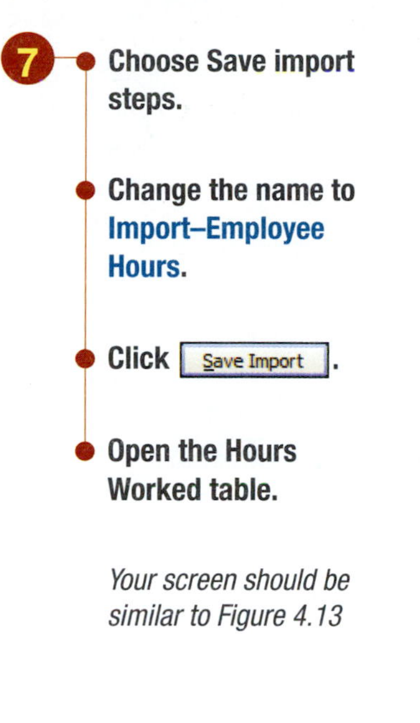

7 • Choose Save import steps.

• Change the name to **Import–Employee Hours**.

• Click Save Import.

• Open the Hours Worked table.

Your screen should be similar to Figure 4.13

New table added to database and contains data imported from Excel

Figure 4.13

The Hours Worked table contains the hours worked for the month of June. Each record has data for the two pay periods during that month.

8 • Use a Find Unmatched Records query against the Personal Data table to verify there are no missing records.

• Close the query results.

• Scroll to the bottom of the Hours Worked table.

Your screen should be similar to Figure 4.14

Your record for week of 6/27/2008 is missing

Figure 4.14

All records in the Hours Worked table have matching records in the Personal Data table. However, your record, 99999, does not yet include the hours worked for June 27, 2008. You will add this information shortly.

Using a Saved Import

The final item you want to import is a table of data containing several new records that your assistant entered for you in a separate database table. You will reuse the import steps you saved for importing an Access table. The only information you will need to change is the name of the file that you want to import.

1 **Click** Saved Imports **in the Import group of the External Data tab.**

- **Click on the name area for the Import-AC04_Employee Pay saved name and change the name to Import-New Records.**
- **Click on the path area and change the file name in the path to ac04_New Records.**

> **Having Trouble?**
> If you accidentally change or delete part of the path information, close the dialog box and begin again.

Your screen should be similar to Figure 4.15

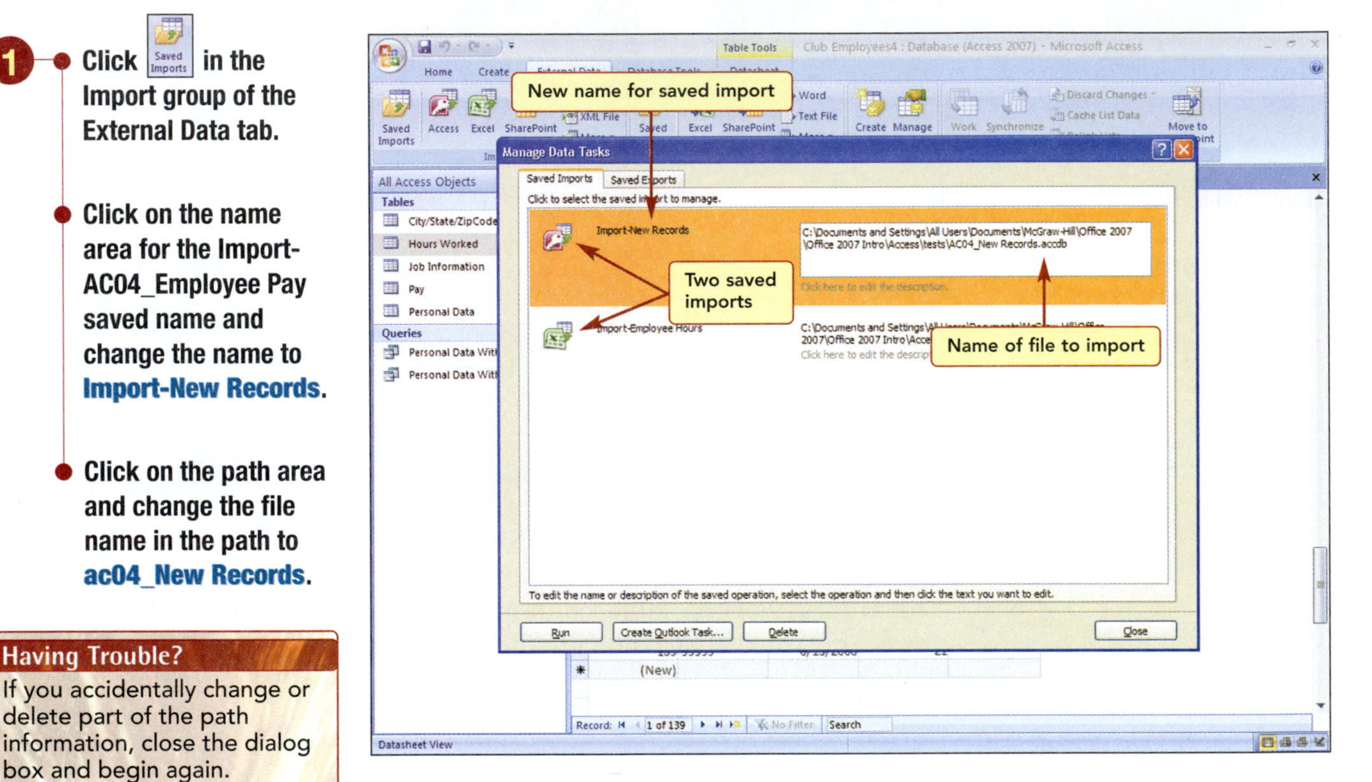

Figure 4.15

The Manage Data Tasks dialog box displays the names of the two saved imports. The name of the file that you want to import is now correctly specified in the path and the saved import step name reflects the new import change. The saved import will look for a file named ac04_New Records and import it to the current database. It also will look for a table named Table1 in the database file.

2

- Click **Run**.
- Click **OK**.
- Click **Close**.
- Rename the Table1 table **New Records**.
- Open the New Records table.

Your screen should be similar to Figure 4.16

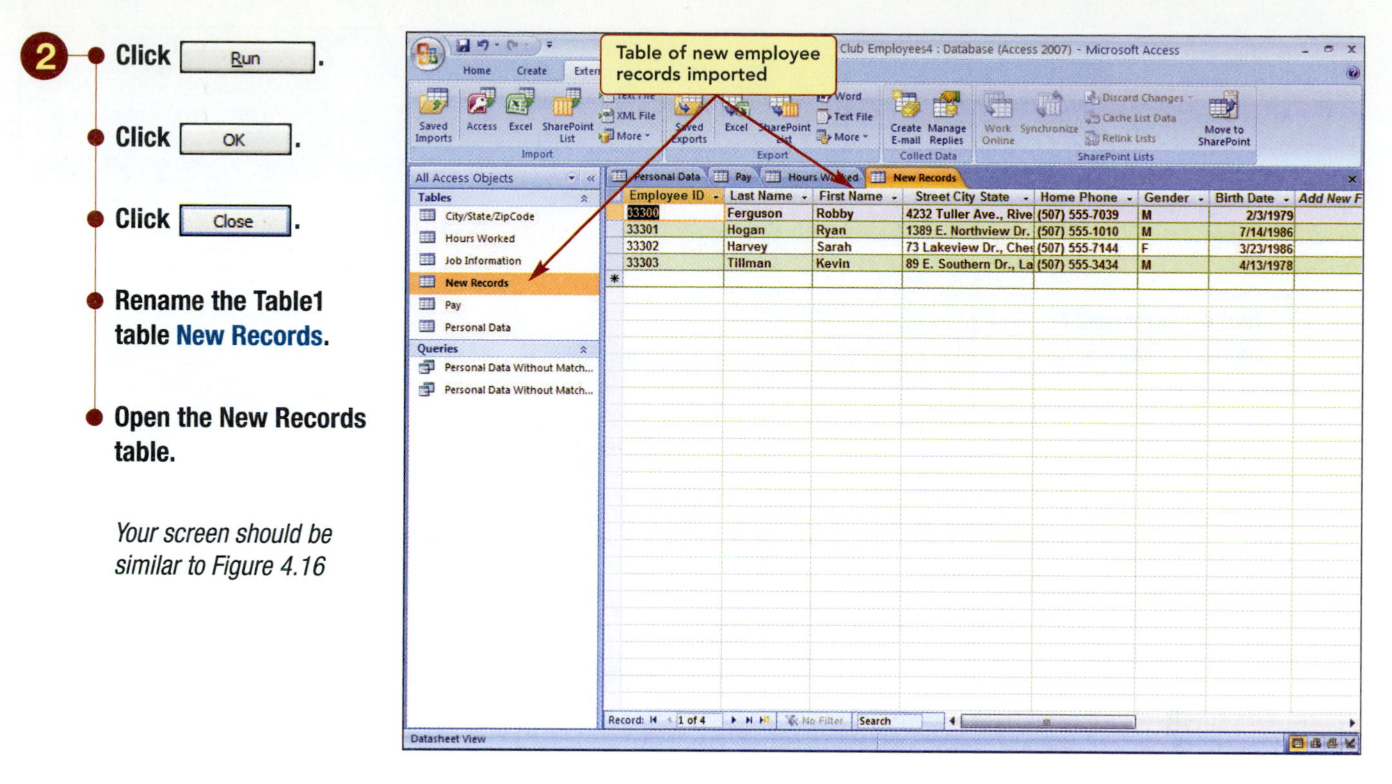

Figure 4.16

The table contains the data for four employees. You will add these records to the Personal Data table shortly.

Generally, saving imports is best for repeating the exact same import operation with files that have the same names and whose contents are the same. In this case, because both databases included a table named Table1, the import was successful. Otherwise, the import specifications will not work.

3

- Close the New Records table.

Controlling Field Input

You have already looked at the table content for the Pay and Hours Worked tables and checked for unmatched records. After importing data, it is also advisable to review the structure of the table in Design view to ensure that the field properties are set correctly and formatted appropriately before using the table.

Changing Field Properties

First, you will look at the Hours Worked table properties.

1 Display the Hours Worked table in Design view.

Select the Employee ID field.

Your screen should be similar to Figure 4.17

Figure 4.17

The four fields have appropriate data types. However, the Employee ID field size is too large and needs to be reduced to five as it is in the other tables to restrict the number of input characters. Additionally you will change the Required property for this field to ensure that it is completed for each employee.

Concept 2

Required Property

2 The **Required property** specifies whether a value is required in a field. If the property is set to Yes for a field, you must enter a value in that field; the value cannot be blank. A field that is empty contains a **Null value.** A field with a value of 0 or that contains a zero-length string is not null. A **zero-length string** is entered by typing two double quotation marks with no space between them. Zero-length strings are used to indicate that you know the field does not contain a value, whereas null values indicate you do not currently know what the value is that should be entered in the field.

If you set the Required property to Yes for a field in a table that already contains data, Access gives you the option of checking whether the field has a value in all existing records. The field must have a value in all instances in which data might be entered in the field—in the table itself as well as in forms, queries, reports, and any other datasheets based on the table.

You can set a Required property for any type of field except a field that has the AutoNumber data type assigned to it. Additionally, a primary key field will not accept null values.

The Indexed property allows duplicates, which is necessary because, in this table, the Employee ID field contains duplicate values.

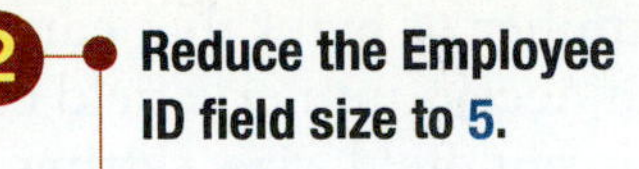

2

- **Reduce the Employee ID field size to 5.**
- **Change the Required property setting to Yes.**

Your screen should be similar to Figure 4.18

Table Tools Club Employees4 : Database (Access 2007) - Microsoft Access

Home Create External Data Database Tools Design

View Primary Key Builder Test Validation Rules Insert Rows Delete Rows Lookup Column Property Sheet Indexes

Views Tools Show/Hide

All Access Objects

Tables

City/State/ZipCode

Hours Worked

Job Information

New Records

Pay

Personal Data

Queries

Personal Data Without Match...

Personal Data Without Match...

Personal Data Pay Hours Worked

Field Name	Data Type	Description
ID	AutoNumber	
Employee ID	Text	
Week Ending	Date/Time	
Hours	Number	

Field Properties

General Lookup

Field Size	5
Format	@
Input Mask	
Caption	
Default Value	
Validation Rule	
Validation Text	
Required	Yes
Allow Zero Length	Yes
Indexed	Yes (Duplicates OK)
Unicode Compression	No
IME Mode	No Control
IME Sentence Mode	None
Smart Tags	

Field size limits number of characters to 5

Field entry is required

Require data entry in this field?

Design view. F6 = Switch panes. F1 = Help.

Figure 4.18

Next, you will check the settings for the last two fields. The Week Ending data type is correctly set to Date/Time. The Hours data type is set to Number. This data type restricts entries to numbers only and can be used in calculations. This is the correct data type.

3

- **Select the Week Ending field.**
- **Select the Hours field.**

Your screen should be similar to Figure 4.19

Table Tools Club Employees4 : Database (Access 2007) - Microsoft Access

Home Create External Data Database Tools Design

View Primary Key Builder Test Validation Rules Insert Rows Delete Rows Lookup Column Property Sheet Indexes

Views Tools Show/Hide

All Access Objects

Tables

City/State/ZipCode

Hours Worked

Job Information

New Records

Pay

Personal Data

Queries

Personal Data Without Match...

Personal Data Without Match...

Personal Data Pay Hours Worked

Field Name	Data Type	Description
ID	AutoNumber	
Employee ID	Text	
Week Ending	Date/Time	
Hours	Number	

Permits up to 15 characters

Field Properties

General Lookup

Field Size	Double
Format	General Number
Decimal Places	Auto
Input Mask	
Caption	
Default Value	
Validation Rule	
Validation Text	
Required	No
Indexed	No
Smart Tags	
Text Align	General

A field name can be up to 64 characters long, including spaces. Press F1 for help on field names.

Design view. F6 = Switch panes. F1 = Help.

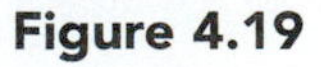

Figure 4.19

Additional Information

For more information about Number size, use Access Help.

The Number Field Size property restricts the number of bytes that can be stored in the field. A **byte** is a unit of storage. An Access numeric field can store values from 0 to 255 in a byte. The current field size setting is Double, which can store up to 15 significant digits. This is much larger than needed. You will change the Hours field size to the smallest size, Byte. You will then add a validation rule to restrict the number of digits to less than 100 to help control the accuracy of the field input.

4

- **Open the Field Size drop-down menu and choose Byte.**
- **Enter <100 as the Validation Rule property setting.**

Your screen should be similar to Figure 4.20

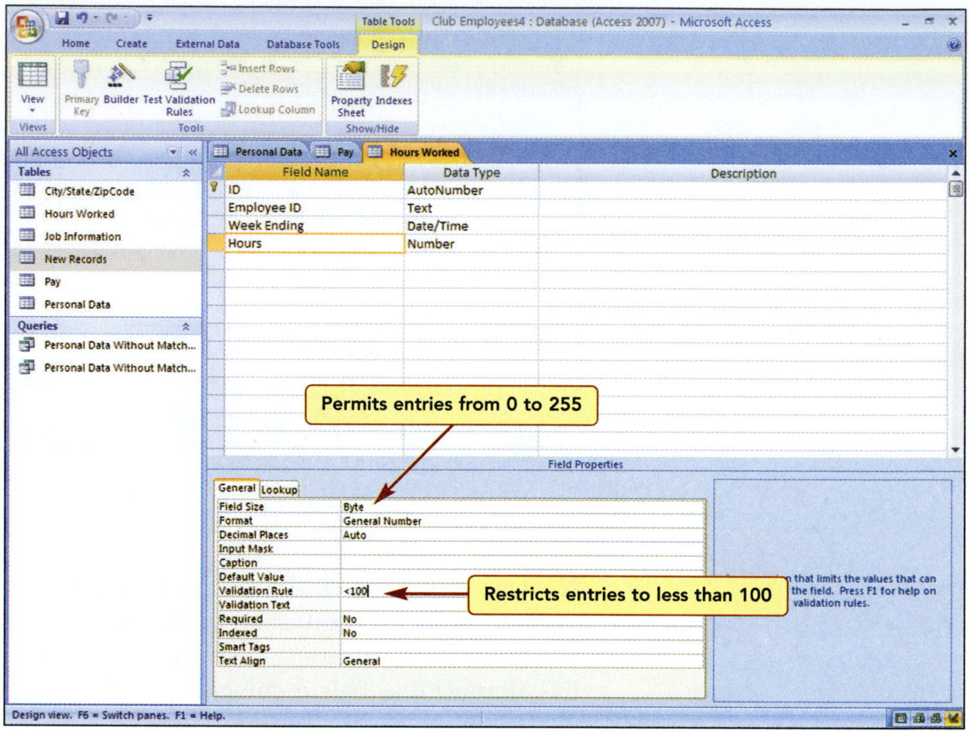

Figure 4.20

Next you will check the properties of the Pay table. When this table was imported, the field definitions and properties as well as the data were imported from the source table.

5 • **Display the Hours Worked table in Datasheet view, save your changes, and click Yes to continue and No to skip testing for data integrity.**

• **Display the Pay table in Design view.**

• **Select the Social Security Number field.**

Your screen should be similar to Figure 4.21

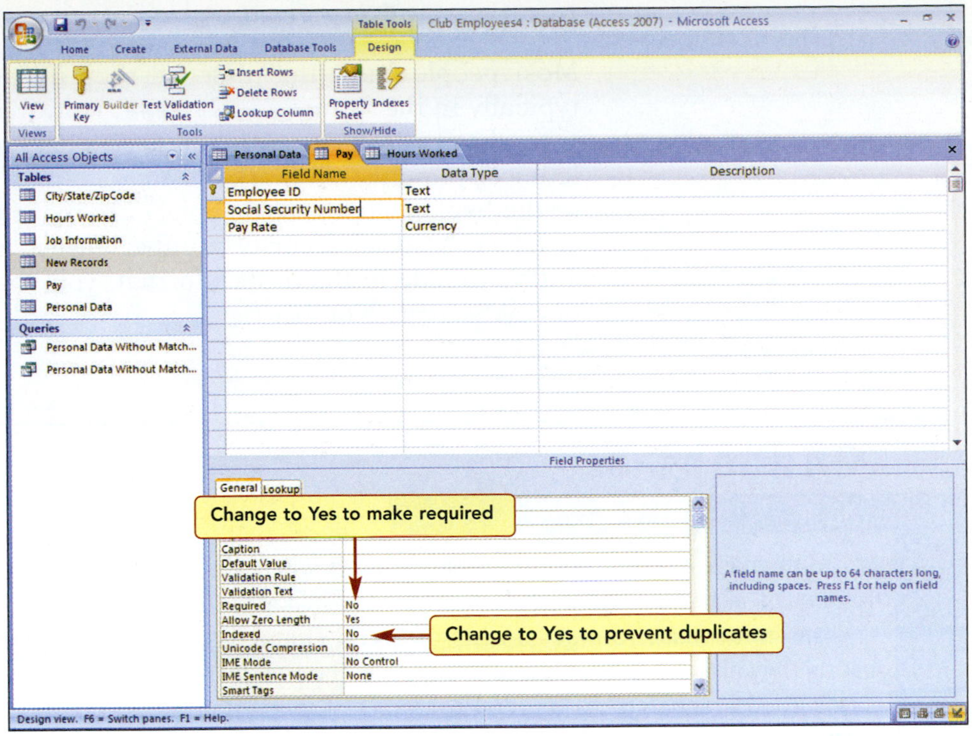

Figure 4.21

The Employee ID field is the primary key field. It will not accept null values by default and automatically requires an entry. As you look at the field properties for the Social Security Number field, you realize that the field should be an indexed field that does not allow duplicates and it should be required.

6 • **Change the Required property to Yes.**

• **Change the Indexed property setting to Yes (No Duplicates).**

Your screen should be similar to Figure 4.22

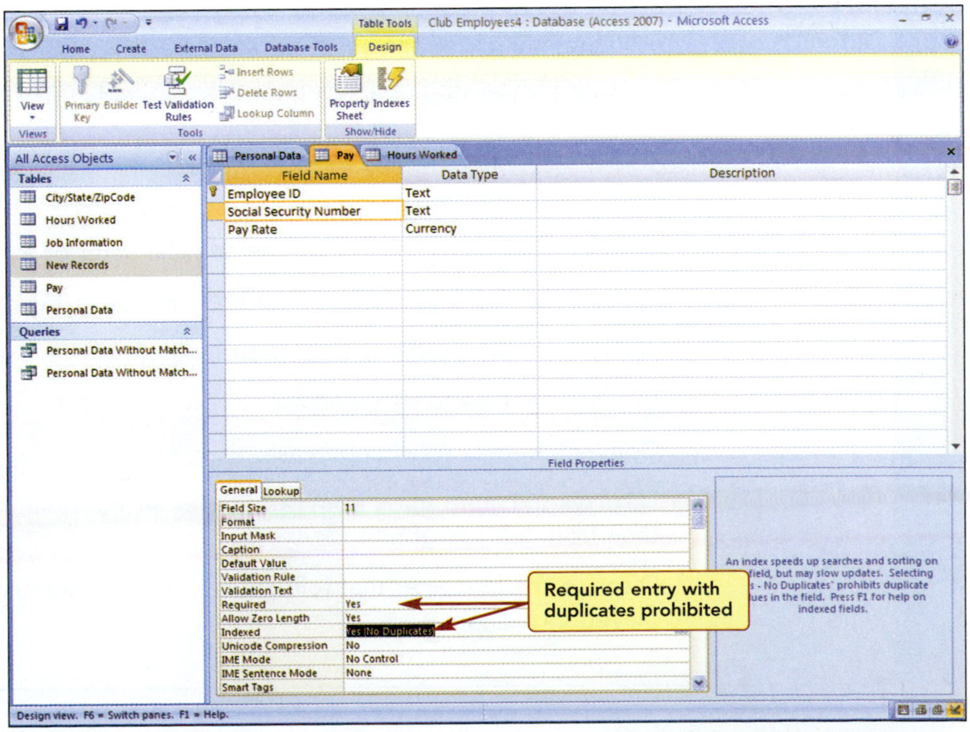

Figure 4.22

Creating an Input Mask

Most people know that a social security number is always nine digits, typically in the format ###-##-####. However, when someone has to enter several records in one sitting, it is very easy to make a mistake and enter a letter or punctuation mark instead of a digit, the wrong number of digits, or the hyphens in the wrong place. To make the task of entering each club employee's social security number easier, as well as to ensure that the entry is made in the proper format, you will apply an input mask to the Social Security Number field.

Concept 3

Input Mask

3 An **input mask** is a field property that controls where data is entered in a field, the kind of data, and the number of allowable characters.

The input mask format consists of **literal characters** such as hyphens and parentheses that display just as they are and **mask characters** that define the characteristics of the input mask. Any character that is not a mask character is a literal character. If you want to use one of the mask characters as a literal, precede it with a backslash (\).

The following mask characters are used to define input masks:

Character	Description
0	Requires that a digit from 0–9 be entered.
9	An entry is not required, but if an entry is made, it must be a digit or space.
#	An entry is not required, but if an entry is made, it must be a digit, space, + (plus sign), or - (minus sign).
L	Requires that a letter from A–Z be entered.
?	An entry is not required, but if an entry is made, it must be a letter from A–Z.
A	Requires that a letter or digit be entered.
a	An entry is not required, but if an entry is made, it must be a letter or digit.
&	An entry is required, and it can be any character or a space.
C	An entry is not required, but if an entry is made, it can be any character or a space.
. , : ; - /	A decimal placeholder and thousand, date, and time separators.
<	Converts entries to all lowercase.
>	Converts entries to all uppercase.
!	Displays the input mask from right to left at the point where the ! is inserted, rather than from left to right.
\	Displays the character that follows as a literal character (for example, \A is displayed as just A).

You will define an input mask for the Social Security Number field to ensure that the correct number and type of characters are entered into the field. Because input masks are sometimes complicated, Access includes a wizard to help you define the input mask. Alternatively, you can type it in directly.

1 • **Click the Input Mask property box for the Social Security Number field.**

Additional Information

The ... button indicates that there is a wizard connected to this property.

Having Trouble?

If the Input Mask Wizard is not installed on your system, type 000-00-0000;;_ in the Input Mask text box and proceed to below Figure 4.29.

• **Click ... (at the end of the property box).**

• **If necessary, click Yes to save the table and click No to skip testing the data integrity rules.**

Your screen should be similar to Figure 4.23

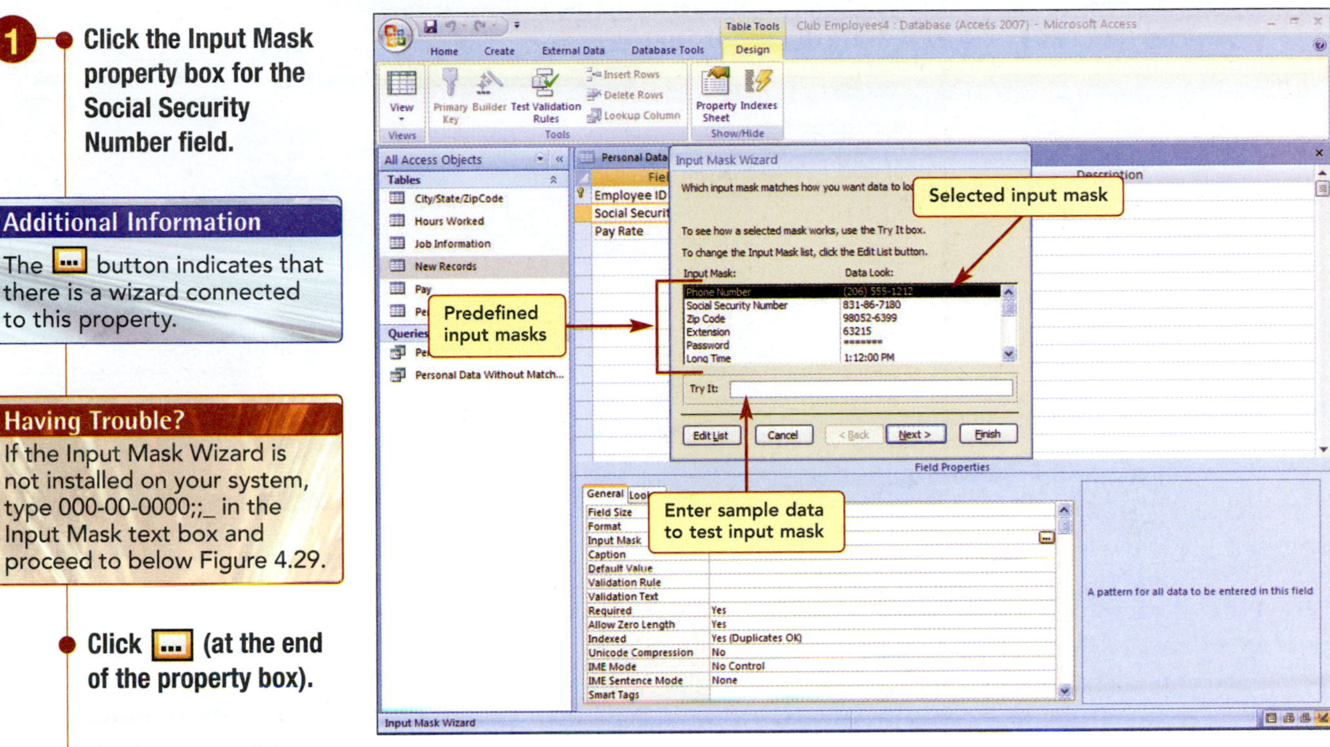

Figure 4.23

The Input Mask Wizard dialog box lists five predefined masks. You also can use this dialog box to try out one of the masks or create your own custom masks for the Input Mask Wizard to display. For your purposes, the Social Security Number input mask is exactly what you want.

Select Social Security Number.

Click in the Try It box.

Your screen should be similar to Figure 4.24

Table Tools Club Employees4 : Database (Access 2007) - Microsoft Access

Home Create External Data Database Tools Design

View Primary Key Builder Test Validation Rules Insert Rows Delete Rows Lookup Column Property Sheet Indexes

Views Tools Show/Hide

All Access Objects

Tables

City/State/ZipCode

Hours Worked

Job Information

New Records

Pay

Personal Data

Queries

Personal Data Without Match...

Personal Data

Field

Employee ID

Social Securit

Pay Rate

Description

Input Mask Wizard

Which input mask matches how you want data to look?

To see how a selected mask works, use the Try It box.

To change the Input Mask list, click the Edit List button.

Input Mask:	Data Look:
Phone Number	(206) 555-1212
Social Security Number	831-86-7180
Zip Code	98052-6399
Extension	63215
Password	********
Long Time	1:12:00 PM

Try It: ___-__-____

Edit List Cancel < Back Next > Finish

Selected input mask

Social Security Number input mask includes hyphens

Field Properties

General Lookup

Field Size	11
Format	
Input Mask	
Caption	
Default Value	
Validation Rule	
Validation Text	
Required	Yes
Allow Zero Length	Yes
Indexed	Yes (Duplicates OK)
Unicode Compression	No
IME Mode	No Control
IME Sentence Mode	None
Smart Tags	

A pattern for all data to be entered in this field

Input Mask Wizard

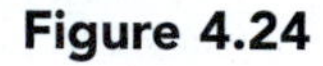

Figure 4.24

Notice that the input mask automatically inserted hyphens in the correct locations for a social security number. This means the social security number can be entered without having to type the hyphens as well. If, however, the user types the hyphens in the correct location, they are accepted. Additionally, if a nonnumeric character is typed, the program beeps and the entry is not accepted. You will test the input mask by entering a social security number a few different ways.

3 • **Position the insertion point at the beginning of the Try It box.**

• **Type 123456789.**

• **Press Esc to clear the entry and type 123-45-6789.**

• **Clear the entry and type 12-345-6 t789.**

Your screen should be similar to Figure 4.25

Test social security number entry

Figure 4.25

In each case, the hyphens were automatically entered in the proper location and the invalid entry was not accepted. Now you want to see what happens when you try to complete an entry that does not have enough numbers.

4 • **Clear the entry and type 12345678.**

• **Press ←Enter.**

Your screen should be similar to Figure 4.26

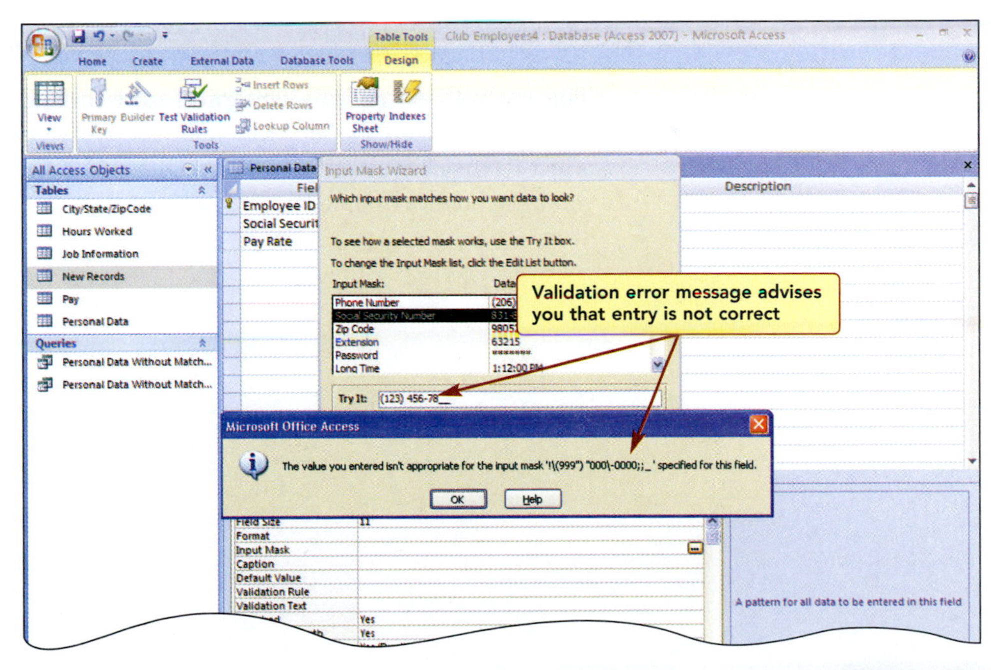

Figure 4.26

A validation error message is displayed advising you that you have made an invalid entry.

Now that you have seen how this feature works, you can complete the entry and continue defining the input mask.

5 Click OK.

- Type 9 to complete the entry.
- Click Next >.

Your screen should be similar to Figure 4.27

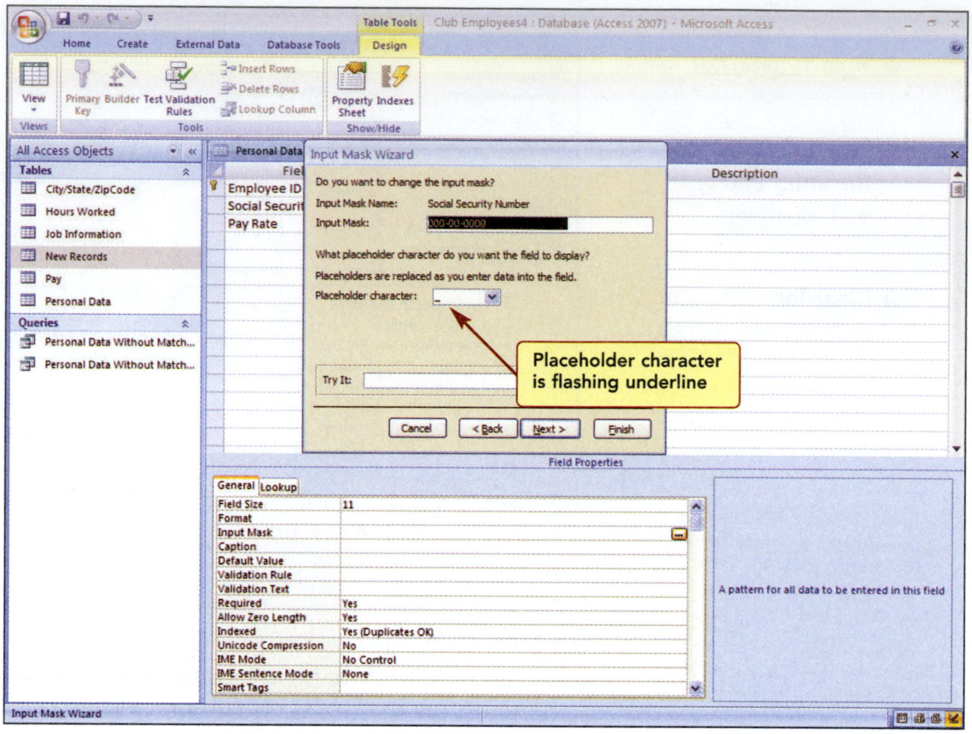

Placeholder character is flashing underline

Figure 4.27

The sample entry was accepted and the next Input Mask Wizard dialog box is displayed. Next, you need to specify the placeholder character you want to display as data is entered into the field. The default is the standard flashing underline, which is acceptable, so you can proceed to the next step.

6 **Click** Next >.

Your screen should be similar to Figure 4.28

Figure 4.28

The Wizard now asks you how you want to store the data that is entered in this field. The default, storing the data without the hyphens, takes up slightly less data storage space. However, storing with hyphens includes the hyphens if you export the data; otherwise, all the digits run together.

7

- **Choose With the symbols in the mask.**
- **Click** Next >.
- **Click** Finish.

Your screen should be similar to Figure 4.29

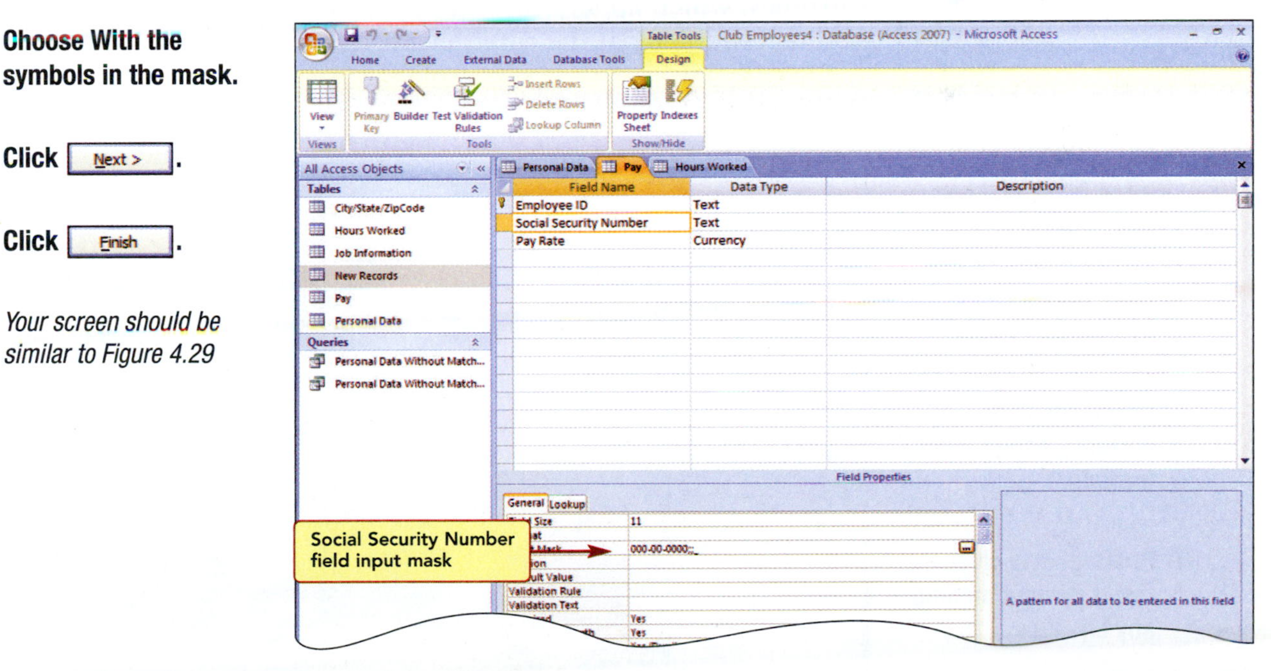

Figure 4.29

The input mask for the Social Security Number field is added to the General properties.

The first section of the input mask, 000-00-0000, specifies a required number entry consisting of nine numbers. The hyphens are literal characters used to separate the parts of the entry. The first semicolon indicates the end of the mask definition. The second semicolon indicates the end of the second part of the input mask definition. Because there is nothing entered between the semicolons, this means that only the characters that are typed will be stored. Adding a 0 between the semicolons (;0;) would store the mask characters as part of the data. Finally, in the third section, the underline identifies the selected placeholder character.

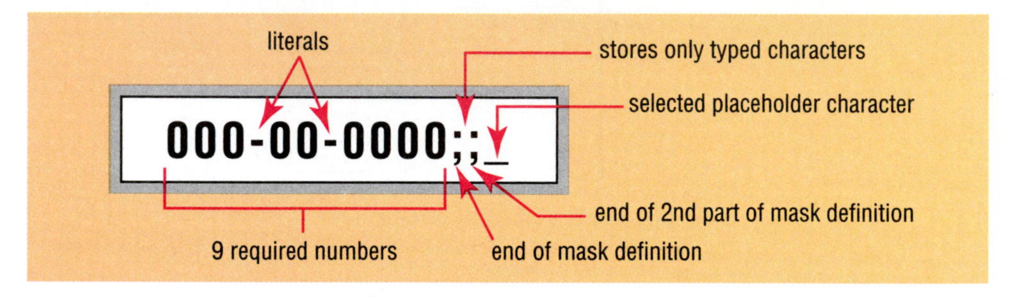

Additional Information

The predefined Currency and Euro formats follow the settings in the regional settings in Windows. These can be overridden by entering your own currency format.

Next, you will create an input mask for the Employee ID field that will allow only numeric entries and prevent the entry of space characters.

The final change you want to make to the Pay table is to require that data be entered into the Pay Rate field. This field's data type is set to Currency, which applies the selected currency format to numeric entries. You will first look at the currency format options and then change it to a required field.

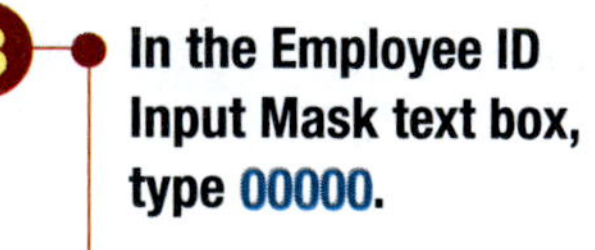

8

- **In the Employee ID Input Mask text box, type 00000.**
- **Open the Pay Rate Format properties drop-down list to see the selection of currency and numeric formats.**
- **Press Esc to close the menu without making any changes.**
- **Change the Required property to Yes for the Pay Rate field.**

Your screen should be similar to Figure 4.30

Table Tools Club Employees4 : Database (Access 2007) - Microsoft Access

Home Create External Data Database Tools Design

View Primary Key Builder Test Validation Rules Insert Rows Delete Rows Lookup Column Property Sheet Indexes

Views Tools Show/Hide

All Access Objects

Tables: City/State/ZipCode, Hours Worked, Job Information, New Records, Pay, Personal Data

Queries: Personal Data Without Match..., Personal Data Without Match...

Personal Data | Pay | Hours Worked

Field Name	Data Type	Description
Employee ID	Text	
Social Security Number	Text	
Pay Rate	Currency	

Field Properties

General Lookup

Format	Currency
Decimal Places	Auto
Input Mask	
Caption	
Default Value	
Validation Rule	
Validation Text	
Required	Yes
Indexed	No
Smart Tags	
Text Align	General

Require data entry in this field?

Pay Rate is a required field entry

Design view. F6 = Switch panes. F1 = Help.

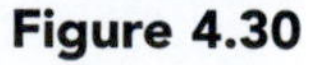

Figure 4.30

Testing the Field Properties

Next you will test the properties you have defined for the tables as you add your own record to them.

1

- **Switch to Datasheet view, saving the table when prompted.**
- **Click No to skip testing for data integrity.**
- **Move to a blank new record row in the Pay table.**
- **Type 9, press Spacebar, type P9999.**
- **Press Tab two times.**
- **Enter 16 as your pay.**
- **Press Enter.**

Your screen should be similar to Figure 4.31

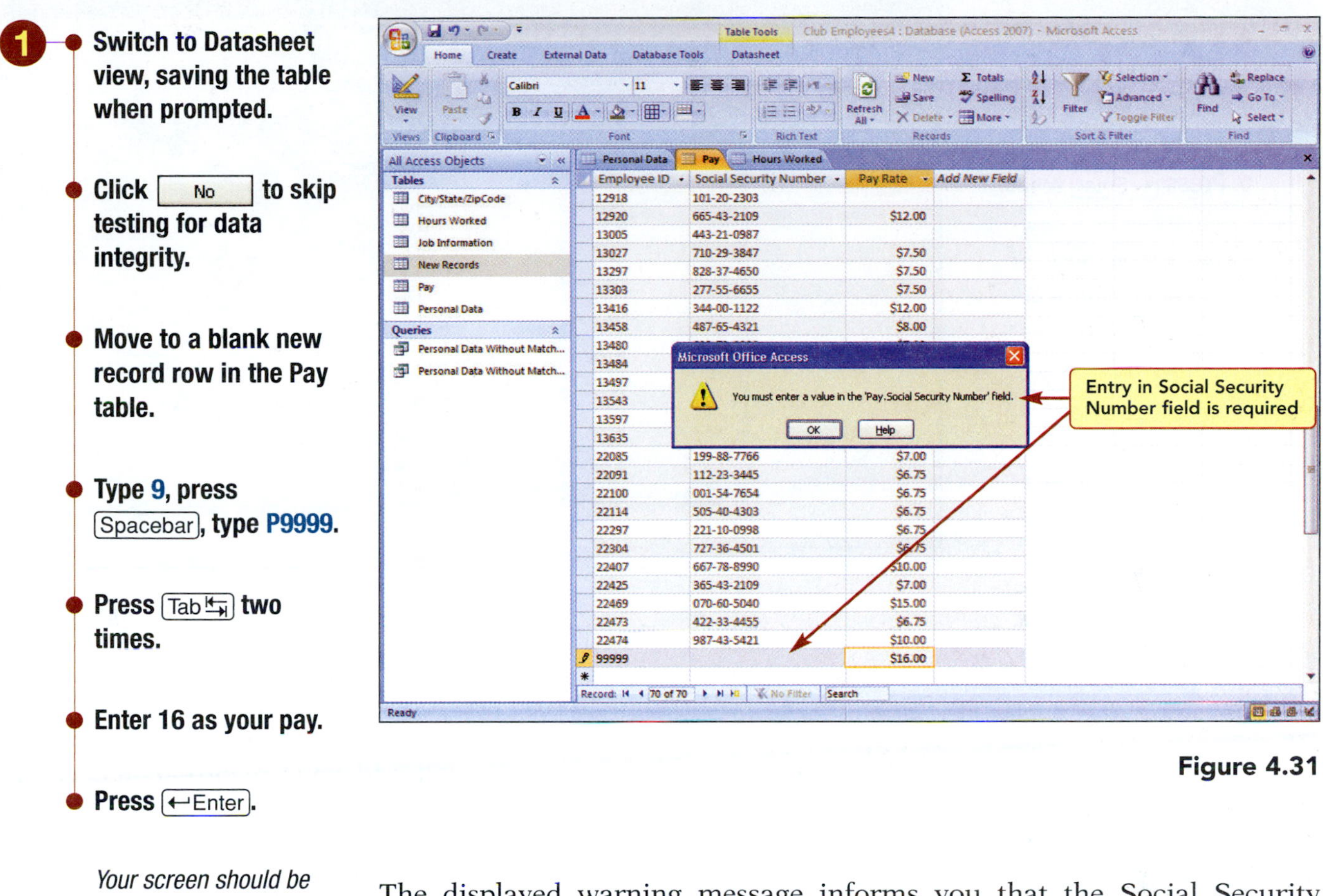

Figure 4.31

The displayed warning message informs you that the Social Security Number field is required and cannot be empty. To complete this record, you need to go back and enter data in this field.

2

- **Click OK to close the warning message box.**
- **Enter 999-99-9999 in the Social Security Number field.**
- **Press ←Enter twice.**

Your screen should be similar to Figure 4.32

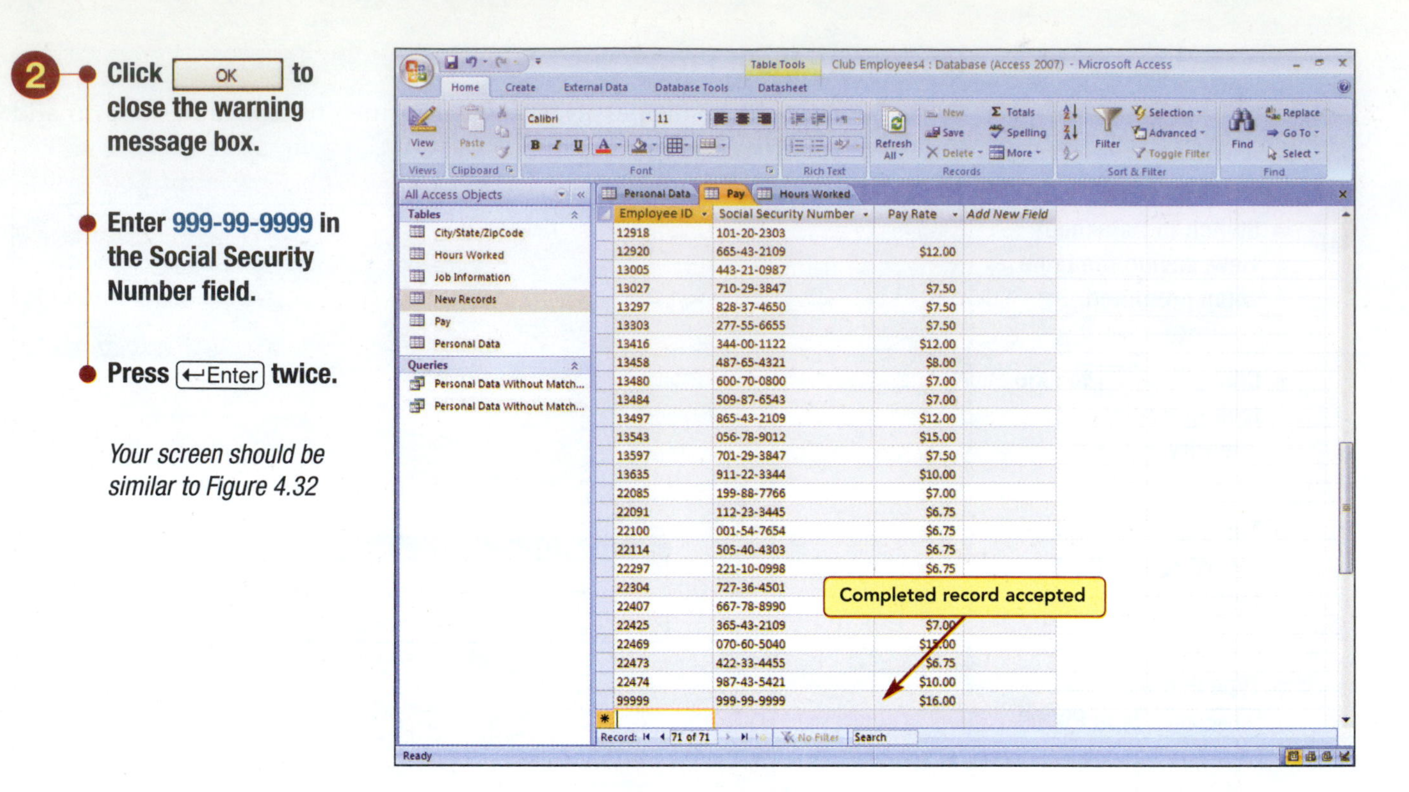

Figure 4.32

The record entry is complete. You are done with the Pay table design and it contains your record. Next, you need to add the Employee ID input mask to the other tables, then you will add your record to the Hours Worked table as well.

3

- **Close the Pay table.**
- **Add the Employee ID input mask to the Hours Worked, Personal Data and Job Information tables.**
- **In the Hours Worked table, enter a new record with the Employee ID of 99999, Week Ending of June 27, 2008, and Hours of 25.**
- **Close all open tables.**

Establishing Relationships

Next, you need to establish relationships between the Pay and Hours Worked tables and the other database tables.

1 **Click** Relationships **on the Database Tools tab.**

- **Click** Show Table.
- **Select the Hours Worked and Pay tables.**

Having Trouble?
Hold down Ctrl while selecting each table name.

- **Click** Add **and close the Show Table dialog box.**

Your screen should be similar to Figure 4.33

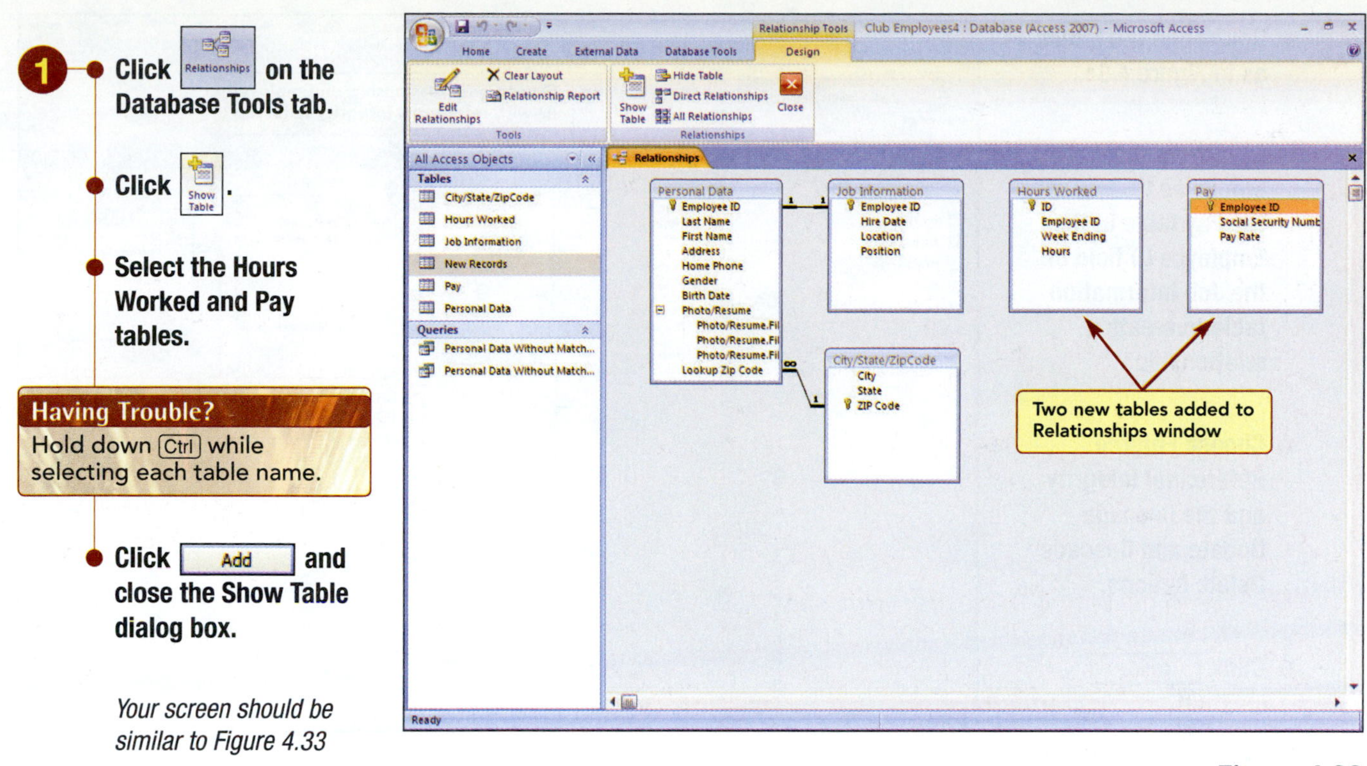

Figure 4.33

The two new tables have been added to the Relationships window. They are not related to any tables in the database. You will join the Job Information table to the Pay table on the common field, Employee ID. Then you will join the Pay table and the Hours table on the same common field.

2

- Rearrange the tables as in Figure 4.34.
- Drag from the Employee ID field of the Pay table to the Employee ID field of the Job Information table to create a relationship.
- Choose Enforce Referential Integrity and the Cascade Update and Cascade Delete options.
- Click Create.
- Create a relationship between the Pay table and the Hours Worked table on Employee ID with referential integrity enforced and the Cascade Update and Cascade Delete features on.

Your screen should be similar to Figure 4.34

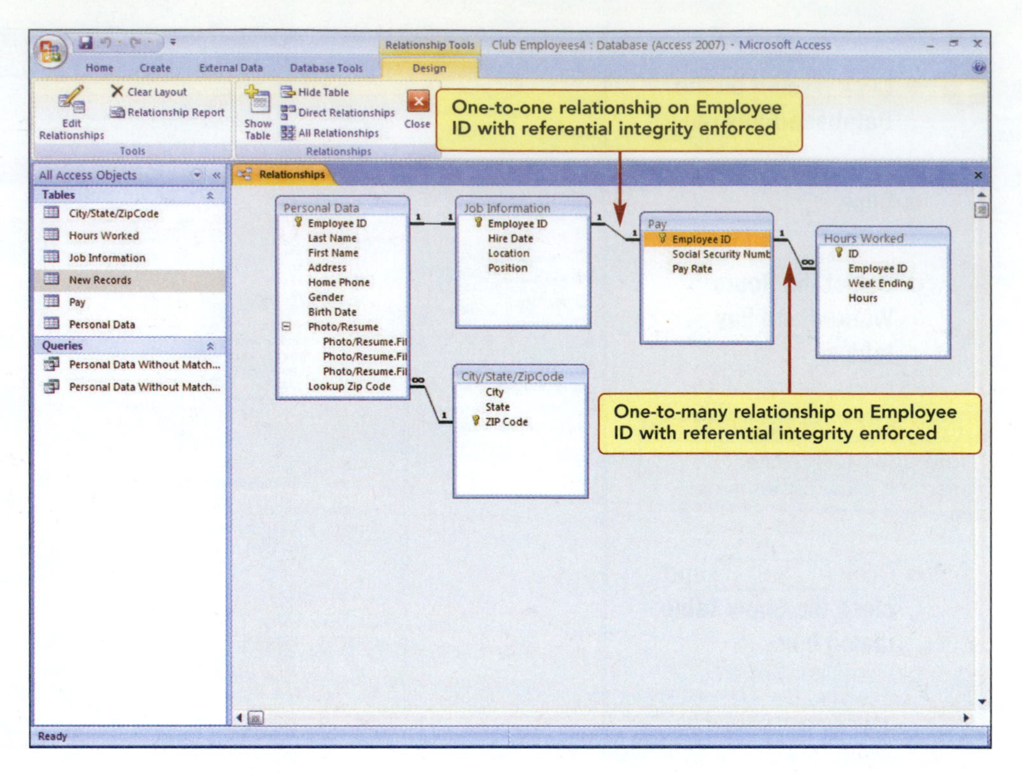

Figure 4.34

A one-to-one relationship was established between the Pay table and the Job Information table. A one-to-many relationship was correctly established between the Hours Worked table and the Pay table because the Employee ID field in the Hours Worked table contains duplicate Employee IDs.

3 Close the Relationships window, saving the layout changes you made.

- Open the Pay table.
- Select the entire table and click on any ⊞ to expand the subdatasheets for all records.

Having Trouble?

Click ◻ in the upper left corner of the table to select the entire table.

Your screen should be similar to Figure 4.35

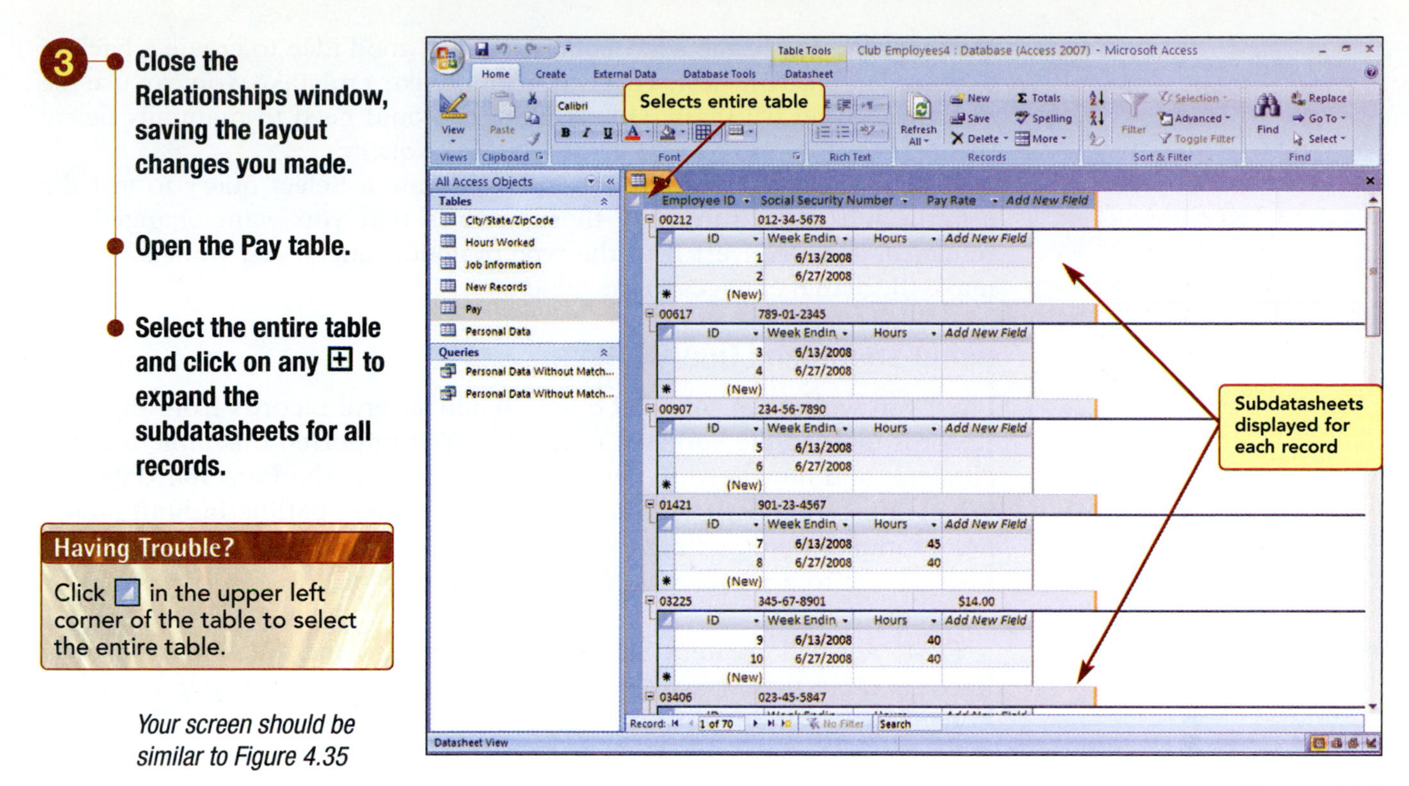

Figure 4.35

The related information from the Hours table for all records is displayed.

4 Select the entire table again and click ⊟ to hide the subdatasheets.

- Close the Pay table.

Using Action Queries

You have used select queries and parameter queries to gather and display data from tables. Now you will use the action queries to help you quickly make changes to large amounts of data at one time. This is in contrast to using a form or table datasheet to move to individual records and manually change data in each record. As introduced in Lab 3, there are four types of action queries:

MORE ABOUT

To learn about using the Make Table query, see 4.1 Create Queries in the More About appendix.

Type	Description
Update	Adds, changes, or deletes data in part (but not all) of one or more existing records.
Append	Adds a group of records from one or more tables in a source database to one or more tables in a destination database.
Make Table	Creates a new table from selected data in one or more tables.
Delete	Removes entire records from a database.

Before using any of the action queries, it is a good idea to create a backup of your database file first. This way, if you make a mistake, you can use the backup file and try again. Otherwise, you would need to manually delete the changes that were made using the action query.

Also, when using action queries, first create a Select query to test the criteria and make sure only those records that you want changed are returned. Then convert it to the type of action query you want to use to make the actual changes to the table.

Using an Append Query

First, you will use an Append query to add several records from the New Records table to the Personal Data table. You imported this table into the database and now need to add the new records to the Personal Data file. When appending data, the data types must be compatible in both tables. For example, numbers can be appended to a text field, but you cannot append text to a number field. The field names in the two tables can be different.

First, you will create a Select query to display the data from the New Records table that you want to append. Then you will convert it to an Append query and perform the append action.

1

- **Back up the database file to your solution file location using the default backup file name.**
- **Use the Query Wizard to create a Select query that displays all seven fields from the New Records table in the design grid.**
- **Run the query.**

Your screen should be similar to Figure 4.36

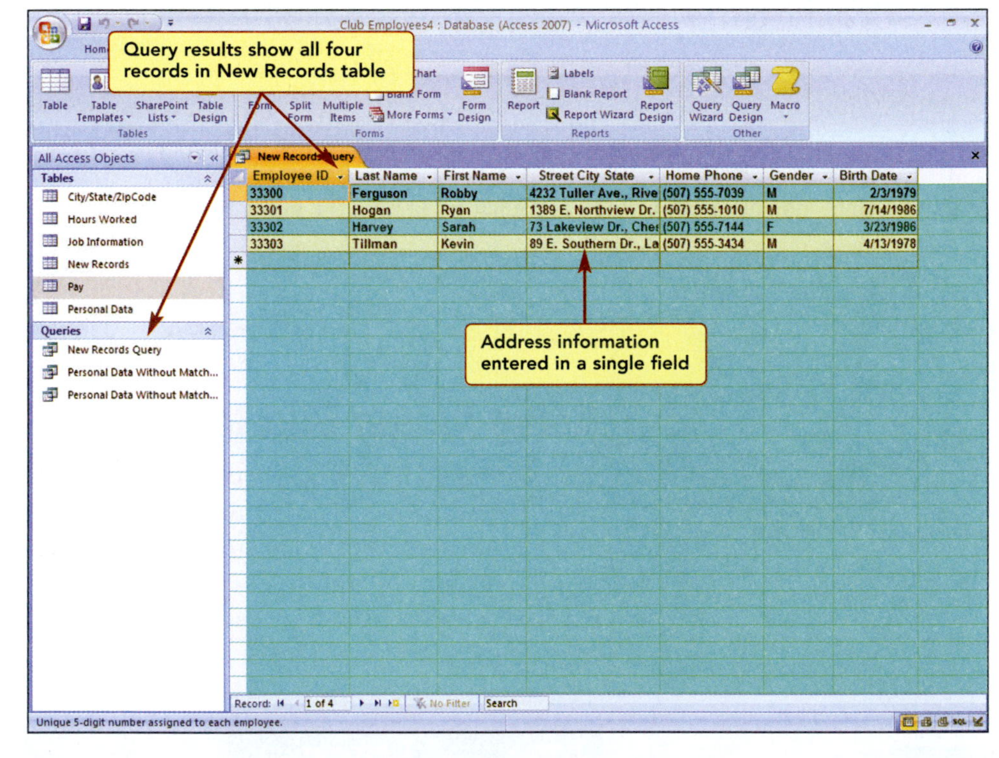

Figure 4.36

The query results display all the information for the four records in the table. Notice the field containing the address information is named Street City State. Your assistant entered all this data into a single field. This data is stored in separate fields in the Personal Data table. Although the two tables are set up differently, the data can still be imported and then moved into the appropriate fields of the destination table.

Now you will convert the select query to an append query. You can append records to a table in the same database or in another database. In this case, you will append the records to the Personal Data table in the current database.

2

- **Display the Query in Design view.**
- **Click Append in the Query Type group of the Design tab.**
- **If necessary, choose Current Database from the Append dialog box.**
- **Select the Personal Data table from the Table Name drop-down list.**
- **Click OK.**

Your screen should be similar to Figure 4.37

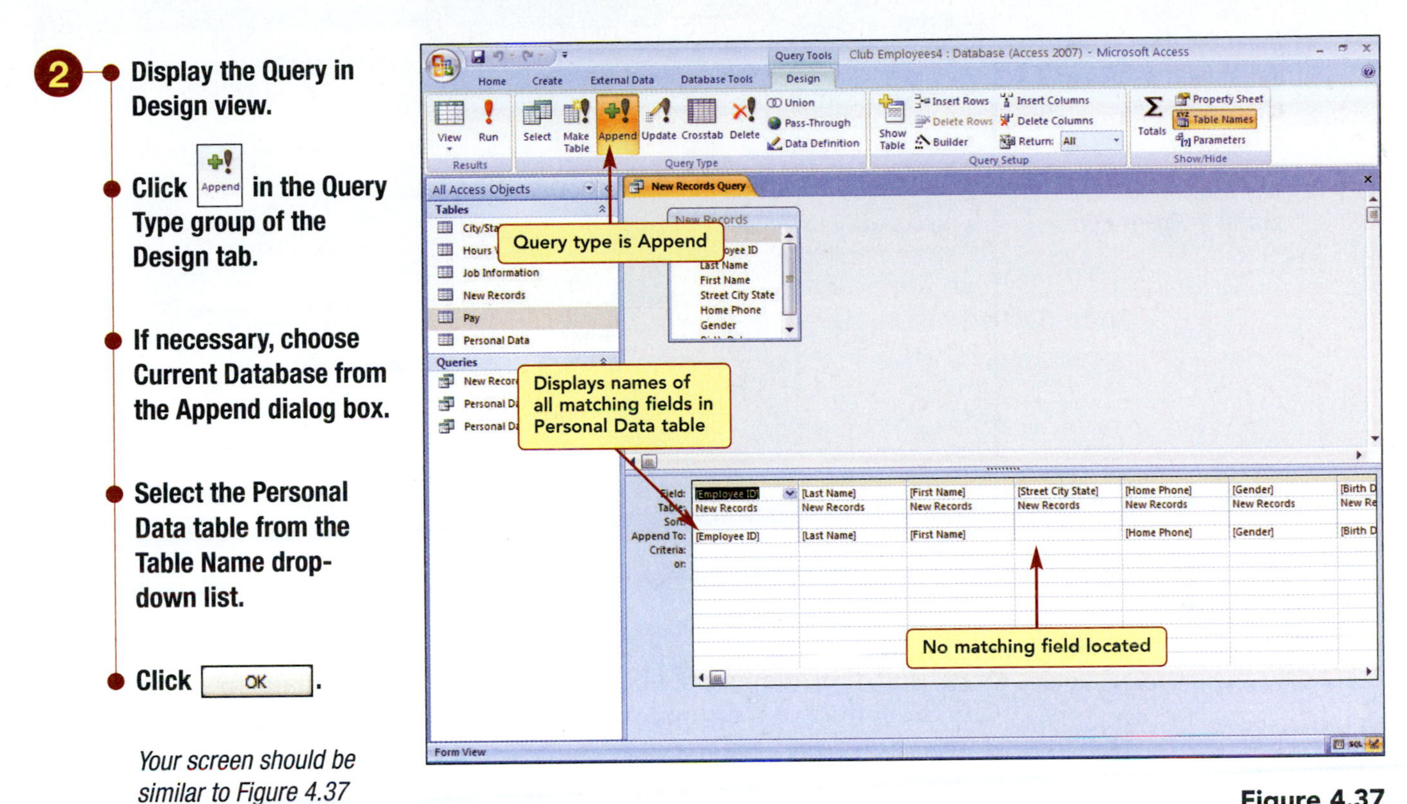

Figure 4.37

A new row, Append To, has been added to the query grid. The names of the matching destination fields in the Personal Data table are displayed in the row. Notice the Street City State column, however, is blank. This is because there is no matching field name in the destination table. You need to select the field from the destination table that you want to use. If you leave it blank, the query will not append data to that field.

3 Click in the Append To row of the Street City State column.

- Open the drop-down list of field names and choose Address.

Your screen should be similar to Figure 4.38

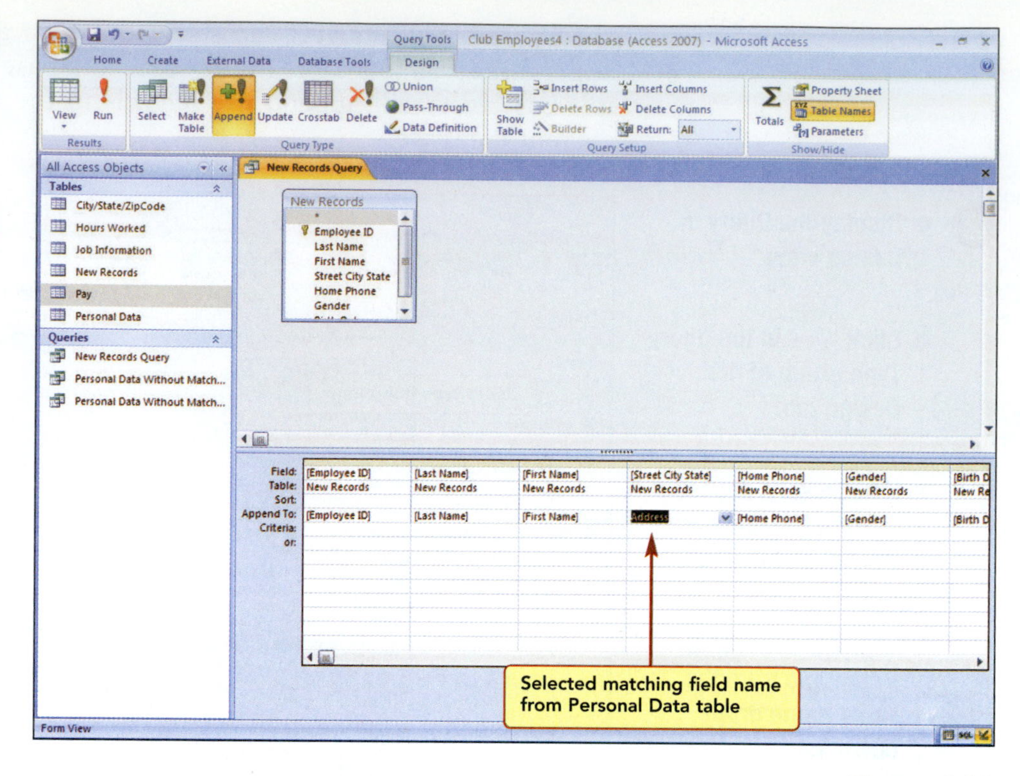

Figure 4.38

Now that the Address field has been specified, the data from the Street City State field in the source table will be added to the Address field of the destination table.

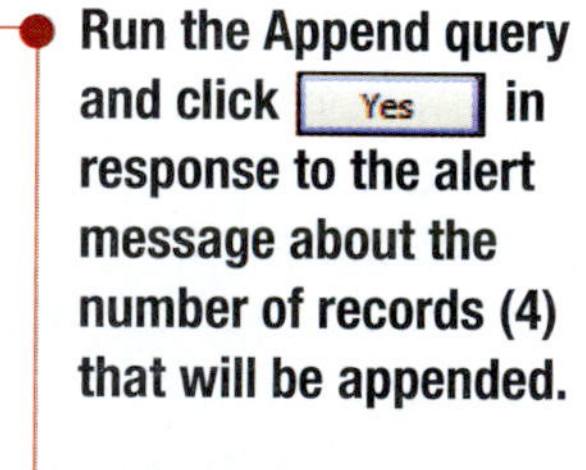

4 Run the Append query and click Yes in response to the alert message about the number of records (4) that will be appended.

- Open the Personal Data table and scroll the datasheet to see the records at the end of the table.

Your screen should be similar to Figure 4.39

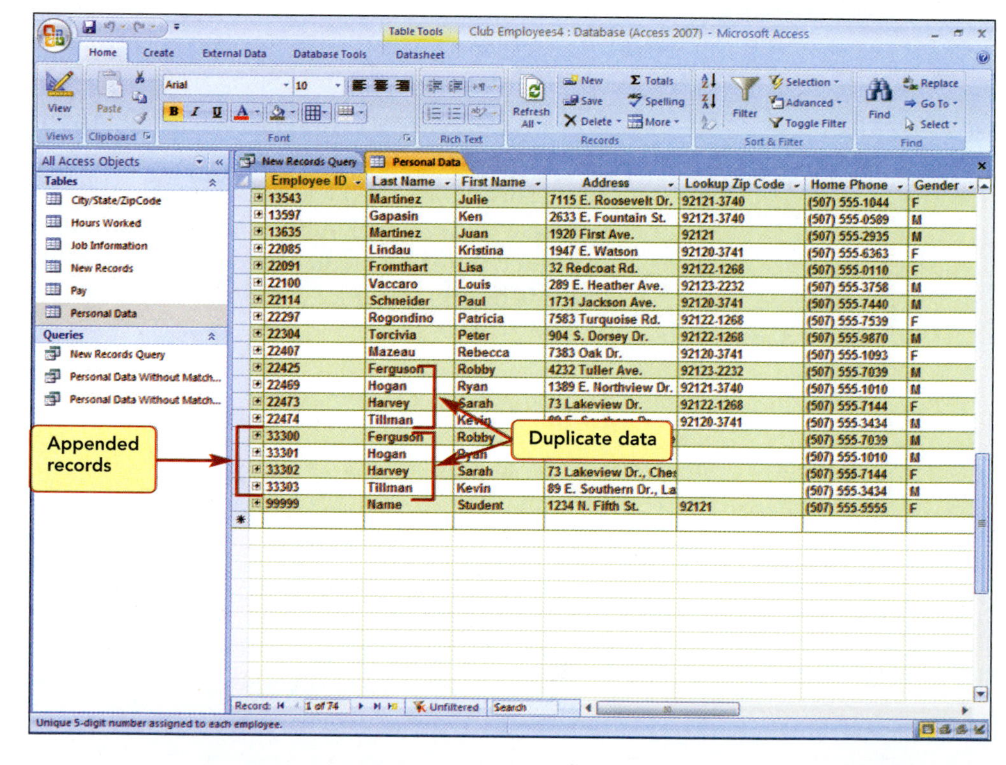

Figure 4.39

The four records from the New Records table were added to the Personal Data table in sorted order by Employee ID. Now, however, you see that these records are duplicates of the four preceding records in the table. Only their Employee ID numbers are different.

Using a Delete Query

The Employee ID numbers of the four appended records all begin with the number 3. You will remove these records using a Delete query to demonstrate how this type of action query works.

1

- **Display the New Records Query in Design view.**
- **Open the Query Tools Design tab.**
- **Remove the New Records table field list.**

> **Having Trouble?**
> Right-click on the table field list and choose Remove Table.

- **Add the Personal Data table to the Query design.**
- **Add the Employee ID, Last Name, and First Name fields to the design grid.**
- **Enter 3* in the Employee ID criteria cell to display only those records with an Employee ID number starting with 3.**

> **Having Trouble?**
> Using the * wildcard character in the criteria allows any characters following the 3 to be included.

- **Click Select to change the type of query to a Select query.**
- **Run the query to view the results.**

Your screen should be similar to Figure 4.40

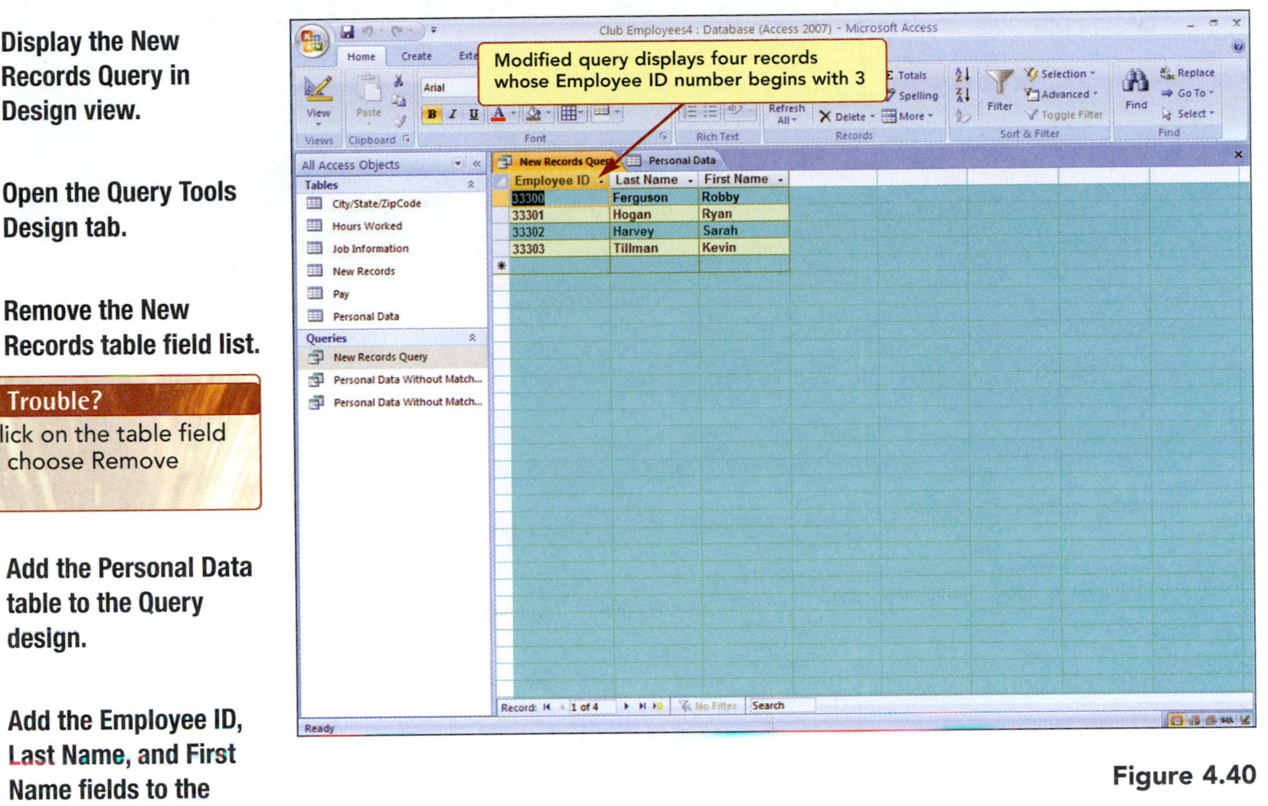

Figure 4.40

The four records with Employee IDs that begin with the number 3 are displayed. These are the four records you want to remove. It is very important to verify that the correct records are identified using a Select query before using the Delete query. Once the records are deleted, the deletions cannot be undone.

2 Switch back to Query Design view.

- Click **Delete** in the Query Type group of the Design tab.
- Run the query and click **Yes** in response to the alert that four rows will be deleted.
- Close the Query window without saving the query.

Your screen should be similar to Figure 4.41

Four records deleted

Figure 4.41

The four records specified in the query are identified as having been deleted from the table.

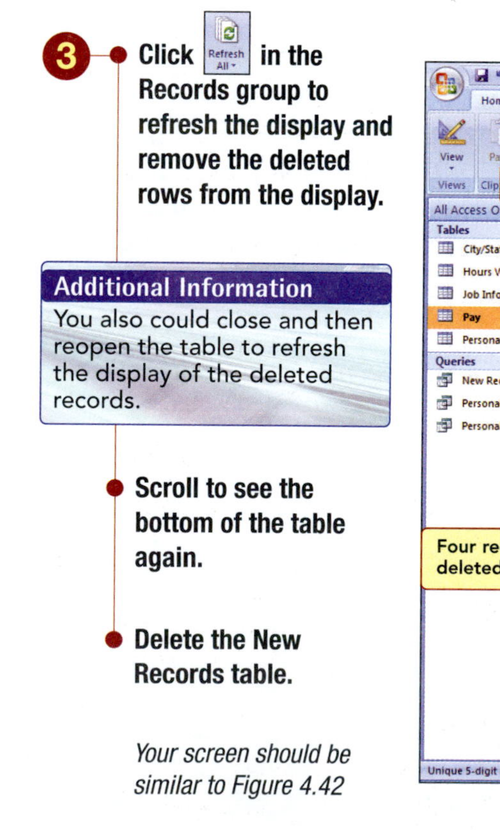

3 Click **Refresh All** in the Records group to refresh the display and remove the deleted rows from the display.

Additional Information

You also could close and then reopen the table to refresh the display of the deleted records.

- Scroll to see the bottom of the table again.
- Delete the New Records table.

Your screen should be similar to Figure 4.42

Updates screen display

New Records table deleted

Four records deleted

Figure 4.42

Generally, use the Update and Delete queries only when large amounts of data need to be changed or removed. Always create a backup copy of the database file and carefully review the Select query results before actually performing the action queries.

Creating a Select Query in Design View

Each year, the club managers determine the pay increases for employees. Although you could manually change each individual record, it is much faster to use an Update query to make changes to many records based on the specified criteria.

You have been given the guidelines for the pay increases and need to update the Pay table appropriately. Specifically, you have been told to award a 3.2 percent increase to all employees. Additionally, recently the club has experienced turnover in Personal Trainer jobs because of market demand. To counteract this turnover, they want to give all personal trainer positions an additional 5 percent pay increase. Pay increases for salaried employees will be individually determined.

Rather than use the Query Wizard to create the Select query first, you will create it directly in Design view.

1

- **Click** 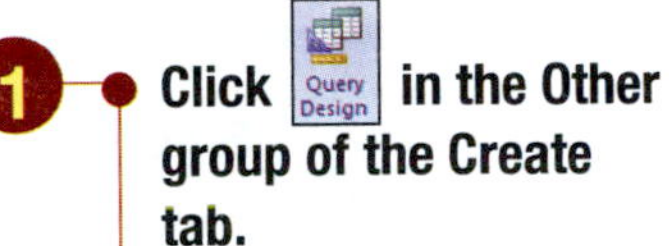

in the Other group of the Create tab.
- **Add the Job Information and Pay tables to the field list.**
- **Close the Show Tables dialog box.**
- **Add the Position and Pay Rate fields to the design grid.**
- **Specify the Pay Rate criteria of not null to eliminate the blank fields for salaried employees.**
- **Run the query.**

Your screen should be similar to Figure 4.43

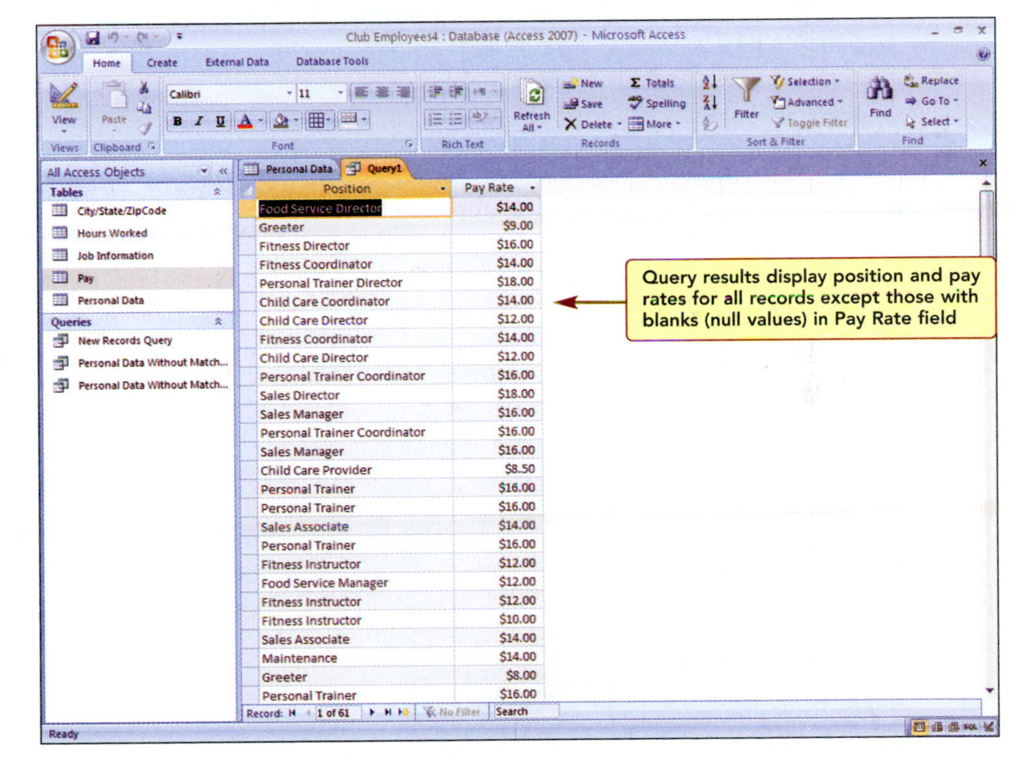

Figure 4.43

The records you want to change are displayed. Those records with blank Pay Rate fields are not included in the results.

Using an Update Query

Now you can convert the Select query to an Update query and enter an expression to calculate the pay increase as the change criteria.

1

- Switch back to Design view.
- Click [Update] in the Query Type group of the Design tab.
- In the Pay Rate cell of the Update To row, enter **[Pay Rate]*1.032**.
- Run the Update query and click [Yes] in response to the warning message about the number of records (61) that will be updated.
- Switch to Datasheet view to see the updated pay rates.

Your screen should be similar to Figure 4.44

Update query increased pay rates by 3.2 percent

Figure 4.44

The query datasheet displays the updated pay rate values. Only the fields that are updated during an Update query are displayed in the results.

Next, you need to update the personal trainers' pay by an additional 5 percent. All records whose job title is Personal Trainer will be affected.

2

- Switch to Design view.
- Click [Select] in the Query Type group to change the type of query back to a Select query.

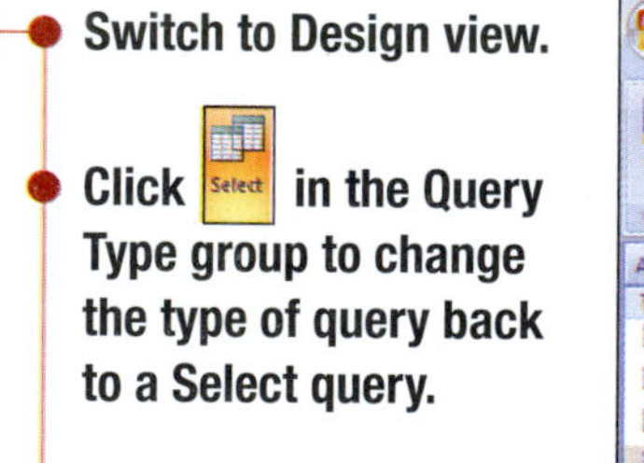

- Enter the criteria **"Personal Trainer"** in the criteria cell of the Position field.
- Run the query.

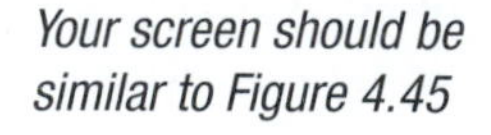

Your screen should be similar to Figure 4.45

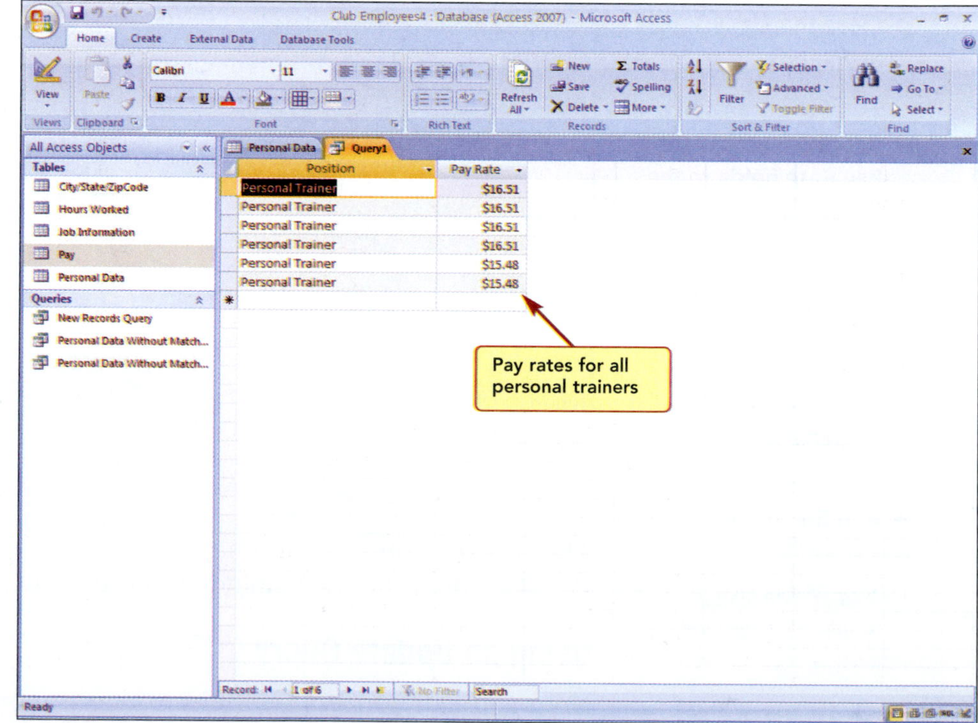

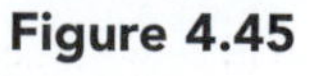

Figure 4.45

All employees with Personal Trainer as their job title are listed. Again, you will convert the query to an Update query and increase the pay rate for these employees by 5 percent.

3 • **Switch back to Design view.**

• **Click** Update **in the Query Type group of the Design tab.**

• **In the Update To row of the Pay Rate field, change the expression to multiply times 1.05.**

• **Run the update query and click** Yes **in response to the alert message about the number of records (6) that will be updated.**

• **Change the query type back to a Select query and run it again.**

Your screen should be similar to Figure 4.46

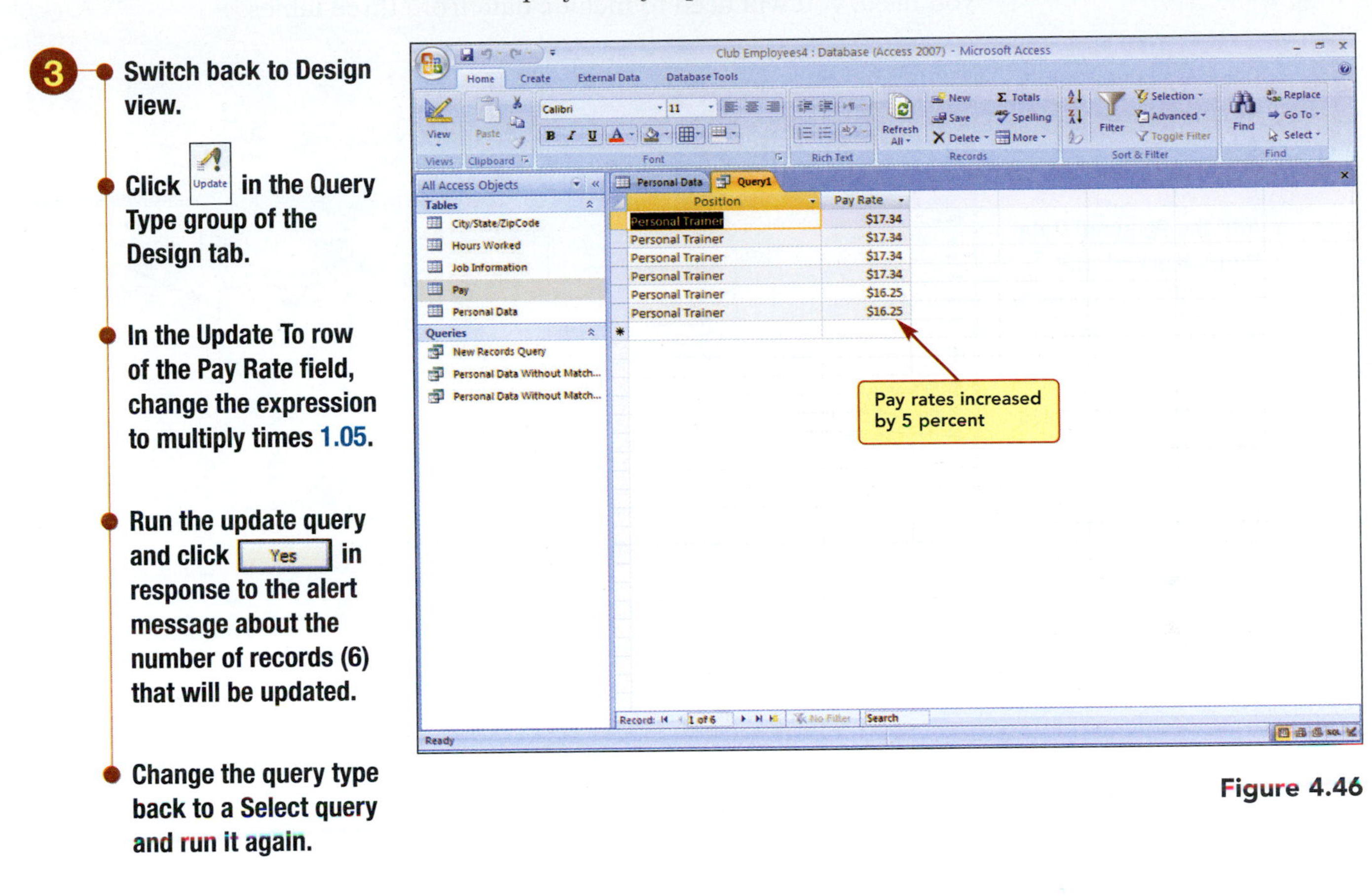

Figure 4.46

The updated pay rates for the selected personal trainers are displayed.

4 • **Close the query and save it as Pay Update.**

Using Calculations in Queries

Now that you have updated the records and have the data you need, you can begin working on the request from the club owners for a report showing the gross pay for all employees sorted by location and job title.

To get this information, you could create a field in the Hours Worked table to calculate and store the gross pay for each record. However, this would be redundant information that wastes space and violates the rules of normalization. Additionally, the calculated field would need to be maintained and can risk data corruption if a value in an underlying field is subsequently edited, resulting in incorrect data in your table and no automatic way to detect that fact.

Instead, you can create a query to calculate these values when needed. Calculating values in a query also allows you to group data and combine information from multiple tables easily. Additionally, the query then can be used as the basis for the report.

Setting Up the Query

You will use Design view to create the query. To obtain the information you need, you will need to include data from three tables.

1 Click [Query Design] in the Other group of the Create tab.

- **Add the Personal Data, Hours Worked, and Pay tables to the query design in that order.**
- **Close the Show Tables dialog box.**

Your screen should be similar to Figure 4.47

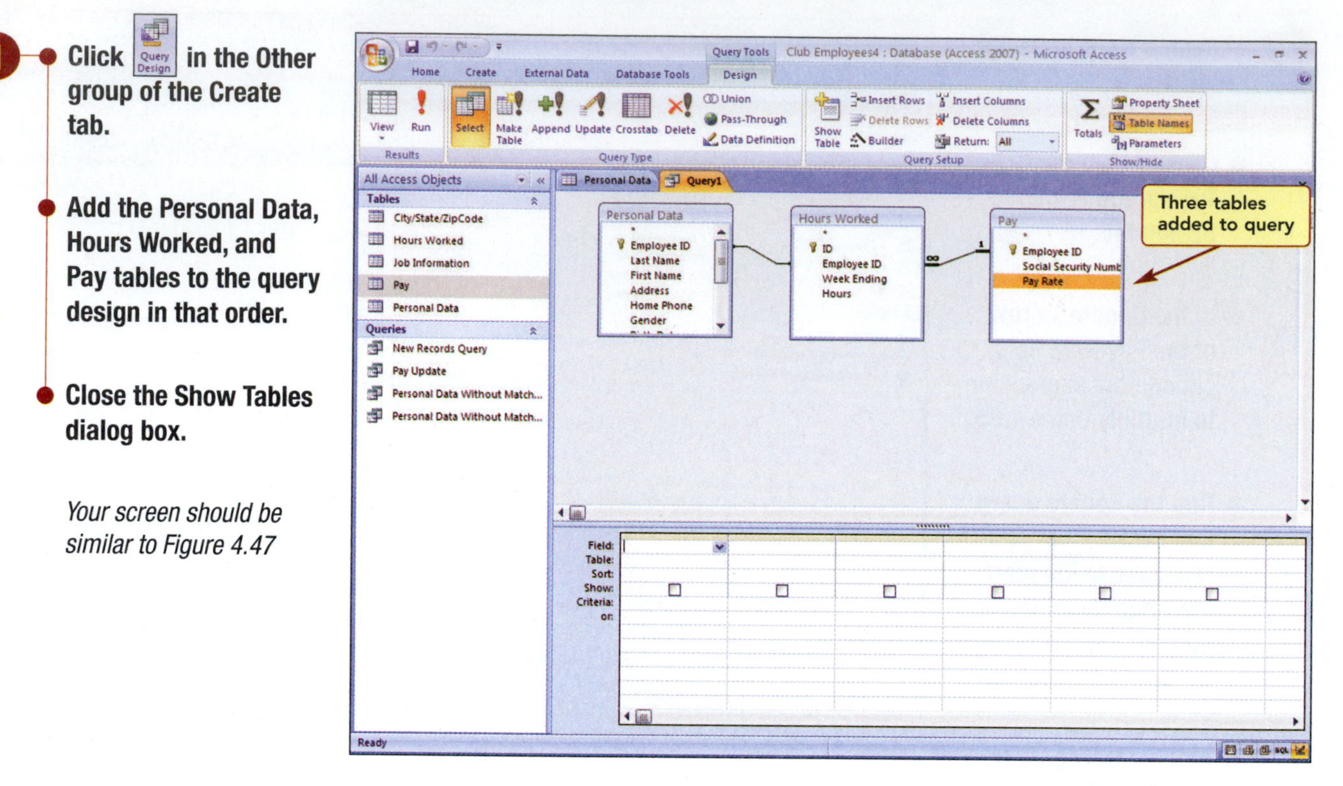

Figure 4.47

The tables are joined and displayed at the top of the design grid. Next, you will add the fields to be included in the query to the grid and sort them in the order requested by the club owners.

2

- **Add Employee ID, Last Name, and First Name from the Personal Data field list.**
- **Add the Pay Rate, Hours, and Week Ending fields to the design grid in that order.**

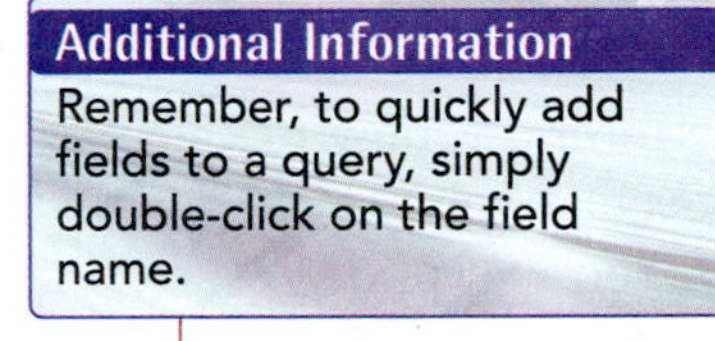
Additional Information
Remember, to quickly add fields to a query, simply double-click on the field name.

- **Run the query.**

Your screen should be similar to Figure 4.48

Query results display specified fields for all records

Figure 4.48

The query shows the selected fields for each record. Next, you need to refine the query so it includes only employees who are paid hourly rates (not those on salary) for the week ending June 27, 2008, only. Also, because the Club owners already know the report is for this date (which is what they requested), you will not show the Week Ending field.

3

- **Return to Design view.**
- **Enter the expression = 6/27/2008 in the Week Ending Criteria cell.**
- **Clear the Show box for the Week Ending field.**
- **Enter not null in the Pay Rate Criteria cell.**
- **Run the query.**

Your screen should be similar to Figure 4.49

Week Ending field not displayed

Query results do not include salaried employees and display only those records with a week ending date of June 27, 2008

Figure 4.49

You are now ready to create a field to perform the pay calculations for the report.

Adding a Calculated Field

To include the gross pay for the week ending June 27, 2008, in your report, you need to add a calculated field that will multiply each employee's hourly rate by the number of hours he or she worked that week.

Concept 4

Calculated Field

4 A **calculated field** displays the results of a calculation in a query. You can perform a variety of calculations in queries. For example, you can calculate the sum of all inventory, the average salary for a department, or the highest sales figures among all sales personnel in the company. You can create your own calculation or use one of Access's seven predefined calculations, called **functions.**

Function	What It Calculates
Sum	Totals values in a field for all records.
Average	Averages values in a field for all records.
Count	Counts number of values, excluding empty cells, in a field for all records.
Minimum	Finds lowest value in a field for all records.
Maximum	Finds highest value in a field for all records.
Standard Deviation	Measures the dispersion of a frequency distribution.
Variance	Square of the standard deviation.

To create a calculated field, you enter an expression in a blank Field cell of the design grid that instructs Access to perform a calculation using the current field values from the specified fields. The expression is preceded by an **alias,** a name that describes the expression. The alias cannot be the same as the name of any field used in the expression. If you do not provide an alias, Access assigns the alias for you, for example, EXPR1. The alias is immediately followed by a colon and then by the expression. An example of a calculated field expression to sum the values in two fields is shown here.

Alias: [Field name1] + [Field name2]

Then the calculated result is displayed in the calculated field column of the datasheet and the alias is used as the column name in the datasheet. The calculated results are not actually stored as data but are recalculated each time the query is run.

Having Trouble?
See Concept 4: Expressions in Lab 2 to review this feature.

You are going to create a calculated field that will multiply the value in the Hourly Rate field (located in the Pay table) by the value in the Hours field (located in the Hours Worked table). You will name the new field Gross Pay.

1 Switch to Design view.

- **Move to the Field cell of the first blank column (to the right of the Week Ending column).**
- **Type Gross Pay:.**
- **Press Spacebar.**
- **Type [Pay Rate]*[Hours].**

Additional Information

Square brackets are used to designate field names in calculations.

- **Press ←Enter.**

Having Trouble?

If you made an error in your calculation entry, a message box will appear advising you of the error. Close the message box and correct the error. A common error is to forget the colon following the field name.

- **Increase the Gross Pay column width to fully display the expression.**

Another Method

You also could press ⇧Shift + F2 to display the cell contents in the Zoom box.

Your screen should be similar to Figure 4.50

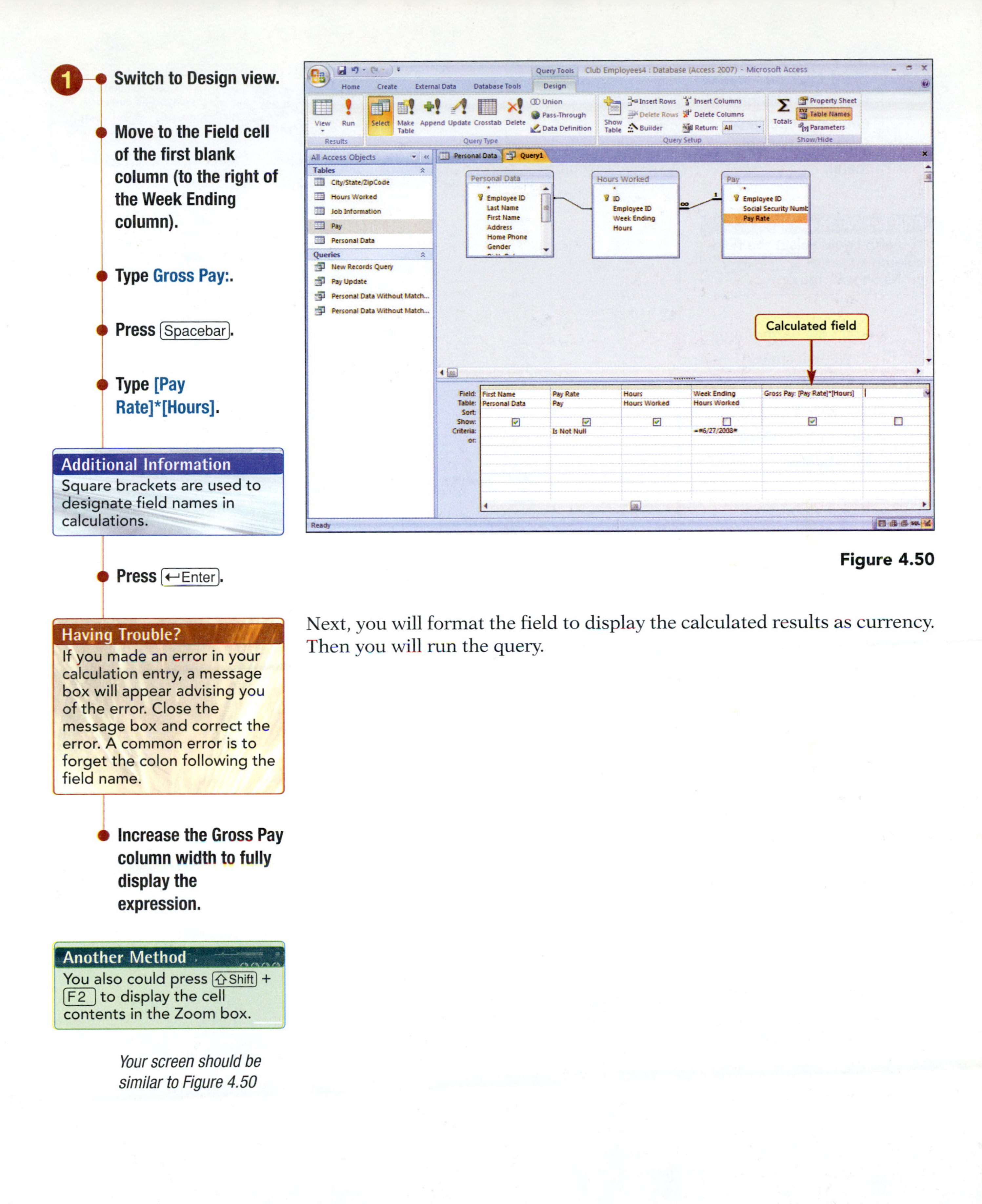

Figure 4.50

Next, you will format the field to display the calculated results as currency. Then you will run the query.

2 **Right-click on the new Gross Pay column and choose Properties from the shortcut menu.**

> **Another Method**
> You also could select the field column and click Property Sheet in the Show/Hide group.

- **From the Format drop-down list, choose Currency.**
- **Close the Property Sheet pane.**
- **Run the query.**

Your screen should be similar to Figure 4.51

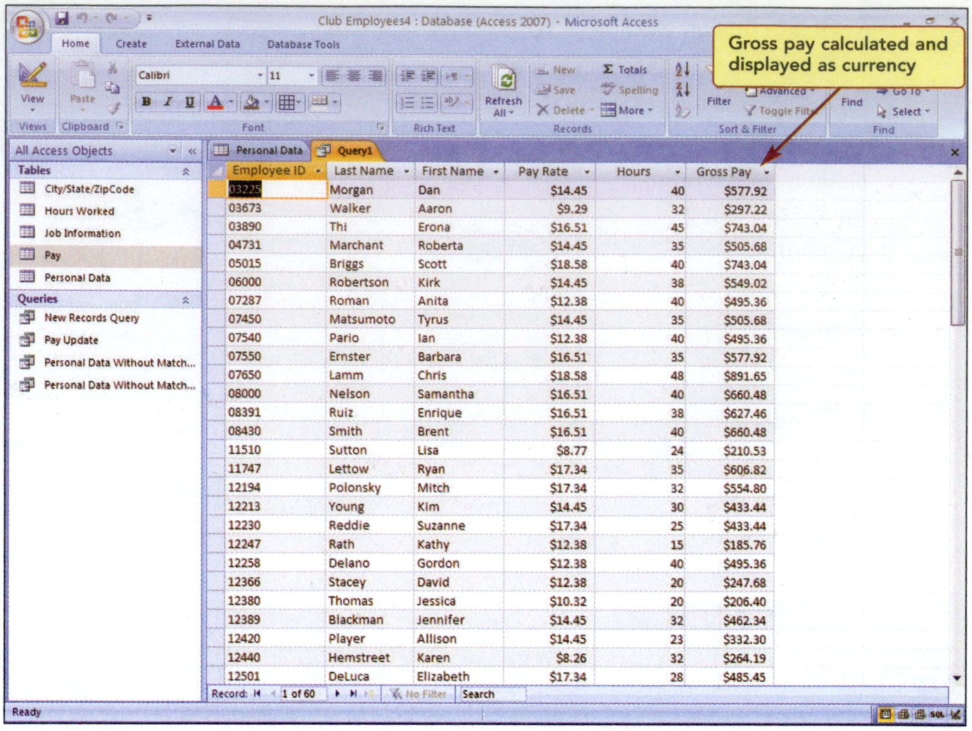

Club Employees4 : Database (Access 2007) - Microsoft Access
Gross pay calculated and displayed as currency
Employee ID Last Name First Name Pay Rate Hours Gross Pay
03225 Morgan Dan $14.45 40 $577.92
03673 Walker Aaron $9.29 32 $297.22
03890 Thi Erona $16.51 45 $743.04
04731 Marchant Roberta $14.45 35 $505.68
05015 Briggs Scott $18.58 40 $743.04
06000 Robertson Kirk $14.45 38 $549.02
07287 Roman Anita $12.38 40 $495.36
07450 Matsumoto Tyrus $14.45 35 $505.68
07540 Pario Ian $12.38 40 $495.36
07550 Ernster Barbara $16.51 35 $577.92
07650 Lamm Chris $18.58 48 $891.65
08000 Nelson Samantha $16.51 40 $660.48
08391 Ruiz Enrique $16.51 38 $627.46
08430 Smith Brent $16.51 40 $660.48
11510 Sutton Lisa $8.77 24 $210.53
11747 Lettow Ryan $17.34 35 $606.82
12194 Polonsky Mitch $17.34 32 $554.80
12213 Young Kim $14.45 30 $433.44
12230 Reddie Suzanne $17.34 25 $433.44
12247 Rath Kathy $12.38 15 $185.76
12258 Delano Gordon $12.38 40 $495.36
12366 Stacey David $12.38 20 $247.68
12380 Thomas Jessica $10.32 20 $206.40
12389 Blackman Jennifer $14.45 32 $462.34
12420 Player Allison $14.45 23 $332.30
12440 Hemstreet Karen $8.26 32 $264.19
12501 DeLuca Elizabeth $17.34 28 $485.45

Figure 4.51

The query datasheet displays the gross pay for all employees except those on salary for the week ending June 27, 2008. You think the information would be more meaningful if you included a Totals row to display several summary statistics about the results.

3

- Click **Σ Totals** to display a Totals row.
- Click on the Pay Rate cell in the Totals row and choose Average from the drop-down list.
- In the Hours column, calculate the Maximum value and, in the Gross Pay column, calculate the Sum.
- Save this query as **Gross Pay 6/27/2008**.
- Print a copy of the query datasheet.

Your screen should be similar to Figure 4.52

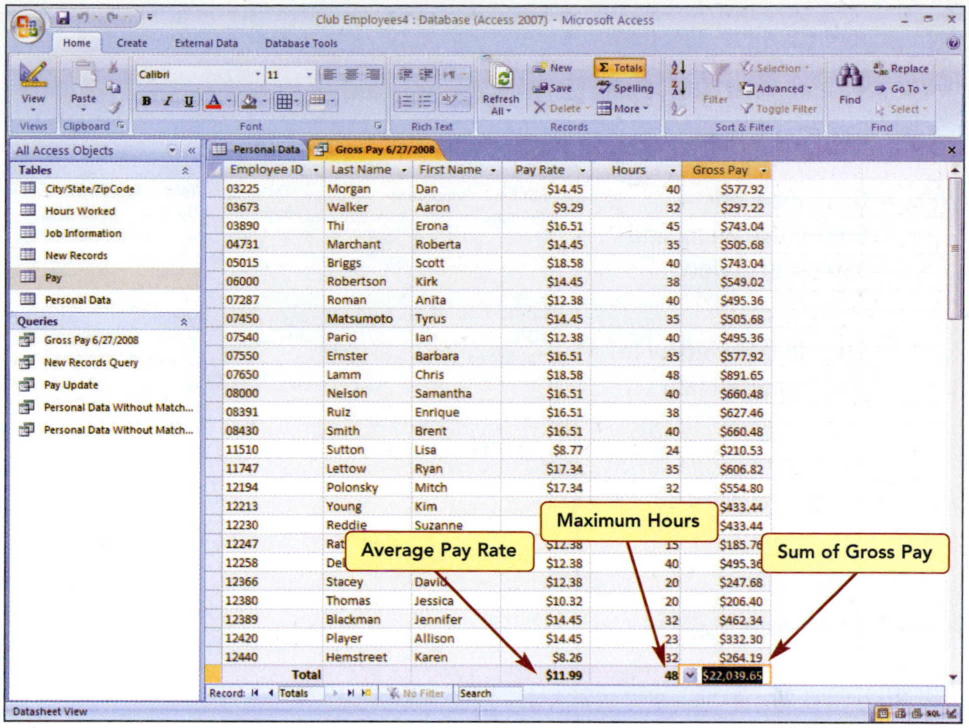

Figure 4.52

Creating a Subquery

Next, you decide to modify the Gross Pay query to display data for only those employees in the Landis location. To do this, you could add the Job Information table to the query design and then specify the criteria you need. However, another way is to create a subquery within the existing (main) query. A **subquery** is an SQL SELECT statement that is inside another select or action query. Subqueries are entered using SQL (Structured Query Language.)

Concept 5

SQL

5

SQL (Structured Query Language) is the most common relational database language. It is generated automatically as you create a query in Design view, but is also used to create subqueries and more advanced queries. SQL uses commands such as SELECT, UPDATE, WHERE, and FROM to instruct Access to perform a task. To create an **SQL statement**, an expression that defines an SQL command, you type the expression in either the criteria row or field row of the Query design grid or in SQL view. Each statement must use the correct format and rules, or **syntax**, which vary with the type of statement. The following is an example of a simple SELECT statement:

(SELECT *fields* FROM *table* WHERE *field criteria expression*)

(SELECT [Employee ID].[Location] FROM [Locations] WHERE [Location] = "Landis")

Traditionally, the SQL command is entered in capital letters so that it is easily identified in the expression. This is followed by the names of the fields or tables, enclosed in brackets and separated by dots. The expression must always be enclosed in parentheses.

Additional Information
Refer to Office Online Help for a more complete discussion of SQL.

To see the SQL statements that were generated for the Gross Pay query, you will use SQL view.

1 **Open the View drop-down menu and choose SQL View.**

Click in the window to clear the selection.

Your screen should be similar to Figure 4.53

Figure 4.53

The SQL language used to create this select query is displayed. It uses the SELECT statement, the most commonly used SQL command. This command allows users to retrieve the data they specify from a database. In this case, it specifies the table name followed by the field name for each displayed field in the design grid. The table names and field names are enclosed in brackets and separated by a dot. The FROM clause establishes the query table joins and the WHERE clause specifies the criteria.

Now you will enter a second SELECT statement in the Employee ID criteria cell to limit the records having the same Employee IDs in the main query to those records that have the same Employee ID and a Location value of Landis in the Job Information table.

Adding a second SELECT statement to the main query creates a subquery. Subqueries are powerful tools to obtain data from tables or other database files that are not included in the main query. A subquery statement consists of three parts:

Part	Description
Comparison	An expression and comparison operator that compares the expression with the results of the subquery.
Expression	An expression for which the result set of the subquery is searched.
SQL statement	A SELECT statement

You will enter the subquery statement in the Employee ID criteria cell. The statement will use the subquery statement as a criterion to limit the data displayed in the field. The subquery SELECT statement will be preceded by an IN clause to identify that the destination table is not included in the query design.

2

- **Display Design view again.**
- **Click in the Criteria cell of the Employee ID column.**
- **Press Shift + F2 to display the Zoom box.**
- **Type IN (SELECT [Employee ID] FROM [Job Information] WHERE [Location] = "Landis") in the Zoom box.**

Your screen should be similar to Figure 4.54

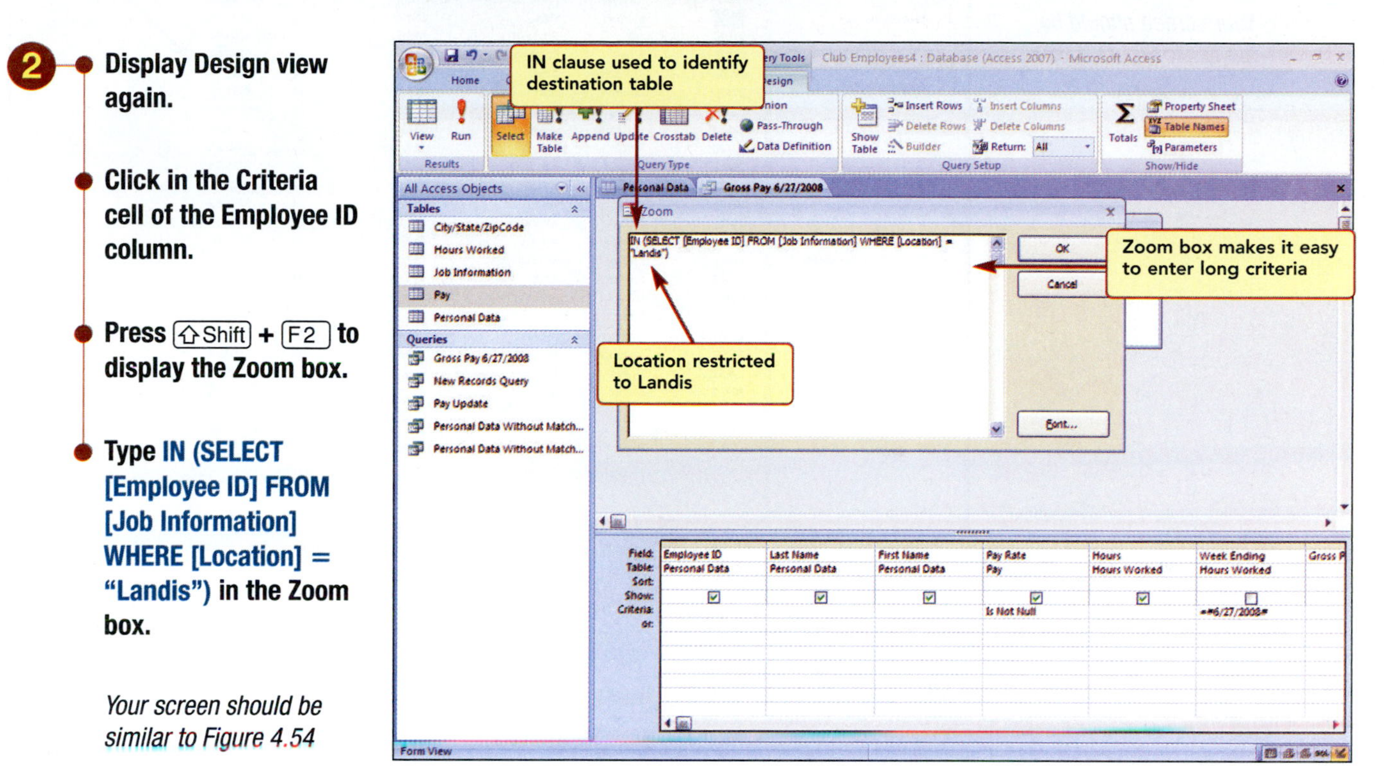

Figure 4.54

Using the Zoom box is particularly helpful when entering long criteria.

3 **Click** OK.

- **Run the query.**

Your screen should be similar to Figure 4.55

Query results display only those records whose location is Landis

Employee ID	Last Name	First Name	Pay Rate	Hours	Gross Pay
03225	Morgan	Dan	$14.45	40	$577.92
03890	Thi	Erona	$16.51	45	$743.04
05015	Briggs	Scott	$18.58	40	$743.04
07287	Roman	Anita	$12.38	40	$495.36
07650	Lamm	Chris	$18.58	48	$891.65
12380	Thomas	Jessica	$10.32	20	$206.40
12389	Blackman	Jennifer	$14.45	32	$462.34
12420	Player	Allison	$14.45	23	$332.30
12501	DeLuca	Elizabeth	$17.34	28	$485.45
12583	Sullivan	Marie	$8.26	24	$198.14
12703	Bader	Jeff	$12.38	24	$297.22
12855	Fachet	Kimberly	$12.38	30	$371.52
12914	Gomez	Alfonso	$12.38	35	$433.44
13027	Kieken	Kimberly	$7.74	24	$185.76
13303	Jensen	Chris	$7.74	30	$232.20
13484	Franklin	Stephanie	$7.22	20	$144.48
13635	Martinez	Juan	$10.32	20	$206.40
22085	Lindau	Kristina	$7.22	24	$173.38
22297	Rogondino	Patricia	$6.97	24	$167.18
22469	Hogan	Ryan	$16.25	12	$195.05
99999	Name	Student	$16.51	25	$412.80
	Total		$12.50	48	$7,955.07

Figure 4.55

Now only those records with Landis in the Location field are displayed.

4 **Display the query in SQL view.**

- **Click in the window to clear the selection.**

Your screen should be similar to Figure 4.56

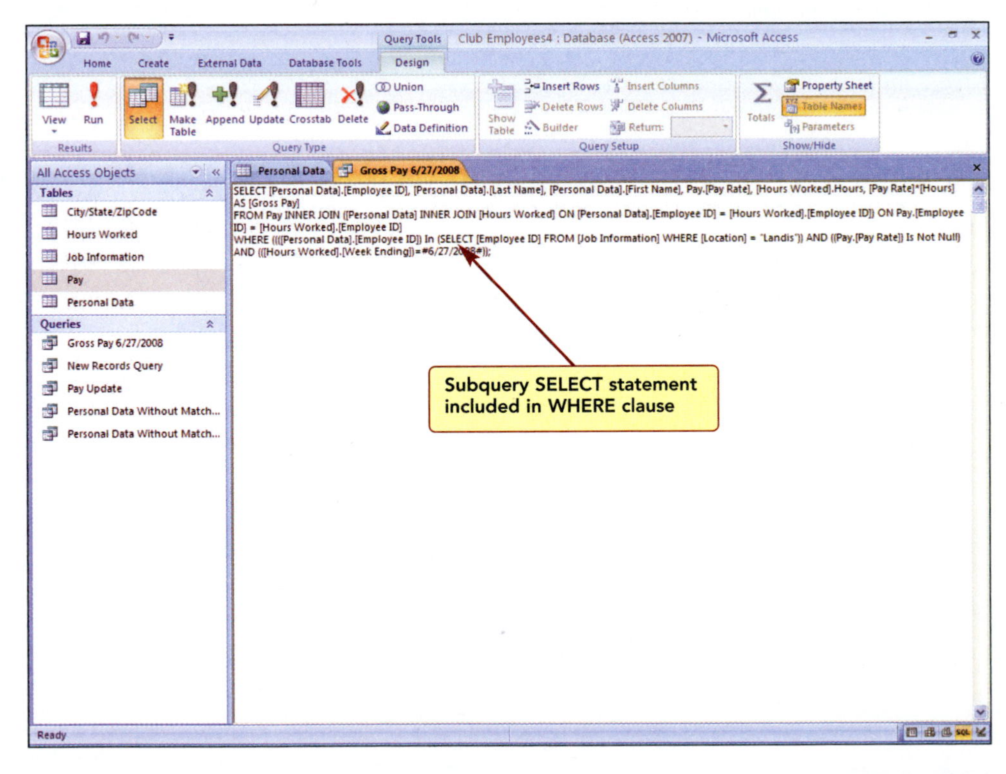

Figure 4.56

The subquery SELECT statement is enclosed in another set of parentheses within the WHERE clause.

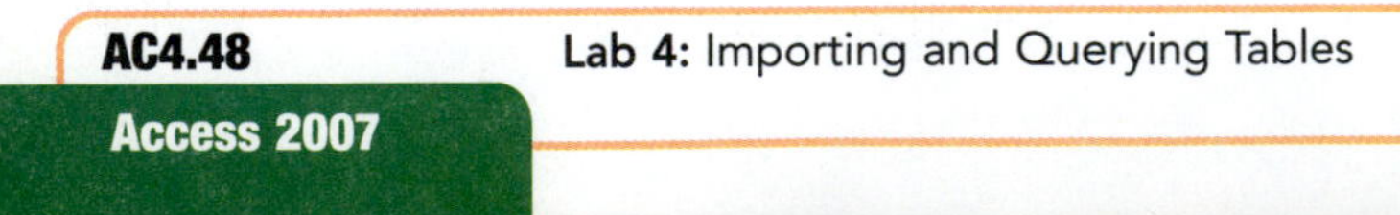

Creating a Top-Values Query

Next, you want to see only those records in the top 25 percent of gross pay earnings. To do this, you can limit the number of records that will display in the query results by specifying an exact number or a percentage. By default, all records that meet the criteria are displayed in the query datasheet. To display only the top number or percentage of records, the results need to be in the correct sorted order first by the field that you want quantified, in this case Gross Pay.

1

- **Display Design view again.**
- **Change the Gross Pay sort order to Descending.**
- **Open the** Return: All **drop-down list in the Query Setup group and choose 25%.**

> **Additional Information**
> You also can type in a value or percentage.

- **Run the query.**

Your screen should be similar to Figure 4.57

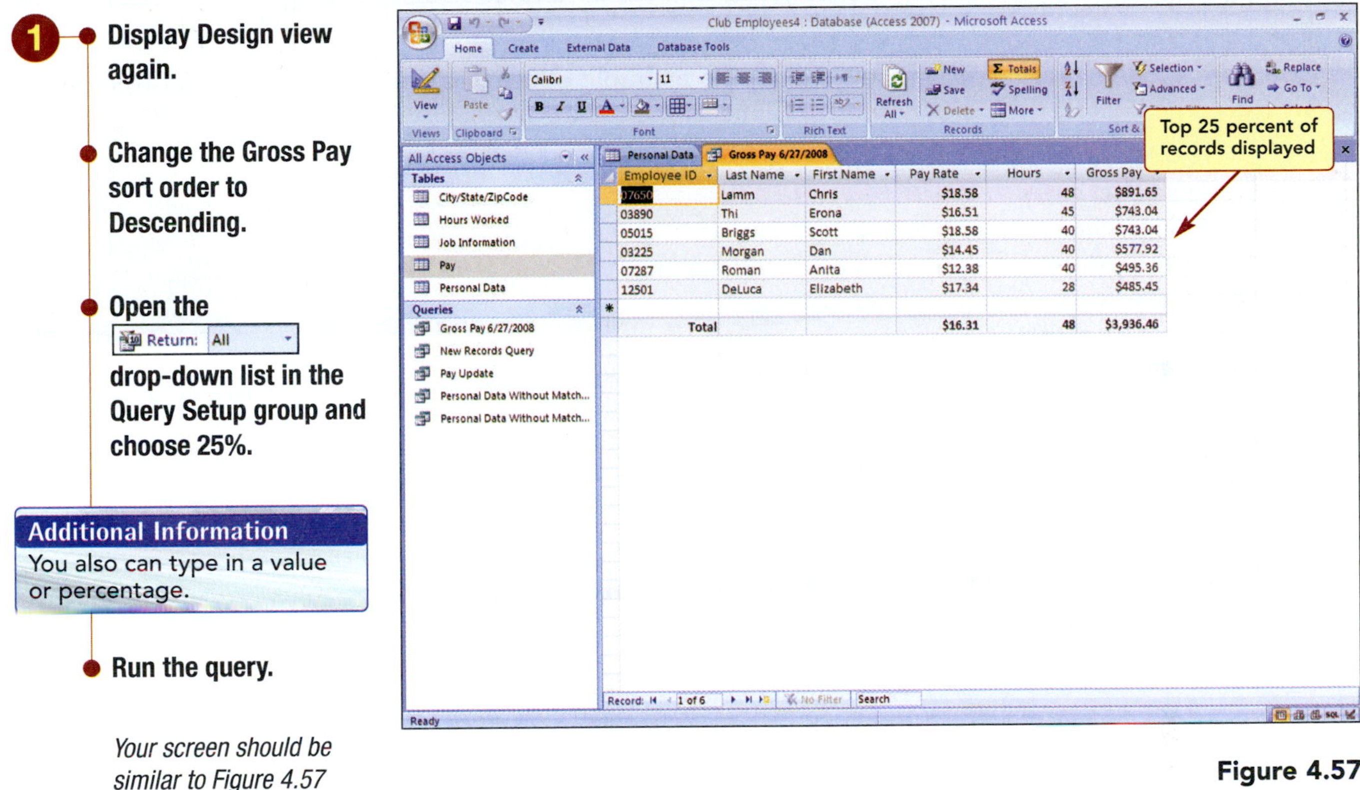

Figure 4.57

The top 25 percent (six) of records are displayed. A Top-Values query was added to the SQL statements to quantify the results.

SQL is a powerful programming language that is created automatically as you use the Query Design interface features. As you have learned, you can use SQL to create even more powerful and complex queries. You can learn much more about SQL through Access online help and other Microsoft Office support features.

2

- **Close and save the changes you made to the query.**

Creating a Crosstab Query

After seeing the gross pay datasheet and the maximum number of work hours, the club owners are curious about the number of hours each employee is working. They have asked you for a simple datasheet that shows the average hours per employee for the last two weeks, excluding the employees on salary. To do this, you will create a crosstab query that will automatically summarize and calculate the data in the Hours query result.

Concept 6

Crosstab Query

6 A **crosstab query** summarizes table data and displays it in a tabular format. In a crosstab query, field values are calculated by sum, average, and count and grouped along the left side and across the top of the datasheet in rows and columns. Being able to see table data grouped both horizontally and vertically is particularly helpful for comparing data in large tables where multiple records are entered one after another down the sheet.

First, you will create a simple query to display only those records that do not contain a blank in the Hours Worked field.

1

- **Create a Select query that includes the Employee ID, Week Ending, and Hours fields from the Hours Worked table.**
- **Set the Hours criteria to not null.**
- **Run the query.**

Your screen should be similar to Figure 4.58

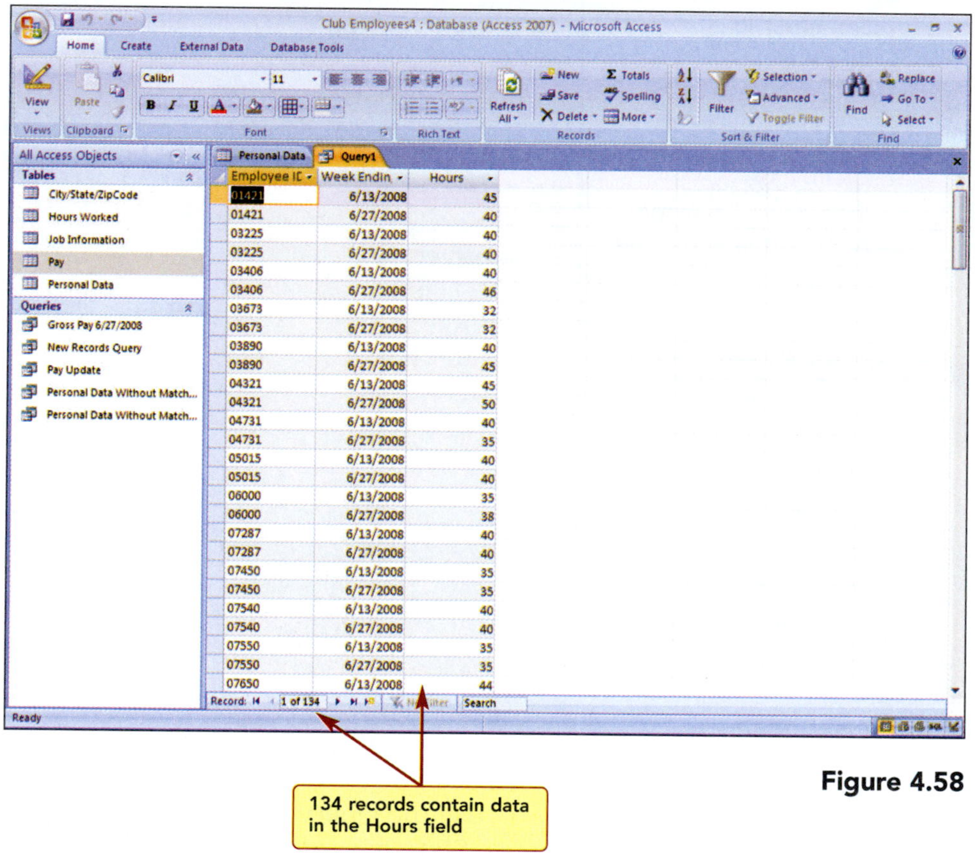

134 records contain data in the Hours field

Figure 4.58

The query results show 134 records that contain entries in the Hours field.

2
- **Save the query as Hours and close the query.**
- **Close the Personal Data table.**

Using the Crosstab Query Wizard

You will use the Crosstab Query Wizard to summarize the hours worked information. The wizard gives you step-by-step instructions on selecting fields for columns and rows and for choosing the way you want the data summarized. Although you can select only one table for the original crosstab query, you can open the query in Query Design view and add more tables and fields if needed.

1
- **Click [Query Wizard] in the Other group of the Create tab.**
- **Choose Crosstab Query Wizard from the New Query dialog box.**
- **Click [OK].**

Your screen should be similar to Figure 4.59

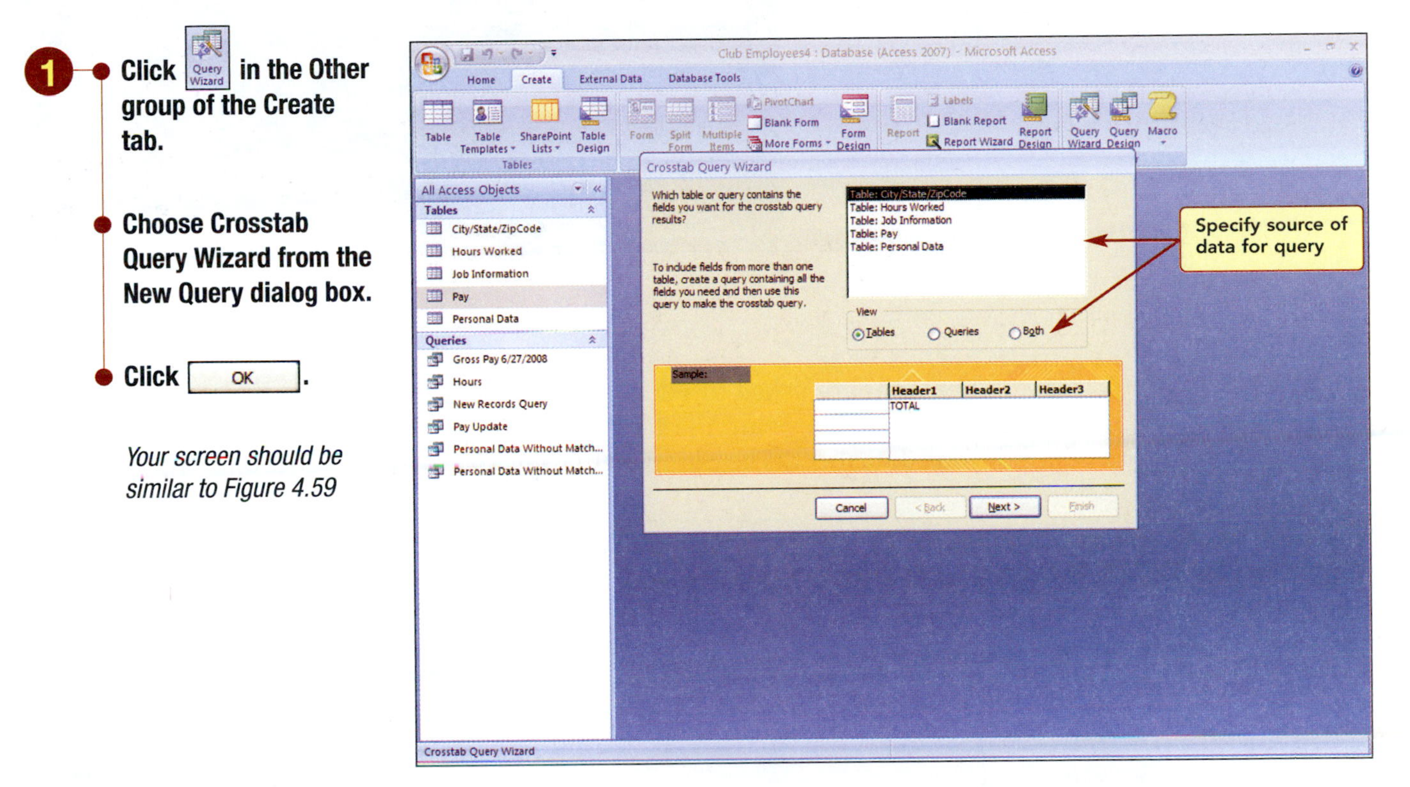

Figure 4.59

The first Crosstab Query Wizard dialog box asks you to select the tables or queries on which you want to base the crosstab query. Because Tables is the selected view, the names of all tables are displayed in the list box. You will use the Hours Worked query.

2 Choose Queries from the View box.

- Choose Query: Hours from the list box.
- Click Next >.

Your screen should be similar to Figure 4.60

Select fields to use as row headings

Figure 4.60

Next you are asked to select the field or fields that you want to use as row headings. These are the fields that will be displayed along the left side of your datasheet. The Sample area shows how your selections will look.

3 Add the Employee ID field to the Selected Fields list.

- Click Next >.

Your screen should be similar to Figure 4.61

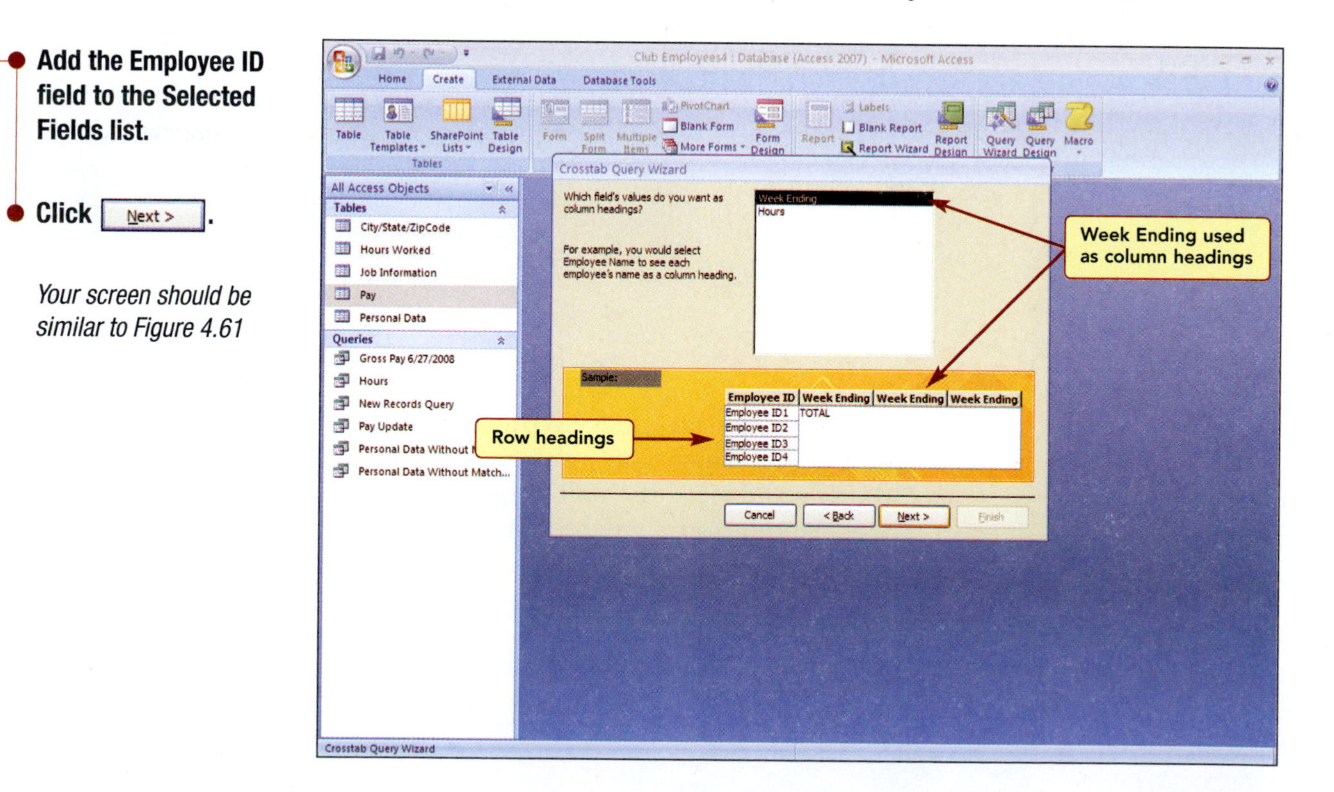

Figure 4.61

You are asked what fields are to be used as column headings (displayed along the top of the datasheet). You want to display the weeks in columns, so the current selection, Week Ending, is acceptable.

Your screen should be similar to Figure 4.62

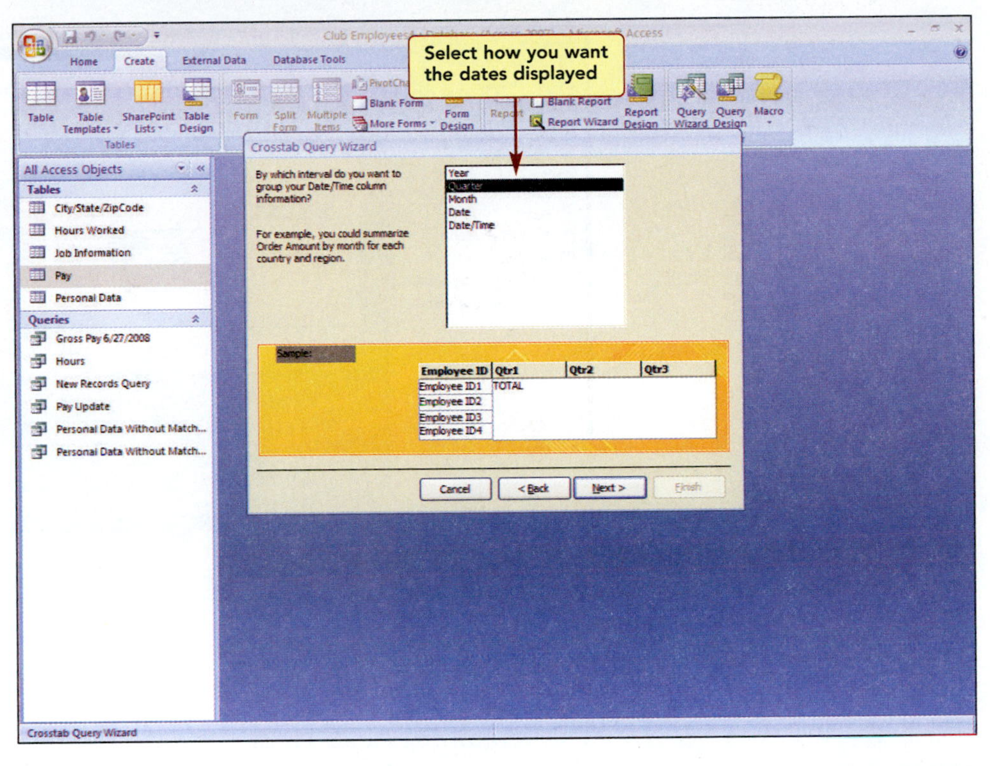

Figure 4.62

Because you selected a date field for the column headings, the wizard asks you how you want the dates displayed: by year, by quarter, by month, by exact date, or by date and time. Because the table contains only two dates, you will use the exact date as the column heading.

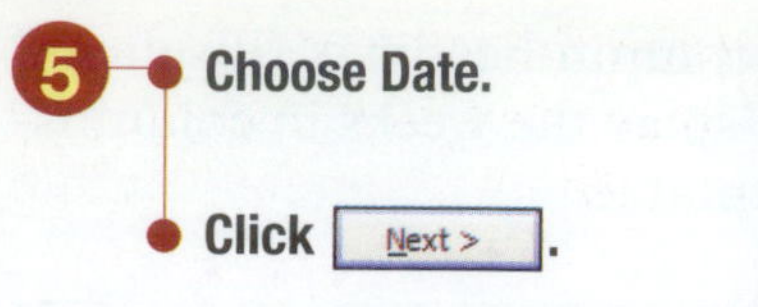

Your screen should be similar to Figure 4.63

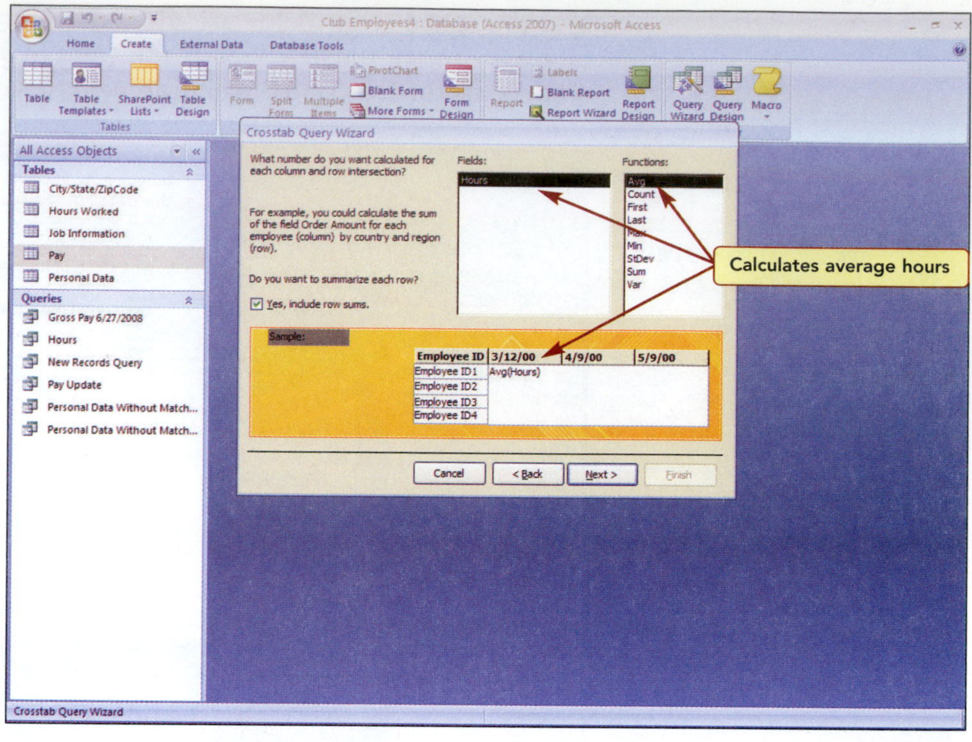

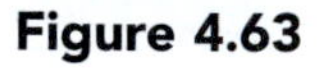

Figure 4.63

The remaining field, Hours, will be the one that is calculated. Since the club owners asked to see an average number of hours for the last two weeks, the current function selection is acceptable. Finally, you will use the default query name and display the query results.

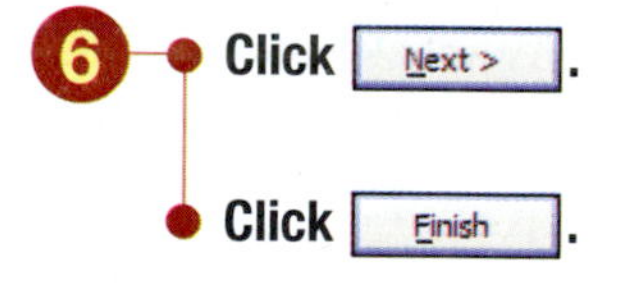

Your screen should be similar to Figure 4.64

Average hours for each employee per week

Hours_Crosstab

Employee ID	Total Of Hou	6/13/2008	6/27/2008
01421	42.5	45	40
03225	40	40	40
03406	43	40	46
03673	32	32	32
03890	42.5	40	45
04321	47.5	45	50
04731	37.5	40	35
05015	40	40	40
06000	36.5	35	38
07287	40	40	40
07450	35	35	35
07540	40	40	40
07550	35	35	35
07650	46	44	48
08000	40	40	40
08391	37	36	38
08430	40	40	40
09430	41	42	40
11510	22	20	24
11747	35	35	35
12194	33	34	32
12213	30	30	30
12230	23.5	22	25
12247	15	15	15
12258	40	40	40
12366	20	20	20
12380	20	20	20

Record: 1 of 67

Figure 4.64

The Hours crosstab query automatically calculated the average number of hours for each employee in each week, which is what the club owners have asked for. However, there are a few things about the query design that you do not like.

Refining the Query Design

First, you would like to change the order of the columns so the average column is last. Also, the Total Of Hours column name does not make it clear that this is an average of the hours worked, not the sum. You will move the columns and rename the column.

1

- **Switch to Design view.**
- **Replace "Total Of Hours:" in the fourth Field cell with Average Hours:.**
- **Switch to Datasheet view.**
- **Move the Average Hours column to the right of the 6/27/2008 column.**
- **Widen the Average Hours column to fully display the field name.**

Your screen should be similar to Figure 4.65

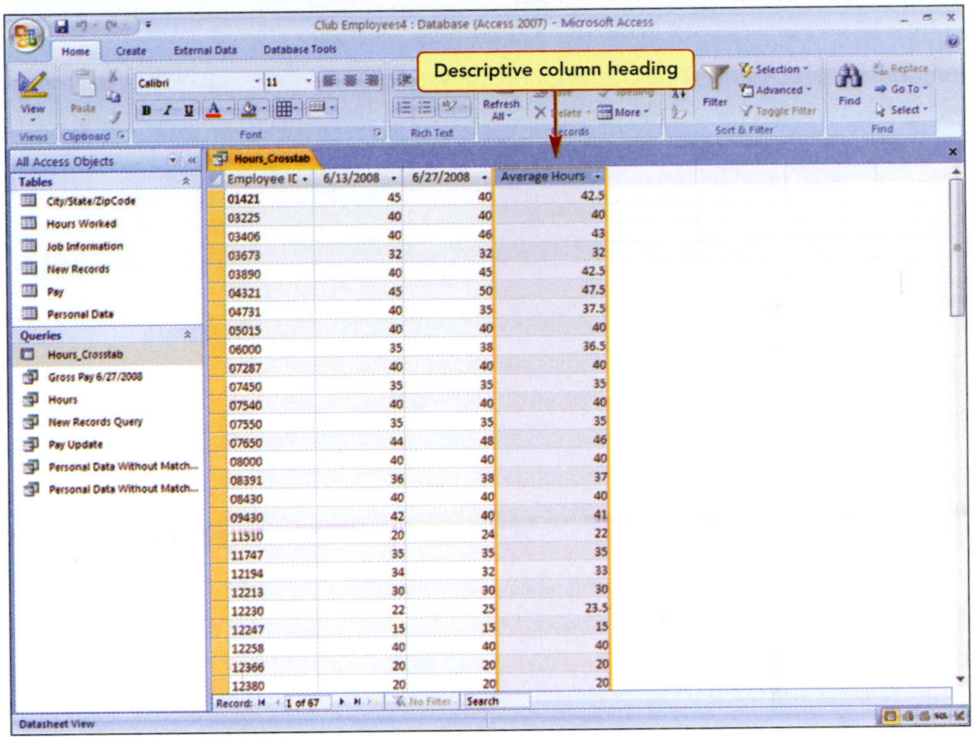

Descriptive column heading

Figure 4.65

The crosstab query results are now easier to understand.

2

- **Print a copy of the crosstab query for the club owners.**
- **Save and close the crosstab query.**
- **Compact and repair the database.**
- **Close the database and exit Access.**

Focus on Careers

EXPLORE YOUR CAREER OPTIONS

Librarian

Have you searched for books at a library lately? Have you ever wondered how libraries keep track of their inventory? Modern libraries use databases to track books and resources. Librarians help develop and maintain these complex databases, and they train new users of the system. They also may use databases maintained by other libraries or institutions. As a librarian, you may be responsible for managing the staff, helping library patrons conduct research, and helping develop reference tools. Although employment of librarians is expected to grow more slowly than the average for all occupations in the future, job opportunities are expected to be very good because a large number of librarians are expected to retire in the coming decade. The typical salary range for a librarian is between $36,000 and $56,000. A master's degree in library science is required in addition to experience in the field.

Concept Summary

LAB 4

Importing and Querying Tables

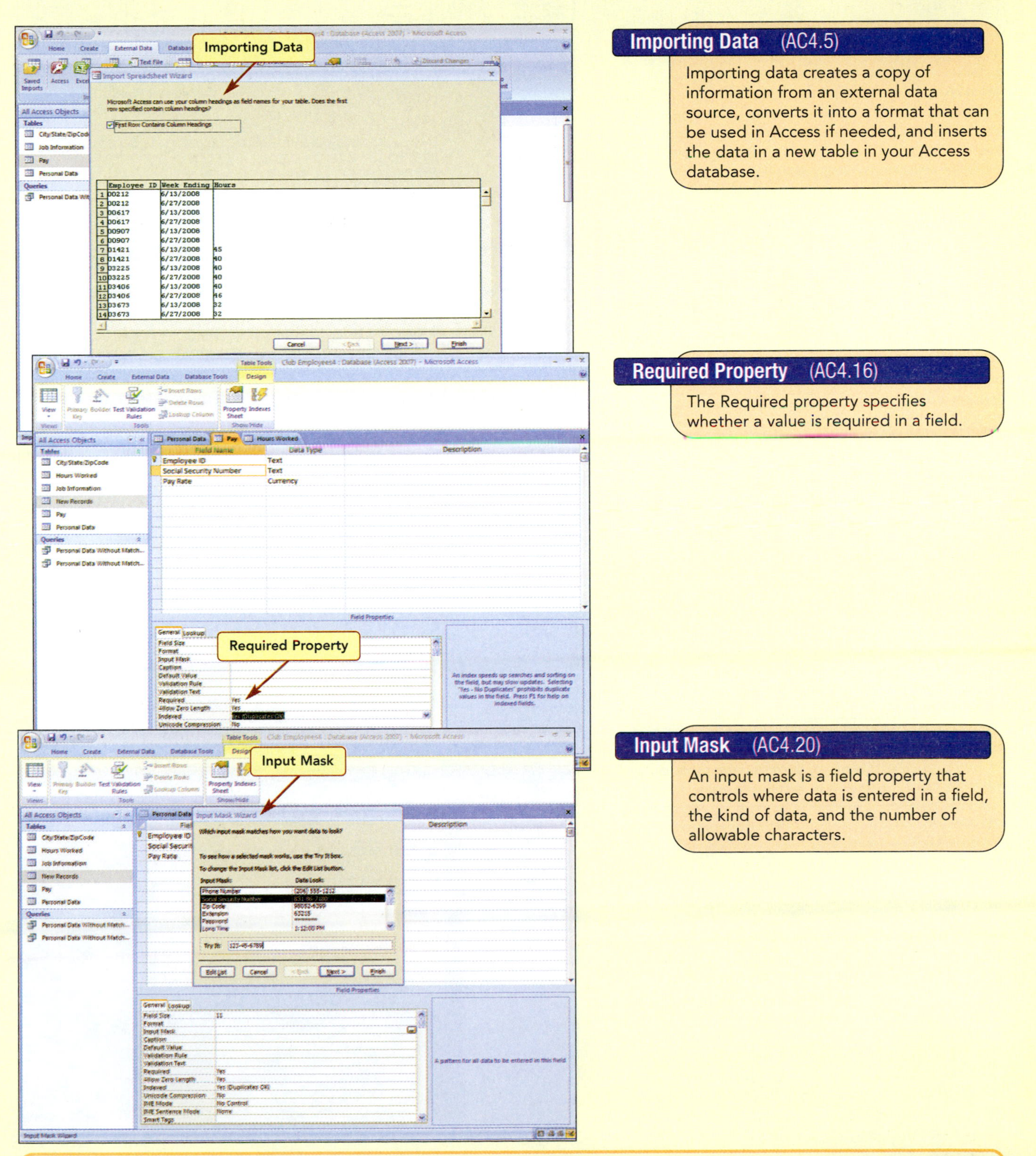

Importing Data (AC4.5)

Importing data creates a copy of information from an external data source, converts it into a format that can be used in Access if needed, and inserts the data in a new table in your Access database.

Required Property (AC4.16)

The Required property specifies whether a value is required in a field.

Input Mask (AC4.20)

An input mask is a field property that controls where data is entered in a field, the kind of data, and the number of allowable characters.

Concept Summary

Calculated Field (AC4.42)

A calculated field displays the result of a calculation in a query.

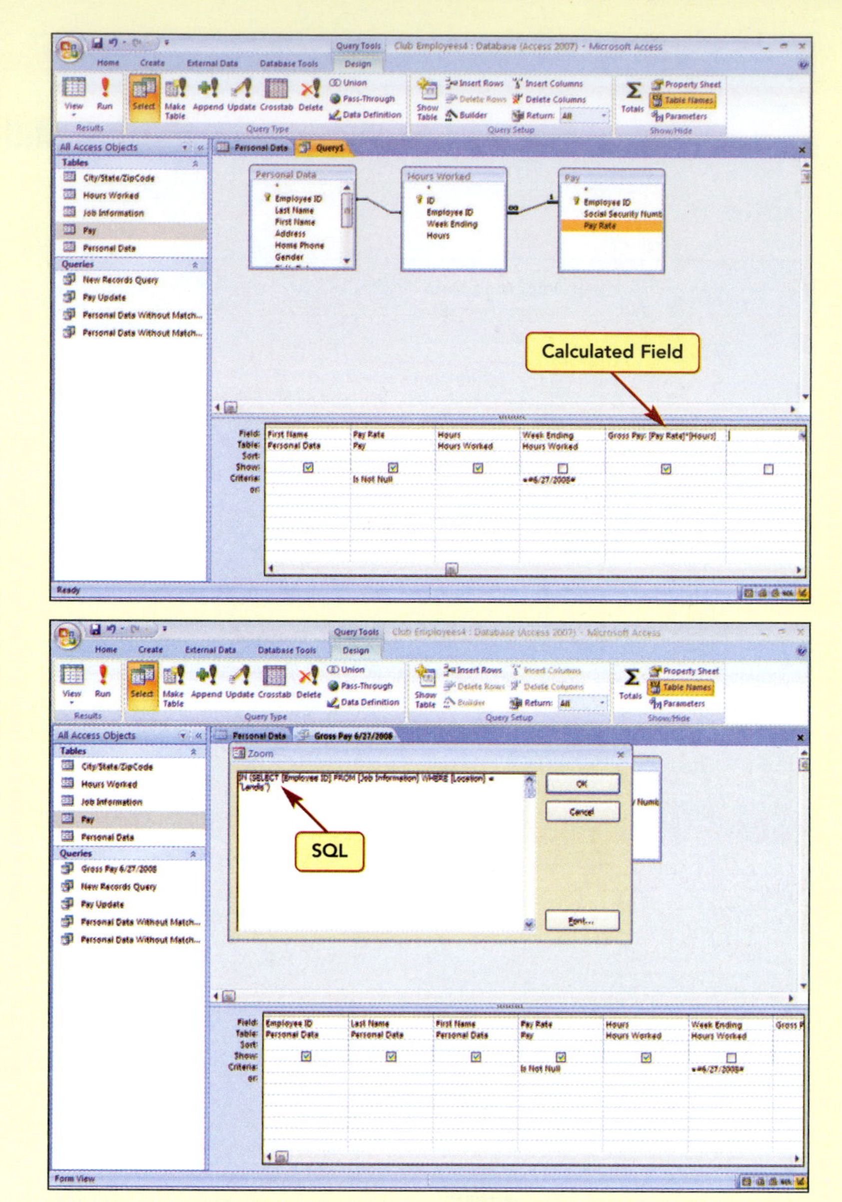

SQL (AC4.45)

SQL (Structured Query Language) is the most common relational database language.

Crosstab Query (AC4.50)

A crosstab query summarizes table data and displays it in tabular format.

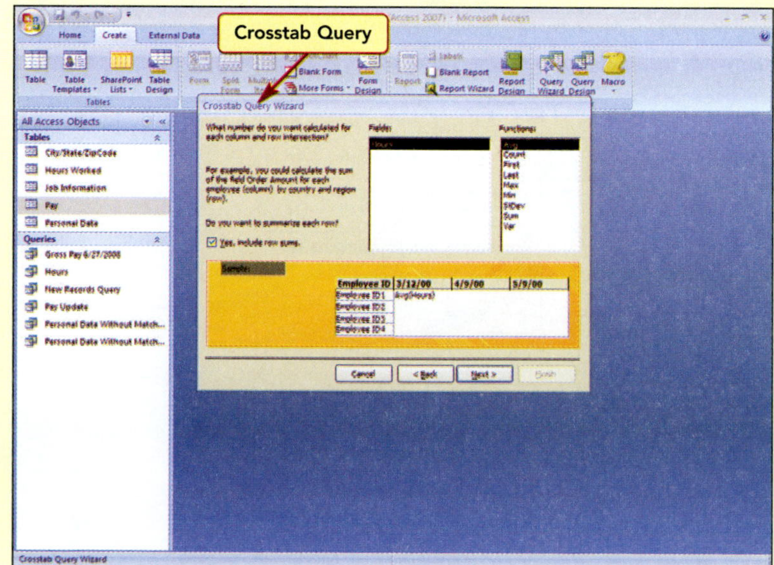

Lab Review

LAB 4

Importing and Querying Tables

key terms

alias AC4.42
byte AC4.18
calculated field AC4.42
crosstab query AC4.50
function AC4.42
import AC4.5
input mask AC4.20
literal character AC4.20
mask character AC4.20
Null value AC4.16
Required property AC4.16
SQL (Structured Query Language) AC4.45
SQL statement AC4.45
subquery AC4.45
syntax AC4.45
zero-length string AC4.16

MCAS Skills

The Microsoft Certified Applications Specialist (MCAS) certification program is designed to measure your proficiency in performing basic tasks using the Office 2007 applications. Certification demonstrates that you have the skills and provides a valuable industry credential for employment. See Reference 2: Microsoft Certified Applications Specialist (MCAS) for a complete list of the skills that were covered in Lab 4.

command summary

Command	Shortcut	Action
Create tab		
Other group		
Query Wizard		Creates a query using the Query Wizard
Query Design		Creates a query using Query Design view
External Data tab		
Import group		
Access		Imports data from or links to data in another Access database
Excel		Imports data from or links to data in an Excel workbook
Saved Imports		Displays a list of previously saved import steps
Query Tools Design tab		
Query Type group		
Select		Defines the current query as a Select query
Append		Defines the current query as an Append query
Update		Defines the current query as an Update query
Crosstab		Defines the current query as a Crosstab query
Delete		Defines the current query as a Delete query
Query Setup group		
Return: All		Allows you to define how much of the total number of valid records should be returned by this query
Show/Hide group		
Property Sheet		Displays (or hides) the Property Sheet for the selected object

Lab Exercises

matching

Match the numbered item with the correct lettered description.

1. import	______	**a.** limits the number of records returned
2. Required property	______	**b.** displays the results of a calculation in a query
3. calculated field	______	**c.** the most common relational database language
4. crosstab query	______	**d.** to copy data that is saved in another format and insert it into an Access table
5. input mask	______	**e.** the name assigned to a calculated field
6. SQL	______	**f.** summarizes table data and displays it in tabular format
7. Action query	______	**g.** makes some change to an existing table
8. subquery	______	**h.** controls how data is entered in a field of a table, query, or form
9. Top-Values query	______	**i.** specifies whether a value is required in a field
10. alias	______	**j.** an SQL SELECT statement that is inside another query

true/false

Circle the correct answer to the following statements.

1. You can use an Append query to create a new table from existing data.	True	False
2. Fields in different tables must have the same name in order to be related.	True	False
3. A calculated field can be created in a query to display the sum of multiple columns.	True	False
4. Data can only be imported from applications that use the same format as Access.	True	False
5. Subqueries must be written in SQL.	True	False
6. If the Required property is set to Yes for a field, the field's value cannot be null.	True	False
7. A crosstab query summarizes query data and displays it in column format.	True	False
8. The < mask character can be used in an input mask to convert entries to lowercase.	True	False
9. You can save the import steps of up to five imports to run from the Saved Imports button.	True	False
10. When using Action queries, it is best to first test using a Select query and then convert it.	True	False

Lab Exercises

fill-in

Complete the following statements by filling in the blanks with the correct key terms.

1. Use a(n) __________ query to return a limited number of valid records.
2. Data that is __________ from another application is converted into a format that can be used in a table.
3. A(n) __________ summarizes table data and displays it in a tabular format.
4. A(n) __________ displays the results of a calculation in a query.
5. __________ is the language used to control and interact with relational databases.
6. Setting the __________ property for a field defines whether or not you must enter a value in the field.
7. An input mask format consists of __________ and __________ characters.
8. Access uses a(n) __________ for calculated fields in order to identify them.
9. SQL statements must use the correct format and rules, or __________, which vary with the type of statement.
10. You can create a(n) __________ by adding an SQL statement in the criteria field of a query.

multiple choice

Circle the letter of the correct response.

1. A field whose Required property is set to No can contain a(n) __________ value.
   - **a.** alphanumeric
   - **b.** null
   - **c.** calculated
   - **d.** any of the above
2. A(n) __________ displays the results of a calculation in a query.
   - **a.** key field
   - **b.** expression
   - **c.** cell
   - **d.** calculated field
3. __________ data duplicates information from an external data source and inserts the data in a new Access table.
   - **a.** Copying
   - **b.** Importing

c. Pasting
d. Exporting

4. The __________ mask character signifies that an entry, if made, must be a letter.
   a. #
   b. /
   c. ?
   d. !

5. A subquery is essentially a(n) __________ statement nested inside another query.
   a. UPDATE
   b. SELECT
   c. APPEND
   d. DELETE

6. Which of the following statements demonstrates the syntax of a calculated field?
   a. [Field1]+[Field2]
   b. MySum=Field1+Field2
   c. =[Field1+Field2]
   d. MySum: [Field1]+[Field2]

7. When using Update or Delete queries, it is a good idea to
   a. use SQL.
   b. back up the database first.
   c. use as many tables as possible.
   d. import the source table.

8. Which of the following is NOT a type of Action query?
   a. Select
   b. Update
   c. Delete
   d. Make Table

9. If the ClientID field from the Clients table is equivalent to the CustomerID field in the Sales table, then the fields have a(n) __________.
   a. alias
   b. relationship
   c. source
   d. calculation

10. Identify the literal character in this input mask: PL?9C#
   a. C
   b. 9
   c. #
   d. P

Hands-On Exercises

rating system
★ Easy
★★ Moderate
★★★ Difficult

step-by-step

Animal Rescue Foundation Database ★

1. The Animal Rescue Foundation database has made life much easier for the directors of this charity organization. The three tables it contains—Rescues, Fosters, and Adopters—have helped them keep track of the animals that come into and are adopted out of their shelter, as well as the individuals who provide foster care or adopt these animals. They would like you to create a new query to show how long the animals that are still being boarded at Animal Angels have been there, which you will accomplish with a calculated field. Your completed Boarded Animals query should be similar to that shown here.

Boarded Animals 1/1/2010

ID #	Type	Name	Current Status	Arrival Date	Days Boarded
B-507	Canary	Tweety	B	2/2/2009	333
C-125	Cat	Lemon	F	6/7/2009	208
C-126	Cat	Student Name	B	7/7/2009	178
C-127	Cat	Ace	B	8/13/2009	141
C-132	Cat		F	9/20/2009	103
C-141	Cat	Lucy	B	10/13/2009	80
D-026	Dog		B	5/7/2009	239
D-027	Dog	Max	F	5/31/2009	215
D-029	Dog	Goldy	B	7/22/2009	163
D-030	Dog	Yappy	B	8/4/2009	150
D-031	Dog		B	8/15/2009	139
D-121	Dog	Lance	F	12/23/2009	9
D-123	Dog	Spreckels	B	12/30/2009	2
H-305	Horse	Beauty	B	7/30/2009	155
P-403	Pig	Babe	B	7/24/2008	526
R-904	Snake	Slither	B	7/16/2009	169

   a. Use Windows to rename the file ac04_ARF as Animal Rescue Foundation.
   b. Open the Animal Rescue Foundation database file.
   c. Create a query in Design view. Add the Rescues table to the design. Add the ID #, Type, Name, Current Status, and Arrival Date fields to the grid, in that order. You want only the records for animals that have not been adopted to be included in this query, so specify the criteria in the Current Status field **not A**.
   d. In the first blank Field column, enter the following equation to calculate the number of days an animal has been boarded at Animal Angels: **Days Boarded: DateDiff('d',[Arrival Date],[Date])**
   e. Make sure the Show box is checked for the calculated field and then run the query. When you are asked to enter a parameter for the Date, enter **01/01/2010**.
   f. Enter your name as the pet with the ID# of C-126. Change the arrival date for Babe, the pig, to **7/24/2008**. Adjust the column widths as necessary to view all displayed data. Apply formatting of your choice to the query results datasheet.
   g. Save the query as Boarded Animals. Print the query results in portrait orientation. Close the query.
   h. Compact and close the database.

Adventure Travel Tours Client Database ★★

2. As the database administrator for Adventure Travel Tours, you have created a database that includes tables of clients and travel tour agents. Personnel currently keep track of reservation information in an Excel spreadsheet. They would like the reservation information to be added to the new database and a table to be prepared for future data entry. Then you will create a query to show the amount due for different events. When you are done, your Amount Due query will be similar to that shown here.

Amount Due 7/1/2010

First Name	Last Name	Phone	Event ID	TotalDue	AmountPaid	AmountDue
Kelly	Musial	555-9936	G-22157	$2,900.00	$1,900.00	$1,000.00
Gerard	Hughes	555-4811	G-22157	$2,900.00	$2,000.00	$900.00
Miguel	Rohmann	555-5566	G-22157	$2,900.00	$1,500.00	$1,400.00
Theresa	Wymore	555-2848	G-22157	$2,900.00	$1,000.00	$1,900.00
June	Thomas	555-2039	G-22157	$2,900.00	$2,900.00	$0.00
Katherine	Gryder	555-6116	G-22157	$2,900.00	$2,500.00	$400.00
Roy	Thieu	555-9559	G-22157	$2,900.00	$2,900.00	$0.00
Jennifer	Zegiel	555-6959	G-22157	$2,900.00	$1,900.00	$1,000.00
Student	Name		G-22157	$4,500.00	$2,000.00	$2,500.00
Total				$27,700.00	$18,600.00	$9,100.00

a. In Windows, rename the ac04_ATT Clients & Agents file ATT Clients & Agents.

b. Open the ATT Clients & Agents database. Import the contents of Sheet1 from the Excel file ac04_ATT Reservations.xlsx into a new table. The first row contains the column headings. Change the Client ID and EmployeeID fields to the Text data type and change the Notes field to the Memo data type. Allow Access to add the primary key. Name the table **Reservations**. Save the import steps as **Import ATT Reservations Worksheet**.

c. Open the Reservations table. The Event ID will always be in the format Uppercase Letter, Dash, five-digit number. Create an input mask for the Event ID field that will enforce this pattern and display and store the literal in the field. Appropriately size the fields in the table.

d. Change the Client ID field to a lookup field based on the Clients table. Similarly, change the EmployeeID field to a lookup field based on the Agents table. Appropriately size all the field columns in the table.

e. Close all tables. Add all three tables to the Relationships window. Edit both relationships to enforce referential integrity and Cascade Update. Close the Relationships window, saving the changes.

f. Add your name as a client with the Client ID of **99999**. Add a new record in the Reservations table using your client ID, today's date as the reservation date, and an Event ID of **G-22157**. Complete the other fields with data of your choice.

g. Create a parameter query on the Event ID field that displays the first and last names and phone of the client, Event ID, Total Due, and Amount Paid in that order for all records. Include a field that will calculate the amount due for each record. Name the field **AmountDue**. Display only those records with an Event ID of G-22157. Include a Totals row and display a sum of the Total Due, Amount Paid, and Amount Due fields. Apply formatting of your choice to the query datasheet. Size the column width to just large enough to display the data. Save the query as **Amount Due**. Print the query result in portrait orientation.

h. Compact and repair the database. Close the database.

Five Points Client Query ★★

3. Kathlyn Frances is the owner of Five Points Health and Wellness Center. She hired you to create a database for the center and is quite pleased with the Clients table that you created in the center's database. She would now like you to create two additional tables: one that contains data about the various spa packages and their costs and another that lists which clients have purchased which package. She also would like you to run a query that shows the package purchased by clients and the total amount spent. When you are finished, you will have the query results similar to those shown here.

Client Purchases 2/3/2008

Last Name	Total Purchases	1	2	3	4	5	6	7	8
Adderson	$515.00	$515.00							
Bkihazi	$300.00				$300.00				
Buchsbaum	$490.00		$315.00			$175.00			
Caniza	$175.00					$175.00			
Cheng	$430.00						$215.00		
Dome	$425.00				$300.00			$125.00	
Downing	$200.00								$100.00
Gajjar	$100.00								$100.00
Gimball	$175.00					$175.00			
Hinds	$440.00		$315.00					$125.00	
Hubert	$275.00					$175.00			$100.00
Johanson	$525.00			$225.00	$300.00				
Kane	$200.00								$100.00
Lindstrom	$215.00						$215.00		
McFrench	$515.00	$515.00							
Name	$225.00			$225.00					
Nichols	$315.00		$315.00						
Pickering	$740.00	$515.00		$225.00					
Radomski	$300.00				$300.00				
Schwartz	$400.00			$225.00		$175.00			
Wright	$425.00				$300.00			$125.00	
Wu	$315.00						$215.00		$100.00

a. In Windows, rename the **ac04_Five Points** file **Five Points Center**. Open the database file. Open the Clients table and enter your first and last names as Client ID **100–24**. Close the Clients table.

b. Use Design view to create a table with the following fields:

Field Name	Data Type
Package #	AutoNumber
Package Name	Text
Description	Text
Price	Currency

c. Name the table **Spa Packages** and keep the default primary key (Package #).

d. Open the Spa Packages table and enter the following records (do not worry about entering a Package #—it is an AutoNumber field):

Package #	Package Name	Description	Price
1	Five Points Rejuvenation	Deep-tissue Massage, Aromatherapy, Body Wrap, Deep-tissue Facial, Sauna	$515.00
2	Five Points Relaxation	Deep-tissue Massage, Facial, Sauna	$315.00
3	Five Points Purification	Aromatherapy, Facial, Sauna	$225.00
4	Five Points Anti-stress	Aromatherapy, Facial, Body Wrap, Sauna	$300.00
5	Five Points Indulgence	Deep-tissue Massage	$175.00
6	Five Points Escential	Aromatherapy	$215.00
7	Five Points Escape	Facial	$125.00
8	Five Points Bliss	Sauna	$100.00

e. Adjust the column widths to fit the data. Then save and close the table.

f. Import the Packages Sold table from the Access file ac04_Five Points Packages Sold.accdb. This will be a one-time import, so you do not need to save the import steps.

g. Open the Packages Sold table and add a new entry with your Client # (100-24) and package 3 (Purification).

h. Create a relationship between the Clients and Packages Sold tables based on the Client No/Client # field and enforce referential integrity. Create a relationship between the Spa Packages and Packages Sold tables based on the Package # field and enforce referential integrity.

i. Create a new query in Design view and include all three tables. Add the Last Name, Package #, and Price fields to the query design grid. Save the query as **Package Revenue**.

j. Use the Crosstab Query Wizard to create a crosstab query based on the Package Revenue query. Select Last Name as the row heading, Package # as the column headings, and Price as the field you want calculated with the SUM function. Name the crosstab query **Client Purchases** and finish the wizard.

k. Rename the Total of Price field **Total Purchases**. Adjust the column widths.

l. Apply formatting of your choice to the datasheet. Print the crosstab query result in landscape orientation. Close and save the query.

m. Compact and repair the database. Close the Five Points Center database.

Downtown Internet Café Inventory Database Improvements ★★★

4. The database you created for the Downtown Internet Café contains a table with information about the café's inventory and vendors. You have used this table to create queries and reports on items that need to be ordered. Evan, the café's owner, has advised you that Fred Wilmington, the contact for By Design, is no longer with the company and that the new contact is Betty Barnton. You will create an Update query to update the database with this new information. Evan also has asked you to create another table that lists the unit costs of the inventory items. You will get this information by importing the information from an Excel worksheet. Finally, Evan also would like you to modify the existing To Be Ordered query to calculate the cost of each order. Your query printout will be similar to that shown here.

Description	In Stock	Supplier	Contact	Phone Number	E-mail	Order Amount	Unit Price	Order Cost
Cups-small	11	ABC Restaurant Supply	Richard Price	(206) 555-0037	brs@email.net	1	$75.00	$75.00
Sugar	6	ABC Restaurant Supply	Richard Price	(206) 555-0037	brs@email.net	6	$65.00	$390.00
Bottled water	9	Aquatics	Lee Branson	(207) 555-1122	thirst@net.com	3	$85.00	$255.00
T-Shirts	12	By Design	Betty Barnton	(502) 555-6973	design@email.com	0	$76.00	$0.00
Coffee Filters	10	Coffee and More	Lon Truman	(206) 555-0037	cof@net.com	2	$60.00	$120.00
Arabian coffee	4	Cuppa Jo	Student Name	(206) 555-9090	jo@dial.com	8	$115.00	$920.00
Ethiopian coffee	9	Cuppa Jo	Student Name	(206) 555-9090	jo@dial.com	3	$135.00	$405.00
Kona coffee	10	Cuppa Jo	Student Name	(206) 555-9090	jo@dial.com	2	$140.00	$280.00
Espresso	11	Cuppa Jo	Student Name	(206) 555-9090	jo@dial.com	1	$185.00	$185.00
Italian Roast	12	Cuppa Jo	Student Name	(206) 555-9090	jo@dial.com	0	$125.00	$0.00
Decaf Guatamala	7	Pure Processing	Nancy Young	(206) 555-5689	pure@ez.com	5	$140.00	$700.00
Coffee mints	12	Sweet Stuff	Su-Chin Lim	(650) 555-3781	sweet@email.net	0	$75.00	$0.00
Total								$3,330.00

a. Rename the ac04_Cafe Purchases database Cafe Purchases. Open the database file and the Suppliers table. Change the contact name for Cuppa Jo to your name. Create an input mask for the Phone Number field. Close the table.

b. Create an Update query to change the contact name for By Design from Fred Wilmington to Betty Barnton. Run the query and then close it. There is no need to save the query as the required action has been performed.

c. Import the Excel file ac04_Prices as a new table named **Inventory Prices**. Change the Data Type for the Item # field to Text. Choose Item # as the primary key for the table. Save the import steps as **Import Price Sheet**.

d. Open the new table in Design view. Check the field properties and adjust as needed. Make both fields required. Format the table to display blue text and gridlines.

e. Close all tables. Open the Relationships window and enforce referential integrity and Update Cascade for both relationships. Close the Relationships window, saving the changes.

f. You are now ready to update the To Be Ordered query to include costs. Open the To Be Ordered query and add the Inventory Prices table to the query. Remove the Special Order field. Change the In Stock criteria to **<= 12**.

g. Next, you need to add a new field that will calculate the number of items that need to be ordered, based on the fact that Evan likes to keep an inventory of less than 12 units of every item on hand. In the blank field cell to the right of the E-mail column, type the following: **Order Amount: 12-[In Stock]**.

h. The next calculation you want to perform is one that will multiply the # To Order value by the Unit Price. Add the Unit Price field from the Inventory Prices table to the blank field cell to the right of the Order Amount calculated field. In the next blank field cell, enter **Order Cost: [Order Amount]*[Unit Price]**. Set the format property to Currency.

i. Run the query. Save the revised query as **Inventory Order Costs**.

j. Display a Totals row that calculates the total order cost. Adjust the column widths to fit the displayed data. Apply formatting of your choice to the datasheet. Change the page orientation to landscape with narrow margins. Print the query and close it.

k. Compact and repair, and then close the database.

LearnSoft Product Database ★★★

5. The database you created for LearnSoft Company currently contains a table that lists the educational software titles produced by the company as well as the subject of each package and the designer who is responsible for developing it. You have created several queries and reports based on this table, which has helped the marketing and development managers immensely. After hearing about the success of this database, the sales manager requested that you add tables that contain data about packages that have been purchased so that queries can be run that show how the packages are selling and what the total monthly, quarterly, and annual purchase amounts are. You decide to start this process by creating a simple order table with product name, order date, and quantity purchased data. Then, by adding a unit cost field to the existing Software Development table, you can use both tables to run a query that calculates the total sales per package to date. When you are finished, you will have a new database table and a query printout that looks similar to that shown here.

Software Package Sales 7/1/2010

ProductID	Developer	Total Packages Sold	Average Price	Total Sales
47-0701	Irene Lee	294	$75.00	$22,050.00
47-0702	Irene Lee	202	$75.00	$15,150.00
63-0101	Juana Jimenez	201	$65.00	$13,065.00
24-0202	Maggie O'Grady	246	$50.00	$12,300.00
57-0703	William Hertzler	161	$75.00	$12,075.00
77-0103	Beth Severs	233	$50.00	$11,650.00
63-0102	Juana Jimenez	177	$65.00	$11,505.00
24-0303	Maggie O'Grady	225	$50.00	$11,250.00
15-0502	Catherine Willis	238	$40.00	$9,520.00
15-0503	Catherine Willis	187	$50.00	$9,350.00
80-0101	Ben Hadden	203	$45.00	$9,135.00
77-0102	Beth Severs	171	$50.00	$8,550.00
24-0103	Maggie O'Grady	189	$45.00	$8,505.00
90-0103	Student Name	264	$30.00	$7,920.00
24-0101	Maggie O'Grady	170	$45.00	$7,650.00
Total				$169,675.00

a. Rename the ac04_LearnSoft database LearnSoft Titles. Open the database and enter your name as the Developer in the last record of the Software table. Create an input mask for the Product Code field that stores the data, including the literals. Close the table.

b. Import the Software Sales table from the ac04_LearnSoft Sales.accdb database. Do not save the import steps.

c. Open the Software Sales table in Design view. Use the Input Mask Wizard to apply the Short Date input mask to the DateSold field. Make all fields in the table required.

d. Create an input mask for the ProductID field that stores the data including the literals. Save the table design and switch to Datasheet view.

e. Enter an order number of **01000**, a Product ID of **15-0602**, a DateSold of **06/15/2010**, and a quantity of **4**. Since this order was for a school's third-grade computer lab, there were two more software packages purchased on the same order. Therefore, you need to enter two more records with the same order number: one for four Read It II (15-0502) packages and another for four Spell It II (15-0202) packages. Enter the same DateSold date for both.

f. Add a final record with your first and last initials followed by **999** as the Order ID and today's date as the DateSold. Enter the software package **90-0103** and a quantity of **25**. Close the table.

g. Open the Relationships window and create a relationship between the Software and Software Sales tables using the Product Code/ProductID fields. Enforce referential integrity. Close the Relationships window, saving the layout.

h. You are now ready to add a field to the Software table that will contain the cost of each software package. Open this table and switch to Design view. Add a field called **Price** with a data type of Currency. Save the design changes and close the table.

i. The prices themselves have already been (mistakenly) entered into the Categories table. To enter the prices in the Software table, you will use an Update query following these steps:

- Create a Select query that includes the Price field from the Software table.
- Add the Categories table.
- Change the query type to Update.
- For the criteria, enter the following: **[Categories]![Product Code]=[Software]![Product Code]**. [Note: Either a dot or an exclamation point (!) can be used to separate the parts of an identifier in an expression.]
- In the Update To row, enter **[Categories]![Price]**.
- Run the Update query. The Software table will now be populated with the correct prices.
- Save the Update query as **Update Prices**. Close the query.

j. Delete the Price field from the Categories table.

k. Next, you will produce the sales-to-date query that the sales manager requested. Use the Simple Query Wizard to create a new query. Include the ProductID and Quantity fields from the Software Sales table and the Developer and Price fields from the Software table. Select Summary as the type of query you would like to create and choose the Sum option for the Quantity field and the Avg option for the Price field. Name the query **Software Package Sales**. Specify that you want to modify the query design and finish the wizard.

l. In the query's Design view, change the Sum of Quantity: calculated field name to **Total Packages Sold:** and the Avg for Price calculated field name to **Average Price**. Then, in the blank field column to the right, enter another calculated field: **Total Sales: [Quantity]*[Price]**. Assign the Currency property to the new field. Change the Total entry from Group By to Sum. Run the query.

m. Next, you will alter the query to display the top 50 percent of titles, in terms of total sales. In Design view, change the Sort property on the Total Sales field to Descending. Set the Return value to **50%**. Run the query. Display a Totals row that sums the Total Sales.

n. Adjust the column widths to fit the displayed data. Apply formatting of your choice and then print the query results.

o. Save and close the query. Compact and repair and then close the database.

on your own

Dental Patient Database ★

1. As manager for a new dental office, you have been maintaining a database named Dental Patients and a table named Personal Information that contains the patient's personal information as well as the dentist to which they are assigned. The bookkeeper has recently requested that you add a table that will track patient payment information. The information for this table has been provided in an Excel worksheet and includes one sample record. Open the database you updated in On Your Own Exercise 3 of Lab 2 (Dental Patients) and import the ac04_Patient Billing worksheet to a new table. Name the table **Billing**.

   Rename the Patient ID field in the Billing table to match the field name that you use for patient identification numbers in the Personal Information table. Review the structure of the table in Design view to ensure that the field properties are set correctly and formatted appropriately before using the table. Make the first four fields required, as well as any other fields that would be essential to each transaction. Change the Patient ID field to a lookup list based on the Personal Data ID field. Do not include a primary key so you can enter more than one record for each patient in this table (which you will do each time they make a payment). Create a one-to-many relationship between the tables. Replace the sample patient ID in the Billing table with an ID from the Personal Information table. Add at least five additional records to the Billing table and enter payment information for each. Print the Billing table.

Lewis & Lewis Query ★

2. The Lewis & Lewis database you modified in On Your Own Exercise 4 of Lab 2 (ac02_Lewis Personnel) has alleviated the paperwork in personnel and helped keep track of employee information. Lewis & Lewis also employs consultants to help on various projects. To make the database even more effective, your manager has requested that the consultant information be included in the database. Import the two tables from the ac04_Lewis Consultants database into the ac02_Lewis Personnel database.

   Review the structure of the two new tables in Design view and modify the field formats as needed. Use an input mask to control the entry of the ZIP Code and Billing Date fields. Create a relationship between the two tables. Enter data for 10 consultants in the Consultant Contact table (include your name as a consultant). Enter 15 records in the Consultant Billing table (a consultant can have multiple billings). Create a query named **Consultant Costs** that displays the Consultant ID, Last and First Names, and all the fields from the Consultant Billing table. Include a field to calculate the total billing amount (Billable Hours * Hourly Rate). Print the query results. Create a crosstab query named **Consultant Hours** to calculate the number of hours per consultant per week. Print the query results. Back up and close the database.

WriteOn! Database ★★

3. WriteOn! distributes writing supplies to many different stationery stores. They would like you to create a database to keep track of the products (writing paper, envelopes, notepads, and so on) they have in stock. Design a relational database named **WriteOn!** that includes the following two tables:

Products

Field Name	Data Type	Notes
Product ID	AutoNumber	Primary Key
Supplier ID	Number	
Description	Memo	
Selling Price	Currency	
Wholesale Price	Currency	
Quantity On Hand	Number	
Reorder Quantity	Number	

Suppliers

Field Name	Data Type	Notes
Supplier ID	AutoNumber	Primary Key
Supplier Name	Text	
Street Address	Text	
City	Text	
State	Text	
Zip Code	Text	

Create an input mask for the supplier Zip Code field. Enter at least 15 records into each table. Establish a relationship between the tables using the supplier ID fields. Query the database for products with a quantity on hand of less than five. In the query, include a calculated field that displays the number of items to order based on the Reorder Quantity – Quantity On Hand. Save the query as **Reorder Query**. Print the query results.

EMP Enterprise Database ★★

4. You are continuing to work on a database for EMP Enterprises to track employee expense requests. This database currently includes two tables: Employee Info and Employee Expenses. Open the database that you last updated in On Your Own Exercise 5 of Lab 3 (**EMP Enterprises**) and

modify the two tables in Design view to include input masks, required fields, and lookup fields where applicable. Then use these tables to create a query that calculates the expense amounts by department. Print the query results. Create a crosstab query that details the expense type and amount by department. Print the query results.

Little League Database ★★★

5. You have been hired as an intern by the Tri-County Little League. They currently maintain a player database in Excel, but they would like to use Access to organize the equipment inventory and the coaches information. Create a new blank database and name it Little League. Import the Excel file ac04_Little League and save the table as **Players**. Create a new table named **Coaches** for the coaches information. Include the fields FirstName, LastName, Title, TeamName, HomePhone, and EmailAddress. Create a lookup field for the Title field using the values Coach, Assistant Coach, Manager, and Team Parent. Make the TeamName field a required property. Apply an input mask to the HomePhone field. Add five records to the Coaches table for the coaches of the following teams: Cubs, Braves, Marlins, Pirates, and Tigers. Make yourself the coach of the Tigers. The Little League would like to have a report that includes the complete rosters for each team. Create a query that shows each player's First Name, Last Name, Team, and Coach. Name it **Roster**. Create a crosstab query that displays the coach's last name and the number of players for which each is responsible. Name the crosstab query **Coach Totals**. Print the crosstab query. Back up and save the database.

Creating Custom Forms

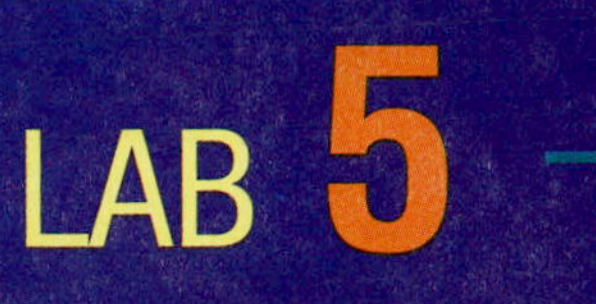

Objectives

After completing this lab, you will know how to:

1. Create a split form.
2. Create a datasheet form.
3. Create a multiple-table form.
4. Add title and label controls.
5. Change fonts, font size, and text colors.
6. Adjust form alignment and spacing.
7. Create and use a subform.
8. Set tab order.
9. Add command buttons to a form.
10. Create page headers and footers.
11. Delete a form.

Case Study

Lifestyle Fitness Club

Now that all the tables for the Lifestyle Fitness Club employee database are complete, you want to create forms to update the tables. You have already created a form to update the Personal Data table. Now, you want to create additional forms to update the other tables. In addition, the owners have asked you to look into creating a single form that could be used to update information in all the tables. This would make updating and viewing the employee data easier, more efficient, and more accurate because you would not need to open and update the records in each table individually.

To do this, you will create a multitable form that will display information from the Personal Data, Job Information, Pay, and Hours Worked tables. After considering the form layout and design, you decide to create a main form that includes the employee data from the Personal Data and Job Information tables. Then you will add a subform to the main form that will display the data from the Pay and Hours Worked tables. Additionally, you will add command buttons to the form to make it easier to add new records and print forms at the click of a button. The completed form is shown here.

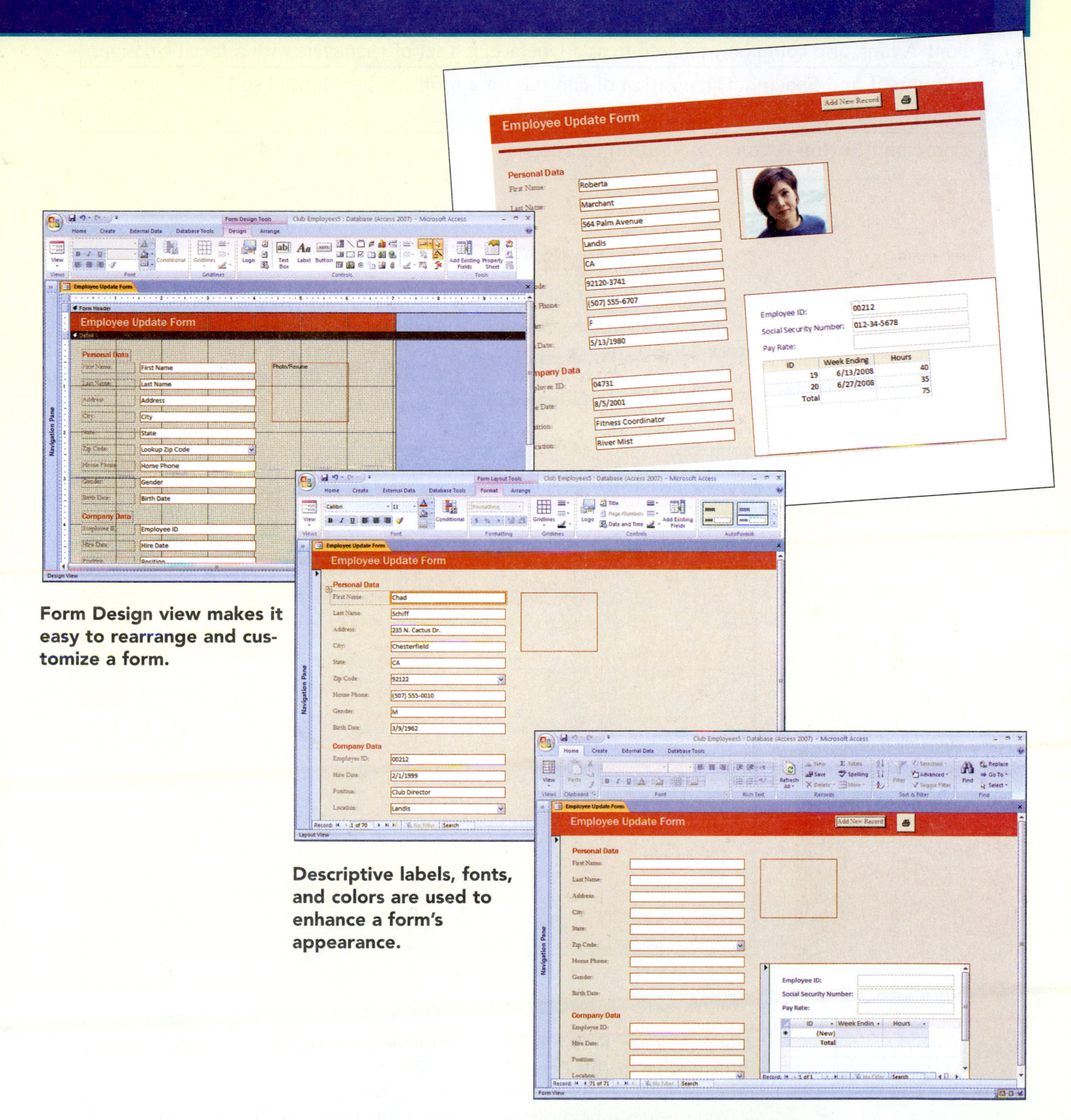

Form Design view makes it easy to rearrange and customize a form.

Descriptive labels, fonts, and colors are used to enhance a form's appearance.

A multitable form and subform make it faster and more efficient to update multiple tables.

Concept Preview

The following concepts will be introduced in this lab:

1. **Subform** A subform is a form that is embedded in another form and is used to show data from another table or query.
2. **Font** A font, also commonly referred to as a typeface, is a set of characters with a specific design.
3. **Alignment and Spacing** The position of controls on a form can be adjusted so that they are evenly aligned and the spacing between them is the same.
4. **Command Button** A command button executes one or more actions on a form.

Creating a Split Form

Your database now includes several tables of employee information that each needs to be opened and updated every time information changes in an existing record or a record is added or deleted. Although you created a form to make entering and editing data easier, this form updates records in the Personal Data table only.

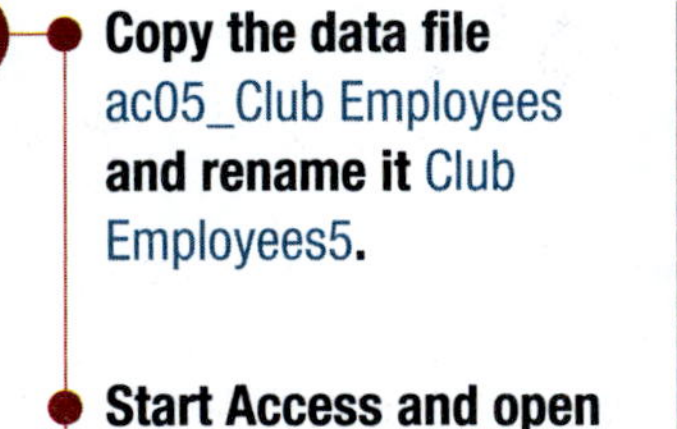

1. **Copy the data file** ac05_Club Employees **and rename it** Club Employees5.

   Start Access and open the database file Club Employees5 **with content enabled.**

   Open the Employee Records form.

   Your screen should be similar to Figure 5.1

Figure 5.1

The Employee Records form works well for viewing and updating the information in the Personal Data file. Now, you want to create several other forms to make updating information in the other tables easier also.

You decide to begin with creating a form for entering new city and zip code information into the City/State/ZipCode table. You decide to use a split form for this purpose. A split form is divided into two areas. The upper area displays the data from the record source table using a simple form design. The lower area of the form displays the record source as a datasheet.

2 **Close the Employee Records form.**

Select the City/State/ZipCode table in the Navigation pane.

Click Split Form **in the Forms group of the Create tab.**

Your screen should be similar to Figure 5.2

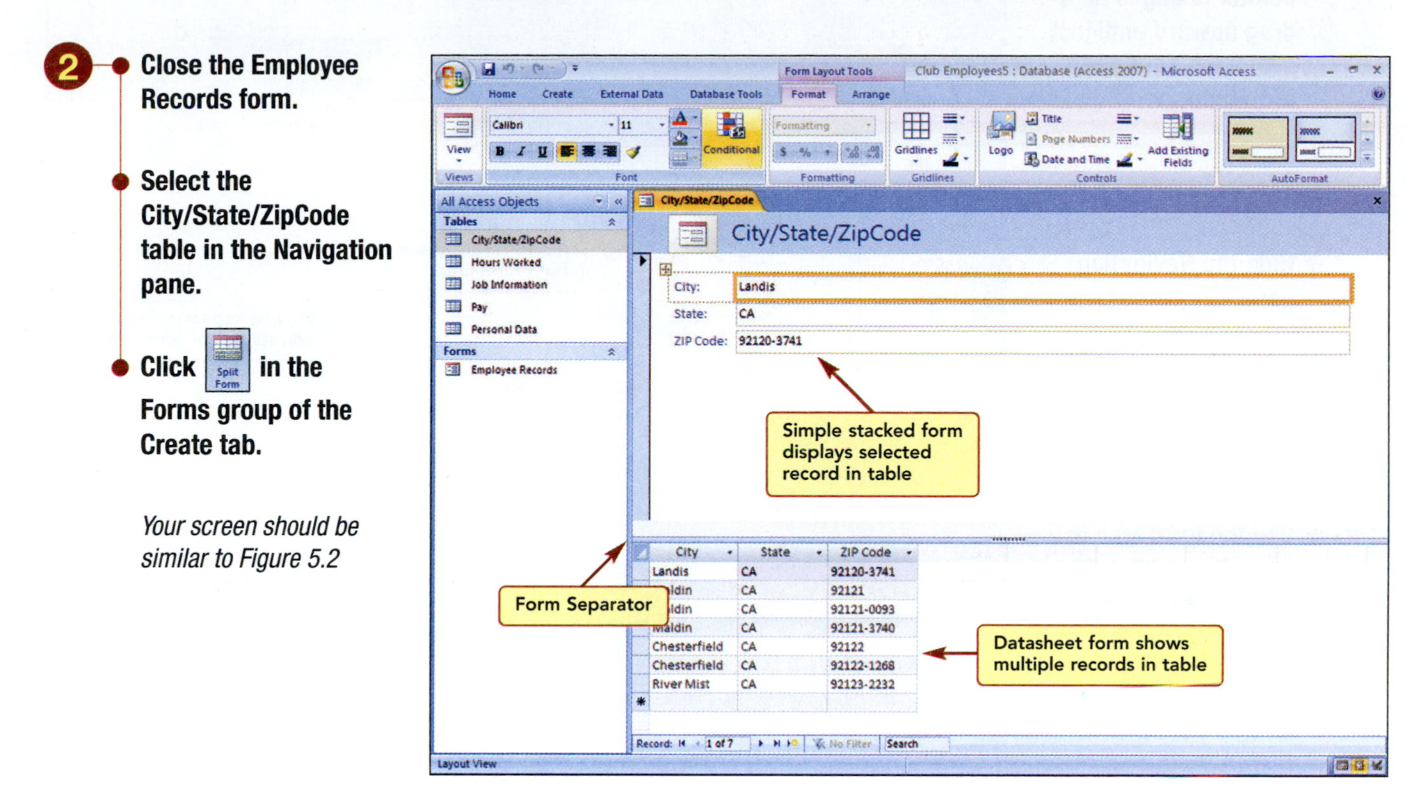

Figure 5.2

The form was quickly created and displayed in Layout view so that you can make changes to the form design. The three fields from the table are displayed as a simple stacked form in the upper section and the same data is displayed in the lower section as a datasheet. This form layout essentially gives you two views of the same data.

A splitter bar, called the **form separator,** separates the two areas of the form. Dragging the splitter bar allows you to resize the form sections, allowing more or less space for display of the datasheet. You will resize the datasheet area and then use the form. When using the form, selecting a field in the form section, selects the same field in the datasheet section. You can add, edit, or delete data using either section of the form. Generally, the form section is used to view and make changes to the data and the datasheet section is used to quickly locate records.

You will add a Zip code for River Mist that does not include an extension, in case this information was not available when entering the employee information.

3

- **Point to the splitter bar and when the mouse pointer changes to ‡, drag upward until just below the ZIP Code form field.**
- **Switch to Form view.**
- **Hide the Navigation pane.**
- **Click New (blank) Record in the Record indicator.**
- **Use the form area to enter River Mist, CA and 92123 in the respective fields.**
- **Click on the first record in the datasheet area.**

Your screen should be similar to Figure 5.3

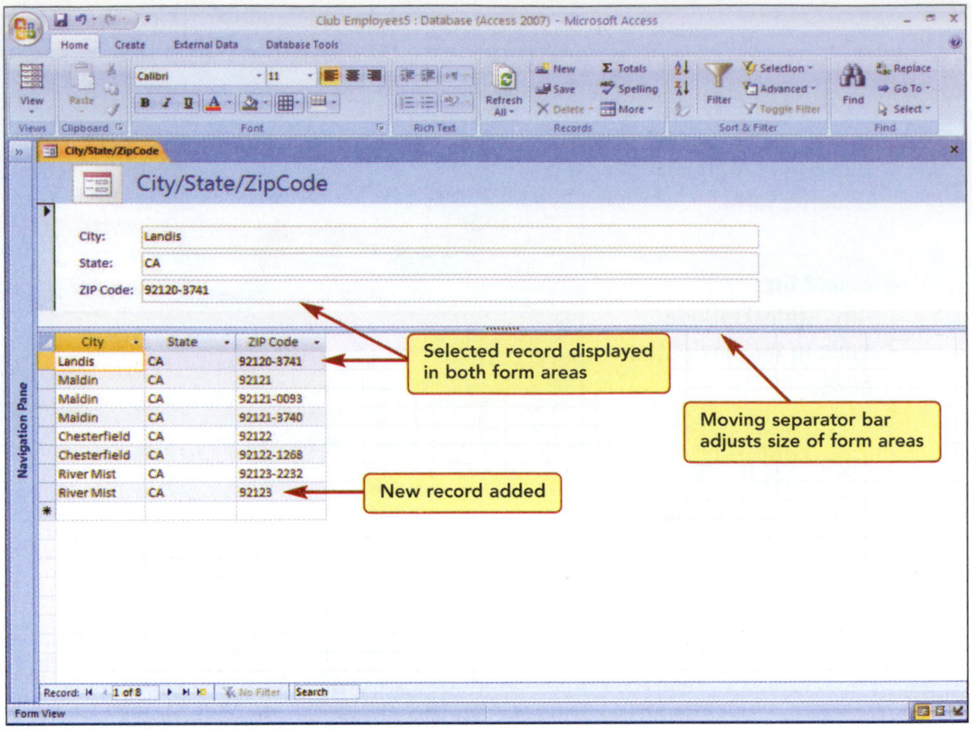

Selected record displayed in both form areas

Moving separator bar adjusts size of form areas

New record added

Figure 5.3

The new Zip code for the city of River Mist was added to the table and is now visible in the datasheet. The new Zip code will be available from the drop-down list when specifying this information in an employee record. As you saw, moving to a record using the datasheet area displays the selected record in the form area. The two views are synchronized at all times.

This form quickly updates the data in a single table and makes viewing and editing the data much easier than using the datasheet.

4

- **Close the form and save it as City/State/ZipCode.**
- **Display the Navigation Pane.**

Creating a Datasheet Form and Subform

Next, you will create a datasheet form for the Pay table. A datasheet form looks just like a table datasheet that you use to view a table, but in a form. The form can be modified like any other form, by moving and sizing controls and adding other controls and design elements. However, it functions much like a table datasheet.

1

- **Select the Pay table in the Navigation pane.**
- **Click More Forms in the Forms group of the Create tab.**
- **Choose Datasheet.**

Your screen should be similar to Figure 5.4

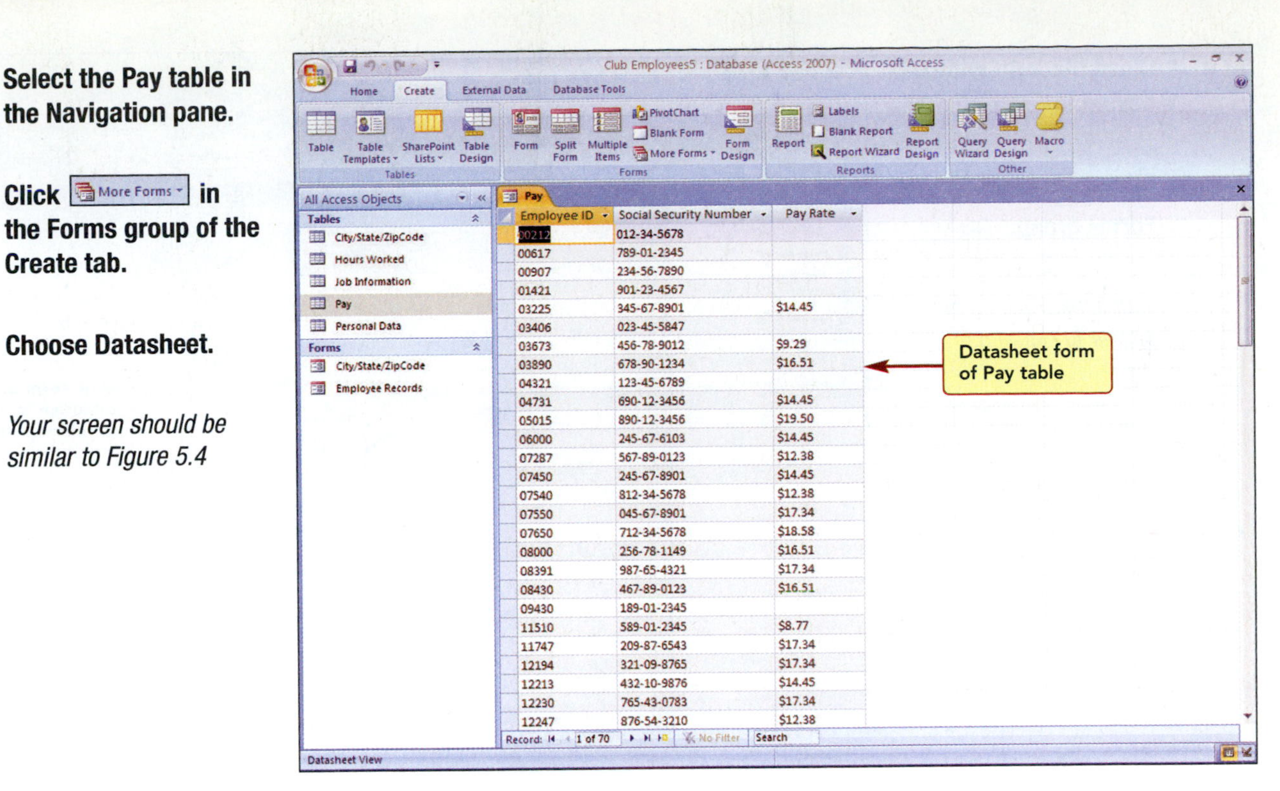

Figure 5.4

The Pay table appears as a datasheet in Form view. It can be modified like any other form by moving and sizing controls and adding other controls and design elements. However, it is not much different than working in a table datasheet. Where datasheet forms work well is when they are used as subforms.

Concept 1

Subform

1 A **subform** is a form that is embedded in another form and is used to show data from another table or query. The form that contains the subform is called the **main form** and the form/subform combination may be referred to as a **hierarchical form**, a **master/detail form**, or a **parent/child form**.

A main form can have multiple subforms. In addition, a subform can contain another subform. Subforms can be embedded within subforms up to 10 levels deep. For example, you could have a main form that displays sales reps, a subform that displays products, another subform that displays product orders, and another subform that displays order details.

Subforms are particularly useful to show data from tables that have a one-to-many relationship. For example, the main form could show the sales representative data (the "one" side of the relationship) and the subform could show all the products the sales representative is responsible for selling (the "many" side of the relationship).

Next, you will create a datasheet subform, again using the Pay table. Before you can create a subform, there must be a preexisting relationship between the main form and the subform. Your database already has a one-to-many relationship established between the Pay table and the Hours Worked table.

2 **Close the form without saving it.**

Click Form in the Forms group.

Your screen should be similar to Figure 5.5

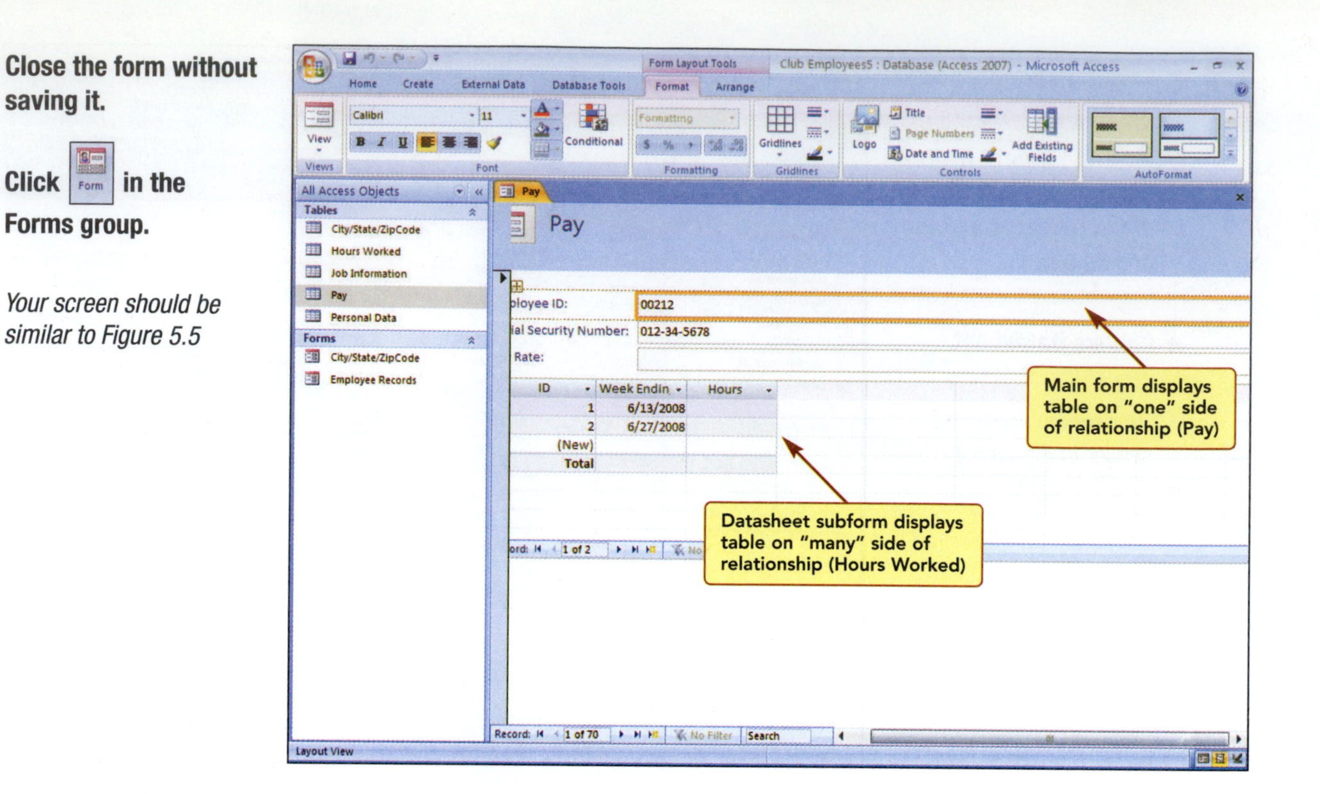

Figure 5.5

When there is a one-to-many relationship established between tables, the Form command will automatically create a main form for the table on the one side of the relationship and a subform for the table on the many side. The main form consists of a simple form that displays the Pay table data. A subform has been embedded in the main form and displays the Hours table data as a datasheet.

Although this form looks very similar to the split form, it is very different in how it works. In the split form, the datasheet area displays data from the same table as in the Form area, whereas a subform displays data from a different, but related, table than the main form. The two tables are also synchronized; moving to a record in the main form will automatically display the related data from the table that is displayed in the subform.

Switch to Form view.

Use the Record indicator at the bottom of the form to display record 5 in the form.

Your screen should be similar to Figure 5.6

Pay information for record 5 in main form

Hours Worked information for same record that is displayed in main form

Figure 5.6

The Pay information for record 5 is displayed in the main form and the Hours Worked information for the same record is displayed in the subform datasheet. Although you do not plan to change the hours worked data, you like being able to display the information from both tables at the same time.

4

Close and save the form as Pay.

Hide the Navigation pane.

Creating a Form for Multiple Tables

Although the subform works well and could be used to update information in the Pay and Hours tables at the same time, you would still need to open and update the Personal Data and Job Information tables individually.

Instead, you want to create a form that will update the Personal Data, Pay, and Job Information tables simultaneously. This will provide one central location for entering and updating the Club employee records.

MORE ABOUT

To learn about creating a form in Design view, see 2.5 Create Forms in the More About appendix.

Another Method

You also could use the Form Wizard to create a multitable form.

Using Form Layout View to Create a Form

You want to create a columnar form like you did when creating the Employee Data form but that will include data from multiple tables. In addition to the Form Wizard, you can create a form directly in Form Layout or Form Design view. You will use Form Layout view, as this allows you to see the data as it is added to the form.

1 Click **Blank Form** in the Forms group of the Create tab.

- If necessary, choose Show all tables from the Field List pane.

Having Trouble?

If the Field List pane is not displayed, press Alt + F8 or click Add Existing Fields in the Form Layout Tools Format tab.

Your screen should be similar to Figure 5.7

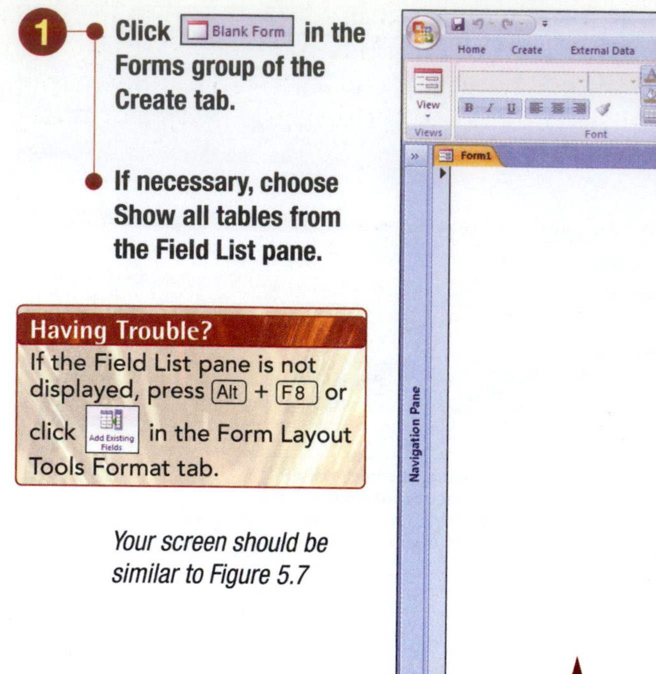

Figure 5.7

A blank form is displayed in Layout view. The Field List pane is automatically displayed so that you can begin adding fields to the form. Generally, when creating forms, it is most efficient to add the bound controls first, especially when they make up the majority of the controls on the form. Then you can add the unbound and calculated controls to complete the design. The Field List initially displays the names of all the tables in the database in alphabetical order.

Your main form will include all the fields from the Personal Data and Job Information tables. When completed, it will be similar to that shown here:

Employee Update Form | Add New Record

Personal Data

First Name: Roberta

Last Name: Marchant

Address: 564 Palm Avenue

City: Landis

State: CA

Zip Code: 92120-3741

Home Phone: (507) 555-6707

Gender: F

Birth Date: 5/13/1980

Company Data

Employee ID: 04731

Hire Date: 8/5/2001

Position: Fitness Coordinator

Location: River Mist

Having Trouble?
Review using the Field List pane in Lab 3.

You will add the fields to the form in the order in which you want them to appear to save some time having to move them around later. Because the Employee ID field is a common field in each table, it will be added only once so that it is not duplicated on the form. Using the Field List pane is the same as in Report Design view.

2 **Expand the Personal Data table to display the field names in the Field List pane.**

Having Trouble?
Click the ⊞ to expand the table.

- **Double-click on the First Name field name to add it to the form.**

Your screen should be similar to Figure 5.8

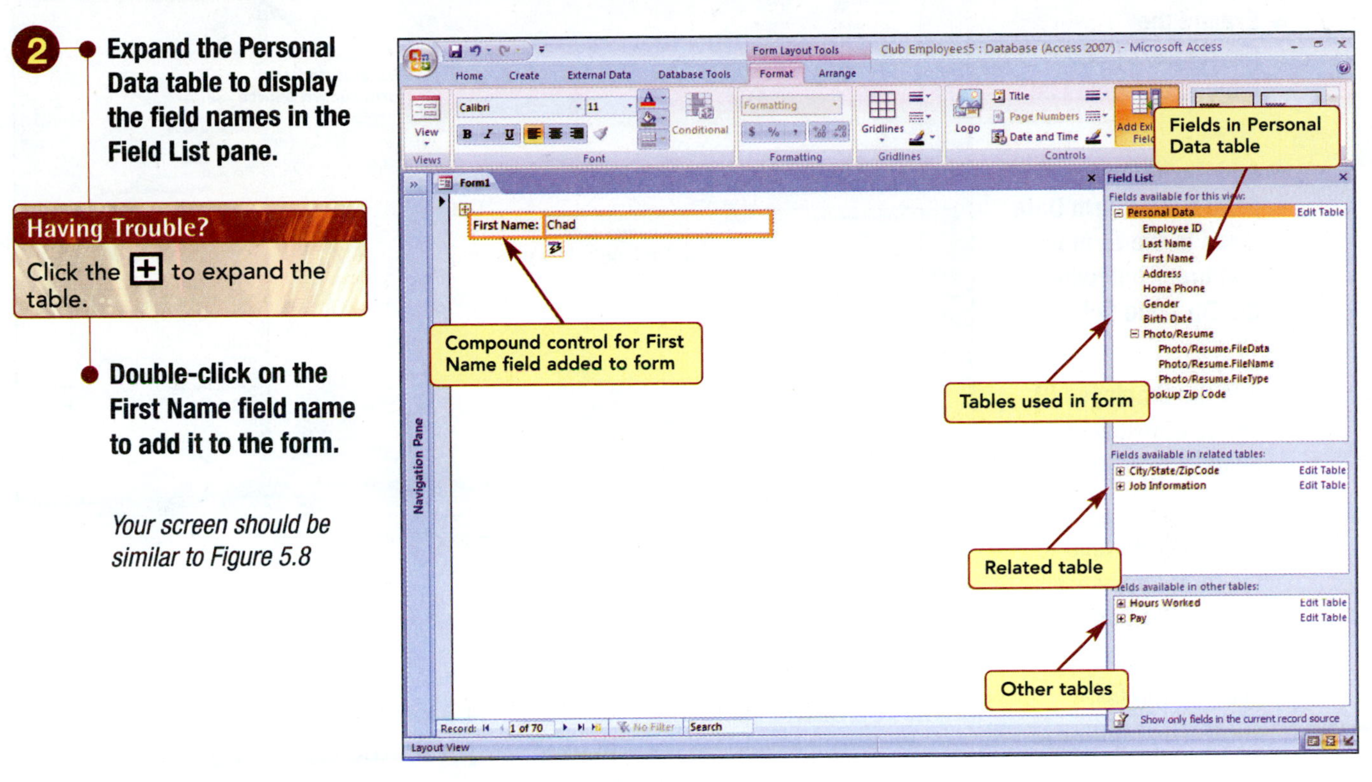

Figure 5.8

The selected field is added to the form. It is a compound control that consists of the label control displayed on the left and the text control on the right in each set of controls. When you select either part of a compound control, its associated control also is selected and the two controls will act as one when manipulated.

The control has been inserted into a stacked design layout. The Field List pane is now divided into three sections. The top section displays the Personal Data table. This section displays the tables or queries that are used as the form's record source. By selecting a field from the Personal Data table, the entire table has automatically been added to the form's record source.

Next, you will select and add several more fields to the form. Then you will add the three fields from the City/State/ZipCode table.

Having Trouble?
Review Form record source in Lab 2.

Additional Information
You can select and add several fields at once by holding down Ctrl while selecting the fields and then dragging them onto the form.

3 **Add the Last Name, Address, and Lookup Zip Code fields to the form in that order.**

- **Expand the City/State/ZipCode table in the Field List.**
- **Add the Home Phone, Gender, and Birth Date fields to the form in that order following the Zip Code field.**
- **Add the Employee ID and Photo/Resume fields.**
- **Drag the City field to the form above the Lookup Zip Code field.**
- **Click on the AutoFormat button.**

Your screen should be similar to Figure 5.9

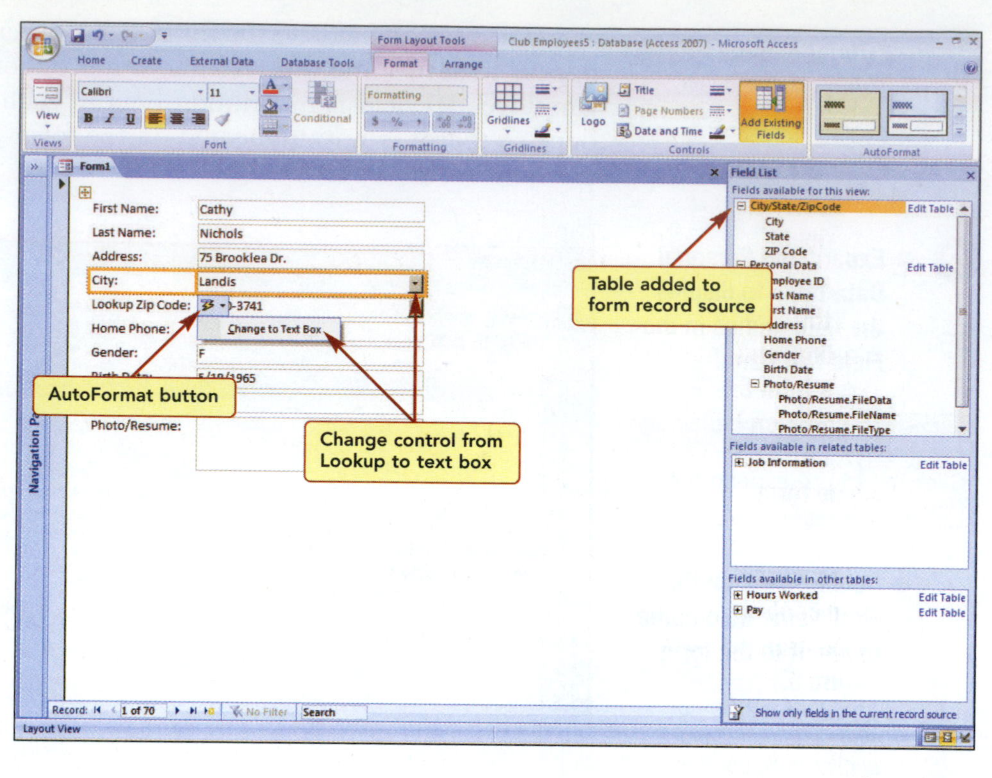

Figure 5.9

The City/State/ZipCode table was added to the record source and appears at the top of the Field List. Notice the AutoFormat button that appears below the City field. It can be used to specify the type of form control that you want associated with the control, in this case, a lookup field or a text box. You want the control to be a plain text box, not a lookup field, because the information in this field is supplied when the Zip Code is selected. You will make this change and then finish adding the fields that make up the Personal Data section of the form next.

4 Choose Change to Text Box.

- Drag the State field to the form below the City field.
- Add the Hire Date, Position, and Location fields from the Job Information table in that order to the end of the form.
- If necessary, move the form controls to the same order as in Figure 5.10.

Having Trouble?
If a field is missing, drag it from the Field List to the location in the form where you want the new field inserted.

Your screen should be similar to Figure 5.10

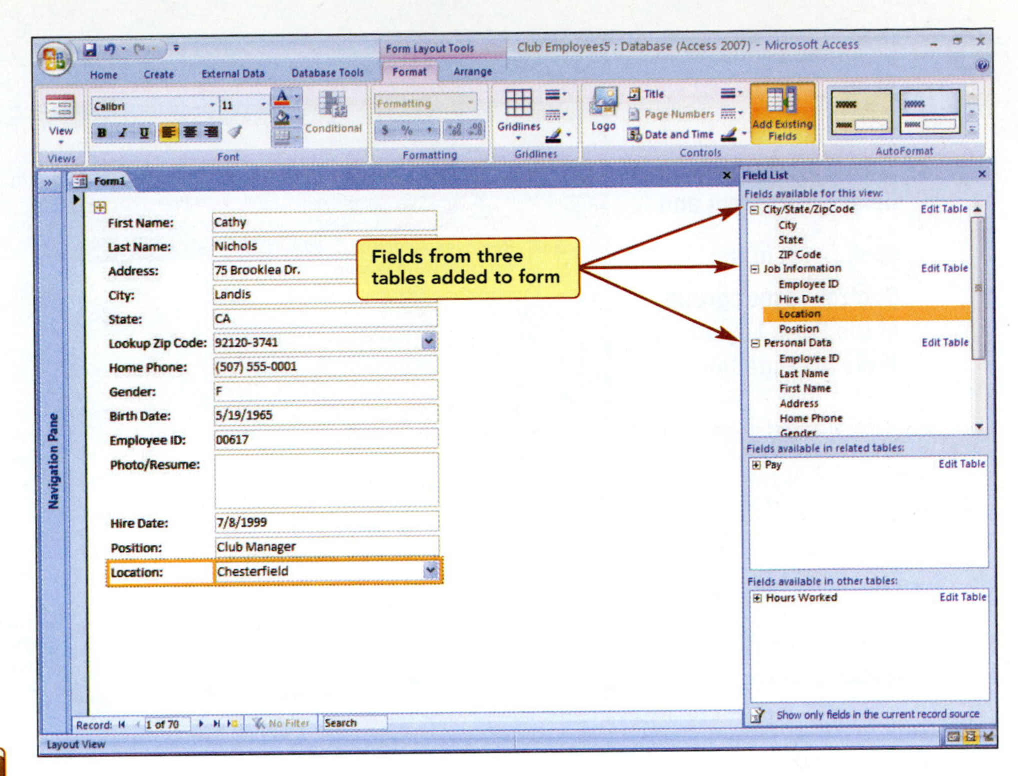

Figure 5.10

The form consists of fields from three tables. You will add the Pay data to the form shortly.

Rearranging Controls

The last five fields in the form make up the information in the Company Data section of the form. Because you want this data in a separate section of the form from the personal data, you will move them to a second stacked layout group. To do this, you remove them from the current stacked layout group and then add them to a new stacked layout group.

1 Close the Field List pane.

- Select the last five fields in the form and click Remove in the Control Layout group of the Form Layout Tools Arrange tab.

Having Trouble?
Hold down Shift while selecting each control.

- Click Stacked to add them to another stacked layout group.

- Drag the selected layout group down to separate the two groups as in Figure 5.11.

Your screen should be similar to Figure 5.11

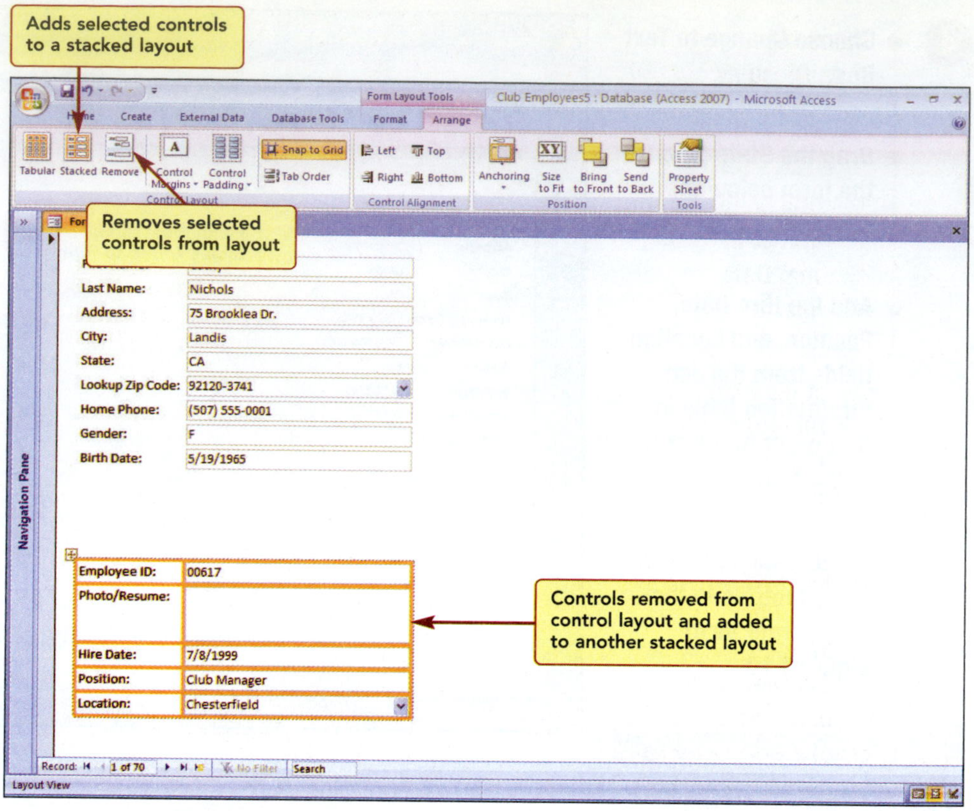

Adds selected controls to a stacked layout

Removes selected controls from layout

Controls removed from control layout and added to another stacked layout

Figure 5.11

As you look at the revised form layout, you decide to move the Photo/Resume control to the top of the form next to the name controls. You also will remove the Photo label control because, when a photo is displayed in the field, the control's content will be obvious.

2

- **Select the Photo/Resume control and click Remove.**
- **Drag the control up to the right of the Personal Data controls.**
- **Select the Photo label control (not the text control) and press Delete.**
- **Display record 3 and size the Photo control by dragging the lower-right corner sizing handle to fit the picture.**
- **Then position the Photo/Resume control as in Figure 5.12.**

Having Trouble?

Do not be concerned about the exact location of the controls. You will adjust them again shortly.

Your screen should be similar to Figure 5.12

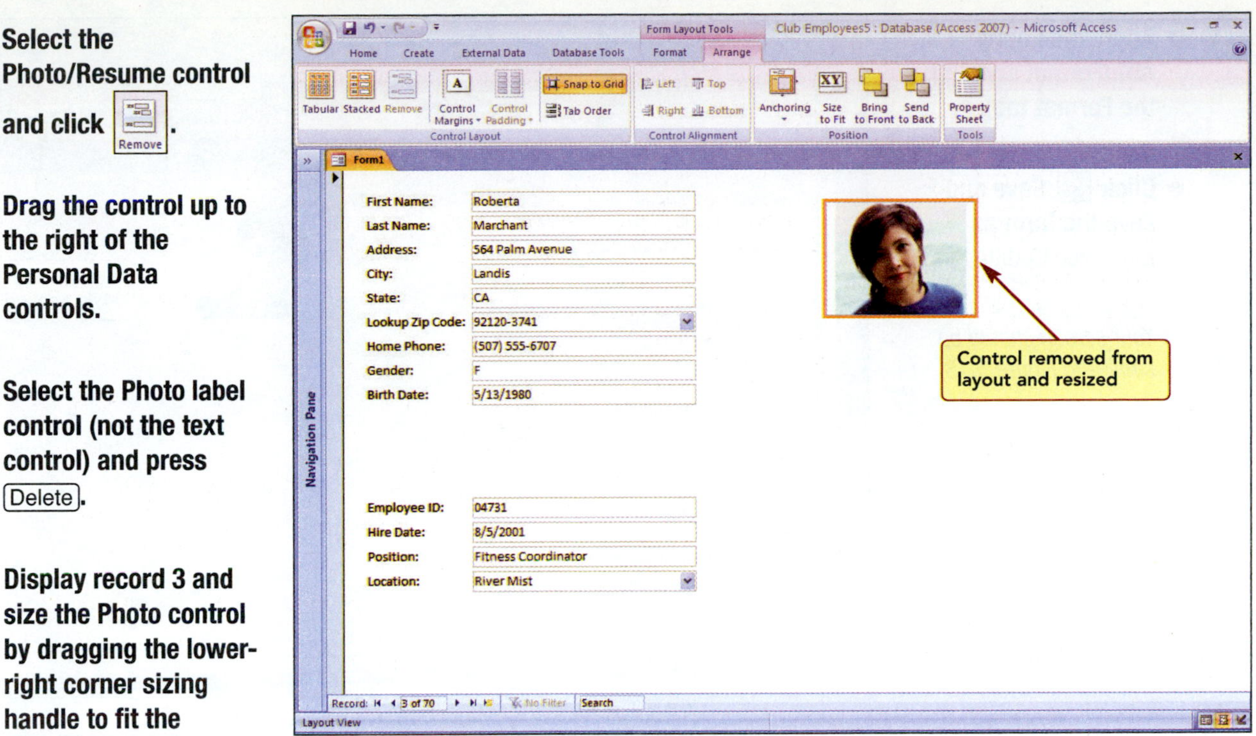

Figure 5.12

The photo size was scaled to the same size as the control when you adjusted the control size.

3 **Apply the Equity AutoFormat style (on the Format tab).**

- **Click Save and save the form as** Employee Update Form.

Your screen should be similar to Figure 5.13

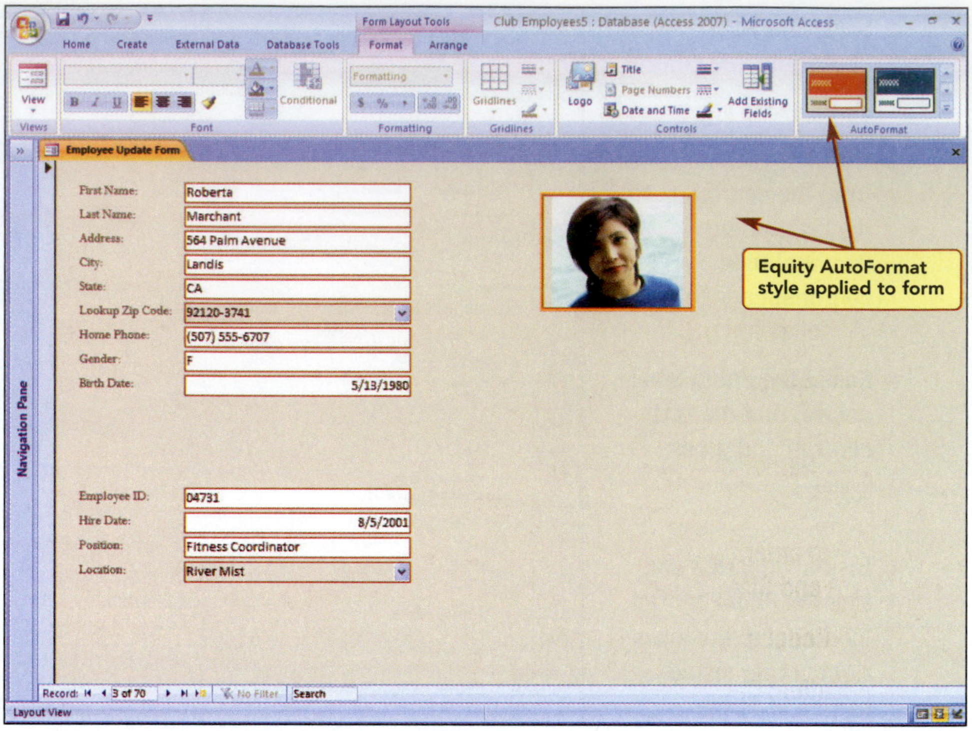

Figure 5.13

Each field you selected from the three tables is displayed in the form. You will continue to modify the form's content and appearance shortly, but first you want to test the form's ability to update the associated tables.

Testing the Form

You will use the new form to make several changes to your record to confirm that the form is operating correctly and see the effect this has on the related tables.

1 Switch to Form view.

- **Move to the Employee ID field and click Ascending.**
- **Display the last record and change the data in the following fields:**

First Name: **Your first name**

Last Name: **Your last name**

Try to enter data in the City and State fields.

Zip Code: **92123**

Location: **Chesterfield**

Your screen should be similar to Figure 5.14

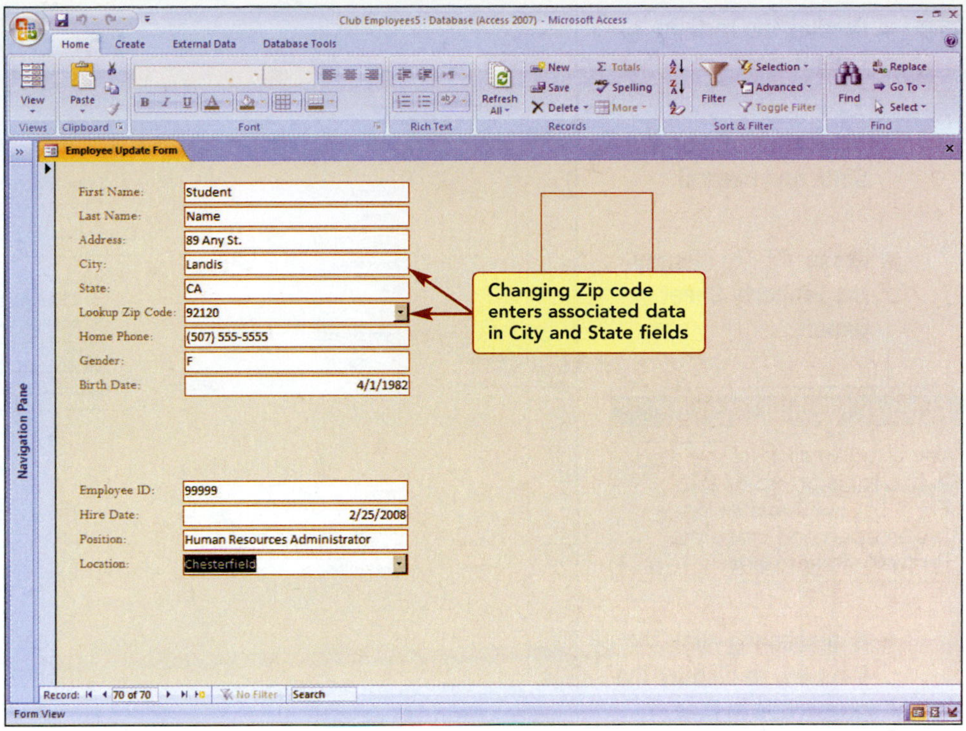

Figure 5.14

The changes were accepted in the name, Zip code, and Location fields but were not allowed in the City and State fields. This is because the City and State controls are locked to prevent entering data in these fields, as their information is determined by the selected Zip code.

Because there is always the possibility that an employee could live in a Zip code that is not listed, you need to change the Lookup Zip Code form control to allow you to add new data to the City/State/ZipCode table from within the form. To do this, you need to change the properties associated with the control.

Changing Control Properties

Every control in the form has properties associated with it that affect how the control looks and acts. The properties are automatically set to appropriate values, for the most part, according to the properties of the field in the record source. These include format settings, input masks, and validation settings. You will look at the property settings associated with the Lookup Zip Code field first and change its setting to allow data entry.

1. Display the form in Layout view.

- Select the Lookup Zip Code text control.
- Press F4 to display the Property Sheet pane.

Another Method

You also can click Property Sheet in the Tools group of the Form Layout Tools Arrange tab to open and close the Property Sheet pane.

- If necessary, click the Data tab to display the properties in that category.

Your screen should be similar to Figure 5.15

Additional Information

The All tab lists all properties.

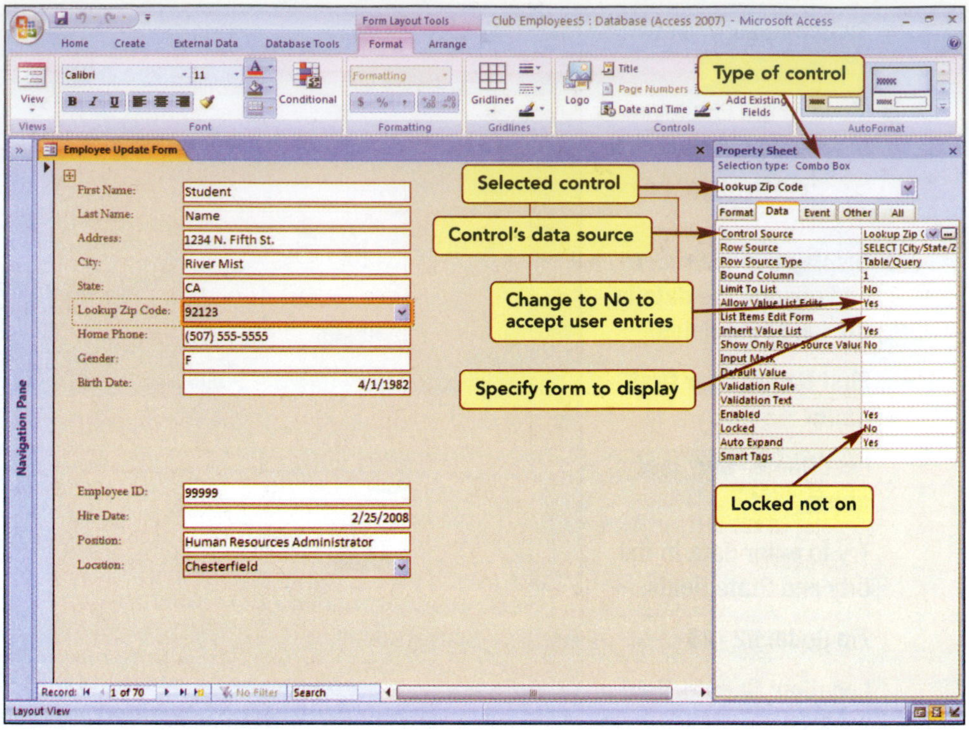

Figure 5.15

The Property Sheet pane is displayed. The type, combo box, and the name of the selected control are identified at the top of the Property Sheet. The control name list box can be used to select and display the properties for another control in the form.

The Property Sheet divides the controls into tabbed categories. The Data tab is open by default and displays a list of the properties associated with the data source for the selected form control. The Control Source identifies the Lookup Zip Code field as the data source. The Row Source identifies the table or query that is the source of the data for the lookup field and the specific row that displays the actual value to be displayed in the form that is the source of the data for the combo box control. The property that stops data entry in a control is the Locked property. It is currently set to No, which is correct for this field.

The properties that need to be set appropriately are Limit to List and List Items Edit Form. The Limit to List property restricts user selection to items in the list when set to Yes. The List Items Edit Form specifies the form to display to edit or add records to the associated combo box table.

2 Change the Limit to List property to Yes.

- Open the List Items Edit Form property and choose City/State/ZipCode.
- Switch to Form view.
- Select the current Zip code entry and type **92120** and press Delete to remove the extension.
- Press ←Enter.
- Click Yes in response to the prompt to edit the items in the list.

Additional Information

You also could open the Lookup Zip Code drop-down list and click Edit List Items... to open the associated form.

Your screen should be similar to Figure 5.16

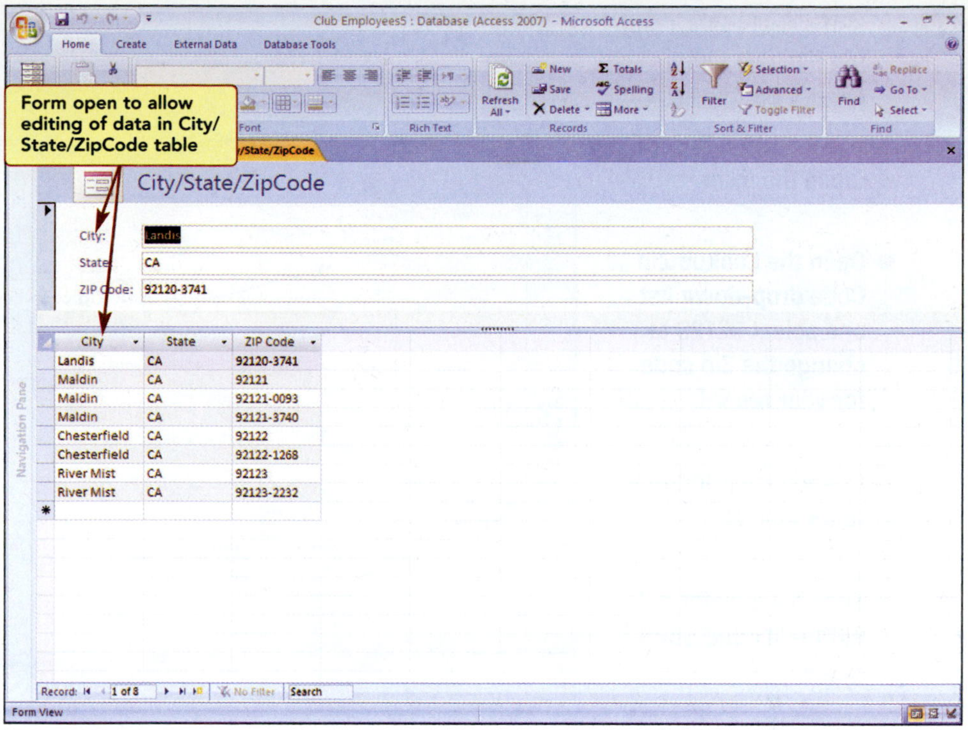

Form open to allow editing of data in City/State/ZipCode table

Figure 5.16

The form you create to add records to the City/State/ZipCode table is displayed. You can now add more zip codes to the list. Then you will use the revised combo box list to select the new zip code for the record.

3 Add a new record with the following data: **Landis CA 92120.**

- Close the form.
- Open the Lookup Zip Code drop-down list and select 92120 to change the Zip code for your record.
- Change your address to **89 Any St.**
- Then try to enter data in the City and State fields.

Your screen should be similar to Figure 5.17

New Zip code accepted and City and State fields updated

Figure 5.17

The form accepted the change in Zip code and automatically updated the City and State fields as needed. You still were unable to make changes directly in the City and State fields because they are locked. Now, you want to make sure each table was updated correctly.

4 Move to any other record to complete your changes.

- Display the Navigation pane.
- To confirm that the changes were made to the tables, open the Personal Data and Job Information tables, go to the last record, and verify the changes.

Your screen should be similar to Figure 5.18

Data in associated tables updated from form

Figure 5.18

As you can see, using a single form to update records in all tables simultaneously is a great time-saving feature.

5
- **Close the open tables.**
- **Hide the Navigation pane.**

Changing the Label Caption

As you look at the form, you decide you also want to change the Lookup Zip Code label control to simply display Zip Code.

1
- **Move to the first record.**
- **Switch to Layout view and select the Lookup Zip Code label control.**
- **Open the All tab of the Property Sheet pane.**

Your screen should be similar to Figure 5.19

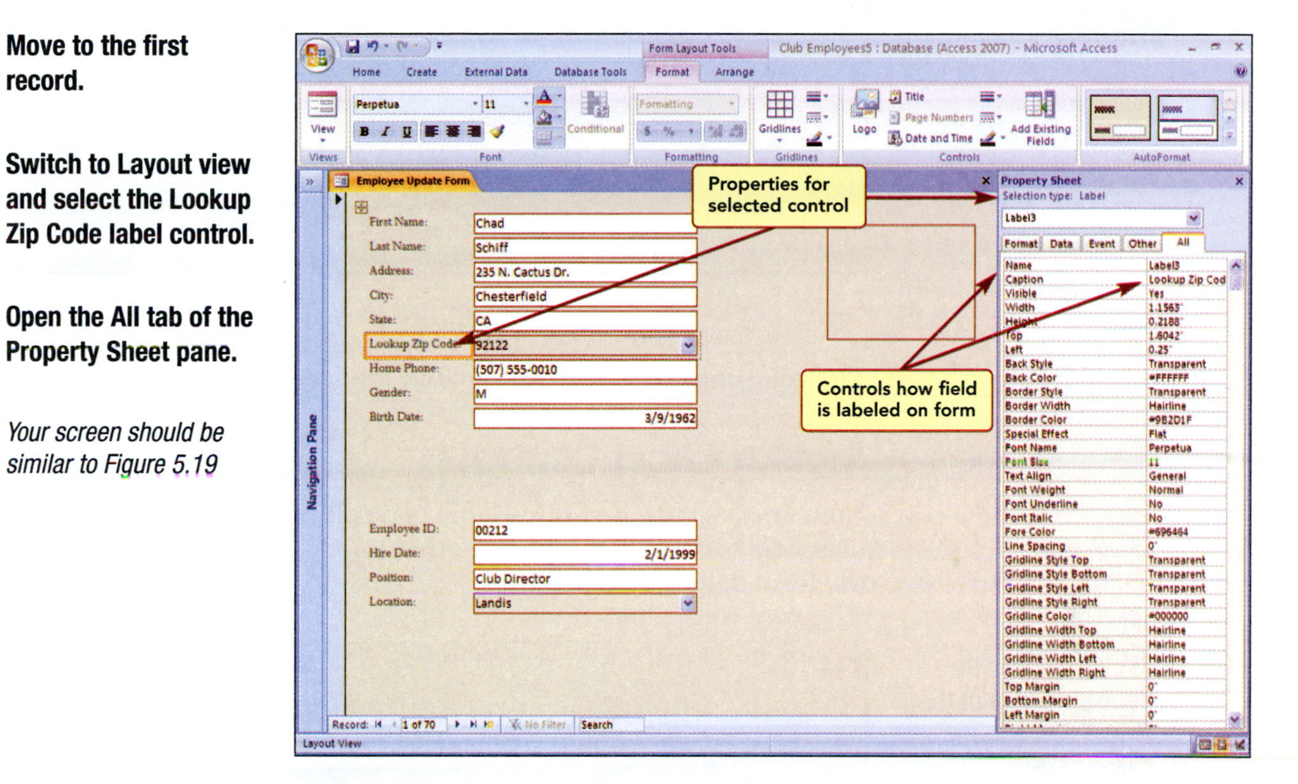

Figure 5.19

The Property Sheet now displays all the properties associated with the selected label control. The Name property identifies the label control from the Personal Data table that is associated with the Lookup Zip Code control. The Caption property controls the way the field is labeled on the form. It is the field name of the Lookup Zip Code combo box control to which it is associated.

2 In the Caption text box, select and delete the word Lookup and the following space.

- Close the Property Sheet pane.

Another Method

You also could edit the label directly in the label control box and the change would be reflected in the control's property sheet.

Your screen should be similar to Figure 5.20

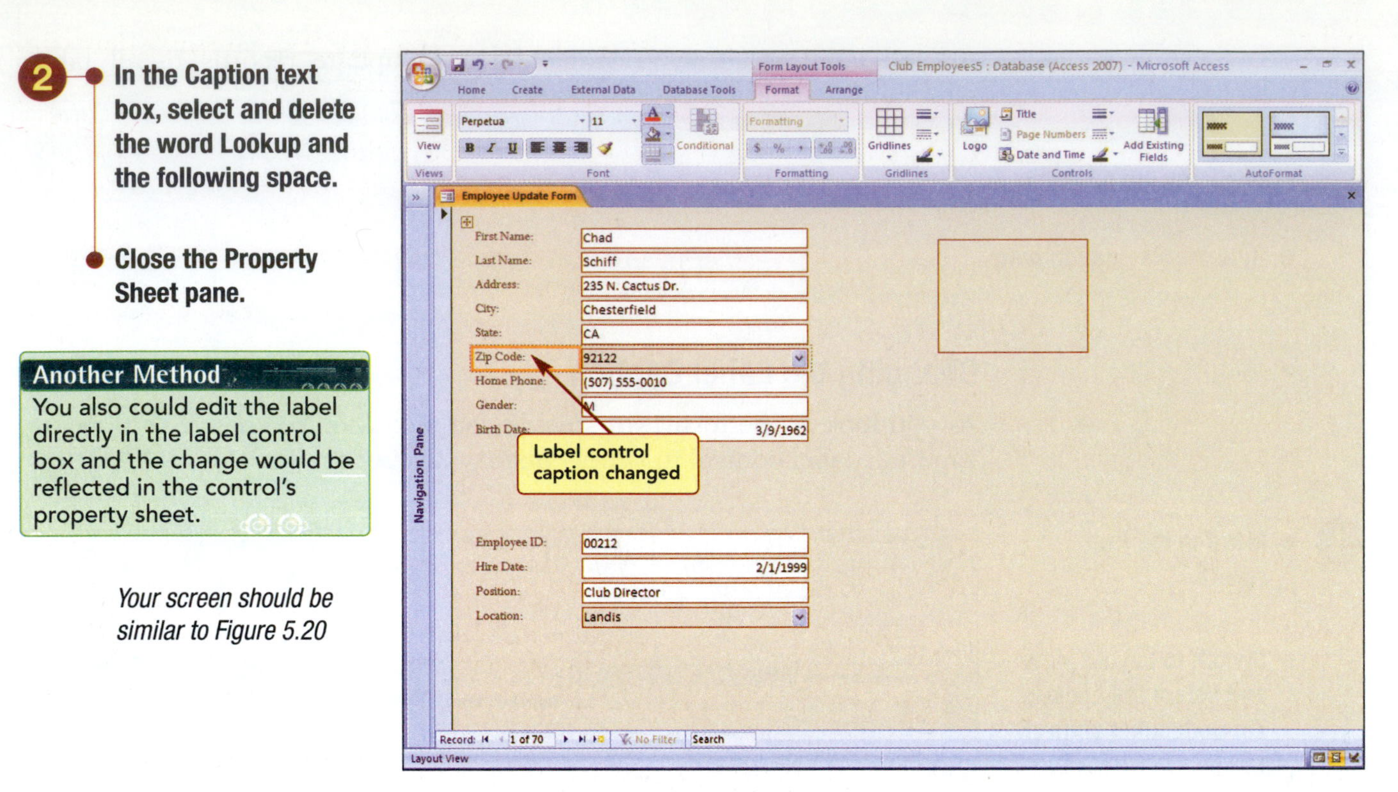

Figure 5.20

The label control reflects the change made to the caption.

Adding Label Controls

Now, you need to add three label controls to the form. The first label will be a title for the form and the other two will identify the two sections of the form.

1 Click Title in the Controls group of the Form Layout Tools Format tab.

- Reapply the Equity AutoFormat style.

Your screen should be similar to Figure 5.21

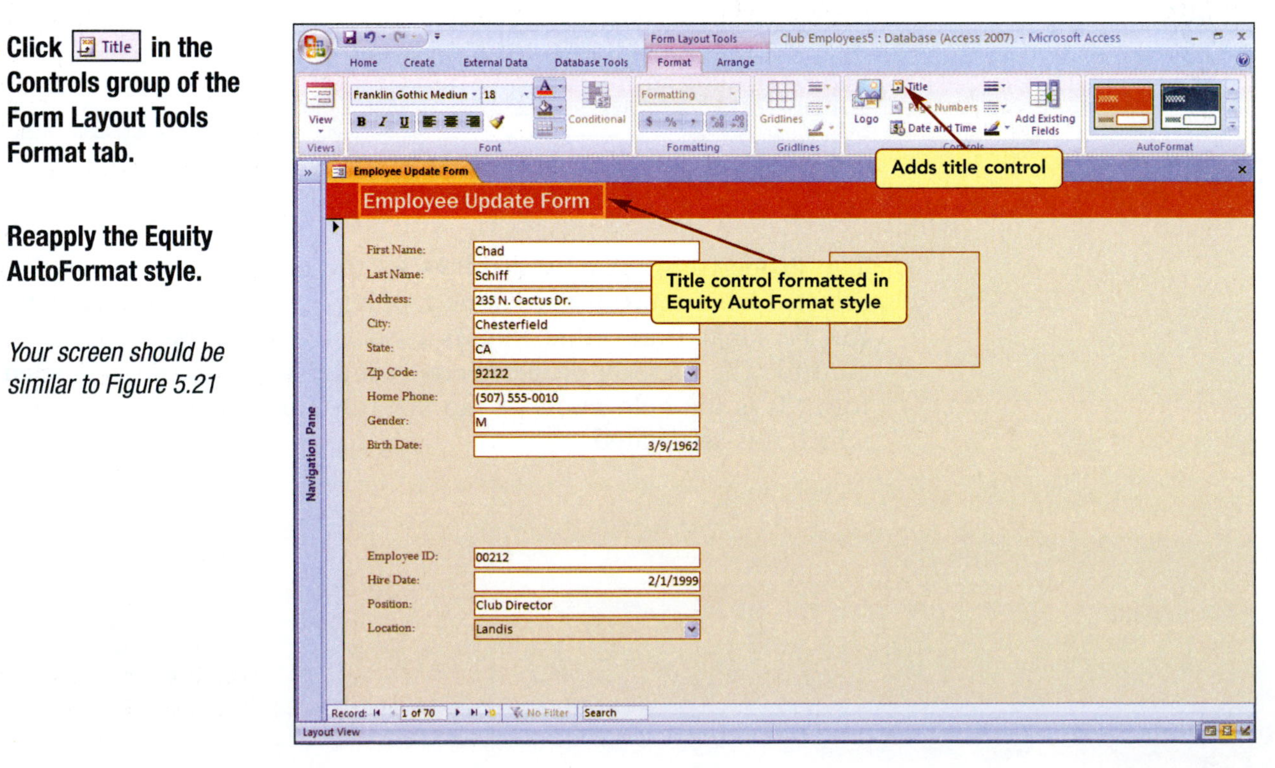

Figure 5.21

Additional Information

You will learn about text formatting shortly.

A title label control displaying the form name is automatically inserted at the top of the form. The text in the title label can easily be changed if you want by selecting the existing text and typing in new text. Also, by reapplying the Equity AutoFormat after adding a title to the form, a background color was added behind the title and the text in the title control was formatted according to the Equity AutoFormat style settings.

Next, you want to add the section label controls. Although many layout changes can be made in Layout view, some types of changes are not available and Design view must be used. To add label controls, you need to work in Design view.

Switch to Design view.

Your screen should be similar to Figure 5.22

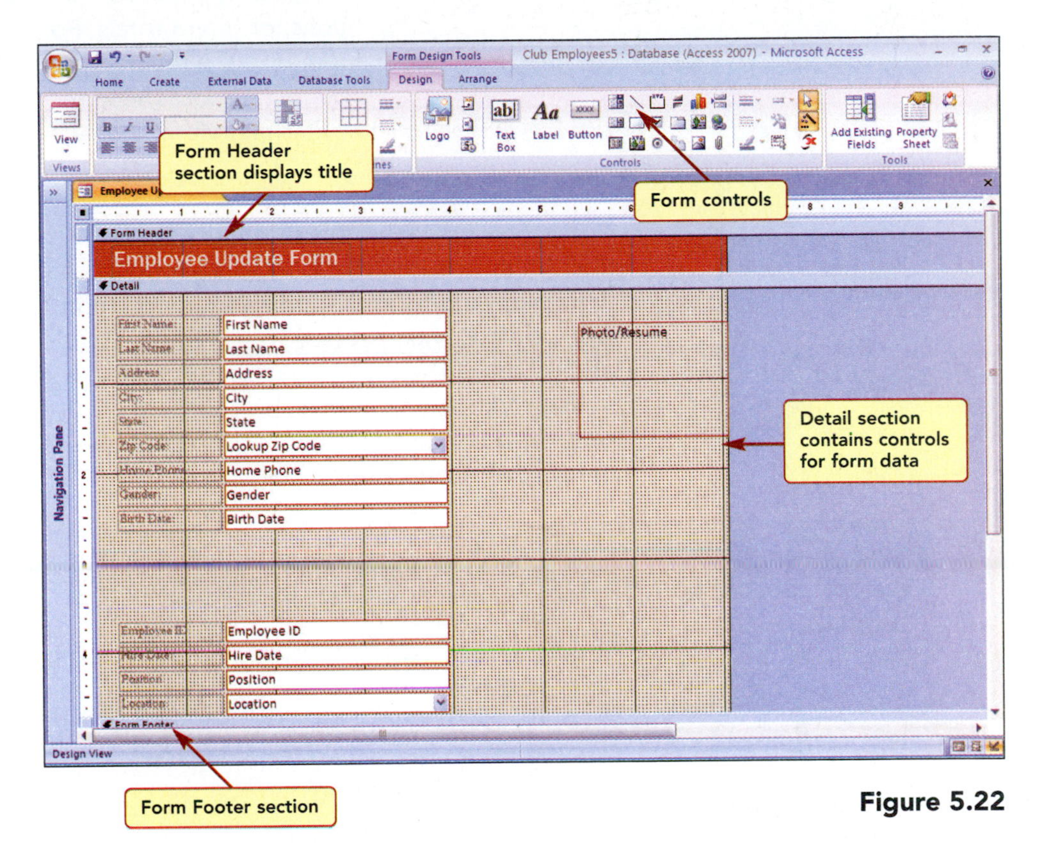

Figure 5.22

The Employee Update Form is displayed in the Form Design view window. Form Design view, like Report Design view, is used to create and modify the structure of a form. In this view, horizontal and vertical rulers are displayed to help you correctly place items in the Form Design window.

The Form Design window is divided into three sections: Form Header, Detail, and Form Footer. The contents of each section appear below the horizontal bar containing the name. The purpose of each of these sections is described in the following table.

Section	Description
Form Header	An optional section that you can include to display information such as the form title, instructions, or graphics. The contents of a form header appear at the top of the screen or, if you print the form, at the top of the first page. Form headers are not visible in Datasheet view and do not scroll as you scroll through records.
Detail	The area where the table data is displayed.
Form Footer	Another optional section that can include notes, instructions, or grand totals. Form footers appear at the bottom of the screen or, if printed, at the end of the last page. Like form headers, form footers do not display in Datasheet view.

Form Design view automatically displays the Form Design Tools Design and Arrange tabs. The Controls group of the Design tab contains tools that are used to add and modify many different types of controls. Notice the title control was inserted in the Form Header section so that it will appear at the top of the form when viewed onscreen.

To make space above the upper group of controls on the form for the section label controls you want to add, you first need to move this group of controls down slightly.

3

- **Click on any control in the upper section to select it.**
- **Click** 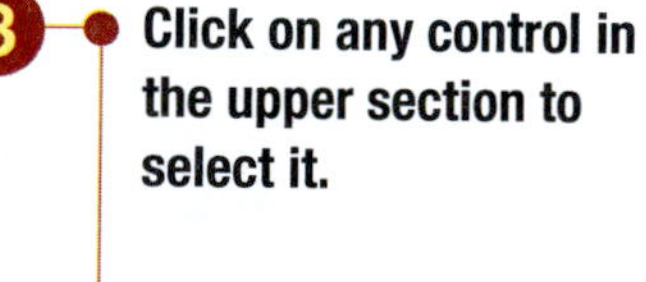 **in the upper left of the layout to select all controls in the control layout.**
- **Drag the group down until the top control in the group is even with the 0.5-inch position on the ruler.**

Your screen should be similar to Figure 5.23

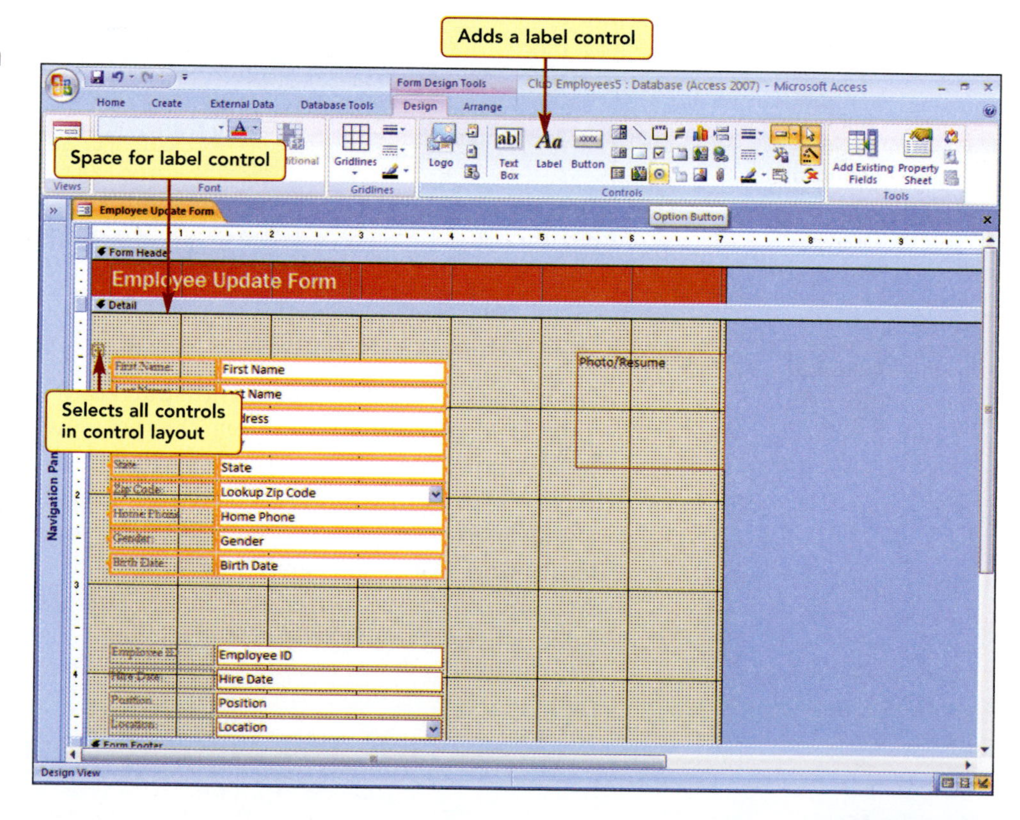

Figure 5.23

You will add a label control that displays the text Personal Data above the First Name control as the section heading. The Aa Label command in the Controls group of the Form Design Tools Design tab is used to add a label control to a form. The mouse pointer changes to $^{+}$A when this feature is in use. You indicate where you want the control to appear by clicking on the location in the window. Then an insertion point is displayed indicating that you can begin typing the descriptive label.

4

- **Click [Aa Label] in the Controls group of the Form Design Tools Design tab.**
- **Click above the First Name control to place the control.**
- **Type Personal Data.**
- **Press ← Enter.**
- **Point to the [◈] to read the advisory message.**

Having Trouble?
Do not be concerned if your control is not evenly aligned with the left edge of the form. You will learn how to adjust the alignment and spacing of controls shortly.

Your screen should be similar to Figure 5.24

Having Trouble?
See Concept 8 in Lab 3 to review controls.

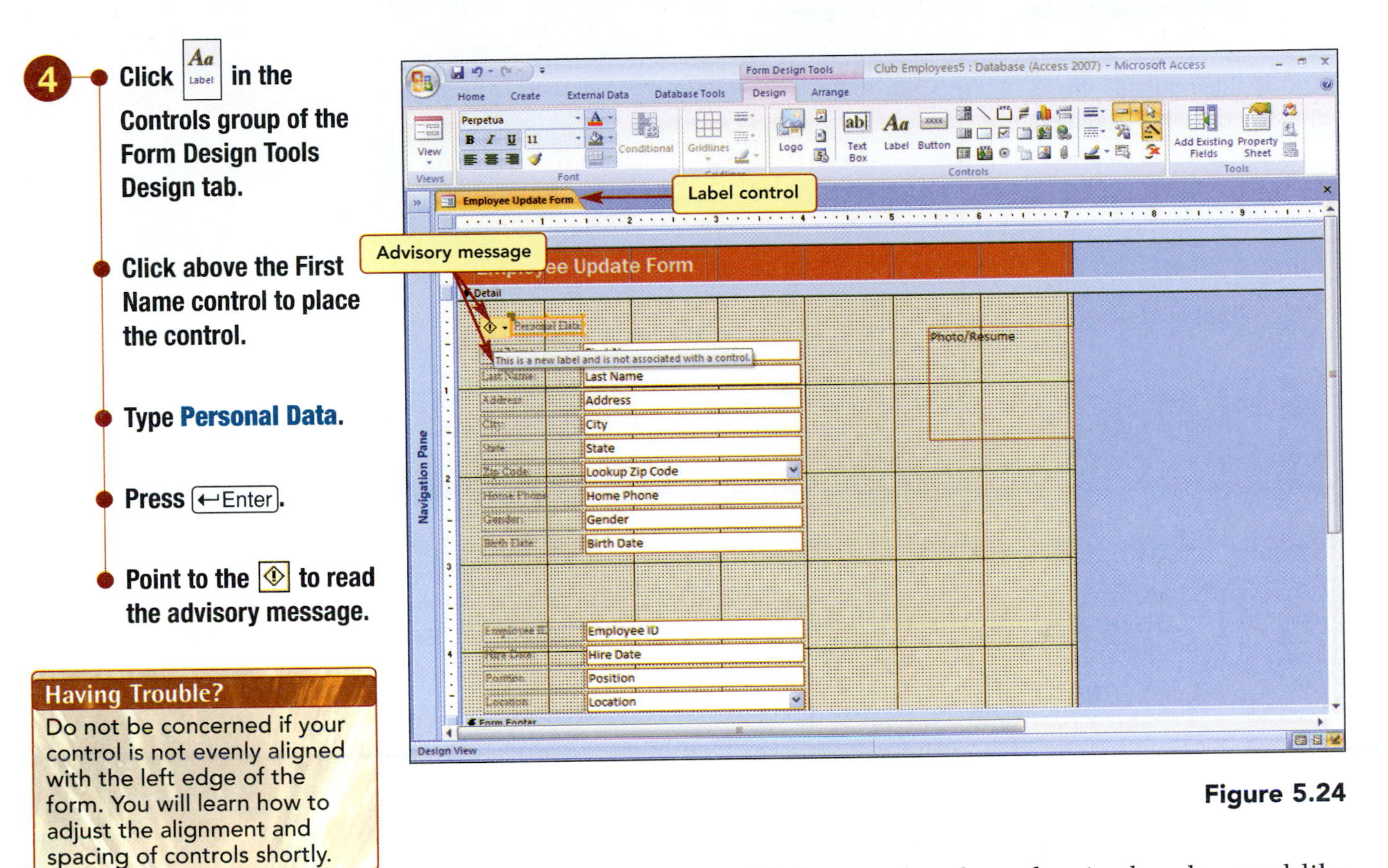

Figure 5.24

The heading appears in a label control and can be sized and moved like any other control. Notice the green triangle in the upper-left corner of the new label control. This is a warning that indicates that the label control is not associated with a text control, as explained in the advisory message. Unlike the label part of a compound control, this label control is a stand-alone control whose purpose, in this case, is simply to clarify the form.

5 In a similar manner, add a label control above the lower layout area that displays the text **Company Data**.

- Click outside the control to deselect it.
- Switch to Layout view.
- Select the Personal Data control.

Your screen should be similar to Figure 5.25

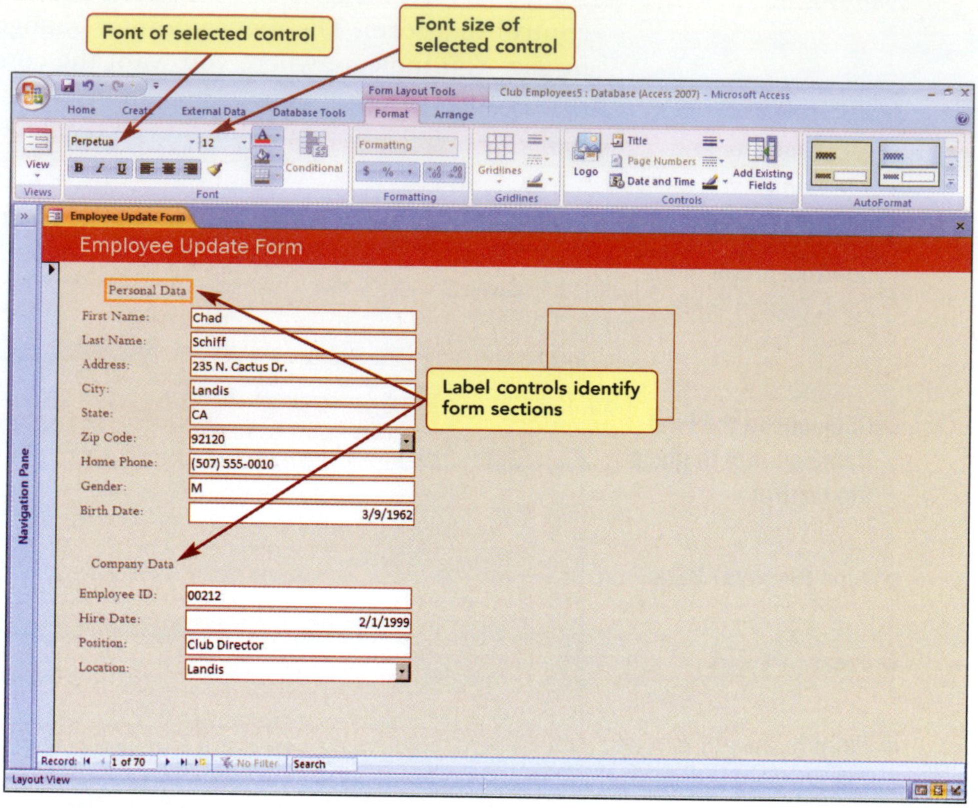

Figure 5.25

Although the two new labels identify the two sections of the form, their appearance needs to be enhanced to make them stand out better.

Enhancing Form Controls

Using a form AutoFormat automatically adds many visual enhancements to the form. In addition, you can apply different font and color enhancements to individual controls to further customize your form. Enhancements you can add include font and font size, text and background colors, and bold, italic, and underline effects.

Changing Font, Font Size, and Color

Because the two section heading controls are the same size and color as the other controls on the form, they do not stand out well. You decide to enhance their appearance by changing the font style, increasing the font size, and adding text color.

Concept 2

Font

2

A **font,** also commonly referred to as a **typeface,** is a set of characters with a specific design. The designs have names such as Times New Roman and Courier. Using fonts as a design element can add interest to your forms and give users visual cues to help users find information quickly.

There are two basic types of fonts: serif and sans serif. **Serif** fonts have a flair at the base of each letter that visually leads the reader to the next letter. Two common serif fonts are Perpetua and Times New Roman. Serif fonts generally are used for text in paragraphs. **Sans serif** fonts do not have a flair at the base of each letter. Calibri and Arial are two common sans serif fonts. Because sans serif fonts have a clean look, they are often used for headings.

Each font has one or more sizes. **Font size** is the height and width of the character and is commonly measured in **points,** abbreviated pt. One point equals about 1/72 inch and text in most documents is 10 pt. or 12 pt.

Several common fonts in different sizes are shown in the following table.

Font Name	Font Type	Font Size
Calibri	Sans serif	This is 10 pt. This is 16 pt.
Arial	Sans serif	This is 10 pt. This is 16 pt.
Perpetua	Serif	This is 10 pt. This is 16 pt.
Times New Roman	Serif	This is 10 pt. This is 16 pt.

Although you must apply font changes to entire controls rather than changing individual characters or words, you can apply multiple font changes to a table, form, or report by selecting and changing fonts for individual controls. You should be careful, however, not to combine too many different fonts and colors. Also, avoid using fancy fonts that might make it difficult to read the screen or are distracting to use for long periods of time.

Currently, the label control font is Perpetua, 12 points, and black font color as you can see in the Perpetua Font and 12 Font Size text boxes in the Font group. These settings were applied by the Equity AutoFormat. You will change the font and font color of the two section headings. You will select and modify both label controls at the same time.

1 **Hold down Shift and click on the Company Data label control.**

Open the Perpetua Font drop-down menu and choose Franklin Gothic Medium.

Additional Information
The font names are listed in ascending alphabetical order.

Open the Font Color gallery and choose Dark Red.

Additional Information
A ScreenTip displays the name of the color as you point to it.

Your screen should be similar to Figure 5.26

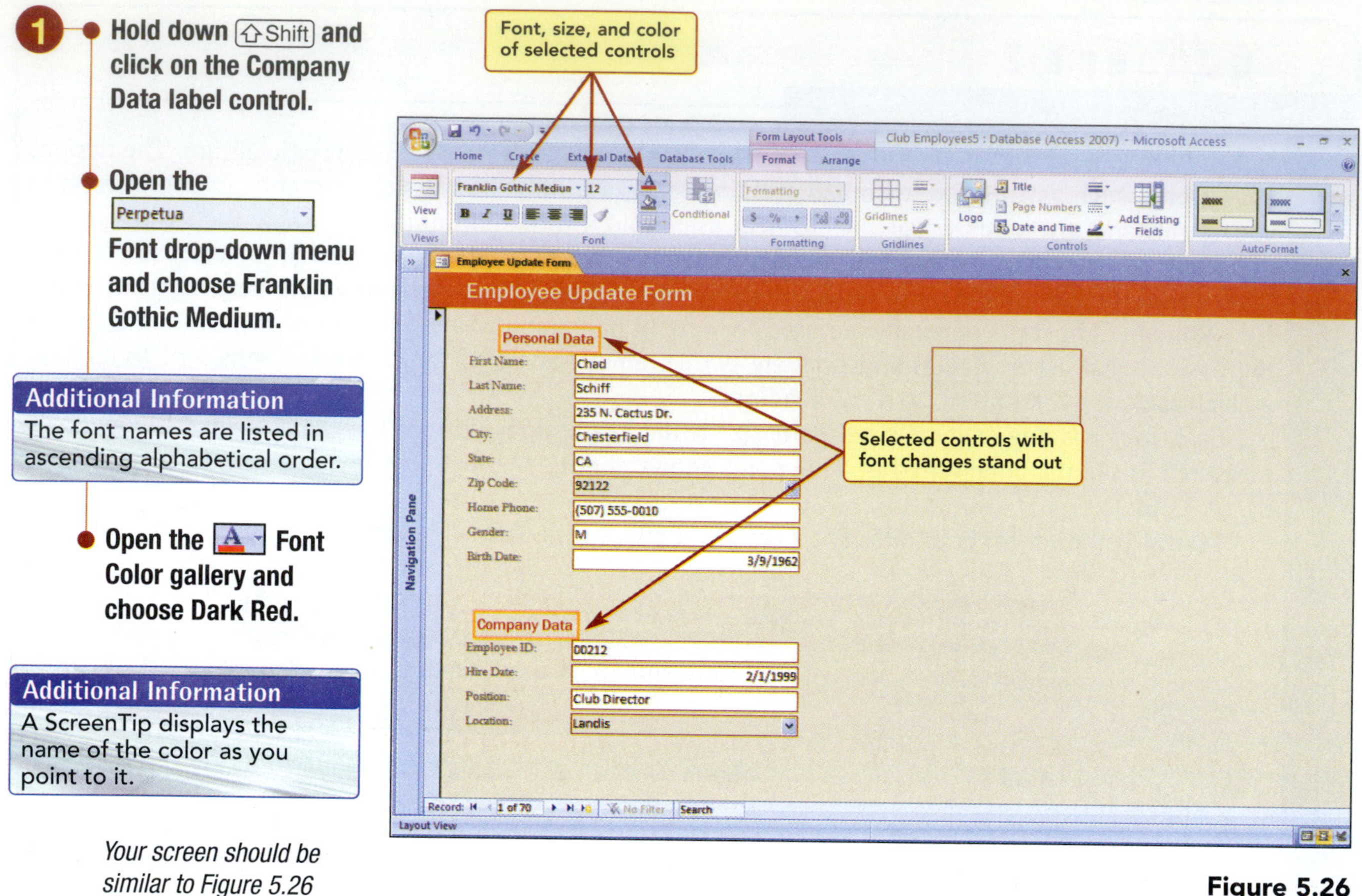

Figure 5.26

The change in font and the addition of color make the headings stand out from the other text in the form and clearly identify the form areas. The label control boxes automatically increased in size to accommodate the larger font. The font size of the label control is 12 points. This setting was applied by the Equity autoformat and looks good.

Changing Text Alignment

The last formatting change you want to make is to change how the text is positioned within the control. Fields that have a Text data type automatically left-align the entry within the control, whereas fields that have a Number data type right-align the entry. Because dates are values (numbers), they are right-aligned. You can change the alignment of an entry within a control to left-aligned, centered, or right-aligned. Changing the alignment does not affect the data type or other formatting settings.

You want to change the alignment of the two date fields to left-aligned so that they are the same as the text fields in the form.

Having Trouble?
If your date fields are already left-aligned, skip this step.

1. Select the Birth Date text control and click Align Text Left in the Font group.
   - In a similar manner, change the Hire Date text control to left-aligned.

Your screen should be similar to Figure 5.27

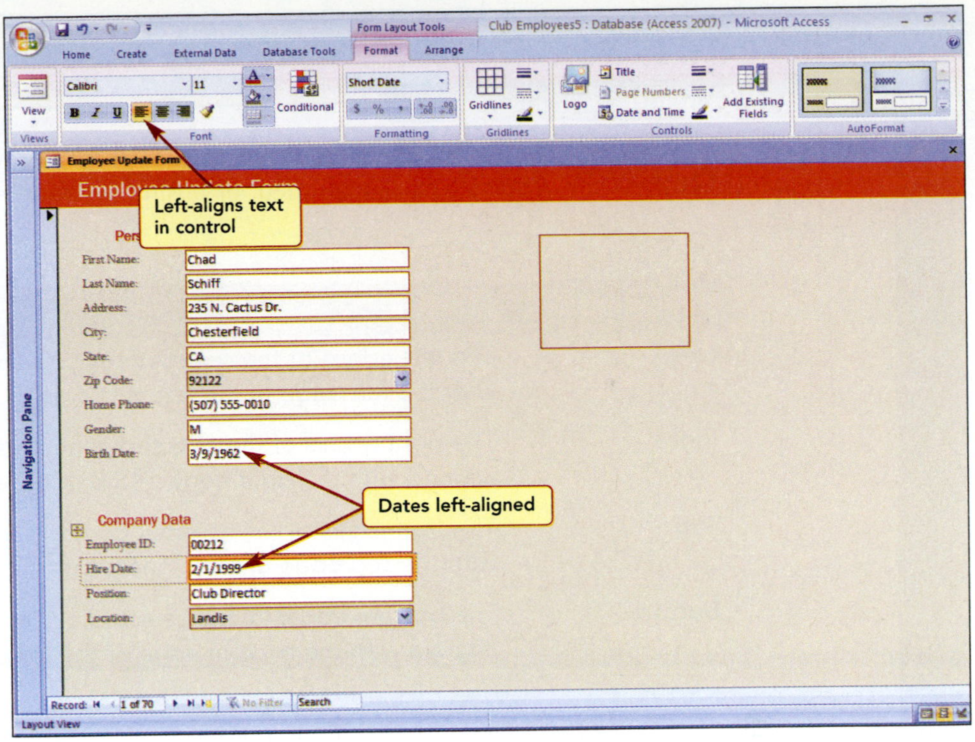

Figure 5.27

Now the date entries are left-aligned, making them consistent with the text entries.

Aligning and Spacing Controls

As you added and moved controls on the form, they are probably not positioned exactly on the form as you want them to be. To precisely position controls, you can adjust their alignment and spacing.

Concept 3

Alignment and Spacing

3 The position of controls on a form can be adjusted so that they are evenly aligned and the spacing between them is the same. Controls can be **aligned**, or positioned relative to other controls, in the following ways:

Alignment	Effect
Left	The left edges of the selected controls are evenly aligned with the left edge of the leftmost control.
Right	The right edges of the selected controls are evenly aligned with the right edge of the rightmost control.
Top	The top edges of the selected controls are evenly aligned with the top edge of the highest control.
Bottom	The bottom edges of the selected controls are evenly aligned with the bottom edge of the lowest control.

The **spacing**, or distance between controls that are not inside a tabular or stacked control layout, can be adjusted horizontally or vertically (see the following table). The Position group of the Form Design Tools Arrange tab contains the commands to make these adjustments.

Spacing	Effect
Equal	The space between selected controls is made equal by changing the space of the middle controls without changing the location of the outside controls.
Increase or Decrease	The spacing is increased or decreased by increments. In horizontal spacing, the leftmost control does not move; in vertical spacing, the highest control does not move.

In a tabular or stacked control layout, the spacing is automatically set between controls. You can quickly adjust the spacing between controls using Control Padding to a narrow, medium, or wide padding amount or to none. The default padding is narrow.

Aligning Controls

You can align controls in Layout or Design view. The advantage to using Design view is that it displays the ruler and a grid to show the exact placement of controls on the form.

 **Switch to Design view.**

Your screen should be similar to Figure 5.28

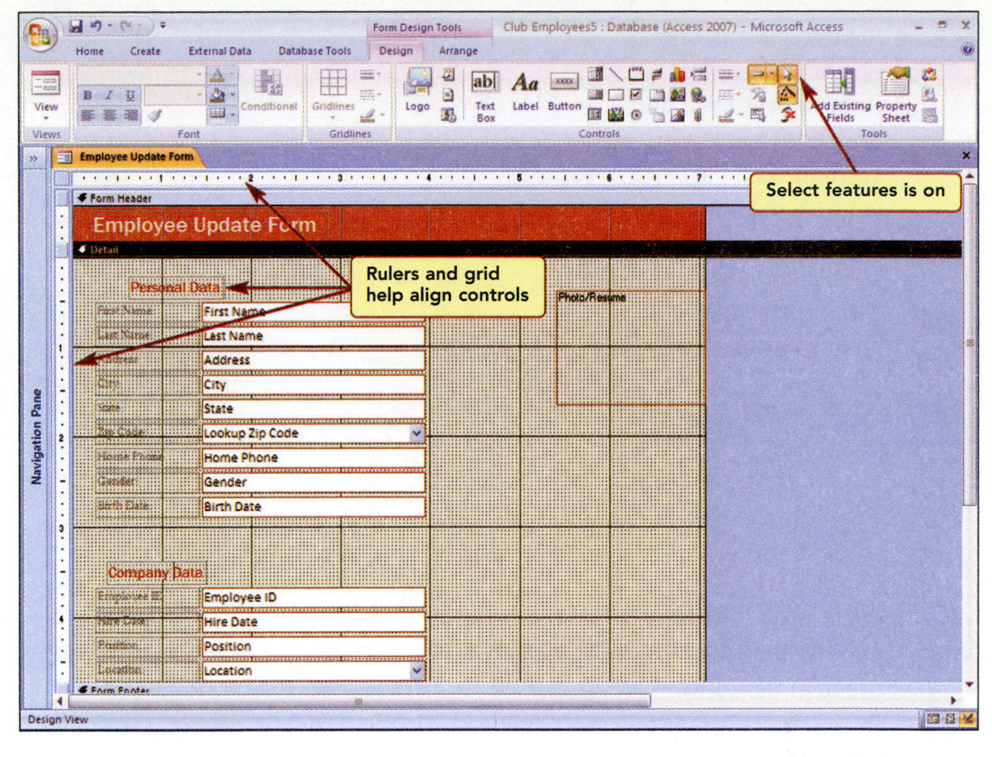

Figure 5.28

The grid behind the controls helps you individually precisely align controls on the form and the ruler identifies the control's vertical and horizontal location as you move it.

To position several controls so that they align with each other on the left or right edges of the controls, you first select the controls that you want to align that are in the same column. To align controls with the top or bottom edges, you first select the controls you want aligned with each other that are in the same row.

Additional Information

If a control is selected in a group that you do not want selected, you can deselect individual controls by holding down ⇧Shift and clicking the control.

A quick way to select a group of adjacent controls is to drag a selection box around the controls. To select the controls using this method, click Select in the Controls group of the Form Design Tools Design tab, point to a blank area above the first control, and click and drag a rectangle over the controls you want to select. The Select button is the default button and is always selected if no other button is in use.

First, you will left-align the two heading label controls with the controls in the two layout groups. The controls in the layout groups are already left-aligned with each other.

2 Point to a blank area above the Personal Data control, click and drag until a box surrounds all the controls in both sections on the left side of the form, and then release the mouse button.

Additional Information

The box does not need to fully enclose the fields. A field that is partially in the box will still be selected.

- Click Left in the Control Alignment group of the Form Design Tools Arrange tab.

Your screen should be similar to Figure 5.29

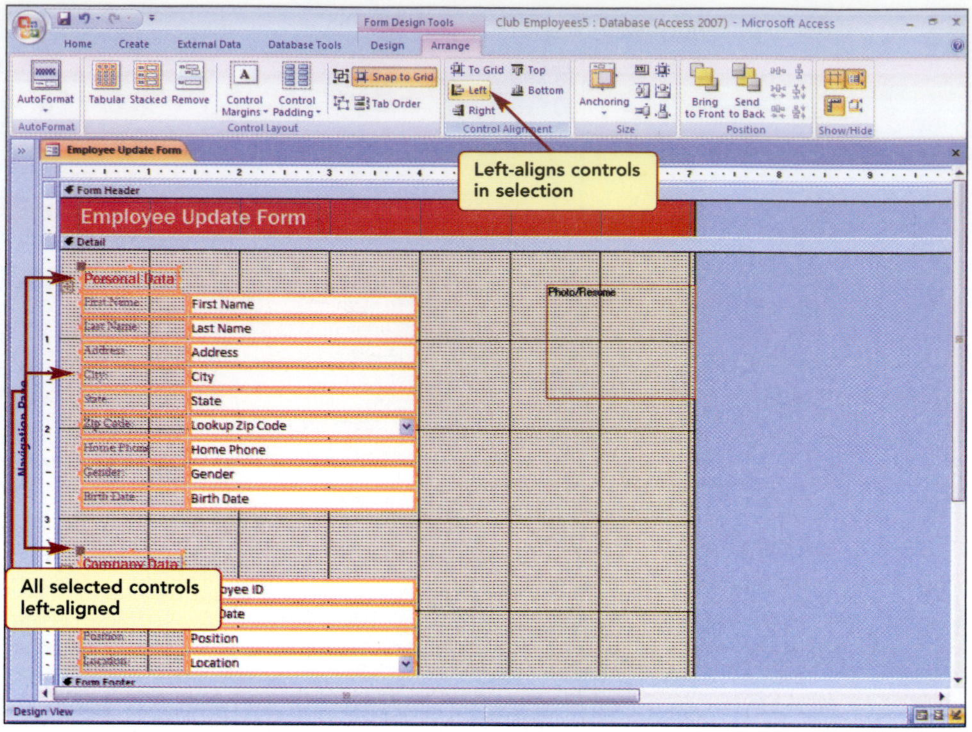

Left-aligns controls in selection

All selected controls left-aligned

Figure 5.29

All the controls in the selection are evenly aligned with the leftmost controls in the selection.

Next, you want to top-align the photo control with the First Name control.

Additional Information

When aligning controls, select only controls that are in the same row or column.

3 Click outside the selected controls to clear the selection.

- Move the Photo/Resume control closer to the Personal Data controls and lower than the first name control if necessary.
- Select the First Name and Photo controls.
- Click Top in the Control Alignment group.

Your screen should be similar to Figure 5.30

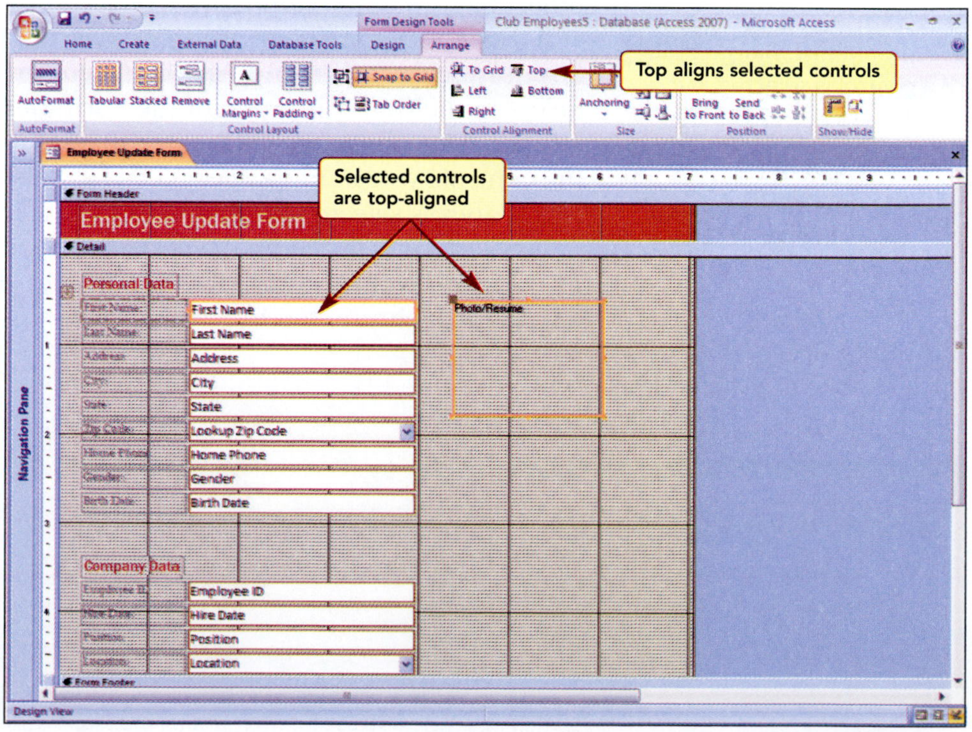

Top aligns selected controls

Selected controls are top-aligned

Figure 5.30

Spacing Controls

Finally, you want to increase the spacing between all the controls in both control layouts. You will move the bottom group of controls down first to create extra space between the control layouts.

1

- **Select the Company Data label control and the four following controls and move them down until the Employee ID control top-aligns with the 4-inch position on the ruler.**
- **Select the controls in both layout groups.**
- **Click  in the Control Layout group of the Form Design Tools Arrange tab.**
- **Choose Medium from the drop-down list.**
- **Deselect the controls.**

Your screen should be similar to Figure 5.31

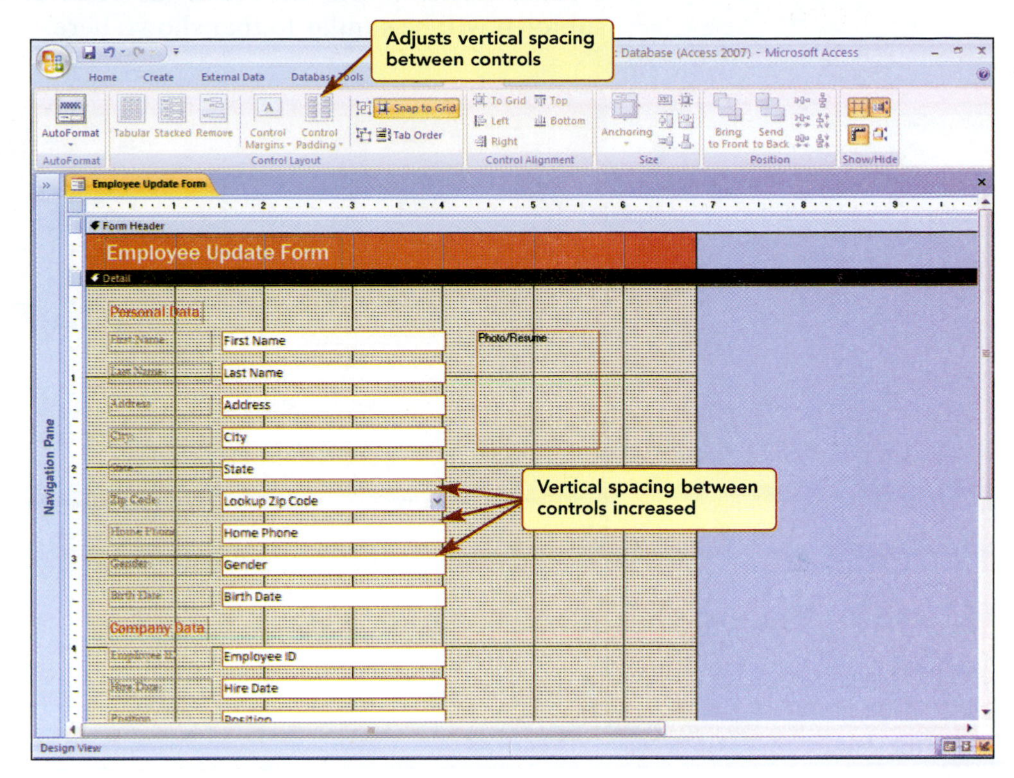

Figure 5.31

The vertical space between controls within each control layout has increased by adding padding space between controls.

2

- **Switch to Layout view.**
- **If necessary, readjust the position of the controls on the form as in Figure 5.32.**
- **If necessary, top-align the Photo and First Name controls again.**

Your screen should be similar to Figure 5.32

Figure 5.32

Adding Subforms

The appearance of the form is much improved. Now that the main form is complete, you want to add the information displayed in the Pay form you created earlier to the form as a subform. Your completed form with the subform will be similar to that shown here.

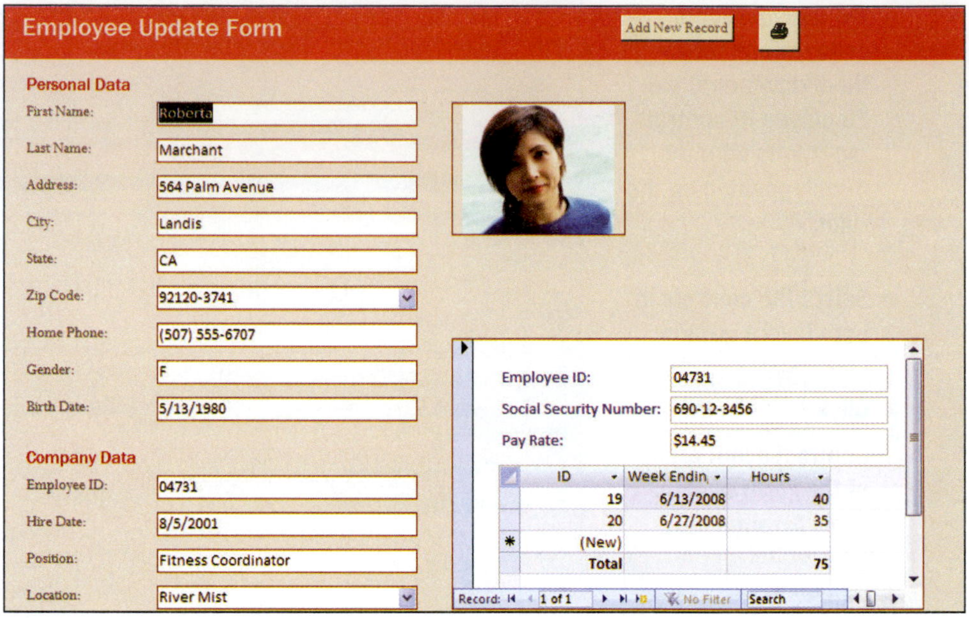

Using Control Wizards

You will use the Control Wizards tool to assist in the process of creating the subform. Control Wizards are available for several of the controls you may want to create. Depending upon the control you select, the related Control Wizard is automatically started.

1 **Switch to Design view.**

- **If necessary, click Control Wizards in the Controls group to turn on this feature.**

Additional Information

The Control Wizard button is highlighted when the feature is on.

- **Click Subform/Subreport in the Controls group.**

Additional Information

The mouse pointer turns to $^{+}$, signifying that the program is ready to create the subform object.

- **Click in the Detail section of the form below the Photo control to create a subform box object.**

Your screen should be similar to Figure 5.33

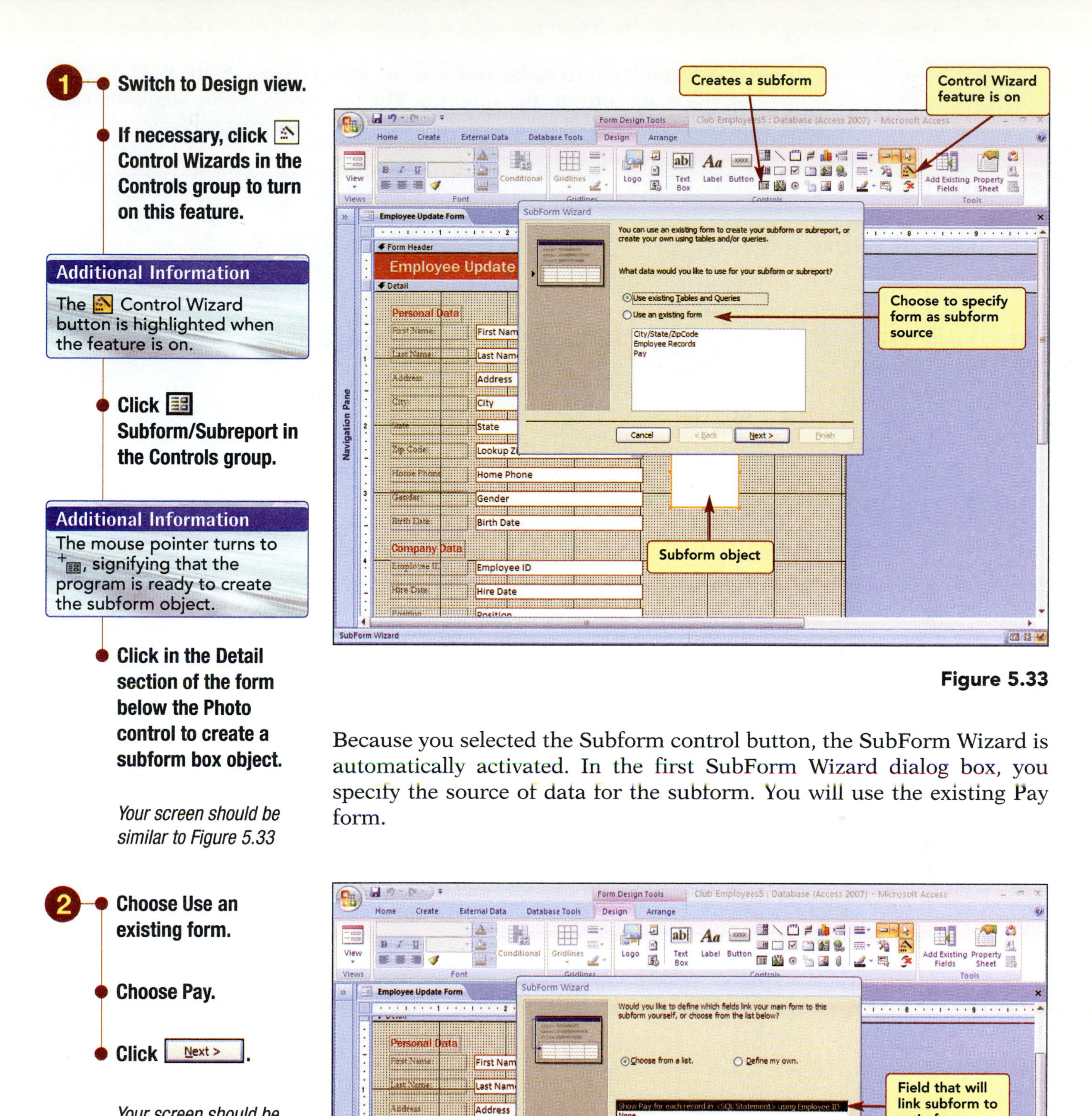

Figure 5.33

Because you selected the Subform control button, the SubForm Wizard is automatically activated. In the first SubForm Wizard dialog box, you specify the source of data for the subform. You will use the existing Pay form.

2 **Choose Use an existing form.**

- **Choose Pay.**
- **Click Next >.**

Your screen should be similar to Figure 5.34

Figure 5.34

In the second wizard dialog box, you are asked to specify the field that will link the main form to the subform. The list box correctly suggests using the Employee ID field that is defined in the Pay form's properties.

3 Click Next >.

Your screen should be similar to Figure 5.35

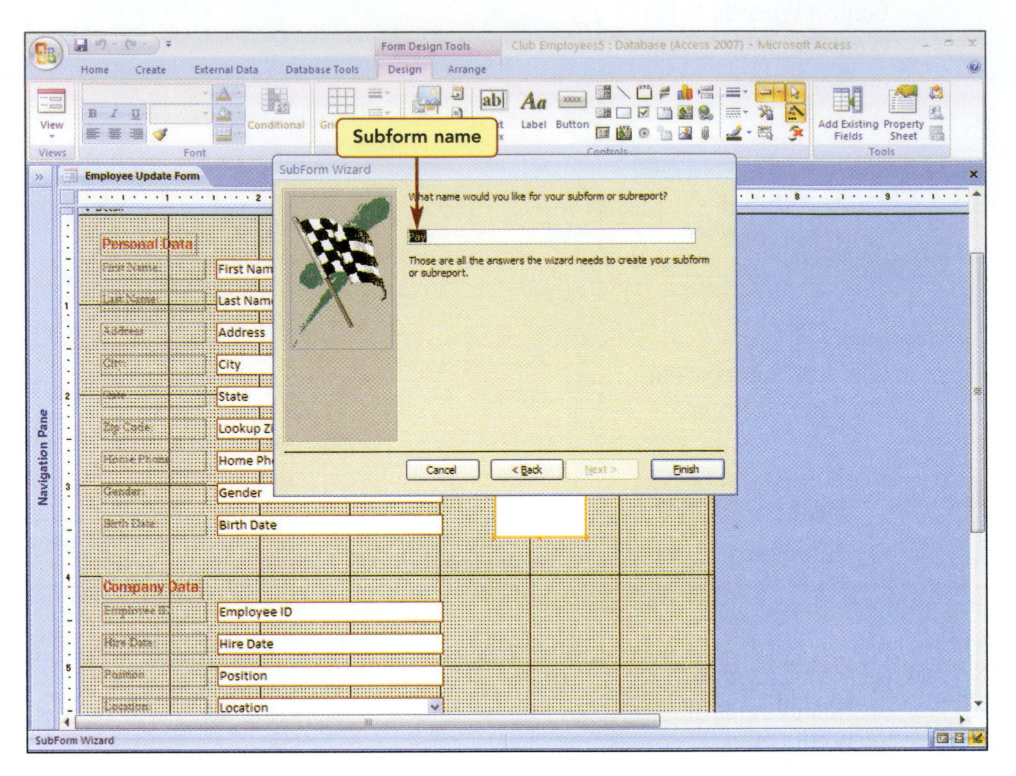

Figure 5.35

Then, in the final wizard dialog box, you will be asked to name the subform. You will accept the default name of Pay.

4 Click Finish.

Your screen should be similar to Figure 5.36

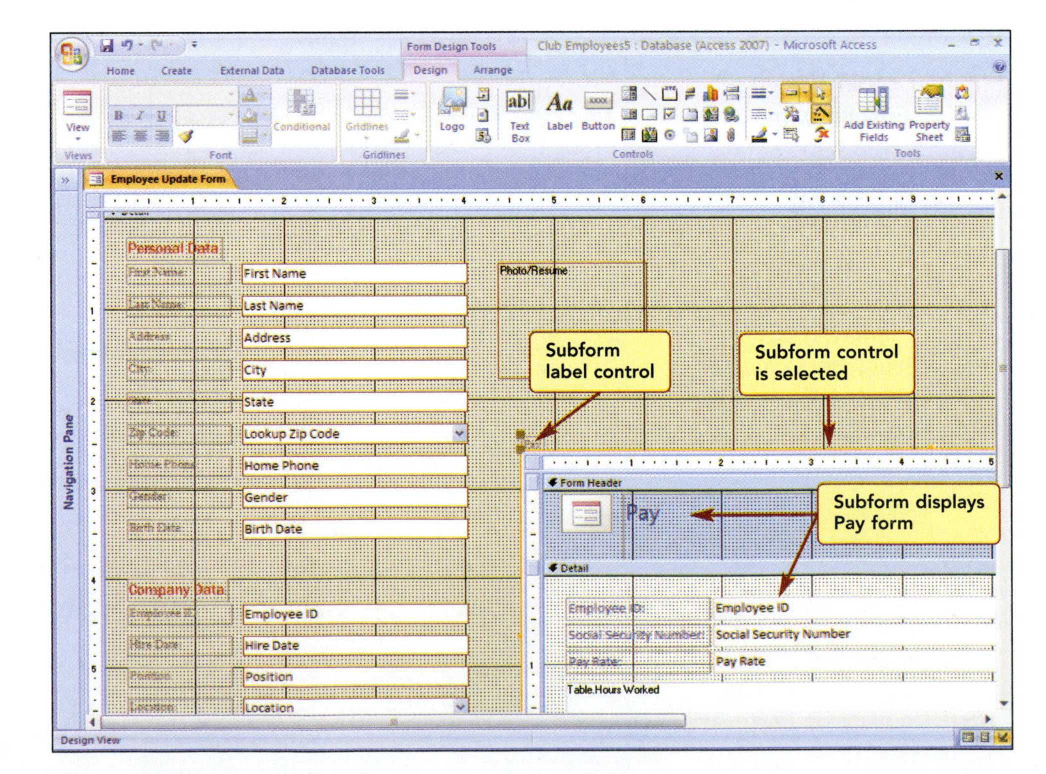

Figure 5.36

The Pay form object has been inserted into the main form. Because the Pay subform contains a datasheet subform, there are actually two subforms embedded in the main form.

Modifying a Subform

Next, you will delete the subform label control and readjust the layout of the subform slightly.

1

- **Select and delete the Pay subform label control.**
- **Select the Pay subform object.**
- **Scroll the main form window horizontally and vertically to see the entire form.**
- **Select the three text controls in the subform.**
- **Scroll the subform window horizontally to see the right edge of the form.**
- **Reduce the size of the three selected controls to the 4-inch ruler position (in the subform window).**
- **Click Form Header/Footer in the Show/Hide group of the Form Design Tools Arrange tab to hide the subform header and respond Yes to the advisory message.**

Your screen should be similar to Figure 5.37

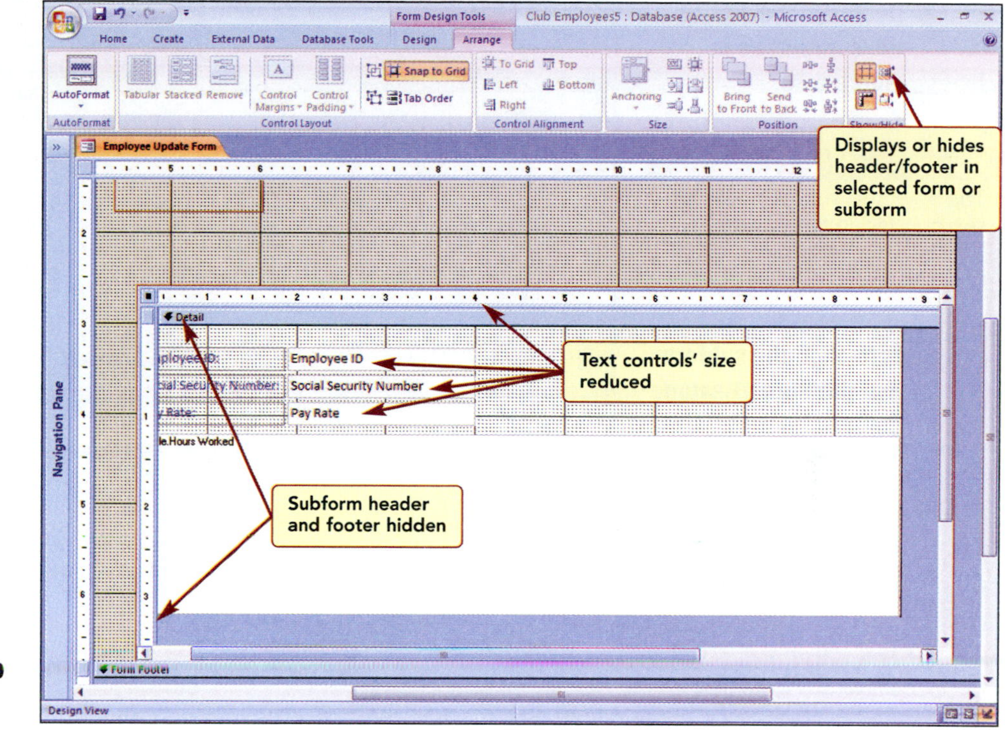

Figure 5.37

The subform header is removed and the controls are more appropriately sized. Next, you need to reduce the overall size of the subform object and then position it appropriately in the main form.

2

- **Select the subform object and move it to the left slightly so that the right edge of the subform is no longer even with the right edge of the main form.**
- **Decrease the size of the subform as in Figure 5.38.**

> **Having Trouble?**
>
> The selected subform will be surrounded in an orange border. Use the sizing handles to size the subform.

- **Left-align the subform and the Photo/Resume control.**
- **Bottom-align the subform and the Location control.**

Your screen should be similar to Figure 5.38

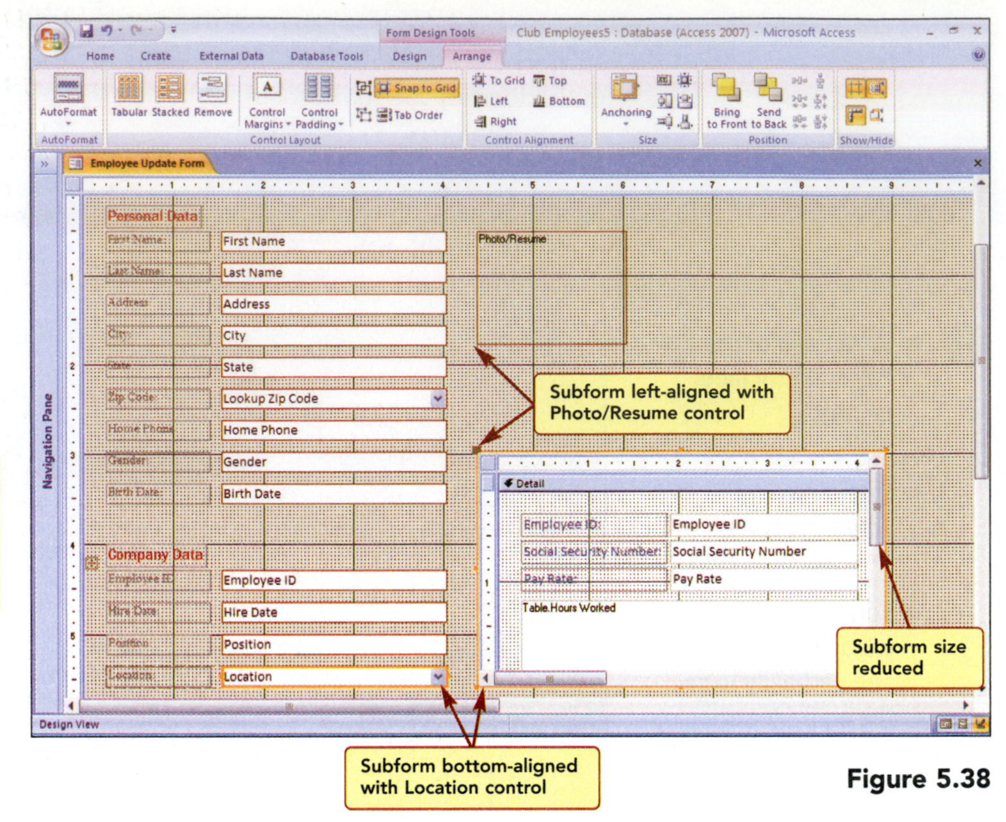

Figure 5.38

Now you will check your changes in Layout view.

3

- **Switch to Layout view.**
- **If necessary, move the Company Data and subform controls up slightly so that the entire form is visible in the window.**
- **Save the form.**
- **Using the scroll bar in the main form window, scroll three records forward to see record 4.**
- **If necessary, increase the size of the subform to display the Total value.**

Your screen should be similar to Figure 5.39

Hours worked data for current record

Figure 5.39

The first three employees' records did not display hours worked in the subform because they are paid on salary. The fourth record shows the hours worked for both weeks recorded in the table for that record.

Setting Tab Order

To test the form and subform, you will switch to Form view and move from one field to another using Tab as if you were entering data in the form. Then you will use the subform to add hours for a new week to your record.

1 Switch to Form view.

- Display your record in the form, move to the First Name control, and press Tab to move from one control to another.
- When the selector is in a new row of the Week Ending field, enter **last Friday's date** in the Week Ending field and **35** in the Hours field.
- Press ←Enter to complete the field entry.

Your screen should be similar to Figure 5.40

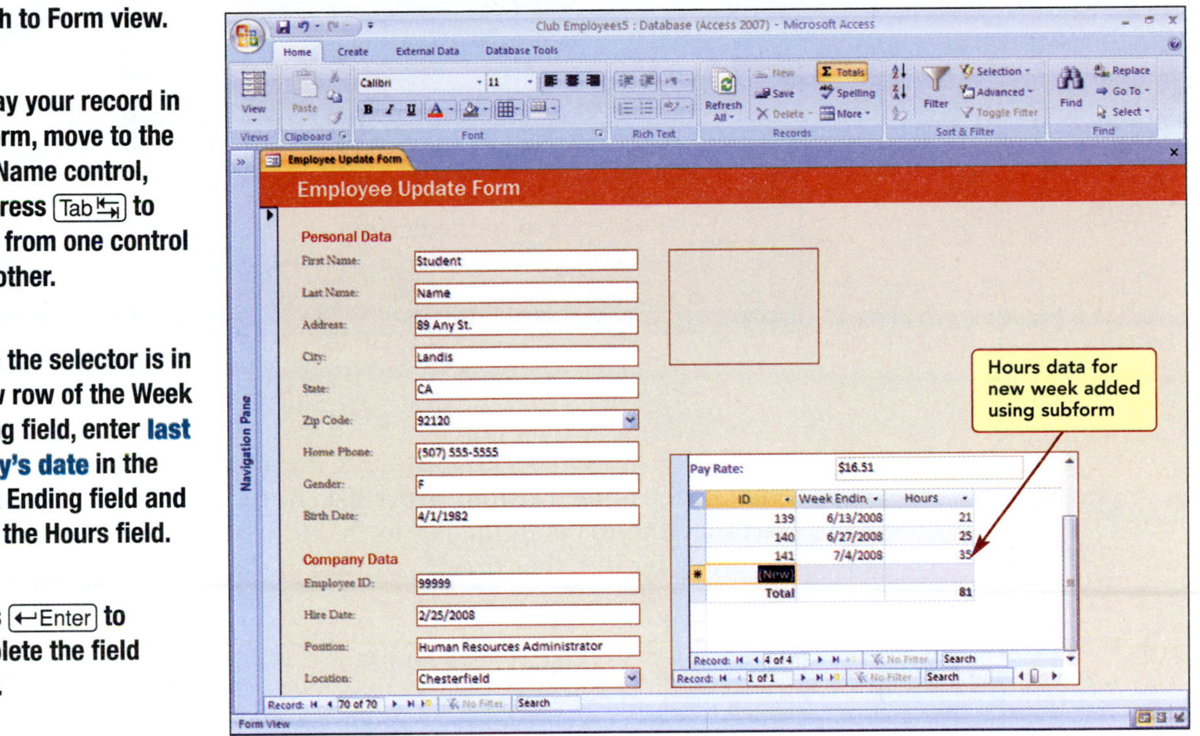

Figure 5.40

The Hours data for the new week has been added to the Hours table. As you tabbed through the fields in the form, you probably noticed that the tabbing sequence was not in the same order as the fields are displayed in the form. Although the order initially is the same as the fields are added to the form, the order changes when fields are moved. You can easily change the tab order of the form to any order you want it to be.

2 **Display Layout view.**

- **Click** Tab Order **in the Control Layout group of the Form Design Tools Arrange tab.**

Your screen should be similar to Figure 5.41

Adjusts tab order of controls in form

Current tab order of form controls

Figure 5.41

The Tab Order dialog box displays the tab order of the controls in the Detail order in the Custom Order list. To change the tab order, you simply rearrange the items in the list to the desired tab order by selecting a row and dragging it to the correct position in the list.

3 **Select and drag the rows in the list until they are in the same order as the controls in the form.**

Additional Information

You also can select and drag multiple rows.

Your screen should be similar to Figure 5.42

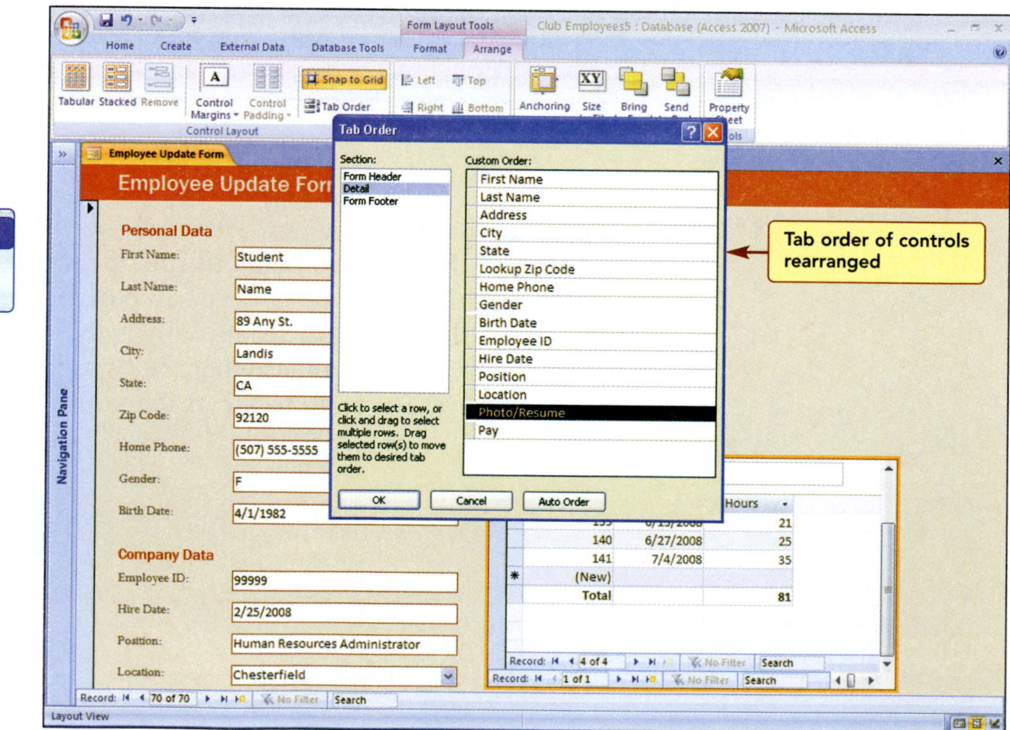

Figure 5.42

- **Click OK.**
- **Switch to Form view and tab through the form to test the order.**
- **Save the form.**

You have finished designing the main form and subform.

Using Command Buttons

Next, you want to make it easier for someone using the form to move to a new blank record and to print the form. To do this, you will add two command buttons to the form.

Concept 4

Command Button

4 A **command button** executes one or more actions on a form. For example, you can create command buttons that perform actions within a form such as moving from record to record and adding, copying, saving, printing, and deleting a record. You also can create a command button that opens another form.

You can create a command button on your own by typing the instructions to be performed in the Properties dialog box or you can select from over 30 types of predefined procedures to create a command button using the Command Button Wizard.

Creating Command Buttons

You will use the Command Button Wizard to add two command buttons to your form: one that displays a blank form for adding a new record and another that prints the current record. You will place them in the Form Header section where they will be visible when viewing each form.

Switch to Design view.

Click Button **in the Controls group of the Form Design Tools Design tab.**

Having Trouble?

To use the Command Button Wizard, the Control Wizard must be activated (the button must be selected). If it is not, click the Control Wizard button to activate it.

Additional Information

The mouse pointer changes to +▭, indicating that the program is ready to create the button.

Click at the 6-inch position in the Form Header section to add the command button.

Having Trouble?

Move the dialog box to see the command button.

Your screen should be similar to Figure 5.43

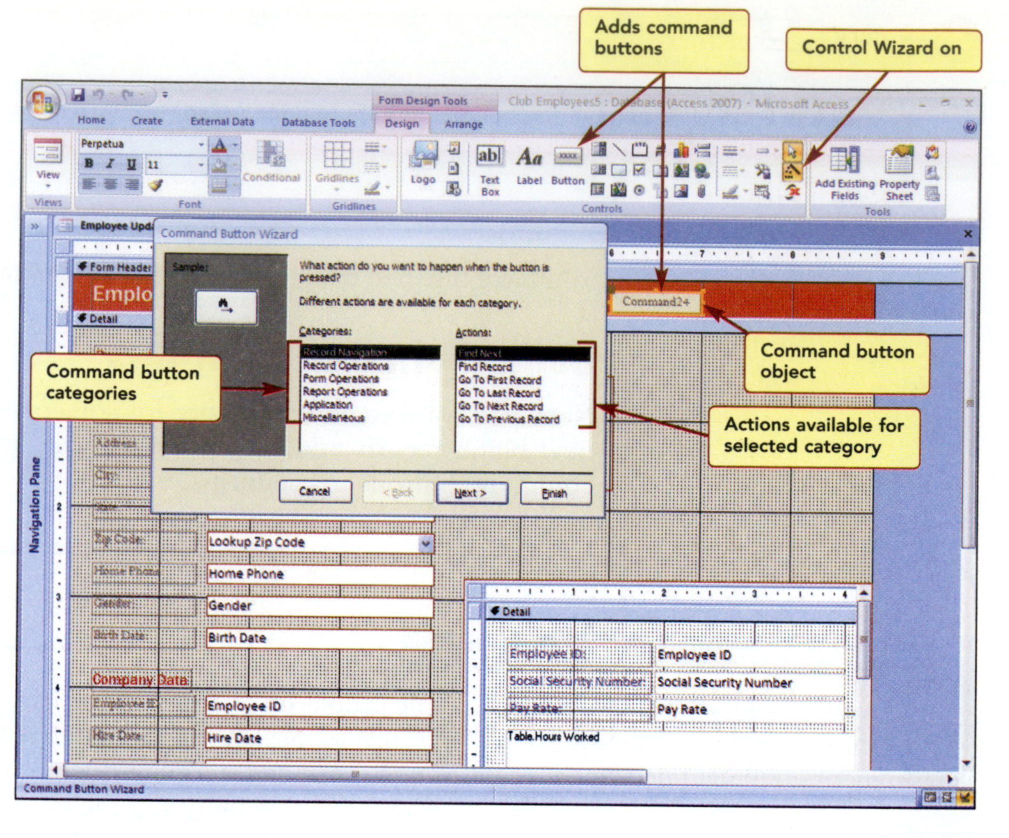

Figure 5.43

The Command Button Wizard dialog box displays a list of six predefined categories and their associated actions that can be assigned to the button. The Record Navigation category is selected and displays six record navigation actions that can be assigned to a button.

You will create the button to display a blank new record for adding a new employee to the database. The action you will use to create this button is in the Record Operations category. However, before selecting the command button category and action, you will take a look at the actions available in all categories.

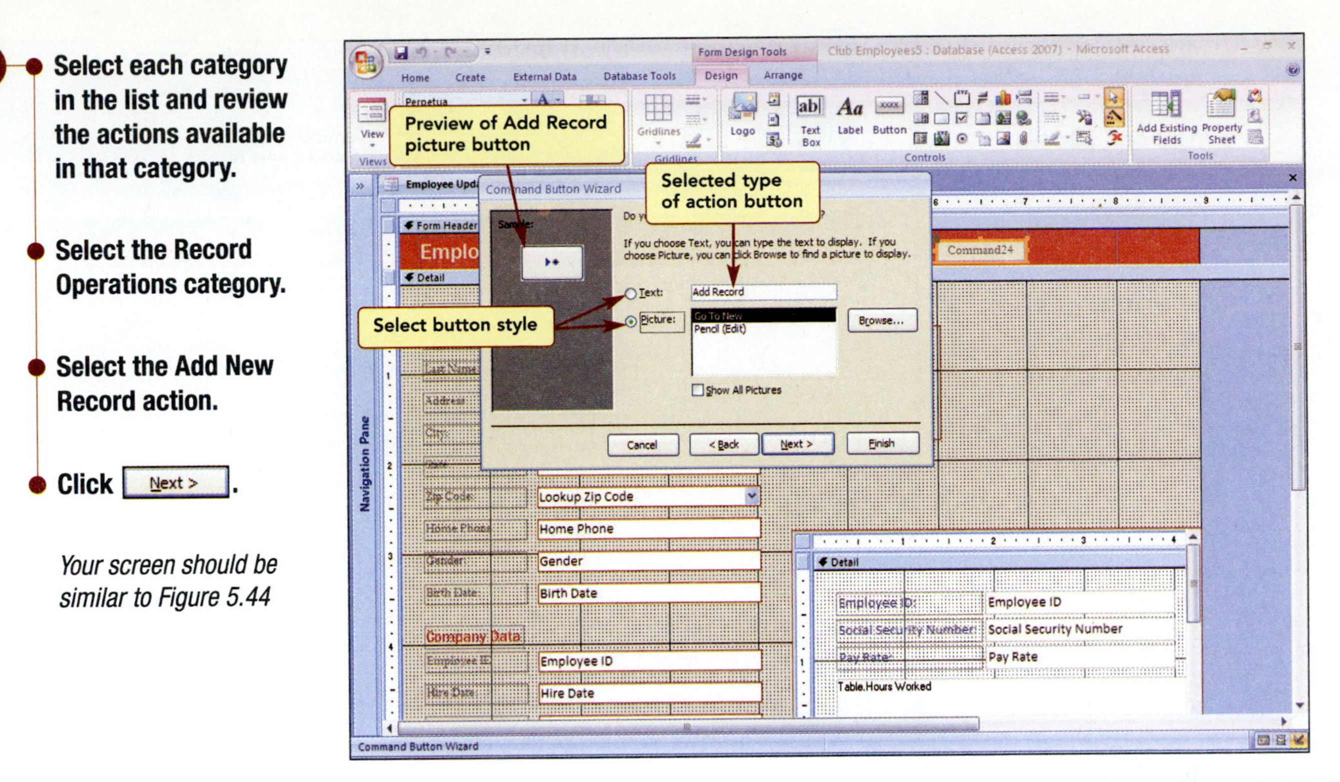

2

- **Select each category in the list and review the actions available in that category.**
- **Select the Record Operations category.**
- **Select the Add New Record action.**
- **Click Next >.**

Your screen should be similar to Figure 5.44

Figure 5.44

The second wizard box gives you a choice of displaying a picture or text on the command button. You want the button to display a text message to identify the action it will perform.

3

- **Choose the Text option.**
- **In the text box, change the default caption to Add New Record.**

Your screen should be similar to Figure 5.45

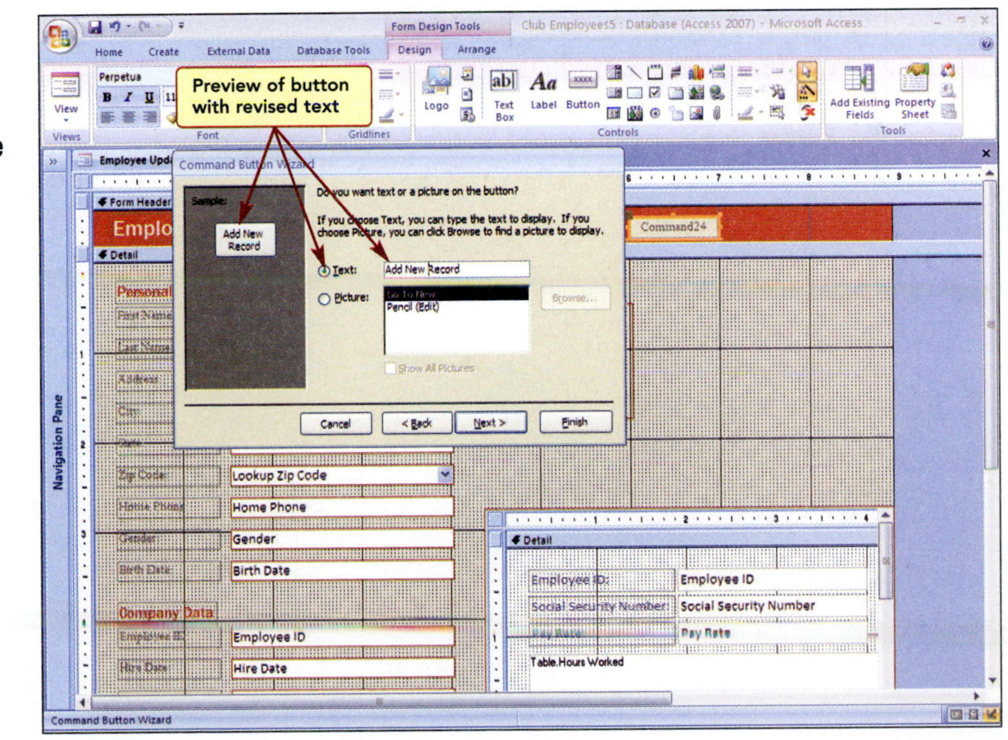

Figure 5.45

The sample area displays the button and text you entered. In the final wizard screen, you will be asked to name the button.

4 Click Next >.

- Type **Add Record**.
- Click Finish.
- If necessary, adjust the position of the button.
- Deselect the button.

Your screen should be similar to Figure 5.46

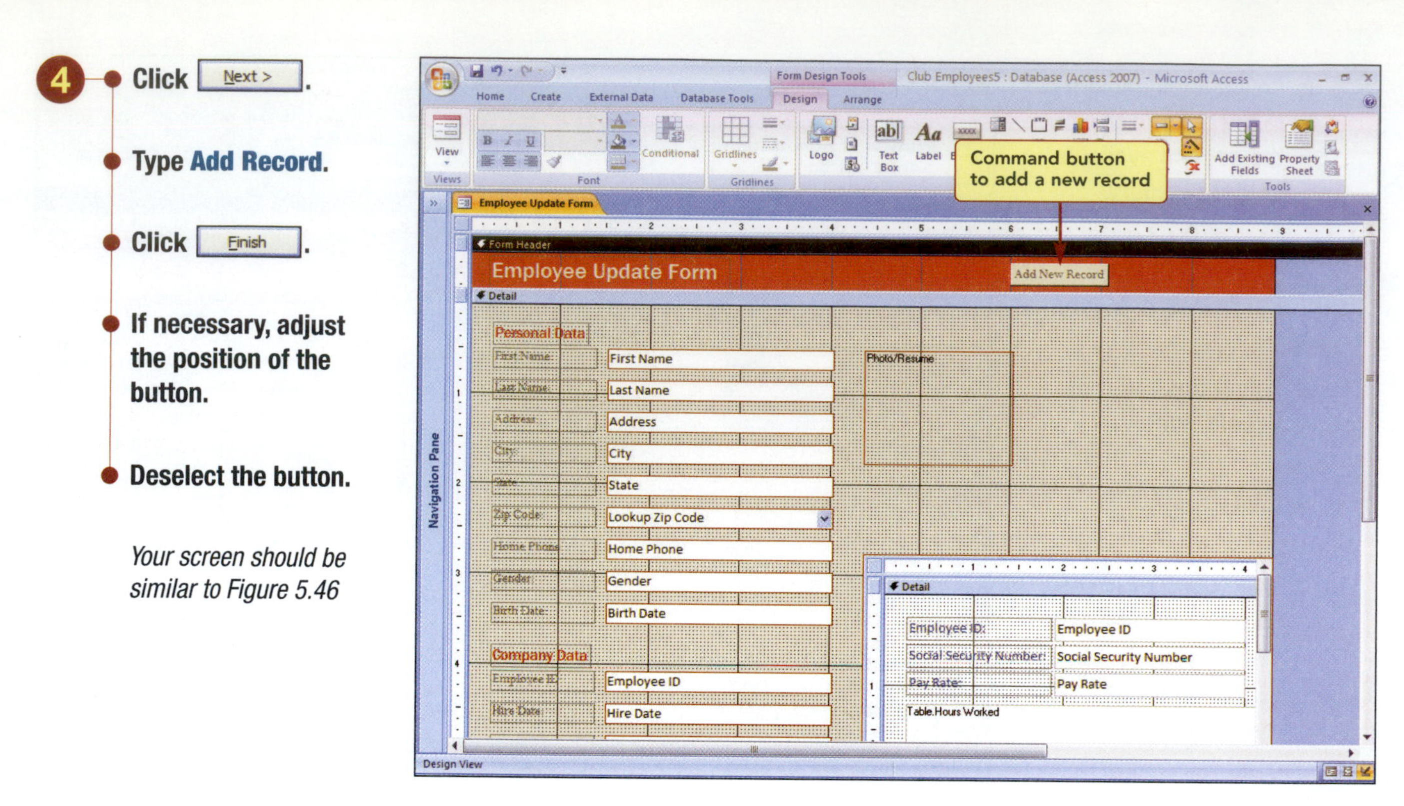

Figure 5.46

The button is now ready to use. The second button you want to add will print the current record. You want this button to display a picture instead of text.

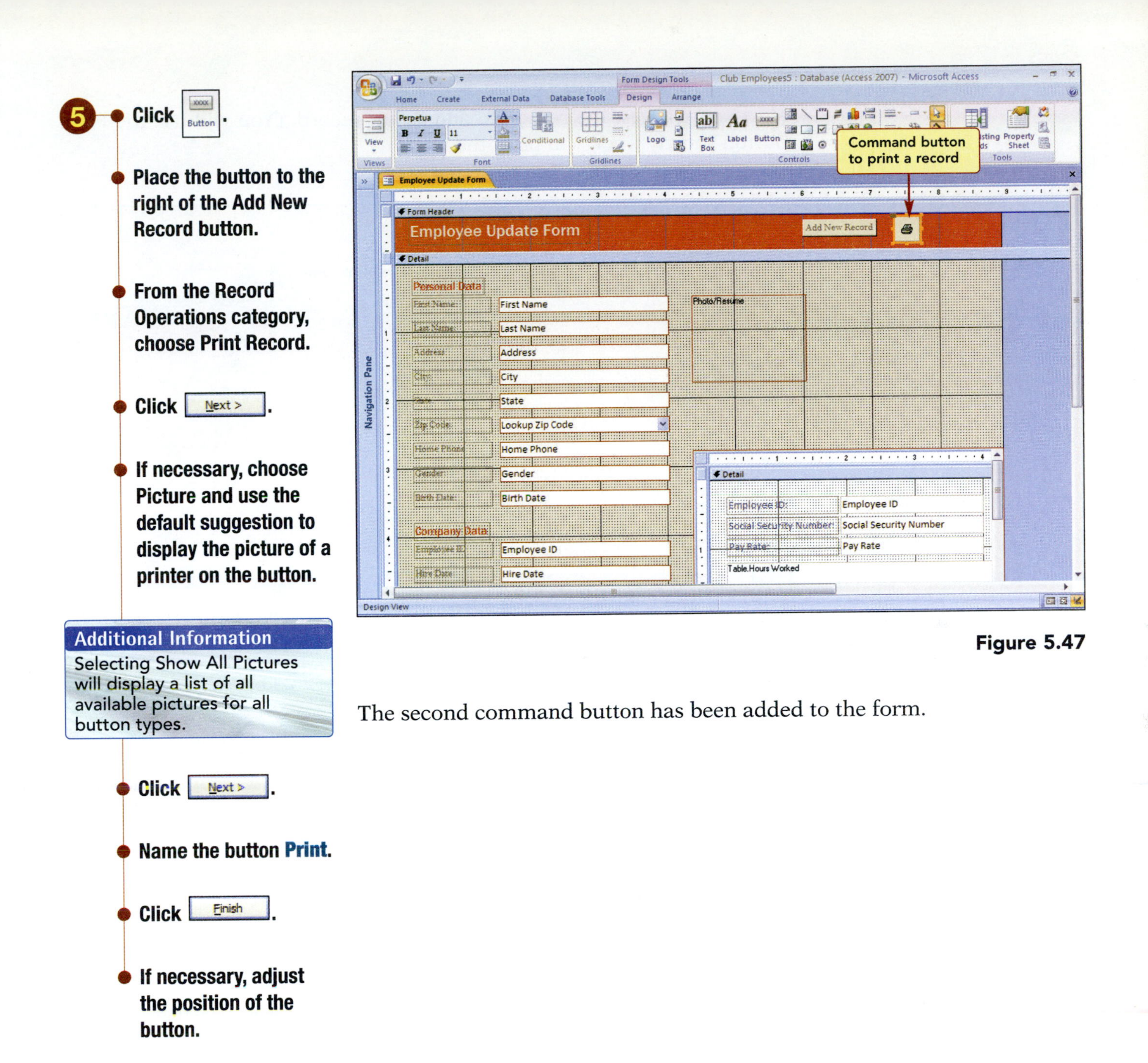

5 Click [Button].

- Place the button to the right of the Add New Record button.
- From the Record Operations category, choose Print Record.
- Click [Next >].
- If necessary, choose Picture and use the default suggestion to display the picture of a printer on the button.

Additional Information

Selecting Show All Pictures will display a list of all available pictures for all button types.

- Click [Next >].
- Name the button **Print**.
- Click [Finish].
- If necessary, adjust the position of the button.

Your screen should be similar to Figure 5.47

Figure 5.47

The second command button has been added to the form.

Using a Command Button

Next you will test the button to add a new record. (You will use the Print button shortly when you print the form.)

1 • **Switch to Form view.**

• **Click** Add New Record.

Additional Information
A ScreenTip displaying the button name is displayed when you point to the button.

Your screen should be similar to Figure 5.48

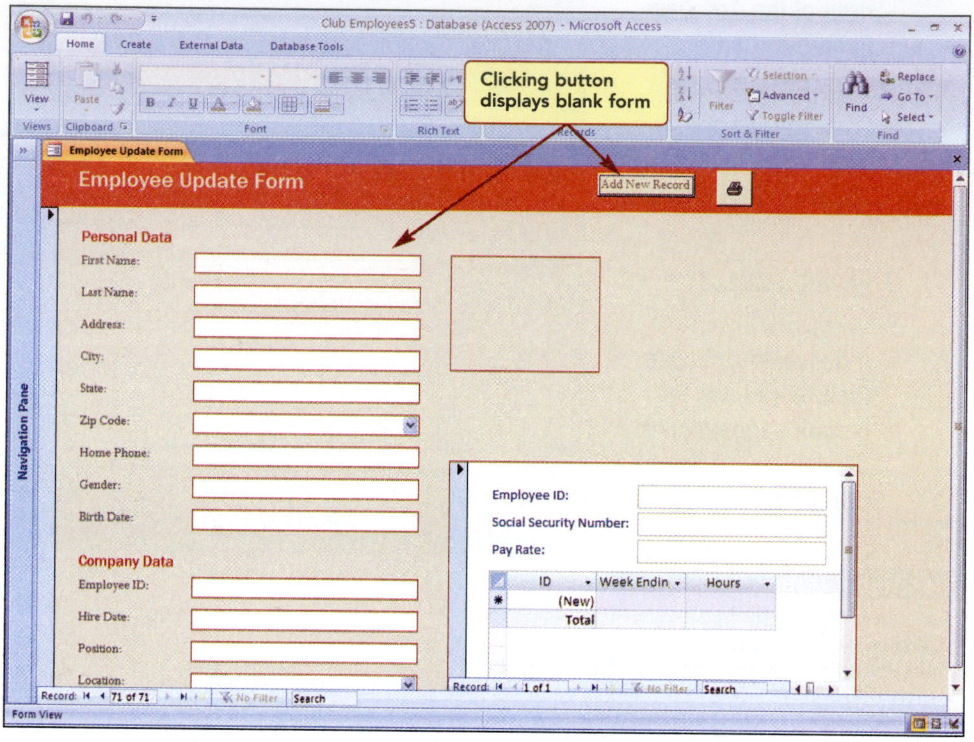

Figure 5.48

A blank form is displayed and ready for entry of a new record, which confirms that the button works.

Creating Page Headers and Footers

The final changes to the form that you want to make are changes that will affect the printed form. You want the form to be printed with a thick borderline at the top and the page number at the bottom of every page.

Adding Page Header and Footer Sections

First, you need to add a Page Header and Page Footer section to the form. Unlike form headers and footers, which print only on the first and last page of a form, page headers and footers print on every page.

- **Switch to Design view.**
- **Click Page Header/Footer in the Show/Hide group of the Form Design Tools Arrange tab.**

Additional Information
You can only add a header and footer as a pair.

Your screen should be similar to Figure 5.49

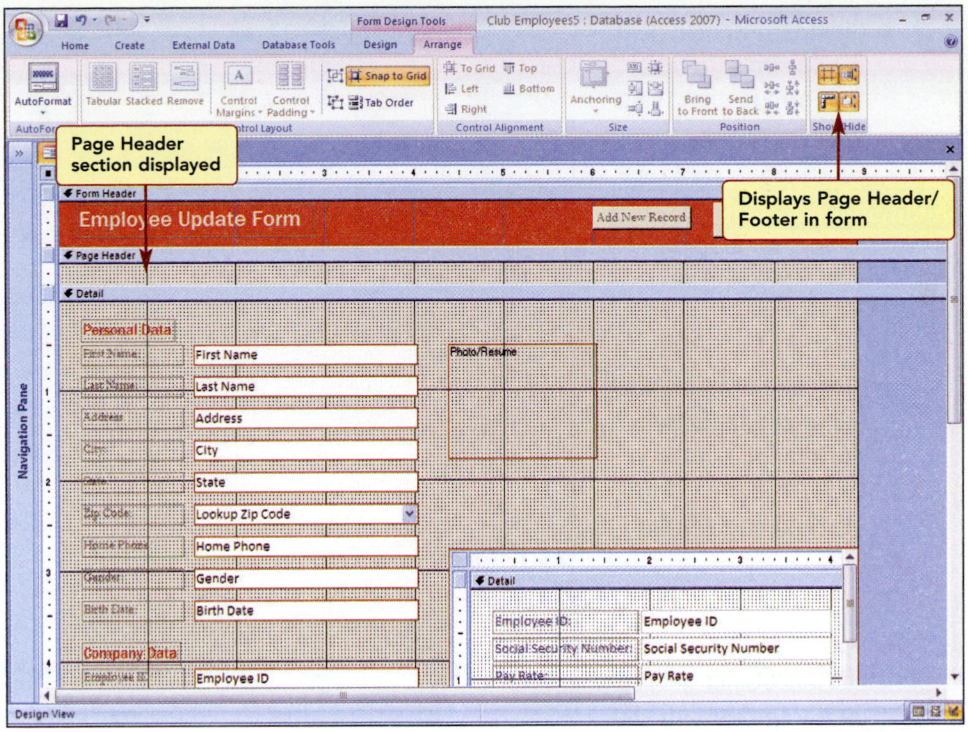

Page Header section displayed

Displays Page Header/ Footer in form

Figure 5.49

Page Header and Page Footer sections are added to the form. You can now adjust the size of these sections and add controls and objects to them just as you can in the other form sections.

Creating a Border Line

In the Page Header, you will create a border line that will appear at the top of every record when the form is printed.

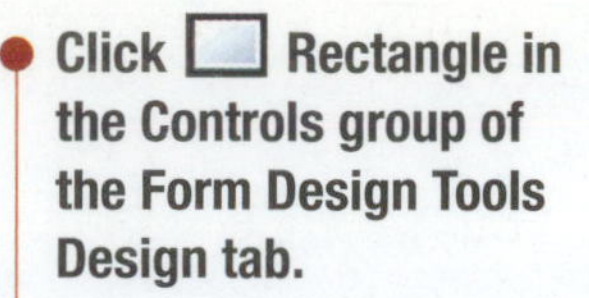

1 Click Rectangle in the Controls group of the Form Design Tools Design tab.

Additional Information
The mouse pointer appears as +□ when creating a rectangle.

- Click and drag to draw a thin rectangle from the left edge of the Page Header section to the right edge of the form.
- Open the Fill/Back Color gallery (in the Font group) and select Dark Red.

Your screen should be similar to Figure 5.50

Figure 5.50

Inserting Page Numbers

Next, you will add the page number in the Page Footer section.

1 Scroll to the bottom of the form to see the Page Footer section.

- Click Insert Page Number in the Controls group.

Your screen should be similar to Figure 5.51

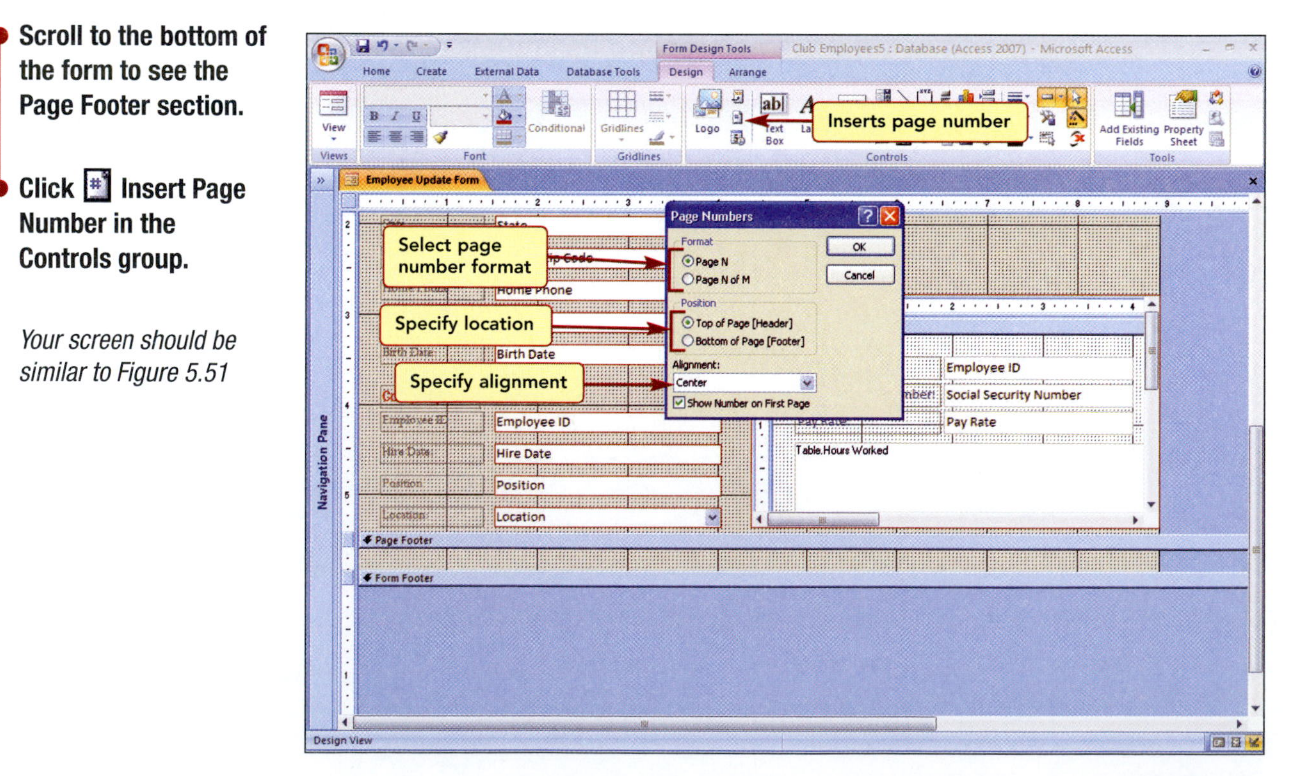

Figure 5.51

The Page Numbers dialog box lets you insert page numbers in your form in either the header or footer in the format "Page N" (which would print out as "Page 2" on the second page) or "Page N of M" (which would print out as "Page 2 of 5" on the second page). You also can choose the alignment of the page number (centered, left, or right) and whether you want the page number printed on the first page or not. You want the single page number centered in the footer and printed on the first and all pages.

2

- **Select the following options (if they are not already selected): Page N, Bottom of Page [Footer], Alignment/Center, and Show Number on First Page.**
- **Click OK.**
- **Save the form.**

Your screen should be similar to Figure 5.52

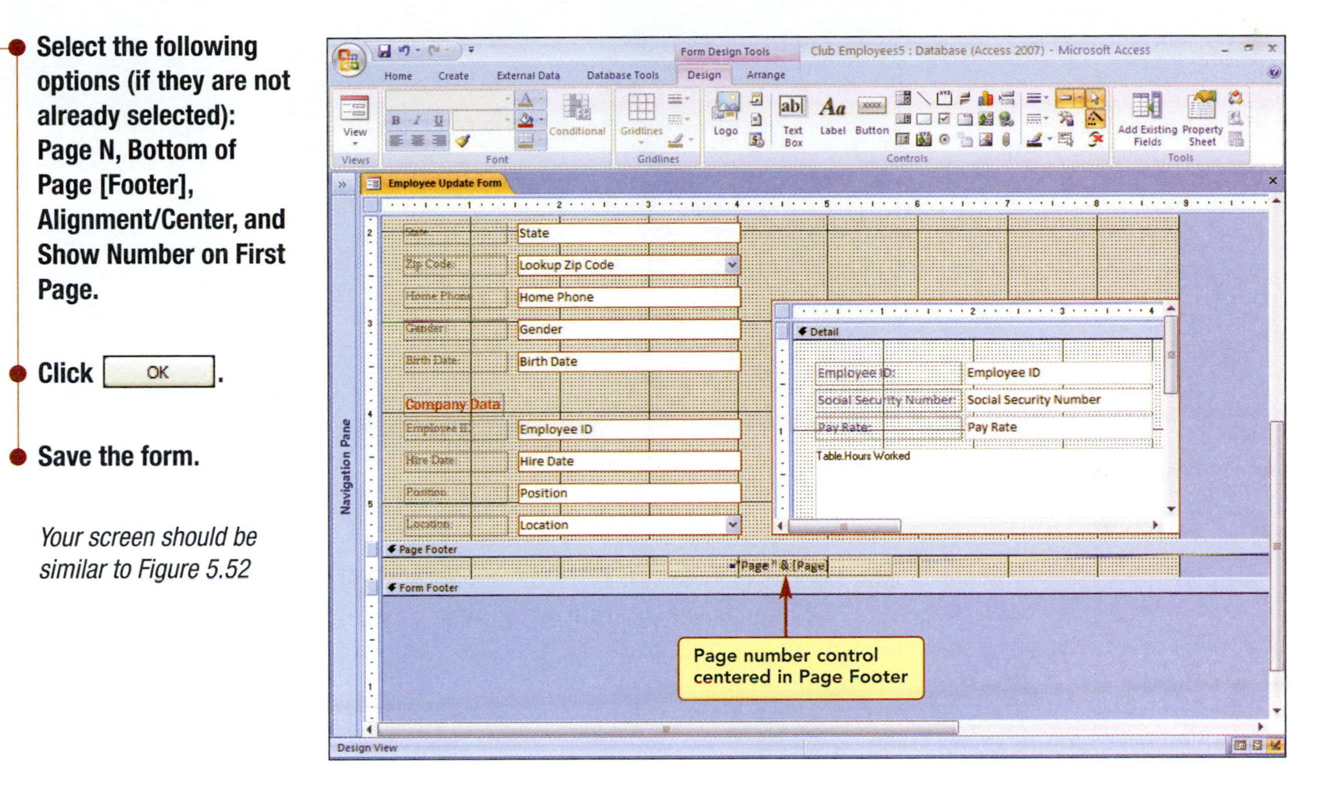

Figure 5.52

A control to display the page number has been added to the Page Footer area of the form.

Previewing a Form

Your customized form has been designed and tested and you are ready to print, save, and close it. Before printing, you will preview how it will appear.

1 **Choose Office Button/Print/Print Preview.**

Your screen should be similar to Figure 5.53

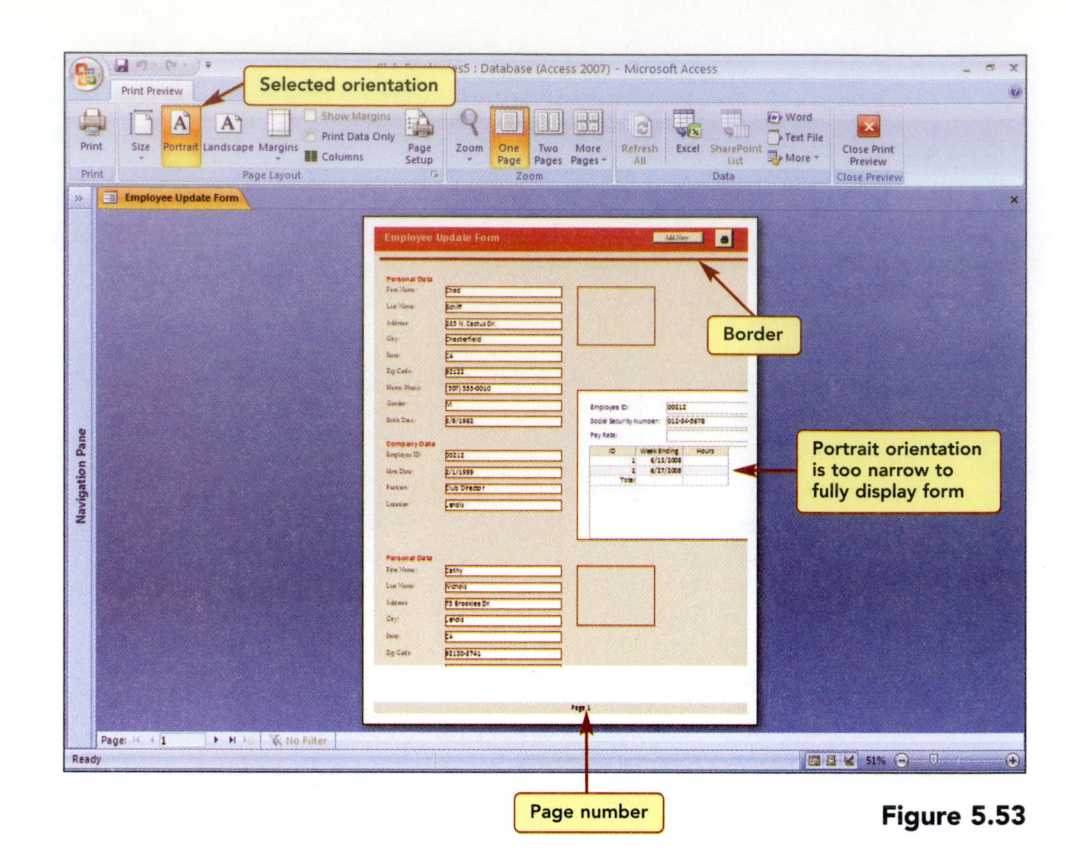

Figure 5.53

The border appears in the Page Header and the page number appears in the Page Footer as you specified. However, because the form is too wide, it does not all fit on one page. To fix this, you will change the orientation of the printout to landscape.

2 **Click** Landscape.

Use the scroll buttons to display page 3.

Your screen should be similar to Figure 5.54

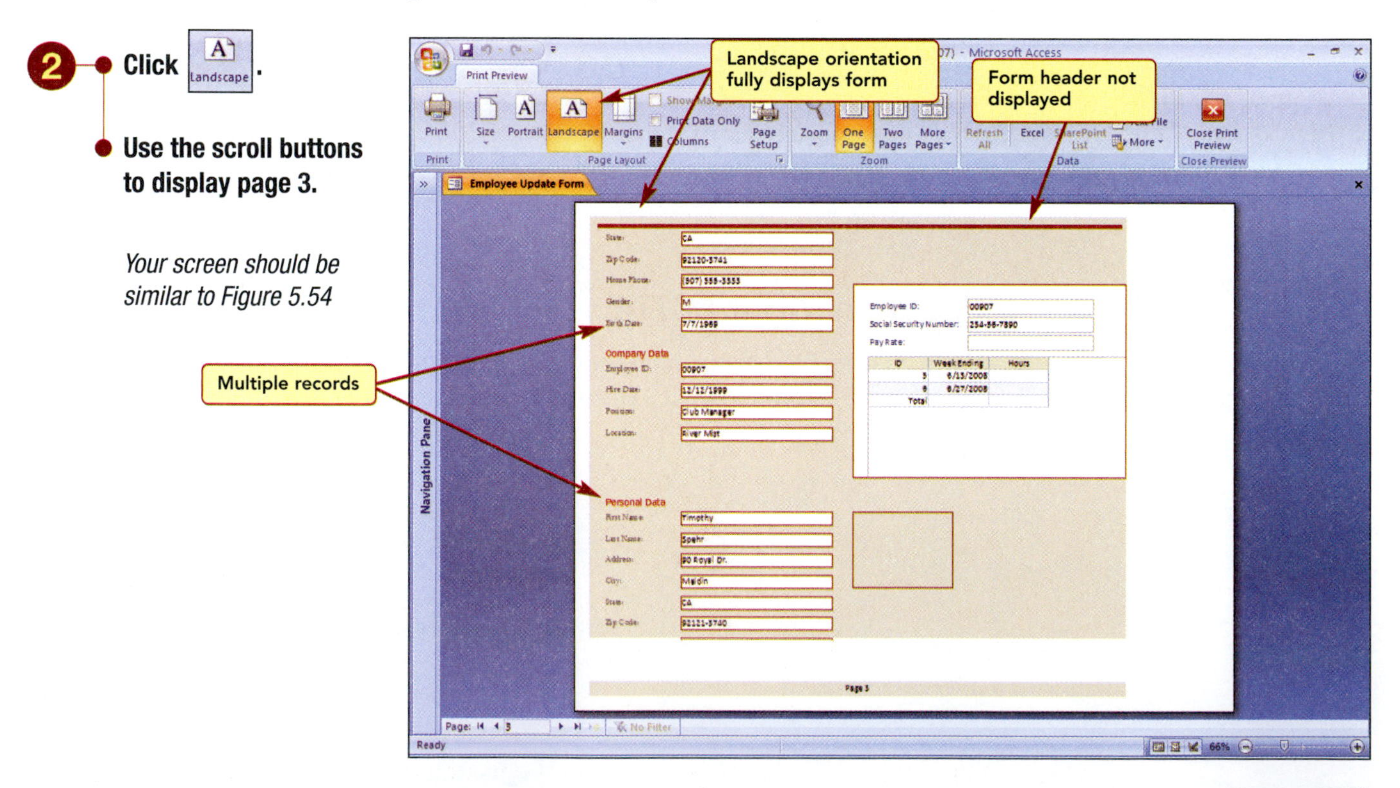

Figure 5.54

The form is displayed in landscape orientation. Notice, however, the form header is no longer displayed. This is because the purpose of the form header is for viewing the form, not printing. Also, the form displays the information for the bottom of one record and the top of another. Again, this is because forms are not designed for printing. However, you can print an individual record in Form view by selecting the record and using the print button.

3
- **Close the preview window and display Form view.**
- **Display your record in the form.**
- **Click the record selector bar and print your record using the Print command button.**
- **Specify the necessary printer settings and click OK.**
- **Close the form, saving the changes.**

Deleting a Form

Now that you have a customized form that will update multiple tables in the database, you no longer need the original form you created to update the Employees table. You can easily delete this form from the database, just as you can all types of database objects.

1
- **Display the Navigation pane.**
- **Select Employee Records in the Forms section of the Navigation pane.**
- **Click Delete in the Records group.**
- **Click Yes to confirm the deletion.**

Your screen should be similar to Figure 5.55

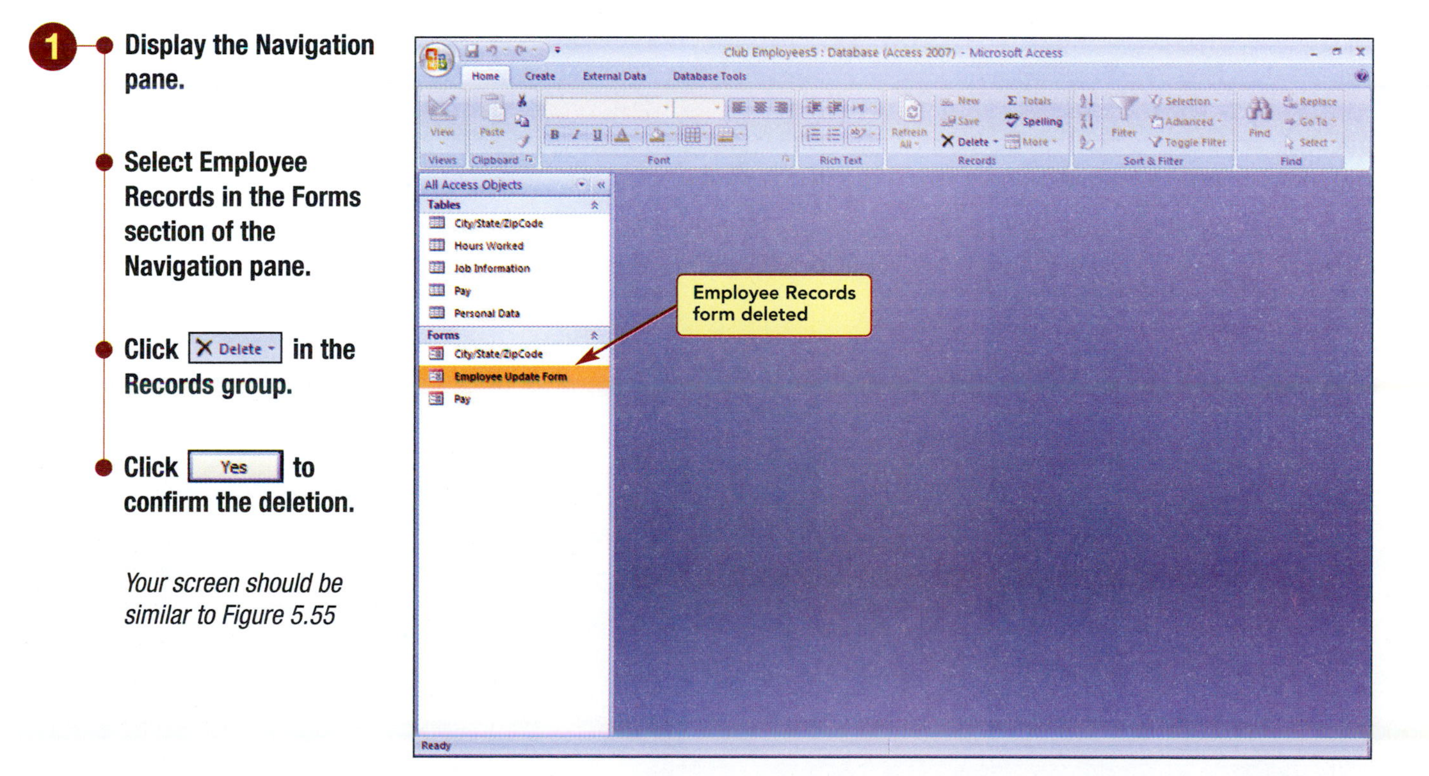

Figure 5.55

The Employee Records form has been deleted and is no longer listed in the Forms objects list.

As a final maintenance task, you will compact and repair the database before you close it.

2 Compact and repair the database.

Exit Access.

Focus on Careers

EXPLORE YOUR CAREER OPTIONS

Claims Adjusters

Have you ever met with an insurance adjuster after a car accident? Have you ever filed a claim after visiting the hospital? Claims adjusters investigate claims, discuss settlement options, and approve payments. As a claims adjuster, you may talk to accident witnesses and law enforcement personnel and review hospital records to make your decision on an insurance claim. Most claims adjusters carry laptops and digital cameras to document information collected on a claim. The details uncovered in this process are often stored in a database. A claims adjuster also may use a database to ensure the applicant is not trying to defraud the insurance company. The typical salary range for a claims adjuster is between $31,000 and $50,000. Employers typically prefer college graduates with excellent communications skills.

LAB 5

Creating Custom Forms

Form Layout Tools Club Employees5 : Database (Access 2007) - Microsoft Access
Home Create External Data Database Tools Format Arrange
View Calibri 11 Conditional Formatting Gridlines Logo Title Page Numbers Date and Time Add Existing Fields
Views Font Formatting Gridlines Controls AutoFormat
All Access Objects
Tables
City/State/ZipCode
Hours Worked
Job Information
Pay
Personal Data
Forms
City/State/ZipCode
Employee Records
Pay
ployee ID: 00212
ial Security Number: 012-34-5678
Rate:

ID	Week Endin	Hours
1	6/13/2008	
2	6/27/2008	
(New)		
Total		

ord: 1 of 2 No Filter Search
Record: 1 of 70 No Filter Search
Layout View

Subform

Subform (AC5.7)

A subform is a form that is embedded in another form and is used to show data from another table or query.

Font

Form Layout Tools Club Employees5 : Database (Access 2007) - Microsoft Access
Home Create External Data Database Tools Format Arrange
View Franklin Gothic Medium 12 Conditional Formatting Gridlines Logo Title Page Numbers Date and Time Add Existing Fields
Views Font Formatting Gridlines Controls AutoFormat
Employee Update Form
Navigation Pane
Employee Update Form
Personal Data
First Name: Chad
Last Name: Schiff
Address: 235 N. Cactus Dr.
City: Chesterfield
State: CA
Zip Code: 92122
Home Phone: (507) 555-0010
Gender: M
Birth Date: 3/9/1962
Company Data
Employee ID: 00212
Hire Date: 2/1/1999
Position: Club Director
Location: Landis
Record: 1 of 70 No Filter Search
Layout View

Font (AC5.27)

A font, also commonly referred to as a typeface, is a set of characters with a specific design.

Alignment and Spacing (AC5.30)

The position of controls on a form can be adjusted so that they are evenly aligned and the spacing between them is the same.

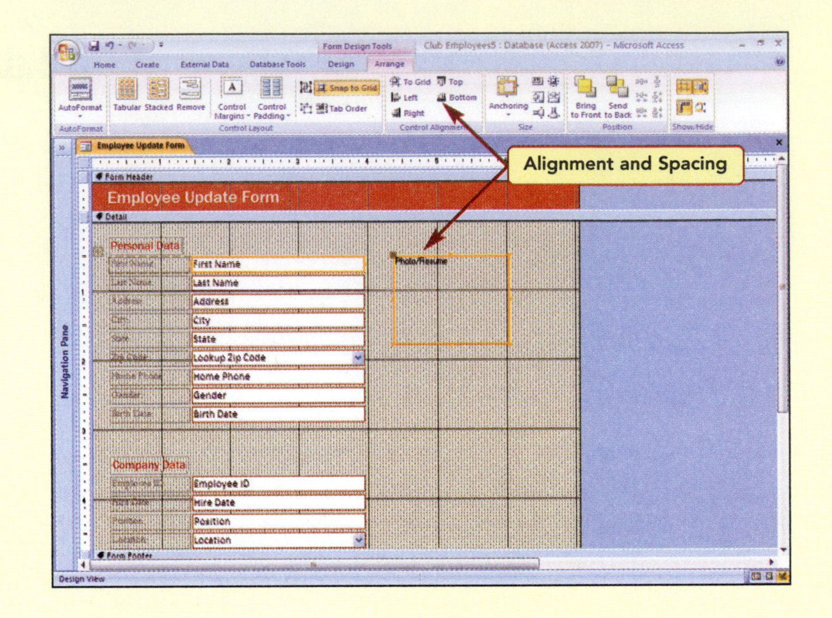

Command Button (AC5.41)

A command button executes one or more actions in a form.

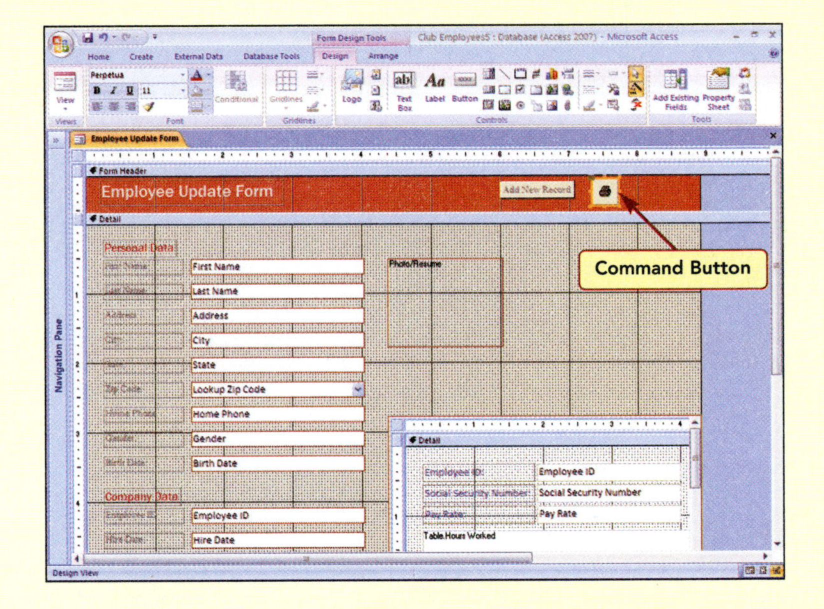

LAB 5

Creating Custom Forms

key terms

align AC5.30
command button AC5.41
font AC5.27
font size AC5.27
form separator AC5.5
hierarchical form AC5.7
main form AC5.7
master/detail form AC5.7
parent/child form AC5.7
point AC5.27
sans serif AC5.27
serif AC5.27
spacing AC5.30
subform AC5.7
typeface AC5.27

MCAS Skills

The Microsoft Certified Applications Specialist (MCAS) certification program is designed to measure your proficiency in performing basic tasks using the Office 2007 applications. Certification demonstrates that you have the skills and provides a valuable industry credential for employment. See Reference 2: Microsoft Certified Applications Specialist (MCAS) for a complete list of the skills that were covered in Lab 5.

Lab Review

command summary

Command	Shortcut	Description
Create tab		
Forms group		
Split Form		Allows for the simultaneous display of a form and its dependent datasheet information
Blank Form		Creates a new blank form
Form Layout Tools Format tab		
Controls group		
Title		Adds a title to the current form
Add Existing Fields		Displays the Field List pane to add fields to a form design
Form Layout Tools Arrange tab		
Control Layout group		
Stacked		Creates a stacked layout with labels to the left of the control
Remove		Removes layouts applied to the selected control
Tab Order		Opens the Tab Order dialog box to control how the Tab key navigates the form
Tools group		
Property Sheet	F4	Opens and closes the Property Sheet pane
Form Design Tools Design tab		
Font group		
Perpetua Font		Chooses a font for the selected control
11 Font Size		Chooses a font size for the selected control
A Font Color		Chooses a font color for the selected control
Controls group		
Page Number		Inserts page number control in header or footer group
Label		Adds a label control to the current form
Button		Adds a command button control to the current form

command summary

Command	Shortcut	Description
Subform/Subreport		Creates a subform
Rectangle		Adds a rectangle control to the current form
Select		Turns Select feature on/off
Control Wizard		Turns wizard feature on/off
Form Design Tools Arrange tab		
Control Layout group Control Padding		Sets the padding (the amount of white space) between controls
Tab Order		Changes the tab order for controls
Control Alignment group Left		Sets the alignment of the selected control to the left side of the form
Top		Sets the alignment of the selected control to the top of the form
Show/Hide group Page Header/Footer		Displays and hides the Page Header and Page Footer sections
Form Header/Footer		Displays and hides the form header and footer sections

Lab Exercises

matching

Match the numbered item with the correct lettered description.

1. font	______	**a.** allows you to see a form and its source at the same time
2. subform	______	**b.** a clean typeface style with little decoration
3. command button	______	**c.** a decorative typeface with flaired characters
4. tab order	______	**d.** controls form keyboard navigation
5. hierarchical form	______	**e.** linked to another control to identify it
6. split form	______	**f.** accesses formatting, data, and event items for a control
7. property sheet	______	**g.** form embedded within another form
8. sans serif	______	**h.** executes one or more actions on a form
9. label control	______	**i.** form/subform combination
10. serif	______	**j.** the design and shape of characters

true/false

Circle the correct answer to the following questions.

1. You can create a form that has the same look and feel as a datasheet.	True	False
2. You can embed a main form within a subform.	True	False
3. Form headers and footers print only on the first and last pages of a form.	True	False
4. Title controls appear in the Page Header section of a form.	True	False
5. Form headers appear at the beginning of the first page when printed.	True	False
6. A split form allows you to see a form and its underlying data simultaneously.	True	False
7. Subforms can be used to show data from tables or queries that have a one-to-one relationship.	True	False
8. You can create your own command buttons by typing the instructions.	True	False
9. To select both a text control and its associated label control, you click the text box control.	True	False
10. You can make your form more intuitive and easier to use by creating a logical tab order.	True	False

fill-in

Complete the following statements by filling in the blanks with the correct key terms.

1. A(n) __________ can be used to show data from tables or queries that have a one-to-many relationship.
2. __________ fonts have a flair at the base of each letter to guide the reader's eye to the next letter.
3. You can create a(n) __________ to open another form, move through records, and print a form.
4. The __________ divides the sections of a split form.
5. You can control the appearance, data source, and event handlers using the __________ pane.
6. A(n) __________ is the design and shape of characters.
7. You can control the placement of form controls by adjusting the control's __________.
8. The Controls group is found under the __________ tab.
9. The form that contains the subform is called the __________.
10. A(n) __________ control is generally tied to and helps identify another control.

multiple choice

Circle the letter of the correct response.

1. In a split form, you can view both the form and a __________.
   - **a.** query
   - **b.** report
   - **c.** datasheet
   - **d.** subform
2. A __________ is embedded in a form to display data from another table or query.
   - **a.** control
   - **b.** subform
   - **c.** split form
   - **d.** label
3. Which of the following is not another term for a form/subform combination?
   - **a.** Split form
   - **b.** Hierarchal form
   - **c.** Master/detail form
   - **d.** Parent/child form

4. Controls on a form can be easily arranged in groups called what?
   a. Collections
   b. Units
   c. Bands
   d. Stacks
5. Items like formatting, data sources, and events are collectively referred to as a form's ___________.
   a. assets
   b. properties
   c. attributes
   d. features
6. What of the following font types has a clean look appropriate for headings?
   a. Sans serif
   b. Fantasy
   c. Serif
   d. Heading
7. Which tab is used to align controls on a form?
   a. Design
   b. Home
   c. Arrange
   d. Database Tools
8. You use what key to quickly navigate back and forth between the fields in a form?
   a. Spacebar
   b. Tab ⭾
   c. ← Enter
   d. End
9. What control is designed specifically to execute one or more actions on a form?
   a. Command button
   b. Subform
   c. Label
   d. Title
10. Which of the following form sections prints only on the last page of a form?
    a. Page Header
    b. Form Footer
    c. Page Footer
    d. Form Header

Hands-on Exercises

rating system

★ Easy

★★ Moderate

★★★ Difficult

step-by-step

Adventure Travel Tours Client Form ★

CONTINUING EXERCISES

1. You have set up a client database for Adventure Travel Tours with tables that contain data on the clients and travel agents at each office location. Next, you need to create a form that will make entering data into these tables easier. You want the form to display the agent data and the records of the clients assigned to them. To do this, you will create a travel agents form with a clients subform. You are also going to customize this form by including different font sizes and colors as well as a form header and footer to make it more attractive. When you are finished, your form will look similar to the form shown here.

   a. Open the ATT Clients & Agents database (which you worked on in Step-by-Step Exercise 2 of Lab 4).

   b. Open the Agents table and expand the subtable to display the Clients table data. (Hint: Click ⊞ and choose Clients.] Close and save the Agents table.

   c. Use the Form command to create a form for the Agents table. Save the form as **Agents**. Close the form.

   d. Use the Form command to create a form for the Clients table. Save it as **Clients**.

   e. Use the Form Wizard to create a new form using all of the fields in the Agents table as well as all of the fields in the Clients table (in that order). Specify that you want to view the data with the Agents table as the main form and the Clients table as the subform. Use the Datasheet layout for the subform. Use the Trek style. Keep the form name as Agents1 and specify that you want to modify the form's design. Finish the wizard.

   f. Remove the First Name and Last Name controls from their current layout and move them to the same line and to the right of the Employee ID control. Move the Office Location and Title controls to the second line. Adjust the size, alignment, and spacing of the controls.

   g. Change the Clients label to **Assigned To:** and move the label and subform up near the line above it.

   h. Change the font size of all labels and text except for the Title control in the main form to 12 points. Size the controls to fit.

   i. Change the Title control to read **ADVENTURE TRAVEL TOURS**. Change the font size to 24. Size and center the title at the top of the form. Apply a font color, border weight and color, background color, and other effects of your choice.

   j. Display the Page Header and Footer sections. In the Page Header section, add a label that reads **Travel Agent Assignments**. Increase the font size to 18. Size the label and center it on the form. Change the font and font color to one of your choice.

k. In the Page Footer area, insert an automatic page number control.

l. In the Form Footer, add a graphic Print Record command button.

m. In Layout view, adjust the column widths in the subform so the entire contents are displayed, if necessary. (You may need to scroll the form horizontally to access all the columns.)

n. Preview the form. If the form is too wide to fit on a single page in portrait orientation with narrow margins, readjust the size and position of controls and the width of the form as needed. Display the agent you selected for your record and print the form for your record only.

o. Save and close the form. Compact and repair the database. Close the database.

Animal Rescue Foundation Animal Tracking Form ★

CONTINUING EXERCISES

2. The director of the Animal Rescue Foundation likes the way the Fosters and Adopters tables show the corresponding animal data from the Animals table; however, he has asked if you can create a form that can be used to track the animal, foster care, and adoption data in one place to make it easier to view and update this information. To do this, you will create a main animal data form with two subforms for the foster and adoption data. Your completed form will look similar to that shown here.

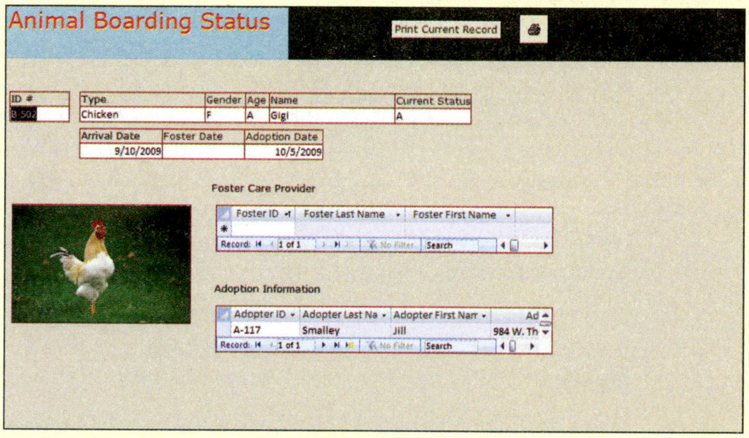

   a. Open the Animal Rescue Foundation database (which you last worked on in Step-by-Step Exercise 1 of Lab 4).

   b. Use the Form Wizard to create a new form and add all of the fields from the Rescues table. Use the Justified layout and Aspect style. Name the form **Animal Status** and open it in Design view.

   c. Delete the Adopter ID and Foster ID text and label controls. In Layout view, decrease the size of the Adoption Date controls to fit entries. Change the sizes of the three Date text control boxes so they are the same size (approximately one inch). Adjust the size of the Photo text control box to approximately 2 inches high by 2–5 inches wide. Delete the Photo Label control.

   d. In Design view, increase the size of the Detail section and use the Subform control to insert a subform at the bottom. Use the Fosters table and all of its fields as the source of the subform. Accept the default link option and name the subform **Foster Care Provider**.

   e. Repeat the previous step to create another subform using the Adopters table and all of its fields. Name the subform **Adoption Information**. Adjust the size of both subforms to $^3/_4$-inch high by $5^1/_2$-inches wide.

   f. In the Form Header section, change the form title control to read **Animal Boarding Status** in a 22-point font of your choice. Assign a font color, border, background color, and other effects of your choice. Resize and left-align the title as necessary.

   g. Add a 12-point label that reads **Created by [your name]** in the Page Header section. Center it below the title. Apply formatting that coordinates with the title. Add an automatic page numbering control in the Page Footer section.

   h. In Form Layout view, adjust the column widths in the subforms so each column's contents are displayed. This may result in a horizontal scroll bar being required for the subform.

i. Rearrange and resize the controls on the form as needed so that they are similar to the form shown above.

j. Switch to Design view. In the right corner of the Form Header section, add a command button to print the current form (found under Form Operations). Use the printer picture on the button and assign the command name **Print Displayed Form**. In the same location, add a second button to print the current record. Make the button a text button containing the words **Print Current Record**. Name the button appropriately. Size and position the buttons appropriately.

k. In Form view, apply an ascending sort to the ID# field. Add Gigi as the name for animal ID# B-502.

l. Preview the form. If the form is too wide to fit on a single page in portrait orientation, readjust the size and position of controls and the width of the form as needed. Use the Print Current Record button to print the form for animal ID# B-502 in portrait orientation.

m. Save and close the form. Compact and repair the database. Close the database.

Five Points Form ★★

3. After reviewing the tables that you created for the Five Points Center, Kathlyn, the owner, has asked you to create a form that will enable users of the database to update information about the spa packages as well as about the clients who have purchased each package. This request will require you to create a multiple-table form using fields from all three tables in the database. She also would like this new form to enable users to access the existing Client Info form quickly so they can update it when necessary. You will provide this access with a command button that links the two forms. The completed form will look similar to the form shown here.

a. Open the Five Points Center database file (which you last worked on in Step-by-Step Exercise 3 of Lab 4).

b. Use the Form Wizard to create a new form using all the fields from the Spa Packages table; the Client No, First Name, and Last Name fields from the Clients table; and the Package# field from the Packages Sold table. Specify that you want to view the data by Spa Packages. Use the Datasheet layout for the form and the Opulent style. Name the form **Spa Package Purchases** and the subform **Purchased by**. Open the form in Form view.

c. Because the Package Name is already displayed on the main form, and the only clients that will display on a package's record will be the ones who purchased that package, you do not need the Package # column to appear in the subform as well. Switch to Layout view and hide the Package # column. Adjust the column widths of the Client No, First Name, and Last Name fields appropriately.

d. Change the text of the Title control to read **Five Points Health and Wellness Center**. Apply a font type, font size, color, background, border, and other effects as desired. Adjust its size to display the entire title on one line.

e. Add a command button in the Form Footer section to open the Purchased by form and show all the records. Specify that you want text to appear on the button and enter **Open Purchased by Form** as the button label. Name the button **OpenFullFormButton**. Resize the button as necessary. Add a second command button to print the current record. Again, use a text label—**Print Current Form**—and give the button a logical name. Resize and align the button so that it appears to the right of the other button.

f. Display the Page Header and Footer sections. In the Page Header, add a label that reads **Spa Package Purchases**. Assign a font size of 14 and a color, border, background color, and other effects of your choice. Size and position the title appropriately.

g. In the Page Footer, insert an automatic page number control.

h. Return to Form view and try out the Open Purchased by Form command button. Change the package purchased for your record from Purification (3) to Rejuvenation (1). Close the Purchased by Form to return to the Spa Package Purchases form. Refresh the form.

i. Preview the form. If the form is too wide to fit on a single page in portrait orientation, readjust the size and position of controls and the width of the form as needed. Print the form for the Five Points Rejuvenation package using the print button. Save and close the form.

j. Compact and repair the database. Close the database.

Downtown Internet Café Form ★★★

CONTINUING EXERCISES

4. The database you created for the Downtown Internet Café contains two tables: one with data regarding the café's inventory and vendors and another with inventory item costs and order information. To make it as easy as possible to review and update all of this data, Evan (the owner of the café) would like you to create a form that combines both tables. He also would like you to include the same order calculations on this form as in the To Be Ordered query you created previously. The completed form will look similar to the form shown here.

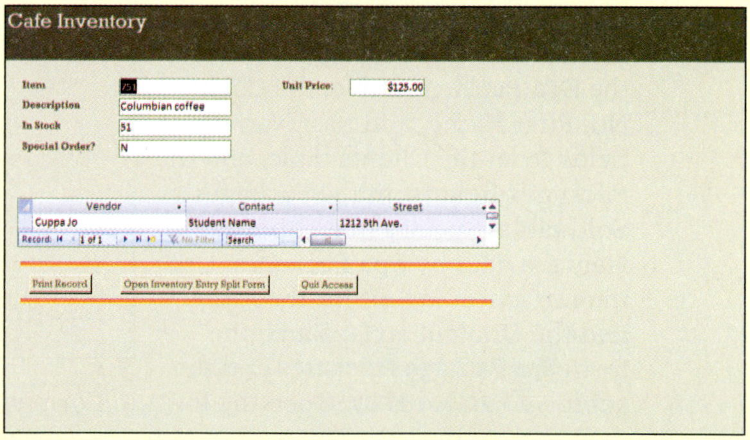

a. Open the Cafe Purchases database (which you last worked on in Step-by-Step Exercise 4 of Lab 4). Open the Suppliers table and expand the subdatasheet. If necessary, first select the Stock subdatasheet. Close and save the table.

b. Use the Form Wizard to create a form based on the Stock table. Use only those fields that Evan feels would be needed to update the inventory on a regular basis—Item #, Description, and In Stock. Use the Justified layout and the Foundry style. Name the form **Inventory Entry** and choose to open it to view or enter information.

c. Evan wants to see the impact of using the form on the underlying table data. Use the Split Form command to change the Inventory Entry form to a split form, resulting in a new form. Using the form in the upper pane, adjust the number of packages of coffee filters in stock to **14** and move to the next record. Close the split form, naming it **Inventory Entry Split**. Close the Inventory Entry form.

d. Use the Form Wizard to create a form with all of the fields from the Stock table. Use the Columnar format and a style of your choice. Name the form **Inventory Item Orders**. Delete the Supplier field controls and add the Unit Price field to the form. Use the Subform control to create a subform that displays all the fields from the Suppliers table.

e. Position, align, vertically space, and size all controls appropriately. Add an appropriate form title and page header that includes your name. Add a color-filled border line below the Suppliers subform to help visually separate the inventory items. Add other enhancements of your choice to the form.

f. Below the line, include text command buttons to print the current record, open the Inventory Entry Split form, and quit the application. Align the controls. Add the same border line below the buttons.

g. Preview the form and make any adjustments needed to print the form in portrait orientation. Switch to Form view and display a the record with your name as the vendor contact. Print that record using the Print button.

h. Save and close the form. Compact and repair the database. Close the database.

LearnSoft Order Form ★★★

5. You are still working on the LearnSoft Company's database. The database currently contains two tables, Software and Software Sales, which you want to combine into one easy-to-use form. The owners also have requested that the form display a total of the quantity sold for each product. Your completed form will be similar to that shown here.

   a. Open the LearnSoft Titles database (which you last worked on in Step-by-Step Exercise 5 of Lab 4).

   b. Using the Form Wizard, create a multiple-table form with all of the fields from the Software table and the Order ID, DateSold, and Quantity fields from the Software Sales table. View the data by Software, use the Datasheet format, and select a style of your choice. Name the form **Software Orders** and name the subform **Software Orders Detail**. Choose to modify the form in Design view.

   c. Move the Developer field and its associated label up in its stack so that it is directly under the Title field.

   d. Switch to Form view and test the tab order. If the move has broken the tab order, return to Design view and correct it if necessary.

   e. Change the Title control to read **LearnSoft Application Software Sales**. Resize the control as necessary.

   f. In Layout view, select the Software Orders Detail subform and display a Totals row that sums the Quantity field.

g. Next, you will create several command buttons in the Software Orders form. Return to Design view and, in the Form Footer section, add command buttons to accomplish the following tasks:
   - Display the top 50 percent selling titles by running the Software Package Sales query (include descriptive text in the command button).
   - Print the displayed record.
   - Close the form.

h. Align and equally space the command buttons. Add automatic page numbers in the Page Footer section.

i. Preview the form and make adjustments as needed to print the form in portrait orientation.

j. Switch to Form view and display the record with your name as the developer. Select and print the record and then save and close the form.

k. Compact and repair the database. Close the database.

on your own

Dental Patients Form ★★

1. You want to enhance the database you developed for the dentist office by creating a form that combines both of its tables. This way, anyone (including you) who has to access or update a patient's contact, insurance, or payment information can do so in one central location. Open the Dental Patients database you updated in On Your Own Exercise 1 of Lab 4 and create a form that displays the patient information in the main form and the patient's billing information in a subform. Format the form to improve its appearance. Include appropriate information in a form header and a page header. Include a form footer with **Created by [your name]** and a page footer with automatic page numbering. Include a command button to display a blank form and another to print a form. Print the first page of the form and then save and close it.

WriteOn! Data Entry Form ★★

2. The WriteOn! database you created in On Your Own Exercise 3 in Lab 4 needs a data entry form. Create a single form that can be used to enter all the data into the underlying tables. Use subforms where necessary. Use the features you learned in these tutorials to enhance the appearance of the form. Create a command button to print the form and any others that enhance the use of the form. Enter your name as one of the suppliers and print the form that displays your name.

Lewis & Lewis Data Entry Form ★★

3. The database you have created for Lewis & Lewis has eased the workload in the personnel department. In order to facilitate data entry in the employee and consultant tables, you have been asked to create a new form. Use the ac02_Lewis Personnel database you updated in On Your Own Exercise 2 of Lab 4. Create a form that includes the information from the Consultant Contact table in the main form and the Consultant Billing table in the subform. Enhance the form's appearance using the techniques you learned in this lab. Add a command button to print the new form. Add your name to the page header. Use the new command button to print the form.

EMP Enterprises Form ★★★

4. As manager for EMP Enterprises, you have created a database (EMP Enterprises) that includes employee and expense request information (On Your Own Exercise 4 in Lab 4). To make it more efficient, you want to be able to update these tables using a single form. Create a form from the Employee Info table and add the Employee Expense table as subform. Display a Totals row in the subform that sums the total expense amount for each employee. Reformat the form as desired. Include your name in the Form Footer and automatic page numbers in the Page Footer. Print one page of this form and then save and close it.

Tri-County Little League Form ★★★

5. The database you created for the Tri-County Little League in On Your Own Exercise 5 in Lab 4 has been a successful upgrade for the league. They would like to use the database to keep an inventory of the league equipment and track the equipment distribution. Open the Little League database and create a multiple-table form named **Team Rosters** that includes the data from the players and coaches tables. Then add a subform to display the equipment allocation for each team. The league hands out a catcher's mitt, a catcher's chest protector, a catcher's mask, six bats, and a case (12) of baseballs to each team. Four teams have received a pitching machine in addition to the standard equipment. Enhance the table's appearance using the skills you learned in the lab. Add a command button to the form to print the form and one that will open the equipment form. Include your name and the current date in the Page Footer. Print the first record in the form.

Creating Custom Reports, Charts, Pivot Charts, and Mailing Labels

LAB 6

Objectives

After completing this lab, you will know how to:

1. Group report records.
2. Calculate group totals.
3. Customize a report's layout.
4. Enhance a report's appearance.
5. Add a calculated control to a report.
6. Apply conditional formatting.
7. Create a chart in a report.
8. Use PivotChart view.
9. Create mailing labels using the Label Wizard.
10. Create a startup form.
11. Secure a database with password protection.
12. Use a database template.

Case Study

Lifestyle Fitness Club

The owners of the Lifestyle Fitness Club are impressed with your ability to use Access to locate and analyze the employee data. You have used the program to automate the updates and changes that occur to the employee tables and to quickly find answers to many different types of queries. Thus far, you have created simple reports from these queries that are quite acceptable for many informal uses.

Next, the club owners would like you to create a more formal status report to be distributed to managers at the various club locations. This report will group and summarize the payroll data in an organized and attractive manner, as shown in the report on the following page. Additionally, you want to display the total gross pay information as a chart.

You also have been asked to use the employee database to create mailing labels. A sample page of the labels you will create is shown on the following page.

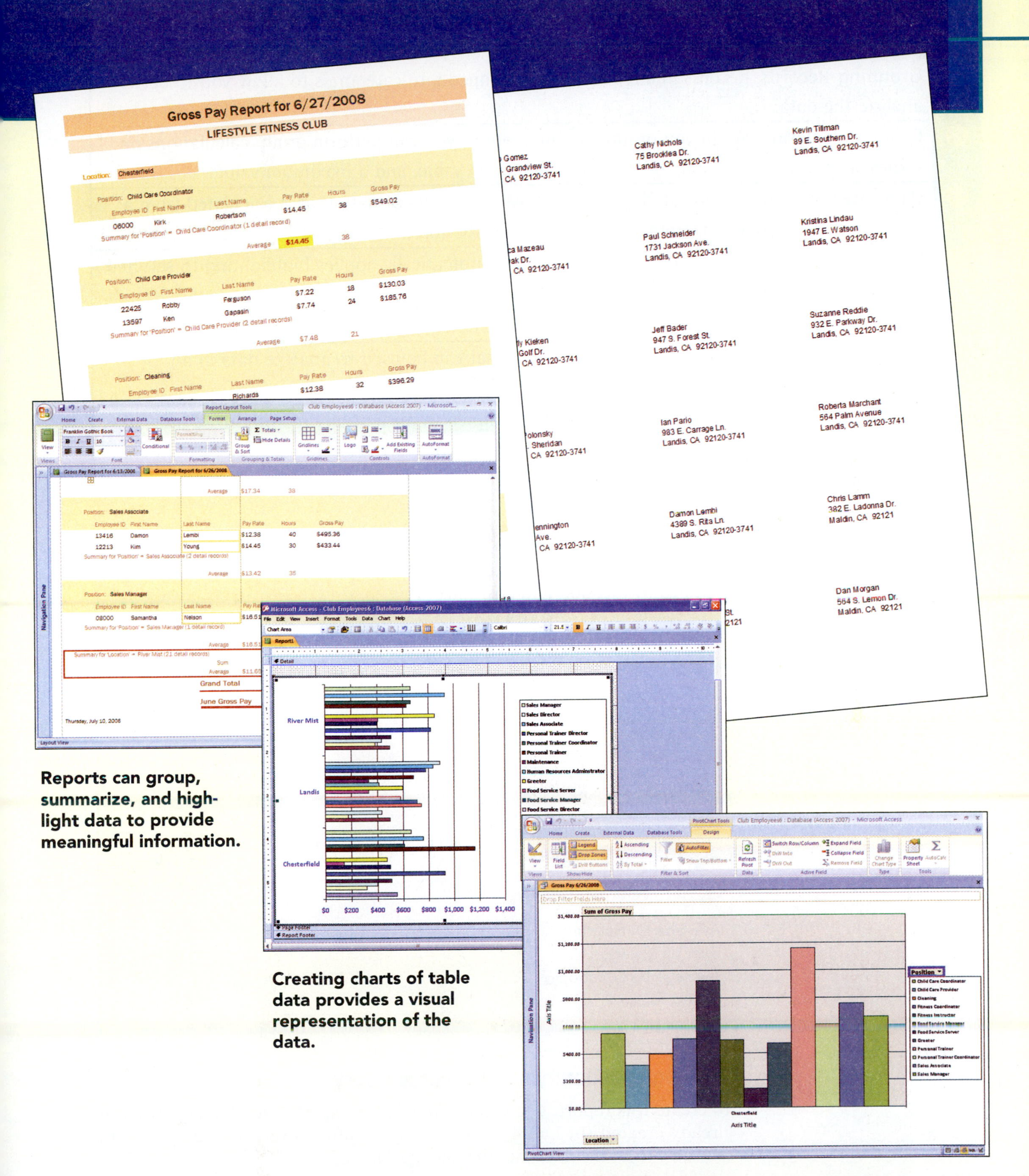

Reports can group, summarize, and highlight data to provide meaningful information.

Creating charts of table data provides a visual representation of the data.

Pivot charts allow users to quickly analyze table data interactively.

Concept Preview

The following concepts will be introduced in this lab:

1. **Grouping Records** Records in a report can be grouped into categories to allow you to better analyze the data.
2. **Group Calculation** When you group data in a report, you can perform group calculations on values such as a group total, an average, a minimum value, and a maximum value.
3. **Calculated Control** A calculated control displays the results of data that is calculated from a field in a table or query or from another control in the form.
4. **Conditional Formatting** Conditional formatting automatically applies highlighting to selected data in text or combo box controls based on a condition that you specify.
5. **Chart** A chart is a visual representation of numeric data.
6. **Pivot Chart** A pivot chart is an interactive chart that can be used to analyze data in a datasheet or form.
7. **Password** A password is a private code that is designed to prevent any unauthorized users from opening the database unless they know the password.

Creating a Grouped Report

The first report you want to create will display the employees' gross pay grouped by location and position.

Planning the Report

You have sketched out the report to look like the one shown below.

Gross Pay Report for xx/xx/xx

Location:	XXXXXX				
Position:	XXXXXX				
Employee ID	First Name	Last Name	Pay Rate	Hours	Gross Pay
XXXX	XXXXXX	XXXXXX	$X.XX	XX	$XXXX.XX
XXXX	XXXXXX	XXXXXX	$X.XX	XX	$XXXX.XX
Average by Position			$X.XX	XX.X	
Sum by Location					$XXXX.XX
Average by Location			$X.XX	XX.X	
Grand Total					$XXXXX.XX

Running and Modifying the Source Query

To create this report, you will use the Gross Pay 6/27/2008 query that you already created (in Lab 4). It is usually helpful to run the query first to remind you of the data that the query gathers.

1

- **Copy the file ac06_Club Employees in your data file location and rename the copy Club Employees6.**
- **Start Access 2007 and open the Club Employees6 database file with content enabled.**
- **Open the Personal Data table and change the first and last names in record 99999 to your name.**
- **Close the Personal Data table.**
- **Open the Gross Pay 6/27/2008 query.**

Your screen should be similar to Figure 6.1

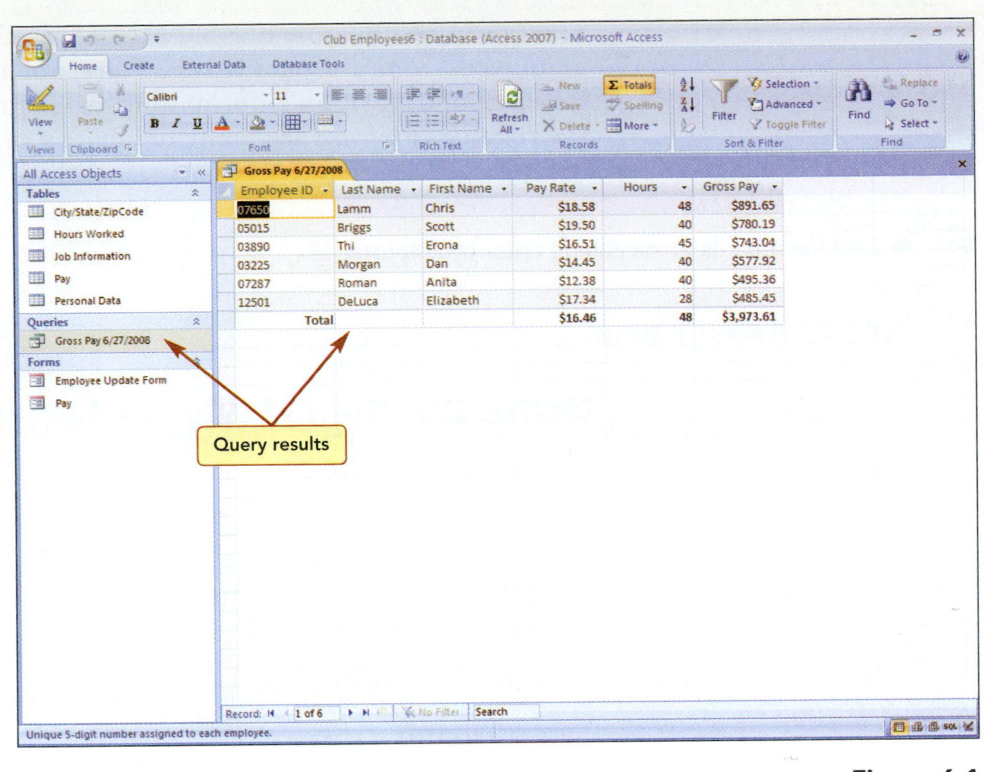

Figure 6.1

The query datasheet displays the Employee ID, Last Name, First Name, Pay Rate, and Gross Pay fields. It also restricts the results to the top 25 percent of those with a location of Landis. You need to modify the query to display all records from all locations. You also want the Position and Location information displayed in the query results.

2

- **Switch to Design view.**
- **Add the Location and Position fields to the design grid in that order after the First Name field.**
- **Remove the SQL subquery statement from the Employee ID criteria cell.**
- **Click Return: 25% and choose All.**
- **Run the query.**

Your screen should be similar to Figure 6.2

Figure 6.2

The query results now display 61 records that meet the criteria. Those employees who are paid a salary are not included in the results. The location and position information for each record also is displayed in the results. Now you are ready to create a report using the data from the query.

3 **Sort the records in ascending order by Employee ID.**

Close and save the query.

Using the Report Wizard to Create a Grouped Report

You have used all the methods to create reports except the Report Design command on the Create tab. This method starts with a blank report that is open in Report Design view. Now that you are much more familiar with using Design view in general from using Form Design view to modify the Employee Update Form, you feel this method also would not be appropriate for creating a complex grouped report. Instead, you think the best method to use is the Report Wizard.

More About

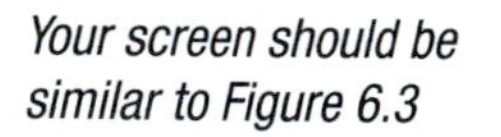

To learn about creating reports in Report Design view, see 2.6 Create Reports in the More About appendix.

1 **Click Report Wizard in the Reports group of the Create tab.**

Your screen should be similar to Figure 6.3

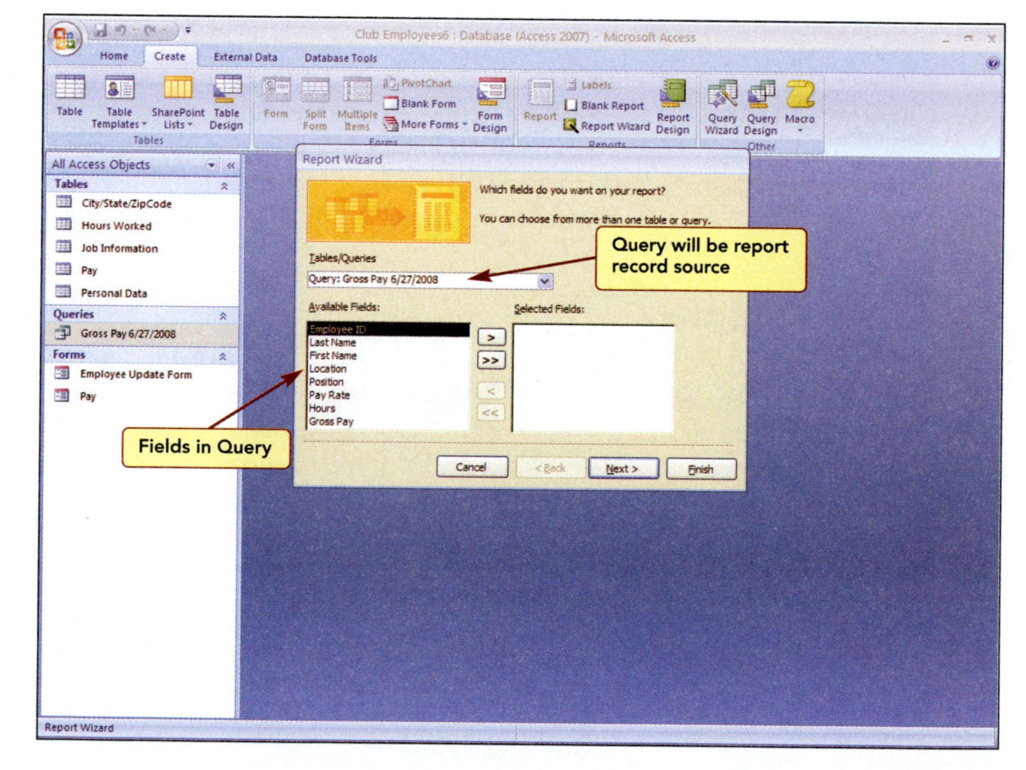

Figure 6.3

The Report Wizard dialog box correctly displays the name of the selected query as the object on which the report will be based and the Available Fields list box displays the fields that are included in the design grid in the Gross Pay 6/27/2008 query. You want to include all the fields in the report.

2 **Click [>>] Add All Fields.**

Click [Next >].

Your screen should be similar to Figure 6.4

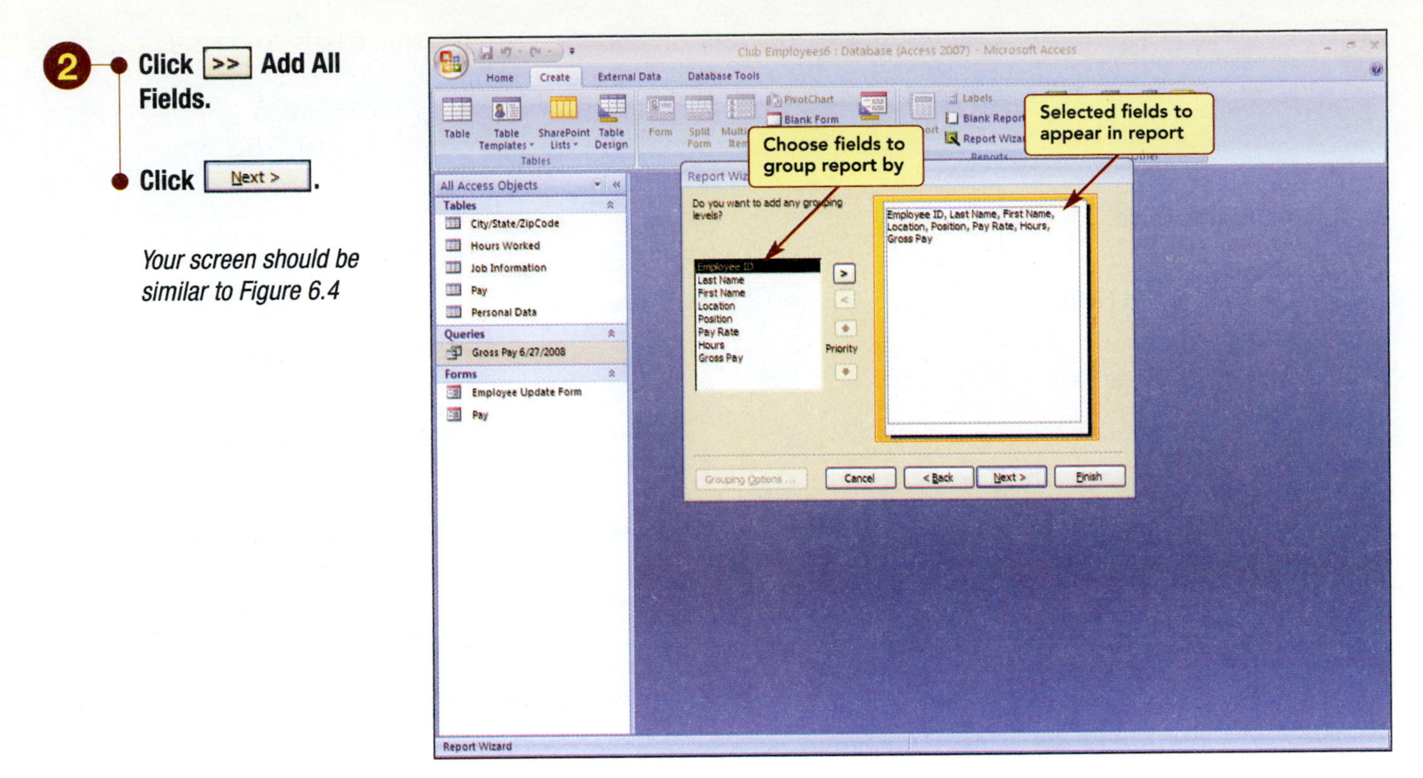

Figure 6.4

In the next dialog box, you need to select the fields on which you want to group the report.

Concept 1

Grouping Records

1 Records in a report can be **grouped** by categories to allow you to better analyze the data. It is often helpful to group records and calculate totals for the entire group. For example, it might be useful for a store manager to group payroll records by department. Then, rather than getting a long list of pay for individual employees, the manager could get a report showing total payroll for each department. A mail-order company might group orders by date of purchase, then by item number to see detailed sales information.

In Access, you can create a report that will automatically group records based on the fields you select. Groups should be created based on priority from the largest to the smallest. You can group by as many as 10 fields in any one report.

You decide that you want to group the records by location and then by position to make it easier for the club owners to assess the staffing and workload and identify any problem areas.

3 Choose Location.

- Click [>] Add Field.
- Choose Position.
- Click [>] Add Field.

Your screen should be similar to Figure 6.5

Figure 6.5

The report will group the data first by location and then by position within the location.

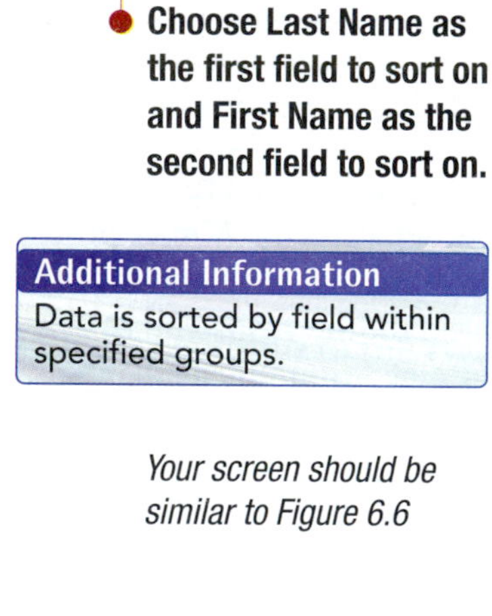

4 Click [Next >].

- Choose Last Name as the first field to sort on and First Name as the second field to sort on.

Additional Information

Data is sorted by field within specified groups.

Your screen should be similar to Figure 6.6

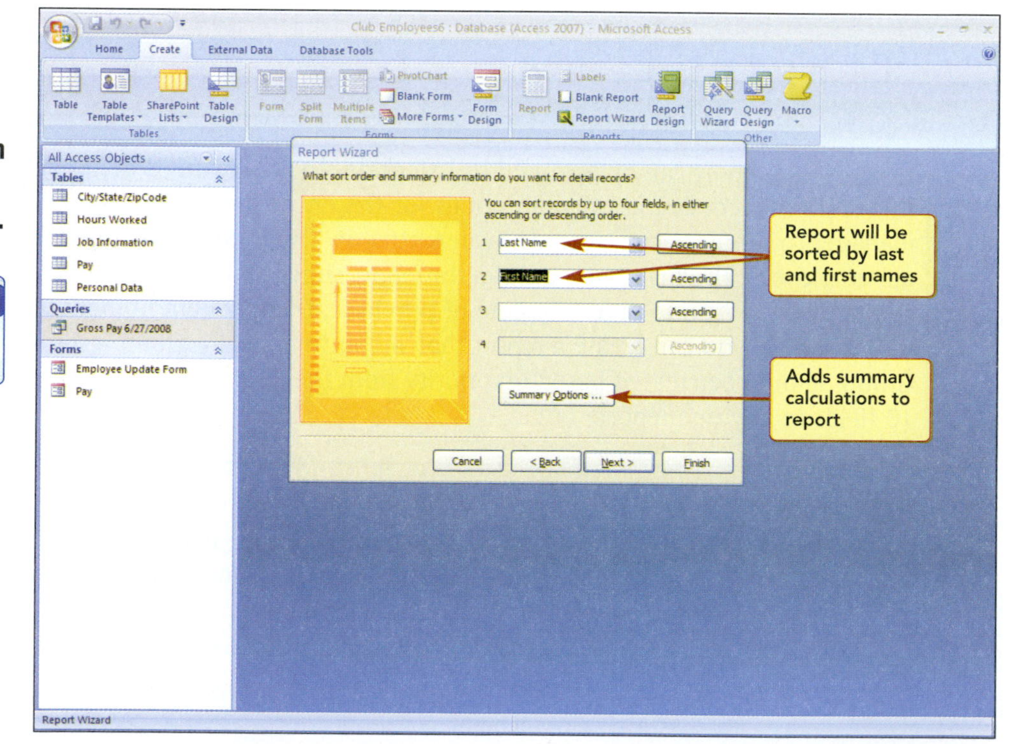

Figure 6.6

Because you have specified groups, you also can include calculations to summarize the grouped data.

5 Click Summary Options ... .

Your screen should be similar to Figure 6.7

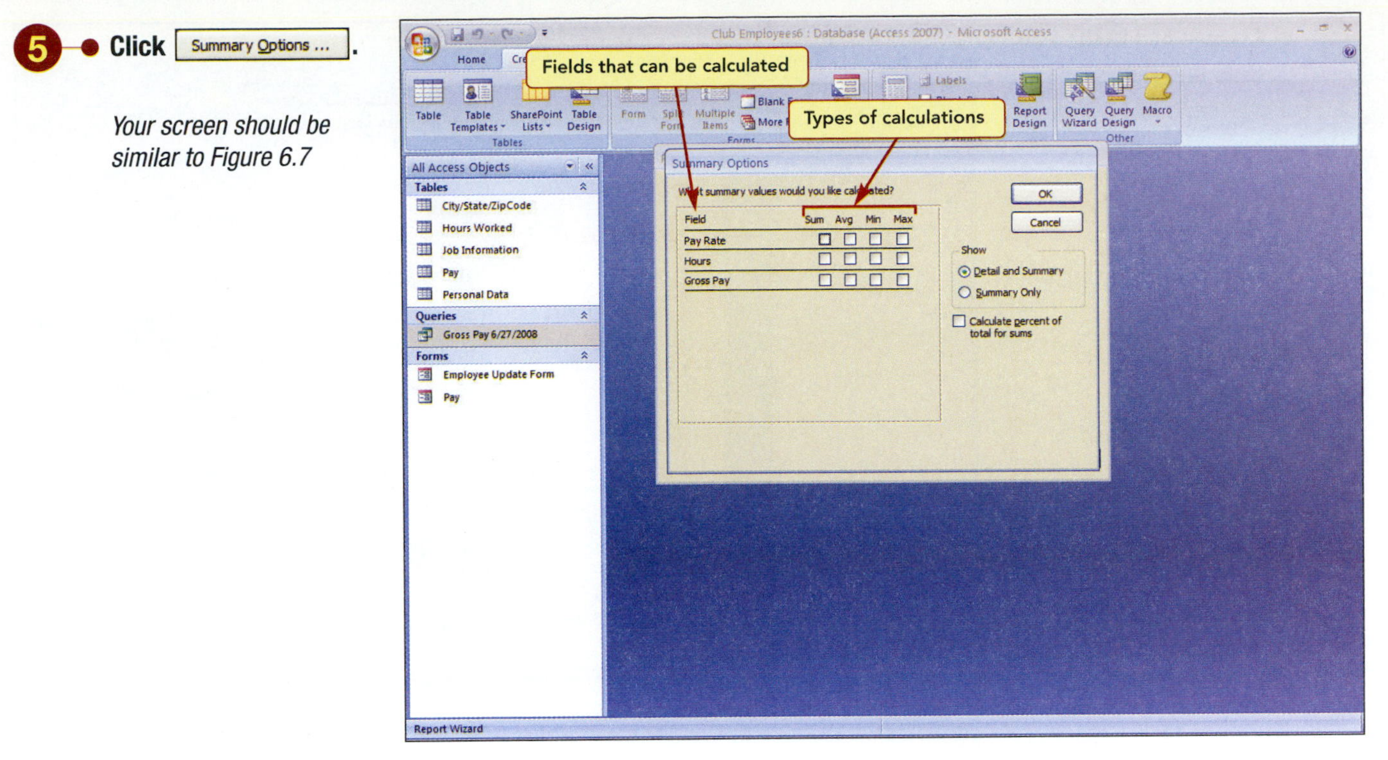

Figure 6.7

This wizard screen asks you to choose the type of calculation you want to use to summarize the grouped data on your report.

Concept 2

Group Calculation

2 When you group data in a report, you can perform **group calculations** on values such as a group total, an average, a minimum value, and a maximum value. The group calculations that can be made on values are Sum (adds all values by group), Avg (calculates the average value for the group), Min (calculates the lowest value for the group), and Max (calculates the highest value for the group).

You can select multiple calculations to complete different analyses of the data. For example, a mail-order company might calculate the sum of different products sold on each day of the month and the average sale for each day. You also can calculate the percent of total for the sums. For example, the mail-order company might want to know what percentage of total sales were made on a specific product for September 15.

You can further customize the report to display both detailed information and the summary information, or just the summary information while hiding the details about the individual items.

You would like the report to display a total and average of the gross pay for each club location and job position.

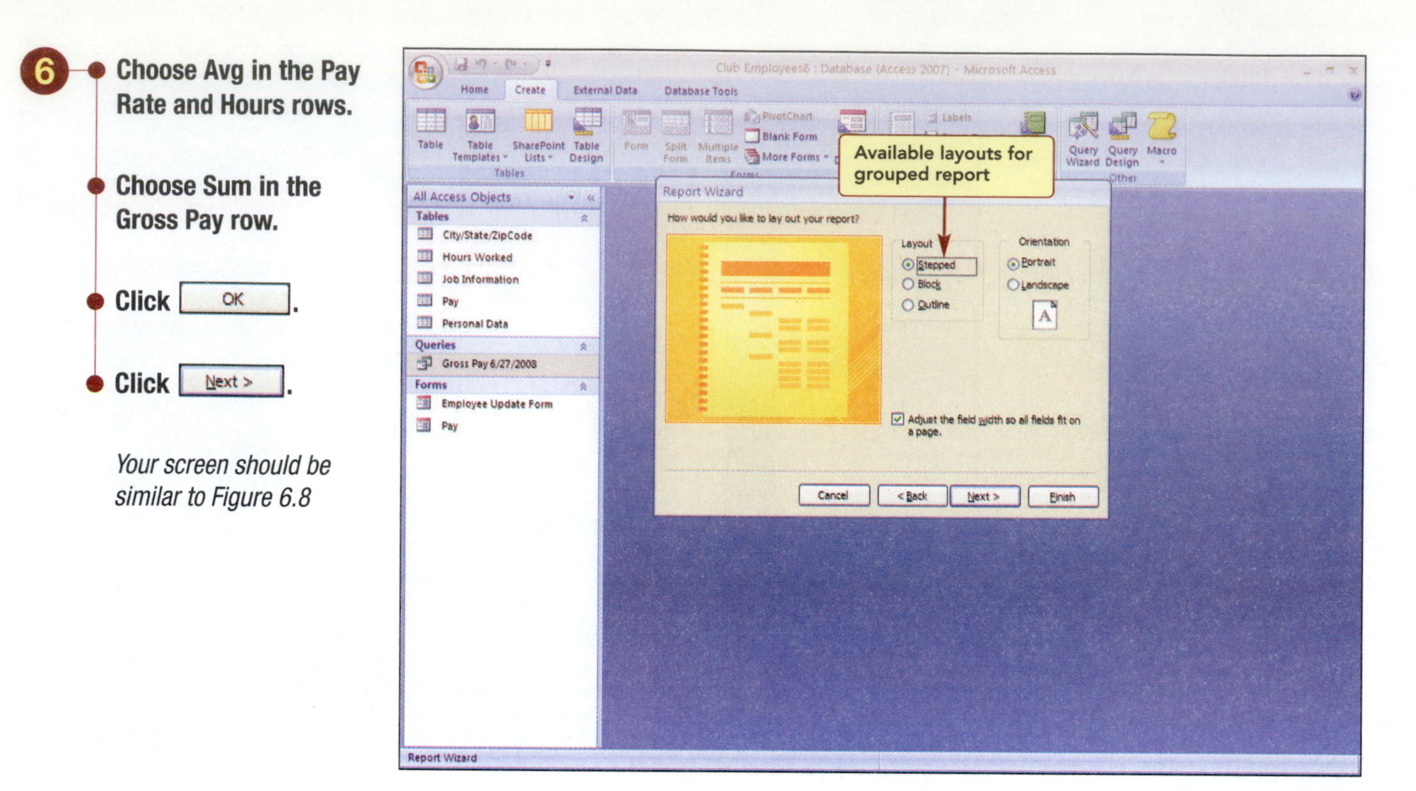

Figure 6.8

In this dialog box you are asked to select from three different layout options for a grouped report.

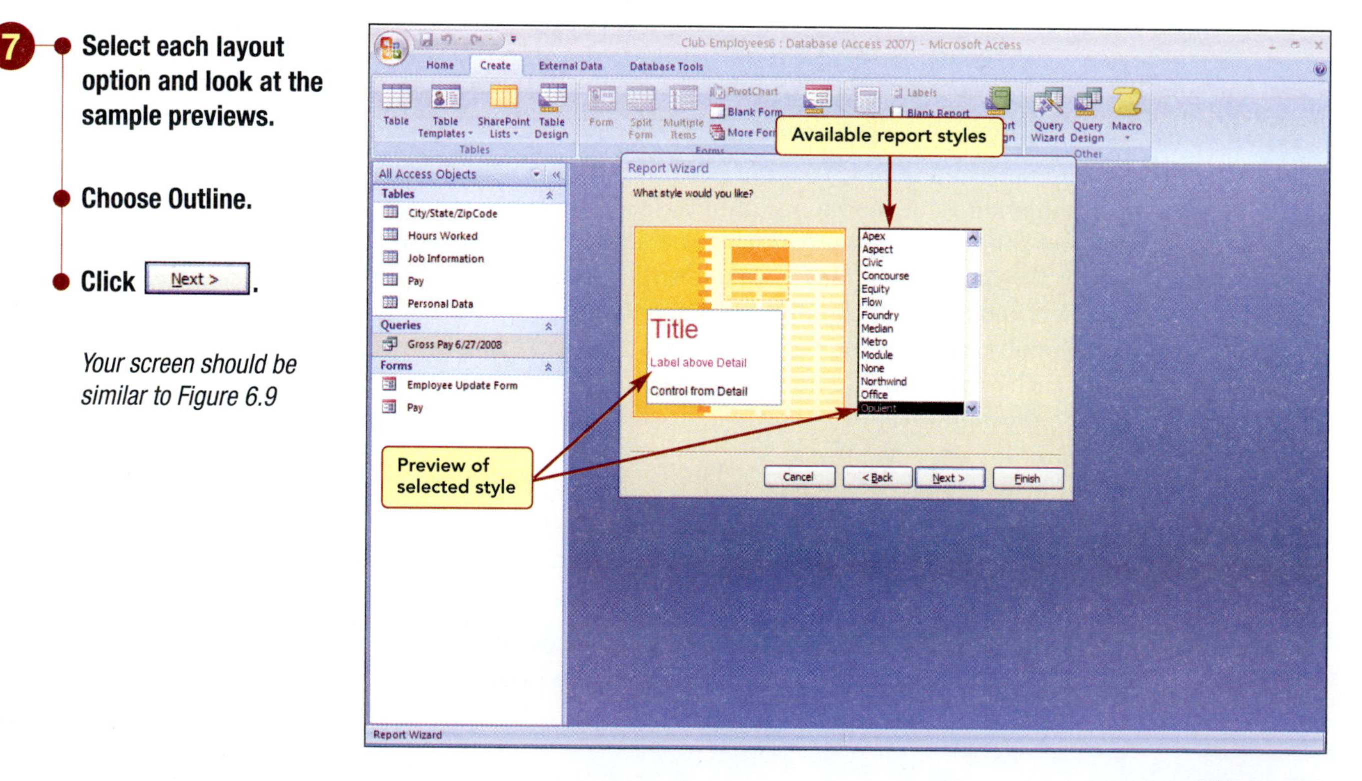

Figure 6.9

You now need to select a style for the report.

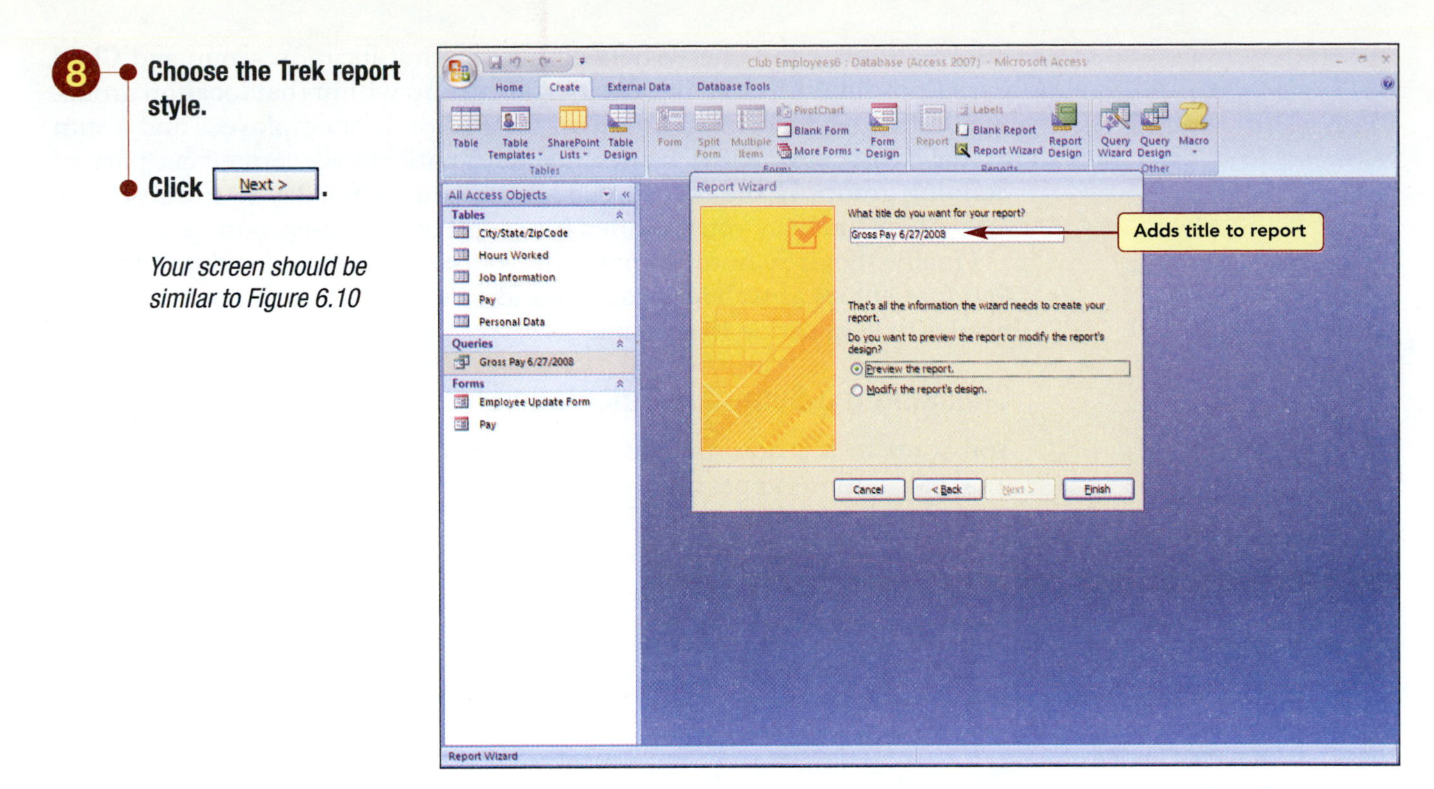

8 **Choose the Trek report style.**

Click Next >.

Your screen should be similar to Figure 6.10

Figure 6.10

The final Wizard screen asks you to enter a title for the report.

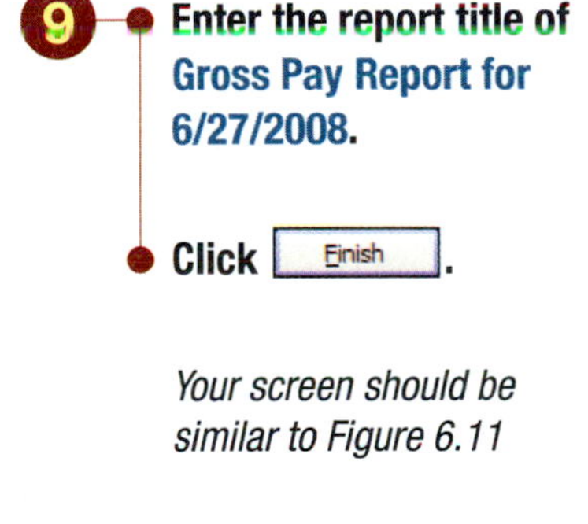

9 **Enter the report title of Gross Pay Report for 6/27/2008.**

Click Finish.

Your screen should be similar to Figure 6.11

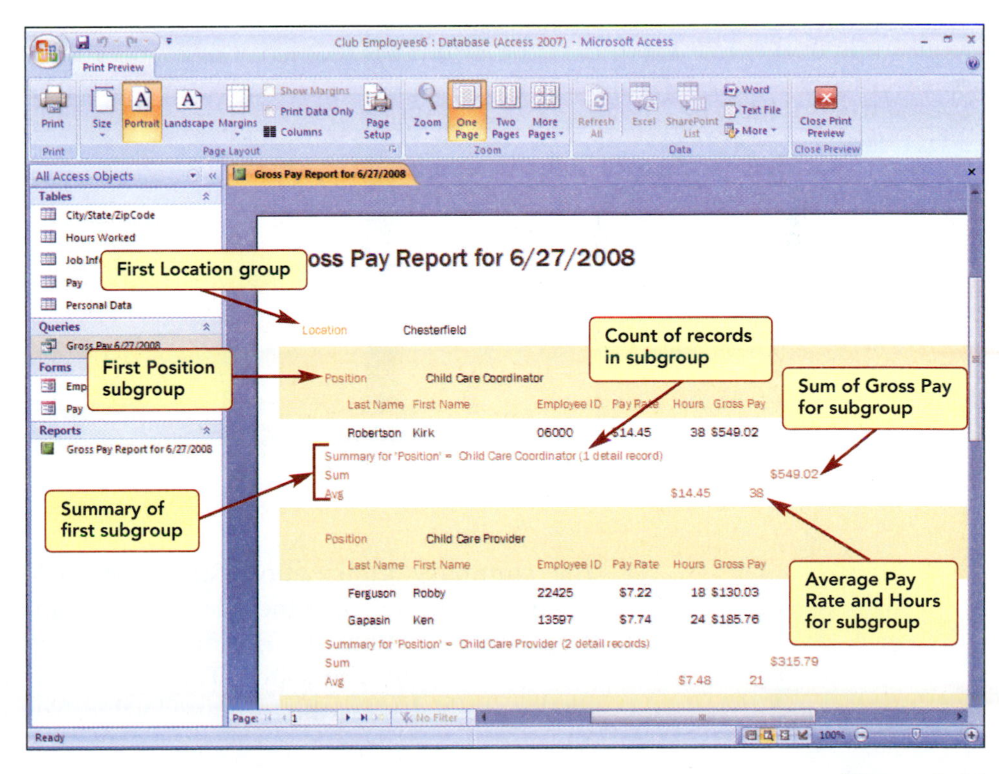

Figure 6.11

The report is displayed in Print Preview. The report name is used as the title for the report. The data in the report is grouped by location and position and the records are alphabetized by last name within groups. The information for the Chesterfield club is the first location group and Child Care Coordinator is the first Position subgroup within that location group. In addition, each location group displays a count of employees and a sum of the gross pay. These values are automatically generated as part of defining groups in the report. The average values for Pay Rate and Hours also are included as you specified for each Position subgroup.

Finally, the Trek AutoFormat style you selected includes different font and font colors as well as a background color behind each Position group header to help define the groups.

Checking the Summary Calculations

You want to see how the location summary calculations and the grand total calculations appear in the report. To do this, move to the report page that displays the summary information for the Chesterfield location. Then you will look at the last page to see the report summary information.

1 **Display page 3 and scroll the page to see the summary information for the Chesterfield location.**

Your screen should be similar to Figure 6.12

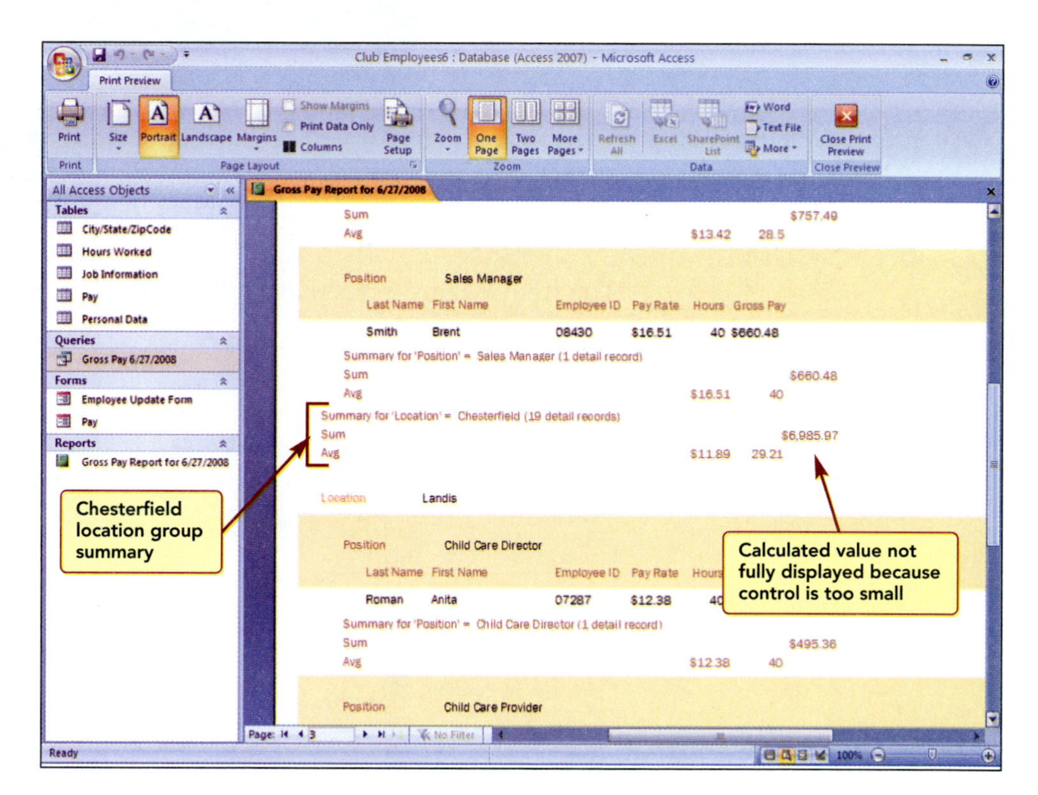

Figure 6.12

The summary information for Chesterfield appears before the Landis location group head. It includes a count value, a total gross pay value, and the average Pay Rate and Hours for that club location. Notice the total gross pay value appears truncated. This is because the control size is slightly too small to fully display the formatted value. You will fix this shortly.

Display the top of the last page of the report (9).

Your screen should be similar to Figure 6.13

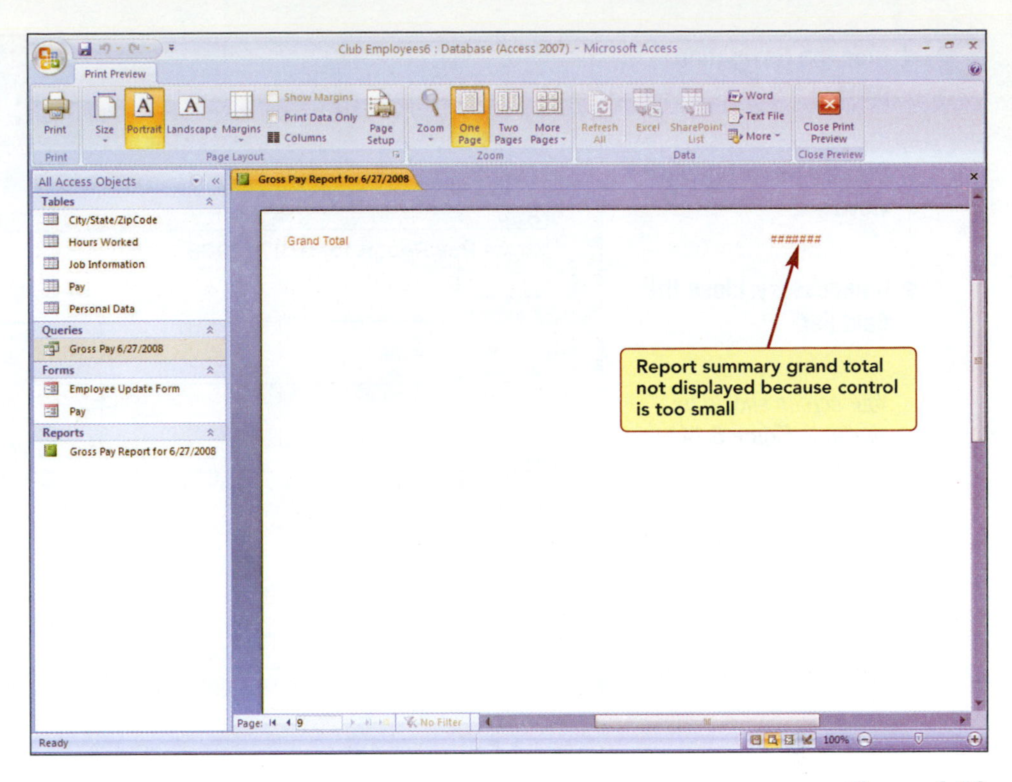

Figure 6.13

A grand total gross pay value for all clubs appears as the last item at the end of the report. Again, the value appears as ####### because the control size is too small.

The report has all the data you requested, but you are not completely pleased with the way the report looks. You will make several changes to the arrangement of controls and add formatting to improve the report's readability and appearance.

Customizing the Report Layout

As you looked through the report, you saw several changes you wanted to make. The first change is to rearrange the order of the fields in the report and to size the fields appropriately. In addition, you want to make the Location group head more noticeable, to change the display of the date in the footer to exclude the day of the week, and to center the title over the report. As you recall from your previous work with reports and forms, most of these changes can be made in Report Layout view. Others will require that you work in Report Design view.

First, you will look at Report Design view to see how a grouped report's structure is different from an ungrouped report.

1

- **Hide the Navigation pane.**
- **Display Report Design view.**
- **If necessary, close the field list.**

Your screen should be similar to Figure 6.14

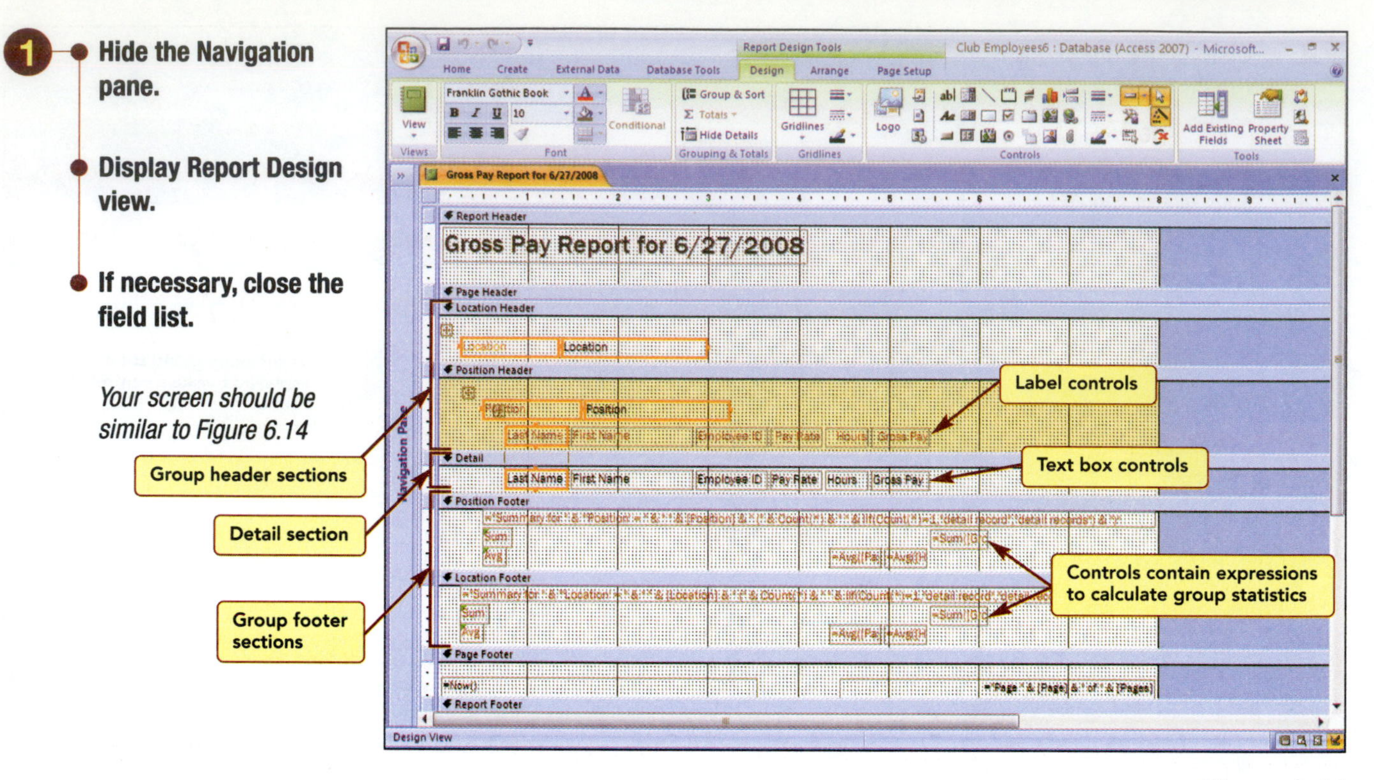

Figure 6.14

Notice that Report Design view includes several additional sections for the grouped information. In addition to the standard Report Header, Page Header, Detail, Page Footer, and Report Footer sections, there are also sections called Location Header and Position Header as well as Location Footer and Position Footer. These are called Group Header and Footer sections and they display group identification information on the report each time the group changes.

The Position Header section displays the label controls for each field column, while the Detail section contains the text box controls. The expressions used to calculate the group and report average and sum values are displayed in the appropriate Position and Location Footer sections. The Report Footer includes the expression to calculate the gross pay grand total.

You want to move and resize several of the report controls first. You will use Report Layout view to make these changes so that you can view the data while making your changes.

Resizing and Rearranging Controls

The first change you will make is to reduce the size of the Location and Position label controls to fit their contents and add a colon after the text in the controls. Working in Report Layout view is just like working in Form Layout view. However, because the report is grouped, selecting and changing a label control affects the display of the labels in each group.

1

- **Switch to Layout view.**
- **Resize the Location and Position label controls to more closely fit their contents.**

> **Additional Information**
>
> Use Size to Fit in the Position group of the Arrange tab to automatically resize the selected control to fit its contents.

- **Add a : following the text in the Location and Position label controls.**

Your screen should be similar to Figure 6.15

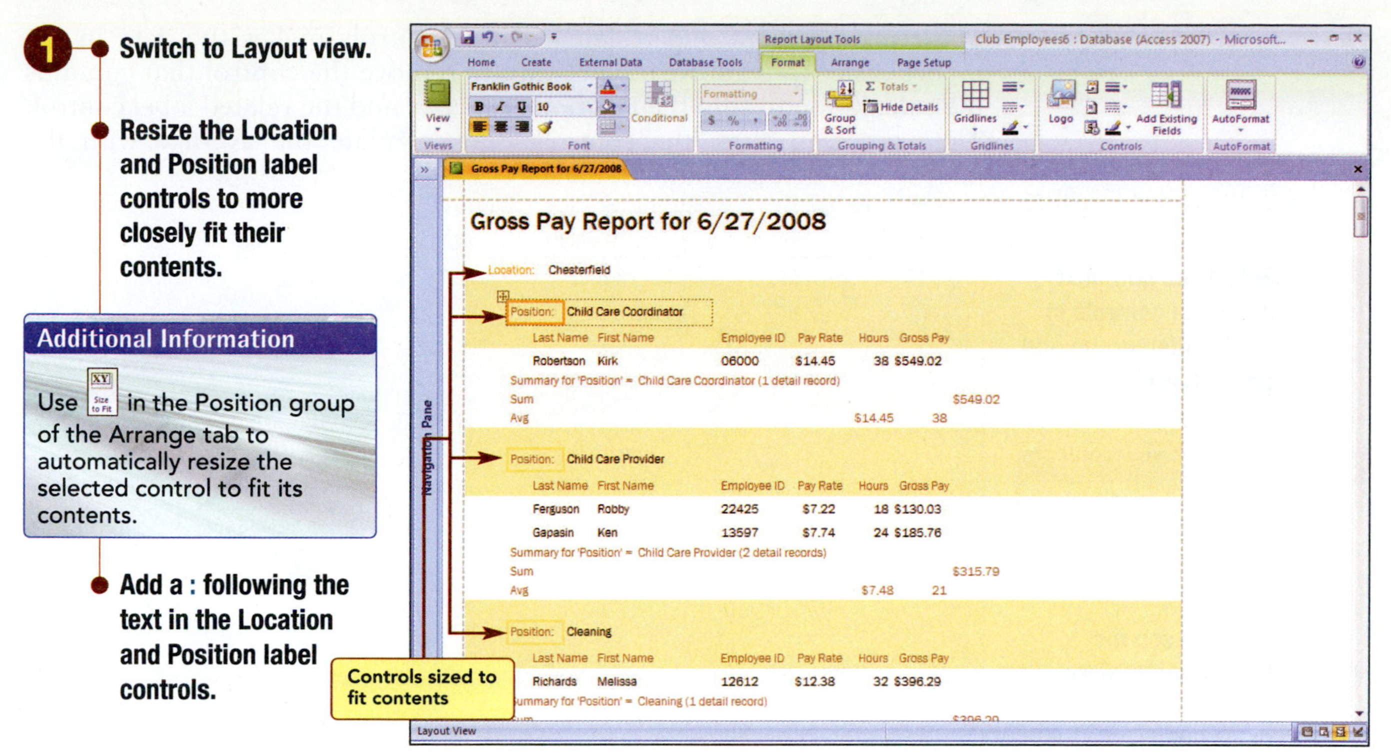

Figure 6.15

The Position and Location label controls are smaller and the bound text controls are now closer to the label control. These changes are reflected in all groups of the report. Next, you will move several of the controls so the report layout is easier to read.

2

- **Move the Employee ID field column before the Last Name column.**
- **Move the First Name column before the Last Name column.**
- **Increase the size of the Last Name, Hours, and Gross Pay controls as in Figure 6.16.**
- **Save the changes you have made to the report.**

Your screen should be similar to Figure 6.16

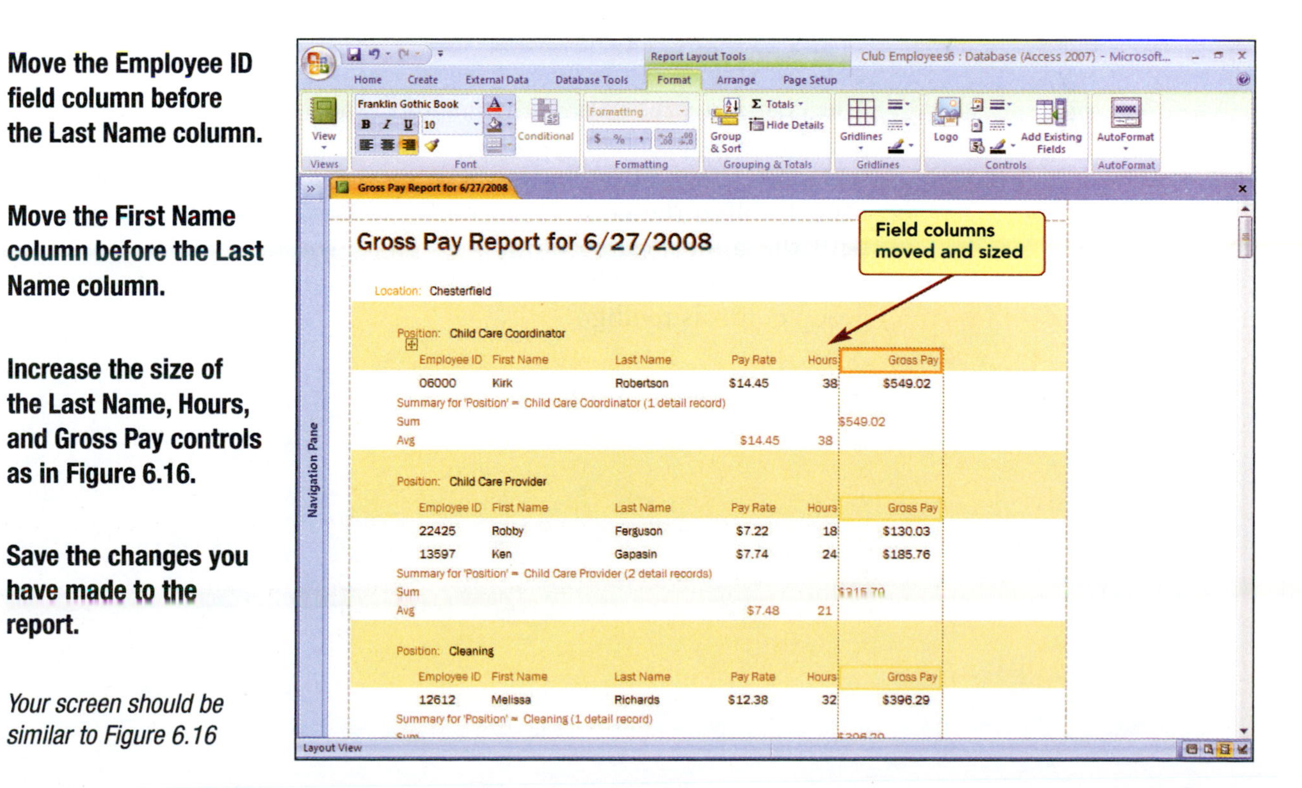

Figure 6.16

The rearrangement and resizing of the controls makes the data in the report easier to read. Next, you want to remove the control that contains the calculation to sum the Position gross pay and the related label control. Then you will align the controls that calculate the average with the appropriate field's column of data.

3 **Select the Sum text and label controls in the Position group and press Delete.**

Having Trouble?

To select multiple controls, hold down Shift while clicking on each control.

- **Scroll to see the Location summary group section for Chesterfield.**

Your screen should be similar to Figure 6.17

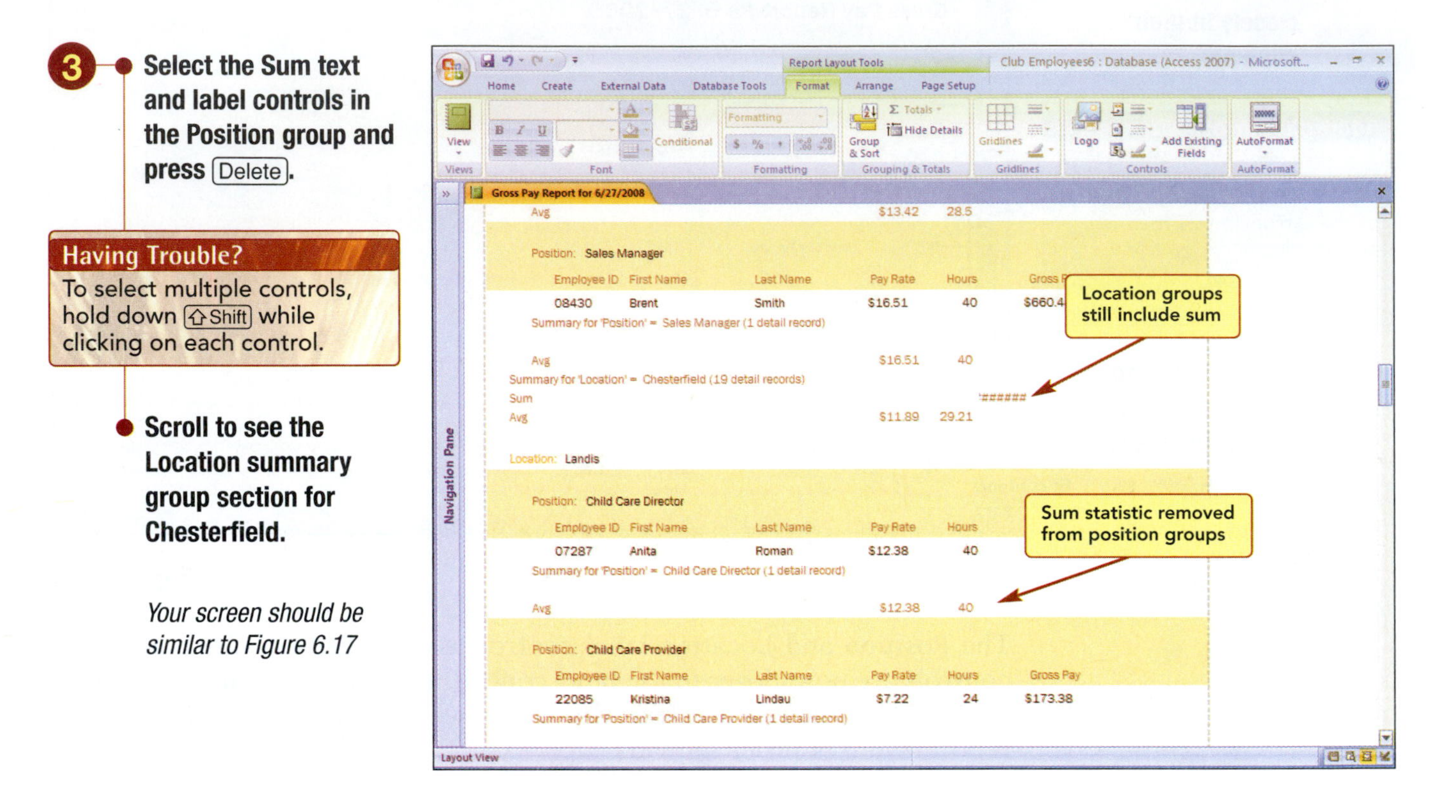

Figure 6.17

The Position summary statistics and labels have been deleted from each position group, leaving only the average statistics. The Location group summary area still includes the sum and average calculations. Next, you want to align the controls in both the Position and the Location groups with the appropriate columns of data. You will make these changes in Report Design view because you will be able to easily identify the correct group controls to align.

4 **Display Design view.**

- **Select the Hours control in the Detail section and the two controls containing the =AVG(Hours) expression in the Position Footer and Location Footer sections.**
- **Click Right in the Control Alignment group of the Report Design Tools Arrange tab.**
- **In a similar manner, select and align the three Pay Rate controls.**

Having Trouble?

Right- or left-align the Pay Rate controls depending on the controls' original relative positions.

Your screen should be similar to Figure 6.18

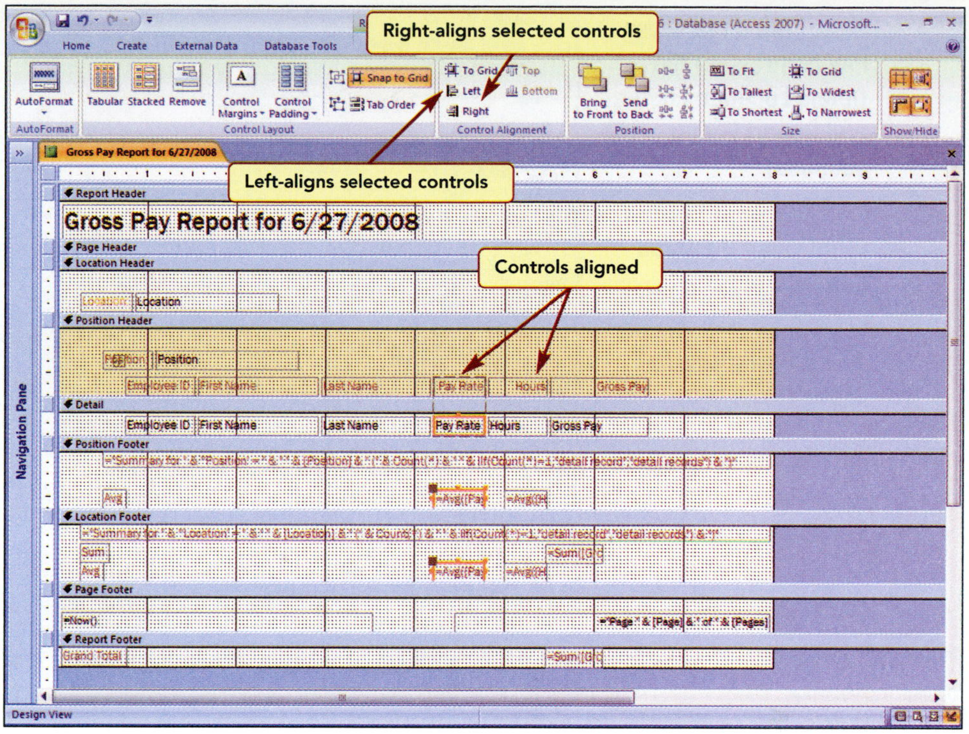

Right-aligns selected controls

Left-aligns selected controls

Controls aligned

Figure 6.18

The controls for the Hours and Pay Rate information are now evenly aligned with the appropriate data in the detail area. Next, you will align the gross pay controls.

5 Select the three Gross Pay controls (in the Detail, Location Footer, and Report Footer sections).

Right-align the three controls.

Your screen should be similar to Figure 6.19

Controls aligned

Figure 6.19

You will look at the changes you have made to the layout and make any further adjustments in Layout view.

6 Switch to Layout view.

Scroll to see the bottom of the report.

Edit the text in the Avg label control of the Position group and the Location group to **Average**.

Your screen should be similar to Figure 6.20

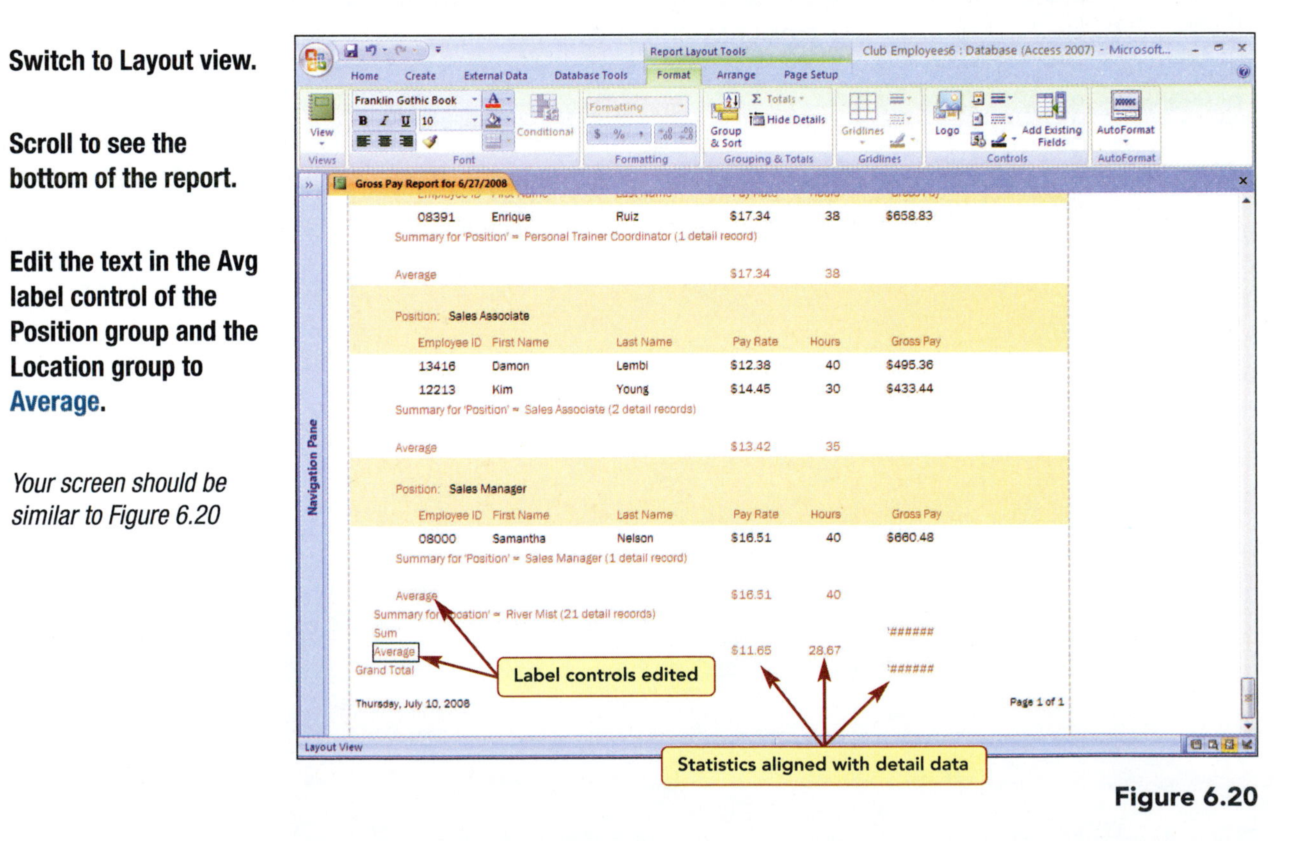

Figure 6.20

The statistics are now aligned appropriately with the columns of data. Next, you want to move the text controls closer to the statistics they describe.

7

- **Move the Location Average text control to the left of the Average Pay Rate data.**
- **Select the other three text controls (Average, Sum, and Grand Total) and right-align them with the Location Average text control.**
- **If necessary, right-align the Sum text control again until it is aligned correctly with the others.**

Your screen should be similar to Figure 6.21

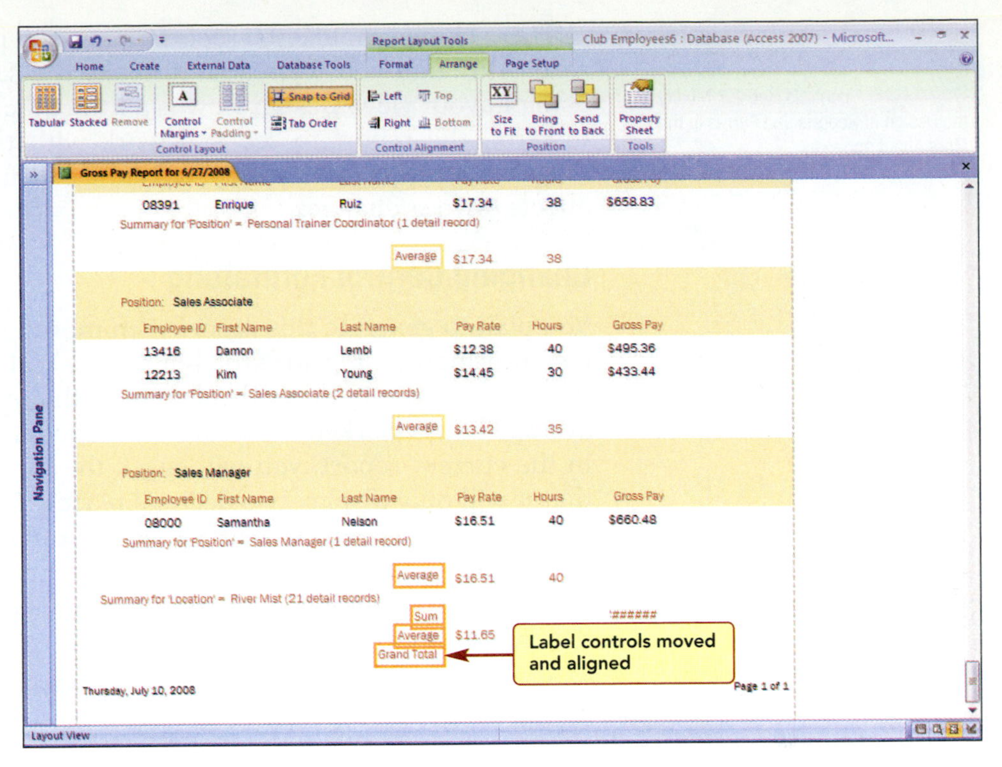

Figure 6.21

Finally, you will increase the size of the Sum and Grand Total text controls to display the values.

8

- **Select the Sum text control and increase the size of the control to fully display the value, including the $ symbol.**
- **Select the Grand Total text control and increase the size of the control to fully display the value, including the $ symbol.**

Your screen should be similar to Figure 6.22

Figure 6.22

The sum and grand total values now display the calculated values and they correctly display in currency format. This is because the report controls inherit the format from the data they use in the underlying table.

More About

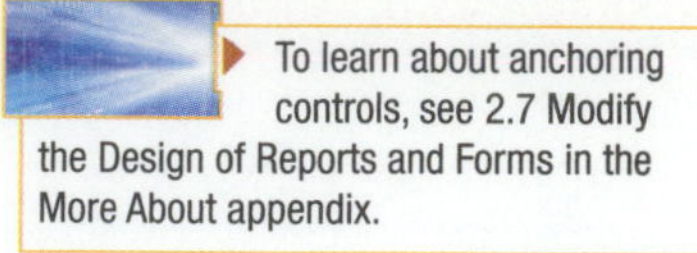

To learn about anchoring controls, see 2.7 Modify the Design of Reports and Forms in the More About appendix.

These changes make the report data much more organized and easier to read. Although you were able to make the same changes to the controls using Layout view, Design view is a little quicker because you do not need to scroll the report to see and work with the different group sections. However, Layout view has the advantage of immediately showing you the effects of your changes.

Changing Control Formatting

You plan to generate this report each month using the updated hours and pay information. Because the hours data will vary, you want to make sure that the report will never display more than two decimal places when the average hours worked is calculated. Although this value displays correctly in the current report, you will check the format of this control to ensure that it will only display two decimal places. The format for each control in a form or report can be changed without affecting the field format of the underlying table. The format choices vary with the data type of the control. Only the appearance of the control changes, not how users enter the data or how the data in the table is stored.

1 **Select the Average Hours control.**

Open the Report Layout Tools Format tab.

Open the General Number Format drop-down list in the Formatting group.

Your screen should be similar to Figure 6.23

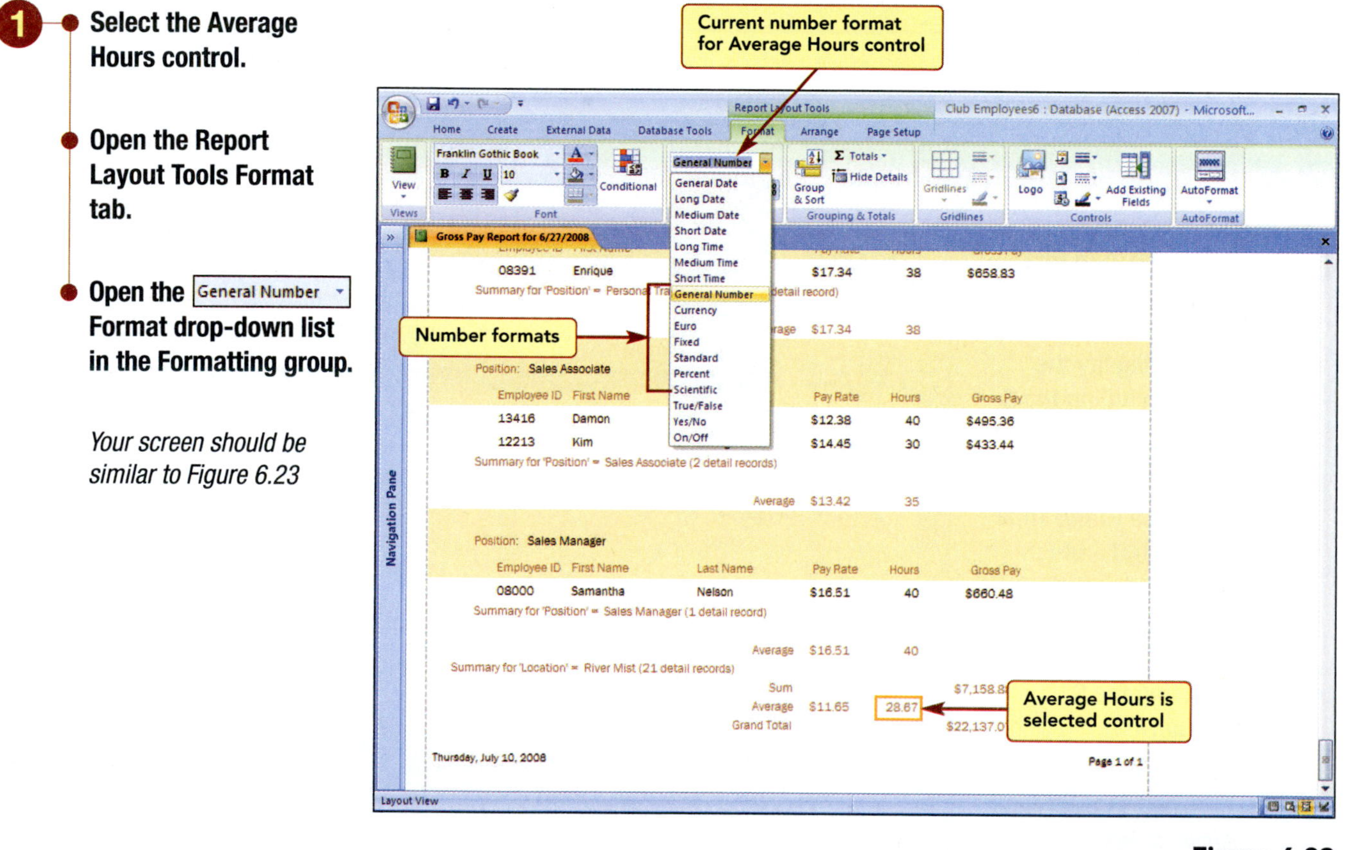

Figure 6.23

This control is formatted using the General Number format. This format displays a number as entered (or calculated) and is the default format. In addition to the date and Currency formats, there are several other number format options as described in the following table.

Setting	Description	Data	Display
General Number	Displays data as entered or calculated	1234.567	1234.567
Euro	Uses the Euro (€) symbol regardless of the Windows regional settings		
Fixed	Displays at least one digit; follows Windows regional settings	1234.567	1234.56
Standard	Uses the thousand separator; follows Windows regional settings	1234.567	1,234.56
Percent	Multiplies value by 100 and adds % sign; follows Windows regional settings	12	1200%
Scientific	Uses standard scientific notation	1234.567	1.23E + 03

You will change the Hours control format to standard.

2 **Choose Standard from the drop-down menu.**

Your screen should be similar to Figure 6.24

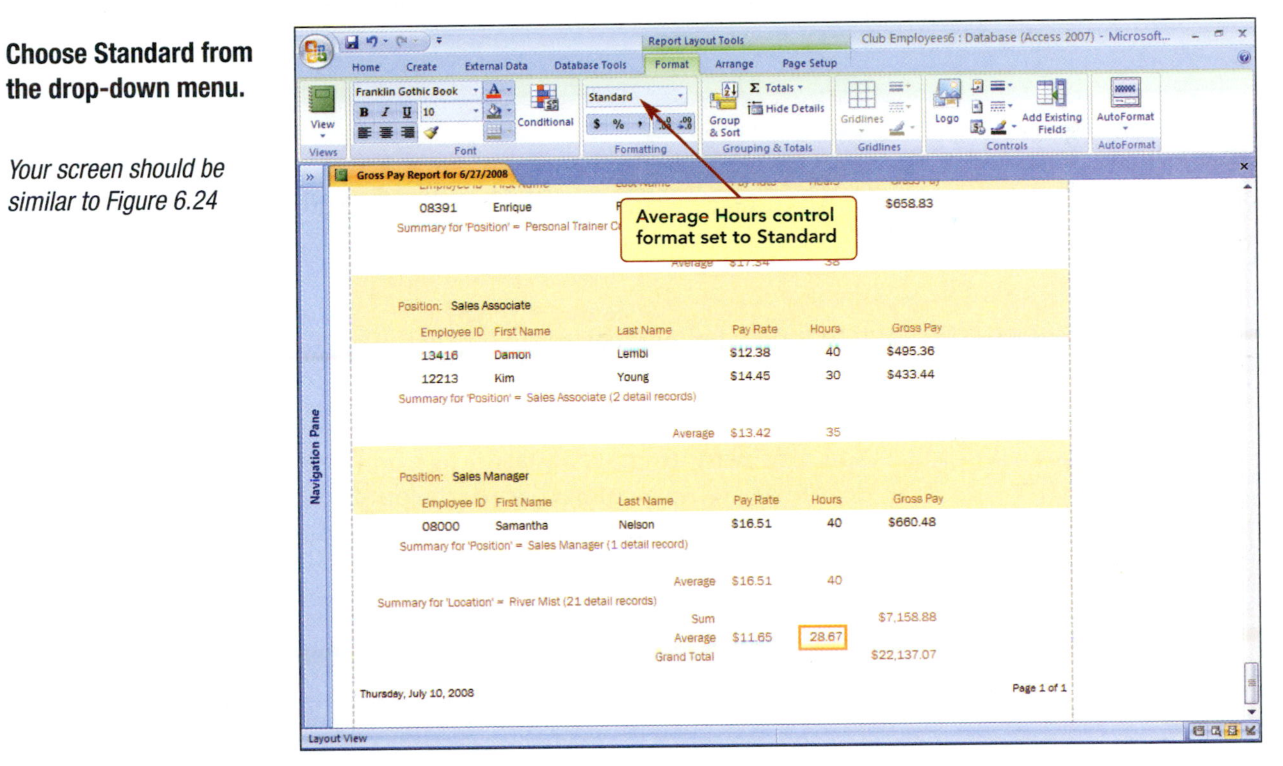

Figure 6.24

The control's format is set to Standard; however, the format of the Hours field in the underlying table remains unchanged.

Enhancing the Report

The report has been improved by adjusting the layout. Next, you want to make the report easier to read by differentiating the report sections using font and background colors.

First, you want the report title to stand out more by adding a background fill color. Then you will use the same fill color for the Location text control and bold the Location label control to make it easier to see each report section.

1

- **Scroll to the top of the report and select the report title control.**
- **Select Brown 3 from the Fill/Back Color gallery.**
- **Apply the same fill color to the Location text control.**
- **Bold the Location label control.**

Your screen should be similar to Figure 6.25

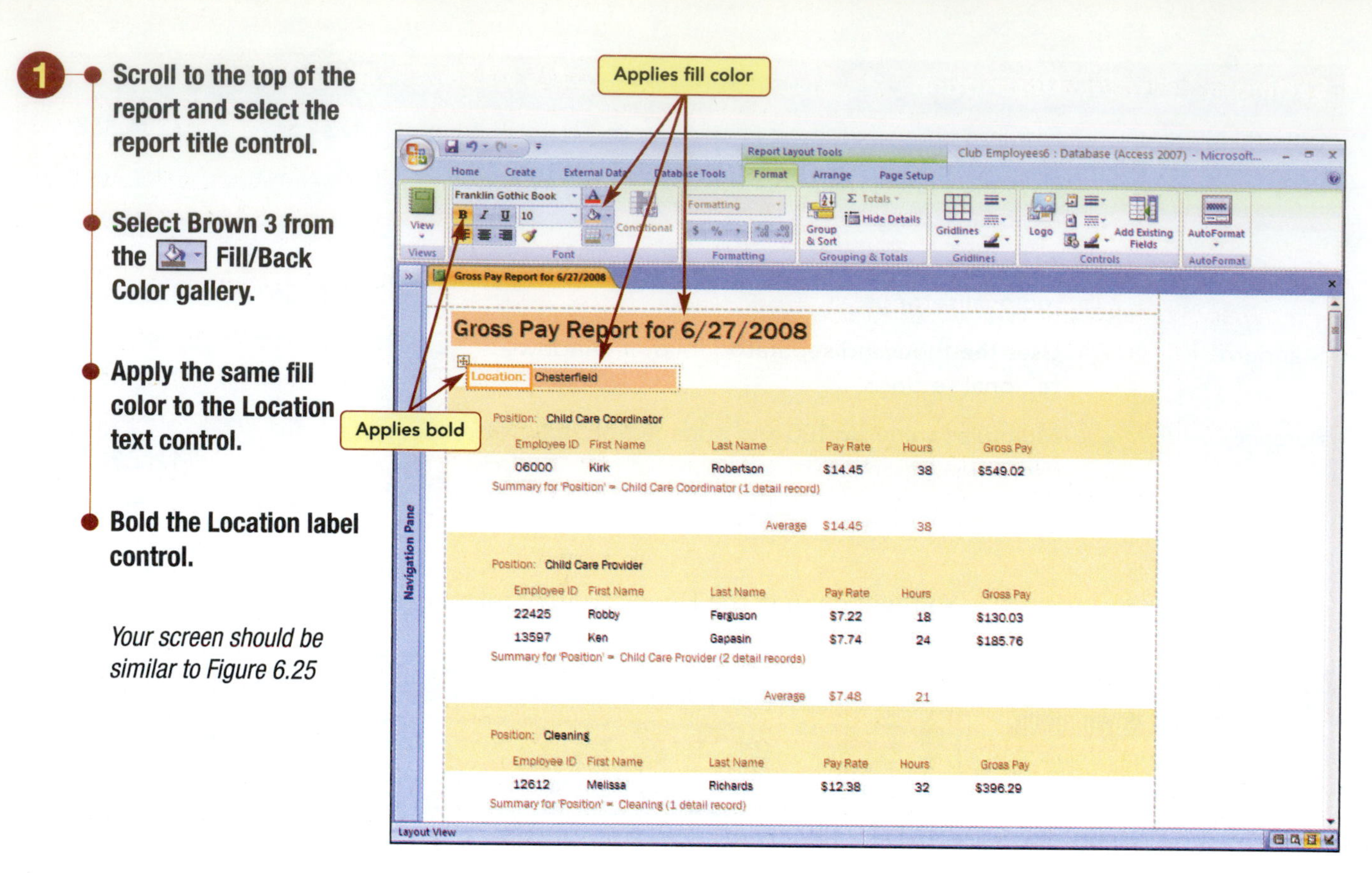

Figure 6.25

It will now be much easier to locate the beginning of a new location section.

Working with Lines and Borders

You also want to make it easier to find the location summary section. You decide to create a colored border around the section and fill it with a light color. Rectangles and lines are controls that are added in Design view.

1. **Switch to Design view.**
   - **Increase the size of the Location Footer slightly.**
   - **Click Rectangle in the Controls group.**
   - **Drag from the top-left corner of the Location Footer to the bottom-right corner to create a rectangle surrounding all the controls in the section.**
   - **Click Line Thickness and choose 2 pt from the drop-down list.**
   - **If necessary, choose Transparent from the Fill/Back Color menu.**
   - **Click Line Color and choose Dark Red.**
   - **Click in the Location Footer area to clear the selection.**

Your screen should be similar to Figure 6.26

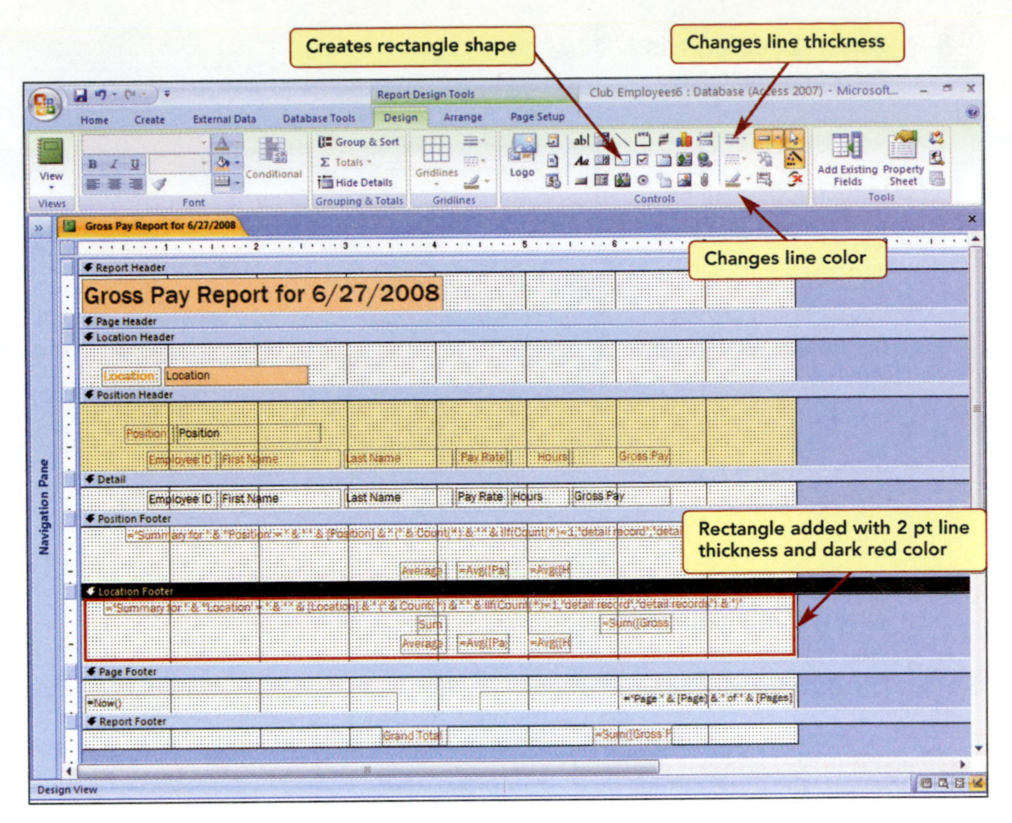

Figure 6.26

Finally, you want to emphasize the Grand Total value by increasing the font size and adding a single heavy line below the Grand Total values.

2

- Select both the Grand Total text and label controls.
- Increase the font size to 12 pt and add bold.
- Increase the size of the Report Footer area slightly.
- Click Line in the Controls group.
- Drag below the Grand Total controls in the Report Footer section to create the line.

Having Trouble?

Hold down Shift while dragging to create a straight line.

- Change the line width to 2 pt and color to Dark Red.
- Switch to Layout view and scroll to the bottom of the report.
- If necessary, enlarge the Grand Total text and label controls to fully display the information.
- If necessary, adjust the length and position of the line.
- Save the report.

Your screen should be similar to Figure 6.27

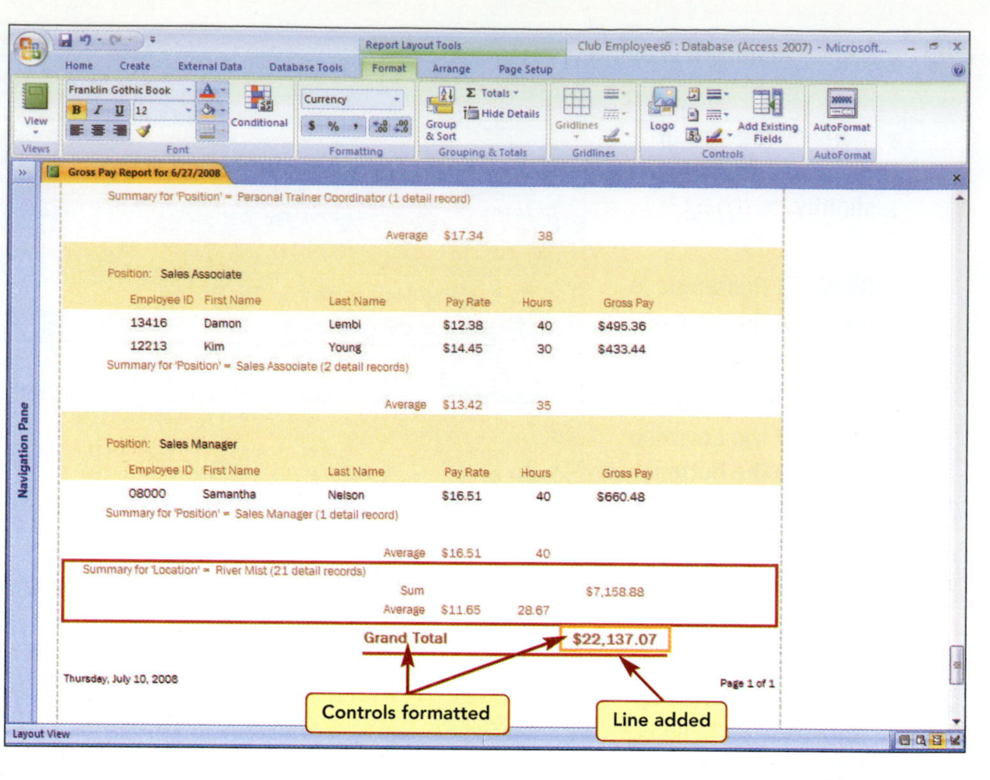

Figure 6.27

The borders and colors enhance the report's appearance quite a bit. Now it is easy to see that the total gross pay for this period is $22,137.07

Adding a Page Header

Finally, you would like the name of the club to appear on every page of the report. To do this, you will add it to the Page Header section. Unlike a report header, which prints only on the first page of a report, a page header will print at the top of every page. You want the page header to display the name of the club using the same formats as the main title.

1 **Switch to Design View.**

- **Increase the size of the Page Header section to 0.5 inch.**
- **Click [Aa] Label and click inside the Page Header section to place the label control.**
- **Type LIFESTYLE FITNESS CLUB and press ←Enter.**
- **Change the font to Franklin Gothic Medium with a font size of 16 pt.**
- **Increase the size of the label control to fully display the label and then extend it the full width of the report.**
- **Center the label within the control.**
- **Apply the Brown 2 background fill to the control.**
- **Center the report title control over the report.**
- **Save the report.**
- **Switch to Print Preview and display the top of the first page.**

Your screen should be similar to Figure 6.28

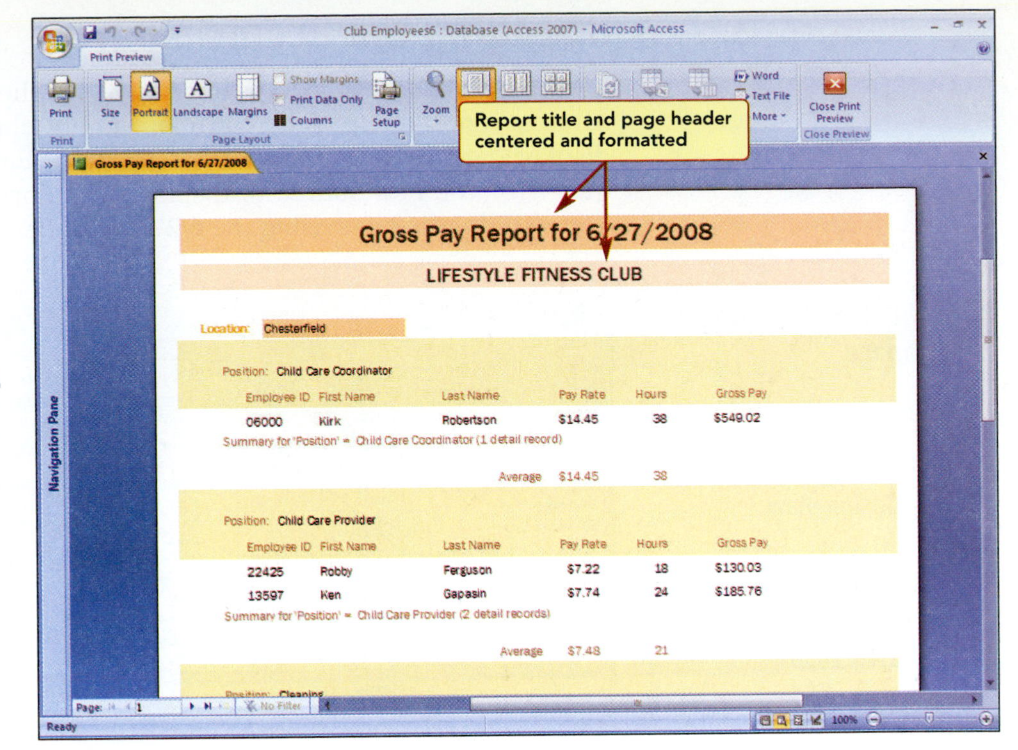

Figure 6.28

The report title appears centered over the report and the club name is displayed under it.

Changing the Record Source

You also want to create the same report for the June 13, 2008, pay period. After a report is created, you can simply change the record source to display data from a different data source. First, you need to create the query for the new source to display the information for this pay period. You will do this by revising the 6/27/2008 query.

1
- **Display the Navigation pane.**
- **Open the Gross Pay 6/27/2008 query in Design view.**
- **Change the Week Ending Criteria to 6/13/2008.**
- **Run the query and save it as Gross Pay 6/13/2008.**

Having Trouble?

Click [Office Button] and choose Save As.

Your screen should be similar to Figure 6.29

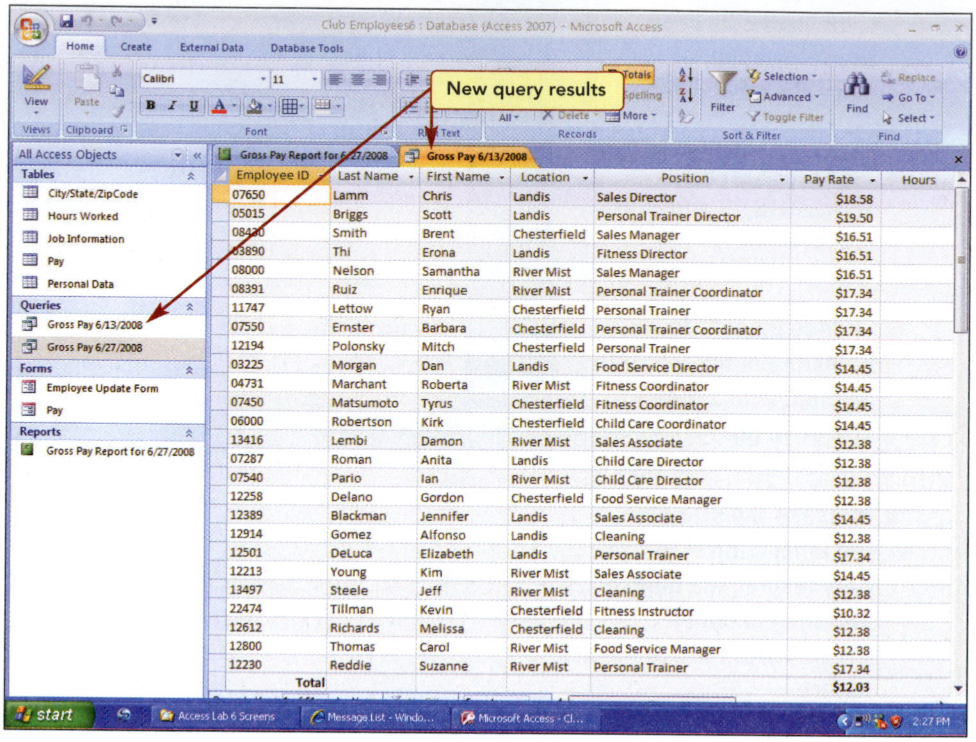

Figure 6.29

Now you are ready to create the new report by changing the record source. To do this, you modify the report properties. A quick way to access the report properties is by clicking the Report Selector box located at the intersection of the rulers in the upper-left corner of the Report Design window.

2 Close the query and hide the Navigation pane.

- Display the Report in Design view.
- Double-click ☐ Report Selector.

Having Trouble?

The ☐ Report Selector is located at the left end of the horizontal ruler.

- If necessary, open the All tab.

Another Method

When no other objects in the report are selected, pressing F4 or clicking Property Sheet in the Tools group of the Form Layout Tools Arrange tab will display the properties for the report in the Property Sheet pane. Alternately, you can select Report from the Property Sheet pane drop-down menu.

Your screen should be similar to Figure 6.30

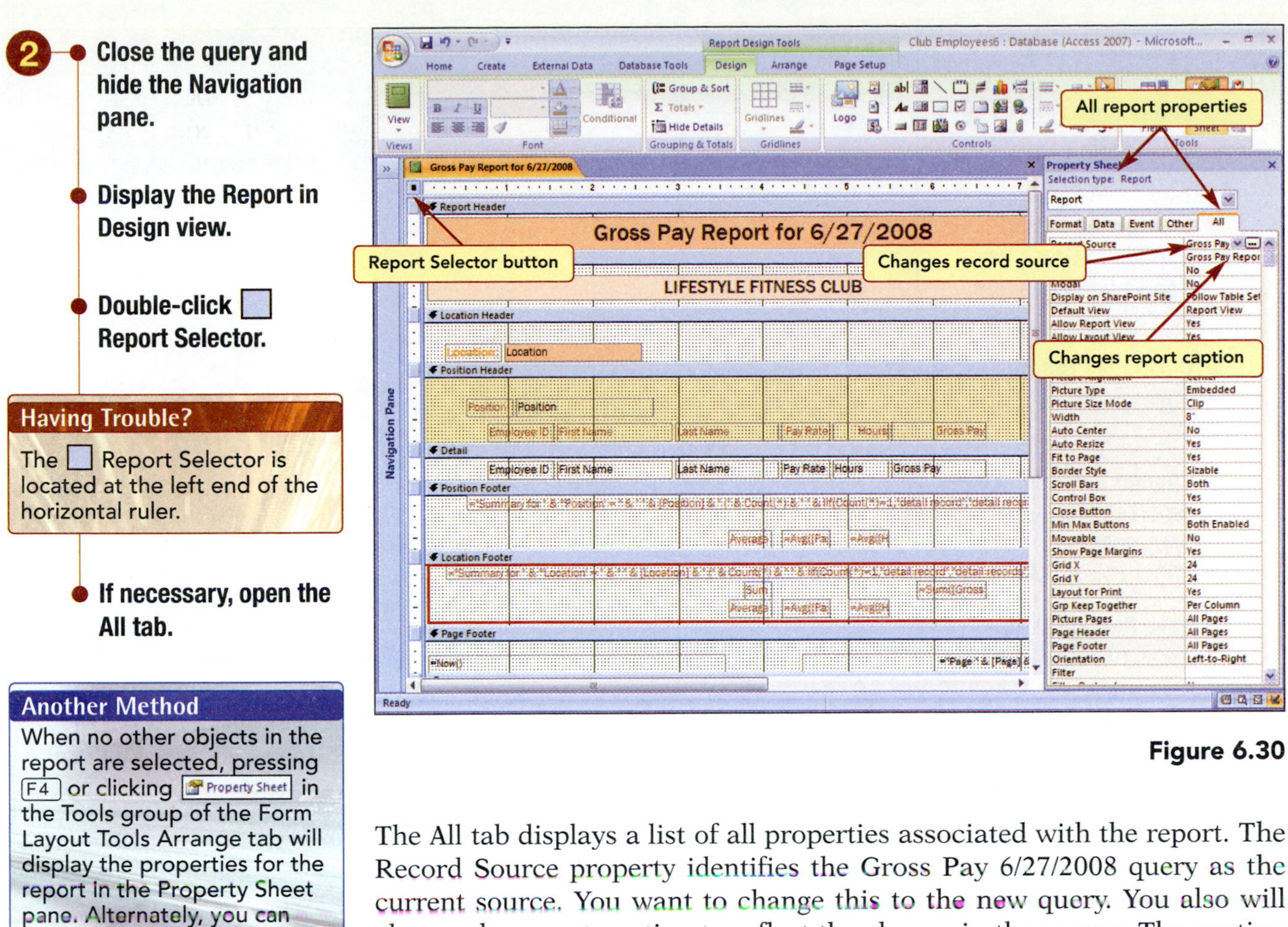

Figure 6.30

The All tab displays a list of all properties associated with the report. The Record Source property identifies the Gross Pay 6/27/2008 query as the current source. You want to change this to the new query. You also will change the report caption to reflect the change in the source. The caption appears in the tab when the report is previewed. Then you will save the new report and preview it.

3 **Open the Record Source drop-down list and choose Gross Pay 6/13/2008.**

- **Change the Report Caption to Gross Pay Report for 6/13/2008.**
- **Close the Property Sheet pane.**
- **Change the date in the report title to 6/13/2008.**
- **Save the report as Gross Pay Report for 6/13/2008.**

Having Trouble?

Click and choose Save As.

- **Display the report in Layout view and scroll to look at all pages of the new report.**
- **Display the grand total on the last page.**

Your screen should be similar to Figure 6.31

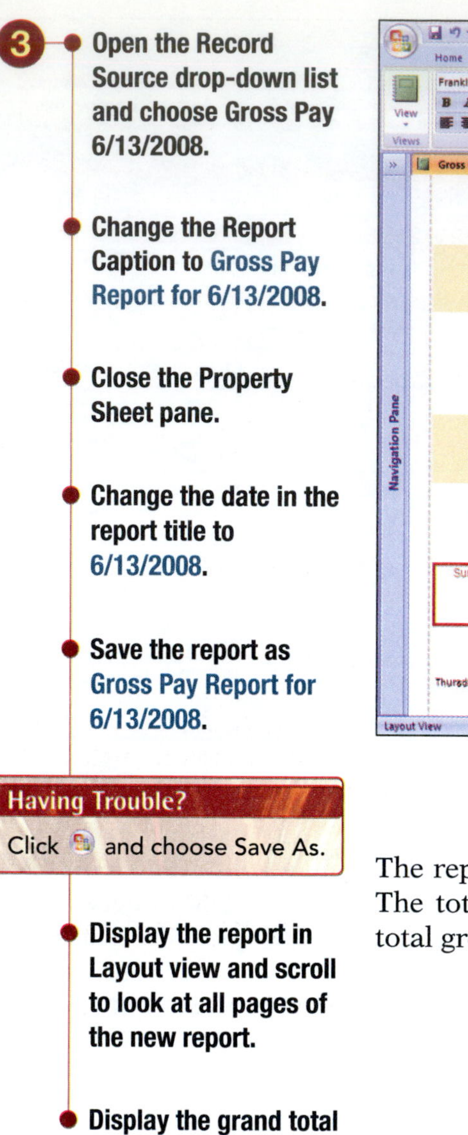

Figure 6.31

The report displays the information from the Gross Pay 6/13/2008 query. The total gross pay for this period was $21,729.12, as compared to the total gross pay of $22,137.07 for the June 27, 2008, pay period.

Using Calculated Controls in a Report

After seeing the two reports, the club owners have asked that the second-period report include the total gross pay for the month of June. To provide this information, you will add a calculated control to the end of the June 27, 2008, report.

Having Trouble?

To review expressions, refer to Lab 2, Concept 4: Expressions and to review calculated fields, see Concept 4: Calculated Field in Lab 4.

Creating a Calculated Control

Creating a calculated control is similar to creating a calculated field in a query except that the expression is entered in a text box control rather than in a query criteria cell.

Concept 3

Calculated Control

3 A **calculated control** displays the results of data that is calculated from a field in a table or query or from another control in the form. The results are recalculated each time there is a change in data on which the calculation depends.

A calculated-control expression is entered in the Control Source property for the control. The Control Source property is used to specify what data appears in a control. The expression always begins with an equal sign (=) and is followed by an identifier. The identifier is the element that refers to the value of a field, control, or property. For example, a calculated control in an Employee Discount field would be =[Price]*.50 if the employees get a 50 percent discount off the merchandise selling price.

A calculated control is typically created from a text box, with the calculation entered in the text box control. You can, however, create a calculated control from any type of control that has a Control Source property.

Creating and Modifying a Text Box Control

You want to display the monthly gross pay at the end of the June 27, 2008, report. You will add a text box control below the Grand Total field in the Report Footer section of the report and then enter the expression to make the calculation. Text box controls are used to display data from a record source like the controls in the Detail section do, or to display any other data.

1

- **Open and display the Gross Pay Report for 6/27/2008 in Design view.**
- **Hide the Navigation pane.**
- **Increase the size of the Report Footer section to 0.75 inch by dragging the bottom border of the report down.**
- **Click abl Text Box in the Controls group of the Report Design Tools Design tab and place the new control under the Grand Total text control.**

Your screen should be similar to Figure 6.32

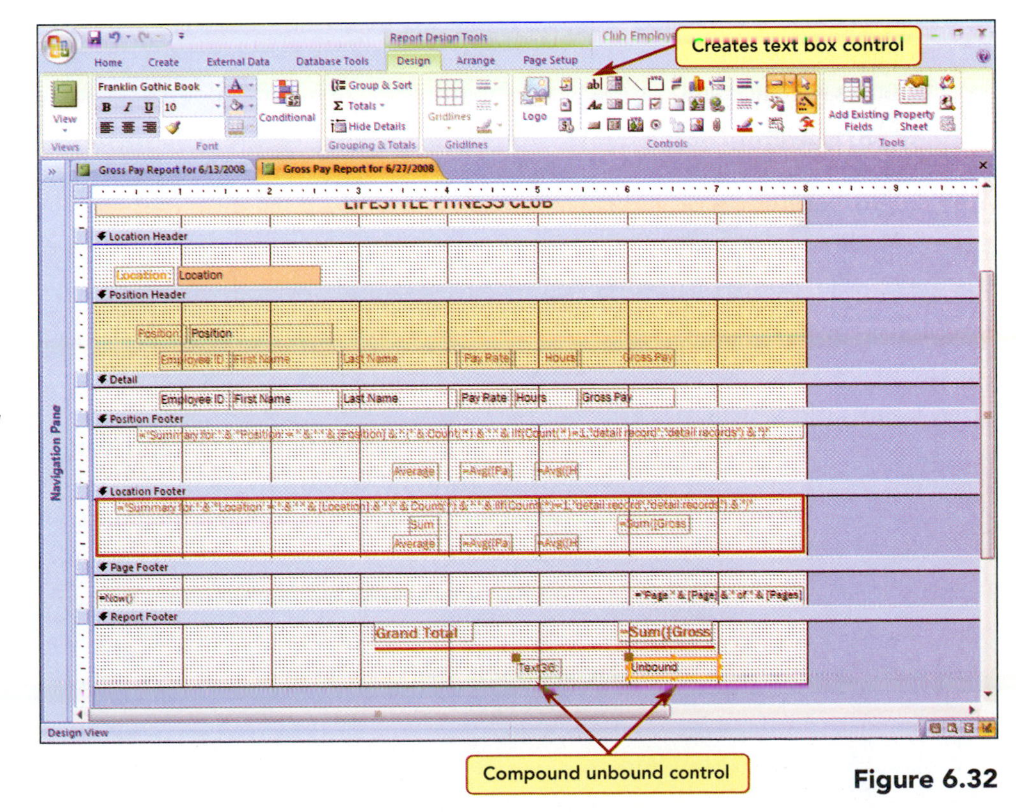

Figure 6.32

A compound control consisting of a label control and a text box control is created. The name "Text" followed by a number is displayed in the label control. This is the default name assigned to the control. The number

Having Trouble?

Do not be concerned if the text control number in your control is different than shown here.

identifies the order in which the control was added to the form. You will rename this control to a more descriptive name.

Then you will format the label and text controls just like the Grand Total label and text controls using the Format Painter feature. This feature copies the formats from the selected control to another control that you select. When activated, the mouse pointer appears as [pointer icon] when pointing to a control that can be formatted and as [pointer icon] when pointing to an area that cannot be formatted. If you single-click on [icon] Format Painter, you can copy a format once and the feature automatically deactivates. If you double-click on [icon] Format Painter, you can copy a format to multiple controls and you need to turn off the feature manually.

2

- **Change the label caption to June Gross Pay.**
- **Select the Grand Total label control and double-click [icon] Format Painter in the Font group of the Report Design Tools Design tab.**
- **Click on the June Gross Pay label and text controls.**

Your screen should be similar to Figure 6.33

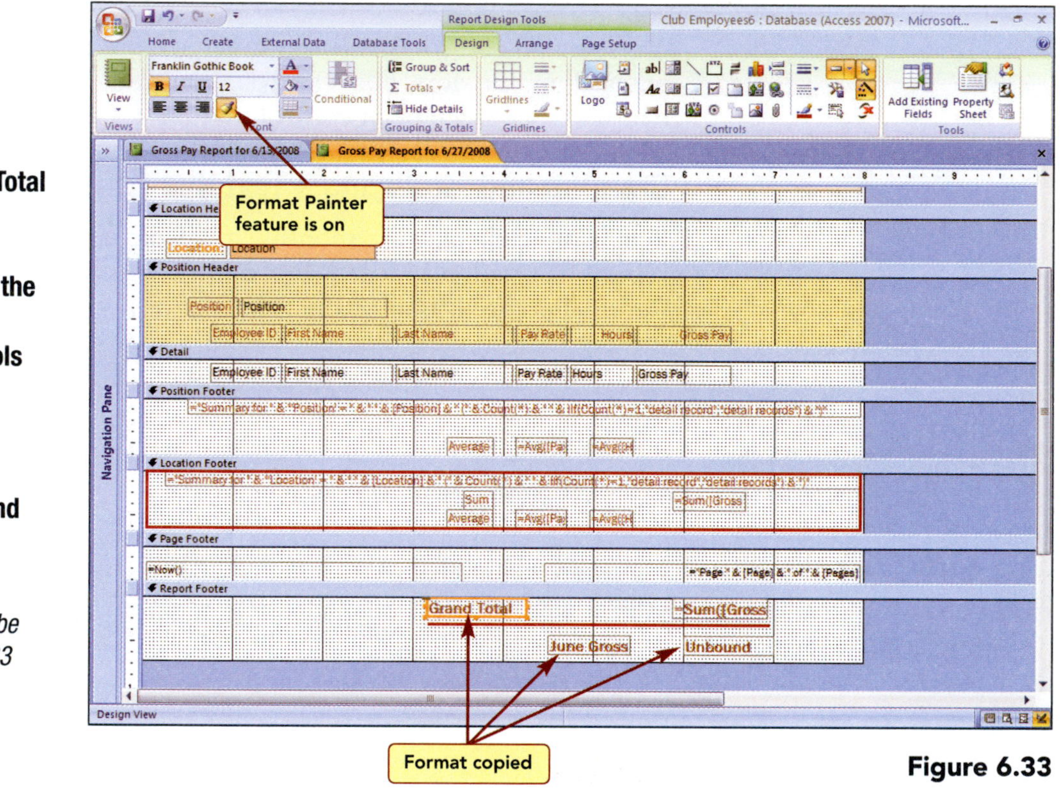

Figure 6.33

The formats associated with the Grand Total label control have been quickly copied to the June Gross Pay label and text controls. Now, you need to turn off this feature and size and align the controls.

3 **Click Format Painter to turn off the feature.**

- **Increase the size of the text control to fully display the label.**
- **Left-align the Grand Total and June Gross Pay label controls.**
- **Right-align the two gross pay text controls.**

Your screen should be similar to Figure 6.34

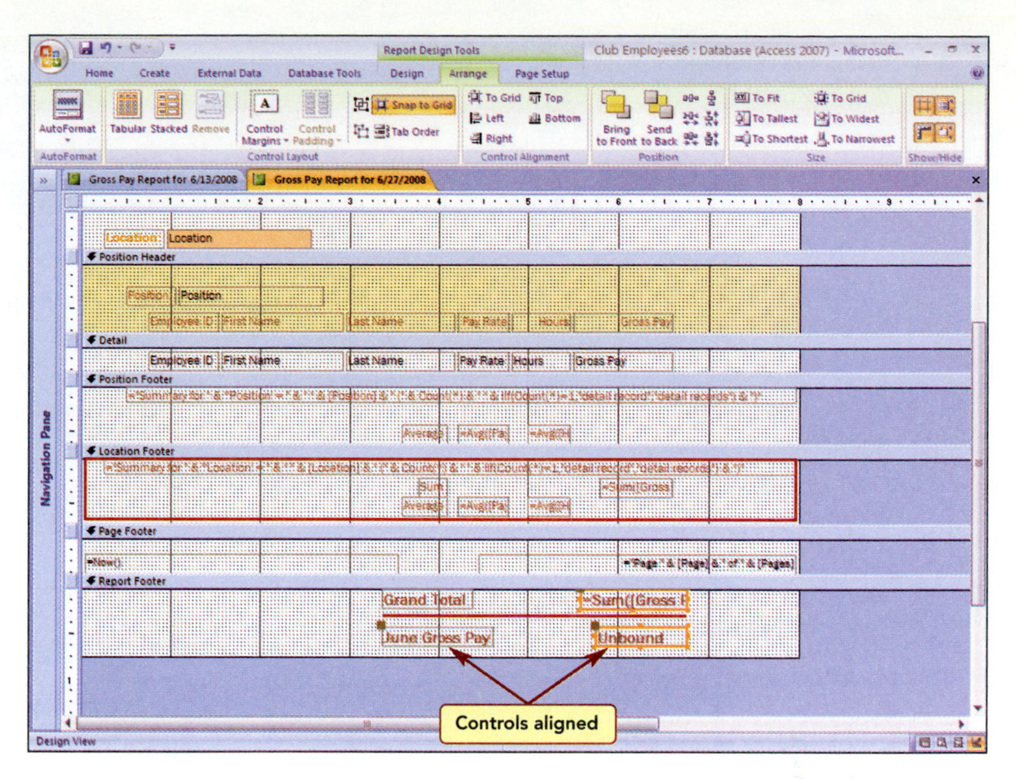

Figure 6.34

Using the Expression Builder

Now you are ready to enter the expression to calculate the total gross pay for the month by adding the total gross pay for this pay period to the total gross pay for the previous period. Notice the text control caption is "Unbound." This identifies the type of control. An unbound text box control can be used to display the results of a calculation or to accept input from a user. Data in an unbound text box is temporary and is not stored anywhere.

The expression is entered by either typing it directly in the box or using the Expression Builder tool. The **Expression Builder** helps you create an expression by providing a list of functions and identifiers from which you select. You will use the Expression Builder to help you enter this expression. You access the Expression Builder from the Control Source property of the text box.

More About

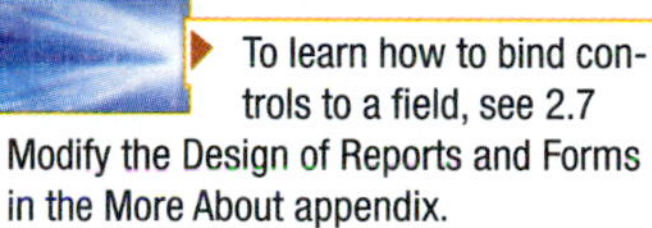

To learn how to bind controls to a field, see 2.7 Modify the Design of Reports and Forms in the More About appendix.

1. Select the Unbound text box control.
   - Press F4 to open the Property Sheet pane.
   - Type June Total in the Name field.
   - Click in the Control Source text box and click [...] to open the Expression Builder.

Your screen should be similar to Figure 6.35

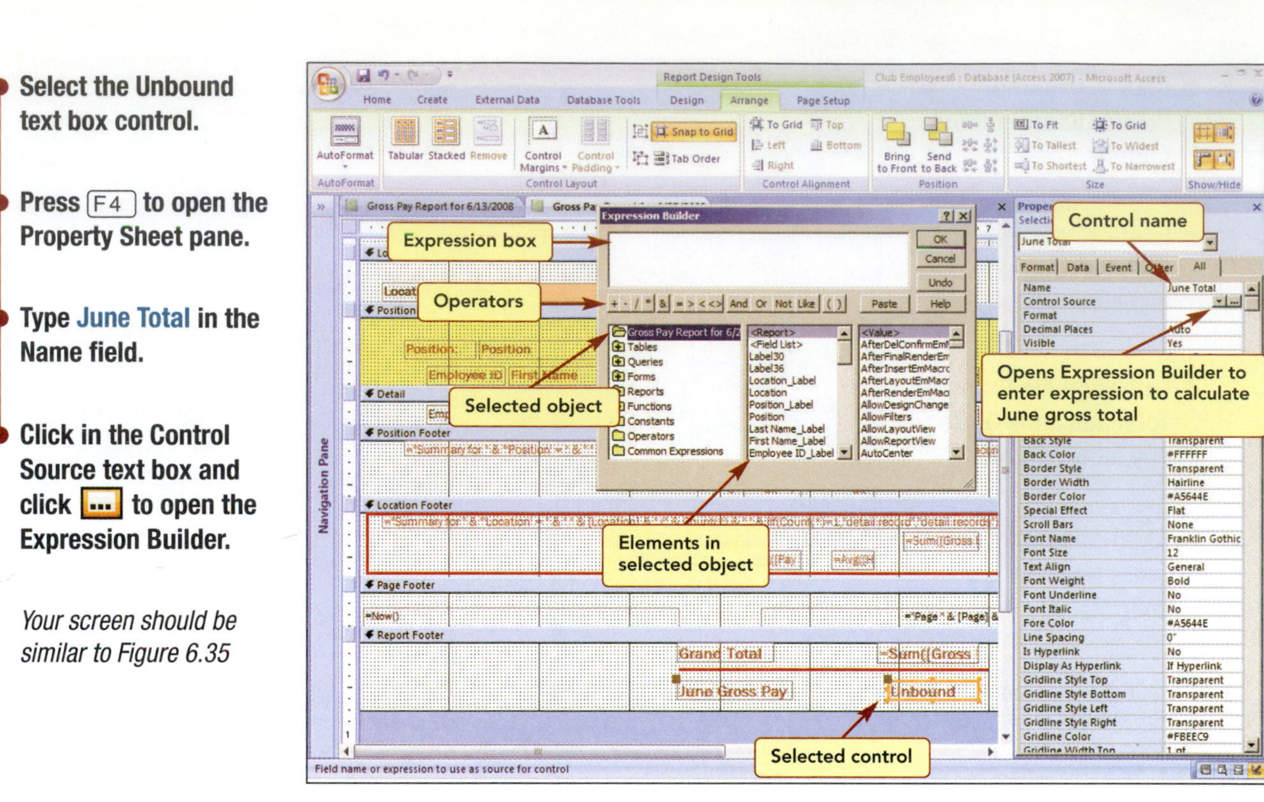

Figure 6.35

The Expression Builder is made up of three main sections, which are described in the following table.

Section	Description
Expression box	Used to build the expression. To build an expression, you select elements from the other two sections and paste them in this box. You also can type parts of the expression directly in the box.
Operator buttons	A toolbar of commonly used operators for the selected expression element. The four types of operators are mathematical, comparison, logical, and reference. Clicking one of these buttons adds it to the expression (in the expression box) at the current insertion point.
Expression elements	This section consists of three list boxes. The left box contains folders that list the objects (tables, queries, forms, and reports) in the database, built-in and user-defined functions, constants (values that do not change such as a specific number or text), operators, and common expressions. The middle box lists specific elements or element categories for the folder that is selected in the left box. The right box lists the values (if any) for the elements selected in the left and middle boxes.

You begin building an expression by specifying the type of operation you want to perform. In this case, you want to enter a formula to add the gross pay data from this report to the total gross pay data in the new Gross Pay Report for 6/13/2008. A formula entry begins with an = sign. You can type the = sign in the expression box or select it from the toolbar of operator buttons. Then you specify the type of object (report, table, query, or form) that contains the data you want to use in the formula. Finally, you specify the object (field or control) within the selected object that contains the data.

2

- **Click [=] in the toolbar of operator buttons.**
- **If necessary, click the Gross Pay Report for 6/27/2008 folder in the left list box to select it.**
- **Double-click Gross Pay Grand Total Sum in the middle list box.**

Your screen should be similar to Figure 6.36

Additional Information

You can type some or all of the formula directly in the expression box or build the expression by selecting the appropriate operator buttons and/or expression elements, or use a combination of both methods.

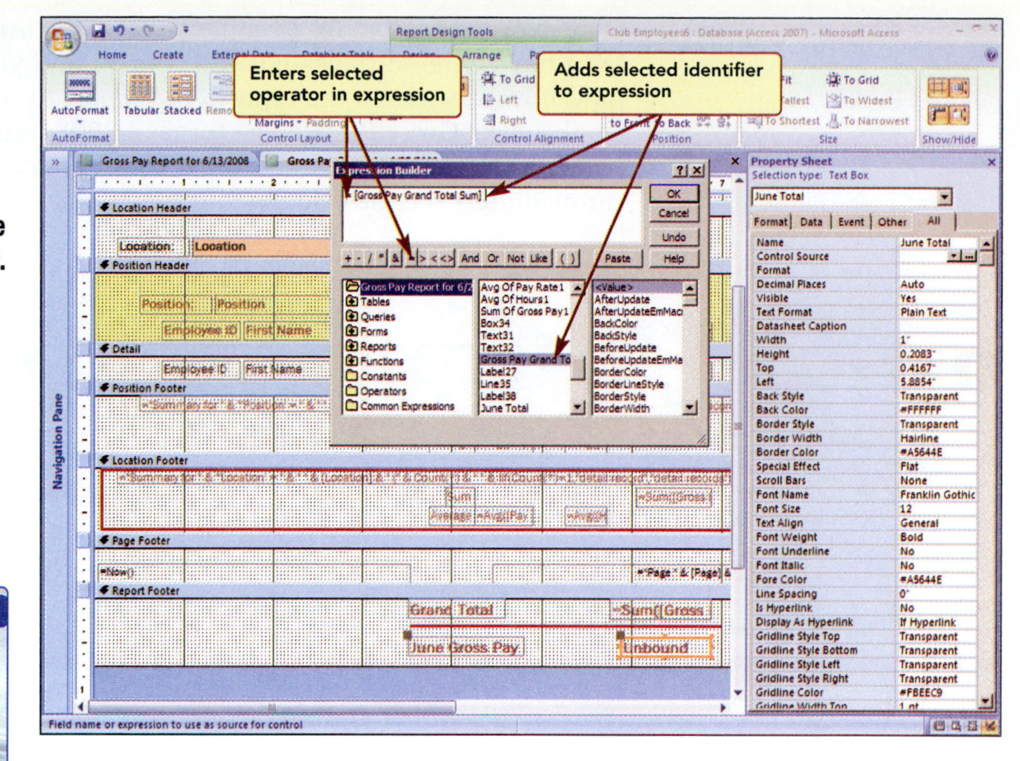

Figure 6.36

You have specified the location of the gross pay value in the Gross Pay Report for 6/27/2008 as the first value in the formula. Next, you need to identify the location of the same value in the Gross Pay Report for 6/13/2008.

3

- **Type + to enter the sum operator.**
- **Double-click Reports in the left list box.**
- **Double-click Loaded Reports and select Gross Pay Report for 6/13/2008.**
- **Double-click Gross Pay Grand Total Sum from the middle list box.**

Your screen should be similar to Figure 6.37

Report Design Tools

Club Employees6 : Database (Access 2007) - Microsoft Access

Home | Create | External Data | Database Tools | Design | Arrange | Page Setup

Expression sums gross pay values from both reports

AutoFormat | Tabular | Stacked | Remove | Control Margins | Control Padding | Snap to Grid | Tab Order | Control Layout | Control Alignment | Position | To Fit | To Tallest | To Shortest | To Grid | To Widest | To Narrowest | Size | Show/Hide

Expression Builder

= [Gross Pay Grand Total Sum] + Reports![Gross Pay Report for 6/13/2008]![Gross Pay Grand Total Sum]

OK | Cancel | Undo | Help | Paste

y Report for 6/27/2008 | ed Reports | ross Pay Report for 6/27 | ross Pay Report for 6/13

Box34 | Text31 | Text32 | Gross Pay Grand To | Label27 | Line35 | Report Header | Page Header | Location Header | Position Header | Detail

<Value> | AfterUpdate | AfterUpdateEmMacr | BackColor | BackStyle | BeforeUpdate | BeforeUpdateEmMa | BorderColor | BorderLineStyle | BorderStyle | BorderWidth

Property Sheet — Selection type: Text Box — June Total

Field name or expression to use as source for control

Figure 6.37

The expression box displays the selected identifiers that will be summed. You have entered the calculated control and you can now check to see if and how it works in the report. The report to which the expression refers, in this case Gross Pay Report for 6/13/2008, must be open in order for the value to be calculated. Because this report is already open, you can immediately see the calculated value by displaying the report.

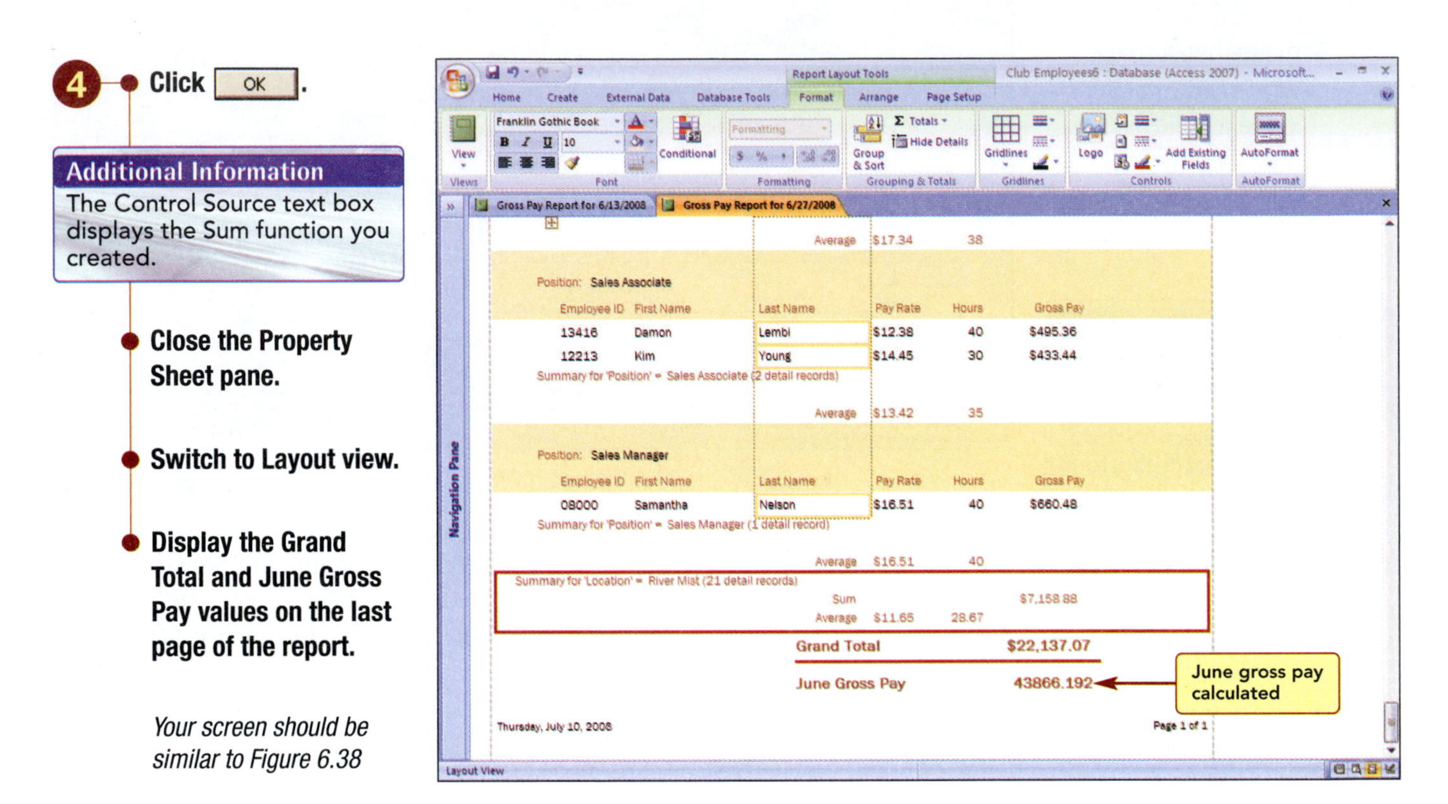

4 **Click** OK.

Additional Information

The Control Source text box displays the Sum function you created.

- **Close the Property Sheet pane.**
- **Switch to Layout view.**
- **Display the Grand Total and June Gross Pay values on the last page of the report.**

Your screen should be similar to Figure 6.38

Figure 6.38

It looks like the calculated control has calculated the June gross pay value just fine. However, it is not displayed as currency. You need to fix the display of this value and also adjust the size. Then you will add a thick red line below the June gross pay value.

5

- Select the June Gross Pay value and change the Format property to Currency.
- Size the text control to fully display the value.
- In Design view, add a 4-pt-weight Dark Red line below the June Gross Pay controls.
- Look at the last page of the report in Layout view again.
- Adjust the position of the line if necessary.

Your screen should be similar to Figure 6.39

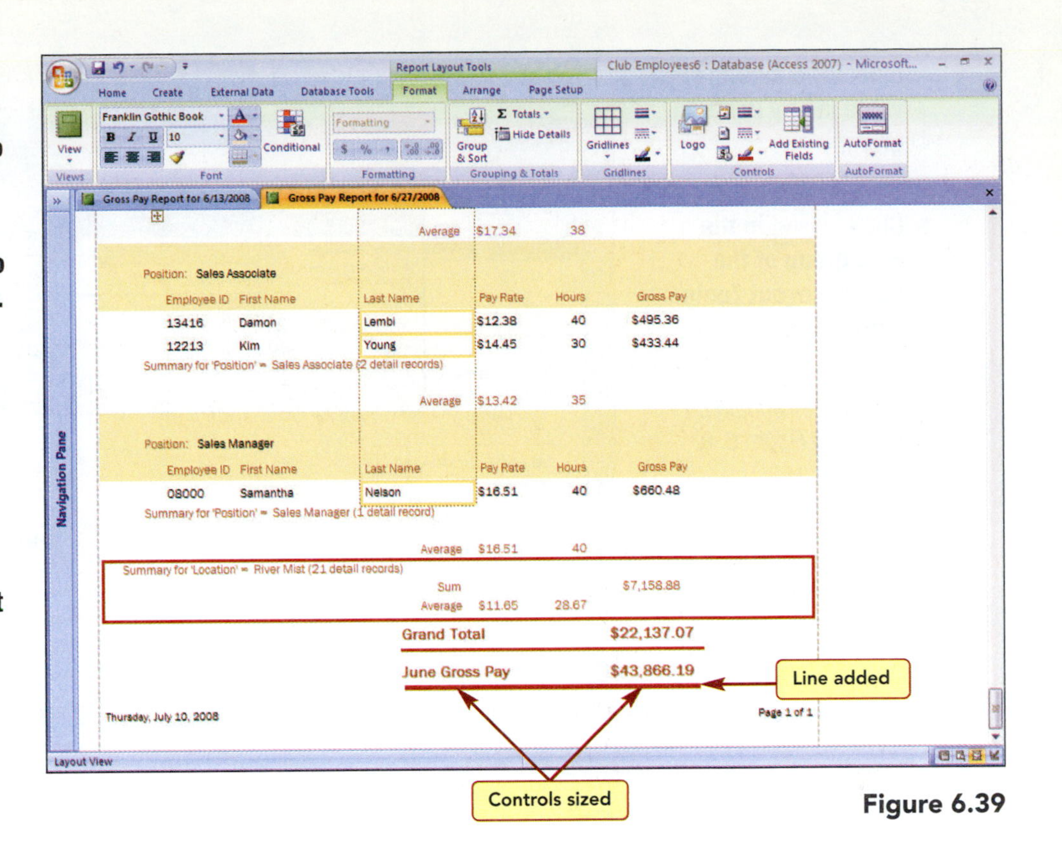

Figure 6.39

Applying Conditional Formatting

The final item the club managers have asked you to do is to identify all average pay rates that are $10.00 or more. You will do this using conditional formatting.

Concept 4

Conditional Formatting

4 **Conditional formatting** automatically applies formatting such as highlighting and font colors to selected data in text or combo box controls based on a condition that you specify. The condition can be based on a field value or on an expression. An expression is used to change the formatting based on the values contained in other fields or controls.

If the data in the control meets the conditions (the conditions are true), the data is formatted. If the data does not meet the conditions (the condition is false), the data remains unformatted. Conditional formatting can be applied based on the value in a text box or combo box control. You can set up to three conditional formats for a single control.

Additionally, in forms, you can use conditional formatting to disable a control or cause the formatting of a control to change when the control is selected based on specified conditions being met.

Specifying Conditions

You will use conditional formatting to highlight all average pay values that are equal to or greater than 10.

1. Select the Average Pay value in any Position group.

   Click Conditional in the Font group of the Report Layout Tools Format tab.

Your screen should be similar to Figure 6.40

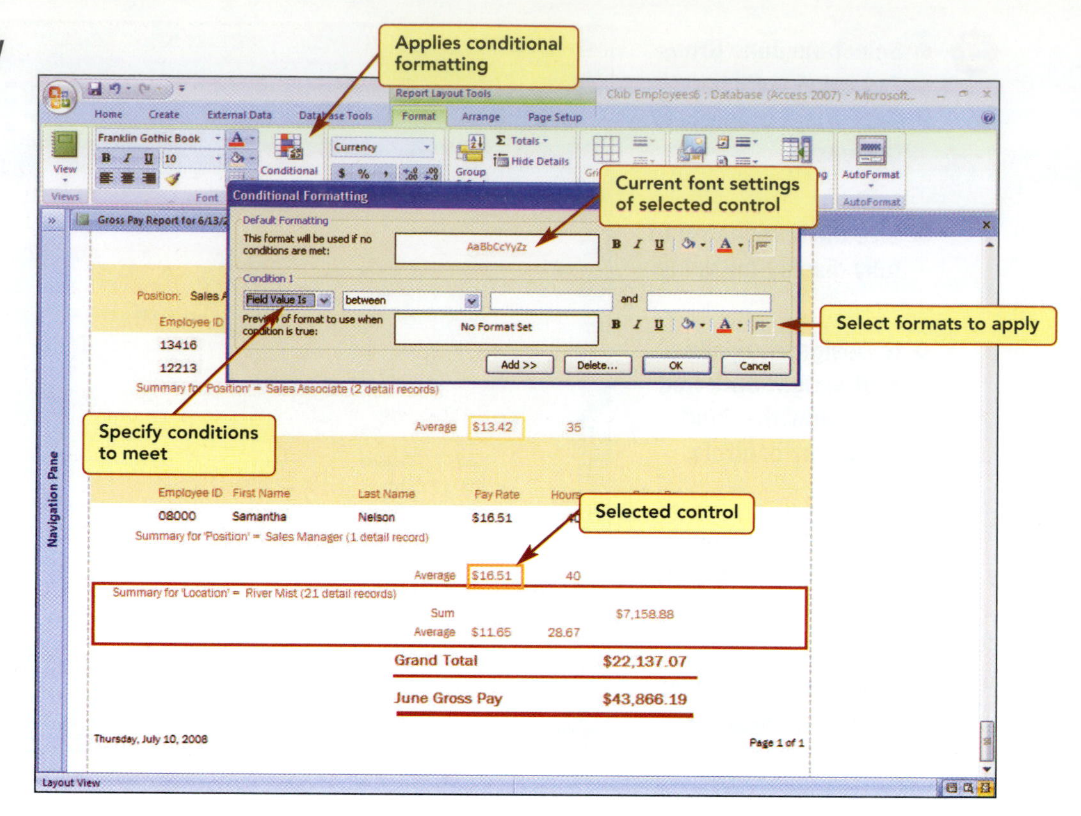

Figure 6.40

The Conditional Formatting dialog box displays the default formatting associated with this control if the conditions are not met. The default settings in this area correspond to the current font settings for the selected control. In the Condition 1 area, you specify the conditions to meet and the formatting to apply. The first text box correctly displays Field Value Is as the source of the conditions. In the second text box, you enter the comparison operator to use for the condition. You will use greater than or equal to. Then you specify the condition value in the third box.

2 Choose Greater than or equal to from the second drop-down list box.

Enter 10 in the third text box.

Your screen should be similar to Figure 6.41

Condition is greater than or equal to 10

Figure 6.41

Now, you are ready to set the format to use when the condition is true. The preview area will display the selections as they are made.

3 Click Fill/Back Fill and choose yellow.

Click Bold.

Click Font/Fore Color and choose Dark Red.

Additional Information

The Add >> button is used to specify additional conditions.

Your screen should be similar to Figure 6.42

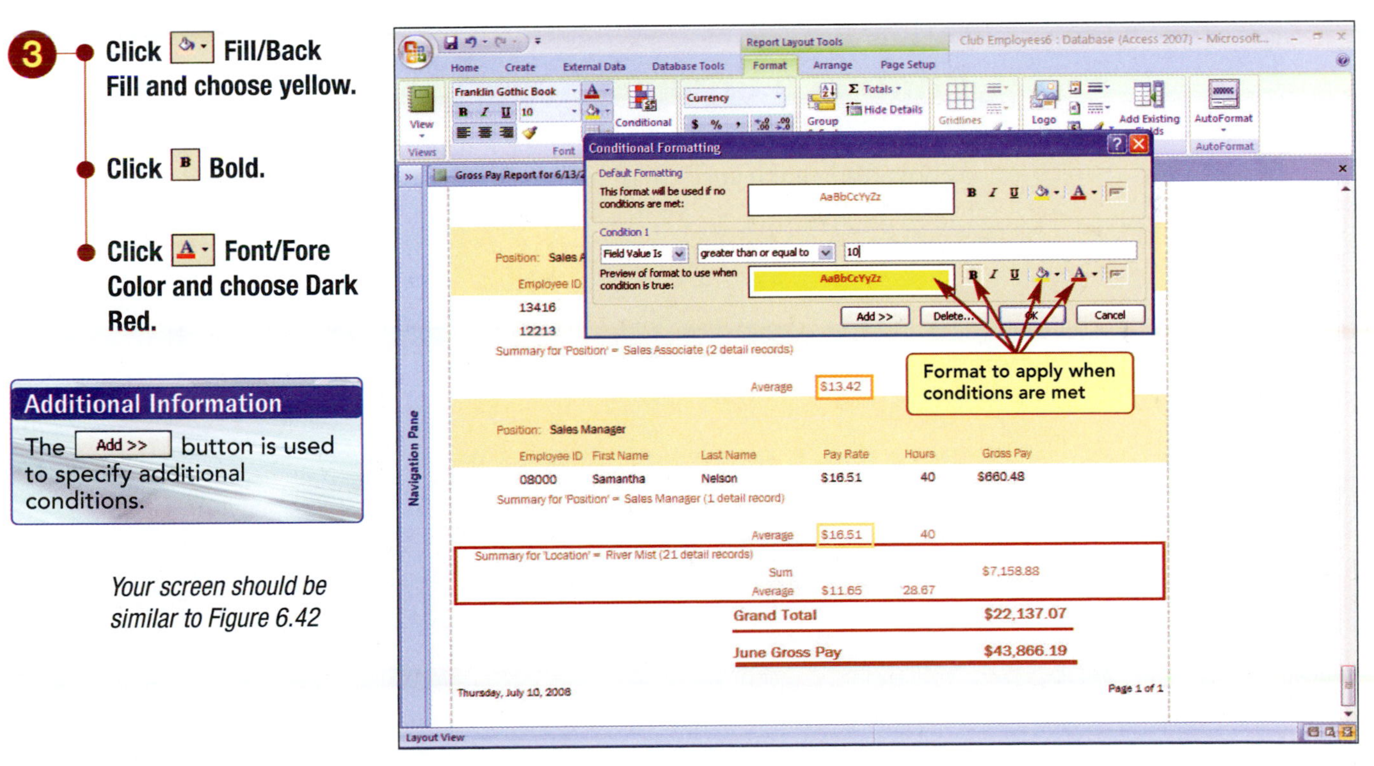

Figure 6.42

The preview area shows how the data that meets the conditions will be formatted.

4 Click OK.

- Increase the size of the control.
- Switch to Print Preview and display the first page of the report.

Your screen should be similar to Figure 6.43

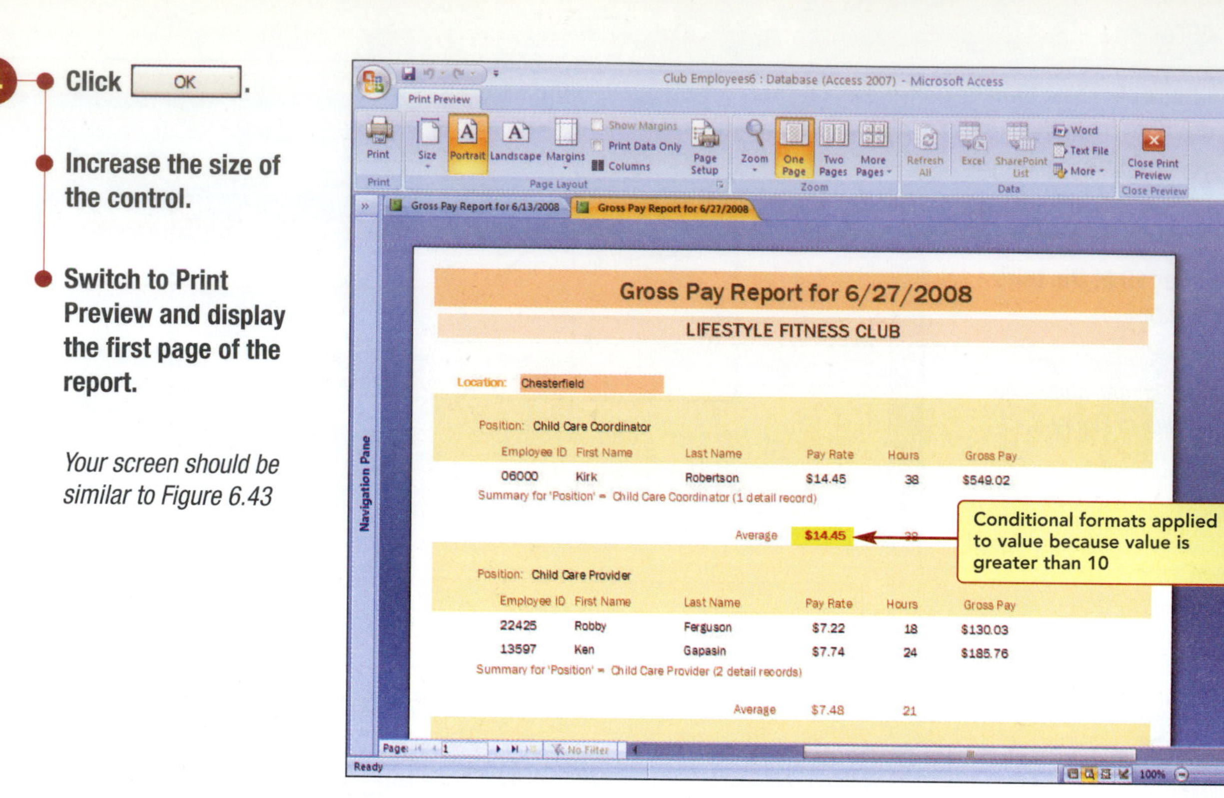

Figure 6.43

The average pay values that are less than 10 are not formatted and those that are 10 and more are formatted using the specified formats. You are now ready to print the report.

Printing a Grouped Report

Before you print your new grouped report, you will preview the entire report and make sure there are no further changes you need to make to it.

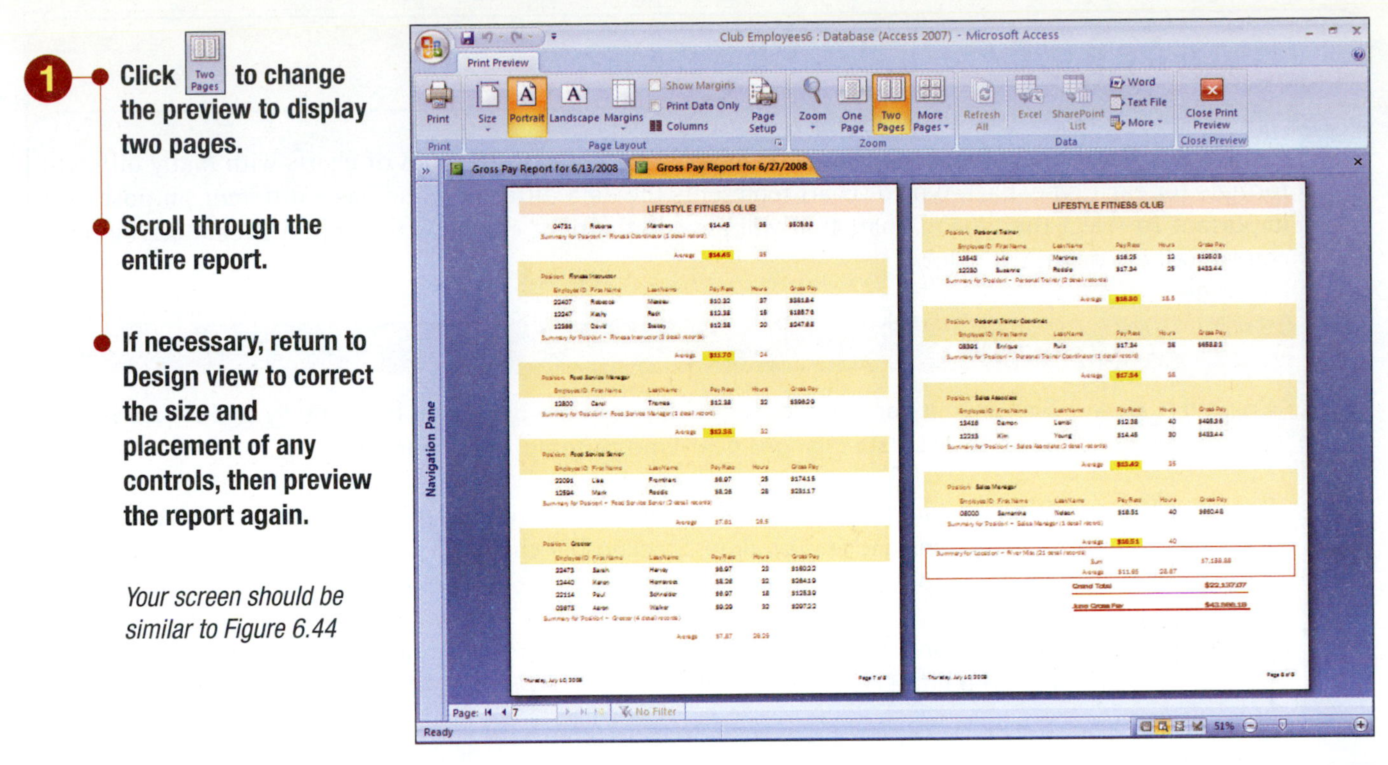

1. Click ![Two Pages] to change the preview to display two pages.
   - Scroll through the entire report.
   - If necessary, return to Design view to correct the size and placement of any controls, then preview the report again.

Your screen should be similar to Figure 6.44

Figure 6.44

You are satisfied with the way the report looks, so you will print and then close it. You will print pages 1, 2, and 8. Because the pages are not consecutive, you will need to send the pages to print to the printer twice.

2. Print pages 1 to 2 of the report

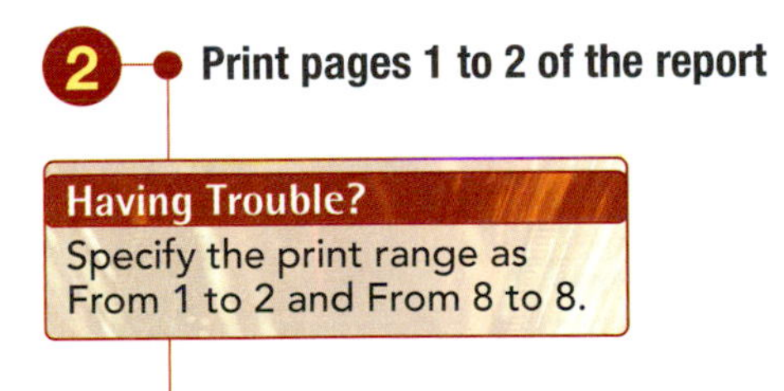
Having Trouble?
Specify the print range as From 1 to 2 and From 8 to 8.

   - Print page 8 of the report.
   - Close Print Preview and close both reports, saving any changes.

Creating a Chart in a Report

The report presents the details and summarizes the payroll information for each club location. However, it is difficult to compare the payroll expenses between clubs. You decide to create a chart of the gross pay data to help the club managers analyze the information.

Concept 5

Chart

5 A **chart** is a visual representation of numeric data. You can create 18 types of charts with many different formats for each type. Each type of chart represents the data differently and has a different purpose. It is important to select the type of chart that will provide the right emphasis to support the data. The basic chart types are described below.

Type of Chart	Description
Column	Similar to a bar chart, except categories are organized horizontally and values vertically. Shows data changes over time or comparison among items.
Bar	Displays categories vertically and values horizontally, placing more emphasis on comparisons and less on time. Stacked-bar charts show the relationship of individual items to a whole by stacking bars on top of one another.
Line	Shows changes in data over time, emphasizing time and rate of change rather than the amount of change.
Pie	Shows the relationship of each value in a data series to the series as a whole. Each slice of the pie represents a single value in a data series.
Area	Shows the relative importance of a value over time by emphasizing the area under the curve created by each data series.

Most charts are made up of several basic parts, as identified and described below.

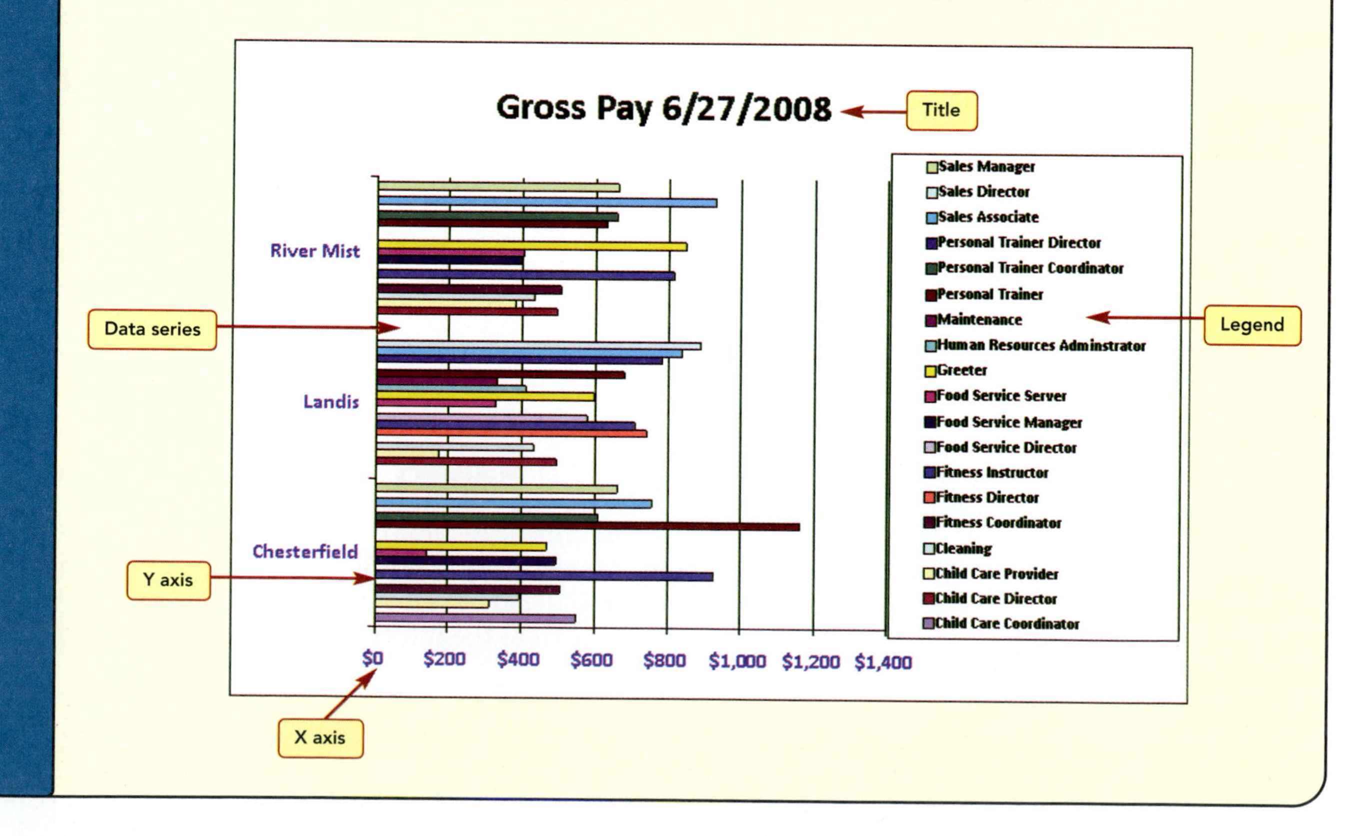

Concept 5

Chart—Continued

5

Part	Description
X axis	The bottom boundary of the chart, also called the category axis, is used to label the data being charted; the label may be, for example, a point in time or a category.
Y axis	The left boundary of the chart, also called the value axis, is a numbered scale whose numbers are determined by the data used in the chart. Each line or bar in a chart represents a data value. In pie charts there are no axes. Instead, the data that is charted is displayed as slices in a circle or pie.
Data Series	Each group of related data that is plotted in a chart.
Legend	A box containing descriptive text that identifies the patterns or colors assigned to the data series in a chart.
Titles	Descriptive text used to explain the contents of the chart.

You will create a second report of the gross pay data for June 27, 2008, that will display the data as a chart. Because the features to create a chart are only available in Design view, you will create the new report using this view.

1 Click [Report Design] in the Reports group of the Create tab.

- If necessary, close the Field List task pane.

Your screen should be similar to Figure 6.45

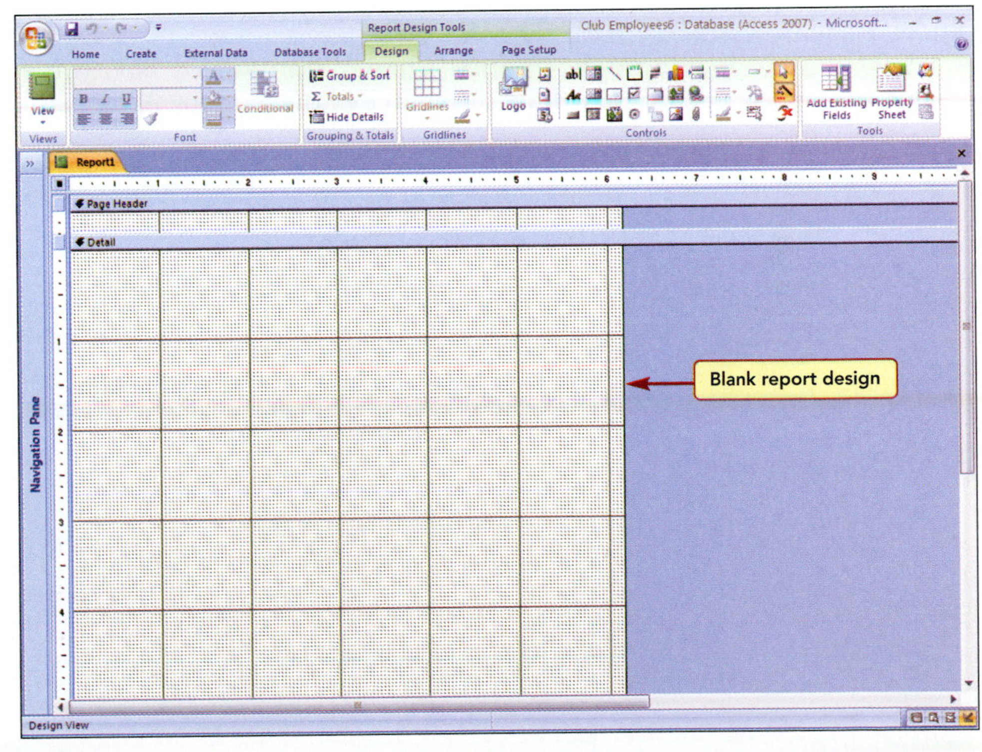

Figure 6.45

Using Chart Wizard

You can create a report from within Design view by dragging fields from the Field List into the appropriate areas of the Design grid. When creating a chart, you do not need to use the Field List. Instead, you use the Chart Wizard to specify the data to appear in the chart. First, you will add a report title. Then you will start the Chart Wizard.

1

- Click Title in the Controls group and type **Gross Pay for June 27, 2008** in the Title control.
- Click Insert Chart in the Controls group and click and drag in the detail area to create a chart control approximately 4 inches high by 6 inches long.

Your screen should be similar to Figure 6.46

Starts Chart Wizard

Adds report title

Selects chart source

Figure 6.46

In the first Chart Wizard dialog box, you specify the table or query that will be the source of the data for the chart.

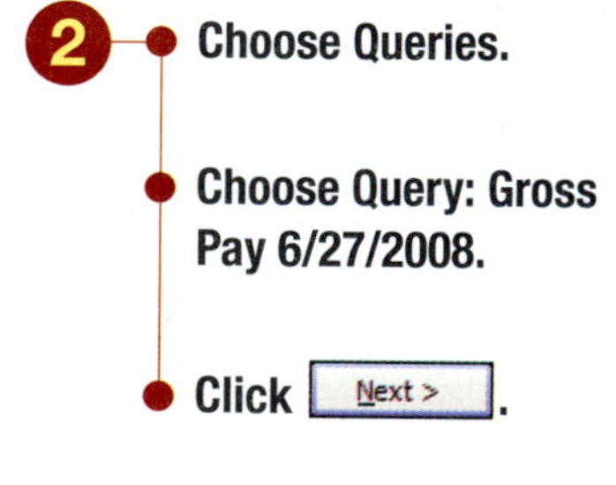

2

- Choose Queries.
- Choose Query: Gross Pay 6/27/2008.
- Click Next >.

Your screen should be similar to Figure 6.47

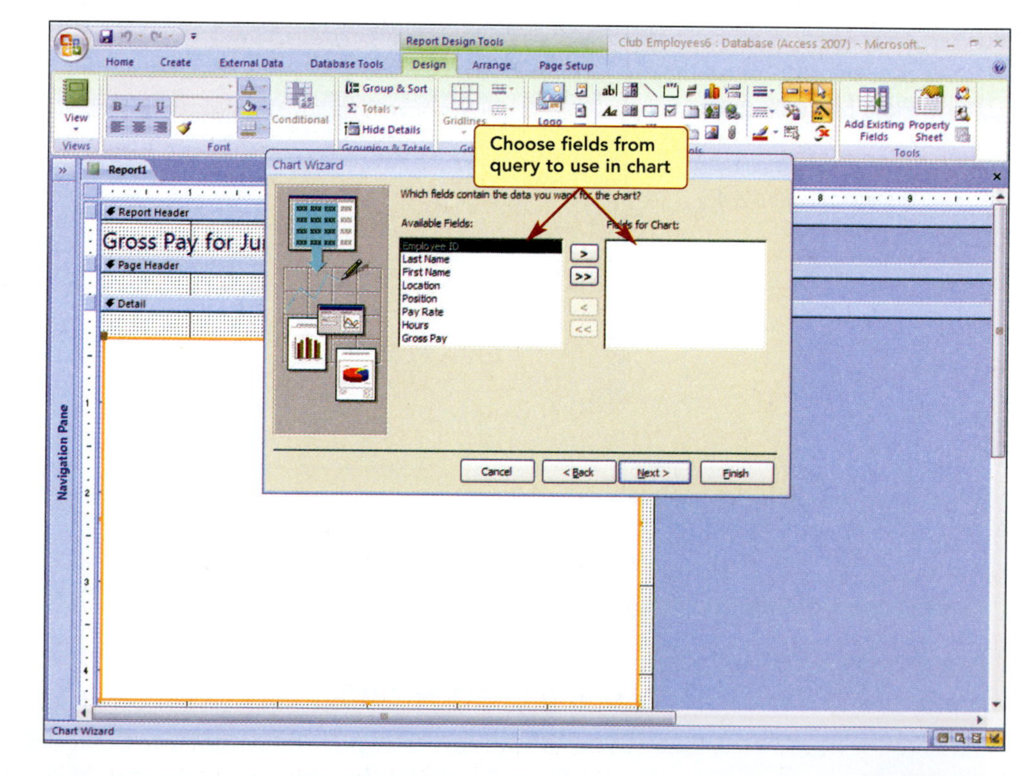

Figure 6.47

Next, you specify the fields containing the information you will use in the chart.

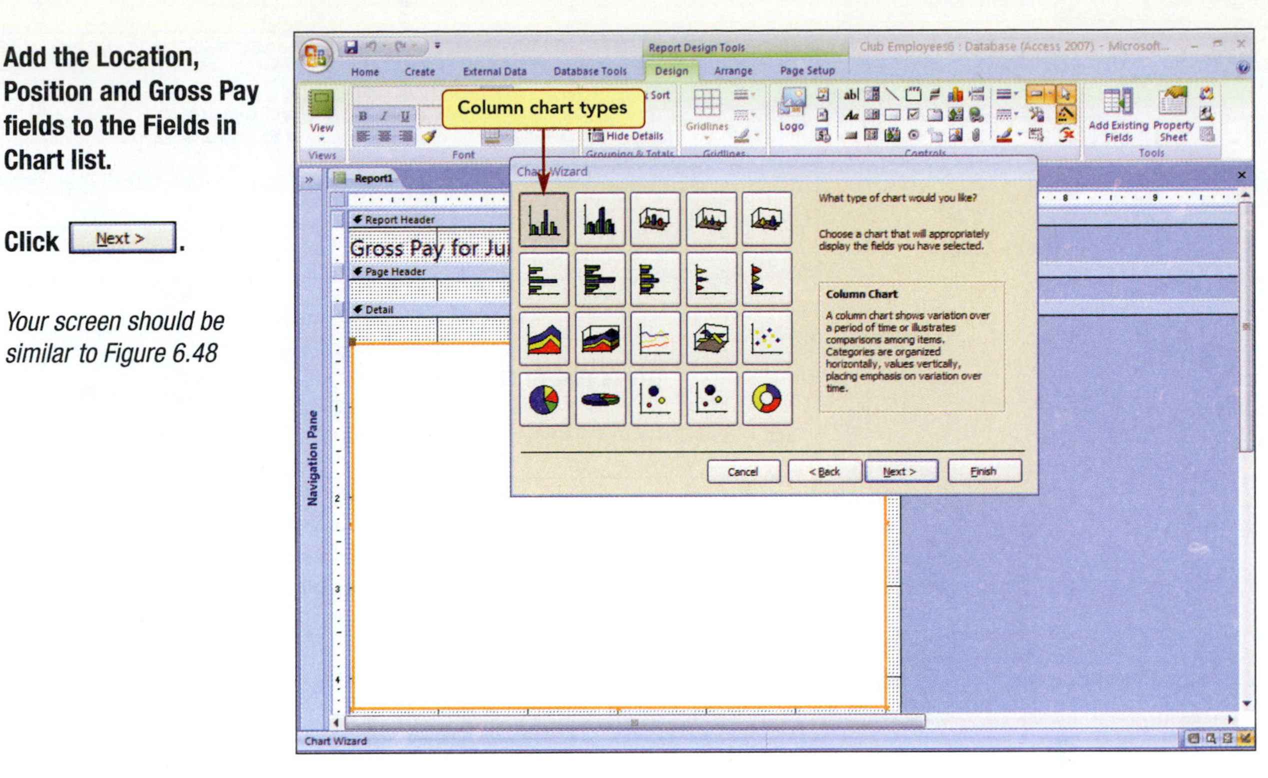

3 ● **Add the Location, Position and Gross Pay fields to the Fields in Chart list.**

● **Click Next >.**

Your screen should be similar to Figure 6.48

Figure 6.48

Next, you select the type of chart. You will use a simple column chart.

4 ● **If necessary, click**

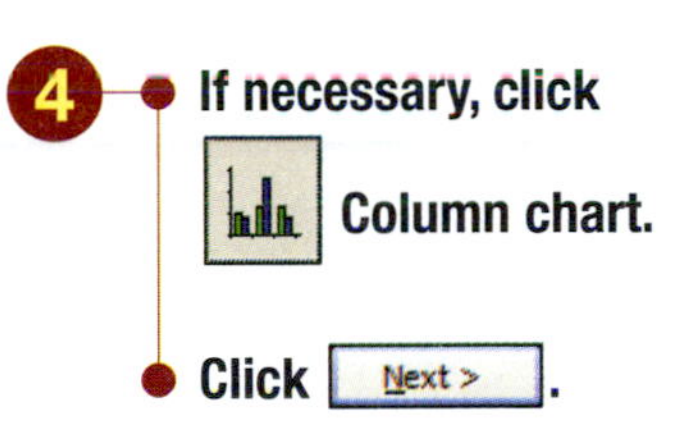

Column chart.

● **Click Next >.**

Your screen should be similar to Figure 6.49

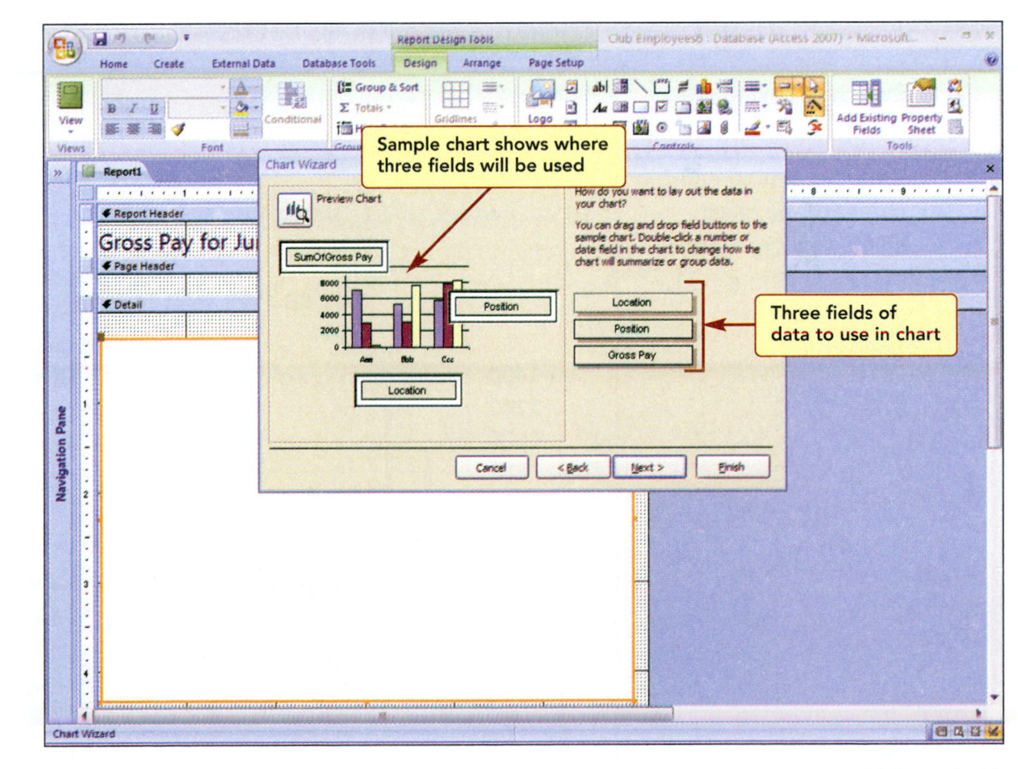

Figure 6.49

A sample chart is displayed and the wizard has placed field buttons along the chart axis and data points to show you how the chart would look with the data represented in this way. You can change the suggested layout of fields by dragging the buttons to other areas on the sample chart. You will go with the wizard's suggestion, as it can always be changed later.

5 Click **Next >**.

Click **Finish**.

Your screen should be similar to Figure 6.50

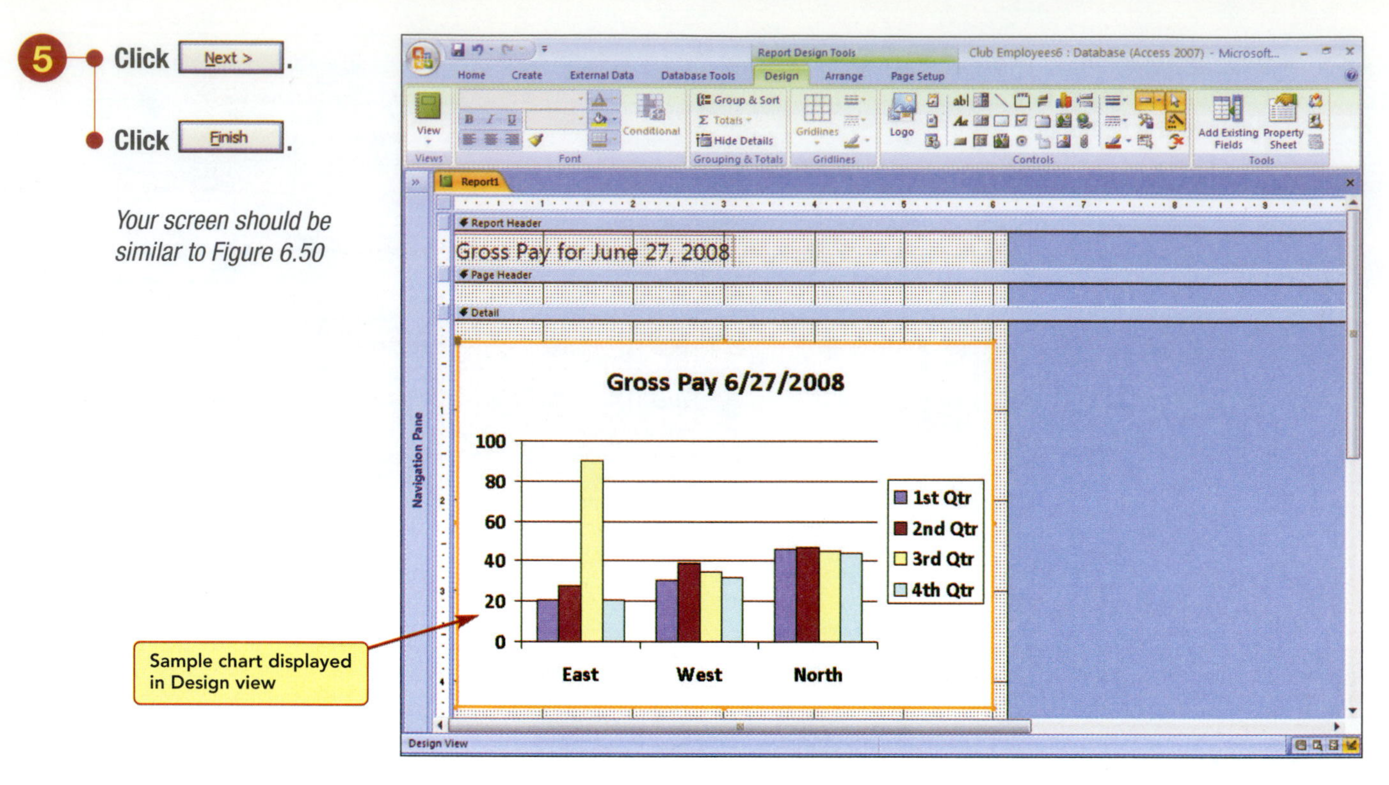

Figure 6.50

A sample chart is displayed in Design view using the query name as the report title. To see the actual chart with data, you switch to Layout view.

6 **Switch to Layout view.**

Drag the bottom-right corner of the chart object to increase the size as in Figure 6.51.

Your screen should be similar to Figure 6.51

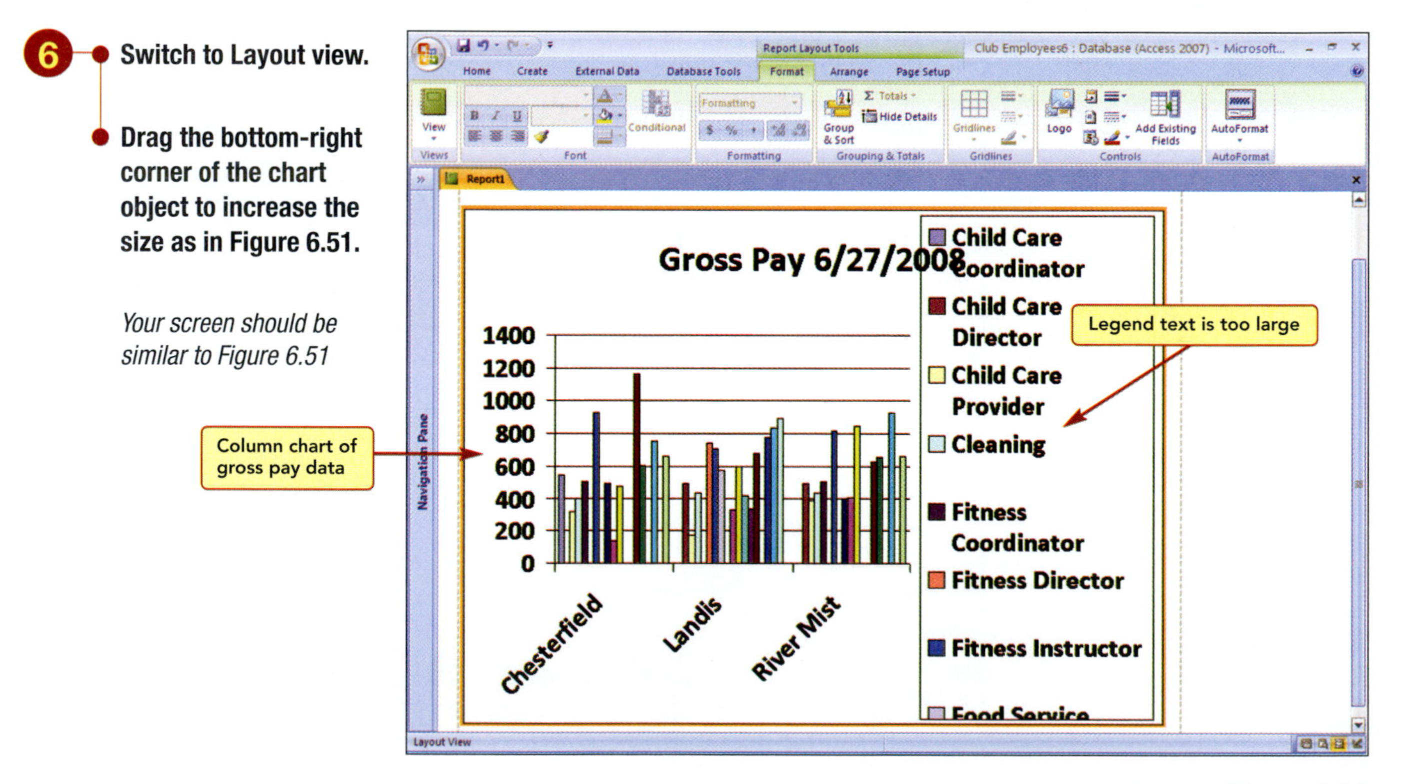

Figure 6.51

The data is displayed as a column chart, but it needs a lot of work. For example, the legend is too large and does not display all the positions and the chart title duplicates the report title.

Formatting the Chart

Changes to the chart format are made in Design view. When you switch back to this view, the actual data will be displayed in the chart so you will be able to immediately see the effects of your changes on the chart as you make them.

1 **Switch to Design view.**

Double-click on the chart object to open it for editing.

Your screen should be similar to Figure 6.52

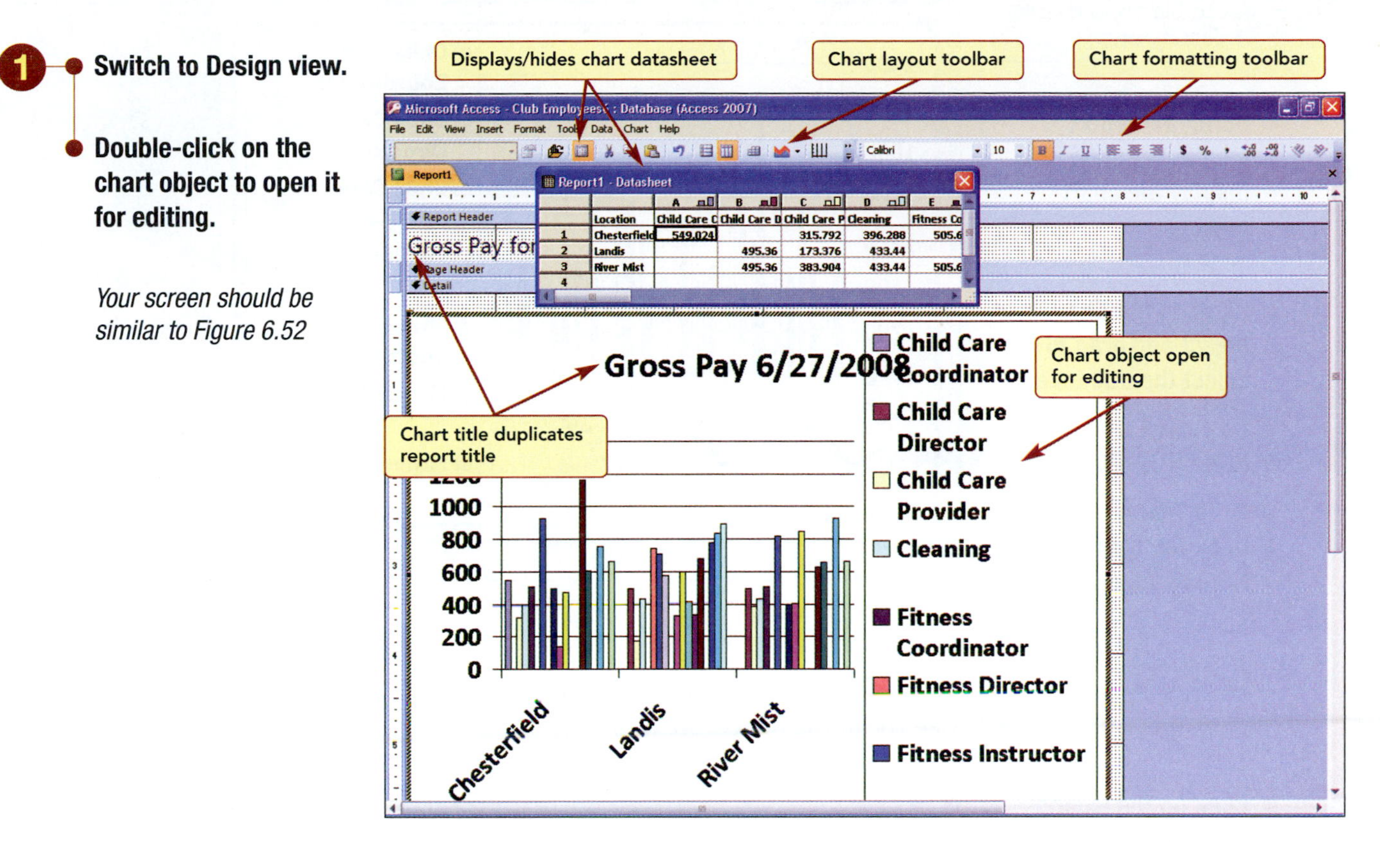

Figure 6.52

A chart datasheet is displayed containing the data that appears in the chart. The Ribbon is replaced with two toolbars that contain commands that can be used to modify the chart. Because you will not be changing the data in the chart, you will close the datasheet. Then, you will delete the chart title to make more space for the data to be displayed.

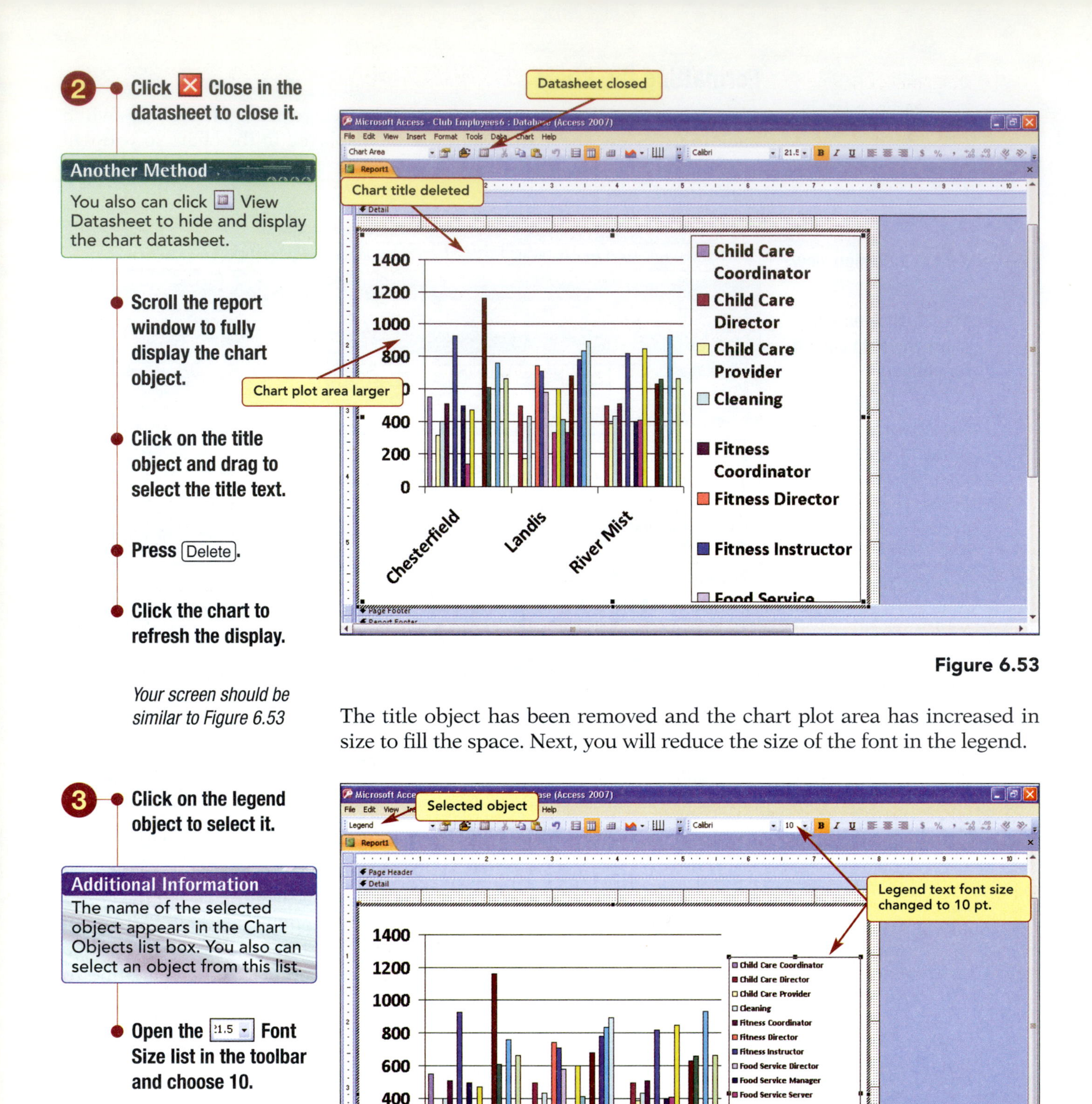

2 • Click ☒ Close in the datasheet to close it.

Another Method

You also can click View Datasheet to hide and display the chart datasheet.

• Scroll the report window to fully display the chart object.

• Click on the title object and drag to select the title text.

• Press Delete.

• Click the chart to refresh the display.

Your screen should be similar to Figure 6.53

Figure 6.53

The title object has been removed and the chart plot area has increased in size to fill the space. Next, you will reduce the size of the font in the legend.

3 • Click on the legend object to select it.

Additional Information

The name of the selected object appears in the Chart Objects list box. You also can select an object from this list.

• Open the 21.5 Font Size list in the toolbar and choose 10.

Your screen should be similar to Figure 6.54

Figure 6.54

Now, all the positions are displayed in the legend. Next, you will select the X axis and reduce the font size and add color to the location names.

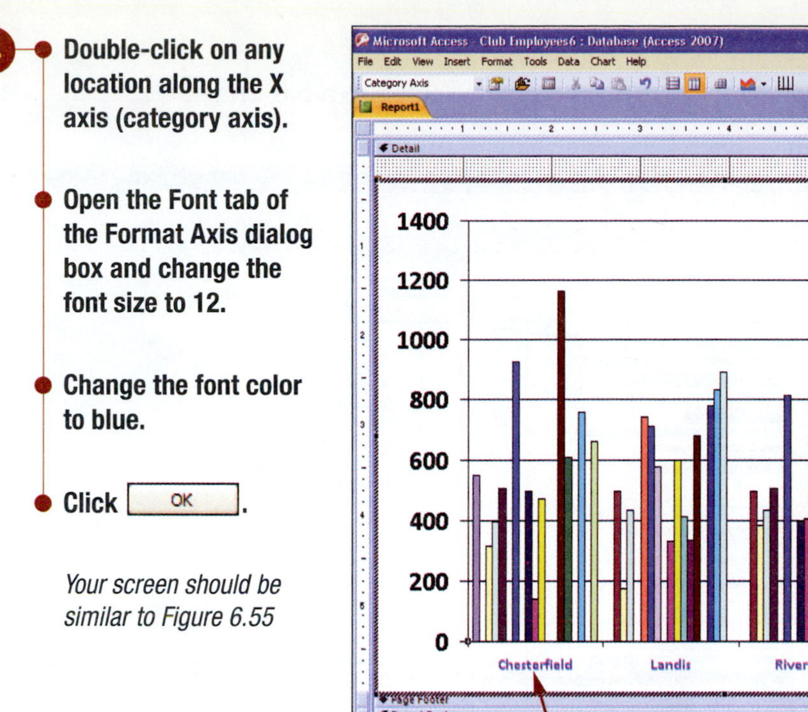

4

- Double-click on any location along the X axis (category axis).
- Open the Font tab of the Format Axis dialog box and change the font size to 12.
- Change the font color to blue.
- Click OK.

Your screen should be similar to Figure 6.55

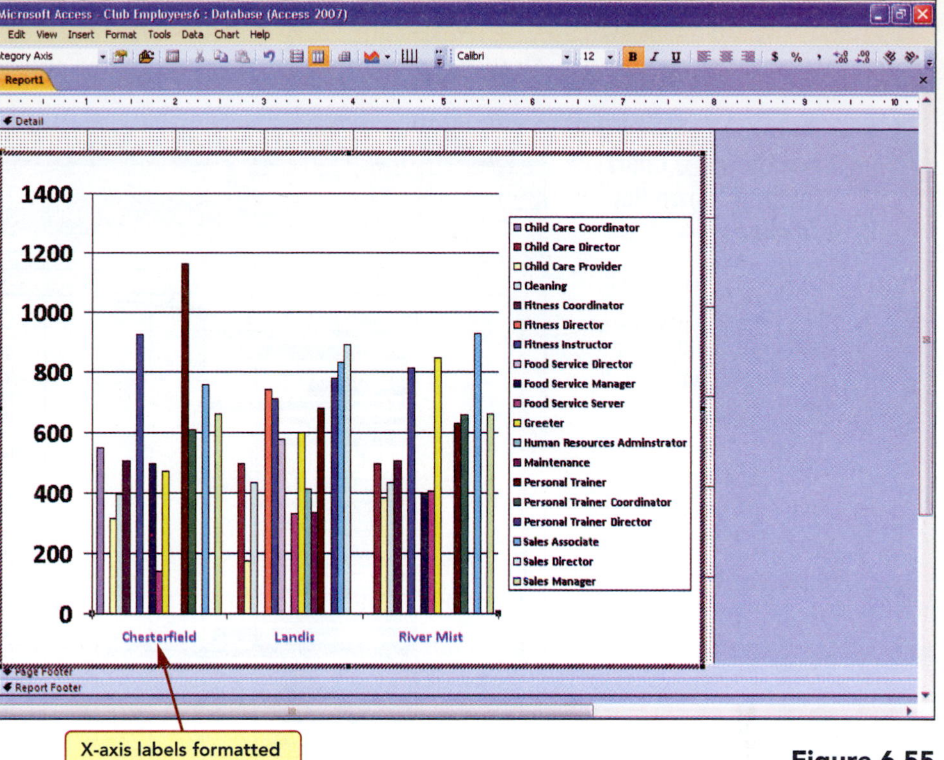

Figure 6.55

Finally, you will format the Y axis to the same font size and color and to display currency.

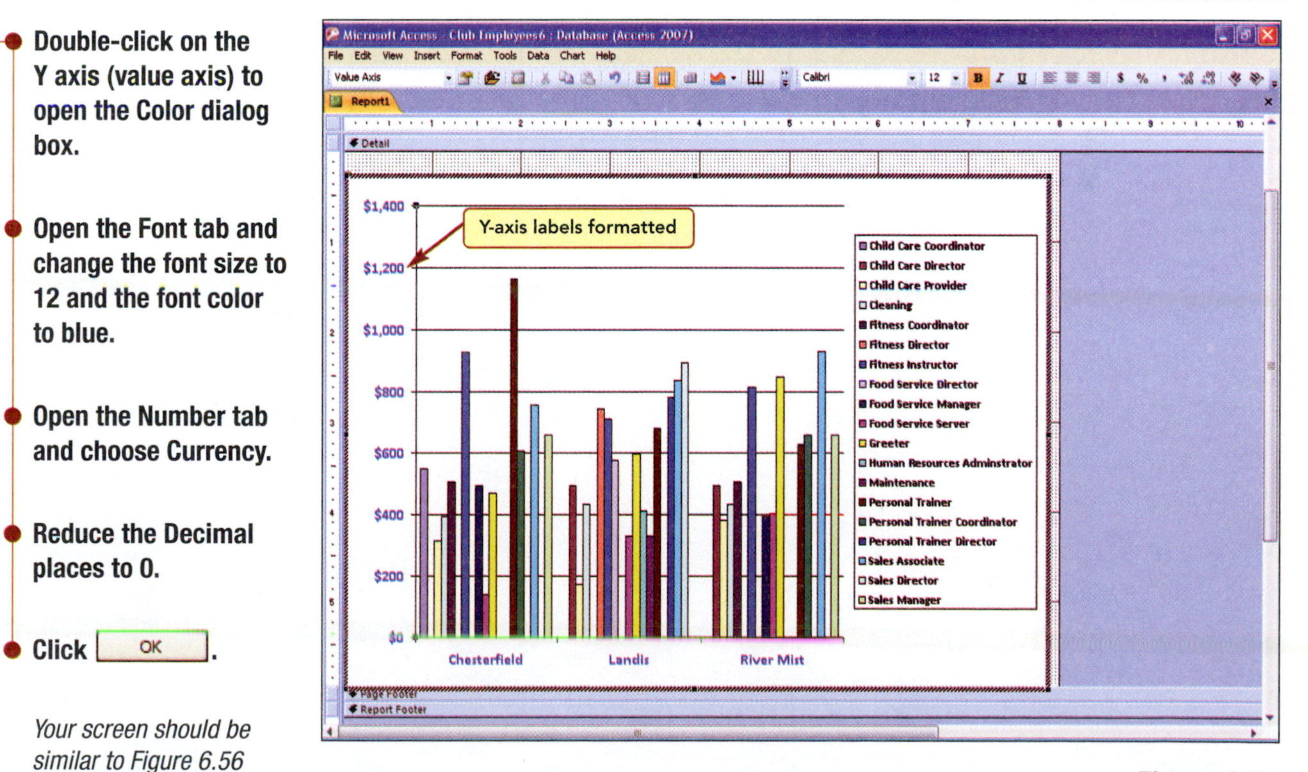

5

- Double-click on the Y axis (value axis) to open the Color dialog box.
- Open the Font tab and change the font size to 12 and the font color to blue.
- Open the Number tab and choose Currency.
- Reduce the Decimal places to 0.
- Click OK.

Your screen should be similar to Figure 6.56

Figure 6.56

The formatting changes have greatly improved the appearance of the chart.

Changing Chart Layout

Now, you want to change the type of chart to a bar chart.

1 Open the Chart Type drop-down list and choose Bar Chart.

Your screen should be similar to Figure 6.57

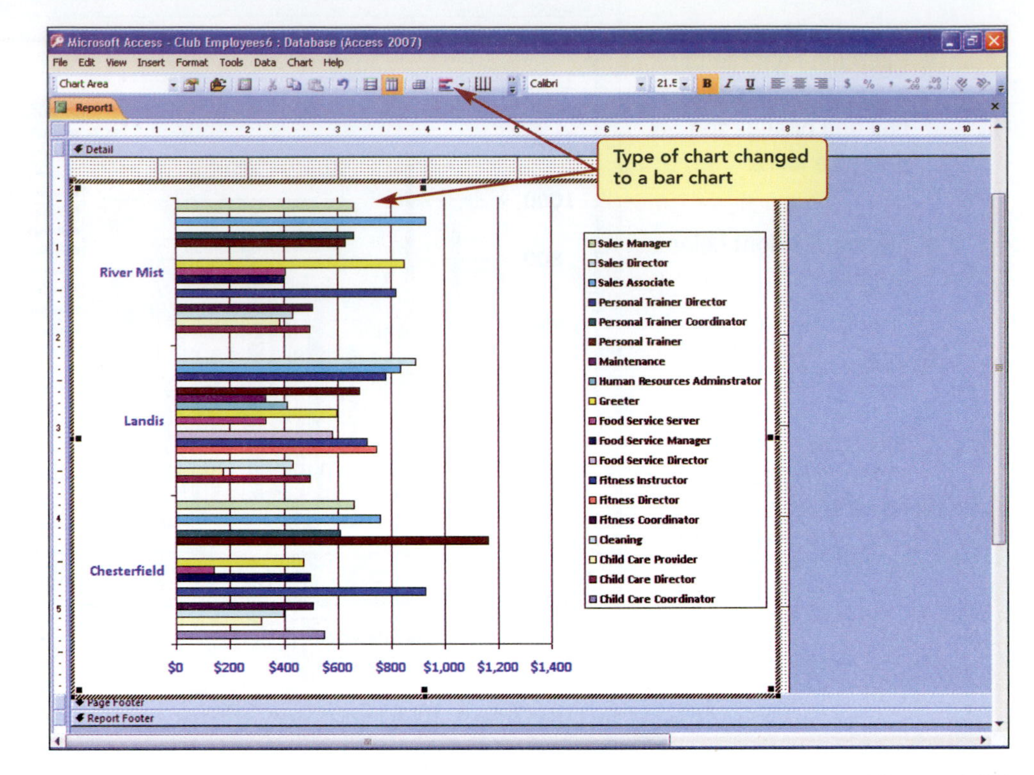

Figure 6.57

Now it is easy to compare the pay rates for each job by location. Notice that the chart is unable to display all the positions. To fix this, you would simply need to increase the chart length. However, because viewing the data by position is not the manager's concern at this time, you will return the chart layout to display the gross pay data by location by switching the position of the axis data.

2

- Click By Row.
- Click outside the chart to exit editing the chart.
- Increase the size of the Page Footer area and add a label control in the footer that displays your name.
- Switch to Layout view and increase the length of the chart object until all positions are displayed.
- Display the report in Print Preview.
- Open the Zoom menu and choose 50%.
- Print the chart.

Your screen should be similar to Figure 6.58

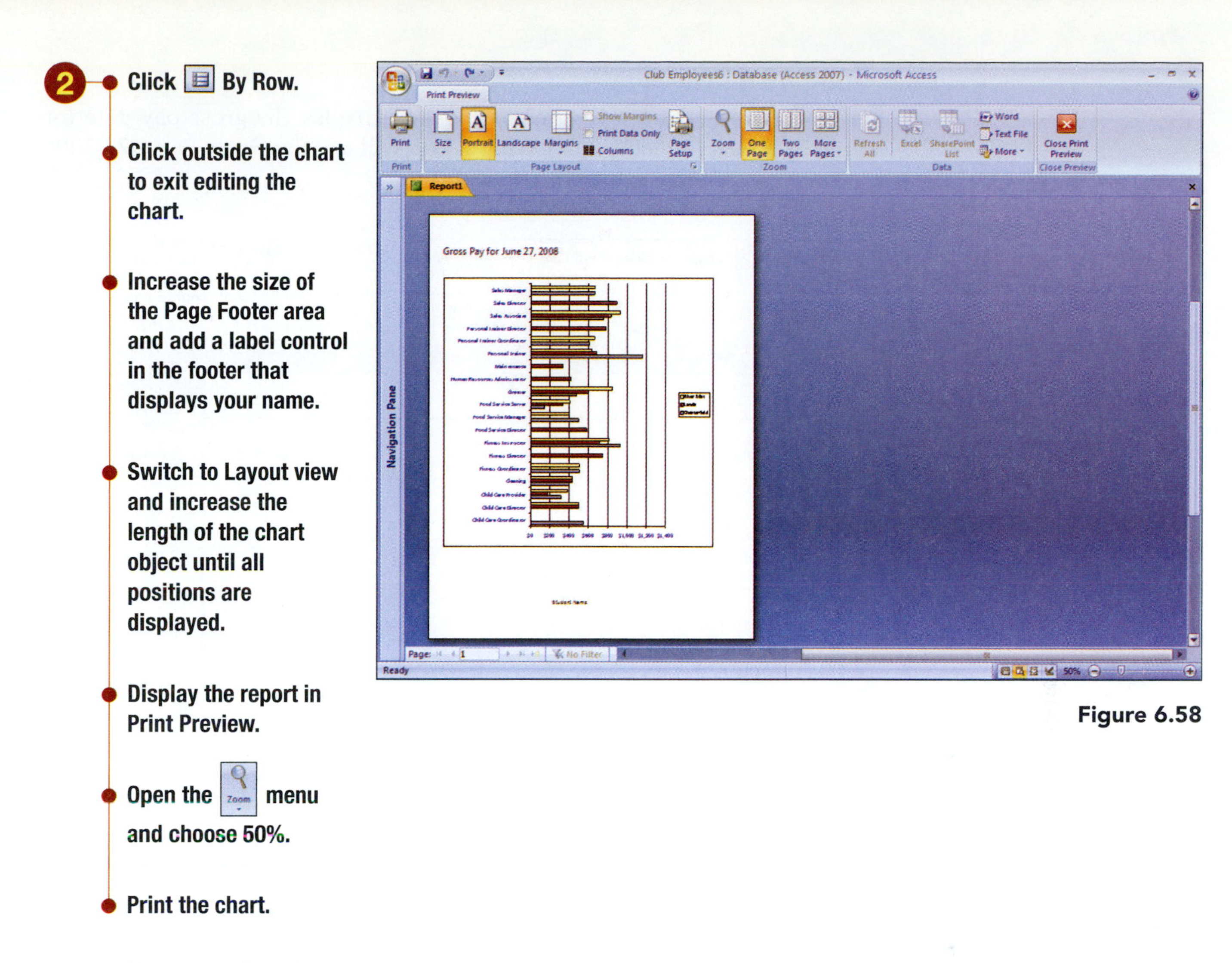

Figure 6.58

Using PivotChart View

Although the chart in the report represents the data, if the managers wanted to see different data in the chart, the chart object would need to be modified in the report. Instead, you decide to create a pivot chart of this data that will allow you to easily view different information in the same chart.

Concept 6

Pivot Chart

6

A **pivot chart** is an interactive chart that can be used to analyze data in a datasheet or form. Using PivotChart view, you can quickly view and rearrange data in the chart. PivotChart view is most useful when you want to change data views quickly to see comparisons and trends in different ways. Using the PivotChart feature, you can create 12 types of charts with many different formats for each type.

A pivot chart is designed for viewing and can be created in a separate form or in PivotChart view. When created as a PivotChart view, the settings are saved with the associated table or query and the pivot chart can quickly be displayed simply by switching views.

Creating a Pivot Chart

You decide to create a pivot chart that will display the gross pay data for June 27, 2008, for each club location. You will use the Gross Pay 6/27/2008 query as the record source for the chart data.

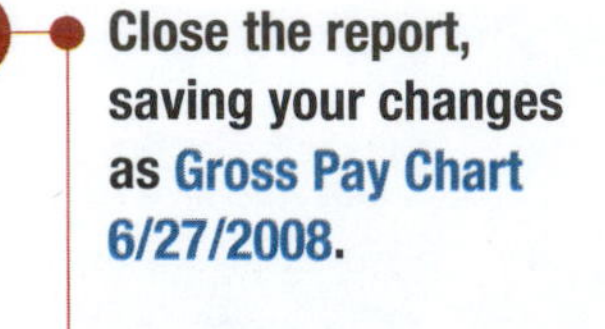

1. - Close the report, saving your changes as **Gross Pay Chart 6/27/2008**.
   - Open the Gross Pay 6/27/2008 query.
   - Hide the Navigation pane.
   - Switch to PivotChart view.
   - If necessary, click Field List in the Show/Hide group of the PivotChart Tools Design tab to display the Chart Field List box.

Additional Information

You also could create a pivot chart by clicking PivotChart in the Forms group of the Create tab. This method creates a pivot chart in a separate form object.

Your screen should be similar to Figure 6.59

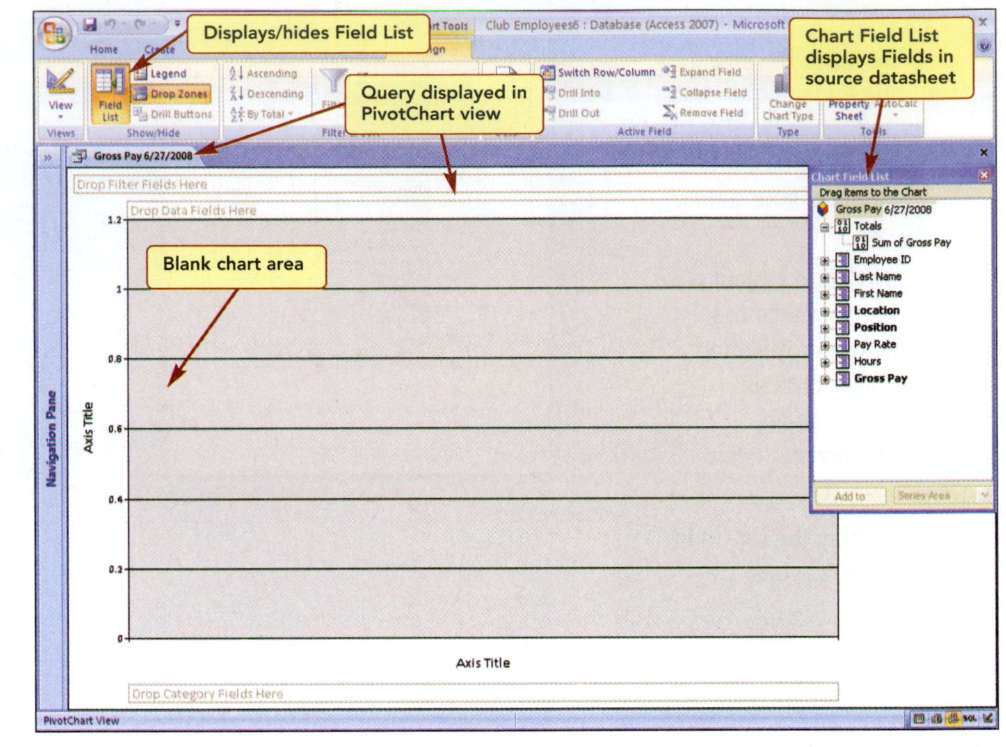

Figure 6.59

When you first open the query datasheet in PivotChart view, it contains a blank chart area. The PivotChart Tools Design tab is displayed automatically and includes commands that are specific to creating and modifying the chart.

In addition, the Chart Field List displays the fields that are available in the source datasheet and is used to add the fields to the areas of the chart. You do this by dragging and dropping the items from the field list onto the appropriate chart location. However, charts can quickly become impossible to read if you try to display too many field values at one time. Consequently, it is common to begin with only one field value as a category (X axis) and one as a series (Y axis). The X axis is the bottom, horizontal boundary of a chart and is used to label the data being charted. In this case, the X axis will be the club locations. The Y axis is the left, vertical boundary and is a numbered scale whose values are determined from the data being plotted. The Y axis will display the gross pay total value for each location.

You will now place the fields onto the pivot chart to create the chart.

2 **Select Gross Pay in the Chart Field List box and drag it to anywhere in the large box labeled "Drop Data Fields Here."**

Your screen should be similar to Figure 6.60

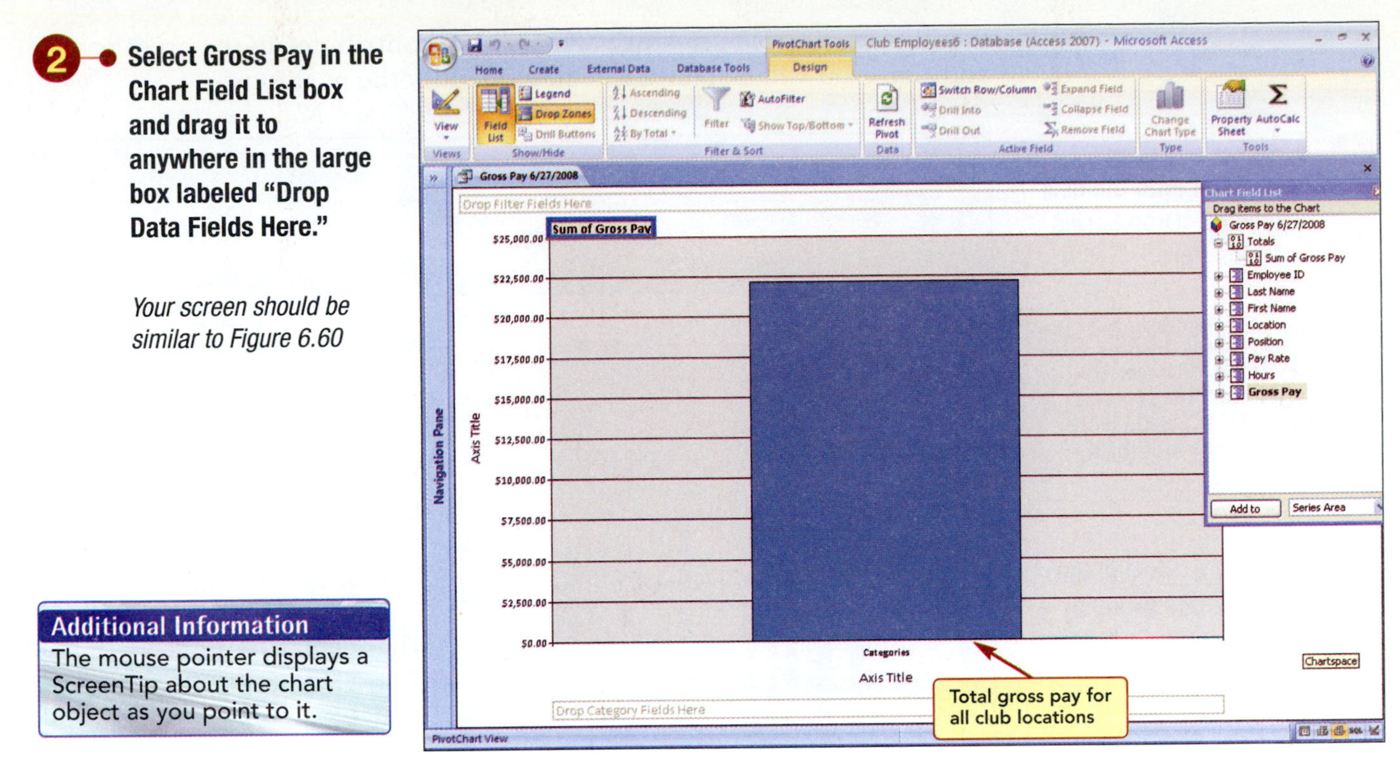

Additional Information

The mouse pointer displays a ScreenTip about the chart object as you point to it.

Figure 6.60

A column chart showing the totals from the source data is displayed by default. It shows the total payroll expense for June 27, 2008, for all clubs. Now you want to see the total gross pay for each of the three club locations.

3 **Select and drag Location in the Chart Field List box onto the box labeled "Drop Category Fields Here."**

Your screen should be similar to Figure 6.61

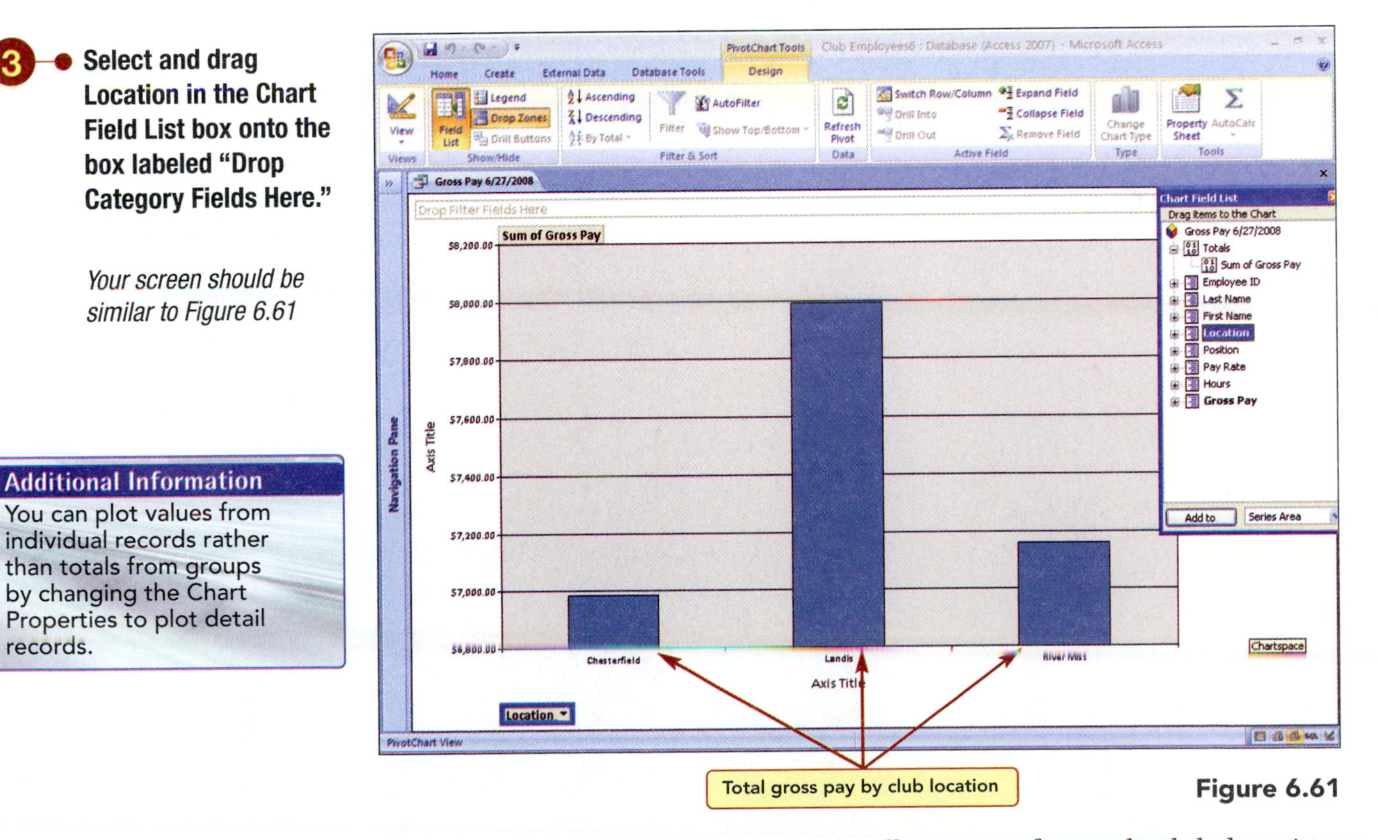

Additional Information

You can plot values from individual records rather than totals from groups by changing the Chart Properties to plot detail records.

Figure 6.61

The chart now shows the total payroll expense for each club location.

Finally, you want to see how each position contributes to the gross pay. In addition, you will display a legend to identify the positions.

4 **Select and drag Position onto the box labeled "Drop Series Fields Here."**

Having Trouble?

You may need to move the Chart Field List box to see the Drop Series Fields Here box on the right side of the chart.

- **Click Legend in the Show/Hide group of the PivotChart Tools Design tab.**
- **Close the Chart Field List box.**

Your screen should be similar to Figure 6.62

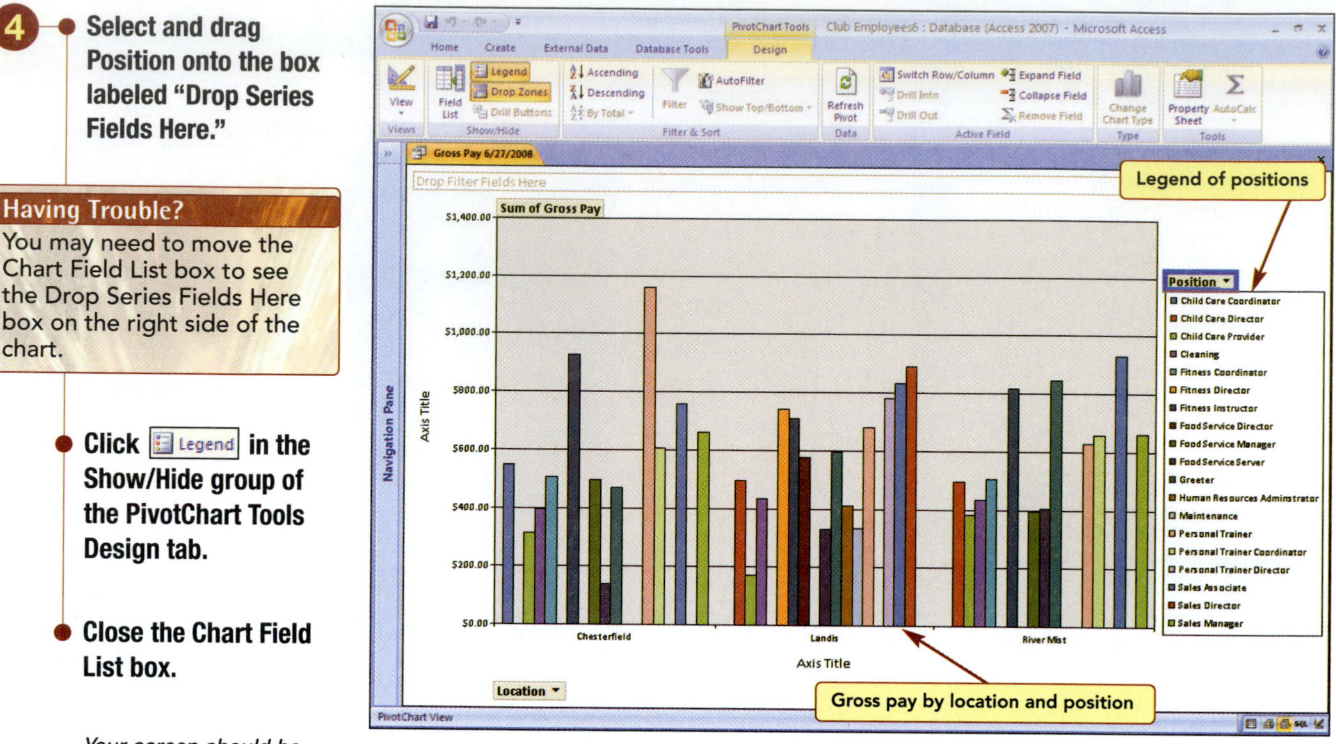

Figure 6.62

Each club location now displays a different colored column showing the total payroll expense for each position. Using PivotChart view, the club owners can now easily change the items displayed on the chart. They could, for example, change the chart to display data for the Chesterfield location only.

5 Open the **Location ▾** drop-down list.

- **Choose All to clear all checkmarks.**
- **Choose Chesterfield.**
- **Click OK.**

Your screen should be similar to Figure 6.63

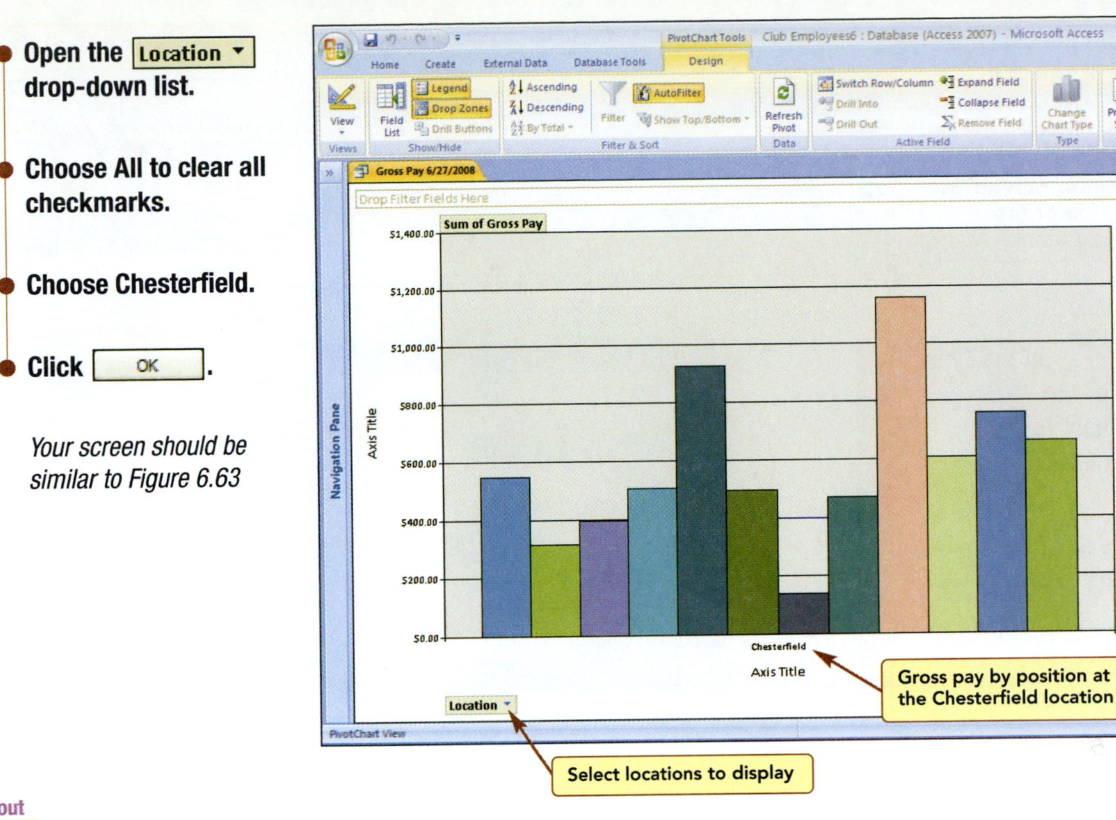

Figure 6.63

More About

To learn about creating a PivotTable form, see 2.5 Create Forms in the More About appendix.

Now the chart displays the gross pay data for each position at the Chesterfield club location only.

Changing the Chart Type

A column chart of the query data was displayed by default. Using PivotChart, you also can quickly change the chart type.

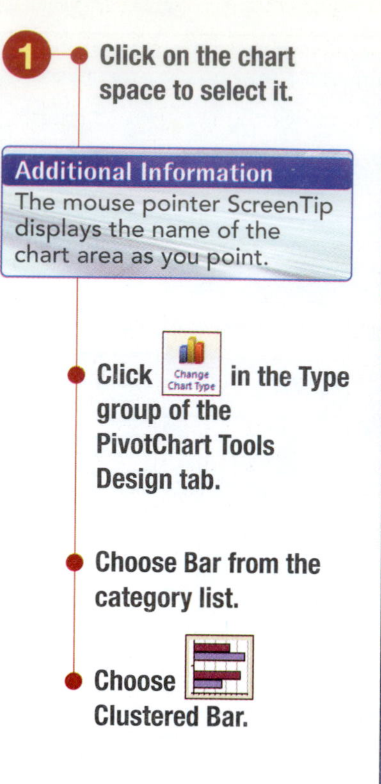

1 Click on the chart space to select it.

Additional Information

The mouse pointer ScreenTip displays the name of the chart area as you point.

- Click **Change Chart Type** in the Type group of the PivotChart Tools Design tab.
- Choose Bar from the category list.
- Choose Clustered Bar.

Your screen should be similar to Figure 6.64

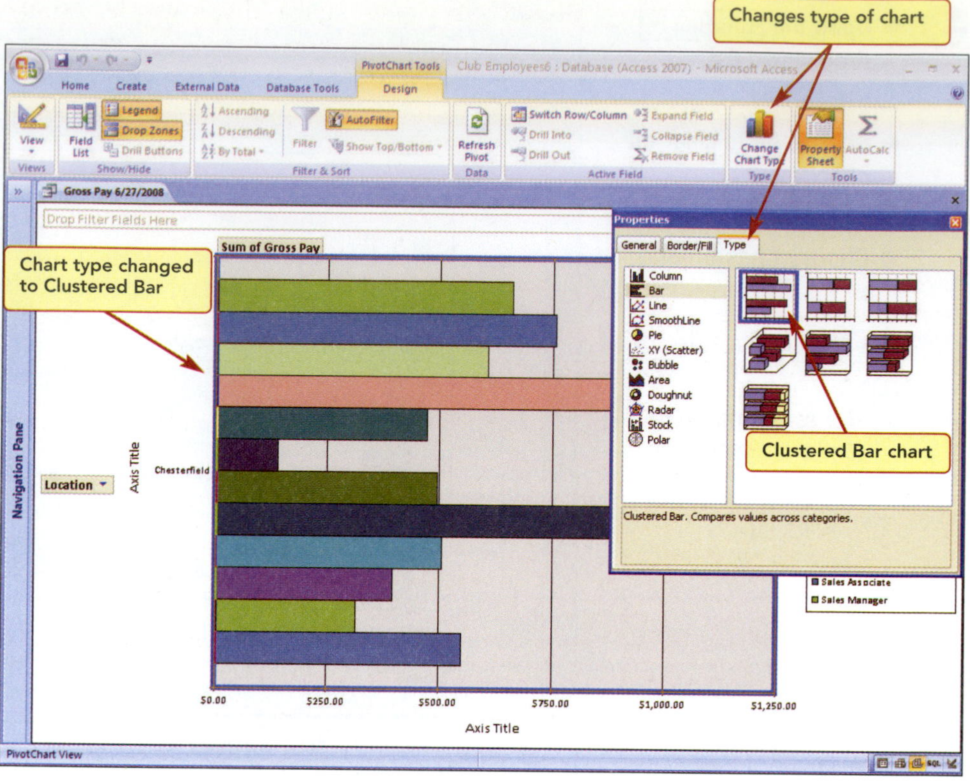

Figure 6.64

You think the bar chart makes it easier to compare the gross pay values.

You decide to remove the positions and return the chart to display the total gross pay for each club.

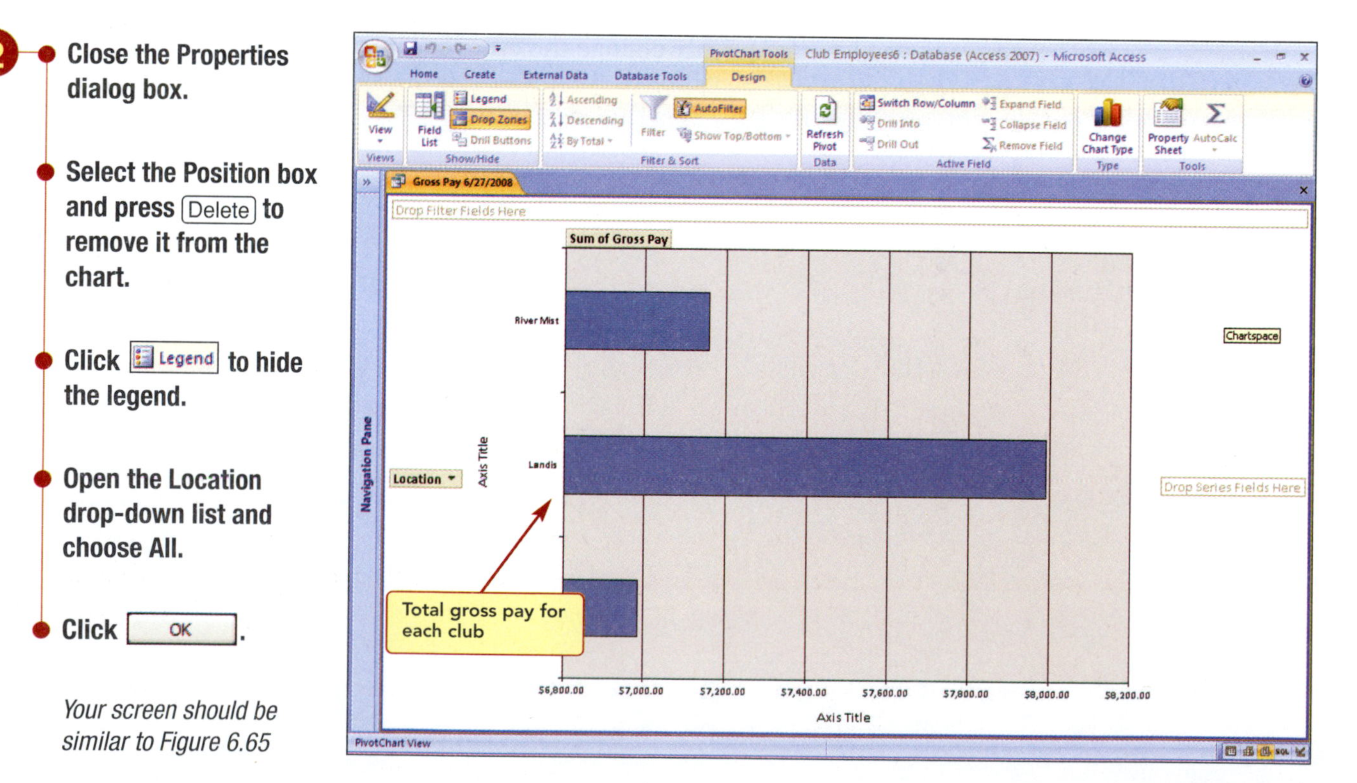

2 Close the Properties dialog box.

- Select the Position box and press Delete to remove it from the chart.
- Click **Legend** to hide the legend.
- Open the Location drop-down list and choose All.
- Click OK.

Your screen should be similar to Figure 6.65

Figure 6.65

PivotChart view again displays the total gross pay for each club as reflected in the report. Next, so that the Position data is available for selection, you will add it to the Filter area. It can then be used to compare gross pay for selected jobs.

3

- **Open the Chart Field List and drag the Position field to the "Drop Filter Fields Here" box.**
- **Close the Chart Field List.**
- **Open the Position Filter drop-down list and select All to clear all selected jobs.**
- **Select the three Fitness job titles and click OK.**

Your screen should be similar to Figure 6.66

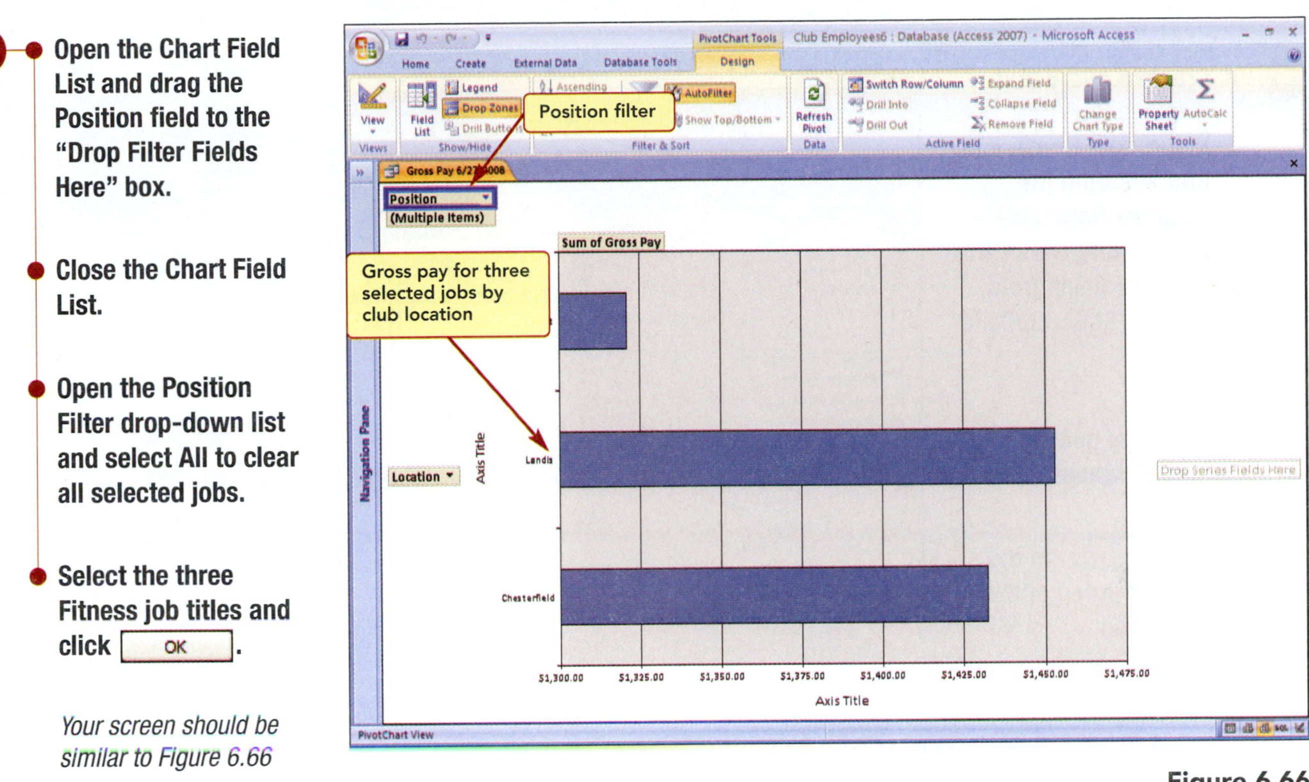

Figure 6.66

Now the pivot chart displays the gross pay for the three selected jobs at each location.

4

- **Change the view to Datasheet view.**
- **Close and save the query.**

The settings that were last viewed in PivotChart view are saved with the query and can quickly be redisplayed by switching to PivotChart view when viewing the query.

Creating Mailing Labels

The final report that the Club owners have requested is one that will print mailing labels for every employee. A sample of a mailing label appears below:

Alfonso Gomez
3429 S. Grandview St.
Landis, CA 92120-3741

Using the Label Wizard

You will use the Label Wizard to create mailing labels for the club employees. You will create a query that will include all the information from both the Personal Data and City/State/ZipCode tables that is needed for the labels.

1 **Create a query that displays the First Name, Last Name, and Address from the Personal Data table and the City, State, and Zip Code fields from the City/State/ZipCode table.**

Name the query Address Label Query.

Click Labels in the Reports group of the Create tab.

Your screen should be similar to Figure 6.67

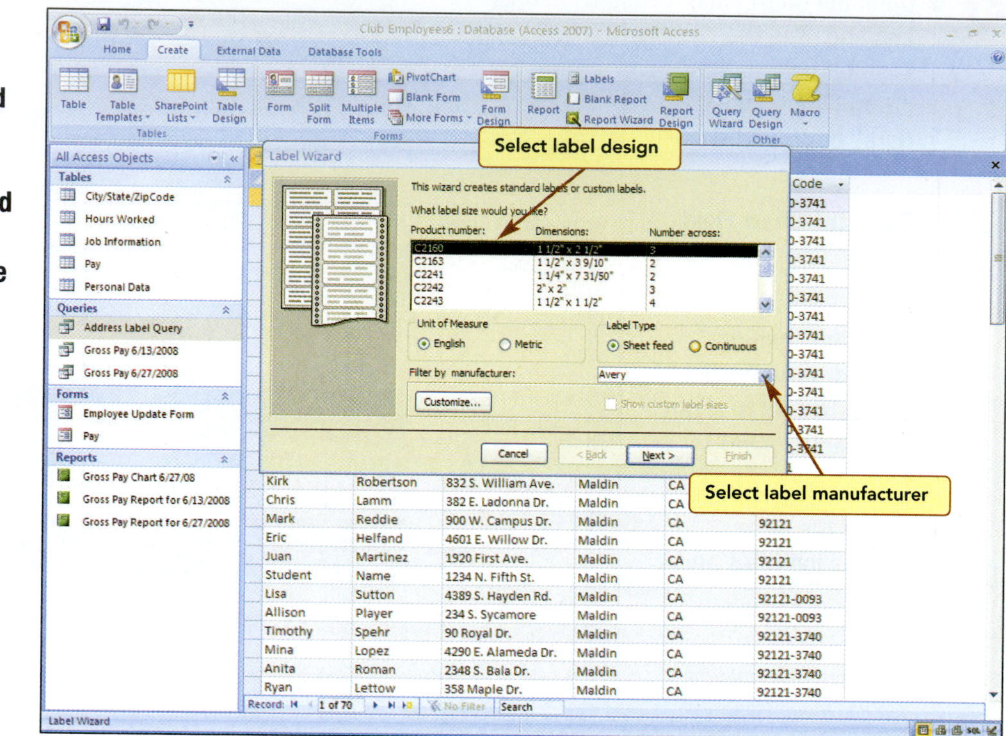

Figure 6.67

In the first Label Wizard dialog box, you specify the type of label you want to create. You can either use a predefined label or create a custom label. The Lifestyle Fitness Club uses predesigned mailing labels made by Avery, number C2160. These labels appear three across the width of the paper.

2 • **If necessary, select English as the Unit of Measure.**

• **Select Avery from the Filter by Manufacturer drop-down list.**

• **Select C2160 as the Product number.**

• **Click Next >.**

Your screen should be similar to Figure 6.68

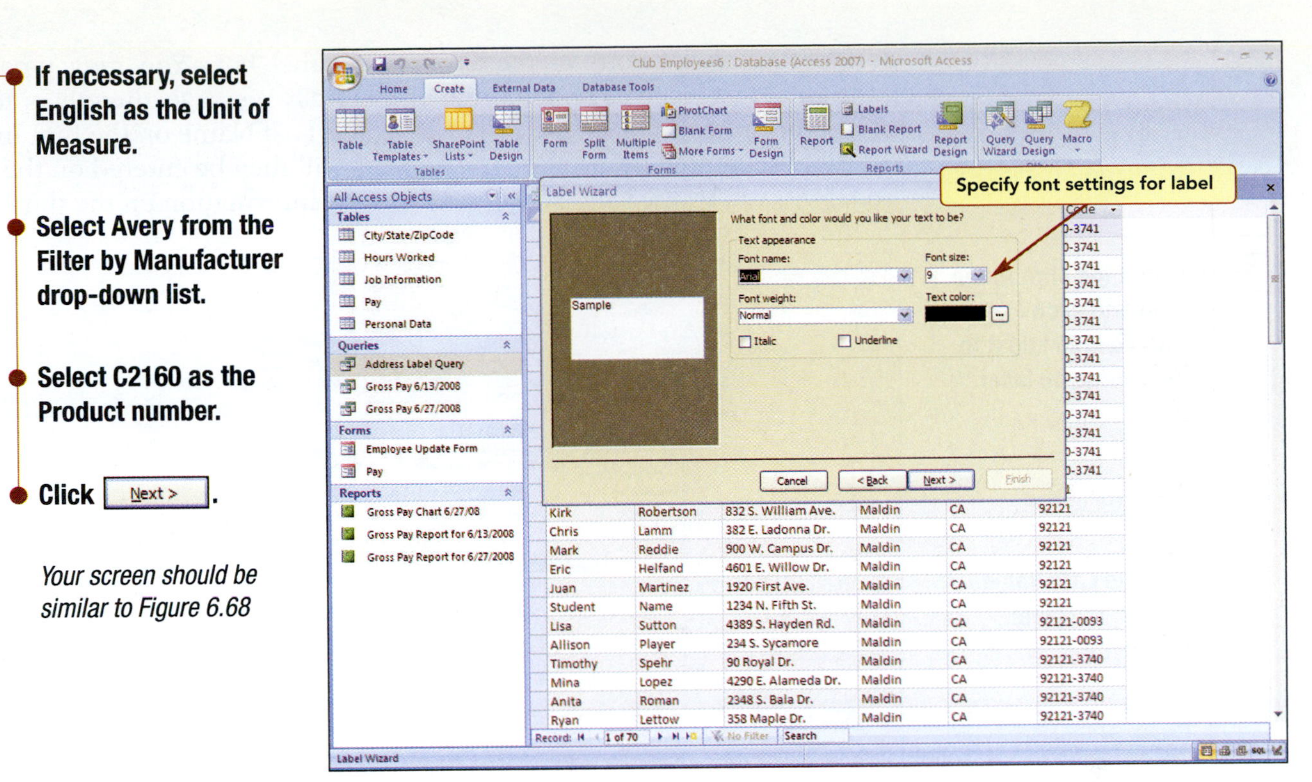

Figure 6.68

In the second step, you specify the font and text color settings for the labels. The default font is Arial and the default font size is 8. Because the Label Wizard remembers previous selections, your font size may be different.

3 • **If necessary, change the font to Arial and the font size to 9.**

• **Choose Normal for the font weight.**

• **Click Next >.**

Your screen should be similar to Figure 6.69

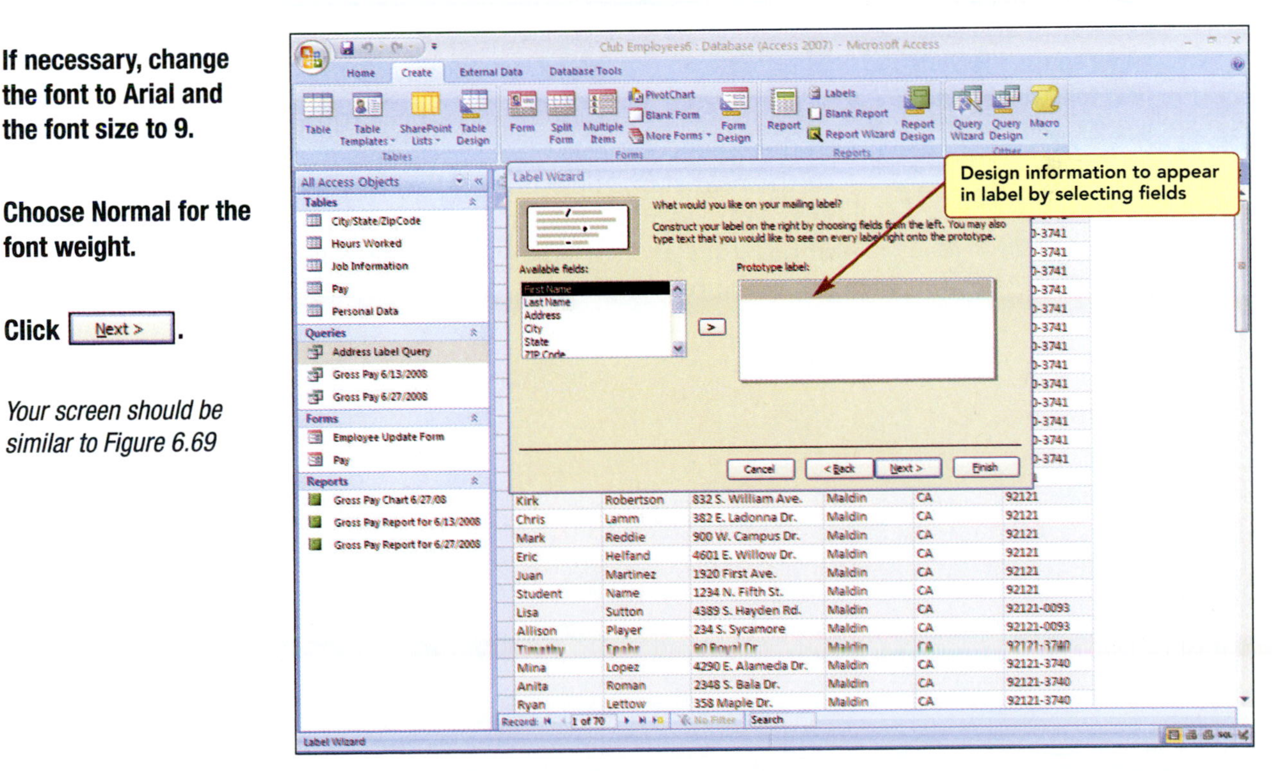

Figure 6.69

Just as with other reports, you select the fields from the table to include in the labels. Unlike other reports, however, as you select the fields, you also design the label layout in the Prototype Label box. You may type any additional text, such as punctuation or a holiday message, directly onto the prototype. You will place the First Name and Last Name on the first line of the label separated by a space. The address will then be entered on the next line, followed by the City, State, and Zip code information on the third line.

4 **Select the First Name field and click [>] Add Field to add it to the Prototype label box.**

- **Press Spacebar.**
- **Add the Last Name field to the label prototype.**
- **Press ←Enter.**
- **Add the Address field to the prototype and press ←Enter.**
- **Add the City field followed by a comma and a space, the State field followed by two spaces, and the ZIP Code field.**

Your screen should be similar to Figure 6.70

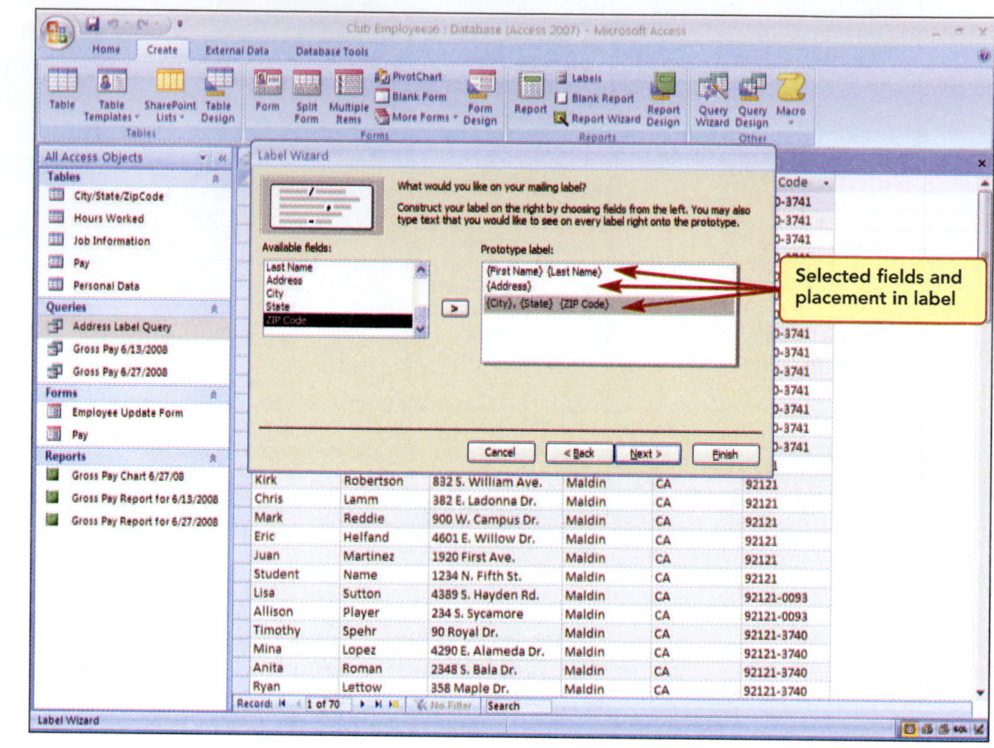

Figure 6.70

You are finished designing the label prototype and are ready to proceed with the label creation.

In the next step, you will be asked to specify a field on which to sort the labels. You want to take advantage of postal discounts resulting from mailings that are sorted by Zip code. Then you will name, finish, and preview the report.

5 Click Next >.

- Add the ZipCode field to the Sort By list box.
- Click Next >.
- Enter **Employee Mailing Labels** as the label report name.
- Click Finish.

Your screen should be similar to Figure 6.71

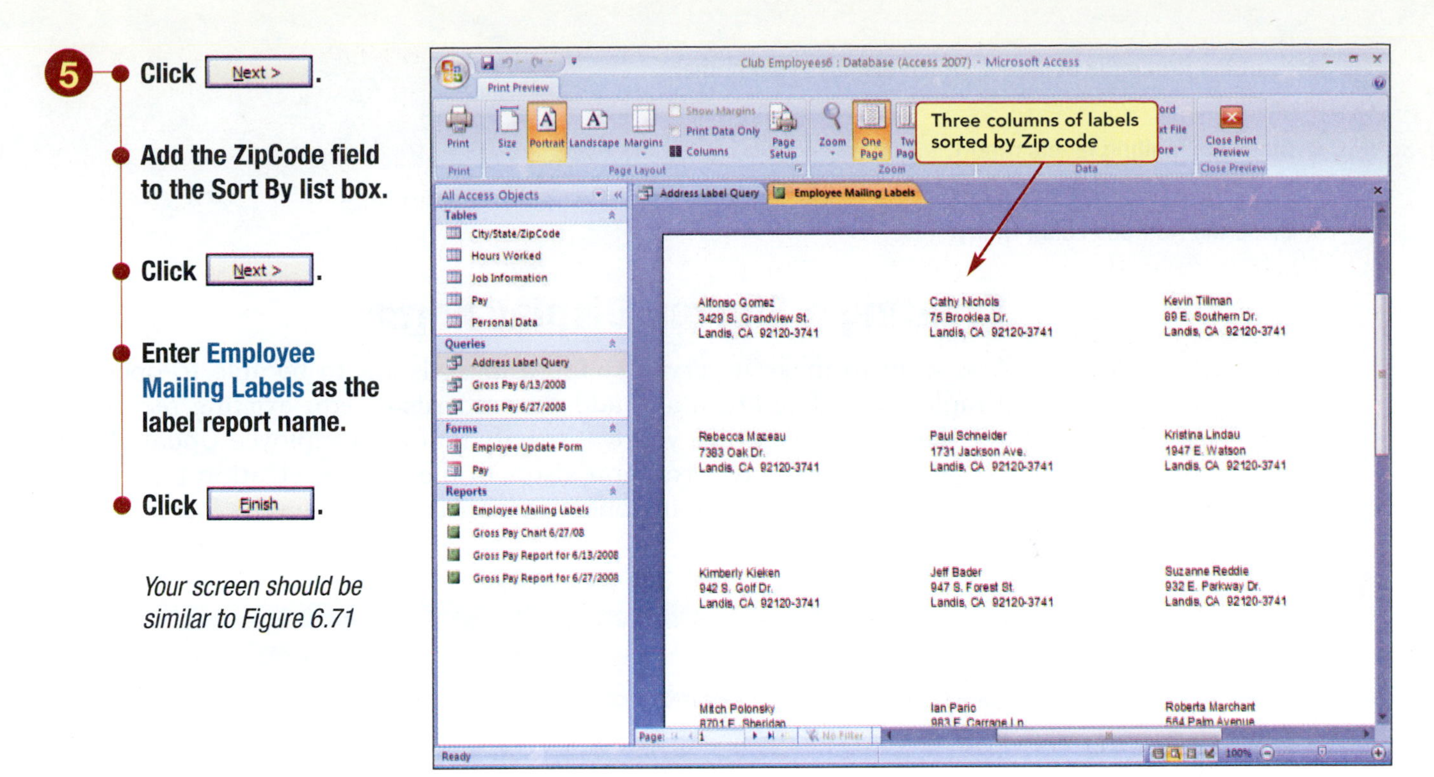

Figure 6.71

Three columns of mailing labels appear across the width of the page. The placement of the labels on the page corresponds to the C2160 Avery labels you selected using the Label Wizard. The labels also are sorted by Zip code, from left to right across the rows, then down the page from top to bottom.

Printing Mailing Labels

You will print one page of the mailing labels on standard printer paper just to see how they look. For an actual club employee mailing, you would print them on Avery C2160 labels (the type of label you specified in the Label Wizard).

6 Print the first page of labels, which displays your name.

Close the mailing labels report.

Close the Address Label Query.

Creating a Startup Display Form

You want to make it very easy for your assistant to be able to open the Employee Update Form and add new records or edit existing records in the database. To do this, you will specify that the Employee Update Form is the startup display form. You also will hide the Navigation pane upon opening this file because it would not be needed to open the form.

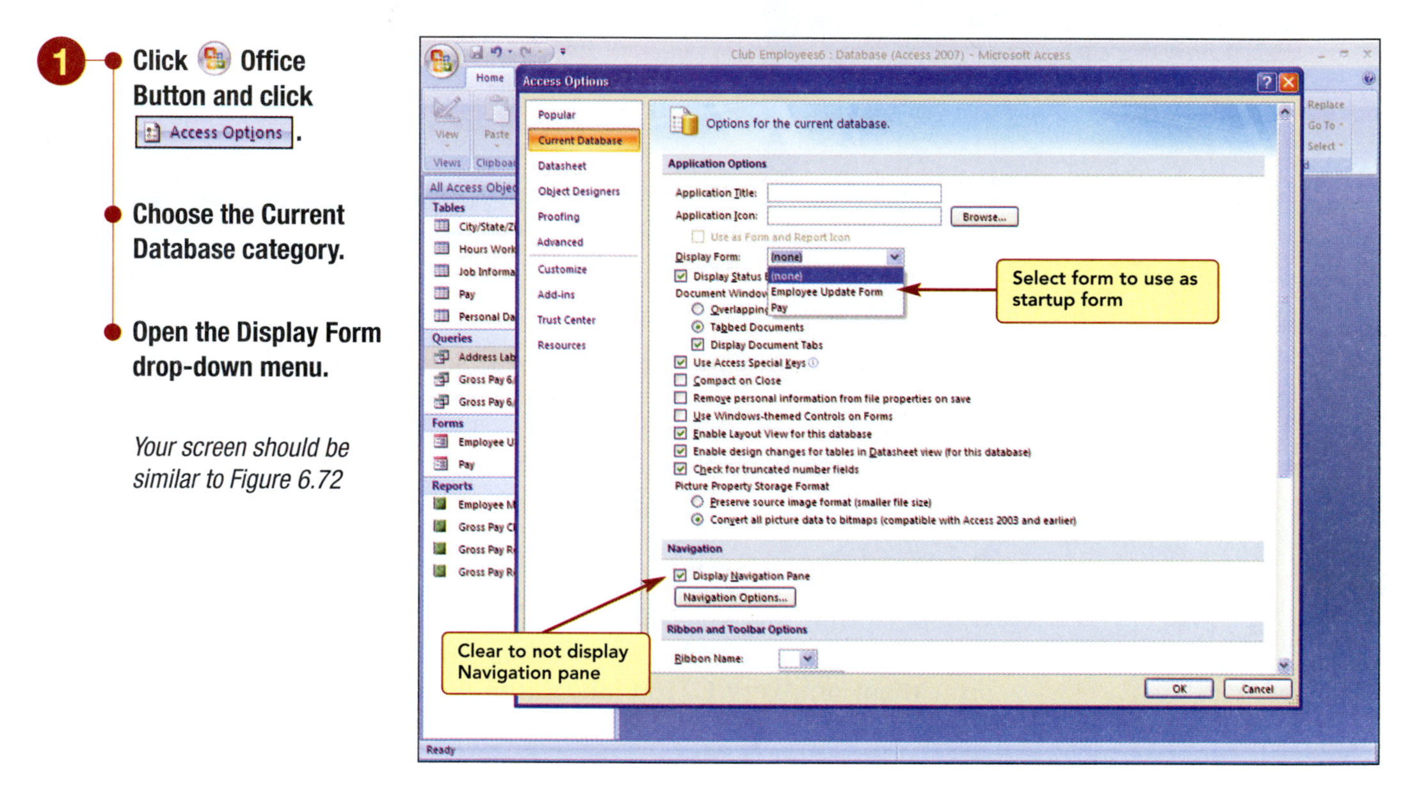

1 Click Office Button and click Access Options.

Choose the Current Database category.

Open the Display Form drop-down menu.

Your screen should be similar to Figure 6.72

Figure 6.72

All forms you have created in the current database are listed.

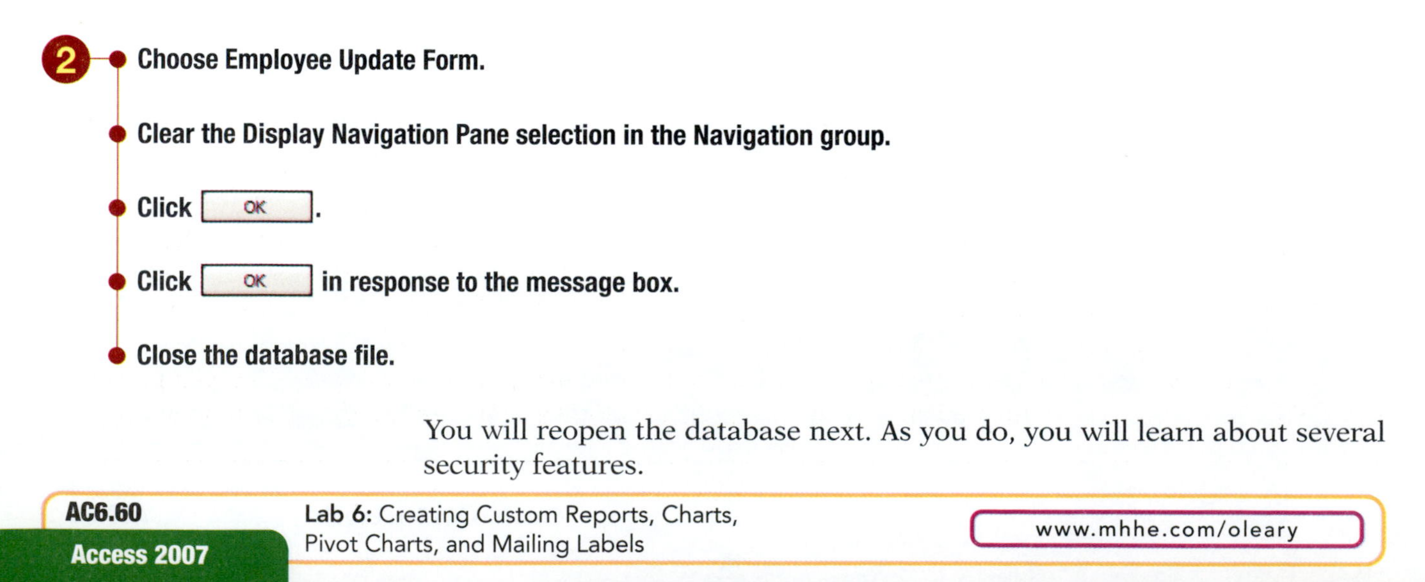

2 Choose Employee Update Form.

Clear the Display Navigation Pane selection in the Navigation group.

Click OK.

Click OK in response to the message box.

Close the database file.

You will reopen the database next. As you do, you will learn about several security features.

Securing a Database

Because much of the information in the Club Employees database is confidential in nature, you want to prevent unauthorized users from opening the database. To do this, you can restrict access to the database by requiring that a password be entered in order to open the database. You also can set the database to **exclusive** access. This means that others in a **multiuser** environment cannot open the database while you are accessing it.

First, you will change the mode of use to exclusive.

Additional Information

You need to set the database to exclusive mode each time you open the file.

1. **Choose Office Button and choose Open.**
   - **Change to your data file location and select the Club Employees6 database file.**
   - **From the Open drop-down menu, choose Open Exclusive.**
   - **Enable content.**

Your screen should be similar to Figure 6.73

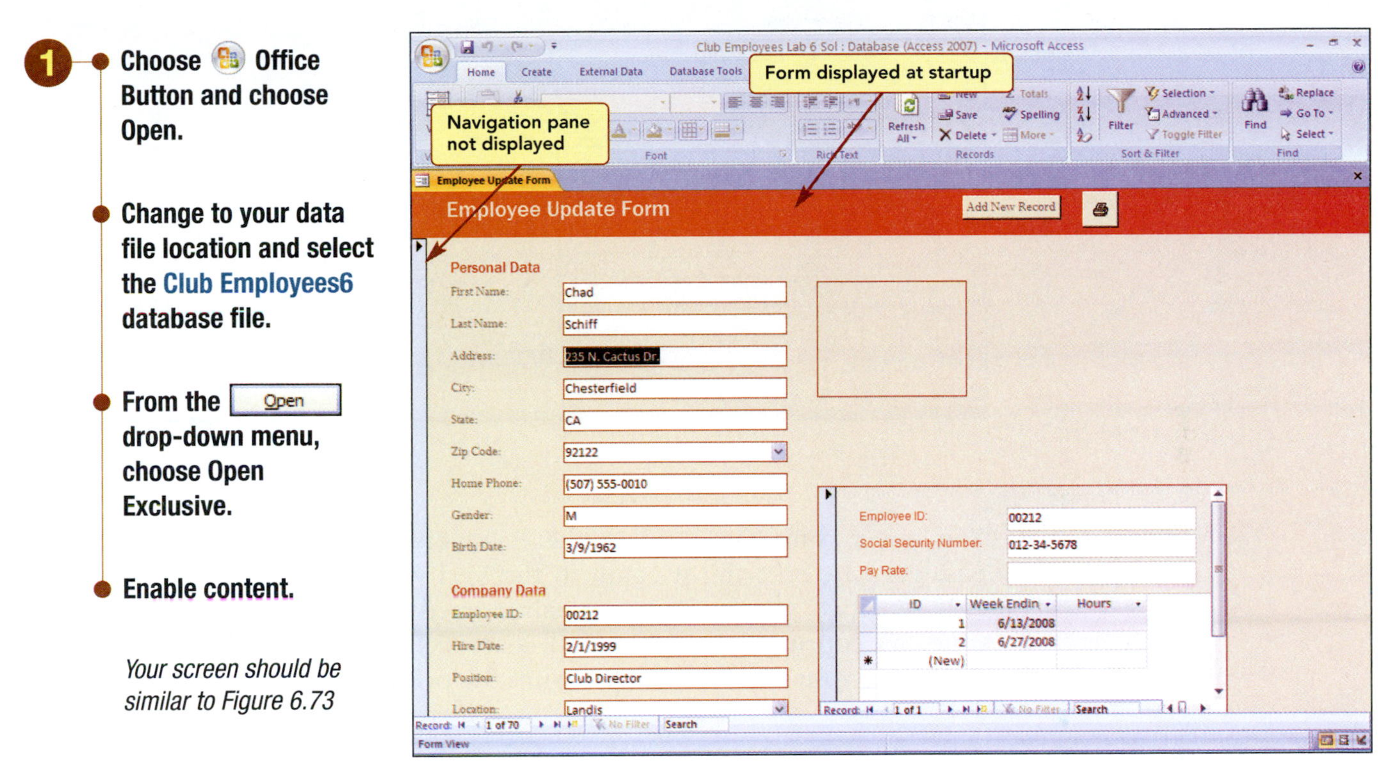

Figure 6.73

The database file opens with the Employee Update Form open and the Navigation pane hidden. The Navigation pane can be opened using F11. It will then operate as usual. In exclusive mode, no other person would be able to open or use this database file while you have it open. However, this only stops others from accessing the file while you have it open. To prevent others from opening the database, you will add a password.

Concept 7

Password

7 A **password** is a private code that is designed to prevent any unauthorized users from opening the database unless they know the password. Using a password encrypts the database, making all data unreadable by other tools, and forces users to enter a password to open the database. It is important that you use strong passwords. A strong password includes combinations of upper- and lowercase letters, numbers, and symbols that are at least eight characters in length. Now you will add a password to protect the database. The longer the password, the more difficult it is to break.

Because passwords cannot be retrieved, it is recommended that you write down and store your passwords in a secure place away from the information they provide or use a strong password that you can remember.

2 Click [Encrypt with Password] in the Database Tools group of the Database Tools tab.

Your screen should be similar to Figure 6.74

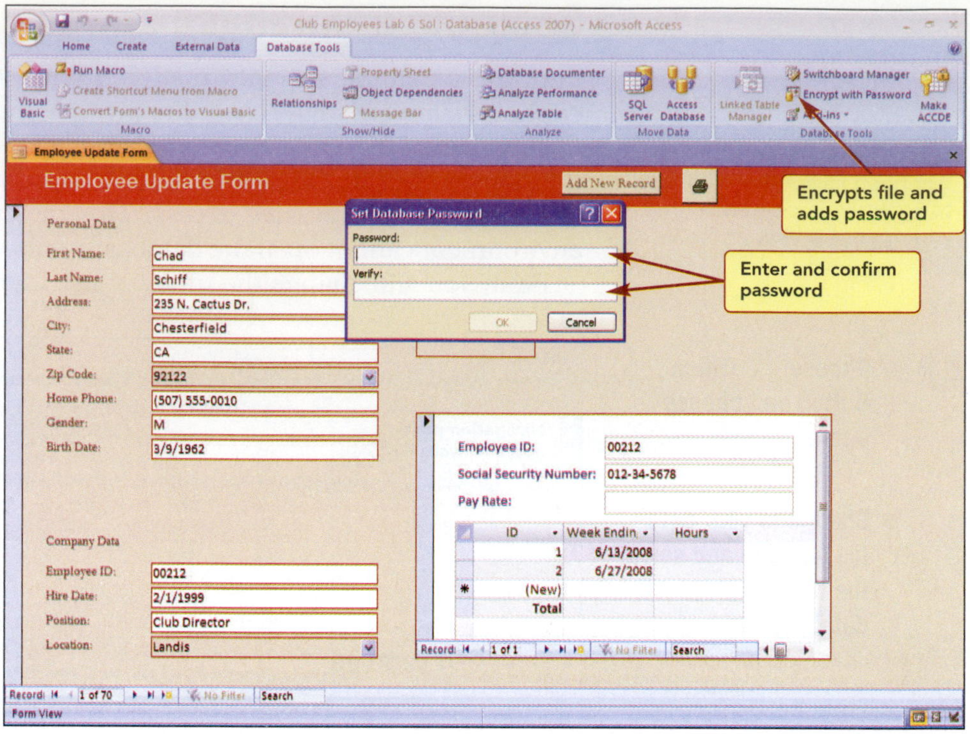

Encrypts file and adds password

Enter and confirm password

Figure 6.74

You enter your password in the Password box and then confirm the password by entering it again in the Verify box. Because passwords are case sensitive, you must enter it using exactly the same capitalization each time. As you enter the password, asterisks are displayed instead of the characters you type to further ensure the privacy of your password.

3 **Enter and then verify your first name as the password for the database file.**

- **Click [OK].**
- **Compact and repair the database file.**
- **Close the database.**
- **Select the Club Employees6 file from the Open Recent Database list.**
- **Enter your password in the Password Required dialog box and click [OK].**
- **Close the database again.**

Additional Information

You can remove a password by opening the database in exclusive use, choosing [Decrypt Database] in the Database Tools group, and entering your password.

After entering your password, the database file opened. Now that you have closed the database file, the Getting Started window is displayed again.

Using Database Templates

You have created, edited, and used tables, queries, forms, and reports while creating the Club Employees database. You created many of the objects from scratch or with the help of one of the wizards. In addition to the methods you have used, Access includes many database templates that you can use to help create complete databases for different types of applications. These templates can be quickly downloaded from the Office Online Web site. Each of the templates creates a database that is specifically designed for the selected type of application.

You decide to look at several of the database templates to see if any may be useful at the club.

Additional Information
More templates are available on the Microsoft Web site by clicking Templates in the Office Online section of the Getting Started window.

1
- **In the Templates section of the Getting Started window, choose Personal.**
- **Choose Nutrition from the Personal templates section.**

Your screen should be similar to Figure 6.75

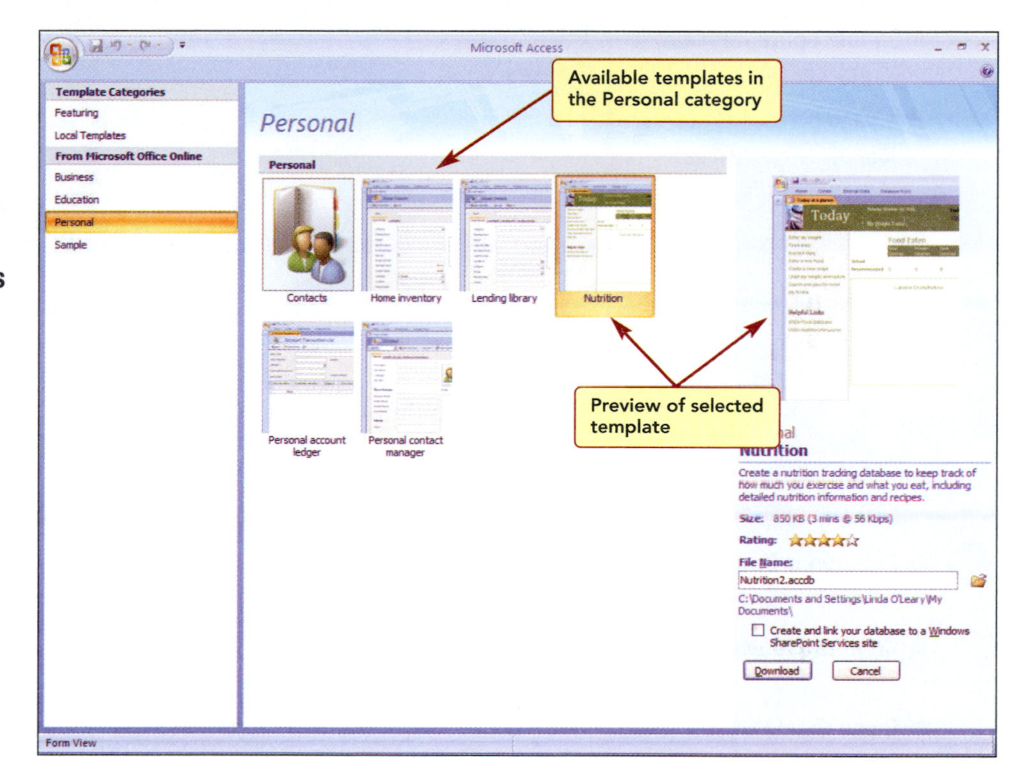

Figure 6.75

A brief description of the purpose of this database template and a larger preview of it help you to decide if the template will suit your needs. Since this template is about nutrition and exercise, you want to look at it more closely to see if it could be used at the club.

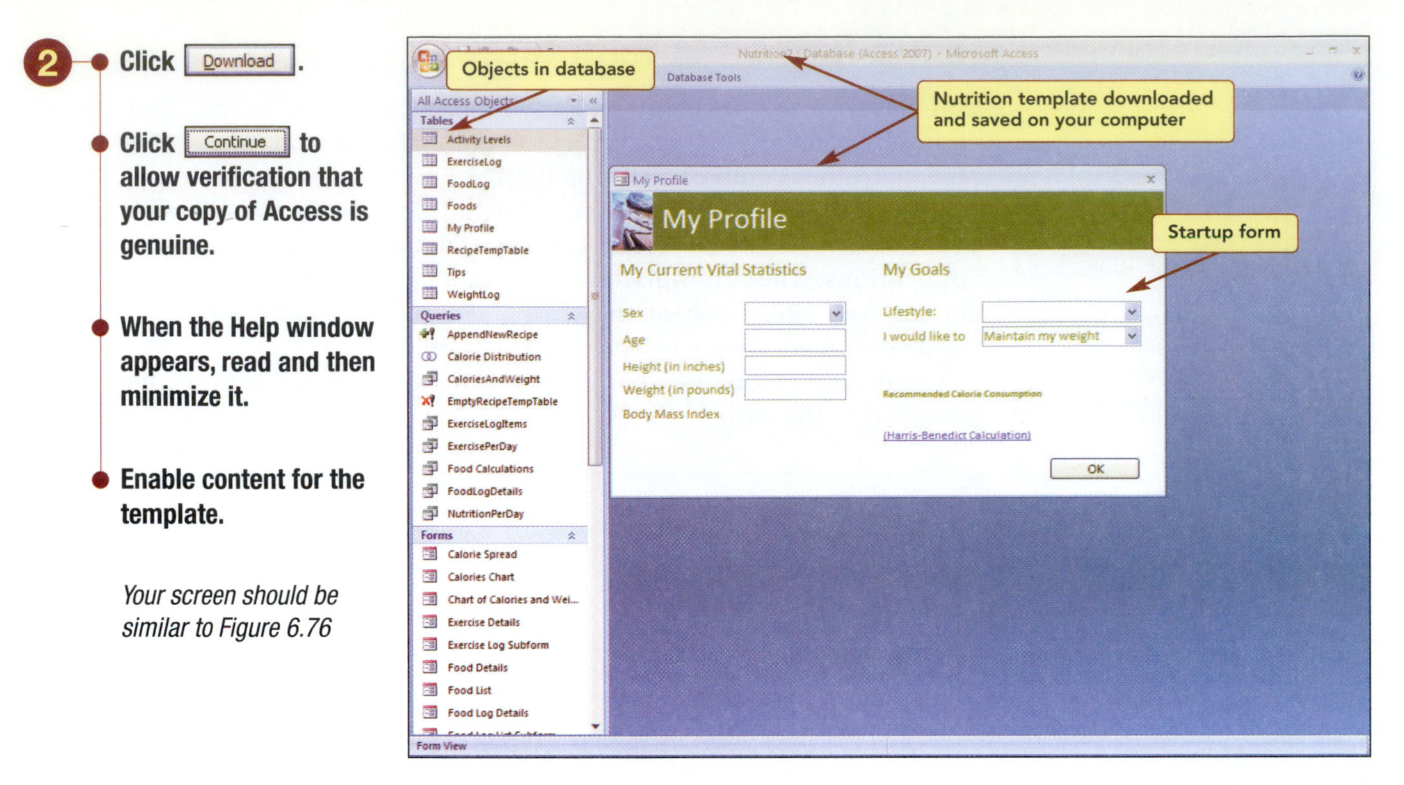

2

- **Click Download.**
- **Click Continue to allow verification that your copy of Access is genuine.**
- **When the Help window appears, read and then minimize it.**
- **Enable content for the template.**

Your screen should be similar to Figure 6.76

Figure 6.76

The Nutrition database opens with a blank My Profile form, ready for you to start recording your vital statistics. The Navigation pane shows you all the objects in the database.

3

- **Enter your information in the form and click OK.**
- **Continue to use and explore the database.**
- **Close the database when you are done.**

The template included many predesigned tables, forms, queries, and reports. You can further refine the database to meet your needs.

Focus on Careers

EXPLORE YOUR CAREER OPTIONS

Museum Curator

Have you ever wondered who keeps track of museum collections? Have you ever thought about who collects and restores artifacts for display? Museum curators plan and catalog museum collections and exhibitions using a database. They also may use a database to do research on an artifact. Many museums now share important historical information in databases. The typical salary range for a museum curator is between $32,700 and $58,280. A master's degree in conservation and experience with computers are essential. Knowledge of a foreign language also may be important. Internships are common and continuing education programs may be required.

LAB 6

Creating Custom Reports, Charts, Pivot Charts, and Mailing Labels

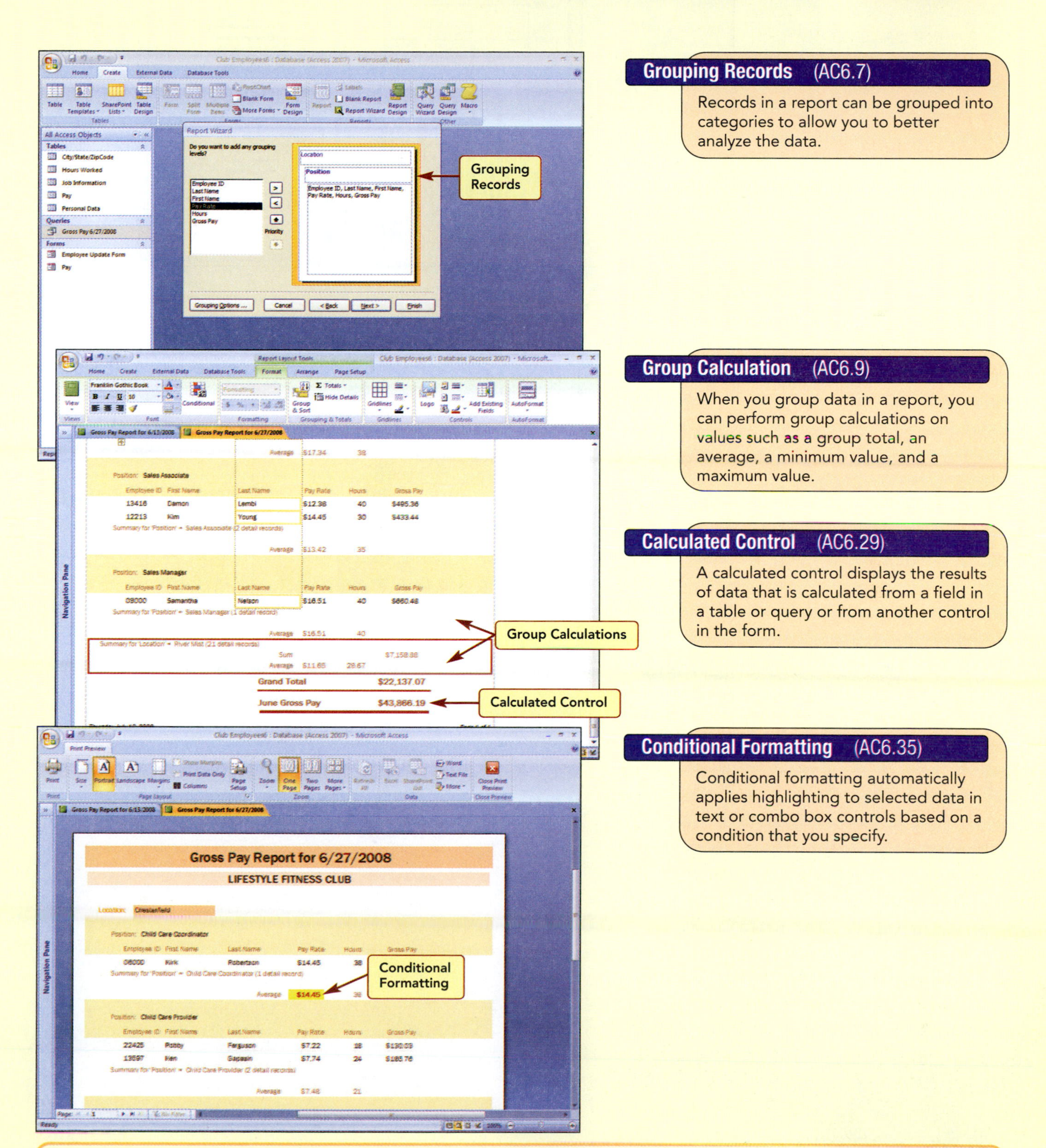

Grouping Records (AC6.7)

Records in a report can be grouped into categories to allow you to better analyze the data.

Group Calculation (AC6.9)

When you group data in a report, you can perform group calculations on values such as a group total, an average, a minimum value, and a maximum value.

Calculated Control (AC6.29)

A calculated control displays the results of data that is calculated from a field in a table or query or from another control in the form.

Conditional Formatting (AC6.35)

Conditional formatting automatically applies highlighting to selected data in text or combo box controls based on a condition that you specify.

Concept Summary

Chart (AC6.40)

A chart is a visual representation of numeric data.

Pivot Chart (AC6.49)

A pivot chart is an interactive chart that can be used to analyze data in a datasheet or form.

Password (AC6.61)

A password is a private code that is designed to prevent any unauthorized users from opening the database unless they know the password.

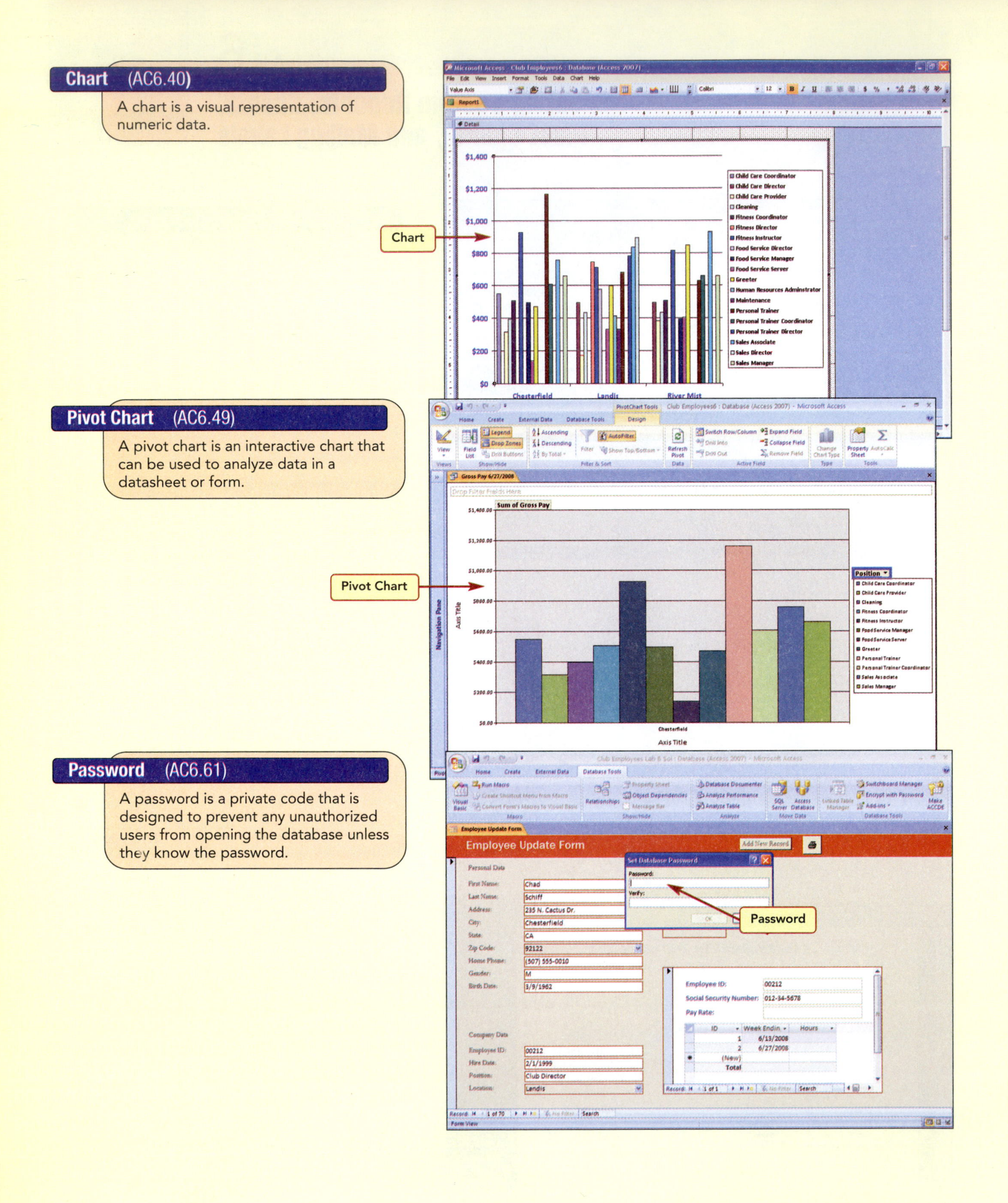

LAB 6

Creating Custom Reports, Charts, Pivot Charts, and Mailing Labels

Key Terms

calculated control AC6.29
chart AC6.40
conditional formatting AC6.35
data series AC6.41
exclusive AC6.61
Expression Builder AC6.31
group AC6.7
group calculation AC6.9
legend AC6.41
multiuser AC6.61
password AC6.61
pivot chart AC6.49
titles AC6.41
X axis AC6.41
Y axis AC6.41

MCAS skills

The Microsoft Certified Applications Specialist (MCAS) certification program is designed to measure your proficiency in performing basic tasks using the Office 2007 applications. Certification demonstrates that you have the skills and provides a valuable industry credential for employment. See Reference 2: Microsoft Certified Applications Specialist (MCAS) for a complete list of the skills that were covered in Lab 6.

command summary

Command	Shortcut	Action
Create tab		
Reports group		
Labels		Opens the Label Wizard to generate mailing labels
Report Design		Opens Design view to create new reports
Report Wizard		Opens the Report Wizard to create new reports
Database Tools tab		
Database Tools group		
Encrypt with Password		Encrypts and password protects a database
Decrypt Database		Decrypts and removes password protection
Report Design Tools Design tab		
Font group		
Font Size		Changes the size of the text in the currently selected control
Fill/Back Color		Allows you to select a background color
Format Painter		Copies the formats from a selected control to multiple other controls that you select
Controls group		
Rectangle		Adds a rectangle to the report
Line Thickness		Selects the line thickness for a graphic element
Line Color		Selects the line color of a graphic element
Line		Adds a line to the report
Title		Adds a title control to the report
Insert Chart		Opens the Chart Wizard to add a chart to the current report
Label Control		Adds a label control
Text Control		Adds a text control
Report Design Tools Arrange tab		
Control Alignment group		
Right		Right-aligns selected controls

command summary

Command	Shortcut	Action
Report Layout Tools Format tab		
Font group		
Conditional		Opens the Conditional Formatting dialog box to specify conditional formatting settings
Fill/Back Color		Selects a background color
Report Layout Tools Arrange tab		
Control Layout group		
Stacked		Adds selected controls to a stacked layout control group
Control Alignment group		
Right		Right-aligns selected controls
Tools group		
Property Sheet	F4	Displays/hides Property Sheet pane
Print Preview tab		
Zoom group		
Zoom		Changes the magnification level of the previewed object
PivotChart Tools Design tab		
Show/Hide group		
Field List		Displays/hides the list of available fields when creating a pivot chart
Legend		Displays/hides the legend on a chart
Type group		
Change Chart Type		Changes the type of chart
Chart Toolbars		
Chart Type		Changes the type of chart
By Column		Changes chart orientation to columns
By Row		Changes chart orientation to rows
Chart Datasheet		Hides/displays the chart datasheet

Lab Exercises

matching

Match the item on the left with the correct description on the right.

1. grouped ______ a. a private code used to access a secure database
2. exclusive access ______ b. prevents users in a multiuser environment from opening the database while you are accessing it
3. group calculations ______ c. a ready-made database suited for a particular purpose
4. Y axis ______ d. data in a report organized on a common attribute
5. pivot chart ______ e. displays the results of a formula in the report
6. X axis ______ f. changes the appearance of text based on what the text says
7. password ______ g. the bottom or horizontal boundary of a chart
8. database template ______ h. an interactive chart used to analyze data in a database
9. calculated control ______ i. the left or vertical boundary of a chart
10. conditional formatting ______ j. performs calculations on values in a group

true/false

Circle the correct answer to the following statements.

1. Groups should be created based on priority from smallest to largest. True False
2. You can select one of the predefined labels in the Label Wizard to create a label prototype for a report. True False
3. Saved PivotChart views are saved with their associated table or query. True False
4. You can group by up to five fields in any one report. True False
5. A calculated control automatically displays the result of an expression in Number format. True False
6. A password is used to allow multiple users to access a database file at the same time. True False
7. The Report Header section contains information that changes every time the group changes. True False
8. A grouped report always displays both detailed information and the summary information. True False
9. The Expression Builder contains a list to access all of the fields in the current database. True False
10. Each slice in a pie chart represents one data series. True False

fill-in

Complete the following statements by filling in the blanks with the correct key terms.

1. A ____________ is a calculation performed on the data in a group in a report.
2. When creating reports, records can be ____________ by categories to allow better analysis of data.
3. You can restrict access to a database with a(n) ____________ that only you know.
4. A(n) ____________ is an interactive tool used to analyze data in a database.
5. It is easiest to adjust the size and alignment of report controls in ____________ view.
6. Rectangles and lines are controls that can be added in ____________ view.
7. ____________ allows you to change the appearance of text based on a specified condition.
8. A(n) ____________ is a visual representation of numeric data.
9. A(n) ____________ is an interactive chart that can be used to analyze data in a datasheet or form.
10. Setting the database to ____________ prevents others from opening it while you have it open.

multiple choice

Circle the letter of the correct answer to the following statements.

1. A(n) ____________ database allows several users to access and modify the database at the same time.
   - **a.** group
   - **b.** multiuser
   - **c.** exclusive
   - **d.** calculated control
2. Displaying a subtotal in red if it is below $125,000 would be an example of what?
   - **a.** conditional formatting
   - **b.** currency format
   - **c.** input mask
   - **d.** subtotal property
3. The ____________ section in a grouped report displays the label control for each field column.
   - **a.** Detail
   - **b.** Group
   - **c.** Group's Header
   - **d.** Footer
4. Sum, Avg, Min, and Max are ____________ that can be used in a report.
   - **a.** arguments
   - **b.** calculated controls
   - **c.** group calculations
   - **d.** actions

5. Which of the following is not one of the operator buttons shown in the Expression Builder?
   a. +
   b.)
   c. And
   d. %

6. A report can be grouped by as many as ___________ fields.
   a. 3
   b. 5
   c. 10
   d. 15

7. A page footer prints at the bottom of ___________.
   a. each group
   b. each page
   c. the first page only
   d. the last page only

8. On a line chart, each line represents one ___________.
   a. query
   b. month
   c. data series
   d. table

9. A calculation in a report is entered in a ___________.
   a. calculated control
   b. rectangle control
   c. label control
   d. option group control

10. Which of the following chart types is ideal for displaying the rate of change in data over time?
   a. Pie
   b. Bar
   c. Line
   d. Column

Hands-On Exercises

rating system
★ Easy
★★ Moderate
★★★ Difficult

step-by-step

Adventure Travel Tours Client Report and Mailing Labels ★

CONTINUING EXERCISES

1. The database that you created for Adventure Travel Tours contains the client and agent tables and forms the manager requested. Now you have been asked to use this data to create some reports. The first report they requested is one that groups the agents by location and lists the clients assigned to each agent. They also would like you to create mailing labels for the clients so they can use them to send out promotional materials. When you are finished, your grouped report will be similar to that shown here.

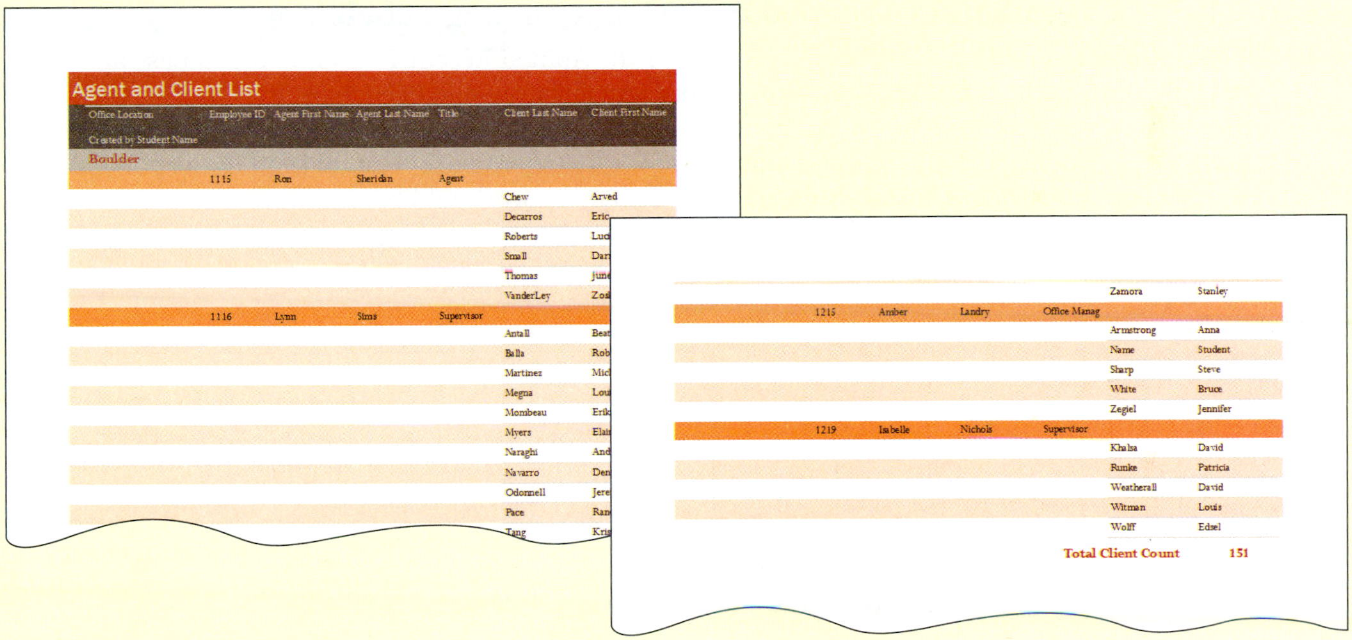

   a. Open the ATT Clients & Agents database (which you last updated in Step-by-Step Exercise 1 of Lab 5).

   b. Use the Report Wizard to create a new report that displays the OfficeLocation, Employee ID, FirstName, LastName, and Title fields (in that order) from the Agents table and the Client ID, First Name, and Last Name fields from the Clients table. View the data by Agents and group the report by Office Location.

   c. Sort the Client records by Last Name and then by First Name. Use the Stepped layout in Portrait orientation. Use the Concourse style and enter the report name **Agent and Client List**.

   d. In Layout view, change the design style to Equity and the OfficeLocation label caption in the Page Header to **Office Location**. Include the word **Agent** before the First Name and Last Name labels for the agents and the word **Client** before the Last Name and First Name labels for the clients. Resize the controls as needed.

   e. In Design view, add a calculated control in the Report Footer to display the total number of clients. Hint: Add a Text Box control with the expression =Count([Client ID]).Change the control caption to **Total Client Count**. Align the calculated control with the Client First Name column and the control caption with the Client Last Name column.

f. Apply font color, fill color, line color, and border color to the report as you like. Adjust the formatting as required.

g. Expand the Page Header section and add a label that reads **Created by your name**. Format the label as necessary.

h. Print the report. Save and close it.

i. Use the Label Wizard to create mailing labels for the Clients table. Use the Agipa 119715 labels. (Hint: If you do not see these labels in the product list, check the Unit of Measure and make sure English is selected.) Increase the font size to 10 and the weight to Normal. Create a prototype by adding the name and address fields in the order they would normally appear in an address, including spacing and punctuation where necessary. Sort the labels by Zip code and name the report **Client Mailing Labels**.

j. Print the page of labels that displays your name as a client and then close the report.

k. Close the database.

Animal Rescue Foundation Grouped Report and Mailing Labels ★★

2. You have finished creating the tables and forms for the Animal Rescue Foundation database and you have asked the directors if there is anything in particular they would like to see. In response, they have asked for a report of the current status of all animals. They also would like to be able to quickly create mailing labels from the foster care and adopter tables so they can use them to send thank you notes and other correspondence. When you are finished, your report should be similar to that shown here.

   a. Open the database named Animal Rescue Foundation (which you last worked on in Step-by-Step Exercise 2 of Lab 5).

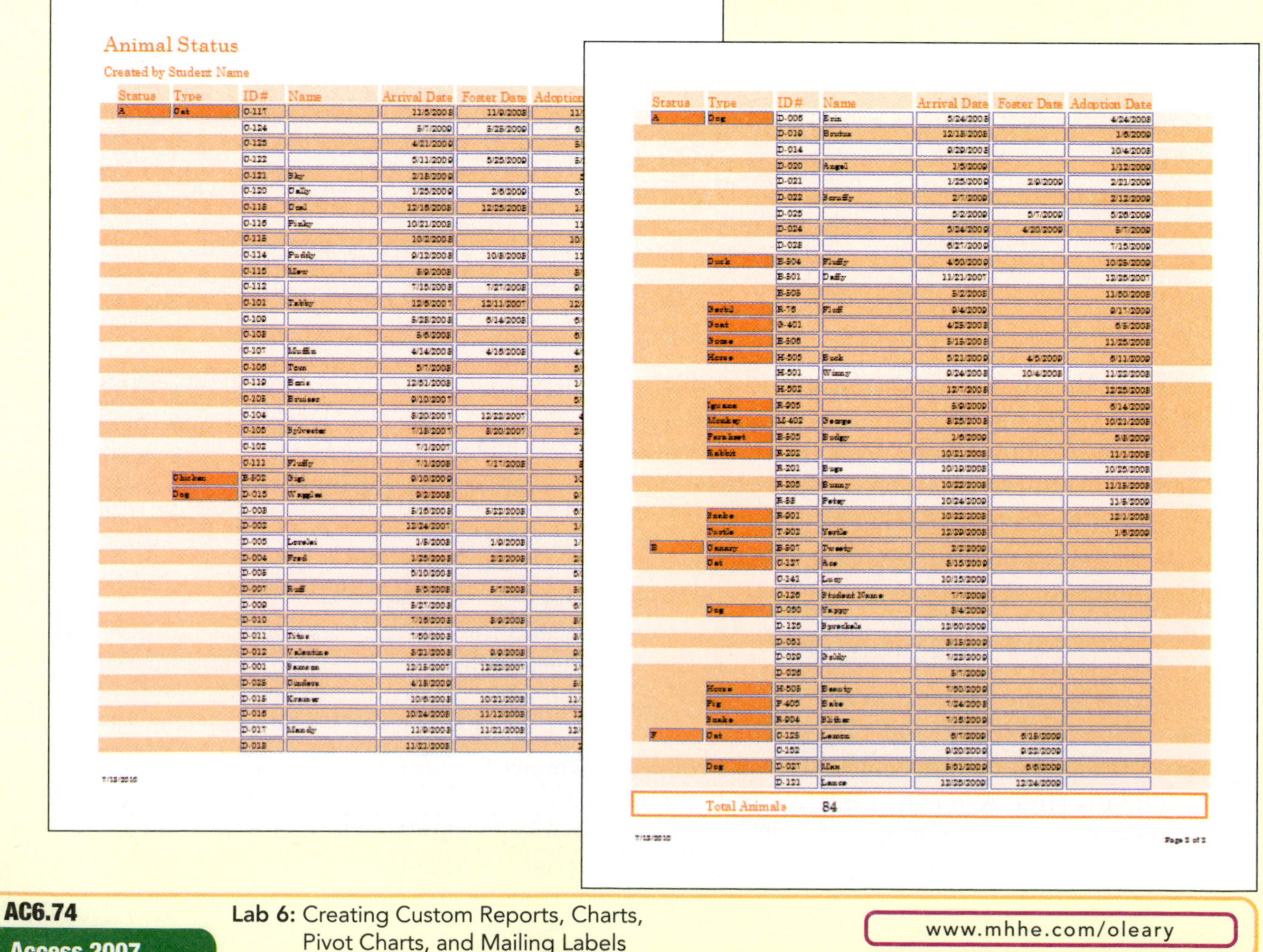

b. Use the Query Wizard to create a new query. From the Rescues table, add the ID#, Current Status, Type, Name, Arrival Date, Foster Date, and Adoption Date fields. Name the query **Animal Status**. Preview and close the query.

c. Use the Report Wizard to create a report using all the fields from the Animal Status query. Group the report by Current Status and then by Type. Do not select any sort fields for this report. Use the Block layout in Portrait orientation. Use the Oriel style and name the report **Animal Status**.

d. Make the following changes to the layout and design of the report:
   - Change the Current Status label control to **Status**. Increase the font size of all the label controls to 12. Size and position the controls appropriately.
   - In the Report Footer, add a calculated control to display the total number of animals. Hint: Add a Text Box control with the expression =Count([ID #]). Change the control caption to **Total Animals**. Increase the font size of both controls to 12 point. Adjust the controls to fit the data. Align the label control with the Type control and align the text control with the Name control.
   - Change the control property of the Now date control in the Page Footer so it displays in Short Date format.
   - In the Report Header section, add a label in 12 point that reads **Created by your name** below the title. Left-align the title and the label control containing your name.
   - Apply font color, fill color, line color, and border color to the report as you like.

e. Preview the report and make any layout changes that are needed to fit the report on two pages. Print both pages of the report. Save and close it.

f. You are now ready to create the two mailing label reports that were requested. Use the Label Wizard to create each report, one with name and address fields from the Fosters table and the other with name and address fields from the Adopters table. Use the Avery 3110 label and create a standard mailing label prototype for each. Change the font to Times New Roman and 12 point. Sort the labels by Zip code and name the first report **Foster Care Mailing Labels** and the second report **Adopters Mailing Labels**.

g. Print the page of labels in the Adopters report that contains your name. Save and close both reports.

h. Close the database.

Five Points Database Reports ★★

3. Kathlyn Frances, the owner of the Five Points Health and Wellness Center, is quite pleased with how the database you created for her has automated what used to be quite time-consuming manual record-keeping tasks. She is particularly pleased with how the data can be used to track the sales of massage packages offered at the spa. Her most recent request is for a report that shows the spa packages that were purchased and by whom, as well as the sales total for each package and the total income generated from these sales. The report will include group calculations as well as a calculated control that will generate the grand total. Your completed grouped report should be similar to that shown here.

   a. Open the Five Points Center database file (which you last worked on in Step-by-Step Exercise 3 of Lab 5).

   b. Use the Report Wizard to create a new report that contains the Package #, Package Name, and Description fields from the Spa Packages table; the Client # from the Packages Sold table; and the First Name and Last Name fields from the Clients table. Specify that you want to view the data by Packages Sold and group the report by Package Name. Do not sort on any fields. Use the Outline layout and the Trek style. Name the report **Spa Packages Sold**.

Spa Packages Sold

Package Name Five Point Indulgence

Client #	First Name	Last Name
100-05	Ky	Hubert
100-22	Joseph	Buchsbaum
100-12	Sally	Gimbell
100-17	Pauline	Caniza
100-18	Sydney	Schwartz

Package Name Five Points Bliss

Client #	First Name	Last Name
100-10	Charlene	Downing
100-05	Ky	Hubert
100-08	Amar	Gajjar
100-20	Lin	Wu
100-10	Charlene	Downing
100-13	Fredrick	Kane
100-13	Fredrick	Kane

Package Name Five Points Escape

Client #	First Name	Last Name
100-07	Barbara	Wright
100-11	Kathleen	Dome
100-18	Pamela	Hinds

Package Name Five Points Escential

Client #	First Name	Last Name
100-19	Debbie	Lindstrom
100-20	Lin	Wu
100-02	Cheng	Cheng

7/13/2010

100-02	Cheng	Cheng

Package Name Five Points Purification

Client #	First Name	Last Name
100-01	Ellen	Pickering
100-18	Sydney	Schwartz
100-04	Karen	Johanson

Package Name Five Points Rejuvination

Client #	First Name	Last Name
100-24	Student	Name
100-09	Bobbi	Adderson
100-01	Ellen	Pickering
100-03	Rachel	McFrench

Package Name Five Points Relaxation

Client #	First Name	Last Name
100-22	Joseph	Buchsbaum
100-18	Pamela	Hinds
100-23	Georgia	Nichols

Package Name Five Ponts Anti-stress

Client #	First Name	Last Name
100-04	Karen	Johanson
100-11	Kathleen	Dome
100-21	Tom	Radomski
100-07	Barbara	Wright
100-06	Denise	Bkihazi

Total Packages Sold: 34

Created by: Student Name

7/13/2010 Page 2 of 2

c. Make the following layout and design changes. (Refer to the figure for an example of how the layout can be modified).

- Delete the Package # and Description controls.
- Adjust the size of the Client # controls.
- Change the font color of the Package Name text controls to purple.
- Size and reposition the three client controls if needed.
- In the Page Footer, change the format property of the date control to Short Date.

d. You are now going to add a calculated control to count the number of packages sold. Expand the Report Footer section and insert a text box control. Change the label caption to Total Packages Sold and size the control to fit the contents. Access the Unbound text control's property settings and use the Expression Builder to create a Count expression that will calculate the number of packages sold. (Hint: You can use any of the fields in the Detail section of the report as the Count expression to produce the desired results.)

e. Apply a font size of 12, purple font color, and shadowed special effect for emphasis to the Total Packages Sold label. Use the Format Painter to apply the same formatting to the Total Packages Sold text control. Size and position the Total Packages Sold controls appropriately.

f. Add a Label control to the Report Footer with **Created By:** and your name.

g. Change the report margins to 1 inch all around. Move any controls that are outside the right margin inside the new page width. Make further enhancements to the report layout as desired (text color, font size and style, special effects). Print the report. Then save and close it.

h. Close the database.

Downtown Internet Café Reports ★★★

4. Evan, the owner of the Downtown Internet Café, is finding the database and its tables, forms, queries, and reports that you created quite useful for keeping track of inventory items and order details. In fact, he would like you to create another report that groups orders by vendor, includes product pricing information, and calculates the order costs. You also have been thinking about automating the database even further by creating command buttons to access its various tables and forms and to centralize the database operations, which you will do after creating the grouped report. Your completed report will be similar to the one shown here.

Stock Orders

Supplier	ABC Restaurant Supply					
Description	Contact	Phone Number	E-mail	Quantity	Unit Price	Order Cost
Sugar	Richard Price	(206) 555-0037	brs@email.net	6	$65.00	$390.00
Cups-small	Richard Price	(206) 555-0037	brs@email.net	1	$75.00	$75.00
				Total Supplier Order		$465.00
Supplier	Aquatics					
Description	Contact	Phone Number	E-mail	Quantity	Unit Price	Order Cost
Bottled water	Lee Branson	(207) 555-1122	thirst@net.com	3	$85.00	$255.00
				Total Supplier Order		$255.00
Supplier	Cuppa Jo					
Description	Contact	Phone Number	E-mail	Quantity	Unit Price	Order Cost
Espresso	Student Name	(206) 555-9090	jo@dial.com	1	$185.00	$185.00
Kona coffee	Student Name	(206) 555-9090	jo@dial.com	2	$140.00	$280.00
Ethiopian coffee	Student Name	(206) 555-9090	jo@dial.com	3	$135.00	$405.00
Arabian coffee	Student Name	(206) 555-9090	jo@dial.com	8	$115.00	$920.00
				Total Supplier Order		$1,790.00
Supplier	Pure Processing					
Description	Contact	Phone Number	E-mail	Quantity	Unit Price	Order Cost
Decaf Guatamala	Nancy Young	(206) 555-5689	pure@ez.com	5	$140.00	$700.00
				Total Supplier Order		$700.00
				Grand Total		$3,210.00

a. Open the Cafe Purchases database (which you last worked on in Step-by-Step Exercise 4 of Lab 5).

b. Open the Inventory Order Costs query. In Query Design view, do not show the In Stock field. (You will not need it for the report.) Run and save the query.

c. Create a new report object using the Report Wizard. Add all fields from the Inventory Order Costs query to the report. Group the report by Supplier. Do not select any sort fields. Open the Summary Options and select the Sum option for the Order Cost field. Select the layout and style of your choice. Name the report **Stock Orders**.

d. Make the following changes to the layout and design:

- Change the Order Amount label to **Quantity**.
- Fix the size, position, and spacing of all controls in the report so that all data is fully displayed.
- In the Supplier Footer, delete the Summary for Supplier control.
- Change the Sum label control to **Total Supplier Order** and move it adjacent to the Sum text control. Add font and fill colors to the controls.
- In the Report Footer, move the Grand Total label control adjacent to the text control. Align the controls in the Supplier Footer and the Report Footer.
- Add emphasis to the Grand Total controls by enlarging the font size and applying the same text and fill color as for the Vendor summary controls. Size the controls to fit.

- Add a rectangle surrounding the Report Footer content. Add other enhancements of your choice to the report.

e. Preview, print, save, and close the report.

f. Open the Inventory Item Orders form and add a command button to preview the Stock Orders report (use a text button).

g. Evenly align and space the buttons.

h. Set the Inventory Item Orders form as the startup form and hide the Navigation pane at startup.

i. Close the database. Reopen it to test your custom options.

j. Test the navigation buttons you created, ending with the one that closes the application.

LearnSoft Reports and Security ★★★

5. As manager for the LearnSoft Company, you get many requests for reports on software titles, development, sales, and so on from the company's department heads and marketing personnel. For example, you just received a request from the product sales manager to create a report that is grouped by software package number, summarizes the sales of each package, and includes a calculated total of all packages sold and a chart showing the sales trend of the most popular series. The completed report will look similar to that shown here. There also has been some concern about unauthorized use of the database, so you are going to assign a password that will be given out upon management approval only.

a. Open the LearnSoft Titles database (which you last worked on in Step-by-Step Exercise 5 of Lab 5).

b. Open the Software Package Sales query and change the Return values setting to All. Close and save the query. Open the Software Sales table and change the date sold for your record to 6/15/2010. Close the table.

c. Create a new report using the Report Wizard and all fields from the Software Package Sales query. Group the report by ProductID. Do not select any sort fields. Select the Sum for the Total Packages Sold and Total Sales fields in the Summary Options. Select the layout and style of your choice. Title the report **Software Package Sales**.

d. Make the following changes to the report:

- Change the Total Packages Sold label to **# Sold**.
- Appropriately size all controls.
- Position the Detail text controls and their corresponding label controls appropriately.
- Delete everything in the Product ID Footer and close the Footer space.

Software Package Sales

ProductID	Developer	Sold	Average Price	Total Sales
15-0101				
	Catherine Willis	174	$30.00	$5,220.00
15-0201				
	Catherine Willis	143	$30.00	$4,290.00
15-0202				
	Catherine Willis	180	$30.00	$5,400.00
15-0301				
	Catherine Willis	195	$35.00	$6,825.00
15-0501				
	Catherine Willis	176	$35.00	$6,160.00
15-0502				
	Catherine Willis	238	$40.00	$9,520.00
15-0503				
	Catherine Willis	187	$50.00	$9,350.00
15-0601				
	Catherine Willis	162	$30.00	$4,860.00
15-0602				
	Catherine Willis	164	$30.00	$4,920.00
15-0603				
	Catherine Willis	192	$30.00	$5,760.00
24-0101				
	Maggie O'Grady	170	$45.00	$7,650.00
24-0102				
	Maggie O'Grady	165	$45.00	$7,425.00
24-0103				
	Maggie O'Grady	189	$45.00	$8,505.00
24-0202				
	Maggie O'Grady	246	$50.00	$12,300.00
24-0302				
	Maggie O'Grady	122	$50.00	$6,100.00
24-0303				
	Maggie O'Grady	225	$50.00	$11,250.00
36-0101				

9/30/2009 Page 1 of 2

- Resize, position, and align the control boxes in the Report Footer so they are in line with their corresponding Detail controls.
- Format the Grand Total controls as you like to make them stand out more.
- Change the properties of the Sold grand total to Standard with zero decimals.
- Change the date format in the Page Footer to Short Date. Make any other layout and format changes you wish.
- Apply conditional formatting to all values whose total sales are equal to or more than $10,000.

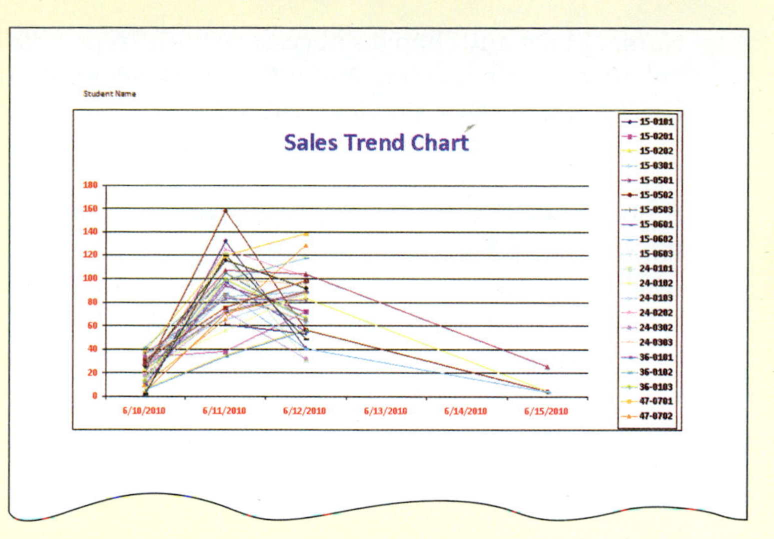

e. Change the report margins to 1 inch all around. Move any controls that are outside the right margin inside the new page width. Preview, print, save, and close the report.

f. Create a new, blank report to hold the line chart. Create a new Chart control in the Detail section of the blank report. Using the Chart Wizard, set the Software Sales table as the source of the chart. Add the Product ID, DateSold, and Quantity fields. Choose Line Chart. Make the Quantity field the Y axis, the Product ID the data series, and the DateSold the X axis. Double-click the DateSold By Month field to change it to DateSold by Day. Save the chart as **Sales Trend Chart**.

g. Appropriately format the chart axes, legend, and title.

h. In Design view, add a label to the Page Header with your name.

i. Change the orientation to landscape and adjust the size of the chart for best readability.

j. Print the chart-based report. Close and save the report.

k. Close the database. Reopen the database in exclusive mode and secure the database by assigning a password to it.

l. Close and save the database.

on your own

Lewis & Lewis Mailing Labels ★

1. The personnel director at Lewis & Lewis has requested mailing labels in order to distribute information on the company's holiday food drive. Use the Lewis Personnel database you worked on in On Your Own Exercise 3 of Lab 5 to create the desired mailing labels. Create a query that can be used to create mailing labels. Create mailing labels for both employees and consultants. Print the mailing label report.

WriteOn! Query and Mailing Labels ★★

2. The WriteOn! database you last worked on in On Your Own Exercise 2 in Lab 5 has been very helpful. Now, you want to create a stock report to show the current stock on hand. Create a report using appropriate fields from both tables to gather this information. Group the report by Supplier

Name. Make any changes necessary to the report layout and design to make it easier to read or enhance its appearance. Add a Report Header with the company name and a Report Footer with **Created by your name**. Preview and then print the report. Create a query that can be used to create mailing labels. Create mailing labels for the suppliers. Print the mailing label report.

Associated Dental Reports and Mailing Labels ★★★

3. Part of your job as manager of the dental office is to maintain the patient database. You just received a request for a report that groups records by dentist and includes the contact and billing information for the patients assigned to each dentist. You also need to create patient mailing labels for appointment reminders. Open the Dental Patients database you updated in On Your Own Exercise 1 of Lab 5 and use the Report Wizard to create a report that includes the dentist name; the patient name, address, and phone fields; and patient amount due from the appropriate tables. Group the report by dentist name and sort it by patient last and first names. Make any changes necessary to the report layout to make it easier to read or enhance its appearance. Add a Report Header with the dental office name and a Report Footer with **Created by your name**. Print the first page of the report and then save and close it. Create a mailing label report using the Label Wizard and the patient contact information table. Print the first page of labels and close the report.

EMP Enterprise Reports ★★★

4. Your job in the accounting department of EMP Enterprises includes updating employee expense records as well as generating reports based on these records. You have recently received a request from the CFO for a report grouped by department that calculates the total expenses for each department and the grand total of expenses incurred to date. Open the EMP Enterprises database that you last updated in On Your Own Exercise 4 of Lab 5 and the expense query you created earlier. Create a report based on this query that is grouped by department and includes a summary showing the expense totals. Format the report as necessary and/or desired and then print, save, and close the report. Add command buttons to the form created in Lab 5 to provide full navigation for the database. Change the database startup options to automatically display this form when the database is opened. Finally, secure the database with a password.

Tri-County Little League Reports ★★★

5. The Tri-County Little League is preparing for the upcoming season and would like to use their new database to distribute registration forms to returning players and advertise the league in the local neighborhoods. The Little League chair has asked for a report that shows the roster for the five teams grouped by team. She also would like to know the average age of the players by team. Using the Little League database you worked on in On Your Own Exercise 5 of Lab 5, modify the Rosters query to include the age of the players. Then create a grouped report on team name based on the Rosters query. Include appropriate group calculations to determine the mean age by team. Format the report as necessary and/or desired and then print, save, and close the report. Add command buttons to the Team Rosters form created in Lab 5 to provide full navigation for the database. Change the database startup options to automatically display this form when the database is opened. Create mailing labels for the returning players. Print the first page of labels. Secure the database with exclusive access to prevent corruption of the rosters. Complete and save the database.

Working Together 2 Linking and Splitting Databases

Case Study

Lifestyle Fitness Club

The Lifestyle Fitness Club payroll department uses the pay data for each employee that you supply to generate payroll. You have decided to make this data available in a separate database file for them to access. Rather than maintain two separate databases, you will link to the new database table from within the existing Club Employees database.

Similarly, you frequently need to access the Hours Worked data that is maintained by the payroll department. Rather than import this data each time into the database, you decide to create a link to the workbook file from within the Club Employees database.

The club also has just established an intranet to share internal information among employees who are authorized to use it, such as the club managers. The owners would like you to make the Club Employees database file available for them to use. To do this, you will split the database to provide access to all authorized users.

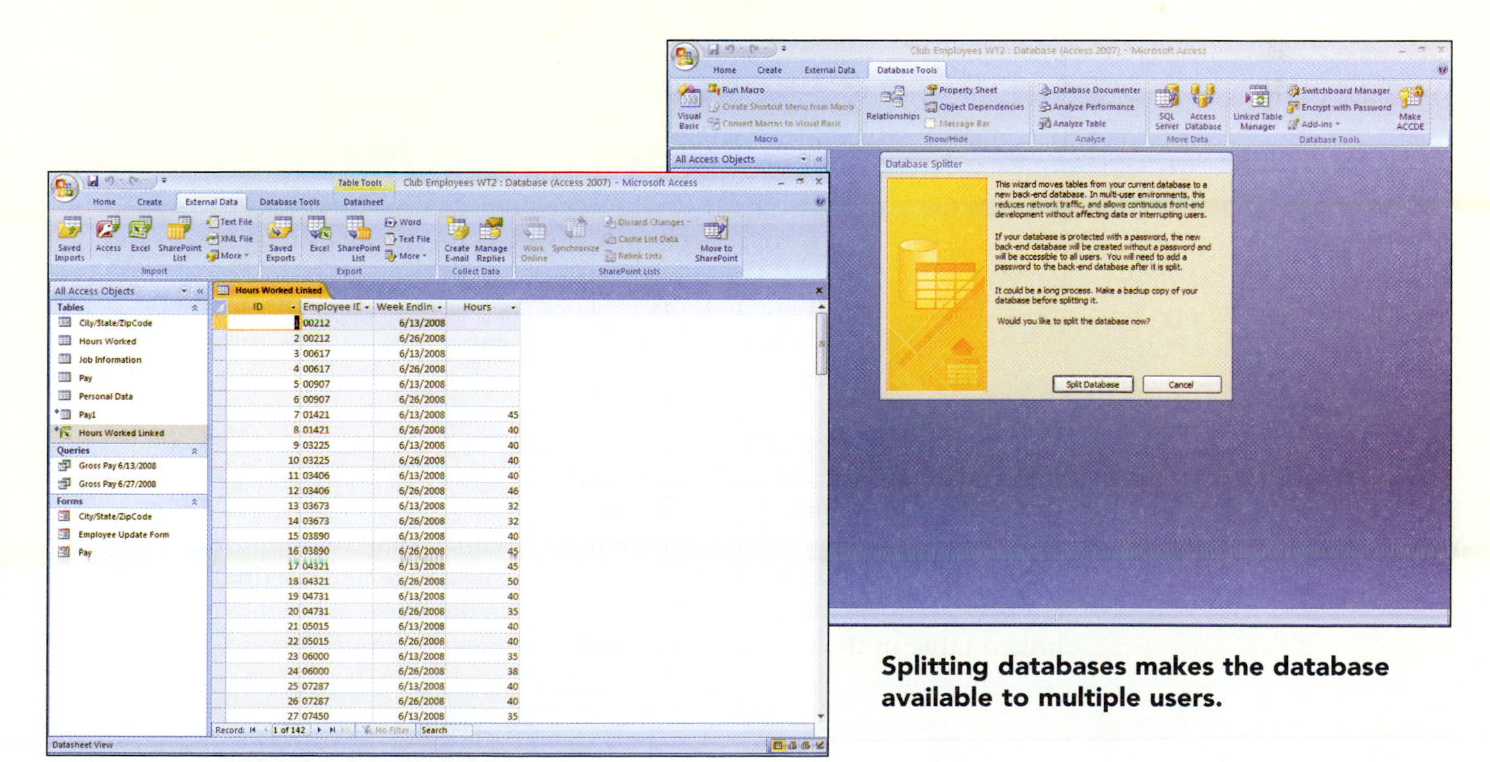

Splitting databases makes the database available to multiple users.

Databases can be linked to tables in external database files and to Excel workbook files.

Linking to External Data Sources

You have decided to maintain the employee pay data in a separate database file so that it can be easily accessed by the payroll department. You will maintain the information in the file and payroll will use the data in the file to generate the payroll. You want the Club Employees database to link to the new database so that you can continue to easily update the data from the one database file and create queries, reports, and forms using this information.

For similar reasons, you also will create a link to the Hours data that is maintained in an Excel workbook by the payroll department.

Creating a Link to a Database Table

You already created a new database file named Club Employees Pay and exported the Pay table from the Club Employees database to the new database. Now you need to create a link to the Pay table in the new database file from the Club Employees database file.

1

- **Create a copy of the acwt2_ Club Employees database file and name it Club Employees WT2.**
- **Open the Club Employees WT2 database file with content enabled.**

Your screen should be similar to Figure 1

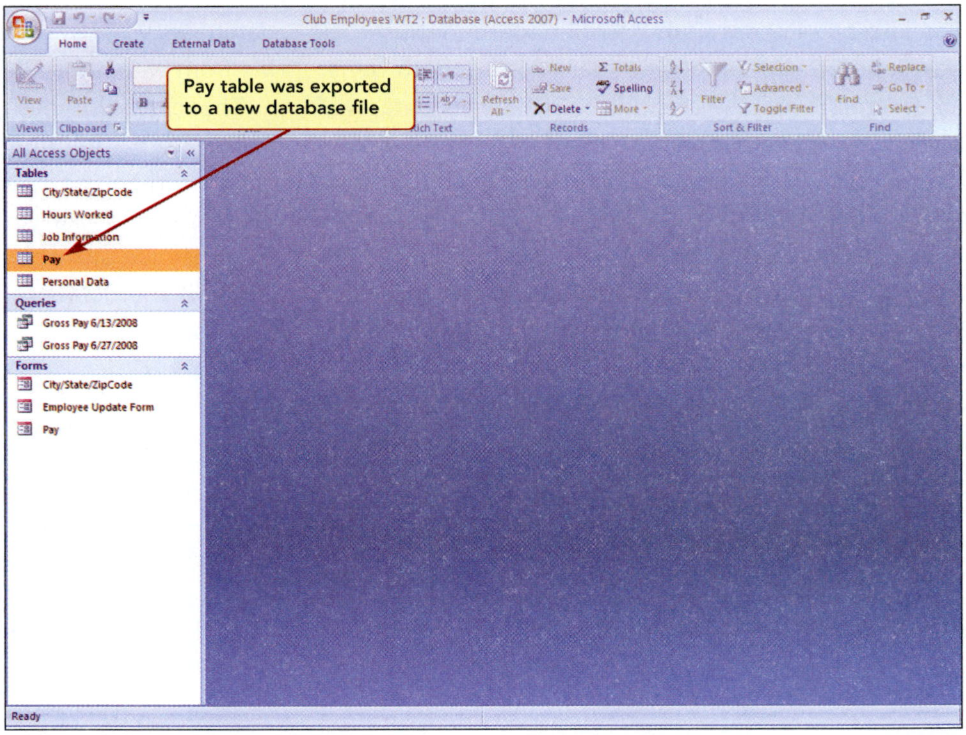

Pay table was exported to a new database file

Figure 1

The Club Employees database still includes the original Pay table. You do not want to delete this table until after you have linked to the Pay table in the new Club Employees Pay database.

Linking lets you connect to data in another database without importing it so you can view and modify data in both the source and destination. Any changes that are made to data in the source database are reflected in the linked table in the destination database. Likewise, any changes you make to this table from within the destination database are reflected in the linked table in the source database. You cannot, however, change the structure of a linked table from within the destination database.

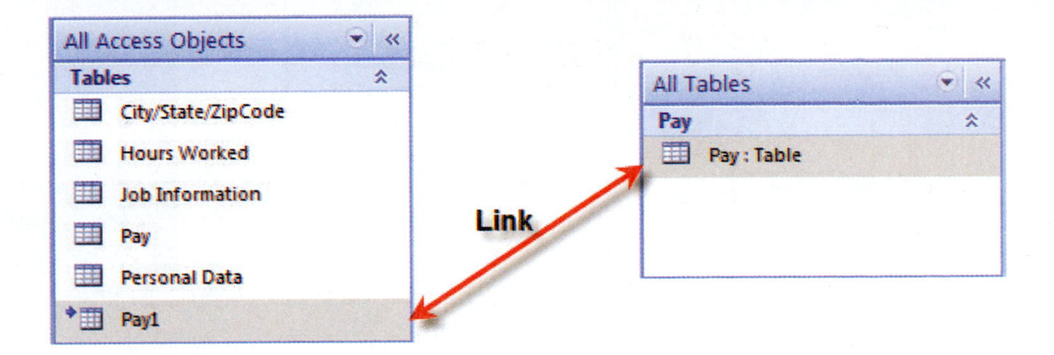

In this case, by creating a separate database file containing only the Pay table data and linking it to the Club Employees database, you are providing only the needed information for the payroll department's use and you can maintain the Pay table from within the Club Employees database. You can only link to tables, not to queries, forms, and reports.

2

- **Click [Access] in the Import group of the External Data tab.**
- **Choose Link to the data source by creating a linked table.**

Your screen should be similar to Figure 2

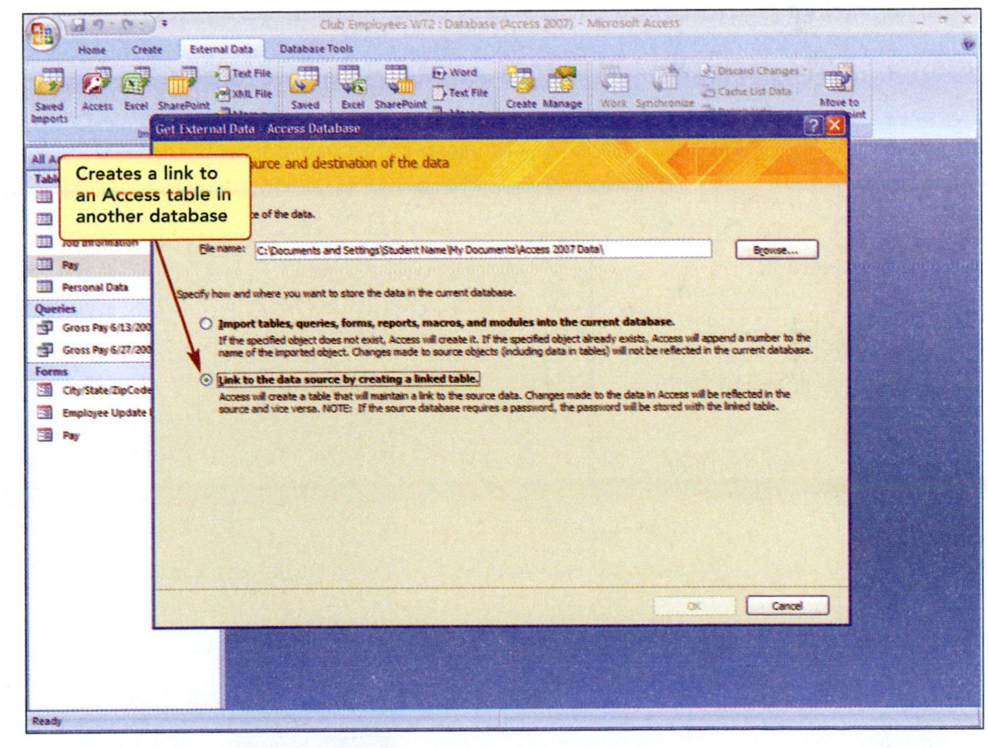

Figure 2

Next, you need to specify the location of the data to link to, in this case acwt2_Club Employees Pay.

3 • **Click** [Browse...] **and change your Look in location to your data file location.**

• **Select** acwt2_Club Employees Pay.

• **Click** [Open].

• **Click** [OK].

Your screen should be similar to Figure 3

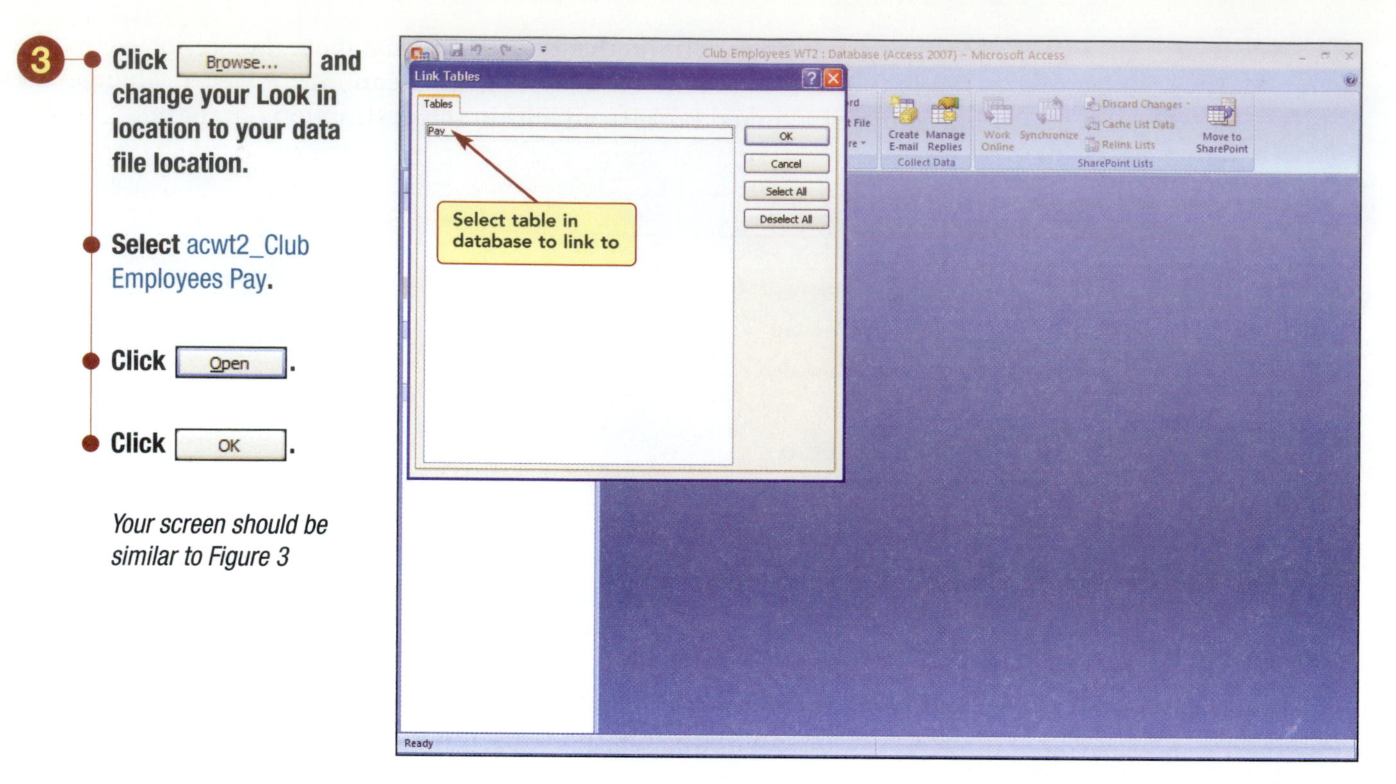

Figure 3

From the Link Tables dialog box, you select the table in the database file to which you want to link. If there were more tables in the database, the name of each table would be listed.

4 • **Click on the Pay table to select it.**

• **Click** [OK] **to link to the selected table.**

Your screen should be similar to Figure 4

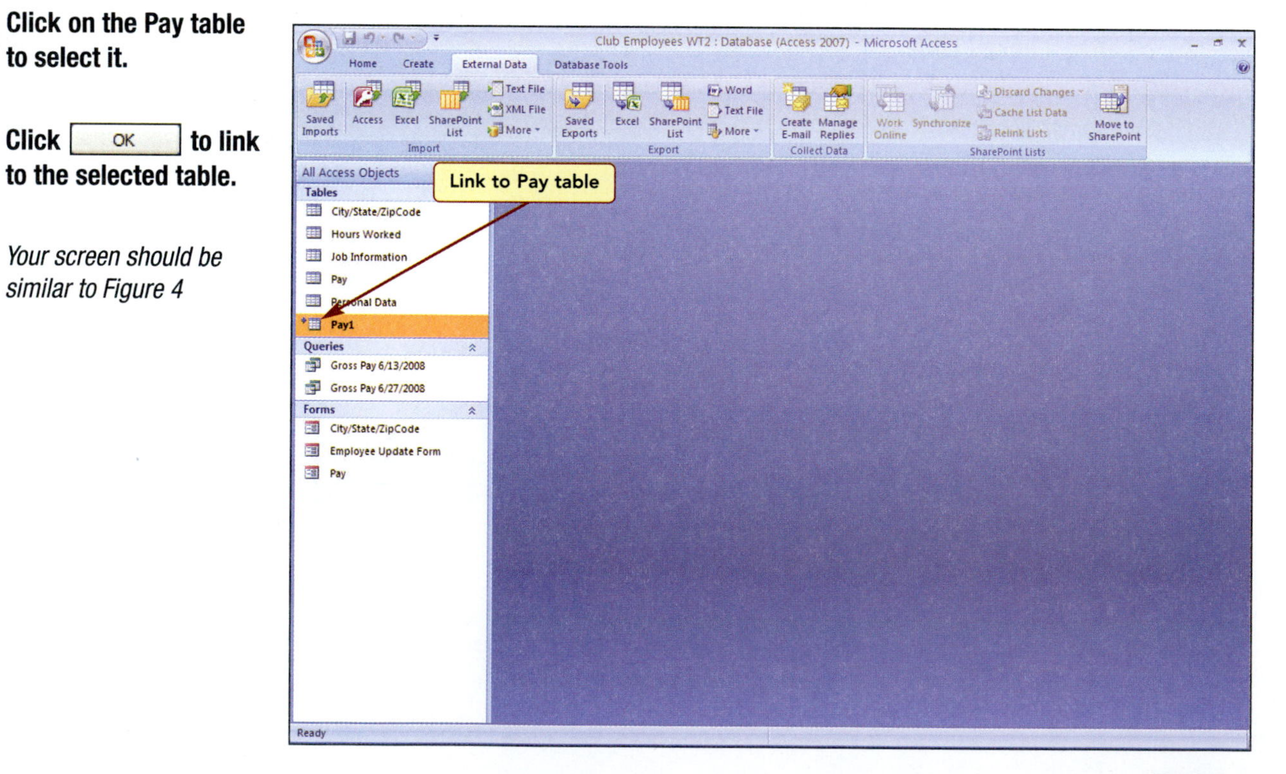

Figure 4

A new table, Pay1, is added to the Tables object list in the Navigation pane. Because the table in the source database had the same name as a table in the destination, Access appended a 1 to the linked table name. The new table is a **linked table,** which maintains a link to the source records and fields. The icon preceding the new table name, Pay1, indicates it is a linked table.

5 **Open the Pay1 table.**

Scroll to see the last record in the table and change the pay rate for Employee ID 99999 to $17.00.

Your screen should be similar to Figure 5

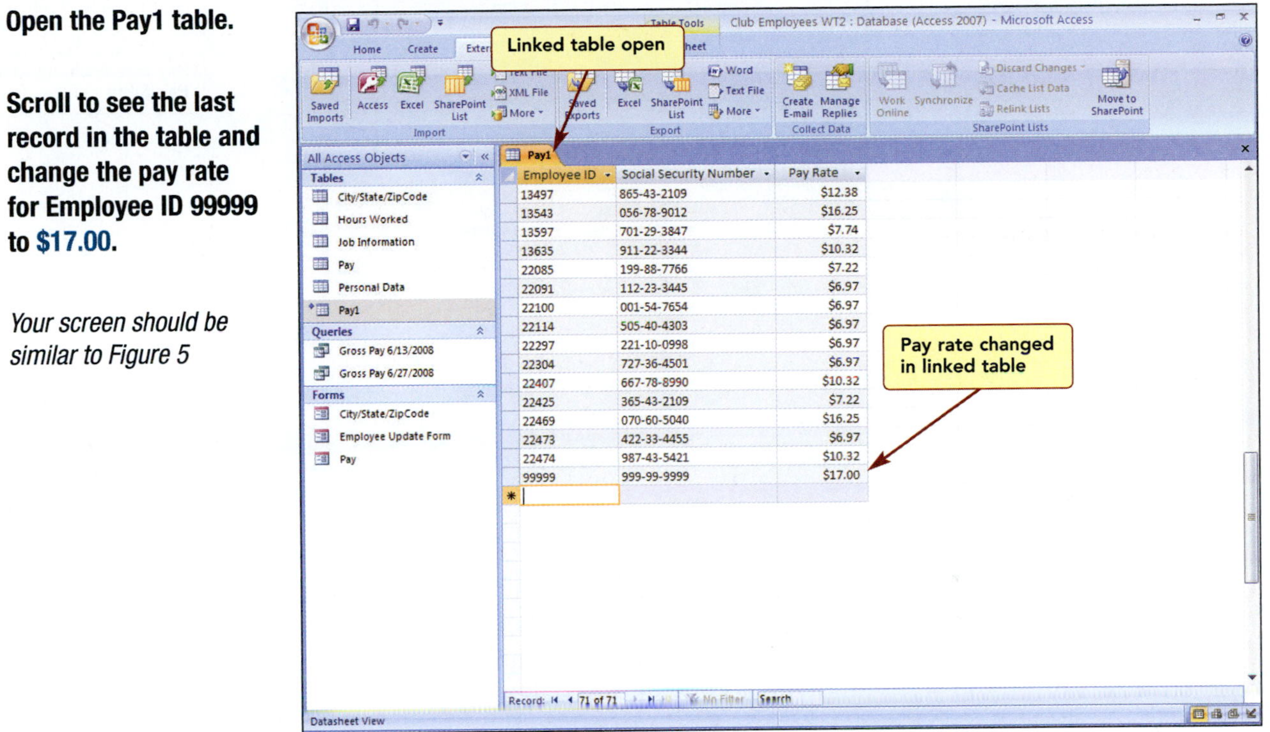

Figure 5

The data from the Pay table in the source database is displayed and the pay data has been updated in the source. It has not been changed in the original Pay table. To confirm this, you will open the Pay table next.

6. • **Close the Pay1 table.**
   • **Open the Pay table and display the last record.**

   Your screen should be similar to Figure 6

Table Tools | Club Employees WT2 : Database (Access 2007) - Microsoft Access

Home | Create | External Data | Database Tools | Datasheet

Import: Saved Imports | Access | Excel | SharePoint List | Text File | XML File | More
Export: Saved Exports | Excel | SharePoint List | Word | Text File | More
Collect Data: Create E-mail | Manage Replies
SharePoint Lists: Work Online | Synchronize | Discard Changes | Cache List Data | Relink Lists | Move to SharePoint

All Access Objects
Tables: City/State/ZipCode, Hours Worked, Job Information, Pay, Personal Data, Pay1
Queries: Gross Pay 6/13/2008, Gross Pay 6/27/2008
Forms: City/State/ZipCode, Employee Update Form, Pay

Pay

Employee ID	Social Security Number	Pay Rate	Add New Field
13484	509-87-6543	$7.22	
13497	865-43-2109	$12.38	
13543	056-78-9012	$16.25	
13597	701-29-3847	$7.74	
13635	911-22-3344	$10.32	
22085	199-88-7766	$7.22	
22091	112-23-3445	$6.97	
22100	001-54-7654	$6.97	
22114	505-40-4303	$6.97	
22297	221-10-0998	$6.97	
22304	727-36-4501	$6.97	
22407	667-78-8990	$10.32	
22425	365-43-2109	$7.22	
22469	070-60-5040	$16.25	
22473	422-33-4455	$6.97	
22474	987-43-5421	$10.32	
99999	999-99-9999	$16.51	

Pay rate unchanged in Pay table

Record: 1 of 70 | No Filter | Search

Datasheet View

Figure 6

The pay rate for this record is unchanged. Your next step would be to modify all the objects in the database that use the Pay table as the record source to the new linked table, Pay1. Until you make these changes at a later time, you will not delete the Pay table.

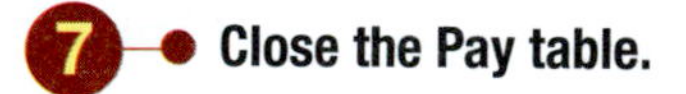

7. • **Close the Pay table.**

Creating a Link to an Excel Workbook

For similar reasons, you want to create a link to the Hours Worked data that is maintained in an Excel workbook by the payroll department.

1 • **Click** [Excel] **in the Import group of the External Data tab.**

• **Choose Link to the data source by creating a linked table.**

Your screen should be similar to Figure 7

Figure 7

Next, you need to specify the location of the data to link to, in this case acwt2_Hours Worked.

2 • **Click** [Browse...] **and change your Look in location to your data file location.**

• **Select** acwt2_Hours Worked**.**

• **Click** [Open]**.**

• **Click** [OK]**.**

Your screen should be similar to Figure 8

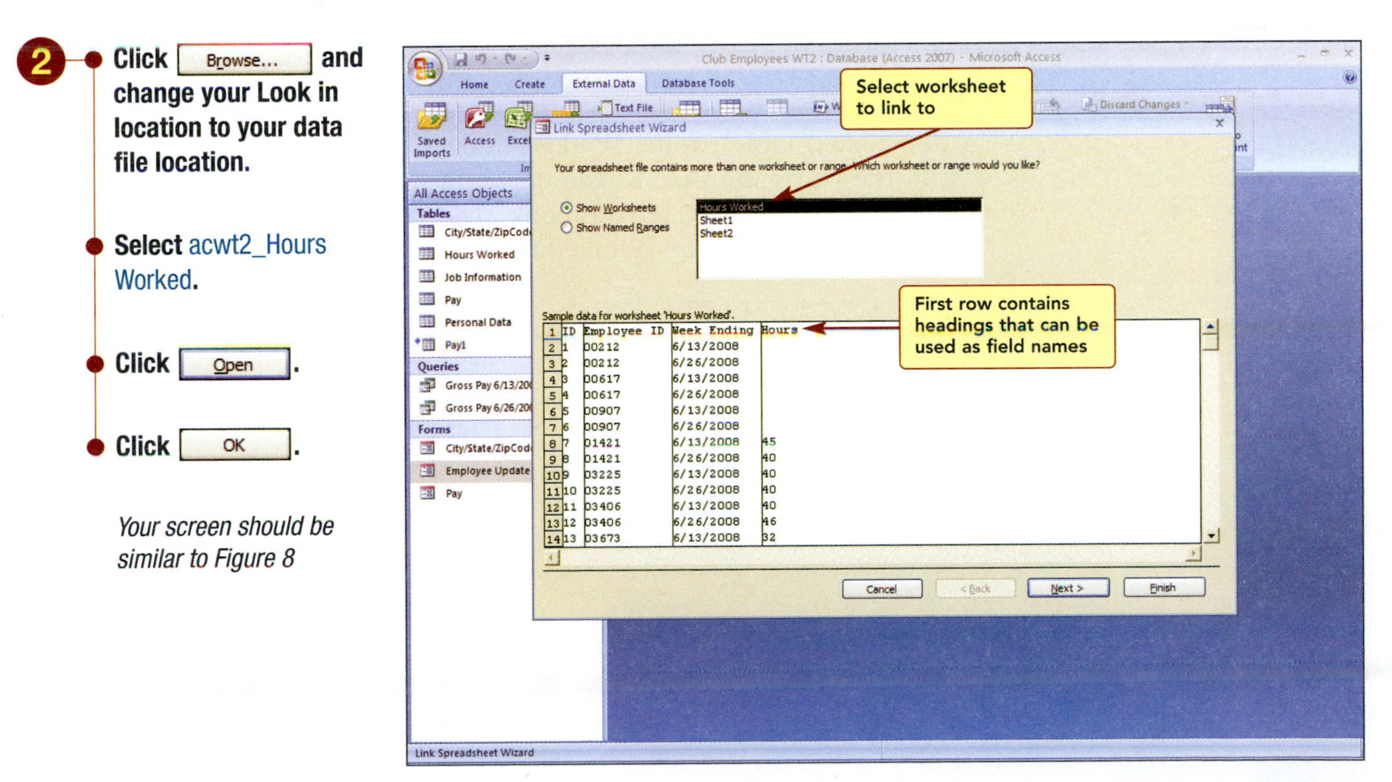

Figure 8

From the Link Spreadsheet Wizard dialog box, you first need to select the worksheet to link to and then confirm that the first row in the worksheet contains column headings that can be used as field names for the linked table.

3

- **Click Next > to use the Hours Worked worksheet.**
- **Click Next > to confirm the column headings.**
- **Revise the name of the linked table to Hours Worked Linked.**
- **Click Finish and click OK in response to the finished linking informational message.**

Your screen should be similar to Figure 9

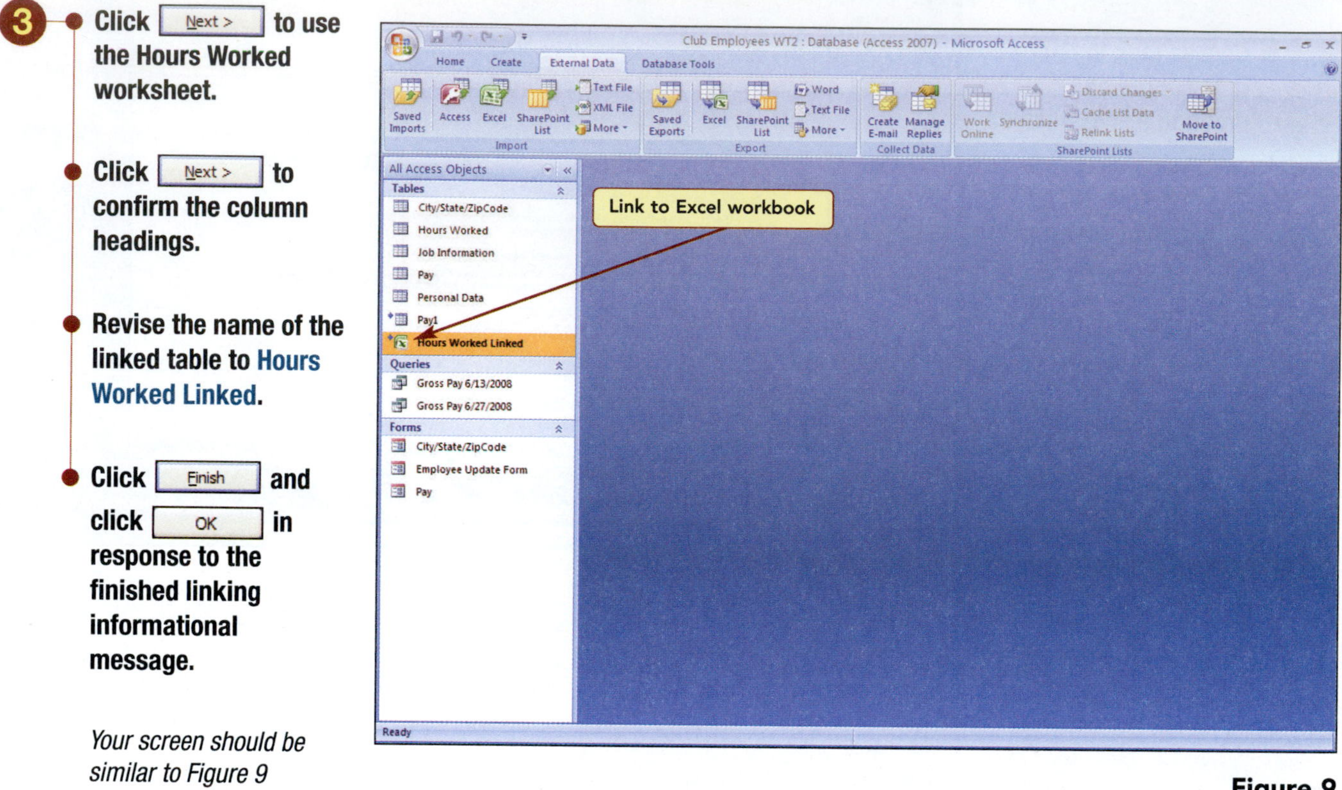

Figure 9

A new linked table, Hours Worked Linked, is added to the Tables object list in the Navigation pane. The new linked table maintains a link to the source data in the Excel workbook. The icon preceding the linked table name indicates it is a linked table to an Excel workbook file.

4 **Open the Hours Worked Linked table.**

Your screen should be similar to Figure 10

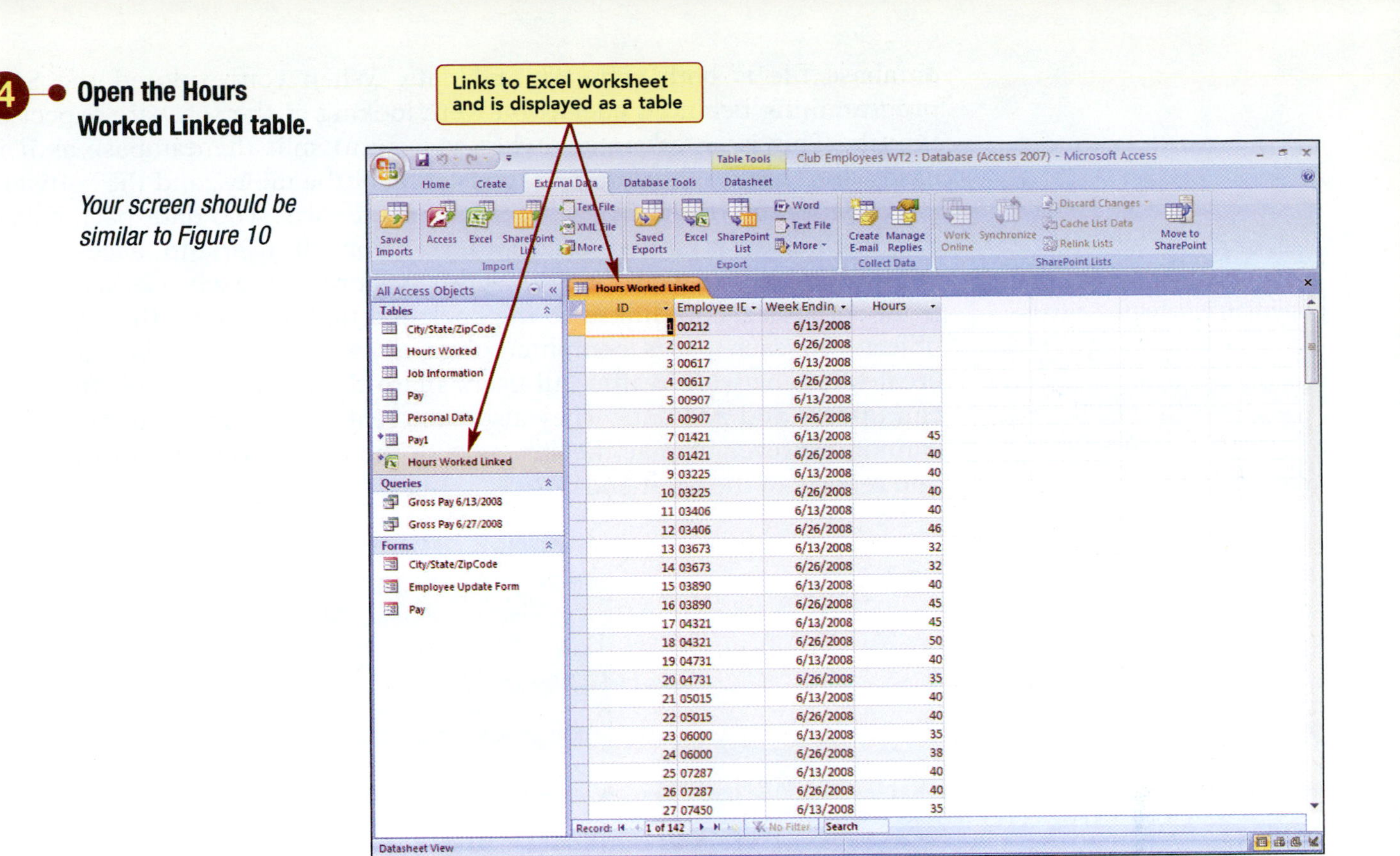

Figure 10

The data from the Excel worksheet is displayed as a table in the database file. You could update the information in this table and it would change the data in the linked worksheet, just as you did with the Pay1 table.

Your next step would be to modify all the objects in the database that use the Pay and Hours Worked tables as the record source to the new linked tables, Pay1 and Hours Worked Linked. Until you make these changes at a later time, you will not delete these tables.

5 **Close the Hours Worked Linked table.**

Splitting a Database

Your plans for the future are to make the database available to the club owners and managers and to your assistant. The best way to do this is to put the database file on the company server where everyone who needs to can access it. When you want multiple users to be able to work on the data in a database file at the same time, you need to split the database.

Splitting the database divides it into two parts: a data part and an application part. The data part is the data or file that is created and used by the application. The application part is the program software that is installed on your computer. All applications consist of these two parts. However, unlike Word and Excel that create document files, an Access database file is both software and data. When you explored the SQL programming behind a query, you were looking at the software aspect of the file. This is an advantage when you go to split the database as it is easily divided into the data part, consisting of the tables, and the software part, consisting of the queries, forms, and reports. The data part, called the **back-end,** is stored on the server for all users to access. The application part, called the **front-end,** is stored on each user's PC. The front-end objects are linked to the back-end tables. Placing the front-end objects on each user's computer gives quicker access to the data and creates less network traffic. All users share the back-end accdb files and can update and add data. They also can create and modify queries. They cannot, however, change the structure of the back-end tables or of forms and reports in the front-end.

Additional Information

Splitting a database also is helpful when the database size is very large and runs slowly. By splitting it into two parts, the size of each part is smaller and the database runs more efficiently.

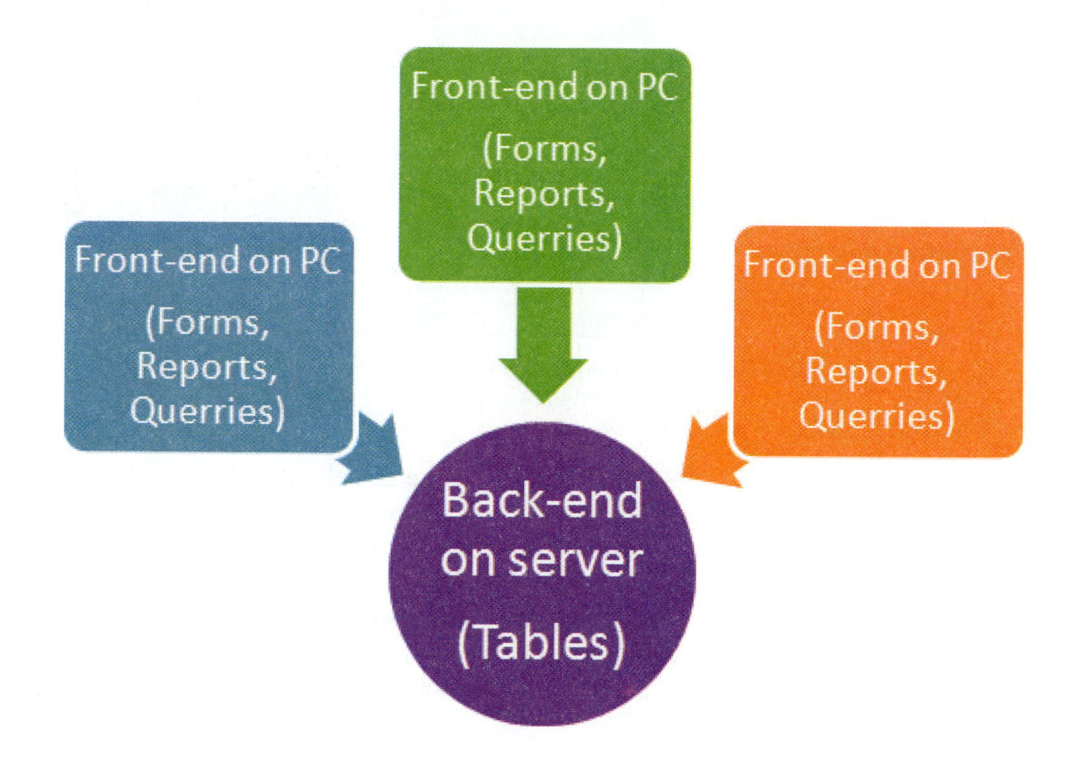

Although the database still needs to be modified to reflect the use of the linked tables, you want to practice splitting the database. When splitting a database, it is a good idea to create a backup copy of the database file first, as you did at the beginning of this lab, in case you encounter problems.

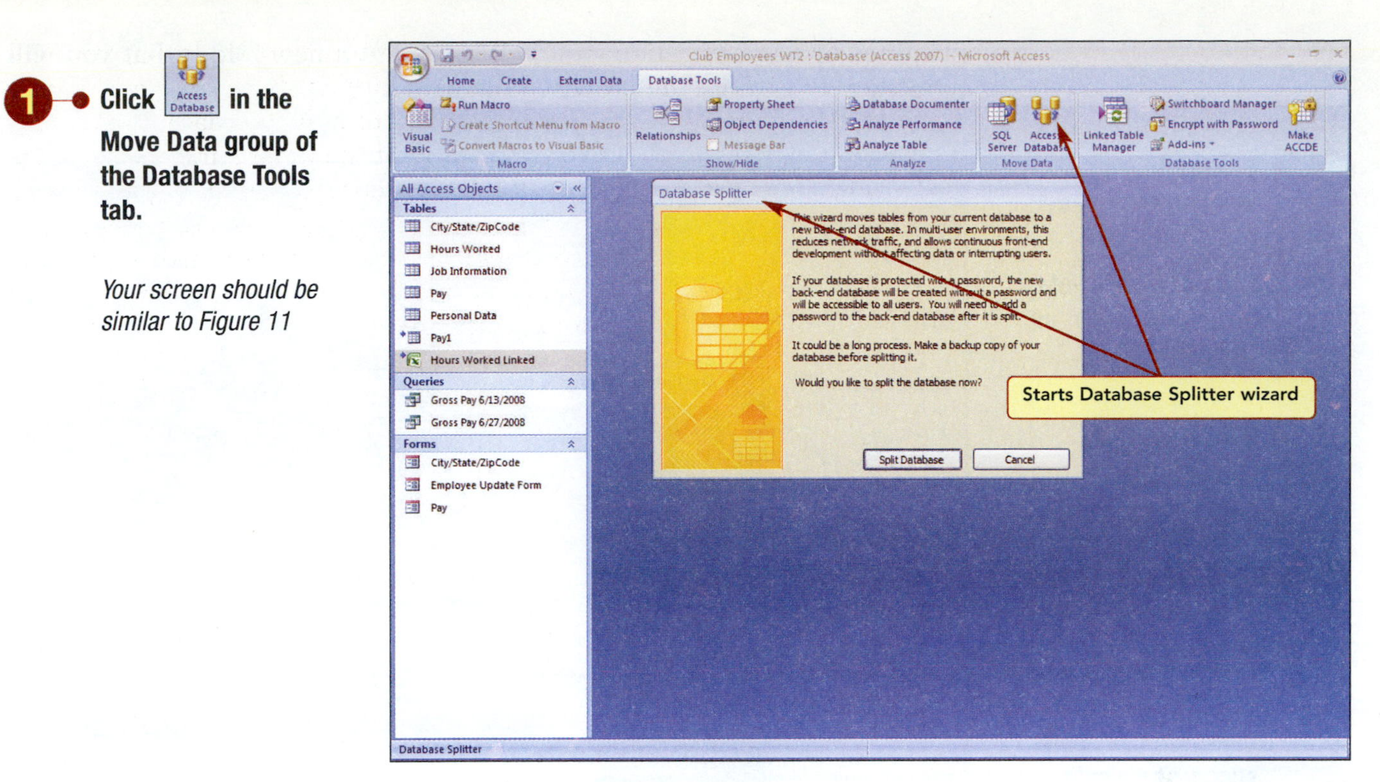

1 **Click** Access Database **in the Move Data group of the Database Tools tab.**

Your screen should be similar to Figure 11

Figure 11

The Database Splitter wizard starts and displays an introductory box explaining the feature.

2 **Click** Split Database.

Your screen should be similar to Figure 12

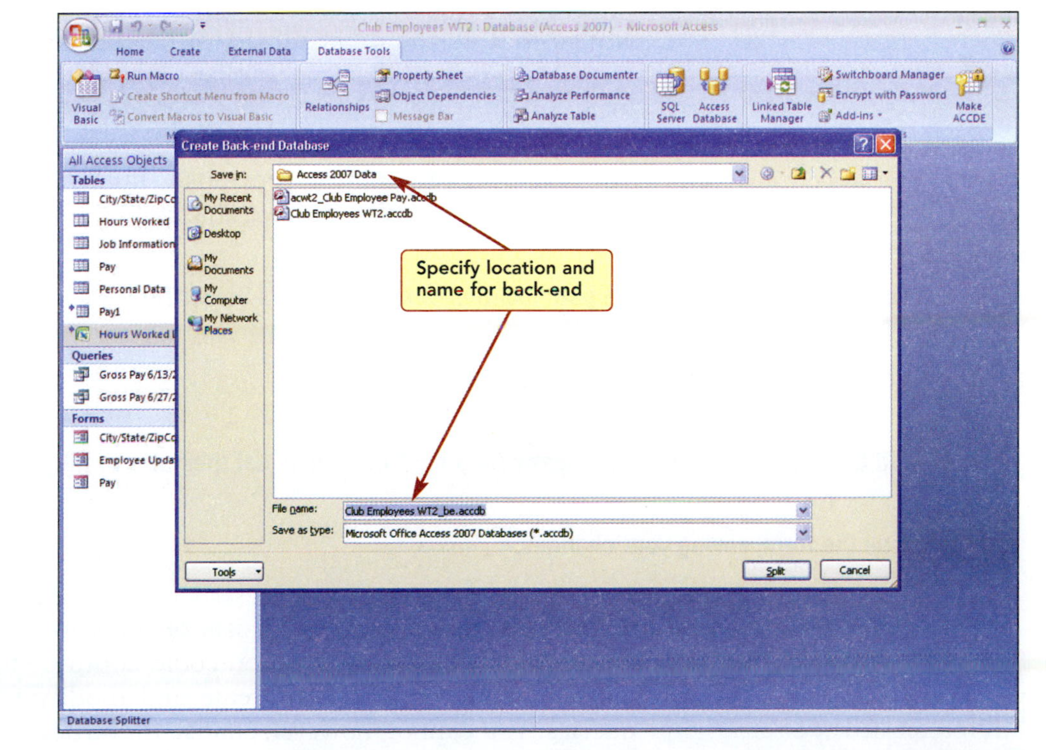

Figure 12

The first step is to create the back-end database by specifying a location where it will be saved and a name. The proposed name is the existing file name with the addition of _be to identify it as the back-end file. For purposes of demonstration, you will save it to a new folder that you will name Server and use the proposed file name.

3

- **Browse to your solution file location.**
- **Click [New Folder] New Folder and enter Server as the folder name.**
- **Click [OK].**
- **Click [Split].**
- **Click [OK] in response to the informational message telling you that the database has been successfully split.**

Your screen should be similar to Figure 13

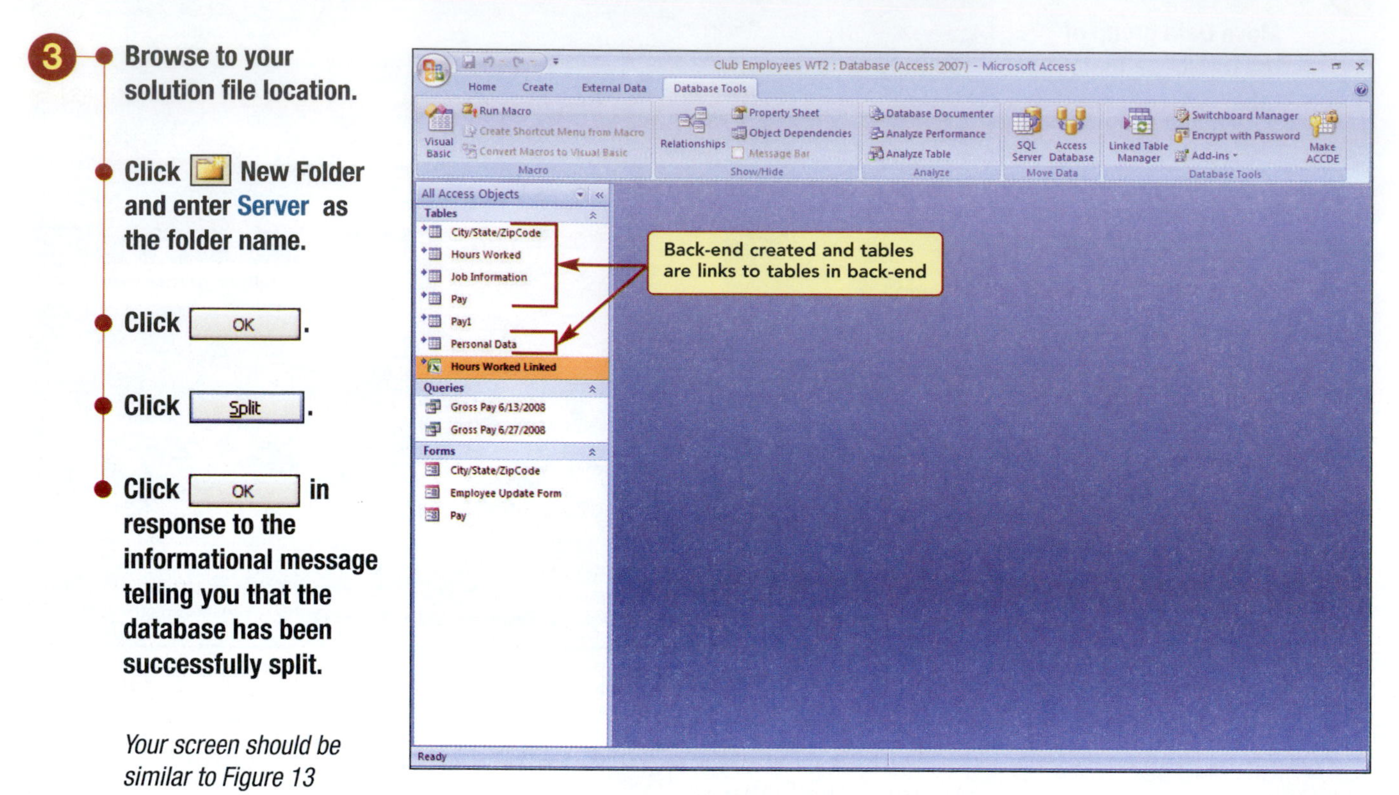

Figure 13

Notice that all the other tables in the Navigation pane are now preceded with a [linked table] symbol. This symbol identifies tables that are in another location and are linked to the database. The five previously unlinked tables have been removed from the database file and copied to the server. The location of the two previously linked tables, the Pay1 and Hours Worked Linked tables, did not change.

4

- **Point to each table to see the path location of the tables in a ScreenTip.**
- **Open the Employee Update Form in Design view.**
- **Bold the Personal Data and Company Data controls and adjust their size to fully display the text.**
- **Close the form, saving your changes.**

Additional Information

Once a database is split, it can be recombined by deleting the links in the front-end database and then importing the back-end tables back into the front-end.

The database file now consists of links to the tables and the database queries, forms, and reports. You could continue to use this database to add and edit table data and to create and modify forms, tables, reports, and queries. You cannot, however, change the structure of the linked tables in the back-end.

In a real split situation, where you are actually placing the tables on a server, do not use a mapped drive to a file share on a server. Instead, you should use UNC (universal naming convention) to link to the back-end files. Do not use linked table manager to navigate to a back-end by a drive letter (c:\student data\backend.accdb). Instead, navigate using Network Places so you will get a UNC path (\\servername\student data\backend.accdb).

Using Linked Table Manager

Next, you will take a closer look at the link between the front- and back-ends using the Linked Table Manager.

1 **Click** [Linked Table Manager] **in the Database Tools group of the Database Tools tab.**

Your screen should be similar to Figure 14

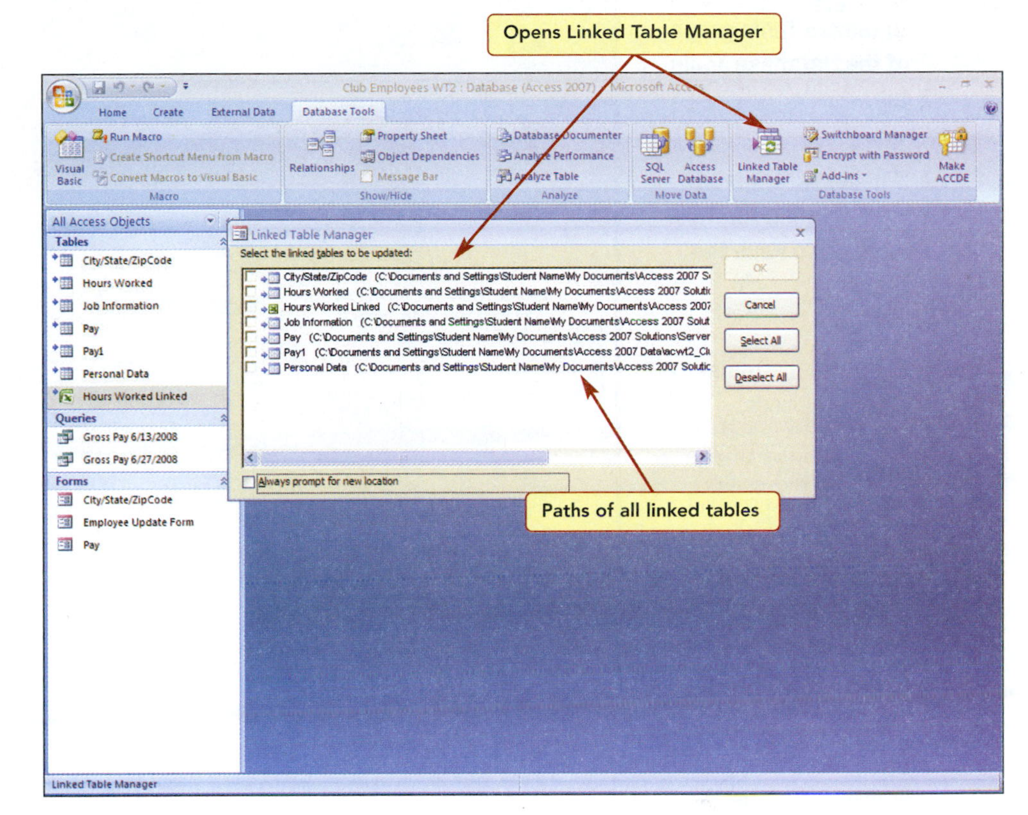

Figure 14

Additional Information
Choose Always prompt for new location to change the path information.

The Linked Table Manager dialog box shows you the path information for each linked table. You use Linked Table Manager when you want to update the linked tables. The need to refresh table content arises when multiple users can update data in a table simultaneously. Linked Table Manager also is used to reestablish the link to a file that may have been moved to another location.

2
- **Select any linked table and click** [OK].
- **Click** [OK] **in response to the informational message telling you that all selected tables were refreshed.**
- **Close the Linked Table Manager dialog box.**

The selected table was refreshed and would display the most current data when opened.

Creating and Using an accde File

Your next step would be to deploy (copy) the front-end to each user's workstation. When you do this, you will want to convert the front-end

Additional Information
When deploying, it is also helpful to include a desktop shortcut on each workstation to launch the accde file.

database to an accde (e stands for executable) file type. The accde file is the end result of your application and is smaller, runs faster, is more reliable, and cannot be modified by users. It locks the form and report objects and prevents changes to their structure. Any changes they make to the table data is automatically updated in the back-end table files on the server.

1 • **Click [Make ACCDE] in the Database Tools group of the Database Tools tab.**

• **If necessary, specify your solution file location to save the file.**

• **Enter the file name** Club Employees.

Additional Information
The accde file extension will be automatically added.

• **Click [Save].**

• **Close the database.**

• **Open the** Club Employees.accde **database file from your solution file location.**

• **If necessary, click [Open] in response to the Security Notice.**

• **Open the Employee Update Form and try to change to Design view.**

Your screen should be similar to Figure 15

Additional Information
Users should add their own passwords to the accde file to provide security against others opening and using the database.

Figure 15

Notice the [Design View] Design View button for the form is dimmed, indicating this view is unavailable. This is because the form is locked for editing.

If you wanted, you could create different accde files for different workstations. For example, you could create a different accde file for your assistant personal computer that will open with the Employee Update Form displayed and the navigation pane closed.

Because the database is not yet complete, you will not place the back-end files on the server, nor will you deploy the front-end. When you have finished modifying the database and it is complete, then you will actually split and deploy the database.

One of the main disadvantages of splitting is that each time you make a change to the front-end objects, you need to deploy the revisions to each of the users' workstations again. When you want to make changes to the back-end, such as modifying table structure or adding tables, always work on a test copy of the back-end when making changes and testing. Then, replace the back-end tables with the newly created or modified tables. Therefore, you do not want to split a database too early in the development process as adding new tables and making changes to existing tables is complicated. Further, do not split a database until it is near the time that other users will start using the database.

2 • **Close the database file and exit Access.**

Lab Review

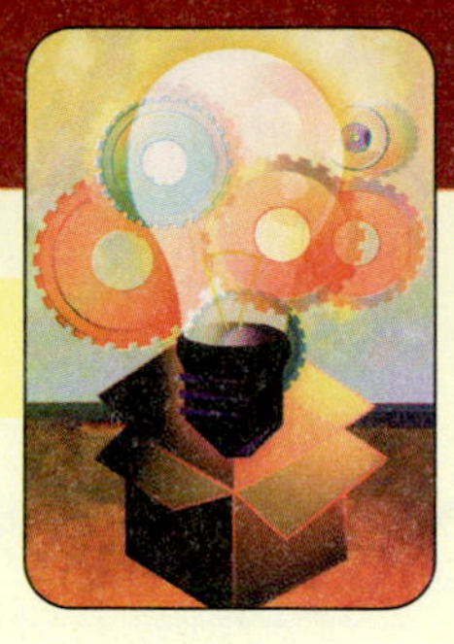

WORKING TOGETHER 2
Linking and Splitting Databases

key terms

back-end ACWT2.10
front-end ACWT2.10
linked table ACWT2.5
linking ACWT2.2
splitting ACWT2.9

MCAS skills

The Microsoft Certified Applications Specialist (MCAS) certification program is designed to measure your proficiency in performing basic tasks using the Office 2007 applications. Certification demonstrates that you have the skills and provides a valuable industry credential for employment. See Reference 2: Microsoft Certified Applications Specialist (MCAS) for a complete list of the skills that were covered in the Working Together 2 lab.

command summary

Command	Shortcut	Action
External Data tab		
Import group		
Access/Link		Creates a linked table to a table in another database
Excel/Link		Creates a linked table to an Excel spreadsheet
Database Tools tab		
Move Data group		
Access Database		Splits a database
Database Tools group		
Linked Table Manager		Opens Linked Table Manager
Make ACCDE		Creates an accde-type database file

step-by-step

rating system
★ Easy
★★ Moderate
★★★ Difficult

Importing Café Email List ★

CONTINUING EXERCISES

1. The Downtown Internet Café Web site offers coupons as an incentive to sign up for the Café's e-mail list. The webmaster has saved the mailing list information in an Excel spreadsheet. Evan would like to incorporate the mailing list information into the database while allowing the webmaster to continue to update it. To accomplish this, you will create a linked table based on the spreadsheet.

   a. Open the Cafe Purchases database (which you last updated in Step-by-Step Exercise 4 of Lab 6).

   b. Import Sheet1 from the acwt2_Cafe Web Signups.xlsx spreadsheet by establishing a link. The first row contains column headings. Save the linked table as **Email List**.

   c. Open the Email List table. Adjust the size of the columns to display all of the data. Close and save the table.

   d. Open the acwt2_Cafe Web Signups.xlsx Excel file and add your name and e-mail address as customer ID #17. Save the Excel file as Web Signups. Exit Excel.

   e. In Access use the Linked Table Manager to update the table location to the Web Signups file. Hint: Choose Always prompt for new location to specify the new file.

   f. Open the Email List table. Print the table and then close it.

   g. Close the database.

Email List 6/11/2010

CustomerID	Customer Name	Customer Email
1	Ronda Davis	ohtwinmom@yahoo.com
2	Brent Bowman	artisticBB@yahoo.com
3	Eric Josephson	eric@buckeye.org
4	Robert Arnold	BuffChuck@bcthinka.com
5	Erin Anderson	HelloKitty@fmerchants.com
6	Savannah Norris	sn@RedNinja.com
7	Bun Pienbun	bunp@gmail.com
8	Pie Pienbun	piep@gmail.com
9	Barbara Pietro	bbp@wingsofsound.com
10	Mariruth Pyles	June10@hk.net
11	Patricia Gephardt	oursounds@gmail.com
12	Tony Maric	ttiger@franlin.edu
13	Stephanie Price	eeyore@gallion.org
14	Trudy Twiest	mom@yahoo.com
15	Mary Bender	sukey@yahoo.com
16	Holli Currier	columbia@rhps.com
17	Student Name	student@college.edu

Deploying the LearnSoft Database ★★

CONTINUING EXERCISES

2. You are ready to deploy the LearnSoft database to be used by the entire sales staff. To improve the database's performance, you will split the database and create an application file.

a. Make a backup copy of the LearnSoft Titles database (which you last updated in Step-by-Step Exercise 5 of Lab 6).

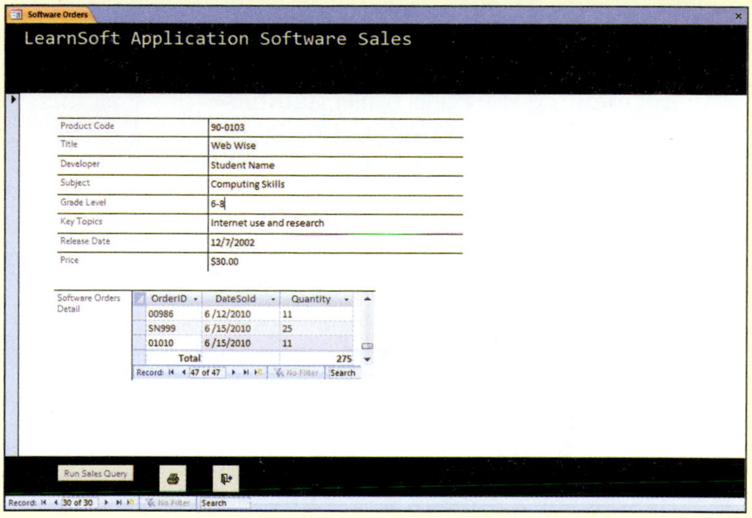

b. Open the LearnSoft Titles database.

c. Split the database. Accept the default name for the back-end file.

d. Set the Software Orders form as the startup form and disable the Navigation pane.

e. Create an accde file in your solution file location using the default file name.

f. Close the database.

g. Test the accde by opening it.

h. Sort the records on Product Code. Navigate to the last record, with your name as the author. Use the Software Orders Detail subform to add an additional order numbered 01010 with today's date and any quantity.

i. Use the form's Print button to print this page of the form.

j. Close the database.

Five Points Expansion ★★★

3. Kathlyn Frances, the owner of the Five Points Health and Wellness Center, is very impressed with the Spa Packages database table that you created. Kathlyn recently acquired the assets of Muncie Beauty LLC, including all the World O' Beauty and Moods locations. She would like you to incorporate the former company's existing locations list into the database and to prepare the database to be deployed across all Five Points locations.

   a. Open the Five Points Center database (which you last updated in Step-by-Step Exercise 3 of Lab 6).

   b. Import Sheet1 from the acwt2_Five Points Locations.xlsx spreadsheet by establishing a link. The first row contains column headings. Save the linked table as **Locations**.

   c. Open the Locations table. Adjust the size of the columns to display all of the data. Close and save the table.

   d. Split the database. Accept the default name for the back-end file.

   e. Set the Spa Package Purchases form as the startup form and disable the Navigation pane.

   f. Create an accde file in your solution file location using the default file name.

   g. Close the database.

   h. Open the accde file. Open the Packages Sold table and add a new record with your client ID number and package number three.

   i. Use the print button to print the page of the form for package number three.

   j. Close the database.

Access 2007 Command Summary

Command	Shortcut	Action
Office Button		**Opens File menu**
New		Opens a new blank database
Open	Ctrl + O	Opens an existing database
Save	Ctrl + S	Saves database object
Save As	F12	Saves database object with a new file name
Print/Print	Ctrl + P	Specifies print settings and prints current database object
Print/Print Preview		Displays file as it will appear when printed
Manage/Compact and Repair		Compacts and repairs database file
Manage/Back Up Database		Backs up database
Manage/Database Properties		Allows changes to database properties
Close Database		Closes open window
Access Options		Specifies program settings
Exit Access		Closes Access 2007 application
Quick Access Toolbar		
Undo	Ctrl + Z	Cancels last action
Save	Ctrl + S	Saves the current object
Home tab		
Views Group		
Design View		Displays object in Design view
Datasheet View		Displays object in Datasheet view
Form View		Changes to Form view
Form Layout View		Changes to Form Layout view

Command	Shortcut	Action
Report View		Displays report in Report view
Report Layout View		Displays report in Layout view
Clipboard group Cut	Ctrl + X	Removes selected item and copies it to the Clipboard
Copy	Ctrl + C	Duplicates selected item and copies to the Clipboard
Paste	Ctrl + V	Inserts copy of item from Clipboard
Font group Bold	Ctrl + B	Applies bold effect to all text in datasheet
Font Color		Applies selected color to all text in datasheet
Gridlines		Changes gridline color of datasheet
Alternate Fill/Back Color		Changes background color of datasheet
Records group Refresh All		Updates display of data
New	Ctrl + +	Adds new record
Save	Shift + Enter	Saves changes to object design
Delete	Delete	Deletes current record
Totals		Displays/hides Totals row
More/Hide Columns		Hides columns in Datasheet
More/Unhide Columns		Redisplays hidden columns
More/Column Width		Adjusts width of selected column
Sort & Filter group Ascending		Changes sort order to ascending
Descending		Changes sort order to descending
Clear All Sorts		Clears all sorts and returns sort order to primary key order
Filter		Allows multiple filter criteria in a single field
Selection/Equals		Displays only those records containing selected value
Advanced/Clear all Filters		Removes all filters from table

Command	Shortcut	Action
Toggle Filter		Applies and removes filter from table
Find group		
Find	Ctrl + F	Locates specified data
Replace	Ctrl + H	Locates specified data and replaces it with specified replacement text
Go To		Moves to First, Previous, Next, Last, or New record location
Select /Select		Selects current record
Select /Select All		Selects all records in database
Create tab		
Tables group		
Table		Creates a new table in Datasheet view
(dropdown arrow)		Creates a new table in Design view
Forms group		
Form		Creates a new form using all the fields from the underlying table
Split Form		Allows for the simultaneous display of a form and its dependent datasheet information
Blank Form		Displays a blank form to which you add the fields from the table that you want to appear on the form
More Forms /Form Wizard		Creates a new form by following the steps in the Form Wizard
Reports group		
Report		Creates a new report using Design view
Labels		Opens the Label Wizard to generate mailing labels
Blank Report		Creates a report using Report Design view
Report Wizard		Creates a report using the Report Wizard
Report Design		Opens Design view to create new reports
Other group		
Query Wizard		Creates a query using the Query Wizard
Query Design		Creates a query using Query Design View

Command	Shortcut	Action
External Data tab		
Import group		
Access		Imports data from or links to data in another Access database
Access/Link		Creates a linked table to a table in another database
Excel		Imports data from or links to data in an Excel workbook
Excel/Link		Creates a linked table to an Excel spreadsheet
Saved Imports		Displays a list of previously saved import steps
Export group		
Saved Exports		View and run saved exports
Excel		Exports selected object to an Excel workbook
Word		Exports selected object to a Rich Text Format file
Database Tools tab		
Show/Hide group		
Relationships		Defines how the data in tables is related
Property Sheet		Specifies general properties associated with the database file
Object Dependencies		Shows the objects in the database that use the selected object
Analyze group		
Database Documenter		Creates a report showing object properties and settings
Analyze Table		Evaluates table design
Move Data group		
Access Database		Splits a database
Database Tools group		
Linked Table Manager		Opens Linked Table Manager
Encrypt with Password		Encrypts and password protects a database
Decrypt Database		Decrypts and removes password protection
Make ACCDE		Creates an accde-type database file

Command	Shortcut	Action
Table Tools Datasheet tab		
Views group		
Design View		Displays table in Design view
Datasheet View		Displays table in Datasheet view
Fields & Columns group		
New Field		Inserts a new field
Delete		Removes selected field column
Rename		Renames selected field
Lookup Column		Creates a lookup column
Data Type & Formatting group		
Data Type: Text		Changes the data type for current field
Table Tools Design tab		
Views group		
Design View		Displays table in Design view
Datasheet View		Displays table in Datasheet view
Tools group		
Primary Key		Makes current field a primary key field
Insert Rows		Inserts a new field in Table Design view
Delete Rows		Deletes selected field row
Form Layout Tools Format tab		
Views group		
Form View		Displays form in Form view
Form Layout View		Displays form in Layout view
Controls group		
Title		Adds a title to the current form
Add Existing Fields		Displays the Field List pane to add fields to a form design
AutoFormat group		
More		Displays gallery of form design styles

Command	Shortcut	Action
Form Layout Tools Arrange tab		
Control Layout group		
Stacked		Creates a stacked layout with labels to the left of the control
Remove		Removes layouts applied to the selected control
Tab Order		Opens the Tab Order dialog box to control how the Tab key navigates the form
Position group		
Bring to Front		Brings selected control to top of stack
Tools group		
Property Sheet	F4	Opens and closes the Property Sheet pane
Form Design Tools Design tab		
Font group		
Perpetua Font		Chooses a font for the selected control
11 Font Size		Chooses a font size for the selected control
Font Color		Chooses a font color for the selected control
Controls group		
Page Number		Inserts page number control in header or footer group
Label		Adds a label control to the current form
Button		Adds a command button control to the current form
Subform/Subreport		Creates a subform
Rectangle		Adds a rectangle control to the current form
Select		Turns Select feature on/off
Control Wizard		Turns wizard feature on/off
Form Design Tools Arrange tab		
Control Padding		Sets the padding (the amount of white space) between controls
Tab Order		Changes the tab order for controls

Command	Shortcut	Action
Control Alignment group Left		Sets the alignment of the selected control to the left side of the form
Top		Sets the alignment of the selected control to the top of the form
Show/Hide group Page Header/Footer		Displays and hides the Page Header and Footer sections
Form Header/Footer		Displays and hides the form header and footer sections
Query Tools Design tab		
Results group Run		Displays query results in Query Datasheet view
Query Type group Select		Defines the current query as a Select query
Append		Defines the current query as an Append query
Update		Defines the current query as an Update query
Crosstab		Defines the current query as a Crosstab query
Delete		Defines the current query as a Delete query
Query Setup group Show Table		Displays/hides Show Table dialog box
Return: All		Allows you to define how much of the total number of valid records should be returned by this query
Show/Hide group Table Names		Displays/hides the Tables row
Property Sheet		Displays (or hides) the Property Sheet for the selected object
Report Layout Tools Format tab		
Views group Report View		Displays report in Report view
Report Layout View		Displays report in Report Layout view

Command	Shortcut	Action
Report Design View		Displays report in Report Design view
Font group Center		Centers text in selected control
Conditional		Opens the Conditional Formatting dialog box to specify conditional formatting settings
Fill/Back Color		Applies selected background color
Controls group Add Existing Fields		Displays/hides Add Existing Fields task pane
AutoFormat group AutoFormat		Applies selected predesigned styles to report
Report Layout Tools Arrange tab		
Control Layout group Stacked		Adds selected controls to a stacked layout control group
Control Alignment group Right		Right-aligns selected controls
Tools group Property Sheet	F4	Displays/hides Property Sheet pane
Report Layout Tools Page Setup tab		
Page Layout group Margins		Sets margins of printed report
Page Setup		Sets features related to the page layout of printed report
Report Design Tools Design tab		
Font group Center		Centers text in selected control
20 Font Size		Changes the size of the text in the currently selected control
Fill/Back Color		Allows you to select a background color
Format Painter		Copies the formats from a selected control to multiple other controls that you select
Controls group Rectangle		Adds a rectangle to the report

Command	Shortcut	Action
Line Thickness		Selects the line thickness for a graphic element
Line Color		Selects the line color of a graphic element
Line		Adds a line to the report
Title		Adds a title control to the report
Insert Chart		Opens the Chart Wizard to add a chart to the current report
Label Control		Adds a label control
Text Control		Adds a text control
Tools group		
Add Existing Fields		Displays/hides the Fields List task pane
Report Design Tools Arrange tab		
Control Alignment group		
Right		Right-aligns selected controls
Relationship Tools Design tab		
Tools group		
Relationship Report		Creates a report of the displayed relationships
PivotChart Tools Design tab		
Show/Hide group		
Field List		Displays/hides the list of available fields when creating a pivot chart
Legend		Displays/hides the legend on a chart
Type group		
Change Chart Type		Changes the type of chart
Print Preview tab		
Print group		
Print		Prints displayed object
Page Layout group		
Portrait		Changes print orientation to portrait
Landscape		Changes print orientation to landscape
Margins		Sets margins of printed output

Command	Shortcut	Action
Zoom group		
Zoom		Changes the magnification level of the previewed object
One Page		Displays one entire page in print preview
Two Pages		Displays two entire pages in print preview
Close Preview group		
Close Print Preview		Closes Print Preview window
Chart Toolbars		
Chart Type		Changes the type of chart
By Column		Changes chart orientation to columns
By Row		Changes chart orientation to rows
Chart Datasheet		Hides/displays the chart datasheet

Glossary of Key Terms

action A self-contained instruction that can be combined with other actions to automate tasks.

Action query A query that is used to make changes to many records in a table at once.

active window The window you can work in when multiple application windows are displayed on the screen at the same time.

aggregate functions Calculations that are performed on a range of data.

alias A name that describes and precedes the expression in a calculated field. It is used as the field name in the query results.

align To position a control relative to other controls.

Allow Zero Length property Specified if an entry containing no characters is valid.

AND operator Used in criteria expression to narrow a search by specifying that a record must meet both conditions to be included.

argument Provides additional information on how a macro is to be carried out.

ascending sort order Data that is arranged in A to Z or 0 to 9 order.

attachment control A control for a field that has an attachment data type.

Attachment data type Data type that allows multiple files of different types to be attached to a field.

AutoNumber data type Data type that enters a unique sequential number for each record as it is added to a table.

back-end The data part of a database file that contains the table data and is stored on the server for all users to access.

Best Fit feature A feature that automatically adjusts column width to fit the longest entry.

bound control A control that is linked to a field in an underlying table.

byte A unit of storage.

calculated control Control that displays data that is calculated from a field in a table or query or from another control in the form.

calculated field A field that contains an expression and displays the results of the calculation in the field column of the query results.

Caption property A property that specifies the field label other than the field name.

cell The intersection of a row and column in a datasheet where field data is entered.

character string A group of text characters.

chart A visual representation of numeric data.

Clipboard A temporary storage area in memory where copied or cut data is stored.

column selector bar In Query Design view, the thin gray bar just above the field name in the grid.

column width The size of a field column in Datasheet view. It controls the amount of data you can see on the screen.

command button User-created button that executes one or more actions on a form.

common field A field that is found in two or more tables. It must have the same data type and the same kind of information in each table but may have different field names.

compact To make a copy of the database file and rearrange how the file is stored on disk for optimal performance.

comparison operator A symbol used in expressions that allows you to make comparisons. The > (greater than) and < (less than) symbols are examples of comparison operators.

composite key A primary key that uses more than one field.

compound control Controls that are associated and act as one when manipulated.

compound criterion Used to instruct the query to locate records meeting multiple criteria. The AND and OR operators are used to create a compound criterion.

conditional formatting Formatting that is applied automatically when specified conditions are met.

control An object in a form or report that displays information, performs actions, or enhances the design.

control reference A second calculated control in the main form that references the calculated control in the subform.

criteria Limiting conditions that are used when specifying the information you want to appear in the query results.

criteria expression An expression that will select only the records that meet certain limiting criteria.

Crosstab query A query that summarizes large amounts of data in an easy-to-read, row-and-column format.

Currency data type Data type that allows entry of digits only and formats them to display decimal places and a currency symbol.

current field The field that is selected and will be affected by any changes you make.

current record The record containing the insertion point and that will be affected by the next action.

data series Each group of related data that is plotted in a chart.

data type Attribute for a field that determines what type of data it can contain.

database An organized collection of related information.

Datasheet view View used to display table data or query results in a row and column format.

Date/Time data type Data type that accepts date and time entries only.

Default Value property A property used to specify a value that is automatically entered in a field when a new record is created.

descending sort order Data that is arranged in Z to A or 9 to 0 order.

design grid The lower part of the Query Design window, which displays settings that are used to define the query.

Design view View that is used to create or modify the structure of a table, form, query, or report.

destination The location where cut or copied data is inserted.

destination file The document in which a linked object is inserted.

drawing object A simple graphic consisting of shapes such as lines and boxes that can be created using a drawing program such as Paint.

exclusive Type of database that prevents others in a multiuser environment from opening the database while you are accessing it.

export The process of copying data, tables, queries, forms, or report objects to a file outside the database.

expression A combination of operators, identifiers, and values that produce a result.

Expression Builder Access feature used to enter expressions in database forms, reports, and queries.

field A single category of data in a table, the values of which appear in a column of a datasheet.

field list In Query Design view, a list box that lists all the fields in the record source table. In Report Design view, a task pane that displays all the fields in the record source table.

field name A label used to identify the data stored in a field.

field property An attribute of a field that affects its appearance or behavior.

Field Size property Field property that limits a Text data type to a certain size or limits numeric data to values within a specific range.

field template A set of predefined fields from which you can select. Each field includes a field name, data type, and format settings that control the behavior and display of the field data.

filter A restriction placed on records in an open form or datasheet to temporarily isolate a subset of records.

Find and Replace A feature that helps you quickly find specific information and automatically replace it with new information.

font A set of characters with a specific design. Also called a typeface.

font size The height and width of the character, commonly measured in points.

foreign key A field that refers to the primary key field in another table.

form A database object used primarily to display records onscreen to make it easier to enter new records and make changes to existing records.

form separator Also called a splitter bar, it separates the two areas of a form.

Form view View used to display records in a form.

format To enhance the appearance of the document to make it more readable or attractive.

Format property A property that specifies the way data is displayed.

front-end The application part of a database file that contains the objects such as forms, reports, and queries and is stored on the users' PC.

function A predefined calculation provided by Access to calculate the sum, average, and so on.

graphic A nontext element or object, such as a drawing or picture, that can be added to a table.

group A way of organizing data on a common attribute. When data is grouped, calculations can be performed on all data in each group.

group calculation A calculation performed on the data in a group in a report.

hard-coded criteria Criteria that are entered in the criteria cell and are used each time the query is run.

header row The row at the top of a datasheet that displays the field names.

hierarchical form A form/subform combination.

Hyperlink data type Data type that accepts hyperlink entries.

identifier A part of an expression that refers to the value of a field, a graphic object, or a property.

import To retrieve data that has been saved in another format and insert it into an Access table.

Indexed property Sets the field to an indexed field that controls the order of the records.

inner join Tells a query that rows from one of the joined tables correspond to rows in the other table on the basis of the data in the joined fields.

input mask Used in fields and text boxes to format data and provide control over what values can be entered into a field.

Input Mask property Restricts data that can be entered in a field to the entries you specify and controls the way the data is displayed.

join An association between fields of the same data type in multiple tables or queries.

join line In the Query Design window, the line that joins the common fields between one or more table field lists.

junction table When an association between two tables is created in which one record in either table can relate to many records in the other table, a third table, called a junction table, is used to hold the primary key fields from the other two tables and serves as a bridge between them.

label control An unbound control that displays descriptive labels.

landscape orientation Printing orientation that prints across the length of the page.

layout Designs that control how data is displayed in a form or report.

Layout view View used to display data while allowing modifications to the design and layout of the table, query, form, or report object.

legend A box containing descriptive text that identifies the patterns or colors assigned to the data series in a chart.

linked table The table created in the destination database that maintains a connection to the source file (database, workbook, or text document).

linking Creating a link lets you connect to data in another database without importing it so you can view and modify data in both the source and destination.

literal characters Characters in an input mask that display just as they appear.

lookup field A field that lets you choose from a list of values you entered or that are from another table or query.

lookup list The list of values from which you select when using a lookup field.

Lookup Wizard Creates a lookup field.

main form The primary form that can have multiple subforms.

many-to-many A type of relationship in which there is an association between two tables where one record in either table can relate to many records in the other table.

margin The blank space around the edge of a page.

mask characters Characters in an input mask that define the characterstics of the input mask.

master/detail form A form/subform combination.

master table The table that holds the subdatasheet.

Memo data type Allows up to 1GB of characters or 2GB of storage in a field of which 65,535 characters can be displayed. Entries in this field can be formatted.

multitable query A query that uses more than one table.

multiuser A type of database that allows multiple users to access and modify the database at the same time.

navigation buttons Used to move through records in Datasheet and Form views. Also available in the Print Preview window.

Navigation pane The pane to the left of the work area that is used to open and manage database objects.

normal form A set of constraints or standards that must be satisfied to meet normalization.

normalization A design technique that identifies and eliminates redundancy by applying a set of rules to your tables to confirm that they are structured properly.

Null value A field that does not contain an entry.

Number data type Data type that allows storage of digits only in a field.

object A table, form, or report that can be selected and manipulated as a unit.

OLE Object data type Use in fields to store an object such as a graphic (picture), sound, document, or graph.

one-to-many A type of relationship in which there is an association between two tables where each record in the first table contains a field value that corresponds to the field value of many records in the other table.

one-to-one A type of relationship in which there is an association between two tables where each record in the first table contains a field value that corresponds to the field value of one record in the other table.

operator A symbol or word used to specify the type of calculation to perform in an expression.

OR operator Used in a criteria expression to broaden a search by specifying that a record may include either condition in the output.

orientation The direction the paper prints, either landscape or portrait.

outer join Specifies that although some of the rows on both sides of the join correspond exactly, the query should include all rows from one table even if there is no match in the other table.

Parameter query A query that displays a dialog box prompting you for the criteria information you want the query to use.

parameter value In a Parameter query, the value that is entered in the criteria cell rather than a specific value. The parameter value tells the query to prompt you for the specific criteria you want to use when you run the query.

parent/child form A form/subform combination.

password A private code that is designed to prevent any unauthorized users from opening the database unless they know the password.

picture An illustration such as a scanned photograph.

pivot chart An interactive chart that can be used to analyze data in a datasheet or form.

point Unit of measure for characters in a font; 1 point equals 1/72 inch.

portrait orientation Printing orientation that prints the report across the width of a page.

primary key One or more fields in a table that uniquely identify a record.

primary table The "one" side of two related tables in a one-to-many relationship.

Print Preview View that displays a datasheet, form, or report as it will appear when printed.

query Used to view data in different ways, to analyze data, and to change data.

record A row of a table, consisting of a group of related fields.

record number indicator A small box that displays the current record number in the lower-left corner of most views. The record number indicator is surrounded by the navigation buttons.

record source The table or query that is the underlying source of data for a form or report.

referential integrity Rules that ensure that relationships between tables are valid and that related data is not accidentally changed or deleted.

relational database A database in which a relationship is created by having a common field in the tables. The common field lets you extract and combine data from multiple tables.

relationship A relationship establishes the association between common fields in two tables.

report Professional-appearing output generated from tables or queries that may include design elements, groups, and summary information.

Report view View that displays the data in a report.

Required property Specifies whether a value must be entered in a field.

row label In the design grid of Query Design view, identifies the type of information that can be entered in the row.

sans serif Fonts that do not have a flair at the base of each letter.

Select All button The square to the left of each row in Datasheet view that is used to select an entire record.

Select query A type of query that retrieves the specific data you request from one or more tables, then displays the data in a datasheet.

serial value Sequential numbers assigned to each day beginning with January 1, 1900, whose serial number is 1, through December 31, 9999, whose serial number is 2958465.

serif Fonts with a flair at the base of each letter that visually leads the reader to the next letter.

Show box A box in the Show row of the design grid that, when checked, indicates that the field will be displayed in the query result.

sort To temporarily reorder table records in the datasheet.

source The data that is copied or cut; the underlying table that provides the values in a lookup list.

source file The document in which a linked object was created.

spacing The vertical distance between controls.

splitting Divides a database file into two parts: an application part called the front-end and a data part called the back-end.

SQL (Structured Query Language) The most common relational database language.

SQL query A query that is created using SQL (Structured Query Language).

SQL statement An expression that defines an SQL command.

stacked layout A layout that arranges data vertically with a field label to the left of the field data.

subdatasheet A data table nested in another data table that contains data related or joined to the table where it resides.

subform A form that is embedded in another form.

subquery An SQL Select statement that is inside another Select or Action query.

syntax The correct format or rules for a statement.

tab order The order in which Access moves through a form or table when the Tab key is pressed.

table Consists of vertical columns and horizontal rows of information about a particular category of things.

tabular layout A layout that arranges data in rows and columns with labels across the top.

template A ready-to-use database file that includes the data structure for a selected type of database.

text control A control that is linked to a field in the record source and displays the information contained in that field.

Text data type Data type that allows up to 255 characters (combinations of letters and numbers not used in calculations) to be entered in a field.

theme colors Combinations of coordinating colors that are used in the default datasheet.

titles Descriptive text used to explain the contents of a chart.

typeface The design and shape of characters such as Times New Roman and Courier.

unbound control A control that is not connected to a field in an underlying table.

unequal join Records to be included in the query results are based on the value in one join field being greater than, less than, not equal to, greater than or equal to, or less than or equal to the value in the other join field.

Validation Rule property An expression that defines the acceptable values in a validity check.

Validation Text property Text that is displayed when a validation rule is violated.

value A part of an expression that is a number, date, or character string.

value list A lookup field that uses fixed values as the source for values in the list.

view One of several windows or formats that Access provides for working with and looking at data.

wildcards Symbols that are used to represent characters when specifying criteria.

wizard A feature that guides you through the steps to create different database objects based upon your selections.

X axis Typically, the bottom boundary of the chart, also called the category axis. It is used to label the data being charted.

Y axis Typically, the left boundary of the chart, also called the value axis, that displays a numbered scale whose values are determined by the data in the chart.

Yes/No data type Data type that accepts only Yes/No, True/False, or On/Off entries.

zero-length string An entry in a field that consists of two double quotation marks with no space between them. It appears empty.

Appendix

MORE ABOUT ACCESS 2007

1 STRUCTURING A DATABASE

1.1 DEFINE DATA NEEDS AND TYPES

WHEN TO USE A MULTIVALUE FIELD

A multivalue field allows you to select and store more than one choice in a field. For example, a multivalue field could be used in a database of horses that are for sale to specify the colors in a horse.

You should consider creating a multivalue field when you want to

- Store a multiple-valued selection from a list of choices and that list of choices is relatively small.
- Export an Access table to a SharePoint site so that it employs the multivalue choice or lookup fields available in Windows SharePoint Services.
- Move an Access database to a SharePoint site so that it employs the multivalue choice or lookup fields available in Windows SharePoint Services.
- Link to a SharePoint list that contains a multivalue choice or multivalue Lookup field.

In addition to the preceding scenarios, you also might want to use a multivalue field when you are relatively sure your database will not be moved to Microsoft SQL Server at a later date. An Office Access 2007 multivalue field is upsized to SQL Server as a memo (ntext) field that contains the delimited set of values. Because SQL Server does not support a multivalue data type that models a many-to-many relationship, additional design and conversion work might be needed.

1.3 ADD, SET, CHANGE, OR REMOVE PRIMARY KEYS

DEFINE AND MODIFY MULTIFIELD PRIMARY KEYS

Most tables have at least one field that is selected as the primary key. Some tables may use two or more fields that, together, provide the primary key of a table. When a primary key uses more than one field, it is called a composite key. The fields do not need to be the same data type.

To define multiple fields as primary keys in a table, follow these steps:

- Open the table in Design view.
- Select (highlight) the two or more fields you want to be primary keys.
- Click .

Now the data in both fields will operate as primary key fields. Multifield primary keys can be removed by selecting the primary key field and clicking Primary Key to turn off this setting.

2 CREATING AND FORMATTING DATABASE ELEMENTS

2.2 CREATE TABLES

CREATE TABLES BY COPYING THE STRUCTURE OF OTHER TABLES

You can copy the structure of a table to another database file as a shortcut to creating a new table. Exporting the definition creates a blank copy of the table in the destination database. Follow these steps to export a table's definitions to another database:

- Open the database file that contains the table whose structure you want to copy.
- Click More in the Export group of the External Data tab.
- Choose Access Database.
- In the File name box, specify the name of the destination database and then click OK.
- In the Export dialog box, change the name of the new object if you do not want to overwrite an existing object with the same name in the destination database.
- Select Table definition only.
- Click OK to finish the operation.
- Choose the Save export steps option if you want to save the steps and click Close; otherwise, simply click Close.

2.4 CREATE FIELDS AND MODIFY FIELD PROPERTIES

CREATE COMMONLY USED FIELDS

The steps to create Memo, Number, Currency, and Yes/No fields is the same, the only difference being the data type that you select. The resulting format and properties associated with each data type, of course, are different. See Concept 3 in Lab 1 to review data types. The following steps are used to create memo, number, currency, and yes/no data types:

- Open the table in which you want to create a new field in Design view.
- Click in a blank Field Name row and enter a new field name.
- Open the Data Type drop-down list and choose the Memo, Number, Currency, or Yes/No data type.

MODIFY FIELD PROPERTIES: SET MEMO FIELDS AS APPEND ONLY

When creating a Memo data type field, you can set the field to Append only. When this feature is on, users can add data to the Memo field, but they cannot change or remove existing data. Follow these steps to enable append only in a memo field:

- Open the table in which you want to change the properties of a Memo field in Design view.
- Click in the memo field's Field Name row.
- Click in the Append Only property box.
- Click Design View to open the drop-down list of options and choose Yes.

By default, when you try to position the mouse pointer in a Memo field with this property enabled, Access hides the text.

CREATE AND MODIFY MULTIVALUE FIELDS

A multivalue field uses check box drop-down lists and check box lists that allow you to select and store more than one value in a table field. You create the multivalue field in Office Access 2007 by using the Lookup Wizard in table Design view. The most common type of multivalue lookup column is one that displays values looked up from a related table or query.

Follow these steps to create a multivalue field:

- Open the table in which you want to create the field.
- Click [Lookup Column] in the Fields & Columns group of the Table Tools Datasheet tab.
- In the first dialog box of the Lookup Wizard, you must decide whether you want to base the lookup column on the values in a table or query or on a list of values that you type in.
- To enter the values:
  - Choose I will type in the values that I want and then click [Next >].
  - Enter the number of columns and then type each value.
  - Click [Next >].
  - If you specified more than one column at step 2, you must choose which column you will use to uniquely identify each value.
  - In the Lookup Wizard, type the label for your lookup column.
  - Choose Allow Multiple Values under Do you want to store multiple values for this lookup?
  - Click [Finish].

To base the lookup column on the values in a table or query:

- Choose Look up the values in a table or query and then click [Next >].
- Select a table or query from the list and then click [Next >].
- Add the field(s) that you want included in your lookup to the Selected Fields list.
- Click [Next >].
- If desired, select one to four fields on which to sort the lookup items and then click [Next >].
- Adjust the width of the columns in your lookup field, if necessary, then click [Next >].
- Choose Allow Multiple Values under Do you want to store multiple values for this lookup?
- Click [Finish].

A lookup column is created whose field properties are set based on the choices you made in the Lookup Wizard.

MODIFYING A MULTIVALUE FIELD

To change the design of a multivalue lookup column, you edit the Lookup field properties in Design view. However, if the lookup column is based on a single-column value list and the Allow Value List Edits property is set to Yes, you can change the list of values in Datasheet view or Form view by right-clicking the multivalue lookup column and then choosing Edit List Items.

2.5 CREATE FORMS

CREATE DATASHEET FORMS

The Datasheet tool is used to create a form using all the fields in the table.

- Open the table in which you want to create a form.
- Open the Create tab.
- Click [More Forms].
- Choose Datasheet.

The newly created form is displayed in Datasheet view. It can be modified just like any other form by adding controls and other design elements.

CREATING FORMS IN DESIGN VIEW

Generally, Design view is used to modify the design of an existing form. However, it also can be used to create a new form. Follow these steps to use Design view to create a stacked form using a table as the record source:

- Click Form Design in the Forms group of the Create tab.
- Click Add Existing Fields in the Tools group of the Report Design Tools Design tab.
- Display the report property sheet and select the table you want to use as the record source.
- Click Add Existing Fields to open the Field List and select Show only fields in the current record source.
- Add the fields you want to appear to the form detail area.
- Select all the fields and click Stacked from the Control Layout group of the Form Layout Tools Arrange tab.

Continue to modify the form just as you would any other form.

CREATE PIVOTTABLE FORMS

PivotTable forms are similar to PivotTable charts in that they provide an interactive way to view table data. Follow these steps to create a PivotTable form:

- Click More Forms in the Forms group of the Create tab and choose PivotTable.
- Display the Field List.
- Drag the fields you want to appear as the row and column data to the appropriate drop areas.
- Drag the field whose data you want to appear in the pivot table to the Detail area.
- Drag a field to the Filter drop area.
- Save the form.

2.6 CREATE REPORTS

CREATING REPORTS USING DESIGN VIEW

Generally, Design view is used to modify the design of an existing report. However, it also can be used to create a new report. Follow these steps to use Design view to create a stacked report using a query as the record source:

- Click Report Design in the Reports group of the Create tab.
- Click Add Existing Fields in the Tools group of the Report Design Tools Design tab.
- Display the report property sheet and select the query you want to use as the record source.
- Click Add Existing Fields to open the Field List and select Show only fields in the current record source.
- Add the fields you want to appear to the report detail area.
- Select all the fields and click Stacked from the Control Layout group of the Report Design Tools Arrange tab.

Continue to modify the report just as you would any other report.

2.7 MODIFY THE DESIGN OF REPORTS AND FORMS

BIND CONTROLS TO FIELDS

If you have added a control to a form that you want to display data from the record source, you can bind the control to the field you want displayed. The control must be the type of control that can display data (a text box or combo box, for example). Follow these steps to bind a control to a field:

- Display the property sheet for the control by clicking the control and then pressing F4.
- On the Data tab of the property sheet, open the Control Source property list and select the field you want displayed in the control. You also can type an expression in the Control Source box.

ANCHORING CONTROLS

Controls in a form can be tied to another control or to a section so that when the parent control moves or resizes, the control that is tied to it moves and resizes in conjunction with it. To anchor controls, follow these steps:

- Display the form in Form Layout view.
- Select the controls that you want to anchor.
- Click Anchoring in the Position group of the Form Layout Tools Arrange tab.
- Specify how you want the controls to move or resize (for example, choosing Stretch Down will make the controls' size change the same when dragging down on the control).

3 ENTERING AND MODIFYING DATA

3.4 ATTACH DOCUMENTS TO AND DETACH FROM RECORDS

EXPORT ATTACHMENTS

Files that have been added to an attachment field can be saved to other locations on your computer. To do this, follow these steps:

Additional Information
If you want to save all the attachments, choose Save All.

- Open the table in Datasheet view and double-click on the Attachment field cell for the record containing the attachment you want to export.
- Select the file you want to export from the Attachments dialog box.
- Choose Save As.
- In the Save Attachments dialog box, specify the name and location where you want a copy of the attached file saved.
- Click Save and then OK.

A copy of the file is saved to the specified location.

3.5 IMPORT DATA

IMPORTING TEXT DATA

You can bring data from a text file into Microsoft Office Access 2007 in two ways:

- To create a copy of the data that you can edit within Access, import the file into a new or existing table by clicking Text File in the Import group of the External Data tab. Then follow the steps in the Import Text Wizard.
- To simply view the latest source data within Access for richer querying and reporting, create a link to the text file in your database by clicking Text File in the Import group of the External Data tab and choosing the Link option. Then follow the steps in the Link Text Wizard.

4 CREATING AND MODIFYING QUERIES

4.1 CREATE QUERIES

CREATE QUERIES BASED ON MORE THAN ONE TABLE

When two tables have fields with the same name, it is important to select the field from the table list that contains the data you want displayed in the query output. To identify which table to draw a field from, follow these steps:

- Create a query that contains multiple tables that use the same field name in at least one field.
- In Query Design view, add the field that has the same name from each table to the grid.
- Run the query to see the content from both fields.
- Remove the field from the grid whose content you do not want displayed.

SAVE FILTERS AS QUERIES

You can save a filter as a query so that the results are always available or to provide a head start in creating a query. To do this, follow these steps:

- Open the table you want to filter and specify the filter criteria.
- Click Advanced in the Sort & Filter group and choose Filter by Form.
- Click Advanced and choose Save as Query.
- Enter a name for the query in the Save As Query dialog box.

USE THE MAKE TABLE QUERY

The Make Table action query can be used to create a new table from selected fields in another table. To use this feature, follow these steps:

- Create a Select query that contains the fields you want in the new table.
- Run the query to make sure it displays the information you want.
- In Design view, click Make Table in the Query Type group of the Query Tools Design tab.
- Name the new table.
- Specify whether the table is to be created in the current database or another database.
- If in another database, browse to select the database file.
- Run the query and click OK to confirm pasting the records in the new table.

The new table is added to the database and the table name appears in the Tables object list.

4.2 MODIFY QUERIES

ADD TABLES TO AND REMOVE TABLES FROM QUERIES

There are times that you may want to add a second copy of a table to a query to produce the results you need. To do this, follow these steps:

- Create a query that contains the table you want to use as the source.
- In Query Design view, open the Show Tables dialog box and select the same table from the list.

The duplicate table is identified with a number following the table name so that you can easily identify from which table you are specifying fields in the design grid.

CREATE JOINS

As you learned in Lab 3, an inner join is created by default. (See Concept 3 in Lab 3 to review this feature.) You also can create a left or right outer join. Left outer joins include all of the records from the first (left) of two tables, even if there are no matching values for records in the second (right) table. Right outer joins include all of the records from the second (right) of two tables, even if there are no matching values for records in the first (left) table. To change the join to a left or right outer join, follow these steps:

- Open the database file that contains the tables you want to join.
- Click Relationships in the Show/Hide group of the Database Tools tab.
- Click All Relationships in the Relationships group of the Relationship Tools Design tab.
- If necessary, first create a relationship between the tables.
- Right-click the relationship line and choose Join Type.
- Select option 2 from the Join Properties dialog box to create an inner join or option 3 to create an outer join.
- Click OK twice.

5 PRESENTING AND SHARING DATA

5.5 SAVE DATABASE OBJECTS AS OTHER FILE TYPES

In addition to the Access 2007 object types, database objects can be saved in other file formats that make it easy to share and print the file and hard to modify. Two common types of files that do this are the Portable Document Format (PDF) file format and the XML Paper Specification (XPS) file types. Both these file formats preserve the original document formatting and make it easy to view the file online and print it. They also make it difficult to change the data in the file.

To save a table (or other Access object) as either a PDF or XPS file, you must have first installed the free add-in to save or export this type of file. Then, to view a PDF file, you must have a PDF reader installed on your computer. One reader is the Acrobat Reader, available from Adobe Systems. To view a file in XPS format, you need a viewer. You or the recipient of your file can download a free viewer from Downloads on Microsoft Office Online.

Follow these steps to learn how to save a database object as a PDF or XPS file type:

- Open the table or report that you want to save as PDF or XPS.
- Click Office Button, select Save As, and then choose PDF or XPS.
- Enter a file name and location to save the file.
- Open the Save as type list and choose XPS Document or PDF.
- Next to Optimize for, do one of the following, depending on whether file size or print quality is more important to you:
  - If the report requires high print quality, click Standard (publishing online and printing).
  - If the print quality is less important than file size, click Minimum size (publishing online).
- Choose Options to specify various options for the file.
- Click OK.
- In the Publish as PDF or XPS dialog box, choose Publish.

6 MANAGING AND MAINTAINING DATABASES

6.1 PERFORM ROUTINE DATABASE OPERATIONS

SAVE DATABASES AS A PREVIOUS VERSION

If you have an Office Access 2007 (.accdb) database that you want to save in an earlier Access file format (.mdb), you can do so as long as your .accdb database does not contain any multivalue lookup fields, offline data, or attachments. This is because older versions of Access do not support these new features. If you try to convert an .accdb database containing any of these elements to an .mdb file format, Access displays an error message.

Follow these steps to save an Access 2007 database file as a previous version:

- Open the database file you want to save as a previous version. Do not have any objects open.
- Click Office Button, select Save As, and from the Save the database in another format section of the menu, choose the appropriate Access file format for your needs.
- In the Save As dialog box, enter a file name for the copy of the database in the File name box and then click Save.

Access creates the copy of the database and then opens the copy. Access automatically closes the original database.

6.2 MANAGE DATABASES

CONFIGURE DATABASE OPTIONS: ENABLE ERROR CHECKING

Access can display error indicators in controls in forms and reports that experience one or more types of errors. The indicators appear as triangles in the upper-left or upper-right corner of the control, depending on how you set the default text direction. The default indicator color is green, but you can change that to suit your needs. Error checking is on by default and clearing this check box disables all types of error checking.

To enable error checking if it is off, follow these steps:

- Click Office Button and click Access Options.
- Open the Object Designer area and choose Enable error checking from the Error Checking section of the dialog box.
- Click OK.

CONFIGURE DATABASE OPTIONS 2: SHOW/HIDE THE NAVIGATION PANE

The Navigation pane is on by default and displayed automatically when you open a database file. If you do not want the pane to appear when you open a specific database file, you can turn off this feature.

To turn on or off the display of the Navigation pane, follow these steps:

- Click Office Button and click Access Options.
- Open the Current database area and choose Display Navigation Pane in the Navigation section to select or deselect this option.
- Click OK.

PRINT DATABASE INFORMATION USING THE DATABASE DOCUMENTER

Access 2007 includes a feature that will quickly create a report showing all the properties and details of the different objects in a database. This report is created using the Database Documenter tool.

To create a database report using the Database Documenter, follow these steps:

- Open the database file on which you want to create a report.
- On the Database Tools tab, click Database Documenter in the Analyze group.
- From the Documenter dialog box, select the tab that corresponds to the type of object on which you want to create a report.
- Select the objects that you want to document and then click OK.

The database report is created, opened, and displayed in Print Preview by default.

Reference 1

Data File List

Supplied/Used	Created/Saved As
Lab 1	
ac01_Roberta.jpg (graphic) ac01_Resume (Word document)	Club Employees: Employee Records (table) Job (table)
Step-by-Step 1.	Oak Ridge School: Students (table)
2. ac01_Guitar.jpg (graphic)	EchoPlex: Records
3.	County Library: Catalog (table)
4. ac01_Flavoring.jpg (graphic)	Cafe Inventory: Stock (table)
5. ac01_Valdez.jpg (graphic)	Kodiak Construction: Jobs, Clients, Foremen (tables)
On Your Own 1.	Valley View News: Advertisers (table)
2.	Music Collection: CD Catalog (table)
3.	Dental Patients: Personal Information (table)
4.	Timeless Treasures: Watches (table)
5.	EMP Enterprises: Employee Expenses, Employee Info (table)
Lab 2	
ac02_Employees ac02_Employees: Records (form) ac02_Carlos.jpg (graphic)	
Step-by-Step 1. ac02_Second Time Around	ac02_Second Time Around: Inventory (form)
2. ac02_Enterprise Employment Agency	ac02_Enterprise Employment Agency: Candidate Information (form)
3. ac02_ARF Database ac02_WhiteDog.jpg (graphic)	ac02_ARF Database: Animals (form)
4. ac02_Kodiak Construction	ac02_Kodiak Construction: Jobs (form)
5. ac02_EchoPlex	ac02_EchoPlex: Records (form)

Supplied/Used	Created/Saved As
On Your Own 1. ac02_ATT Database	ac02_ATT Database: Travel Packages (form)
2. EMP Enterprises (from Lab 1)	EMP Enterprises: Expenses (form)
3. Dental Patients (from Lab 1)	Dental Patients: Patient Data (form)
4. ac02_Lewis Personnel	ac02_Lewis Personnel: Phone List (form)
5. Timeless Treasures (from Lab 1)	Timeless Treasures: Watches (form)
Lab 3	
ac03_Personnel	ac03_Personnel: City/State/Zip Code (table) Car Pool Query (query) Location Query (query) Find duplicates for Personal Data (query) Personal Data without Matching Job Information (query) Maldin to Landis Car Pool Report (report) Job Position Report (report) ac03_Personnel/current date
Step-by-Step 1. ac03_Scensations Spa	ac03_Scensations Spa: City/State/Zip 40+ Clients (query) 40+ Clients Report (report)
2. ac02_EchoPlex (from Lab 2)	ac02_EchoPlex: Shipping List (query)
3. ac03_Cafe Inventory	ac03_Cafe Inventory: Low Stock (query) Stock Report (report)
4. ac02_Kodiak Construction (from Lab 2)	ac02_Kodiak Construction: Priority (query) Job Priority Report (report)
5. ac03_ARF3	ac03_ARF3: 2008 Foster Parents (query) 2008 Foster Parents Report (report)
On Your Own 1. ac03_LearnSoft	ac03_Learnsoft: Project Manager Report
2.	P&P Employees: Employees (table) Employee Addresses (report)
3. EMP Enterprises (from Lab 2)	EMP Enterprises: Pending Payment (query) Open Expense Reports (report)
4. ac03_ARF3	ac03_ARF3: Adopters (query) 2008 Adoptions Report (report)
5. Timeless Treasures (from Lab 2)	Timeless Treasures: Clocks (table) Timeless Treasures Inventory (report)
Working Together 1 acwt1_Personnel	Landis Job Positions (Excel) River Mist Job Positions (Excel) Job Position Report (Word document)
acwt1_Job Positions (Word document)	Job Positions (Word document)

Supplied/Used	Created/Saved As
Step-by-Step	
1. ac03_Scensations Spa (from Lab 3)	40+ Spa Clients (Word document)
2. ac03_Cafe Inventory (from Lab 3)	ac03_Cafe Inventory: Special Orders (query) Special Orders (Excel worksheet)
3. ac02_Kodiak Construction (from Lab 3)	ac02_Kodiak Construction: Top Priority (query) Kodiak Top Priority (Word document)
Lab 4	
ac04_Club Employees ac04_Employee Pay ac04_Employee Hours.xls ac04_New Records	Club Employees4 Pay (table) Hours Worked (table) Hours_Crosstab (query) Hours (query) New Records Query Gross Pay 6/27/2008 (query) Pay Update (query) Personal Data Without Matching Hours Worked (query) Personal Data Without Matching Pay (query)
Step-by-Step	
1. ac04_ARF	Animal Rescue Foundation Boarded Animals (query)
2. ac04_ATT Clients & Agents ac04_ATT Reservations.xlsx	Clients & Agents Reservations (table) Amount Due (query)
3. ac04_Five Points ac04_Five Points Packages Sold	Five Points Center Spa Packages (table) Packages Sold (table) Package Revenue (query) Client Purchases (crosstab query)
4. ac04_Cafe Purchases ac04_Prices	Café Purchases Inventory Order Costs
5. ac04_LearnSoft ac04_LearnSoft Sales	LearnSoft Titles Update Prices (query) Software Package Sales (query)
On Your Own	
1. Dental Patients (Lab 2, OYO 3) ac04_Patient Billing.xls	Dental Patients Billing (table)
2. ac02_Lewis Personnel (Lab 2, OYO 4) ac04_Lewis Consultants	ac02_Lewis Personnel Consultant Contact (table) Consultant Billing (table) Consultant Costs (query) Consultant Hours (crosstab query)
3.	WriteOn! Products (table) Suppliers (table) Reorder Query (query)

Supplied/Used	Created/Saved As
4. EMP Enterprises (Lab 3, OYO 3)	EMP Enterprises Departments Expenses Department Expenses (query) Expenses by Manager (query and subquery)
5. ac04_Little League.xls	Little League Players Coaches Roster (query) Coach Totals (crosstab query)
Lab 5	
ac05_Club Employees	Club Employees5: Record Form (form) City/State/ZipCode (form) Pay (form) Employee Update Form (form)
Step-by-Step 1. Clients & Agents (Lab 4, PE 1)	Clients & Agents Agents (form)
2. Animal Rescue Foundation (Lab 4, PE 3)	Animal Rescue Foundation Animal Status (form)
3. Five Points Center (Lab 4, PE 2)	Five Points Center Spa Package Purchases (form)
4. Café Purchases (Lab 4, PE 4)	Café Purchases Inventory Entry (form) Inventory Entry Split (form) Inventory Item Orders
5. LearnSoft Titles (Lab 4, PE 5)	LearnSoft Titles Software Orders (form)
On Your Own 1. Dental Patients (Lab 4, OYO 1)	Dental Patients Multitable form
2. WriteOn! (Lab 4, OYO 5)	WriteOn! Form and subform
3. Lewis Personnel (Lab 4, OYO 3)	Lewis Personnel Multitable form
4. EMP Enterprises (Lab 4, OYO 4)	EMP Enterprises Form and subform
5. Little League (Lab 4, OYO 5)	Little League Team Rosters (form)

Supplied/Used	Created/Saved As
Lab 6	
ac06_Club Employees	Club Employees6 Gross Pay Report for 6/27/2008 (report) Gross Pay Report for 6/13/2008 (report) Gross Pay 6/13/2008 (query) Gross Pay Chart (report) Employee Mailing Labels
Step-by-Step	
1. Clients & Agents (Lab 5, PE 1)	Clients & Agents Agent and Client List (report) Client Mailing Labels
2. Animal Rescue Foundation (Lab 5, PE 2)	Animal Rescue Foundation Animal Status (query) Animal Status (report) Foster Care Mailing Labels Adopters Mailing Labels
3. Five Points Center (Lab 5, PE 3)	Five Points Center Spa Package Sold (report)
4. Café Purchases (Lab 5, PE 4)	Café Purchases Stock Orders (report)
5. LearnSoft Titles (Lab 5, PE 5)	LearnSoft Titles Software Package Sales (report) Sales Trend Chart (report)
On Your Own	
1. Lewis Personnel (Lab 5, OYO 3)	Lewis Personnel Mailing labels
2. WriteOn! (Lab 5, OYO 5)	WriteOn! Stock report Mailing labels
3. Dental Patients (Lab 5, OYO 1)	Dental Patients Billing report and mailing labels
4. EMP Enterprises (Lab 5, OYO 4)	EMP Enterprises Department expenses report
5. Little League (Lab 5, OYO 5)	Little League Roster report Mailing labels
Working Together 2	
acwt2_Club Employees acwt2_Club Employees Pay acwt2_Hours Worked.xls	Club Employees WT2 Club Employees WT2.accde Club Employees WT2_be.accdb

Supplied/Used	Created/Saved As
Step-by-Step	
1. Cafe Purchases (Lab 6, PE 4) acwt2_Cafe Web Signups.xlsx	Café Purchases Email List (table) Web Signups.xlsx
2. LearnSoft Titles (Lab 6, PE 5)	LearnSoft Titles.accde LearnSoft Titles_be.accdb
3. Five Points Center (Lab 6, PE 3) acwt2_Five Points Locations.xlsx	Five Points Center Locations (table) Five Points Center.accde Five Points Center_be.accdb

Reference 2

Microsoft Certified Applications Specialist (MCAS)

Microsoft Office Access 2007

The Microsoft Certified Applications Specialist (MCAS) certification program is designed to measure your proficiency in performing basic tasks using the Office 2007 applications. Getting certified demonstrates that you have the skills and provides a valuable industry credential for employment.

After completing the labs in the Microsoft Office Access 2007 Introductory edition, you have learned the following MCAS skills:

Skill	Lab
1. Structuring a Database	
1.1 Define data needs and types	Labs 1, 3, 4, More About
1.2 Define and print table relationships	Labs 3, 4
1.3 Add, set, change, or remove primary keys	Labs 1, 4, More About
1.4 Split databases	Working Together 2
2. Creating and Formatting Database Elements	
2.1 Create databases	Labs 1, 6
2.2 Create tables	Labs 1, 4, 6, More About
2.3 Modify tables	Labs 1, 2, 3, 4, 5, 6, More About
2.4 Create fields and modify field properties	Labs 1, 2, 3, 4, 5, More About
2.5 Create forms	Labs 2, 5, More About
2.6 Create reports	Labs 3, 6, More About
2.7 Modify the design of reports and forms	Labs 2, 3, 5, 6, More About
3. Entering and Modifying Data	
3.1 Enter, edit, and delete records	Labs 1, 2, 3, 4, 5, 6
3.2 Navigate among records	Labs 1, 2, 3, 4, 5, 6
3.3 Find and replace data	Lab 2
3.4 Attach documents to and detach from records	Lab 1, Working Together 1, More About
3.5 Import data	Lab 4, Working Together 2, More About
4. Creating and Modifying Queries	
4.1 Create queries	Labs 3, 4, 6, More About
4.2 Modify queries	Labs 3, 4, 6, More About

Skill	Lab
5. Presenting and Sharing Data	
5.1 Sort data	Labs 2, 3
5.2 Filter data	Labs 2, 3
5.3 Create and modify charts	Lab 6
5.4 Export data	Working Together 1
5.5 Save database objects as other file types	More About
5.6 Print database objects	Labs 1, 2, 3, 4, 5, 6, Working Together 1, Working Together 2
6. Managing and Maintaining Databases	
6.1 Perform routine database operations	Labs 1, 2, 3, 4, 5, 6, More About
6.2 Manage databases	Labs 2, 6, More About

Index

D

E

G

H

I

J

K

L

M

N

O

P

Q

R

S

T

U

V

W

X

Y

Z

Credits

AccessLab1	dynamicgraphics/Jupiterimages
AccessLab2	Ryan McVay/Getty Images
AccessLab3	Russell Illig/Getty Images
AccessLab4	dynamicgraphics/Jupiterimages
AccessLab5	Ryan McVay/Getty Images
AccessLab6	Getty Images

Notes